SPORT
second edition
PSYCHOLOGY

THEORY, APPLICATIONS AND ISSUES

EDITED BY:
TONY MORRIS
JEFF SUMMERS

WILEY

John Wiley & Sons Australia, Ltd

Second edition published 2004 by
John Wiley & Sons Australia, Ltd
33 Park Road, Milton, Qld 4064

Offices also in Sydney and Melbourne

First published 1995

Typeset in 10/12 pt Plantin

© John Wiley & Sons Australia, Ltd 1995, 2004

National Library of Australia
Cataloguing-in-Publication data:

Sport psychology: theory, applications and issues.

> 2nd ed.
> Includes index.
> For tertiary students
> ISBN 0 470 80008 9.

> 1. Sports — Psychological aspects. 2. Exercise —
> Psychological aspects. I. Morris, Tony (Tony M.).
> II. Summers, J. (Jeff).

796.01

Front cover image: © PhotoDisc, Inc.

Internal images: © Digital Stock/Corbis Corporation,
© PhotoDisc, Inc.

Printed in Singapore by
Kyodo Printing Co (S'pore) Pte Ltd

10 9 8 7 6 5 4 3 2 1

To Felicity, Rachel and Adam, whose patience and
support have carried me through.

TM

To Avril and the family, for everything.

JS

Brief contents

Contents

Preface

In the preface to the first edition of *Sport Psychology: Theory, Applications and Issues*, we stated that the rapid development of sport psychology made it ever more difficult for teachers and students to keep up with all aspects of the discipline and the profession. During the 10 years since we made that claim, sport and exercise psychology, as the field is now termed, has expanded at an even faster rate. As well as a wider range of general texts, books on specific aspects of sport and exercise psychology have proliferated. The field now boasts five specialist journals, with many more research articles appearing in numerous sport and exercise science periodicals and mainstream psychology publications. It is therefore ever harder for the student and scholar to examine the published materials comprehensively. Nonetheless, there are few texts that cover the main theoretical, research and applied aspects of sport and exercise psychology at an advanced level, with education as the priority. Our aim in this book is to help to remedy this deficiency.

Probably the single most significant change in the academic world over the past 10 years is the globalisation of scholarship. International congresses, books and journals and academic exchanges are no longer the preserve of a small number of scholars from the world's wealthy countries. Students from North America, Europe and Australia interact regularly with those from Asia, Africa and South America through exchange programs and overseas study. Academic colleagues from around the world meet at international congresses annually. Information is communicated instantly to all corners of the world via the Internet. Our perspective cannot be parochial; our writing must reflect the needs of the discipline and the profession globally.

In the first edition of *Sport Psychology: Theory, Applications and Issues*, we acknowledged the maturing of sport and exercise psychology in Australia. Our main aim was to reflect this in a text that was written by researchers and applied sport psychologists who were based in Australia. In recognition of the tremendous developments in the field since, we have made substantial changes in the second edition. Many of our Australian-based contributors from the first edition have gained international repute as the globalisation process has evolved. Others have faded from the scene, most choosing alternative career paths. Sadly, two contributors, Chris Madden and Rob Kirkby, are no longer with us. Their contributions to sport and exercise psychology in Australia and around the world, not to mention in this book, are sorely missed.

To fill the gaps left by Australian-based colleagues, we have invited contributions from leading overseas experts. Most of the content in the second edition covers the same topics as the first edition. In some cases, however, the approach is quite different — see, for example, the treatment of psychological characteristics in chapter 1, anxiety in chapter 3, confidence in chapter 7, goal setting in chapter 10, stress management in chapter 11, building confidence in chapter 12, exercise in chapters 17 and 18, and injuries in chapter 21. In other cases, new content has been added to reflect the developments in the field. For examples of this, see emotion and mood in chapter 2, intrinsic–extrinsic motivation in chapter 5, achievement goal orientations in chapter 6, flow in chapter 15, professional issues in chapter 16, and psychophysiology in chapter 19. This is a substantial catalogue of change, yet we have largely maintained the structure of the first edition.

Given our conviction that the Australian focus of the first edition was no longer appropriate, the perspective of the authors of each chapter of this new text is intentionally international. Both in its content and in its contributors, this book intentionally takes on the flavour of an international text. We are delighted with the wide range of world-renowned sport and exercise psychology scholars who have agreed to contribute. Part 1 covers the major areas of theory and research; part 2, the most widely practised applications; and part 3, some of the key current issues in the field. We have had to make some hard decisions. For example, the topics of attributions and social facilitation have been omitted from this edition, because there appears to have been little research activity in these areas during the past 10 years. Issues such as substance abuse and eating disorders in sport might justifiably have been included in part 3. Themes such as psychological momentum, overtraining and burnout might also have been suitable candidates for the second edition, but none has quite attained the depth needed to replace the chapters included. In the applied part of the book, team building has not survived, while counselling is discussed in a section of chapter 9, as is the application of sport psychology in areas beyond sport and exercise such as the performing arts and business.

Accepting that there are other topics we could have included, we are confident that the second edition of *Sport Psychology: Theory, Applications and Issues* is an exciting addition to the literature in sport and exercise psychology, providing a considered coverage of major theoretical and applied topics in the field, as well as many crucial issues of concern to those in sport. These areas are reviewed at an advanced level by authors who are world leaders on the topics they consider. We trust that students and teachers, researchers and practitioners — indeed, all scholars and informed non-professionals — will enjoy and benefit from the result.

Tony Morris and Jeff Summers
December 2003

About the contributors

Eugene Aidman is a senior research scientist with the Defence Science and Technology Organisation in South Australia, where his current research focuses on human factors in Army training systems. He is also Visiting Research Fellow at the Department of Psychology, University of Adelaide. His academic career in psychology spans 18 years, with successive appointments at Moscow State University, LaTrobe University, and the Universities of Melbourne, Ballarat and Adelaide. Dr Aidman is a member of the APS College of Sport Psychologists and editor of its national newsletter, *The Sporting Mind*. His practice and research in sport psychology are informed by years of experience as a national-level competitor in decathlon, and by his extensive state-based and international consultancy work in athletics, swimming, basketball, golf, equestrian and numerous other sports.

Mark B Andersen is an associate professor in the School of Human Movement, Recreation and Performance at Victoria University in Melbourne. He is also the convenor of the sport and exercise psychology stream of the master's of applied psychology program in the Department of Psychology. He teaches in the areas of rehabilitation psychology, statistics and research design, and the professional practice of psychology. His research interests include psychosocial factors and injury, exercise and quality of life for those with chronic diseases, and the supervision and training of psychologists. Mark is a registered psychologist in Australia and licensed to practise in the United States. He received his PhD from the University of Arizona in 1988 and immigrated to Australia in 1994. He has published more than 80 journal articles and book chapters, and his edited text *Doing Sport Psychology* is now a standard used in the training of sport psychologists worldwide.

Jeffrey W Bond has been involved in sport psychology teaching and practice since 1972, and has been Head of the Sport Psychology Department at the Australian Institute of Sport since early 1982. He has provided sport psychology services to many AIS sports and national and professional teams, and has held sport psychology positions at nine Olympic Summer and Winter Games. Jeffrey was the founding President of the Australian Applied Sport Psychology Association and a founding member and later Chair of the Australian Psychological Society's College of Sport Psychologists. His research interests lie in the area of attention high-performance issues.

Stephen H Boutcher is an associate professor in the School of Medical Sciences at the University of New South Wales. His major research interest focuses on the effects of exercise on stress reactivity and health. He is particularly interested in the ability of acute and chronic exercise to reduce risk factors underlying hypertension. He is a keen jogger and golfer and also carries out research examining the psychophysiology of golf.

Likang Chi is the director in the Graduate Institute of Coaching Science at National College of Physical Education and Sports in Taiwan. He received his PhD in sport and exercise psychology in 1993 from Purdue University, Indiana. He received the dissertation award from the Association for the Advancement of Applied Sport Psychology. He is now a full professor. He has been a member of the Managing Council of the

International Society of Sport Psychology, vice-president of the Asian South Pacific Association of Sport Psychology and vice-president of the Society of Sport Psychology of Taiwan. Professor Chi has more than 50 research and professional publications. His areas of research interest include exercise and sport motivation, and anxiety in sport. For more than 10 years he has been involved in applied work with athletes and coaches from a variety of sports and at various competitive levels. Since 2000 he has been the sport psychology consultant for the Taiwan Olympic team. He enjoys playing tennis, basketball and golf.

Kerry S Courneya is a professor in the Faculty of Physical Education at the University of Alberta in Edmonton, Canada. He received his BA (1987) and MA (1989) in physical education from the University of Western Ontario (London, Canada) and his PhD (1992) in kinesiology from the University of Illinois (Urbana, Illinois). His research program focuses on the role of exercise in cancer prevention and rehabilitation including addressing motivational issues. His motivational research has been guided primarily by the theory of planned behaviour, but he has also published on the transtheoretical model, social cognitive theory and protection motivation theory. Dr Courneya received the Early Career Distinguished Scholar Award from the North American Society for the Psychology of Sport and Physical Activity in 1998 and the Young Investigator Award from the Society of Behavioral Medicine in 1999. He currently holds an Investigator Award from the Canadian Institutes of Health Research and serves as Associate Editor for the *Journal of Sport and Exercise Psychology* and Section Editor (Psychology) for *Research Quarterly for Exercise and Sport.*

Christina M Frederick-Recascino is an associate professor in the Department of Human Factors and Systems at Embry-Riddle Aeronautical University, Florida, where she teaches in both the undergraduate and graduate programs. She received her PhD in 1991 from the University of Rochester, New York, with a major in Psychological Development. She has taught in the psychology departments of a number of academic institutions including the University of Rochester, Southern Utah University and the University of Central Florida. Her research interests focus on motivational processes as they affect participation and performance in applied domains such as aviation, work and sport. She has also published in the areas of sport psychology, motivation, creativity, diversity issues, communicative negotiations, aviation and cognitive processing. Dr Frederick-Recascino is the author of more than 25 research publications, four book chapters and over 45 conference presentations. She is active in a number of regional and national psychological associations and is a Consultant for Psi Chi, the National Honor Society in Psychology. She lives in Ormond Beach, Florida.

Sandy Gordon is a senior lecturer in the School of Human Movement and Exercise Science at the University of Western Australia, where he teaches undergraduate and postgraduate courses in sport and exercise psychology and sport sociology. In addition to career transitions in competitive sport, Dr Gordon's current research interests include the psychosocial aspects of sport injuries, exercise promotion among elderly cohorts and evaluation of mental skills programs.

J Robert Grove is an associate professor in the School of Human Movement and Exercise Science at the University of Western Australia, Perth. He is a member of the College of Sport Psychology and College of Health Psychology within the Australian Psychological Society and a fellow of the AAHPERD Research Consortium. His general area of research interest is the social psychology of exercise, health and sport. Specific areas of current interest include personality factors, coping processes and the psychology of exercise.

Stephanie J Hanrahan is an associate professor in sport and exercise psychology in the Schools of Human Movement Studies and Psychology at the University of Queensland. Her research interests are in achievement motivation, attribution theory and applications of sport psychology. As a registered psychologist she works with athletes and coaches from a number of sports, as well as non-sport performers such as dancers, actors and singers.

Keith Henschen is a professor in the Department of Exercise and Sport Science at the University of Utah with an expertise in the psychosocial aspects of sports. He has been a member of the University of Utah faculty for the past 31 years. His research interests include psychology of performance, psychological interventions in sports, and sport psychology for special populations. He has published more than 200 articles, 25 book chapters and five monographs, and is the co-author of four textbooks. He is a frequent research presenter and conference speaker. He also works with numerous college and professional teams in a variety of sports. Dr Henschen has consulted with numerous world-class, professional and elite athletes as well as five National Governing Boards for the USOC. He was the sport psychology consultant for the US track team at the Sydney Olympics. During the Salt Lake City Olympics, he worked with three US teams — aerialists, short track speed skaters and long track speed skaters. From 1997 to 1998 he served as President of the American Alliance of Health, Physical Education, Recreation and Dance. He is currently President of the International Society of Sport Psychology.

Ken Hodge is a senior lecturer in sport psychology at the School of Physical Education, University of Otago, New Zealand (NZ). His research focuses primarily on the psychosocial effects of participation in sport. In particular, he has investigated issues such as life skills, self-esteem and moral development through sport. He has worked as a consultant, with a particular interest in team building, in several sports. He is currently a staff coach for the NZ Rugby Union, and has worked for Netball NZ, NZ Swimming and NZ Golf, providing psychological skills training for a number of different teams and individuals. In 1992 he was team psychologist for the NZ Olympic team at the Barcelona Games. In 1994 he worked in the same capacity for the NZ Commonwealth Games team at the Victoria Games. Ken is the author of *Sport Motivation: Training Your Mind for Peak Performance* and co-author of three other sports training books aimed at athletes and coaches, *Smart Training for Peak Performance: A Complete Sport Training Guide for Athletes*, *Thinking Rugby: Training Your Mind for Peak Performance* and *Smart Training for Rugby: The Complete Rugby Training Guide*. He served as President of the NZ Sport Psychology Association from 1992 to 1996 and deputy chairman of the NZ Federation of Sports Medicine from 1993 to 1995.

Susan A Jackson has developed a program of research in the area of flow, and is recognised as an international authority on flow in sport and exercise. Her research has focused on ways of helping make the flow concept understandable and attainable by individuals and teams. *Flow in Sports: The Keys to Optimal Performances and Experiences*, co-authored with Mihaly Csikszentmihalyi, is an example of this application. Dr Jackson lives in Brisbane, where she divides her time between a research position at the University of Queensland and raising her two sons.

Stefan Koehn is completing his PhD in the School of Human Movement, Recreation and Performance, at Victoria University, Melbourne. He received his master's degree at the Ruhr University, Bochum, Germany. His main research interests include the flow experience, confidence, action control and volition in sport. Mr Koehn is actively competitive in tennis, volleyball and soccer. For the past several years he has also coached tennis in Germany and Australia. He has recently also developed a keen interest in golf.

David Lavallee is a Reader in Exercise and Sport Psychology in the Scottish School of Sports Studies at the University of Strathclyde, Scotland. A chartered psychologist with the British Psychological Society, he has research and applied interests in counselling in sport and exercise settings. He received his master's degree in counselling psychology from Harvard University and his PhD in sport and exercise psychology from the University of Western Australia.

Daryl B Marchant is a senior lecturer at Victoria University, Melbourne, where he teaches undergraduate and postgraduate sport psychology subjects. He received his master's degree from the University of Alberta and his PhD from Victoria University. During the past nine years Dr Marchant has consulted extensively for professional Australian Rules football teams, including the Essendon, Port Adelaide and Geelong football clubs. He is a registered psychologist and former Victorian section Chair of the College of Sport Psychologists. His research interests are primarily in competitive anxiety, psychometrics, psychology of coaching, personality and applied sport psychology delivery.

Aidan P Moran is Professor of Psychology and Director of the Psychology Research Laboratory at University College, Dublin. His research lies in the field of cognitive sport psychology, especially the areas of attention, mental imagery and expertise. His books include *The Psychology of Concentration in Sport Performers: A Cognitive Analysis* (1996) and *Sport and Exercise Psychology: A Critical Introduction* (2004). A chartered psychologist of the British Psychological Society, he is a former official psychologist to the Irish Olympic squad. He is a consultant to many of Ireland's leading athletes and teams.

Tony Morris is Professor of Sport and Exercise Psychology in the Centre for Ageing, Rehabilitation, Exercise and Sport (CARES) and the School of Human Movement, Recreation and Performance at Victoria University, Melbourne. In more than 25 years in the field he has taught widely across the sport and exercise psychology curriculum, worked as a sport psychology service provider to individual athletes and squads, and participated in research in most of the areas addressed in this book, leading to a wide range of publications and presentations around the world. His main research interests centre on imagery; anxiety, stress, and coping; confidence; and motivation in sport and physical activity. He has been on the editorial board of several major journals in psychology and the sports sciences. He was inaugural Chair of the College of Sport Psychologists (CoSP), in the Australian Psychological Society. He currently serves as a member of the Managing Council of the International Society of Sport Psychology (1997 to 2005) and as President of the Asian South Pacific Association of Sport Psychology (1998 to 2007).

Maria Newton is an assistant professor in the Department of Exercise and Sport Science at the University of Utah, specialising in the psychosocial aspects of sports. She received her PhD from Purdue University, Florida, in 1994. Her research focuses on examining how personal and situational factors influence motivation; her work examines antecedents of motivation and the effectiveness of interventions designed to maximise motivation. Her most recent work has focused on the importance of feeling cared for and caring in underserved youth involved in physical activity. Dr Newton has more than 15 publications and has presented many times at national and international conferences. She currently consults with the University of Utah Women's Volleyball and Tennis teams as well as a number of individual athletes of all ages and skill levels.

Frank Perna is a licensed psychologist and an associate professor in the Division of Psychiatry at Boston University School of Medicine. Dr Perna maintains an active program of nationally funded research and a small clinical practice in the areas of exercise and health psychology, performance enhancement and the psychology of athletic injury.

Clark Perry is a psychologist in private practice in Canberra. He was trained in the United States, where he gained a PhD at Temple University in the area of imagery in sport. He has researched and published on this topic. Until recently he was sport psychologist at the Australian Institute of Sport, where for 10 years he provided support for a wide range of elite athletes and sports teams. For much of that time he worked closely with the powerful Australian swimming team. He has attended several Olympic Games and many World Championships as sport psychologist to Australian teams in a range of sports. He has presented and published widely on aspects of the application of psychology in sport.

Trent A Petrie received his PhD in Psychology from Ohio State University in 1991. Since then he has been on the faculty in the Department of Psychology at the University of North Texas. Now a full professor, he is Director of the university's Center for Sport Psychology and Performance Excellence. He is also a licensed psychologist and certified consultant. He has published more than 50 articles and book chapters in the areas of the psychology of injury, eating disorders, professional issues in sport psychology and academic excellence. He is co-author of two books, *Strategic Learning in College* and *A Student Athlete's Guide to College Success: Peak Performance in Class and Life, 2nd edition*.

Gregory Sargent graduated from the University of Melbourne, completing his research on marathon running and motor control under the direction of Jeff Summers. He then gained sport science qualifications and undertook a clinical master's program at ANU.

He was a student counsellor and teacher of psychology and physical education at McKinnon Secondary College before undertaking a postgraduate scholarship at the Australian Institute of Sport under the supervision of Jeff Bond. After three years at the AIS as both a postgraduate and staff member, Greg consulted with the Victorian Institute of Sport's program and then for three years with the Australian national netball team. He has written some thirty sport psychology articles, most of them for the national coaching magazine, *Sports Coach*. His research interests are related to effectiveness and mental skills programs. He continues to be involved in a wide variety of sports.

Grant Schofield is a sport and exercise psychologist at Auckland University of Technology, New Zealand. He has spent several years working in tertiary settings in Australia and is a member of the Australian Psychological Society's College of Sport Psychologists. His present research interest is in the area of athletic goal setting and wellbeing, and in physical activity health promotion. Dr Schofield has spent several years counselling athletes and sport teams at all levels. His expertise is mainly focused around endurance-based sports. He has been a national representative triathlete, competing over many distances including the Hawaii Ironman triathlon.

Ronald E Smith is Professor of Psychology in the Department of Psychology, University of Washington, Seattle. An undoubted leader of the discipline of sport and exercise psychology, he has made major contributions to the development of that field and to the psychology of coaching over 30 years. He is a prolific researcher, with many publications in the major sport and exercise psychology journals, as well as the mainstream psychology literature. His main areas of interest are stress and anxiety, coaching behaviour, and children and youth in sport. He has also developed several key measures that are widely used in sport and exercise psychology research and practice. He has contributed chapters on these topics to many of the major texts in the field and has published more than 15 books. He has substantial experience of working with athletes at a range of ages and levels, including professional baseball and major league soccer. He has delivered keynote addresses at all the major sport and exercise psychology conferences, including the ISSP World Congress of Sport Psychology and the AAASP annual conference. He is a Fellow of the American Psychological Association and a past president of AAASP.

Frank L Smoll is Professor of Psychology in the Department of Psychology, University of Washington, Seattle. He is a noted researcher in sport and exercise psychology and the psychology of coaching. He has published widely in these fields for about 30 years. His main areas of research interest are children and adolescents in sport, coaching behaviour, and stress and coping. He has been involved in the development of several widely used instruments in research and practice in the field. He is author or co-author of a wide range of book chapters on aspects of sport and exercise psychology. He is a Fellow of the American Psychological Association and the AAASP. As well as consulting with athletes at many levels, he has conducted many coaching clinics and workshops for parents of young athletes.

Michael Spittle is a lecturer in motor learning and control in the School of Human Movement and Sport Sciences at the University of Ballarat, Victoria. A participant in many sports and activities including cricket, Australian Rules football and soccer, he is also a dedicated runner and has coached cricket extensively. Michael completed his PhD at Victoria University, investigating imagery perspectives and performance of open and closed motor skills. He is an active researcher in motor learning and sport psychology with many papers and presentations at both national and international level. His research interests include imagery and mental practice, attention and concentration, information processing and decision making, cognitive and human performance factors, agility, learning and skilled performance, and physical activity participation.

Jeff Summers is Professor of Psychology and Head of the School of Psychology at the University of Tasmania. He undertook his higher education at the University of Oregon, gaining his doctorate in Psychology in 1974. He spent 18 years at the University of Melbourne before becoming the Foundation Professor of Psychology at the University of Southern Queensland, a position he held until 1998. He has published extensively in the fields of human motor control and learning, and sport psychology. In the latter field his research interests include attentional mechanisms in sport, the stress–performance relationship, predisposition to injury, and exercise addiction.

Peter C Terry is Professorial Research Fellow in the Department of Psychology, University of Southern Queensland. Author of more than 100 publications, he is on the Editorial Board of *The Sport Psychologist* and has guest edited the *Journal of Applied Sport Psychology*. An applied practitioner since 1983, he has worked as a psychologist at six Olympic Games and more than 50 other major international events around the world. He is the Psychology Coordinator at the Queensland Academy of Sport. He is also the current Chair of the Australian Psychological Society's College of Sport Psychology, and is a Fellow of the British Association of Sport and Exercise Sciences. He has served on the Psychology Steering Committee of the British Olympic Association, the Advisory Council to the Women's Tennis Association and the Board of Directors of the British Bobsleigh Association. In the distant past he played at representative level in rugby, football and athletics, skydived with the Red Devils, competed in the British bobsleigh championships and ran a three-hour marathon. He has now migrated to golf and tennis.

Patrick Thomas is an associate professor at Griffith University, Brisbane, where he is Head of School in the Faculty of Education and a member of the Applied Cognitive Neuroscience Research Centre. He teaches undergraduate courses in sport psychology and research methods, and a postgraduate course aimed at enhancing human performance at work and in other settings. In 1990 he was Visiting Professor at the United States Olympic Training Center, Colorado Springs. He has since provided psychological services to individual athletes and teams in a range of sports, but particularly golf. He edited the book *Optimising Performance in Golf*, was one of the international panel of judges for *GOLF Magazine*'s Science in Golf prize, is on the Steering Committee of the World Scientific Congress of Golf, and is a member of the College of Sport Psychologists, in the Australian Psychological Society.

Bob Tremayne has worked as a physical and health educator in a range of schools in New South Wales and, more recently, as a teacher educator in tertiary institutions. While recognising the importance of elite performance in different movement areas, Bob's main professional concern has been in investigating and encouraging reasonable and meaningful access to health activities for all groups in society, including people with disabilities and people from diverse cultural backgrounds.

Patsy Tremayne is an associate professor and Regional Head of the School of Psychology at the University of Western Sydney. She is a member of the Professional Development Advisory Group for the Australian Psychological Society and an executive member of the Australian College of Sport Psychologists. Patsy is well known for her clinical and practical work in sport psychology, particularly relating to performance enhancement with children and adults in sport and other domains. Her research interests include psychophysiology as it relates to attention and activation in sport, and the effectiveness of mental skills for children.

Robert Weinberg is a professor in the Department of Physical Education, Health, and Sport Studies at Miami University, Oxford, Ohio. He has been voted by his peers as one of the top 10 sport psychologists in North America. He has published extensively in the psychology of tennis on such topics as goal setting, imagery, arousal and performance, mental preparation and mental skills training. He has written many books, including the widely acclaimed *Foundations of Sport and Exercise Psychology* (now in its third edition). His applied tennis books include his most recent publication, *Tennis: Winning the Mental Game*. A former collegiate tennis player and coach, he has consulted extensively with numerous tennis players of all ages and skill levels and given many tennis presentations and workshops. He is past president of the two major sport psychology associations in North America and is editor-in-chief of the *Journal of Applied Sport Psychology*.

William J Wrigley is a clinical psychologist in private practice in Brisbane specialising in performance psychology in sport and the performing arts. He is soon to complete his PhD dissertation investigation into the association between the flow state experience and music performance.

Nadine Zillmann graduated from the University of Leipzig with a master's degree in sport science. She contributed to this publication while working as a research assistant within the School of Human Movement and Exercise Science at the University of Western Australia.

Acknowledgements

First, we would like to thank our families for all their help and understanding during the period of intensive work on this book and through all our personal ups and downs. Next, we want to express our gratitude to the staff at John Wiley & Sons in Brisbane for their thorough, professional work on this edition of the book. In particular, we extend our appreciation to Rebecca Gollan, whose patience, perseverance and encouragement carried us through difficult times. The support and guidance of Lucy Russell and Jem Bates have also been valuable.

We would also like to thank all our contributors, who stood by us during those difficult periods and delivered what we requested whenever we asked for it. We are proud of the book that has resulted, which we believe makes a significant contribution to the field. The excellent content of this book is due largely to the high quality of our colleagues' contributions.

Tony Morris and Jeff Summers

I want to acknowledge the contributions of Drs Mark Andersen, Jean Williams and Ron Smith. Their work has inspired me and provided a road map for investigations into the psychology of sport injury. I also want to thank my children, Kyla and Braeden, for their love and support, and the joy they bring to my life.

Trent A Petrie

Dr Kerry Courneya is supported by an Investigator Award from the Canadian Institutes of Health Research and a Research Team Grant from the National Cancer Institute of Canada (NCIC), with funds from the Canadian Cancer Society (CCS) and the CCS/NCIC Sociobehavioural Cancer Research Network.

The authors and publisher would also like to thank the following copyright holders, organisations and individuals for permission to reproduce copyright material in this book.

Images:
• Figure 1.1(a) and (b), page 24: © PhotoDisc, Inc. • Figure 1.4, page 31: © 'In the dawn of the new millennium', vol. 3, 10th World Congress of Sport Psychology, 31 May. • Figure 2.1, page 51: © 1998 American Psychological Association. Reproduced with permission. • Figure 2.2, page 52: © 2000 *Journal of Applied Sport Psychology*, Lane and Terry. Reproduced by permission of Taylor & Francis, Inc., www.routledge-ny.com. • Figure 2.5, page 63: 'Revised conceptual framework for the prediction of responses to motivational asynchronous music is exercise and sport', from Costa I Karageorghis, Peter C Terry and Andrew M Lane 1999, 'Development and initial validation of an instrument to assess the motivational qualities of music in exercise and sport: the Brunel Music Rating Inventory', *Journal of Sport Sciences*, vol. 17, no. 9, p. 721, www.tandf.co.uk/journals/titles/02640414.html. • Figure 2.6, page 64: © 2000 *Journal of Applied Sport Psychology*, Berger and Motl. Reproduced by permission of Taylor & Francis, Inc., www.routledge-ny.com. • Figure 8.1, page 222: from WN Widmeyer, LR Brawley and AV Carron 1985, *The measurement of cohesion in sport teams: the Group Environment Questionnaire*, p. 18, Spodym Publishers, Eastbourne, UK. Reproduced

with permission of Fitness Information Technology, Inc. • Figure 12.2, page 328: © Robin S Vealey. • Figure 13.1, page 347: adapted with permission from Martin, Moritz and Hall 1999, 'Imagery use in sport: a literature review and applied model', *The Sport Psychologist*, 13 (3) 245–68. • Figure 15.1, page 429: adapted from S Jackson and M Csikszentmihalyi 1999, *Flow in sports: the keys to optimal experiences and performances*, Human Kinetics, Champaign, IL, and from Jackson and Csikszentmihalyi 1988, *Optimal experience — psychological studies of flow in consciousness*, Cambridge University Press. Reproduced with joint permission from Human Kinetics and Cambridge University. Based on the original by F Massimini. • Figure 18.1, page 495: from Norman, Abraham and Connor 2000, *Understanding and changing health behaviour from health beliefs to self-regulation*, fig. 13.2, p. 306, Harwood Academic Publishers. • Figure 18.2, page 499: reproduced from Icek Ajzen 1991, 'The theory of planned behaviour', *Organisational Behaviour and Human Decision Processes*, 50, p. 182, with permission from Elsevier. • Figure 21.1, page 549: © 2003 *Journal of Applied Sport Psychology*. Reproduced by permission of Taylor & Francis, Inc., www.routledge-ny.com.

Text:
• Page 85: from Susie O'Neill 1999, *Choose to win: achieving your goals, fulfilling your dreams*, Pan Macmillan Australia Pty Ltd. • Page 154: text extracts from the *Journal of Sport & Exercise Psychology*, 1992. The authors are with the Department of Health, Kinesiology, and Leisure Studies, Purdue University, Lambert 113, West Lafayette, IN 47907. Reprint requests should be sent to Joan L Duda. • Page 155: reprinted by permission of the publisher from John G Nicholls 1989, *The competitive ethos and democratic education*, p. 21, Harvard University Press Cambridge, MA, © 1989 by the president and Fellows of Harvard College. • Pages 457–8: reproduced by permission from Andersen, Van Raalte and Brewer 1994, 'Assessing the skills of sport psychology supervisors', *The Sport Psychologist*, 8 (3) 238–47. • Page 497: © 1992 *American Journal of Health Promotion*.

Every effort has been made to trace the ownership of copyright material. Information that will help to rectify any error or omission in subsequent editions will be welcome. In such cases, please contact the Permissions Section of John Wiley & Sons Australia, Ltd, which will be happy to pay the usual permission fee.

INTRODUCTION

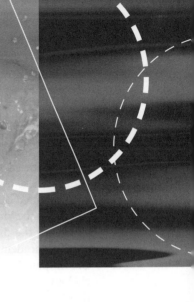

THE DEVELOPING DISCIPLINE OF SPORT AND EXERCISE PSYCHOLOGY

Sport, in its many forms, is one of the most ubiquitous institutions in the world. Through its natural evolution from play, and by the more artificial route of the missionary activities of various nations, many peoples from all parts of the globe have come to share a range of activities involving physical effort and skill, played competitively according to widely agreed rules. Sports are enjoyed by children, adults and older people, by males and females, by the able-bodied and people with disabilities. Participation in some form of sport at an appropriate level is denied to few.

Given the universal interest in play and games, which has been rapidly translated into a world of sport over the past century, it is hardly surprising that sport has come to play such a significant role in economic and political realms, or that it has attracted the interest of academic scholars. That this latter interest focused first on the biological and then the mechanical and motor aspects of sport is also predictable; the physical demands and the production of skill are the most obvious elements that many sports have in common. Still, some people recognised that other, psychological factors affect sport behaviour. Many of us have observed the player with all the skills and physical attributes, the outstanding favourite for an Olympic or world championship gold, who falls at the first hurdle against a lesser opponent. We have watched performers in the heat and emotion of competition producing a superhuman feat of endurance or strength to achieve their goals. Everybody knows someone, whether a player, coach, administrator or even spectator, who shows a level of commitment to his or her sport that borders on the fanatical, even when they know they will never achieve fame or glory. What makes millions of people exhibit such devotion to activities that typically have little or no instrumental value? Why does the overwhelming favourite crash in a major competition? How can athletes display resources of strength or endurance far beyond their normal capacities? It is an interest in seeking answers to questions like these that led some scholars to focus on the application of psychological principles to sport, and thus to create sport psychology.

The relationship between sport and psychology has a long history, going back at least as far as Triplett's (1897) study of coaction effects in racing cyclists, which has been acknowledged as the first social psychological experiment (Williams 2001). Triplett used sport to examine social psychological processes. Psychologists studied sport for its own sake or as an exemplar of human behaviour in general for several decades before the field was recognised and expanded into a specialism, originally within Physical Education. Over the past 40 years the specialist area of sport psychology (and more recently sport and exercise psychology) has developed from its hesitant beginnings to become a confident, mature academic discipline. Sport psychology is now supported by a plethora of texts, several international journals, and national and international professional associations. These associations host conferences at which new theories, research and practice are presented and discussed, and the sport psychology community meets to shape the future of the discipline. In this section we will summarise the development of these aspects of the discipline around the world.

The academic study of sport psychology was a comparatively late starter. Coleman Griffith, an American coach and academic, is often called the 'grandfather of sport psychology'. Griffith, a physical educator and coach, worked at the University of Illinois in the 1920s, producing two books titled *Psychology of Coaching* (1926) and *Psychology of Athletics* (1928). His main role was to facilitate the work of university coaches, and he studied motor learning as much as sport psychology (Williams & Straub 1993). Despite his pioneering example, Griffith is not considered the 'father' of sport psychology, because a whole generation would pass before the field blossomed.

Development and activities of a world body

It was in the 1960s that interest developed on a scale that was to provide the foundation for an academic area of study. Probably the first formal development that heralded the arrival of sport psychology as a discipline was the foundation of the International Society of Sport Psychology (ISSP) in 1965 (Morris, Lidor & Hackfort 2003a). In fact, the impetus for this development came from an Italian psychiatrist, Feruccio Antonelli, who organised the 1st World Congress of Sport Psychology in Rome during that year. The congress was attended by about 500 delegates, most of whom were medical, psychiatric or physical education experts (Morris et al. 2003a). The main reason for this was that Antonelli was associated with the International Sports Medicine Federation (FIMS). During the congress a business meeting was held, ISSP was founded and Antonelli was elected its first president, a position he held for eight years (Morris et al. 2003a). The inaugural managing council of ISSP included members from all around the world, but few of them could claim, then or later, to be sport psychologists by discipline or profession.

The 2nd World Congress of Sport Psychology, by then under the auspices of ISSP, was held in Washington, DC in 1968. This was a signal meeting in two respects. First, because the Americans were responsible for running the event, they quickly established a national sport psychology organisation, the North American Society for the Psychology of Sport and Physical Activity (NASPSPA) in 1967 (Morris et al. 2003a). Second, the French and other Europeans, especially representatives from Eastern Europe, felt they received a cool reception. In fact, many people from the Soviet Union, East Germany and other countries in the Communist bloc were not permitted to attend by their own governments. In 1968 these sport psychologists formed their own body, the European Federation of Sport Psychology (FEPSAC) (Morris et al. 2003a). The three-year gap between the 1st and 2nd World Congress placed the event in an

Olympic year, which was considered to be inappropriate (Morris et al. 2003a). Thus, there was a five-year gap until the 3rd World Congress, which took place in 1973 in Madrid.

Since the 3rd World Congress, the ISSP has organised congresses every four years — these being in Prague in 1977, Ottawa in 1981, Copenhagen in 1985, Singapore in 1989, Lisbon in 1993, Israel in 1997 and Greece in 2001 (Morris et al. 2003a). These events have been the principal foci for the meeting of sport psychology scholars from around the world. At the 1973 event, a Czech sport psychologist, Miroslav Vanek, was elected president of ISSP; he remained in the position for 12 years. During that period the membership of the society, as well as its managing council, were increasingly identified as individuals who specialised in sport psychology. Gradually, differences with FEPSAC were resolved and it was agreed, as Vanek put it, that FEPSAC was for Europe and ISSP was for the world (Morris et al. 2003a). Thus, FEPSAC evolved into a regional body, whereas ISSP clarified its mission as the development of sport psychology around the world.

In addition to sponsoring ten world congresses to promote sport psychology worldwide, ISSP has fulfilled its mission in several ways. First, it has fostered the development of regional bodies that can pay more attention to the development of sport psychology in their own geographical area. Indirectly, as already suggested, ISSP was responsible for the creation of NASPSPA, the first North American continental group, and FEPSAC, the European federation. In the late 1980s ISSP encouraged leading Asian sport psychologists to develop their own regional group. The Asian South Pacific Association of Sport Psychology (ASPASP) was founded, appropriately, during the 7th World Congress of ISSP in Singapore (Lidor, Morris, Bardaxoglou & Becker 2001). In the early years of the new millennium ISSP has provided support for sport psychologists in Africa to form a regional organisation. Sport psychologists in South America have tried for many years to form a viable regional body there, but its fortunes have waxed and waned (Lidor et al. 2001). Second, ISSP published the first academic journal focusing specifically on sport psychology, the *International Journal of Sport Psychology* (IJSP), which first appeared in 1970. Third, ISSP has arranged for its managing council to hold its annual meetings in a wide range of countries, where members of the council also present symposia or participate in conferences.

Development of sport psychology in North America

Although the development of ISSP preceded the creation of a specific sport psychology organisation in North America, it was probably the spread of sport psychology among the physical education departments of North American universities that established a critical mass of scholars and scholarly work. This quantum of scholarly activity created sufficient momentum for the formation of the North American Society for the Psychology of Sport and Physical Activity (NASPSPA) in 1967. It is interesting to note that NASPSPA held its first meeting prior to the conference of the American Alliance for Health, Physical Education, Recreation and Dance (AAPHERD), the professional body for physical educators in the USA. Because the new sport psychologists were largely physical educators who would be congregating for the AAPHERD meeting anyway, it was no doubt assumed that this timing would ensure a large attendance of interested parties.

A similar relationship between a nascent sport psychology group and a parent physical education body was the vehicle to establish a sport psychology association in Canada just two years later, in 1969. Here the connection was even closer, as the Canadian Society for Psychomotor Learning and Sport Psychology (CSPLSP) was actually part of the Canadian Association for Health, Physical Education and Recreation (CAHPER) until 1977, when it became independent. It is noteworthy that not only was the parent a physical education association, but in both cases the 'older sibling' represented motor learning.

As well as maintaining the motor learning emphasis, the first established North American groups, especially NASPSPA, adopted a research orientation. By the early 1980s the emergence of applied work in sport psychology in North America had led many NASPSPA members to seek opportunities for discussion of issues related to practice as well as research. To cater for this demand, the practitioners set up a separate body from the research-oriented NASPSPA, creating the Association for the Advancement of Applied Sport Psychology (AAASP) in 1985. AAASP has rapidly developed as a national organisation for the promotion of applied sport psychology, gaining sufficient support to establish a certification program for practitioners in 1991. The very demanding criteria for certification, including some form of proposed accreditation of doctoral programs, led Williams and Straub (1993) to comment that 'whether or not the AAASP's certifying criteria and procedures will be widely accepted remains to be seen' (p. 5). Although AAASP has generated substantial momentum, it is not formally a part of the organisational structure of either of the 'parent' disciplines, namely physical education or psychology. The American Psychological Association (APA), a very large and powerful pressure group, officially recognised sport psychology by establishing Division 47, the Division of Exercise and Sport Psychology, as an interest group in this area in 1987. AAASP is entirely separate from this body, as is NASPSPA. Thus, the North Americans must consider three organisations when reflecting on their professional development in sport psychology. NASPSPA has an active sport psychology section, but its large motor learning and motor development sections tend to reflect its current strength. APA has retained its interest group, but is not involved in licensing or accreditation of sport psychologists or sport psychology programs. AAASP has grown into a strong and vibrant organisation. It has a large membership and exerts substantial influence on training and practice in sport psychology in North America, yet it stands alone, with no links to either the major psychology or physical education organisations. All these groups also hold annual conferences. The sport and exercise psychology content of APA conferences plays a small part in the biggest psychology event in the world, yet it maintains good support. NASPSPA annual conferences still attract good numbers. Today, however, AAASP conferences represent the largest scholarly gatherings of sport and exercise psychologists worldwide. In recent years they have drawn more international delegates to swell the substantial support from the North American sport psychology community.

Development of sport psychology in Europe and the United Kingdom

As already stated, sport psychology in Europe gained coherence through the establishment of the European federation, FEPSAC, in 1968. In the early days, FEPSAC was dominated by the French and the Eastern Europeans. Geron, from Bulgaria, was the first president, and Vanek was involved in this organisation as well as ISSP. Information on developments in the Soviet bloc countries was rarely clear at this time and there were few strong national organisations in Europe; rather, there were highly active individuals and groups that linked up with FEPSAC. The European federation also began to organise congresses. These fell into a pattern of four-yearly meetings that took place two years after (or before) ISSP congresses. Until quite recently delegates to the

FEPSAC events came predominantly from the countries of continental Europe. During much of the 1990s, which saw an increase in attendance by British sport psychologists, Stuart Biddle, from the UK, was president of FEPSAC.

The development of sport psychology in the United Kingdom reflected the British approach in several ways. There was a reluctance to participate fully in European developments, and an eye on what was happening in North America, without ever committing completely in that direction either. The British focused on their own developments, which have led to the evolution of a strong national body. During the 1970s the nascent sport psychology organisation in the UK was the British Society of Sport Psychology (BSSP). In 1985, BSSP federated with its sports sciences cousins, physiology and biomechanics, to form the British Association of Sports Sciences (BASS). In recognition of the growing emphasis on physical activity research and practice, BASS changed its name to BASES, the British Association of Sport and Exercise Sciences. The early 1990s saw a massive expansion of sports sciences undergraduate programs in Britain. These typically included a substantial curriculum in sport and exercise psychology. Based on the large number of staff needed to teach these programs, as well as on developments in government funding of research in sport psychology, research and publications increased dramatically.

In the first instance, these sports sciences programs emerged from physical education departments, as in North America. The expansion took exercise science into other realms, such as health and science departments. Nonetheless, the training of sport psychologists at the postgraduate level has remained primarily the province of physical education. Representatives of the sport psychology section of BASS/BASES have held discussions with the British Psychological Society (BPS) over the years, but at present BPS has an interest group in sport and exercise psychology and BASES remains the principal organisation to which sport psychologists affiliate in the UK.

Development of sport and exercise psychology in Australia

Certainly on a smaller scale, but all the same pioneering in its conception, has been the progress of sport psychology in Australasia. In Australia, a small cadre of academics have been studying sport psychology since the 1960s, as in North America. Again, many were based in physical education or human movement departments, although some were based in psychology (Lidor et al. 2001; Morris 1995). Glencross's *Psychology and Sport* (1978) was a contemporary of the classic North American texts of Martens (1975), Cratty (1981) and Fisher (1976), for example. Applied sport psychology was a particularly early starter in Australia.

Morris (1995) reported that sport psychology in Australia took a massive leap forward in 1991 with the formation of the College (originally Board) of Sport Psychologists (CoSP), a professional body within the Australian Psychological Society (APS). This gave sport psychology direct recognition as one of only eight professional areas of psychological practice recognised by APS. Not only does individual membership of CoSP confer tacit professional status, but the APS controls accreditation of all tertiary psychology courses and APS colleges approve programs as professional training. The nascent College let it be known that it would follow the APS model of four years of general psychology training followed by a two-year specialist master's degree, and this led to the development of such master's programs in psychology departments around Australia (Lidor et al. 2001; Morris 1995). Those programs, along with the introduction or expansion of sport psychology at other levels, especially in departments of psychology, led to a virtual doubling of sport psychology positions in tertiary education in Australia in the early 1990s (Morris 1995), an expansion that has slowed down only in recent years. Sport psychology in Australia now has a strong foundation on which to build the discipline and the profession. It is an established part of a strong professional society, the Australian Psychological Society (APS), which has more than 13 000 members. The APS provides sport psychology with status and credibility in the psychology profession, in sport and in the community. It also offers an established infrastructure for the operation of a truly national organisation and provides the support of a powerful national pressure group (Lidor et al. 2001).

Development of sport and exercise psychology in Asia

Although every region of the world has shown variations in the development of sport psychology, the distinctions have been more marked in Asia than elsewhere. Morris et al. (2003a) reported that Japan has been involved in ISSP from its inception. Typically, until quite recently the Japanese interest came from motor learning specialists. The Japanese Society of Sport Psychology (JSSP) is the largest and longest established in the Asian region (Lidor et al. 2001). Japan's close neighbour South Korea has also developed a strong national sport psychology society, KSSP. China was a slow starter, but progress has been rapid since the world's most populous nation adopted a more outward-looking perspective, including a major commitment to international sport success. This political development appears to have been based more on economic foundations than on the ideological approach of the past. India falls into a similar category. Communities with a Western colonial tradition, such as Hong Kong, Taiwan, Macao and Singapore, have embraced sport psychology but have limited opportunities for its application, so numbers of sport psychologists remain small (Lidor et al. 2001). Developing countries such as Thailand, Malaysia, Indonesia and the Philippines focused on their own traditional sports and physical activities for many years. In recent times they have started developing their national efforts in sports played around the world, and sport psychologists are now emerging in these countries (Lidor et al. 2001).

The Asian regional body, ASPASP, shows evidence of this development. At its inception there were only a handful of member countries, including Japan, Korea, China, India and Australia. Today its 15 members include all the places named in the previous paragraph, along with New Zealand. It is perhaps in this region of the world that the most rapid developments will be observed over the next few years (Lidor et al. 2001).

Development of sport and exercise psychology in South America and Africa

The region that shows perhaps the most perplexing pattern of development in sport psychology is South America. Representatives from this continent have been involved in the ISSP managing council since its early years. In addition, individuals from South American countries have regularly attended world congresses (Morris et al. 2003a). Some of the early involvement might have been linked to the involvement of Spanish and Portuguese sport psychologists in the world body, providing a language link to countries like Mexico, Brazil and Argentina. At the same time, reports from a South

American association of sport psychology are to be found in early editions of the IJSP (Morris et al. 2003a). However, a viable regional association does not presently exist, and the fortunes of the South American region seem to ebb and flow with the involvement of specific individuals (Lidor et al. 2001).

Africa reflects a different pattern. Very little organised activity was evident in that continent until quite recently. The involvement of a number of African sport psychologists in ISSP congresses and other international meetings encouraged the ISSP managing council to invite several leading figures from African nations to develop a regional body. Knowing the difficulties of the developing countries in the region, ISSP offered some financial support. The African Sport Psychology Association has been formed. Currently its membership is modest, with a small number of sport psychologists from Nigeria, Morocco, South Africa and Egypt leading the way (Lidor et al. 2001).

There is no doubt that the establishment of sport psychology as an academic discipline owes much to developments in North America. The US, in particular, has been the focus of academic sport psychology since the 1960s, both in terms of numbers of trained people involved and the quantity of publications produced. Until recently only the Europeans and Australasians supported the North American development of the field. Now more activity is evident in Asia too. We await the expansion of sport psychology in Africa and South America.

Development of sport psychology books and journals

The development of sport psychology as an academic discipline is reflected in the proliferation of published materials that address the field, or aspects of it, from a theoretical, research or applied perspective. The first texts that specifically referred to the psychology of sport, such as those by Martens (1975), Fisher (1976) and Cratty (1981), which appeared in the late 1970s (Griffith's books of the 1920s aside), were the forerunners of an ever-increasing range of books. Aside from general texts that aim to reflect the whole field (e.g. Gill 2000; Horn 2002; Weinberg & Gould 2001), there is now a voluminous edited *Handbook of Sport Psychology* (Singer, Hausenblas & Janelle 2001). Writers have produced books that focus on applied sport psychology, such as Williams' (1986, 1993, 1998, 2001) seminal edited text and authored publications that adopt a more descriptive approach to applied sport psychology (e.g. Gauron 1984; Harris & Harris 1986; Orlick 2000; Weinberg 1988). As the field of sport psychology has blossomed, more exponents have produced books on specific topics. An early example was the text on competitive anxiety in sport by Martens, Vealey and Burton (1990), which was followed by books on topics including motivation (Roberts 1992), attention (Moran 1996), emotions (Hanin 1999), sports injuries (Heil 1993; Pargman 1993, 1999), career transitions (Lavallee & Wylleman 2000), flow in sports (Jackson & Csikszentmihalyi 1999), exercise psychology (Berger, Pargman & Weinberg 2002; Biddle & Mutrie 2001; Buckworth & Dishman 2002), and aspects of applied sport psychology practice and delivery (Andersen 2000; Van Raalte & Brewer 2002; Murphy 1996; Tenenbaum 2001). Morris and Thomas further discuss resources in applied sport psychology in chapter 9. It is reassuring to note that, although the majority of these books have been produced by publishers whose focus is on sport, such as Human Kinetics and Fitness Information Technology, a range of academic publishers, notably John Wiley & Sons, have committed to publishing in sport psychology.

Until 1970 sport psychology research had to be published in general physical education and sports science and medicine journals. In that year the ISSP first published the *International Journal of Sport Psychology*. After one or two false starts with other publishers, this journal was published in Italy under the editorship of the ISSP president Antonelli (Morris et al. 2003a). Interestingly, it was not until 1979 that the first American-based, sport psychology specific journal, the *Journal of Sport Psychology* (JSP), which became the *Journal of Sport and Exercise Psychology* (JSEP) from 1988, was published. IJSP and JSP were predominantly research-oriented journals, so it was not long before the expansion of applied sport psychology led to the publication of journals that focused on applied issues. Papers in these journals described the application of psychological skills training programs and techniques, as well as reporting on research to test such applied methods. First to be published, in 1987, was *The Sport Psychologist* (TSP), which was sponsored by ISSP for many years from its inception. That association was terminated in the late 1990s. In 1989 the then relatively young American applied sport psychology group, AAASP, sponsored its own journal, the *Journal of Applied Sport Psychology* (JASP). It was more than ten years before it was considered that there was room for another journal. In 2000 the *Psychology of Sport and Exercise* was published, under the auspices of FEPSAC. Reluctant to change the name of the first journal to be published in sport psychology, in 2003 ISSP finally introduced the *International Journal of Sport and Exercise Psychology* to replace the IJSP. These remain the only journals that focus on publication of sport and exercise psychology content. Sport psychologists continue to publish in the more generic sport science journals, such as *Research Quarterly for Exercise and Sport*, the *Journal of Sports Sciences* and the *Journal of Sport Behaviour*, as well as incursions into a range of general psychology journals.

Taken together, the developments of national, regional and world bodies, the international congresses and national conferences that they host, the array of texts and the range of journals now on offer support the contention that sport and exercise psychology is now a well-established discipline, particularly in post-industrial societies around the world (Lidor et al. 2001). It is a healthy sign for the future of the discipline that major organisations such as ISSP and AAASP have stated their commitment to the development of sport psychology around the world (Lidor et al. 2001).

Development of sport psychology practice

The practice of sport and exercise psychology has developed concurrently with the establishment of the academic discipline. On some occasions, practice has evolved out of theory and research. On others, practitioners have responded to novel issues and problems by creating innovative strategies and techniques, which have then been examined by researchers. Perhaps too often, however, practice and theory have developed in isolation. Because chapter 9 examines the practice of sport and exercise psychology in detail, here we will comment only briefly on three main issues. These are the links between sport psychology practitioners and the sports organisations to which they provide support, the training and accreditation of sport psychologists around the world, and the theory–practice nexus to which we have just referred.

Links with sports organisations

Accounts written by experienced practitioners in sport psychology suggest that, from the inception of applied work in the late 1960s and 1970s, links between sports organisations and sport psychologists have developed in two main ways (e.g. Murphy

1996; Tenenbaum 2001). First, some practitioners have adopted an entrepreneurial strategy, approaching professional sports organisations or Olympic sports to inform them of the benefits to be gleaned from the inclusion of a sport psychologist as a member of their team. Second, clubs, associations and other national bodies have approached sport psychology practitioners to employ their services, based on the recognition that psychological support is important for personal development and/or performance. Murphy (1996) proposed that increasing professionalism was a key factor that opened the door to elite sport service provision for sport psychologists. The increasingly organised and systematic approach to Olympic as well as professional sport, according to Murphy, was related to two major developments, at least in the United States. These were the development of televised sport and the growth of sport as a medium for advertising. Murphy acknowledged the economic basis of this observation; it was the influx of big money into American sport that stimulated the practice of applied sport psychology at the elite level. Experience suggests that increasing professionalism, whether associated with the growth of funding or with the recognition that such an approach was a prerequisite for success, has been a major factor in the approach of sport to all the sports sciences. Perhaps sport psychology was a latecomer to this party, as suggested in chapter 9, but it has gradually become a regular guest. By way of example, Henschen (2001) described an invitation he received and the way he responded to it.

In the third edition of the *World Sport Psychology Sourcebook*, Lidor et al. (2001) brought together reports submitted by national sport psychology organisations from around the world. In describing the involvement of sport psychologists in service provision to elite sport, there was almost universal agreement that sport psychologists were involved in this work. What varied was the mode through which practitioners were employed or otherwise involved. It was reported that in many countries sports organisations or the government employed sport psychologists to support elite athletes, mainly in Olympic sports, on a full-time, continuing basis. In other cases, practitioners were brought in on short contracts or for stand-alone sessions. The prevalence of sport psychology service provision to professional sport varied even more widely, depending on the structure of professional sport in each country. As Murphy (1996) noted, professional sport is very big business in the United States, so there are opportunities there. In a range of Asian and African countries there is little professional sport. Countries in Europe vary, but typically they fall between the two extremes, as do Canada, Australia, New Zealand and some South American countries (Lidor et al. 2001).

There is no doubt that the pattern of inclusion of applied sport psychology in elite sport has changed substantially from the early 1980s to the early years of the twenty-first century. There is a much greater acceptance of sport psychology among the present generation of athletes and coaches than was the case in the past. Nonetheless, opportunities to develop a full-time career in sport psychology remain limited. In a survey of graduates of sport psychology training programs in North America between 1989 and 1994, carried out under the auspices of AAASP, Andersen, Williams, Aldridge and Taylor (1997) found that virtually none of the individuals whom they were able to contact were working in applied sport psychology on a full-time basis. One factor that confounds this issue is that expanding numbers and size of sport psychology training programs has led to more graduates being attracted to academic positions. Many of those in academic positions offer their services, on a part-time basis, from the security of their university jobs and with the advantage of the perceived status attributable to their university affiliations. Given the limited opportunities in other countries, the way in which the sport psychology profession has developed in the US does not promise a great deal. Unless a different approach can be identified and developed, full-time employment in applied sport psychology might become, or remain, the preserve of a lucky few.

Training and accreditation in sport and exercise psychology

Training and accreditation are closely related to the involvement of applied sport psychologists in the provision of services. For national sport psychology associations, the identification of a training path that provides some form of accreditation has at least two important functions. The first is quality control. For any professional association, there is a need to ensure, and to be seen to ensure, that the services provided by individuals representing that profession meet the highest professional and ethical standards. Thus it is important that clients perceive that those professionals will provide the required service effectively and efficiently, and that they will do so with the minimum of risk. The second function of accreditation is that it provides a mechanism to ensure that clients preferentially employ members of the professional association or group. The medical and legal professions in many countries have been particularly adept at 'protecting their turf'. Zizzi, Zaichkowsky and Perna (2002) provided a clarification of terms related to the assignment of credentials, such as certification, registration, licensing and accreditation. Zizzi et al. went on to discuss the range of processes that apply to sport psychology in the US, with brief comment on a small number of other countries. In a worldwide survey of national organisations in sport and exercise psychology, Morris, Alfermann, Lintunen and Hall (2003b) reported that training and accreditation vary widely from country to country. Only a small number of respondents indicated that there was a recognised training path to becoming a sport psychologist in their country. Those with such training included the US, Canada, the United Kingdom and Australia. Even in those countries, it was rare, according to respondents, for the training to be recognised by the national psychology organisation. For example, although the APA (in the United States) and the BPS (in the United Kingdom) include formal interest groups in sport and exercise psychology, these major organisations for the profession of psychology do not recognise the accreditation offered by AAASP or BASES as the basis for licensing as a psychologist (called chartering in the UK). Australia is the exception. In 1990 Australia's sport psychologists agreed to form a national group. A steering committee of leaders in the field made the crucial decision to bid for acceptance within the Australian Psychological Society. Sport psychology in Australia added to its growing credibility by achievement of College status in the APS in May 1991 (Morris 1995). The new College of Sport Psychologists (CoSP) was able to establish a six-year training path, equivalent to other areas of psychology, including a fifth- and sixth-year professional master's specialising in sport psychology, that was accredited by the APS, as are all undergraduate and postgraduate programs in psychology in Australia. Licensing of individuals to practise, called registration in Australia, is separate from accreditation of programs and, based on the American model, involves a statutory process at the state level. Although registration includes a certain amount of supervised practice following graduation from the master's program, it is largely based on the accredited training. Thus sport psychologists are eligible to be registered as psychologists in their home state once they had completed their supervision to a satisfactory level. Morris et al. (2003b) indicated that contributors to their survey from many countries around the world reported that sport psychology was given little recognition by the psychology profession in their country. It will be interesting to see if national sport psychology organisations continue to be denied accreditation within their country's psychology profession. Currently most sport psychology organisations appear to look to well-established, national physical education and sport science organisations to legitimise their guidelines for training and certification in sport psychology, rather than to national psychology organisations, which are often unwelcoming. At the same time, responses to the survey on sport psychology accreditation around the world (Morris et al. 2003b) suggested that sport psychologists in a wide range of responding countries resent the lack of recognition afforded them by their national psychology organisation, as well as its individual members.

Theory–practice nexus

The nexus between theory and practice is an issue that is of great concern in sport psychology. The foregoing discussion, and the structure of this book itself, reflect this concern: theory and research are discussed in one part of the book, and the areas of practice, both well-established and developing, are considered in the other two parts. Although there are few texts that cover the ground that this one does, comparable books tend to be structured in a similar way. Much consideration was given to alternative ways of presenting sport psychology, particularly thematic approaches that would bring together all the theory, research and practice on, for example, self-confidence or stress management, in an integrated discussion. Unfortunately, a substantial proportion of the theory and research on topics related to applied issues was not executed in the applied setting, and its applicability is therefore questionable. Conversely, applied practice often has its foundation in what has worked in other areas of psychology or in related areas such as meditation and the martial arts. Practice has also been based on what has appeared intuitively to be the appropriate action and what has proved successful on a trial-and-error basis. This is less the case with respect to the topics in part 3 of the book, most of which are recent developments that have evolved through the interplay of theory, research and practice.

On the other hand, much in the theoretical area has little directly to do with the applied field, especially in the context of elite athletes. Theoretical issues frequently concerned mass participation, addressing questions such as 'What makes people participate in sports and exercise activities, and what makes them stop?' and 'Do particular types of people play specific sorts of sports?' Theoretical issues were also related to the outcomes of mass participation sport, such as 'Does sport build character?' and 'Does sport involvement make people more aggressive?' Even when the issues were relevant to practice, the research has often been of questionable applicability. Much research has employed high-school or college students as participants; it is doubtful whether they think, feel or behave like Olympic rowers, professional footballers or big-money golfers and tennis players in many of the contexts of interest.

A concern for the lack of articulation between theory and practice was evident in two seminal papers by Martens. In the first issue of the *Journal of Sport Psychology*, Martens (1979) wrote an article entitled 'About smocks and jocks'. Martens (1980) wrote a similar chapter, 'From smocks to jocks: a new adventure for sport psychologists', in an edited text. In these papers, Martens argued that it was important for the ecological validity of research in sport psychology that sport psychology researchers should leave their symbolically white-coated laboratories (smocks) for the training fields and competition pitches of sport (jocks). Some years later, by no coincidence in the first issue of *The Sport Psychologist*, Martens (1987) considered methodological and epistemological issues related to the need for research to be carried out in real-world sport. In particular, Martens noted the difficulty that the traditional, positivist paradigm of science has in providing a framework to answer many of the questions of interest to practitioners. He encouraged researchers in sport psychology to consider other ways of knowing about sport that were not based on the positivist construction of the world.

One reason for this poor integration between theory and practice in sport psychology relates to the historical development of theoretical and applied sport psychology, which was touched on earlier and is discussed again in chapter 9. Briefly, it is suggested that many of the early sport psychologists came from a physical education background and a philosophy that related to the value of sport and physical activity for everyone in the population. Hence, sport psychology theory and research reflected this interest in issues such as participation and drop-out, aggression and character. Applied sport psychology had an abrupt start, which was driven by organised, elite sport. The research on performance enhancement was largely absent, because of the broad focus of theoretical sport psychology on sport for all, and because there was no time for elaborate research projects; the sports needed action immediately.

Another major factor, particularly related to the slow response of sport psychology in establishing research to address the issues of concern in practice, was the nature of elite sport. Although benefits can be gleaned from the application of psychology to the training ground, practitioners appreciate that the crunch comes with competitive performance, especially in major competition. They are also aware that it is in the intensity of the Olympics, world championships, grand finals or grand slam events that the psychological 'glue' typically comes unstuck. Many psychologists have ethical reservations about executing invasive research in these situations; even if they didn't, most coaches would oppose any activity the psychologist proposed that might disrupt the performer. Thus the best that could often be hoped for was arm's-length activity, such as observation or the use of tests or interviews well before or after the event. Similarly, where sport psychologists have the opportunity to apply interventions, it is often not possible to employ traditional experimental designs. First, it would not be ethical, for example, to employ half an Olympic squad as the control group, who would be denied a potentially important psychological strategy. Second, as noted in chapter 9, most practitioners adopt individualised approaches to performance enhancement — that is, interventions vary between individuals who receive them. Clearly it would be equally unethical to give all athletes exactly the same intervention, whether it is considered appropriate for them or not.

These concerns about the difficulty of executing research where it counts, in the major competitive setting of elite performers, limited the amount of applied research that was done for some years. More recently a number of developments have increased the potential for such research. First, perhaps lacking the confidence of a mature discipline, for many years sport psychology adopted a conservative perspective on what constituted acceptable research. It copied the sciences and its closer relatives the other sports sciences by predominantly employing traditional experimental methods and occasionally using correlational research methods. Aware of the need for research in real-world settings, sport psychologists began to acknowledge the value of other research methods, such as in-depth interviews and single-case design studies. Concurrently, the applied sport psychology community has created its own journals to promote the communication of good practice and research in the applied field. *The Sport Psychologist* and the *Journal of Applied Sport Psychology* are now well established. The publication of research on elite athletes in competitive settings has expanded and has also been published more frequently in the *Journal of Sport and Exercise Psychology* in recent times. This shift in the ethos of sport psychology does reduce the ethical problems, as well as many of the logistical ones, associated with research on elite athletes. In addition, the patient years of practice of many sport psychologists have also created a high degree of trust in top coaches and administrators. The more senior coaches have seen the benefits that can accrue from the involvement of a sport psychologist without any threat to their own positions, and the newer generation of coaches has entered an environment in which sport psychology is typically an established part of the support system. Such trust is the basis for acceptance of the need for research, and that recognition is helping to resolve problems of access to elite athletes in real competitive environments. Together, these developments are leading to a much richer research base for the applied area.

Sport and exercise psychology is a dynamic young discipline that is now well enough established to have the confidence to develop its own theories and perspectives, to use the broadest range of appropriate research methods and to generate distinctive modes of practice. As the chapters of this book demonstrate, interest and attention in sport psychology has moved away from less fruitful issues, such as the role of traditional personality traits in determining sport involvement (see chapter 1 by Aidman and Schofield for a discussion of the latest approaches to 'personality' in sport) or the trait of achievement motivation as the key to direction and intensity of sport activity (see chapter 6 by Chi for a current review of goal orientation theory in sport). As well as embracing an interactionist perspective (Williams & Straub 1993), sport psychology has broadly adopted a cognitive phenomenological approach (Straub & Williams 1984) in such areas as attribution theory (Weiner 1972, 1979), cognitive evaluation theory (Deci 1975) and goal orientations (Duda 1987; Nicholls 1984). The cognitive phenomenological approach recognises that human behaviour is based not on what is misleadingly called the 'objective' situation — that is, the situation as perceived by the psychologist — but on the interpretation of the situation in the head of the performer. Similarly, applied sport psychology, in taking up a broader range of research methods, recognises the importance of the subjective experience of individual athletes and is in its best-ever position to study this in the field. Today researchers not only employ different techniques to examine specific issues separately; they also address an individual research problem using a number of research methods to gain the richest understanding of the issue under investigation. The growth areas reviewed in part 3 of this book further show the way in terms of more integrated research and practice. As a result of these forces, which all appear to be pulling in the same direction, perhaps in the not too distant future we will see a comfortably integrated thematic text on sport psychology.

FUTURE OF SPORT PSYCHOLOGY

The main aim of this book is to present a view of the current status of theory, research and practice in sport and exercise psychology as a foundation for those who will develop the field in the future. Sport and exercise psychology is a young discipline that has developed rapidly over the past 40 years. With changes in the experiences of the people working in the field and the forces acting on sport and exercise activities, no doubt it will continue to evolve. A snapshot of these kinds of changes can be seen in the way this second edition of *Sport Psychology: Theory, Applications and Issues* has been developed.

In part 1, on theory and research, almost every chapter has changed. For chapter 1, we invited two experts on the study of the latest personality-oriented characteristics, Aidman and Schofield, to write about the area, acknowledging the long history of personality and sport research, but focusing on current concepts. Recognising the development of the thinking and study of emotions, including mood, we have added a chapter on this topic by Terry, a leader in research on mood and emotions. Chapter 3 has also changed shape, now including consideration of stress and coping, alongside anxiety, to reflect the development of work in these closely linked areas. To update chapter 4, we have brought in Moran, a leading expert on attention, especially from a cognitive perspective, to expand the perspective. In the area of motivation, change has been substantial. Rather than having one general chapter that mainly focused on participation motives, we have provided two separate contributions. For chapter 5 Frederick was invited to lead the examination of intrinsic and extrinsic motivation, including participation motivation. Recognising the development of the achievement goal orientations approach to motivation, Chi has reviewed this area in chapter 6. We have replaced the chapter on self-efficacy in the first edition with a chapter on self-confidence. Chapter 7 retains a substantial section on self-efficacy as an approach to the understanding of confidence in sport, but also considers sport confidence and state self-confidence, two approaches developed by sport psychologists, to present a more comprehensive picture. Research on attributions in sport seems to have lost momentum in the past 10 years. With little new in this field, we have removed the topic from the book and refer interested readers to the chapter by Hanrahan in the first edition for a historical account. In the final chapter in part 1, chapter 8, Hodge reports on the latest developments in the area of group dynamics that he first addressed in the first edition.

The least change in topics is found in part 2 of this book, although this does not mean that applied sport psychology has remained unchanged. In fact, the area of practice is especially dynamic. We have restricted much of the reflection of the evolution, perhaps even revolution, in applied sport psychology to chapter 9. The original authors address the development of performance enhancement work and the shift in the balance of practitioner functions, including a much more substantial review of counselling support for the range of personal and professional issues that athletes experience. They also report on the expansion of consulting by sport psychologists to non-athlete groups, especially performing arts and business professionals. In this edition, the issues of counselling and 'moving beyond sport psychology' are also handled only in chapter 9, but we believe that they are likely to warrant separate chapters in the future. The psychological skills training areas of goal setting, stress management, confidence, imagery and concentration remain the backbone of part 2. We are fortunate to welcome contributions by our eminent colleagues Weinberg, Smith and Smoll, and Henschen and Newton, in chapters 10, 11 and 12. They add to the insights of leading Australian-based practitioners from the first edition Perry and Bond (with Sargent) in chapters 13 and 14. The two chapters that complete part 2 are new to this book. Flow is a concept that applies both to the reasons why we participate in sport, those peak experiences of pleasure and enjoyment that remove us from the everyday world, and to the achievement of peak performance. Jackson, who has largely been responsible for developing research and practice related to flow in the sport context, leads the contribution on it in chapter 15. As is reflected in the whole of part 2, and is dealt with in some detail in chapter 9, sport and exercise psychology has now become a complex area of practice, for which substantial education and training is required, both pre-service and during practice. It is appropriate that chapter 16, by Andersen, an eminent writer on this topic, addresses professional and ethical concerns related to training of sport psychologists and their practice.

In part 3 we have removed two topics. The first is the consideration of gender in sport and exercise psychology. This does not indicate our belief that considerations related to gender are no longer important. Rather, we argue that it is now well acknowledged that a concern for gender pervades all we do. Thus, we expect the authors of all chapters of the book to consider gender as appropriate to their topic. The second topic that has not been carried over from the first edition as a separate chapter is on the topic of qualitative research. Once again, the reason for omitting this area from the second edition is that it is now well accepted that researchers in sport and exercise should consider the full range of research methods, using the most appropriate methods to address their research question. This recognition is largely due to the pioneering work of the sport psychology researchers who introduced methods such as in-depth interviews (e.g. Gould, Eklund & Jackson 1992a, 1992b; Gould, Jackson & Finch 1993a, 1993b; Scanlan, Ravizza & Stein 1989; Scanlan, Stein & Ravizza 1989, 1991) and single-case designs (e.g. Elko & Ostrow 1991; Kendall, Hrycaiko, Martin & Kendall 1990) into the sport psychology literature. We trust that the chapters on gender and qualitative research methods in the first edition played some small role in changing the perspectives of our colleagues, and that it is no longer necessary to address the issues in specific chapters. In place of those chapters, we have two new additions to the book. The application of psychological theory, research and practice to exercise and physical activity in the whole community is probably the area that has expanded most within the field over the past 10 years. This is particularly the case in terms of the publication of new books devoted to the topic and the appearance of research articles in the sport and exercise psychology journals. It seemed unreasonable to expect that this could all be conveyed adequately in one chapter, as in the first edition. Thus, with advice from Grove, who wrote the chapter in the first edition and leads chapter 18, on the psychological consequences of physical activity, we have added a second chapter on exercise psychology, chapter 17, in which Courneya, a leading authority on theories about what motivates people to undertake physical activity, addresses that topic. For many years, sport and exercise psychologists have delved into psychophysiology. As the name suggests, this is a field that is closely related to psychology. Although we have seen the application of psychophysiology in some areas, including arousal and anxiety, attention, imagery, and motor skill research and practice in sport psychology, it is probably its recent application in the area of exercise psychology that has brought this topic to the fore again. In chapter 21 Boutcher, an eminent sport psychology and psychophysiology researcher, reviews the latest developments in this field. We also welcome contributions by three other sport psychologists of international repute, Petrie, Perna and Lavallee, in part 3.

These amendments to *Sport Psychology: Theory, Applications and Issues* reflect the kinds of changes that have taken place in the field of sport and exercise psychology in less than 10 years. Although we, and others, anticipated some of these developments, many were not predicted. We have asked all contributors to the present edition to include a section in which they discuss likely future directions for the topic they have considered. To many of our readers, these sections should be of great interest, yet we must expect that today's students will be the sport and exercise psychologists who develop the field in the future. They should never feel hamstrung by the methods or perspectives of the present generation of researchers or practitioners. Reading this book should provide a solid foundation of understanding of the thinking, the testing of ideas, and the applied activities that sport and exercise psychologists have undertaken in the past. The next generation of researchers and practitioners in our discipline should move forward with more confidence, based on this knowledge, while remaining aware that science often progresses through challenges to orthodoxy. Remember Galileo, Pasteur, Einstein and Freud! In chapter 24 we will suggest some of the issues, concerns and ideas that we perceive will have currency over the next few years. We will be happy to be contradicted by exciting new ideas, revelations and approaches to this fascinating field of study and practice.

References

Andersen, MB (ed.) 2000, *Doing sport psychology*, Human Kinetics, Champaign, IL.

Andersen, MB, Williams, JM, Aldridge, T & Taylor, T 1997, 'Tracking the training and careers of graduates of advanced degree programs in sport psychology 1989 to 1994', *The Sport Psychologist*, 11, 326–44.

Berger, BG, Pargman, D & Weinberg, RS 2002, *Foundations of exercise psychology*, Fitness Information Technology, Morgantown, WV.

Biddle, SJH & Mutrie, N (eds) 2001, *Psychology of physical activity*, Routledge, London.

Buckworth, J & Dishman, RK 2002, *Exercise psychology*, Human Kinetics, Champaign, IL.

Cratty, BJ 1981, *Social psychology in athletics*, Prentice Hall, Englewood Cliffs, NJ.

Deci, EL 1975, *Intrinsic motivation*, Plenum Press, New York.

Duda, JL 1987, 'Toward a developmental theory of children's motivation in sport', *Journal of Sport Psychology*, 9, 130–45.

Elko, PK & Ostrow, AC 1991, 'Effects of a rational-emotive education program on heightened anxiety levels of female collegiate gymnasts', *The Sport Psychologist*, 5, 235–55.

Fisher, AC 1976, *Psychology of sport*, Mayfield, Palo Alto, CA.

Gauron, EE 1984, *Mental training for peak performance*, Sport Science Associates, Lansing, NY.

Gill, DL 2000, *Psychological dynamics of sport and exercise*, 2nd edn, Human Kinetics, Champaign, IL.

Glencross, DJ 1978, *Psychology and sport*, McGraw-Hill, East Roseville, NSW.

Gould, D, Eklund, RC & Jackson, SA 1992a, '1988 USA Olympic wrestling excellence I: mental preparation, precompetitive cognition, and affect', *The Sport Psychologist*, 6 (4) 358–82.

Gould, D, Eklund, RC & Jackson, SA 1992b, '1988 USA Olympic wrestling excellence II: competitive cognition, and affect', *The Sport Psychologist*, 6 (4) 383–402.

Gould, D, Jackson, SA & Finch, LM 1993a, 'Life at the top: the experiences of US national figure skaters', *The Sport Psychologist*, 7 (4) 354–74.

Gould, D, Jackson, SA & Finch, LM 1993b, 'Sources of stress in national champion figure skaters', *Journal of Sport & Exercise Psychology*, 15 (2) 134–59.

Griffith, CR 1926, *Psychology of coaching*, Scribner, New York.

Griffith, CR 1928, *Psychology of athletics*, Scribner, New York.

Hanin, Y (ed.) 1999, *Emotions in sport*, Human Kinetics, Champaign, IL.

Harris, DV & Harris, BL 1986, *The athlete's guide to sport psychology*, Leisure Press, Champaign, IL.

Heil, J 1993, *Psychology of sports injury*, Human Kinetics, Champaign, IL.

Henschen, KP 2001, 'Lessons from sport psychology consulting', in G Tenenbaum (ed.), *The practice of sport psychology*, Fitness Information Technology, Morgantown, WV, pp. 77–88.

Horn, T 2002, *Advances in sport and exercise psychology*, 2nd edn, Human Kinetics, Champaign, IL.

Jackson, S & Csikszentmihalyi, M 1999, *Flow in sports*, Human Kinetics, Champaign, IL.

Kendall, G, Hrycaiko, D, Martin, GL & Kendall, T 1990, 'The effects of an imagery rehearsal, relaxation, and self-talk package on basketball game performance', *Journal of Sport & Exercise Psychology*, 12, 157–66.

Lavallee, D & Wylleman, P (eds) 2000, *Career transitions in sport: international perspectives*, Fitness Information Technology, Morgantown, WV.

Lidor, R, Morris, T, Bardaxoglou, N & Becker, B 2001, *World sport psychology sourcebook*, 3rd edn, Fitness Information Technology, Morgantown, WV.

Martens, R 1975, *Social psychology and physical activity*, Harper & Row, New York.

Martens, R 1979, 'About smocks and jocks', *Journal of Sport Psychology*, 1, 94–9.

Martens, R 1980, 'From smocks and jocks: a new adventure for sport psychologists', in P Klavora & KAW Wipper (eds), *Psychological and sociological factors in sport*, Schools of Physical and Health Education, University of Toronto, Toronto, pp. 20–6.

Martens, R 1987, 'Science, knowledge and sport psychology', *The Sport Psychologist*, 1, 29–55.

Martens, R, Vealey, RS & Burton, D 1990, *Competitive anxiety in sport*, Human Kinetics, Champaign, IL.

Moran, AP 1996, *The psychology of concentration in sports performers: a cognitive analysis*, Psychology Press, Brighton, UK.

Morris, T 1995, 'Sport psychology in Australia: a profession established', *Australian Psychologist*, 30, 128–34.

Morris, T, Lidor, R & Hackfort, D 2003a, 'From pope to hope: the first twenty years of ISSP', *International Journal of Sport and Exercise Psychology*, 1, 119–38.

Morris, T Alfermann, D, Lintunen, T & Hall, H 2003b, 'Training and selection of sport psychologists: an international review', *International Journal of Sport and Exercise Psychology*, 1, 139–54.

Murphy, SM (ed.) 1996, *Sport psychology interventions*, Human Kinetics, Champaign, IL.

Nicholls, JG 1984, 'Achievement motivation: conceptions of ability, subjective experience, task choice and performance', *Psychological Review*, 91, 328–46.

Orlick, T 2000, *In pursuit of excellence*, Human Kinetics, Champaign, IL.

Pargman, D 1993, *Psychological bases of sport injuries*, 1st edn, Fitness Information Technology, Morgantown, WV.

Pargman, D 1999, *Psychological bases of sport injuries*, 2nd edn, Fitness Information Technology, Morgantown, WV.

Roberts, GC (ed.) 1992, *Motivation in sport and exercise*, Human Kinetics, Champaign, IL.

Scanlan, TK, Ravizza, K & Stein, GL 1989, 'Sources of enjoyment in elite figure skaters', *Journal of Sport & Exercise Psychology*, 11, 65–83.

Scanlan, TK, Stein, GL & Ravizza, K 1989, 'An in-depth study of former elite figure skaters: introduction to the project', *Journal of Sport & Exercise Psychology*, 11, 54–64.

Scanlan, TK, Stein, GL & Ravizza, K 1991, 'Sources of stress in elite figure skaters', *Journal of Sport & Exercise Psychology*, 13, 103–20.

Singer, RN, Hausenblas, HA & Janelle, CM (eds) 2001, *Handbook of sport psychology*, 2nd edn, John Wiley & Sons, New York.

Straub, WF & Williams, JM 1984, *Cognitive sport psychology*, Sports Science Associates, Lansing, NJ.

Tenenbaum, G (ed.) 2001, *The practice of sport psychology*, Fitness Information Technology, Morgantown, WV.

Triplett, N 1897, 'The dynamogenic factors in pacemaking and competition', *American Journal of Psychology*, 9, 507–53.

Van Raalte, JL & Brewer, B (eds) 2002, *Exploring sport and exercise psychology*, 2nd edn, American Psychological Association, Washington, DC.

Weinberg, RS 1988, *The mental advantage*, Leisure Press, Champaign, IL.

Weinberg, RS & Gould, D 2001, *Foundations of sport and exercise psychology*, 3rd edn, Human Kinetics, Champaign, IL.

Weiner, B 1972, *Theories of motivation: from mechanism to cognition*, Rand McNally, Chicago.

Weiner, B 1979, 'A theory of motivation for some classroom experiences', *Journal of Educational Psychology*, 71, 3–25.

Williams, JM (ed.) 1986, *Applied sport psychology: personal growth to peak performance*, 1st edn, Mayfield, Mountain View, CA.

Williams, JM (ed.) 1993, *Applied sport psychology: personal growth to peak performance*, 2nd edn, Mayfield, Mountain View, CA.

Williams, JM (ed.) 1998, *Applied sport psychology: personal growth to peak performance*, 3rd edn, Mayfield, Mountain View, CA.

Williams, JM (ed.) 2001, *Applied sport psychology: personal growth to peak performance*, 4th edn, Mayfield, Mountain View, CA.

Williams, JM & Straub, WF 1993, 'Sport psychology', in JM Williams (ed.), *Applied sport psychology: personal growth to peak performance*, 2nd edn, Mayfield, Mountain View, CA.

Zizzi, S, Zaichkowsky, L & Perna, FM 2002, 'Certification in sport and exercise psychology', in JL Van Raalte & B Brewer (eds), *Exploring sport and exercise psychology*, 2nd edn, American Psychological Association, Washington, DC, pp. 459–78.

PART 1

THEORY AND RESEARCH IN SPORT PSYCHOLOGY

>>

Sport and exercise psychology developed as a research discipline largely in the schools of human movement of North American universities. Much of the work in the 1960s and 1970s involved the application of psychological theories and principles to phenomena in sport and physical activity. Major issues addressed by scholars of that generation examined basic questions, such as whether people who participate in physical activity have a particular personality type, what motivates people to participate, whether sport competition is stressful and, if so, how might this affect performance, what impact audiences have on sport behaviour, and what makes a team stick together. During the past 20 years, succeeding generations of sport and exercise psychology academics have developed the discipline, sometimes by extending the application of theories from mainstream psychology, at other times by modifying established theories to fit the sport environment, and occasionally by developing new approaches specific to sport. Part 1 includes contributions that consider the development of these major theoretical topics, which provide the foundation for much of the applied work in the profession. In chapter 1 Aidman and Schofield describe the development of thinking on psychological characteristics from the early attempts to match personality type to sport involvement and success, to the recent emergence of more specific dispositional conceptions. Terry, in chapter 2, addresses emotions and mood, an area of long of interest to people involved in sport but only quite recently structured into a more coherent field of theory and research. In chapter 3, Marchant and Morris consider the vast field of anxiety theory and research, probably the most intensively developed topic in the discipline of sport and exercise psychology. In discussing the theme of attention in chapter 4, Summers and Moran illustrate the interplay between the ever more sophisticated theory and research in mainstream psychology and the more down-to-earth issues of facilitating concentration for optimal sports performance. Motivation is divided into two topics. In chapter 5, Frederick and Morris examine the integration of intrinsic and extrinsic motivation into sport and physical activity research, largely based on the mainstream psychology development of self-determination theory. In chapter 6, Chi reports on the growth of theory and research on achievement goal orientations, an area that originated in the field of education but expanded substantially in sport and exercise research over the past 25 years. In chapter 7, Morris and Koehn address the concept of self-confidence, intuitively considered by many to be central to sport and exercise. To conclude part 1, Hodge reflects on theory and research related to group dynamics, which has principally been applied to sport through the study of teams.

CHAPTER 1

PERSONALITY AND INDIVIDUAL DIFFERENCES IN SPORT

Eugene Aidman & Grant Schofield

Why do some people enjoy playing sport and others avoid physical activity, especially when it is competitive? Are those who prefer individual sports, such as swimming or marathon, more self-sufficient and less group-oriented in other life pursuits than those who play sport only as part of a team? Might our choice of sport or exercise activity — as well as our ultimate achievements in it — be linked to certain personal characteristics, such as extroversion, emotionality or self-esteem? Such questions have inspired research about the role of personality in sport for more than 40 years. Their intuitive appeal, coupled with the relative transparency and accessibility of personality measurement instruments, has generated one of the most prolific research streams in sport psychology, ranging from investigations of the choice of sport (e.g. Franken, Hill & Kierstad 1994; Sadalla, Linder & Jenkins 1988) to personality factors in sport performance (e.g. Silva 1984) and long-term athletic achievement (e.g. Kirkcaldy 1982; Schurr, Ashley & Joy 1977). As extensive reviews of the field are available elsewhere (see Fisher 1984; Fisher, Horsfall & Morris 1977; Tenenbaum & Bar-Eli 1995; Vealey 1989, 1992), this chapter will concentrate on current issues and on the developments in mainstream research on personality and individual differences that have informed it. The chapter will summarise current views regarding the fundamental characteristics of personality, outlining established personality dimensions and their role in the overall pattern of factors influencing sport-related behaviours. Several important dimensions will be examined in detail, including the latest research on stress resistance and self-concept. The chapter will introduce an important distinction between the 'actor' and 'observer' perspectives in describing personality and the consequent differences in methods of studying identity and reputation. New trends in the measurement of personality will be examined, including cognitive and performance-based assessment, and contrasted with conventional questionnaire-based methods. Finally, the chapter will discuss recent conceptual models, such as the big five personality factors model (Digman 1989; McCrae & Costa 1985), that have proven useful in refining personality measurement, as well as improving predictions of important and meaningful outcomes of sport behaviour, such as individual performance, reactions to failure and long-term athletic achievement.

PERSONALITY PSYCHOLOGY: THE SCIENCE OF INDIVIDUALITY

Have you noticed how vastly different the reactions of two different athletes can be in almost identical situations? For example, compare the careers of two talented American athletes, swimmer Pablo Morales and long-distance runner Kathy Love Ormsby. Morales was one of the swimming stars of the 1984 Olympic Games in Los Angeles. Although he won three medals in Los Angeles, an individual title eluded him as he was upset in his speciality, the 100-metre butterfly, by German swimmer Michael Gross. Four years later, in 1988, Morales failed to make the US team. However, he did not quit there. After a brief retirement from the sport he returned in 1992 to make the US Olympic team and went on to capture the gold in the 100-metre butterfly at the Barcelona Olympic Games. By contrast, Kathy Love Ormsby, who was favoured to win the 10 000 metres race at the 1986 NCAA track meet, displayed a very different response to failure that was less typical of an athlete at the elite level of competition. After falling to fourth place during the championship race, Ormsby dropped out of the competition and subsequently attempted suicide by jumping off a bridge (see Baumeister 1991, pp. 89–90).

On the other hand, individual athletes tend to show remarkable consistency of behaviour across vastly different situations. Australian swimming sensation Ian Thorpe has captured the world's attention not only with his record-breaking performances, but also with his trademark composure: he appears just as calm, laid-back and relaxed during his media interviews as he is in the pool. NBA star Dennis Rodman has always been just as bubbly and eccentric on the basketball court as he has been off it (Rodman & Keown 1996).

The examples above illustrate — and confirm — two basic assumptions that underpin the general notion of personality. First, people behave (think, feel and act) *differently* — we are not like anyone else! Second, people behave *consistently* across different settings — we remain ourselves across a range of circumstances. These differences are also assumed to be measurable: according to Thurstone's law, if something exists, it exists in some amount and can therefore be measured. Personality research is therefore conceived as the study of measurable individual differences.

Personality has been defined as a unique pattern of 'characteristic *thoughts, feelings, and behaviours* that distinguish one person from another and that *persist over time and situations*' (Phares & Chaplin, 1997, p. 9; emphasis added). This definition captures the essence of several competing definitions that only recently began to converge. It highlights three important properties of personality characteristics: (a) they are unique, (b) they are stable across time and situations, and (c) they set each individual apart from others. In addition, the term personality may have two fundamentally different meanings:

- personality from the *actor's perspective* — 'my view of myself' or 'your view of yourself'
- personality from the *observer's perspective* — others' views of the person: 'my/our view of you' or 'your view of me'.

This distinction between actor and observer is critical to understanding personality, and it is far from being purely academic — it has major practical implications. 'Is it me, or is it me as I think others view me? This question has important implications in relation to exercising or playing sport. For example, imagine yourself competing in your sport in front of a capacity crowd. Which view did you choose — the view from the stands (similar to figure 1.1a) or the one from inside your head (figure 1.1b)?

Figure 1.1 (a) The observer's view (b) the actor's view

Clearly, the pictures are not the same. Psychologically, their roles are fundamentally different. As will be seen later (chapter 13), when the aim is to improve skill by mental rehearsal, the 'view from the stands' — the observer's view — is not as effective as the actor's view. In relation to personality, these perspectives are fundamentally distinct and only modestly related empirically (Hogan 1998).

Personality from the actor's perspective — 'me from my own perspective' — is not very well understood. In general, personality *from the inside* concerns the story people tell themselves and others about their hopes and dreams, their fears and aspirations, their successes and failures. The story defines their identity and gives certain thematic unity to their actions, and their life in general. In a sense, being a citizen, parent or athlete is as much an identity choice as being criminal, homeless or an addict.

The effort to understand personality 'from inside out' requires an *idiographic approach* (Allport 1961; Shoda, Mischel & Wright 1994), which emphasises the unique-ness of individual personality and relies on 'person-centred' methods of research, such as case studies. This approach began with Freud's (1949) psychoanalytic 'interpretive psychology' and was further developed in humanistic models of personality (Maslow 1970; Rogers 1980). Personal construct theory (Kelly 1955) and its *repertory grid tech-nique* (Neimeyer 1985) have dramatically improved the methodology of personality assessment in this approach. Yet, its applications in sport and exercise remain limited (e.g. Butler & Hardy 1992).

On the other hand, the observer's perspective has dominated personality research, both in mainstream and sport psychology. Not surprisingly, personality from the observer's perspective is well understood. This understanding is derived predominantly from *nomothetic research*, which is based on rigorous and (usually) large-sample analysis of group and individual differences on various personality traits. In this context, a trait is defined as a predisposition to act in a certain way, and is assumed to be the building block of personality (Pervin 1996).

Personality traits are organised in a structural hierarchy. For example, in Eysenck's model specific behaviours are linked through habits to the underlying fundamental dif-ferences in personality types, such as *extroversion* and *neuroticism* (Eysenck & Eysenck 1985). Cattell's model utilised a factor-analytic approach to distinguish between surface, source and global traits, measured by the Sixteen Personality Factors inventory (Cattell, Cattell & Cattell 1993). Interestingly, Cattell's global factor structure is quite consistent with Eysenck's types, indicating a degree of convergence between trait constructs generated from different theoretical perspectives. The emergence of the big five model (McCrae & Costa 1985) has completed the convergence, with the emergence of a robust five-factor structure, repeatedly confirmed for both self-report and observer ratings of personality, across languages and cultures (Borkenau 1988; Digman & Takemoto-Chock 1981) as well as age groups (Digman 1989). These five *supertraits* and their defining dispositions are summarised in figure 1.2.

The big five model provides a clear conceptual framework, based on a great deal of underlying research, and a correspondingly clear measurement framework. Notably, global factors in the last edition of the Sixteen Personality Factor Inventory (Cattell, Cattell & Cattell 1993) are almost identical to the five supertraits in figure 1.2, with only minor variations in terminology. Eysenck's dimensions are also well aligned with the big five factors (Draycott & Kline 1995). There is, in fact, a growing consensus that any new dispositional measure has to be defined in relation to the big five dimensions (cf. Digman 1997). This has coincided with the resurgence of interest within a range of applied psychology disciplines in the role personality may play in important life outcomes such as academic achievement (Ferguson, Sanders, O'Hehir & James 2000; Zuckerman, Miyake, Osborne & Koestner 1991), vocational choice (Raymark & Schmit 1997) and work-related behaviour (Robertson et al. 2000), as well as sport- and exercise-related behaviours (Vealey 1992; Aidman & Woollard 2003).

- **Neuroticism vs Stability**
  worrying/calm; nervous/at ease; high-strung/relaxed; insecure/secure; vulnerable/hardy
- **Extroversion vs Introversion**
  sociable/retiring; fun-loving/sober; affectionate/reserved; talkative/quiet; joiner/loner
- **Openness to experience**
  original/conventional; creative/uncreative; independent/conforming; untraditional/traditional; daring/unadventurous
- **Agreeableness vs Antagonism**
  likeability (reflects the person's efforts to get along): good-natured/irritable; courteous/rude; lenient/critical; flexible/stubborn; sympathetic/callous
- **Conscientiousness vs Undirectedness**
  dependable/unreliable; careful/careless; hardworking/lazy; punctual/late; persevering/quitting

---

Figure 1.2 The big five factor model   (*Source:* Summarised from McCrae & Costa 1987)

Person versus situation

It is important to note that while personality traits exert profound influences on behaviour, they are not the only influence. The situations people are in also play a role. For example, a highly extroverted basketball player would behave in a different way with the coach at a pre-game briefing compared with at a post-game party. In other words, how we behave is a function of consistent individual differences in our personality, but it is also a function of the situation we find ourselves in. By and large, the most important features of situations are other people. Furthermore, the situations that arise do not arise by chance: for the most part, we have some degree of choice about where we go, what we do and who we interact with. Through this choice, situational influences depend — at least in part — on personality. Our behaviour may also have an impact on the situations we are in. These three key sets of variables — behaviour, personal qualities and situation — interact in a mutually reciprocating way. This interconnectedness, termed *reciprocal determinism* (Bandura 1982, 1991), is critical to understanding the role of personality in sport.

The observer's view of personality is summarised in terms of disposition traits making up a person's reputation. We think about ourselves in terms of our identities. We think about other people in terms of their reputations. Other people translate our social behaviour (which is guided by our identities) into our reputation, which may in turn influence our identities. Reputation is a summary of the accounting process carried out in every interaction. A person's reputation tells us at a glance how well this person is liked and how much status or power that person has in a community of people with whom they choose to interact.

There are several key points to note about reputation. First, contrary to Gordon Allport's (1961) assertion that reputation had nothing to do with personality, reputations are vastly consequential. Most people understand this and make strenuous efforts to keep their reputations in good shape. In addition, the individual differences approach suggests that some people care more about their reputations than others, and that some are better at managing their reputations than others; and these individual differences are likely to be related to individual differences in social status and acceptance. Second, reputations are based on past social performance. Because the best predictor of future behaviour is past behaviours, reputations are quite useful in predicting a person's behaviour in the future. Third, the big five factor model, proposed as a universal terminology for personality description, is effectively a taxonomy of reputations (Hogan 1998).

MEASURING PERSONALITY

The study of personality is inextricably linked to, and dependent on, the discipline of personality measurement. Personality assessment techniques are typically classified into objective tests and projective tests. Most objective personality tests take the form of a self-report questionnaire (alternative forms include repertory grid techniques, already mentioned above, semantic differential and other ratings scales, as well as automated behaviour observations [cf. Aidman & Shmelyov 2002]). Two types of questionnaires have emerged in the field: those designed for clinical personality assessment, and those measuring so-called 'normal' personality. Clinical personality assessment has been dominated by one instrument, the Minnesota Multiphasic Personality Inventory (MMPI), which measures dispositions related to psychopathology, such as depression and anti-social behaviour (see Butcher 1995 for review). Assessment of the normal range of personality traits has evolved into a well-integrated theoretical endeavour driven by the big five factor model of personality (McCrae & Costa 1987) and its related instruments (NEO-FFI) (Costa & McCrae 1992), complemented by a range of well-established instruments such as the Eysenck Personality Questionnaire (EPQ) (Eysenck & Eysenck 1991) and the Sixteen Personality Factor Inventory (Cattell, Eber & Tatsuoka 1970; Cattell, Cattell & Cattell 1993).

Despite their widespread use in personality assessment, self-report techniques have substantial limitations. Most of these limitations stem from the following two assumptions: (a) the test taker is assumed to be *able* to self-report and (b) the test taker is assumed to be *willing* to self-report. In other words, the test taker is assumed to have sufficient insight into what is being measured yet no intention (or unintended propensity) to distort his or her responses. However, the widely known self-presentation distortions, ranging from impression management (deliberate faking) to self-enhancement (e.g. claiming virtue), self-deception (favourably biased but honestly held self-views) and denial (Cohen, Swerdlik & Phillips 1996), call for caution in using personality questionnaires. Violations of either of these two assumptions can compromise the validity of personality assessment. While it is relatively safe to accept assumption (a) in dispositional trait assessment — most trait markers tend to be universally understood (McCrae & Costa 1985) — assumption (b) remains wide open and, as such, should be examined in each individual measurement. Ideally, self-report should be complemented with alternative personality measurement techniques.

An important alternative to self-report techniques, with a largely untapped potential in sport psychology, is projective personality testing. Projective techniques require the test taker to respond to various ambiguous stimuli, for example to describe an inkblot in the Rorschach Inkblot Test (Exner 1993), to create a story on the basis of a thematically vague picture in the Thematic Apperception Test (TAT) (Murray 1943), to complete a sentence stem in the Rotter Incomplete Sentences Blank (Rotter & Rafferty 1950), to categorise an ambiguous joke in Aidman's (1996, 1997) Humour Apperception Test, to fill in a speech bubble in a frustration-provoking cartoon in Rosenzweig's (1945) Picture Frustration Study, or even to sketch a tree, a person or a whole family in various projective drawing tests (Knoff 1990). According to the *projective hypothesis* (Frank 1939), careful interpretation of such material can reveal inner feelings, unspoken motives and other implicit personality characteristics the test taker might not be fully aware of. Despite the historical problems with reliability, most of the currently used projective tests are well quantified and validated (cf. Cohen, Swerdlik & Phillips 1996). However, their applications in sport psychology have been limited — partly because of their highly labour-intensive administration and analysis procedures, but perhaps more importantly because of the paucity of substantive hypotheses generated in the field that call for projective personality assessment. With the growing recognition of the importance of the implicit processes that underlie behaviour (for a review, see Greenwald & Banaji 1995), applications of projective testing can be expected to grow, particularly in future research on implicit attitudes and self-esteem (cf. Aidman 1999; Aidman & Carroll 2003; Greenwald & Farnham 2000; Meagher & Aidman, in press), implicit motivation and implicit learning (Kihlstrom 1999).

Personality assessment is such a strong and dynamic field that an assertion that 'personality exists because personality measures work' would not be a big overstatement. But why do personality tests work? First, it is important to understand that our thinking about ourselves is necessarily more complex than our thinking about others. We think about ourselves in terms of our ongoing agendas; we think about others in terms of their traits. However, all our social behaviour is symbolic: it is a 'text' to be interpreted. Other people watch us, make inferences about what they see and then construct our reputations. Regardless of how mindless you think you are being at any point in time, others will see what you are doing as meaningful (Hogan 1998).

Second, when people respond to personality tests, interviews or psychological experiments, they are likely to engage in the same kind of impression management that characterises the rest of their life. That means that responses to personality questionnaires are not 'self-report' in the strictest sense; they are a demonstration of what the actor wishes to portray — and as such, these responses should never be treated at their face value. The predictive power of well-constructed personality inventories is due to the fact that they tap into the person's reputation by sampling from a limited set of that person's self-presentation behaviour. In that sense, item endorsements are merely samples of social behaviour, whose meaning needs to be discovered empirically. Those empirical links, when established, become instrumental in predicting future behaviours.

PERSONALITY IN SPORT PERFORMANCE

Being in the 'right frame of mind' is essential to performing well, especially in sport as the standard of competition increases (Williams & Krane 1998). It is well documented that athletes commonly recall feelings of inner calmness, supreme confidence, control of emotions, immersion in the activity and an absence of fear while recording their greatest performances (Ravizza 1977; Loehr 1982; Cohn 1991; see chapter 15 for further discussion). Consistency in achieving these mental states in athletic performance may make the difference between excellence and mediocrity at an elite level where little separates the top athletes in terms of technical and physical ability (Orlick & Partington 1988).

This consistency may be affected either by transient situational factors or by stable characteristics of the performer (e.g. ability and personality dispositions). Among transient factors, mood states have been directly implicated in the quality of sport performance: athletes tend to report being less anxious, depressed or angry immediately before successful performances (Morgan 1968, 1979; Morgan & Hammer 1974; Renger 1993; Terry 1995; see chapter 2 for more detail). The logic of mood profiling was extended to the *typical mood* assessment in the 'iceberg profile' (Morgan & Johnson 1978; Morgan 1980b), which has been used, with mixed success, in performance prediction across a range of sports and levels of achievement (for a review, see Rowley et al. 1995). On the other hand, personality is a key factor, along with skill, that affects performance over and above the situational influences.

Predicting sport performance from personality characteristics has long been considered one of the most attractive applications in sport psychology (Apitzch 1995; Deary & Matthews 1993; Diamant, Byrd & Himelein 1991; Eysenck 1995; Greenberg & Greenberg 1992). A wide range of personality traits have been found to be associated with levels of achievement in a number of sports, such as basketball (Evans & Quarterman 1983), hockey (Williams & Parkin 1980), American football (Daus, Wilson & Freeman 1986; Kroll & Petersen 1965; Kroll & Crenshaw 1968; Schurr, Ruble, Nisbet & Wallace 1984), rowing (Morgan & Johnson 1978) and other endurance sports (Egloff & Jan Gruhn 1996; Morgan et al. 1988). However, the specific personality predictors found in earlier research vary so dramatically from study to study that they make generalisations impossible. Not surprisingly, despite substantial progress towards its resolution, the debate continues between the 'sceptical' and the 'credulous' views on personality and sport (Morgan 1980a). Is personality really so irrelevant in sport, as suggested by the sceptics? Or has the earlier research just been unable to detect its influence effectively, as would be argued from a 'credulous' point of view?

The widely acknowledged lack of methodological and conceptual rigour in 'sports personology' (Vealey 1992) seems to confirm the latter suggestion. In particular, sport psychologists' brave but often simplistic pursuit of personality seems to have largely ignored the fundamental developments in mainstream personality research. The two most commonly overlooked principles are (a) the long-term nature of personality influences (Hogan 1998; Hogan & Shelton 1998; Pervin 1996) and (b) their moderating — rather than direct — effects in predicting outcomes of importance, such as job performance (Barrick & Mount 1991) and educational attainment (Zuckerman et al. 1991). Regarding the former, personality does matter when critical long-term issues such as career prospects (Hogan 1998; Hogan & Shelton 1998) or health risks (Eysenck 1995) are at stake. This fundamental influence is also likely to reveal itself if the personality–performance relationship is examined in the context of the life span (Vealey 1992). However, any serious life-span operationalisation of personality influences on sport behaviour requires rigorous application of expensive longitudinal methodology, which has been repeatedly called for (Morris 1995), while the cross-sectional approach remains less than convincing.

Second, the latter principle explains why most reported direct personality effects on athletic performance are so small — in fact, it is surprising that there is any effect at all. Personality is known as a source of moderator variables, and the search for their effects in sport has largely been misplaced. Personality variables are more likely to appear in interaction — rather than direct — effects, such as influencing the likelihood of *converting one's ability into achievements*. In other words, personality makes a difference when other factors, such as ability, are controlled for. For example, no amount of group orientation and emotional stability can help someone with a small body frame to become a rugby or basketball star, or someone with limited lung capacity to make it onto an Olympic rowing crew or swimming squad. Some remarkable exceptions from this rule are well known (e.g. NBA star Tyrone 'Muggsy' Bogues is only 1.60 m tall). What is most interesting about such exceptions is that they are almost always attributable to personality. On the other hand, for two athletes of similar ability (having the same 'physical potential'), personality is what is likely to make a difference in their ultimate sporting achievements.

Informed by these two principles, a recent study confirmed the existence of both long-term and moderating personality effects on athletic achievement among Australian Rules football players (Aidman 2000). A group of elite junior players with a leading Australian Football League (AFL) club were profiled using the Sixteen Personality Factor Inventory (Cattell, Eber & Tatsuoka 1970) at the peak of their junior playing career, immediately after the season they won the National Championship in their age group. The same players were followed up seven years later with an assessment of their progress in the sport. Personality variables showed only weak associations with players' performance as junior champions (at the time of initial profiling), but produced strong longitudinal effects on several achievement measures in the ensuing seven years as senior players. For example, personality measurement achieved remarkable accuracy in predicting whether or not the player made it to senior AFL (84.2 per cent correct discrimination, compared with 59.4 per cent accuracy achieved based on coach ratings of the players' performance and ability shown in juniors and 50 per cent obtainable by flipping a coin). Moreover, combining personality factors with coach ratings of players' physical ability achieved a perfect 100 per cent accuracy for the same prediction (see figure 1.3).

The general findings of the current literature point to several specific personality characteristics that predict athletic performance and discriminate between athletes and non-athletes, as well as between elite, sub-elite and non-elite athletes. The constructs of emotional stability, conscientiousness (e.g. discipline), self-concept (e.g. confidence) and anxiety appear to be central to overall performance prediction. Anxiety is examined in detail in chapter 3. The next section will examine the remaining constructs more closely.

Emotional stability is a construct reflecting the ability to withstand stress and to control impulses. An opposite construct often used in the literature, *neuroticism*, is characterised by a propensity to experience negative affect including fear, sadness, guilt, anger, embarrassment and disgust (Costa & McCrae 1992). Neuroticism is associated with an overreactive autonomic nervous system, leading to increased sensitivity and lower emotional stability (Eysenck 1967).

An adequate level of arousal is a key to performing at athletes' full potential (Bond & Nideffer 1992; Landers & Boutcher 1998). According to the Yerkes-Dodson law of optimal motivation, both over-arousal and under-arousal lead to weaker performances (Hardy 1990; Sonstroem & Bernardo 1982). As a result of increased arousal levels, people high in neuroticism are less likely to be able to withstand stressful situations without losing control over their impulses and experiencing the resulting negative affect (Eysenck & Eysenck 1985). Elite athletes clearly need greater emotional stability in order to withstand the increased levels of stress inherent in sport competition.

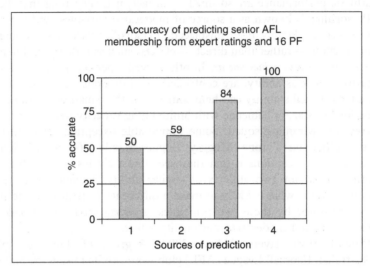

Sources of prediction: 1 = flipping a coin; 2 = coach ratings of ability and performance as juniors; 3 = personality profile; 4 = personality profile combined with coach ratings of ability.

Figure 1.3 Predicting whether or not junior champions make it to senior football league

There is evidence to suggest that emotional stability is associated with athletic success (Garfield & Bennett 1984; Morgan 1980b; Singer 1986, 1988; Terry 1995; Williams 1986). Higher levels of competitive stress were found to be associated with greater performance deficits in athletes with lower levels of emotional stability (Williams 1986). These findings suggest that emotional stability is particularly important in close contests and, as a disposition trait, is likely to have a major impact on athletes' progress in their sport.

Achievement orientation

Achievement motivation and *will to achieve* form an important segment of the *conscientiousness* factor in the big five model (Digman 1989). Individuals with high levels of conscientiousness are known to have a high level of aspiration and to work hard to achieve their goals. They tend to be self-disciplined and able to carry out tasks despite boredom or distractions. Their motivation is self-derived, their behaviour is organised and purposeful, and they tend to adhere strictly to self-determined ethical and moral principles (Costa & McCrae 1992). Achievement orientation is a well-established factor that influences individuals' career prospects (Barrick & Mount 1991), while its umbrella factor, conscientiousness, has been found to predict performance in employment (Robertson et al. 2000) and to discriminate between successful and less successful entrants in education settings (Wolfe & Johnson 1995).

Achievement orientation has been widely used by sport psychologists in their attempts to predict levels of athletic success (Davis & Mogk 1994). This research has met with limited success — mostly owing to a lack of sophistication in predictions developed so far. For example, despite clear differences between elite and non-elite athletes on measures of achievement orientation, no significant differences have been found between elite and sub-elite athletes; neither have any associations been established between conscientiousness and performance statistics or coach's ratings (Piedmont, Hill & Blanco 1999).

However, conscientiousness is likely to interact with emotional stability in predicting athletes' frustration response. Athletes low on conscientiousness are known to be lower on self-discipline, and those lower on emotional stability are prone to impulsive behaviour, anger and aggression under stress (Costa & McCrae 1992). A recent study has uncovered predictable interactive effects of personality and playing conditions on player performance in Australian Rules football: neuroticism significantly predicted the overall effort to produce an effective play (measured by aggregating game statistics of contested marks, tackling/obstructing opposition and protecting the ball handler) both in 'close' (highly contested) games and in 'easy-win' games (Aidman & Bekerman 2001), with emotionally stable players performing better than the unstable in both game conditions. Player performance was further influenced by self-discipline in the easy-win games, and by self-esteem in the close games (Aidman & Bekerman 2001). Furthermore, in the games classified as 'bad losses' (when the team was not in contention for most of the game), player performance was not related to personality at all. The study also discovered that sub-elite performers may show stronger personality differences from the elite than non-elite performers do. Thus, a group of players who played for both seniors and reserves teams (identified as 'swingers') reported significantly lower achievement striving and self-discipline than either top senior players or the core reserves team (see figure 1.4). The data indicate that while ability is what creates an opportunity to play at an elite level (it is what the reserves lack), it needs to be complemented by achievement striving and self-discipline, in order to produce consistent elite performances (these are what the swingers lack).

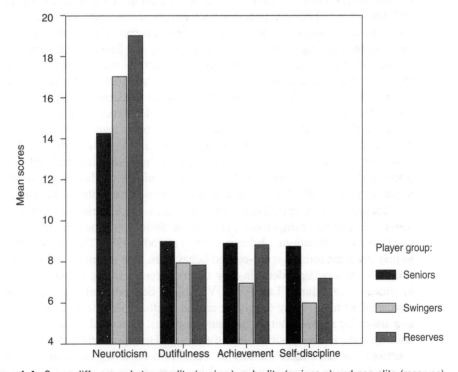

Figure 1.4 Group differences between elite (seniors), sub-elite (swingers) and non-elite (reserves) Australian Rules football players on personality measures

(*Source:* Aidman & Bekerman 2001, © 'In the dawn of the new millennium', vol. 3, 10th World Congress of Sport Psychology, 31 May)

Self-concept

The concept of *self* represents a core structure in one's personality, comprising self-perceptions and the resulting self-feelings and self-views. Self-feelings are usually generalised as self-esteem (Rosenberg 1979); self-views form a system of self-attributions termed self-concept (Marsh 1994). Five aspects of self have been identified:

- the physical self: the body and its biological processes
- the self-as-actor: perception and action components of self
- the social self: the roles taken (student, athlete, wife, daughter etc.)
- the self-concept: mental self-portrait made of self-descriptions
- self-ideal: what the person would like to be if all obstacles were removed.

Self-concept includes three components: cognitive, affective and behavioural. The *cognitive* component involves a system of self-attributions (e.g. bright, attractive, athletic, slow etc.). The *affective* component determines how we feel about these self-attributions (evaluation): self-esteem has been defined as an affective evaluation of self (Rosenberg 1979). Self-esteem is therefore a very special type of attitude, representing the attitude towards self. Self-esteem derives from two main sources: (a) experiences of being competent, and (b) experiences of being accepted (Aidman 1998; Tafarodi & Swann 1995). The *behavioural* component involves our tendencies to behave in accordance with self-image. In that sense, self-concept involves more than self-descriptions, it may operate as a commitment to continue being oneself 'as described'.

Theorised as a key performance-related personality characteristic, self-esteem has eluded sport psychologists for decades: to date empirical evidence of its role in an athlete's life and achievements is scarce and often conflicting. To a large extent this is due to the well-known gap between people's declarations about their self-esteem and their actual self-attitudes (Farnham et al. 1999). Self-presentation effects, ranging from social desirability to malingering in the general population, are further exacerbated in elite athletes by the extra pressure they experience to project — and protect — the image of a role model. These confounding effects can be effectively addressed with indirect measurement of implicit self-attitudes (Aidman 1999; Aidman & Carroll 2003; Greenwald & Farnham 2000; Meagher & Aidman, in press). For example, a recent study, conducted at the Australian Institute of Sport with the national swimming team (Perry & Marsh 2000), found the swimmers' ISPs (international performance ratings produced by FINA) to be associated with their implicit self-appraisals of strength, but not with declared self-esteem. More importantly, these implicit self-appraisals were highly predictive of the swimmers' ability to improve their ISP during a major international competition (Aidman & Perry 2000).

Theoretical conceptualisation of self-esteem as comprised of generalised feelings of self-worth and self-competence (Tafarodi & Swan 1995) has stimulated a new stream of research and applications (Aidman 1998; Tafarodi 1998). The two components are likely to play different roles in sport-related behaviours. For example, feelings of self-worth help people to be less dependent on how others perceive them, influencing people's reactions to success and failure (Tafarodi & Vu 1997). Self-positivity has also been found to be associated with an ability to receive critical feedback and benefit from it, rather than getting upset by it (Meagher & Aidman, in press). Extended to athletic populations, these findings suggest that positive self-attitudes — both declared and implicit — are likely to contribute to the athlete's ability to learn from mistakes and acquire new skills. This is often referred to as 'coachability' and has been shown to be predictive of athletic success (Piedmont et al. 1999; Smith & Christensen 1995). Indeed, the coachability construct, rated by Australian Rules football coaches as an ability to listen and learn from instruction, was found to be related to the players' self-esteem (Aidman & Bekerman 2001).

BOOSTING SELF-ESTEEM: ISSUES FOR CONSIDERATION

Practices of 'boosting self-esteem' are largely counterproductive (Baumeister 1991), as they often take the form of self-flattery leading to uncritical self-celebration as an entitlement, instead of applauding hard-earned achievement. Awarding trophies to all contestants or 'socially promoting' students who have not learned the skill, deprives them of the opportunity to develop a well-founded sense of self-competence. Such practices may in fact deplete self-competence as the key element of self-esteem and instead cultivate inflated views of self and entitlements — a dangerous form of high self-esteem, linked to violence and aggression (Sutton 1994). Recent research suggests that the development of self-control skills (controlling emotions, impulse, actions, thoughts) is ultimately better for self-esteem than indiscriminate self-flattery (Baumeister 1999).

A key element of self-concept, in the context of sport behaviour, is *self-confidence*. Self-confidence reflects the degree to which an individual believes she or he has the capacity to perform. When athletes are confident in their skills and ability to perform a task, they do so with reduced pressure and fewer negative emotions (Horsley 1995). Athletes high in self-confidence will have a greater belief in their ability to perform well and will derive greater enjoyment from participating in their sport. As a result, they will be more likely to persevere and enjoy longevity in that sport. Where survival, or continued participation, in elite sport is considered success in its own right, self-confidence is predictive of success. Smith and Christensen (1995), in a study of survival in professional baseball, found that that confidence was the most consistent predictor of both batting and pitching performance. Although self-confidence reflects a transient state, it has been shown to be a strong predictor of athletic success (Gould, Weiss & Weinberg 1981; Highlen & Bennett 1979; Krane & Williams 1987; Martin & Gill 1991).

Cognitive self-complexity

The way in which we construct and describe ourselves plays a very important role in the way in which we handle success and failure in sport. This section is focused on recent theory in self-concept, which suggests that an individual with a more complex self-definition will have a better protection from negative affect following adverse events in life and sport.

What is cognitive self-complexity?

Self-complexity is a structural characteristic of people's views of themselves. The self may be viewed as being composed of a number of aspects (Linville 1985; 1987). Linville defined self-complexity as a 'function of two things: the number of aspects that one uses to cognitively organize knowledge about the self, and the degree of relatedness of these aspects' (1985, p. 97). According to Linville, more complex individuals are char- acterised by a greater number of aspects in their self-description, and these aspects tend to have less overlap. The organisation of self according to Linville, illustrated in figure 1.5, involves different aspects of self — which are, in turn, characterised by various attributes. These attributes may be shared with other aspects. The number of aspects combined with the degree of shared attributes defines self-complexity. For example, Roger might define himself as a tennis player and a husband. In these roles he may also have some shared attributes. He may see himself as outspoken, aggressive and hard- working in both roles. On the other hand, Rachael, a more complex individual, sees herself in several different roles — as a tennis player, a coach, a wife, a mother, a pet owner and an office assistant. She sees herself as assertive and confident in some roles but subdued and shy in other roles.

Linville (1985, 1987) operationalised self-complexity through the dimensionality statistic H, derived from the results of a trait-sorting task similar to Q-sort (Rogers 1961). Calculation of this statistic is beyond the scope of this chapter.

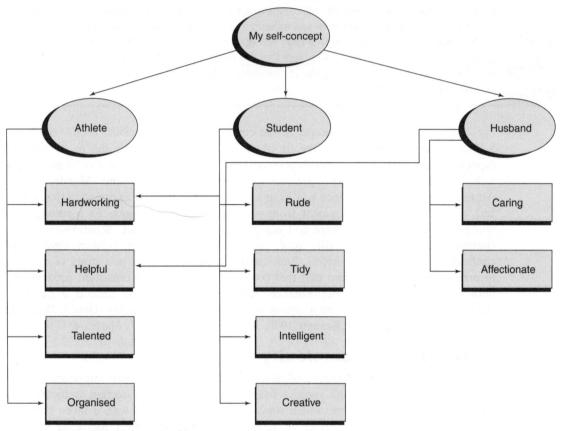

Figure 1.5   A model of self-complexity   (*Source:* Linville 1985)

Why is a complex view of the self beneficial?

Linville (1985, 1987) proposed that increased levels of self-complexity may act as a buffer against extreme affective reactions to stressful life events. Linville predicted that when a stressful life event occurs, it affects the self-aspect most related to the stressor. For those with many self-aspects, the affected aspect is one of many, and therefore only a small proportion of the 'total' self will be affected. Conversely, those with few self-aspects will have a greater proportion of their entire 'self' affected by the stressor. This postulate, known as the *affective-extremity hypothesis*, is equally true for positive and negative life events.

Additionally, when there is overlap between self-aspects there may be a spill-over effect, which occurs when 'feelings and inferences associated with the originally activated self-aspect, spill over and colour feelings and inferences regarding associated self-aspects' (Linville 1987, p. 664). Several empirical studies have confirmed the relationship between self-complexity and reactions to stress as predicted by Linville (Dixon & Baumeister 1991, Linville 1987; Niedenthal, Setterlund & Wherry, 1992, Showers, Abramson & Hogan

1998). None of this research, however, has been related to sport or exercise. Furthermore, several measurement-related problems have been identified. Kalthoff and Neimeyer (1993) found no significant correlations between three different measures of self-complexity — Linville's trait sort, the repertory grid and a text-analysis measure derived from a self-description task. Only Linville's (1985, 1987) trait-sort measure supported the stress-buffering hypothesis. Conversely, Stroot (1999) found no confirmation of the affective-extremity hypothesis from Linville's own trait-sort measure of self-complexity, whereas Messer and Harter's (1986) measure of self-concept was consistent with it.

Self-complexity and the athlete

There is a considerable amount of self-complexity research in mainstream psychology. However, findings specific to sport and exercise are sparse. The notion of self-complexity and its potential to buffer stress is appealing to athletes, coaches and sport psychologists. Competitive sport is typically a stressful environment. The athlete's reaction to a stressful event — be it success or failure — could be either facilitating or debilitating. Elite athletes and coaches are well advised to stay composed both with the joys of success and the trauma of failure. This state of composure comes more naturally to someone who has a greater number of relatively independent self-aspects, according to self-complexity theory.

Unfortunately, however, it is not that simple. Top-level sport has a reputation for being time-consuming in terms of training and competition. As a result, it is quite normal for athletes and coaches to talk about 'sacrificing' other aspects of their lives in order to succeed on the sporting field. In general, 'putting all your eggs into one basket' is not advisable from the self-complexity theory point of view. Translating this generic advice into improvements in athletes' psychological wellbeing will require more sport and exercise–contextualised research on self-complexity. In addition, this new research will face the challenge of finding more valid and reliable self-complexity measures (Rafaeli Mor, Gotlib & Revelle 1999; Stroot 1999).

Athletic identity

Research on athletic identity has discovered that those with a strong and exclusive athletic identity are likely to suffer more negative affect in relation to a stressful or negative sporting outcome — for example losing an important match, not making a team, injury or retirement from sport (Brewer 1993, Brewer, Van Raalte & Linder 1993; Horton & Mack 2000; Sparkes 1998). To explain this, Brewer et al. (1993) hypothesised that a strong athletic identity might force an athlete to neglect other aspects of life in order to fulfil the athlete role. Confirming this hypothesis, Brewer (1993) showed that athletes' affective responses (defined as depressed mood) to both hypothetical and actual athletic injuries were higher when the athletic identity was stronger and more exclusive. Similarly, an idiographic study by Grove, Lavallee and Gordon (1997) showed how detrimental a permanent termination of athletic career can be to a person with a strong and exclusive athletic identity.

There is evidence, however, that a strong athletic identity may be beneficial. In a sample of marathon runners, Horton and Mack (2000) showed that high athletic identity was associated with better performance, greater commitment to running, and an expanded social network. The same study found that runners with high athletic identity reported both positive and negative aspects of marathon training more frequently than those with lower athletic identity. This finding is mixed news, although consistent with the predictions of self-complexity theory.

STRESS, RESILIENCE AND VULNERABILITY

Sport is inherently unpredictable. A very thin line often separates winning from losing. In many professional sports there is a lot at stake for the competitors, as well as coaching and support staff. Lucrative contracts may be won or lost in matches decided by judgement calls and other uncontrollable factors. Such an environment can be very stressful. In this section we will examine some of the factors that may 'protect' an individual from the various negative psychosocial and physical outcomes associated with stress and sport.

Athletic careers are filled with fluctuations of fortune that allow athletes to experience both the highs of victory and the lows of defeat or poor performances. Recall the examples of Morales and Ormsby at the beginning of this chapter. Their stories offer just two extreme and well-known examples of individual response to poor athletic performance. Given the uncertainty of outcome that is the nature of sporting events, what leads individuals to produce dramatically different responses to failure? Why is it that some people are able to bounce back from adversity, while others simply give up or drop out? It is clear that failure can be either motivating or disruptive depending on how one deals with it.

The widely variable ability to cope with adversity is, at least in part, due to the existence of moderator variables — that is, characteristics of persons or their environments that make them more or less vulnerable to the negative effects of stressful life events (Anthony 1987). The variables that moderate a behavioural response to a stressful situation can help us understand why one person reacts with negative symptoms to an objectively minor event, while others maintain their composure even when facing major disruptions. According to Rutter (1987), resilience refers to a set of protective factors that have the capacity to improve a person's typically maladaptive responses to environmental hazards. Braddock, Royster, Winfield and Hawkins (1991) employed the term in a similarly general way, conceptualising it as an individual's positive response to situations of stress and adversity. This perspective presents resilience as a protective mechanism that is thought to emerge from specific personality characteristics, such as self-esteem, self-complexity or adaptive coping resources and strategies. In general, resilient persons are believed to possess the ability to remain unaffected by adversity or — more realistically — to rebound from it and carry on, to bounce back and get on with life.

A review of research into stress-resistant individuals by Garmezy (1987) identified three broad sets of variables that promote resilience: individual factors, social factors and other external support mechanisms. Personality characteristics (self-esteem), social factors (family and peer support) and the availability of coping resources contribute to individuals' ability to develop problem-solving strategies needed to achieve an optimal response to adversity. A recent meta-analytic review (Crawford et al. 1998) identified a number of specific factors that contribute to a resilient response (see figure 1.6).

Resilience in sport

The examination of performance slumps is one way of studying resilience in sport. The study of success after failure in sport is not new. Performance slumps (Taylor 1988) are behavioural manifestations of extended poor performance, which may be caused by physical or technical changes within the individual. However, the individual's ability to cope with these extended periods of poor performance has a number of known psychological precursors. For example, Grove and Heard (1997) found that dispositional optimism and sport confidence were positively related to the use of problem-focused strategies (typically classed as adaptive) and negatively related to the use of emotion-focused coping strategies (classed as maladaptive). Underlying the study of psychological precursors of performance slumps is the desire to reverse the extended poor performance trend by inoculating the individuals against the negative consequences of the initial poor performance, and by effectively using a range of mental skills.

INDIVIDUAL FACTORS	SOCIAL FACTORS
• Positive self-perception	• **Family factors**
• Coping style	– Social support from family
• Self-esteem	– Both parents attend dinner
• Self-concept	– Family composition
• Explanatory style/locus of control	– Parental education
• Intelligence	– Parental substance use
• Sensation seeking	– Parents' marital status
• Perceived competence	– Positive father–adolescent relations
• Various socio-demographics (age, ethnicity, gender, gender role)	– Positive mother–adolescent relations
• Low anxiety	• **Factors outside the family**
• Career/educational goal and stage	– Communication with significant adult
	– Mentorship experiences
	– Social support from peers
	– Participation in sport

Figure 1.6 Resilience as a combination of protective factors that modify, ameliorate, or alter a person's response to environmental hazards

There is evidence that a single poor performance may trigger poor performances in the future. Seligman, Nolen-Hoeksema, Thornton and Thornton (1990) administered measures of attributional style to predict swimming performance after perceived failure. As part of the study the researchers manipulated performance feedback given to a group of college swimmers to induce perceptions of relative success or failure. They found that participants exhibiting negative or pessimistic attributional patterns experienced greater reduction in subsequent performance efforts following perceived failure than did their optimistic counterparts.

The term resilience has been predominantly used in sport-related literature with regard to sport injuries (Patterson, Smith, Everett & Ptacek 1998; Smith, Smoll & Ptacek 1990; Smith, Ptacek & Patterson 2000). In this context resilience has mostly been operationalised in terms of the time required to return to competition (or participation) following injury. Smith et al. (1990) studied the moderating effects of social support and psychological coping skills on the total number of days of non-participation due to sport-related injury in a sample of adolescent athletes. The results indicated that individuals who had low levels of social support combined with low coping skills took longer to recover from injury. Similar results were found by Patterson et al. (1998) in their study of injury resilience in ballet dancers. Finally, Smith (2000) showed that trait anxiety may be a contributing factor in ballet dancers' vulnerability to injury (defined through injury time loss).

In a recent extension of resilience research, participation in sport and physical activity has itself been emphasised as an independent variable, which may help to protect against negative life outcomes. This is consistent with the traditional health psychology model of resilience and health-protective factors. In particular, a recent review (O'Neal, Dunn & Martinsen 2000) found that physical activity may reduce an individual's risk of suffering from depression. Similarly, Tomori and Zalar (2000) found a relationship between self-reported suicide attempts and sport-related attitudes and behaviours among adolescents. Overall, attempted suicide reports were associated with attitudes that sport is not important for health. Further, suicide risk factors included non-involvement in sport in girls and low frequency of sport activity in boys (Tomori & Zalar 2000).

The protective effects of sport and physical activity have also been shown in intervention studies (e.g. McClendon, Nettles & Wigfield, 2000). This study noted several positive outcomes of the Promoting Achievement in School through Sport (PASS) program. The program was specifically designed to promote resilience through the transfer of coping skills learned in the sporting environment to the academic environment. It may be argued that such resilience qualities can be generalised even further.

FUTURE DIRECTIONS

One of the greatest challenges facing future research on personality in sport is the issue of measurement. In particular, impression management, unintentional distortions and other limitations of self-report methodology have highlighted the need for alternative measurement approaches, such as projective testing, and cognitive and behavioural assessment, which are likely to be the growth areas in future research on personality and individual differences in sport. Further development and refinement of the instruments measuring self-concept and self-complexity can also be anticipated.

Research on stress, resilience and vulnerability in sport has suffered from definitional circularity. Negative events have often been defined as those with observable adverse consequences. As a result, athletes who were able to cope successfully tended to be excluded from studies. Future research will need to close this gap, as well as refine the operational definitions of resilient responses. One can also expect terminological refinements on the *vulnerability–resilience* continuum. The term *hardiness* has often been used to describe stress-resistant individuals (e.g. Ford, Eklund & Gordon, 2000), but its status as an independent predictor is often confused with one of an outcome variable.

Overall, research on personality in sport seems to have accumulated sufficient critical mass to convert it into quality, hypothesis-driven research programs. An emphasis on theory and sound conceptual models can be expected, with particular attention to the 'person vs situation' controversy, specific analyses of direct and interactive personality effects, and a clearer distinction between long-term and 'here-and-now' performance predictions.

CONCLUSIONS

Following recent developments in mainstream personality and individual differences research, the field of 'sports personology' is poised to embrace — and benefit from — a unified taxonomy of personality descriptions. The big five personality factors model provides solid grounds for the streamlining of operational definitions, refining the measurement protocols and focusing the creative research effort on the production of substantive, theory-driven predictions. In particular, evidence is mounting in support of conscientiousness as a long-term predictor of athletic achievement and emotional stability/neuroticism as a key factor moderating situational influences (e.g. contest intensity, level of stress) on individual performances.

The combination of the progressively aligned personality description models with the converging empirical evidence connecting these descriptions with key elements of sport behaviour is a promising indicator that our understanding of personality from the observer/spectator perspective is approaching what Kuhn (1970) termed 'paradigmatic' knowledge that characterises advanced scientific disciplines. This may yet be only an early indication, but it is clearly ahead of our knowledge about 'personality from the actor perspective', which is largely based on the notions of *self* and *identity*.

The idea of personal self in sport and exercise psychology remains somewhat fragmented. When studying the relationship between self and sport, one needs to consider how the multiple facets of self — and not just physical self — contribute to individual behaviour in sporting environments. In particular, researching athletic identity is likely to benefit from considerations of self-complexity in order to advance a fuller understanding of the connection between self-concept and affect in sport.

SUMMARY

Personality does matter when important things in life are at stake. Despite some enduring bouts of scepticism about this intuitive conviction, it has been thoroughly supported in relation to a number of important life outcomes such as academic performance, vocational choice, job performance and satisfaction, and even life expectancy. Research summarised in this chapter confirms the validity of this observation in sport psychology: personality factors exert a profound influence on sport behaviour, including such critical outcomes as individual performance, reaction to failure and long-term athletic achievement. In order to detect these influences, however, one needs to combine the intimate knowledge of sport with sharp, theory-driven conceptual predictions and refined methodology that take into account the predominantly long-term and moderating effects of personality in sport.

REVIEW QUESTIONS

1 Compare and contrast the actor and observer perspectives on personality. Which is more complex?

2 What is the difference between identity and reputation? How are the two connected?

3 What are the main assumptions of self-report personality assessment? What are the alternatives?

4 Why is the role of personality traits more visible in long-term predictions?

5 How do moderating effects of personality on athletic performance operate?

6 What factors are important in rebounding after an adverse event?

7 Is there any evidence that involvement in sport and exercise itself might protect against negative life events?

8 Why is a complex view of the self beneficial?

9 How can a complex self-concept be detrimental to an elite-level athlete?

References

Aidman, EV 1996, 'Apperceptive categorisation of humour in the assessment of motivation and personality: preliminary validation', paper presented at 15th International Conference on Personality Assessment, Melbourne, March.

Aidman, EV 1997, *Humour Apperception Test: technical manual*, InterMind Consulting, Melbourne.

Aidman, EV 1998, 'Analysing global dimensions of self-esteem: factorial structure and reliability of the Self-Liking/Self-Competence Scale', *Personality and Individual Differences*, 24, 735–7.

Aidman, EV 1999, 'Measuring individual differences in implicit self-concept: initial validation of the Self-Apperception Test', *Personality and Individual Differences*, 27 (1) 211–28.

Aidman, EV 2000, 'Converting ability into achievement: personality factors in long term prediction of elite junior players' transition into senior AFL competition', paper presented at 2000 APS Conference, Canberra, 2–6 October (abstracted in *Australian Journal of Psychology*, 52, 66).

Aidman, EV & Bekerman, M 2001, 'Predicting achievement and performance in Australian Rules football: the role of self-concept, emotional stability, achievement orientation and stress appraisal', paper presented at 10th World Congress of Sport Psychology, Skiathos, Greece, 28 May–2 June.

Aidman, EV & Carroll, SM 2003, 'Implicit individual differences: relationships between implicit self-esteem, gender identity and gender attitudes', *European Journal of Personality*, 17, 19–37.

Aidman, EV & Perry, C Jr 2000, 'Declared versus implicit self-esteem in elite swimmers: exploring conceptual distinctions between self-report and indirect measurement of self-appraisal', paper presented at 2000 APS Conference, Canberra, 2–6 October.

Aidman, EV & Shmelyov, AG 2002, 'Mimics: a symbolic conflict/cooperation simulation program, with embedded protocol recording and automatic psychometric assessment', *Behavior Research Methods, Instruments & Computers*, 34 (1) 83–9.

Aidman, EV & Woollard, S 2003, 'The influence of self-reported exercise addiction on acute emotional and physiological responses to brief exercise deprivation', *Psychology of Sport & Exercise*, 4 (3) 225–36.

Allport, GW 1961, *Pattern and growth in personality*, Holt, Rinehart & Winston, New York.

Anthony, EJ 1987, 'Risk, vulnerability and resilience: an overview, in EJ Anthony & B Kohler (eds), *The invulnerable child*, Guildford Press, New York, pp. 3–48.

Apitzsch, E 1995, 'Psychodynamic theory of personality and sport performance', in SJH Biddle (ed.), *European perspectives on exercise and sport psychology*, Human Kinetics, United Kingdom, pp. 111–27.

Bandura, A 1982, 'Self-efficacy mechanism in human agency', *American Psychologist*, 37, 122–47.

Bandura, A 1991, 'Human agency: the rhetoric and the reality', *American Psychologist*, 46 (2) 157–62.

Barrick, MR & Mount, MK 1991, 'The big five personality dimensions and job performance: a meta-analysis', *Personnel Psychology*, 44, 1–26.

Baumeister, RF 1991, *Escaping the self: alcoholism, spirituality, machoism, and other flights from the burden of selfhood*, Basic Books, New York.

Baumeister, RF 1999, 'Low self-esteem does not cause aggression', *Monitor of the American Psychological Association*, January, p. 7.

Bond, JW & Nideffer, RM 1992, 'Attentional and interpersonal characteristics of elite Australian athletes', *Excel*, 8, 101–10.

Borkenau, P 1988, 'The multiple classification of acts and the big five factors of personality', *Journal of Research in Personality*, 22 (3) 337–52.

Braddock, JH, Royster, DA, Winfield, LF & Hawkins, R 1991, 'Bouncing back: sports and academic resilience among African-American males', *Education and Urban Society*, 24, 113–31.

Brewer, BW 1993, 'Self-identity and specific vulnerability to depressed mood, *Journal of Personality*, 61 (3) 343–64.

Brewer, BW, Van Raalte, JL & Linder, DE 1993, 'Athletic identity: Hercules' muscles or Achilles heel?', *International Journal of Sport Psychology*, 24 (2) 237–54.

Brown, DR, Morgan, WP & Kihlstrom, JF 1989, 'Comparison of test construction strategies in an attempt to develop an athletic potential scale', *International Journal of Sport Psychology*, 20, 93–113.

Butcher, JN (ed.) 1995, *Clinical personality assessment: practical approaches*, Oxford University Press, New York.

Butler, RJ & Hardy, L 1992, 'The performance profile: theory and application', *The Sport Psychologist*, 6, 253–64.

Cattell, RB, Cattell, RGB & Cattell, HEP 1993, *16PF, fifth edition*, Institute for Personality and Ability Testing, Champaign, IL.

Cattell, RB, Eber, HW & Tatsuoka, M 1970, *Handbook for the Sixteen Personality Factors questionnaire (16PF)*, Institute of Personality and Ability Testing, Champaign, IL.

Cohen, RJ, Swerdlik, ME & Phillips, SM 1996, *Psychological testing and assessment*, Mayfield Publishing Company, Mountain View, CA.

Cohn, PJ 1991, 'An exploratory study on peak performance in golf', *The Sport Psychologist*, 5, 1–14.

Costa, PT Jr & McCrae, RR 1992, *NEO PI-R professional manual*, Psychological Assessment Resources, Odessa, FL.

Crawford, C, Ho, R, Lietz, P, Mummery, K & Schofield, G 1998, 'You've lost ... so you give up?', paper presented at the 'Issues of Regional Youth' conference, Mackay, Qld.

Daus, AT, Wilson, J & Freeman, WM 1986, 'Psychological testing as an auxiliary means of selecting successful college and professional football players', *Journal of Sports Medicine*, 26, 274–8.

Davis, C & Mogk, JP 1994, 'Some personality correlates of interest and excellence in sport', *International Journal of Sport Psychology*, 25, 131–43.

Deary, IJ & Matthews, G 1993, 'Personality traits are alive and well', *The Sport Psychologist*, 6, 299–311.

Diamant, L, Byrd, JH & Himelein, MJ 1991, 'Personality traits and athletic performance', in L Diamant (ed.), *Mind-body maturity: psychological approaches to sports, exercise, and fitness*, Hemisphere Publishing Corporation, New York, pp. 227–36.

Digman, JM 1989, 'Five robust trait dimensions: development, stability and utility', *Journal of Personality*, 57, 195–214.

Digman, JM 1997, 'Higher-order factors of the big five', *Journal of Personality and Social Psychology*, 73 (6) 1246–56.

Digman, JM & Takemoto-Chock, NK 1981, 'Factors in the natural language of personality: re-analysis, comparison and interpretation of six major studies', *Multivariate Behaviour Research*, 16, 149–70.

Dixon, TM & Baumeister, RF 1991, 'Escaping the self: the moderating effect of self-complexity', *Personality and Social Psychology Bulletin*, 17 (4) 363–8.

Draycott, SG & Kline, P 1995, 'The big three or the big five — the EPQ-R vs the NEO-PI: a research note, replication and elaboration', *Personality and Individual Differences*, 18, 801–4.

Egloff, B & Jan Gruhn, A 1996, 'Personality and endurance sports', *Personality and Individual Differences*, 21 (2) 223–9.

Evans, V & Quarterman, J 1983, 'Personality characteristics of successful and unsuccessful black female basketball players', *International Journal of Sport Psychology*, 14, 105–15.

Exner, JE 1993, *The Rorschach: a comprehensive system, volume 1, basic foundations*, 3rd edn, John Wiley & Sons, New York.

Eysenck, HJ 1967, *The biological basis of personality*, Charles C Thomas, Springfield, IL.

Eysenck, HJ 1995, 'Science and psychology of sport: the place of theory', *Sportonomics*, 1 (1) 3–9.

Eysenck, HJ & Eysenck, MW 1985, *Personality and individual differences: a natural science approach*, Plenum, New York.

Eysenck, HJ & Eysenck, SBG 1991, *Manual for the EPQ-R*, Hodder & Stoughton, Sevenoaks, UK.

Eysenck, HJ, Nias, DK & Cox, DN 1982, 'Sport and personality', *Advances in Behaviour Research and Therapy*, 4 (1) 1–56.

Farnham, SD, Greenwald, AG & Banaji, MR 1999, 'Implicit self-esteem', in D Abrams & MA Hogg (eds), *Social cognition and social identity*, Blackwell, London, pp. 230–48.

Ferguson, E, Sanders, A, O'Hehir, F & James, D 2000, 'Predictive validity of personal statements and the role of the five-factor model of personality in relation to medical training', *Journal of Occupational and Organizational Psychology*, 73 (3) 321–44.

Fisher, AC 1984, 'New direction in sport personality research', in JM Silva III & RS Weinberg (eds), *Psychological foundations of sport*, Human Kinetics, Champaign IL, pp. 70–80.

Fisher, AC, Horsfall, JS & Morris, HH 1977, 'Sport personality assessment: a methodological reexamination', *International Journal of Sport Psychology*, 8 (2) 92–102.

Ford, IW, Eklund, RC & Gordon, S 2000, 'An examination of psychosocial variables moderating the relationship between life stress and injury time-loss among athletes of a high standard, *Journal of Sports Sciences*, 18 (5) 301–12.

Frank, LK 1939, 'Projective methods for the study of personality', *Journal of Psychology*, 8, 389–413.

Franken, RE, Hill, R & Kierstad, J 1994, 'Sport interest as predicted by the personality measures of competitiveness, mastery, instrumentality, expressivity, and sensation-seeking, *Personality and Individual Differences*, 17 (4) 467–76.

Freud, S 1949, *An outline of psychoanalysis*, Norton, New York.

Garfield, CA & Bennet, HZ 1984, *Peak performance: mental training techniques of the world's greatest athletes*, Jeremy P. Tarcher, Los Angeles.

Garmezy, N 1987, 'Stress, competence, and development: continuities in the study of schizophrenic adults, children vulnerable to psychopathology and the search for stress resilient children', *American Journal of Orthopsychiatry*, 57, 159–74.

Gould, D, Weiss, M & Weinberg, R 1981, 'Psychological characteristics of successful and nonsuccessful big ten wrestlers', *Journal of Sport Psychology*, 3, 69–81.

Greenberg, H & Greenberg, J 1992, 'Predicting athletic performance: psychology of a winner', *USA Today Magazine*, 121 (2568) 90–3.

Greenwald, AG & Banaji, R 1995, 'Implicit social cognition: attitudes, self-esteem and stereotypes', *Psychological Review*, 102 (1) 4–27.

Greenwald, AG & Farnham, SD 2000, 'Using the Implicit Association Test to measure self-esteem and self-concept', *Journal of Personality and Social Psychology*, 79 (6) 1022–38.

Grove, JR & Heard, NP 1997, 'Optimism and sport confidence as correlates of slump related coping among athletes', *The Sport Psychologist*, 11, 400–10.

Grove, JR, Lavallee, D & Gordon, S 1997, 'Coping with retirement from sport: the influence of athletic identity', *Journal of Applied Sport Psychology*, 9 (2) 191–203.

Hardy, CJ 1990, 'Social loafing: motivational losses in collective performance', *International Journal of Sport Psychology*, 21 (4) 305–27.

Highlen, PS & Bennett, BB 1979, 'Psychological characteristics of successful and non-successful elite wrestlers: an exploratory study', *Journal of Sport Psychology*, 1, 123–37.

Hogan, R 1998, 'Reinventing personality', *Journal of Social and Clinical Psychology*, 17 (1) 1–10.

Hogan, R & Shelton, D 1998, 'A socioanalytic perspective on job performance', *Human Performance*, 11 (2–3) 129–44.

Horsley, C 1995, 'Confidence and sporting performance', in T Morris & J Summers (eds), *Sport psychology: theory, applications and issues*, John Wiley & Sons, Brisbane, pp. 311–38.

Horton, RS & Mack, DE 2000, 'Athletic identity in marathon runners: functional focus or dysfunctional commitment?', *Journal of Sport Behavior*, 23 (2) 101–19.

Kalthoff, RA & Neimeyer, RA 1993, 'Self-complexity and psychological distress: a test of the buffering model', *International Journal of Personal Construct Psychology*, 6 (4) 327–49.

Kelly, GA 1955, *The psychology of personal constructs*, Norton, New York.

Kihlstrom, J 1999, 'The rediscovery of the unconscious', keynote address presented at the 34th Conference of the Australian Psychological Society, Hobart, Tasmania, September.

Kirkcaldy, BD 1982, 'Personality profiles at various levels of athletic participation', *Personality and Individual Differences*, 3, 321–6.

Knoff, HM 1990, 'Evaluation of projective drawings', in CR Reynolds & TB Gutkin (eds), *Handbook of school psychology*, 2nd edn, John Wiley & Sons, New York, pp. 898–946.

Krane, V & Williams, J 1987, 'Performance and somatic anxiety, cognitive anxiety, and confidence changes prior to competition', *Journal of Sport Behavior*, 10 (1) 47–56.

Kroll, W & Petersen, KH 1965, 'Personality factor profiles of collegiate football teams', *Research Quarterly*, 36, 433.

Kroll, WP & Crenshaw, W 1968, 'Multivariate personality profile analysis of four athletic groups', in G Kenyon (ed.), *Contemporary psychology of sport*, Athletic Institute, Chicago.

Kuhn, TS 1970, *The structure of scientific revolutions*, 2nd edn, University of Chicago Press, Chicago.

Landers, DM & Boutcher, SH 1998, 'Arousal-performance relationships', in JM Williams (ed.), *Applied sport psychology: personal growth to peak performance*, 3rd edn, Mayfield, Mountain View, CA.

Linville, PW 1985, 'Self-complexity and affective extremity: don't put all of your eggs in one cognitive basket', *Social Cognition*, 3 (1) 94–120.

Linville, PW 1987, 'Self-complexity as a cognitive buffer against stress-related illness and depression', *Journal of Personality and Social Psychology*, 52 (4) 663–6.

Loehr, JE 1982, *Athletic excellence: mental toughness training for sports*, Forum, Denver, CO.

Marsh, H 1994, 'The importance of being important: theoretical models of relations between specific and global components of physical self-concept', *Journal of Sport & Exercise Psychology*, 16, 306–25.

Martin, JJ & Gill, DL 1991, 'The relationships among competitive orientation, sport-confidence and self-efficacy, anxiety and performance', *Journal of Sport & Exercise Psychology*, 13, 149–59.

Maslow, A 1970, *Motivation and personality*, 2nd edn, Harper & Row, New York.

McClendon, C, Nettles, SM & Wigfield, A 2000, 'Fostering resilience in high school classrooms: a study of the PASS program (Promoting Achievement in School through Sport)', in MG Sanders (ed.), *Schooling students placed at risk: research, policy, and practice in the education of poor and minority adolescents*, Lawrence Erlbaum, Mahwah, NJ, pp. 289–307.

McCrae, RR & Costa, PT, Jr 1985, 'Validation of the five-factor model of personality across instruments and observers', *Journal of Personality and Social Psychology*, 52, 81–90.

Meagher, BE & Aidman, EV 2001, 'Self-esteem and sensitivity to negative feedback: the role of individual differences in implicit and declared self-attitudes', paper presented at 1st Australian Conference on Individual Differences, Woollongong, NSW, 15 February.

Meagher, B & Aidman, E (in press), 'Individual differences in implicit and declared self-esteem as predictors of response to negative performance evaluation: validating Implicit Association Test as a measure of self-attitudes', *International Journal of Testing*.

Messer, B & Harter, S 1986, *Manual for the Self-Perception Profile*, University of Denver, Denver, CO.

Morgan, WP 1968, 'Personality characteristics of wrestlers participating in the world championships', *Journal of Sport Medicine*, 8, 212–16.

Morgan, WP 1979, 'Prediction of performance in athletics', in P Klavora & JV Daniel (eds), *Coach, athlete, and the sport psychologist*, University of Toronto, Toronto, pp. 173–86.

Morgan, WP 1980a, 'The trait psychology controversy', *Research Quarterly for Exercise and Sport*, 51, 50–76.

Morgan, WP 1980b, 'Test of champions: the iceberg profile', *Psychology Today*, July, pp. 92–9.

Morgan, WP & Hammer, WM 1974, 'Influence of competitive wrestling upon state anxiety', *Medical Science and Sports*, 6, 58–61.

Morgan, WP & Johnson, RW 1978, 'Personality characteristics of successful and unsuccessful oarsmen', *International Journal of Sport Psychology*, 9, 119–33.

Morgan, WP, O'Connor, PJ, Ellickson, KA & Bradley, PW 1988, 'Personality structure, mood states, and performance in elite distance runners', *International Journal of Sport Psychology*, 19, 247–63.

Morris, T 1995, 'Psychological characteristics and sports behaviour', in T Morris & J Summers (eds), *Sport psychology: theory, applications and issues*, John Wiley & Sons, Brisbane, pp. 3–27.

Murray, HA 1943, *Thematic Apperception Test manual*, Harvard University Press, Cambridge, MA.

Neimeyer, RA 1985, 'Personal constructs in clinical practice', in PC Kendall (ed.), *Advances in cognitive-behavioural research and therapy*, vol. 4, Academic Press, New York, pp. 275–339.

Niedenthal, PM, Setterlund, MB & Wherry, MB 1992, 'Possible self-complexity and affective reactions to goal-relevant evaluation', *Journal of Personality and Social Psychology*, 63 (1) 5–16.

O'Neal, HA, Dunn, AL & Martinsen, EW 2000, 'Depression and exercise', *International Journal of Sport Psychology*, 31 (2) 110–35.

Orlick, T & Partington, J 1988, 'Mental links to excellence', *The Sport Psychologist*, 2, 105–30.

Patterson, EL, Smith, RE, Everett, JJ & Ptacek, JT 1998, 'Psychosocial factors as predictors of ballet injuries: interactive effects of life stress and social support', *Journal of Sport Behavior*, 21, 101–12.

Perry, C Jr & Marsh, HW 2000, 'Listening to self-talk, hearing self-concept', in M Andersen (ed.), *Doing sport psychology*, Human Kinetics, Champaign, IL, pp. 61–76.

Pervin, LA 1996, *The science of personality*, John Wiley & Sons, New York.

Phares, EJ & Chaplin, WF 1997, *Introduction to personality*, Longman, New York.

Piedmont, RL, Hill, DC & Blanco, S 1999, 'Predicting athletic performance using the five-factor model of personality', *Personality and Individual Differences*, 27, 769–77.

Rafaeli Mor, E, Gotlib, IH & Revelle, W 1999, 'The meaning and measurement of self-complexity', *Personality and Individual Differences*, 27 (2) 341–56.

Ravizza, K 1977, 'Peak experiences in sport', *Journal of Humanistic Psychology*, 17, 35–40.

Raymark, PH & Schmit, MJ 1997, 'Identifying potentially useful personality constructs for employee selection', *Personnel Psychology*, 50 (3) 723–37.

Renger, R 1993, 'A review of the profile of mood states (POMS) in the prediction of athletic success', *Journal of Applied Sport Psychology*, 5, 78–84.

Robertson, IT, Baron, H, Gibbons, P, MacIvor, R & Nyfield, G 2000, 'Conscientiousness and managerial performance', *Journal of Occupational and Organizational Psychology*, 73 (2) 171–81.

Rodman, D & Keown, T 1996, *Bad as I wanna be*, Bantam, New York.

Rogers, C 1980, *A way of being*, Houghton Mifflin, Boston.

Rosenberg, M 1979, *Conceiving the self*, Basic Books, New York.

Rosenzweig, S 1945, 'The picture-association method and its applications in a study of reactions to frustration', *Journal of Personality*, 14, 3–23.

Rotter, JB & Rafferty, JE 1950, *The manual for the Rotter Incomplete Sentences Blank*, New York: Psychological Corporation, New York.

Rowley, AJ, Landers, DM, Kyllo, B & Etner, JL 1995, 'Does the iceberg profile discriminate between successful and less successful athletes? A meta-analysis', *Journal of Sport & Exercise Psychology*, 17, 185–99.

Rutter, M 1987, 'Psychosocial resilience and protective mechanisms', *American Journal of Orthopsychiatry*, 57, 316–31.

Sadalla, EK, Linder, DE & Jenkins, BA 1988, 'Sport preference: a self-presentational analysis, *Journal of Sport & Exercise Psychology*, 10, 214–22.

Schurr, KT, Ashley, MA & Joy, KL 1977, 'A multivariate analysis of male athlete characteristics: sport type and success', *Multivariate Experimental Clinical Research*, 3, 53–68.

Schurr, KT, Ruble D, Nisbet MA & Wallace, DE 1984, 'Myers-Briggs type inventory characteristics of more and less successful players on an American football team', *Journal of Sport Behaviour*, 7, 47–57.

Seligman, ME, Nolen-Hoeksema, S, Thornton, N & Thornton, KM 1990, 'Explanatory style as a mechanism of disappointing athletic performance', *Psychological Science*, 1 (2) 143–6.

Shoda, Y, Mischel, W & Wright, JC 1994, 'Intraindividual stability in the organization and patterning of behaviour: Incorporating psychological situations into the idiographic analysis of personality', *Journal of Personality and Social Psychology*, 67, 674–87.

Showers, CJ, Abramson, LY & Hogan, ME 1998, 'The dynamic self: how the content and structure of the self-concept change with mood', *Journal of Personality and Social Psychology*, 75 (2) 478–93.

Silva, JM 1984, 'Personality and sport performance: controversy and challenge', in JM Silva & RS Weinberg (eds), *Psychological foundations of sport*, Human Kinetics, Champaign, IL, pp. 59–69.

Singer, RN 1986, *Peak performance ... and more*, Mouvement Publications, Ithaca, NY.

Singer, RN 1988, 'Psychological testing: what value to coaches and athletes?', *International Journal of Sport Psychology*, 19, 87–106.

Smith, RE & Christensen, DS 1995, 'Psychological skills as predictors of performance and survival in professional baseball', *Journal of Sport and Exercise Psychology*, 17, 399–415.

Smith, RE, Ptacek JT & Patterson E 2000, 'Moderator effects of cognitive and somatic trait anxiety on the relation between life stress and physical injuries', *Anxiety, Stress & Coping: An International Journal*, 13 (3) 269–88.

Smith, RE, Smoll, FL & Ptacek, JT 1990, 'Conjunctive moderator variables in vulnerability and resiliency research: life stress, social support and coping skills, and adolescent sport injuries', *Journal of Personality and Social Psychology*, 58 (2) 360–70.

Sonstroem, RJ & Bernardo, P 1982, 'Intraindividual pregame state anxiety and basketball performance: a re-examination of the inverted-U curve', *Journal of Sport Psychology*, 4 (3) 235–45.

Sparkes, AC 1998, 'Athletic identity: an Achilles' heel to the survival of self', *Qualitative Health Research*, 8 (5) 644–64.

Stroot, EA 1999, 'Self-complexity and adjustment to the first semester of college', unpublished PhD thesis, University of Delaware, Delaware.

Sutton, J 1994, 'Aggression and violence', in J McKnight & J Sutton (eds), *Social psychology*, Prentice Hall, Sydney, pp. 303–58.

Tafarodi, RW 1998, 'Paradoxical self-esteem and selectivity in the processing of social information', *Journal of Personality and Social Psychology*, 74 (5) 1181–96.

Tafarodi, RW & Swann, WB 1995, 'Self-liking and self-competence as dimensionality of global self-esteem: initial validation of a measure', *Journal of Personality Assessment*, 65, 322–42.

Tafarodi, RW & Vu, C 1997, 'Two-dimensional self-esteem and reactions to success and failure', *Personality and Social Psychology Bulletin*, 33, 626–35.

Taylor, J 1988, 'Slumpbusting: a systematic analysis of slumps in sports, *The Sport Psychologist*, 2, 39–48.

Tenenbaum, G & Bar-Eli, M 1995, 'Personality and intellectual capabilities in sport psychology', in DH Saklofske & M Zeidner (eds), *International handbook of personality and intelligence*, Plenum Press, New York, pp. 687–710.

Terry, P 1995, 'The efficacy of mood state profiling with elite performers: a review and synthesis', *The Sport Psychologist*, 9, 309–24.

Tomori, M & Zalar, B 2000, 'Sport and physical activity as possible protective factors in relation to adolescent suicide attempts', *International Journal of Sport Psychology*, 31 (3) 405–13.

Vealey, RS 1989, Sport personology: a paradigmatic and methodological analysis', *Journal of Sport & Exercise Psychology*, 11, 216–35.

Vealey, RS 1992, 'Personality and sport: a comprehensive overview', in TS Horn (ed.), *Advances in sport psychology*, Human Kinetics, Kingswood, pp. 25–59.

Williams, JM 1986, 'Psychological characteristics of peak performance', in JM Williams (ed.), *Applied sport psychology*, Mayfield, Palo Alto, CA, pp. 123–31.

Williams, JM & Krane, V 1998, 'Psychological characteristics of peak performance', in JM Williams (ed.), *Applied sport psychology: personal growth to peak performance*, Mayfield, Palo Alto, CA.

Williams, LRT & Parkin, WA 1980, 'Personality factor profiles of three hockey groups', *International Journal of Sport Psychology*, 11, 113.

Wolfe, RN & Johnson, SD 1995, 'Personality as a predictor of college performance', *Educational and Psychological Measurement*, 55 (2) 177–84.

Zuckerman, M, Miyake, K, Osborne, JJ & Koestner, R 1991, 'Some new moderator variables, *Differential Assessment of Persons: A Methodological and Substantive Reappraisal. APA Division 5 Invited Symposium. The Score*, XIII (4) 5–6.

CHAPTER 2

MOOD AND EMOTIONS IN SPORT

Peter C Terry

Sport generates powerful emotional responses among participants and spectators alike. The sight of professional soccer players and their supporters overwhelmed by euphoria or reduced to despair during penalty shoot-outs is testament to this fact. There is also strong anecdotal and scientific evidence that the emotions experienced by athletes before and during sport performance have a profound effect on the quality of their performances (Jones & Hardy 1990; Hanin 2000). The purpose of this chapter, which is divided into four sections, is to explore the nature of the link between emotional responses and sport performance.

The first section considers conceptual issues, in particular the distinction between the related constructs of emotion and mood, and presents some of the conceptual models put forward by theoreticians. The second section looks at measurement issues, giving an overview of the different measures available and discussing some of the variables that influence mood responses. The third section synthesises research on the relationship between mood and athletic performance. The fourth section explores a range of mood management strategies.

CONCEPTUAL ISSUES

A necessary first step in the exploration and elaboration of any psychological construct is to establish conceptual clarity; to answer the question 'what exactly are we talking about here?'

Definitions and distinctions

According to Richard Lazarus, after half a century of research in the area, emotion represents one-third of what he terms the 'trilogy of mind', sharing a complex interaction and interdependence with cognition and motivation to shape human functioning. Lazarus (1999) proposed that, in general terms, emotion is a response to the meaning we attach to our interactions with the environment — meaning that results from cognitive processes and is mediated by personal motives.

Describing emotion in more specific terms, Ekman (1999) proposed several characteristics of basic emotions that help distinguish emotions from one another and from other related phenomena such as moods or emotional traits. First, emotions are seen to have *distinctive universal signals*, such as the facial expressions associated with anger or hostility. By contrast, moods and emotional traits are not necessarily associated with such distinctive signals but instead tend to be inferred from the signals of one or several emotions. The second proposed characteristic of basic emotions is their *specific physiology*; that is, distinctive patterns of activity in the autonomic nervous system are associated with different emotions, such as those shown for anger, fear and disgust (Ekman, Levensen & Friesen 1983; Levensen, Ekman & Friesen 1990) and sadness (Levensen, Carstensen, Friesen & Ekman 1991). The third proposed characteristic is an *automatic appraisal mechanism*, whereby a particular stimulus (perhaps a thought or something said by another person) produces an emotional response almost immediately and without conscious consideration, whereas other emotional responses are more consciously appraised and depend on the meaning attached to the incident. For example, disgust may result from appraising a comment as offensive. The fourth proposed characteristic of basic emotions is that of *universal antecedent events*. This refers to the notion of common antecedents for specific emotions; for example, concern about physical or psychological harm is a common antecedent for fear (Boucher 1983).

Ekman (1999) ventured further on the nature of emotions to highlight their rapidity of onset, their relatively short duration (in the realm of minutes and seconds rather than hours and days), and the uniqueness of the subjective feelings and physical sensations associated with different emotions. He proposed that moods 'have different causes and last much longer, and are highly saturated with emotions' (p. 55). Ellis and Moore (1999, p. 193) distinguished an emotion as 'having the properties of a reaction, sometimes an intense response to a specific stimulus', whereas mood is 'a more subtle, longer-lasting and less intense experience (that) tends to be more general or non-specific'.

Considering moods from a functional perspective, Parkinson, Totterdell, Briner and Reynolds (1996) argued that they 'reflect changing, non-specific psychological dispositions to evaluate, interpret, and act on past, current, or future concerns in certain patterned ways' (p. 216). Further, Morris (1992) suggested that a person's mood signals the likelihood of success or failure in dealings with the environment and plays an adaptive role in mobilising personal resources to cope with environmental demands (see also Batson, Shaw & Oleson 1992; Brehm 1999).

Lane and Terry (2000) defined mood as 'a set of feelings, ephemeral in nature, varying in intensity and duration, and usually involving more than one emotion' (p. 17). This definition implies that mood represents a cumulative process, through which a series of emotional responses to daily events combine to form a mindset that persists until gradually or suddenly changed by future events.

From the views presented thus far, it is apparent that emotion and mood are commonly distinguished in the literature in terms of the intensity and duration of responses and the specificity of their antecedents. Emotions are seen as relatively brief but intense experiences activated by cognitive appraisals of situational factors. Mood is generally conceptualised as of lower intensity, longer duration and more diffuse origins (see also Vallerand & Blanchard 2000). Further, the consequences of emotion are mostly behavioural, whereas those of mood are mostly cognitive (Ekman & Davidson 1994). The characteristics of emotions and moods are summarised in table 2.1.

Both emotions and moods, it is proposed, have an evaluative component, in terms of the degree to which feelings are perceived as pleasant or unpleasant, and an arousal component, characterised by varying degrees of activity (Parkinson et al. 1996). Parkinson et al. also argued that the relationship between emotions and moods is transactional in nature, whereby an existing mood influences the emotional reaction to a situation, and the subsequent emotional experience, in turn, contributes to mood.

An emotion is not easily distinguished from a mood. For example, a tennis player, already feeling moderately tense, becomes very tense when she learns that her next opponent has won two recent tournaments. The increase in tension is a result of a specific environmental cue (information about an opponent) and therefore could be described as an emotion. However, the search for environmental information associated with perceptions of threat is characteristic of pre-existing tension, so the underlying mood can be seen to have acted as a catalyst for the emotional response. The transactional nature of the process suggests that mood influences cognition, and emotional responses to specific situations continue to reinforce or modify the intensity of the underlying mood.

Given the proposed complexity of the emotion–mood distinction, it may seem perverse to differentiate them on the basis of a simple analogy. However, many elements of the relationship between emotional traits (what we might call temperament), moods and emotions can be compared to changing weather patterns. Temperament is analogous to the climate of a place; that is, weather patterns that repeat over the years. Just as a climate may include hot, dry summers and cool, wet winters, so an athlete's temperament may be characterised by a confident, happy disposition. This is not to say that the athlete always feels confident and happy but that these feelings are characteristic of that person.

A mood, however, is analogous to the prevailing weather front, which lasts a few hours or several days and may or may not be consistent with normal climatic conditions. For example, just as a summer storm may blow in, so the normally upbeat mood of an athlete may darken, and feelings of anger, tension and unhappiness may prevail temporarily.

Continuing the analogy, emotions represent brief changes to the weather, such as a cloud passing in front of the sun, a sudden gust of wind or a light shower of rain. Similarly, a generally buoyant mood may be threatened by brief but intense emotional responses to specific incidents: a soccer player may be irritated by a referee's decision, frustrated by missing a scoring opportunity or angered by an opponent's illegal tackle. These emotions do not necessarily erode the general positivity of the player's mood, unless the frequency and intensity of negative emotional responses is sufficient to precipitate a downturn in mood, in the same way that increasing cloud cover and frequent showers might signal a new weather front.

TABLE 2.1 Characteristics of emotions and moods

Characteristic	Emotions	Moods
Duration	Shorter (seconds/minutes)	Longer (hours/days)
Speed of onset	Faster	Slower
Intensity	Greater	Lesser
Visibility	Distinctive facial signals	Inferred from general signals
Physiology	Distinctive patterns of CNS activity	No distinctive patterns
Function	Distinct functions	General adaptive role
Antecedents	Greater specificity	Lesser specificity
Consequences	Specific behaviours	General patterns of behaviour and cognition

Conceptual models of emotion and mood

It should be made clear from the start that there is little consensus in the literature about how best to represent the structure of emotions and moods. There are many proponents of two-dimensional, bio-psychological models, whereby the constructs of emotion, mood or affect (different authors use different terms) are organised on two orthogonal dimensions. Larsen and Diener (1992) proposed the dimensions of pleasant–unpleasant and high–low activation; Thayer (1989, 1996) suggested energy-tiredness and tension–calmness dimensions; and Russell (1980) put forward pleasure-misery and arousal–sleep. However, these models vary more in terminology than in essence. Usually, the two-dimensional models are presented as a circumplex, with emotions arranged around the perimeter of a circle (see figure 2.1). Although circumplex models are pervasive in the recent literature (Russell & Feldman Barrett 1999; Watson, Wiese, Vaidya & Tellegen 1999; Yik, Russell & Feldman Barrett 1999), there is disagreement about where on the circumplex particular emotions should be placed.

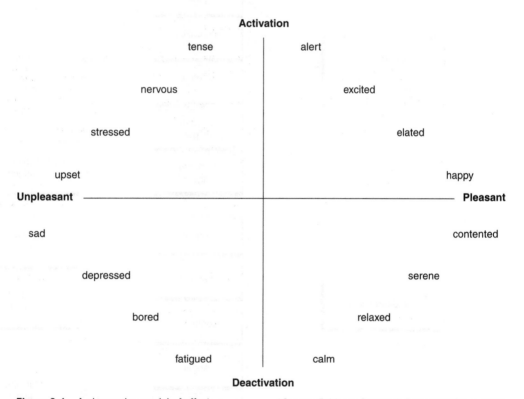

Figure 2.1   A circumplex model of affect   (*Source:* Feldman Barrett & Russell 1998, p. 970)

Circumplex models of emotion have rarely been applied to research in sport and exercise. More commonly, researchers in these domains have used models based in particular on a series of unipolar dimensions such as tension, depression and anger. (McNair, Lorr & Droppelman 1971, 1992; Terry, Lane, Lane & Keohane 1999), but also on bipolar opposites such as happy–sad or relaxed–tense (Lorr & McNair 1988), or on broad orthogonal dimensions, such as negative and positive affect (Watson & Tellegen 1985). In taking on the huge challenge of trying to understand the nature of emotions ('dissecting the elephant', as Russell and Feldman Barrett (1999) referred to it), equally compelling arguments can be made to support different models. Watson et al. (1999) called on future researchers to use 'a variety of approaches in seeking to understand this extraordinarily complex domain' (p. 836).

Generally, investigations of mood in sport and exercise have been blighted by a lack of theory to underpin research questions. A recent model of mood–performance relationships (Lane & Terry 2000) emphasised the pivotal role of the depression component of mood (see figure 2.2). Lane and Terry proposed that the negative cognitive generalisations that characterise depression have a pervasive effect and act as a catalyst for other unpleasant dimensions of mood. A depressed mood also promotes a focus on negative previous experiences, which may reduce perceptions of ability and coping (Rokke 1993), and requires more regulation than other moods, reducing the capacity for alternative types of regulation such as physical performance (Muraven, Tice & Baumeister 1998).

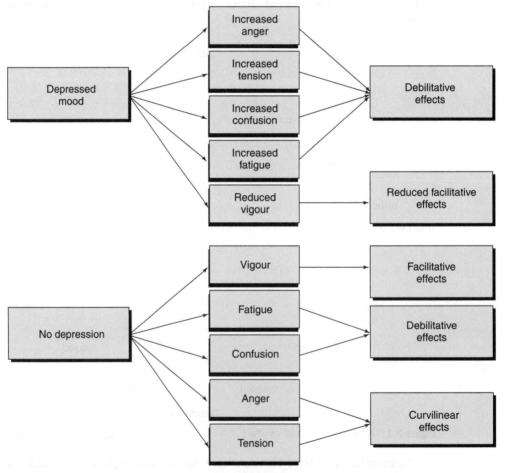

Figure 2.2 A conceptual model to predict performance from pre-competition mood

(*Source:* Lane & Terry 2000, p. 24)

Crucial to the Lane and Terry model is the notion that depressed mood moderates the mood–performance relationship for anger and tension. In contrast, even though depressive symptoms are proposed to reduce vigour and increase confusion and fatigue, vigour remains facilitative of performance and confusion and fatigue remain debilitative.

The proposed moderating influence of depressed mood on some mood–performance relationships but not others can be explained by the nature of anger and tension.

Spielberger (1991) suggested that anger-related thoughts are directed either inwardly towards the self (suppressed) or externally towards other individuals or objects (expressed). The distinction between suppressed and expressed anger is important for sport performance. According to Spielberger, the self-blame element of suppressed anger intensifies feelings of hopelessness and thus leads to poorly motivated behaviour causing performance decrements. By contrast, expressed anger tends to be directed at the source of the original frustration, or else displaced towards another object or person. Although this process will not in itself benefit performance, the anger may be channelled into, or manifest as, determination to succeed. Importantly, the tendency to suppress anger is closely associated with depression.

Tension, like anger, is associated with heightened arousal. Schwarz and Bless (1991) contended that states such as tension serve a functional role by signalling whether conditions warrant action. Pre-performance tension may signal the likelihood of poor performance unless some form of action is taken, such as increased effort or concentration. In this instance, tension may provide a motivating effect if performance outcome is considered by the individual to be important. In a depressed mood, rather than initiating a search for solutions, tension is directed towards negative self-thoughts, engendering a demotivating effect.

The model proposes four testable hypotheses. First, anger, confusion, fatigue and tension will be higher and vigour will be lower among athletes experiencing depressed mood than among those experiencing no symptoms of depression. Second, interrelationships among anger, confusion, fatigue, tension and vigour will be stronger for athletes experiencing depressed mood. Third, vigour will facilitate performance, and confusion and fatigue will debilitate performance, regardless of the presence or absence of depressed mood. Fourth, anger and tension will debilitate performance among individuals reporting symptoms of depression, whereas anger and tension will show a curvilinear relationship with performance among individuals reporting no symptoms of depression.

During preliminary tests of the model (Lane & Terry 1998, 1999a, 1999b; Lane, Terry, Karageorghis & Lawson 1999; Owens, Lane & Terry 2000), the first and second hypotheses were strongly supported, the third and fourth hypotheses partially so. Recent, more comprehensive tests of the model by Lane, Terry, Beedie, Curry and Clark (2001) and Janover and Terry (2002) have provided further support. Lane et al. (2001) assessed mood among 451 schoolchildren taking part in running competitions. They found that, compared with those who reported no symptoms of depression, a depressed mood group reported higher scores for anger, confusion, fatigue and tension, lower scores for vigour, and stronger correlations among these mood dimensions. Also, the depressed mood group set easier goals and performed less well than the no-depression group. Vigour was associated with facilitated performance regardless of depression, whereas anger was associated with debilitated performance in the depressed mood group and with facilitated performance in the no-depression group. Some support was shown for a moderating effect of depressed mood on the tension–performance relationship, although the hypothesised curvilinear anger–performance and tension–performance relationships in the no-depression group did not emerge. However, a more recent test of the model among 354 age-group (junior) swimmers (Janover & Terry 2002) provided more robust support for all four hypotheses. Collectively, early tests of the model suggest it has the potential to help increase understanding of the relationship between mood and athletic performance.

MEASUREMENT ISSUES

The measurement of any psychological construct is a key challenge in the process of testing theory or investigating hypothesised relationships.

Types of measures

Measures vary substantially in terms of their scientific rigour, psychometric integrity, degree of invasiveness (and therefore viability in the athletic context), influence by confounding variables, cost and so on.

An obvious way to find out how someone feels is to ask him or her to complete a self-report measure. However, there are other strategies for measuring emotional states (Parrott & Hertel 1999) including several behavioural, cognitive and psychophysiological indices. For example, there is a tradition of assessing emotional states from the behavioural patterns, such as facial expressions, associated with them (Keltner & Ekman 1996), although this measurement strategy demands sensitivity to social context. Similarly, emotional states such as embarrassment can be gauged from behaviours such as gaze aversion and blushing (Asendorpf 1990). Alternatively, some emotions can be assessed via cognitive patterns in the form of psychomotor retardation, indexed for example by reductions in writing speed, which is associated with feelings of sadness (Clark 1983).

In the field of psychophysiology, indices such as heart rate, blood pressure, galvanic skin response, finger temperature, respiration rate and eye movement are commonly used to infer emotional change (Wagner & Manstead 1989). Further, the use of EEG has facilitated the identification of changes in blood flow to various areas of the brain during emotional and non-emotional states. Also, EMG has been used to investigate the muscle activity responsible for facial expressions and has been shown not only to detect muscle movements too slight to be visible to the naked eye but to discriminate among emotions from the combined activity of different facial muscles (Sinha & Parsons 1996).

However, self-report measures are undoubtedly the most common method of assessing moods and discrete emotions. Typically, respondents are presented with a series of Likert or analogue scales and rate the extent to which they feel particular emotions or mood descriptors. The more common self-report measures of affect used in the sport and exercise environments include the Profile of Mood States (POMS) (McNair et al. 1971, 1992) and its derivatives (Shacham 1983; Grove & Prapavessis 1992; Terry et al. 1999), the Positive and Negative Affect Scale (PANAS) (Watson, Clark & Tellegen 1988), the Activation–Deactivation Adjective Checklist (Thayer 1986), the Multiple Affective Adjective Checklist — Revised (Zuckerman & Lubin 1985) and measures developed specifically for the exercise environment, such as the Exercise-induced Feeling Inventory (Gauvin & Rejeski 1993) and the Subjective Exercise Experience Scale (McAuley & Courneya 1994).

Self-reports have the obvious advantage of simplicity and convenience. They are also relatively inexpensive and minimally invasive when used appropriately. Further, when a researcher is interested in the conscious experience of moods and emotional states, self-reports offer the most direct route to what a person felt. However, there are potential hazards in the use of self-report mechanisms. Response distortion may occur owing to the effects of social desirability, reactivity to the researcher, disinterest, lack of insight, faking good or bad, and order effects — all of which should be considered before assessment. Moreover, on all standardised tests important issues of psychometric integrity come into play; namely, validity, objectivity and reliability. Further threats to the integrity of the data are associated with the assessment of emotional responses retrospectively, and these receive particular attention in the following section.

ADVANTAGES AND DISADVANTAGES OF SELF-REPORT MEASURES

Advantages	*Disadvantages*
Simple	Social desirability effects
Convenient	Reactivity to researcher
Relatively inexpensive	Disinterest of participant
Direct route to emotions	Order effects
Minimally invasive (if used appropriately)	Lack of insight
	Faking good or bad

Psychometrically, a clear distinction between emotions and moods is problematic. Some feelings, such as anger and anxiety, occur as both emotions and moods (Lazarus 1999), and distinctions based on intensity and duration are not always possible because individuals can experience intense but brief moods or low-intensity emotions. Theoretical and empirical distinctions between the two constructs may therefore require some reference to context — that is, the relative awareness of the antecedents, focus and likely consequences of the feelings. Beedie, Lane and Terry (2001) recently developed a measure to assess the context in which athletes experience mood and emotional states. 'I am nervous about the event', for example, represented emotions associated with anxiety, whereas 'I feel nervous at the moment for no particular reason' represented mood. Model testing supported the discrimination of emotion from mood by contextualising feelings.

The most appropriate measure of mood or emotions depends primarily on exactly what needs to be assessed for the purposes of the investigation but also on the psychometric rigour applied to the development of the measure. Researchers and practitioners are encouraged to give careful consideration to both of these factors.

Response time frame

The reference period included in instructions to respondents is one of several important considerations in the assessment of mood or emotions. This reference period is known as the response time frame. McNair et al. (1971) offered four alternative response time frames for the original POMS: (1) 'How have you felt over the past week including today?' (2) 'How do you feel generally?' (3) 'How do you feel today?' and (4) 'How do you feel right now?' The PANAS (Watson et al. 1988) offers a similar range of response time frames.

Watson (1988) is one of very few researchers to have addressed the impact of response time frame on mood assessments. Watson found that, although the factor structure of mood remained constant, correlations among mood dimensions and test–retest coefficients varied as a function of the time frame used. Correlations were weakest and test–retest coefficients highest with a 'past year' time frame, suggesting that a trait-like construct was being assessed, whereas a 'right now' time frame was associated with high correlations among mood dimensions and low test–retest coefficients, appearing to reflect person–environment interactions at the time of testing.

More recently, Winkielman, Knauper and Schwarz (1998) found that with a short response time frame such as 'Have you felt angry today?' participants reported less intense experiences compared with longer time frames such as 'Have you felt angry this week?' The authors suggested that respondents interpret longer time frames as an inference that the researcher is interested primarily in intense reactions, as it would seem unrealistic to list every incident that generated a mild response. This perception appeared to strengthen as the response time frame grew longer, for example to six months or a year; therefore, mood summaries over a long time period may be influenced unduly by relatively short but intense feelings, which inflate scores for the assessed moods.

The literature generally indicates that retrospective measures have limited accuracy. For example, Rasmussen, Jeffrey, Willingham and Glover (1994) showed that an 'over time' assessment of mood for a period of three days differed significantly from the mean of 18 'right now' assessments collected during the same time period. The questionable accuracy of retrospective recall has also been identified in many other areas of investigation (Cohen & Java 1995; Eich, Reeves, Jaeger & Graff-Radford 1985; Ptacek, Smith, Espe & Raffety 1994) and is explained variously as resulting from faulty or incomplete encoding, memory decay or distorted recollections (Smith, Leffingwell & Ptacek 1999). Recall of mood over time appears especially problematic given the proposed influence on memory of ambient mood (i.e. mood at the time of recall). Mood-congruency effects have been postulated, whereby people tend to seek information from memory that is consistent with ambient mood (Bower 1981; Parrott & Sabini 1990); moreover, memories are more readily accessible when mood is similar to when the memories were originally encoded (Blaney 1986).

Recent research in sport has further illustrated the impact of response time frame on measures of mood. Stevens, Lane and Terry (2001) conducted two studies to compare mood scores using different time frames. In both studies, 'past week' mood assessments yielded higher scores than multiple 'right now' assessments, and were particularly associated with ambient mood for confusion, depression and vigour. It may be concluded that retrospective reports should not be treated as equivalent to measures taken in closer temporal proximity to the experience of interest. It is therefore essential that researchers consider the influence of response time frame on mood assessments.

Moderating variables

As part of the assessment process, it is important to consider variables that may have the potential to influence mood responses among athletes and are therefore possible confounds. These variables include, but are not restricted to, individual differences, gender, age, level of competition, situation and time of day.

Effects of individual differences on mood

Individual differences in mood responses are self-evident and simply show that different people have different temperaments. Such differences have been clearly identified by researchers both in terms of absolute differences between individuals (Terry & Lane 2000) and significant changes over time within individuals (Cowdry, Gardner, O'Leary, Leibenluft & Rubinow 1991). Further, patterns of mood variability, in particular the frequency and extent of mood fluctuations, have been shown to vary significantly between individuals (Cowdry et al. 1991; Penner, Shiffman, Paty & Fritzsche 1994). Interestingly, though, it is suggested that the patterns of mood variability show temporal and situation stability (Penner et al. 1994). Therefore, it appears that although different individuals report very different moods and the volatility of mood change varies greatly, there is some consistency in the degree to which moods are stable or volatile. In other words, it is well understood that people have different moods and that some people are more 'moody' than others, but it should also be understood that these differences in mood fluctuations are trait-like and may therefore be somewhat predictable.

From a practitioner's perspective, such evidence points to a need to understand not only the typical pattern of mood change of individual athletes leading up to a competition but also the typical extent of mood stability or volatility, and ultimately the 'ideal' pre-competition mood for each athlete. The regular monitoring of mood responses may facilitate such insights and provide a systematic basis for implementing mood management strategies.

Effects of gender on mood

Gender stereotypes might suggest that females are more volatile in their mood responses than males. By extension, such stereotypes suggest that cross-gender comparisons would show significant differences in mood responses between male and female athletes. However, the research evidence points to a general consistency in reported mood across gender groups. For example, no differences in mood responses between males and females were found in the original validation studies of the POMS by McNair et al. (1971), or in subsequent sport-focused investigations by Fuchs and Zaichkowsky (1983), Craighead, Privette, Vallianos and Byrkit (1986), and Terry and Lane (2000), although a study of mood responses among adolescent athletes did report significant gender differences (Terry et al. 1999). It appears that in terms of mood responses, as with many other psychological variables, male and female athletes can be considered more alike than different.

Effects of age on mood

There is a relative paucity of research investigating the effects of age on mood. In a study by McNeil, Stone, Kozma and Andres (1994) older adults reported more positive moods than younger adults, and in the athletic environment, Riddick (1984) reported that varsity (adult) swimmers reported more positive moods than age group (junior) swimmers. Beyond this suggested tendency for moods to be more positive among older groups, there are no longitudinal investigations of how moods change as people get older. Therefore, although age may be related to mood change, the nature of its effects is not well understood.

Effects of level of competition on mood

The idea that the typical personality characteristics of athletic champions can be identified scientifically has been a strong tradition in the field of sport psychology, spawning much of the personology research during the 1960s and 1970s (Fisher 1984). From this tradition, it has been very common over recent decades for researchers to search for patterns of mood responses that differentiate among athletes at different levels of competition, such as international, club or novice levels (LeUnes & Burger 1998).

From the pioneering work of William Morgan and his colleagues (Morgan 1974; Morgan & Johnson 1978; Morgan & Pollock 1977, Nagle, Morgan, Hellickson, Serfass & Alexander 1975), an association was proposed between athletic success and a mood profile, based on the POMS, typified by above-average scores for vigour and below-average scores for tension, depression, anger, fatigue and confusion — a pattern of mood responses referred to by Morgan as an iceberg profile (Morgan 1980). Over recent years there has been a growing realisation that any link between athletic achievement and mood responses is probably more subtle and complex than can be explained readily by the iceberg profile. For example, narrative reviews by Renger (1993) and Terry (1995) have cast doubt on whether it is reasonable to expect mood profiles to predict athletic achievement, and a meta-analysis of pertinent studies by Rowley, Landers, Kyllo and Etnier (1995) concluded that the iceberg profile accounted for less than 1 per cent of the variance in performance outcome and that the 'utility of the POMS in predicting athletic success is questionable' (p. 185).

Further, normative mood data for athletes published by Terry and Lane (2000) showed that, when plotted against the psychiatric outpatient or student norms (McNair et al. 1971) that were used as the point of reference by almost all previous studies, an iceberg profile is typical of athletes regardless of their level of competition. Collectively, the more recent evidence does not mean that previous emphasis on the desirability of the iceberg profile was misplaced but, given the normality of such a profile among athletes, perhaps its importance was overstated (Morgan 1980).

Nevertheless, some findings continue to support the notion that athletic achievement can be differentiated from mood scores (Morgan, Brown, Raglin, O'Connor & Ellickson 1987; Trafton, Meyers & Skelly 1998). Two recent meta-analyses by Beedie, Terry and Lane (2000) summarised the findings of 13 published studies investigating whether mood responses can differentiate athletes of varying degrees of achievement and 16 published studies investigating whether mood responses can differentiate performance outcome among athletes of similar ability. Beedie et al. concluded that mood responses have significant utility in the prediction of performance outcome but not in the prediction of level of achievement.

Effects of situation on mood

By definition, moods are influenced by situational factors. The emotional responses that underlie mood change are initiated by our interaction with other individuals and by environmental forces that we encounter as we move from situation to situation. Few studies have investigated the effects of situational factors on mood, particularly in athletic environments, although in a cross-sectional study of the mood responses of more than 2000 athletes assessed either before competition, after competition or away from the competition environment, Terry and Lane (2000) found that athletes reported higher tension, depression, anger and confusion before competition than at the post-competition stage. Away from the competition environment, such feelings were at levels midway between the pre- and post-competition situations.

Just as the prospect of public speaking or a visit to the dentist has the capacity to change a person's mood, so, it would appear, has the prospect of impending athletic competition. For example, research conducted at the 1993 World Rowing Championships (Hall & Terry 1995), in which the moods of 12 athletes were monitored daily during the pre-event training camp and throughout the competition period, revealed significant mood fluctuations as the competition drew nearer. In all 12 cases, the eventual performance of the athletes could be dichotomised into 'performance to expectations' or 'underperformance' from the mood profiles taken on the eve of competition, with the better performances associated with higher vigour and lower anger, confusion, depression and fatigue. Those athletes who underperformed reported more mood volatility and a deteriorating mood as the competition approached, whereas those athletes who performed to expectations showed greater mood stability and a gradually improving mood.

The authors suggested that these data might reflect the success or failure of the final preparation period, during which the training load was increased and then tapered before the start of competition. Based on unsolicited comments from some of the rowers, the authors speculated that the significant fluctuations in anger, depression and confusion among underperforming athletes, and their general mood disturbance, appeared to be associated with difficulties meeting the physical demands of training.

Specific examples of the effects of situation on mood responses are drawn from my applied work with elite athletes. Figure 2.3 shows the mood profiles of a medal-winning athlete taken periodically during the 1998 Olympic Winter Games in Nagano, from the day the team arrived in Japan until the competition days. It was apparent to me from his mood profiles that the athlete was experiencing a degree of mood disturbance, evidenced particularly by uncharacteristically low levels of vigour, high levels of anger and depression, and a general volatility of mood responses. Discussion with the athlete revealed the huge impact of situational factors on his mood, in particular the travel fatigue and jet lag associated with the journey, the unsettling experience of being in an Olympic environment and a family-related issue. His mood profile returned to what was, for him, the ideal only on the second day of competition, when the medals were being decided.

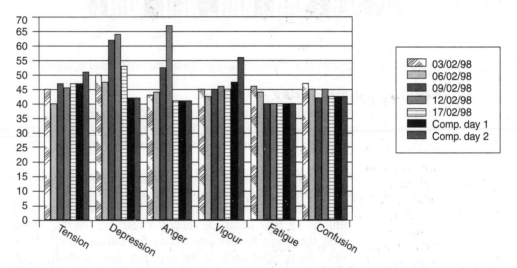

Figure 2.3 Mood profiles of a medal-winning athlete during the 1998 Olympic Winter Games

Figure 2.4 shows the mood profiles of an Olympic champion at the 2000 Olympic Games in Sydney, assessed from the day after arriving in Australia from Europe until the morning of competition. In this instance, the pattern is one of an early adjustment to the fatiguing effects of travel and jet lag followed by an extended period of mood stability, with a slight increase in tension as competition approached. It should be noted that the scores for this performer, which are plotted against athlete norms in standard score format (Terry & Lane 2000; Terry, Lane & Fogarty 2003), represent raw scores of zero on the scales of depression, anger and confusion throughout the assessment period and on the tension and fatigue scales for the vast majority of the assessment period. Moreover, given that the optimal pre-competition mood profile for this athlete had been identified during previous events, the challenge was to identify when the optimal mood was achieved (in this case, as early as the first week in Australia) and to attempt to maintain emotional stability thereafter using some of the mood management strategies identified later in the chapter.

The critical importance of situational factors in managing the Olympic experience was recognised by this athlete. He had found the experience of the 1996 Olympic Games in Atlanta to be an emotionally overwhelming occasion. In 2000, therefore, he opted out of the Olympic Village environment, stayed in a house in the Sydney suburbs with a fellow athlete, their coaches and the sport psychologist, used his own transport and generally tried to create a 'home away from home' atmosphere.

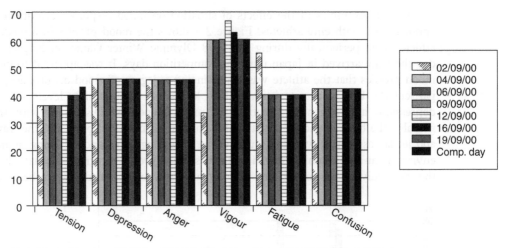

Figure 2.4 Mood profiles of an Olympic champion during the 2000 Games in Sydney

Effects of time of day on mood

People appear to acknowledge regular patterns of mood change during the course of a day. An individual may describe himself or herself as, for instance, 'an early bird' or 'a night owl'. Research has also identified diurnal fluctuations in mood, characterised by improved mood from early morning to midday, a post-lunch dip, and then mood enhancements later in the afternoon or early evening (Atkinson & Reilly 1996; Clark, Watson & Leeka 1989; Hill & Hill 1991; McNeil et al. 1994).

A study by Karageorghis, Dimitriou and Terry (1999), which assessed the mood responses of 58 athletes on four occasions during a rest day (08.00, 12.00, 16.00 and 20.00 hours), showed significant fluctuations during the testing period. Mood was most positive at noon and least positive early in the morning. Also, a study of cyclists found that, before exhaustive exercise, vigour was significantly higher in the afternoon than in the morning (Koltyn, Lynch & Hill 1998).

In summary, an important implication of these findings for the applied practitioner is that, in order to control for potential diurnal fluctuations in mood, the monitoring of emotional responses should ideally occur at the same time on each assessment day.

MOOD–PERFORMANCE RELATIONSHIPS

A link between mood and sport performance may have strong intuitive appeal but researchers have not had great success in elaborating what constitutes the 'ideal mood' for best performance. Indeed, it is difficult from the body of research to conclude even that mood and performance are closely related (Renger 1993; Rowley et al. 1995). It is possible, however, that much of the equivocality that typifies findings in this area can be explained by methodological factors. Although this author has elaborated some of these concerns previously (Terry 1995) they will be briefly summarised here.

Firstly, researchers have not always distinguished adequately between level of performer and level of performance. Given the transient nature of mood, there is no compelling reason why mood profiles should distinguish between performers at different levels of achievement. Elite athletes do not have a monopoly on positive moods. However, its very transience suggests a link with performance, in that an individual would be more likely to perform optimally when in their 'ideal' mood than in any other mood. Unfortunately, some research designs, ostensibly addressing the mood-performance link, have lacked precision in their research question.

Secondly, several potential confounds have been generally overlooked by researchers. Task characteristics such as increasing duration, complexity and number of co-acting performers have the potential to restrict the impact of mood on performance and should be considered carefully (Terry 1995). Similarly, personal characteristics such as skill and conditioning clearly have a major impact on performance and therefore need to be controlled for if the effects of mood are to be identified.

Finally, the measure(s) of performance used is critical in investigating mood–performance relationships. It appears likely that the use of objective performance indicators, such as win–loss record or selection to a national team, that are insensitive to the relative quality of performance for a particular athlete, may often have masked the effects of pre-performance mood.

The meta-analysis of Beedie et al. (2000) showed that, when studies investigating level of achievement and studies using inappropriate methods were excluded, the mean effect of mood on performance was small-to-moderate (mean ES = .31). Effects were moderate for vigour, confusion and depression, small for anger and tension, and very small for fatigue. All effects were in the direction predicted by Morgan's (1985) Mental Health Model. Notably, effects were larger in sports of short duration, in sports involving open skills, and where performance was judged using self-referenced criteria such as achievement of performance goals or percentage of personal best. Overall, it appears that when certain conditions are met, mood profiles taken at the pre-performance stage are significant predictors of subsequent performance.

Several commentators on the literature (e.g. Hanin 1997; Prapavessis 2000) have endorsed the advantages of an idiographic rather than a nomothetic approach to unravelling the complexities of the effects of human emotions on performance. Although the results of more than 300 cross-sectional studies conducted in the area have offered many insights into the mood–performance link, there is little doubt that models that emphasise an intra-individual focus, such the Individual Zone of Optimal Functioning (Hanin 1997), offer great potential for refining our understanding.

MOOD MANAGEMENT STRATEGIES

Evidence on mood management strategies in sport is scarce. Although some texts hint at the mood benefits for athletes of mental training techniques, almost all the systematic investigations of this topic have been conducted in the sphere of general psychology. There is a consensus in the literature that people tend to monitor and evaluate their own moods, and develop and implement self-regulation strategies (Wegner & Pennebaker 1993). Often the role of the applied practitioner is to monitor and help direct this naturally occurring process.

Of course, the list of strategies used by different individuals is long and varied. A study by Thayer, Newman and McClain (1994), which investigated the incidence and efficacy of different categories of mood-regulating behaviours among the general population, found that the most common behaviours to reduce nervousness, tension or anxiety in the short term were affiliative-communicative (e.g. calling, talking to or being with someone), exercise, relaxation techniques, rest, music and food. Thayer et al. found that the most effective strategies for enhancing the energy component of mood were to control thoughts through self-talk, listen to music, take a shower, exercise, take a nap, do something to keep busy, eat something or drink a caffeinated beverage. Stevens and Lane (2000) found that athletes reported exercise, listening to music, talking to or being with someone, and thought control as the most common mood-regulating strategies, although their relative effectiveness was not established in this study.

Several gender and age differences in the use of mood management strategies have been identified. Women are more likely to use food as a mood regulator (Grunberg & Straub 1992; Thayer et al. 1994), to seek social interaction (Houtman 1990; Thayer et al. 1994), to go shopping (Thayer et al. 1994) or to vent their feelings (Thayer et al. 1994), whereas men are more likely to resort to alcohol or drugs (Berger & Adesso 1991; Engs & Hanson 1990), to engage in a hobby, to use humour, to have sex, or to control their thoughts (Thayer et al. 1994). People in the 16–34 age range are more likely to control bad moods by being alone, listening to music, indulging in pleasant activities, eating something or venting their feelings, whereas people aged 35 years and above are more likely to tend to chores or seek spiritual or religious help (Thayer et al. 1994).

Given the extensive range of potential mood management strategies, the present chapter will focus on three readily implemented behaviours that have been shown to be both commonly used and effective; music, food and exercise.

Effects of music on mood

Music pervades many aspects of society; it has, for example, become an ubiquitous element in the modern exercise experience. The psychophysical effects of music in sport and exercise are numerous. For example, it appears that the synchronisation of submaximal physical activity with music tempo can reduce perceived exertion and increase work output (for reviews, see Lucaccini & Kreit 1972; Karageorghis & Terry 1997). The effects of asynchronous (background) music are less clear, but research has shown that well-chosen music has the potential to generate significant improvements in mood (Boutcher & Trenske 1990; Karageorghis & Terry 2000; Kodzhaspirov, Zaitsev & Kosarev 1988).

Several factors influence the effectiveness of music as a mood enhancer, some associated with the characteristics of the music and others associated with the characteristics of the listener. A study by Karageorghis, Terry and Lane (1999) identified four key features, which they termed *rhythm response*, *musicality*, *cultural impact* and *association*. Rhythm response refers to the characteristics of the music that inspire movement, such as its rhythm, tempo, stimulative qualities and 'danceability'. Musicality refers to the melodic and harmonic aspects of the music that shape the listener's interpretation and thereby influence his or her emotional response. Cultural impact refers to the familiarity and preferences of a particular musical piece or genre in the cultural context of the listener. Association refers to the extra-musical associations evoked by the music — the images generated by particular pieces that, for example, relax, motivate or inspire. Karageorghis et al. (1999) proposed that these four factors determine the motivational qualities of music, and this in turn mediates the psychophysical effects (see figure 2.5).

In an applied context, music often plays an important role in pre-competition routines. Specific examples from my work include using stimulative music combined with verbal suggestions as part of an energising strategy, using music with sedative qualities as a backdrop to relaxation techniques, or using music with associations of glory in the face of adversity to inspire athletes before important international competitions. The music used by three gold medallists from the 2000 Olympic Games in Sydney illustrates its potential to influence pre-competition mood. For rowing champion James Cracknell, listening to *Blood Sugar Sex Magik*, an album by the Red Hot Chilli Peppers, proved an effective pre-competition strategy for optimising the arousal and aggression components of mood and shutting out potential distractions. Audley Harrison, the super-heavyweight boxing champion, listened to Japanese classical music to ease his pre-fight nerves coming into the final. Richard Faulds, winner of the double trap shooting competition, was inspired to seize the moment, in the tensest of shoot-offs, by Whitney Houston's classic 'One moment in time'.

In summary, music can act as a potent mood enhancer, but choice of music demands great sensitivity to the personal preferences of the athlete, the match between the characteristics of the music and the target emotion, and the associations engendered by a particular piece of music.

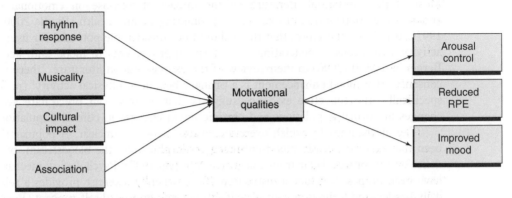

Figure 2.5 Conceptual framework for the prediction of responses to music in exercise and sport
Note: RPE = rate of perceived exertion.

(*Source:* Adapted from Karageorghis, Terry & Lane 1999, *Journal of Sport Science*, vol. 17, no. 9, p. 721. Taylor & Francis)

Dietary effects on mood

There is a longstanding intuitive link between food and mood. Such a link is illustrated by the notion that favourite 'comfort foods' such as cakes or chocolate can make us feel better. A more fundamental link, however, captured in the maxim 'you are what you eat', suggests that dietary intake has a profound effect on all aspects of human functioning. The food–mood link represents a complex relationship (Somer 1995) and is not one that can be elaborated fully in this chapter. However, given its proposed significant potential for mood enhancement and the relative ease with which diet can be modified, a brief overview follows.

Effective human functioning requires effective communication among the billions of neurons that make up the human nervous system. Communication around the nervous system requires electrical impulses to bridge the gap between neurons, using chemicals known as neurotransmitters. There are dozens of different types of neurotransmitters, each with a slightly different role in the regulation of nerve cell functions, and all physical, emotional and cognitive processes can be affected dramatically if the correct neurotransmitter is in short supply. Effective memory functioning, for example, depends on the neurotransmitter acetylcholine; depression is associated with reduced levels of the neurotransmitters dopamine, norepinephrine and seratonin.

The production and release of specific neurotransmitters, in particular the four mentioned above, is related to the ingestion of different food types and nutrients. For example, seratonin levels in the brain, which help regulate sleep patterns and pain tolerance as well as mood, are closely related to diet and can be boosted by eating a carbohydrate-rich meal. Similarly, high dopamine and norepinephrine levels, which may guard against depressive symptoms and enhance alertness and vigour, may be boosted by a protein-rich meal high in tyrosine, an amino acid from which these neurotransmitters are manufactured.

Given the substantial individual differences in body metabolism and brain chemistry, and the complexity associated with dose responses and ingestion patterns, it would be inappropriate to propose specific foods to enhance different aspects of mood. The point to be emphasised here is that mood and food are linked chemically; mood management strategies, therefore, may very likely have a dietary component. More comprehensive discussions of this topic can be found in Somer (1995) and Wurtman (1988).

Effects of exercise on mood

Most of the substantial literature on the impact of exercise on emotional responses endorses the contribution of exercise in promoting mental health (Biddle 2000; Morgan 1997). It follows, therefore, that there should be considerable potential for using physical activity as a means of generating short-term improvements to mood and, according to Berger and Motl (2000) in their review of the exercise–mood literature, 'there is a strong consensus that mood enhancement is a primary benefit of physical activity' (p. 71). More specifically, the collective evidence suggests that exercise can precipitate acute mood changes in normal populations and chronic mood changes in clinical populations.

The mechanisms by which exercise elevates mood are unclear. A popular theory has been that exercise releases mood-enhancing endorphins into the bloodstream, but the evidence on this process is far from conclusive (Morgan 1997). Psychological mechanisms that have been proposed include a distraction effect, whereby exercise provides a release from daily hassles, and feelings of control, self-efficacy and improved self-concept (Berger 1996). Janelle (1999) provided an interesting alternative explanation for the mood benefits of exercise. Using a model of ironic mental processes (Wegner 1994), Janelle suggested that some people know they should exercise but don't want to and, by overcoming the urge to avoid exercising, mood-elevating effects are derived 'from the unconscious relief of realising that the negative consequences of ironic processes were avoided' (p. 210).

Berger and Motl (2000, p. 78) presented a taxonomy to help guide the maximisation of mood benefits, in which they emphasised that mood enhancement depends on the interaction between participant, exercise mode and practice conditions (see figure 2.6). Berger and Motl proposed that a key requirement for short-term improvements in mood to occur is the personal enjoyment attached to the exercise. For example, Motl, Berger and Leuschen (2000) showed that mood enhancement was negated if unpleasant environmental conditions, such as high temperatures, detracted from the enjoyment of the exercise.

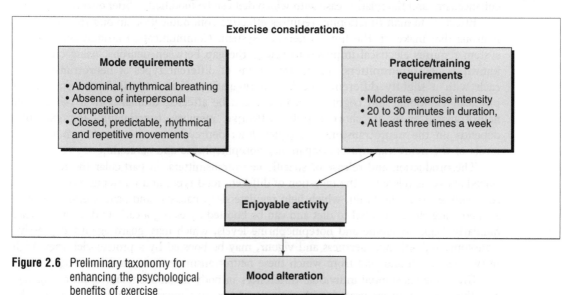

Figure 2.6 Preliminary taxonomy for enhancing the psychological benefits of exercise

(*Source:* Berger & Motl 2000, p. 78, © 2000 *Journal of Applied Sport Psychology* by Berger & Motl. Reproduced by permission of Taylor & Francil Inc., www.routledge-ny.com)

As for type of exercise, it appears that mood enhancement is associated particularly with exercise that promotes rhythmical and abdominal breathing, including meditation, tai chi and yoga, as well as a whole range of aerobic activities (Berger 1996; Berger & Owen 1992a; Jin 1992). Also, given the detrimental effects on mood associated with losing in athletic competitions (Grove & Prapavessis 1992; Hassmén & Blomstrand 1995; Hoffman, Bar-Eli & Tenenbaum 1999), a relative absence of interpersonal competition may help promote mood improvements. Further, Berger and Motl (2000) speculated that the predictable and repetitive nature of many aerobic activities (e.g. cycling, jogging, rowing and swimming) encourages introspection and creative thinking that may, in turn, engender mood enhancements.

In terms of the optimal practice conditions to maximise mood improvements, Berger and Motl (2000) recommended that exercise should be regularly included in a weekly schedule, especially given that mood benefits following exercise may last only 2 to 4 hours (Raglin 1997; Thayer 1996), of moderate intensity, and 20 to 30 minutes in duration. There is some evidence that even short-duration exercise of 5 to 10 minutes can promote desirable mood change (Thayer 1996) although a previous meta-analysis by Petruzello, Landers, Hatfield, Kubitz and Salizar (1991) raises a question mark over the generalisability of this finding. Berger and Motl noted that even low-intensity exercise, such as brisk walking, has been shown to engender significant mood improvements (Berger & Owen 1988; Steptoe & Cox 1988; Thayer 1996), whereas high-intensity exercise generally has not, even among trained athletes (Berger & Owen 1992b; O'Connor 1997), although individual preferences for low-, moderate- or high-intensity exercise may influence the relationship between exercise intensity and mood enhancement.

It is clear that exercise has great potential for enhancing mood, but the evidence presented suggests that the exercise characteristics associated with maximum mood improvements may not be identical to those associated with maximum health benefits. As with many applied interventions, the challenge for practitioners is carefully to match the judicious use of exercise as a mood enhancer to the individual needs of the athlete.

FUTURE DIRECTIONS

The study of emotion and mood in sport and exercise settings shows no sign of abating. If anything, the burgeoning literature in the area (see LeUnes 2000) suggests that interest is increasing. However, the type of investigation will probably change. For example, it appears likely that the number of descriptive studies conducted in this area of research will decline. In particular, it is difficult to see a compelling rationale for further cross-sectional group comparisons of mood responses, except perhaps for those that investigate specialised or marginalised populations. Instead, there are likely to be more intra-individual and longitudinal investigations, and an increasing use of qualitative techniques to enrich our understanding of emotional processes.

There is a particular need for the further development of theoretical models to explain the structure and function of emotions and moods, and how they influence performance in sport. In turn, there is considerable potential for testing existing and future conceptual models in the sport domain. Along with these theoretical developments is the need to review and refine measures. This process should include rigorous evaluation of the validity of existing measures of emotions and moods, some of which will be found wanting, and the subsequent development of new measures based on revised theoretical positions.

From an applied perspective, there is much scope for innovation in the systematic monitoring of emotional responses among athletes and evaluation of the effectiveness of mood management strategies. To this end, normative datasets for specific athletic populations are needed, as are intervention studies to assess the efficacy of particular mood management techniques and the mechanisms by which mood enhancements occur.

CONCLUSIONS

The first conclusion to be drawn is that the need for conceptual clarity when investigating and especially when measuring moods and emotions is paramount but seemingly problematic. Consensus among researchers of the distinction between what constitutes a mood and an emotion is still to be achieved, although there are signs that researchers in the sport and exercise domains are seeking to reconcile conceptual differences.

Secondly, the evidence leaves little doubt that emotions, moods and sport performance are closely linked, even if the exact nature of the relationship is still to be fully elucidated. Much of the research in the area has given insufficient consideration to important measurement issues and has overlooked important individual and situational variables that may have confounded results.

Finally, there appear to be benefits in monitoring the emotional responses of athletes on a regular basis in the lead-up to competition. The potential uses of mood profiling in sport have been elaborated elsewhere (Terry 1995, 1997), and applied practitioners are encouraged to consider its implementation.

SUMMARY

This chapter provided an overview of selected conceptual and measurement issues relevant to the areas of emotion and mood. These two constructs are generally differentiated on the basis of the intensity and duration of feelings, and their cause, function and consequences. In addressing these conceptual issues, the complexity of understanding something as fundamental and pervasive as emotions was emphasised. There is a range of two-dimensional, unipolar and bipolar models in the literature to explain the structure of emotion and mood but no genuine consensus about which best represents each construct. The sport domain, in particular, suffers from a paucity of theoretical models to explain the effects of mood on performance. As another indication of an absence of consensual thinking, a wide range of relevant but diverse measures is available to the researcher, some of which have been thoroughly validated while others have received only cursory scrutiny. Important measurement issues, such as the response time frame used in instructions to participants, are rarely given due consideration. Similarly, many potential confounds are frequently overlooked by researchers, including individual and situational differences, gender, age, level of competition and time of day.

The chapter also contained a synthesis of the evidence pertaining to mood–performance relationships. There is collective evidence (Beedie et al. 2000) that when certain conditions are met, pre-competition mood is a significant predictor of athletic performance, especially for the mood dimensions of vigour, confusion and depression. Recent theoretical developments by Lane and Terry (2000) have suggested that performance is influenced by the interactive rather than independent effects of specific mood dimensions. Finally, a series of mood-regulation strategies was reviewed. It was suggested that several of these strategies, notably music, nutrition and exercise, offer considerable potential for the applied practitioner who is seeking to assist athletes in their quest to achieve optimal performance.

REVIEW QUESTIONS

1   What are the main distinguishing features between emotions and moods?

2   According to the Lane and Terry (2000) conceptual model, how does depressed mood affect sport performance?

3   What are the key measurement issues in the assessment of emotional responses?

4   Which individual and situational variables have been shown to moderate mood responses?

5   What are the main variables to consider when using music to improve mood?

6   How does food influence mood state?

7   What characteristics of exercise are associated with improvements to mood?

8   What are the proposed mechanisms by which exercise enhances mood?

References

Asendorpf, J 1990, 'The expression of shyness and embarrassment', in WR Crozier (ed.), *Shyness and embarrassment: perspectives from social psychology*, Cambridge University Press, Cambridge, UK, pp. 87–118.

Atkinson, G & Reilly, T 1996, 'Circadian variations in sport performance', *Sports Medicine*, 21, 292–312.

Batson, CD, Shaw, LL & Oleson, KC 1992, 'Differentiating affect, mood, and emotion: toward functionally based conceptual distinctions', in MS Clark (ed.), *Review of personality and social psychology: emotion*, Sage, Newbury Park, CA, pp. 294–326.

Beedie, CJ, Lane, AM & Terry, PC 2001, 'Distinguishing emotion from mood in psychological measurement: a pilot study examining anxiety', (abstract), *Journal of Sports Sciences*, 19, 69.

Beedie, CJ, Terry, PC & Lane, AM 2000, 'The Profile of Mood States and athletic performance: two meta-analyses', *Journal of Applied Sport Psychology*, 12, 49–68.

Berger, BG 1996, 'Psychological benefits of an active lifestyle: what we know and what we need to know', *Quest*, 48, 330–53.

Berger, BD & Adesso, VJ 1991, 'Gender differences in using alcohol to cope with depression', *Addictive Behaviors*, 16, 315–27.

Berger, BG & Motl, RW 2000, 'Exercise and mood: a selective review and synthesis of research employing the Profile of Mood States', *Journal of Applied Sport Psychology*, 12, 69–92.

Berger, BG & Owen, DR 1988, 'Stress reduction and mood enhancement in four exercise modes: swimming, body conditioning, hatha yoga, and fencing', *Research Quarterly for Exercise and Sport*, 59, 148–59.

Berger, BG & Owen, DR 1992a, 'Mood alteration with yoga and swimming: aerobic exercise may not be necessary', *Perceptual and Motor Skills*, 75, 1331–43.

Berger, BG & Owen, DR 1992b, 'Preliminary analysis of a causal relationship between swimming and stress reduction: intense exercise may negate the effects', *International Journal of Sport Psychology*, 23, 70–85.

Biddle, SJH 2000, 'Exercise, emotions, and mental health', in YL Hanin (ed.), *Emotions in sport*, Human Kinetics, Champaign, IL, pp. 267–91.

Blaney, PH 1986, 'Affect and memory: a review', *Psychological Bulletin*, 99, 229–46.

Boucher, JD 1983, 'Antecedents to emotions across cultures', in SH Irvine & JW Berry (eds), *Human assessment and cultural factors*, Plenum, New York, pp. 407–20.

Boutcher, SH & Trenske, M 1990, 'The effects of sensory deprivation and music on perceived exertion and affect during exercise', *Journal of Sport & Exercise Psychology*, 12, 167–76.

Bower, GH 1981, 'Mood and memory', *American Psychologist*, 36, 129–48.

Brehm, JW 1999, 'The intensity of emotion', *Personality and Social Psychology Review*, 3, 2–22.

Clark, DM 1983, 'On induction of depressed mood in the laboratory: evaluation and comparison of the Velten and musical procedures', *Advances in Behavior Research and Therapy*, 5, 27–49.

Clark, LA, Watson, D & Leeka, L 1989, 'Diurnal variation in the positive affects', *Motivation and Emotion*, 13, 205–34.

Cohen, G & Java, R 1995, 'Memory for medical history: accuracy of recall', *Applied Cognitive Psychology*, 9, 273–88.

Cowdry, RW, Gardner, DL, O'Leary, KM, Leibenluft, E & Rubinow, DR 1991, 'Mood variability: a study of four groups', *American Journal of Psychiatry*, 148, 1505–11.

Craighead, D, Privette, G, Vallianos, F & Byrkit, D 1986, 'Personality characteristics of basketball players, starters and non-starters', *International Journal of Sport Psychology*, 17, 110–19.

Eich, E, Reeves, JL, Jaeger, B & Graff-Radford, SB 1985, 'Memory for pain: relation between past and present pain intensity', *Pain*, 23, 375–80.

Ekman, P 1999, 'Basic emotions', in T Dalgleish & M Power (eds), *Handbook of cognition and emotion*, John Wiley & Sons, New York, pp. 45–60.

Ekman, P & Davidson, RJ (eds) 1994, *The nature of emotion*, Oxford University Press, Oxford, UK.

Ekman, P, Levensen, RW & Friesen, WV 1983, 'Autonomic nervous system activity distinguishes between emotions', *Science*, 221, 1208–10.

Ellis, HC & Moore, BA 1999, 'Mood and memory', in T Dalgleish & M Power (eds), *Handbook of cognition and emotion*, John Wiley & Sons, New York, pp. 193–210.

Engs, RC & Hanson, DJ 1990, 'Gender differences in drinking patterns and problems among college students: a review of the literature', *Journal of Alcohol and Drug Education*, 35, 36–47.

Feldman Barrett, L & Russell, JA 1998, 'Independence and bipolarity in the structure of current affect', *Journal of Personality and Social Psychology*, 74, 967–84.

Fisher, AC 1984, 'New directions in sport personality research', in JM Silva & RS Weinberg (eds), *Psychological foundations of sport*, Human Kinetics, Champaign, IL, pp. 70–80.

Fuchs, C & Zaichkowsky, L 1983, 'Psychological characteristics of male and female bodybuilders: the iceberg profile', *Journal of Sport Behavior*, 6, 136–45.

Gauvin, L & Rejeski, WJ 1993, 'The Exercise-induced Feeling Inventory: development and initial validation', *Journal of Sport & Exercise Psychology*, 15, 403–23.

Grove, JR & Prapavessis, H 1992, 'Preliminary evidence for the reliability and validity of an abbreviated Profile of Mood States', *International Journal of Sport Psychology*, 23, 93–109.

Grunberg, NE & Straub, RO 1992, 'The role of gender and taste class in the effects of stress on eating', *Health Psychology*, 11, 97–100.

Hall, A & Terry, PC 1995, 'Predictive capability of pre-performance mood profiling at the 1993 World Rowing Championships, Roundnice, the Czech Republic' (abstract), *Journal of Sports Sciences*, 13, 56–7.

Hanin, YL 1997, 'Emotions and athletic performance: individual zones of optimal functioning model', *European Yearbook of Sport Psychology*, 1, 29–72.

Hanin, YL 2000, *Emotions in sport*, Human Kinetics, Champaign, IL.

Hassmén, P & Blomstrand, E 1995, 'Mood state relationships and soccer team performance', *The Sport Psychologist*, 9, 297–308.

Hill, CM & Hill, DW 1991, 'Influence of time of day on responses to the Profile of Mood States', *Perceptual and Motor Skills*, 72, 434.

Hoffman, JR, Bar-Eli, M & Tenenbaum, G 1999, 'An examination of mood changes and performance in a professional basketball team', *Journal of Sports Medicine and Physical Fitness*, 39, 74–9.

Houtman, ILD 1990, 'Personal coping resources and sex differences', *Personality and Individual Differences*, 11, 53–63.

Janelle, CM 1999, 'Ironic mental processes in sport: Implications for sports psychologists', *The Sport Psychologist*, 13, 201–20.

Janover, M & Terry, PC 2002, 'Relationships between pre-competition mood and swimming performance: test of a conceptual model with an emphasis on depressed mood', paper presented at the XXV International Congress of Applied Psychology, Singapore, July.

Jin, P 1992, 'Efficacy of tai chi, brisk walking, meditation, and reading in reducing mental and emotional stress', *Journal of Psychosomatic Research*, 36, 361–70.

Jones, JG & Hardy, L 1990, *Stress and performance in sport*, John Wiley & Sons, New York.

Karageorghis, CI & Terry, PC 1997, 'The psychophysical effects of music in sport and exercise: a review', *Journal of Sport Behavior*, 20, 54–68.

Karageorghis, CI, Dimitriou, LA & Terry, PC 1999, 'Effects of circadian rhythms on mood among athletes' (abstract), *Journal of Sports Sciences*, 17, 56–7.

Karageorghis, CI, Terry, PC & Lane, AM 1999, 'Development and initial validation of an instrument to assess the motivational qualities of music in exercise and sport: the Brunel Music Rating Inventory', *Journal of Sports Sciences*, 17, 713–24.

Karageorghis, CI & Terry, PC 2000, 'Affective and psychophysical responses to asynchronous music during submaximal treadmill running' (abstract), *Journal of Sports Sciences*, 18, 218.

Keltner, D & Ekman, P 1996, 'Affective intensity and emotional responses', *Cognition and Emotion*, 10, 323–8.

Kodzhaspirov, YG, Zaitsev, YM & Kosarev, SM 1988, 'The application of functional music in the training sessions of weightlifters', *Soviet Sports Review*, 23, 39–42.

Koltyn, KF, Lynch, NA & Hill, DW 1998, 'Psychological responses to brief exhaustive cycling exercise in the morning and the evening', *International Journal of Sport Psychology*, 29, 145–56.

Lane, AM & Terry, PC 1998, 'Prediction of athletic performance from mood: test of a conceptual model' (abstract), *The Psychologist*, August, 109.

Lane, AM & Terry, PC 1999a, 'Mood states as predictors of performance: test of a conceptual model' (abstract), *Journal of Sports Sciences*, 17, 606.

Lane, AM & Terry, PC 1999b, 'The conceptual independence of tension and depression' (abstract), *Journal of Sports Sciences*, 17, 605–6.

Lane, AM & Terry, PC 2000, 'The nature of mood: development of a conceptual model with a focus on depression', *Journal of Applied Sport Psychology*, 12, 16–33.

Lane, AM, Terry, PC, Karageorghis, CI & Lawson, J 1999, 'Mood states as predictors of kickboxing performance: a test of a conceptual model' (abstract), *Journal of Sports Sciences*, 17, 61–2.

Lane, AM, Terry, PC, Beedie, CJ, Curry, DA & Clark, N 2001, 'Mood and performance: test of a conceptual model with a focus on depressed mood', *Psychology of Sport and Exercise*, 2, 157–72.

Larsen, RJ & Diener, E 1992, 'Promises and problems with the circumplex model of emotion', in MS Clark (ed.), *Review of personality and social psychology: vol. 13. emotion*, Sage, Newbury Park, CA, pp. 25–9.

Lazarus, RS 1999, 'The cognition-emotion debate: a bit of history', in T Dalgleish & M Power (eds), *Handbook of cognition and emotion*, John Wiley & Sons, New York, pp. 3–19.

LeUnes, A 2000, 'Updated bibliography on the Profile of Mood States in sport and exercise psychology', *Journal of Applied Sport Psychology*, 12, 110–13.

LeUnes, A & Burger, J 1998, 'Bibliography on the Profile of Mood States in sport and exercise, 1971–1995', *Journal of Sport Behavior*, 21, 53–70.

Levensen, RW, Carstensen, LL, Friesen, WV & Ekman, P 1991, 'Emotion, physiology, and expression in old age', *Psychology and Aging*, 6, 28–35.

Levensen, RW, Ekman, P & Friesen, WV 1990, 'Voluntary facial expression generates emotion-specific nervous system activity', *Psychophysiology*, 27, 363–84.

Lorr, M & McNair, DM 1988, *Manual for the Profile of Mood States — Bipolar form*, Educational and Industrial Testing Service, San Diego, CA.

Lucaccini, LF & Kreit, LH 1972, 'Music', in WP Morgan (ed.), *Ergogenic aids and muscular performance*, Academic Press, New York, pp. 240–5.

McAuley, E & Courneya, KS 1994, 'The Subjective Exercise Experience Scale (SEES): development and preliminary validation', *Journal of Sport & Exercise Psychology*, 16, 163–77.

McNair, DM, Lorr, M & Droppelman, LF 1971, *Manual for the Profile of Mood States*, Educational and Industrial Testing Services, San Diego, CA.

McNair, DM, Lorr, M & Droppelman, LF 1992, *Revised manual for the Profile of Mood States*, Educational and Industrial Testing Services, San Diego, CA.

McNeil, JK, Stone, MJ, Kozma, A & Andres, D 1994, 'Age differences in mood: structure, mean level, and diurnal variation', *Canadian Journal on Aging*, 13, 201–20.

Morgan, WP 1974, 'Selected psychological considerations in sport', *Research Quarterly for Exercise and Sport*, 45, 374–90.

Morgan, WP 1980, 'Test of champions: the iceberg profile', *Psychology Today*, 14, 92–108.

Morgan, WP 1985, 'Selected psychological factors limiting performance: a mental health model', in DH Clarke and HM Eckert (eds), *Limits of human performance*, Human Kinetics, Champaign, IL, pp. 70–80.

Morgan, WP (ed.) 1997, *Physical activity and mental health*, Taylor & Francis, Washington, DC.

Morgan, WP, Brown, DR, Raglin, JS, O'Connor, PJ & Ellickson, KA 1987, 'Psychological monitoring of overtraining and staleness', *British Journal of Sports Medicine*, 21, 107–14.

Morgan, WP & Johnson, RW 1978, 'Personality characteristics of successful and unsuccessful oarsmen', *International Journal of Sport Psychology*, 9, 119–33.

Morgan, WP & Pollock, ML 1977, 'Psychologic characterisation of the elite distance runner', *Annals of the New York Academy of Sciences*, 301, 383–403.

Morris, WN 1992, 'A functional analysis of the role of mood in affective systems', in MS Clarke (ed.), *Review of personality and social psychology: emotion*, Sage, Newbury Park, pp. 257–93.

Motl, RW, Berger, BG & Leuschen, PS 2000, 'The role of enjoyment in the exercise–mood relationship', *International Journal of Sport Psychology*, 31, 347–63.

Muraven, M, Tice, DM & Baumeister, RF 1998. 'Self-control as a limited resource: regulatory depletion patterns', *Journal of Personality & Social Psychology*, 74, 774-89.

Nagle, F, Morgan, WP, Hellickson, R, Serfass, R & Alexander, J 1975, 'Spotting success traits in Olympic contenders', *Physician and Sports Medicine*, 3, 31–4.

O'Connor, PJ 1997, 'Overtraining and staleness', in WP Morgan (ed.), *Physical activity and mental health*, Taylor & Francis, Washington, DC, pp. 145–60.

Owens, AJN, Lane, AM & Terry, PC 2000, 'Mood states as predictors of tennis performance: a test of a conceptual model' (abstract), *Journal of Sports Sciences*, 18, 559–60.

Parkinson, B, Totterdell, P, Briner, RB & Reynolds, S 1996, *Changing moods: the psychology of mood and mood regulation*, Longman, London.

Parrott, WG & Hertel, P 1999, 'Research methods in cognition and emotion', in T Dalgleish & M Power (eds), *Handbook of cognition and emotion*, John Wiley & Sons, New York, pp. 61–81.

Parrott, WG & Sabini, J 1990, 'Moods and memory under natural conditions: evidence for mood congruent recall', *Journal of Personality and Social Psychology*, 59, 321–36.

Penner, LA, Shiffman, S, Paty, JA & Fritzsche, BA 1994, 'Individual differences in intraperson variability in mood', *Journal of Personality and Social Psychology*, 66, 712–21.

Petruzello, SJ, Landers, DM, Hatfield, BD, Kubitz, KA & Salizar, W 1991, 'A meta-analysis on the anxiety-reducing effects of acute and chronic exercise: outcomes and mechanisms', *Sports Medicine*, 11, 143–82.

Prapavessis, H 2000, 'The POMS and sports performance: a review', *Journal of Applied Sport Psychology*, 12, 34–48.

Ptacek, JT, Smith, RE, Espe, K & Raffety, B 1994, 'Limited correspondence between daily reports and retrospective coping recall', *Psychological Assessment*, 6, 41–8.

Raglin, J 1997, 'Anxiolytic effect of physical activity', in WP Morgan (ed.), *Physical activity and mental health*, Taylor & Francis, Washington, DC, pp. 107–26.

Rasmussen, PR, Jeffrey, AC, Willingham, JK & Glover, TL 1994, 'Implications of the true score model in assessment of mood state', *Journal of Social Behavior and Personality*, 9, 107–18.

Renger, R 1993, 'A review of the Profile of Mood States (POMS) in the prediction of athletic success', *Journal of Applied Sport Psychology*, 5, 78–84.

Riddick, C 1984, 'Comparative psychological profiles of three groups of collegians: competitive swimmers, recreational swimmers, and inactive swimmers', *Journal of Sport Behavior*, 7, 160–74.

Rokke, PD 1993, 'Social context and perceived task difficulty as mediators of depressive self-evaluation', *Emotion and Motivation*, 17, 23–40.

Rowley, AJ, Landers, DM, Kyllo, LB & Etnier, JL 1995, 'Does the iceberg profile discriminate between successful and less successful athletes? A meta-analysis', *Journal of Sport & Exercise Psychology*, 16, 185–99.

Russell, JA 1980, 'A circumplex model of affect', *Journal of Personality and Social Psychology*, 39, 1161–78.

Russell, JA & Feldman Barrett, L 1999, 'Core affect, prototypical emotional episodes, and other things called emotion: dissecting the elephant', *Journal of Personality and Social Psychology*, 76, 805–19.

Schwarz, N & Bless, H 1991, 'Happy and mindless, but sad and smart? The impact of affective states on analytic reasoning', in P Forgas (ed.), *Emotion and social judgement*, Pergamon, Oxford, UK, pp. 55–71.

Shacham, S 1983, 'A shortened version of the Profile of Mood States', *Journal of Personality Assessment*, 47, 305–6.

Sinha, R & Parsons, OA 1996, 'Multivariate response patterning of fear and anger', *Cognition and Emotion*, 10, 173–98.

Smith, RE, Leffingwell, TR & Ptacek, JT 1999, 'Can people remember how they coped? Factors associated with discordance between same-day and retrospective reports', *Journal of Personality and Social Psychology*, 76, 1050–61.

Somer, E 1995, *Food and mood: the complete guide to eating well and feeling your best*, Henry Holt, New York.

Spielberger, CD 1991, *Manual for the State-Trait Anger Expression Inventory*, Psychological Assessment Resources, Odessa, FL.

Steptoe, A & Cox, S 1988, 'Acute effects of aerobic exercise on mood', *Health Psychology*, 7, 329–40.

Stevens, M & Lane, AM 2000, 'Mood-regulating strategies used by athletes' (abstract), *Journal of Sports Sciences*, 18, 58–9.

Stevens, M, Lane, AM & Terry, PC 2001, 'The impact of response set on measures of mood' (abstract), *Journal of Sports Sciences*, 19, 82.

Terry, PC 1995, 'The efficacy of mood state profiling with elite performers: a review and synthesis', *The Sport Psychologist*, 9, 309–24.

Terry, PC 1997, 'The application of mood profiling with elite sport performers', in R Butler (ed.), *Sport psychology in performance*, Butterworth-Heinemann, Oxford, UK, pp. 3–32.

Terry, PC & Lane, AM 2000, 'Development of normative data for the Profile of Mood States for use with athletic samples', *Journal of Applied Sport Psychology*, 12, 69–85.

Terry, PC, Lane, AM & Fogarty, GJ 2003, 'Construct validity of the Profile of Mood States — Adolescents for use with adults', *Psychology of Sport and Exercise*, 4, 125–39.

Terry, PC, Lane, AM, Lane, HJ & Keohane, L 1999, 'Development and validation of a mood measure for adolescents', *Journal of Sports Sciences*, 17, 861–72.

Thayer, RE 1986, 'Activation–Deactivation Adjective Checklist: current overview and structural analysis', *Psychological Reports*, 58, 607–14.

Thayer, RE 1989, *The biopsychology of mood and arousal*, Oxford University Press, New York.

Thayer, RE 1996, *The origin of everyday moods: managing energy, tension, and stress*, Oxford University Press, New York.

Thayer, RE, Newman, JR & McClain, TM 1994, 'Self-regulation of mood: strategies for changing a bad mood, raising energy, and reducing tension', *Journal of Personality and Social Psychology*, 67, 910–25.

Trafton, T, Meyers, M & Skelly, W 1998, 'Psychological characteristics of the telemark skier', *Journal of Sport Behavior*, 20, 465–75.

Vallerand, RJ & Blanchard, CM 2000, 'The study of emotion in sport and exercise: historical, definitional, and conceptual perspectives', in YL Hanin (ed.), *Emotions in sport*, Human Kinetics, Champaign, IL, pp. 3–37.

Wagner, HL & Manstead, A (eds) 1989, *Handbook of social psychophysiology*, John Wiley & Sons, New York.

Watson, D 1988, 'The vicissitudes of mood measurements: the varying descriptors, time frames, and response formats on the study of positive and negative affect, *Journal of Personality and Social Psychology*, 55, 128–41.

Watson, D, Clark, LA & Tellegen, A 1988, 'Development and validation of brief measures of positive and negative affect: the PANAS scales', *Journal of Personality and Social Psychology*, 54, 1063–70.

Watson, D & Tellegen, A 1985, 'Toward a conceptual structure of mood', *Psychological Bulletin*, 98, 219–35.

Watson, D, Wiese, D, Vaidya, D & Tellegen, A 1999, 'The two general activation systems of affect: structural findings, evolutionary considerations, and psychobiological evidence', *Journal of Personality and Social Psychology*, 76, 820–38.

Wegner, DM 1994, 'Ironic processes of mental control', *Psychological Review*, 16, 34–52.

Wegner, DM & Pennebaker, JW (eds) 1993, *Handbook of mental control*, Prentice Hall, Englewood Cliffs, NJ.

Winkielman, P, Knauper, B & Schwarz, N 1998, 'Looking back at anger: reference periods change the interpretation of emotion frequency questions', *Journal of Personality and Social Psychology*, 75, 719–28.

Wurtman, JJ 1988, *Managing your mind and mood through food*, Grafton, London.

Yik, MSM, Russell, JA & Feldman Barrett, L 1999, 'Structure of self-reported current affect: integration and beyond', *Journal of Personality and Social Psychology*, 77, 600–19.

Zuckerman, M & Lubin, B 1985, *Manual for the Multiple Affect Adjective Checklist — revised*, Educational and Industrial Testing Services, San Diego, CA.

CHAPTER 3

STRESS AND ANXIETY IN SPORT

Daryl B Marchant & Tony Morris

Sports performers at all levels of competition face the constant challenge of regulating their emotions. For instance, athletes often talk in colloquial terms of being 'over the top' (over-aroused) or of not being able to 'get up for competition' (under-aroused). It has long been recognised that anxiety is one of the most powerful factors affecting participation and performance. More than seventy years ago McHale, Chadwick and Taylor (1931) described the negative effects of anxiety on performance in Australian football.

> You say that 'Smith can't play before a crowd because he is nervous' ... Some people are naturally calm; even in the most exciting moments they have such a complete mastery over their feelings; others have so trained themselves that they are able to stand the strain, while others again are categorized as incurable ... We have seen players in a dressing room before an important game showing distinct signs of 'the needle'. They walk about uneasily, they cannot keep still, their faces pale, all unmistakable signs of nervousness, and yet ten minutes after the game has started in many cases the 'disease' has disappeared. (p. 117)

Anxiety is a fundamental part of the sport experience for many athletes. McHale et al. allude to aspects of anxiety, such as trait anxiety, anxiety management, crowd effects and behavioural anxiety. In subsequent years sport psychologists have investigated anxiety and related concepts of stress and arousal in minute detail. Indeed, anxiety, stress and arousal remain among the most heavily researched and widely discussed themes in sport psychology.

Frequently researched topics related to sport anxiety include the multidimensional aspects of anxiety and the development and evaluation of anxiety measures. In this chapter we consider how sport psychology researchers of stress and anxiety have also raised a number of questions relating to anxiety processes, such as causal factors, consequences of anxiety, the choking phenomenon and interventions designed to minimise the negative consequences of anxiety. Although anxiety is the central focus of this chapter, over the past 10 years or more sport psychologists have paid increasing attention to *coping* as an alternative approach to stress management. Thus, the last section of the chapter discusses stress and coping. The chapter ends by reviewing future directions for theory and research.

Anxiety remains a conundrum because, despite impressive advances in conceptual understanding, there exists a gulf between knowledge gleaned from research and the delivery of treatments to anxious athletes. Burton (1990) stated candidly, 'l learned early on in my work as an educational sport psychologist that anxiety is a topic that is easier to theorise about than to apply effectively' (p. 171). Despite the vast amount of accumulated research examining the structure of anxiety, we still cannot confidently predict performance based on current theories and measures of anxiety, or ensure that sports participants can enjoy the experience of competing free from overpowering and unpleasant anxieties. In a wider context, anxiety and stress also affect many students, public speakers and performing artists (e.g. musicians, dancers and actors). A number of the sport-anxiety topics covered in this chapter are relevant to a broad range of performance situations. The aim of this chapter is to provide a summary of the theoretical study of stress, anxiety and arousal in sport, an issue on which whole books have been written (e.g. Jones & Hardy 1993; Martens, Vealey & Burton 1990). The chapter is interspersed with quotes from prominent athletes and discussion issues to allow readers to connect theory and research with their own experiences. Applied sport psychologists have developed many approaches to the management of stress and anxiety. Smith and Smoll consider the management of stress and anxiety in chapter 11 of this text.

DISTINGUISHING BETWEEN AROUSAL, STRESS AND ANXIETY

Although some writers have used the terms *stress, arousal* and *anxiety* virtually interchangeably, they have important distinctions.

Arousal

There are a number of ways to interpret arousal; however, generally it is used to reflect the level of activity of various physiological indicators in the body, such as heart rate, respiration rate, galvanic skin response, hormonal activity, brain wave activity (EEGs) and temperature. These physiological indicators can be affected by a range of circumstances including physical activity, sexual arousal, excitement, anger or fear. Higher levels of arousal may be associated with positive or negative experiences. How the individual interprets the situation determines whether arousal is a pleasant or unpleasant experience. Bridges (1971) stated that arousal constitutes a continuum that includes relaxed drowsiness, wakefulness, curiosity and attentiveness. Increased levels of arousal may result in stronger emotions, such as joy, exhilaration, anxiety, panic, anger or rage.

Stress

Stress relates to the force applied to a system that invariably brings about some change or modification. Psychological stress is often thought of as the perceived demands of a situation in relation to the resources of the individual to cope with those demands. When the demands are judged to outweigh the person's resources, stress is the result. McGrath (1970) suggested that stress results when there is 'a substantial imbalance between [environmental] demand and response capability, under conditions where failure to meet the demands has important consequences' (p. 20). Some psychologists prefer to think of stress as the process itself; various emotional reactions might result from the stressor (i.e. the demand itself). For example, 'facing a tough opponent' (the stressor) is appraised as stretching one's resources (the stress process).

Anxiety

Anxiety normally refers to an unpleasant emotional state consisting of apprehension, tension, worry and nervousness. Anxiety is generally classified as having state and trait components. The differentiation between trait anxiety and state anxiety, as proposed by Cattell and Scheier (1961), was a major breakthrough in anxiety research. *Trait anxiety* is a predisposition to experiencing anxiety in a range of situations, whereas *state anxiety* refers to temporal and transitory feelings of anxiety associated with a specific situation. While it is important to understand the fundamental differences between arousal, stress and anxiety, many situations involve elements of all three.

KEY HISTORICAL DEVELOPMENTS

Anxiety has held an enduring fascination for sport psychologists. Sport anxiety research has advanced both methodologically and conceptually in the past four decades. For the sake of brevity, we have included a timeline that demonstrates some of the most critical advances in understanding anxiety, stress and arousal in sport (see figure 3.1).

MULTIDIMENSIONAL ANXIETY

From the early 1960s psychologists became aware that anxiety wasn't a unidimensional construct. We have already discussed the trait–state distinction. The multidimensional nature of anxiety can be further appreciated by discussing the cognitive–somatic and intensity–direction distinctions.

Cognitive–somatic anxiety distinction

Liebert and Morris (1967) were the first to draw a distinction between worry and emotionality or, as they are generally termed, cognitive anxiety and somatic anxiety. Cognitive anxiety is defined by Martens et al. (1990) as 'the mental component of anxiety and is caused by negative expectations about success or by negative self-evaluation' (p. 6). Cognitive anxiety is manifested in persistent worries and ruminations and an inability to concentrate. Martens et al. refer to somatic anxiety as 'the physiological and affective elements of the anxiety experience that develop directly from autonomic arousal' (p. 6). Somatic anxiety is reflected in responses such as rapid heart rate, shortness of breath, clammy hands, butterflies in the stomach and tense muscles.

Research shows that cognitive and somatic anxiety are likely to covary. Martens et al. (1990) argued that many situations elicit both cognitive and somatic elements of anxiety. For example, an athlete may exhibit conditioned somatic responses to a particular environment or event such as a locker room, a pre-contest warm-up routine or even a particular opponent. The conditioned somatic response may then trigger the athlete to start worrying. In contrast, Hatfield and Landers (1983) proposed that many individuals are primarily either cognitive 'responders' or somatic 'responders'. This idea ties in with the research of Davidson and Schwartz (1976), who developed a matching hypothesis — a diagnostic approach that assesses the anxiety sufferer as either cognitive or somatic anxiety dominant, and left hemisphere or right hemisphere dominant.

According to some theorists, somatic anxiety should influence performance less than cognitive anxiety, because it reaches its peak before and during the early stages of competition and then declines (Martens et al. 1990). In contrast, cognitive anxiety is hypothesised to be a better predictor of performance, because it is likely to persist for a greater part of the competition. Gould, Petlichkoff, Simons and Verera (1987) suggested that somatic anxiety influences performance primarily when the performer becomes preoccupied with the internal functions of his or her body, as often occurs with fine motor activities such as rifle shooting or golf putting and chipping. In these fine motor activities, physical effects such as hand tremor are detrimental to performance.

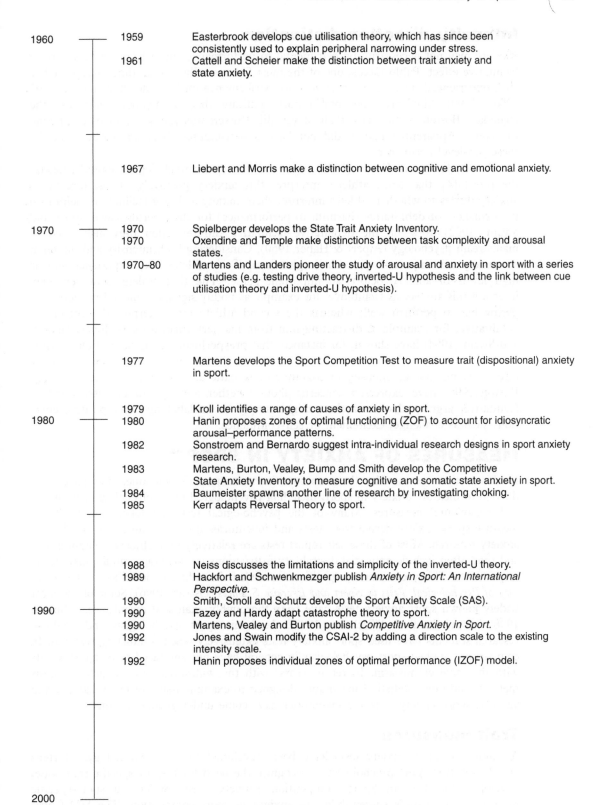

Figure 3.1   Key developments in sport anxiety research

Intensity–direction distinction

Anxiety may not necessarily be detrimental to performance. In fact, anxiety can have a facilitative effect. Pablo Casals, one of the most famous cellists of all time, is reported to have experienced strong anxiety with every performance until his death at the age of 97 (Plaut 1990). Similarly, anecdotal reports indicate that throughout his career the legendary Boston Celtics basketball player Bill Russell was physically ill before taking the court. Apparently anxiety did not have a detrimental effect on performance for these top-level performers.

Parfitt, Jones and Hardy (1990) suggested that sport psychologists should consider the possibility that some athletes interpret this anxiety positively. Thus, directional anxiety relates to whether athletes interpret their anxiety as being facilitative (helpful to performance) or debilitative (harmful to performance) for their performance. Jones and Swain (1992) drew on the debilitative–facilitative differentiation previously used in mainstream psychology (Alpert & Haber 1960). Considering both intensity and direction of anxiety has important practical implications. Two athletes may experience similar high levels of anxiety before an important game. The first athlete, however, may interpret this anxiety as facilitative, for example as bodily signals or mental triggers preparing her to perform well, whereas the second athlete may interpret the anxiety as debilitative, for example as distracting him from his performance focus. Jones, Hanton and Swain (1994) have shown, for instance, that pre-performance anxiety of elite swimmers differed from that of non-elite swimmers in both cognitive and somatic anxiety directions, but not in intensity of cognitive or somatic anxiety. Some researchers (e.g. Burton 1998) have expressed concerns about whether anxiety can be interpreted as facilitative, arguing that researchers might simply be mislabelling other positive emotions such as challenge, excitement or self-confidence.

MEASURES OF ANXIETY IN SPORT

In this section we consider the numerous instruments and techniques that have been devised to measure anxiety in sport, including psychological tests, physiological measures and behavioural measures. Many of the psychological tests developed specifically to measure sport anxiety derive from tests and inventories used in mainstream psychology anxiety research. Most of these self-report tests are relatively time efficient to administer, and they often include antisocial desirability instructions to encourage candid answers by respondents. Thirty-one anxiety-specific tests are listed and briefly described in the *Directory of Psychological Tests in Sport and Exercise Sciences* (Ostrow 1996). Some of the most widely known sport anxiety tests have been thoroughly examined recently (e.g. Burton 1998; Smith, Smoll & Wiechman 1998). Academic sport psychologists and graduate research students have used sport anxiety tests extensively when conducting research. In comparison, applied sport psychologists in general have not embraced sport anxiety tests with the same enthusiasm. In recent years, with the widespread use of factor analysis methods and other statistical techniques designed to examine issues of test reliability and validity, sport anxiety tests and inventories have come under greater scrutiny.

Trait measures

A number of trait anxiety tests have been developed in sport psychology. Martens (1977), the first sport psychologist to recognise the need for a sport-specific trait scale, developed the 15-item Sport Competition Anxiety Test (SCAT), a sport-specific measure of a person's susceptibility to anxiety in sport competition. The SCAT was especially popular in the 1980s as a research instrument. More recently Smith, Smoll and Schutz (1990) developed the Sport Anxiety Scale (SAS), which has superseded the SCAT as the most frequently used sport-specific measure of trait anxiety. The SAS is a multidimensional instrument consisting of 21 items grouped into three factors (worry, somatic anxiety and concentration disruption).

State measures

Martens, Burton, Vealey, Bump and Smith (1983) developed the 27-item Competitive State Anxiety Inventory–2 (CSAI-2) to measure athletes' perceived intensity of cognitive and somatic state anxiety and self-confidence. The reliability of the cognitive and somatic subscales was demonstrated using factor analysis. As discussed earlier, Jones and Swain (1992) provided a persuasive argument that state anxiety is governed by direction in addition to intensity. Thus, Jones and Swain developed the Directional Modification — Competitive State Anxiety Inventory–2 (DM-CSAI-2), which included a direction component permitting athletes to report on whether they perceive their anxiety as facilitative or debilitative. The directional interpretation of anxiety is a significant development and has considerable implications for practice. Nonetheless we should be cautious. We felt the same confidence about the distinction between state and trait anxiety 20 to 25 years ago, and then again about somatic and cognitive anxiety 10 to 15 years ago. Neither conceptualisation provided the complete answer, although each generated research that has enhanced our understanding of the relationship between emotions and performance.

Qualitative assessment of anxiety

There is so much diversity in anxiety responses that paper and pencil tests capture an incomplete range of the feelings people experience. Researchers have responded to this shortfall by using qualitative research methods in an effort to gain more in-depth information regarding individuals' anxiety experiences (e.g. Cohn 1990; Scanlan, Stein & Ravizza 1991). By using qualitative research methodologies, Strean (1998) wrote, '[Researchers] investigating sport might examine failures, choking and big disappointments more thoroughly' (p. 339). By widening the methodological paradigm, sport psychologists can potentially gain a richer and more well-rounded understanding of anxiety in sport.

When first meeting with an athlete, the applied sport psychologist conducts an intake interview. Intake interviews normally cover a broad range of topics, including sporting background, family, general health, personality and issues relating to sport performance such as perceived susceptibility to anxiety. For example, the sport psychologist might ask an athlete to describe situations in which he managed nerves and anxiety either well or poorly. After specific descriptions of anxiety-evoking situations have been described, the sport psychologist might then probe further by asking more specific anxiety-related questions. Because anxiety experiences are relatively complex, practical assistance for athletes needing to better manage anxiety depends on a thoughtful, well-conducted assessment (see highlighted feature on page 80).

Physiological assessments of anxiety are sometimes used in preference to paper and pencil questionnaires, but as with questionnaires these methods present their own advantages and disadvantages. For example, Landers et al. used physiological measures in a number of studies with elite rifle shooters and archers (e.g. Landers, Boutcher & Wang 1986). The researchers measured a number of physiological parameters and then applied them practically. For example, shooters were taught via biofeedback techniques to shoot in the middle of their cardiac cycle (i.e. r-spike) to reduce hand tremor. With ongoing improvements in technology and instrumentation, psychophysiological instruments can provide objective and accurate measurement not always possible with the more reactive psychological measures (e.g. paper and pencil tests).

DEVELOPMENT OF AN INTERVIEW PROTOCOL FOR ASSESSING ANXIETY

Working either individually or in small groups, place yourself in the position of the sport psychologist meeting for the first time with a talented junior golfer (Sarah). Sarah has been referred by her coach who says: 'Sarah has an excellent long game and also putts well, but at times her short game (chipping and pitching) is inconsistent. She has worked hard on her short game and has improved, but in competition she can't reproduce the quality shots she hits in practice.' While conducting the intake interview you ask Sarah about how her golf game is going. She replies, 'If only I didn't get so nervous when I am pitching the ball'. How will you respond to Sarah to initiate a thorough assessment of anxiety susceptibility? Listed below are some related issues and topics that might affect your assessment.

Client comfort level	Performance level
Non-verbal behaviour during interview	Goals and expectations
Trait anxiety	Anxiety inventory
Cognitive, physical and behavioural anxiety	Specific questions
Self-talk	Optimal arousal
Self-consciousness	Relaxation
Pressure	Concentration–anxiety connections

Finally, conduct a three-way anxiety assessment role-play with an 'observer', a 'sport psychologist' and a 'client'. Incorporate some of the issues above that you have already discussed.

When casually assessing whether team-mates or opponents are nervous, coaches and athletes normally use behavioural methods. Behavioural signs of anxiety include fidgeting, vomiting, talking about nerves, physiognomic (facial) changes, excessive sweating and pacing around the room. Observational assessments of anxiety can be less intrusive than either paper and pencil or psychophysiological techniques, but they suffer from the difficulty of making universal associations between particular behaviours and anxiety.

Despite the range of anxiety measurement options available to sport psychologists, including behavioural observation, in-depth interviews and physiological assessment, more often than not paper and pencil tests are administered as the sole method of assessing competitive anxiety. Very little research has been directed towards assessing the interrelationship between various measures of competitive anxiety. This type of research is necessary because considerable evidence has accumulated that competitive anxiety is multidimensional and idiosyncratic. In addition, the majority of research in anxiety to date has utilised quantitative methodologies, with a lack of published research examining anxiety from a qualitative perspective. Qualitative research designs often give participants a chance to reflect on their experiences, with the opportunity to express their anxiety experience in depth, rather than having to respond to predetermined questionnaires.

Some of the most recent anxiety research has taken a broader, more holistic approach. Cern (2003), for example, assessed anxiety in the context of a constellation of differential emotions. Cern concludes that assessment of athletes' emotional states should not be exclusively based on anxiety measures and recommends a broader approach that also encompasses such emotions as anger, guilt, shame and fear. Hanin (1995) initiated this emotion-focused approach by developing his individual zones of optimal performance (IZOF) approach, described later in this chapter, through which a spectrum of emotions are examined in addition to anxiety.

AROUSAL–PERFORMANCE AND ANXIETY–PERFORMANCE THEORIES

Sport psychologists have applied a number of unidimensional theories to explain the relationship between arousal and performance. Frequently cited theories include *drive theory* (Hull 1943) and *the inverted-U hypothesis* (Yerkes & Dodson 1908). At present there is little evidence to suggest that researchers are united in subscribing to any one of these theories as an adequate explanation of how anxiety affects performance. Furthermore the recent development of alternative explanations, such as *zone of optimal performance* (ZOF) (Hanin 1980), the *cusp catastrophe model* (Fazey & Hardy 1990) and *reversal theory* (Kerr 1985), perhaps reflects a dissatisfaction with more traditional arousal theories. Changes in allegiance over the years to different arousal theories may reflect a lack of confidence in their predictive validity. In this section we outline a number of these theories, moving from the more simplistic early theories to more sophisticated recent theories.

Inverted-U hypothesis and drive theory

The inverted-U hypothesis (Yerkes & Dodson 1908) is an interpretation of very early experimental findings. Yerkes and Dodson proposed that when arousal level is low, performance is also low. As arousal level increases, performance increases up to an optimal point. As arousal continues to increase to high and very high levels, performance is expected to gradually decline. The inverted-U hypothesis has intuitive appeal in sport; most sports performers are familiar with the experience of playing poorly because they felt either under-aroused or over-aroused. Although the inverted-U has intuitive appeal, however, most sport psychologists nowadays consider it simplistic and limited in its explanatory power. Traditionally the inverted-U hypothesis was cited and adopted widely, probably well beyond the supporting experimental evidence. Readers should be aware that sport psychology researchers have enumerated a number of issues and problems associated with the inverted-U hypothesis.

In the 1960s, when sport psychology was rapidly expanding as a field of research and practice, largely in the United States, the prevailing perspectives in mainstream psychology were behaviourism and trait psychology. Hull's (1943) drive theory was still a strong influence. Hull proposed that behaviour is a function of habit strength (previous learning) and drive. Applying drive theory to human behaviour, habit strength refers to the extent of prior learning of a skill. When people start learning a task, they usually make numerous mistakes; thus incorrect responses are dominant. As learning proceeds, the learner makes the correct response more often, until finally the correct response is dominant. Based on drive theory, resultant behaviour depends on habit strength multiplied by the level of drive (operationalised as anxiety). Thus, if a skill is well learned, behaviour (performance) is optimal when drive is high, because the correct response is dominant and high drive increases production of the dominant response. Conversely, for skills that are still being learned, behaviour (performance) is predicted to be optimal when drive is low. In these early stages of learning, performance is predicted to decline as drive level increases. Although some early research with relatively simple tasks provided support for the drive theory predictions, further research in sport was not favourable.

Cusp catastrophe theory

The cusp catastrophe model (CCM) is based on a set of mathematical models that reflect complex relationships between variables in which otherwise smooth relationships suddenly shift in a dramatic fashion. Hardy and Fazey (1987) applied a relatively simple

CCM to explain the relationships between cognitive state anxiety, somatic state anxiety and performance. Hardy and Fazey developed a sport adaptation of catastrophe theory for a number of reasons. First, they pointed out that the right-hand side of the inverted-U curve does not seem to correspond well to situations in which sports performers experience high levels of anxiety. Quite frequently performers suffer a dramatic (catastrophic) decline in performance rather than a gradual decline, as the inverted-U depicts. Second, Hardy and Fazey observed that, although such catastrophic effects can be seen in the performance of any athlete, they do not always occur. An adequate model must explain why high arousal is sometimes catastrophic and on other occasions just a minor nuisance. Third, Hardy and Fazey argued that explanations that posited two separate relationships, one between cognitive state anxiety and performance and the second between somatic state anxiety and performance, were too simplistic. In the CCM, Hardy and Fazey found a single framework that was capable of explaining more of the complexities of how arousal affects performance. The technical details of CCM are more fully expounded by Hardy (1990). The capacity of CCM to explain performance catastrophes varies, reflecting the equivocal research findings to date (see Cohen, Pargman & Tenenbaum 2002; Hardy 1996).

Reversal theory

Apter (1982) developed a wide-ranging theory relating motivation to emotion. Kerr (1985) then adapted this perspective in the context of anxiety in sport. *Reversal theory* is based on the concept of meta-motivational states that are considered to be broad, underlying ways of viewing the world. Apter called them telic and paratelic states. The telic state is a serious, goal-directed perspective, whereas the paratelic state is a fun-loving, non-directional way of being. Although Apter proposed that individuals are predisposed to experience the world through one perspective, he argued that everyone switches between these ways of viewing their environment at various times. It is this switching that creates reversals — that is, emotional states such as anxiety. Low arousal is interpreted as relaxation in the telic state and high arousal is experienced as anxiety. For the individual in a paratelic state, however, low arousal corresponds to boredom, whereas high arousal is experienced as excitement. Thus a switch from telic to paratelic state for a person whose arousal level is low means a reversal of experience from relaxation to boredom. When an individual switches from telic to paratelic under conditions of high arousal, the reversal changes experience from anxiety to excitement.

Individual zones of optimal functioning (IZOF)

Hanin (e.g. 1980, 1995) has long been working on the concept of *individual zones of optimal functioning* (IZOF). Hanin's model is particularly interesting because it is more practical in orientation than some approaches to arousal and performance. Hanin proposed that performance is optimal within a zone of plus or minus a half standard deviation on the arousal continuum. The zone of optimal functioning varies from athlete to athlete, and thus is mostly relevant for intra-athlete rather than inter-athlete comparison. To identify the IZOF for a specific athlete, Hanin proposed that it is necessary to measure arousal or state anxiety and performance on a number of occasions until the pattern of arousal/anxiety levels at which performance is good, moderate and poor emerges. Woodman, Albinson and Hardy (1997) have suggested that a sample of two or three best scores might provide the foundation for retrospectively identifying an IZOF. Most research has provided support (e.g. Hanin & Syrja 1995) or qualified support (e.g. Prapavessis & Grove 1991) for the IZOF model. The IZOF continues to hold promise as a useful, practical method for identifying emotional states that are helpful or unhelpful before and during performance. As sport psychology has become more open to individualised approaches in recent years, Hanin's work has begun to receive more attention and appreciation.

Much has changed since the early days of sport anxiety research, when the approach was often mechanistic — that is, x must be right and y must be wrong. Nowadays there is a greater appreciation and willingness to consider several perspectives simultaneously. The cusp catastrophe model, zones of optimal performance and reversal theory, for example, might best be viewed as alternative explanations, each of which is capable of explaining important aspects of the complex relationship between anxiety and sports performance.

Process issues

Early sport psychology researchers frequently conducted studies to test whether global-unidimensional anxiety predicted global performance measures, such as game score, race or time. Not surprisingly, results were equivocal, because performance outcome has been shown to be affected by a wide range of variables (e.g. physical, technical, mental and tactical). With the benefit of hindsight and an appreciation of anxiety as a multidimensional construct, these early attempts to study how anxiety affects performance now appear rather crude and naive. Despite the development of multidimensional state anxiety theory, sport-specific measures and more sophisticated arousal–performance models, by the late 1980s and early 1990s the level of prediction achieved in research on the anxiety–performance relationship in sport was still proving to be moderate at best. An alternative approach to the study of how anxiety affects performance is to examine performance process components. The next section reviews the many variables that have been identified as potential causes of anxiety and how, specifically, the athlete is affected by anxiety. Following this, intervention strategies often used by applied sport psychologists to assist athletes in better managing anxiety are briefly reviewed. The choice of anxiety management strategies to a large degree depends on a thorough understanding of these process issues. Thus an integrated model (see figure 3.2) is presented that brings together the huge range of causes, effects and interventions in the sport anxiety area.

CAUSES, EFFECTS AND TREATMENT OF COMPETITIVE ANXIETY

As a result of more than forty years of sport anxiety research we have seen a number of conceptual breakthroughs in explaining links between anxiety and performance. An associated challenge has been to draw together the sometimes disparate and multifaceted anxiety research into workable models that practitioners can readily adopt. In this section we discuss competitive anxiety from a sequential diagnostic perspective by outlining, first, the causes or antecedents of anxiety; second, the effects or manifestations of anxiety; and third, the treatments or interventions typically used to work with anxious athletes. This approach, we believe, might reflect the methods used by applied sport psychologists, who need to assess a broad range of interrelated causes and effects of anxiety before proceeding to teach athletes anxiety management strategies.

Causes of anxiety in sport

Research to enumerate the underlying causes of performance anxiety in sport has been intermittent. Causes of anxiety seem to emanate from athlete characteristics and situational factors. Athletes can quickly move from relaxed to anxious states, or vice-versa, depending on their perceptions of how well they are playing and the context of the game or match.

Predisposition to experiencing anxiety, which is frequently included as a dimension in personality inventories (e.g. NEO-PIR; Costa & McCrae 1992), is referred to as trait anxiety. Research has consistently found that a predisposition to experience high levels of sports-specific trait anxiety is correlated to state anxiety in the $r = .5$ to .6 range (Weinburg & Genuchi 1980). Thus trait anxiety is a logical starting point for predicting those athletes who are likely to frequently experience high levels of state anxiety. Ego threat, perceived uncertainty of outcome and perceived importance of outcome are frequently cited as causes of anxiety. Dunn and Nielsen (1993) found that situations in which attention was focused negatively on soccer and ice hockey players were consistently perceived as sources of threat. The types of situations included being benched, receiving criticism from the coach and making a bad pass that led to an opposition goal. Another prevalent source of anxiety relates to the internal pressure associated with not performing to expectation and not improving on previous performance. Gould and Weinberg (1985) identified 33 separate sources of worry with wrestlers. Two of the top four perceived worries related directly to performance expectations. Perceived uncertainty is 'the inability to predict the future, especially if the doubt centers on the experience of potentially unpleasant events like punishment, physical harm, failure, or rejection' (p. 52). Perceived importance of outcome relates to the perceived value of attaining a favourable result. According to Martens et al. (1990), the perceived value is a combination of the intrinsic and extrinsic consequences of the result. Extrinsic consequences include tangible rewards, such as money or positive reinforcement, whereas intrinsic consequences include a sense of mastery, feelings of competence and increased self-esteem. A number of researchers have found high levels of perceived importance to be a source of competitive anxiety (e.g. Marchant, Morris & Andersen 1998; Prapavessis, Cox & Brooks 1996).

In a study of university basketball players, Gruber and Beauchamp (1979) found game difficulty to be closely related to state anxiety. Mean scores for global state anxiety were significantly different for two practice situations ($M = 19.5$, $SD = 3.9$), compared with three easy games ($M = 22.0$, $SD = 6.7$), and three crucial games ($M = 25.4$, $SD = 6.5$), thus demonstrating that as task difficulty increased, so did state anxiety. A number of studies have shown how the presence of others can lead to anxiety. Cohn (1990) reported that the first tee shot was a significant stressor for nine out of the ten collegiate golfers interviewed. The stress of teeing up is exemplified by the following quote: 'The biggest is the first tee, whether I am in a match or just playing with friends; you just have a lot of pressure to start well, and usually if I do well it will cut down the stress' (p. 101). In another qualitative study by Scanlan et al. (1991), skating in front of people and falling in front of a crowd were mentioned as sources of stress for some skaters. In addition, the comments, expectations and attitudes of coaches and parents can be a source of stress for some athletes. Apart from the constancy of sport-related stressors, other unexpected stressful events may produce anxiety responses. Although many general life stressors, such as daily hassles and life events, are not directly linked to competition, they can negatively influence an athlete's preparation, and hence represent a potential source of anxiety that may affect competition. The opportunity to hit the game-winning run, hole the tournament-winning putt or defy the opposition with a buzzer-beating jump shot represent critical moments in sport contests. Krane, Joyce and Rafeld (1994) investigated the effects of situation criticality with collegiate softball players. Krane et al. found a significant increase in cognitive state anxiety when the score differential in competition was close and when a player was on third base, compared with when there was a two-run or more score differential and when third base was not occupied.

Effects of anxiety

Sport psychologists have identified an array of specific somatic, cognitive and behavioural effects relating to competitive anxiety (see Hackfort & Schwenkmezger 1989 and Harris & Harris 1984 for extensive lists of anxiety effects). Apart from direct physical manifestations, somatic effects may also indirectly contribute to injury susceptibility (Andersen & Williams 1988).

COGNITIVE, SOMATIC AND BEHAVIOURAL EFFECTS OF COMPETITIVE ANXIETY

Early sports anxiety research found that coaches are unable to predict accurately which of their athletes will experience competitive anxiety. Perhaps this is because the effects of anxiety are so diverse and not necessarily readily observable. Compile three separate lists of the types of cognitive, somatic or physical, and behavioural effects that an anxious athlete might experience. Which of these effects would an astute coach identify either before or during competition?

The intensity and manifestation of anxiety symptoms differ from person to person and situation to situation. In addition, each subsystem (i.e. somatic, cognitive or behavioural) triggers the others. For example, thinking about a particularly challenging opponent may first induce worrying thoughts, followed by an increase in heart rate and breathing and, finally, a change in facial expression. In addition, each subsystem is connected, allowing for a multitude of feedback loops. Symptoms of anxiety are further mediated by a number of sport- and person-related variables. Sport-related variables include task complexity, task duration, type of sport (i.e. team or individual, contact or non-contact, open skills or closed skills, direct or indirect opposition) and skill level. Examples of individual-related variables are experience level and quality of past experiences. Consider the experiences of elite Australian swimmer Susie O'Neill (see highlighted feature below). Two-time Olympic gold medallist O'Neill, in her book *Choose to Win: Achieving Your Goals, Fulfilling Your Dreams*, discusses how self-doubt and anxiety plagued the early part of her swimming career — first when competing as a nine-year-old in a regional carnival, and later before the 1994 Commonwealth Games trials.

ELITE SWIMMER OVERCOMES EARLY CAREER ANXIETY TO WIN OLYMPIC GOLD MEDALS

'Nothing would get rid of the nervous feeling that was overtaking me. I was so petrified I started to feel sick. I dived in and I knew I would not be able to reach the other side ... I felt overwhelmed and became physically sick at the thought of putting my head under the water. My breathing started to shorten and then I seemed to forget to breathe. I felt a claustrophobic sensation ... This wasn't a one-off situation. I barely finished one freestyle race in three years ... It was weird because I had no problem in training, but things changed once it got to the racing stage.' (pp. 22–3)

'... Mr Wakefield [her coach] really made a difference. I worked on being relaxed before races and he gave me breathing exercises to practise. He would tell me to concentrate on my breathing before I dived in ... but the focus on relaxation and on my breathing worked. I was so busy trying to breathe properly I forgot about my fears.' (p. 24)

(continued)

'... before all my races I had this awful sickly feeling. My nerves were uncontrollable. I had lost my confidence after a time trial the day before the trials. I knew then I was not going to have a good meet. I felt lethargic and heavy in the water and my arms felt weak and brittle, as though they were twigs. Something I called "twiggy". I was trying hard but it felt like I was going backwards.' (pp. 6–7)

Discuss with other students a situation in which you experienced severe debilitating anxiety and yet later became successful. Also, consider the link between the probable causes and the manifestations of the anxiety.

Treatment of anxiety

Mahoney and Meyers (1989) suggested there is considerable room for improvement in the treatment of sport-related anxiety. Assuming the practitioner correctly diagnoses the source of the anxiety, a successful treatment outcome is still contingent on a thorough understanding of likely symptoms. Finally, a comprehensive knowledge of anxiety reduction techniques and their delivery is necessary before selecting the 'treatment of choice'. The range of cognitive approaches available to practitioners includes rational emotive therapy (Ellis 1970), cognitive behaviour therapy (Beck 1976), systematic desensitisation (Wolpe 1958), stress inoculation therapy (Meichenbaum 1985) and stress management training (Smith 1980). Somatic treatments include progressive muscle relaxation (Jacobson 1938), relaxation response, a derivative of transcendental meditation (Benson 1975), hypnosis, autogenic training and biofeedback. The wide range of treatments available permits many possible strategies to combat anxiety.

Figure 3.2 shows an integrated flow diagram of the many variables and factors that relate to the causes, effects and treatment of anxiety in sport. The diagram could easily be expanded to include additional information; nevertheless the multidimensionality of anxiety in sport is easily demonstrated.

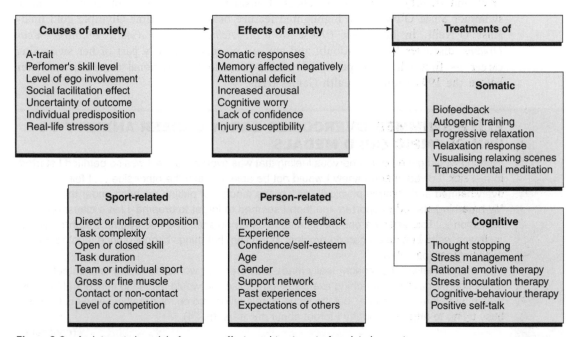

Figure 3.2 An integrated model of causes, effects and treatment of anxiety in sport

Anxiety in sport is a very complex emotion. We have deliberately shown that there are many factors that an applied sport psychologist will need to understand to work effectively to help athletes better manage anxiety. In the next section we turn our attention to special cases — in particular the intense and severe anxiety experiences that are described as 'choking'. We explain the choking phenomenon from an anxiety–attention perspective.

CHOKING

With victory in sight, a golfer inexplicably misses what would normally be an easy putt. After being in a commanding position, a tennis player repeatedly produces unforced errors. Some of the most experienced and talented athletes talk openly about choking. For example, tennis player Pete Sampras confessed after winning his seventh Wimbledon title, 'We all choke ... No matter who you are, you just feel pressure in the heat of the moment ... I really felt it slipping away ... From a matter of feeling like I was going to lose the match, I felt like I was going to win within two minutes' (Sampras 2000). Athletes are often accused of choking when they fail to perform well in important competitions or when, after being in a winning position, they suffer a dramatic decline in form. Sports reports in newspapers and magazines often describe situations in which high-profile performers have purportedly choked under pressure. In such reports, journalists speculate that athletes such as golfer Greg Norman or tennis player Jana Novotna, after enjoying a commanding position, have choked and subsequently lost in major events and competitions. The media frequently report such incidents, and typically base their accusations of choking on conjecture, rather than on hard evidence or a clear notion of what actually constitutes a choke.

The following discussion proposes that choking is a complex issue. Although the research to date has advanced our understating of choking, a number of unresolved issues remain. First, several definitions exist, none of which appears adequate. Second, a number of theoretical explanations have been advanced and tested, with no one theory gaining universal support from researchers. Third, the fundamental role of self-consciousness in choking is frequently discussed, yet some researchers have supported the view that high self-conscious individuals are more susceptible to choking, whereas other researchers have proposed that low self-conscious individuals are more susceptible. Fourth, although some researchers have suggested that choking may be related to an inability to cope with pressure, no studies have examined coping processes in detail. Sport psychologists generally agree, however, that choking is a combined anxiety–attention problem.

A problem for researchers investigating choking has been the lack of definitional agreement. Baumeister (1984) defined choking as 'performance decrements under pressure circumstances' (p. 610) and defined pressure as 'any factor or combination of factors that increases the importance of performing well on a particular occasion' (p. 610). Since poor performance can be caused by a myriad reasons, it becomes difficult to isolate choking as the actual reason for the performance decrement. Furthermore, the Baumeister definition is limited in the sense that even a relatively small performance decrement under pressure could be interpreted as choking. Arguably, popular opinion defines only relatively large decrements in performance under pressure as choking. From a research perspective, the Baumeister definition is relatively easy to operationalise, but it may run the risk of false negatives (i.e. including people as chokers who have not choked). Hall and Marchant (2003) have recently redefined choking as 'an elevation in anxiety and arousal levels under perceived pressure leading to a critical deterioration in the execution of habitual performing'.

A number of theoretical models have been put forward to explain the choking phenomenon. The distraction model is based on the belief that, under pressure, athletes become concerned about their performance, which diverts attention from the performance task and results in performance decrements (e.g. Nideffer 1992). The distraction model may involve one of two processes. First, the performer chokes, because he or she ceases to filter cues selectively and attempts to process an increased amount of information. Second, the performer processes a normal amount of information but shifts his or her focus of attention to task-irrelevant cues, thereby neglecting the critical features of the task. Nideffer and Sagal (1998) have suggested that over-attention to task-irrelevant factors, such as internal distractions (e.g. self-doubt, self-evaluation, awareness of fatigue or pain, anxiety) results in physiological changes (e.g. increases in muscle tension, heart rate, respiration) and attentional changes (e.g. narrowing of attention, internal focus of attention), which then affect performance.

Another widely researched theory, proposed by Baumeister (1984) and Masters (1992), is based on the belief that choking occurs when the automatic execution of a well-learned task is inhibited. When individuals first attempt a task they have to attend to the particulars of the task (controlled processing). With repeated practice, less and less attention to those task particulars is required for successful completion. The expert athlete, for example, can perform the task without conscious control of the steps that make up the performance (i.e. automatic processing). According to proponents of the automatic execution model of choking, performers under pressure typically refocus on the specific steps of execution during performance. Paradoxically, the attempt to consciously control performance processes inhibits automatic skill processing. Beilock and Carr (2001) recently completed a sophisticated series of studies that showed conclusively that attending to proceduralised skills diminished performance on a golf-putting task (i.e. support for the automatic execution model). In general, to prevent athletes from choking, sport psychologists who subscribe to the distraction model are likely to promote the importance of focusing on task-relevant cues under pressure. Based on the fundamentals of the automatic execution model, athletes who focus on task-relevant cues under pressure, such as the mechanics of skill execution, may increase their chances of choking. Conceivably, either model may explain choking, depending on factors such as the type of task, skill level, attentional demands and skill demands.

A personality characteristic that has been consistently linked with choking is self-consciousness (S-C). According to Fenigstein (1979), self-conscious individuals believe themselves to be the target of others' observations, and this oversensitivity leads to further self-focus. Self-consciousness takes the form of private S-C (e.g. a tendency to focus on inner thoughts, feelings, moods and attitudes) or public S-C (e.g. a tendency to focus on outwardly observable aspects of the self, such as physical appearance). Baumeister (1984) found that low S-C individuals were more likely to choke in a series of non-sport experiments. Baumeister claimed that high self-conscious people find it easier to cope with situations that promote self-awareness because they are accustomed to performing while focusing on themselves. In contrast, sport-specific studies (e.g. Beilock and Carr 2001; Wang 2002) have found that high self-conscious people are more susceptible to choking in sport than low self-conscious people. A closer examination of Baumeister's (1984) study, however, shows that a relatively simple task was used, which is probably inappropriate because inhibition of automatic execution typically occurs in complex skill tasks.

Coping style is another variable that seemingly affects choking susceptibility. The most common categorisation of coping styles in sport research has been through approach and avoidance styles. An approach coping style refers to the typical use of coping strategies that direct cognitive and behavioural efforts towards reducing the intensity of stress. Conversely, avoidance coping style refers to the typical use of coping strategies that direct the activity away from the threat-related stimulus (Anshel & Weinberg 1999). Wang, Marchant and Morris (in press) found that approach coping style was negatively associated with performance under pressure on a basketball free throw task. Anshel and Weinberg (1999) have found that 'approachers' are more likely to become distracted from the task by becoming immersed in a process of explanation. The old adage 'paralysis by analysis' seems to sum up much of what approachers engage in. Conversely, 'avoiders' under pressure avoided thinking about the threatening information.

To gain a more thorough understanding of choking in sport, researchers need to address a number of current issues and limitations. We need to develop a more comprehensive definition of choking in sports. In addition, researchers will no doubt pursue other possibilities, such as coping processes and choking, specific interventions for athletes susceptible to choking, and whether choking resembles established arousal–performance theories (e.g. catastrophe theory). Alternatively, some researchers might choose to examine participants who are resistant to choking even under extreme pressure.

The media have reinforced the use of the term choking, and this has produced unfortunate connotations and associations. Consider the well-documented story of Jean Van de Velde, an athlete golfer who (according to media analysts) choked when in a position to win the prestigious British Open Golf Championship (see the following highlighted feature).

CHOKING: A COMBINED ANXIETY–ATTENTION PROBLEM

During the closing stages of the 1999 British Open golf tournament, Frenchman Jean Van de Velde, ranked outside the top 100 golfers at the time, held a three-stroke lead going into the 72nd and last hole. After performing superbly over 71 holes, Van de Velde's performance deteriorated rapidly. His first shot was a wayward drive, followed by a shot that ricocheted off the grandstand and into long grass. It was at this point that the slide really began, Van de Velde's next stroke dropping squarely into a lateral waterway. After removing his shoes and socks and wading in, Van de Velde eventually took a one-stroke penalty drop, and proceeded to place his next stroke into a greenside bunker. The result was a triple bogey, and Van de Velde subsequently lost in a playoff. At face value, Van de Velde's performance appears to be a clear case of choking. An interview with the Frenchman, however, perhaps suggested otherwise, and certainly points up the need for caution before making accusations of choking without investigating the athlete's perceptions. Van de Velde apparently later suggested in an interview that he intentionally aimed at the green with his second shot rather than 'laying up', as commentators continually suggested he should have done. Van de Velde felt a poor shot or mishit into the surrounding grandstands would result in a 'free drop' into a relief zone next to the green. Whether Van de Velde choked is arguable; however, the incident highlights the importance of considering the athlete's perceptions before applying the choking label.

Consider the following debatable points and questions:

- Choking is sad because highly skilled athletes fail to convert their abilities.
- Choking is given too much attention by the mass media.
- Choking probably happens to sub-elite athletes more than elite athletes.
- Choking is likely to be most prevalent in which sports? Why?
- How would you define choking?
- Have you ever choked in a performance domain?
- Assuming you have experienced choking, would you openly discuss it? Why? Why not?

STRESS AND COPING

For many years the concept of stress was confused with anxiety. More recently stress has been conceptualised as a process that is linked to coping. In this section we briefly consider the development of the theoretical concept of stress in general psychology, then we link stress to coping. We discuss the measurement of stress and coping, then we look at the ways in which these concepts have been applied to sport, including in qualitative research that has substantially developed our understanding of stress and coping in sport.

Conceptualising stress and coping

Selye (1975), a physiologist, first defined 'stress' in terms of the demands placed on a person in relation to his or her resources. When the demands are greater than the person's resources, stress is experienced. Selye also pointed out that stress can be subjectively perceived to be positive or negative. It is individuals' interpretation that determines whether they experience *eustress* (i.e. positive stress) or *distress* (i.e. negative experience). The adoption of the term in everyday language has caused much confusion in psychology. People commonly refer to their job, a divorce or a tough match as stressful. This broad use of the term to mean a *stimulus* that leads to stress can be avoided by using the term *stressor* to identify something that creates stress. Similarly, people talk about feeling stress or being stressed; in this case, stress is employed to denote a *response* to a stressor. The conceptualisation of stress as a stimulus or a response has been largely replaced by the view of stress as a process.

Lazarus (1991) proposed a transactional theory of stress, which he linked to the concept of coping. In this cognitive approach, people perceive and appraise the demands facing them. There are two kinds of cognitive appraisal. The primary appraisal process involves a judgement that there is a demand to be met. The secondary appraisal process involves the individual's judgement of whether they possess the resources to handle that demand. This process results in a decision about whether and how the person might cope; it is transactional, because repeated interpretations of the situation and one's resources lead to reappraisals of the demand and coping capacity. Thus, stress changes from moment to moment as the person considers new information about demands and resources.

As an example, imagine playing the crucial match in an Olympic team event final to decide whether your team wins gold or silver in front of a large crowd in your home country. One would need to be extraordinarily self-controlled not to feel those demands (primary appraisal). Perhaps your initial thought is that you can't cope (secondary appraisal). Then the coach reminds you that you have performed at this level several times before, that you have prepared better than ever and that you have performed superbly throughout the competition. This should alleviate some concerns about whether you have sufficient physical and technical resources (reappraisal). Team-mates come over and wish you well, saying that you can only do your best. This reduces some of the pressure you feel about letting down the team (further reappraisal). Finally, a colleague points out that the crowd is right behind you. A third aspect of the demands is reduced, as your perception that the crowd is a source of pressure is changed (more reappraisal). Each additional piece of information leads to a transaction between your perception of the demands and your view of the resources you possess to meet those demands — in this case, reducing the level of stress and giving you greater confidence that you can cope.

Coping with stress

One major appeal of process theories is that it is immediately evident how interventions might be developed. When a process has several stages, this usually increases the points at which interventions might be introduced. For example, in the transactional theory of stress and coping, interventions can be applied to change the person's perception of the demands of situations experienced (primary appraisal), whereas interventions that build up the performer's confidence in his or her resources should help in the secondary appraisal process, and interventions that increase coping resources could further alleviate stress (secondary reappraisal). To facilitate the development of interventions, it is clear that understanding coping is an important issue for the management of stress.

Coping can be either *adaptive* or *maladaptive.* Adaptive coping improves the situation. For example, if a basketball player feels the coach is picking on her, a discussion of this might clear the air (adaptive). A maladaptive coping strategy might be to quit the team to escape the particular coach. This would be maladaptive, unless she found a team of equivalent standing, but it could be adaptive if the coach really did have a grudge against her. Thus, coping strategies cannot be considered adaptive or maladaptive *in themselves.* It is the outcomes that determine how useful a strategy turned out to be on that occasion. This still leaves one possible source of confusion — namely, what one considers to be the outcome. One outcome in the examples just presented is the person's sport success, whether as an individual or team player. Another is the level of stress experienced. A soccer player experiencing intense stress because he is about to play in the World Cup final could reduce the stress considerably by the avoidance strategy of not playing. That would not be a desirable sport outcome at all! Coping has also been classified as *approach* or *avoidance* in style. When an individual enters the stressful situation to try to deal with it, as in the case of the basketball player talking to the coach, approach coping style is being employed. Leaving the team is an example of avoidance coping style. Again, neither is inherently correct; rather, the context determines what will work best. There is some confusion between coping styles and coping strategies. Broad ways of handling stressful situations are generally termed coping styles, whereas more specific techniques are called coping strategies.

Lazarus and Folkman (1984) proposed that coping strategies could be classified as problem-focused or emotion-focused. Problem-focused strategies are those by which the person tries to identify and resolve the problem. For individuals with financial problems, a problem-focused coping strategy might be to go to the bank, work through their expenditures with an expert, and develop strategies to manage their income. Although problem-focused strategies often reduce stress, they are not always adaptive. For example, if a rugby player incurs a career-ending injury, he cannot solve the problem. Believing that he can recover and play again could lead to greater heartache in the long run. Emotion-focused coping involves the use or management of emotion to cope with a situation. Becoming angry about the financial situation is unlikely to help the person in debt, whereas venting his feelings of frustration at the loss of a sport career could help the injured rugby player to move forward.

Measuring coping

Folkman and Lazarus (1985) developed the Ways of Coping Checklist (WOCC) to examine problem- and emotion-focused coping strategies. Items refer to various coping strategies, each category (problem or emotion) being summed to reflect relative use of problem- and emotion-focused strategies. Endler and Parker (1990) acknowledged the problem- and emotion-focused categories of coping strategy and added a separate avoidance category in their 44-item Multidimensional Coping Inventory (MCI). In their 60-item Coping Skills Questionnaire (CSQ), Roger, Jarvis and Najarian (1993) included a fourth category of strategy, detachment coping, after they had observed that some people seem to detach their emotions so they can enter stressful situations without reacting emotionally.

Stress and coping in sport

Madden (1987), one of the first researchers to apply Lazarus's approach to sport, developed the Ways of Coping in Sport (WOCS) questionnaire, based on another way of looking at Folkman and Lazarus's (1985) Ways of Coping Checklist (WOCC), which reveals eight functionally different coping scales. Madden's WOCS has eight subscales, measuring problem-focused coping, seeking social support, general emotionality, increased effort and resolve, detachment, denial, wishful thinking and emphasising the positive. The WOCS has been employed to examine coping in basketball (Madden, Summers & Brown 1989) and running (Madden, Kirkby & McDonald 1989). Crocker has applied a different instrument, the COPE (Carver, Scheier & Weintraub 1989), a 13-subscale measure based on theory and function, to examine coping in sport (Crocker 1992; Crocker & Graham 1995). Recently a new instrument has emerged from research in Korea. Yoo and Park (1998) developed the Korean Coping in Sport Inventory (KCSI), drawing on Folkman and Lazarus's (1985) WOCC as well as the MCI (Endler & Parker 1990). Yoo and Park identified four coping strategies in the KCSI. They added transcendental coping, which appears to be similar to detachment, to problem, emotion and avoidance coping. Questionnaire research on stress and coping in sport has been sporadic, while the appeal of qualitative methods has grown.

Scanlan, Stein and Ravizza (1991) were among the first to examine sources of stress in sport, using an interview research design. Scanlan et al. interviewed 26 former US elite figure skaters, using open-ended interview questions and inductive content analysis. Skaters were asked what they recalled as the 'major causes or sources of stress pertaining to your skating experience' (p. 105). Probes were then used to identify any additional sources of stress and to elaborate on sources mentioned. Tape-recorded responses of the skaters were content analysed, using an inductive procedure. Scanlan et al. identified five major categories of sources of stress: negative aspects of competition; negative significant other relationships; demands/costs of skating; personal struggles; and traumatic experiences, including competition and, for others, non-competition aspects of skating. Two aspects of their study should be noted. First, although they claimed that the skaters were elite, only eight of 26 former skaters interviewed had participated at world championship level, whereas the others had competed at senior, junior or even novice level. Second, the research relied on retrospective reports, sometimes looking back over long periods.

Gould, Jackson & Finch (1993) used a similar approach in a study of 17 elite current and former US national figure skating champions. They asked the participants about two phases of their career — before they won a national championship and after they won a national. From the responses, six major themes emerged relating to the time before winning a national title and seven themes emerged for the skaters' experience of stress after becoming a national champion. In studies conducted in the same sport in the same country, Gould et al. identified the stress sources 'too much media attention', 'undesirable training situations' and 'pressure to skate up to national champion standards', which were not reported by Scanlan et al. This might have been because the skaters in the Gould study were all elite performers. James and Collins (1997) and Nasution, Morris and Fortunato (1999) have carried out similar studies. The Nasution study was conducted with Indonesian elite badminton players, thus extending research beyond the usual Western athlete samples.

Sport psychology researchers have also explored the ways in which sports performers cope with the stress of competition. Gould et al. (1993) interviewed 20 US wrestlers who were part of the 1988 US Olympic team. Gould et al. asked how the wrestlers coped with the stress that they experienced. They identified four general dimensions that summarised the ways in which wrestlers coped. These were thought control strategies, such as blocking distractions, positive thinking and coping thoughts; task-focused strategies, mainly comprising the maintenance of a narrow focus on aspects of the task, such as goals; emotion control strategies, primarily involving efforts to control feeling states or activation level; and behavioural strategies, which involved acting out various behaviours that changed or controlled the environment. Gould et al. noted that strategies from different dimensions frequently occurred together and that coping processes were constantly changing, as proposed by Folkman and Lazarus (1985) in their transactional model. Gould et al. also proposed that coping effectiveness should be examined in future research.

Gould et al. (1993) examined how US national champion figure skaters coped with the stress of competition. Common coping strategies used by the skaters included rational thinking and self-talk, positive focus and orientation, social support, time management and prioritisation, pre-competitive mental preparation and anxiety management, training hard and smart, isolation and deflection, and ignoring the stressors. Gould et al. also reported that although rational thinking was employed most, skaters employed a wide range of strategies, depending on the specific stressor. Nasution et al. (1999) identified 14 categories of coping employed by 16 Indonesian elite badminton players to manage the stress associated with being an elite sport performer. These were social support and relationships; positive thinking and orientation; training hard, preparing and playing smart; personal mental strategies; rational thinking and self-talk; leisure activities; determining solutions to problems; personal physical fitness strategies; detachment; reactive behaviours; religious orientation; isolation; inability to cope; and preparing for the future. This list is longer than that found by Gould et al. (1993), because Nasution et al. asked their participants about coping with life as an elite performer, whereas the studies by Gould and his colleagues focused only on coping with competition. Nasution et al. (1999) also investigated the effectiveness of coping strategies. They demonstrated the complexity of the stress–coping process, finding that each coping strategy was effective to varying degrees for different stressors with different players. Even the most effective category of coping strategy — use of personal mental strategies — was reported to be ineffective by some players when they were facing hostile crowds.

The application to sport of models and measures of stress and coping, as well as the use of interview methods to explore the experience of stress and examine the way people cope, shed light on the experience and management of negative emotion that complements the vast array of theory and research on anxiety in sport. From a practical perspective, an appreciation of the sources of stress and the (sometimes maladaptive) ways athletes try to cope with the environments in which they perform and the demands they experience in their lives, can help sport psychologists to devise individually tailored stress management programs.

FUTURE DIRECTIONS

Sport psychology researchers have made significant advances in understanding the complexity of stress, arousal and anxiety in sport. Future research will undoubtedly further refine this understanding. A number of studies have been conducted to examine the efficacy of sport anxiety interventions. However, additional studies are needed before we have a complete understanding of how interventions work. For example, researchers might consider the ways sport psychology practitioners go about choosing interventions, the repertoire of anxiety management strategies that practitioners have at their disposal, the nuances and micro-details of how practitioners deliver interventions, and athlete perceptions of sport anxiety management strategies. The publication of case studies and vignettes (e.g. Rotella 1998; Thompson, Vernacchia & Moore 1998) allows readers to reflect on how some sport psychologists draw from theory in helping anxious athletes with practical strategies. With more applied sport psychologists working with elite and sub-elite athletes than ever before, we anticipate more extensive and detailed case accounts of successful and unsuccessful interventions. In recent years there has been a sharp upswing in the use of qualitative research designs to investigate aspects of stress and anxiety from the athlete's perspective. We expect qualitative designs to remain popular, but we recommend more 'multi-method' research in which researchers use a broader range of research methods within a single project. In the past decade there has been considerable interest in the relative contributions that anxiety intensity and anxiety direction make to performance. Researchers are likely to continue to tease out the differential contributions that intensity and direction have on performance. Because of the media and consequent public interest in choking, we expect the amount of research published in this area to increase in the coming years. Although some choking research has been conducted by sport psychologists, we recommend that definitional issues, and some incompatibilities between automatic execution theory and distraction theory, need to be fully resolved. A closer examination of why some athletes are relatively resilient to choking is also needed. The one constant in sport anxiety research has been continued interest in the relationship between arousal and performance. Individual zones of optimal performance (ZOF) and catastrophe theory have evoked the closest interest and scrutiny in recent years. It remains for researchers to demonstrate more specifically how applied practitioners can use current arousal–performance theories to facilitate positive change for anxious athletes. Arousal–performance theories that can be readily adapted to applied settings should have a better chance of staying in vogue. Finally, the connections between subdomains such as stress, arousal, anxiety and attention are more frequently being linked to a broader range of coping strategies.

CONCLUSIONS

The constant developments in stress, arousal and anxiety research over the past 40 years have paralleled the growth and maturity of the field of sport psychology. Literally hundreds of studies have shaped our present understanding of stress, arousal and anxiety as extremely complex and multidimensional constructs. In this chapter we have condensed and simplified much of this research, providing readers, many of whom will have experienced the types of stresses and anxieties that have been discussed here, with opportunities for critical-reflective thinking.

SUMMARY

We began this chapter by showing how stress, arousal and anxiety are constant elements in the sport experience. In the early 1900s writers were discussing, albeit using different terminology, many of the subdomains that researchers have subsequently pursued. Sport psychology researchers began investigating stress, arousal and anxiety in earnest in about 1960. Figure 3.1 presented a timeline that logs many of the landmark developments that have taken place. The heavy reliance on mainstream anxiety research in the early years was discussed, as were the various aspects of multidimensional anxiety theory. Sport psychologists have developed or applied a number of arousal–performance and anxiety–performance theories to sport. No examination of the area would be complete without a summary of the inverted-U hypothesis, drive theory, catastrophe theory, reversal theory and individual zones of optimal performance. From a process perspective, we identified many causes, effects and interventions related to anxiety and we presented a summary, integrative model. The current understanding of how choking affects performance was reviewed from the theoretical perspective. Finally, the connections between stress and coping were also reviewed.

REVIEW QUESTIONS

1 How have sport psychologists refined the developments of mainstream psychologists in multidimensional anxiety theory and the measurement of anxiety?

2 What are the major advantages and disadvantages of using paper and pencil tests to measure anxiety?

3 In what way does socially desirable responding on paper and pencil tests threaten reliability?

4 Catastrophe theory has been developed to rectify the limitations of the inverted-U hypothesis. How is catastrophe theory different from the inverted-U hypothesis?

5 What is meant by social debilitation in the context of causes of anxiety?

6 In what ways did swimmer Susie O'Neill experience debilitating anxiety in the early part of her career?

7 Has recent research supported the automatic execution theory of choking or the distraction model of choking?

8 What happens to attention under conditions of high arousal, and why?

9 What is primary and secondary cognitive appraisal? How do they affect the experience of stress in sport?

10 What is meant by adaptive and maladaptive coping? Give an example of how the same behaviour is an adaptive coping strategy in one situation but maladaptive in another.

11 What are approach and avoidance coping? Explain why approaching the stressful situation is effective sometimes, whereas on other occasions avoidance is more beneficial.

12 What are problem-focused, emotion-focused, avoidance and detachment coping?

References

Alpert, R & Haber, RN 1960, 'Anxiety in academic achievement situations', *Journal of Abnormal and Social Psychology*, 61, 207–15.

Andersen, MB & Williams, JM 1988, 'Stress and athletic injury: prediction and prevention', *Journal of Sport & Exercise Psychology*, 10, 294–306.

Anshel, MH & Weinberg, RS 1999, 'Re-examining coping among basketball referees following stressful events: implications for coping interventions', *Journal of Sport Behavior*, 22, 141–61.

Apter, MJ 1982, *The experience of motivation: the theory of psychological reversals*, Academic Press, London.

Baumeister, RF 1984, 'Choking under pressure: self-consciousness and paradoxical effects of incentives on skillful performance', *Journal of Personality and Social Psychology*, 46, 610–20.

Beck, AT 1976, *Cognitive therapy and the emotional disorders*, International Universities Press, New York.

Beilock, SL & Carr, TH 2001, 'On the fragility of skilled performance: what governs choking under pressure?', *Journal of Experimental Psychology: General*, 130, 701–25.

Benson, H 1975, *The relaxation response*, Avon Books, New York.

Bridges, PK 1971, 'Attention and arousal: some factors influencing physiological responses to arousal', *Proceedings of the Fifth Conference of the British Society of Sport Psychology*, Leeds, UK, pp. 212–23.

Burton, D 1990, 'Multimodal stress management in sport: current status and future directions', in JG Jones & L Hardy (eds), *Stress and performance in sport*, John Wiley & Sons, Chichester, UK, pp. 171–201.

Burton, D 1998, 'Measuring competitive state anxiety', in JL Duda (ed.), *Advances in sport and exercise psychology measurement*, Fitness Information Technology, Morgantown, WV, pp. 129–48.

Carver, CS, Scheier, MF & Weintraub, JK 1989, 'Assessing coping strategies: a theoretically based approach', *Journal of Personality and Social Psychology*, 56, 267–83.

Cattell, RB & Scheier, IH 1961, *The meaning and measurement of neuroticism and anxiety*, Ronald Press, New York.

Cern, E 2003, 'Anxiety versus fundamental emotions as predictors of perceived functionality of pre-competitive emotional states, threat, and challenge in individual sports', *Journal of Applied Sport Psychology*, 15, 223–38.

Cohen, A, Pargman, D & Tenenbaum, G 2002, 'Critical elaboration and empirical investigation of the cusp catastrophe model: a lesson for practitioners', *Journal of Applied Sport Psychology*, 15, 144–59.

Cohn, PJ 1990, 'An exploratory study on sources of stress and athlete burnout in youth golf', *The Sport Psychologist*, 4, 95–106.

Costa, PT & McCrae, RR 1992, *Professional manual for the NEO Personality Inventory*, Psychological Assessment Resources, Odessa, FL.

Crocker, PRE 1992, 'Managing stress by competitive athletes: ways of coping', *International Journal of Sport Psychology*, 23, 161–75.

Crocker, PRE & Graham, TR 1995, 'Coping by competitive athletes with performance stress: gender differences and relationships with affect', *The Sport Psychologist*, 9, 325–38.

Davidson, RJ & Schwartz, GE 1976, 'The psychobiology of relaxation and related states: a multiprocess theory', in DI Mostofsky (ed.), *Behavior control modification of physiological activity*, Prentice Hall, Englewood Cliffs, NJ.

Dunn, GH & Nielsen, AB 1993, 'A between-sport comparison of situational threat perceptions in ice hockey and soccer', *Journal of Sport & Exercise Psychology*, 15, 449–65.

Easterbrook, JA 1959, 'The effect of emotion on cue utilization and the organization of behavior', *Psychological Review*, 66, 183–201.

Ellis, A 1970, *The essence of rational psychotherapy: a comprehensive approach to treatment*, Institute for Rational Living, New York.

Endler, NS & Parker, JA 1990, 'Multidimensional assessment of coping: a critical evaluation', *Journal of Personality and Social Psychology*, 58, 844–54.

Fazey, JA & Hardy, L 1990, 'The inverted-U hypothesis: catastrophe for sport psychology', *British Association of sports sciences monograph No. 1*, The National Coaching Council, Leeds.

Fenigstein, A 1979, 'Self-consciousness, self-attention, and social interaction', *Journal of Personality and Social Psychology*, 37, 75–86.

Folkman, S & Lazarus, RS 1985, 'If it changes it must be a process: study of emotion and coping during three stages of a college examination', *Journal of Personality and Social Psychology*, 48, 150–70.

Gould, D, Eklund, B & Jackson, S 1993, 'Psychological foundations of Olympic wrestling excellence: reconciling individual differences and nomothetic characterization', *Journal of Applied Sport Psychology*, 5, 35–47.

Gould, D, Jackson, S & Finch, L 1993, 'Sources of stress in national champion figure skaters', *Journal of Sport & Exercise Psychology*, 15, 134–59.

Gould, D, Petlichkoff, L, Simons, J & Veera, M 1987, 'Relationship between competitive state anxiety inventory-2 subscale scores and pistol shooting performance', *Journal of Sport Psychology*, 9, 33–42.

Gould, D & Weinberg, RS 1985, 'Sources of worry in successful and less successful intercollegiate wrestlers', *Journal of Sport Behavior*, 8, 115–27.

Gruber, JJ & Beauchamp, DB 1979, 'Relevancy of the competitive state anxiety inventory in a sport environment', *Research Quarterly*, 50, 207–14.

Hackfort, D & Schwenkmezger, P 1989, 'Measuring anxiety in sports: perspectives and problems', in D Hackfort & CD Spielberger (eds), *Anxiety in sports: an international perspective*, Hemisphere Publishing, New York, pp. 261–6.

Hall, E & Marchant, D 2003, 'Defining choking: a qualitative examination', *The Sport Psychologist*.

Hanin, YL 1980, 'A study of anxiety in sports', in WF Straub (ed.), *Sport psychology: an analysis of athlete behavior*, Mouvement, Ithaca, NY, pp. 236–49.

Hanin, YL 1995, 'Individual zones of optimal functioning (IZOF) model: an idiographic approach to performance anxiety', in K Henschen & W Straub (eds), *Sport psychology: an analysis of athlete behavior*, Movement, Longmeadow, MA, pp. 103–19.

Hanin, YL & Syrja, P 1995, 'Performance affect in junior ice hockey players: an application of the individual zones of optimal functioning model', *The Sport Psychologist*, 9, 167–87.

Hardy, L 1990, 'A catastrophe model of performance in sport', in JG Jones & L Hardy (eds), *Stress and performance in sport*, John Wiley & Sons, Chichester, UK, pp. 43–80.

Hardy, L 1996, 'Testing the predictions of the CCM of anxiety and performance', *The Sport Psychologist*, 10, 140–56.

Hardy, L & Fazey, J 1987, 'The inverted-U hypothesis: a catastrophe for sport psychology', *Journal of Applied Psychology*, 72, 161–82.

Harris, DV & Harris, BL 1984, *The athlete's guide to sports psychology: mental skills for physical people*, Leisure Press, New York.

Hatfield, BD & Landers, DM 1983, 'Psychophysiology — a new direction for sport psychology', *Journal of Sport Psychology*, 5, 243–59.

Hull, CL 1943, *Principles of behavior*, Appleton-Century Co., New York.

Jacobson, E 1938, *Progressive relaxation*, 2nd edn, University of Chicago Press, Chicago.

James, B & Collins, D 1997, 'Self-presentational sources of competitive stress during performance', *Journal of Sport & Exercise Psychology*, 19, 17–35.

Jones, G & Swain, ABJ 1992, 'Intensity and direction dimensions of competitive state anxiety and relationships with competitiveness', *Perceptual and Motor Skills*, 74, 467–72.

Jones, G, Hanton, S & Swain, A 1994, 'Intensity and interpretation of anxiety symptoms in elite and non-elite sports performers', *Personality and Individual Differences*, 17, 657–63.

Jones, JG & Hardy, L 1993, *Stress and performance in sport*, John Wiley & Sons, Chichester, UK.

Kerr, JH 1985, 'The experience of arousal: a new basis for studying arousal effects in sport', *Journal of Sport Science*, 16, 169–79.

Krane, V, Joyce, D & Rafeld, J 1994, 'Competitive anxiety, situation criticality, and softball performance', *The Sport Psychologist*, 8, 58–72.

Kroll, W 1979, 'The stress of high performance athletes', in P Klavora & JV Daniel (eds), *Coach, athlete, and the sport psychologist*, University of Toronto Press, Toronto, pp. 211–19.

Landers, DM, Boutcher, SH & Wang, MQ 1986, 'A psychobiological study of archery performance', *Research Quarterly for Exercise and Sport*, 57, 236–44.

Lazarus, RS 1991, *Emotion and adaptation*, Oxford University Press, New York.

Lazarus, RS & Folkman, S 1984, *Stress, appraisal, and coping*, Springer, New York.

Liebert, RM & Morris, LW 1967, 'Cognitive and emotional components of test anxiety: a distinction and some initial data', *Psychological Reports*, 30, 975–8.

Madden, CC 1987, 'Ways of coping', unpublished doctoral thesis, University of Melbourne.

Madden, CC, Kirkby, RJ & McDonald, D 1989, 'Coping styles of competitive middle distance runners', *International Journal of Sport Psychology*, 20, 287–96.

Madden, CC, Summers, JJ & Brown, DF 1989, 'The influence of perceived stress on coping with competitive basketball', *International Journal of Sport Psychology*, 21, 21–35.

Mahoney, MJ & Meyers, AW 1989, 'Anxiety and athletic performance: traditional and cognitive-developmental perspectives', in D Hackfort & CD Spielberger (eds), *Anxiety in sports: an international perspective*, Hemisphere Publishing, New York, pp. 261–6.

Marchant, DB, Morris, T & Andersen, MA 1998, 'A test of perceived importance of outcome as a contributing factor in competitive state anxiety', *Journal of Sport Behavior*, 21, 71–91.

Martens, R 1977, *Sport Competition Anxiety Test*, Human Kinetics, Champaign, IL.

Martens, R, Burton, D, Vealey, RS, Bump, LA & Smith, DE 1983, 'Competitive State Anxiety Inventory-2', symposium conducted at the meeting of the North American Society for the Psychology of Sport and Physical Activity, College Park, MD.

Martens, R & Landers, DM 1970, 'Motor performance under stress: a test of the inverted-U hypothesis', *Journal of Personality and Social Psychology*, 16, 29–37.

Martens, R, Vealey, RS & Burton, D 1990, *Competitive anxiety in sport*, Human Kinetics, Champaign, IL.

Masters, RSW 1992, 'Knowledge, knerves and know-how: the role of explicit versus implicit knowledge in the breakdown of a complex motor skill under pressure', *British Journal of Psychology*, 83, 343–8.

McGrath, JE 1970, 'Major methodological issues', in JE McGrath (ed.), *Social and psychological factors in stress*, Holt, Rinehart & Winston, New York, pp. 19–49.

McHale, JM, Chadwick, AE & Taylor, ECH 1931, *The Australian game of football*, Hartley, Melbourne.

Meichenbaum, D 1985, *Stress inoculation training*, Pergamon, New York.

Nasution, Y, Morris, T & Fortunato, V 1999, 'Coping with stress in Indonesian elite badminton players', abstract in *Australian Journal of Psychology*, 49, Supplement.

Neiss, R 1988, 'Reconceptualizing arousal: psychological states in motor performance', *Psychological Bulletin*, 103, 3, 345–66.

Nideffer, RM 1992, *Psyched to win*, Leisure Press, Champaign IL.

Nideffer, RM & Sagal, MS 1998, 'Concentration and attention control training', in JM Williams (ed.), *Applied sport psychology: personal growth to peak performance*, 3rd edn, Mayfield, Mountain View, CA, pp. 296–315.

O'Neill, S with Chappell, F 1999, *Choose to win: achieving your goals, fulfilling your dreams*, Pan Macmillan, Sydney.

Ostrow, A 1996, *Directory of psychological tests in the sport and exercise sciences*, 2nd edn, Fitness Information Technology, Morgantown, WV.

Oxendine, JB 1970, 'Emotional arousal and motor performance', *Quest*, 13, 23–32.

Parfitt, CG, Jones, JG & Hardy, L 1990, 'Multidimensional anxiety and performance', in JG Jones & L Hardy (eds), *Stress and performance in sport*, John Wiley & Sons, Chichester, UK, pp. 43–80.

Plaut, EA 1990, 'Psychotherapy of performance anxiety', *Medical Problems of Performing Artists*, 5, 58–63.

Prapavessis, H, Cox, H & Brooks, L 1996, 'A test of Martens, Vealey, and Burton's theory of competitive anxiety', *Australian Journal of Science and Medicine in Sport*, 28, 24–9.

Prapavessis, H & Grove, JR 1991, 'Precompetitive emotions and shooting performance: the mental health and zone of optimal function models', *The Sport Psychologist*, 5, 223–34.

Rotella, B 1998, *Case studies in sport psychology*, Jones and Bartlett, Boston, MA.

Roger, D, Jarvis, G & Najarian, B 1993, 'Detachment and coping: the construction and validation of a new scale for measuring coping strategies', *Personality and Individual Differences*, 15, 619–26.

Sampras, P 2000, 'Historic win for Sampras', *The Advertiser*, 11 July, p. 68.

Scanlan, TK, Stein, G & Ravizza, K 1991, 'An in-depth study of former elite figure skaters: 111 sources of stress', *Journal of Sport & Exercise Psychology*, 13, 103–20.

Selye, H 1975, *Stress without distress*, New American Library, New York.

Smith, RE 1980, 'A cognitive-affective approach to stress management training for athletes', in CH Nadeau, WR Halliwell, KM Newell & GC Roberts (eds), *Psychology of motor behavior and sport — 1979*, Human Kinetics, Champaign, IL, pp. 54–72.

Smith, RE, Smoll, FL & Wiechman, SA 1998, 'Measurement of trait anxiety in sport', in JL Duda (ed.), *Advances in sport and exercise psychology measurement*, Fitness Information Technology, Morgantown, WV, pp. 105–28.

Smith, RE, Smoll, FL & Schutz, RW 1990, 'Measurement and correlates of sport specific cognitive and somatic trait anxiety: the Sport Anxiety Scale', *Anxiety Research*, 2, 263–80.

Sonstroem, RJ & Bernardo, P 1982, 'Intraindividual pre-game state anxiety and basketball performance: a re-examination of the inverted-U curve', *Journal of Sport Psychology*, 4 (3) 235–45.

Spielberger, CD, Gorsuch, RI & Lushene, RL 1970, *Manual for the State–Trait Anxiety Inventory*, Consulting Psychologists, Palo Alto, CA.

Strean, B 1998, 'Possibilities for qualitative research in sport psychology', *The Sport Psychologist*, 12, 333–45.

Thompson, RA, Vernacchia, RA & Moore, WE 1998, *Case studies in applied sport psychology: an educational approach*, Kendall/Hunt Publishing, Dubuque, IA.

Wang, J 2002, 'Developing and testing an integrated model of choking in sport', unpublished doctoral thesis, Victoria University, Melbourne.

Wang, J, Marchant, D & Morris, T (in press), 'Coping style and susceptibility to choking', *Journal of Sport Behavior*.

Weinberg, RS & Genuchi, M 1980, 'Relationship between competitive trait anxiety, state anxiety, and golf performance: a field study', *Journal of Sport Psychology*, 2, 148–54.

Wolpe, J 1958, *Psychotherapy by reciprocal inhibition*, Stanford University Press, Palo Alto, CA.

Woodman, T, Albinson, JF & Hardy, L 1997, 'An investigation of the zones of optimal functioning hypothesis with a multidimensional framework', *Journal of Sport & Exercise Psychology*, 19, 131–41.

Yerkes, RM & Dodson, JD 1908, 'The relation of strength of stimulus to rapidity of habit formation', *Journal of Comparative Neurology and Psychology*, 18, 459–82.

Yoo, J & Park, SJ 1998, 'Development of a sport coping scale', *Korean Journal of Physical Education*, 37, 151–68.

CHAPTER 4

ATTENTION IN SPORT

Aidan P Moran & Jeff Summers

> At this level, it's all about focus ... The level of concentration was very high.

Tennis player Andre Agassi after his thrilling 6–4, 3–6, 6–7, 7–6, 6–1 victory over Pete Sampras in the semifinal of the 2000 Australian Open (27 January 2000), cited in Ramsay 2000, p. 20

> I was in my own little world, focusing on every shot. I wasn't thinking what score I was on or anything ... But today was probably as good as I have ever played.

Golfer Darren Clarke after shooting a record-equalling score of 60 in the 1999 European Open championship (31 July 1999), cited in Otway 1999, p. 13

Andre Agassi and Darren Clarke are among the many athletes who believe that attentional factors play a crucial role in producing optimal performance in sport. These anecdotal insights are supported by objective evidence. For example, Durand-Bush, Salmela and Green-Demers (2001) found that a large sample ($n = 335$) of athletes perceived *focusing* as a mental skill that is vital in achieving successful performance in their sport. Indeed, Cox (2002) argued that 'in sport, nothing can be more important than paying attention' (p. 132). Not surprisingly, therefore, attentional skills training has become a major concern in applied sport psychology in recent years (Moran 2003, 2004). But what exactly is *attention*? How has it been studied in psychology? Is it possible to measure attentional processes? What has research revealed about the relationship between attention and athletic performance? The purpose of this chapter is to provide some answers to these and other relevant questions. Overall, we will show that, despite James' much-cited remark that 'everyone knows what attention is' (1890, p. 404), there is still a great deal of uncertainty about the nature and status of this construct in contemporary sport psychology.

The chapter is organised as follows. To begin with, we will analyse what the term *attention* means in psychology. Then we will review the main theoretical perspectives on attention in sport psychology. Next, three dimensions of attention — direction, intensity and flexibility — will be reviewed, and the relationship between attention and arousal in sport will be examined. Finally, we will identify the principal unresolved issues in research on attention and outline some future directions for this field.

WHAT IS ATTENTION?

At first glance, attention, or the 'concentration of mental activity' (Matlin 2002, p. 51) on sensory or mental events, appears to be a fertile construct in psychology. After all, it has a venerable scientific ancestry that can be traced back to the writings of James (1890). Also, references to attentional terms, such as *concentration* and *focus*, are common in everyday sporting discourse. For example, the snooker star Stephen Hendry attributed his narrow (18–17) defeat by Peter Ebdon in the 2002 world championship final to a mental lapse — 'my concentration went' (cited in Everton 2002, p. 25). Unfortunately, despite its popularity, the term 'attention' is deceptively slippery. To illustrate, consider the profusion of metaphors (e.g. a 'filter', 'spotlight' or 'zoom lens') to which it has given rise over the past 50 years (see review in Fernandez-Duque & Johnson 1999). Before we analyse such metaphors, however, we need to clarify at least three different meanings of attention in sport psychology.

First, when players are asked to 'pay attention' to a move illustrated by a coach at a training session, they are required to concentrate on, or exert mental effort in absorbing, the information presented to them. Of course, in such situations, the players' minds may wander and their focus could shift elsewhere (see the following highlighted feature for a practical exercise on distractions).

EXPLORING DISTRACTIONS IN SPORT: A PRACTICAL EXERCISE

The purpose of this exercise is twofold. First, it will encourage you to find out what the term 'concentration' means to athletes. In addition, it will help you to understand the main types of distractions that affect their performance.

Instructions

Find three athletes who compete regularly in different sports (e.g. golf, soccer or swimming). Request their permission to record an interview with them on a dictaphone or audiocassette machine. Then ask them the following questions.

1. What does the term *concentration* mean to you?
2. On a scale of 0 ('not at all important') to 5 ('extremely important'), how important do you think the skill of concentration is for successful performance in your sport?
3. What sort of distractions tend to upset your concentration *before* a game/match? Describe the situation and the distraction that results from it.
4. What distractions bother you *during* the event itself? Describe the situation and the distraction that results from it.
5. Give a specific example of how a distraction changed your focus and/or affected your performance. What was the distraction, how did it occur and how did you react to it?
6. What techniques, if any, do you use to cope with distractions?

Analysis

Compare and contrast the athletes' answers to your questions. The word *focus* will probably feature in responses to question 1. You should also find that athletes regard concentration as being very important for successful performance in their sport (question 2). After you have compiled a list of distractions (questions 3 and 4), you should find that they fall into two main categories — external and internal. In your view, is there any connection between the type of sport played and the distractions reported? If you find a pattern, what is the best explanation for it? Finally, what techniques do your athletes use to deal with distractions? How do they compare with those reported in the literature?

There is a second meaning of *attention* in the context of sport. For example, when a tennis player scrutinises the ball-toss of an opponent who is about to serve, the receiver demonstrates *selective attention*, or the ability to 'zoom in' on relevant information while ignoring irrelevant details (e.g. the colour of the server's shirt). In a third application of the term, when a basketball player dribbles with the ball while scanning the court for a team-mate to pass it to, she or he is engaging in a form of mental time-sharing ability called *divided attention*. In summary, attention refers to at least three distinct processes — concentration or effortful awareness, selectivity of perception, and the ability to coordinate two or more concurrent tasks successfully.

Unfortunately, these components of attention are not always delineated clearly in sport science. For example, whereas researchers tend to interpret 'concentration' as paying attention to a small number of task-relevant stimuli at any given time, sport performers tend to regard it as attending to a task in *any* manner — as long as it is completed successfully.

HOW HAS ATTENTION BEEN STUDIED IN PSYCHOLOGY? THEORETICAL PERSPECTIVES

The construct of attention has been investigated from three main theoretical perspectives in psychology — the cognitive approach, the neuroscientific tradition and the 'individual difference' paradigm.

1. The cognitive perspective

Since the cognitive revolution of the 1950s the mind has been regarded as a limited-capacity information processing system (Matlin 2002). From this tradition, three key metaphors of attention have emerged. First came the idea that attention was a physical device (or *filter*) that screened the flow of information into the mind (Broadbent 1958). Unfortunately, the filter metaphor encountered both conceptual and methodological difficulties. For example, researchers could not agree on either the location or the timing of the hypothetical filtering mechanism (Matlin 2002). Furthermore, as experimenters could measure the presentation times of visual stimuli more accurately than their auditory equivalents, a new and more dynamic metaphor emerged — that of attention as a *spotlight* or *zoom lens*. According to this visual metaphor, our minds pick up information as if by directing a beam of light at target stimuli around us. In a related perspective, the zoom lens model (Eriksen & St James 1986) suggests that the attentional beam can be broadened or narrowed as if one were adjusting the focus of a camera (Cave & Bichot 1999). As with its predecessor, however, the spotlight and zoom lens metaphors have several weaknesses. For example, spotlight theorists have not explained adequately the mechanisms by which people control their attentional focus. Also, most spotlight models fail to address the fact that people's attentional 'beam' can be directed *inwards* as well as outwards.

Whereas filter theories of attention were concerned mainly with identifying *how* and *where* selective perception occurred in the information processing system, 'resource' theories of attention (Kahneman 1973) were developed to explain how people can manage to perform two or more simultaneous actions successfully. Briefly, according to the resource metaphor, attention resembles a pool of undifferentiated mental energy that can be allocated flexibly to task demands according to certain psychological principles; for example, motivation, arousal and practice increase 'spare' attentional capacity. Navon & Gopher (1979), however, argued that people may have *multiple* attentional resources, rather than a single resource. Furthermore, they suggested, each of these multiple pools has its own specialised functions. For example, the attentional resources required for selecting a finger to make a movement may be separate from those required to facilitate jaw movements in saying a word (Schmidt & Lee 1999). Therefore, these two operations may possibly run concurrently without any interference between them.

A major contribution of resource theories of attention has been the idea that task performance is constrained by available mental resources. To explain, in most sporting situations, athletes face the challenge of selecting task-relevant information from a surfeit of stimulation while simultaneously ignoring distractions. Figure 4.1 shows the attentional processes operating in a typical sporting situation (a fast break in basketball). One way of reducing the danger of 'cognitive overload' in such situations is to practise one or more of the skills to be executed. But what exactly does practice achieve? To answer this question, we need to explain the distinction between *controlled* and *automatic* processes (Schneider & Shiffrin 1977).

Figure 4.1 Attention in sport — basketball

In general, cognitive processes are believed to range along a continuum depending on the degree to which they require conscious attentional control for their execution. At one end of this continuum lie automatic processes (e.g. for most adults, reading), which are largely unconscious and consume few attentional resources. At the other end are controlled processes, which are effortful and attentionally demanding. Research shows that the key to *automaticity* of performance is extensive practice. In other words, practice produces a significant reduction in the perceived difficulty of a given task, although some degree of concentration is still usually required to perform it. For example, driving a car, no matter how practised you are, always requires some mental effort. That is why you probably stop talking to passengers and/or turn down the radio in order to concentrate better when traffic is heavy or when driving conditions are hazardous. Under automatic control, performance is usually fast, fluent, effortless and error-free. Indeed, most top-class athletes report being in a state of automaticity or 'empty-mindedness' when they perform optimally. For example, after Pete Sampras won the 1999 Wimbledon tennis championship he told reporters 'there was absolutely nothing going on in my mind at that time ... I don't know how I do it, to be honest with you. I really don't' (cited in Barnes 1999, p. 14). Clearly, this quotation reveals that athletes are truly focused only when there is no difference between what they are doing and what they are thinking.

Evaluation of cognitive perspectives on attention in sport

Despite their intuitive appeal, cognitive models of attention have two main limitations. First, they tend to focus only on objective determinants of attention, thereby neglecting the fact that 'internal' sources of information (e.g. people's own thoughts and feelings) provide a powerful source of distraction for athletes (Moran 1996). Happily, some progress has been made recently in assessing the effects of self-generated distractions among athletes. For example, Hatzigeorgiadis (2002) and Hatzigeorgiadis and Biddle (2000) have used psychometric tools to measure cognitive interference in sport performers. Also, Wegner (1994, 2002) has developed the *ironic processes* model in an effort to understand why people sometimes end up thinking about and/or doing the *opposite* of what they had intended. For example, a golfer may inadvertently steer the ball towards a hazard that she or he had consciously tried to avoid. According to Wegner, such 'ironic' lapses occur most frequently when people are tired, anxious or otherwise cognitively overloaded. In such situations, people's attentional resources are depleted and hence unable to prevent the ironic intrusion into consciousness of previously suppressed thoughts or actions. As a result, negative self-commands (such as 'don't double-fault' in tennis or 'don't overshoot the hole' in golf putting) may produce counterintentional behaviour (see Wegner, Ansfield & Pilloff 1998). Interestingly, some support for this theory comes from Janelle, Singer and Williams (1999), who found that under conditions of high cognitive load, drivers who had participated in an auto-racing simulation were *more* likely to focus on irrelevant cues in comparison with baseline conditions.

The second major weakness of cognitive models of attention is that they tend to ignore the influence of emotional states, such as anxiety. This neglect is disappointing because there are strong theoretical reasons for believing that anxiety impairs attentional processing even among expert athletes. For example, consider the phenomenon of *choking* under pressure in sport (Graydon 2002). Here, athletic performance is suddenly impaired — mainly as a consequence of excessive self-consciousness, which, in turn, encourages performers to try to gain control over previously automatic skills. Typically, such attempts lead to an unravelling of the skills concerned in a cycle of 'paralysis by analysis'.

2. The neuroscientific perspective

The second theoretical perspective on attentional processes emerged from the field of cognitive neuroscience, which is broadly concerned with the identification of the neural substrates of mental processes. Recent technical advances have facilitated the 'real-time' analysis of cortical activity in normal or 'intact' brains. For example, *event related potential* (ERP) recordings allow researchers to measure tiny changes in the brain's spontaneous electrical activity from the scalp of participants (see review by Luck,

Woodman & Vogel 2000). In addition, neuroscientific techniques such as *electroencephalography* (EEG), *functional magnetic resonance imaging* (fMRI) and *positron emission tomography* (PET scanning) can reveal which parts of the brain 'light up' when a person is paying attention to designated stimuli (Kolb & Whishaw 2003).

Although PET scans can answer questions concerning the *where* of attention, issues concerning the *how* of attention require methods (such as EEG) that assess changes in patterns of the brain's neurological activity over time. A considerable body of research has accumulated on the pre-event patterns of EEG activity in certain athletes (Hatfield & Hillman 2001; Lawton, Hung, Saarela & Hatfield 1998). For example, there is evidence that just as expert shooters and archers prepare to fire, their EEG records reveal a marked shift from left-hemisphere to right-hemisphere activation. This shift may signify a change in executive control from the verbally based left hemisphere to the visiospatially specialised right hemisphere. More speculatively, a reduction in left-hemisphere activity may indicate a deliberate suppression of 'self-talk' on the part of the shooters in an effort to achieve a truly focused state of automaticity (Boutcher 2002).

Evaluation of the neurocognitive perspective

Despite the impressive technology underlying its insights, the neurocognitive approach to attention in sport is hampered by two main problems. First, the collection of neurocognitive data is both expensive and extremely time-consuming. In addition, there is a danger that studies in this field often resemble atheoretical 'fishing expeditions'. Thus Lawton et al. (1998) complained that neurocognitive research in sport amounts to 'little more than an unguided search process in which investigators seek to find psychological explanations for observed electrophysiological patterns' (p. 48).

3. The 'individual differences' perspective: attentional style

The final theoretical approach to the study of attention is the differential perspective. Here, attention is regarded as an 'individual difference' variable that can be measured psychometrically. A popular tool for this purpose is the Test of Attentional and Interpersonal Style, or TAIS (Nideffer 1976), which involves a self-report, paper-and-pencil inventory.

According to Nideffer, people's attentional focus varies simultaneously along two independent bipolar dimensions — *width* and *direction*. With regard to width, attention is believed to range along a continuum from a 'broad' focus (where one is aware of many stimulus features at the same time) to a 'narrow' one (where irrelevant information is filtered out). Attentional direction denotes the *target* of one's focus, whether external or internal. These dimensions of width and direction may be combined factorially to yield four different attentional *styles*. For example, a *narrow external* focus in sport is believed to be necessary when an archer focuses on the bullseye on the target before shooting. Conversely, a *narrow internal* focus is used when a performer mentally rehearses a specific skill (e.g. a back flip in gymnastics) before a competition.

A number of studies have been conducted on the relationship between attentional style (as measured by the TAIS) and athletic performance. These studies have tested two main hypotheses. First, Nideffer proposed that different sport skills require different types of attentional foci. For example, a point-guard in basketball may need to display a *broad external* attentional style, whereas a golf putter may require a *narrow external* focus. In support of this idea, significant relationships have been reported between athletes' scores on the TAIS and their performance in such sports as swimming (Nideffer 1976) and golf (Kirschenbaum & Bale 1984). Second, Nideffer suggested that successful performance in sport depends on the degree to which the athlete's preferred attentional style matches the cognitive requirements of the skill in question. If a mismatch exists, lapses in performance may occur. For example, a tennis player who is about to serve (hence needing a narrow attentional focus) may become distracted if she or he scans the crowd for her or his coach (broad attentional focus) before commencing the ball-toss.

Evaluation of individual differences perspective

Although Nideffer's model has considerable intuitive appeal and has received some empirical support (Nideffer 1993), research on attentional style has been plagued by several difficulties. The main problem has been not with the model per se, but rather with the instrument used to measure attentional style, the TAIS. First, the TAIS assesses *perceived*, rather than actual, attentional skills. The problem here is that few researchers have tried to validate people's beliefs about their attentional processes against objective evidence of attentional performance. It is also questionable whether athletes are capable of evaluating their own attentional processes accurately using self-report instruments, especially when such tests are not conducted under the time pressure that characterises most everyday sporting activities. Specifically, studies of 'meta-attention' (i.e. people's knowledge of, and control over, their own attentional processes) suggest that people are unreliable judges of their own concentration skills (Reisberg & McLean 1985). Second, some aspects of the attentional style model are not adequately measured by the TAIS. For example, there is no assessment of attentional flexibility — that is, athletes' capacity to adapt their attentional style to situational demands. Finally, concerns over the psychometric properties of the TAIS (Ford & Summers 1992) suggest that the test may have limited value in assessing attentional processes in athletes. Although the development of new self-report instruments may be warranted (see Abernethy, Summers & Ford 1998), other methodologies may provide a more valid way of examining attention in sport. For example, thought-sampling techniques, in which an athlete's thoughts during an actual performance are tape-recorded, may be appropriate in sports such as golf, cricket and motor racing (Boutcher & Rotella 1987).

DIMENSIONS OF ATTENTION

So far we have explained that the functioning of attention can be regarded as involving three major aspects: where attention is directed (direction), how much attention is devoted to the direction chosen (intensity), and alteration of intensity and direction as required (flexibility). The first two aspects can be broken down to reveal further distinctions that are useful in guiding our understanding of attention and its application to sport. For example, the issue of whether attention is directed to a large number of stimuli or to only a few relates to the span or width of attention (i.e. distributed or focused attention). Which particular stimuli receive attention (some having greater relevance for the task) relates to the selectivity of attention. Concepts such as mental workload, alertness and overall processing capacity are related to the intensity of attention. Attentional flexibility, in a more refined sense, can usually be conceived as altering attention along any of these subdimensions.

Direction

The *direction* dimension refers to the source of the stimuli — whether they originate in the environment (external attention) or internally (Nideffer 1976). Examples of external attention include tracking a ball, focusing on a target or watching a play develop.

Internal attention refers to thoughts, self-talk, imagery and internal sensations (e.g. kinaesthetic cues). As previously mentioned, becoming too focused on thoughts and feelings appears to be one cause of an athlete's 'choking' when under pressure.

Width

The *width* of attention refers to the number of cues analysed at one time. As indicated earlier, Nideffer (1976) viewed width as a continuous dimension ranging from broad (many cues receiving attention) to narrow (a small number of cues attended to). Some writers have suggested that broad attention should be broken into scanning and broad 'snapshot' forms (Wachtel 1967). *Scanning* relates to serially searching across a field of cues, whereas *broad attention* relates to a snapshot that processes a great number of cues at one glance.

Selectivity

As noted earlier, a major feature of attention is its selectivity. Selective attention, however, is not merely reducing the number of stimuli that receive further processing (narrowing or focusing attention); it also relates to the task relevance of the cues attended. For example, a soccer goalkeeper defending a penalty could focus on the ball as the kick is taken or on the kicker's leg angle and foot orientation before contact. Although in both instances, attention is selective, focusing on the leg swing might be more beneficial for successful task performance (defending the goal), because it would yield earlier information on the likely direction of the ball. Thus, selective attention has two major aspects: the ability to focus attention without being overloaded or distracted, and the ability to direct that focus to the most important stimuli for successfully performing the task.

In recent years, selectivity has been the main focus in sport research on visual attention in athletes. Most of these studies have compared elite with novice athletes on various perceptual tasks (Williams 2002). One issue of interest in this field has been the degree to which expertise in fast-ball sports depends on the ability of the athlete to utilise contextual information to anticipate future events. In such sports, because of the inherent limitations on an individual's reaction and movement time, attending to advance sources of information to make predictions is essential. A typical approach used in laboratory-based research on advance cue usage is to show participants films of an athlete (seen from the perspective of an opponent) performing various sporting actions, such as a tennis serve, a badminton smash or a volleyball offensive play. In the temporal occlusion condition, the film is cut at various times before and after a critical event (e.g. ball contact). In a spatial occlusion condition, different regions of the player's body are occluded by masking (e.g. arm and racquet, head and face). Commonly, the task given to the film viewer is to predict direction and the location where they believe the opponent's shot would land by marking it on a scaled version of the playing area (for a review of this research, see Lavallee, Kremer, Moran & Williams 2004).

Another method for determining the cues used by experts is the recording of eye movements to assess visual search strategies (Williams 2002; Lavallee et al. 2004). When our eyes move, a sequence of images of target stimuli is conveyed to the fovea (a central region of the retina that promotes high resolution) and maintained there for as long as is required by the attentional system. Whereas little information processing occurs during saccadic eye movements (high-speed jumps of the eyes from one gaze location to another), foveal fixation facilitates detailed visual consideration of target stimuli. In such research, the location and duration of the perceiver's visual fixations provide clues to his or her attentional focus. For example, the *location* of a fixation may indicate the relative importance of a given cue within a stimulus display. Thus, when viewing a series of slides of opponents' pre-serve behaviour, an experienced tennis player may focus on the ball-toss, rather than on the position of the racket.

Consistent findings across studies of selective attention in a variety of sports suggest that, relative to novices, highly skilled performers are: (1) faster and more accurate in recognising and recalling patterns of play in their particular sport, and (2) better able to anticipate the actions of opponents through the use of efficient visual search strategies that allow the detection of advanced cues (see Williams, Davids & Williams 1999 for review). For example, whereas inexperienced soccer players tend to fixate mainly on the ball and the player passing the ball, expert players concentrate more frequently on players 'off the ball' (Williams, Davids, Burwitz & Williams 1994). Experts, therefore, are better able to recognise the redundancy of many cues (such as the ball) and focus on extracting meaning from more pertinent cues. This effectively reduces the quantity of information to manageable proportions within the time constraints. The ability to use earlier cues also results in more time to choose, organise and execute a response.

Various factors have been shown to influence selective attention in team sport players. For example, in their study of baseball batters, Paull and Glencross (1997) described the game context for some of the film clips, but not for others. Results showed that knowing the strategic context decreased decision time and errors in predicting the final position of the pitch over the plate. These results applied to both experts and novices, although experts were still superior on both aspects. Thus it appears that strategic knowledge helps players in setting up prior probabilities for certain types of pitches.

Importantly, the above findings are unlikely to be due to 'hardware' differences between elite and novice athletes; that is, elite athletes do not appear to possess a superior nervous system to less talented sportspersons. There is little empirical evidence, for example, to support the link between visual-perceptual abilities such as stereoacuity, dynamic visual acuity or processing speed (e.g. reaction time) and sport skill (Williams et al. 1999). It is possible, of course, that the hardware factors previously examined are not the same as those used by the central nervous system in skilled performance. Proponents of direct perception theories, for example, have argued that the expert performer may be someone who has learned to accurately pick up directly relevant optical information, such as *tau* — visual information specifying time to contact (see Bootsma 1999 for review).

Some caution must be exercised in interpreting the findings of film occlusion studies, however, because of the questionable ecological validity of this approach. For example, these simulated situations do not contain factors known to affect attentional processes, such as contextual information and the stressors or the motivation encountered in a competitive situation. Recent advances in technology, such as electronically controlled liquid crystal occlusion spectacles, however, may allow for the examination of perceptual anticipation in situations more akin to the 'real game' (Starkes, Edwards, Dissanayake & Dunn 1995). A further problem relates to the determination of the direction of attention from eye movements and fixations. Although it appears that shifts in eye fixation are usually accompanied by shifts in attention (Zelinsky, Rao, Hayhoe & Ballard 1997), there is evidence to suggest that the locus of attention can be detached from the locus of fixation (Posner, Nissen & Ogden 1978). Thus studies of covert attentional orienting (determining the direction of attention when the focus of the eyes does not move) have found that the focus of attention need not be where the eyes are centred, and that attention can move flexibly during a fixation. For example, Castiello and

Umilta (1992) found that professional volleyball players could split focal attention between non-contiguous regions of space better than novices. Despite these reservations, studies using the film occlusion paradigm do suggest that cognitive skills, such as selective attention and memory, differentiate elite from non-elite athletes, at least for fast action sports.

Can selective attention skills be trained?

An important question for coaches and athletes is whether or not the perceptual anticipation skills displayed by expert performers can be trained. Although some visual training programs claiming to enhance visual functioning in sport have been promulgated (Revien 1987), there is little evidence that they actually improve selective attention skills (Williams 2002). More encouraging results, however, have been obtained from training programs focusing on the detection of advanced cues using the film occlusion paradigm mentioned previously. In these studies, stopping the video at specific times during an action (e.g. a tennis serve) is accompanied by explicit instructions highlighting the link between key early information cues and the eventual outcome of the action displayed (see Williams & Grant 1999 for a review). Significant improvements in anticipatory performance have been reported from such perceptual training programs (Farrow, Chivers, Hardingham & Sachse 1998). The use of virtual reality technology to provide even more real world–like, multisensory, three-dimensional environments offers exciting prospects for the training of perceptual anticipation in sport. In chapter 14, Bond and Sargent examine attentional skills training programs that are frequently used by sport psychologists to assist athletes in maintaining concentration in the face of external and internal distractions.

Intensive aspects of attention

The question of how much attention is devoted to a task is related to the assumption that the information processing system has limits on the amount of information that can be processed at one time.

Capacity limits on attention

As previously discussed, capacity limitations evident under controlled processing may not apply when the task becomes automated. It is not clear, however, how the performance of a task progresses from being a controlled process to an automatic one. One possibility is that part of the automatisation process involves *chunking*, or perceptual grouping whereby separate stimuli are organised into meaningful units. A major advantage of chunking is that a number of stimuli, previously processed independently and serially, are analysed as one stimulus group. This not only speeds up processing, because more can be taken in at a glance, but the patterns of stimuli can be more easily interpreted.

Research on chunking by athletes has used the paradigm originally developed by de Groot (1965) and Chase and Simon (1973) to study chess masters. Most of this research has compared elite and non-elite athletes on how much information can be extracted in a short period of time. For example, Allard, Graham and Paarsalu (1980) required basketballers and non-basketballers to view slides of structured and unstructured basketball situations for 4 seconds and then to recall the position of the players on a scaled-down version of the court. Results revealed that the basketballers were more accurate in their recall of the positions of players in structured situations (e.g. a point guard about to initiate a play from the top of the key), but not in unstructured situations (e.g. a scramble for a loose ball). The same pattern of results has been reported across a variety of team and individual sports including soccer, figure skating and snooker (Williams et al. 1999).

Support for the hypothesis that the stimuli are being perceptually chunked has come from investigating how the game elements are recalled. For example, the encoding advantage displayed by experts was evident in a study monitoring eye movements in chess players (Reingold, Charness, Pomplun & Stampe 2001). Experts in this field were shown to have a larger visual span than lesser skilled players when processing structured, but not random, chess positions. That is, experts exhibited fewer fixations, extracted more perceptual information from a single fixation, and made greater use of information from parafoveal regions.

Although experts exhibit superior performance in these recall tasks, it is not clear whether this ability is an important aspect of skilled performance or merely a by-product of an expert's greater experience and familiarity with the sport. To answer this question, Williams and Davids (1995), in a study of declarative knowledge in soccer players, included a group of physically disabled spectators who had watched an average of 600 soccer matches but had never played the game. The results showed that experienced soccer players (over 600 games played) outperformed the disabled spectators on recall, recognition and anticipation tasks. It appears, therefore, that playing the sport facilitates the acquisition of sport-specific knowledge and that such knowledge is a basic component of expertise.

Alertness

The term *alertness* has been used in many ways in the attention literature. Most commonly it has been defined as the responsivity or sensitivity of a person to stimuli. Kahneman (1973), for example, associated alertness with the situational capacity of an individual (the amount of available capacity at any one time), or the amount of conscious sensitivity to task-related information. With greater alertness, individuals have more acute attentional capabilities. Clearly, momentary increases in alertness (e.g. when receiving a serve in tennis) and sustained alertness (e.g. over a long, five-set tennis match) are crucial requirements in many sports.

In the laboratory, sustaining alertness has been typically studied using vigilance tasks. In such tasks, people's ability to detect stimuli that occur infrequently and irregularly over a long period of time is measured (e.g. watching a clock face for occasional jumps of the sweep hand). In sport, outfielders in cricket, baseball and softball are engaged in vigilance tasks, as are line and net cord judges in tennis. The ability to maintain sufficient sensitivity to the environment (or maintain general awareness) is also important in fast-ball sports (e.g. soccer, rugby, hockey), where one lapse of concentration at the wrong moment can result in a missed tackle or dropped ball and a game-winning score for the opposition. As maintaining a high level of concentration for long periods of time can be mentally tiring, players need to develop strategies to increase their level of alertness at the right moments during their sport. So the batsman learns to relax mentally between balls to delay mental fatigue. However, turning on attention to focus on the next delivery is crucial after this 'time-out'. On a longer time scale, the professionalism of sport in recent years has meant that athletes must be tougher, more athletic and more resilient than ever before and, in many sports, must be able to turn on intense concentration to perform at an extremely high standard week after week.

Arousal and attention

Fluctuations in a person's level of alertness have been seen as being related to, or synonymous with, changes in arousal level. *Arousal* refers to a person's physiological and psychological activation. In most sports, arousal level is affected not only by the physical exercise involved, but also by psychological factors such as anxiety and motivation.

The relationship between arousal and performance has typically been hypothesised to follow the shape of an inverted-U curve (see chapter 3); that is, as arousal increases it facilitates performance up to a point beyond which further increases lead to a decrement in performance. The most common explanation of the inverted-U curve suggests that changes in arousal level produce changes in attentional processes. Easterbrook's (1959) cue utilisation hypothesis, for example, suggests that poor performance when under-aroused is a result of indiscriminate processing of stimuli. As arousal increases, attention narrows to cues pertinent to the task, and irrelevant stimuli (e.g. crowd movement) are ignored — hence performance improves. Further increases in arousal produce further attentional narrowing, and eventually important task-relevant cues (e.g. position of team-mates) begin to be neglected leading to a decrement in performance. Support for the attention-narrowing explanation has come from a number of studies, including one of rifle shooters (Landers, Wang & Courtet 1985), which showed a narrowing of peripheral vision under stress.

As mentioned earlier, there is growing evidence that increases in anxiety/arousal produce attentional narrowing and, at high levels of stress, heightened susceptibility to peripheral distraction. For example, in a study examining visual search strategies in karate (Williams & Elliott 1999), increases in anxiety were accompanied by an increase in the scanning rate and number of fixations on an opponent's peripheral body areas. The attentional effects accompanying high levels of stress/anxiety have also been linked to the occurrence of athletic injury; that is, athletes suffering psychological stress, often from factors outside the sport environment (e.g. home life), have been found to be more susceptible to injury, with increased distractibility and peripheral narrowing being cited as possible causes (e.g. Fawkner, McMurray & Summers 1999).

Although the effects of arousal on attentional processes are clear, the mechanisms that underlie these effects are not well understood. One problem is that much of the research has been based around optimal arousal theory proposing an inverted-U relationship between arousal and performance. We know, however, that high arousal does not always have a deleterious effect on performance. Rather, athletes' interpretation of their arousal level is the crucial factor. For example, although high-risk sporting activities (e.g. motor racing or hang gliding) involve extremely high levels of arousal, they may be experienced as exciting and pleasant by most participants (Kerr 1997). As a consequence of increasing criticism of the inverted-U hypothesis, other models, such as multidimensional anxiety theory (Martens, Vealey & Burton 1990), reversal theory (Kerr 1997) and catastrophe theory (Hardy 1996) have been proposed (see chapter 3 for further discussion of these models).

Flexibility

Flexibility, or switching, of attention, is vital in most sporting contexts (Nideffer 1976). It is particularly important in activities in which the environment is continually changing (e.g. soccer), requiring athletes to move or alter their attention to meet changing task demands. Even in more static sports, such as pistol shooting, the performer must shift attention between internal cues (monitoring relaxation levels) and external cues (observing the target).

According to Etzel (1979), attentional flexibility is the ability to direct and alter the scope (width) and focus (direction) of attention (i.e. along a broad to narrow as well as an internal to external continuum). It is reasonable to extend this definition to include other aspects of attention that also require flexibility. One is the ability to switch between cues that are optimally task-relevant, including refocusing after becoming distracted. For example, in fast-ball sports a player will need to quickly switch attention between opponents and to unexpected events, such as a full-back entering the attacking back line in rugby. An athlete must also learn to quickly regain control and refocus on the task at hand following errors during a performance (e.g. missed shots or double faults), and after distraction from external sources (e.g. crowd noise, public address systems or the taunts of an opponent) or internal sources (e.g. task-irrelevant thoughts). Some specific techniques for monitoring and improving the flexibility of attentional skills are outlined in chapter 14.

A person's ability to shift attention can be viewed as lying along a continuum, ranging from complete control over the alteration of attentional processes to 'perseveration', or the inability to relinquish a particular attentional focus despite wanting to do so. In Nideffer's (1976) theory, for example, it is argued that detriments in performance may occur because an individual is dominated by a particular attentional style and is unable to adopt one that is more appropriate to the situation. The consequences of various types of attentional mismatch are dealt with fully in chapter 14.

Intuitively, one might expect that the ability to respond quickly to unexpected events is a characteristic of highly skilled performers in open sports played in rapidly changing environments. Some support for attention-switching ability as an ingredient of skilled performance came from Kahneman, Ben-Ishai and Lotan (1973), who found that low-accident bus drivers and successful pilots performed better on dichotic listening tasks that require switching of attention than high-accident bus drivers and less successful pilots. It is also useful to distinguish between voluntary and automatic shifts in attention (Nougier & Rossi 1999). In many situations, we can use our knowledge of the probabilities with which different events will occur to voluntarily orient our attention to certain events or locations. Our attention, however, can also be drawn automatically to certain stimuli (e.g. unexpected sounds or movements of spectators). Voluntary and automatic attention have been studied in the laboratory using a reaction-time task (RT) in which subjects either are cued in advance (voluntary mode) towards a location at which 80 per cent of stimuli will be presented or are drawn automatically to a location by the unexpected presentation of a stimulus at a location. In the voluntary mode, attentional benefits and costs can be measured by comparing RT for cued (benefit) and non-cued (cost) locations to a neutral condition in which attention was not cued to a specific location.

The trade-off between attentional cost and benefits has been regarded as a measure of an individual's attentional flexibility (Keele & Hawkins 1982); that is, smaller costs and benefits are associated with an ability to rapidly switch attention between information sources (high attentional flexibility). This RT pattern has been obtained with elite athletes engaged in open skills (e.g. volleyball, water-polo and fencing), whereas closed-skill performers (e.g. swimmers) behave like non-athletes (Nougier, Rossi, Alain & Taddei 1996). Automatic orienting effects have also been found to be smaller in skilled athletes than control participants. This strategy of minimising attentional costs through 'expecting the unexpected' appears to be a general ability acquired by people who are constantly faced with attentionally demanding situations in which the environment is rapidly changing (Nougier & Rossi 1999). There also appear to be task-specific abilities that have developed in response to the particular attentional requirements of the sport. For example, subtle differences in the event-related brain potentials of expert skeet and trap clay-pigeon shooters have been observed (Rossi & Zani 1991), as have directional effects in the costs associated with responding to unexpected stimulus locations in volleyball players (Castiello & Umiltà 1992). In summary, there is good evidence that a characteristic of highly skilled performers in certain sports is the development of both general attentional expertise and sport-specific attentional skills. Put simply, experts are more efficient than non-experts in modulating the allocation of attentional resources to meet specific task demands (Lavallee et al. 2004).

FUTURE DIRECTIONS

Despite the progress made by attentional researchers in psychology, some questions remain about the extent to which research findings gained from the study of contrived tasks (e.g. dichotic listening) in controlled laboratory environments can ever accurately simulate real-life sporting demands. For example, it is difficult to study experimentally the disruptive effects of internal distractions that are common in competitive sport settings (e.g. when golfers experience negative thoughts as they face a tricky putt in a competition). In this section, therefore, we shall sketch some new directions for research on attention in athletes.

First, there is a lot to be gained by studying the attentional processes of expert athletes in field settings. Whereas early research on attention emphasised the *constraints* in people's performance that occurred under conditions of imposed cognitive load, studies of experts have restored the balance by exploring how structural performance limitations can be bypassed or overcome through extensive practice (Summers 2002). For example, recent evidence suggests that expert performers in fast-action sports like cricket and tennis manage to overcome daunting time constraints by using anticipatory strategies gained from experience and training (Starkes, Helsen & Jack 2001). In the light of such findings, an optimistic conclusion about human performance emerges. Specifically, it seems that the most significant limitations on skilled performance are not 'hardwired' but come instead from people's reluctance to engage in extensive practice of the tasks to be mastered. On a cautionary note, however, it is naïve to expect that average athletes can 'fast-track' their path to expertise simply by copying the attentional strategies used by more proficient performers in their sport (Williams 2002).

A second new direction in research concerns the study of *meta-attentional* processes in athletes — or the informal theories that these performers have developed about how to regulate their own concentration system. These theories may be elicited from interviews with sports stars about their psychological preparation for important athletic events. For example, consider the views of Garry Sobers, the former West Indies cricket star, who suggested that 'concentration's like a shower. You don't turn it on until you want to bathe ... You don't walk out of the shower and leave it running. You turn it off, you turn it on ... It has to be fresh and ready when you need it' (cited in White 2002, p. 20). As yet, however, we know little about the nature and malleability of athletes' mental models of their own psychological processes.

Third, there is an urgent need for systematic analysis of the attentional requirements of various sports. Interestingly, although a great deal is known about the physical demands of athletic pursuits — for example, Brewer (1997) claimed that runners in the London marathon suffer such 'feet-to-pavement' impact that the muscles in their spines compress by up to 1 centimetre as a result of the race! — little is known about their psychological demands. Against this background, do untimed games such as golf require different types of attentional skills from performers than timed activities (e.g. soccer)? A similar question could be asked for endurance sports (e.g. marathons) as opposed to 'explosive' sports (e.g. sprints). If evidence of different attentional requirements emerges, what theoretical mechanisms could account for them? Although there has been some speculation about the different types of attentional focus needed to execute various sport skills, surprisingly little research has been conducted on the precise task demands of athletic activities. Until this type of study is undertaken, we are left with the questionable assumption that generic attentional skills training 'packages' are equally applicable to all sports (Moran 2003).

Fourth, until recently psychologists largely ignored 'internal' distractions — or the effect of people's own thoughts, feelings and emotions on their attentional processes. Following the development of Wegner's (1994) model of mental control, however, sport psychologists have begun to explore the nature and implications of ironic effects in athletic performance — situations in which people either think or do the opposite of what they had intended (e.g. double-faulting at match point in tennis). Clearly, a comprehensive program of research is now required to establish precisely when such effects occur and what causes them (see also Janelle 1999).

A fifth fruitful avenue for research on attention in sport comes from cognitive neuroscience. As mentioned earlier, this field is concerned with understanding the biological substrates of cognitive processes through the use of psychophysiological measures (e.g. EEG, ERP, PET and fMRI) collected during real-time performance of various tasks. Already, electrophysiological techniques have proved valuable in identifying the main attentional networks in the brain (Posner & Peterson 1990), exploring whether visual search processes operate in a serial (one at a time) or parallel (all at once) manner (Woodman & Luck 1999), and in identifying differences in attentional processes in athletes (see Boutcher, chapter 19). Although these techniques have limitations (Cowey 2001), they offer intriguing possibilities for the study of attentional processes in athletes.

Finally, as an alternative to the hegemony of the cognitive tradition, some research in the field of motor control is offering exciting new possibilities for understanding the role of attention in the performance of athletic skills. As we have indicated, most of our knowledge about attention in sport has been gained within an information processing perspective. In the last decade the motor control field has seen the emergence of a radically different approach to the study of motor behaviour. The dynamic or emergent properties approach, exemplified in the work of Kelso and Turvey (Kelso 1995; Kugler & Turvey 1987), seeks to explain goal-directed behaviour in terms of physical laws and emphasises the action system's capacity for self-organisation. In this formulation, cognition and action are inseparable and must be analysed together. The basic tenet is that attention represents an intervening variable in the stabilisation and modification of behavioural patterns. Interestingly, the study of attention within this approach has used the traditional dual-task method in which participants perform two tasks simultaneously: a *primary task*, about which understanding of attention is sought; and a *secondary task*, often a discrete reaction-time (RT) task that directly reflects the attention demands of the primary task. In several studies, involving the concurrent performance of a rhythmic, bimanual coordination task and a discrete RT task, bimanual pattern stability and attention demands were found to covary strongly: the more stable (less variable) pattern was also the less 'demanding' to perform, and vice versa (Summers, Byblow, Bysouth-Young & Semjen 1998; Temprado, Zanone, Mono & Laurent 2001). This research suggests that attention may modify the stability of coordinated behaviour by changing the strength of the coupling between motor system components (e.g. the two arms). Although still in its infancy, the dynamical systems approach may provide new insights into the phenomenon of attention and the operation of cognition.

CONCLUSIONS

William James, as long ago as 1890, remarked, 'Everyone knows what attention is' (p. 404). As the quotes that begin this chapter illustrate, elite athletes clearly recognise the importance of attention in their sport. A review of the literature on attention reveals a multifaceted phenomenon that has been studied from a variety of perspectives. In the previous edition of this book, it was suggested that the systematic study of attention in applied settings such as sport should provide valuable information towards a better understanding of the phenomenon. This research has now begun, and recent theoretical developments in cognitive psychology and cognitive neuroscience suggest that we may be getting closer to understanding what attention really is.

SUMMARY

In this chapter we have given an overview of the theoretical perspectives and research related to the concept of attention. Our current understanding of attention has emerged predominantly from the fields of cognitive psychology and neuroscience. We discussed three theoretical perspectives from which attention has been studied: the cognitive, the neuroscientific, and the individual differences perspective. A key assumption of the laboratory-based approaches is that the mind is a limited-capacity system for processing information. Initial studies of attention in the 1950s tackled the questions of where and when these processing limitations occur by exploring deteriorations in people's performance in laboratory situations where they had been deliberately 'overloaded' with information. From such research, two important aspects of attention were revealed. On the one hand, the fact that the mind engages in selective or preferential processing in order to avoid cognitive overload was captured by the *filter* and *spotlight* metaphors of attention. On the other hand, the interference people experience when trying to perform two similar tasks at the same time was attributed to an apparent paucity of hypothetical attentional 'resources' or mental energy (Kahneman 1973). So, by exploring certain limitations in people's performance, cognitive psychologists discovered that attention is at once selective and divisible. More recently, neuroscientific research has indicated that attention is also required to help people to prepare and sustain alertness in situations demanding vigilance.

REVIEW QUESTIONS

1 What are the three different meanings of the term *attention* in cognitive psychology? Why is the ability to 'focus' effectively so important for athletic success?

2 Are there different types of attention? What are they? Can you think of examples to illustrate the differences between them? What selective attention tasks have you performed within the past day? What divided attention tasks have you tackled in the same period?

3 What are the main theoretical traditions from which attention has been studied in psychology? Can you explain at least one benefit that has arisen from each of them?

4 List three neuroscientific techniques used by researchers to explore attentional processes.

5 Why do athletes 'lose' their concentration? Explain the distinction between *external* and *internal* distractions.

6 Scanning the sports pages of your national press, can you find examples of each of these different categories of distractions?

7 What is meant by the *direction* of an athlete's attention?

8 Can attentional skills be trained in athletes?

9 In what ways are *arousal* and *attention* related in sport?

10 What are the main topics that need to be addressed in future research on attention in athletes?

References

Abernethy, B, Summers, JJ & Ford, S 1998, 'Issues in the measurement of attention', in JL Duda (ed.), *Advancements in sport and exercise psychology measurement*, FIT Press, Morgantown, WV, pp. 173–93.

Allard, F, Graham, S & Paarsalu, ME 1980, 'Perception in sport: basketball', *Journal of Sport Psychology*, 2, 14–21.

Barnes, S 1999, 'Awesome aces sink the marketing gurus', *Irish Independent*, 5 July, p. 14.

Bootsma, RJ 1999, 'Information and movement in interception tasks', in R Lidor & M Bar-Eli (eds), *Sport psychology: linking theory and practice*, Fitness Information Technology, Inc., Morgantown, WV, pp. 151–63.

Boutcher, SH 2002, 'Attentional processes and sport performance', in T Horn (ed.), *Advances in sport psychology*, 2nd edn, Fitness Information Technology, Morgantown, WV.

Boutcher, SH & Rotella, RJ 1987, 'A psychological skills educational program for closed-skill performance enhancement', *The Sport Psychologist*, 1, 127–37.

Brewer, J 1997, 'Pushed to the limit', *Sunday Times Magazine* (Lifestyle section), 13 April, pp. 31–3.

Broadbent, DA 1958, *Perception and communication*, Pergamon, New York.

Castiello, I & Umilta, C 1992, 'Orienting of attention in volleyball players', *International Journal of Sport Psychology*, 23, 301–10.

Cave, KR & Bichot, NP 1999, 'Visuospatial attention: beyond a spotlight model', *Psychonomic Bulletin and Review*, 6, 204–23.

Chase, WG & Simon, HA 1973, 'Perception in chess', *Cognitive Psychology*, 4, 55–81.

Cowey, A 2001, 'Functional localisation in the brain: from ancient to modern', *The Psychologist*, 14, 250–4.

Cox, RH 2002, *Sport psychology: concepts and applications*, 5th edn, McGraw-Hill, Boston, MA.

De Groot, AD 1965, *Thought and choice in chess*, Mouton, The Hague.

Durand-Bush, N, Salmela, JH & Green-Demers, I 2001, 'The Ottawa Mental Skills Assessment Tool (OMSAT-3)', *The Sport Psychologist*, 15, 1–19.

Easterbrook, JA 1959, 'The effect of emotion on cue utilization and the organization of behavior', *Psychological Review*, 66, 183–201.

Eriksen, CW & St James, JD 1986, 'Visual attention within and around the field of focal attention: a zoom lens model', *Perception and Psychophysics*, 40, 225–40.

Etzel, EF 1979, 'Validation of a conceptual model characterizing attention among international rifle shooters', *Journal of Sport Psychology*, 1, 281–90.

Everton, C 2002, 'Ebdon's regime pays off', *Irish Times*, 8 May, p. 25.

Farrow, D, Chivers, P, Hardingham, C & Sachse, S 1998, 'The effect of video-based perceptual training on the tennis return of serve', *International Journal of Sport Psychology*, 29, 231–42.

Fawkner, HJ, McMurray, NE & Summers, JJ 1999, 'Athletic injury and minor life events: a prospective study', *Journal of Science and Medicine in Sport*, 2, 117–24.

Fernandez-Duque, D & Johnson, ML 1999, 'Attention metaphors: how metaphors guide the cognitive psychology of attention', *Cognitive Science*, 23, 83–116.

Ford, SK & Summers, JJ 1992, 'The factorial validity of the TAIS attentional-style sub-scales', *Journal of Sport & Exercise Psychology*, 14, 283–97.

Graydon, J 2002, 'Stress and anxiety in sport', *The Psychologist*, 15, 408–10.

Hardy, L 1996, 'Testing the predictions of the cusp catastrophe model of anxiety and performance', *The Sport Psychologist*, 10, 140–56.

Hatfield, BD & Hillman, CH 2001, 'The psychophysiology of sport: a mechanistic understanding of the psychology of superior performance', in RN Singer, HA Hausenblas & CM Janelle (eds), *Handbook of sport psychology*, 2nd edn, John Wiley & Sons, New York, pp. 362–88.

Hatzigeorgiadis, A 2002, 'Thoughts of escape during competition: relationships with goal orientation and self-consciousness', *Psychology of Sport and Exercise*, 3, 195–207.

Hatzigeorgiadis, A & Biddle, SJH 2000, 'Assessing cognitive interference in sport: development of the Thought Occurrence Questionnaire for Sport', *Anxiety, Stress, and Coping*, 13, 65–86.

James, W 1890, *Principles of psychology*, Holt, New York.

Janelle, CM 1999, 'Ironic mental processes in sport: implications for sport psychologists', *The Sport Psychologist*, 13, 201–20.

Janelle, CM, Singer, RN & Williams, AM 1999, 'External distraction and attentional narrowing: visual search evidence', *Journal of Sport & Exercise Psychology*, 21, 70–91.

Kahneman, D 1973, *Attention and effort*, Prentice Hall, Englewood Cliffs, NJ.

Kahneman, D, Ben-Ishai, R & Lotan, M 1973, 'Relation of test attention to road accidents', *Journal of Applied Psychology*, 58, 113–15.

Keele, SW & Hawkins, HL 1982, 'Explorations of individual differences relevant to high level skill', *Journal of Motor Behavior*, 14, 3–23.

Kelso, JAS 1995, *Dynamic patterns: the self-organisation of brain and behaviour*, MIT Press, Cambridge, MA.

Kerr, JH 1997, *Motivation and emotion in sport: Reversal theory*, Psychology Press, Brighton, UK.

Kirschenbaum, DS & Bale, RM 1984, 'Cognitive-behavioural skills in golf', in RM Suinn (ed.), *Psychology of sports: methods and application*, Burgess, Minneapolis, MN, pp. 334–43.

Kolb, B & Whishaw, IQ 2003, *Fundamentals of human neuropsychology*, 5th edn, Worth Publishers, New York.

Kugler, PN & Turvey, MT 1987, *Information, natural law, and the self-assembly of rhythmic movement*, Erlbaum, Hillsdale, NJ.

Landers, DM, Wang, MQ & Courtet, P 1985, 'Peripheral narrowing among experienced and inexperienced rifle shooters under low- and high-time stress conditions', *Research Quarterly for Exercise and Sport*, 56, 122–30.

Lavallee, D, Kremer, J, Moran, AP & Williams, AM 2004, *Sport psychology: contemporary themes*, Palgrave Macmillan, Basingstoke, UK.

Lawton, GW, Hung, TM, Saarela, P & Hatfield, BD 1998, 'Electroencephalography and mental states associated with elite performance', *Journal of Sport & Exercise Psychology*, 20, 35–53.

Luck, SJ, Woodman, GF & Vogel, EK 2000, 'Event-related potential studies of attention', *Trends in Cognitive Sciences*, 4, 432–40.

Martens, R, Vealey, RS & Burton, D (eds) 1990, *Competitive anxiety in sport*, Human Kinetics, Champaign, IL.

Matlin, MW 2002, *Cognition*, 5th edn, Harcourt Brace, Fort Worth, TX.

Moran, AP 1996, *The psychology of concentration in sport performers: a cognitive analysis*, Psychology Press, Brighton, UK.

Moran, AP 2003, 'The state of concentration skills training in applied sport psychology', in I Greenlees and AP Moran (eds), *Concentration skills training in sport*, The British Psychological Society, Leicester, UK, pp. 7–19.

Moran, AP 2004, *Sport and exercise psychology: a critical introduction*, Psychology Press/Routledge, London.

Navon, D & Gopher, D 1979, 'On the economy of the human processing system', *Psychological Review*, 86, 214–55.

Nideffer, RM 1976, 'Test of Attentional and Interpersonal Style', *Journal of Personality and Social Psychology*, 34, 394–404.

Nideffer, RM 1993, 'Attention control training', in RN Singer, M Murphey & LK Tennant (eds), *Handbook of research in sport psychology*, Macmillan, New York, pp. 542–56.

Nougier, V & Rossi, B 1999, 'The development of expertise in the orienting of attention', *International Journal of Sport Psychology*, 30, 246–60.

Nougier, V, Rossi, B, Alain, C & Taddei, F 1996, 'Evidence of strategic effects in the modulation of orienting of attention', *Ergonomics*, 9, 1119–33.

Otway, G 1999, 'Clarke enjoys special K day', *The Sunday Times*, 1 August, p. 13.

Paull, G & Glencross, DJ 1997, 'Expert perception and decision making in baseball', *International Journal of Sport Psychology*, 28, 35–56.

Posner, MI, Nissen, M & Ogden, W 1978, 'Attended and unattended processing modes: the role of set for spatial location', in HL Pick & E Saltzman (eds), *Modes of perceiving and processing information*, Erlbaum, Hillsdale, NJ, pp. 128–81.

Posner, MI & Peterson, SE 1990, 'The attention system and the human brain', *Annual Review of Neuroscience*, 13, 25–42.

Ramsay, A 2000, 'Agassi focus forces Sampras surrender', *Irish Independent*, 28 January, p. 20.

Reingold, EM, Charness, N, Pomplun, M & Stampe, DM 2001, 'Visual span in expert chess players' *Psychological Science*, 12, 48–55.

Reisberg, D & McLean, J 1985, 'Meta-attention: do we know when we are being distracted?', *Journal of General Psychology*, 112, 291–306.

Revien, L 1987, *Eyerobics*, Visual Skills Inc., Great Neck, NY.

Rossi, B & Zani, A 1991, 'Timing of movement-related decision processes in clay-pigeon shooters as assessed by event-related brain potentials and reaction times', *International Journal of Sport Psychology*, 22, 128–39.

Schmidt, RA & Lee, TD 1999, *Motor control and learning: a behavioural emphasis*, 3rd edn, Human Kinetics, Champaign, IL.

Schneider, W & Shiffrin, RM 1977, 'Controlled and automatic human information processing: I. detection, search, and attention', *Psychological Review*, 84, 1–66.

Starkes, JL, Edwards, P, Dissanayake, P & Dunn, T 1995, 'A new technology and field test of advance cue usage in volleyball', *Research Quarterly for Exercise and Sport*, 66, 162–7.

Starkes, JL, Helsen, W & Jack, R 2001, 'Expert performance in sport and dance', in RN Singer, HA Hausenblas & CM Janelle (eds), *Handbook of sport psychology*, 2nd edn, John Wiley & Sons, New York, pp. 174–201.

Summers, JJ 2002, 'Practice and training in bimanual coordination tasks: strategies and constraints', *Brain and Cognition*, 48, 166–78.

Summers, JJ, Byblow, WD, Bysouth-Young, D & Semjen, A 1998, 'Bimanual circle drawing during secondary task loading', *Motor Control*, 2, 106–13.

Temprado, JJ, Zanone, PG, Monno, A & Laurent, M 2001, 'A dynamical framework to understand performance tradeoffs and in dual-task performance', *Journal of Experimental Psychology: Human Perception and Performance*, 27, 1303–13.

Wachtel, P 1967, 'Conceptions of broad and narrow attention', *Psychological Bulletin*, 68, 417–29.

Wegner, DM 1994, 'Ironic processes of mental control', *Psychological Review*, 101, 34–52.

Wegner, DM 2002, 'Thought suppression and mental control', in L Nadel (ed.), *Encyclopaedia of cognitive science*, vol. 4, Nature Publishing Company, London, pp. 395–7.

Wegner, DM, Ansfield, M & Pilloff, D 1998, 'The putt and the pendulum: ironic effects of the mental control of action', *Psychological Science*, 9, 196–9.

White, P 2002, 'Interview: Garry Sobers', *Guardian*, 10 June, pp. 20–1.

Williams, AM 2002, 'Perceptual and cognitive expertise in sport', *The Psychologist*, 15, 416–17.

Williams, AM & Davids, K 1995, 'Declarative knowledge in sport: a byproduct of experience or a characteristic of expertise?', *Journal of Sport & Exercise Psychology*, 17, 259–75.

Williams, AM, Davids, K, Burwitz, L & Williams, J 1994, 'Visual search strategies in experienced and inexperienced soccer players', *Research Quarterly for Exercise and Sport*, 65, 127–35.

Williams, AM, Davids, K & Williams, JG 1999, *Visual perception and action in sport*, E & FN Spon, London, pp. 395–7.

Williams, AM & Elliott D 1999, 'Anxiety, expertise, and visual search strategy in karate', *Journal of Sport & Exercise Psychology*, 21, 362–75.

Williams, AM & Grant, A 1999, 'Training perceptual skill in sport', *International Journal of Sport Psychology*, 30, 194–220.

Woodman, GF & Luck, SJ 1999, 'Electrophysiological measurement of rapid shifts of attention during visual search', *Nature*, 400, 867–9.

Zelinsky, GJ, Rao, RPN, Hayhoe, MM & Ballard, DH 1997, 'Eye movements reveal the spatiotemporal dynamics of visual search', *Psychological Science*, 8, 448–53.

CHAPTER 5

INTRINSIC AND EXTRINSIC MOTIVATION IN SPORT AND EXERCISE

Christina M Frederick-Recascino & Tony Morris

Traditionally motivation has been an area of great interest to theorists, researchers and students in psychology. Why do we do the things we do, and how do certain activities come to be preferred over others? This is the essence of motivation. In sport, these issues have been explored by examining why and how people are motivated to begin or maintain their participation, as well as how different motivational states influence performance and psychological outcomes. This chapter will explore the concepts associated with two different types of motivation: intrinsic and extrinsic motivation. In particular, we will explore the characteristics of each type of motivation, examining how contingencies in the environment can modify motivational states, and relating motivation to psychological and performance outcomes. In addition, we will present tips for coaches and individuals involved in sport that will help foster better motivational states in athletes and sport participants.

DEFINING MOTIVATION

Motivation has been defined as energy and direction of behaviour (Deci 1980; Deci & Ryan 1985; Roberts 1992). The energy component of motivation reflects the amount of effort or attention we choose to devote to an activity or task. Greater energy is usually associated with a greater amount of motivation. As will be discussed in this chapter, motivation can also be conceptualised as existing on a continuum, with extrinsic motivation anchoring one end and intrinsic motivation at the opposite end (Pelletier, Fortier, Vallerand, Tuson, Briere & Blais 1995).

A definition of motivation would not be complete without mention of the concept of *amotivation*. Amotivation is believed to fall outside the continuum of motivation. In an amotivated state, individuals feel that they cannot interact effectively or competently in their environment. Pelletier et al. (1995) likened the amotivated state to that of learned helplessness (Abramson, Seligman & Teasdale 1978) and predict that it will lead to decreased involvement in a chosen domain of activity.

The direction of behaviour reflects the individual's unique level of personal interest in a specific task or activity. Some individuals are motivated to paint beautiful pictures; some are motivated to fly; and others turn their attention to sports, exercise and other physical activities. The direction of motivation is determined by the opportunities to which one is exposed and the outcome of initial attempts at performance in those domains (Harter 1978). In sport, the external environment helps to shape the direction of athletes' interests. For example, it would be quite common to find athletes from colder climates motivated to engage in sports such as cross-country and downhill skiing. Indeed, we sometimes find it amusing when this commonsense prediction does not hold true and we are presented with athletes, such as the Jamaican Bobsled Team, whose motivational direction would not have been predictable given their home environment.

The importance of motivation in sport and exercise domains

Sport, exercise and physical activity in general provide numerous benefits for individuals living in today's high-stress, fast-paced world. There can be no argument that sports offer an opportunity to engage in activities that not only help relieve physical stress but enhance our cardiovascular health, help us maintain a healthy weight and muscle mass, and provide psychological benefits (ACSM 1990; Pate et al. 1995). We also know that the energy and direction of our behaviour, or our motivation, can be sustained over a short or a long period of time. It is in the best interest of sport psychologists, coaches and trainers to study and understand motivation in order to help their clients sustain motivation and engagement in sport activities over extended periods of time. With the correct motivational elements in place, it is quite possible for an individual to acquire a lifelong love of physical activity, and to reap the benefits of this participation.

Knowledge of motivational states: correlation and prediction

Although important, it is not enough for sport researchers and practitioners to understand only whether or not an athlete is motivated. Researchers strive to understand how motivation is associated with other personal and psychological factors (Frederick & Ryan 1993). With this knowledge, practitioners can attempt to build interventions that enhance motivational states in the athletes they serve. For example, for many years researchers have sought to understand the differences between male and female athletes' motivational states (Biddle & Bailey 1985; Mathes & Battista 1985). One finding that emerges from this line of inquiry is that female sport participants are more motivated by the social elements (friendship, contact with others interested in the same activity) associated with physical activities than men (Biddle & Bailey 1985). This information can then be translated into practice by offering female athletes more within-sport opportunities for social contact, as well as by providing a climate of interpersonal support for female athletes.

Beyond understanding the personal variables related to motivational states, researchers have also tried to understand the psychological correlates of motivation. Psychological characteristics such as happiness, self-esteem, depression and anxiety have all been associated with motivation for sport and exercise (Frederick & Ryan 1993; Vallerand & Losier 1999). Later in the chapter we will explore these associations in greater detail.

INTRINSIC VERSUS EXTRINSIC MOTIVATION

Researchers have always been interested in studying motivation and its correlates. However, early research often adopted either a Freudian perspective (Hull 1943; Freud 1923) that focused on how instinctual needs or drives motivated behaviour, or a behavioural perspective, focused on how external environmental contingencies formed the basis for motivating behaviour (Skinner 1971). It was not until the late 1950s that a newer approach for thinking about motivation was developed (White 1959). In 1959 White published a now well-known paper titled 'Motivation reconsidered: the concept of competence'. In this monograph, based on his own research, he argued that humans and other mammals can be motivated by more than just drive satisfaction, instinctual urges or external contingencies. White observed that humans are active explorers of their environments, endowed with an innate curiosity and a need to be effective in their interactions. He called this need *effectance motivation* and proposed that effectance or competence was crucial for task mastery and continued motivation. In addition, White indicated that this self-initiated motivation formed the basis for our experience of domain-specific competence, or self-efficacy. White's work formed the foundation for the current conceptualisation of intrinsic motivation.

Drawing from White's seminal work and the related motivational and conceptual work of other researchers (Blasi 1998; deCharms 1968; Deci 1980; Heider 1958), Deci and Ryan (1985) presented a theoretical approach specifically directed towards the study of intrinsic and extrinsic motivational processes. This theoretical perspective is today known as *self-determination theory* (Deci & Ryan 1991, 1985).

Self-determination theory begins with the premise that there are three primary psychological needs that motivate human behaviour across domains (Deci 1980; Deci & Ryan 1985, 1991). These needs are autonomy, competence and relatedness with others. As individuals, we strive to fulfil these needs in order to create a healthy psychological environment in which to exist. Sport and exercise activities provide participants with many opportunities to fulfil the three proposed needs. Since sport and exercise are usually self-initiated and are not requisites of human life, they tend to have some element of autonomy associated with them. Mastering a sport skill or developing ever greater expertise in an activity fulfil the need for competence. Playing on a team with like-minded individuals and experiencing the camaraderie associated with such play infuse us with a sense of relatedness.

Of these three proposed needs, research has focused on the needs for autonomy and competence, which, combined, form the basis for understanding states of intrinsic and extrinsic motivation. When individuals are in a state of *intrinsic motivation*, they experience choice in their behavioural options, thereby fulfilling their need for autonomy. Additionally they are at a level of optimal challenge, which fulfils their competence need. A state of intrinsic motivation is associated with feelings of satisfaction, enjoyment, competence and a desire to persist at the activity. Sports and exercise for many individuals provide domains in which intrinsic motivation can be experienced fairly frequently.

On the other hand, when one loses optimal challenge or autonomy, a state of *extrinsic motivation* is created (Deci & Ryan 1985; Ryan & Connell 1989; Ryan, Koestner & Deci 1991). In sport, motives reflecting pressure to participate, and those resulting from the need for status or approval, reflect an extrinsic motivational orientation. Unfortunately, for some athletes a sport that was initially intrinsically motivated can, through pressure to perform, conformity to parents' or coaches' desires, or even self-initiated demands for performance, become extrinsically motivated.

SELF-DETERMINATION THEORY: LEVELS OF SELF-REGULATION

Self-determination theory addresses both intrinsic and extrinsic motivation. However, it also goes further to explain that non-intrinsically motivated activities actually exist on a continuum ranging from those that are entirely externally directed to those that, although still extrinsic in origin, have become self-regulated. This model of motivation is based on perceived locus of causality (PLOC) (Ryan & Connell 1989). PLOC refers to the beliefs individuals hold about whether forces internal or external to self initiate their behaviours.

At the base level of the PLOC motivational continuum is external regulation, or behaviour that is entirely controlled by external forces. At an externally regulated level, individuals feel they have little or no choice about the direction their behaviour may take. As a result, they may experience feelings of frustration and a lack of interest in the activity.

As an individual moves towards self-determination, behaviours are internalised. The individual experiencing the initial stage of internalisation makes decisions about behaviour based on an internal awareness of the wishes and desires of others. The first level of internalisation is referred to as *introjected regulation*. At this level, the individual regulates his or her behaviour in order to gain social approval, avoid disapproval or alleviate feelings of guilt.

At the next level of self-regulation the individual moves from seeking social approval into more self-determined behavioural choices based on perceptions of the value, benefits and importance of a behaviour to one's self. This level of regulation is referred to as *identified regulation*. At the last and most self-determined level of regulation, *integrated regulation*, motivation is not only perceived as being self-determined and desirable, but the individual has come to associate his or her personal identity with the motivational domain (Deci & Ryan 1991). For instance, in an integrated state, a college baseball player will not only report enjoyment of his involvement in baseball, but will develop personal behaviours, other interests and hobbies that centre on his identity as a baseball player. Table 5.1 provides a direct example of each level of self-regulation as experienced in a sport domain.

TABLE 5.1   Examples of levels of self-regulation (for a baseball or basketball player)

External regulation	'I go to practice because the coach requires it.'
Introjected regulation	'I go to training because I know the coach expects me to be there.'
Identified regulation	'I play baseball because I can use my skills to earn a college scholarship.'
Integrated regulation	'Baseball is my life and I identify myself as a baseball player before anything else.'

Research examining levels of self-regulation has been undertaken across a variety of domains (Blais, Sabourin, Boucher & Vallerand 1990; Plant 1990; Ryan & Connell 1989; Vallerand, Blais, Briere & Pelletier 1989). Across studies, results clearly indicate that greater self-determination (e.g. identified and integrated regulation) is associated with positive affect, as well as greater achievement, persistence and effort expenditure. On the other hand, external and introjected regulatory styles are associated with higher levels of anxiety and less activity persistence.

The PLOC approach has been used to address issues of motivation within the sport and exercise domain. A shortened version of the Perceived Locus of Causality Scale, developed by Goudas, Biddle and Fox (1994) for use with children, measures level of self-regulation in physical education classes. Another assessment tool that uses the PLOC approach is the Sport Motivation Scale (SMS) (Pelletier, Fortier, Vallerand, Tuson, Briere & Blais 1995; Fortier, Vallerand, Briere & Provencher 1995), a self-report scale with seven subscales. The subscales assess three types of intrinsic motivation towards sport as well as levels of external, introjected and identified regulation. The seventh subscale provides a measure of amotivation. Results of initial work with the SMS indicate outcomes similar to those found within other domains (Pelletier et al. 1995). The SMS has been used to study many aspects of behaviour within the sport domain, including gender- and sport-related differences in motivation (Chantal, Guay, Dobreva-Martinova & Vallerand 1996; Fortier, Vallerand, Briere & Provencher 1995; Losier & Vallerand 1994; Vallerand & Losier 1999).

Sport and exercise researchers have also used a more inductively driven approach to the study of intrinsic and extrinsic motivation in sport. This approach uses the Motivation for Physical Activities Measure — Revised (MPAM-R) (Ryan, Frederick, Lepes, Rubio & Sheldon 1997; Frederick & Ryan 1993). The MPAM-R focuses on specific outcome-oriented goals that are thought to drive exercise engagement. Through repeated empirical studies, these outcomes have been organised and discussed in terms of the self-regulatory level or psychological need they most closely address.

More specifically, the MPAM-R is a self-report scale assessing five sport participation motives: interest/enjoyment motives, competence motives, fitness motives, appearance-based motives and social motives. Of these, interest/enjoyment and competence motives reflect intrinsic motivation towards physical activity, whereas fitness and appearance-based motives are extrinsic in nature, most closely relating to identified and introjected regulation respectively. Social motives reflect the need for relatedness. The MPAM-R has been used to relate participation motives to adherence variables, emotional attitudes associated with sport, and personality characteristics of participants (Frederick & Morrison 1996; Frederick, Morrison & Manning 1996; Ryan et al. 1997).

ASSOCIATED CONCEPTS — FLOW AND BEING 'IN THE ZONE'

Experiencing 'flow', or being 'in the zone', both widely discussed in athletic experience (Csikszentmihalyi 1975, 1990, 1997), can be understood in self-determination theory as part of the heightened awareness and sense of wellbeing associated with intrinsic motivation. Specifically, Csikszentmihalyi has proposed that the experience of flow occurs in situations where one's skill level is high and the optimal amount of challenge is being provided to the participant. He called these high-challenge, high-skill moments. Csikszentmihalyi contrasted the flow experiences with three others, more indicative of experiences associated with extrinsic motivation. Using the same challenge–skill dichotomy, he described boredom-producing activities as low challenge, high skill. Apathy-producing activities are characterised by low-skill, low-challenge situations, and anxiety-producing activities result from low-skill, high-challenge situations.

In research with American teenagers, Csikszentmihalyi (1997) found that the greatest percentage of flow experiences occur when teens are actually engaged in games and sports (44 per cent of the time), as compared with other activities such as hobbies, socialising or watching television. Interestingly, and perhaps paradoxically, the highest percentage of anxiety-producing situations are also associated with sport and game participation, with anxiety occurring 24 per cent of the time during sport participation. This research supports the belief that, although sport participants can reap the benefits of their intrinsic motivation, for others extrinsic factors may create less than optimal personal and psychological conditions.

COGNITIVE EVALUATION THEORY

Using the concepts of intrinsic and extrinsic motivation to think about and understand motivation for sport and exercise has led to the development of a body of knowledge about how factors such as rewards, feedback and competition enhance or undermine intrinsic motivation. This subtheory of self-determination theory is referred to as *cognitive evaluation theory* (Deci & Ryan 1985; Frederick & Ryan 1995; Ryan, Vallerand & Deci 1984).

Cognitive evaluation theory begins with the premise that since intrinsic motivation is driven by the needs for autonomy and competence, any event that affects these needs has an influence on intrinsic motivation. Experiences like rewards, positive and negative feedback, and the competitive nature of a sporting event all provide participants with information about their autonomy and competence. To the extent that autonomy and competence are undermined, intrinsic motivation will be negatively affected. Furthermore, the potential for intrinsic motivation to be affected is based on how the event is interpreted by the individual participant, either in a controlling manner or in an informational one (Ryan et al. 1984).

Sport participants who perceive their experience to be controlled or pressure-filled lose a sense of self-determination. For example, if a coach tells a young athlete that she must practise harder because she lacks the required level of skill, this information could be interpreted as controlling and could undermine the player's intrinsic motivation; on the other hand, it could provide knowledge to the athlete that will benefit, rather than reduce, her intrinsic motivation levels. If she can take the advice and use it to guide her behaviour in order to increase her level of competence, then her intrinsic motivation will not be affected negatively.

Research on cognitive evaluation theory has focused on how specific types of events affect intrinsic motivation for sport. The three most widely researched events are use of positive and negative feedback, use of rewards and direct versus indirect competition. Each of the factors will be discussed in turn.

Use of feedback

According to cognitive evaluation theory, any feedback that promotes a sense of competence in the participant will have a beneficial impact on intrinsic motivation. Conversely, if feedback is provided that undermines perceived competence, then intrinsic motivation will suffer. Vallerand (1983) and Vallerand and Reid (1984) have tested the effects of feedback on intrinsic motivation in children and young athletes. Vallerand and Reid found that positive feedback about performance on a balancing task increased intrinsic motivation towards the task, while negative performance feedback decreased intrinsic motivation. Vallerand (1983) found similar results in 50 youth hockey players. Compared with no-feedback groups, groups that received positive feedback showed increases in intrinsic motivation, although those groups receiving more feedback did not show greater increases in intrinsic motivation than those receiving less feedback.

Use of rewards

In many countries around the world, professional athletes are highly rewarded for their performances. Young athletes on recreational teams are also rewarded using trophies or treats such as candy or ice-cream. What effects do such rewards have on players' levels of intrinsic motivation? According to cognitive evaluation theory, if a reward is perceived as controlling, in that it takes away one's self-determination for a task or it refocuses the participant's attention on the task outcome (receiving the reward) and away from enjoyment associated with task engagement, intrinsic motivation will be undermined. If an athlete can perceive a reward informationally as a positive reflection of competence, intrinsic motivation will be unaffected. Orlick and Mosher (1978) tested the influence of rewards in children's play behaviour and found that children who were rewarded for play later showed decreased interest in playtime in subsequent testing sessions. Additionally, in a set of two studies Ryan (1980, 1977) showed similar effects of rewards on intrinsic motivation of college athletes. In the first study, he compared intrinsic motivation levels of male scholarship and non-scholarship athletes. The scholarship athletes had significantly lower levels of intrinsic motivation than their peers who were not receiving scholarships. In the second study, Ryan (1980) compared intrinsic motivation levels of male and female college athletes, either receiving or not receiving scholarships. For the male athletes, the 1980 results were the same as those shown in the earlier study. For the women, however, receiving a scholarship had no negative effect on the athletes' intrinsic motivation levels.

Competition

As was the case with rewards and feedback, competitive situations can either enhance or undermine intrinsic motivation for sport activities. If the competitive situation is perceived to provide competence feedback about one's abilities (e.g. as a result of winning or achieving a self-set standard), then intrinsic motivation will be enhanced. If, on the other hand, competition provides feedback about one's incompetence through losing, and the competitive situation becomes pressure-laden or ego-driven, then intrinsic motivation levels would be expected to decrease.

In research testing the effects of competition on intrinsic motivation, Vallerand, Gauvin and Halliwell (1982) found that even in situations involving indirect competition (i.e. not face to face), participants felt pressured to beat the scores of other participants. In a direct competition task, Deci, Betley, Kahle, Abrams and Porac (1981) had participants compete at a puzzle-solving task. In the Deci et al. study, the negative effect of competition on performance was noted and was especially strong for women. Similar results were found in studies using competition involving a simple motor task. Vallerand, Gauvin and Halliwell (1986) and Reeve, Olson and Cole (1985) found that losing at a task undermined participants' intrinsic motivation. In an applied sport setting, Fortier, Vallerand, Briere and Provencher (1995) compared the motivation of competitive and recreational athletes. They found that competitive athletes had lower levels of intrinsic and higher levels of extrinsic motivation than the recreational sport group.

In two more recent studies, the importance of the outcome of the competitive athletic endeavour and the athlete's achievement orientation have been linked to intrinsic motivation. McAuley and Tammen (1989) examined changes in intrinsic motivation during a basketball jump-shot competition. Their results indicated that individuals who were successful at the event had significantly higher intrinsic motivation and perceived themselves as more competent than those who were unsuccessful. Tauer and Harackiewicz (1999) also showed that high achievement-oriented individuals were able to maintain more enjoyment of a game during competition than those individuals low in achievement motivation. It appears from this study that achievement motivation may moderate the effects of competition as predicted by cognitive evaluation theory.

THE PRACTICAL APPLICATION OF COGNITIVE EVALUATION THEORY

Given the predictions of, and supporting research related to, cognitive evaluation theory, student readers may wonder whether it is ever appropriate to use rewards, negative feedback or pressured, competitive sport experiences when working with athletes. The answer, of course, cannot be as simple as yes or no, and one must take into consideration the player's age and level of ability as well as the goals associated with the sport.

For children and in recreational sport settings, a high-pressure, controlling environment is likely to lead to a loss of intrinsic motivation even before perceptions of competence are legitimately established. The primary goal of sport for these types of athletes is not to beat an opponent, but to develop basic competency, to promote fitness and future interest in the activity, and to provide a socialisation experience for those involved. With this goal in mind, a high-pressure environment in which competition is stressed and rewards are emphasised for high achievers would probably decrease most participants' levels of intrinsic motivation.

On the other hand, in professional sports participation and performance are the athlete's job and winning is the goal of the endeavour. In this case rewards, feedback and a focus on the outcome are not only appropriate, but may be most desirable. Without a solid reward structure in place, it is possible that most professional athletes would no longer feel the urge to participate that may have once driven their sport behaviour. Indeed, this situation may be partly to blame for the escalation in player salaries and demands in recent years. Professional athletes are rewarded handsomely for their performances. Over time, however, rewards must be continually increased in order for athletes to feel adequately compensated and to ensure continued participation. When performance and participation are solely driven by the rewards one receives, then last year's reward for a successful season almost guarantees that a larger reward will be needed this year to maintain the same level of commitment. Thus, player salaries continue to escalate, resulting in higher ticket prices for the consumer and a sense of astonishment at the discrepancy between the salary of an ordinary working individual and the enormous salaries some athletes receive.

MOTIVATION AND ITS ASSOCIATION WITH RELATED SPORT OUTCOMES: WHAT DOES THE RESEARCH TELL US?

Based on information derived from domains such as education and work (Deci, Connell & Ryan 1989; Illardi, Leone, Kasser & Ryan 1993), predictions can be made about how the type of motivation an individual has for an activity influences factors such as participation rates, adherence, psychological variables and emotion. It can be predicted that intrinsic participation motives would relate to higher levels of positive affect, satisfaction and competence. Participants with higher levels of intrinsic motivation should also persist in the activity for a greater amount of time, and might report higher levels of adherence. An extrinsic orientation would relate to lower levels of positive affect, satisfaction and/or competence, and less adherence to the activity. An examination of the literature relating motivation to a variety of variables of interest will shed further light on these predictions.

Motivation, adherence and levels of participation

Perhaps one of the most important and compelling reasons for studying motivation in the sport and exercise domain is the desire to link motivation with adherence variables, such as amount of participation. Frederick and Ryan (1993) found clear relationships between participation motivation and self-reports of adherence in exercise. This study involved two samples of participants, a group of 35 male and 114 female college students ranging in age between 17 and 32 years and a general sample of 376 adults ranging in age from 18 to 75 years with a mean age of 39 years. Intrinsic motives were positively related to the numbers of hours a week one exercised. In contrast, extrinsic motives were positively related to days a week of exercise, but negatively related to hours a week of exercise, self-reported length of participation in the current activity and estimated length of future participation.

Ryan et al. (1997) showed results in line with these earlier studies. In this work, 24 tae kwon do participants showed greater adherence to their activity than did a comparable age group of 16 aerobics class participants. Analysis comparing the role of motivation in predicting adherence found that these differences in adherence were explained by the greater intrinsic motivation expressed by the tae kwon do participants.

This research showed a clear link between motivational orientation towards exercise and adherence-related variables. Self-determination theory can be used to explain why this relationship exists. It appears that when individuals experience intrinsic motivation for sport they may enter a state of absorption in the activity in which time becomes irrelevant. This state, similar to a sense of flow (Csikszentmihalyi 1975, 1990), could easily explain the relationship between intrinsic participation motives and increased levels of adherence and participation. In contrast, extrinsic motivation is often characterised by a sense of external control, guilt or pressure to participate (Deci & Ryan 1985), but not by a sense of enjoyment or fulfilment. Extrinsically oriented athletes may feel external and internal pressures to practise or work out, but once these pressures are lifted their participation wanes.

Research with exercise participants exhibiting higher levels of extrinsic motivation has shown that they report a lower overall length of participation (months or years) in their activity and don't foresee themselves persisting in this activity into the future (Frederick & Ryan 1993). Although these individuals may temporarily be ritualistic in their participation, their motivational attitudes may not bode well for their long-term physical health. The research addressing motivational issues as they relate to adherence and participation suggest that exercise settings foster an intrinsic motivational orientation and help promote greater engagement in, and adherence to, physical activity. Research by Pelletier, Briere, Blais and Vallerand (1988) supports this proposition. Pelletier et al. developed an intervention with young athletes designed to encourage intrinsic motivation. After 18 months the athletes' attendance rates increased and the team dropout rate decreased by approximately 30 per cent.

Descriptive research on motives for participation in sport and physical activity

Another way to explore the relationship between intrinsic and extrinsic motivation and participation in sport and physical activity is to examine the reasons people give for participating in various activities. The substantial dropout rate from organised sport during adolescence provided the impetus for descriptive research on participation motives. Researchers began to examine the phenomenon of youth sport participation and dropout in North America during the 1970s and 1980s. A popular approach was to ask adolescents the reasons why they participated, the assumption (later shown to be erroneous) being that dropout reflected an absence or low level of those motives that underlie participation. Gill, Gross and Huddleston (1983) developed a questionnaire to examine motives for participation. First, they asked adolescents to state their own reasons for participating, using open-ended questions. Then Gill et al. devised a questionnaire that presented those reasons preceded by the phrase 'I want to' or 'I like to' — for example, 'I like to have fun' and 'I want to develop my skill'. Response was on a five-point Likert scale from 1 (*not at all important*) to 5 (*very important*). After some refinement, Gill et al. administered the 30-item Participation Motivation Questionnaire (PMQ) to 1138 male and female children and adolescents at a multi-sport summer camp. They found that the individual items, or reasons for participating, that were rated most highly were to improve skill, for fun, to learn new skills, for the challenge and for fitness. Gill et al. performed an exploratory factor analysis on the data. They identified eight underlying factors, each of which accounted for a number of items. These were achievement, team (affiliation/social), fitness, energy release, to be with others, skill, friends and fun.

The PMQ approach has been used by a number of researchers in the sport and exercise domain to examine the motives for participation in a range of contexts. Reviewers often group all these studies together, but it is helpful to appreciate the variety of activities and types of participant that have been studied. Table 5.2 summarises the characteristics of the major descriptive studies that have used versions of the PMQ. In that table, studies are grouped into those that examined motives for participation in youth sport in a single culture, mostly the United States, those that compared participation motives in youth sport across cultures, and those that considered participation motives across the life span. Most of the research that followed the initial work by Gill et al. also examined youth sport. Some studies focused on a single sport, such as swimming (Gould, Feltz & Weiss 1985) or gymnastics (Klint & Weiss 1987). Klint and Weiss did not perform a factor analysis, probably because their sample was too small, but grouped the items under six categories of motives for participation in youth sport identified by pre-PMQ research. These were skill development, affiliation (including with the team and with friends), success/status, energy release, fitness and excitement/challenge. The Klint and Weiss study involved a very small sample for this kind of participation motivation research, even for the examination of one sport. It was, however, one of the first studies to perform discriminant function analysis to distinguish between the key motives of different groups, in this case males and females.

TABLE 5.2 Summary of research using the Participation Motivation Questionnaire

Authors	Date	PMQ version	Country	Sample size	Age range	Activity type(s)	Top-rated items	Factor analysis
Youth sport								
Gill, Gross & Huddleston	1983	Original 30-item 5-point Likert scale	USA	1138	8–18	Multi-sport	Improve skill, fun, learn new skills, challenge, fitness	Achievement, team (affiliation/social), energy release, to be with others, fitness, skill, friends, fun

Authors	Date	PMQ version	Country	Sample size	Age range	Activity type(s)	Top-rated items	Factor analysis
Gould, Feltz & Weiss	1985	30-item original 3-point Likert scale, modified for swimming	USA	365	8–19	Swimming	Fun, fitness, team, skill, excitement	Achievement/status, team atmosphere, excitement/challenge, fitness, energy release, skill development, friendship
Klint & Weiss	1987	32-item 5-point Likert scale	USA	67	8–16	Gymnastics	Learn skills, get in shape, improve skills, fun, stay in shape, challenge	No factor analysis
Longhurst & Spink	1987	27-item 5-point Likert scale	Australia	404	8–18	Netball, cricket, athletics, Australian Football	Improve skills, fitness, competition, learn skills, challenge	Team/achievement, situational, status, fitness
Buonamano, Cei & Mussino	1995	32-item Italian 7-point Likert scale	Italy	2589	9–18	Multi-sport	No ranking reported	Success/status, fitness/skill, extrinsic rewards, team, friendship/fun, energy release
Sutherland & Morris	1997	50-item 5-point Likert scale, Morris et al. version	Australia	293	13–15	Multi-activity	Fun, health, stay in shape, good at, action, improve skill, go to high level, new skills, challenge	Health, challenge, relaxation, status, social, environment, fun, affiliation, skills
Cross-cultural								
Kirkby, Kolt & Liu	1999	30-item original 3-point Likert scale, modified	Australia, China	383	8–15	Gymnasts	Improve skills, go to high level, be fit, learn new skills, exercise, fun	Excitement, affiliation, social cohesion, action, miscellaneous, somatic (fitness/exercise), status (win/energy release/be important)

(continued)

TABLE 5.2 (*continued*)

Authors	Date	PMQ version	Country	Sample size	Age range	Activity type(s)	Top-rated items	Factor analysis
Cross-cultural (*continued*)								
Kolt, Kirkby, Bar-Eli, Blumenstein, Chadha, Liu & Kerr	1999	300-item original 3-point Likert scale, modified	Australia, Canada, China, India, Israel	701	8–15	Gymnasts	Improve skills, be fit, learn new things, challenge, fun, go to high level	Team/affiliation, popularity/ energy release, challenge/fun, skills, achievement, recognition/ excitement, miscellaneous
Weinberg, Tenenbaum, McKenzie, Jackson, Anshel, Grove & Fogarty	2000	22-item 3-point Likert scale, Gould et al. version	USA, Australia, New Zealand	1472	13–18	Multi-sport	Fun, stay in shape, improve skills, be physically fit, do something good at	*Sport* competition, social energy, fitness/fun, teamwork *Exercise* intrinsic, extrinsic, fitness, energy release
Life span								
Brodkin & Weiss	1990	35-item 5-point Likert scale	USA	100	6–74	Swimming	Differences between age groups in top-ranked items (see text)	Health/fitness, social status, affiliation, energy release, significant others, fun, 'characteristics of competitive swimming'
Morris & Han	1991	40-item original 5-point Likert scale, modified from Gill et al.	Australia	228	9–70+	Tai chi	Mental relaxation, beauty and grace, gentle movements, exercising body /mind together, health, skill, social	Aesthetic, philosophical, improve existing medical condition, exercising body and mind together, non-competitive, health, skill, energy release, social, status, fun

Authors	Date	PMQ version	Country	Sample size	Age range	Activity type(s)	Top-rated items	Factor analysis
Morris, Power & Pappalardo	1993	44-item 5-point Likert scale, Morris & Han, plus compete items	Australia	346	10–80+	Table tennis	Fun, health/ fitness, improve skills, challenge, competition	Health/fitness, fun, challenge, social, skill development, aesthetic/ philosophy, status, relaxation
Morris, Clayton, Power & Han	1995	50-item 5-point Likert scale, modified from Morris & Han	Australia	2601	6–80+	Multi-sport	Variations between age groups (see text); but health, fun, challenge, skill development	Skills, challenge, fun, health, affiliation, relaxation/ aesthetic, status, environment, to be occupied

Other researchers examined a range of sports. For example, Longhurst and Spink (1987) studied athletics, netball, cricket and Australian Football. This diversity makes precise comparisons between studies difficult. Longhurst and Spink conducted probably the first PMQ study in a culture outside North America. It should be noted that Longhurst and Spink chose a particularly stringent cut-off for the determination of factors, so 11 items were not included in any of the four factors they reported. Recently youth studies of participation motivation have been conducted in a number of countries, broadening the cultural base of the research. The study by Buonamano et al. (1995) is noteworthy because it involved a large sample and a range of Italy's major national sports. Contrary to convention, Buonamano et al. did not report the top-ranking items. A concern with this study is that, in the factor analysis, two factors, fitness/skill and friendship/fun, each reflect two motives that typically resolve as separate factors.

In the past few years researchers have also conducted the first cross-cultural studies on participation motivation in youth sport using versions of the PMQ (e.g. Kirkby, Kolt & Liu 1999; Kolt, Kirkby, Bar-Eli, Blumenstein, Chadha, Liu & Kerr 1999; Weinberg, Tenenbaum, McKenzie, Jackson, Anshel, Grove & Fogarty 2000). Using a Multivariate Analysis of Variance, Kolt et al. found that cross-cultural differences were complex, because of the large number of countries from which samples were recruited. Kolt et al. noted the major differences. Indian gymnasts rated team/affiliation as a more important reason for participation than the rest of the sample, whereas Canadian gymnasts rated this as a less important motive than gymnasts from other cultures. Chinese gymnasts rated challenge/fun as less important than gymnasts from the other four countries. Skill-related reasons for participation were considered more important by Australian and Indian gymnasts than those from Canada and China. Israeli participants rated achievement higher as a motive than gymnasts from other Western countries. Kirkby et al. also studied gymnasts and used the same version of the PMQ. Their results for Australian and Chinese athletes were similar to those obtained by Kolt et al. A drawback with these studies is that they examined only one activity, as did many of the earlier studies. Weinberg et al. studied athletes from the United States, Australia and New Zealand who participated in a range of activities. They found few cross-cultural differences, but their selection of cultures seems to have been less strategic than that of Kolt et al. Weinberg et al. also measured frequency of participation. They found that adolescents who participated at a high frequency rated a range of intrinsic and extrinsic motives to be more important as reasons for their participation than did lower frequency participants.

Brodkin and Weiss (1990) introduced a life span approach to the descriptive research on motives for participation. In 6- to 74-year-old swimmers they found that different motives were rated highly by different age groups. Broadly, very young participants were motivated by social and health motives, older children and adolescents were interested in skills development as well as health, and adults emphasised health and fitness. All groups, except the youngest, rated fun as an important reason for participating. A weakness of the study by Brodkin and Weiss is that the samples in several age groups were quite small, being as low as 14 for younger children (6 to 9 years), 10 for high-school/college (15 to 22 years), 17 for younger adults (23 to 39 years), 14 for middle adults (40 to 59 years), and 13 for older adults (60 to 74 years). The age groups employed (the terms used were coined by Brodkin and Weiss) were also somewhat arbitrary.

Morris and Han (1991) examined a life span sample in the first PMQ study on a non-competitive, physical activity, tai chi. Their study of beginners in 20 tai chi classes, employing an extended version of the PMQ, was based on a preliminary study in which different participants in introductory tai chi classes gave open-ended reasons for participating. Those that were stated repeatedly and were not among the 30 PMQ items in the Gill et al. version of the questionnaire were added, using the same stems. Competitive items were removed, a single, non-competitive item was added, and team items were revised to refer to 'group'. The highest rated motives were all items generated specifically for tai chi. They were followed by the health, skill and social reasons common in other studies. Factor analysis identified four new factors — aesthetic, philosophical, exercising body and mind together, and a single-item 'improve an existing medical condition' factor. Also, the non-competitive item resolved as a separate factor. This study examined motives for a sample that comprised people whose outlook typically was quite different from that of the competitive sports performers in most previous studies. Many of the tai chi participants were mid-life females, who had never played competitive sport. They chose to do physical activity that was gentle and non-competitive.

Morris, Power and Pappalardo (1993) employed the version of the PMQ that was developed in the tai chi study to examine whether the new items were relevant to competitive sport. Morris et al. put the competitive items back in the PMQ and reverted to group/team items to use of the word 'team'. Three interesting findings from their factor analysis supported the suggestion that the more wide-ranging version of the PMQ had good integrity. First, the non-competitive item that was generated for tai chi loaded as a negative item on the challenge factor, which was also the factor on which competition items loaded positively. Second, the medical treatment item loaded on the health and fitness factor. Third, the items specific to martial arts formed one factor. Morris et al. also asked the table tennis players in this study to list any reasons for participation that were not included in the predetermined items.

It is clear from table 5.2 and this brief summary of descriptive research on participation motivation that studies have largely been unsystematic. Some have selected a single sport, whereas others have examined several activities. Often the choice of type of activity appears to have been based on opportunity or a specific interest in the activity, rather than a conceptually based rationale. In addition, the level of participation varies greatly from study to study. This is likely to influence the order of items.

For example, the young gymnasts who participated in the cross-cultural study by Kolt et al. were serious competitors. Not surprisingly these young, committed sports performers rated skill development and going to a high level to be important motives, whereas the older beginners in tai chi in the study by Morris and Han (1991) considered these items to be much less important reasons for their participation. Sample sizes have varied greatly, with some studies employing samples that would be considered small for the use of exploratory factor analytic techniques. Klint and Weiss (1987) did not try to perform a factor analysis on their sample of 67 young gymnasts. Many studies have considered gender and age, but comparisons are often clouded by differences in other factors, such as activities and levels of experience. The following highlighted text describes a large-scale study of participation motives that addressed a number of these criticisms of the previous research.

A LARGE, LIFE SPAN PMQ STUDY

In a major study of participation motives for physical activity in Australia, Morris and colleagues aimed to examine age, gender and activity type in a more systematic way than most earlier studies (Clayton, Morris, Power & Han 1995; Morris, Clayton, Power & Han 1995a, 1995b, 1996a, 1996b). Morris et al. added new items to the PMQ, which had already been expanded (Morris & Han 1991; Morris et al. 1993). Morris et al. (1995a) identified the additional items on the basis of discussions among a focus group of experts on physical activity. The experts considered the PMQ items that had been used in the table tennis study and the suggestions from participants for additional items in the open-ended question at the end of that study.

A 50-item version of the PMQ resulted. This begs the question of whether a questionnaire with 67 per cent more items, covering a much wider range of motives, should still be considered to be a version of the original PMQ. Morris et al. administered this 'revised version' of the PMQ to 2601 participants (1164 males and 1437 females), aged between 6 and over 80 years, who were involved in 14 different kinds of physical activity. The activities were chosen to represent five categories of physical activity, namely body movement sports (gymnastics, swimming), racquet sports (tennis, table tennis, squash), team ball games (lacrosse, netball, basketball, volleyball), exercise activities (aerobics, weight training), and martial arts (karate, tae kwon do, tai chi). Although the gender balance, average age and skill level varied between activities, there was a substantial sample for each activity, covering males and females, a broad age range and a wide variety of skill levels because the total sample was so large.

Morris et al. (1996b) carried out an exploratory factor analysis, which revealed nine factors. These were consistent with previous research, being skills, challenge, fun, health, relaxation/ aesthetic, affiliation, status, the environment and to be occupied. Consistent with Klint and Weiss (1987), Morris et al. conducted discriminant function analyses for gender and age. For gender, seven factors discriminated between males and females in the sample. The strongest discriminators were challenge, affiliation, health and status, with affiliation and health rated higher by females than males, and challenge and status being more important motives for males than females. For age, participants in each age group were compared with the rest of the sample in separate analyses. The youngest age group (6- to 14-year-olds) was discriminated from the sample on eight of the nine factors. The strongest discriminators were status and skills/movements, both rated higher by this group than the sample. Seven factors discriminated 15- to 18-year-olds from the sample. This group scored higher on status and challenge than the sample, but lower on atmosphere. For 19- to 22-year-olds, six factors were significant discriminators. The most highly rated discriminating factor by participants in this age group was health, with fun next, whereas affiliation and relaxation/aesthetic were not as important for these participants as they were for the sample as a whole.

(continued)

In the 23- to 39-year-olds, six factors significantly discriminated between this group and the sample. Status and skills were the strongest discriminators, both being lower in this age group than the sample. Health was the next highest discriminating factor, being rated more highly by 23- to 39-year-olds than the sample as a whole. Eight factors discriminated 40- to 59-year-olds from the sample. The strongest discriminators were status, skills and challenge, all of which were rated higher by the rest of the sample. Relaxation/aesthetic was the next strongest discriminator, being rated as a more important motive by this group than for the sample. Finally, seven factors discriminated the over-60-year-old group from the sample. This group was again more motivated by relaxation/aesthetic than the whole sample, but less interested in the fun and challenge of participation, in particular. To summarise the results for age, young participants were motivated by skill learning/improvement and status; in adolescence challenge also became important; by adulthood these motives were replaced by health/fitness as the primary motivation; and in middle to late adulthood relaxation/aesthetic joined health as a key motive for physical activity.

In terms of the main focus of this study, type of activity, Morris et al. conducted discriminant function analyses, comparing each sport type with the rest of the sample to identify the motives that were particularly strong reasons for participation in that activity. These analyses largely supported predictions made by Morris et al. For racquet sports, challenge, including competing, was the main discriminator. This makes sense, because one goes head-to-head, one-on-one in these activities, thus maximising the personal challenge. Challenge was also important in team ball games, and so was fun. Importantly, affiliation was higher for these activities than for any other activities examined, as would be expected because these are all group activities. There was no discriminating function for the body movement activities. The strongest discriminators for the exercise activities were affiliation, health and challenge. Exercisers rated health/fitness as a more important motive than the rest of the sample for their participation. Significantly, they were less interested in affiliation and challenge than the sample as a whole. Only the relaxation/aesthetic motive distinguished martial arts from the other activities. The picture that emerges here is consistent with expectations. The patterns identified here need to be replicated in studies that examine sports from each category, especially sports that were not employed in the Morris et al. study. Given support for the major motives that characterise different types of activity, Morris et al. proposed that people could be matched to a type of activity based on their principal motives. This would leave choice, based on access, costs, culture, preferences and the like, but reduce the risk of mismatches that lead to rapid drop-out.

The descriptive PMQ study by Morris et al. (Clayton et al. 1995; Morris et al. 1995a, 1995b, 1996a, 1996b) reported patterns of motives for participation that are consistent with much of the literature, but for a very large and diverse sample. That study demonstrated that these patterns still emerged from a much larger list of motives. This is noteworthy, because a criticism that could be levelled at much of the research is that it is based on a list of motives developed by Gill et al. (1983) from a rather narrow sample of US youth sport participants. Motives not included in the original list certainly do gain some pre-eminence in particular groups, for example the aesthetic and 'philosophical' motives in Tai Chi and martial arts, and the medical motive in older adults. Nonetheless health, fun, challenge and skill development were found to be the most important motives across the whole sample of 2601 participants. Following Klint and Weiss (1987), Morris et al. employed a more rigorous technique than many other researchers to determine the motives that were particularly distinctive in various groups (activity types, age groups, genders). Most PMQ studies have simply compared order of rating for different groups. Morris et al. showed that discriminant function analysis could tease out meaningful distinctions, involving not only those motives that are more important for a group than for other participants, but also those motives that are less important, for example health for children and fun for older adults.

Despite the systematic approach adopted by Morris et al. (1995a, 1995b, 1996a, 1996b), their study does have limitations. One problem that Morris et al. identified is that even groups of activities predetermined on the basis of commonalities do not always prove to have common motives. For example, gymnastics and swimming did not form a coherent category. Certainly they share the characteristic that body movement is central to the activity and each is a competitive sport, but otherwise they are quite different. Another limitation of the study is that participation in various activities reflects different profiles by age and gender.

Linking participation motivation and intrinsic–extrinsic motivation

Rogers and colleagues conducted a research program that drew the descriptive participation motivation research into the intrinsic–extrinsic motivation framework of self-determination theory in a different way (Rogers & Morris 2000a, 2000b; Rogers, Tammen & Morris 1999a, 1999b). To examine the reasons why people participate in non-competitive physical activities, Rogers et al. conducted in-depth, semi-structured interviews with 11 recreational exercisers. This study was conducted within an achievement goal orientation framework (see chapter 6). Participants were asked to nominate their goals for exercise and to say what they felt constituted success in their activity. The terms *goals* and *success* were used throughout, and the researchers avoided the term 'motive' to focus on achievement goals. Nonetheless Rogers et al. found that many of the responses given could only be interpreted as motives. They identified 13 first-order themes, which they reduced to seven second-order themes — namely (with first-order themes in parentheses), competition/ego (competition/ego, social comparison, appearance), extrinsic rewards (same), social (others' expectations, affiliation/social), physical and psychological health (fitness, medical, psychological wellbeing, self-esteem, relaxation/stress release), mastery (same) and enjoyment (same). Rogers et al. acknowledged that the mastery and ego orientations of the achievement goal orientation approach did emerge, but emphasised that the goals of or reasons for participation that they found included a much wider range of goals/motives. They argued that the motives of mastery and enjoyment could be grouped into an intrinsic motivation general dimension, whereas all the other second-order categories were extrinsic motives, so they proposed that self-determination theory would provide a more appropriate theoretical framework for their results.

Rogers and Morris (2000a) observed that many of the motives that emerged in the interview study were consistent with the items and factors in the 50-item version of the PMQ (Morris et al. 1995b). Although this questionnaire was originally developed for use in youth competitive sport, the expansion to 50 items included a number of items that made the measure more suitable for use in non-competitive physical activity settings. Rogers and Morris also noted that the MPAM (Frederick & Ryan 1993) and the MPAM-R (Ryan et al. 1997) covered some of the same ground. With permission of the authors of these measures, Rogers et al. systematically checked which items fell into each of the 13 first-order categories they had identified. By selecting these items and adding items to represent motives not covered by the other questionnaires, Rogers and Morris developed a new scale, which they called the Recreational Exercise Motivation Measure (REMM). Following refinement, Rogers and Morris examined the reliability of the 73-item REMM in a study involving 750 recreational exercise participants aged 14 to 84 years ($M = 38.5$, $SD = 13.2$). Participants responded to items with the stem 'I exercise to ...' or 'I exercise because ...' on a 5-point Likert scale that ranged from 1 (*strongly disagree*) to 5 (*strongly agree*). An exploratory factor analysis produced eight factors. These were identified as mastery, physical condition/health, psychological condition/wellbeing, affiliation, appearance, others' expectations, enjoyment and competition/ego. In view of the concern reported earlier with the single fun item on the PMQ, it is interesting to note that the item 'It is fun ...' had equal highest loading (.78) on the REMM enjoyment factor, which consisted of eight items. Other high-loading items on this factor were 'I have a good time ...' (.78), 'I enjoy exercising ...' (.67) and 'It is interesting ...' (.59). Because there were noteworthy correlations between some of these factors, Rogers and Morris conducted a second-order factor analysis on the factor scores for each factor for the whole sample. Three second-order factors emerged. Rogers et al. identified these as (with first-order factors in parentheses) intrinsic motives (mastery, enjoyment/fun), social motives (affiliation, competition/ego, others' expectations) and body/mind motives (health/physical condition, wellbeing/psychological condition, appearance). It can be seen that all the factors in the social motives category depend on other people, whereas the body/mind motives are all about the individual. None of these motives concern the activity itself, so they are all extrinsic, whereas mastery and fun are both about the activity — that is, they are intrinsic motives. Thus Rogers and Morris concluded that the two factor analyses together support their proposition that the range of participation motives fit clearly into an intrinsic–extrinsic motivation framework, consistent with self-determination theory. Rogers and Morris also provided support for the internal consistency and test–retest reliability of the REMM (Rogers & Morris 2000a) and for its construct validity (Rogers & Morris 2000b).

The development and initial research with the REMM has been useful in clarifying some issues raised in previous participation motivation research. In terms of measurement, it has brought together the descriptive PMQ approach to the measurement of participation motivation, which was developed empirically by Gill et al. (1983) and Morris et al. (1995a, 1995b) and the theoretically driven MPAM approach of Ryan and Frederick (Frederick & Ryan 1993; Ryan et al. 1997). Research on the REMM has also supported the claim by Frederick and Ryan that the participation motivation research fits into the intrinsic–extrinsic motivation framework of self-determination theory.

Motivation and age

Research within the sport and exercise domain has found age-related differences in motivation. In studies involving youth athletes (Buonamano, Cei & Mussino 1995; Gill, Gross & Huddleston 1983; Klint & Weiss 1987; Morris et al. 1996a; Sapp & Haubenstricker 1978; Whitehead 1995), evidence suggests that intrinsic motives such as fun, enjoyment, skill development and challenge supersede other motives in explaining youth sport participation. Research with young and middle-aged adults, however, indicates that a more diverse set of motives drives these older sport and exercise participants (Biddle & Bailey 1985; Gill, Williams, Dowd, Beaudoin & Martin 1996; Mathes & Battista 1985; Summers, Sargent, Levey & Murray 1982; Morris et al. 1996a; Morris & Han 1991; Morris et al. 1993; Summers, Machin & Sargent 1983). Adults, although maintaining aspects of intrinsic motivation, include other motives as influential in their participation. These additional motives tend to reflect a more extrinsic orientation and include fitness motivation, stress release and weight control.

For older adults, questions related to motivation and sport participation are still unanswered. Although older adults are living longer and are in better physical condition than in previous generations (Kolata 1996; Horn & Meer 1987), they also tend to engage in regular physical exercise less than younger age groups (Leventhal, Prochaska & Hirschman 1985). Furthermore, Mobily, Lemke, Ostiguy and Woodard (1993) failed to find a correlation between elderly individuals' intrinsic leisure motivation attitudes and their exercise behaviours. Based on just these findings, overall motivation for exercise appears to decline as individuals reach older age. However, there is a large and growing group of older adults who spend a great deal of their free time engaged in sport and physical activities. Some even retire to specialised communities that offer an active lifestyle centred around sports like golf, tennis and swimming. Are these active older individuals the ones who have successfully maintained a focus on intrinsic motives for sport, and who are enjoying the benefits of that motivation into older age? Another perspective on this question comes from the studies by Morris and colleagues, who found consistently that treatment of an existing medical condition was a primary motive for participation in older adults across a range of physical activities (Morris et al. 1996a; Morris & Han 1991; Morris et al. 1993). Although people in Western societies are living longer, many older adults have chronic illnesses for which physical activity is part of the treatment. Future research will be important in understanding motivational issues in sport and exercise across the life span.

Motivation and gender

Do women and men experience the same motivational styles and preferences with regard to their sport participation? This question has interested sport researchers for a number of years. We know that a greater number of women are participating in sport than ever before; however, their numbers are still not equal to those of their male counterparts (Weinberg & Gould 1995). Second, women are experiencing more equality with men in nearly every element of their sport participation (LeUnes & Nation 1996). Have these changes created a climate in which similar motivational needs will be displayed by both male and female athletes?

Results from research in the 1980s indicated that men and women exhibited differing motives for sport participation. For example, Mathes & Battista (1985) found in a college-age sample that although the primary participation motives for both men and women were desire for competition, fitness and health motives, and need for social experience, men favoured competition as a motive and women favoured social experience. Biddle and Bailey (1985) found results similar to Mathes and Battista in a sample of 17 male and 24 female adult exercisers. In the Biddle and Bailey study, men had significantly higher competition-based motives than women, whereas women rated social experience, tension release, and the feelings of affiliation and group cohesion they experienced as part of the class as motivating their participation to a greater extent than men.

Early research exploring gender differences using an intrinsic–extrinsic motivation distinction found that gender differences existed for competence and body-related types of motivation (Frederick 1991). Men showed significantly higher intrinsic motivation, based in desire to achieve mastery, than women. On the other hand, for extrinsic motives related to physical attractiveness and appearance, women showed higher scores (Frederick 1991). Using the same measurement strategy as the 1991 study, Frederick and Ryan (1993) showed a similar pattern of results. Although in this sample, there were no gender differences in competence motivation, women did show significantly higher scores for extrinsic, body-related motivation than did men.

In two more recent studies, sex differences in participation motivation occurred in both investigations. In a study primarily designed to address the relationship between motivation and exercise affect in 38 men and 80 women ranging in age from 17 to 52 years, Frederick, Morrison and Manning (1996) found differences in body-appearance and fitness motives, with women showing higher scores than men on both of these dimensions. Both of these motives are considered to be reflective of extrinsic motivation. No gender differences were shown for intrinsic or social motives. In Frederick and Morrison's (1996) study of college-age fitness centre members, which related social physique anxiety to motivation, gender differences in motivation were also apparent. Identical to the Frederick, Morrison and Manning (1996) study, results indicated that women (n = 199) reported higher levels of body-related, extrinsic motivation than their male peers (n = 127). Again, no gender differences were found for intrinsic sport participation motives. Morris et al. (1995a) examined gender differences in 1264 males compared with 1437 females in the largest life span gender comparison in the descriptive PMQ literature. Differences between males and females were limited. In discriminant function analysis, females rated affiliative motives as more important than males did, whereas males rated winning and competition higher than females did. Weinberg et al. (2000) examined 822 male and 650 female adolescents across three Western cultures. Their results were very similar to those of Frederick et al. and Morris et al. Among those involved in competitive sport, females rated fun/fitness and teamwork as more important motives than did males, who reported competition and social/energy release motives more highly than females. Among exercisers, females rated staying in shape as a more important motive than males, whereas males indicated that extrinsic and energy release were more important reasons for participation than they were for females.

Sutherland and Morris (1997) adopted a different approach to the study of gender and participation motives. In all the PMQ research that has been identified, researchers have accessed samples from people involved in sports and other physical activities. This tells us something about what motivates those who are participating, which is clearly of interest. It does not tell us what motivates those who are not participants in formal sport and exercise activities. Sutherland and Morris explored the physical activity participation motives of 13- to 15-year-old adolescents. This age range was chosen because it is a time during which biological and psychosocial changes are taking place that influence thoughts and behaviour. Because those who do participate in organised or systematic physical activity form a biased sample, Sutherland and Morris recruited their sample of 293 (134 males, 159 females) adolescents from several secondary schools. More substantial differences in PMQ motives were found for the genders than have typically been found with samples recruited from regular participants in various activities. Females rated fun, to stay in shape and health as their top three, but then rated to get out of the house as the fourth most important motive (rated 22 by males) and to get more energy sixth (rated 20 by males). Males aged 13 to 15 also rated fun first, but health was rated eleventh and to stay in shape was fifteenth. For this group of males, the second most important motive was to win (rated thirty-fourth by females), with to improve skill third (rated seventh by females). Other large discrepancies, in which females rated motives substantially higher than males, arose for exercise (eighth for females and twenty-third for males) and for something to do (ninth for females and sixteenth for males). Males rated the action (fourth for males and twentieth for females) and challenge (sixth for males and eighteenth for females) notably higher than females. Once again, these results indicate that we need to interpret findings with the PMQ carefully, taking note of a range of characteristics of the sample, such as age, gender, activity and level of involvement.

Overall, the conclusion can be drawn that females evidence more appearance and fitness-related motivation than do their male counterparts. These body-related motives are considered to be extrinsic in nature, owing to their basis in sociocultural pressures to be thin and fit, which are typical in many countries across the world. What should also be noted is that recent studies in sport have not found the same difference in competence motivation between sexes that was evidenced in earlier works. A motive for competence reflects intrinsic motivation. It includes a desire to master sport skills and engage in situations involving optimal challenge. In the 1970s, theorists believed that competent women athletes were not viewed as desirable role models (Griffin 1973). Later research shows no such effects (Brown 1988; Kingsley, Brown & Seibert 1977; Vickers, Lashuk & Taerum 1980). As such, female sport participants may now feel that it is acceptable to express their intrinsic desires to achieve and become competent as motivating factors in their participation, without experiencing social stigma. At the same time, research using broader samples has shown differences between males and females in terms of motivation for competition and winning. Recent research that has considered non-competitive exercise activities (Morris et al. 1995a; Sutherland & Morris 1997) indicates a preference for these activities among women, primarily because they are non-competitive and also because of the appearance and health/fitness motives that emerged in the sport research.

Motivation, emotion and personality in physical activity

Motivation, emotion and personality have often been studied together within self-determination theory (Deci & Ryan 1985; Ryan, Connell & Plant 1990; Ryan & Frederick 1997). Typically, an intrinsic orientation has fostered expression of positive affect and healthy personality traits. Extrinsic states have been associated with negative affective states, such as feeling frustrated, tense, pressured or controlled, as well as personality deficits, such as low self-esteem. For sport and exercise these relationships are believed to be the same (Vallerand & Losier 1999).

Using both French and English versions of the Sport Motivation Scale, researchers have found that happiness, enjoyment and satisfaction correlated positively with intrinsic and identified levels of self-regulation (Briere et al. 1995; Pelletier et al. 1995). The Briere et al. study was conducted with approximately 600 athletes with a mean age of 18 years, and the Pelletier et al. study included 593 college athletes (274 women and 319 men) with a mean age of 19 years. Conversely, in both studies measures of positive affect were negatively related to amotivation and external regulation. Negative affect, expressed as anxiety, was also found to be positively related to amotivation and external regulation.

Frederick and Ryan (1993) found significant correlations between exercise motivation and aspects of emotion and personality, using the Motivation for Physical Activities Measure. Interest/enjoyment and competence motivations were positively related to feelings of perceived satisfaction about one's chosen activity. Competence motives were also negatively related to global self-esteem and positively related to anxiety within a fitness population. Body-related motives were negatively related to body appearance self-esteem and global self-esteem, but positively related to anxiety and depression. A later study (Frederick & Morrison 1996) also showed motivation to relate directly to physique anxiety. More specifically this research indicated that high body appearance motivation led to higher levels of social physique anxiety.

The results of this type of research indicated that the motives underlying athletes' sport involvement not only are important in predicting variables like adherence, but go beyond that to influence basic personality and affective characteristics. In general, studies showed that intrinsic motivation for sport is related to positive affect, while extrinsic motivation is related to constructs such as anxiety, depression and lack of self-esteem. With findings such as these the importance of one's motivational orientation cannot be underestimated.

MOTIVATING ATHLETES: WHERE THEORY MEETS APPLICATION

A variety of writers and researchers have discussed the application of motivational principles in real-world domains such as education or sport (Deci, Koestner & Ryan 1999; Kohn 1999; Whitehead 2001). Whitehead (2001) provided a concise list of principles to use to enhance intrinsic motivation in athletes and decrease the negative consequences associated with extrinsic motivation. Whitehead's guidelines are particularly applicable to children's sport, although with minor modifications; taking into account level of skill and expertise they could be used for a wider range of age groups.

Two of Whitehead's tips focus on concepts related to competence development, which is critical in maintaining intrinsic motivation in sport (Deci & Ryan 1985). As Deci and Ryan (1985) explain in cognitive evaluation theory, feedback that undermines an athlete's sense of competence also works to undermine his or her intrinsic motivation for that activity. Based on this premise, Whitehead advises coaches to try to emphasise personal competence through honest and positive, mastery-based feedback. Giving praise when a skill is done correctly is an example of application of this concept. When skilled activities are not performed correctly, teach the correct skill and don't dwell on earlier failure. Second, Whitehead advises not to overemphasise peer comparisons, especially those that give the athlete a sense of incompetence. This is especially important for athletes who are just beginning their sport engagement and those with lower levels of ability. One of the ways in which children during middle childhood glean information about their own competence is by comparing themselves with others across a variety of areas, including the domain of physical activity (Harter 1993). Coaches are thus advised to work with each individual child to develop basic skills, while trying to limit peer-based comparisons. Whitehead also addressed issues related to support of autonomy in order to foster intrinsic motivation in athletes. First, remember to promote choice, or at least the perception of choice. Individual choice can be promoted in a variety of ways, such as allowing the athlete to pick practice times, or allowing choice of specific activities or exercises within a prescribed fitness environment.

Unfortunately, in competitive athletics, such as those played at high school or college level, it is not always possible to promote choices about practice times or activities. In more competitive athletes, it appears that choice may not be as crucial a factor in maintaining intrinsic motivation as it once appeared (Frederick-Recascino and Schuster-Smith 2003). Frederick-Recascino and Schuster-Smith found high levels of intrinsic motivation in competitive adult bicycle racers. It is believed that athletes in highly competitive environments accept that in order to maintain a competitive edge, their activities related to sport may be more controlled (e.g. they must practise a prescribed number of hours to maintain performance; and they must eat a certain diet). As a result, competitive athletes focus on building personal competence and optimal challenge in order to maintain their intrinsic motivation for sport.

Furthermore, Whitehead suggested that in using motivational principles in applied settings, the focus should be on the fun and excitement of sport participation. With this emphasis, an intrinsic orientation will be the norm. In order to help facilitate this perspective, make sure sport does not become repetitive, boring and ordinary. He suggested adding variety to practices and workouts. This suggestion may be especially important for trainers working in an exercise setting. Frederick & Ryan (1993) found an interesting pattern of behavior in fitness centre participants who reported working out for more days per week but fewer hours per week than their sport-oriented peers. In interpreting this information, Frederick and Ryan believed that fitness participants were likely becoming bored with the repetitive nature of their activities (stair-climbing, circuit training), and in order to maintain their participation and enjoyment of exercise they rotated through a variety of fitness activities.

In a set of three principles, Whitehead focused attention on the different levels of self-regulation. Whitehead advised coaches to use rewards carefully. As elaborated in cognitive evaluation theory (Deci & Ryan 1985), overuse of rewards can undermine intrinsic motivation and place attention on the outcome of a sport event rather than the satisfaction associated with participation. Rewards may, however, be used under certain conditions. First, they should never become an expected outcome of practice or performance. Second, honest praise about hard work, good performance or increased competence in an area can also be rewarding. Praise given sincerely and based on actual performance does not seem to undermine intrinsic motivation.

Next, Whitehead recommends emphasising the importance of physical activity in promoting health. When greater internalisation of exercise motives can be fostered, participants move away from external regulation of activity to more identified self-regulation. This type of motivation reflects self-determination, if not true intrinsic motivation.

Last, Whitehead suggests moving away from providing misinformation about training fads, fitness gimmicks or supplements. The basic goal of most coaches and trainers is to facilitate development of competence and health in people, which is realised through attention to mastery activities, through lasting effort and through the provision of a stimulating fitness environment. However, every day individuals are bombarded with gimmicks that claim to be fitness miracles. When fads don't work, exercise participants may lose motivation to continue athletic involvement. It is better to emphasise techniques that, through effort and practice, do achieve results, than to promote fads that are inevitably amotivating.

FUTURE DIRECTIONS

Theory and research related to intrinsic and extrinsic motivation in sport have had a robust history, but there are also opportunities to expand our knowledge base in this area. Discussed below are avenues that may prove fruitful for research in the future.

Cross-cultural differences in motivation

Most of the research done today examines motivation within a specific culture. However, participation in sport and exercise is universal. Cultures vary in fundamental ways. For instance, Hofstede (1980) discusses the differences between collectivist and individualist cultures, as well as between feminine-oriented and masculine-oriented cultures. Based on these and other cultural differences, it may be fruitful to examine motivational differences associated with different aspects of sport participation across cultures.

Developmental studies of sport motivation

From the literature, we know that as children move toward adulthood, their sport motivation changes. Children tend to report higher intrinsic motivation than adult sport participants. How does this change occur and when does it occur? If we can understand the process of motivational change, then perhaps we can intervene to decrease the high drop-out rates experienced in many youth sports (Vallerand & Losier 1999).

At the other end of the developmental continuum, very little is known about motivation in older adult exercisers. In many countries the older population is increasing as birth rates decline and medical care increases the life span. Engagement in physical activity is one way to increase the health and quality of life of individuals as they age. However, in order to move in that direction, we also must understand older adults' exercise motives and habits.

Intervention studies

Intervention research is difficult to do. However, we can never know which motivational techniques and principles are most effective in engaging adults in sport and exercise activities until such studies are completed. Studies should systematically test treatments designed to increase intrinsic motivation and decrease extrinsic motivation, until a full body of effective motivational interventions can be created.

These are just a few of the possible directions in which researchers may increase the knowledge base related to sport motivation. Although this list is important, it is by no means exhaustive of the potential set of topics that focus on intrinsic and extrinsic sport motivation.

CONCLUSIONS

This chapter has provided an overview of the topic of intrinsic and extrinsic motivation in the domain of sport and exercise. Using self-determination theory (Deci & Ryan 1985, 1991) as the focal point of the discussion, intrinsic motivation was defined as the unique combination of autonomy and optimal challenge. Under conditions of intrinsic motivation, athletes report greater sport enjoyment, positive affect and even enhanced levels of self-esteem (Frederick & Ryan 1993; Vallerand & Losier 1999). In contrast, extrinsic motivation is characterised by loss of autonomy and/or loss of optimal challenge. Extrinsic motives can range from those that are entirely externally regulated to those that, although not fundamentally intrinsically motivated, do have degrees of self-determination. In general, the greater the self-determination associated with motives, the better the outcomes associated with such motives. In sport, this means that athletes who express motives associated with fun, enjoyment, challenge and satisfaction are more likely to persist in their activity and reap positive psychological benefits. Those athletes who are extrinsically motivated are more likely to feel pressured and controlled, and would be expected to experience higher drop-out rates.

In a major section of the chapter, cognitive evaluation theory (Deci & Ryan 1985) was discussed. This theory addresses how rewards, feedback and competition can either enhance or undermine intrinsic motivation for sport. Specifically, it is believed that any event that undermines athletes' feelings of competence or creates an external perceived locus of causality will undermine intrinsic motivation. For instance, negative feedback tends to undermine intrinsic motivation. Likewise, competitive sports that focus on winning and losing can certainly undermine feelings of competence and intrinsic motivation, especially in those who lose the contest. Rewards can undermine intrinsic motivation because they foster an external locus of causality in athletes. Overuse of rewards can lead athletes to perform for the reward received and not for the satisfaction of engagement in the activity.

The chapter also discussed correlates of sport motivation, such as adherence issues, gender and age. The research has shown that better adherence and greater persistence in sport is associated with intrinsic motives such as competence, interest and enjoyment. Likewise, happiness, self-esteem and lower levels of depression are also associated with greater intrinsic motivation. Extrinsic motivation is associated with fewer hours a week of exercise, as well as with less positive affect and greater levels of depression and anxiety.

In addition, the chapter considered motivational differences across age groups, and for men and women. Children are more likely to report intrinsic motives for their sport participation, whereas adults report a wider array of both extrinsic and intrinsic motives. Men and women also show slightly different types of participation motivation, with men displaying more competence-based motivation and women displaying greater body-related motivation. This is not surprising given the continuing pressure on women in many cultures to achieve an almost unachievable ideal of thinness and fitness.

The chapter ended with two discussions, one applied and one research-based. In the applied section, motivational principles were presented that could be used to enhance intrinsic motivation in sport participants. The second discussion focused on potential areas for future research. Research in sport motivation has been a fruitful area of inquiry for years, and it continues to evolve as our societies and cultures change. Future research will focus on application, intervention and innovation.

SUMMARY

This chapter focused on intrinsic and extrinsic motivation as it is conceptualised in the sport and exercise domain. The chapter reviewed the body of research related to conceptualisation of motivational attitudes in sport, measurement of sport motivation, correlates of motivational orientation in sport and individual differences in sport motivation. Last, the chapter provided motivational principles for use with athletes in applied sport domains and future directions for sport motivation research.

 REVIEW QUESTIONS

1 Define intrinsic and extrinsic motivation.

2 Explain the central tenet of self-determination theory.

3 What are introjected, identified and integrated regulation?

4 What are the controlling and informational aspects of cognitive evaluation theory?

5 How does competition affect intrinsic motivation?

6 What are the highest ranked motives for participation in youth sport and physical activity? Do they remain the same in adults and older people? If not, how do they change?

7 What are the eight motivational factors identified in the Recreational Exercise Motivation Measure (REMM)?

8 What advice did Whitehead give for enhancing motivation?

9 What is the significance of studying motivation in different cultures?

10 Why should we do intervention studies on motivation for sport and exercise?

References

Abramson, LY, Seligman, ME & Teasdale, JD 1978, 'Learned helplessness in humans: critique and reformulation', *Journal of Abnormal Psychology*, 87, 49–74.

American College of Sports Medicine 1990, 'The recommended quality and quantity of exercise for developing and maintaining cardiorespiratory and muscular fitness in healthy adults', *Medicine & Science in Sports & Exercise*, 22, 265–74.

Biddle, S & Bailey, C 1985, 'Motives toward participation and attitudes toward physical activity of adult participants in fitness programs', *Perceptual and Motor Skills*, 61, 831–4.

Blais, MR, Sabourin, S, Boucher, C & Vallerand, RJ 1990, 'Toward a motivational model of couple happiness', *Journal of Personality and Social Psychology*, 59, 1021–31.

Blasi, A 1998, 'Loevinger's theory of ego development and its relationship to the cognitive-developmental approach', in P Westenberg & A Blasi (eds), *Personality development: theoretical, empirical and clinical investigations of Loevinger's conception of ego development*, LEA, Mahwah, NJ, pp. 13–25.

Briere, NM, Vallerand, RJ, Blais, MR & Pelletier, LG 1995, 'Developement et validation d'une mesure de motivation intrinseque, extrinseque et d'amotivation en contexte sportif: l'Echelle de Motivation dans les Sports (EMS)', *International Journal of Sport Psychology*, 26, 465–89.

Brodkin, P & Weiss, MR 1990, 'Developmental differences in motivation in competitive swimming', *Journal of Sport & Exercise Psychology*, 12, 248–63.

Brown, B 1988, 'Study: girls find activities for a lifetime', *USA Today*, 8 June, 9C.

Buonamano, R, Cei, A & Mussino, A 1995, 'Participation motivation in Italian youth sport', *The Sport Psychologist*, 9, 265–81.

Chantal, Y, Guay, F, Dobreva-Martinova, T & Vallerand, R 1996, 'Motivation and elite performance: an exploratory investigation with Bulgarian athletes', *International Journal of Sport Psychology*, 27, 173–82.

Chatzisarantis, N & Biddle, S 1996, 'A self-determination theory approach to the study of intentions and the intention-behaviour relationship in children's physical activity', unpublished manuscript, University of Exeter, UK.

Clayton, H, Morris, T, Power, H & Han Jin-song 1995, 'Examination of motives for involvement in sport and exercise', paper presented at Three Decades of Science and Practice: 30th Annual Conference of the Australian Psychological Society, Perth, September.

Csikszentmihalyi, M 1975, *Beyond boredom and anxiety*, Jossey-Bass, San Francisco.

Csikszentmihalyi, M 1990, *Flow: the psychology of optimal experience*, HarperCollins, New York.

Csikszentmihalyi, M 1997, *Finding flow: the psychology of engagement with everyday life*, Basic Books, New York.

De Charms, R 1968, *Personal causation: the internal affective determinants of behaviour*, Academic Press, New York.

Deci, EL 1980, *The psychology of self-determination*, Lexington Books, Toronto.

Deci, EL & Ryan, RM 1985, *Intrinsic motivation and self-determination in human behaviour*, Plenum, New York.

Deci, EL & Ryan, RM 1991, 'A motivational approach to self: integration in personality', in R Dienstbier (ed.), *Nebraska symposium on motivation 1990: perspectives on motivation*, University of Nebraska Press, Lincoln, NE, pp. 237–88.

Deci, EL, Betley, G, Kahle, J, Abrams, L & Porac, J 1981, 'When trying to win: competition and intrinsic motivation', *Personality and Social Psychology Bulletin*, 7, 79–83.

Deci, EL, Connell, JP & Ryan, RM 1989, 'Self-determination in a work organization', *Journal of Applied Psychology*, 74, 580–90.

Deci, EL, Koestner, R & Ryan, RM 1999, 'A meta-analytic review of experiments examining the effects of extrinsic rewards on intrinsic motivation', *Psychological Bulletin*, 125, 627–68.

Fortier, MS, Vallerand, RJ, Briere, NM & Provencher, PJ 1995, 'Competitive and recreational sport structures and gender: a test of their relationship with sport motivation', *International Journal of Sport Psychology*, 26, 24–39.

Frederick, CM 1991, 'An investigation of the relationship among participation motives, level of participation, and psychological outcomes in the domain of physical activity', unpublished doctoral dissertation, University of Rochester, NY.

Frederick, CM & Morrison, CS 1996, 'Social physique anxiety: personality constructs, motivations, exercise attitudes, and behaviours', *Perceptual and Motor Skills*, 82, 963–72.

Frederick, CM, Morrison, CS & Manning, T 1996, 'Motivation to participate, exercise affect, and outcome behaviours toward physical activity', *Perceptual Motor Skills*, 82, 691–701.

Frederick, CM & Ryan, RM 1995, 'Self-determination in sport: a review using cognitive evaluation theory', *International Journal of Sport Psychology*, 26, 5–23.

Frederick, CM & Ryan, RM 1993, 'Differences in motivation for sport and exercise and their relations with participation and mental health', *Journal of Sport Behaviour*, 16, 124–46.

Frederick-Recascino, CM & Schuster-Smith, H 2003, 'Competition and intrinsic motivation in physical activity: a comparison of two groups', *Journal of Sport Behavior*, 26 (3).

Freud, S 1923, *The ego and the id*, Norton, New York.

Gill, DL, Gross, JB & Huddleston, S 1983, 'Participation motivation in youth sports', *International Journal of Sport Psychology*, 14, 1–14.

Gill, DL, Williams, L, Dowd, DA, Beaudoin, CM & Martin, JJ 1996, 'Competitive orientations and motives of adult sport and exercise participants', *Journal of Sport Behaviour*, 19, 307–18.

Goudas, M, Biddle, S & Fox, K 1994, 'Perceived locus of causality, goal orientations and perceived competence in school physical education classes', *British Journal of Educational Psychology*, 64, 453–63.

Gould, D, Feltz, D & Weiss, M 1985, 'Motives for participating in competitive youth swimming', *International Journal of Sport Psychology*, 16, 126–40.

Griffin, P 1973, 'What's a nice girl like you doing in a profession like this?' *Quest*, 19, 96–101.

Harter, S 1978, 'Effectance motivation reconsidered: toward a developmental model', *Human Development*, 1, 34–64.

Harter, S 1993, 'Visions of self: beyond the me in the mirror', in J Jacobs (ed.), *Developmental perspectives on motivation*, University of Nebraska Press, Lincoln, NE, pp. 99–144.

Heider, F 1958, *The psychology of interpersonal relations*, John Wiley & Sons, New York.

Hofstede, G 1980, 'Motivation, leadership and organizations: do American theories apply abroad?', *Organizational Dynamics*, 3, 42–63.

Horn, JC & Meer, J 1987, 'The vintage years', *Psychology Today*, May, pp. 76–84, 89–90.

Hull, CL 1943, *Principles of behaviour*, Appleton-Century-Crofts, New York.

Ilardi, BC, Leone, D, Kasser, T & Ryan, RM 1993, 'Employee and supervisor ratings of motivation: main effects and discrepancies associated with job satisfaction and adjustment in a factory setting', *Journal of Applied Social Psychology*, 23, 1789–1805.

Kingsley, J, Brown, F & Seibert, M 1977, 'Social acceptance of female athletes by college women', *Research Quarterly*, 48, 727–33.

Kirkby, RJ, Kolt, GS & Liu, J 1999, 'Participation motives of young Australian and Chinese gymnasts', *Perceptual and Motor Skills*, 88 (2) 363–73.

Klint, K & Weiss, M 1987, 'Perceived competence and motives for participating in youth sports: a test of Harter's competence motivation theory', *Journal of Sport Psychology*, 9, 55–65.

Kohn, A 1999, *Punished by rewards*, Houghton Mifflin, Boston, MA.

Kolata, G 1996, 'New era of robust elderly belies the fears of scientists', *New York Times*, 27 February, A1, C3.

Kolt, GS, Kirkby, RJ, Bar-Eli, M, Blumenstein, B, Chadha, NK, Liu, J & Kerr, G 1999, 'A cross-cultural investigation of reasons for participation in gymnastics', *International Journal of Sport Psychology*, 30, 381–98.

LeUnes, A & Nation, J 1996, *Sport psychology*, 2nd edn, Nelson-Hall, Chicago.

Leventhal, H, Prochaska, TR & Hirschman, RS 1985, 'Preventive health behaviour across the lifespan', in JC Rosen & LJ Solomon (eds), *Prevention in health psychology*, University Press of New England, Hanover, NH, pp. 191–235.

Li, F 1999, 'The Exercise Motivation Scale: its multifaceted structure and construct validity', *Journal of Applied Sport Psychology*, 11, 97–115.

Lindner, KJ 2001, 'Banding effects in physical activity participation: extent and reasons therefor of Hong Kong secondary school pupils', *Hong Kong Journal of Sports Medicine and Sports Science*, 12, 21–33.

Longhurst, K & Spink, KS 1987, 'Participation of Australian children involved in organized sport', *Canadian Journal of Sport Sciences*, 12, 24–30.

Losier, GF & Vallerand, VJ 1994, 'The temporal relationship between perceived competence and self-determined motivation', *Journal of Social Psychology*, 134, 793–801.

Mathes, S & Battista, R 1985, 'College men's and women's motives for participation in physical activity', *Perceptual and Motor Skills*, 61, 719–26.

McAuley, E & Tammen, V 1989, 'The effects of subjective and objective competitive outcomes on intrinsic motivation', *Journal of Sport & Exercise Psychology*, 11, 84–93.

Mobily, KE, Lemke, JH, Ostiguy, LJ & Woodard, RJ 1993, 'Leisure repertoire in a sample of midwestern elderly', *Journal of Leisure Research*, 25, 84–99.

Morris, T, Clayton, H, Power, H & Han Jin-Song 1995a, 'Gender and motives for participation in sport and exercise', *Proceedings of the FEPSAC IXth European Congress of Sport Psychology*, FEPSAC, Brussels, pp. 364–73.

Morris, T, Clayton, H, Power, H & Han Jin-song 1995b, 'Activity type differences in participation motives', *Australian Journal of Psychology*, 47, Supplement, 101–2.

Morris, T, Clayton, H, Power, H & Han Jin-song 1996a, 'Age differences in participation motives', poster presented at the International Pre-Olympic Congress, Dallas, Texas, August.

Morris, T, Clayton, H, Power, H & Han Jin-song 1996b, 'Participation motivation for different types of physical activity', poster presented at the International Pre-Olympic Congress, Dallas, Texas, August.

Morris, T & Han Jin-Song 1991, 'Motives for taking up tai chi', paper presented at the First Asian South Pacific Association of Sport Psychology International Congress, Melbourne.

Morris, T, Power, H & Pappalardo, B 1993, 'Motivation for participation in table tennis', paper presented at the VIIIth World Congress in Sport Psychology, Lisbon, June.

Orlick, TD & Mosher, R 1978, 'Extrinsic awards and participant motivation in a sport related task', *International Journal of Sport Psychology*, 9, 27–39.

Pate, RR, Pratt, M, Blair, SN, Haskell, WL, Macera, CA, Bouchard, C, Buchner, D, Ettinger, W, Heath, GW, King, AC, Kriska, A, Leon, AS, Marcus, BH, Morris, J, Paffenbarger, RS, Patrick, K, Pollock, ML, Rippe, JM, Sallis, J & Wilmore, JH 1995, 'Physical activity and public health', *Journal of the American Medical Association*, 273, 402–7.

Pelletier, LG, Briere, NM, Blais, MR & Vallerand, RJ 1988, 'Persisting versus dropping out: a test of Deci and Ryan's theory', *Canadian Psychology*, 29a, 600.

Pelletier, LG, Fortier, MS, Vallerand, RJ, Tuson, KM, Briere, NM & Blais, MC 1995, 'Toward a new measure of intrinsic motivation, extrinsic motivation, and amotivation in sports: the Sport Motivation Scale (SMS)', *Journal of Sport & Exercise Psychology*, 17, 35–53.

Plant, RW 1990, 'Motivation, expectation and psychiatric severity in predicting early dropout from outpatient alcoholism treatment', unpublished doctoral dissertation, University of Rochester, NY.

Reeve, J, Olson, BC & Cole, SG 1985, 'Motivation and performance: two consequences of winning and losing in competition', *Motivation and Emotion*, 9, 291–8.

Roberts, GC 1992, 'Motivation in sport and exercise: conceptual constraints and convergence', in GC Roberts (ed.), *Motivation in sport and exercise*, Human Kinetics, Champaign, IL, pp. 3–29.

Rogers, H, Tammen, V & Morris, T 1999a, 'Goals of recreational exercise participants: an interview-based study', *Proceedings of the 3rd International Congress of the Asian South Pacific Association of Sport Psychology*, ASPASP, Wuhan, China, pp. 258–60.

Rogers, H, Tammen, V & Morris, T 1999b, 'Motivation in recreational exercise participants', paper presented at the 5th International Olympic Committee World Congress on Sport Sciences, Sydney, November.

Rogers, H & Morris, T 2000a, 'Assessing the structure and reliability of the Recreational Exercise Motivation Measure (REMM)', paper submitted to the 2000 Pre-Olympic Congress, Brisbane, September.

Rogers, H & Morris, T 2000b, 'Motivational differences between recreational sport and exercise participants', paper presented at The Brain Games (35th Annual Conference of the Australian Psychological Society in Association with the International Society of Sport Psychology), Canberra, October.

Ryan, ED 1977, 'Attribution, intrinsic motivation, and athletics', in LI Gedvilas & ME Kneer (eds), Proceedings of the National College Physical Education Association for Men/National Association for Physical Education of College Women, National Conference, Office of Publications Services, University of Illinois at Chicago Circle, Chicago.

Ryan, ED 1980, 'Attribution, intrinsic motivation, and athletics: a replication and extension', in CH Nadeau, WR Halliwell, KM Newell & C Roberts (eds), *Psychology of motor behaviour and sports*, Human Kinetics, Champaign, IL, pp. 19–26.

Ryan, RM & Connell, JP 1989, 'Perceived locus of causality and internalization: examining reasons for acting in two domains', *Journal of Personality and Social Psychology*, 57, 749–61.

Ryan, RM & Frederick, CM 1997, 'On energy, personality and health: subjective vitality as a dynamic reflection of well-being', *Journal of Personality*, 65, 529–64.

Ryan, RM, Connell, JP & Plant, RW 1990, 'Emotions in non-directed text learning', *Learning and Individual Differences*, 2, 1–17.

Ryan, RM, Frederick, CM, Lepes, D, Rubio, N & Sheldon, K 1997, 'Intrinsic motivation and exercise adherence', *International Journal of Sport Psychology*, 28, 335–54.

Ryan, RM, Koestner, R & Deci, EL 1991, 'Varied forms of persistence: when free-choice behaviour is not intrinsically motivated', *Motivation and Emotion*, 15, 185–205.

Ryan, RM, Vallerand, R & Deci, EL 1984, 'Intrinsic motivation in sport: a cognitive evaluation theory interpretation', in WF Straub & JM Williams (eds), *Cognitive sport psychology*, Sport Science Associates, Lansing, NY, pp. 231–41.

Sapp, M & Haubenstricker, J 1978, 'Motivation for joining and reasons for not continuing in youth sports programs in Michigan', paper presented at the American Alliance for Health, Physical Education, Recreation and Dance National Conference, Kansas City, Missouri, 7 April.

Skinner, BF 1971, *Beyond freedom and dignity*, Penguin, New York.

Summers, J, Machin, V & Sargent, G 1983, 'Psychosocial factors related to marathon running', *Journal of Sport Psychology*, 5, 314–31.

Summers, J, Sargent, G, Levey, A & Murray, K 1982, 'Middle-aged, non-elite marathon runners: a profile', *Perceptual and Motor Skills*, 54, 963–9.

Sutherland, G & Morris 1997, 'Gender and participation motivation in 13- to 15-year-old adolescents', in R Lidor & M Bar-Eli (eds), *Proceedings of the IX World Congress of Sport Psychology*, ISSP, Netanya, Israel, pp. 676–8.

Tauer, JM & Harackiewicz, JM 1999, 'Winning isn't everything: competition, achievement orientation, and intrinsic motivation', *Journal of Experimental Social Psychology*, 35 (3) 209–38.

Vallerand, RJ 1983, 'The effects of differential amounts of positive verbal feedback on the intrinsic motivation of hockey players', *Journal of Sport Psychology*, 5, 100–7.

Vallerand, RJ & Losier, GF 1999, 'An integrative analysis of intrinsic and extrinsic motivation in sport', *Journal of Applied Sport Psychology*, 11, 142–69.

Vallerand, RJ & Reid, G 1984, 'On the causal effects of perceived competence on intrinsic motivation', *Journal of Sport Psychology*, 6, 94–102.

Vallerand, RJ, Blais, MR, Briere, NM & Pelletier, LG 1989, 'Construction et validation de l'echelle de motivation en education (EME)', *Canadian Journal of Behavioural Sciences*, 21, 323–49.

Vallerand, RJ, Gauvin, LI & Halliwell, WR 1982, 'When you're not good enough: the effect of failing to win a performance-contingent reward on intrinsic motivation', unpublished manuscript, University of Montreal, Quebec.

Vallerand, RJ, Gauvin, LI & Halliwell, WR 1986, 'Effects of zero-sum competition on children's intrinsic motivation and perceived competence', *Journal of Sport Psychology*, 6, 465–72.

Vickers, J, Lashuk, M & Taerum, T 1980, 'Differences in attitude toward the concepts "male", "female", "male athlete" and "female athlete"', *Research Quarterly for Exercise and Sport*, 51, 407–16.

Weinberg, RS & Gould, D 1995, *Foundations of sport and exercise psychology*, Human Kinetics, Champaign, IL.

Weinberg, R, Tenenbaum, G, McKenzie, A, Jackson, S, Anshel, M, Grove, R & Fogarty, G 2000, 'Motivation for youth participation in sport and physical activity: relationships to culture, self-reported activity levels, and gender', *International Journal of Sport Psychology*, 31, 321–46.

White, RW 1959, 'Motivation reconsidered: the concept of competence', *Psychological Review*, 66, 279–333.

Whitehead, J 1995, 'Multiple achievement orientations and participation in youth sport: a cultural and developmental perspective', *International Journal of Sport Psychology*, 26, 431–52.

Whitehead, JR 2001, 'Physical activity and intrinsic motivation', from the President's Council on Physical Fitness and Sports website, www.fitness.gov/activity/activity7/intrinsic/intrinsic.html (accessed 1 October 2001).

CHAPTER 6

ACHIEVEMENT GOAL THEORY

Likang Chi

The woods would be silent if only the best birds were allowed to sing.

— Chinese proverb

The issue of maximising motivation is one that has long been important for physical educators, coaches and sport psychologists. Not everyone in the sport and exercise field is fully motivated, with the result that some fail to reach their potential. If you become a physical educator, an exercise leader, a coach or even a sport psychologist, you will probably encounter the following sorts of situations.

John coaches the boys basketball team at high school. Lately the team's star centre, Tony, has not played as hard as he can during practice. Although talented, Tony doesn't seek out challenges — he is not motivated. John really wants to know what he can do to motivate Tony.

Hanna, an instructor at a fitness centre, runs an aerobic fitness program for overweight women. She feels she needs help, because some participants don't stick with their exercise programs after a few weeks.

James has just begun a job teaching physical education classes at high school. His goal is to teach lifelong physical activity skills and to get the sedentary students motivated to engage in fitness activities. However, James feels frustrated because many students show little interest in learning skills or participating in fitness activities. James wonders what he can do to achieve his goal.

Motivation is an interesting and pervasive topic in sport and exercise psychology. Why do some people become intensively involved and continue their involvement in sport and exercise over time, while others lose interest and withdraw their efforts, even dropping out of sport and exercise? Why do people choose or avoid certain sport tasks that differ in their degree of challenge? How can athletes' and exercisers' motivation be enhanced? To answer these questions, theoretical frameworks are needed to investigate the antecedents and consequences of achievement motivation in the sport setting. Over the years a variety of theoretical frameworks have guided sport-specific motivation research (Roberts 1992). These include Atkinson's (1964) achievement need theory, Weiner's (1979, 1985) attribution theory, Harter's (1978) theory of competence motivation, Locke's theory of goal setting (Locke & Latham 1984) and Bandura's (1977, 1986) self-efficacy theory.

In the past 20 years research into achievement motivation has primarily adopted a social cognitive approach. A social cognitive perspective places an emphasis on the cognitive mediators of behaviours — that is, how people construe an achievement situation, interpret events in the situation and process information about the situation. As one of the theories emerging from the social cognitive approach, achievement goal theory (Ames 1984, 1992; Ames & Archer 1988; Dweck 1986; Dweck & Leggett 1988; Maehr & Braskamp 1986; Nicholls 1984a, 1989) was originally formulated to foster understanding of variations in educational achievement patterns and to provide a model for motivation enhancement in the academic domain. Over the past decades an extensive body of literature has evolved that tests and extends this theoretical framework in sport settings (Roberts 1992; Duda 1992, 1993; Duda & Whitehead 1998; Duda & Hall 2000).

THE TENETS OF ACHIEVEMENT GOAL THEORY

Achievement goal theory proposes that people's main achievement concern is to demonstrate high ability and avoid demonstrating low ability. The salience of perceptions of ability is therefore a central feature of achievement striving. In other words, how individuals construe and interpret achievement events and define success affects and gives meaning to their actions. Furthermore, the goals for demonstrating ability that individuals emphasise guide their thoughts, feelings and subsequent behaviours. The two major goal states, task and ego involvement (this terminology is from Nicholls), reflect how individuals judge their ability or define their subjective success. For example, for an athlete, 'success' is defined not simply by winning and losing in a match or coming first in a race. Success in a person's first marathon could be simply finishing, even if in fiftieth place. When involved in a task, people's perceptions of ability are self-referenced and their subjective success is based on the experience of personal improvement. On the other hand, ego-involved people are concerned with demonstrating ability compared with others. The theory of achievement motivation assumes that three factors determine whether a person is task-involved or ego-involved in a particular setting (Nicholls 1989). These factors are individual differences, the situational factor and the developmental factor.

Individual differences

Nicholls (1989) suggests there are dispositional tendencies that predispose individuals to adopt task or ego involvement. As defined by Nicholls, task and ego orientations are 'the individual differences in proneness to the different type of involvement' (Nicholls 1989, p. 95). Previous research in sport settings has indicated that task and ego orientations are orthogonal or independent of each other. In other words, people might be either 'high task-oriented, low ego-oriented' or 'low task-oriented, high ego-oriented'. Alternatively they could both be high or low on task orientation and ego orientation (Chi & Duda 1995; Duda 1989; Duda & Nicholls 1992; Duda & White 1992). As suggested by Nicholls (1989), individual differences in dispositional goal orientation are a consequence of socialisation experiences within the achievement domain. A proneness to task or ego involvement is established when children interact with significant others who constantly reinforce a particular goal perspective. In order to assess individual differences in the proneness to task and ego involvement, Duda (1989) first developed the Task and Ego Orientation in Sport Questionnaire (TEOSQ). Later, Roberts and his colleagues (Roberts & Balague 1991; Roberts, Treasure & Balague 1998) developed the Perceptions of Success Questionnaire (POSQ) to assess dispositional goal orientation. In accord with Nicholls' theory regarding the measurement of achievement goal orientation, both instruments determine sport participants' differential emphasis on achievement-related criteria underlying subjective success. That is, when completing the TEOSQ and POSQ, sport participants are asked to think of when they felt successful in a particular sport and then indicate their agreement with a series of items reflecting task or ego criteria.

The situational factor

Situational factors can also influence how people construe their perceived competence and subjectively define success. When the environment emphasises learning from one's mistakes, personal skill mastery and participation tend to evoke task involvement. On the other hand, in situations characterised by an emphasis on interpersonal competition, normative feedback and social evaluation, ego involvement is more likely to emerge (Ames & Archer 1988; Nicholls 1989). Ames (1992) has been particularly interested in the study of the motivational climate in the academic setting. According to Ames's work, classroom environments can be characterised as more or less task-involving (a mastery goal) or ego-involving (a performance goal), in the view of students. Ames and Archer (1988) also found that students' perceptions of the classroom goal structure predicted important motivational indices. Specifically, perceptions of a mastery climate were related to the reported use of more effective learning strategies, a preference for more challenging tasks, a more positive attitude towards the class and the belief that effort leads to success. Extending the work of Ames and her colleagues, a major component of the motivational climate operating on sport teams is the goal structures represented in the actions and reactions of the coach. The Perceived Motivational Climate in Sport Questionnaire (PMCSQ) was developed to measure athletes' perceptions of the degree to which their coaches created a mastery and/or performance climate (Seifriz, Duda & Chi 1992). When perceived as a mastery climate, athletes characterised their environment in terms of, for example, emphasis on cooperation, reinforcement of effort and personal improvement, and fostering the view that all players can make a contribution to team outcomes. Performance climate was characterised in terms of rivalry between team members being encouraged, or the coach paying more attention to the 'stars' or responding to mistakes with punishment. In more recent work from Newton, Duda & Yin (2000), the PMCSQ was revised as a multi-subscale version of the Perceived Motivational Climate in Sport Questionnaire (PMCSQ-2).

SAMPLE ITEMS FROM THE PERCEIVED MOTIVATIONAL CLIMATE IN SPORT QUESTIONNAIRE (PMCSQ)

On this team ...

Performance climate

- Players feel good when they do better than team-mates.
- Doing better than others is important.
- Players are afraid to make mistakes.
- The coach pays most attention to the 'stars'.

Mastery climate

- Trying hard is rewarded.
- The coach focuses on skill improvement.
- Players are encouraged to work on weaknesses.
- Players try to learn new skills.

(*Source:* Seifriz, Duda & Chi 1992, p. 7)

The developmental factor

Development factors are another key determinant of whether a person is task-involved or ego-involved in a particular setting. Nicholls (1989) suggested that most children acquire a mature understanding of ability around the age of twelve. Until this time children are by nature task-involved, as the adoption of an ego orientation requires a mature understanding of ability. As shown in table 6.1, Nicholls (1989) contended that a mature understanding of ability is a result of an individual distinguishing three components: effort and ability, task difficulty and ability, and luck and ability. Research conducted in the academic setting has found that at approximately 12 years of age children begin to progress developmentally through the stages of distinguishing these concepts (Nicholls 1976, 1978, 1992; Nicholls 1978; Nicholls & Miller 1983; Nicholls & Miller 1984; Nicholls & Miller 1985). Table 6.1 shows levels of differentiation of the concept of ability from difficulty, luck and effort.

TABLE 6.1   Levels of differentiation of the concept of ability from difficulty, luck and effort

Difficulty and ability	Luck and skill	Effort and ability
At ages up to 7		
(1) Children's own expectations of success are the basis for judging task difficulty and ability.	(1) Tasks are not distinguished in terms of the dependence of outcomes on luck versus skill. Children focus on the apparent difficulty of mastering a task.	(1) Accomplishment with higher effort means higher ability. Effort and outcomes are imperfectly distinguished as cause and effect.
(2) Concrete properties of tasks (such as complexity) are the basis for judging task difficulty and the ability indicated by outcomes.		
At ages 7 to 11		
	(2) Effort is expected to improve performance on luck and skill tasks, but skill tasks are seen as more affected by effort.	(2) Effort is the cause of outcomes. Equal effort by different students is expected to lead to equal outcomes.
(3) Task difficulty and ability are judged in relation to the performance of others. Tasks that few can do are seen as hard and success on these is viewed as indicating high ability.	(3) It is recognised that luck tasks do not offer a means of using one's senses to influence outcomes. Yet some faith remains that outcomes can be influenced.	(3) Ability (as a cause of outcomes) is partially differentiated from effort.
At ages 11 and older		
	(4) Luck and skill are clearly differentiated. Effort is expected to have no impact on outcomes dependent on luck.	(4) Ability is conceived as capacity; the effect of effort on performance relative to others is limited by capacity.

(*Source:* Nicholls 1989)

The implications of this developmental process are extremely relevant to educators. Also, an understanding of how children acquire a mature understanding of ability as it relates to academic activity has provided important information about the motivational processes children experience. In the physical domain, however, only a few studies have been conducted on the developmental issue of goal perspectives (Walling 1994; Chi 1996; Chi 2001). The results of the studies by Walling (1994) and Chi (1996) indicated that, as expected, there was a positive correlation between age and level of understanding of effort and ability. In addition, there was no significant gender difference in the levels of understanding of effort and ability in the physical domain. In Chi's study (2001), he replicated Nicholls' research on how children acquire a mature understanding of ability with respect to the physical domain. Specifically, the focus of this study was on examining the levels of understanding of the concepts of task difficulty and ability, and luck and ability. In addition, gender differences in the development of the concepts of difficulty and luck were also examined. The results of the Piagetian structural method of analysis were consistent with Nicholls' four levels of differentiation of difficulty and ability in the academic domain. Specifically, at Level 1 (up to 7 years) tasks are not distinguished in terms of the dependence of outcomes on luck versus skill. At Level 2 (7 to 11 years) effort is expected to improve performance on luck and skill tasks, but skill tasks are seen as more affected by effort. At Level 3 (7 to 11 years) children recognise that luck tasks do not offer a means of using their senses to influence outcomes, yet some faith remains that outcomes can be influenced. At Level 4 (11 years and older) luck and skill are clearly differentiated; effort is expected to have no impact on outcomes dependent on luck. However, the results were not completely in accord with Nicholls' three levels of differentiation of difficulty and ability in the academic domain. Specifically, the results suggested that one more level should be included. This additional level was referred to as a level between Level 2 and Level 3. At age 7 to 11, children might not be able to fully differentiate task difficulty and ability. In other words, between Level 2 and Level 3 might be a level at which ability is partially differentiated from task difficulty. Moreover, there were positive correlations between age and level of understanding of task difficulty and ability as well as luck and ability. Again, there was no significant gender difference in the levels of understanding of task difficulty and ability as well as luck and ability.

ACHIEVEMENT GOALS AND CORRELATES OF MOTIVATIONAL PROCESSES AND BEHAVIOURS

Contemporary achievement goal theory provides a valuable framework for identifying the means by which goals influence subsequent achievement-related cognitions, affects and behaviours. The motivation model of achievement goal theory is shown in figure 6.1. Specifically, it is suggested that an individual's goal perspective will affect self-evaluations of demonstration of ability, expended effort, and attributions for success and failure. In turn, these cognitions are assumed to influence achievement-related effects, such as anxiety, satisfaction, enjoyment and strategy use, as well as subsequent behaviours, such as effort exertion, task choice, persistence and performance (Duda 1992).

Achievement goal theory has also made an elaborate prediction about motivational patterns. Over the past 20 years an extensive body of literature has evolved that examines the relationships of achievement goals and correlates of motivational processes and behaviours and investigates the impact of goal perspectives on achievement-related cognitions, affects and behaviours in sport settings (Duda 1992, 1993; Duda & Hall 2000; Duda & Whitehead 1998; Roberts 1992).

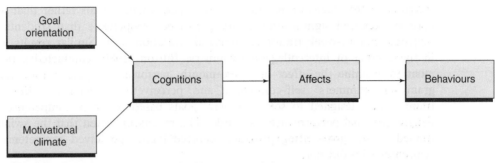

Figure 6.1 The motivation model of achievement goal theory

Achievement goals and motivational processes

Previous research examining the impact of achievement goals and motivational processes in sport settings has focused on cognitions and affects, such as perceived competence, attribution, intrinsic motivation and anxiety.

Goals and perceived competence

According to achievement goal theory (Dweck 1986; Nicholls 1989, 1992), task-involved people emphasise mastering the task; their perceptions of demonstrated competence are self-referenced. Therefore it is assumed that task-involved people will sustain or increase their perceived competence when they perceive that they have learned something new or improved their skill. On the other hand, ego-involved people experience competence through outperforming others. Learning and improvement are not enough for them to experience high competence. Consequently it is assumed that ego involvement is more likely to be associated with feelings of incompetence, especially after being outperformed by others or after failures.

Previous studies in sport-related contexts support these predictions. Duda, Chi and Newton (1990) conducted a study to examine the relationships of dispositional goal orientation and perception of competence before and after tennis games. The results indicated that task-oriented people tended to maintain their competence after losing the game. Huang and Chi (1994) examined the relationships of intercollegiate basketball players' perceived motivational climates, perceived competence, pre-competition anxiety and satisfaction. The results indicated that perception of a mastery climate was positively associated with perceived competence. In other words, athletes who perceived that the environment emphasised cooperation, reinforcement of effort and personal improvement, and fostered the view that all players can make a contribution to team outcomes, tended to report higher perceived competence.

Field experimental studies also support the prediction of achievement goal theory that task involvement and a mastery environment are related to perceived competence. Duda and Chi (1989) conducted a study to examine the effects of pre-game perceived competence, objective outcome and a mastery versus performance game condition on post-game perceived competence. College students enrolled in physical education skill classes were recruited. The results indicated that, regardless of winning or losing, low pre-game perceived competence participants who were in a mastery condition tended to report higher post-game perceived competence than those who were in a performance condition. Similar findings emerged in a study by Newsham (1989), who examined the effect of a task-oriented physical education program on the perceived competence of elementary school children. The results indicated that students who participated in a 12-week task-oriented physical education program (with a focus on meeting personal performance goals rather than social comparison) reported significantly higher perceived competence than students who participated in a 12-week traditional physical education class. Similar results were found in the context of intercollegiate swimmers. Burton (1989) conducted a field experiment to examine the effect of a five-month 'performance' goal-setting training program on swimmers' self-confidence and perceived competence. The goal-setting training was designed to set swimmers' goals based on their competence and challenging personal performance standards. The results indicated that the swimmers who trained by the goal-setting program reported higher perceived competence than the swimmers who did not.

Two experimental studies also provided evidence supporting the predictions of relationships between achievement goals and perceived competence. Hall (1988) determined the impact of task- versus ego-involving conditions, perceived competence, and success/failure feedback on stabilometer task performance and perception of competence. The participants were randomly assigned to a task-involving or ego-involving condition. Their perceived competence was manipulated by telling participants that they had performed in either the bottom 18 per cent or the top 82 per cent of all participants following a baseline measure of stabilometer performance. For participants assigned to the task-involving condition, only individualised performance feedback was given. Participants in the ego-involving condition received both personal performance feedback and normative feedback. The results indicated that goal structure and perceived competence affect participants' perceptions of competence before, during and following task performance. Participants who received negative feedback and were in the ego-involving condition reported lower perceived competence than participants who received negative feedback and were in the task-involving condition. Similar findings were revealed in Chi's (1993) study.

Goals and attribution

Previous classroom-based research (Ames 1992; Nicholls, Cheung, Lauer & Patashnick 1989; Nicholls, Cobb, Wood, Yackel & Patashnick 1990) has revealed consistent relationships between achievement goals and attributional focus. In general, the findings were congruent with achievement goal theory that task involvement is linked to effort attributions while ego involvement is associated more with ability attributions. Much research in sport settings has been conducted to examine the relationships between goals and beliefs about causes of success across age and competitive level groups. Duda and Nicholls (1992) examined the relationships between dispositional goal orientations and beliefs about causes of success in sport among high-school students. The results indicated that task orientation was positively correlated with the belief that sport success is the result of hard work and effort. Task orientation was negatively correlated with the belief that sport success is caused by deception and external factors. In contrast, ego orientation was positively correlated with the belief that sport success is the results of talent and skills. Moreover, ego orientation was positively correlated with the belief that deception and external factors will create success in sport. Similar findings of the relationships between goal orientations and beliefs about causes of success in sport were reported in studies of children (Biddle, Akande, Vlachopoulos & Fox 1996), 8- to 15-year-old young sport participants (Hom, Duda & Miller 1993), elite adolescent tennis athletes (Newton & Duda 1993), senior Olympic Games participants (Newton & Fry 1998) and intercollegiate skiers (Duda & White 1992).

In recent years much research has also been conducted to examine the relationships between motivational climate and beliefs about causes of success in sport settings.

Seifriz, Duda & Chi (1992) assessed the relationships of perceived motivational climate to intrinsic motivation and beliefs about success among high-school basketball players. The results indicated that there was a significant difference between high- and low-mastery climate groups in belief in effort as a cause of success, with belief in effort being higher in the mastery climate group. Moreover, there was a significant difference between high- and low-performance climate groups in belief in ability as a cause of success, with a greater belief in the role of ability in the high-performance climate group. Similar findings were reported in studies by Kavussanu and Roberts (1996) and Newton and Duda (1995). Both studies indicated that perceptions of a mastery environment were positively associated with the belief that effort creates success. In contrast, perceptions of a performance climate were positively linked to the belief that ability leads to success in sport.

To better understand the impact of achievement goals on attributional patterns after outcome, Duda and Chi (1989) conducted a field experiment examining the effect of a mastery versus performance game condition and objective outcome on performance attributions in one-on-one basketball games. The results of this study indicated that the situational manipulation of goal perspective had an impact on effort attribution among objective winners and losers. Specifically, in terms of effort attribution there was no difference between mastery and performance conditions for winners. However, losers in the performance condition attributed less to effort than losers in the mastery condition.

Peng and Chi (1996) examined the impact of dispositional goal orientation and objective outcome on performance attribution after a one-on-one basketball game. Participants were categorised as high task-, low ego-oriented or high ego-, low task-oriented by using the median split of task and ego scores on the TEOSQ. The results did not support the prediction of achievement goal theory. There was no significant difference in participants' effort and ability attributions, when comparing with high task-, low ego-oriented or high ego-, low task-oriented participants.

Goals and intrinsic motivation

Vallerand and Fortier (1998) suggested that engagement in sport and physical activities is characterised by two forms of motivation. Intrinsic motivation is related to behaviour performed for itself in order to experience the pleasure and satisfaction inherent in the activities. This form of motivation is likely to occur when the activity is interesting and challenging, and provides people with clear feedback and freedom with which to perform the task (Deci & Ryan 1985). The second type of motivation, which involves engaging in the activity in order to receive social approval and rewards or to avoid punishment, has been called extrinsic motivation. These two forms of motivation are important antecedents that influence subsequent behaviours.

Achievement goal theory suggests that goals influence intrinsic motivation in achievement-related activities such as academic settings and sport. Nicholls (1989) argued that, when people are task-involved, engagement in activity is experienced more as 'the end in itself'. Therefore people high in task involvement work hard at a task for its own sake and foster intrinsic motivation. In contrast, ego-involved people, who participate in activities, experience the task more as 'a means to an end'. Consequently a decrease in intrinsic motivation is expected for ego-involved people.

A number of studies have attempted to examine the relationship between dispositional goal orientations and intrinsic motivation. Duda, Chi and Newton (1990) examined this relationship among college students who enrolled in a tennis skills class. They were asked to complete the TEOSQ and Intrinsic Motivation Inventory (IMI) (Plant &

Ryan 1985). The results indicated that task orientation was positively correlated to enjoyment, effort and the composite intrinsic motivation score. In two studies reported by Duda, Chi, Newton, Walling and Catley (1995), task orientation was positively correlated to enjoyment and interest in physical education skills classes. On the other hand, an ego orientation was negatively related to enjoyment and interest in activities.

Much of the research on this issue has also attempted to examine the combined relationships of dispositional goal orientations and perceptions of motivational climates to intrinsic motivation. For example, Seifriz et al. (1992) found that a high mastery and low performance climate was related to greater enjoyment and intrinsic interest in high-school basketball players. However, when both dispositional goal orientations and perceptions of motivational climate were used to predict intrinsic motivation, goal orientations accounted for more explained variance in terms of prediction of enjoyment, effort and competence, whereas the climate contributed more to the prediction of the pressure/tension that participants experienced. Similar findings were reported in the studies of a sample of novice tennis players (Kavussanu & Roberts 1996) and a sample of 345 volleyball players (Newton & Duda 1999). Both these studies indicated that perceptions of mastery climate, performance climate and perceived competence contributed significantly to the prediction of enjoyment and interest in sport. Specifically, the higher level of intrinsic motivation was predicted by high mastery climate, low performance climate and high perception of competence. In addition, a low ego and high task orientation positively predicted perceived effort exertion. Moreover, Newton and Duda suggested that goal orientations appeared to be the best predictors of effort, whereas the climates seemed to be the best predictors of affective responses. In a study of a sample of 439 elite male youth soccer players, Treasure, Standage and Lochbaum (1999) also examined the relationship between perceptions of motivational climate and sport motivation. The Sport Motivation Scale (SMS) (Pelletier, Fortier, Vallerand, Tuson, Briere & Blais 1995) was used to assess participants' sport motivation from high to low levels of self-determination moving from intrinsic motivation, identified regulation, introjected regulation and external regulation to amotivation. The results indicated that a high perceived mastery and low perceived performance climate were associated with higher intrinsic motivation and identified regulation and lower external regulation and amotivation. In contrast, a strong perceived performance climate and low mastery climate were related to higher external regulation, identified regulation and amotivation.

Although much of the research to date has been consistent with the predictions of achievement goal theory, not all studies in the sport setting have demonstrated that an ego orientation is negatively related to intrinsic motivation. For example, studies of young athletes (Hom et al. 1993) and undergraduate physical activity students (Roberts 1996) reported that both task and ego orientations were positively related to enjoyment and interest in sport. In a series of studies, Chi and his colleagues (Chi, Lai & Chen 1995; Chiou & Chi 1999; Dongfung & Chi 2001) examined the relationships between dispositional goal orientations and sport motivation in different competitive levels of intercollegiate tennis and basketball players in Taiwan. The SMS was used to measure athletes' intrinsic motivation, extrinsic motivation and amotivation in sport. Similar findings were reached across three studies. The results indicated that a task orientation was positively related to intrinsic motivation. An ego orientation was positively related to both intrinsic and extrinsic motivation. Amotivation showed no relationship with task or ego orientation. Chi and his colleagues suggested that athletes' perceived competence and the different competitive levels at which athletes were involved might play an important role in the relationships between achievement goals and sport motivation. Specifically, positive correlation between ego orientation and intrinsic motivation might be expected for highly competitive sport athletes rather than for low-competitive sport participants.

Goals and anxiety

As pointed out by Duda and Hall (2000), only a few sport researchers have examined the impact of achievement goals on competitive anxiety, although achievement goal theory has proposed that achievement goals provide a framework for understanding athletes' cognitions, affects and behaviours. Based on achievement goal theory, task-involved people are self-referenced when they judge their perceptions of ability, and their subjective success is based on the experience of personal improvement. Therefore they are expected to have a higher sense of control and less sense of threat, regardless of their levels of perceived competence. On the other hand, ego-involved people are concerned with demonstrating ability compared with others. When they doubt their ability or experience low perceived competence, they are more concerned to avoid demonstrating low ability than to demonstrate high ability. Consequently they tend to experience higher competitive anxiety (Roberts 1986).

Research has been conducted to examine the effect of the relationship between dispositional goal orientation and perceived motivational climate on competitive anxiety. For example, Vealey and Campbell (1988) examined the relationship between goal orientation and state anxiety among adolescent figure skaters. The results indicated that task orientation was negatively correlated with state anxiety. White and Zellner (1996) examined the relationship between goal orientations and multidimensional trait anxiety among male and female high-school, intercollegiate and recreational athletes. The results indicated that a high ego orientation and low task orientation were related to high cognitive anxiety in athletes. In a study of male and female adolescent athletes, White (1998) also found that athletes who were high in ego orientation and low in task orientation scored higher on trait anxiety. Similar results were found in another study conducted by Ommundsen and Pedersen (1999). Task orientation and perceived ability emerged as negative predictors of cognitive trait anxiety. In summary, not all the studies have found that task orientation was negatively related to anxiety and that ego orientation was positively related to anxiety.

Some studies also examined the situational effect of achievement goals on competitive anxiety. For example, Walling, Duda and Chi (1993) examined the relationship between perceived motivational climates and performance worry among tennis players. The results indicated that perception of a mastery climate was negatively related to performance worry and perception of a performance climate was positively correlated with performance worry. Huang and Chi (1994) used goal orientation, perceived motivational climate and perceived competence in an attempt to predict multidimensional state anxiety. The results indicated that perception of a mastery climate and perceived competence were negative predictors for cognitive and somatic anxiety among intercollegiate basketball players. Neither task orientation nor ego orientation could significantly predict athletes' state anxiety.

Ntoumanis and Biddle (1998) combined dispositional goal orientation and perceived motivational climate to examine their influences on the intensity and direction of cognitive anxiety and somatic anxiety in student athletes. The results indicated that neither task orientation nor a mastery climate was related to state anxiety. However, an ego orientation and a performance climate were found to correlate with both intensity and direction of cognitive and somatic anxiety. The structural equation model showed that athletes' confidence was a mediator of the effect of ego orientation and performance climate on state anxiety.

Achievement goals and behaviours

Achievement goal theory also made an elaborate prediction of interrelationships between achievement goals, perceived competence and achievement-related behaviours, such as effort exertion, task choice, persistence and performance (Maehr 1984; Nicholls 1989) (see table 6.2). Depending on an individual's achievement goals (task involvement or ego involvement) and perceived competence, different achievement-related behaviours are predicted. According to achievement goal theory, people's major concern in an achievement setting is to demonstrate high ability and avoid demonstrating low ability. In a state of task involvement, conceptions of ability are based on self-improvement. The more individuals feel they have learned and improved, the more competent they feel. In this case, regardless of the level of perceived competence, people are not concerned with 'looking good' or capable, and their sense of competence is less likely to be in jeopardy. In other words, individuals focus on demonstrating high ability, but not to avoid demonstrating low ability. Consequently an adaptive achievement pattern is expected to emerge, such as the exertion of effort, the choosing of moderately challenging tasks, sustained or improved performance, and participating persistently. An ego-involved individual who has a high level of perceived competence would have the same adaptive behaviours as a task-involved person because she or he is still focusing on demonstrating high ability. However, once individuals are ego-involved and experience lack of competence, they tend to focus on avoiding the demonstration of low ability. They perceive little chance to beat others in order to demonstrate high ability. Therefore they indulge in maladaptive behaviours, such as withdrawing effort, choosing either extremely hard or extremely easy tasks, performance impairment and lack of persistence.

TABLE 6.2   The interrelationships between achievement goal, perceived competence and achievement-related behaviours

Achievement goal	Perceived competence	Achievement-related behaviours
Task	High	Adaptive behaviours: • Exerting effort • Choosing moderate challenging task • Sustained or improved performance • Persistence
Task	Low	Adaptive behaviours
Ego	High	Adaptive behaviours
Ego	Low	Maladaptive behaviours: • Withdrawing effort • Choosing too easy or too difficult task • Performance impairment • Lack of persistence

Effort exerting, task choice, persistence and performance are considered the most important indices of achievement-related behaviours (Maehr 1984; Roberts 1992). Many studies have been conducted that support the impacts of achievement goals on achievement-related behaviours in academic settings (Ames 1984; Dweck 1986; Nicholls 1989). However, little research has been conducted in sport settings.

Goals and exerting effort

Duda (1988) examined the relationship between goal orientations and exercise intensity among recreational sport participants. The results indicated that intramural athletes who were high in task orientation reported that they spent more time in practice than those who were high in ego orientation. In a study of the predictors of adherence to athletic injury rehabilitation, Duda, Smart and Tappe (1989) found that task orientation was positively related to the effort exerted by athletes while completing their prescribed exercises.

Several experimental studies have been conducted to examine the effects of achievement goals and perceived competence on achievement-related behaviours. Hall (1988) examined the mediating effects of situationally induced achievement goals and perceived ability on effort exerted during stabilometer task performance. Exerted effort was assessed by a self-reported measure of perceived exerted effort on the task. The results indicated that the perceived exerted effort significantly differed among the groups. Specifically, ego-involved participants who had low manipulated perceived ability reported that they did not try as hard as those who were in the task-involving condition and had low manipulated perceived ability. Chi (1993) examined the effects of dispositional goal orientation and manipulated perceived competence on effort exerted during exercise. Eighty college students predetermined as high task-, low ego-oriented or high ego-, low task-oriented by TEOSQ were recruited as participants. Participants were asked to assess their VO_2 max by exercising on a cycle ergometer for five minutes. After completing the exercise trial, participants were given either positive or negative bogus feedback via a computer monitor. After a ten-minute rest, participants were asked to compete against each other on an adjacent cycle ergometer for six minutes. Their workload was set at 50 per cent of their estimated VO_2 max. The results indicated that participants who were high task-, low ego-oriented reported that they tried harder than participants who were high ego-, low task-oriented. Similar findings were revealed in Lin's (1995) study.

Goals and task choice

Nicholls (1984a, 1989) proposed that an individual's goal perspective and perceived ability have an impact on patterns of task choice. In a state of task involvement, conceptions of ability are based on self-improvement. The more individuals feel they have learned and improved, the more competent they feel. Therefore, a preference for choosing a moderately challenging level of task is predicted for high task-involved people. On the other hand, ego-involved people judge their ability depending on the ability of others. Task difficulty is based on the performance of others and the demonstration of high ability demands success on tasks where others fail. As long as ego-involved people have high competence, they are assumed to believe that they can master moderately difficult tasks and then move up in level of difficulty, thus gaining in perceived competence. For ego-involved people who have low perceived competence, it is expected that they will want to avoid moderate difficulty tasks, because failure in such tasks is more likely to reflect low ability. In this case, they are predicted to choose the extreme levels of difficulty (i.e. very easy or very difficult tasks) in order to avoid demonstrating low ability. By choosing very easy tasks, ego-involved individuals with low competence avoid demonstrating low ability by the high probability of securing a victory or success, thus preserving their sense of competence. Demonstrating low ability is also avoided by choosing very difficult tasks. In this case, most individuals would fail at the task because it is too difficult.

Although seeking challenge has long been an important achievement behaviour for sport psychology researchers and applied sport psychologists, little sport research has been done on this issue to date. Chi and his colleagues (Chi 1993; Lee & Chi 1998) conducted a series of studies to examine the impact of dispositional goal orientation, perceived competence and commitment on task choice in the physical domain. In the Chi (1993) cycle ergometer competition study, the results indicated that there was an interaction effect of goal orientation, outcome and phase of assessment on participants' task choice. The participants who were high ego-, low task-oriented and lost the races tended to select less challenging opponents than the participants who were high ego-, low task-oriented and won the races and the high task-, low ego-oriented participants regardless of race outcome. A similar finding was revealed in a study of elementary school children (Lee & Chi 1998). In that study, fifth- and sixth-grade students were asked to perform on an eye–hand coordination test. Participants received bogus normative feedback regarding their performance on the test; then they were asked to choose a different level of challenge to compete with. Participants' commitment to demonstrating ability was also assessed. The results were consistent with the hypothesis that ego-oriented participants who had low perceived competence would tend to select normatively difficult or easy tasks. In this case, most of them tended to choose much less challenging tasks.

Goals and persistence

Persistence is an important index of achievement behaviours. Lack of persistence or drop-out (especially after failure) indicates lack of achievement motivation. Nicholls (1989) argued that when people are task-involved, engagement in an activity is experienced more as 'the end in itself'; therefore people who are task-involved should work hard at a task for its own sake. Further, they tend to enjoy continuously participating in the activity regardless of their levels of perceived competence. In contrast, ego-involved people who participate in activities are more involved as 'a means to an end'. Consequently a lack of enjoyment is expected for ego-involved people when they feel incapable. In order to avoid demonstrating low ability, ego-involved people tend to drop out.

Most research on achievement goals and persistence in sport settings has been correlational in nature (Duda 1992). Most of the correlational studies in the physical domain have shown a positive relationship between task involvement and persistence. Ego involvement, on the other hand, has been negatively associated with persistence (Duda 1988, 1989). Weitzer (1989) conducted a study to predict involvement in physical activities by linking goal perspectives and perceptions of competence. The results indicated that fourth-grade children who emphasised task-involving goals, regardless of their levels of perceived competence, tended to participate more in physical activities.

Although the previous studies supported the predictions of achievement goal theory, longitudinal studies are needed to examine the impact of achievement goals on persistence. Recently a few longitudinal studies have been conducted, and the results have been consistent with the theory. Andree & Whitehead (1996) conducted a two-year study to examine interactive effects of perceived ability and goal orientations or perceived motivational climates on persistence in young athletes. The results indicated that those who did not continue participating in sport had low perceived competence and perceived their sport environment to have a high performance climate.

Goals and performance

Theorists of achievement goal theory (Ames & Archer 1988; Dweck 1986; Elliott & Dweck 1988; Nicholls 1989) have proposed that when people are task-involved, their perceptions of demonstrated competence are self-referenced and their success is defined as learning and improvement. Therefore task-involved people tend to perform effectively regardless of their levels of perceived competence. Alternatively, when people are ego-involved, their major concern is to demonstrate superior ability or to avoid showing a lack of ability. If they have high perception of competence, they are concerned with performing well compared with others, and they expect to be able to do so. Such people, it is predicted, will exhibit effective performance on the task. Low perceived ability people who are ego-involved do not expect success, and exerting effort following a failure reflects lack of ability. Therefore it is predicted that they will stop trying once they fail and impaired performance is expected as a consequence.

Much research has supported the predictions of goal perspective and perceived competence on performance in academic-related settings (Elliott & Dweck 1988; Miller 1985). However, only a few studies have been conducted to test the sports performance predictions emanating from achievement goal theory. In a field experimental study, Burton (1989) examined the effect of a goal-setting training program on collegiate swimmers' performance. During a season-long training period the athletes were taught to set goals based on personal performance standards rather than outcome. The results support the predictions of achievement goal theory. Compared with the swimmers who were not in the training program and swimmers who were in the training program but did not set accurate goals, swimmers who set accurate personal performance goals had superior performance during a mid-season dual meet and the league championship.

Hall (1988) examined the influence of situationally induced achievement goals and perceived ability on the performance of a motor skill. The participants were randomly assigned to a task-involving or ego-involving condition, and their perceived ability was manipulated by telling participants that they had performed in either the bottom 18 per cent or the top 82 per cent of all participants their age, following a baseline measure of stabilometer performance. The results indicated that participants who were in the ego-involving condition with low perceived ability performed worse than participants who were in the ego-involving condition with high perceived ability and participants who were in the task-involving condition regardless of their level of perceived ability.

Similar findings were revealed in Jourden, Bandura and Banfield's (1991) study. They examined the impact of conception of ability on motor skill acquisition. To manipulate the conception of ability, participants were randomly assigned to either the acquirable condition (task-involving) or the inherent aptitude condition (ego-involving). In the inherent condition, participants were led to believe that the task measured one's basic natural capacity for processing and translating dynamic information into proficient action. In the acquirable skill condition, participants were informed that the task was a learnable skill and one could learn from errors to perform the task better. The results indicated that participants who believed that the task was an acquirable skill exhibited significantly better performance than the participants who were in the inherent aptitude condition.

In the Chi (1993) cycle ergometer competition study, the results indicated that there was an interaction effect of goal orientation, manipulated competence, outcome and phase of assessment on participants' performance. The participants who were high task-, low ego-oriented with high manipulated competence and told that they won the races significantly improved their cycling performance across the competitions. In contrast, participants who were high ego-, low task-oriented with low manipulated competence and told that they lost the races showed significantly impaired performance.

PRACTICAL APPLICATIONS OF ACHIEVEMENT GOAL THEORY IN SPORT

Achievement goal theory has provided a valuable framework for understanding the practical applications of achievement motivation in sport settings. Research related to the antecedents and consequences of goal involvement has also provided sufficient information to draw out some practical applications for sport. Much research has indicated that the prevailing situational goal structure or motivational climate will influence the goals sport participants adopt as well as their perceptions, attitudes and behaviours in sport settings. Sport participants' perceptions of a mastery climate are positively related to enjoyment, intrinsic motivation, the belief that effort leads to achievement (Seifriz et al. 1992), team satisfaction (Walling et al. 1993) and group cohesion (Chi & Lu 1995). On the other hand, athletes' perception of a performance climate positively related to performance worry (Walling et al. 1993), state anxiety (Huang & Chi 1994) and negatively related to task cohesion (Chi & Lu 1995).

To ensure the effects of situational goal structure or motivational climate influence the goals sport participants adopt, as well as their perceptions, attitudes and behaviours in sport settings, longitudinal intervention studies are badly needed. Only a few studies have been done in the physical domain. Chang (1996) conducted a study to examine the effects of dispositional goal orientation and mastery teaching on children's self-concept, intrinsic motivation and performance in basketball physical education class. Sixth-grade elementary school students and six physical education teachers were recruited as participants. After Chang received informed consent from school administrators, students and parents, participants were asked to complete the TEOSQ and then were assigned to either a mastery teaching class or a traditional teaching class. In the mastery teaching class, teachers were trained by using TARGET (Ames 1992; Epstein 1989) to set the motivational strategies for three months. The motivational strategies created by TARGET include six areas — Task, Authority, Recognition, Grouping, Evaluation and Time (see feature table on p. 167). Children's physical self-concept, intrinsic motivation and basketball performance were assessed before and after the four-month class. The results indicated that ego-oriented children in traditional teaching classes revealed lower physical self-concept than ego-oriented children who were in mastery teaching classes and task-oriented children, regardless of whether they were in traditional or mastery teaching classes. Regarding the participants' intrinsic motivation, both goal orientation and mastery teaching showed significant influences. Students who were in mastery classes reported greater intrinsic motivation than students who were in traditional teaching classes. In addition, high task-, high ego-oriented and high task-, low ego-oriented children reported higher intrinsic motivation than high ego-, low task-oriented and low ego-, low task-oriented children. With respect to basketball performance, students who were in mastery teaching classes performed significantly better than students who were in traditional teaching classes. Intervention studies have also demonstrated that students who perceive the motivational climate to be mastery-oriented are more likely to display adaptive affect and behaviour than those who perceive the climate to be performance-oriented (Ames & Archer 1988; Chang 1996; Powell 1990).

Within sport, the role of the parent, teacher and coach in the active construction of an individual's perception of the motivational climate should be emphasised: How do they design practice sessions? How do they evaluate performance? What behaviours do they consider desirable? Do they congratulate players on ability or good effort? How do they react when the team loses? Persuasive evidence exists to suggest that by making certain cues, rewards and expectations salient, a coach can encourage a particular goal involvement, and in so doing significantly affect the way an athlete perceives the sport experience. The evidence also clearly suggests that, if we want athletes to employ effortful strategies, seek challenging tasks, persist in the sport and improve performance, we must move towards enhancing the mastery climate of the competitive environment. When the environment is characterised as a mastery climate, athletes are more likely to have fun and experience satisfaction. In conclusion, it is important to encourage coaches and parents to focus on criteria that emphasise a mastery climate and de-emphasise a performance climate for athletes.

ENHANCING MASTERY CLIMATE: TARGET STRUCTURE AND STRATEGIES

TARGET descriptions	Strategies
Task Training activities, design of practice drills	Design activities for variety, individual challenge and active involvement. Assist athletes to set appropriate goals.
Authority Athletes' participation in the instructional process	Involve athletes in decision-making and leadership roles. Help athletes develop self-management and self-monitoring skills.
Recognition Reasons for recognition, distribution of rewards, opportunities for rewards	Recognise individual effort, progress and improvement. Ensure equal opportunities for reward. Focus on each athlete's self-worth.
Grouping The way in-groups are created during practice	Use flexible and heterogeneous grouping arrangements. Provide for multiple grouping arrangements.
Evaluation Standards for performance, monitoring of performance, evaluative feedback	Use criteria of individual progress, improvement and mastery. Involve athletes in self-evaluation. Make evaluation private and meaningful.
Timing Schedule flexibility, pace of learning, management of time and training schedule	Provide opportunities and time for improvement. Help athletes establish training and competition schedule.

FUTURE DIRECTIONS

In general, research has provided support for achievement goal theory's relevance to the physical education and sport domain. As Duda and Hall (2000) pointed out, the past several years have been an exciting time in the evolution of achievement goal research. New extensions and applications of the theory and existing empirical literature seem to be emerging quickly. However, much more work is still needed to understand the antecedents, consequences and processes of achievement goals in the sport realm. Several important directions for future research based on achievement goal theory are proposed:

1. One promising direction in achievement goal theory research in the sport domain is reflected in efforts to combine the constructs from other models of achievement motivation theory, such as cognitive evaluation theory, self-determination theory, self-efficacy theory, attribution theory and goal-setting theory. Research comparing and integrating achievement goal theory with other achievement motivation theories in the physical domain appears warranted.

2. To determine the causal effects of achievement goals on subsequent cognitions, affects and behaviours, longitudinal studies are strongly needed. Qualitative studies are also recommended to observe the impacts of achievement goals on sport behaviours.

3. Most previous studies assessed achievement goals by using a dispositional measure (i.e. goal orientation) and a measure of motivational climate. Dispositional goal orientation and perceptions of the motivational climate are presumed to influence subsequent cognitions, affects and behaviours. However, researchers have not considered the possible interaction between personal and situational goals. From the research standpoint, to consider dispositional goal orientation and perception of motivational climate simultaneously in one study would be too complex and might not reflect an individual's goal state in a particular setting. However, little has been done with respect to the assessment of goal states in the physical domain. Future research in development of assessment of goal states is warranted.

4. As suggested by Duda (2001), achievement goal theory provides insight not only into differences in achievement striving but also into the potential facilitating or debilitating influence of this realm on people's physical and mental welfare. Future research might examine the possible links between achievement goals and healthful sport in areas such as physically active lifestyles and eating disorders.

CONCLUSIONS

During the past decade achievement goal theory has dominated the literature related to achievement motivation in sport and exercise, and this theory has provided a useful framework for understanding and enhancing achievement motivation in sport and exercise settings. Diverse research in terms of samples (such as age group, gender, culture and methodology) has provided consistent findings on the relationships between achievement goal and cognitive, affective and behavioural factors. From a practical standpoint, research has revealed that motivation in athletes, exercisers and students in physical education classes will be enhanced by the promotion of a mastery climate and a task orientation in children.

SUMMARY

This chapter has reviewed the major tenets of achievement goal theory and outlined the recent research based on achievement goal theory, providing a framework for organising and understanding the basic mechanisms underlying motivation in sport settings. Preliminary findings have indicated that dispositional goal orientation and motivational climate influence motivational processes such as attributions, perceived competence and intrinsic motivation; affects such as anxiety and enjoyment; and sport behaviours such as effort exerting, task choice, persistence and performance. This research offers an integrated understanding of the current knowledge to inform physical educators and coaches, so they can enhance people's motivation in the sport setting.

REVIEW QUESTIONS

1   Compare task involvement and ego involvement. Why do they play important roles in achievement motivation?

2   Distinguish goal involvement, goal orientation and motivational climate by giving examples in sport settings.

3   Describe the major tenets of achievement goal theory, including antecedents, achievement-related cognitions, affects and behaviours.

4   Describe three factors that help to determine whether a person is task-involved or ego-involved in a particular setting.

5   Describe the major findings relating to predicting achievement-related behaviours.

6   Discuss the practical implications and principles that can be drawn from the literature on achievement goal theory.

7   List three findings each from studies about the antecedents and the consequences of achievement goal theory in sport.

8   Describe TARGET strategies used by physical education teachers and coaches to foster mastery climate.

References

Ames, C 1984, 'Competitive, cooperative and individualistic goal structures: a motivational analysis', in R Ames & C Ames (eds), *Research on motivation in education: student motivation*, Academic Press, New York, pp. 177–207.

Ames, C 1992, 'Achievement goals, motivational climate and motivational processes', in G Roberts (ed.), *Motivation in sport and exercise*, Human Kinetics, Champaign, IL, pp. 161–76.

Ames, C & Archer, J 1988, 'Achievement goals in the classroom: students' learning strategies and motivation processes', *Journal of Educational Psychology*, 80, 260–7.

Andree, KV & Whitehead, J 1996, 'The interactive effect of perceived ability and dispositional or situational achievement goals on persistence in young athletes', paper presented at the annual meeting of the North American Society for Sport and Physical Activity, Asilomar, CA, June.

Atkinson, JW 1964, *An introduction to motivation*, Van Nostrand, Princeton, NJ.

Bandura, A 1977, 'Self efficiency: toward a unifying theory of behavioral change', *Psychological Review*, 84, 191–215.

Bandura, A 1986, *Social foundations of thought and action: a social cognitive theory*, Prentice Hall, Englewood Cliffs, NJ.

Biddle, SJH, Akande, A, Vlachopoulos, S & Fox, KR 1996, 'Toward an understanding of children's motivation for physical activity: achievement goal orientations, beliefs about the causes of success, and sport emotion in Zimbabwean children', *Psychology and Health*, 12, 49–55.

Burton, D 1989, 'Winning isn't everything: examining the impact of performance goals on collegiate swimmers' cognitions and performance', *The Sport Psychologist*, 2, 105–32.

Chang, J 1996, 'The effects of goal orientations and mastery basketball teaching on elementary school students' self-concept, intrinsic motivation, and performance', unpublished master's thesis, National College of Physical Education and Sports, Taiwan.

Chi, L 1993, 'Prediction of achievement-related cognitions and behaviors in the physical domain: a test of the theories of goal perspective and self-efficacy', unpublished doctoral dissertation, Purdue University, West Lafayette, IN.

Chi, L 1996, 'The differentiation of the concepts of effort and ability in the physical domain', *Taiwan Bulletin of Physical Education*, 22, 83–94.

Chi, L 2001, 'The differentiation of the concepts of difficulty and ability, luck and ability in the physical domain', paper presented at the International Society of Sport Psychology 10th World Congress of Sport Psychology.

Chi, L & Duda, JL 1995, 'Multi-sample confirmatory factor analysis of the Task and Ego Orientation in Sport Questionnaire', *Research Quarterly for Exercise and Sport*, 66, 1–8.

Chi, L, Lai, S & Chen, M 1995, 'The relationships of task and ego orientation to intrinsic motivation, extrinsic motivation, and amotivation among tennis players', *Taiwan Bulletin of Physical Education*, 20, 1–12.

Chi, L & Lu, S 1995, 'The relationships between perceived motivational climates and group cohesiveness in basketball', paper presented at the annual meeting of the North American Society for Sport and Physical Activity, Monterey, CA.

Chiou, Z & Chi, L 1999, 'The relationships of goal orientation and perceived motivational climate to men's basketball players' sport motivation', *Proceedings of Annual Conference of Chinese Taipei Sport Federation*, 333–6.

Deci, E & Ryan, R 1985, *Intrinsic motivation and self-determination in human behavior*, Plenum, New York.

Dongfung, G & Chi, L 2001, 'The relationships of goal orientation, perceived motivational climate, perceived competence, sport motivation, and satisfaction among basketball players', *Journal of Physical Education in Higher Education*, 3 (1) 1–10.

Duda, JL 1988, 'The relationship between goal perspectives and persistence and intensity among recreational sport participants', *Leisure Sciences*, 10, 95–106.

Duda, JL 1989, 'The relationship between task and ego orientation and perceived purpose of sport among male and female high school athletes', *Journal of Sport & Exercise Psychology*, 11, 318–35.

Duda, JL 1992, 'Sport and exercise motivation: a goal perspective analysis', in G Roberts (ed.), *Motivation in sport and exercise*, Human Kinetics, Champaign, IL, pp. 57–91.

Duda, JL 1993, 'Goals: a social cognitive approach to the study of motivation in sport', in RN Singer, M Murphey & LK Tennant (eds), *Handbook on research in sport psychology*, Macmillan, New York, pp. 421–36.

Duda, JL 1997, 'Perpetuating myths: a response to Hardy's 1996 Coleman Griffith address', *Journal of Applied Sport Psychology*, 9, 307–13.

Duda, JL & Chi, L 1989, 'The effect of task- and ego-involving conditions in basketball', paper presented at the annual meeting of the Association for the Advancement of Applied Sport Psychology, University of Washington, Seattle, WA, September.

Duda, JL, Chi, L & Newton, M 1990, 'Psychometric characteristics of the TEOSQ', paper presented at the annual meeting of the North American Society for the Psychology of Sport and Physical Activity, University of Houston, TX.

Duda, JL, Chi, L, Newton, M, Walling, MD & Catley, D 1995, 'Task and ego orientation and intrinsic motivation in sport', *International Journal of Sport Psychology*, 26, 40–63.

Duda, JL & Hall, HK 2000, 'Achievement goal theory in sport: recent extensions and future directions', in RN Singer, HA Hausenblas & CM Janelle (eds), *Handbook of sport psychology*, 2nd ed., John Wiley & Sons, New York, pp. 417–43.

Duda, JL & Nicholls, JG 1992, 'Dimensions of achievement motivation in schoolwork and sport', *Journal of Educational Psychology*, 84, 1–10.

Duda, JL, Smart, A & Tappe, M 1989, 'Personal investment in the rehabilitation of athletic injuries', *Journal of Sport & Exercise Psychology*, 11, 367–81.

Duda, JL & White, SA 1992, 'The relationship of goal perspectives to beliefs about success among elite skiers', *The Sport Psychologist*, 6, 334–43.

Duda, JL & Whitehead, J 1998, 'Measurement of goal perspectives in the physical domain', in J Duda (ed.), *Advances in sport and exercise psychology measurement*, Fitness Information Technology, Morgantown, WV, pp. 21–48.

Dweck, CS 1986, 'Motivational processes affecting learning', *American Psychologist*, 41, 1040–8.

Dweck, CS & Leggett, EL 1988, 'A social cognitive approach to motivation and personality', *Psychological Review*, 95, 1–18.

Elliott, ES & Dweck, CS 1988, 'Goals: an approach to motivation and achievement', *Journal of Personality and Social Psychology*, 46, 26–43.

Epstein, J 1989, 'Family structures and student motivation: a developmental perspective', in C Ames & R Ames (eds), *Research on motivation in education*, vol. 3, Academic Press, New York, pp. 259–95.

Hall, HK 1988, 'A social-cognitive approach to goal setting: the mediating effects of achievement goals and perceived ability', unpublished doctoral dissertation, University of Illinois at Urbana, Champaign, IL.

Harter, S 1978, 'Effectance motivation reconsidered: toward a developmental model', *Human Development*, 1, 34–64.

Hom, H, Duda, JL & Miller, A 1993, 'Correlates of goal orientations among young athletes', *Pediatric Exercise Science*, 5, 168–76.

Huang, I & Chi, L 1994, 'The relationships of perceived motivational climate and perceived ability to competitive state anxiety and team satisfaction in basketball', *Taiwan Bulletin of Physical Education*, 18, 321–32.

Jourden, FJ, Bandura, A & Banfield, J 1991, 'The impact of conceptions of ability on self-regulatory factors and motor skill acquisition', *Journal of Sport & Exercise Psychology*, 8, 213–26.

Kavussanu, M & Roberts, GC 1996, 'Motivation in physical activity contexts: the relationship of perceived motivational climate to intrinsic motivation and self-efficacy', *Journal of Sport & Exercise Psychology*, 18, 254–80.

Lee, Z & Chi, L 1998, 'The effects of goal orientation, perceived competence, and commitment on task choice after failures', *Taiwan Bulletin of Physical Education*, 25, 219–28.

Lin, S 1995, 'The effects of goal orientation and perceived competence on effort and performance in a stabilometer task', unpublished master's thesis, National College of Physical Education and Sports, Tauyuan, Taiwan.

Locke, EA & Latham, GP 1984, *A theory of goal setting and task performance*, Prentice Hall, Englewood Cliffs, NJ.

Maehr, ML 1984, 'Meaning and motivation: toward a theory of personal investment', in R Ames & C Ames (eds), *Research on motivation in education, volume 1: student motivation*, Academic Press, New York, p. 144.

Maehr, ML & Braskamp, L 1986, *The motivation factor: a theory of personal investment*, Lexington Books, Lexington, MA.

Miller, A 1985, 'A developmental study of the cognitive basis of performance impairment after failure', *Journal of Personality and Social Psychology*, 49, 529–38.

Newsham, S 1989, 'The effects of a task-oriented physical education program on the self-perception of third, fourth, and fifth grade students', unpublished doctoral dissertation, University of Southern California, Los Angeles.

Newton, ML & Duda, JL 1993, 'Elite adolescent athletes' achievement goals and beliefs concerning success in tennis', *Journal of Sport & Exercise Psychology*, 15, 437–48.

Newton, ML & Duda, JL 1995, 'The relationship of goal orientations and expectations on multi-dimensional state anxiety', *Perceptual and Motor Skills*, 81, 1107–12.

Newton, ML & Duda, JL 1999, 'The interaction of motivational climate, dispositional goal orientation and perceived ability in predicting indices of motivation', *International Journal of Sport Psychology*, 30, 63–82.

Newton, ML, Duda, JL & Yin, Z 2000, 'The Perceived Motivational Climate in Sport Questionnaire–2: a test of the hierarchical factor structure', *Journal of Sport Science*, 18, 275–90.

Newton, ML & Fry, MD 1998, 'Senior Olympians' achievement goals and motivational responses', *Journal of Aging and Physical Activity*, 6, 256–70.

Nicholls, JG 1976, 'Effort is virtuous, but it's better to have ability: evaluative responses to perceptions of effort and ability', *Journal of Research in Personality*, 10, 306–15.

Nicholls, JG 1978, 'The development of concepts of effort and ability, perception of academic attainment, and the understanding that difficult tasks require more ability', *Child Development*, 49, 800–14.

Nicholls, JG 1984a, 'Achievement motivation: conceptions of ability, subjective experience, task choice, and performance', *Psychological Review*, 91, 328–46.

Nicholls, JG 1984b, 'Conceptions of ability and achievement motivation', in R Ames & C Ames (eds), *Research on motivation in education: student motivation*, vol. 1, Academic Press, New York, pp. 39–73.

Nicholls, JG 1989, *The competitive ethos and democratic education*, Harvard University Press, Cambridge, MA.

Nicholls, JG 1990, 'What is ability and why are we mindful of it? A developmental perspective', in RL Sternberg & J Kolligian, Jr (eds), *Competence considered*, Yale University Press, New Haven, CT, pp. 11–40.

Nicholls, JG 1992, 'The general and the specific in the development and expression of achievement motivation', in G Roberts (ed.), *Motivation in sport and exercise*, Human Kinetics, Champaign, IL, pp. 31–56.

Nicholls, JG, Cobb, P, Wood, T, Yackel, E & Patashnick, M 1990, 'Assessing students' theories of success in mathematics: individual and classroom differences', *Journal for Research in Mathematics Education*, 21, 109–22.

Nicholls, JG, Cheung, P, Lauer, J & Patashnick, M 1989, 'Individual difference in academic motivation: perceived ability, goals, beliefs, and values', *Leaning and Individual Differences*, 1, 63–84.

Nicholls, JG, Jagacinski, CM & Miller, AT 1986, 'Conceptions of ability in children and adults', in R Schwarzer (ed.), *Self-related cognitions in anxiety and motivation*, Lawrence Erlbaum Associates, Hillsdale, NJ, pp. 262–84.

Nicholls, JG & Miller, AT 1983, 'The differentiation of the concepts of difficulty and ability', *Child Development*, 54, 951–9.

Nicholls, JG & Miller, AT 1984, 'Reasoning about the ability of self and others: a developmental study', *Child Development*, 55, 1990–9.

Nicholls, JG & Miller, AT 1985, 'Differentiation of the concepts of luck and skill', *Developmental Psychology*, 21, 76–82.

Ntoumanis, N & Biddle, SJH 1998, 'The relationship between competitive anxiety, achievement goals, and motivational climates', *Research Quarterly for Exercise and Sport*, 69, 176–87.

Ommundsen, Y & Pedersen, BH 1999, 'The role of achievement goal orientations and perceived ability upon somatic and cognitive indices of sport competition trait anxiety: a study of young athletes', *Scandinavian Journal of Medicine and Science in Sports*, 9, 333–43.

Pelletier, LG, Fortier, MS, Vallerand, RJ, Tuson, KM, Briere, NM & Blais, MR 1995, 'Toward a new measure of intrinsic motivation, extrinsic motivation, and amotivation in sports: the Sport Motivation Scale (SMS)', *Journal of Sport & Exercise Psychology*, 17, 35–53.

Peng, W & Chi, L 1996, 'The effects of goal orientations on attributions and emotions after a one-on-one basketball game', paper presented at the annual meeting of the North American Society for the Psychology of Sport and Physical Activity, Ontario, Canada.

Plant, R & Ryan, RM 1985, 'Self consciousness, self-awareness, ego involvement, and intrinsic motivation: an investigation of internally controlling styles', *Journal of Personality*, 53, 435–49.

Powell, B 1990, 'Children's perceptions of classroom goal structure and related motivational processes', unpublished master's thesis, University of Illinois, Urbana, IL.

Roberts, GC 1986, 'The perception of stress: a potential source and its development', in MR Weiss & DR Gould (eds), *Sport for children and youths*, Human Kinetics, Champaign, IL, pp. 119–26.

Roberts, GC 1992, 'Motivation in sport and exercise: conceptual constraints and convergence', in G Roberts (ed.), *Motivation in sport and exercise*, Human Kinetics, Champaign, IL, pp. 3–30.

Roberts, GC & Balague, G 1991, 'The development and validation of the Perception of Success Questionnaire', paper presented at the FEPSAC Congress, Cologne, Germany, September.

Roberts, GC, Treasure, DC & Balague, G 1998, 'Achievement goals in sport: the development and validation of the Perception of Success Questionnaire', *Journal of Sport Science*, 16, 337–47.

Seifriz, J, Duda, JL & Chi, L 1992, 'The relationship of perceived motivational climate to intrinsic motivation and beliefs about success in basketball', *Journal of Sport & Exercise Psychology*, 14, 375–91.

Treasure, DC & Roberts, GC 1998, 'Relationship between female adolescents' achievement goal orientations and perceptions of the motivation climate, belief about success and sources of satisfaction in basketball', *International Journal of Sport Psychology*, 29, 211–30.

Treasure, DC, Standage, M & Lochbaum, M 1999, 'Perceptions of the motivational climate and situational motivation in elite youth sport', paper presented at the annual meeting of the Association for the Advancement of Applied Sport Psychology, Banff, Canada, October.

Vallerand, RJ & Fortier, MS 1998, 'Measures of intrinsic and extrinsic motivation in sport and physical activity: a review and critique', in J Duda (ed.), *Advancements in sport and exercise psychology measurement*, Fitness Information Technology, Morgantown, WV, pp. 83–100.

Vealey, RS & Campbell, JL 1988, 'Achievement goals of adolescent figure skaters: impact on self-confidence, anxiety and performance', *Journal of Adolescent Research*, 3 (2) 227–43.

Walling, MD 1994, 'Children's conceptions of effort and ability in the physical and academic domain', unpublished doctoral dissertation, Purdue University, Indiana.

Walling, MD, Duda, JL & Chi, L 1993, 'The Perceived Motivational Climate in Sport Questionnaire: construct and predictive validity', *Journal of Sport & Exercise Psychology*, 15, 172–83.

Weiner, B 1979, 'A theory of motivation for some classroom experiences', *Journal of Educational Psychology*, 71, 3–25.

Weiner, B 1985, 'An attribution theory of achievement motivation and emotion', *Psychological Review*, 92, 548–73.

Weitzer, JE 1989, 'Childhood socialization into physical activity: parental roles in perceptions of competence and goal orientation', unpublished master's thesis, University of Wisconsin, Milwaukee.

White, SA 1998, 'Adolescent goal profiles, perceptions of the parent-initiated motivational climate, and competitive trait anxiety', *The Sport Psychologist*, 12, 16–28.

White, SA & Zellner, S 1996, 'The relationship between goal orientation, beliefs about the causes of sport success, and trait anxiety among high school, intercollegiate, and recreational sport participants', *The Sport Psychologist*, 10, 58–72.

CHAPTER 7

SELF-CONFIDENCE IN SPORT AND EXERCISE

Tony Morris & Stefan Koehn

Confidence is an essential element of successful performance in any sphere, not least sport and exercise. Examples abound of sport players and teams who have demonstrated their ability but whose performance goes through troughs that seem like they will never end. Rehabilitation from heart attack provides a ready example of the role of confidence in the area of exercise activity. Although knowledge is gradually increasing in the community, the reaction of many people to suffering a heart attack is to believe that they are invalids. The last thing they would imagine they can do in the future is vigorous exercise. Their confidence is low and their return to health-supporting physical activity levels must be a slow, gradual process in which confidence is built on the achievement of small, step-by-step goals.

Although sport and exercise psychologists have long been aware of the important role of confidence, it is only recently that conceptual frameworks have begun to emerge from within sport psychology. Martens and colleagues (Martens, Burton, Vealey, Bump & Smith 1983; Martens, Vealey & Burton 1990) identified a state self-confidence construct in the work on multidimensional state anxiety. They also included a measure of state self-confidence in the instrument they developed to assess cognitive and somatic anxiety — namely, the Competitive State Anxiety Inventory–2 (CSAI-2) (Martens et al. 1990). Sport psychologists have done little to develop the state self-confidence concept directly; the focus over much of the past 20 years has been on somatic and cognitive anxiety. Nonetheless substantial evidence about state self-confidence has emerged, largely owing to its inclusion in much of the research on state anxiety, which has typically employed the CSAI-2. Jones and Swain (1992) proposed that inclusion of a directional measure of state anxiety (facilitative–debilitative) would enhance theory and research. Jones and Hanton (2001) have argued that self-confidence should be conceived as a moderator of state anxiety. In such a conceptualisation, self-confidence would play a central role in the cognitive processes that influence motivation and affect in athletes. Vealey (1986), one of Martens' colleagues, developed a state–trait conceptualisation of self-confidence in sport, which she termed sport confidence, and examined scales to measure the trait and the state components separately. Vealey included a third variable, competitive orientation, in a carefully specified model, which she tested in a number of studies. Although the underlying rationale for Vealey's trait–state approach seemed promising, researchers were slow to take it up. Ultimately, Vealey, Hayashi, Garner-Holman and Giacobbi (1998) proposed a new conceptualisation of sport confidence, integrating the trait and state components. Vealey's work represents the most concerted attempt to develop a sport-specific theoretical framework that will help us understand the role of self-confidence in sport.

One approach to self-confidence that has proved fruitful in sport is based on the concept of self-efficacy, which has gained substantial support from research (Feltz & Lirgg 2001). Bandura (1977, 1982) developed the concept of self-efficacy as a central construct in his social learning theory and then in his reframed social cognitive theory (Bandura 1986). Feltz applied self-efficacy to sport as early as 1979 (Feltz, Landers & Raeder 1979), and she has since been a major contributor to the development of the concept (e.g. Feltz 1982, 1988a; Feltz, Chase, Moritz & Sullivan 1999; Feltz & Lirgg 1998; Feltz & Mugno 1983; Feltz & Riessinger 1990; Garza & Feltz 1998; George, Feltz & Chase 1992). She has written a number of reviews of the theoretical base, the measurement of self-efficacy and empirical work in sport (Feltz 1988b; Feltz 1992; Feltz & Chase 1998; Feltz & Lirgg 2001). Self-efficacy has also been the subject of promising research in exercise psychology, particularly in relation to sedentary populations, obesity, heart problems and diabetes (Feltz & Lirgg 2001; McAuley 1992a; Morris 1995).

In this chapter we aim to address the three main approaches to self-confidence that have emerged in the sport and exercise psychology literature during the past 25 years. We will consider self-efficacy first, because it was developed before the other conceptions and was the first approach to be examined in sport (Feltz et al. 1979). State self-confidence will be considered next, because Martens et al. (1983) identified it during the development of the CSAI-2 in the early 1980s. Then we will examine Vealey's (1986; Vealey et al. 1998) conceptions of sport confidence, because the trait–state model was developed in Vealey's doctoral work, which was conducted in parallel with her involvement in the development of the CSAI-2 and seems to reflect a similar underlying notion to Martens' trait–state conception of anxiety in sport. In considering each approach to self-confidence in sport, we will first define the central confidence concept(s) and distinguish between it and the other conceptions, then we will discuss theory relating to the concept and measurement of it, and finally we will review research that has focused on or employed that conception of self-confidence. To conclude the chapter we will consider future directions in self-confidence in sport, and draw some conclusions.

SELF-EFFICACY IN SPORT AND EXERCISE

Definition

Bandura (1986) defined self-efficacy as the belief that individuals have in their capability to perform a particular task. It is a cognitive process by which the individuals form a subjective judgement of their ability to meet certain environmental demands. The point that self-efficacy is a subjective perception — that is, it reflects what the person believes, rather than accurately representing the true state of affairs — is crucial to the role of self-efficacy as a conceptualisation of self-confidence. Thus a swimmer standing on a diving board may well have the physical capability to perform an acceptable dive, but while he believes that he cannot — that is, while his self-efficacy is low — he is unlikely to launch off towards the water. Observers would probably say that he lacked the confidence to perform the dive. Conversely, many people whose self-efficacy is clearly higher than their capability are observed to jump from the diving board. The mismatch between self-efficacy and ability is obvious from their disorganised and often painful entry into the water; this condition is commonly called 'overconfidence'!

Self-efficacy and true capability are usually not very different for tasks with which the person is familiar, as previous performance is a major source of information for the cognitive, self-referential process of self-efficacy. Thus, for example, the gymnast who performed several successful back somersaults on the beam in her previous training session is likely to have a high level of self-efficacy for the back somersault when asked to perform it in the present session. It is the gymnast who fell on her last attempt in the previous session or the one who is being asked to perform this advanced move for the first time whose self-efficacy is likely to be low, with a consequent negative effect on performance.

Self-efficacy is considered by Bandura (1977, 1986) to be task-specific. A person can have high self-efficacy for tennis and low self-efficacy for football, perhaps based on self-assessment that, although his ball skills are strong, he finds it difficult to pay attention to all the stimuli operating in a football match, and his fear of hard physical contact makes him hesitant. Further, it is a rare performer of a multi-skill task like tennis whose confidence in performance of every skill in the game is equally high. For example, a great serve and volley exponent such as Mark Philippoussis might have felt much lower self-efficacy for his backhand drive from the baseline, if pinned back there on a clay court by the hard, deep groundstrokes of a player of the style and class of Andre Agassi.

As well as being an indicator of self-confidence, self-efficacy is also considered to have a close relationship with motivation. Bandura (1986) argued that level of self-efficacy will influence individuals' choice of activity, high self-efficacy tasks being preferred to low ones; the amount of effort they expend on the activity, greater self-efficacy leading to greater effort; and the level of persistence in the activity when faced with adversity, higher self-efficacy being associated with greater persistence. Choice, effort and persistence are all major elements of motivation.

To summarise, self-efficacy refers to individuals' belief in their capability to execute a specific task or sub-component of a multi-component task. It influences both motivation and actual performance. People's perception of their self-efficacy for a task, at any time, results from a cognitive process, involving past experience and the current context. That cognitive process is part of a larger network of processes, which Bandura (1986) described as social cognitive theory.

Self-efficacy theory

Self-efficacy is part of a complex social cognitive theory, within which its action is linked to a number of other variables (Bandura 1986). It is not appropriate to delineate Bandura's social cognitive theory in detail here. Instead, we will discuss two key elements that are particularly relevant to the application of the theory in sport and exercise. These are the relationship between self-efficacy and outcome expectancy and the antecedents of self-efficacy.

Self-efficacy and outcome expectancy

In sports research, self-efficacy has frequently been examined independently — that is, without accompanying analysis of the other major aspects of Bandura's (1986) theory (e.g. Feltz & Riessinger 1990; Fitzsimmons, Landers, Thomas & van der Mars 1991; McAuley 1985a). Less often, outcome expectation is also studied, most commonly in exercise research (e.g. Dzewaltowski 1989; Godding & Glasgow 1985).

Bandura (1977, 1986) has long argued that an incentive, as well as sufficient self-efficacy, is necessary for behaviour to occur. That incentive is often outcome expectancy, a person's belief that their behaviour will lead to certain outcomes. In the exercise context, Dzewaltowski (1989) argued that people can have different outcome expectancies, such as that exercise will make them healthy, improve their appearance or reduce stress. When that outcome is desirable, it adds incentive. Dzewaltowski has measured outcome expectation as a multiplicative function of the expected outcomes and their respective values to the individuals being studied. One reason why outcome expectation has not often been considered in the competitive sports context could be that most sports performers, especially at the elite level, have high outcome expectancy, and when a variable is uniformly high or low it can hardly act as a sensitive predictor. Research on self-efficacy in areas other than sport has typically found that only efficacy expectations play a significant explanatory role (e.g. Dzewaltowski 1989; Kingery & Glasgow 1989). Bandura (1986) expressed the view that in activities in which efficacy perceptions are directly linked to task outcomes, outcome expectation will not add information, but where efficacy and outcome are dissociated, outcome expectation may add significant variance. So far, as Dzewaltowski (1989) concluded, research on exercise has not revealed the expected dissociation.

Antecedents of self-efficacy

Self-efficacy has been shown to be a key variable in successful performance in sport and in exercise behaviour (Feltz & Lirgg 2001; McAuley 1992a, 1992c). Thus the issue of raising self-efficacy is central to interventions designed to increase confidence and enhance performance. Bandura (1986) proposed four major antecedents of self-efficacy — that is, factors that influence the level and strength of self-efficacy. These are performance accomplishments, vicarious experience, verbal persuasion and physiological state.

Performance accomplishments

The most convincing source of information in the cognitive process of self-assessment or self-persuasion (Feltz 1992), which produces self-efficacy beliefs, is performance accomplishments (Bandura 1997). Experiences of success provide direct evidence of capability, whereas failure experiences raise doubts. Bandura (1986) also proposed that success in a more difficult task will enhance self-efficacy to a greater extent than success in an easy one. Similarly, achieving success independently will be more efficacious than achieving the same level of success attained with support from other people. When success is attained without expending a great deal of effort, it implies greater ability than when great effort must be expended. Tasks performed well on the first few attempts engender greater efficacy than those where failures occur early in learning.

Vicarious experience

In sport and exercise, individuals must perform skills they have never performed before, perhaps involving an element of risk or a new technique. In competition, a person may face an opponent for the first time. Self-efficacy in these situations cannot be based on the individual's own previous experience. Observing somebody else perform the new skill successfully or beat the unknown opponent can enhance that observer's self-efficacy for the task, especially if the person watched, called the model, is similar to the observer in skill and other relevant characteristics. Bandura did a great deal of research on this social comparison process, called vicarious experience (e.g. Bandura 1969; Bandura, Blanchard & Ritter 1969; Bandura, Ross & Ross 1961) before the first publication of his social learning theory (Bandura 1977). The potency of vicarious experiences is diminished when the individual has some personal experience of the task, but it is important in situations like those described earlier, where the person is going into unknown territory. George, Feltz and Chase (1992) and Weiss, McCullagh, Smith and Berlant (1998) demonstrated that the gender and skill of the model affected vicarious experience, but when the model had a level of ability similar to that of the participant, ability was a more important characteristic than the gender of the model.

A technique that is now commonly used by elite sports performers is to repeatedly watch videotapes of their best performances. Bandura (1997) argued that it is through its impact on self-efficacy beliefs that 'self-modelling' affects performance. Feltz and Lirgg (2001) noted that research on self-modelling is limited and unclear. In a study in which collegiate hockey players watched self-modelling videotapes for several weeks, shooting accuracy increased more than in a control condition and self-efficacy for performance was higher (Singleton & Feltz 1999). Winfrey and Weeks (1993) found no increase in self-efficacy for balance beam performance among female gymnasts using self-modelling videotapes. Feltz and Lirgg emphasised that Singleton and Feltz followed Bandura's microanalytic method of measurement whereas Winfrey and Weeks did not.

Verbal persuasion

Coaches and team-mates often spend time persuading players that they have the capability to meet specific task demands, such as to beat the next opponent or to make the next qualifying standard. This is a common application of Bandura's (1986) third antecedent of self-efficacy, verbal persuasion. The persuasion is likely to be more effective if the person presenting it is perceived to be trustworthy as a source of information and credible — that is, if the persuader is perceived to possess the knowledge or expertise required to make the judgement. The potential for achievement of the task must also be realistic. Even when all these criteria apply, the effect of verbal persuasion is still likely to be weaker than the impact of performance accomplishments. Imagery involving successful performance is another means of communicating ideas. Imagery has been shown to enhance self-efficacy and performance of muscular endurance tasks (Feltz & Riessinger 1990), but performance of such tasks could be improved simply by an increase in effort. Callery and Morris (1997a, 1997b) and She and Morris (1997) found that self-efficacy and performance were enhanced for football and baseball batting skills respectively among high-level performers. The effect of imagery on self-efficacy and performance was noteworthy here, because the participants had high levels before they performed imagery of successful performance, so a ceiling effect might have been expected. Maddux (1995) proposed that imaginal experiences should be considered to be a separate source of self-efficacy.

Physiological state

A common experience in sport is the heightened physiological arousal that is associated with the period immediately before performance. Performers often interpret this as a sign that they are anxious about the performance, thus they begin to suffer from self-doubts. In other words, such physiological arousal can lead to reduced self-efficacy. Where the same physical sensations are interpreted as a signal that the body has been activated and the person is therefore ready to perform optimally, self-efficacy can be enhanced. Feltz (1992) noted that other physiological states, such as fitness, fatigue and pain, can influence judgements of self-efficacy. Some researchers have found that emotional experiences represent a separate category of self-efficacy antecedents. Feltz and Lirgg (2001) reported that Maddux and Meier (1995) indicated that positive affect, such as happiness, exhilaration and tranquillity, is more likely to enhance self-efficacy than negative affect, such as sadness, anxiety and depression.

Bandura (1977) proposed that a reciprocal relationship exists between self-efficacy and performance accomplishments — that is, previous experience of performance influences present level of self-efficacy, and this in turn affects the person's next performance and so on. He called this phenomenon reciprocal determinism. Feltz (1982) found that, although self-efficacy was a strong predictor of the first performance of a back dive, for succeeding dives previous performance became the strongest predictor. More recently, Bandura (1990) has suggested that a similar reciprocal relationship exists between self-efficacy and thought processes. Because the influence of all four antecedents is cognitively mediated, it is likely that all the antecedents of self-efficacy at some point become consequences of self-efficacy later.

Measurement of self-efficacy

Measurement is a crucial factor in the successful development of any concept. Bandura (1977, 1986) took special care to delineate the way in which self-efficacy should be measured. He proposed that a 'microanalytic technique' should be used to assess self-efficacy cognitions. In the area of sport, some researchers have developed rating-scale measures of self-efficacy. We focus on the microanalytic approach, briefly considering rating scale measurement of physical self-efficacy.

The microanalytic approach involves measuring three aspects of self-efficacy — level, strength and generality — for each specific task or each component of a multi-component skill. *Level* of self-efficacy is a measure of the degree of difficulty of the task that individuals believe they can perform successfully. For example, in golf putting, a one-metre putt on a flat green is easier that a 15-metre putt across three levels of a sloping green. Many levels of difficulty exist between these easy and very difficult putts. Golfers could establish a graduated list of eight levels of difficulty of putts. A self-efficacy questionnaire on aerobic exercise for older adults might ask whether a person believes he or she can walk one, two, five or ten kilometres twice a week, representing four levels of self-efficacy for this task. Bandura (1986) proposed that once a list of levels is established, individuals simply check those that they believe they can perform. Substantial pilot work should be carried out to ensure the levels of any task are meaningful to the people to be studied. For example, asking recent heart attack survivors whether they can jog five, seven, ten or twelve kilometres would clearly be inappropriate.

A problem that has not received adequate attention in the measurement of self-efficacy is the distinction between ability and intention. It is possible that the typical instructions of self-efficacy level scales do not make it clear that the issue is whether the individuals are *capable* of performing the activity, not whether they intend to do it. This could add variability to responses, as those making an interpretation based on their intention would say 'no' to levels that they believe themselves capable of performing but that they have no intention of actually performing.

Although the list of levels is already a grading of the task, Bandura (1986) recognised that people do not move from the simplest version of the task up to their limit of self-assessed capability with an equal level of assurance, and then suddenly have no belief at all in the next step. To reflect the way in which confidence varies for different levels that an individual expresses a capability to perform, Bandura included a measure of *strength* of self-efficacy. Strength of self-efficacy assesses the certainty individuals have that they will successfully attain each level or component task. It is usually measured on a scale from 10 to 100, where response is made at 10-point intervals, representing the person's strength of confidence as a percentage. A score of zero is excluded in Bandura's original scoring method, because only those levels of the activity to which the person answered 'yes' are included in the strength measure. Because Bandura used only 10 per cent steps, it is questionable whether the scores are true percentages. An alternative that has been used in research is to employ a scale from 0 to 100 (Dzewaltowski 1989) or even −100 to +100 (e.g. Kingery 1988; Kingery & Glasgow 1989).

It is not entirely clear whether tasks that a person cannot perform should be included in the strength assessment. McAuley (1992a) indicated that 'overall strength of self-efficacy is determined by summing the confidence ratings and dividing by the total number of items comprising the target behavior' (p. 109). Inclusion of the zero scoring items in the final arithmetical division will make a big difference for those with low levels of self-efficacy, greatly reducing their final scores relative to more efficacious respondents. Dzewaltowski (1989) cited the results from two studies by Bandura (Bandura & Cervone 1983, 1986) as support for his decision to exclude level and simply measure strength on a 100-point scale with a zero point.

Bandura considered *generality* of self-efficacy as a measure of the number of domains in which individuals believe they are capable of successful performance. For a highboard diver, level and strength of self-efficacy may be assessed for each specific dive they perform. General diving self-efficacy would then be the average of these. In the exercise context, walking, swimming and bicycle riding would be considered to be different tasks, all of which would have their own self-efficacy level and strength. Again, a global measure of generality could be derived. Some evidence does support generalisation of self-efficacy across sports events (Holloway, Beuter & Duda 1988; McAuley, Courneya & Lettunich 1991). Feltz and Chase (1998) reported that researchers have employed single-item measures of self-efficacy, but they appear to be less sensitive. Ryckman, Robbins, Thornton & Cantrell (1982) produced a global measure of physical self-confidence, the Physical Self-Efficacy Scale (PSES). This 22-item scale, assessing two subscales, perceived physical ability (PPA) and physical self-presentation confidence (PSPC), contradicts Bandura's (1986) advice that a microanalytic approach is most effective. Feltz and Lirgg (2001) reported that research has generally supported Bandura's position with task-specific measures producing larger correlations with performance than global measures (e.g. LaGuardia & Labbe 1993; Mueller 1992; Slanger & Rudestam 1997). There are some ambiguities in the measurement of self-efficacy. Feltz and Chase (1998) and Feltz and Lirgg (2001) consider these issues in more detail.

Research on self-efficacy in sport and exercise

The popularity of research on self-efficacy is reflected in the wide range and large number of studies conducted. In this chapter we can only summarise research on self-efficacy in sport and exercise. We recommend recent reviews and meta-analyses (Feltz & Lirgg 2001; Moritz, Feltz, Fahrbach & Mack, in press). The present summary addresses research on the antecedents of self-efficacy for sport and exercise, studies of self-efficacy and sports performance out of sports competition, research on the self-efficacy–performance relationship during sports competition, and research on self-efficacy and exercise or physical activity.

Antecedents of self-efficacy in sport and exercise

Primarily because self-efficacy is proposed to be an important factor influencing behaviour, including performance, the determination of techniques that reliably enhance self-efficacy has been a central issue for sport and exercise psychologists interested in performance enhancement and exercise promotion. Research has been carried out on the effects of all four antecedents on self-efficacy in a range of sport and exercise settings. A number of studies have looked at more than one antecedent, some actually comparing their relative influence on self-efficacy.

Performance accomplishments

Research considering the influence of performance accomplishments on self-efficacy has consistently found that techniques involving performance accomplishments enhance self-efficacy (e.g. Hogan & Santomier 1984; McAuley 1985b). Feltz, Landers and Raeder (1979) also found that performance accomplishments, in the form of participant modelling, where the learner makes an attempt after the model, strengthened self-efficacy more than modelling alone, whether that modelling was live or recorded on videotape. Lirgg, George, Chase and Ferguson (1996) reported that conceptions of ability and the sex-type of the task (typically suited to males or females) affected the impact of performance accomplishments on self-efficacy. Feltz and Lirgg (2001) indicated that amount of effort expended, perceived difficulty and extent of guidance affect the influence of performance accomplishments. In addition, early success on a task has a positive effect on self-efficacy (Feltz & Lirgg 2001).

Vicarious experience

Vicarious experience has been widely researched, mainly because physical education had a well-established interest in observational learning. Most studies supported modelling as an antecedent of self-efficacy (George, Feltz & Chase 1992; Lirgg & Feltz 1991; McAuley 1985a). George, Feltz and Chase (1992) required female college students to watch a videotaped model perform a leg-extension endurance task and then perform the same task. The five conditions were an athletic male model, an athletic female model, a non-athletic male model, a non-athletic female model and a non-model control condition. A similar model and similarity of ability were more influential than similarity of sex. Weiss, McCullagh, Smith and Berlant (1998) also demonstrated a greater effect of similar models on self-efficacy. Singleton and Feltz (1999) added a dimension by using self-modelling.

Verbal persuasion

Although the use of persuasion is common in sport, few studies have looked at the effect of persuasion on self-efficacy directly. Feltz (1992) included research on the use of self-talk and imagery in her review of 'persuasory efficacy information' (p. 98), as did Feltz and Lirgg (2001). At best, these seem to be examples of self-persuasion. Verbal persuasion by coaches is more common. Another form of persuasion is false feedback. The results of the studies on this are equivocal. Yan Lan and Gill (1984) tried to persuade participants in one group that heightened arousal levels were indicative of superior performance. There was no effect of increasing self-efficacy through this manipulation, but it may have been that participants didn't believe the false feedback. Performance accomplishment has the strongest influence on self-efficacy, so it is difficult to persuade a performer that they have high ability for a task they have failed to accomplish on the last three attempts. Fitzsimmons, Landers, Thomas and van der Mars (1991) considered whether false feedback affected experienced weight-lifters, arguing that much of the previous work was carried out with novices and might not transfer easily to experienced performers. The participants were randomly assigned to one of three conditions: accurate performance information, false positive feedback (lifted more than they had) or false negative feedback (lifted less than they had). Fitzsimmons et al. (1991) found that performance was enhanced by the false positive manipulation, but that previous weight-lifting performance accounted for most of the variance in subsequent performance. Feltz and Riessinger (1990) provided further support for the primacy of performance experiences over persuasion.

Physiological state

Bandura's (1986) fourth antecedent has not often been systematically examined. Fe. (1982, 1988a; Feltz & Mugno 1983) measured physiological arousal and perceiveu autonomic arousal in back diving, a high-avoidance task. The former did not significantly predict self-efficacy, but the latter did. Since both perceived physiological arousal and self-efficacy involve cognitive processing, it is not surprising that they are related, but contextual factors could positively bias the interpretation of actual arousal level. Chase, Feltz, Tully and Lirgg (1994) found that physiological state influenced self-efficacy more in sport and exercise than in non-physical tasks. Schunk (1995) distinguished between the effect of physiological state on self-efficacy and the effect of emotional state. Induction of happy and sad moods was used by Kavanagh and Hausfeld (1986), who induced happy and sad moods to manipulate self-efficacy in strength tasks. They found no consistent pattern of change in self-efficacy associated with mood changes. Maddux and Meier (1995) did find that positive affective states were more likely to enhance self-efficacy than negative affective states. Maddux and Meier did not try to manipulate affective states but measured the states that occurred in the situations.

In summary, research suggests that self-efficacy is influenced by Bandura's (1986) four antecedents. The evidence clearly indicates that performance accomplishments provide the most potent information for judgements of self-efficacy. In many situations where other aspects have been manipulated, incidental information about actual performance has overridden the experimental manipulation. Vicarious experience seems to be a fairly reliable source of effective information on the self-efficacy process, but the research on persuasion, physiological states and affective states is not as substantial or convincing.

Self-efficacy and performance outside competition

A substantial proportion of the research on self-efficacy has considered sport tasks outside of actual sports competition. Reasons include the longstanding pre-eminence of 'experimental' research in sport psychology, involving the need for a high degree of control. This kind of approach is difficult to introduce into the competitive environment. Coaches railed against control conditions. If a manipulation was expected to have a positive effect, they wanted all their athletes to benefit from it. The use in research of manipulations that might have negative effects is, of course, unethical. As a consequence, sport psychology researchers spent a lot of time trying to devise 'field studies'.

The work of Feltz (1982, 1988a; Feltz & Mugno 1983) on back diving stands out in the research on performance of sports skills out of competition, not only because of its seminal position in determining the roles of self-efficacy and performance accomplishments, but also for its early use of sophisticated methods and analysis. Feltz (1982, 1988a; Feltz & Mugno 1983) examined the relationship between self-efficacy, performance accomplishments and physiological arousal, employing causal modelling; her model predicted that self-efficacy would be the strongest predictor of performance on each of four dives. Feltz proposed a reciprocal relationship between self-efficacy and back-diving performance. Results of path analyses revealed that self-efficacy was indeed the major determinant of diving performance on the first dive. For dives two, three and four, however, the major predictor of performance was participants' performance on the previous dive. From trial to trial, previous performance became a stronger predictor of self-efficacy than self-efficacy was of performance. Feltz (1992) noted that 'although a reciprocal relationship between self-efficacy and diving behavior was evidenced, they were not equally reciprocal' (p. 100).

:Auley (1985a) tested models during examination of the relationship of self- and state anxiety to performance of a dive forward roll on the gymnastics beam, ιovice, female undergraduates selected because their pre-task anxiety was high. ⋅ms of modelling were used: aided participant, where a model demonstrated the .ᴗᴏʀ, then supported the participant physically during training trials; and unaided, where the demonstration was made, then participants attempted the move without physical support during training. These conditions were compared with a control group, shown an instructional film on uneven bar exercises. A task-specific self-efficacy measure and the Competitive State Anxiety Inventory (CSAI) (Martens, Burton, Rivkin & Simon 1980) were employed. Results showed that both aided and unaided modelling increased self-efficacy, reduced state anxiety and enhanced performance. McAuley (1985a) also compared two models of the process. The self-efficacy model, based on Bandura's (1977) social learning theory, proposed that self-efficacy is the direct mediator between the modelling treatments and performance. Reduced anxiety is simply a result of increased self-efficacy. For high avoidance tasks, others proposed that anxiety is the mediating variable and self-efficacy is an epiphenomenon — that is, a by-product of the anxiety reduction process. Using path analysis, McAuley (1985a) examined these models. Results favoured the interpretation that self-efficacy was the direct mediating variable.

Self-efficacy and performance in competitive sport

A number of studies have considered the relationship between self-efficacy and performance in competitive sport (Feltz, Bandura & Lirgg 1989; Gayton, Matthews & Burchstead 1986; Lee 1982; McAuley & Gill 1983; Weiss, Weise & Klint 1989). In general, these studies have indicated that higher levels of self-efficacy are associated with superior performance. Weiss, Weise and Klint (1989) measured self-efficacy and performance in young female gymnasts. The gymnasts were competing in state championships. A significant correlation was found between self-efficacy and performance. Feltz's (1982) research indicates that, as personal experience of performance increases, its predictive influence on further performance increases relative to the influence of self-efficacy. At the same time, because performance accomplishment is the most potent antecedent of self-efficacy expectations, self-efficacy becomes a much closer reflection of previous performance, as the individual has more experience of performance. This would explain the correlation found by Weiss et al. between self-efficacy and competitive performance in high-level sports performers.

Studies like the one conducted by Weiss et al. (1989) simply measured self-efficacy and performance and examined the correlation between them. Recently researchers have given interventions to athletes to examine their effects of self-efficacy and performance. In a single-case design, Callery and Morris (1997a) gave elite footballers an imagery program three times a week over much of a season. Self-efficacy was measured weekly using Bandura's (1977) microanalytic technique. Both self-efficacy and performance improved. She and Morris (1997) conducted a very similar study of baseball batters, again over a full competitive season, finding that self-efficacy and performance both increased. Callery and Morris (1997b) raised the idea that self-efficacy might moderate the effect of imagery on performance. To test this, they conducted a field study, but with elite players, performing a key closed football skill, goal kicking. Compared with a control condition, imagery led to an increase in self-efficacy, after four sessions and further increases after eight and 10 sessions. Performance also increased from pre- to post-intervention. Structural equation modelling, a sophisticated causal modelling technique, did not show a significant causal path between self-efficacy, on any occasion,

and performance. Once again, however, Callery and Morris moved from rea.
tition to performance in a controlled environment, in order to examine causal re..
ships between self-efficacy and sports performance.

Self-efficacy and physical activity

Physical activity in the shape of sport and exercise is now recognised as an important
factor in primary health care (Dishman 1988; Haskell 1984) — that is, in preventing a
range of health problems and reducing the risk of contracting debilitating and life-
threatening diseases. It is also a specific component of the treatment in a number of
common diseases — that is, in secondary health care. Its role in such illnesses as coronary heart disease, diabetes, stroke and hypertension is critical (Buckworth & Dishman
2002). In addition, substantial research now indicates that exercise positively influences
mood state and psychological wellbeing (Biddle & Mutrie 2001; Buckworth & Dishman
2002). Although people of all ages and backgrounds do play sport or take regular exercise by choice, a large proportion of the population does not participate in regular
health-promoting physical activity. Often these people are precisely those most at risk
for the diseases already mentioned, because they are overweight, sedentary and older, or
because they lead hectic, stressful lives. As sport psychology has expanded its interest
into the general exercise area, the application of self-efficacy to the problems of
initiation of and adherence to exercise has proved to be a very fruitful avenue for
research and applied interventions.

McAuley (1992a) presented a substantial review of the research on self-efficacy and
exercise behaviour. Among prominent findings are those that relate to the influence of
self-efficacy on exercise in cardiac rehabilitation. Ewart et al. (1986) found that post-
myocardial infarction patients with higher levels of self-efficacy for exercise complied
with prescribed exercise programs more closely than those with lower self-efficacy. The
finding that the physical capabilities of these patients did not predict their compliance
supported Bandura's (1986) proposal that it is the individual's belief in what they are
able to do rather than their actual physical capabilities that is the important factor. Further support for the influence of self-efficacy on effort in treadmill exercise (Ewart,
Taylor, Reese & DeBusk 1983) and cardiac rehabilitation (Taylor, Bandura, Ewart,
Miller & DeBusk 1985) has come from Ewart's group.

Research has also shown self-efficacy to be related to exercise activity in middle-
aged and older adults (McAuley 1991, 1992b; Sallis et al. 1986), sedentary adult women
and self-professed 'unfit' young females (McAuley & Jacobson 1991; McAuley &
Rowney 1990). In addition, self-efficacy explained a significant amount of the variance
in studies where self-reported exercise behaviour was the independent variable
(Dzewaltowski 1989; Dzewaltowski, Noble & Shaw 1990). McAuley (1989) found that
self-efficacy related to adherence to an exercise program. He examined exercise participation during a 10-week program using SEM. Participants were followed up three
months later. Self-efficacy positively affected attendance during the program and perceptions of success when it was over. In addition, self-efficacy influenced self-reported
exercise behaviour, when the participants were questioned about this after three
months.

Self-efficacy remains the most strongly supported approach to self-confidence in
sport and physical activity, reflecting its pre-eminent position in psychology generally.
The four antecedents and their relative potency are well established, as is the concept of
reciprocal determinism between self-efficacy and performance. Applied researchers have
demonstrated that self-efficacy can be enhanced by interventions, such as appropriate
goal setting, mastery experiences and imagery, and that this typically leads to enhanced

performance. While our understanding of self-efficacy and the capacity to manipulate it are encouraging, other approaches to self-confidence in sport deserve mention, and it is to these that we now turn.

COMPETITIVE STATE SELF-CONFIDENCE

Based on the distinction between state and trait anxiety (Spielberger 1966), Martens, Burton, Rivkin and Simon (1980) developed a sport-specific measure of state anxiety in sport, which they called the Competitive State Anxiety Inventory (CSAI). Psychometric properties of this measure were weak, however, so Martens and colleagues then developed a questionnaire based on the distinction made between worrying thoughts or cognitive anxiety and bodily reactions or somatic anxiety (Davidson & Schwartz 1976; Liebert & Morris 1967). The Competitive State Anxiety Inventory–2 (CSAI-2) (Martens, Burton, Vealey, Bump & Smith 1990) was developed to measure cognitive and somatic state anxiety, but Martens et al. found that reversed items intended to measure cognitive anxiety formed an independent factor. Thus the CSAI-2 is situation (sport) specific, measuring cognitive and somatic anxiety and self-confidence as state variables, which has made it one of the most frequently utilised questionnaires in the sport anxiety context (Woodman & Hardy 2001).

Martens, Vealey and Burton (1990) defined cognitive anxiety as the 'mental component of anxiety ... [it] is caused by negative expectations about success or by negative self-evaluation' (p. 6). Athletes' performance is debilitated through negative mental processes (e.g. worry, negative expectations) and intense physiological responses (e.g. increased respiration and heart rate, muscle tension). The somatic component 'refers to the physiological and affective elements of the anxiety experience' (p. 6). Martens et al. (1990) asserted that the cognitive and somatic anxiety components are 'always negative in direction due to their links with negative affect' (p. 6).

In contrast to state anxiety, self-confidence is characterised by positive expectations of success (Lane, Sewell, Terry, Bartram & Nesti 1999). Emerging from a factor analysis, Martens, Burton, Vealey, Bump and Smith (1990) viewed self-confidence 'as the absence of cognitive A[nxiety]-state, or conversely, cognitive A-state as being the lack of self-confidence' (p. 129). Martens et al. hypothesised that self-confidence and cognitive anxiety are located on opposite ends of the same continuum, which means that as athletes' levels of cognitive anxiety rise, the level of self-confidence declines. Correlations between these two measures, however, have typically been not more than moderate, suggesting that CSAI-2 self-confidence is more than simply the inverse of cognitive anxiety.

Martens et al. (1990) hypothesised the conceptual independence of the CSAI-2 subcomponents. Self-confidence and cognitive anxiety were proposed to have a stronger impact on performance than somatic anxiety. So far researchers who employed the CSAI-2 in their studies have focused on state anxiety outcomes. Self-confidence has appeared to be a by-product or a concomitant of multidimensional anxiety theory. Here, however, we consider the status of competitive state self-confidence, as operationalised by the CSAI-2 self-confidence subscale, in its own right.

Theory of competitive state anxiety

To describe and explain the relationship between anxiety and performance was the aim of various models within sport psychology research. Among these theories are the inverted-U hypothesis (Yerkes & Dodson 1908), drive theory (Spence & Spence 1966), zones of optimal functioning (Hanin 1980, 1986), multidimensional anxiety theory (Martens et al. 1990), the catastrophe model (Hardy 1990), and reversal theory (Kerr

1985). In the context of examining the contribution of CSAI-2 self-confidence to the understanding of confidence in sport, the theoretical background for this part of the chapter is based mainly on the development of multidimensional state anxiety theory.

Multidimensional state anxiety was utilised as a theoretical base to assess the influences of physiological and cognitive factors on performance. The inclusion of self-confidence in multidimensional anxiety theory was largely the result of the iterative factor analysis conducted by Martens et al. (1990). Besides the expected factors of cognitive and somatic anxiety, a third component was extracted that was independent from the other components. Negatively and positively phrased items of the cognitive anxiety subscale were found to resolve into separate factors. Once the stability of this factor structure had been demonstrated, theory and research progressed on the three components, namely cognitive anxiety, somatic anxiety and self-confidence.

The multidimensional anxiety theory in sport is underlined by several predictions (Martens et al. 1990). Martens et al. proposed that (a) cognitive anxiety, somatic anxiety and self-confidence are predicted by different antecedents; (b) each component shows a different temporal pattern in anticipation of upcoming competition; and (c) each component reveals a different relationship with performance. Athletes' expectation of success and perceived ability are thought to be the main antecedents for cognitive anxiety and self-confidence (Martens et al. 1990). Jones, Swain and Cale (1990) commented that an uncertainty or decrease of expectations would lead to a lower level of self-confidence and a rise of cognitive anxiety. Martens et al. (1990) proposed that the CSAI-2 subcomponents are based on common antecedents, as well as antecedents that are unique to each component.

Martens et al. (1990) hypothesised that temporal changes of the CSAI-2 subcomponents occur in reference to the proximity of the competition. Self-confidence and cognitive anxiety are predicted to remain relatively stable before competition. Owing to the assumption that both constructs are based on performance expectancies, an increase of either self-confidence or cognitive anxiety is expected when new information changes expectancy. Multidimensional anxiety theory predicts that the constructs of self-confidence, cognitive anxiety and somatic anxiety affect performance in different ways. Martens et al. (1990) hypothesised that cognitive anxiety and self-confidence have a stronger relationship to performance, because both factors are connected to expectancies and social evaluation, which might be present during the entire performance. The effect of somatic anxiety on performance is supposedly less powerful, because of the prediction that somatic anxiety will lower with the onset of physical activity. Martens et al. proposed that self-confidence and performance have a positive linear relationship — that is, the higher the level of confidence, the stronger the actual performance. Contrary to self-confidence, Martens et al. hypothesised that cognitive anxiety shows a negative linear relationship with performance, whereas somatic anxiety and performance are connected in an inverted-U pattern. Emerging out of the development of the CSAI-2, a measure created to assess state anxiety, much less attention has been given to state self-confidence than to cognitive and somatic anxiety. Martens et al. (1990) emphasised the need to conduct more intervention studies to elicit the cause-and-effect relationships among state self-confidence, state anxiety and performance.

Measurement of competitive state anxiety

State self-confidence in sport has been measured as one component of the CSAI-2. The items of the CSAI-2 originated from the first CSAI inventory (Martens et al. 1980), newly composed items and modified items from general state anxiety questionnaires (Liebert & Morris 1967; Schwartz, Davidson & Goleman 1978). The aim was to establish a situation-specific measure of state anxiety in sport (Martens et al. 1990). Factor and discriminant analyses shaped the final CSAI-2 version, with three nine-item subscales termed CSAI-cog (cognitive anxiety subscale), CSAI-som (somatic anxiety subscale) and CSAI-sc (self-confidence subscale). Reliability was measured by Cronbach's alpha in three different samples, ranging from .79 to .90 for each subscale (Martens et al. 1990). All three alpha values for CSAI-2 self-confidence (sample 1 = .88; sample 2 = .87; sample 3 = .90) were higher than the internal coefficients of the state anxiety subscales. Concurrent validity examination between CSAI-2 subscales and anxiety state inventories (the revised Worry-Emotionality Inventory, WEI, Morris, Davis & Hutchings 1981; the Cognitive-Somatic Anxiety Questionnaire, CSAQ, Schwartz et al. 1978; the State Anxiety Inventory, SAI, Spielberger et al. 1970; and the Affect Adjective Checklist, AACL, Zuckerman 1960) revealed negative correlations for CSAI-2 self-confidence, ranging from $r = -.40$ to $r = -.77$ for all scales except the AACL, $r = .66$, which was the only state inventory that did not show a positive relationship with CSAI-cog and CSAI-som.

Critique of the CSAI-2 measure

Although the CSAI-2 has been the measure of choice for studies on state anxiety in sport, researchers have questioned its use and validity (Lane et al. 1999; Woodman & Hardy 2001). Woodman and Hardy argued that evaluations of the intensity scores of the CSAI-2 might be limiting. For instance, athletes who scored similarly on state anxiety scales, but revealed significant differences on state self-confidence, might experience pre-competitive anxiety from different points of view. Thus athletes high in state confidence might be concerned and look forward to an upcoming event, whereas equal levels of state anxiety appear more threatening in connection with low levels of confidence. In order to thoroughly examine the anxiety–performance relationship, Woodman and Hardy advocated a measure that includes intensity, frequency and directionality.

The structural validity of the CSAI-2 was questioned by Lane et al. (1999). Their objections are based on methodology as well as concerns about computer calculation. First, Lane et al. observed that none of the four exploratory factor analyses employed a ratio of participants to items of at least 5:1, as proposed by Tabachnick and Fidell (2001). The ratios in the four studies ranged from 1.5:1 to a maximum of 4.5:1. Martens et al. (1990) included a homogeneous group of undergraduate participants for the validation. Instead of checking the responses in a cross-validation, the re-analysis was based on the same data set. Second, Lane et al. proposed that confirmatory factor analyses are more efficient than the exploratory techniques employed in all the original validation studies of the CSAI-2. The identification of the self-confidence scale was an outcome of the exploratory validation research on cognitive anxiety. Thus it seems to lack a detailed theoretical background. In concordance with Mulaik (1987), Lane et al. (1999) underlined that psychological measures should emerge from theory and not data analyses.

On the one hand, the critiques of the development and validation of CSAI-2 suggest that a re-evaluation of this measure seems to be necessary, and thus findings generated so far by the CSAI-2 seem to be questionable. On the other hand, results for state self-confidence have not been the focus of researchers employing the CSAI-2. Further research needs to be conducted to shed more light on the relationship between state self-confidence and state anxiety.

Directional CSAI-2

Martens et al. (1990) indicated that the CSAI-2 measures state anxiety in terms of intensity and directionality. Martens et al. asserted that the direction of state anxiety is 'always' negative. Swain and Jones (1992) modified the CSAI-2 by adding a direction scale to each of the original items to measure whether the CSAI-2 subcomponents are experienced as facilitative or debilitative. The 7-point directional scale ranges from +3 ('very facilitative') to −3 ('very debilitative'), with 0 as 'unimportant'. Thus the overall score for each CSAI-2 directional scale varies from +27 to −27. When the directional scale was used in combination with the CSAI-2, correlational analyses revealed that the directional measure is more efficient for interpretations on state anxiety than state self-confidence. Jones, Swain and Hardy (1993) found a positive connection between intensity of self-confidence and direction of self-confidence ($r = .80$). This result, supported by recent studies (Fletcher & Hanton 2001), led to the conclusion that both scales essentially measure the same state (Jones & Hanton 2001). The Cronbach alpha coefficients for the direction subscales ranged from .72 to .90 (Jones & Hanton 2001; Jones, Swain & Hardy 1993).

Research in sport

The relationship between CSAI-2 self-confidence and performance has been examined intensively. The studies conducted that included self-confidence will be reviewed in terms of antecedents, temporal patterning, performance and directional perception of state anxiety.

Antecedents of CSAI-2 self-confidence

One of the first studies to focus on antecedents of self-confidence was carried out by Gould, Petlichkoff and Weinberg (1984) on intercollegiate wrestlers. Gould et al. examined various potential precursors of the CSAI-2 subcomponents, such as perceived ability, previous match results, years of experience and trait anxiety (SCAT). Altogether, self-confidence, cognitive anxiety and somatic anxiety were not predicted by one single antecedent. A standardised regression showed a weak relationship between trait anxiety (SCAT) and cognitive anxiety ($r = .32$, $p < .05$) and somatic anxiety ($r = .34$, $p < .05$). Years of experience was negatively related with cognitive anxiety ($r = −.51$, $p < .01$). The strongest relationship, however, was exposed between perceived ability as a predictor of self-confidence ($r = .55$, $p < .01$). The findings of Gould et al. (1984) confirmed Martens et al.'s (1990) hypothesis that the CSAI-2 subcomponents are not based on one single antecedent. The more precise prediction of Martens et al. that perceived ability would predict cognitive anxiety was not corroborated, but the correlation of perceived ability with CSAI-2 self-confidence is noteworthy.

Jones, Swain and Cale (1990) examined situational antecedents of multidimensional competitive state anxiety and self-confidence among intercollegiate middle-distance runners. Jones et al. employed the CSAI-2 and the Pre-Race Questionnaire (PRQ), consisting of five factors, which were perceived readiness, position goal, attitude towards previous performance, external environment and coach influence. Separate stepwise multiple regression analysis revealed that none of the PRQ factors predicted somatic anxiety significantly. Perceived readiness accounted for 23 per cent of the variance, attitude towards performance 3.5 per cent, and position goal another 3.3 per cent of the total variance in cognitive anxiety. All precursors showed a negative relationship with this CSAI-2 subcomponent, which means that the higher the perceived readiness the lower the level of cognitive anxiety. Perceived readiness also accounted for 34.9 per cent of the total variance of self-confidence, and external environment accounted for an additional 4.8 per cent. In contrast to the results on cognitive anxiety, perceived readiness and external environment revealed a positive relationship with self-confidence. Jones et al. summarised that self-confidence and cognitive anxiety are based on common as well as unique situational antecedents. Hanton and Jones (1995), Hardy et al. (1996),

Lane, Terry and Karageorghis (1995), and Martens et al. (1990) supported these findings in general. Lane et al. (1995) proposed that researchers should intensify study of antecedents of anxiety and confidence across sport, between genders and on various competition levels to understand more clearly the relationship between precursors and responses on CSAI-2 self-confidence and state anxiety.

In a similar study, Hanton and Jones (1995) compared antecedents between elite competitive swimmers and intercollegiate middle-distance runners (Jones et al. 1990) by employing the PRQ and the CSAI-2. Hanton and Jones pointed out that data were collected at the Olympic swimming trials, which indicates a higher competitive standard than manifested within the runners' sample (Jones et al. 1990). The mean scores showed that the elite swimmers scored four points higher on the CSAI-2 self-confidence scale than the middle-distance runners (Hanton & Jones 1995). Perceived readiness was the main predictor for both cognitive anxiety and self-confidence, accounting for 5.6 per cent and 30.3 per cent respectively of the total variance. Additionally, cognitive anxiety revealed a negative, and self-confidence a positive, relationship with perceived readiness, whereas somatic anxiety did not show any significant connections.

Temporal patterns of CSAI-2 self-confidence

The CSAI-2 subcomponents of self-confidence, cognitive and somatic anxiety have been examined frequently in terms of pre-competition changes. In several studies, researchers measured the CSAI-2 constructs on various occasions before competition in a time-to-event paradigm (Gould et al. 1984; Jones, Swain & Cale 1991; Martens et al. 1990; Swain & Jones 1993). For instance, participants were repeatedly asked to answer the CSAI-2 in a time frame of two weeks, one week, two days, one day and within one hour before the start of competition. Martens et al. (1990) investigated temporal changes within the validation research of the CSAI-2. They found that self-confidence and cognitive anxiety remained relatively stable as the competition neared. Somatic anxiety, however, showed an increase before the start of competition. Gould et al. (1984) supported these results by questioning 63 female high-school volleyball players on five different occasions before competition. Only somatic anxiety increased significantly before competition. The hypothesis by Martens et al. (1990) that somatic anxiety would increase whereas cognitive anxiety and self-confidence would remain constant before competition was confirmed (Gould et al. 1984).

Jones et al. (1991) conducted a study on temporal patterning and gender differences within university athletes. The athletes, 28 males competing in field hockey and rugby and 28 females competing in field hockey and netball, were questioned one week, two days, one day, two hours and 30 minutes before competition. The results revealed that male athletes generally experienced a higher level of confidence, whereas female athletes reached higher scores on cognitive anxiety. Particularly, the results of male and female athletes on self-confidence and cognitive anxiety appeared contradictory. The confidence level of both genders dropped marginally as the competition approached. The amount of confidence lowered significantly for male athletes between two hours and 30 minutes before competition. The confidence curve of the female athletes proceeded in the same way, except that confidence decreased one day before competition. In terms of cognitive anxiety, male athletes showed a stable pattern, whereas female players revealed a significant increase two hours and 30 minutes before match onset. Also unexpected, no significant variations in the progress of somatic anxiety between genders were found. Jones et al. concluded that temporal patterning might be influenced by the type of sport, in terms of team versus individual sports. Swain and Jones (1993) investigated gender differences within 22 female and 27 male track and field athletes.

Athletes were tested on four occasions in a similar time frame as that applied by Jones et al. (1991) except for the one-week stage. Swain and Jones found few noteworthy results for self-confidence, but the somatic anxiety of both genders increased significantly on every occasion as competition approached.

CSAI-2 self-confidence and performance

The relationship between the CSAI-2 subcomponents and performance is characterised in different ways. Martens et al. (1990) hypothesised a positive linear relationship between self-confidence and motor performance, whereas cognitive anxiety and performance should be linked by a negative linear relationship. Martens et al. predicted that somatic anxiety and performance would show an inverted-U relationship. Cognitive anxiety and self-confidence are hypothesised to have a stronger impact on performance, because both variables were connected with expectancies and social evaluation, which might be present during the entire performance. The effect of somatic anxiety on performance was proposed to be less powerful, because in most sports somatic anxiety was expected to disperse once performance started owing to the effect of intensive physical activity.

Burton (1988) examined the anxiety–performance relationship by employing the CSAI-2 in 28 collegiate swimmers on three different occasions in early season, at mid season and at a Big Ten Championships. Self-confidence and cognitive anxiety were significantly related with performance throughout the various measurements, whereas somatic anxiety reached significance only at mid season. In regression analysis, self-confidence significantly predicted performance on all three occasions. Additionally, cognitive anxiety and somatic anxiety were significant predictors of performance at the mid-season event. Overall, somatic anxiety showed the weakest relationship to performance at all three events. Using trend analysis, Burton did identify the predicted negative linear relationship of cognitive anxiety, the positive linear relationship of self-confidence, and the inverted-U relationship of somatic anxiety and performance.

Gould, Petlichkoff, Simons and Vevera (1987) and Perreault and Marisi (1997) also carried out trend analyses to shed more light into the anxiety–performance relationship. Gould et al. administered the CSAI-2 to 39 students of the University of Illinois Police Training Institute and then measured their shooting performance. Performances were assessed on five different occasions, which included head-to-head and simultaneous competitions for all participants. Trend analyses showed a significant effect for the inverted-U relationship between somatic anxiety and performance. No interpretable trend emerged between cognitive anxiety and performance. Contrary to the hypothesis of Martens et al. (1990), self-confidence and performance had a significant negative linear relationship. Inconsistencies were also reported by Perreault and Marisi (1997) in a sample of 37 elite male wheelchair basketball players. The trend analyses on the CSAI-2 subcomponents did not reveal any significant results as hypothesised by multiple anxiety theory. Neither a linear nor a quadratic trend was found between self-confidence or cognitive anxiety and performance. No quadratic relationship emerged between performance and somatic anxiety. Pointing out the problematic relationship of the anxiety and performance, Jones (1995) asserted that an anxiety measurement acquired some time before competition will not predict performance accurately.

CSAI-2 Self-confidence and the directional perception of anxiety

Because of the inconsistent results of research on pre-competitive state anxiety, state self-confidence and performance, Jones and Swain (1992) added a directional scale to the CSAI-2. To date, research with the directional scale has been illuminating. Jones and Hanton (2001) pointed out that a high level of confidence and anxiety occurring at the same time might still result in successful performance. Jones and Hanton (2001) examined 190 high-standard swimmers employing a modified CSAI-2 and a checklist of feeling state labels. The CSAI-2 subscales of cognitive and somatic anxiety contained a directional scale. Jones and Hanton did not supplement the self-confidence intensity scale with a directional scale. Previous studies revealed that the intensity and direction-ality scores on state self-confidence were highly correlated (e.g. Jones et al. 1993). Jones and Hanton suggested that the intensity and directional components measured essen-tially the same state for self-confidence. The checklist of feeling states was used to reflect on athletes' pre-competitive feeling states as being positive or negative. Both questionnaires were applied one hour or less before competition. Jones and Hanton reported that athletes who experienced cognitive anxiety as facilitative scored signifi-cantly higher on positive feeling states than athletes experiencing cognitive anxiety as debilitative. Conversely, athletes debilitated in cognitive anxiety scored higher on nega-tive labels than facilitated participants. Athletes, whose state anxiety was facilitative experienced more confidence than debilitated athletes. Jones and Hanton (2001) con-cluded that self-confidence might be a crucial mediator in the assessment and interpret-ation of pre-competitive anxiety symptoms. This suggests that athletes' debilitative interpretations might be overcome by increasing their self-confidence.

Research on directionality of anxiety has revealed consistent support for the debili-tative and facilitative interpretations of anxiety (Jones & Swain 1992; Jones, Swain & Hardy 1993; Jones & Hanton 2001). In contrast to the equivocal findings of the original CSAI-2 on intensity of anxiety, the direction scale appears to have value for under-standing the relationship between state self-confidence, state anxiety and performance (Jones 1995). The recent proposal by Jones and Hanton (2001) that self-confidence plays a key moderating role in the determination of state anxiety direction is certainly worthy of further study.

SPORT CONFIDENCE

Sport confidence is a comparatively new term in sport psychology that is defined as 'the belief or degree of certainty individuals possess about their ability to be successful in sport' (Vealey 1986, p. 222). Previous examinations on self-confidence in sport have depended on the adaptation of general theoretical concepts. Self-confidence was largely based on the concept of self-efficacy, which was part of Bandura's social learning and social cognitive theory (Bandura 1977, 1986), as well as perceived competence (Harter 1978), movement confidence (Griffin & Keogh 1982) and expectancy theory (Nelson & Furst 1972; Corbin 1981). In pursuit of a sport-specific approach to confidence, Hardy, Jones and Gould (1996) distinguished between self-efficacy and sport confidence as a 'micro level' and 'macro level of self-confidence, respectively. Whereas the micro-level of self-confidence, as described in self-efficacy theory, is connected with specific skills in practice — for example, the tee shot compared to the putting shot in golf, or serving contrasted with receiving shots in tennis — sport confidence focuses predominantly on the global level of self-confidence that is one's belief in one's ability in golf or tennis (trait sport confidence) or in success in the upcoming golf round or tennis match (state sport confidence).

Incorporating past research into a sport-specific context, Vealey (1986) introduced the conceptual framework of sport confidence. Vealey differentiated sport confidence into two one-dimensional constructs termed trait sport-confidence (SC-trait) and state sport-confidence (SC-state). SC-trait is defined as the belief or degree of certainty indi-viduals *usually* possess about their ability to be successful, whereas SC-state is defined as the belief or degree of certainty individuals possess *at one particular moment* about their ability to be successful in sport (Vealey 1986). The construct of competitive orientation, in terms of outcome- and performance-oriented goals, complemented the sport confidence concept. Over time, athletes are supposed to develop one of these goals more strongly. Attaining a certain type of goal reflects competence and success, and also shows what athletes are confident about (Vealey 1986).

Examinations of the initial dichotomous SC-trait and SC-state approach revealed several limitations that led to a re-conceptualisation of the original model. Instead of dealing with a dispositional and state construct of confidence that promoted incongruities in predicting performance, Vealey (2001) developed the integrated model to view sport confidence as a single construct lying on a continuum that varies from trait-like to state-like. Vealey, Hayashi, Garner-Holman and Giacobbi (1998) also extended the original model of sport confidence from a situational into a sociocultural context, including the athlete's characteristics and the organisational culture on which sport confidence is built. Furthermore, Vealey et al. (1998) proposed that various sources of sport confidence mediate the actual level of sport confidence. Vealey (2001) viewed sport confidence as a multidimensional construct that represents the athletes' confidence in their ability to accomplish physical, perceptual and psychological skills, as well as physical fitness, training status and learning potential and, ultimately, to improve their own abilities.

There have been substantive efforts in the development and extension of the sport-specific construct of confidence, which culminated in the integrative model of sport confidence. Several authors (Hardy et al. 1996; Vealey 1988; Weinberg & Gould 2003) addressed one main issue in the research of confidence in sport as the 'catch-22 dilemma'. The catch-22 dilemma refers to the correlation between whether athletes possessed a certain amount of self-confidence that enabled them to compete at a high level and whether they developed a high confidence level because of high performance achievements. Breaking this impasse may be one of the main challenges within sport confidence research. It is to be hoped that future investigations based on the conceptual framework as offered by the new sport confidence model will find fruitful ways out of this quandary.

Theory of sport confidence

The sport confidence model has evolved over the years through three distinctive stages. The foundation of the original conceptual framework of sport confidence was spurred on by the insufficiencies of applying general psychological concepts in a sport context. Vealey (1986) argued that, 'based upon this past research, it seems that a valid, parsimonious operationalization of self-confidence would allow more consistent prediction of behaviors across different sport situations' (p. 222). Extending this early approach, Vealey et al. (1998) included several sources of sport confidence. These sources are hypothesised to influence the level of confidence, which subsequently influences the performance outcome. Finally, Vealey (2001) has developed an integrative model of sport confidence. Although the innovations and adjustments of the final model are minor, the pursuit of sport confidence as a 'unifying framework' (p. 555) for both researchers and practitioners indicated a change of perspective to promote further possibilities for fruitful research.

The original model of sport confidence (Vealey 1986) consists of three main constructs. These were conceptualised as trait sport confidence (SC-trait), state sport confidence (SC-state) and competitive orientation. Vealey viewed SC-trait as a dispositional and SC-state as a state construct of self-confidence, whereas she included competitive orientation to measure the specific goal upon which sport confidence is based. That is, athletes are expected to develop either a performance- or an outcome-oriented disposition on which their evaluations of ability and success are based. Vealey (1986) proposed that SC-trait in conjunction with competitive orientation will influence the SC-state for any given sport situation. Based on the interaction of SC-trait and competitive orientation goals, SC-state mediates behavioural responses, which subsequently results in subjective outcomes. Subjective outcomes are manifested as causal attributions, perceived success and emotions. Vealey (1986) underlined the crucial position of subjective outcomes within the model, interacting with SC-trait and competitive orientation in a reciprocal manner.

In terms of reconceptualising and extending the original model, Vealey et al. (1998) incorporated two innovations to the extended model. First, Vealey et al. identified and discriminated between different sources of confidence underlying and affecting the level of sport confidence. Second, Vealey et al. viewed athletes as functioning within a unique sociocultural background. The sociocultural background is implicated by the organisational culture and the individual characteristics of the athletes. Both components are thought to have significant influences on the sources of sport confidence. Depending on the organisation, Vealey et al. (1998) asserted that the competitive level, the motivational climate, coaching behaviour and expected athletic commitment have a certain impact on the sources of sport confidence. The athletes' characteristics include personal (e.g. attitudes, values), demographic (e.g. gender, age) and ethnic (e.g. origin) features. Competitive orientation that was also conceptualised in the original model of sport confidence (Vealey 1986) appears in this context as one of the main personality characteristics.

Vealey et al. (1998) established nine sources of sport confidence, which are categorised into domains of achievement (Mastery, Demonstration of Ability), self-regulation (Physical and Mental Preparation, Physical Presentation) and social climate (Social Support, Coaches' Leadership, Vicarious Experience, Environmental Comfort, Situational Favourableness). The first domain includes sources of achievement termed as Mastery and Demonstration of Ability, which means that confidence can be derived from improving individual skills or mastering. In correspondence to self-efficacy theory, this domain emerged from Bandura's (1986) source of performance accomplishments (Vealey 2001). In association with improvement in individual skill level, athletes can also gain confidence from demonstrating their skills against opponents in competition. The mastery and demonstration of ability sources are related to achievement goal orientations (see chapter 6).

Vealey et al. (1998) separated the second domain, embracing aspects of self-regulation, into Physical/Mental Preparation and Physical Self-presentation. The former facilitates level of confidence through the belief in being physically and mentally prepared to perform well. Physical self-presentation represents the athlete's body image. Issues of self-presentation and self-perception are often illustrated in terms of physical conditioning and appearance.

The third domain, which Vealey et al. (1998) referred to as social climate, focuses on social processes that are inherent in achievement situations. Social support is perceived to be one of the most important sources for building confidence. The support of family, coaches and team-mates, especially in teenage years, constitutes a high amount of athletes' sources of self-confidence. Coaches' decision making is a crucial aspect of the relationship between coach and athlete. Weinberg and Gould (2003) pointed out that coaches' inaccurate and inflexible expectations may lead to inappropriate behaviours of the coach, which in turn may affect athletes' confidence disadvantageously. Environmental comfort refers to athletes' feelings about the competitive environment and venue where the competition takes place (Vealey 2001). The final source of sport confidence, situational favourableness, refers to athletes' perception that the entire situation, including breaks, is favourable for the competition outcome. In this context, the level of confidence and the psychological momentum might be crucial components of athletes' performance.

The integrated model of sport confidence (Vealey 2001) primarily focuses on the constructs of sport confidence, sources of sport confidence and consequences of sport confidence. These consequences are athletes' affect (A), behaviour (B) and cognition (C), which Vealey labelled the ABC triangle. Within the integrative model, Vealey viewed sport confidence as a multidimensional construct — that is, confidence about physical, psychological and perceptual skills, adaptability, current fitness and training level, learning potential, decision making and the ability to improve.

Vealey (2001) observed that the background for this model includes demographic and personality characteristics, as well as organisational aspects that are predicted to have an influence on the sources and consequences of sport confidence. Vealey proposed that the identified source domains of confidence, achievement, self-regulation and social climate would predict the present level of sport confidence and interact with the ABC triangle. The athletes' response in terms of affect, behaviour and cognition is a crucial point within the theoretical model. The ABC response, the way the athlete feels, thinks and acts, manifests how and why the level of confidence might have influenced athletes' performance. The constructs constituting the ABC triangle are hypothesised to influence the outcome of performance most directly. Thus they are proposed to be important for performance enhancing interventions (Vealey 2001).

Vealey (2001) hypothesised that the interaction between sources of sport confidence, the actual level of sport confidence and the ABC triangle would follow a reciprocal relation. Vealey also hypothesised that athletes' level of sport confidence would continuously interplay with affect, behaviour and cognition. Hence, high levels of confidence would have a certain effect on the way athletes feel, behave and think, which in turn influences the level of confidence. A result of the interaction between sources and levels of confidence, as well as related affects, cognitions and behaviours, is athletes' performance. The performance outcome is also thought to re-influence the constructs from which it emerged, echoing Bandura's (1977) concept of reciprocal determinism that was discussed earlier in this chapter.

In summary, the integrative model of sport confidence proposed by Vealey and colleagues (Vealey et al. 1998; Vealey 2001) offers a more comprehensive view of confidence in sport than her earlier trait–state model. Interrelations between sources and levels of sport confidence and subsequent affects, behaviours and cognitions offer a wide range of research opportunities to understand why and how confidence has such a distinctive effect on performance.

Measurement of sport confidence

Parallel to the development and extensions of the sport confidence model, several questionnaires have been introduced. On the operational level, the original model of sport confidence was measured by three inventories. These are the Trait Sport Confidence Inventory (TSCI), the State Sport Confidence Inventory (SSCI) and the Competitive Orientation Inventory (COI). In exploring the revised model, Vealey et al. (1998) developed and employed the Sources of Sport Confidence Questionnaire (SSCQ).

Trait and state confidence inventories

Focusing on the initial measures of self-confidence, the TSCI assesses athletes' dispositional sport confidence, whereas the SSCI measures athletes' confidence level in sport-specific situations (e.g. upcoming competition). Both inventories ask the participants to compare themselves to the 'most confident athlete you know' (Vealey 1986, pp. 244–6), either in general (TSCI) or with reference to a specific competition (SSCI). The inventories each consist of 13 items, both utilising a 9-point Likert scale anchored by 1 (*low*) and 9 (*high*). Final scores are obtained by adding up scores for the 13 items. The wording of the 13 items is identical for the TSCI and SSCI, but the trait and state context differentiates between the two inventories (Feltz & Chase 1998).

Vealey (1986) validated the questionnaires in a five-phase study. Vealey reported that the TSCI and SSCI revealed adequate results in terms of item discrimination, test–retest reliability, internal consistency, concurrent validity and content validity. The results showed that the TSCI and SSCI each measures a one-dimensional construct. Cronbach's alpha coefficient was measured as .93 for the TSCI and .95 for the SSCI. Test–retest reliability for the TSCI was reasonable, being between .83 and .86 on each occasion. As hypothesised, the results revealed SC-trait and competitive orientation were predicting SC-state. However, the interaction between SC-trait and competitive orientation was not evident for the subjective outcomes. Also unexpected, no significant relationship was found between SC-trait and performance or between SC-state and performance. Some criticism has emerged based on these incongruities.

Critique of the TSCI and SSCI measures

Feltz and Chase (1998) have criticised the format that is inherent in the TSCI and SSCI measures. The respondents are asked to compare their confidence level with that of another athlete who is believed to be the most outstanding. Feltz and Chase pointed out that the format of the TSCI and SSCI might generate unsystematic variance, because respondents are most likely to compare their standard of confidence with the confidence level of different athletes they consider being most confident. Short and Vadocz (2002) quoted Kauss (1980), who asserted that the sole comparison with other athletes could undermine the athletes' own confidence level. As a result of such criticism, Short and Vadocz (2002) have examined the modifiability of the State Sport Confidence Inventory by removing the 'comparison' component from the inventory. The original and the modified version of the SSCI were given to a rather small sample consisting of 31 female figure skaters and the results of both inventories compared afterwards. In accordance with Kauss's critique, the modified version revealed higher scores in total and for every single item than the original version. Short and Vadocz (2002) found incongruities within the variances of both SSCI versions. Scores of the modified items accounted for 9 to 59 per cent of the variances in original item scores. Based on these findings, Short and Vadocz concluded that the modified version is not an adequate representation of the original version, because both are meant to measure the same construct.

The Sources of Sport Confidence Questionnaire

Vealey et al. (1998) established the Sources of Sport Confidence Questionnaire (SSCQ) consisting of nine subscales (Mastery, Demonstration of Ability, Physical/Mental Preparation, Physical Self-Presentation, Social Support, Coach's Leadership, Vicarious Experience, Environmental Comfort and Situational Favourableness), with 43 items overall. Participants responded on a 7-point Likert scale anchored by 1 (*not at all important*) and 7 (*of highest importance*). The internal consistency values, measured by Cronbach's Alpha, were beyond the .70 criterion for all subscales, except for the variable Physical Self-Presentation. At that stage only two items were loaded on the Physical Self-Presentation scale. Vealey et al. (1998) decided to keep the scale and add further items to increase reliability.

Confirmatory factor analysis (CFA) supported the nine-factor structure. The 'goodness-of-fit' of the overall model was not well supported. The correlations between the SSCQ subscales ranged between .02 and .61. Vealey et al. (1998) pointed out that subscales that correlated more highly were expected to show a correspondence because of their conceptual proximity. For instance, Mastery and Physical/Mental Preparation stemmed from the same achievement domain and therefore showed the highest correlation. Although support was found for the SSCQ's being a reliable and valid measure of multidimensional sources of sport confidence, a weakness was the relatively low ratio between variables and participants. To overcome this shortcoming, further verification of the SSCQ as a valid measure of sources of sport confidence is necessary.

Research in sport

The research conducted by Vealey and colleagues (1986, 1988, 2001; Vealey, Hayashi, Garner-Holman & Giacobbi 1998) embraced several aspects of sport confidence. We briefly consider validation of the TSCI, SSCI and SSCQ, testing the theory, examining correlates of sport confidence, and investigating the relationship between confidence and performance.

Validating the measures

TSCI and SSCI

Vealey (1986) assessed the psychometric properties of the constructs of trait sport confidence (SC-trait), state sport confidence (SC-state) and competitive orientation through a five-phased study. To assess the internal structure of the TSCI and SSCI, 99 high-school and 101 college/adult athletes of both genders were involved in Phase 1. Vealey carried out a factor analysis including oblique and varimax rotations. Factors that showed eigenvalues less than 1.0 were removed from the validation. The factor analysis revealed no separate factors indicating that the TSCI and SSCI measure a unidimensional construct. In Phase 2, all items revealed acceptable values on item discrimination coefficients, item-total correlation coefficients (< .50), variability and items contributed positively to alpha. Phase 3 indicated acceptable values (> .60) on the test–retest reliability for the TSCI. Concurrent validity was measured in Phase 4 (Vealey 1986), correlating the TSCI and SSCI with related constructs (see page 199 on correlates of sport confidence). In Phase 5, Vealey (1986) examined construct validity — that is, whether the operational constructs of TSCI and SSCI are valid instruments to measure the theoretical constructs of sport confidence. A sample of 48 elite gymnasts was included to examine the relationship between SC-trait, SC-state, competitive orientation and performance. TSCI and COI were administered 24 hours before competition and athletes completed the SSCI within two hours before and after the competition. The results corroborated the hypothesis that SC-trait and competitive orientation have an influence on SC-state. A strong correlation was found between performance-orientation, outcome-orientation and SC-trait with pre-competitive SC-state. Actual performance was rated by the first-round mean scores obtained from the judges. A median split divided the group into high and low SC-trait participants and high and low COI-performance participants. Athletes high in SC-trait and performance orientation showed significantly higher performance scores than high SC-trait athletes with outcome orientation or athletes low in SC-trait. Subsequent multiple regression analysis between SC-trait and performance with post-competitive SC-state, as criterion variable, revealed a significant relationship. Performance accounted for 13 per cent and SC-trait for 20 per cent of the variance, respectively, in post-competitive SC-state scores. In correspondence with Feltz (1982), Vealey (1986) concluded that the prediction from performance to subsequent self-confidence levels was stronger than the prediction from self-confidence to performance. Even though the results revealed adequate support for the hypothesised constructs in terms of item discrimination, internal consistency, test–retest reliability, concurrent validity and content validity, the predictions and interactions between the components remained largely unclear in this research.

SSCQ

Vealey et al. (1998) conducted a four-phase study to identify preliminary sources of confidence, to examine the perceived importance of these sources, to validate the questionnaire's psychometric properties, and to evaluate the relationship between sources of sport confidence and SC-trait. Throughout the phases, the initial items were revised until the final version of nine sources of confidence emerged. Data of 208 male and female high-school basketball players (Vealey et al. 1998) were utilised to evaluate the multidimensional factor structure of the Sources of Sport Confidence Questionnaire (SSCQ). Adequate scores were found for the goodness-of-fit index, the adjusted goodness-of-fit and the root mean square residual. The internal consistency coefficients for all scales were higher than .70, except for Physical Self-Presentation. Vealey et al. increased the alpha value for Physical Self-Presentation by generating additional items. Initial results look promising, but more work is needed to thoroughly examine the psychometrics of the SSCQ.

Testing the theory

Sport confidence

In an addendum to the sport confidence construct, Vealey (1988) focused on gender differences in individual and team sports. As indicated by previous research (Corbin 1981), the expectation was that female athletes experience lower confidence levels than male athletes in association with motor performances. Vealey's (1988) examination included a sample of 103 male and 144 female athletes from various sports, such as tennis, track and field, baseball, softball, basketball and gymnastics. The Trait Sport Confidence Inventory (TSCI) was applied to high-school ($n = 103$), college ($n = 96$), and elite athletes ($n = 48$) of different performance levels. Female athletes at high-school and college level revealed lower SC-trait scores than males, but there was no significant difference between the SC-trait scores of female and male participants at an elite level. Therefore, Vealey (1988) suggested that in the context of gender differences and confidence, the performance level should be taken into consideration.

Sources of sport confidence

Vealey et al. (1998) hypothesised that athletes develop a competitive orientation that, in turn, might influence the sources of sport confidence. In a sample of 187 athletes of both genders and from various sports, a multivariate analysis of variance revealed a significant difference between outcome-oriented athletes and performance-oriented athletes in relation to the SSCQ subscales. Differences between the two groups were investigated by a discriminant function analysis. Physical/Mental Preparation, Demonstration of Ability and Environmental Comfort discriminated most between the two groups. Athletes with performance orientation favoured Physical/Mental Preparation, whereas outcome-oriented athletes proposed that Environmental Comfort and Demonstration of Ability were more important.

The conceptual model of sport confidence predicts that the level of SC-trait has an effect on the athlete's cognition, affect and behaviour. To examine this, Vealey et al. (1998) investigated whether SC-trait influences the variables of intrinsic motivation, self-confidence, cognitive anxiety and somatic anxiety. High- and low-confidence athletes who scored in the upper and lower 40 per cent of the sample were included in further investigations. MANOVA and discriminant function analyses revealed significant differences between high- and low-confidence athletes. Athletes high in SC-trait experienced a higher state of self-confidence, more intrinsic motivation, and less cognitive and somatic anxiety than their low confident counterparts. A significant link between sources of sport-confidence and the constructs of intrinsic motivation, self-confidence, cognitive anxiety and somatic anxiety was not confirmed. Clearly, more research is needed to understand sources and levels of confidence and subsequent influences on athletes' affect, behaviour and cognition.

Correlates of sport confidence

Vealey (1986) examined correlates of trait and state confidence in terms of concurrent validity, namely the SCAT (Martens 1977), the CSAI-2 (Martens et al. 1990), the Physical Self-Efficacy Scale (Ryckman, Robbins, Thornton & Cantrell 1982) and Internal-External Control Scale (Rotter 1966). Pearson's correlation coefficients revealed significant results for all tested constructs except for perceived physical ability, external locus of control and the SSCI. The strongest positive relationships were found between the CSAI-2 self-confidence and SSCI, and the CSAI-2 self-confidence and the TSCI. Negative relationships were revealed between CSAI-2 cognitive anxiety and SSCI. Competitive A-trait was more strongly related to trait sport confidence than to state sport confidence. Significant correlations were also found between the TSCI and physical self-presentation confidence and self-esteem.

Vealey et al. (1998) examined the relationship between sources and levels of sport confidence in 84 female and 103 male athletes from various sports. A regression equation was applied between SSCQ subcomponents and SC-trait. Physical/Mental Preparation emerged as the only significant predictor, accounting for 8 per cent of the variance of SC-trait in male and 10 per cent of variance of SC-trait in female athletes. This means a higher amount of sport confidence was linked with the focus on mental and physical preparation before competition than with other variables measured.

Relating sport confidence to performance

Vealey's (1986) hypothesis that pre-competitive SC-state was a strong predictor of performance could not be confirmed within the validation study. Hoffman (2000), however, confirmed the contention that male high-school basketball players experienced a significantly higher trait and state sport confidence level than female athletes. In contrast, Caserta's (2002) investigation on male and female high-school tennis players revealed that female players reported significantly higher trait and state sport confidence than male tennis players. One explanation for the equivocal results was indicated by Gayton and Nickless (1987), who examined trait and state sport confidence as predictors of performance outcomes for male ($n = 25$) and female ($n = 10$) marathon runners. Both male and female trait and state scores showed a significant relationship to predicted and actual finishing times. The study by Gayton and Nickless (1987) revealed no corroborating results for Vealey's (1986) hypothesis that SC-trait would predict performance more accurately than SC-state. Based on these outcomes, Gayton and Nickless (1987) questioned the utility of Vealey's (1986) concept of separating sport confidence into a trait and state construct.

Vealey (1986) proposed the first sport-specific model of self-confidence, which received relatively little attention, despite its meticulous development in the state–trait mould, so popular at the time. Recently Vealey (2001) has developed a revised model that appears to hold promise, particularly in terms of the early research with the SSCQ.

FUTURE DIRECTIONS

This chapter has considered three conceptualisations of sport confidence, adding discussion on state self-confidence and sport confidence to a review of the substantial work done on self-efficacy in the sport and exercise context. Inclusion of the self-confidence and sport confidence conceptions recognises the efforts of leading sport psychology researchers to develop sport-specific theory and measures. Nonetheless the stage of development of theory and research on self-efficacy is far in advance of the progress made on state self-confidence or sport confidence. In addition, self-efficacy is the only approach that has been applied to non-competitive physical activity at this stage. At this time, it appears that the three conceptions might be applied in different ways, so the continued development of all three seems to be warranted.

The antecedents of self-efficacy are well established, as is its relationship to behaviour, whether in competitive sports or in recreational exercise. There is still potential for further research on the application of self-efficacy interventions. A perspective that has perhaps been neglected is the influence of personal and situational variables on the effectiveness of self-efficacy interventions. Especially in the context of sport, the examination of collective efficacy, such as that of teams, as discussed by Feltz and Lirgg (2001), appears to be a fruitful approach. Another area that has great potential, as noted by Feltz and Lirgg, relates to the examination of the self-efficacy of coaches. How this relates to the self-efficacy of individual athletes, as well as to team efficacy, in team sports is worthy of research. A particular focus here could be the link between coach efficacy, verbal persuasion and athlete efficacy. The more distant connection between coach efficacy and athlete performance might also be examined.

The measurement of competitive state self-confidence is now well established. Introduction of the directional component has helped to clarify why intensity measures did not produce predictable relationships with behaviour and, in particular, performance. At the same time, the role of competitive state self-confidence has not been fully developed, although it has emerged from the status of by-product of the measurement of competitive state anxiety. Our view is that a promising direction is the examination of the role of state self-confidence as a moderator of directional state anxiety. Perhaps a focus on this issue would lead to more research that examines aspects of state self-confidence in its own right, independent of state anxiety.

The original trait–state approach to sport confidence, developed by Vealey (1986), did not receive the attention it deserved. It was theoretically well constructed and Vealey's initial research held promise. More data from a range of sources would have helped to point the direction forward. In the event, Vealey et al. (1998) proposed a new direction for research on sport confidence, moving away from the trait–state conception to a more integrated approach. Given the recognised importance of confidence to athletes, and the need for theory on central variables like sport confidence to be developed in sport psychology (Martens 1987), it is to be hoped that more researchers will study the sources of sport confidence and their links to performance and personal growth.

Confidence is a key element in the pattern of factors that affect involvement in sport, successful performance and, most importantly, enjoyment of the sport experience. It is healthy for research that there is a diversity of conceptions to examine. Practice must also benefit from a wider range of research that increases our understanding of how to develop self-confidence in ways that will enhance the satisfaction that people get from their involvement in sport and physical activity.

CONCLUSIONS

In this chapter we have considered the major theoretical and research approaches to the concept of self-confidence in sport. We noted that the perspectives have different origins — self-efficacy in mainstream psychology, competitive state self-confidence in the study of competitive anxiety, and sport confidence as the development of a theoretically driven view of self-confidence in sport. We have argued that there is strength in this diversity; with different ways of looking at an issue tending to raise a variety of useful insights. We have also pointed out that the three conceptions of self-confidence in sport are at different stages of development. Research support for the antecedents of self-efficacy and for the relationship between self-efficacy and performance is strong. Perhaps the weakness of self-efficacy in practice is its specificity. Strictly, to apply self-efficacy with maximum effectiveness, self-efficacy must be measured separately for every component of each task. Development of the concept of global self-efficacy within a domain such as sport or physical activity is being considered, but is not strongly supported (Feltz & Lirgg 2003). Competitive state self-confidence has been measured reliably and widely in sport research, but mainly as an adjunct to the study of state anxiety. It has been given little attention at a theoretical level. Perhaps the most promising opportunity for this is Jones and Hanton's (2001) suggestion that state self-confidence is a moderator of anxiety direction. Vealey's (1986) original trait–state sport confidence model attracted relatively little research, despite its roots in the Martens et al. (1990) approach to anxiety in sport. The recent integrated conception of sport confidence deserves to fare better, given the need for the development of sport-specific theory. Self-confidence is recognised today to be one of the, if not the, most important and ubiquitous factors in enjoyment and success in sport and physical activity. We look forward to continued development of approaches to help us understand it more deeply.

SUMMARY

In this chapter we have identified three approaches to self-confidence in sport and physical activity, which have been relatively widely developed — these are self-efficacy, competitive state self-confidence and sport confidence. In each case, we reviewed the approach's definition, theory, measurement and research. We pointed out strengths and weaknesses and proposed future directions for work on each concept. We concluded that it is healthy for researchers to be exploring diverse conceptions and advised practitioners to take advantage of insights deriving from the study of each approach to self-confidence in sport.

 REVIEW QUESTIONS

1   What is self-efficacy? How is it related to effort and persistence?
2   What are the four antecedents of self-efficacy?
3   What is the microanalytic technique?
4   What is the relationship between self-efficacy and sport performance?
5   Define competitive state self-confidence. How is it usually measured?
6   What role do Jones and Hanton (2001) propose that self-confidence plays in determination of the direction of state anxiety?
7   How would you define sport confidence?
8   How are trait sport confidence, state sport confidence and competitive orientation related?
9   What are the proposed sources of sport confidence?

References

Bandura, A 1969, *Principles of behavior modification*, Holt, Rinehart & Winston, New York.

Bandura, A 1977, 'Self-efficacy: toward a unifying theory of behavior change', *Psychological Review*, 84, 191–215.

Bandura, A 1982, 'Self-efficacy mechanism in human agency', *American Psychologist*, 37, 122–47.

Bandura, A 1986, *Social foundations of thought and action*, Prentice Hall, Englewood Cliffs, NJ.

Bandura, A 1990, 'Perceived self-efficacy in the exercise of human agency', *Journal of Applied Sport Psychology*, 2, 128–63.

Bandura, A 1997, *Self-efficacy: the exercise of control*, WH Freeman, New York.

Bandura, A, Blanchard, EB & Ritter, B 1969, 'The relative efficacy of desensitization and modeling approaches for inducing behavioral, affective and attitudinal changes', *Journal of Personality and Social Psychology*, 13, 173–99.

Bandura, A & Cervone, D 1983, 'Self-evaluative and self-efficacy mechanisms governing the motivational effects of goal systems', *Journal of Personality and Social Psychology*, 45, 1017–28.

Bandura, A & Cervone, D 1986, 'Differential engagement of self-reactive influences in cognitive motivation', *Organizational Behaviors and Human Decision Processes*, 38, 92–113.

Bandura, A, Ross, D & Ross, S 1961, 'Transmission of aggression through imitation of aggressive models', *Journal of Abnormal and Social Psychology*, 63, 575–82.

Biddle, SJH & Mutrie, N 2001, *Psychology of physical activity: determinants, well-being, and interventions*, Routledge, New York.

Buckworth, J & Dishman, RK 2002, *Exercise psychology*, Human Kinetics, Champaign, IL.

Burton, D 1988, 'Do anxious swimmers swim slower? Reexamining the elusive anxiety-performance relationship', *Journal of Sport & Exercise Psychology*, 10, 45–61.

Callery, P & Morris, T 1997a, 'The effects of an imagery program on self-efficacy and performance of an Australian Rules football skill', in R Lidor & M Bar-Eli (eds), *Proceedings of the IX World Congress of Sport Psychology*, ISSP, Netanya, Israel, pp. 175–7.

Callery, P & Morris, T 1997b, 'Imagery, self-efficacy and goal-kicking performance', in R Lidor & M Bar-Eli (eds), *Proceedings of the IX World Congress of Sport Psychology*, ISSP, Netanya, Israel, pp. 169–71.

Caserta, RJ 2002, *Sport-confidence as related to performance in male and female tennis players*, Microform Publications, University of Oregon, Eugene, OR.

Chase, MA, Feltz, DL, Tully, DC & Lirgg, CD 1994, 'Sources of collective and individual efficacy in sport', *Journal of Sport & Exercise Psychology*, 16, S18.

Corbin, CB 1981, 'Sex of subject, sex of opponent, and opponent ability as factors affecting self-confidence in a competitive situation', *Journal of Sport Psychology*, 3, 265–70.

Davidson, RJ & Schwartz, GE 1976, 'The psychobiology of relaxation and related states: a multi-process theory', in D Mostofsky (ed.), *Behavioral control and modification of physiological activity*, Prentice Hall, Englewood Cliffs, NJ, pp. 399–442.

Dishman, RK (ed.) 1988, *Exercise adherence: its influence on public health*, Human Kinetics, Champaign, IL.

Dzewaltowski, DA 1989, 'Toward a model of exercise motivation', *Journal of Sport & Exercise Psychology*, 11, 251–69.

Dzewaltowski, DA, Noble, JM & Shaw, JM 1990, 'Physical activity participation: social cognitive theory versus the theories of reasoned action and planned behavior', *Journal of Sport & Exercise Psychology*, 12, 388–405.

Ewart, CK, Stewart, KJ, Gillian, RE, Keleman, MH, Valenti, SA, Manley, JD & Kaleman, MD 1986, 'Usefulness of self-efficacy in predicting overexertion during programmed exercise in coronary artery disease', *American Journal of Cardiology*, 57, 557–61.

Ewart, CK, Taylor, CB, Reese, LB & DeBusk, RF 1983, 'Effects of early post myocardial infarction exercise testing on self-perception and subsequent physical activity', *American Journal of Cardiology*, 51, 1076–80.

Feltz, DL 1982, 'Path analysis of the causal elements of Bandura's theory of self-efficacy and an anxiety-based model of avoidance behavior', *Journal of Personality and Social Psychology*, 42, 764–81.

Feltz, DL 1988a, 'Gender differences in the causal elements of self-efficacy on a high avoidance motor task', *Journal of Sport & Exercise Psychology*, 10, 151–66.

Feltz, DL 1988b, 'Self-confidence and sports performance', in KB Pandolf (ed.), *Exercise and Sports Science Reviews*, 16, 423–58.

Feltz, DL 1992, 'Understanding motivation in sport: a self-efficacy perspective', in GC Roberts (ed.), *Motivation in sport and exercise*, Human Kinetics, Champaign, IL, pp. 93–105.

Feltz, DL, Bandura, A & Lirgg, CD 1989, 'Perceived collective efficacy in hockey', in D Kendzierski (Chair), 'Self-perceptions in sport and physical activity: self-efficacy and self-image', symposium conducted at the meeting of the American Psychological Association, New Orleans, August.

Feltz, DL & Chase, MA 1998, 'The measurement of self-efficacy and confidence in sport', in JL Duda (ed.), *Advances in sport and exercise psychology measurement*, FIT Press, Morgantown, WV, pp. 65–80.

Feltz, DL, Chase, MA, Moritz, SE & Sullivan, PJ 1999, 'Development of the Multi-dimensional Coaching Efficacy Scale', *Journal of Educational Psychology*, 91, 765–76.

Feltz, DL, Landers, DM & Raeder, U 1979, 'Enhancing self-efficacy in high avoidance motor tasks: a comparison of modeling techniques', *Journal of Sport Psychology*, 1, 112–22.

Feltz, DL & Lirgg, CD 1998, 'Perceived team and player efficacy in hockey', *Journal of Applied Psychology*, 83, 557–64.

Feltz, DL & Lirgg, CD 2001, 'Self-efficacy beliefs of athletes, teams, and coaches', in RN Singer, HA Hausenblas and CM Janelle (eds), *Handbook of sport psychology*, 2nd edn, John Wiley & Sons, New York, pp. 340–61.

Feltz, DL & Mugno, DA 1983, 'A replication of the path analysis of the causal elements in Bandura's theory of self-efficacy and the influence of autonomic perception', *Journal of Sport Psychology*, 5, 263–77.

Feltz, DL & Riessinger, CA 1990, 'Effects of in vivo emotive imagery and performance feedback on self-efficacy and muscular endurance', *Journal of Sport & Exercise Psychology*, 12, 132–43.

Fitzsimmons, PA, Landers, DM, Thomas, JR & van der Mars, H 1991, 'Does self-efficacy predict performance in experienced weightlifters?', *Research Quarterly for Exercise and Sport*, 62, 424–31.

Fletcher, D & Hanton, S 2001, 'The relationship between psychological skills usage and competitive anxiety responses', *Psychology of Sport and Exercise*, 2, 89–101.

Garza, DL & Feltz, DL 1998, 'Effects of selected mental practice on performance, self-efficacy, and competition confidence in figure skaters', *The Sport Psychologist*, 12, 1–15.

Gayton, WF, Matthews, GR & Burchstead, GN 1986, 'An investigation of the validity of the Physical Self-efficacy Scale in predicting marathon performance', *Perceptual and Motor Skills*, 63, 752–4.

Gayton, WF & Nickless, CJ 1987, 'An investigation of the validity of the trait and state sport-confidence inventories in predicting marathon performance', *Perceptual and Motor Skills*, 65, 481–2.

George, TR, Feltz, DL & Chase, MA 1992, 'Effects of model similarity on self-efficacy and muscular endurance: a second look', *Journal of Sport & Exercise Psychology*, 14, 237–48.

Godding, PR & Glasgow, RE 1985, 'Self-efficacy and outcome expectancy as predictors of controlled smoking status', *Cognitive Therapy and Research*, 9, 591–3.

Gould, D, Petlichkoff, L, Simons, J & Vevera, M 1987, 'Relationship between competitive state anxiety inventory–2 subscale scores and pistol shooting performance', *Journal of Sport Psychology*, 9, 33–42.

Gould, D, Petlichkoff, L & Weinberg, RS 1984, 'Antecedents of, temporal changes in, and relationships between CSAI-2 subcomponents', *Journal of Sport Psychology*, 6, 289–304.

Griffin, NS & Keogh, JF 1982, 'A model for movement confidence', in JAS Kelso & J Clark (eds), *The development of movement control and coordination*, John Wiley & Sons, New York, pp. 213–36.

Hanin, YL 1980, 'A study of anxiety in sport', in WF Straub (ed.), *Sport psychology: an analysis of athletic behavior*, Movement, Ithaca, NY, pp. 236–49.

Hanin, YL 1986, 'State trait anxiety research on sports in the USSR', in CD Spielberger & R Diaz (eds), *Cross-cultural anxiety*, vol. 3, Hemisphere, Washington, DC, pp. 45–64.

Hanton, S & Jones, G 1995, 'Antecedents of multidimensional state anxiety in elite competitive swimmers', *International Journal of Sport Psychology*, 26, 512–23.

Hardy, L 1990, 'A catastrophe model of anxiety and performance', in GJ Jones & L Hardy (eds), *Stress and performance in sport*, John Wiley & Sons, Chichester, UK, pp. 81–106.

Hardy, L, Jones, JG & Gould, D 1996, *Understanding psychological preparation for sport*, John Wiley & Sons, Chichester, UK.

Harter, S 1978, 'Effectance motivation reconsidered: toward a developmental model', *Human Development*, 21, 34–64.

Haskell, WL 1984, 'Overview: health benefits of exercise', in JD Matarrazzo, SM Weiss, JA Herd, WE Miller & SM Weiss (eds), *Behavioral health: a handbook of health enhancement and disease prevention*, John Wiley & Sons, New York, pp. 409–23.

Hoffman, JD 2000, *Sport-confidence and perceptions of coaching behavior of male and female high school basketball players*, Microform Publications, University of Oregon, Eugene, OR.

Hogan, PI & Santomier, JP 1984, 'Effects of mastering swim skills on older adults' self-efficacy', *Research Quarterly for Exercise and Sport*, 56, 284–96.

Holloway, JB, Beuter, A & Duda, JL 1988, 'Self-efficacy and training for strength in adolescent girls', *Journal of Applied Social Psychology*, 18, 699–719.

Jones, JG 1995, 'More than just a game: research developments and issues in competitive anxiety in sport', *British Journal of Psychology*, 86, 449–78.

Jones, JG & Hanton, S 2001, 'Pre-competitive feeling states and directional anxiety interpretations', *Journal of Sport Sciences*, 19, 385–95.

Jones, JG & Swain, ABJ 1992, 'Intensity and direction dimensions of competitive anxiety and relationships of competitiveness', *Perceptual and Motor Skills*, 74, 467–72.

Jones, JG, Swain, ABJ & Cale, A 1990, 'Antecedents of multidimensional competitive state anxiety and self-confidence in elite intercollegiate middle-distance runners', *The Sport Psychologist*, 4, 107–18.

Jones, JG, Swain, ABJ & Cale, A 1991, 'Gender differences in precompetition temporal patterning and antecedents of anxiety and self-confidence', *Journal of Sport & Exercise Psychology*, 13, 1–15.

Jones, JG, Swain, ABJ & Hardy, L 1993, 'Intensity and direction dimensions of competitive state anxiety and relationships with performance', *Journal of Sports Sciences*, 11, 525–32.

Kauss, DR 1980, *Peak performance: mental game plans for maximizing your athletic potential*, Prentice Hall, Englewood Cliffs, NJ.

Kavanagh, D & Hausfeld, S 1986, 'Physical performance and self-efficacy under happy and sad moods', *Journal of Sport Psychology*, 8, 112–23.

Kerr, JH 1985, 'A new perspective for sport psychology', in MJ Apter, D Fontana & S Murgatroyd (eds), *Reversal theory: applications and developments*, University College Cardiff Press, Cardiff, UK, pp. 89–102.

Kingery, PM 1988, 'Self-efficacy and outcome expectations in the self-regulation of non insulin dependent diabetes mellitus', unpublished doctoral dissertation, University of Oregon, Eugene, OR.

Kingery, PM & Glasgow, RE 1989, 'Self-efficacy and outcome expectations in the self-regulation of non-insulin dependent diabetes mellitus', *Health Education*, 20, 13–19.

LaGuardia, R & Labbe, EE 1993, 'Self-efficacy and anxiety and their relationship to training and race performance', *Perceptual and Motor Skills*, 77, 27–34.

Lane, AM, Sewell, DF, Terry, PC, Bartram, D & Nesti, MS 1999, 'Confirmatory factor analysis of the Competitive State Anxiety Inventory–2', *Journal of Sports Sciences*, 17, 505–12.

Lane, AM, Terry, P & Karageorghis, C 1995, 'Antecedents of multidimensional competitive state anxiety and self-confidence in duathletes', *Perceptual and Motor Skills*, 80, 911–19.

Lee, C 1982, 'Self-efficacy as a predictor of performance in competitive gymnastics', *Journal of Sport Psychology*, 4, 405–9.

Liebert, RM & Morris, LW 1967, 'Cognitive and emotional components of test anxiety: a distinction and some initial data', *Psychological Reports*, 20, 975–8.

Lirgg, CD & Feltz, DL 1991, 'Teacher versus peer model revisited: effects on motor performance. *Research Quarterly for Exercise and Sport*, 62, 217–24.

Lirgg, CD, George, TR, Chase, MA & Ferguson, RH 1996, 'Impact of conception of ability and sex-type of task on male and female self-efficacy', *Journal of Sport & Exercise Psychology*, 18, 426–43.

Maddux, JE (ed.) 1995, 'Self-efficacy theory: an introduction', in JE Maddux (ed.), *Self-efficacy, adaptation, and adjustment: theory, research, and application*, Plenum, New York, pp. 3–33.

Maddux, JE & Meier, LJ 1995, 'Self-efficacy and depression', in JE Maddux (ed.), *Self-efficacy, adaptation, and adjustment: theory, research, and application*, Plenum, New York, pp. 143–72.

Martens, R 1977, *Sport competition anxiety test*, Human Kinetics, Champaign, IL.

Martens, R 1987, 'Science, knowledge, and sport psychology', *The Sport Psychologist*, 1, 29–55.

Martens, R, Burton, D, Rivkin, F & Simon, J 1980, 'Reliability and validity of the Competitive State Anxiety Inventory (CSAI)', in CH Nadeau, WR Halliwell, KM Newell & GC Roberts (eds), *Psychology of motor behavior and sport — 1979*, Human Kinetics, Champaign, IL.

Martens, R, Burton, D, Vealey, RS, Bump, LA & Smith, DE 1983, 'The Competitive State Anxiety Inventory–2', unpublished manuscript, University of Illinois, Urbana, IL.

Martens, R, Burton, D, Vealey, RS, Bump, LA & Smith, DE 1990, 'Development and validation of the Competitive State Anxiety Inventory–2', in R Martens, RS Vealey & D Burton (eds), *Competitive anxiety in sport*, Human Kinetics, Champaign, IL, pp. 117–90.

Martens, R, Vealey, RS & Burton, D 1990, *Competitive anxiety in sport*, Human Kinetics, Champaign, IL.

McAuley, E 1985a, 'Modeling and self-efficacy: a test of Bandura's model', *Journal of Sport Psychology*, 7, 283–95.

McAuley, E 1985b, 'Success and causality in sport: the influence of perception', *Journal of Sport Psychology*, 7, 13–22.

McAuley, E 1989, 'Efficacy cognitions and exercise behaviour in young females', unpublished manuscript, Department of Kinesiology, University of Illinois.

McAuley, E 1991, 'Efficacy and attributional determinants of affective reactions to exercise participation', *Journal of Sport & Exercise Psychology*, 14, 237–48.

McAuley, E 1992a, 'Understanding exercise behavior: a self-efficacy perspective', in GC Roberts (ed.), *Motivation in sport and exercise*, Human Kinetics, Champaign, IL, pp. 107–27.

McAuley, E 1992b, 'The role of efficacy cognitions in the prediction of exercise behavior in middle-aged adults', *Journal of Behavioral Medicine*, 15, 65–88.

McAuley, E 1992c, 'Self-referent thought in sport and physical activity', in TS Horn (ed.), *Advances in sport psychology*, Human Kinetics, Champaign, IL, pp. 101–18.

McAuley, E, Courneya, KS & Lettunich, J 1991, 'Effects of acute and long-term exercise responses in sedentary, middle-aged males and females', *The Gerontologist*, 31, 534–42.

McAuley, E & Gill, DL 1983, 'Reliability and validity of the physical self-efficacy scale in a competitive sport setting', *Journal of Sport Psychology*, 5, 410–18.

McAuley, E & Jacobson, LB 1991, 'Self-efficacy and exercise participation in sedentary adult females', *American Journal of Health Promotion*, 5, 185–91.

McAuley, E & Rowney, T 1990, 'The role of efficacy cognitions in adherence and intent to exercise', in L VanderVelden & JH Humphrey (eds), *Psychology and sociology of sport: current selected research*, vol. 2, AMS, New York, pp. 3–15.

Moritz, SE, Feltz, DL, Fahrbach, K & Mack, D (in press), 'The relation of self-efficacy measures to sport performance: a meta-analytic review', *Research Quarterly for Exercise and Sport*.

Morris, L, Davis, D & Hutchings, C 1981, 'Cognitive and emotional components of anxiety: literature review and revised worry-emotionality scale', *Journal of Educational Psychology*, 75, 541–55.

Morris, T 1995, 'Self-efficacy in sport and exercise', in T Morris and J Summers (eds), *Sport psychology: theory, applications and issues*, 1st edn, John Wiley & Sons, Brisbane, pp. 143–72.

Mueller, LM 1992, 'The effect of general and task specific self-efficacy on the performance of a fine motor task', *Journal of Sport Behavior*, 15, 130–40.

Mulaik, SA 1987, 'A brief history of the philosophical foundations of exploratory factor analysis', *Multivariate Behavioural Research*, 22, 267–305.

Nelson, L & Furst, M 1972, 'An objective study of the effects of expectation on competitive performance', *Journal of Psychology*, 81, 69–72.

Perreault, S & Marisi, DQ 1997, 'A test of multidimensional anxiety theory with male wheelchair basketball players', *Adapted Physical Activity Quarterly*, 14, 108–18.

Rotter, JB 1966, 'Generalized expectancies for internal and external control of reinforcement', *Psychological Monographs*, 80 (1) 609.

Ryckman, RM, Robbins, MA, Thornton, B & Cantrell, P 1982, 'Development and validation of a physical self-efficacy scale', *Journal of Personality and Social Psychology*, 42, 891–900.

Sallis, JF, Haskell, WL, Fortnam, SP, Vranisan, MS, Taylor, CB & Solomon, DS 1986, 'Predictors of adoption and maintenance of physical activity in a community sample', *Preventive Medicine*, 15, 331–41.

Schunk, DH 1995, 'Self-efficacy and education and instruction', in JE Maddux (ed.), *Self-efficacy, adaptation, and adjustment: theory, research, and application*, Plenum, New York, pp. 281–303.

Schwartz, GE, Davidson, RJ & Goleman, DJ 1978, 'Patterning of cognitive and somatic processes in the self-regulation of anxiety: effects of meditation versus exercise', *Psychosomatic Medicine*, 40, 321–8.

She, WJ & Morris, T 1997, 'Imagery, self-confidence, and baseball hitting', in R Lidor & M Bar-Eli (eds), *Innovations in sport psychology: linking theory and practice: Proceedings, IXth World Congress of Sport Psychology*, The Wingate Institute for Physical Education and Sport, Netanya, Israel, pp. 626–8.

Short, ES & Vadocz, EA 2002, 'Testing the modifiability of the state sport confidence inventory', *Perceptual and Motor Skills*, 94, 1025–8.

Singleton, DA & Feltz, DL 1999, 'The effect of self-modeling on shooting performance and self-efficacy among intercollegiate hockey players', unpublished manuscript, Michigan State University, East Lansing.

Slanger, E & Rudestam, KE 1997, 'Motivation and disinhibition in high risk sports: sensation seeking and self-efficacy', *Journal of Research in Personality*, 31, 355–74.

Spence, JT & Spence, KW 1966, 'The motivational components of manifest anxiety: drive and drive stimuli', in CD Spielberger (ed.), *Anxiety and behavior*, Academic Press, New York, pp. 291–326.

Spielberger, CD 1966, 'Theory and research on anxiety', in CD Spielberger (ed.), *Anxiety and behavior*, Academic Press, New York, pp. 3–20.

Spielberger, CD, Gorsuch, RI & Lushene, RL 1970, *Manual for the State-Trait Anxiety Inventory*, Consulting Psychologists, Palo Alto, CA.

Swain, ABJ & Jones, G 1992, 'Relationships between sport achievement orientation and competitive state anxiety', *The Sport Psychologist*, 6, 42–54.

Swain, A & Jones, G 1993, 'Intensity and frequency dimensions of competitive state anxiety', *Journal of Sports Sciences*, 11, 533–42.

Tabachnick, BG & Fidell, LS 2001, *Using multivariate statistics*, 2nd edn, Harper & Row, New York.

Taylor, CB, Bandura, A, Ewart, CK, Miller, NH & DeBusk, RT 1985, 'Exercise testing to enhance wives' confidence in their husbands' cardiac capabilities soon after clinically uncomplicated acute myocardial infarction', *American Journal of Cardiology*, 55, 6335–8.

Vealey, RS 1986, 'Conceptualization of sport confidence and competitive orientation: preliminary investigation and instrument development', *Journal of Sport Psychology*, 8, 221–46.

Vealey, RS 1988, 'Sport-confidence and competitive orientation: an addendum on scoring procedures and gender differences', *Journal of Sport & Exercise Psychology*, 10, 471–8.

Vealey, RS, Hayashi, SW, Garner-Holman, M & Giacobbi, P 1998, 'Sources of sport-confidence: conceptualization and instrument development', *Journal of Sport & Exercise Psychology*, 20, 54–80.

Vealey, R 2001, 'Understanding and enhancing self-confidence in athletes', in RN Singer, HA Hausenblas, CM Janelle (eds), *Handbook of sport psychology*, 2nd edn, John Wiley & Sons, New York, pp. 550–65.

Weinberg, RS & Gould, D 2003, *Foundations of sport and exercise psychology*, Human Kinetics, Champaign, IL.

Weiss, MR, McCullagh, P, Smith, AL & Berlant, AR 1998, 'Observational learning and the fearful child: influence of peer models on swimming skill performance and psychological responses', *Research Quarterly for Exercise and Sport*, 69, 380–94.

Weiss, MR, Weise, DM & Klint, KA 1989, 'Head over heels with success: the relationship between self-efficacy and performance in competitive youth gymnastics', *Journal of Sport & Exercise Psychology*, 11, 444–51.

Winfrey, ML & Weeks, DL 1993, 'Effects of self-modeling on self-efficacy and balance beam performance', *Perceptual and Motor Skills*, 77, 907–13.

Woodman, T & Hardy, L 2001, 'Stress and anxiety', in RN Singer, HA Hausenblas & CM Janelle (eds), *Handbook of Sport Psychology*, 2nd edn, John Wiley & Sons, New York, pp. 290–319.

Yan Lan, L & Gill, DL 1984, 'The relationships among self-efficacy, stress responses, and a cognitive feedback manipulation', *Journal of Sport Psychology*, 6, 227–38.

Yerkes, RM & Dodson JD 1908, 'The relation of strength of stimulus to rapidity of habit formation', *Journal of Comparative Neurology and Psychology*, 18, 459–82.

Zuckerman, M 1960, 'The development of an affect adjective check list for the measurement of anxiety', *Journal of Consulting Psychology*, 24, 457–62.

CHAPTER 8

TEAM DYNAMICS

Ken Hodge

> Most leaders tend to view teamwork as a social engineering problem: take x group, add y motivational technique and get z result. But working with the Bulls I've learned that the most effective way to forge a winning team is to call on the players' need to connect with something larger than themselves. Even for those who don't consider themselves 'spiritual' in a conventional sense, creating a successful team — whether it's an NBA champion or a record-setting sales force — is essentially a spiritual act. It requires the individuals involved to surrender their self-interest for the greater good so that the whole adds up to more than the sum of its parts.
>
> Phil Jackson (Chicago Bulls basketball coach, six-time NBA champions; LA Lakers coach, two-time NBA champions), outlining the 'soul of teamwork' (Jackson & Delehanty 1995)

Many of the most popular sports worldwide (such as soccer, basketball, volleyball, rugby, hockey) are team sports; consequently the nature, status and functioning of 'teams' is a logical area in which to apply the principles of sport psychology. By definition, the successful performance of a team, and of individuals within a team, depends on effective team dynamics (e.g. team motivation, cohesion, leadership and communication). Even individual sports, such as swimming, golf, and track and field, are often organised to include team events (e.g. relays, foursomes). In addition, most sportspeople train and practise in squads or teams even if theirs is an individual sport or event.

A common cliché about team sports is that 'a champion team will always beat a team of champions'. A considerable amount of coaching wisdom is reflected in this claim. In interactive team sports each player relies totally on his or her team-mates (including those on the reserves bench and coaches), but the integrated, coordinated effort required to be successful in a team sport can be achieved only by a high degree of 'teamwork'. A 'team of champions' may be more a loose, uncoordinated group of talented players than a real *team*. This raises the interesting and important question, how does a coach or captain identify the key differences between these two types of teams? As a leader, how can you develop a *champion team*? (Hardy & Crace 1997). In this chapter we will examine various theoretical and research issues regarding team dynamics.

There is certainly no shortage of topics to investigate in the area of 'team dynamics'. For example, team or group influences are the basis of team cohesion (Prapavessis, Carron & Spink 1996), team motivation (Hodge & McKenzie 1999), collective efficacy (Spink 1990a, 1990b) and social facilitation (Harkins 1987). Group setting influences such as team-mates, coaches and spectators are significant sources of stress for many players (Prapavessis & Carron 1996; Schellenberger 1990). In addition, teams, squads or groups play an important role in creating a *motivational* climate for individual athletes (Pensgaard & Roberts 2000; Walling, Duda & Chi 1993); and groups or teams play an important *socialising* role, since they act as significant reference groups in sport socialisation (Estrada, Gelfand & Hartmann 1988; Greendorfer 1992).

Despite the clear conceptual rationale for considering the role of group/team dynamics in a number of areas of sport psychology, this role has been neglected for the most part in multivariate investigations. As Widmeyer, Brawley and Carron (1992) observed, sport psychologists often fail to recognise that the group/team has a major influence on individual behaviour and performance in sport. Many of the 'individual-ised' areas in sport psychology (e.g. achievement motivation, goal orientation, attribution, self-confidence, stress and anxiety) are directly influenced by group processes such as social evaluation, social facilitation, expectations by significant others and team cohesion (Hoffman, Bar-Eli & Tenenbaum 1999). Indeed, Widmeyer et al. (1992) concluded that the failure to examine the influence of the group on the individual excludes a major source of variance in the sport behaviour equation.

Notwithstanding this comparative lack of research interest, the issue of team/group dynamics is central to many topic areas in the social psychology of sport, and it is particularly applicable to team sports (Schellenberger 1990; Weinberg & Gould 1999). Consequently more research is needed that examines the group/team setting influences on behaviour. Sport psychologists often use the *interactional* model as a framework for examining social psychological issues in sport — that is, *Behaviour is a function of the Person interacting with the social Environment*, or $B = f(P \times E)$. However, we have been less diligent in investigating situational or *environmental* elements (e.g. team/group setting) than the individual or *person* elements of this model. Given that the interactional model is grounded in social learning theory, we should logically be examining sport issues from an environmental perspective as well as the interactional perspective (Weinberg & Gould 1999). Yet sport psychology has been guilty over the years of an almost exclusive interest in person and, to some extent, interactional issues. The environmental aspects of sport have typically been relegated to the level of a means-to-the-end for understanding the individual, rather than as an important end to be investigated in their own right.

Although it has a clear theoretical base, this chapter is grounded in both pure and applied research (for extensive reviews of the literature, see Carron & Hausenblas 1998; and Widmeyer, Brawley & Carron 1992). Consequently, the following discussion will provide readers with links to 'practical' suggestions for improving team/group processes and, ultimately, team/group performance.

HISTORICAL RETROSPECTIVE

> In a team sport I am a great believer in attitude. Now, how do you motivate a team, considering that all of us have so many different reasons for doing things? For me, that's where the fun was, getting all the players *linked together and thinking as one in a game* ... It's always back to attitude. You can always improve your skills, as a player or a coach, if you've got an open mind, but at international level the key thing is mental.
>
> Lois Muir (New Zealand netball coach, 1974–1987)

In this section the historical literature regarding team dynamics will be reviewed as a precursor to a discussion of current research perspectives in team dynamics. Compared with other areas in sport psychology, team/group dynamics had been the subject of relatively little study until recent years. Nevertheless, there is now a significant body of research, and some clear and important conclusions can be drawn from this literature.

Introduction to 'the' team

Most sport activities involve groups or teams. Even individual sports such as golf and lawn bowls are often conducted as team competitions (e.g. pairs or fours). In addition, even those athletes who compete in individual sports usually practise and train in groups or squads. So we need to understand how teams work from a psychological perspective in order to increase enjoyment, enhance participation and achieve peak performance (Partington & Shangi 1992).

> Road cycling is a team sport as much as hockey is, and I don't think the public realises that. In fact, to be honest, I didn't realise it much myself until I tried it.
>
> Sarah Ulmer (New Zealand cyclist; World Track Cup 'Individual Pursuit' champion, 2000 and 2001; gold medallist, 'Individual Pursuit', 1998 Commonwealth Games)

Team dynamics is clearly an appropriate concern for all athletes in team sports, but it is particularly useful for leaders (i.e. captains and coaches) in team sports (Hodge & McKenzie 1999; Murray & Mann 2001). To achieve effective team building requires an understanding of the principles underlying teamwork and team spirit in sport. However, before we examine team dynamics we need to understand the broader issue of group dynamics, since most of the research has examined team issues in sport from a group dynamics perspective.

Definition of a group

In their classic work on the subject, Cartwright and Zander (1968) defined a group as 'a collection of individuals who have relations to one another that make them interdependent to some significant degree' (p. 46). The key requirements of a group are interaction, mutual awareness, interdependence and continuity over time. In addition, Carron and Dennis (2001) stated that 'groups are dynamic, not static. They exhibit life and vitality, interaction and activity' (p. 129).

A collection of individuals is not necessarily a group (Zander 1982). The defining characteristic of a group is that of *interaction and mutual awareness*; group members must be aware of each other and able to interact and communicate with each other (McGrath 1984). Consequently, a collection of swimmers who swim for fitness during their lunch hour is not a group — they are not necessarily aware of each other, nor do they interact in a structured manner. On the other hand, a collection of competitive swimmers who meet for early-morning swim training is a group — they have a shared purpose (training for competition), they are aware of each other (they belong to the same swim team/club), and they interact with each other (they pace each other and share coaches and training programs).

What is a team?

A team is a special type of group. A team is a group who have a well-developed collective identity and who work together to achieve a specific goal or set of goals: the goal(s) makes the team members *interdependent* to a significant degree. Miller (1992), former sportpsych consultant at the Australian Institute of Sport primarily working with team sports, argues that 'a team must have a shared sense of purpose, structured patterns of interaction, interpersonal attraction, personal interdependence, and a collective identity' (p. 165). Each team member views membership of the team as rewarding and satisfying, and believes that such rewards and satisfaction would not be attainable without membership of the team (Murrell & Gaertner 1992).

Rugby is also the contentment of being part of a team which has through mental collusion and diligent training been able to coordinate its action to overcome that of 15 men with the same ideal ... Rugby to the players is not just the game, it is the complete atmosphere surrounding the enjoyment of a team sport ... Afterwards having shared such a self-inflicted stressful situation, what more human thing is there than to share and enjoy each other's company, especially if the match has been satisfactorily resolved.

Graham Mourie (former New Zealand rugby captain, 1977–1982;
Super 12 rugby coach, 2000–)

A 'common' assumption about team performance

It is often assumed that the best individual players will make the best team. The assumed relationship between individual abilities and team performance is not always straightforward, however. Simply summing the abilities of individual team members will not help in accurately predicting the team performance. In order to understand team performance one must consider the team/group process as well as individual ability (Steiner 1972). For example, team motivation (George & Feltz 1995; Zander 1975), team cohesion (Grieve, Whelan & Meyers 2000; Salminen & Luhtanen 1998), and leadership (Gardner, Light-Shields, Light-Bredemeier & Bostrom 1996; Riemer & Chelladurai 1995) are processes that have a significant impact on team performance.

General observation of any team sport reveals that few teams consistently perform to their potential. It is typically assumed that the team that, 'on paper', appears to have the best players will perform best, but this is often not the case. Team dynamics research focuses on explaining why teams do not always effectively harness the individual abilities of their players for consistent team performance. One useful model applied in team dynamics research has been Steiner's (1972) model of group performance.

Steiner's (1972) model of group performance

This general model has been useful in providing a framework for team dynamics research in sport; it is expressed in the following equation.

Actual productivity = Potential productivity – Losses due to faulty process

Actual productivity (or performance) is what the group actually does. *Potential productivity* is the group's best possible performance given those of its resources that are relevant to the task and the demands of that task. *Process* is everything the group does while transforming its resources into a product or performance (Steiner 1972). In sport, process relates to each player's individual skill development combined with teamwork skills developed by the coach, including team tactics and strategies.

I did not have a single Olympic yachtsman with me. And we were off to face the inevitable boatload of them in America. In the absence of stars, there was but one commodity we could develop, and that was team spirit. In every walk of life, a tightly grouped, determined, well-trained team will so often overcome pure genius. All they need is an explicit belief that they can fight and win, that they can overcome opposing cleverness with unshakeable determination, tireless work, and the desire to back each other, to cover each other's mistakes, and ultimately to triumph through sheer sense of communal purpose ... I decided to start with the word *democracy. Australia II* would be a completely democratic environment.

John Bertrand (skipper of *Australia II*, in 1983 the first team to win the America's Cup from
the USA in its 132-year history)

Faulty process is the ineffective use of available resources to meet task demands. It can result from two types of 'losses' — coordination losses and motivation losses. *Coordination losses* include poor timing, teamwork or strategy. *Motivation losses* occur when all or some members of the team lack effort and desire (Steiner 1972).

Steiner's model has been used effectively to assess team performance in sport (Ingham, Levinger, Graves & Peckham 1974; Latene, Williams & Harkins 1979). Nevertheless, while this conceptualisation of group productivity is a useful heuristic device, it lacks sufficient detail to be able to fully explain and predict team performance. In particular, the general conceptions of coordination losses and motivation losses are loosely defined and difficult to operationalise for assessment in the sport setting. This lack of specificity poses a serious problem for explanatory and predictive research. Notwithstanding these problems, Steiner's model is useful as a general description of team productivity. It is the role of team leaders and coaches to decrease faulty process by developing and practising organisational strategies that reduce coordination losses (i.e. teamwork) and maintain optimal motivation levels (i.e. team motivation). Of course, this is nowhere near as easy to achieve as it sounds! So why do teams not always perform up to their potential?

Research on team performance

Steiner's (1972) model has been used to investigate the relationship between individual performance or ability and group performance (e.g. Ingham et al. 1974; Latene et al. 1979).

Team process and team performance

The classic work commonly referred to as a precursor to this research is that of a French psychologist, Ringelmann, who examined individual and group performance in a rope pulling task (i.e. a tug-of-war). He discovered that the average individual performance decreased with increases in group size; this finding is commonly referred to as the *Ringelmann effect*.

Steiner (1972) interpreted the Ringelmann effect as the result of coordination losses; that is, as the group size increases it becomes more difficult to coordinate effort and skill execution. However, considerable research demonstrates that the Ringelmann effect is primarily the result of motivation losses (Hardy & Crace 1991; Ingham et al. 1974; Latene et al. 1979; see Hardy 1990 for a review). This phenomenon is commonly referred to as social loafing. *Social loafing* means that the average individual performance decreases with increases in team size. Coordination losses may partly account for decreased performance, but the key psychological reason seems to be motivation losses, especially social loafing (Hardy, 1990).

Social loafing

Social loafing occurs when the identifiability of individual performances is lost in a team/group performance; performance decreases because of the diffusion of responsibility (Hardy & Latene 1988; Harkins 1987). If individuals believe that their own performance within the team can be identified (e.g. individual statistics, lap times, assists, tackles), and that they will be held accountable for their contribution, then social loafing typically does not occur (Latene et al. 1979; Swain 1996). Therefore players' individual performances should be monitored and they need to be made accountable for their personal contribution to the team performance.

If monitoring individual performances can eliminate social loafing, then clearly other factors can increase individual effort in teams (Everett, Smith & Williams 1992).

Teams can provide social incentives such as peer pressure and social support from team-mates (Huddleston, Doody & Ruder 1985). For example, studies in swimming have found that when individual lap times were announced (high identifiability), individuals swam faster in relays than in individual races. When lap times were not announced (low identifiability), individuals swam faster in individual races than they did in the relays (Latene et al. 1979).

> Playing for yourself wins trophies; playing for your team wins championships.
>
> Tommy Lasorda (US baseball manager, LA Dodgers)

General implications for sport teams

Individual skill performance should *not* be the only factor for team member selection. Most team sports require high interaction and communication skills that are not present in individual performance. Also, motivation losses can be avoided by identifying and rewarding the individual and teamwork behaviours that contribute to desired team performance (Swain 1996). Contrary to the common coaching cliché, it may be useful to put the 'I' back into 'team', so that individual contributions are identified and desired teamwork behaviours (e.g. positive communication and assists) are recognised, encouraged and rewarded for each team member (Hodge 1994; Riley 1993).

Team motivation

Teamwork and team process are necessary but not sufficient for peak performance in team sports. We also need to consider team motivation if a team is to consistently perform to its potential. The basis of team motivation is the team's goal(s) and the team members' *desire for group success*.

The desire for group success (Dgs)

Desire for group success (Dgs) (Zander 1975) is a team-oriented motive or goal, the basis of which is the team members' desire to derive pride and satisfaction from the team if it is successful in accomplishing its goal(s). Unlike the analogous 'motive to approach success' (Ms) in Atkinson's (1974) model of achievement motivation, the Dgs is situation-specific. Like the Ms trait, however, the Dgs encourages team members to set and strive to achieve a challenging goal(s).

The fundamental factor to consider in developing team motivation is the identification of a single, unifying team goal; that is, a goal that all team members agree on and commit themselves to achieving (Murrell & Gaertner 1992; Widmeyer & Ducharme 1997). The team members have to freely agree to redefine their self-esteem to include membership of the team as being important to them as individuals.

The stages in developing Dgs (increasing team motivation) are as follows: First, emphasise a 'pride-in-team' approach (Zander 1975). With input from each team member, set a unifying team goal and objectives to achieve that single goal (these should be performance (not outcome) objectives — see Weinberg, chapter 10). Second, ensure that each member's individual contribution is valued and recognised by both coach and team-mates (Zander 1975). Keep reserves and substitutes involved. Third, place strong emphasis on good *leadership* from the coach, and from the team captain(s) (Westre & Weiss 1991). Fourth, actively work to encourage and develop team *cohesion* — that is, both social cohesion (team spirit) and task cohesion (teamwork). Fifth, encourage unified commitment to the team effort; team members have to be prepared to invest time and energy to achieve the overall team goal (Zander 1975). Expect and reward the pursuit of high standards of excellence. Finally, it is vital that *effective communication* is utilised to keep all team members informed and feeling 'part of the team' (Yukelson 2001).

It helps young guys to come into a team containing players who've got it right mentally and to be surrounded by guys who've achieved and are successful ... To be able to communicate and help guys through is one of the big things about team unity ...

John Wright (former New Zealand cricketer; Indian cricket coach, 2000–)

However, while the team members need to feel a strong identification with the team, they also need to feel accountable and responsible for playing their key part in the team's success of achieving its unifying goal. This sense of responsibility is related to the important issue of team cohesion.

CAREER BEST EFFORT

Pat Riley, coach of the LA Lakers basketball team in the 1980s, used a team motivation technique called the Career Best Effort program to increase identifiability and to reward individual contributions to his all-star team. During the 1986–1987 NBA season the LA Lakers initiated 'Career Best Effort' to improve team motivation and team performance. They went on to win back-to-back NBA Championships in 1987 and 1988 — the first team in 19 years to do so.

'Career Best Effort was a system steeped in numbers and measurement, but we weren't just talking about points and statistics. Like any true quest for excellence it reached for the best in body, mind, and spirit. Unlike most reviews of player performance, which arbitrarily rake people over the coals, this system focuses on the positive use of information. We were out to give our players a clear picture of how they were doing, where they stood, and where to focus their fullest concentration' (Riley 1993; p. 161).

Riley reasoned that complacency (and social loafing) could not exist in an environment of knowledge and accountability. The core of the Career Best Effort program was a detailed record-keeping system. When players first joined the team, the coaches tracked their basketball statistics all the way back to high school. They used this information to create an accurate gauge both of what the players could do and what they had to achieve in order to help the team achieve excellence. Instead of ranking players against each other, the Lakers compared them to players on opposing teams with similar positions and similar role definitions (e.g. point guard against point guard; first reserve power forward against first reserve power forward). Every player on the team had a category in which they could — potentially — rank number one in the NBA. The other comparison was for each player's monthly statistics to be compared against his stats from the same month in the previous season — his own personal yardstick.

'The numbers were used to define a goal that was simple and realistic, yet they could thrust ahead toward an incredible improvement. From a list of fifteen possible measures we selected five ... These defined five "trigger points", five areas which comprised the basis of basketball performance for each role and position. We challenged each player to put forth enough effort to gain just one percentage point in each of those five areas ... A one percent improvement in five areas for twelve players gave us a 60 per cent increment!' (p. 163).

One of the key areas was a category for 'unsung hero' deeds — taking a charge at full force, diving on the floor for loose possession, going after rebounds whether you get them or not. As Pat Riley concluded, 'morale is the lifeblood of any team ... [and] the Career Best Effort system was a way to address morale' (p. 170).

Excellence is the way. Mastery is the way. Challenge is the way (p. 181).

Pat Riley (coach, LA Lakers NBA basketball team, 1981–1989; four times NBA champions; 'Team of the Decade')

Cohesion and team performance

Team cohesion is a 'dynamic process which is reflected in the tendency for a group to *stick together* and remain united in the pursuit of its goals' (Carron & Dennis 2001; p. 123). Indeed, Carron and Dennis (2001) concluded that the 'terms "cohesion" and "group" are tautological — if a group exists, cohesion is present' (p. 123). Cohesive teams are able to ignore distractions and avoid disruptions while staying firmly focused on their team goal(s) (Brawley, Carron & Widmeyer 1988; Carron, Brawley & Widmeyer 1998).

There are two general dimensions associated with team cohesion. *Social cohesion* (interpersonal attraction) reflects the degree to which the members of a team like each other and enjoy each other's company (Brawley 1990; Carron & Hausenblas 1998). In sport this is often referred to as *team spirit*. *Task cohesion* reflects the degree to which members of a team work together to achieve a specific and identifiable task or goal (Brawley 1990; Carron & Hausenblas 1998). This instrumental goal or task is usually associated with the purpose for which the team was formed. Task cohesion is the basis of *teamwork* (Brawley, Carron & Widmeyer 1987).

Antecedents of cohesion

Carron (1988) has developed a model that offers four general antecedents of cohesion: environmental (situational), personal, leadership and team factors (for reviews see Carron & Hausenblas 1998; Carron, Brawley & Widmeyer 1998).

Environmental

These antecedents include potential factors such as the availability of team sports, eligibility, geographic restrictions, and sporting body organisational structures. Aspects of the social environment, such as family expectations, peer pressures, socialisation, spectators and home advantage, also play a role (Bray 1999; Bray & Widmeyer 2000; Moore & Brylinsky 1993). Another social environmental variable is team size (Carron 1990; Widmeyer, Brawley & Carron 1990). Brawley (1990) contends that team size affects the level of cohesion (i.e. small to moderate-sized groups of less than nine members have higher interaction and therefore greater cohesion) and the type of cohesion (i.e. task or social).

Personal

Each team member's personal characteristics influence the type of cohesion developed and the 'perceived cohesion' of team members (Crace & Hardy 1997; Granito & Rainey 1988). Brawley (1990) reports that social background, gender, attitudes, ability, level of competition, commitment and personality have differential influences on cohesion. Significant similarity on any or all of these factors creates the opportunity for consensus on the goals and tasks of the team. Cohesion rests on agreement on these issues among team members.

> Good teams become great ones when the members trust each other enough to surrender the 'me' for the 'we'.
>
> Phil Jackson (Chicago Bulls basketball coach, six-time NBA Champions; LA Lakers coach, two-time NBA champions) (Jackson & Delehanty 1995)

Leadership

The role of leaders is vital in developing team cohesion (Curtner-Smith, Wallace & Wang 1999; Westre & Weiss 1991). Clear, consistent, unambiguous communication from coaches and captains regarding team goal(s), team tasks and team member roles plays a very influential role in cohesiveness (Carron & Dennis 2001; Yukelson 2001). In addition, leaders who involve team members in team decisions (e.g. goal setting or selection of tactics) help to develop cohesion by increasing each player's feelings of 'ownership and investment' in the team (Westre & Weiss 1991).

With the talent and *think power* we had, we were able to open up the court and let one or two guys penetrate, then feed off of them. In the fourth quarter your leadership, your unity, your understanding of personnel, your fulfilment of roles — all those things come out. And I think that's the way we won.

Michael Jordan (US basketball player, Chicago Bulls, six-time winners of the NBA Championship)(Jackson & Delehanty 1995)

Team

Finally, Brawley (1990) outlined the role that shared team experiences play in developing or maintaining cohesion. For example, common experience of a series of successes or failures creates a 'shared experience', and the act of unifying as a team to counter the threat of the opposing team can create a climate for increased cohesion (Boone, Beitel & Kuhlman 1997). Moreover, Carron and Dennis (2001) claimed that aspects of the team such as team structure, position, status, roles, norms, stability and communication significantly affect cohesion (Munroe, Estabrooks, Dennis & Carron 1999).

Consequences of cohesion

While considerable research has examined the antecedents of cohesion, the focus of most research in this area has addressed the consequences of cohesion; in particular the consequences of team performance and success. Although numerous studies have investigated the relationship between cohesion and performance success, the results are equivocal. Some studies have found a positive relationship, with greater cohesion leading to success (Davids & Nutter 1988; Shangi & Carron 1987). Other studies have revealed more limited levels of cohesion leading to success (Landers & Lueschen 1974; Lenk 1969); and some studies have not found any relationship (Williams & Hacker 1982). The inconsistency in this research has led investigators to consider the possible mediating variables in the cohesion–performance relationship. Mediating variables such as satisfaction, collective efficacy and team motivation will be considered later.

Team motivation, another possible consequence of cohesion, usually depends on a strong sense of cohesion within the team (Carron & Hausenblas 1998). Motivation, or intention to continue participation in a sport, may also be influenced by team cohesion. For example, Spink (1995) found that social cohesion was a significant predictor of intention to participate the following season for both recreational and elite female team athletes.

Team climate: keeping everyone focused and happy

Hodge and McKenzie (1999) used this term to describe the team member's perceptions of the conditions and relationships among team members. Team climate perceptions dictate the level and type of cohesion within the team and also have a major influence on team motivation and team member satisfaction (Carron, Prapavessis & Grove 1994; Ryska, Yin & Boyd 1999). Players are attracted to team sports and to particular teams for a number of reasons. If they are to build trust among team members and effectively harness their skills and enthusiasm, coaches and leaders need to understand each team member's reasons for being involved with the team (McLure & Foster 1991). Some of the major reasons are as follows.

- *Interpersonal attraction* among members refers to the level of friendship within the team. It is often the case that the stronger the friendship, the more cohesive the team (Klein & Christiansen 1969; Weiss & Smith 1999).
- *Attractiveness of the team* as a whole refers to the benefit each player receives from being a member of the team. This is sometimes but not always related to the level of interpersonal attraction (Carron, Widmeyer & Brawley 1985; Brawley, Carron & Widmeyer 1987).

* *Closeness of identification with the team* refers to the extent to which someone describes herself or himself as a member of the team. The greater the sense of belonging, identification and team integration, the greater the cohesiveness of the team (Carron et al. 1985).

> There is no doubt that I will miss rugby and there is also a vague suspicion that nothing I may do in the next 10 years will cause me the same pleasure. The sense of belonging, of comradeship through a common team aim with its ability to meld many diverse personalities into a cohesive group is a rare thing; one which I imagine many people never experience ... Only those who play a team sport can fully appreciate the sense of pride in belonging to a team of renown, the trust in the ability of your teammates.
>
> Graham Mourie (former New Zealand rugby captain; Super 12 rugby coach, 2000–)

Cohesiveness undoubtedly involves a *combination* of these components, and others as well. Indeed, thinking of team cohesion solely in terms of attraction is often not enough for consistent peak team performance. Teams form for reasons other than attraction; the team goal must be compatible with each individual's goals, and a person may expect personal payoffs or rewards as a result of a team's endeavours (e.g. selection in representative teams/squads or winning a championship).

For example, Team New Zealand won the America's Cup (the supreme international competition for sailing) in 1995 and successfully defended the Cup in 2000. They became only the second non-American team to win the America's Cup since the first regatta in 1851, and they are the only non-American team to successfully defend the Cup. Team New Zealand placed enormous importance on team building and team cohesion as the basis of their successes in winning and then defending the America's Cup (Coutts & Larsen 1996; Mazany 1995). See the highlighted example of their team vision and team values below.

TEAM NEW ZEALAND — AMERICA'S CUP, 1995

'What is our vision?'

'These were the words we tried to live by for the next two years (1993–1995): *"To build a challenge in which we could be proud; a challenge of which all New Zealanders could be proud."*

'It sounds simple, but it was sincere. It also served as a motivational goal. There was more to the full statement. Each individual present was asked to read the entire statement and sign it, signifying his agreement. It read:

' *"We want a small, informed and fully motivated team that:*

* *works in an environment which encourages every member to make a meaningful contribution*
* *has a high degree of personal integrity and group honesty*
* *recognises personal goals but not hidden agendas*
* *continuously monitors and improves its performance*
* *is fun to be in."*

'The last point may seem a bit frivolous, but in many ways it was of more importance than each of the others. Having fun, enjoying ourselves and each other may have been the one characteristic that most distinguished the 1995 challenge from each of its three predecessors.'

Russell Coutts (skipper, Team New Zealand; winners of the America's Cup in 1995 and 2000)

(*Source:* Coutts & Larsen 1995, pp. 166–7)

CURRENT PERSPECTIVES

In this section the most recent research developments and the most promising theoretical perspectives are discussed. Finally, this current work will be used as the basis for a number of recommendations regarding future research in the area of team dynamics.

Controlling social loafing

Hardy (1990) suggested that social loafing is consistent with the social facilitation phenomenon in that 'evaluation' of performance is the key issue. In social loafing the absence of performance evaluation contributes to motivation losses, whereas in social facilitation the presence of others (i.e. co-actors) increases performance evaluation and therefore contributes to an increase in motivation (Harkins 1987). However, the important issues of co-actor/partner ability, cohesion, task difficulty and the incentive value of the task need to be investigated further to determine the full extent of the complementary relationship between social loafing and social facilitation (Hardy 1990). Moreover, social loafing may not be the only form of possible motivation loss in sport (Hardy 1990).

Hardy (1990) has suggested that social loafing can be controlled so that team performance is maintained or increased. First, the coach and team leaders need to develop ways to identify, recognise, evaluate and reward each team member's role and her or his individual contributions to the team performance (Hodge & McKenzie 1999). Second, leaders need to seek to increase each team member's sense of responsibility for the team performance by increasing team interaction, commitment to the team goal(s) and task cohesion (Hodge 1994; Hodge & McKenzie 1999). Third, leaders should ensure that the team effort and team success is personally involving for each team member by developing a sense of team pride and a collective team identity (Hodge & McKenzie 1999; Zander 1975). Fourth, systematic goal setting needs to be utilised for the team as a whole and for individual team members (Hodge 1994; Swain 1996; see also Weinberg, chapter 10).

The relationship between team cohesion and performance

Despite the lack of consistency in the cohesion–performance research, there is a definite feeling among those involved in sport that there is a connection between team cohesion and the quality of performance. The common assumption is that it is a direct and positive relationship; that is, greater cohesion is associated with greater success. There are at least two problems with this assumption.

First, high cohesion is sometimes related to success, but sometimes it is not. The relationship is more complex than it first appears (Matheson, Mathes & Murray 1996; Rainey & Schweickert 1988; Salminen & Luhtanen 1998; Slater & Sewell 1994). It has been assumed that there is a cause–effect relationship, with cohesion the cause and success the effect. However, research has demonstrated that this assumption may not always be valid. Indeed the relationship may be circular rather than linear (see Carron & Hausenblas 1998 for a review). Second, the relationship between cohesion and performance seems to depend on the type of sport task (Williams & Widmeyer 1991). For example, East German Olympic and world championship rowing teams experienced success despite strong internal conflicts and minimal social cohesion (Lenk 1969). The rowers had high task cohesion, however.

When considering the different types of sport tasks one can distinguish between sport tasks involving independence, coactive dependence, reactive/proactive dependence and interactive dependence (Carron & Hausenblas 1998; Weinberg & Gould 1999). *Independent* tasks (e.g. archery, rifle shooting, triathlon) do not require coordinated action between individuals for performance success. *Coactive dependent* tasks (e.g.

rowing) are those in which members perform similar tasks simultaneously and a collective performance contributes directly to team effectiveness. In *reactive and proactive dependent* tasks (e.g. softball/baseball pitcher and catcher; cricket bowler and wicket-keeper) one member of a team initiates the action while another completes the action. Finally, *interactive dependent* tasks are those in which members are mutually dependent on each other (e.g. basketball, soccer, rugby and hockey).

For independent, coactive dependent and proactive/reactive dependent sports, cohesion and performance appear to be relatively unrelated (Carron & Dennis 2001). Nevertheless, research by Williams and Widmeyer (1991) has provided preliminary evidence that cohesion can be positively related to performance in a coacting sport (i.e. golf). For interactive dependent sports there is a clear positive relationship between *task* cohesion and performance (Davids & Nutter 1988; Grieve, Whelan & Meyers 2000; Matheson, Mathes & Murray 1996; Salminen & Luhtanen 1998; Slater & Sewell 1994). Interaction between members enhances the opportunity for team success. Finally, for interactive team sports, where team members depend on their team-mates for mutual success through continuous interaction (e.g. in soccer, basketball or volleyball), *social* cohesion and performance also appear to be positively related (Klein & Christiansen 1969). Social interaction between members in these types of team sports appears to enhance the opportunity for team success.

Even when cohesion and performance are positively related, the issue of whether or not cohesion is the cause and team success the effect is not clear. Indeed, the relationship seems to be circular: cohesion contributes to performance success, and performance success brings an increase in cohesion (Carron & Dennis 2001). Williams and Hacker (1982) have suggested that satisfaction may be a mediating variable between team cohesion and performance success. Both cohesion and satisfaction can be either a cause or an effect of performance. Successful teams express greater satisfaction with participation, and a consequence of satisfaction is increased cohesiveness. Playing on a cohesive team may be more satisfying than playing on a non-cohesive team.

Carron and Hausenblas (1998), in their extensive review of the group/team dynamics literature, concluded that *cohesion* is a vital aspect of group and team effectiveness (i.e. success or performance) and an important group property worth developing. While the results of these cohesion–performance studies do not provide consistent findings regarding the cause–effect relationship between cohesion and team effectiveness or performance, Carron (1988) argued that 'the overall pattern of results does support a conclusion that when groups are more cohesive they are more effective' (p. 170).

> As I grew to understand the structure of the game I was more and more absorbed by its reliance on teamwork with player working for player, a mutual reliance which placed team before individual.
>
> Brian Lochore (New Zealand rugby player, 1963–1971; coach, 1985–1987)

A model of team cohesion

This model of cohesion is based on the premise that cohesion is *dynamic*: it develops and then declines slightly, renews itself and increases again, and then declines slightly (Brawley, Carron & Widmeyer 1987). According to Carron and Dennis (2001), this pattern is repeated throughout the course of a team's existence. Cohesion has a number of dimensions and is perceived in multiple ways by different groups and their members.

The model of team cohesion proposed by Carron et al. (1985) and Brawley et al. (1987) suggests that these multiple perceptions of the team are organised and integrated by team members into two general categories. The first category is labelled *group integration*, and is designed to represent each individual's perceptions of the team as a total unit. The second category, *individual attractions*, represents each individual's personal attractions to the team. Both of these categories of cohesion are assumed to consist of *task* and *social* aspects of the team. As figure 8.1 demonstrates, team cohesion is considered to have four facets: individual attractions to the group — task (ATG-T), individual attractions to the group — social (ATG-S), group integration — task (GI-T), and group integration — social (GI-S).

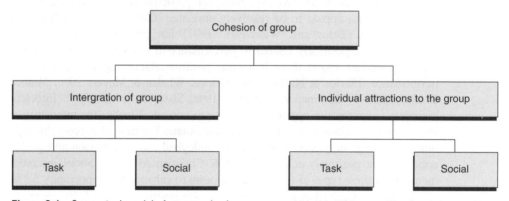

Figure 8.1 Conceptual model of group cohesion (*Source:* Widmeyer, Brawley & Carron 1985)

Group integration represents 'the closeness, similarity, and bonding within the group as a whole — the degree of unification of the group' (Carron et al. 1985, p. 248). *Individual attractions* to the group represent 'the interaction of the individual member's feelings about the group, their personal role involvement, and involvement with other group members' (Carron et al. 1985, p. 248). It is assumed that these four facets of cohesion are correlated through the perceived interaction of the various task and social aspects of the group by team members (Carron et al. 1985).

These two important distinctions — individual versus the group, and task versus social — are vital aspects of this model of team cohesion. The model predicts that team members possess views of what personally attracts them to the team, and also of how the team functions as a unit. These combined perceptions help to bind the team into a cohesive unit. Brawley (1990) concludes that the four related dimensions of the cohesion model are likely to be the product of a complex person–environment interaction. The team athlete develops these perceptions over time, for example during the course of a sport season. 'It is assumed that the process of a team becoming cohesive is one that is dynamic and socially learned' (Brawley 1990, p. 365).

> We are trying to establish a culture that it is in everyone's interests to develop the highest standard we can, rather than worrying about self-interest ... We don't want people holding back ideas.
>
> Russell Coutts (skipper, Team New Zealand sailing team, winners of the America's Cup in 1995 and 2000)

Carron et al. (1985) and Brawley et al. (1987) developed the Group Environment Questionnaire (GEQ) as an operationalised measure of their model. The GEQ is an 18-item, four-scale instrument with demonstrated psychometric properties of reliability and validity (Brawley et al. 1987; Carron et al. 1985). It has been used to examine issues in the contexts of both sport (Brawley et al. 1988; McLure & Foster 1991; Westre & Weiss 1991) and exercise (e.g., Carron & Spink 1992; Carron, Widmeyer & Brawley 1988; Estabrooks & Carron 2000; Spink & Carron 1992, 1993).

Cohesion

As Spink (1990a) pointed out, a number of explanations have been put forward to explain inconsistent findings regarding the cohesion–performance relationship (e.g. measurement and methodological reasons, or difficulty in establishing causality); however, until recently little research had examined the role of mediating variables in the cohesion–performance relationship. Spink (1990a) suggested that one such variable may be collective efficacy. For example, he found that individual perceptions of team/group cohesiveness (both task and social cohesion) were positively related to collective efficacy for elite volleyball players, but not for recreational players.

Collective efficacy

Collective efficacy is a term created by Bandura (1986) to reflect the observation that groups often have collective expectations for success (George & Feltz 1995; Paskvich, Brawley, Dorsch & Widmeyer 1999). Bandura (1986) developed the motivational concept of self-efficacy to describe an individual's confidence and expectations of success at a particular task. The concept of collective efficacy is the group-level equivalent of such confidence and expectations of success. Spink (1990b) suggested that the Desire for Group Success (Dgs) can be construed as a general measure of collective efficacy. Consequently, collective efficacy is a useful concept to employ when discussing team motivation.

Furthermore, Spink (1990b) suggested that collective efficacy is particularly relevant to the sporting situation as it influences every individual's choice of team goal(s), how much effort they will expend in pursuit of that goal(s), and their persistence in the face of slow progress towards the goal(s) or failure in achieving the goal(s). Indeed, there is initial support for the role of collective efficacy in influencing group goal selection and group goal commitment (Greenlees, Graydon & Maynard 2000), and collective efficacy has been found to have a positive effect on effort and persistence on a group task (Greenlees, Graydon & Maynard 1999a). In addition, there is preliminary evidence that collective efficacy influences the pre-competition affect and state anxiety of individuals engaged in a team task (Greenlees, Graydon & Maynard 1999b). Finally, collective efficacy itself appears to be influenced by game location factors and 'home advantage' (Bray & Widmeyer 2000).

A number of studies have indicated that collective efficacy is positively related to team performance (Feltz, Corcoran & Lirgg 1989; Hodges & Carron 1992; Lichacz & Partington 1996; Spink 1990a). Nevertheless, while a positive relationship appears to exist, considerable research is still needed to fully determine the nature of this relationship and to identify specific methods or strategies to develop collective efficacy. For example, collective efficacy appears to be more than just the summation of the confidence/efficacy levels of individual team members (Bandura 1986; Feltz et al. 1989; Gould, Hodge, Peterson & Giannini 1989). If, as Spink (1990b) claimed, collective efficacy is found to represent more than the sum of individual efficacies, then *team cohesion* seems a useful area to pursue in an attempt to understand the relationship between team performance and collective efficacy. Another area in need of further investigation is the relationship between the coach's efficacy expectations of his or her team and the team's collective efficacy (Chase, Lirgg & Feltz 1997).

Spink (1990b) concluded that the area of cohesiveness holds the most promise owing to the commonality between cohesion and collective efficacy. Indeed, the concepts of cohesion and collective efficacy have both been linked to performance success (George & Feltz 1995; Spink 1990a).

FUTURE DIRECTIONS

Brawley (1990) and Widmeyer et al. (1992) outlined the following 'research pitfalls' that need to be avoided if team dynamics research is to advance significantly. First, there is a need to base studies consistently on a guiding theory or conceptual framework (see Widmeyer et al. 1992 for greater detail). Second, longitudinal studies over the period of a complete sport season are needed if the *dynamic*, social learning aspects of team dynamics are to be fully investigated (McCarroll 2001). Moreover, Widmeyer (1986) advocated the use of more sophisticated statistical techniques, such as path analysis, to directly examine issues of causality in longitudinal research.

Third, team dynamics research needs to investigate multiple aspects of the team dynamic equation concurrently rather than in univariate, discrete studies of single issues such as cohesion, team process or leadership (Widmeyer 1986). Multivariate team dynamics research is clearly lacking. For example, Brawley (1990) pointed out that much of the research regarding cohesion focuses on *performance success*, yet the complex outcome referred to as 'performance success' typically depends on far more than cohesion alone. A direct, one-to-one relationship is implicitly assumed when in reality team performance depends on more than one factor. For example, cohesion, tactics, strategies and skill/ability level all play a role in performance success (Grove & Webb 1990). Consequently, it is important to differentiate the team's cohesive behaviour from other team factors involved in producing the desired performance (Brawley 1990). This need for multivariate research applies to all the areas of team dynamics.

Fourth, as Brawley (1990) concluded, researchers need to carefully consider the appropriate 'unit of analysis' for their particular research question; that is, should the researcher use individual athletes on a team or the team itself as the unit of analysis. For example, the average task cohesion score for a team may be quite different from the 'collective efficacy' for that team as a whole — the whole may represent something quite different from the sum of its parts. As Widmeyer (1986) pointed out, 'Recognizing that the group is more than its mean score is not only recognizing that variations in member characteristics are significant and that compatibility of member characteristics are important. It is also recognizing that the group exhibits properties of its own rather than simply being the sum of its members' (p. 186).

Finally, there is a need to study a variety of 'teams'; that is, different sports, different levels of competition and non-sport groups in the physical activity environment (e.g. exercise groups, recreational activity groups, physical education classes, dance classes). Non-sport groups differ significantly from sport teams. Sport teams are unique and different from other groups since sport is competitive by definition, possesses unique and specified rules, is time-bound, and is formally organised via sporting bodies, clubs and leagues. Consequently, as Widmeyer et al. (1992) stated, the study of teams alone leads to a narrow view of group dynamics in the sport and physical activity domain. Indeed, the issue of group dynamics has been examined in a number of exercise adherence studies in recent years (Carron & Spink 1993; Carron, Hausenblas & Mack 1996; Estabrooks & Carron 2000; Spink & Carron 1993).

A number of specific areas are still in need of concerted investigation. For example, the broad issue of team motivation is poorly understood, as are the specific relationships between cohesion and team motivation, and cohesion and the motivation of individual team members. Team dynamics during training and practice is another area of interest that we know very little about (McCarroll 2001; McCarroll & Hodge 2001). Is the training/preparation phase for sport different from the competition phase with respect to team dynamics? In addition, we know virtually nothing about inter-team dynamics in sport — do relationships between opposing, competing teams significantly influence intra-team dynamics?

Another issue in need of investigation is the phenomenon of *team momentum*. Many individual athletes report the perception of being 'on a roll' in the sense of gaining control, feeling confident and capturing the initiative in the game, event or race (Perreault, Vallerand, Montgomery & Provencher 1998; Vallerand, Colavecchio & Pelletier 1988). The concept of psychological momentum is defined as a perception on the athlete's part that she or he is progressing towards his/her goal. Generally such a goal is winning, although personal best performance is also a common goal. Vallerand et al. (1988), in their model of psychological momentum, contended that the perception of 'progression toward the goal is associated with heightened levels of motivation and enhanced perceptions of control, confidence, optimism, energy, and synchronism' (p. 94). Vallerand et al.'s model suggests that the crucial variable that determines whether psychological momentum will be perceived is the degree of perceived *control* inherent in the situation. One volatile 'control' variable in team sports is the performance of team-mates, captains and coaches, and the effectiveness of 'team processes' (McTeer, White & Persad 1995); thus the possibility of a group-level *team momentum* perception is one that needs to be investigated further. Preliminary research indicates that the notion of team momentum does indeed exist and is linked to team cohesion (Burke, Burke & Joyner 1999; Eisler & Spink 1998).

In addition to team momentum, the related psychological construct of *flow* or *peak performance* in sport is one that has received considerable attention at the individual level of analysis (Jackson 1992; Jackson, Thomas, Marsh & Smethurst 2001), yet we know little about this phenomenon at the group/team level of analysis.

Another aspect of sport in which a team dynamics perspective needs to be employed is the psychological aspects of injury. There is significant evidence demonstrating the important role of *social support* as a mediating variable in the life stress–injury relationship (Hardy, Richman & Rosenfeld 1991; Petrie 1993). Social support has also been recognised as an important facet of an athlete's psychological rehabilitation and recovery from sporting injury (Williams, Rotella & Scherzer 2001). Nevertheless, while social support has been identified as an important variable, studies so far have not directly investigated social support from a team dynamics perspective (Rosenfeld & Richman 1997).

Finally, aspects of team dynamics exert a powerful influence through psychosocial variables such as aggression, cheating and moral reasoning (Shields, Bredemeier, Gardner & Bostrom 1995). Future research that integrates aspects of team dynamics with the influence of *motivational climate* should provide new insights into the influence of the social environment on these and other psychosocial variables.

CONCLUSIONS

The literature reviewed in this chapter has provided a clear theoretical and empirical basis for links to 'practice', with suggestions for improving team/group processes and, ultimately, team/group performance (see Carron & Hausenblas 1998 and Widmeyer, Brawley & Carron 1992 for extensive reviews of this literature). Thus, this chapter has particular application to team sports and training squads (Carron & Dennis 2001; Hodge & McKenzie 1999; Schellenberger 1990). However, it also has implications for any 'group' in the sport or physical activity environment — the practical focus should not be limited to *elite* sport or sport performance enhancement. For example, school physical education classes (Carlson & Hastie 1997; Ebbeck & Gibbons 1998), exercise groups (Carron, Hausenblas & Mack 1996; Estabrooks 2000), recreation groups (Karlis 1998; Shivers 1986), and dance classes (Fensham 1997) can all benefit from the practical implications of team dynamics.

SUMMARY

As Carron and Dennis (2001) concluded, 'groups are dynamic, not static. They exhibit life and vitality, interaction, and activity' (p. 132). Sports teams are a special type of group; consequently 'teams' are open to frequent change, growth and improvement. The team captain or coach who wishes to exert some control over this dynamic team/group process and produce positive improvements needs to be aware of the principles of team dynamics outlined in this chapter. Team dynamics issues discussed in this chapter, such as team process and performance (Steiner 1972), social loafing (Hardy 1990), team motivation (George & Feltz 1995), cohesion and team performance (Grieve, Whelan & Meyers 2000), and cohesion and collective efficacy (Greenlees, Graydon & Maynard 2000) all need to be considered if team effectiveness and performance is to be maximised.

 ## REVIEW QUESTIONS

1 Describe the key aspects of a 'group' and differentiate a group from a 'team'.

2 Discuss Steiner's model of group performance.

3 Explain the *Ringelmann effect* and the related issue of social loafing.

4 Define 'cohesion' and its two major subdimensions.

5 Discuss the 'antecedents' and 'consequences' of team cohesion.

6 Discuss the relationship between team cohesion and team performance. Ensure that you identify the differential effects of the two dimensions of cohesion and the mediating impact of different sport tasks.

7 Summarise Carron's model of team cohesion and its elements.

8 Define 'collective efficacy' and explain its relationship with team performance.

References

Atkinson, J 1974, 'The mainsprings of achievement-oriented activity', in JW Atkinson & JO Raynor (eds), *Motivation and achievement*, Halstead, New York: Halstead, pp. 13–41.

Bandura, A 1986, *Social foundations of thought and action: a social cognitive theory*, Prentice Hall, Englewood Cliffs, NJ.

Boone, KS, Beitel, P & Kuhlman, JS 1997, 'The effects of the win/loss record on cohesion', *Journal of Sport Behavior*, 20, 125–34.

Brawley, LR 1990, 'Group cohesion: status, problems and future directions', *International Journal of Sport Psychology*, 21, 355–79.

Brawley, LR & Paskevich, DM 1997, 'Conducting team building research in context of sport and exercise', *Journal of Applied Sport Psychology*, 9, 11–40.

Brawley, LR, Carron, AV & Widmeyer, WN 1987, 'Assessing the cohesion of teams: validity of the Group Environment Questionnaire', *Journal of Sport Psychology*, 9, 275–94.

Brawley, LR, Carron, AV & Widmeyer, WN 1988, 'Exploring the relationship between cohesion and group resistance to disruption', *Journal of Sport & Exercise Psychology*, 10, 199–213.

Bray, SR 1999, 'The home advantage from an individual team perspective', *Journal of Applied Sport Psychology*, 11, 116–25.

Bray, S & Widmeyer, N 2000, 'Athletes' perceptions of the home advantage: an investigation of perceived causal factors', *Journal of Sport Behavior*, 23, 1–10.

Burke, K, Burke, M & Joyner, A 1999, 'Perceptions of momentum in college and high school basketball: an exploratory, case study investigation', *Journal of Sport Behavior*, 22, 303–9.

Carlson, T & Hastie, P 1997, 'The student social system within sport education', *Journal of Teaching in Physical Education*, 16, 176–95.

Carron, AV 1988, *Group dynamics in sport: theoretical and practical issues*, Spodym, London, Ontario.

Carron, AV 1990, 'Group size in sport and physical activity: social psychological and performance consequences', *International Journal of Sport Psychology*, 21, 286–304.

Carron, AV & Dennis, P 2001, 'The sport team as an effective group', in J Williams (ed.), *Applied sport psychology: personal growth to peak performance*, 4th edn, Mayfield, Mountain View, CA, pp. 120–34.

Carron, AV & Hausenblas, H 1998, *Group dynamics in sport*, 2nd edn, Fitness Information Technology, Morgantown, WV.

Carron, AV & Spink, KS 1992, 'Internal consistency of the Group Environment Questionnaire modified for an exercise setting', *Perceptual and Motor Skills*, 74, 304–6.

Carron, AV & Spink, K 1993, 'Team building in an exercise setting', *The Sport Psychologist*, 7, 8–18.

Carron, AV, Brawley, LR & Widmeyer, WN 1990, 'The impact of group size in an exercise setting', *Journal of Sport & Exercise Psychology*, 12, 376–87.

Carron, AV, Brawley, LR & Widmeyer, WN 1998, 'The measurement of cohesiveness in sport groups', in JL Duda (ed.), *Advances in sport and exercise psychology measurement*, Fitness Information Technology, Morgantown, WV, pp. 213–26.

Carron, A, Hausenblas, H & Mack, D 1996, 'Social influence and exercise: a meta-analysis', *Journal of Sport & Exercise Psychology*, 18, 1–16.

Carron, A, Prapavessis, H & Grove, R 1994, 'Group effects and self-handicapping', *Journal of Sport & Exercise Psychology*, 16, 246–57.

Carron, AV, Widmeyer, WN & Brawley, LR 1985, 'The development of an instrument to assess cohesion in sport teams: the Group Environment Questionnaire', *Journal of Sport Psychology*, 7, 244–66.

Carron, AV, Widmeyer, WN & Brawley, LR 1988, 'Group cohesion and individual adherence to physical activity', *Journal of Sport & Exercise Psychology*, 10, 127–38.

Cartwright, D & Zander, A 1968, *Group dynamics: research and theory*, Harper & Row, New York.

Chase, MA, Lirgg, CD & Feltz, DL 1997, 'Do coaches' efficacy expectations for their teams predict team performance?', *The Sport Psychologist*, 11, 8–23.

Coutts, R & Larsen, P 1996, *Russell Coutts: course to victory*, Hodder Moa Beckett, Auckland, NZ.

Crace, RK & Hardy, CJ 1997, 'Individual values and the team building process', *Journal of Applied Sport Psychology*, 9, 41–60.

Csikszentmihalyi, M & Csikszentmihalyi, IS 1988, *Optimal experience: psychological studies of flow in consciousness*, Cambridge University Press, New York.

Curtner-Smith, MD, Wallace, SJ & Wang, MQ 1999, 'Relationship of coach and player behaviors during practice to team performance in high school girls' basketball', *Journal of Sport Behavior*, 22, 203–20.

Davids, K & Nutter, A 1988, 'The cohesion–performance relationship of English national league volleyball teams', *Journal of Human Movement Studies*, 15, 205–13.

Ebbeck, V & Gibbons, S 1998, 'The effect of a team building program on the self-conceptions of grade 6 and 7 Physical Education students', *Journal of Sport & Exercise Psychology*, 20, 300–10.

Eisler, L & Spink, K 1998, 'Effects of scoring configuration and task cohesion on the perception of psychological momentum', *Journal of Sport & Exercise Psychology*, 20, 311–20.

Estabrooks, P 2000, 'Sustaining exercise participation through group cohesion', *Exercise & Sport Science Reviews*, 63–7.

Estabrooks, P & Carron, A 2000, 'Predicting scheduling self-efficacy in older adult exercisers: the role of task cohesion', *Journal of Aging & Physical Activity*, 8, 41–50.

Estrada, AM, Gelfand, DM & Hartmann, DP 1988, 'Children's sport and the development of social behaviours', in FL Smoll, RA Magill & MJ Ash (eds), *Children in sport*, Human Kinetics, Champaign, IL, pp. 251–62.

Everett, J, Smith, R & Williams, K 1992, 'Effects of team cohesion and identifiability on social loafing in relay swimming performance', *International Journal of Sport Psychology*, 23, 311–24.

Feltz, D, Corcoran, J & Lirgg, C 1989, 'Relationships among team confidence, sport confidence, and hockey performance', *Psychology and motor behaviour in sport — 1989: abstracts*, North American Society for the Psychology of Sport and Physical Activity.

Fensham, R 1997, 'Dance and the problems of community', in H Poynor & J Simmonds (eds), *Dancers and communities*, Australian Dance Council, Walsh Bay, pp. 14–19.

Gardner, DE, Light-Shields, DL, Light-Bredemeier, BJ & Bostrom, A 1996, 'The relationship between perceived coaching behaviors and team cohesion among baseball and softball players', *The Sport Psychologist*, 10, 367–81.

George, TR & Feltz, DL 1995, 'Motivation in sport from a collective efficacy perspective', *International Journal of Sport Psychology*, 26, 98–116.

Gould, D, Hodge, K, Peterson, K & Giannini, J 1989, 'An exploratory examination of strategies used by elite coaches to enhance self-efficacy in athletes', *Journal of Sport & Exercise Psychology*, 11, 128–40.

Granito, VJ & Rainey, DW 1988, 'Differences in cohesion between high school and college football teams and starters and nonstarters', *Perceptual and Motor Skills*, 66, 471–7.

Greendorfer, S 1992, 'Sport socialisation', in T Horn (ed.), *Advances in sport psychology*, Human Kinetics, Champaign, IL, pp. 201–18.

Greenlees, I, Graydon, J & Maynard, I 1999a, 'The impact of collective efficacy beliefs on effort and persistence in a group task', *Journal of Sports Sciences*, 17, 151–8.

Greenlees, I, Graydon, J & Maynard, I 1999b, 'The relationship between collective efficacy and precompetitive affect in rugby players: testing Bandura's model of collective efficacy', *Perceptual and Motor Skills*, 89, 431–40.

Greenlees, I, Graydon, J & Maynard, I 2000, 'The impact of individual efficacy beliefs on group goal selection and group goal commitment', *Journal of Sports Sciences*, 18, 451–9.

Grieve, F, Whelan, J & Meyers, A 2000, 'An experimental examination of the cohesion–performance relationship in an interactive team sport', *Journal of Applied Sport Psychology*, 12, 219–35.

Grove, JR & Webb, S 1990, 'Descriptive models for team performance in international baseball competition', *Australian Journal of Science and Medicine in Sport*, 22, 44–8.

Hardy, CJ 1990, 'Social loafing: motivational losses in collective performance', *International Journal of Sport Psychology*, 21, 305–27.

Hardy, CJ & Crace, RK 1991, 'The effects of task structure and teammate competence on social loafing', *Journal of Sport & Exercise Psychology*, 13, 372–81.

Hardy, CJ & Crace, RK 1997, 'Foundations of team building: introduction to the team building primer', *Journal of Applied Sport Psychology*, 9, 1–10.

Hardy, CJ & Latene, B 1988, 'Social loafing in cheerleaders: effects of team membership and competition', *Journal of Sport & Exercise Psychology*, 10, 109–14.

Hardy, CJ, Richman, JM & Rosenfeld, LB 1991, 'The role of social support in the life stress/injury relationship', *The Sport Psychologist*, 5, 128–39.

Harkins, SG 1987, 'Social loafing and social facilitation', *Journal of Experimental Social Psychology*, 23, 1–18.

Hodge, KP 1994, *Sport motivation: training your mind for peak performance*, Reed, Auckland.

Hodge, K & McKenzie, A 1999, *Thinking rugby: training your mind for peak performance*, Reed, Auckland.

Hodges, L & Carron, A 1992, 'Collective efficacy and group performance', *International Journal of Sport Psychology*, 23, 48–59.

Hoffman, JR, Bar-Eli, M & Tenenbaum, G 1999, 'An examination of mood changes and performance in a professional basketball team', *Journal of Sports Medicine and Physical Fitness*, 39, 74–9.

Huddleston, S, Doody, S & Ruder, M 1985, 'The effect of prior knowledge of the social loafing phenomenon on performance in a group', *International Journal of Sport Psychology*, 16, 176–82.

Ingham, A, Levinger, G, Graves, J & Peckham, V 1974, 'The Ringelmann effect: studies of group size and group performance', *Journal of Experimental Social Psychology*, 10, 371–84.

Jackson, SA 1992, 'Athletes in flow: a qualitative investigation of flow states in elite figure skaters', *Journal of Applied Sport Psychology*, 4, 161–80.

Jackson, P & Delehanty, H 1995, *Sacred hoops: spiritual lessons of a hardwood warrior*, Hyperion, New York.

Jackson, S, Thomas, P, Marsh, H & Smethurst, C 2001, 'Relationships between flow, self-concept, psychological skills and performance', *Journal of Applied Sport Psychology*, 13, 129–53.

Karlis, G 1998, 'Social cohesion, social closure, and recreation: the ethnic experience in multicultural societies', *Journal of Applied Recreation Research*, 23, 3–21.

Klein, M & Christiansen, G 1969, 'Group composition, group structure and group effectiveness of basketball teams', in J Loy & G Kenyon (eds), *Sport, culture, and society*, Macmillan, Toronto, pp. 397–408.

Landers, D & Lueschen, G 1974, 'Team performance outcome and the cohesiveness of competitive coaching groups', *International Review of Sport Sociology*, 9, 57–71.

Latene, B, Williams, K & Harkins, S 1979, 'Many hands make light work: the cause and consequences of social loafing', *Journal of Experimental Social Psychology*, 37, 822–32.

Lenk, H 1969, 'Top performance despite internal conflict: an antithesis to a functional proposition', in J Loy & G Kenyon (eds), *Sport, culture, and society*, Macmillan, Toronto, pp. 393–7.

Lichacz, FM & Partington, JT 1996, 'Collective efficacy and true group performance', *International Journal of Sport Psychology*, 27, 146–58.

McCarroll, N 2001, 'Training motivation in elite rugby players', unpublished master's thesis, University of Otago, Dunedin, New Zealand.

McCarroll, N & Hodge, K 2001, 'Training motivation in elite rugby: feedback for players and fitness trainers', unpublished summary report, University of Otago, Dunedin, New Zealand.

McGrath, J 1984, *Groups: interaction and performance*, Prentice Hall, Englewood Cliffs, NJ.

McLure, BA & Foster, CD 1991, 'Group work as a method of promoting cohesiveness within a women's gymnastics team', *Perceptual and Motor Skills*, 73, 307–13.

McTeer, W, White, PG & Persad, S 1995, 'Manager/coach mid-season replacement and team performance in professional team sport', *Journal of Sport Behavior*, 18, 58–68.

Matheson, H, Mathes, S & Murray, M 1996, 'Group cohesion of female intercollegiate coacting and interacting teams across a competitive season', *International Journal of Sport Psychology*, 27, 37–49.

Mazany, P 1995, *Team think — Team New Zealand: the 'black magic' of management behind the 1995 America's Cup success*, VisionPlus Developments, Auckland.

Miller, B 1992, 'Team athletes', in J Bloomfield, P Fricker & K Fitch (eds.), *Textbook of science and medicine in sport*, Blackwell, Melbourne, pp. 165–75.

Moore, JC & Brylinsky, JA 1993, 'Spectator effect on team performance in college basketball', *Journal of Sport Behavior*, 16, 77–84.

Munroe, K, Estabrooks, P, Dennis, P & Carron, A 1999, 'A phenomenological analysis of group norms in sports teams', *The Sport Psychologist*, 13, 171–82.

Murray, M & Mann, B 2001, 'Leadership effectiveness', in J Williams (ed.), *Applied sport psychology: personal growth to peak performance*, 4th edn, Mayfield, Mountain View, CA, pp. 82–106.

Murrell, AJ & Gaertner, SL 1992, 'Cohesion and sport team effectiveness: the benefit of a common group identity', *Journal of Sport and Social Issues*, 16, 1–14.

Partington, JT & Shangi, GM 1992, 'Developing an understanding of team psychology', *International Journal of Sport Psychology*, 23, 28–47.

Paskvich, D, Brawley, L, Dorsch, K & Widmeyer, N 1999, 'Relationship between collective efficacy and team cohesion: conceptual and measurement issues', *Group Dynamics*, 3, 210–22.

Pensgaard, AM & Roberts, GC 2000, 'The relationship between motivational climate, perceived ability and sources of distress among elite athletes', *Journal of Sports Sciences*, 18, 191–200.

Perreault, S, Vallerand, R, Montgomery, D & Provencher, P 1998, 'Coming from behind: on the effect of psychological momentum on sport performance', *Journal of Sport & Exercise Psychology*, 20, 421–36.

Petrie, TA 1993, 'The moderating effects of social support and playing status on the life stress-injury relationship', *Journal of Applied Sport Psychology*, 5, 1–16.

Prapavessis, H & Carron, A 1996, 'The effect of group cohesion on competitive state anxiety', *Journal of Sport & Exercise Psychology*, 18, 64–74.

Prapavessis, H, Carron, A & Spink, K 1996, 'Team building in sport', *International Journal of Sport Psychology*, 27, 269–85.

Rainey, DW & Schweickert, GJ 1988, 'An exploratory study of team cohesion before and after a spring trip', *The Sport Psychologist*, 2, 314–17.

Riemer, H & Chelladurai, P 1995, 'Leadership and satisfaction in athletics', *Journal of Sport & Exercise Psychology*, 17, 276–93.

Riley, P 1993, *The winner within: a life plan for team players*, GP Putnam, New York.

Rosenfeld, LB & Richman, JM 1997, 'Developing effective social support: team building and the social support process', *Journal of Applied Sport Psychology*, 9, 133–53.

Ryska, TA, Yin, Z & Boyd, M 1999, 'The role of dispositional goal orientation and team climate on situational self-handicapping among young athletes', *Journal of Sport Behavior*, 22, 410–25.

Salminen, S & Luhtanen, P 1998, 'Cohesion predicts success in junior ice hockey', *Perceptual and motor skills*, 87, 649–50.

Schellenberger, H 1990, *Psychology of team sports*, Sport Books, Toronto.

Shangi, G & Carron, A 1987, 'Group cohesion and its relationship with performance and satisfaction among high school basketball players', *Canadian Journal of Sport Sciences*, 12, 20.

Shields, D, Bredemeier, B, Gardner, DE & Bostrom, A 1995, 'Leadership, cohesion, and team norms regarding cheating and aggression', *Sociology of Sport Journal*, 12, 324–36.

Shivers, JS 1986, *Recreational leadership: group dynamics and interpersonal behavior*, 2nd edn, Princeton Publishers, Princeton, NJ.

Slater, M & Sewell, D 1994, 'An examination of the cohesion-performance relationship in university hockey teams', *Journal of Sports Sciences*, 12, 423–31.

Spink, KS 1990a, 'Group cohesion and collective efficacy of volleyball teams', *Journal of Sport & Exercise Psychology*, 12, 301–11.

Spink, KS 1990b, 'Collective efficacy in the sport setting', *International Journal of Sport Psychology*, 21, 380–95.

Spink, KS 1995, 'Cohesion and intention to participate of female sport team athletes', *Journal of Sport & Exercise Psychology*, 17, 416–27.

Spink, KS & Carron, AV 1992, 'Group cohesion and adherence in exercise classes', *Journal of Sport & Exercise Psychology*, 14, 78–86.

Spink, KS & Carron, AV 1993, 'The effects of team building on the adherence patterns of female exercise participants', *Journal of Sport & Exercise Psychology*, 15, 39–49.

Steiner, I 1972, *Group processes and group productivity*, Academic Press, New York.

Swain, A 1996, 'Social loafing and identifiability: the mediating role of achievement goal orientations', *Research Quarterly for Exercise & Sport*, 67, 337–44.

Vallerand, RJ, Colavecchio, PG & Pelletier, LG 1988, 'Psychological momentum and performance inferences: a preliminary test of the antecedents–consequences psychological momentum model', *Journal of Sport & Exercise Psychology*, 10, 92–108.

Walling, M, Duda, J & Chi, L 1993 'The perceived motivational climate questionnaire: construct and predictive validity', *Journal of Sport & Exercise Psychology*, 15, 172–83.

Weinberg, R & Gould, D 1999, *Foundations of sport and exercise psychology*, 2nd edn, Human Kinetics, Champaign, IL.

Weiss, M & Smith, A 1999 'Quality of youth sport friendships: measurement development and validation', *Journal of Sport & Exercise Psychology*, 21, 145–66.

Westre, KR & Weiss, MR 1991, 'The relationship between perceived coaching behaviors and group cohesion in high school football teams', *The Sport Psychologist*, 5, 41–54.

Widmeyer, WN 1986, 'Theoretical and methodological perspectives of group dynamics in the study of small groups in sport', in CR Rees and AM Miracle (eds), *Sport and social theory*, Human Kinetics, Champaign, IL, pp. 171–87.

Widmeyer, N & Ducharme, K 1997, 'Team building through team goal setting', *Journal of Applied Sport Psychology*, 9, 97–113.

Widmeyer, WN, Brawley, LR & Carron, AV 1985, *The measurement of cohesion in sport teams: the Group Environment Questionnaire*, Spodym, Eastbourne; UK.

Widmeyer, WN, Brawley, LR & Carron, AV 1990, 'The effects of group size in sport', *Journal of Sport & Exercise Psychology*, 12, 177–90.

Widmeyer, WN, Brawley, LR & Carron, AV 1992, 'Group dynamics in sport', in T Horn (ed.), *Advances in sport psychology*, Human Kinetics, Champaign, IL, pp. 163–80.

Williams, J & Hacker, C 1982, 'Causal relationships among cohesion, satisfaction, and performance in women's intercollegiate field hockey teams', *Journal of Sport Psychology*, 4, 324–37.

Williams, JM & Widmeyer, WN 1991, 'The cohesion–performance outcome relationship in a coacting sport', *Journal of Sport & Exercise Psychology*, 13, 364–71.

Williams, J, Rotella, RJ & Scherzer, C 2001, 'Injury risk and rehabilitation: psychological considerations', in J Williams (ed.), *Applied sport psychology: personal growth to peak performance*, 4th edn, Mayfield, Mountain View, CA, pp. 456–79.

Yukelson, D 2001, 'Communicating effectively', in J Williams (ed.), *Applied sport psychology: personal growth to peak performance*, 4th edn, Mayfield, Mountain View, CA, pp. 135–49.

Zander, A 1975, 'Motivation and performance of sports groups', in DM Landers (ed.), *Psychology of sport and motor behaviour II*, Pennsylvania State University Press, University Park, PA.

Zander, A 1982, *Making groups effective*, Jossey-Bass, San Francisco, CA.

PART 2

APPLICATIONS IN SPORT PSYCHOLOGY

The application of psychological theories, research and measures to a range of sport and physical activity settings had relatively slow beginnings in the 1970s, but has rapidly picked up pace over the past 20 years. In some cases, applied sport psychology developed in a closely integrated way with theory and research. In other areas, practitioners have long adopted an eclectic approach, borrowing from mainstream psychology practice, and from other areas such as counselling, meditation and the martial arts. In part 2, contributors describe current best practice in a range of major areas of applied sport psychology. In chapter 9, Morris and Thomas discuss the development of the field, reflecting on the dominance of the performance enhancement role of applied sport psychologists during the 1980s and early 1990s. In this chapter, Morris and Thomas also draw attention to two developing trends in sport and exercise psychology. First, there has been a considerable shift from pure performance enhancement work at elite and developing levels in sport, to the provision of more broadly based counselling support. Second, sport and exercise psychology practitioners have matured sufficiently that they are now applying their expertise in other performance contexts, such as the performing arts and business. In the third edition of this book, no doubt these will be worthy of separate chapters. Chapters 10 to 14 address the main components of psychological skills training for sport performance enhancement. Weinberg, in chapter 10, describes the well-developed area of goal setting, where theory, research and practice originated in business but have been developed substantially in sport and exercise contexts. Smith and Smoll consider the management of stress and anxiety in chapter 11. This is such a broad field that they necessarily focus on major approaches. In chapter 12, Henschen and Newton explain techniques to build confidence, especially in the context of high-level sport. Imagery is a very widely used technique in sport and exercise psychology. In chapter 13, Morris, Spittle and Perry briefly consider underlying theory and research, before describing a wide range of uses of imagery and strategies to facilitate its effective application. In chapter 14, Bond and Sargent address ways to enhance concentration, based on theory and research on attention. They give plenty of examples from their extensive experience in elite sport. Flow is a conceptualisation of peak experience that has been widely applied to sport, especially during the past 10 years. In chapter 15, Jackson and Wrigley describe the development of the concept and its application for increased enjoyment and enhanced performance in sport and exercise. As sport and exercise psychology training and practice have developed, it has become important to reflect on the way we train future generations and the support we provide via supervision in order to ensure that novice practitioners and our experienced peers deliver services effectively. To conclude part 2 on the application of sport and exercise psychology, Andersen considers these matters in chapter 16.

CHAPTER 9

APPLIED SPORT PSYCHOLOGY

Tony Morris & Patrick Thomas

The discipline of sport psychology has much of practical value to offer sports performers. The profession of sport psychology developed during the 1970s and 1980s based on this premise. Before that time academics examined how psychological constructs such as motivation, personality, anxiety and group processes affected people's involvement in sport at all levels. When psychologists were invited to work with elite athletes, many focused on developing ways to practise sport psychology. Because of the priorities of coaches, administrators and athletes, the most prominent function of applied sport psychologists, especially at the elite level, has been performance enhancement, as reflected in the professional activities of sport psychologists around the world (K Cogan, personal communication, 4 December 2003; Lidor, Morris, Bardaxoglou & Becker 2001; Morris, Alferman, Lintunen & Hall 2003). This chapter discusses work on psychological skills training techniques and programs to enhance performance, treating this aspect of applied sport psychology in depth. Largely as a result of the efforts of pioneer practitioners, this role of the applied sport psychologist is widely accepted and valued by athletes, coaches and administrators (Lidor et al. 2001; Morris et al. 2003). In this chapter we first delineate the nature of applied sport psychology, placing performance enhancement in context. In considering the breadth of applied sport psychology, we reflect on the diverse developments within the profession. A detailed analysis of approaches to psychological skills training, as the most prominent aspect of performance enhancement, is then presented. The chapter draws together consistencies and highlights significant contradictions concerning the application of mental skills training, and raises issues currently facing practitioners.

As sport psychologists practised in a range of elite sport settings, they became aware that factors other than psychological skills affected athletes' performance and development (e.g. Henschen 2001; Serpa & Rodrigues 2001). Coping with injuries, worrying about life after sport and handling an elite athlete's world are just some factors that affect elite sports performers (Andersen 2001). Some sport psychologists believe these concerns must be addressed because they affect athletes' performance (Andersen 2000). For other sport psychologists the main issue is individual wellbeing, so they also prioritise personal development (Andersen 1992; Balague 1999). Counselling athletes who are dealing with various personal problems is a growing part of the work of applied sport psychologists (Andersen

2000; Tenenbaum 2001; Van Raalte & Brewer 2002; Williams 2001). Therefore we briefly consider psychological counselling of athletes.

We like to think of sport as a unique part of our lives, yet sport psychologists have recognised that many sport psychology issues — including the development of physical and psychological skills, the need to cope under pressure and produce optimal performance, and the importance of being able to work cooperatively with others — also apply to other areas of life (Hays 2000). There are obvious parallels with artistic performance activities such as dance, drama and music, which involve complex skills that must be produced optimally in stressful situations, often as part of an ensemble. Many other kinds of work also involve maximum performance, working under pressure and cooperation. Recently, experienced sport psychologists have started to provide services for the performance arts and the world of business (Hays 2000; Jones 2002). The skills and knowledge that expert sport psychologists possess are transferable to these other domains, and the practitioners often gain credibility from their work with elite sports performers (Jones 2002). In a later section of this chapter we consider the potential for expanding the knowledge and skills of sport psychologists into other domains such as artistic performance and the world of work.

As the skills and knowledge needed to practise professionally as a sport and exercise psychologist have expanded, we have become interested in the course of our development as practitioners, through training to our first tentative steps into practice, and on to that high level of expertise we observe in our esteemed colleagues (Andersen 2002a; Andersen, Van Raalte & Harris 2000; Petitpas, Danish & Giges 1999; Van Raalte & Andersen 2000; see also chapter 16). The chapter outlines a stage theory of professional development and considers the implications of this theory for the development of expertise in applied sport psychology. Based on the foregoing analysis, the chapter proposes a number of future directions for professional practice by applied sport psychologists in the performance enhancement area and suggests several areas of research that should be addressed with some urgency.

Recently the discipline of exercise psychology has gained increased attention. A number of professional associations (e.g. the British Association of Sports Sciences and the British Association of Sport and Exercise Science) and journals in sport psychology (e.g. the *Journal of Sport Psychology*, the *Journal of Sport & Exercise Psychology*, the *International Journal of Sport Psychology* and the *International Journal of Sport and Exercise Psychology*) have recognised that 'exercise' is a major area of scientific study with important implications for health and wellbeing in the whole community. Similarly, new bodies (e.g. the American Psychological Association Division 42, Exercise and Sport Psychology) and periodicals (e.g. *Psychology of Sport and Exercise*) have included sport and exercise in their titles. The quantum of research on psychological aspects of physical activity is growing rapidly. Further, more work is focusing on interventions to increase involvement of various groups, such as children, older adults, women and people with disabilities. Nonetheless we have yet to see sport psychologists working substantively in the role of exercise service providers, so we have not included the practice of exercise psychology in this chapter or in part 2 of the book. Two chapters in part 3 are devoted to psychological theory and research on exercise and physical activity (see chapters 17 and 18).

PRACTICE OF APPLIED SPORT PSYCHOLOGY

Sport and exercise psychology is now considered by many researchers and practitioners to be a diverse discipline involving psychological theory and research directed to the understanding of human behaviour in and through sport (e.g. Williams 2001). Applied sport and exercise psychology is just one part of the discipline — the part concerned with the application of theories, principles and techniques from psychology to the enhancement of performance and the personal growth of athletes and physical activity participants (Williams 2001; Williams & Straub 2001). Some new aspects of applied sport psychology have arisen as a consequence of the experiences of sport psychologists in the applied field and the awareness that a viable profession with jobs to offer must diversify its product (Andersen 2002a). This section discusses the major areas in which the practice of applied sport psychology is well established and then considers some fields in which sport psychologists have begun to apply their skills.

Performance enhancement

The first substantial application of sport psychology was in the area of performance enhancement, and this is still a major area of consultant involvement with Olympic athletes (Gould, Tammen, Murphy & May 1989; Van Raalte & Brewer 2002; Williams 2001). The most widely practised approach to performance enhancement is mental or psychological skills training, which has been called the educational approach to sport psychology practice (US Olympic Committee 1983; Zizzi, Zaichkowsky & Perna 2002). Early research in applied sport psychology identified a limited number of psychological characteristics that appeared to be associated with peak performance (Highlen & Bennett 1979; Mahoney & Avener 1977; Ravizza 1977). The psychological skills training approach instructs performers in a range of techniques intended to emulate these psychological characteristics. The aim is to replicate the peak performance state, based on the assumption that this makes superior performance more likely. The following sections discuss the performance enhancement and mental skills training field in some detail.

Sports injuries

Sports injuries cost the Australian community around $1.5 billion a year, and injuries are still growing despite advances in technique, safety of equipment, physical fitness and preparation, and new technology to reduce risks (Bond, Miller & Chrisfield 1988; Gordon, Milios & Grove 1991; Medibank Private 2003). A similar picture has emerged from North America (Heil 1993; Pargman 1999). Prevention of injuries would save individuals from pain and inactivity and reduce the nation's medical bill. Various psychological factors are also important, particularly life stress levels, coping resources and social support (Williams & Andersen 1998). Interventions involving stress management techniques, coping strategies and mobilisation of social support, for example through education, can help. Faster rehabilitation would also achieve the aims cited earlier. Research is limited here, as noted in Green's (1992) consideration of the area, but there is evidence that some applied sport psychology techniques can speed up recovery (e.g. Ievleva & Orlick 1991) and support for the application of psychology in sports injury rehabilitation from a survey of athletic trainers (Wiese, Weiss & Yukelson 1991). Whether to an elite player just before Olympic trials or to a daily jogger, injury in sport can be very distressing. An understanding of the psychological processes involved and a number of techniques that can help the injured person to cope have provided sport psychologists with a start in this field, but much remains to be done. Furthermore, an athlete may be considered by medical experts to be recovered from injury but may still be unable to perform adequately. Alongside physical recovery, psychological readiness for return from injury is an important consideration (Rotella & Heyman 1993). In chapter 21, Petrie and Perna review work on sports injury, describing the rapid development of this aspect of the practice of sport psychology.

Overtraining

In many sports, endurance, power, speed and technique, or their combination, is critical to success. As sports have become more professional and human limits have been pushed ever further, training demands have been relentlessly forced upwards. This has led to the phenomenon called overtraining. Ironically it is the sheer weight of training to be faster, stronger or more accurate that appears to lead to a reduction in physiological functioning, a downturn in performance at training and in competition, and a negative psychological profile. A range of techniques, including periodisation, has been developed or applied to minimise the chances of becoming overtrained and to cope with and recover from it. Again, prevention is considered to be preferable to cure. If it is not recognised quickly, overtraining can increase in severity to reach the state referred to as burnout, which requires a much longer rehabilitation period and can lead to permanent drop-out. This area is not the subject of substantial consideration in the present text, but is treated by Henschen (2001) and by Mackinnon and Hooper (1992).

Career transitions

Despite the adulation and financial rewards given to our elite amateur and professional athletes, many suffer from doubts during their careers and experience serious problems in adapting to life after sport (e.g. Blann & Zaichkowsky 1989; Petitpas, Danish, McKelvain & Murphy 1992). Sport psychologists' interest in and research on career transitions has expanded at a great pace (Lavallee & Wylleman 2000). During their careers, many athletes worry about what they will do when their time at the top inevitably comes to an end. The ethos of many top-level sports environments has focused on total commitment to sports success. Taking time to study, get work experience or undergo career training would have been unthinkable in some regimens; such pursuits might even have been considered an admission that one was not wholehearted about achieving in sport. The irony is that worrying about lack of career preparation can actually lead to inferior performance, because of the stress felt by the individual athlete (Taylor & Ogilvie 2001). In addition to the effects on the performance of elite athletes during their careers, many outstanding sports performers find the transition out of elite sport to be traumatic as a consequence of the lack of career preparation. The degree of personal investment in their sport can also present problems for some athletes. Elite sport was alerted to these phenomena; early responses included the Lifeskills Education for Athletes Program (LEAP) run by the Australian Institute of Sport, and the Athlete Career Education (ACE) program of the Victorian Institute of Sport. Anderson and Morris (2000) reported on a range of programs that followed in different parts of the world. Gordon and Lavallee provide a detailed review of career transitions and career training in chapter 23.

Interpersonal and organisational issues

Applied sport psychologists have reported being sensitised to the group dynamics in particular elite sport contexts. Once trust was established, athletes, either individually or as a group, often looked to the psychologist to resolve problems with a coach or administrator, or with other athletes, whereas coaches were often concerned with disunity in their squads. This has led to an interest in the application of a number of principles of group dynamics to sports teams (Carron & Hausenblas 1999). Research and applied work is now well established on the facilitation of communication within teams, and between players and officials (Yukelson 2001), the development of leadership styles that are most effective in specific situations (Chelladurai & Trail 2000; Murray & Mann

2001), and the creation and maintenance of cohesion within teams (Carron & Dennis 2001). Hodge considers theory and research on this issue in chapter 8.

The experiences gained from working with elite athletes have also led to awareness that organisational issues at various levels sometimes limit the potential of the team or individual athletes. Again, some applied sport psychologists have addressed issues of organisational structure, training and competition schedules, time management, when and how to travel, where to stay when on tour or overseas, how to spend time when not training and competing, how to minimise the effects of jet lag, and so on (e.g. Baillie & Ogilvie 2002; Gordon 2001).

Special needs groups

Applied sport psychologists have also recognised the needs of other groups, particularly those that can benefit from different kinds of psychological support to help them compete at the highest level and those who may require special support to undertake any type of physical activity (Cogan 2000; Petrie & Sherman 2000). The feats of high-level disabled athletes match anything able-bodied performers achieve, as does their dedication. It is not yet clear, however, whether they require the same psychological support as elite able-bodied athletes, or when such support is best provided (Cogan & Petrie 2002). The current state of research and applied work with disabled athletes receives attention from Hanrahan in chapter 22. Although youth sport has been the focus of substantial research in theoretical sport psychology, particularly with respect to issues of motivation, it has received little systematic attention in the applied area (Smith & Smoll 2002). Tremayne and Tremayne report on the issues and current activities in this field in chapter 20. Sport or exercise is prescribed in the treatment of a number of chronic diseases, such as heart disease, diabetes and asthma. As Morris and Koehn point out in chapter 7, many lack the confidence to undertake physical activities, whereas compliance with regimens also presents problems. These are issues that can be addressed by practitioners in sport psychology.

Health and wellbeing

The physical and psychological benefits of sport and exercise apply to everybody, not just to people with chronic illnesses. Research has indicated that, in addition to producing positive change in physical indicators of health, sport and exercise are associated with psychological wellbeing (e.g. Berger, Pargman & Weinberg 2002; Biddle & Mutrie 2001; Buckworth & Dishman 2002; Hayden, Allen & Camaione 1986; Morgan & Goldston 1987). This appears to be the case with some clinically depressed groups (McCullagh, North & Mood 1988; North & McCullagh 1988), as well as with those who are considered to be psychologically healthy. At the same time, there is a recognition that, as with the compliance problems in special groups, there are many barriers to adherence to exercise in the general population. Exercise psychology is becoming a substantial interdisciplinary area, with contributions from sport psychology and health psychology, as well as from other areas of psychology. Sport psychology is currently playing a major role in theory and practice (Berger, Pargman & Weinberg 2002; Biddle, Fox & Boutcher 2000; Biddle & Mutrie 2001; Buckworth & Dishman 2002), and the potential of this area for future applied work is immense. The massive growth of research work on physical activity is reflected by the inclusion of two chapters on aspects of exercise psychology in this book. Courneya discusses reasons why people do and don't undertake physical activity in chapter 18, and Grove and Zillmann examine research on the outcomes of physical activity in chapter 17.

New applications of sport and exercise psychology are also emerging in the performing arts and business areas, as will be discussed later in this chapter. The examples presented here are broad enough to make the point that there is more than one area in which applications can be made and research needs to be executed. It is this diversity that holds out the hope for those enthusiasts of sport who also have an interest in human behaviour and mental processes to train to become sport psychologists in a vibrant profession.

PERFORMANCE ENHANCEMENT AND PSYCHOLOGICAL SKILLS TRAINING

Sport psychology was an established discipline for some time before sport psychologists became widely involved in performance enhancement in elite sport. The application of psychology to sport was largely the realm of physical educators, whose primary aim was to understand this aspect of human activity, rather than to manipulate and control it. The various political and economic pressures for sport success in the international arena led to demands for higher levels of performance. Elite sport administrators introduced technique-oriented coaches, followed by physiologists with expertise in physical conditioning, to their squads and teams. Many athletes arrived at major events with superb technique and excellent physical conditioning, and still performed poorly. It was at this point that sport began to look to psychology for the 'mental advantage', as Weinberg (1988) called his applied text on performance enhancement in tennis. Claims that 'sport at the elite level is 90 per cent mental' and the like were soon heard from coaches and athletes, but sport psychologists were ill prepared for the development. Few had thought about how psychological characteristics could be applied to sport, so research on techniques and programs was lacking.

Feeling the need to respond quickly to the call from elite sport, some sport psychologists adopted a common approach. To find out what psychological factors help athletes to perform at their best, they asked the athletes. Mahoney and Avener (1977) employed a questionnaire approach with US Olympic gymnasts. Highlen and Bennett (1979) used a similar questionnaire to study Canadian national wrestlers. Using the same kind of design, Meyers, Cooke, Cullen and Liles (1979) studied a university racquetball team. Interview research to address similar questions originated around the same time. Ravizza (1977) interviewed athletes from a number of sports about their 'greatest moments'. Loehr (1984) and Garfield and Bennett (1984) employed large-scale interviews involving hundreds of performers. The studies that employed interviews typically examined the subjective experience of elite performers in depth to determine the psychological characteristics that occur during peak experiences in sport. The questionnaire studies, on the other hand, largely addressed the issue of what psychological factors were important by providing athletes with lists of behaviours, thoughts and feelings to determine those factors that distinguished between successful and unsuccessful performers, as operationally defined in their particular study. Williams and Krane (1993) described these and related approaches in greater detail. They appear to be based on the assumption that what the elite performers subjectively experience must be the best psychological preparation for peak performance. This begged the question whether these performers had reached the top because of other factors, regardless of their mental skills! Fortunately the results revealed that a number of characteristics were repeatedly associated with elite performance. Williams and Krane (1993) listed these as self-regulation of arousal (being energised but relaxed); higher levels of confidence; concentration (being focused on the relevant cues); in control, but not forcing it;

positive preoccupation with sport (through imagery and thoughts); and determination and commitment. Williams and Krane observed:

> Thus, even though adequate cause-and-effect data are lacking, current thinking and practice in applied sport psychology tend to assume that level of performance is a direct reflection of the way one is thinking and feeling rather than that the emotional state is a consequence of performance outcome. In actuality, both could be correct: a circular relationship would be quite logical — that is, optimal mental states lead to better performance, and being successful enhances desirable mental states. (p. 145)

In any event, these characteristics became established as the main elements of the mental state it was perceived that performers must attain as a basis for achievement of peak performance. The 'ideal performance state', as Loehr (1983) dubbed it, was considered to be a necessary, but not sufficient, condition for optimal performance. What quickly became the basic working principle for applied sport psychology in the area of performance enhancement was generated from self-report questionnaire and interview-based research, using retrospective techniques. Substantial experimental research in support of these claims was lacking for some time. Elite sport had appealed for prompt psychological support, and the view of sport psychologists appeared to be that a positive response was needed for the successful future professional development of the discipline.

The major preoccupation of applied sport psychologists for some time was to develop techniques to increase the mental characteristics identified by the peak performance research. Mental skills training was considered primarily to involve stress management for the attainment of the relaxed but energised state; various confidence-building techniques, including positive self-talk and positive imagery; techniques to enhance concentration or focus attention, such as centring and attention control training; imagery, as a technique to see oneself in control, without great effort, as well as to mentally rehearse performance; and goal setting to increase determination and commitment (e.g. Gould, Tammen, Murphy & May 1989). The perspectives that pervaded the field for many years influenced research on the efficacy of various techniques for competitive performers in their sports. It is possible that the breadth of application of relaxation and imagery techniques in applied work biased researchers to choose to study these techniques. Although it may seem logical to determine whether these techniques work, as they have been the most widely used techniques, there may be other techniques that would work more effectively but that have not been studied, because the spotlight remained on relaxation and imagery.

Reflection and early experience in consulting with teams and individuals indicated that it is important to gain early commitment from performers who are undergoing mental skills training. This ensures the athletes understand why the psychological work on performance enhancement is important. This is a major aspect of what is called the orientation stage in a number of programs and models to be discussed. Presenting the characteristics as mental skills that can be developed, just as physical skills are learned, is one way of placing them in a context that performers readily understand. This approach also emphasises the positive nature of the process, focusing on developing new skills to optimise performance, not on finding ways to overcome problems or cover up weaknesses. The term *psychological* replaced 'mental', to produce the phrase Psychological Skills Training (PST).

The methods and techniques that have come to be standard elements of PST were, in the first instance, gleaned in eclectic fashion from a wide range of sources. These included other applied areas of psychology, such as behaviour modification (e.g. Wolpe 1958), cognitive theory and therapy (e.g. Beck 1967, 1976), and rational emotive therapy (Ellis 1958, 1962). As well, Eastern mystical traditions, such as yoga and meditation, and even the martial arts, were tapped. For example, probably the most widely used technique in PST, progressive muscle relaxation (Jacobson 1930), was long employed in Wolpe's (1958) behavioural process of Systematic Desensitisation, as well as being a major induction technique in hypnosis (e.g. Karle & Boys 1987; Waxman 1989). The Relaxation Response was developed by Benson (1975) from his study of transcendental meditation and then adopted by sport psychology. Nideffer's (1985) process of centring emerged from his personal experience with the martial arts.

Thus the central methods and techniques of the performance enhancement area developed in a somewhat piecemeal fashion from the urgent needs of the new practitioners. Practitioners aimed to create the conditions identified by the questionnaire and interview-based research as those most likely to be associated with an 'ideal performance state', using the best methods of which they were aware. A number of characteristics of a typical PST program until quite recently have been, at least in part, consequences of this historical development process, and these are worthy of note. First, many of the general approaches to PST that are reported in the literature reflect procedures associated with the development of particular skills, such as relaxation and imagery for stress management, or positive self-talk and imagery for confidence. There is little or no mention of how the techniques can be effectively implemented in practice — that is, during training and competition. This weakness was ameliorated when Weinberg and Williams contributed a chapter specific to 'Integrating and implementing a Psychological Skills Training program' (p. 347) to the second and succeeding editions of Williams' seminal applied text (Weinberg & Williams 1993, 2001). Second, the specific way in which an intervention is to be learned and practised is often based on imitation of earlier monographs by more recent publications, rather than empirically determined principles. Thus, for example, many writers who have described relaxation procedures followed the original Jacobson (1930) approach closely, without questioning whether this is appropriate for active athletes. This then became the standard procedure, which cannot be questioned on the grounds of research, because little criticism exists, being rejected only by reference to this consensual orthodoxy. These specific skills-based approaches are reviewed first in the following section.

There have been few attempts to produce a general framework or model for PST until quite recently. Those models that have been produced tend to describe broad stages without referring to the actual procedures involved. Often the models themselves may be too general to be of great practical value. Perhaps a watershed in the development of applied sport psychology was the publication of Murphy's (1996a) book *Sport Psychology Interventions*.

In this text Murphy gathered together reports by a number of eminent practitioners who discussed their approaches to sport psychology practice. The book reflected a diversity of underlying perspectives and began to question the orthodoxy of rigidly applied models. Recently two texts have amplified on this work. Andersen (2000) chose the title *Doing Sport Psychology* for his book specifically to indicate that the content is about what sport psychologists actually *do*, rather than the models they profess to follow. Andersen encouraged his contributors to include the sort of dialogue that occurs in sessions with athletes. Tenenbaum (2001) adopted a similar perspective in his text *The Practice of Sport Psychology*. The earlier mode of discourse in applied sport psychology that involved reporting models and the recent trend towards narrative about the experiences of 'doing' sport psychology are both reflected in the third part of the review of approaches. Finally, it may be that the PST approach, which emerged from the urgent demands of sport and the response of those sport psychologists who were prepared to try to put their skills and knowledge into practice, is not the most appropriate way to approach performance enhancement services. We note some problems with the PST approach and consider alternatives.

APPROACHES TO PSYCHOLOGICAL SKILLS TRAINING

Information on PST can be found in at least four different types of literature. A number of sport psychologists have written texts on the performance enhancement area. Most of these are basic, often couched in lay language and intended for athletes and coaches more than scientific colleagues (e.g. Gauron 1984; Harris & Harris 1984; Orlick 1986, 2000; Weinberg 1988). Some adhere to the academic conventions, being intended, like this book, for the use of students in training and colleagues in the profession (e.g. Andersen 2000; Hardy, Jones & Gould 1996; Tenenbaum 2001; Van Raalte & Brewer 1996, 2002; Williams 1986, 1993). Practitioners have reported the nature of programs that they have offered to specific groups. Before the launch of *The Sport Psychologist* and the *Journal of Applied Sport Psychology* in the late 1980s, it had proved difficult to find an appropriate forum for the publication of such material. The development of applied journals in the field has opened one avenue for this valuable type of communication, as exemplified by the papers in special issues (e.g. *Australian Psychologist* 1995; *The Sport Psychologist* 1989, 1990). Some practitioners have published the materials developed in their PST programs, providing athletes, coaches and sport psychologists with training manuals, worksheets, audiocassettes and videotapes (e.g. Suinn 1986; Winter & Martin 1991). Although there is great variability in these training materials, they nevertheless represent another useful source of information on PST. General models have been proposed in a range of contexts — occasionally, but not frequently, within texts, sometimes in a wider review of the field, but again only rarely in specific papers (e.g. Boutcher & Rotella 1987; Martens 1987; Tenenbaum 2001; Thomas 1990; Vealey 1988). These four types of literature reflect rather different approaches, and are therefore considered separately.

Skills without a framework

Much of the early applied sport psychology literature consisted of texts written by eminent or high-profile sport psychologists, especially those with strong credentials of practice in the elite sphere (Sachs 1991). Although various approaches have been adopted in these books to retain the reader's attention or to make books more readily applicable, the typical structure is to assign one, occasionally two, chapters to each of the major areas identified in the peak performance literature. Usually this material includes an explanation of the importance of the characteristic in optimal sports performance, followed by a description of a number of techniques to enhance the athlete's functioning in terms of that characteristic, often with examples. Some or all of the techniques might then be presented in the form of exercises. Frequently it is at this point that the book leaves that topic. The exercises are usually to be conducted outside the sport context. There is little guidance on how to integrate the techniques into practice or competition; and, aside from whatever examples of typical situations are used to explain the importance of the skill for optimal functioning, it is not made very clear when to use the technique.

Many of these texts have been pioneering work. As far as they go, they provide thorough and well-informed material, but they miss an important link between the development of the skill and its effective application in the performer's sport context (e.g. Gauron 1984; Harris & Harris 1984). Weinberg (1987) wrote specifically in the context of tennis, and his examples were most relevant to practice, but the text still stops short. Orlick (1986), as much as anyone, spent time considering more specific implementation, with chapters on mental plans, pre-competition plan, competition focus plan, pre-competition refocusing, refocusing at the event and implementing the plans.

Williams' (1986, 1993, 1999, 2001) book *Applied Sport Psychology: Personal Growth to Peak Performance* has been widely accepted as the seminal academic text on applied sport psychology. The core material on 'mental training for performance enhancement' provides perhaps the strongest evidence available that the peak performance–based approach still plays a dominant role in the practice of sport psychology. Following an updated version of the chapter on psychological characteristics of peak performance (Williams & Krane 1993, 2001) and one on awareness in athletes (Ravizza 1993, 1999, 2001), chapters consider goal setting, arousal, stress and relaxation, imagery, confidence and attention. Although updated, these chapters on specific psychological skills reflect little change in the orthodoxy. Later editions of the book conclude with a chapter on PST programs for coaches (Smoll & Smith 2001) and a chapter co-authored by Weinberg and Williams (1993, 2001) that has increasingly provided specific detail on the integration and implementation of PST programs. The evolution of that chapter illustrates the development of applied sport psychology, at least in the premier area of psychological skills training.

There is still a need for field-based research on PST using competitive athletes as participants. The advent of the applied journals has encouraged such research and provided a forum for its dissemination and critical appraisal. Intervention-based research has increased substantially over the past decade, and there is now a substantial body of literature on each psychological skill. Although the number of studies of elite performers in competition contexts has increased, much of the literature has focused on North American college athletes, leaving questions about the validity of its application to elite performers. It is therefore still difficult to draw any firm conclusions on the optimal conditions for the application of any of the psychological skills in Olympic or professional sport, or to confidently identify the mechanisms on which their action is based. There is still room for more research on PST, particularly carefully designed and theoretically based work conducted with elite athletes in competition. Understanding the underlying mechanisms of psychological skills will provide the most flexible, adaptable and effective interventions for athletes and coaches in high-level sport.

Specific programs

For many years there was little alternative to the publication of a book as a means to present ideas about applied work or reports of practice. The major journals in the field, the *Journal of Sport Psychology* and the *International Journal of Sport Psychology*, were primarily empirical in nature, reporting formal research. Much of that research, moreover, did not address applied issues. The need for publications that encouraged discussion of topics relevant to applied sport psychology was recognised in the late 1980s by the International Society of Sport Psychology (ISSP), which became affiliated with *The Sport Psychologist* (TSP) from its inception in 1987 (an affiliation that lapsed in the late 1990s), and the Association for the Advancement of Applied Sport Psychology (AAASP), which began publication of the *Journal of Applied Sport Psychology* in 1989. *The Sport Psychologist* includes major sections focusing specifically on *applied research*, which often evaluates programs or techniques, and *professional practice*, which encourages the report of innovative programs, packages or methods, with no requirement to include a research or evaluation component. Early issues of the *Journal of Applied Sport Psychology* addressed the status of sport psychology around the world and specific issues, such as training stress and gender in sport. The editors of this journal have continued to publish topic-focused issues, such as those in the early issues on flow in sport and applying social psychological theories to health and exercise.

Typical of the early content of TSP was an applied research paper by Gould, Murphy, Tammen and May (1991), which evaluated the effectiveness of sport psychologists associated with the US Olympic effort in Seoul in 1988. Gould et al. were able to report that individualising sport psychology strategies was considered to be important by athletes and administrators, as well as by sport psychologists and other sport scientists. Drawing on athletes' strengths was seen to be a positive characteristic of consultants, as was fitting in with the team. That research threw light on the applied process by evaluating a cross-section of sport psychologists operating at the highest level, whereas other research has examined specific programs. An early program intervention study was reported in a paper by Elko and Ostrow (1991), who investigated the effects of a rational-emotive therapy (RET) program on the anxiety levels of female gymnasts. A single-case design was used, allowing flexibility in the application of RET and monitoring of the effects of the program in the competitive setting. Although RET principles are widely used in sport psychology, few studies have examined a formal program. The originator, Ellis (1958, 1962), typically receives no formal recognition for the use of his techniques. Elko and Ostrow (1991) selected high-anxiety gymnasts as participants and were able to show that the RET program reduced cognitive anxiety in five of the six gymnasts, while not affecting somatic anxiety. Ravizza and Osborne's (1991) description of the University of Nebraska football team's '3 Rs' pre-performance routine exemplifies contributions to the professional practice section of TSP. The '3 Rs' refers to 'Ready', a cue to focus attention, 'Respond', denoting the switch to automatic response, and 'Refocus', a brief period to review the play, including acknowledging positive and negative feelings, and then move on to the next play. Ravizza and Osborne (1991) went on to apply this routine in a 'one-play-at-a-time' technique (p. 260), describing a number of typical situations in which it can enhance performance, such as dwelling on mistakes, coping with distractions and not paying attention in a huddle.

Particularly interesting in the context of the present discussion are the special theme issues included in TSP in its first years of publication. In 1989 the journal dedicated a whole issue to the delivery of sport psychology services at the two 1988 Olympic Games in Calgary and Seoul. To start the issue, Gould, Tammen, Murphy and May (1989) presented a general examination of services, and to end it Murphy and Ferrante (1989) described the on-site services at the Summer Games, a somewhat different situation, where a small number of sport psychologists are thrown together with a large number of athletes, with most of whom they are not familiar, in the most intense cauldron of sport on Earth. In between were papers on the specific Olympic preparation programs offered to the Canadian sailing team (Halliwell 1989), the US alpine ski team (May & Brown 1989), the US women's volleyball team (Gipson, McKenzie & Lowe 1989), the Canadian men's gymnastics team (Salmela 1989), the US track and field team (Nideffer 1989), and the US women's gymnastics team (Gordin & Henschen 1989). Orlick (1989) also contributed a paper based on his experience with 'athletes in a dozen different sports over the past two Olympic games' (p. 358). Most of these papers discussed the philosophy underlying their service delivery, the range of services provided and the problems they encountered, as well as giving specific details of programs.

A year later, the December 1990 issue of TSP was devoted to working with professional athletes. A brief, generally similar to that followed by the Olympic contributors, was given to the nine authors. Several contributors wrote papers specific to one sport, namely baseball (Dorfman 1990; Ravizza 1990; Smith & Johnson 1990), ice hockey (Botterill 1990; Halliwell 1990), tennis (Loehr 1990) and cricket (Gordon 1990). Two authors reported on their work across a number of athletes, teams and sports (Neff 1990; Rotella 1990).

The main patterns that emerged from an examination of the Olympic and professional issues included that performance enhancement was the most frequent occupation, although crisis intervention and personal counselling were recognised; that most practitioners espoused an educational sport psychology philosophy, recognising the need for a sound referral system; that more than half the expert practitioners avoided the use of formal tests, their preferred methods being interview and observation; and that they mostly operated on a one-on-one basis with athletes. Few of these expert applied sport psychologists used structured programs or models, preferring to be flexible and to 'go with the flow' (Rotella 1990, p. 416), although several practitioners then proposed models to present areas of training. The question of how to apply the psychological skills in competition was rarely addressed in detail. Many experts proposed that athletes should learn psychological skills before they reached the elite level, and that the skills should be integrated with training. These practitioners, who worked with elite Olympic and professional performers, gave various views on the topic of problems they encountered. Some played down problems, whereas others listed them while giving no account of how they had been handled. One widely identified problem was a lack of sufficient time with players. In general philosophy, the practitioners showed much greater agreement, stating their commitment to athlete fulfilment.

These two special issues appeared at a critical time in the development of applied sport psychology and had a seminal influence on the shape of work for much of the 1990s. This is reflected in the continued publication of PST programs in the sport psychology literature. One trend that has been observed during this period is for the programs to be more specifically focused. Another trend encouraged by the early writers in the applied journals was for sport psychology researchers to study the effectiveness of their programs. The efficacy of PST programs has since been examined in a wide range of activities, including major sports, such as golf (Thomas & Fogarty 1997; Ulrich-Suss 1999), swimming (Gallagher 1999), tennis (Gould, Damarjian & Medbury 1999; Gould, Medbury, Damarjian & Lauer 1999), cycling (Kress, Schroeder, Potteiger & Haub 1999) and ice-hockey (Rogerson & Hrycaiko 2002), and in lower profile sports like scuba (Fields 1997), water running (Brewer & Helledy 1998), gymnasium triathlon (Thelwell & Greenlees 2001), equestrianism (Bloom & Stevens 2002), and those performed by athletes with disabilities (Gorley, Lobling, Lewis & Bruce 2002). Although this trend seems set to continue, an alternative perspective has emerged in recent years, as some very experienced applied sport psychology practitioners have argued that much of their work involves counselling for psychological problems often, but by no means exclusively, related to performance (e.g. Andersen 2000; Giges & Petitpas 2000; Henschen 2001; Murphy 1996a; Petitpas 2002). This development is examined in more detail in the section on counselling in applied sport and exercise psychology later in this chapter.

Training materials and resources

Various psychological skills training programs have been developed in North America. Suinn (1986) was one of the first to produce a mental training manual for athletes. The seven steps in his program began with training in relaxation techniques. Progressive muscle relaxation was followed by instruction in centring techniques, which were then implemented in different situations including competition. The second step trained the athlete to recognise the signs of stress, prevent stress from getting out of hand, and learn how to use centring techniques to control high levels of stress. Step 3 provided training in a number of thought-control techniques, including using negative thoughts to trigger positive and corrective action, changing negative thoughts to positive thoughts, countering, reframing and thought stopping. Training was also provided in developing and using positive affirmation statements. Personal best performances were reviewed in Step 4, in order to develop self-regulation skills. Training in visual-motor behaviour rehearsal — relaxation followed by visualisation of performance in competition and achievement of goals — was provided in Step 5. Step 6 incorporated earlier developed relaxation and mental rehearsal techniques in a routine for controlling and directing concentration during competition, and for refocusing attention after distraction. Finally, Suinn trained athletes to recognise their own energy and to harness this energy, so that it could be directed for maximum use.

Martens (1987) published a psychological skills training program primarily for the use of Level 2 coaches in the American Coaching Effectiveness Program, with an accompanying study guide and workbook (Bump 1989). The program provided training materials in six major areas: imagery skills, managing psychic energy, stress management, attentional skills, self-confidence and goal setting. The study guide and workbook presented questions and exercises that further developed understanding in each area and provided a range of useful resource materials.

Rushall (1992) adopted a behavioural orientation in his psychological skills training manual, which extended his previous handbook on imagery training in sports (Rushall 1991). This program provided training through a series of exercises in each of the following areas: promoting a positive approach to the sporting experience, goal setting, developing commitment, performance enhancement imagery, relaxation skills, precompetition mental skills, competition mental skills and team building. For example, training in competition strategies included exercises on performance segmenting, task-relevant thinking, using mood words to control action, positive thinking, switching attention, coping with the unexpected and combating fatigue. This area concluded with a performance debriefing exercise, which trained athletes to evaluate the adequacy of their pre-competition preparations and use of competition strategies.

Hardy and Fazey (1990) produced a mental training program for the National Coaching Foundation in the United Kingdom. The four audiocassettes and accompanying booklets provided training in goal setting (six sessions, each lasting about 30 minutes), relaxation/anxiety control (18 sessions spread over three weeks), mental rehearsal (seven sessions) and concentration (six sessions). Taking concentration training as an example, the initial session emphasised the need to focus attention on the present and introduced training in dissociation techniques for use with distractions. The subsequent training exercises promoted a narrow focus of attention and further desensitised athletes to distractions. Athletes were encouraged to simulate competition conditions at practice and develop skills in handling negative feedback during performance. The final session directed athletes' attention to performance or process-oriented goals and recommended the use of competition tapes containing appropriately positive statements and verbal triggers associated with effective concentration.

Winter and Martin (1991) produced a basic training program in sport psychology for the South Australian Sports Institute, together with a practical guide for coaches. The program, which was expected to take between five and ten weeks to complete, consisted of seven modules presented to athletes through a workbook and accompanying audiocassette tapes. These modules provided athletes with information and training activities in goal setting, relaxation and the relationship between arousal and performance in different sports, concentration, self-confidence, visualisation and motivation. The final module combined the skills of relaxation, visualisation and planning to establish a mind-set conducive to optimal performance in competition. Athletes were encouraged to reflect on previously successful performances to identify effective pre-competition routines. They were encouraged to plan their pre-competition schedule carefully, beginning with positive thoughts and feelings from the moment they wake on the day of competition. In preparing for competition, athletes implemented relaxation techniques as they mentally rehearsed important aspects of their performance in the specific competition environment. One objective of these mental rehearsals was to establish a set of performance cues that would later trigger appropriate reactions in competition.

Although applied sport psychologists have continued to develop generic documentary training programs in book, manual, audiotape or videotape format, in recent years there has been a move towards the presentation of sport-specific programs. A promising example of this is the 'Sport Psychology Library', which is under development by Fitness Information Technology (FIT). *Sport Psychology Library: Basketball* (Burke & Brown 2002), one of the first books in this series, demonstrates the model. Burke is a well-known sport psychologist and Brown is a renowned college basketball coach. Together they outlined 'mental skills training that is critical to all-round success, both on and off the court' (abstract). Publications by particular sports provide another source of resource materials. For example, Heil and Zeland (2001) published the *Psychological Skills Training Manual* for the US Fencing Association. Wann and Church (1998) described a method for enhancing the psychological skills of track and field athletes in *Track Coach*. Kluge and Savis (1998) reported on a systematic and situational approach to mental skills training in *Coaching Women's Basketball*. Other sport psychologists have focused specifically on school sport or school-age participants (e.g. Haslam 2002; Hogg 1997; Malinauskas 2002; Smith 2000; Tingley 1998), and athletes with disabilities (e.g. Hanrahan 1999; Harlick & McKenzie 2000). The trend is not all in this direction, however. For instance, Sargent (1997a, 1997b, 1997c) wrote a series of generic articles for *Sports Coach*, a journal produced in Australia, on developing a mental skills training program. As these kinds of publications have proliferated in recent years, it is not possible to cover them comprehensively. They can be found by searching Internet sites of publishers, sports organisations and sport psychology groups.

Other useful resources include a number of videotapes that can be integrated very effectively in a psychological skills training program. Some address generic skills (e.g. Curtis 1988; Jacobs 1988), whereas others focus on specific skills such as visualisation (Botterill 1988). Videotapes have also been produced for training psychological skills in specific sports, such as Australian football (Stewart 1990), figure skating (Martin 1989), golf (Fine 1993; Hogan 1988) and tennis (Loehr 1989). A more recent example of an audiotape is *Inner sports: mental skills for peak performance: psyching to perform your best* (Ievleva 1997). *The Sport Psychologist* regularly includes reviews of new books and videotapes, as does *Sports Coach*. Once again, non-book resources are expanding rapidly as publishers respond to the growth in interest of sports performers and coaches at all levels in the potential of applied sport psychology, especially mental skills training.

General models

Applied sport psychology practitioners have not proposed many general models of the performance enhancement or PST process. Three of the earliest attempts to be found are those of Martens (1987), Boutcher and Rotella (1987), and Vealey (1988). Martens' proposed program had three phases. In the first, the education phase, athletes learned about various psychological skills, how they influence performance and how they can be developed. The second phase was called acquisition and involved structured training on the skills required. Phase 2 was assumed to take place away from the sport, as the third phase involved practice of the skills to make them habitual and integrate them into competition. It was called the practice phase.

Vealey (1988) also proposed a three-phase approach. The first phase in Vealey's model, *attainment*, combined the education and acquisition phases in Martens' conceptualisation, referring to understanding and developing proficiency in the skills. *Sustainment* then involved incorporation into daily practice and competition routines, like Martens' practice phase. Vealey (1988) added a *coping* phase, during which strategies were developed for coping with situations when the skill proved inadequate or when skills weakened — that is, lost their effectiveness. Vealey emphasised the importance of preparing athletes for the possibility that established competition plans would fail under certain circumstances and back-up coping strategies would be needed. Vealey (1988) also stressed the importance of distinguishing between skills and the methods or techniques used to develop them. Thus, the attainment of optimal arousal for performance or arousal control is a skill that may be supported by a range of techniques, such as muscular relaxation, the relaxation response, imagery to reduce or increase arousal level, positive self-talk, thought stopping, centring, meditation, and listening to stirring or relaxing music.

Boutcher and Rotella (1987) referred to their educational program as the enhancement of closed skills, although they acknowledged that much of it would apply to open skills as well. They stated that the program has four phases, sport analysis, assessment, conceptualisation and skill development, but their diagrammatic representation also included a final program evaluation. The sport analysis phase involved an analysis of the skills needed in the sport from a number of disciplinary perspectives, including sport psychology. Based on this, assessment would be conducted to determine the individual's strengths and weaknesses, which could be profiled. From the profile, Boutcher and Rotella proposed that it was possible to draw out implications for performance, leading to the use of a goal-setting strategy in the conceptualisation phase to gain commitment from the athlete to behaviour change. The fourth stage involved the development of the skills identified in the conceptualisation phase — first as general skills, then applied specifically to the performer's situation, and finally incorporated in performance routines. Boutcher and Rotella (1987) proposed the use of routines before, during, after and between performances. Interestingly, although Boutcher and Rotella (1987) espoused an educational philosophy, the flavour of their description was problem-oriented, especially in the example interview schedule they presented.

Drawing on these general models as well as his observations of the practices of prominent North American sport psychologists, Thomas (1990) outlined seven phases of performance enhancement processes, as shown in figure 9.1. Thomas proposed that, when an athlete sought the help of a sport psychologist to enhance performance, the initial orientation meeting needed to clarify the purpose of the consultation, set objectives to be achieved and determine whether the level of commitment to the task is sufficient. Often there is no 'quick fix' to the problem identified, and the athlete needs to know and accept that time and effort will be required to understand, develop and integrate psychological skills to the point at which they can be utilised effectively in competition.

Once the task has been defined, Thomas suggested that the sport psychologist needs a detailed analysis of the specific domain involved, an analysis that draws on research in psychology, biomechanics and exercise physiology, as well as knowledge of the situation drawn from personal experience. Boutcher and Rotella (1987) argued that the sport psychologist needed to be skilled, for example, in determining whether a flawed golf swing derives from an underlying biomechanical problem or, as the golfer may initially suggest, a result of ineffective concentration. Because the performance enhancement process sometimes begins with an analysis by the athlete (or coach) that precedes the request for help from a sport psychologist or some other professional, arrows in either direction are shown between the first two phases in figure 9.1.

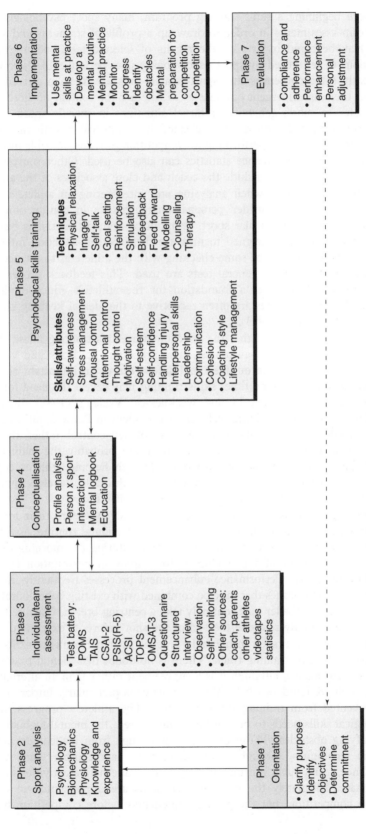

Figure 9.1   Performance enhancement processes in applied sport psychology: Thomas's model

Before beginning a skills training program, many sport psychologists conduct individual/team assessments in order to draw up a profile of strengths and weaknesses. The profile may be based in part on the results of selected tests and inventories. Detailed descriptions of tests used by sport psychologists may be found in Ostrow (1996). There is currently some consensus that sport-related tests are to be preferred over non-sport tests, but there are divergent opinions as to whether the content of those test instruments should refer to sports generally or target situations in specific sports. Test results are usually supplemented with material gleaned from interviews with the athlete. Personal observation of the athlete performing in competition provides valuable insights, but videotapes, diaries and performance statistics can also be used. Other sources of information for this profiling exercise include the coach and close associates of the athlete.

Thomas stated that, when analysing and interpreting an athlete's profile, a sport psychologist needs to consider personal characteristics in conjunction with the situational demands of a particular sport. It might be argued that this is best done through use of tests specifically designed to measure these person–situation interactions. At the very least, there ought to be some checking with the athlete as to the accuracy of profile interpretation when more general tests are used. This feedback process enhances conceptualisation and provides a foundation for the athlete's education in psychological skills. At this point athletes are often receptive to the idea of keeping a mental logbook, as outlined by Ravizza (1993).

Martens (1987) argued that the psychological skills training phase should begin by developing an athlete's self-awareness. The process of feedback and verification of the athlete's assessment profile outlined in Phase 4 serves an important role in improving self-awareness. At the same time, skills training may reveal the need for further assessment of an athlete's strengths and weaknesses. Vealey's (1988) distinction between psychological skills and training techniques is evident in Phase 5, although thought control is considered a skill like other aspects of self-control rather than a technique. Relaxation, imagery, self-talk and goal setting are probably the main techniques currently being used to enhance performance through helping athletes cope with stress, find an optimal arousal level, focus attention on the task, develop appropriate motivation for training and competition, and improve self-efficacy.

Psychological skills need to be practised extensively before their implementation in competition. Most athletes have well-developed behavioural routines associated with their sport, ranging from consistent patterns of activity during the morning of a competition, through to the waggle of a golf club or the wiping of perspiration from the forehead before kicking a goal. Performance enhancement processes frequently involve the development of mental routines that may be combined with existing behavioural routines. Thus the golfer or the footballer may routinely take a centring breath, visualise the ball reaching its target and mentally rehearse the feel of the shot before its execution.

Athletes are encouraged to mentally practise their performance skills away from the competition arena or training track. There is no doubt that mental practice significantly enhances performance, although it is a supplement rather than an alternative to physical practice (Feltz & Landers 1983). Mental practice is particularly important for those athletes prevented from training through injury. The athlete's progress in implementing psychological skills needs to be constantly monitored, the mental logbook proving useful in identifying obstacles. Those obstacles may range from inadequate understanding of the basic techniques, through to an inability to handle other team members or the coach. Once again, such information may lead to alternative activities in the implementation phase. Ultimately the psychological skills are implemented to enhance performance in competition, but the period immediately before competition has a substantial effect on the subsequent outcome. To ensure optimal performance, psychological skills need to be implemented during this period of preparation. Ravizza (1988) and Weinberg (1984) provided useful accounts of various mental preparation strategies.

Sound evaluation of the performance enhancement processes used by sport psychologists is needed for the good of the athlete and the discipline (Greenspan & Feltz 1989). Various evaluation procedures can be used, ranging from large group studies (e.g. Gould, Petlichkoff, Hodge & Simons 1990) to single-subject designs (Bryan 1987; Smith 1988). In evaluating the effectiveness of intervention processes, it is essential to determine initially the athlete's level of compliance and adherence to aspects of the training program. Ideally one would wish to find clear evidence of performance enhancement in those athletes participating fully in the program, but other goals of the program should not be overlooked, such as evidence of improved personal adjustment in athletes. The end result of such evaluations will subsequently help the athlete and sport psychologist set appropriate objectives in the initial orientation phase.

The model proposed by Thomas (1990) appeared to include most of the elements of other models and added some interesting stages to cover most aspects of a structured process. Few general models have been proposed recently. This might reflect recognition that Thomas's model is effective. At the same time, as reported elsewhere in this chapter, recently there has been a shift towards the counselling approach (e.g. Andersen 2000; Tenenbaum 2001; Van Raalte & Brewer 2002), with its more intuitive and individualised ethos. The next section considers other limitations of general models.

Limitations of models

The general models of psychological skills training share some of the same limitations as the specific programs discussed earlier. There are common logistical difficulties, for example, in getting quality time with individuals and balancing this with sessions for the whole team. Fitting the training program around the schedules of other professionals working with the athletes can also pose difficulties. Working with the team coach is essential. Initially the sport psychologist might experience difficulty in gaining acceptance from both coach and players, and a relationship of trust needs to be developed before any meaningful assessment can be conducted. Ravizza (1988) offered some particularly sound advice on gaining acceptance as a consultant.

Not all athletes will be well served by formal assessment in the initial phases of intervention. Indeed, appropriate assessment instruments often do not exist. Initially, slow progress in performance enhancement is just as much a problem with the general models as the specific programs. This problem may arise if the orientation, assessment and program design stages are protracted, thus preventing the athlete from actually getting to practise any psychological skills. Similarly, frustration will be experienced by some athletes who have worked on developing stress management skills through progressive muscle relaxation techniques, or thinking more positively through self-talk exercises, only to find little evidence of immediate improvement in their sport performance.

The general models may not adequately represent the performance enhancement processes appropriate in some sports, nor should it be assumed that the same processes are appropriate for elite athletes and beginners. This is perhaps the greatest limitation of the general models — their implicit suggestion that performance enhancement through psychological skills training is accomplished through a single, sequential set of procedures. This lack of flexibility predisposes the sport psychologist to one approach, when others may be more suited to the demands of a particular situation. In situations where the proposed sequence is hard to maintain because of logistical or personal circumstances, applying the model may be both difficult and ultimately ineffective.

A number of alternative perspectives on psychological skills training have been published recently, and these warrant careful consideration.

Performance profiling

The performance-profiling approach advocated by Butler and Hardy (1992) and illustrated by Jones (1993) and Butler, Smith and Irwin (1993) incorporates most of the processes typically found in psychological skills training programs. The approach begins with an orientation meeting between sport psychologist and athlete, followed by an assessment phase. The athlete identifies characteristics required by elite performers in their sport and receives a visual profile of their self-ratings on each of these characteristics. Discussion of the results of this assessment provides guidelines for the design of a psychological skills training program that meets each athlete's specific needs. There follows a phase in which the newly learned skills are implemented in practice before their use in competition. Finally, the effectiveness of the intervention is evaluated.

The performance-profiling approach is distinctive in the assessment phase. Sport psychologists typically exercise professional judgement in selecting appropriate techniques to assess the athlete's initial strengths and weaknesses and subsequent changes in those areas. They may choose to use standardised tests or questionnaires developed specifically for sport, interview the athlete, observe performance in competition, or consider information obtained from other sources (coaches, performance records etc.). The performance-profiling approach, on the other hand, shifts the responsibility for determining which constructs will be assessed from the sport psychologist to the athlete.

There are both advantages and disadvantages in this approach to psychological skills training. Athletes are actively engaged, rather than passive participants, in the assessment phase. It is argued that this will lead to the identification of pertinent needs and avoid irrelevant measurement. The process of goal setting is likely to increase the athlete's motivation to bring about improvement in selected areas. Adherence and compliance to the training program are thus likely to increase. The constructs are subjective and tacitly defined by the athlete, however. Whereas the items on a questionnaire explicitly define the constructs selected by the sport psychologist, the athlete's interpretation of constructs will need further elaboration. Those interpretations may well change over time, making it difficult to measure progress in an area. Subjective interpretations also make it difficult if not impossible to compare and contrast self-ratings among athletes or to refute an athlete's inaccurate self-ratings.

Inviting athletes to identify the attributes to be assessed assumes that they have knowledge of the psychological skills required for high levels of performance in their sport. Although such knowledge may develop with expertise, it is often the case that athletes are unaware of some psychological skills that may well enhance their performance. How are these skills or attributes to be included in the program?

Limitations of psychological skills training role

Apart from limitations to the models of psychological skills training, there is the much broader issue of limitations to the role of the psychological skills trainer. It is clear from the thrust of this chapter, and indeed that of other chapters in this book, that provision of psychological skills training is a crucial role of the applied sport psychologist. However, Jeff Bond, Head of the Sport Psychology Department at the Australian Institute of Sport, cautioned psychologists not to restrict themselves to this role:

> If Australian sport psychologists continue to see themselves and/or promote themselves as purely educational sport psychologists or performance enhancement mental skills trainers, then in my opinion, they are selling themselves and their

profession short and are doomed as far as future involvement in elite sport is concerned ... Our training must surely have equipped us with knowledge and competencies which enable us to offer something more than basic mental skills training ... it is no longer appropriate for sport psychologists to hang their professional hat on, or be seen to be the teachers of, basic mental skills for sport. We must continue to do some of that work, continue to teach coaches to do some of that work, but we must practise psychology if we are to continue to advance our profession and to contribute to Australian sport.

(Bond 1993, pp. 8–9)

This issue was also addressed in a report on how the roles of sport psychologists working with gymnasts in the British national squads broadened beyond that of an expert psychological skills trainer (Parfitt & Hardy 1993). As *educators*, Parfitt and Hardy proposed that they taught specific psychological skills, as required, to individuals who had determined their own needs. Coaching workshops and clinics were also conducted throughout the country to develop an understanding of sport psychology at all levels of the sport, enabling others to perform this role. Parfitt and Hardy stated that they also acted as *facilitators*, building group cohesion and a social support network among gymnasts and coaches, and assisting them to construct personal profiles that would be used to develop performance enhancement strategies. As *mediators*, the psychologists addressed difficulties that threatened effective interactions among gymnasts and coaches. As *counsellors*, Parfitt and Hardy described how they worked with gymnasts experiencing a range of problems, including injury, disappointing performances in competition, non-selection for a team and low motivation. As *problem-solvers*, they were instrumental in helping gymnasts overcome psychological difficulties in performing certain moves. Performance profiles proved helpful in this role, discrepancies between a gymnast's self-ratings and those provided by the coach being used to devise appropriate training programs. Finally, Parfitt and Hardy (1993) acknowledged the '*tea person*' role, in which psychologists performed a range of menial tasks, from fetching popcorn to minding baggage, tasks that were much appreciated and helpful in the development of friendly relations with their clients. Evaluations of the effectiveness of the sport psychologists adopting this revised consultant approach were very positive, with many items showing significant improvement from the more traditional approach initially adopted.

COUNSELLING IN APPLIED SPORT AND EXERCISE PSYCHOLOGY

Applied sport psychologists have long been involved in counselling athletes. Henschen (2001) described his experience many years earlier, when, during pre-season training, a coach told a veteran basketball player that he had been excluded from the squad for the season. Henschen reported that he had watched the player walk out the opposite end of the hall, as his former team-mates returned to the dressing room. Henschen followed the lone player, sat with him in silence for several minutes, then grieved with him for nearly half an hour, before the player spoke, asking 'What do I do now?' Henschen just knew the player needed support and counselling. This story appeared in Tenenbaum's (2001) book, *The Practice of Sport Psychology*, which is full of anecdotes by eminent applied sport psychologists from around the world, many focusing on counselling, rather than PST.

In the introductory chapter of his book *Sport Psychology Interventions*, Murphy (1996a) was perhaps the first to highlight the counselling role explicitly. He reported that more than 60 per cent of the 1000-plus issues that athletes at the US Olympic Training Centre in Colorado Springs brought to the sport psychologists there involved performance concerns, criticising the view that PST is what most performers need. Murphy stated, 'the reality is that athletes operate in a stressful world with challenges that few of us can imagine. Athletes encounter a variety of problems in their sports participation, and the interventions described in this book have grown out of a need to help athletes with these problems.' (p. 6). *Sport Psychology Interventions* includes chapters by a range of applied sport psychologists, each describing a different approach to applied sport psychology consulting, including the application of life development, multisystemic, family systems, organisational and developmental models. Part 2 of Murphy's book, 'Special issues in counselling athletes', examines counselling for injuries (Petitpas & Danish 1996), substance abuse (Carr & Murphy 1996), eating disorders and weight management (Swoap & Murphy 1996), career transitions (Murphy 1996c), and overtraining and burnout (McCann 1996).

Andersen's (2000) book, *Doing Sport Psychology*, represents the most substantial collection of reports by experienced and eminent applied sport psychologists about their counselling practice. The book does include some chapters on PST, or what Andersen calls 'the applied sport psychology canon' (p. v), but these four chapters focus on how the practitioners deliver relaxation, imagery, self-talk and goal-setting interventions, not on the techniques per se. The other 15 chapters in the book focus on counselling across a wide range of sport psychology issues, providing clear illustrations of Murphy's point.

Van Raalte and Brewer's (2002) recent text *Exploring Sport and Exercise Psychology* also reflects the growth of counselling. Petitpas (2002), in discussing counselling interventions, distinguished counselling psychology as being psychoeducational and developmental, whereas clinical psychology is remedial and pathology oriented. Petitpas considered both the opportunities for development offered by the sport experience, which can be programmed into athletes' lives, and the unexpected events that athletes must cope with, such as injury. In a chapter of *Exploring Sport and Exercise Psychology* on helping college student-athletes, Andersen (2002b) discussed a range of issues, including transitions, substance use and abuse, sexuality issues, academic performance issues, such as time management and test anxiety, sport injury, dealing with the media, depression, adjustment disorders and eating disorders.

Giges and Petitpas (2000) pointed out another aspect of counselling, arguing that the literature has paid little attention to the brief interventions that applied sport psychologists frequently face when they work in the field. Athletes often present with issues that have to be dealt with on the spot. This might be because the athlete must soon perform in a major event or because the issue is so devastating that it must be addressed quickly to minimise suffering. Giges and Petitpas discussed brief counselling interventions, as well as a framework within which they can be used. They also presented several examples of cases handled in this way.

The development of counselling across a range of sport and life issues is a strong trend in sport and exercise psychology. In the future, a chapter devoted to this topic is likely to be appropriate in any collection of contributions about applied sport psychology. For now, the interested reader is directed to the coverage of aspects of counselling found in Murphy (1996a), Andersen (2000), Tenenbaum (2001), and Van Raalte and Brewer (2002), along with papers, like the one by Giges and Petitpas (2000), that can be found in recent issues of *The Sport Psychologist* and the *Journal of Applied Sport Psychology*.

MOVING BEYOND SPORT PSYCHOLOGY

Although expertise does not always transfer across unrelated domains, recent reports suggest that the knowledge, skills and professional experience of sport psychologists may well transfer to other domains of performance excellence. Such a transfer would not only open up significant new employment options for sport psychology graduates, but also provide opportunities to test the generalisability of our theories, methods and research findings, and enable us to learn from the work being undertaken in those other domains (Gould 2002). It is often argued that performers other than athletes stand to benefit greatly from psychological skills training, particularly those in vigilance and emergency related roles such as police officers, firefighters, and ambulance and other medical personnel (Botterill, Patrick & Sawatzky 1996). Lester (2000) urged psychologists to take on performance enhancement roles to increase the combat effectiveness of defence force personnel, and called for more research to support such interventions. Le Scanff and Taugis (2002) recently reported the benefits derived from a stress management program conducted for French police special forces. Other papers in the special issue of the *Journal of Applied Sport Psychology* (2002) devoted to moving beyond the psychology of athletic excellence focused on excellence in the performing arts and business, and the contribution sport psychologists can make to enhancing performance in those domains.

Applying sport psychology to the performing arts

There are many similarities between sport and the performing arts. The performance arena is common to both, and practitioners who understand performance issues in sport are well placed to work with people who face difficult performance challenges in other domains (Heil, Sagal & Nideffer 1997; Murphy 2000). Hays (2002) argued that 'applied sport psychologists may have a strong theoretical and practical base to transfer their knowledge into work within the domain of performance psychology or performing arts psychology' (p. 300). Hays has recommended such application of sport psychology principles and techniques for a number of years now (Hays 1995), but she warns that if sport psychology can be said to be in its adolescence, performing arts psychology is still in its infancy (Hays 2002). Nevertheless there is research in this area that identifies the similarities and differences with sport and guides the work of the practitioner.

We know, for example, that imagery techniques can be used effectively to enhance dance performance. Using a pretest–post-test control group design, Hanrahan, Tetreau and Sarrazin (1995) showed that imagery facilitated performance of the *battement* and *arabesque* movements, though not the *developpe*. Subsequent research revealed that professional modern dancers make multiple uses of imagery in creating and rehearsing a choreographed movement at practice, and before, during and after a performance (Hanrahan & Vergeer 2000–01). Qualitative analyses identified eight imagery categories, including rehearsal of specific movements, that can be included in dance instruction. It is interesting to note that dance teachers, figure skating coaches and soccer coaches differ significantly in how they use mental imagery, particularly in the use of kinaesthetic and metaphorical imagery (Overby, Hall & Haslam 1997–98).

Palmer (1997) conducted a detailed analysis of research on music performance, one of the most complex forms of human motor skill, and concluded that the cognitive mechanisms underlying music performance are similar to those in other domains. This review examined the components of performance excellence in music, such as interpretation and expression, rhythm and movement. Palmer noted there were few studies of long-term changes in performance ability. She suggested that differences in performance levels across individuals are largely a function of experience and practice (Ericsson

1996), and she anticipated further research on individual differences and skill acquisition in this domain.

Sport psychologists have been actively engaged in overcoming obstacles to performance in music and enhancing performance in that domain, demonstrating the effectiveness of treatment programs incorporating relaxation training, breathing techniques, affirmations, attentional focus, imagery, reframing, and associative and dissociative thinking (Hays 2000). It has long been known that music performance can be a very stressful experience, the state anxiety levels of young band soloists being higher than those associated with academic tests, participation in competitive physical education classes, and competitive individual or team sports (Simon & Martens 1979). Stage fright is a significant impediment to performance for musicians and actors. Dealing with performance anxiety is therefore one of several major issues in working with performing artists. Other issues identified by Hays (2002) include the effects of thousands of hours of dedicated practice on the social and emotional development of young performers, parental 'overengagement', gender stereotyping of particular activities, overuse injuries and eating disorders.

Although these issues are common to both sport and the performing arts, Hays (2002) identified subtle differences that need to be considered by consultants. For example, winning in sport is often an end in itself, but winning a part in a play or dance, or a chair in an orchestra is more often viewed as a means to an end. There are also important differences in the nature of the relationship between the performer and the audience. Hays (2002) provided valuable insights into the similarities and differences in the consultation process. The consultant needs good relational skills; knowledge, interest and experience in the domain in which the performer works; and an understanding of the specific demands made by dance, music and acting. Performing artists are likely to view coaching, consultation and therapy differently from athletes, being more comfortable with psychotherapy because of tradition, but hesitating before seeking performance enhancement training (Schoen & Estanol-Johnson 2001). Mental skills techniques need to be adapted and careful consideration given before examples from sport are used.

Our understanding of performance excellence in dance, music, singing and acting is significantly advanced by recent studies comparing the coping strategies of athletes and performing artists (Poczwardowski & Conroy 2002), and exploring flow in actors (Martin & Cutler 2002). We need further research of this type — examining, for example, whether the dimensions of flow are the same or different in music and sport — if we are to be effective in working with performing artists. Already, however, there are a number of useful publications guiding such professional practice (Emmons & Thomas 1998; Hamilton 1997; Hays & Brown 2003; Taylor & Taylor 1995; Wilson 2002).

Applying sport psychology to the world of business

The psychology of performance excellence has long been of interest in sport and is now the focus of attention in business (Weinberg & McDermott 2002). Coaches and sport psychologists have responded to the demand from business for the principles underlying performance success. For example, Murphy (1996b) described how the skills used by elite athletes to perform at their peak under pressure can be applied to achieve success in business and other domains. Similarly, Nideffer (1996) and Orlick (2000) have explored the application of sport psychology principles to enhance performance in business and other fields of work. Indeed, Orlick (2000) reported, 'Exceptional surgeons and astronauts in North America had performance perspectives and mental strengths similar to those of exceptional classical musicians in Europe and Scandinavia' (p. 15). Loehr and Schwartz (2001) argued that the ideal performance state is characteristic of success in both sport and business; they have established a training program for business executives based on their experience of working with athletes. Jones (2002) recently provided an interesting account of his transition from sport psychologist to business consultant.

The term *executive coaching* emerged in the late 1980s, and the literature on coaching applications grew substantially during the 1990s, although Kilburg (1996, 2000) cautioned that the scientific basis for these applications was extremely limited. Two special issues of the *Consulting Psychology Journal: Practice and Research* in 1996 and 2001 have significantly shaped this emerging field. Various theoretical frameworks are adopted by those engaged in executive coaching, including psychodynamic (Kilburg 1996, 2000; Levinson 1996), social psychological (Smither & Reilly 2001) and cognitive-behavioural orientations (Grant 2001; Richard 1999). Kampa-Kokesch and Anderson's (2001) review of the literature concluded that it provided some basis for understanding the definition, purpose, process, methodologies, clients and service providers of executive coaching. It is an emerging field, however, with no clear and widely accepted definition. As a consequence, there is still uncertainty as to whether lawyers, doctors and other professionals qualify as recipients of executive coaching, and no clear agreement on who should be delivering executive coaching services. Brotman, Liberi and Wasylyshyn (1998) have argued that psychologists are uniquely qualified as executive coaches because of their tactics, tools and training. Given the nature of their work with athletes, sport psychologists are particularly well placed to deliver executive coaching services. However, Garman, Whiston and Zlatoper (2000) found that psychologists were not always highly regarded as executive coaches; they suggested that some psychologists were entering this field without appropriate retraining.

Given that 50 per cent of those in executive positions fail at some time in their careers (Hogan, Curphy & Hogan 1994), it is perhaps not surprising that executive coaching originally focused on the remediation of problems, mostly maladroit behaviour (Levinson 1996), and helping executives develop essential skills. The present focus, however, is on the upside of an individual's potential, and the stigma attached to needing a coach's help to develop has been replaced by the opposite — the status of being important enough to the organisation's future to warrant the investment of individual attention (Frisch 2001). Various authors have outlined the steps or stages in their interventions as executive coaches (Saporito 1996; Weinberger 1995). Smither and Reilly (2001) proposed a five-stage model of effective coaching that is similar to the phases of performance enhancement in applied sport psychology discussed earlier in this chapter: (a) establishing the coaching relationship, (b) assessment, (c) goal setting and development planning, (d) implementation, and (e) evaluating progress and the coaching relationship.

The proposal to expand the target populations for executive coaching by including high performers in other fields, such as lawyers, physicians, religious leaders and sports executives, is one of several issues currently being addressed (Richard 1999). Kampa-Kokesch and Anderson (2001) have asked: is it the clientele that makes executive coaching unique, is it the executive coaching process, or is it a combination of the two? Diedrich (2001) questioned whether executive coaching should be defined as a one-on-one process, offering guidelines for coaching executive teams. Frisch (2001) described the emerging role of the internal coach, a professional within an organisation whose job it is to coach managers and executives. Another issue now receiving considerable attention is the distinction between coaching and therapy.

Attempts have been made to clarify the roles of a consultant, mentor, trainer, coach, counsellor and therapist. There is some overlap in roles (Witherspoon & White 1996) and inconsistency in terminology; indeed, Jones (2002) suggested the one-on-one session involving an athlete and sport psychologist that is commonly referred to as consulting in sport is the same process as that referred to as coaching in business. Kilburg (2000) argued there are no sharp lines distinguishing consulting, coaching and counselling or psychotherapy, viewing these types of helping relationships as zones for which the boundaries are fluid rather than fixed. He referred to his work with a client on the direct problems of the organisation and its systems as consulting. He engaged in coaching when working on the client's behaviourally mediated interactions with the organisation's systems and people, as well as the client's adaptation to the role of manager or executive. When the work involves the client's inner psychological world and problems in dealing with a difficult set of circumstances, counselling or therapy is required, and coaches need to proceed carefully, making appropriate referrals. Mentoring is the process of passing down expert knowledge in a specific domain, and is distinct from coaching in that the coach does not need to be an expert in the client's specific area (Grant 2001). Training is often a rigid process of instruction designed to impart predetermined competencies to the trainee. In contrast, coaching facilitates learning through fostering the development of metacognitive skills, recognising prior knowledge and experience, and giving adult learners responsibility for setting their own agenda and goals.

Kilburg (2000) warned that knowledge and skills in one of these areas may not transfer to another when he stated, 'I do not think that the majority of therapists could work successfully as consultants or coaches in organisational contexts' (p. 17). Later he acknowledged the emergence of life coaching (Hudson 1999) as a counterpart to counselling and psychotherapy, but wanted to distinguish such generic life-enhancing approaches to coaching from the services provided in executive coaching (Diedrich & Kilburg 2001).

Hart, Blattner and Leipsic (2001) reported how 30 qualified and experienced professionals perceived coaching and therapy. Although there were some similarities (e.g. methods of inquiry), there were also distinct differences. Participants reported that therapy often involves a retrospective focus on past injuries to promote insight and interpersonal health, whereas coaching involves a prospective orientation focusing on goals to enhance human performance. There are profound differences in how therapists and coaches relate to their clients, with coaching seen as a more flexible, collaborative process. Interestingly, these practitioners were concerned that coaches who lack clinical training would fail to recognise danger signals requiring referral. At the same time, therapists need to understand how business organisations function and appreciate the role of the individual in the context of the organisation, if they are to make a successful transition into coaching. Being a good therapist does not necessarily make one a good coach.

The research and professional experience of sport psychologists indicate there are many more similarities than differences in the factors associated with performance excellence in sport and business (Jones 2002; Weinberg & McDermott 2002). Organisational issues have a major impact on performance in both domains. Sport psychology graduates whose training programs included courses in organisational psychology are particularly well placed to enhance the performance of those with leadership responsibilities in business organisations. As is the case for anyone practising executive coaching, those applying the principles of elite sport to business must ensure their coaching is evidence-based, using theory and techniques that have been shown to be effective (Grant 2003). Further research is needed on factors that link performance excellence in sport and business, such as motivation, goal setting and organisational culture (Weinberg & McDermott 2002). The characteristics of high-performance environments in sport and business need to be investigated, as do the effects of different leadership styles, the coping strategies of leaders in both domains, the similarities and differences of high-performing teams, and the key mechanisms through which consulting and coaching have their beneficial effects (Jones 2002). A better understanding of these issues based on evidence of how they can be addressed effectively will lead to the transfer of knowledge and skills across domains. If sport psychology continues to broaden its scope to study high performance across a variety of areas, it will continue to meet the growing needs of society, and its future is assured (Murphy 2000).

DEVELOPMENT OF EXPERTISE IN APPLIED SPORT PSYCHOLOGY

Stages of professional development

Clearly there are important differences in how applied sport psychologists approach the task of helping athletes. In part, those differences reflect alternative premises on which the approaches are based. Equally important, however, are the differences that emerge as practitioners develop expertise within a specific domain. Berliner (1988) proposed a general theory of the development of expertise based on the model presented by Dreyfus and Dreyfus (1986). Berliner proposed five stages in skill development as ignorance is overcome and expertise achieved. His theory has implications beyond the field of pedagogy in which it was formulated. We would contend that Berliner's model of expertise development provides a useful framework for understanding the professional evolution of applied sport psychologists, although there is as yet little evidence to substantiate the duration of each stage in the context of the practice of sport psychology. The model may be summarised as follows:

Stage 1: Novice. In order to perform tasks that will be expected of them, students and beginning practitioners focus initially on learning the meanings of terms and concepts. They acquire a set of context-free rules and procedures that guide behaviour, which they tend to follow relatively inflexibly. The novice seeks the 'objective facts' and features of situations and typically places higher value on gaining real-world experience than on verbal information.

Stage 2: Advanced Beginner. After two or three years of work experience, many practitioners begin to allow contexts to guide their behaviour. As episodic knowledge develops with experience and combines with verbal knowledge, the practitioner recognises similarities across contexts and starts to act strategically, knowing when to break or ignore rules and when to follow them. But, like the novice, the advanced beginner often acts in a detached way, having no sense of what is important and often failing to accept personal responsibility for what is happening.

Stage 3: Competent. After three or four years of work experience, competent practitioners have two distinctive characteristics. Firstly, they make conscious choices about their activities, setting priorities and rational goals, and planning how those goals will be achieved. Secondly, they exercise judgement about what is important and draw on experience to determine what to attend to and what to ignore. Competent practitioners tend to feel personally responsible for what happens, but at this stage they are not yet fast, fluid or flexible in their behaviour.

Stage 4: Proficient. Some practitioners reach the proficient stage of development after about five years of work experience. Intuition or know-how becomes prominent at this stage. The proficient individual develops an intuitive sense of a situation and can predict events more precisely through a holistic awareness and recognition of similarities and patterns. The proficient individual is typically analytic and deliberative when deciding what to do, however.

Stage 5: Expert. Experts have the ability to perform a task effortlessly and fluidly. They grasp a situation intuitively and seem to sense the appropriate action to take in non-analytic, non-deliberative ways. In contrast to novices, advanced beginners and competent performers, who are rational, and proficient performers, who are intuitive, experts are described by Berliner (1988) as 'arational' in that their behaviour typically involves neither calculation nor deliberative thought. Experts rarely appear to reflect on their performance when things are going smoothly, but bring deliberate analytical processes to bear when anomalies occur.

In concluding his account of this theory of the development of expertise, Berliner (1988) made some important observations. As in other stage theories of development, wide variations are to be expected in the duration of time individuals spend in a stage. Someone who is typically at one stage of development may display characteristics associated with another stage in particular situations. Finally, expertise is thought to be highly contextualised. Expertise in one domain may not transfer very well to another, unrelated domain.

Application of stages of expertise to applied sport psychology

If we extrapolate from Berliner's (1988) theory to the development of skills in the applied sport psychologist, we can see how different interpretations may be placed on the training models and programs we have presented. Those new to the field of applied sport psychology may well use the materials to familiarise themselves with the terms and concepts that define the field. Initially they are likely to expect to learn rules and procedures for intervening with athletes that can be adopted regardless of the specific features of the context in which they are working. As practitioners become more knowledgeable in their field, comfortable with their techniques and confident in their professional role, their expertise develops. Work experience is integrated with subject knowledge, and the professional behaviour of applied sport psychologists becomes much more strategic and flexible. In many cases, they are capable of getting quickly to the nub of the problem without recourse, for example, to the results of diagnostic tests. Clearly they do not work in the same way with all athletes. They are sensitive to how athletes prefer to process information and consequently are able to offer suggestions that readily effect improvement in the targeted area.

FUTURE DIRECTIONS

Applied sport psychology has developed rapidly in the past 20 years, changing its identity as it has matured. This chapter has reflected the shift from a focus on highly structured psychological skills training to a more wide-ranging role in the provision of psychological support for athletes and, more recently, others in performance contexts. The chapter has noted that an emphasis on personal development often supersedes the search for optimal performance. Sport psychologists functioning within this context will assess the needs of each individual with whom they consult, operating flexibly to address that person's unique psychological profile. Research that explores the issues and concerns that athletes and coaches face will sensitise practitioners to the range of needs of athletes. Understanding and enhancing the sensitivity of sport psychologists to client needs is an important issue for research into the practice of sport psychology. Not only will athletes be poorly served by practitioners who do not respond to those performers' reports of their subjective experience of the problem, but the negative impression given may lose the practitioner valuable credibility in the athletes' eyes.

One dilemma long recognised by applied sport psychologists is to work out who is the client. The psychological growth of athletes is typically the focus of attention for practitioners, but the coach is directly responsible for the performer's overall physical, psychological and performance state, and the administrators of the association pay the bills. It is important for practitioners to be sensitive to the needs of these different groups to understand better what coaches and administrators, as well as athletes, expect. In-depth research on the dynamics that operate between athlete, coach, administrator and sport psychologist will benefit the practice of sport psychology.

The future directions for research on practice that have been discussed to this point reflect the need for practitioners to be able to operate in a highly flexible manner. This allows them to adapt to new or changing situations as they arise. The way in which many of the practitioners in the TSP special issues described their mode of operation suggests that they were functioning at Berliner's (1988) 'Stage 5: Expert' level of professional practice. For the most effective future training of applied sport psychologists, it is important for research to examine the process of acquiring this level of expertise in sport psychology. It is helpful if novices have an understanding of how expertise develops. Educators of future sport psychologists who are aware of the developmental process from beginning practitioner to expert can take steps in the formative years of novices to advance their professional development, facilitating progress through Stages 1 to 5 of Berliner's model. Further, there is a need for more research examining the process of training the deliverers.

The role of the applied sport psychologist has changed, despite its short history. As sport psychologists undertake less of the basic psychological skills training, the relatively straightforward, mechanical skills development being led by coaches and other members of the support team, their role in counselling for a wide range of personal problems is increasing. An understanding of that role is needed. A good starting point seems to be the sort of narrative research that is reflected in the recent texts on doing sport psychology (Andersen 2000; Murphy 1996a; Tenenbaum 2001). As our knowledge of this role increases, we must include more guidance about the specifics of counselling athletes, especially those at the elite level, in sport psychology professional training programs.

The application of performance enhancement and personal development techniques that have evolved in the cauldron of elite sport psychology to the equally pressurised world of performance arts such as dance, drama and music at the highest levels is attracting successful sport psychologists. Recognising that dance and drama are not the same as sport, just as we have acknowledged that gymnastics is not the same as wrestling, there does still seem to be an assumption that what worked in sport will work equally well in the arts. It is important for research to be carried out to confirm that this is the case. Otherwise this could be a very costly assumption, especially for elite dancers, actors, singers and musicians who follow the guidance of sport psychology practitioners. This word of caution also applies to those who propose to apply sport psychology assumptions to the world of business.

We should also ask where the niche for our skills and knowledge is to be found in the realm of exercise. Research has exploded in the field of physical activity promotion, but this is not being translated into employment opportunities for sport and exercise psychologists. It is important for the sport and exercise psychology profession to quickly gain insight into how the promising research results that are currently being reported can be converted into wide recognition in the community of the valuable role sport and exercise psychologists can play in the promotion of physical activity.

CONCLUSIONS

In this chapter we have addressed the development and current status of applied sport psychology. Although we acknowledged the central role of performance enhancement, and especially psychological skills training, recent trends towards diversification were recognised and supported for the future viability of the profession. In accepting Rejeski and Brawley's (1988) call for tighter definition of the field of sport psychology, it was argued that careful definition of function and an increasing range of applications within that function are not incompatible. There is a great diversity of contexts in which sport psychologists can and should function, but they should always use the skills and knowledge they have been trained to apply; they must practise sport psychology in those diverse contexts.

In reviewing books on applied sport psychology, programs proposed in journal articles and models of the PST process, the recurring theme was of the flexible and adaptive mode of operation of the most experienced practitioners, compared with the rather rigid sequences represented by current models. Greater flexibility is needed in future models, yet there must be sufficient structure for the novice practitioner to lean on. Moving new applied sport psychologists through the stages of development of expertise in professional practice is a challenge that research-minded sport psychologists should address as soon as possible. A recognition of the needs of performers and coaches is essential for effective consultancy in applied sport psychology. An adaptability to different needs and contexts should be reflected in the professional training that practitioners receive, a training that must encourage practitioners to become innovative problem-solvers. This adaptability is evident in the way that sport and exercise psychologists have broadened their realm of activity over the past 10 years both with respect to their work with elite athletes and in their exploration of the fields of the performing arts and business. We await the application of the burgeoning research effort in the realm of exercise to practice in the promotion of physical activity, which has great potential for the profession. Then the title and role of sport and exercise psychologist will attain its full maturity.

SUMMARY

This chapter set the scene for part 2 of the book by considering some of the essential elements of applied sport psychology. We began by examining the nature of applied sport psychology and pointing to the range of issues now considered in an applied context. The chapter then focused on the major area of psychological skills training (PST). It reflected on a number of approaches to the communication of PST, including the description of skills without a framework for their operation, common to earlier texts in the applied field; the description of programs designed specifically for a particular sports context, such as work with an Olympic or professional team; and the presentation of a general model that should apply to many contexts. The chapter then raised a number of the limitations of the applied sport psychologist's role. The broadening of the role of applied sport psychologists to counselling for sport-related and personal issues was then considered. The chapter then addressed recent trends for sport psychologists to apply their skills and knowledge in other performance contexts, such as the performing arts and business. Finally, we described a model of professional development that appears to be applicable to applied sport psychology, according to which novice professionals are likely to depend on models of procedure, whereas expert professionals will use their experience of many applied contexts to generate original programs, adapting to each new situation they meet.

REVIEW QUESTIONS

1 How did the practice of sport psychology develop?

2 What are the main components of psychological skills training for performance enhancement? How were they identified?

3 Identify some specific programs in the context of applied sport psychology. What are their advantages and disadvantages?

4 Identify some general models for the implementation of psychological skills training. Describe a model that you consider has good applicability.

5 What are some of the main limitations of models of PST?

6 What other sorts of support can applied sport psychologists give to athletes?

7 Should sport psychologists in practice undertake a range of counselling activities?

8 How might techniques of sport psychology practice be applied to other performance contexts, such as dance, drama and music?

9 What is the potential for applied sport psychologists to offer services to business?

10 How does this chapter suggest that expertise in applied sport psychology might develop? How might this be applied to the training of sport psychologists?

References

Andersen, MB 1992, 'Sport psychology and procrustean categories: an appeal for synthesis and expansion of service', *Association for the Advancement of Applied Sport Psychology Newsletter*, 7, 8–9, 15.

Andersen, MB (ed.) 2000, *Doing sport psychology*, Human Kinetics, Champaign, IL.

Andersen, MB 2001, 'When to refer athletes for counselling or psychotherapy', in JM Williams (ed.), *Applied sport psychology: personal growth to peak performance*, 4th edn, Mayfield, Palo Alto, CA, pp. 401–15.

Andersen, MB 2002a, 'Comprehensive sport psychology services', in JL Van Raalte & B Brewer (eds), *Exploring sport and exercise psychology*, 2nd edn, American Psychological Association, Washington, DC, pp. 13–24.

Andersen, MB 2002b, 'Helping college student-athletes in and out of sport', in JL Van Raalte & B Brewer (eds.), *Exploring sport and exercise psychology*, 2nd edn, American Psychological Association, Washington, DC, pp. 373–94.

Andersen, MB, Van Raalte, JL & Harris, G 2000, 'Supervision II: a case study', in MB Andersen (ed.), *Doing sport psychology*, Human Kinetics, Champaign, IL, pp. 167–80.

Anderson, D & Morris, T 2000, 'Athlete lifestyle programs', in D Lavallee & P Wylleman (eds), *Career transitions in sport: international perspectives*, Fitness Information Technology, Morgantown, WV, pp. 59–80.

Baillie, PHF & Ogilvie, B 2002, 'Working with elite athletes', in JL Van Raalte & B Brewer (eds), *Exploring sport and exercise psychology*, 2nd edn, American Psychological Association, Washington, DC, pp. 395–415.

Balague, G 1999, 'Understanding identity, meaning, and value when working with elite athletes, *The Sport Psychologist*, 13, 89–98.

Beck, AT 1967, *Depression*, Hoeber-Harper, New York.

Beck, AT 1976, *Cognitive therapy and the emotional disorders*, International Universities Press, New York.

Benson, H 1975, *The relaxation response*, Avon Books, New York.

Berger, BG, Pargman, D & Weinberg, RS 2002, *Foundations of exercise psychology*, Fitness Information Technology, Morgantown, WV.

Berliner, DC 1988, 'The development of expertise in pedagogy', Charles W. Hunt Memorial Lecture at the Annual Meeting of the American Association of Colleges for Teacher Education. New Orleans, LA, February.

Biddle, SJH & Mutrie, N (eds) 2001, *Psychology of physical activity: determinants, well-being, and interventions*, Routledge, London.

Biddle, SJH, Fox, KR & Boutcher, SH (eds) 2000, *Physical activity and psychological well-being*, Routledge, London.

Blann, W & Zaichkowsky, L 1989, 'National Hockey League and Major League baseball players' post-sport career transition surveys', final report for the National Hockey League Players' Association.

Bloom, GA & Stevens, DE 2002, 'Case study: a team-building mental skills training program with an intercollegiate equestrian team', *Athletic Insight: The Online Journal of Sport Psychology 4*, www.athleticinsight.com.

Bond, J 1993, 'Controversy corner', *Australian Sport Psychology Association Bulletin*, 2 (1) 8–9.

Bond, JW, Miller, BP & Chrisfield, PM 1988, 'Psychological prediction of injury in elite swimmers', *International Journal of Sports Medicine*, 9, 345–8.

Botterill, C 1988, *Visualization: what you see is what you get*, Ottawa, Coaching Association of Canada, Ontario.

Botterill, C 1990, 'Sport psychology and professional hockey', *The Sport Psychologist*, 4, 358–68.

Botterill, C, Patrick, T & Sawatzky, M 1996, *Human potential*, Lifeskills Inc., Winnipeg, Canada.

Boutcher, SH & Rotella, RJ 1987, 'A psychological skills educational program for closed-skill performance enhancement', *The Sport Psychologist*, 1, 127–37.

Brewer, BW & Helledy, KI 1998, 'Off (to) the deep end: psychological skills training and water running', *Applied Research in Coaching and Athletics Annual*, 13, 99–118.

Brotman, LE, Liberi, WP & Wasylyshyn, KM 1998, 'Executive coaching: the need for standards of competence', *Consulting Psychology Journal: Practice and Research*, 50, 40–6.

Bryan, AJ 1987, 'Single-subject designs for evaluation of sport psychology interventions', *The Sport Psychologist*, 1, 283–92.

Buckworth, J & Dishman, RK 2002, *Exercise psychology*, Human Kinetics, Champaign, IL.

Bump, L 1989, *Sport psychology study guide and workbook*, Human Kinetics, Champaign, IL.

Burke, KL & Brown, DF 2002, *Sport psychology library: basketball*, Fitness Information Technology, Morgantown, WV.

Butler, RJ & Hardy, L 1992, 'The performance profile: theory and application', *The Sport Psychologist*, 6, 253–64.

Butler, RJ, Smith, M & Irwin, I 1993, 'The performance profile in practice', *Journal of Applied Sport Psychology*, 5, 48–63.

Carr, CM & Murphy, SM 1996, 'Alcohol and drugs in sport', in SM Murphy (ed.), *Sport psychology interventions*, Human Kinetics, Champaign, IL, pp. 283–306.

Carron, AV & Dennis, PW 2001, 'The sport team as an effective group', in JM Williams (ed.), *Applied sport psychology: personal growth to peak performance*, 4th edn, Mayfield, Mountain View, CA, pp. 120–34.

Carron, AV & Hausenblas, HA 1999, 'Group dynamics in sport', in G. Tenenbaum (ed.) *The practice of sport psychology*, 2nd edn, Fitness Information Technology, Morgantown, WV, pp. 101–28.

Chelladurai, P & Trail, G 2000, 'Styles of decision-making in coaching', in JM Williams (ed.), *Applied sport psychology: personal growth to peak performance*, 4th edn, Mayfield, Mountain View, CA, pp. 107–19.

Cogan, KD 2000, 'The sadness in sport: working with a depressed and suicidal athlete', in MB Andersen (ed.), *Doing sport psychology*, Human Kinetics, Champaign, IL, pp. 107–20.

Cogan, KD & Petrie, TA 2002, 'Diversity in sport', in JL Van Raalte & B Brewer (eds), *Exploring sport and exercise psychology*, 2nd edn, American Psychological Association, Washington, DC, pp. 417–36.

Curtis, J 1988, *The mindset for winning*, Athletic Visions, Bloomington, MN.

Diedrich, RC 2001, 'Lessons learned in — and guidelines for — coaching executive teams', *Consulting Psychology Journal: Practice and Research*, 53, 238–9.

Diedrich, RC & Kilburg, RR 2001, 'Further consideration of executive coaching as an emerging competency', *Consulting Psychology Journal: Practice and Research*, 53, 203–4.

Dorfman, HA 1990, 'Reflections on providing personal and performance enhancement consulting services in professional baseball', *The Sport Psychologist*, 4, 341–6.

Dreyfus, HL & Dreyfus, SE 1986, *Mind over machine*, The Free Press, New York.

Elko, PK & Ostrow, AC 1991, 'Effects of a rational-emotive education program on heightened anxiety levels of female collegiate gymnasts', *The Sport Psychologist*, 5, 235–55.

Ellis, A 1958, 'Rational psychotherapy', *Journal of General Psychology*, 59, 35–49.

Ellis, A 1962, *Reason and emotion in psychotherapy*, Lyle Stuart, Secaucus, NJ.

Emmons, S & Thomas, A 1998, *Power performance for singers: transcending the barriers*, Oxford University Press, London.

Ericsson, KA (ed.) 1996, *The road to excellence: the acquisition of expert performance in the arts and sciences, sports and games*, Erlbaum, Mahwah, NJ.

Feltz, DL & Landers, DM 1983, 'The effects of mental practice on motor skill learning and performance: a meta-analysis', *Journal of Sport Psychology*, 5, 25–57.

Fields, BR 1997, 'Two case studies of the effects of a clinically oriented psychological skills training program on perceived anxiety, perceived efficacy, scuba performance, and progress in therapy of scuba diving clients', unpublished doctoral thesis, Temple University.

Fine, A 1993, *Mind over golf*, BBC Enterprises, London.

Frisch, MH 2001, 'The emerging role of the internal coach', *Consulting Psychology Journal: Practice and Research*, 53, 240–50.

Gallagher, M 1999, 'Psychological skills training programs of successful Division I women's swim programs', unpublished master's thesis, Ball State University.

Garfield, CA & Bennett, HZ 1984, *Peak performance: mental training techniques of the world's greatest athletes*, Tarcher, Los Angeles.

Garman, AN, Whiston, DL & Zlatoper, KW 2000, 'Media perceptions of executive coaching and the formal preparation of coaches', *Consulting Psychology Journal: Practice and Research*, 52, 201–5.

Gauron, EF 1984, *Mental training for peak performance*, Sport Science Associates, Lansing, NY.

Giges, B & Petitpas, A 2000, 'Brief contact interventions in sport psychology', *The Sport Psychologist*, 14, 176–87.

Gipson, M, McKenzie, T & Lowe, S 1989, 'The sport psychology program of the USA women's national volleyball team', *The Sport Psychologist*, 3, 330–9.

Gordin, RD & Henschen, KP 1989, 'Preparing the USA women's artistic gymnastics team for the 1988 Olympics: a multimodel approach', *The Sport Psychologist*, 3, 366–73.

Gordon, S 1990, 'A mental skills training program for the Western Australian state cricket team', *The Sport Psychologist*, 4, 386–99.

Gordon, S 2001, 'Reflections on providing sport psychology services in professional cricket', in G. Tenenbaum (ed.), *The practice of sport psychology*, Fitness Information Technology, Morgantown, WV, pp. 17–36.

Gordon, S, Milios, D & Grove, R 1991, 'Psychological aspects of the recovery process from sport injury', *Australian Journal of Science and Medicine in Sport*, 6, 53–9.

Gorley, T, Lobling, A, Lewis, K & Bruce, D 2002, 'An evaluative case study of a psychological skills training program for athletes with intellectual disabilities', *Adapted Physical Education Quarterly*, 19, 350–63.

Gould, D 2002, 'Moving beyond the psychology of athletic excellence', *Journal of Applied Sport Psychology*, 14, 247–8.

Gould, D, Damarjian, N & Medbery, R 1999, 'An examination of mental skills training in junior tennis coaches', *The Sport Psychologist*, 13, 127–43.

Gould, D, Medbery, R, Damarjian, N & Lauer, L 1999, 'A survey of mental skills training knowledge, opinions, and practices of junior tennis coaches', *Journal of Applied Sport Psychology*, 11, 28–50.

Gould, D, Murphy, S, Tammen, V & May, J 1991, 'An evaluation of U.S. Olympic sport psychology consultant effectiveness', *The Sport Psychologist*, 5, 111–27.

Gould, D, Petlichkoff, L, Hodge, K & Simons, J 1990, 'Evaluating the effectiveness of a psychological skills educational workshop', *The Sport Psychologist*, 4, 249–60.

Gould, D, Tammen, V, Murphy, S & May, J 1989, 'An examination of the U.S. Olympic sport psychology consultants and the services they provide', *The Sport Psychologist*, 3, 300–12.

Grant, AM 2001, *Towards a psychology of coaching*, www.psych.usyd.edu.au/psychcoach/Coaching_review_AMG2001.pdf (retrieved 30 June 2003).

Grant, AM 2003, *Evidence-based coaching: what, how and why?* Paper presented at the First Australian Evidence-Based Coaching Conference, University of Sydney, July.

Green, LB 1992, 'The use of imagery in the rehabilitation of injured athletes', *The Sport Psychologist*, 6, 416–28.

Greenspan, MJ & Feltz, DL 1989, 'Psychological interventions with athletes in competitive situations: a review', *The Sport Psychologist*, 3, 219–36.

Halliwell, W 1989, 'Delivering sport psychology services to the Canadian sailing team at the 1988 summer Olympic games', *The Sport Psychologist*, 3, 313–19.

Halliwell, W 1990, 'Providing sport psychology consulting services in professional hockey', *The Sport Psychologist*, 4, 369–77.

Hamilton, LH 1997, *The person behind the mask: a guide to performing arts psychology*, Ablex, Greenwich, CT.

Hanrahan, C & Vergeer, I 2000–01, 'Multiple uses of mental imagery by professional modern dancers', *Imagination, Cognition and Personality*, 20, 231–55.

Hanrahan, C, Tetreau, B & Sarrazin, C 1995, 'Use of imagery while performing dance movement', *International Journal of Sport Psychology*, 26, 413–30.

Hanrahan, S 1999, 'Mental skills training for athletes with disabilities', in *Vista downunder '98: International conference on athletes with disabilities*, Australian Sports Commission, Belconnen, ACT, pp. 99–104.

Hardy, L & Fazey, J 1990, *Mental training programme*, National Coaching Foundation, Beckett Park, Leeds.

Hardy, L, Jones, JG & Gould, D 1996, *Understanding psychological preparation for sport*, John Wiley & Sons, Chichester, UK.

Harlick, M & McKenzie, A 2000, 'Psychological skills training for athletes with disabilities: a review', *New Zealand Journal of Sports Medicine*, 28, 64–6.

Harris, DV & Harris, BL 1984, *The athlete's guide to sports psychology: mental skills for physical people*, Leisure Press, Champaign, IL.

Hart, V, Blattner, J & Leipsic, S 2001, 'Coaching versus therapy: a perspective', *Consulting Psychology Journal: Practice and Research*, 53, 229–37.

Haslam, IR 2002, 'Psychological skills education for school aged athletes', *Journal of the International Council for Health, Physical Education, Recreation, Sport and Dance*, 38, 53–7.

Hayden, RM, Allen, GJ & Camaione, DN 1986, 'Some psychological benefits resulting from involvement in an aerobic fitness program from the perspectives of participants and knowledgeable informants', *Journal of Sports Medicine*, 26, 67–76.

Hays, KF 1995, 'Putting sport psychology into (your) practice', *Professional Psychology: Research and Practice*, 26 (1) 33–40.

Hays, KF 2000, 'Breaking out: doing sport psychology with performing artists', in MB Andersen (ed.), *Doing sport psychology*, Human Kinetics, Champaign, IL, pp. 261–74.

Hays, KF 2002, 'The enhancement of performance excellence among performing artists', *Journal of Applied Sport Psychology*, 14, 299–312.

Hays, KF & Brown, CH 2003, *You're on! Consulting for peak performance*, American Psychological Association, Washington, DC.

Heil, J 1993, 'Sport psychology, the athlete at risk, and the sports medicine team', in J Heil (ed.), *Psychology of sport injury*, Human Kinetics, Champaign, IL, pp. 1–13.

Heil, J & Zealand, C 2001, *Psychological skills training manual*, United States Fencing Association Technical Report 2001–01.

Heil, J, Sagal, M & Nideffer, R 1997, 'The business of sport psychology consulting', *Journal of Applied Sport Psychology*, 9 (Supplement), S109.

Henschen, KP 2001, 'Lessons from sport psychology consulting', in G Tenenbaum (ed.), *The practice of sport psychology*, Fitness Information Technology, Morgantown, WV, pp. 77–88.

Highlen, PS & Bennett, BB 1979, 'Psychological characteristics of successful and non-successful elite wrestlers: an exploratory study', *Journal of Sport Psychology*, 1, 123–37.

Hogan, C 1988, *Nice shot*, Sports Enhancement Associates, Sedona, AZ.

Hogan, R, Curphy, GJ & Hogan, J 1994, 'What we know about leadership: effectiveness and personality', *American Psychologist*, 49, 493–504.

Hogg, JM 1997, *Mental skills for young athletes: a mental skills workbook for athletes 12 years and under*, Sport Excel Publishing, Edmonton, AB.

Hudson, FM 1999, *The handbook of coaching: a comprehensive resource guide for managers, executives, consultants, and human resource professionals*, Jossey-Bass, San Francisco.

Ievleva, L 1997, *Inner sports: mental skills for peak performance: psyching to perform your best*, Human Kinetics, Champaign, IL.

Ievleva, L & Orlick, T 1991, 'Mental links to enhanced healing: an exploratory study', *The Sport Psychologist*, 5, 25–40.

Jacobs, A 1988, *Sports psychology: the winning edge in sports*, The Winning Edge, Kansas City, MO.

Jacobson, E 1930, *Progressive relaxation*, University of Chicago Press, Chicago.

Jones, G 1993, 'The role of performance profiling in cognitive behavioral interventions in sport', *The Sport Psychologist*, 7, 160–72.

Jones, G 2002, 'Performance excellence: a personal perspective on the link between sport and business', *Journal of Applied Sport Psychology*, 14, 268–81.

Kampa-Kokesch, S & Anderson, MZ 2001, 'Executive coaching: a comprehensive review of the literature', *Consulting Psychology Journal: Practice and Research*, 53, 205–28.

Karle, HWA & Boys, JH 1987, *Hypnotherapy: a practitioner's handbook*, Free Association Books, London.

Kilburg, RR 1996, 'Toward a conceptual understanding and definition of executive coaching', *Consulting Psychology Journal: Practice and Research*, 48, 134–44.

Kilburg, RR 2000, *Executive coaching: developing managerial wisdom in a world of chaos*, American Psychological Association, Washington, DC.

Kluge, MA & Savis, JC 1998, 'A systematic and situational approach to mental skills training for collegiate women's basketball', *Coaching Women's Basketball*, 12, 30–5.

Kress, J, Schroeder, J, Potteiger, JA & Haub, M 1999, 'The use of psychological skills training to increase 10 km cycling performance: an exploratory investigation', *International Sports Journal*, 3, 44–54.

Lavallee, D & Wylleman, P 2000, *Career transitions in sport: international perspectives*, Fitness Information Technology, Morgantown, WV.

Le Scanff, C & Taugis, J 2002, 'Stress management for police special forces', *Journal of Applied Sport Psychology*, 14, 330–43.

Lester, KS 2000, 'The psychologist's role in the garrison mission of combat stress control units', *Military Medicine*, 165, 459–62.

Levinson, H 1996, 'Executive coaching', *Consulting Psychology Journal: Practice and Research*, 48, 115–23.

Lidor, R, Morris, T, Bardaxoglou, N & Becker, B Jr (eds) 2001, *The world sport psychology sourcebook*, 3rd edn, Fitness Information Technology, Morgantown, WV.

Loehr, JE 1983, 'The ideal performance state', *Science Periodical on Research and Technology in Sport*, Coaching Association of Canada, Ottawa.

Loehr, JE 1984, 'How to overcome stress and play at your peak all the time', *Tennis*, March, 66–76.

Loehr, JE 1989, *Mental toughness training for tennis: 'the 16 second cure'*, FTM Sports, Miami, FL.

Loehr, JE 1990, 'Providing sport psychology consulting services to professional tennis players', *The Sport Psychologist*, 4, 400–8.

Loehr, J & Schwartz, T 2001, 'The making of a corporate athlete', *Harvard Business Review*, January, 120–8.

Mackinnon, LT & Hooper, S 1992, 'Overtraining: state of the art review no. 26', *Excel*, 8, 3–12.

Mahoney, MJ & Avener, M 1977, 'Psychology of the elite athlete: an exploratory study', *Cognitive Therapy and Research*, 1, 135–41.

Malinauskas, R 2002, 'Implementing psychological skills training program in sports school teams', *Exercise and Society Journal of Sports Science*, 31, 289.

Martens, R 1987, *Coaches guide to sport psychology*, Human Kinetics, Champaign, IL.

Martin, G 1989, *Sport psyching for figure skaters*, Communication Systems, Winnipeg, Manitoba.

Martin, JJ & Cutler, K 2002, 'An exploratory study of flow and motivation in theatre actors', *Journal of Applied Sport Psychology*, 14, 344–52.

May, JR & Brown, L 1989, 'Delivery of psychological services to the U.S. alpine ski team prior to and during the Olympics in Calgary', *The Sport Psychologist*, 3, 320–9.

McCann, S 1996, 'Overtraining and burnout', in SM Murphy (ed.), *Sport psychology interventions*, Human Kinetics, Champaign, IL, pp. 347–68.

McCullagh, P, North, TC & Mood, D 1988, 'Exercise as a treatment for depression: a meta-analysis', paper presented at the meeting of the North American Society for the Psychology of Sport and Physical Activity, Knoxville, TN.

Medibank Private 2003, 'Sports injuries report', http://secure.medibank.com.au/uploads/user/Sports_injuries_report.pdf (retrieved 17 September 2003).

Meyers, AW, Cooke, CJ, Cullen, J & Liles, L 1979, 'Psychological aspects of athletic competitors: a replication across sports', *Cognitive Therapy and Research*, 3, 361–6.

Morgan, WP & Goldston, SE 1987, 'Summary', in WP Morgan & SE Goldston (eds), *Exercise and mental health*, Hemisphere, New York, pp. 155–9.

Morris, T, Alfermann, D, Lintunen, T & Hall, H 2003, 'Training and selection of sport psychologists: an international perspective', *International Journal of Sport and Exercise Psychology*, 1, 139–54.

Murphy, SM (ed.) 1996a, *Sport psychology interventions*, Human Kinetics, Champaign, IL.

Murphy, SM 1996b, *The achievement zone*, Berkley, New York.

Murphy, SM 1996c, 'Transitions in competitive sport: maximizing individual potential', in SM Murphy (ed.), *Sport psychology interventions*, Human Kinetics, Champaign, IL, pp. 331–46.

Murphy, SM 2000, 'Afterword', in MB Andersen (ed.), *Doing sport psychology*, Human Kinetics, Champaign, IL, pp. 275–9.

Murphy, SM & Ferrante, AP 1989, 'Provision of sport psychology services to the U.S. team at the 1988 summer Olympic games', *The Sport Psychologist*, 3, 374–85.

Murray, MC & Mann, BL 2001, 'Leadership effectiveness', in JM Williams (ed.), *Applied sport psychology: personal growth to peak performance*, 4th edn, Mayfield, Mountain View, CA, pp. 82–106.

Neff, F 1990, 'Delivering sport psychology services to a professional sport organization', *The Sport Psychologist*, 4, 378–85.

Nideffer, RM 1976, 'Test of attentional and interpersonal style', *Journal of Personality and Social Psychology*, 34, 394–404.

Nideffer, RM 1985, *Athletes' guide to mental training*, Human Kinetics, Champaign, IL.

Nideffer, RM 1989, 'Psychological services for the U.S. track and field team', *The Sport Psychologist*, 3, 350–7.

Nideffer, RM 1996, 'Meeting the challenges of a global market place', www.enhancedperformance.com/nideffer/articles/article11.html (retrieved 30 June 2003).

North, TC & McCullagh, P 1988, 'Aerobic and anaerobic exercise as a treatment for depression: a meta-analysis', paper presented at the meeting of the Association for the Advancement of Applied Sport Psychology, Nashua, NH, August.

Orlick, T 1986, *Psyching for sport: mental training for athletes*, Leisure Press, Champaign, IL.

Orlick, T 1989, 'Reflections on sportpsych consulting with individual and team sport athletes at summer and winter Olympic games', *The Sport Psychologist*, 3, 358–65.

Orlick, T 2000, *In pursuit of excellence*, 3rd edn, Human Kinetics, Champaign, IL.

Ostrow, AC (ed.) 1996, *Directory of psychological tests in the sport and exercise sciences*, 2nd edn, Fitness Information Technology, Morgantown, WV.

Overby, LY, Hall, C & Haslam, I 1997–98, 'A comparison of imagery used by dance teachers, figure skating coaches, and soccer coaches', *Imagination, Cognition and Personality*, 17, 323–37.

Palmer, C 1997, 'Music performance', *Annual Review of Psychology*, 48, 115–38.

Parfitt, G & Hardy, L 1993, 'Sport psychology and the BAGA', *Coaching Focus*, 22, 22–23.

Pargman, D (ed.) 1999, *Psychological bases of sport injuries*, 2nd edn, Fitness Information Technology, Morgantown, WV.

Petitpas, AJ 2002, 'Counselling interventions in applied sport psychology', in JL Van Raalte & B Brewer (eds), *Exploring sport and exercise psychology*, 2nd edn, American Psychological Association, Washington, DC, pp. 253–68.

Petitpas, AJ, Danish, S, McKelvain, R & Murphy, S 1992, 'A career assistance program for elite athletes', *Journal of Counseling and Development*, 70, 383–6.

Petitpas, A & Danish, SJ 1996, 'Caring for injured athletes', in SM Murphy (ed.), *Sport psychology interventions*, Human Kinetics, Champaign, IL, pp. 255–82.

Petitpas, A, Danish, SJ & Giges, B 1999, 'The sport psychologist–athlete relationship: implications for training', *The Sport Psychologist*, 13, 344–57.

Petrie, TA & Sherman, RT 2000, 'Counseling athletes with eating disorders: a case example', in MB Andersen (ed.), *Doing sport psychology*, Human Kinetics, Champaign, IL, pp. 121–38).

Poczwardowski, A & Conroy, DE 2002, 'Coping responses to failure and success among elite athletes and performing artists', *Journal of Applied Sport Psychology*, 14, 313–29.

Ravizza, K 1977, 'Peak experiences in sport', *Journal of Humanistic Psychology*, 17, 35–40.

Ravizza, K 1988, 'Gaining entry with athletic personnel for season-long consulting', *The Sport Psychologist*, 2, 243–54.

Ravizza, K 1990, 'Sportpsych consultation issues in professional baseball', *The Sport Psychologist*, 4, 330–40.

Ravizza, K 1993, 'Increasing awareness for sport performance', in JM Williams (ed.), *Applied sport psychology*, 2nd edn, Mayfield, Mountain View, CA, pp. 148–57.

Ravizza, K & Osborne, T 1991, 'Nebraska's 3 R's: one-play-at-a-time preperformance routine for collegiate football', *The Sport Psychologist*, 5, 256–65.

Rejeski, WJ & Brawley, LR 1988, 'Defining the boundaries of sport psychology', *The Sport Psychologist*, 2, 231–42.

Richard, JT 1999, 'Multimodal therapy: a useful model for the executive coach', *Consulting Psychology Journal: Practice and Research*, 51, 24–30.

Rogerson, LJ & Hrycaiko, DW 2002, 'Enhancing competitive performance of ice hockey goaltenders using centering and self-talk', *Journal of Applied Sport Psychology*, 14, 14–26.

Rotella, RJ 1990, 'Providing sport psychology consulting services to professional athletes', *The Sport Psychologist*, 4, 409–17.

Rotella, RJ & Heyman, SR 1993, 'Stress, injury, and the psychological rehabilitation of athletes', in JM Williams (ed.), *Applied sport psychology*, 2nd edn, Mayfield, Mountain View, CA, pp. 338–55.

Rushall, BS 1991, *Imagery training in sports*, Sports Science Associates, Spring Valley, CA.

Rushall, BS 1992, *Mental skills training for sports*, Sports Science Associates, Spring Valley, CA.

Sachs, ML 1991, 'Reading list in applied sport psychology: psychological skills training', *The Sport Psychologist*, 5, 88–91.

Salmela, JH 1989, 'Long-term intervention with the Canadian men's Olympic gymnastic team', *The Sport Psychologist*, 3, 340–9.

Saporito, TJ 1996, 'Business-linked executive development: coaching senior executives', *Consulting Psychology Journal: Practice and Research*, 48, 96–103.

Sargent, G 1997a, 'Developing a mental skills training program: imagery part two', *Sports Coach*, 19, 32–3.

Sargent, G 1997b, 'Developing a mental skills training program 5', *Sports Coach*, 20 (1) 33–5.

Sargent, G 1997c, 'Developing a mental skills training program 7: periodising mental training programs', *Sports Coach*, 20 (3) 24–7.

Schoen, C & Estanol-Johnson, E 2001, 'Assessment of the applicability of sport psychology implementation to ballet and dance', paper presented at the 10th World Congress of Sport Psychology, Skiathos, Greece, May.

Serpa, S & Rodrigues, J 2001, 'High performance sports and the experience of human development', in G Tenenbaum (ed.), *The practice of sport psychology*, Fitness Information Technology, Morgantown, WV, pp. 101–28.

Simon, J & Martens, R 1979, 'Children's anxiety in sport and nonsport evaluative activities', *Journal of Sport Psychology*, 1, 160–9.

Smith, DE 2000, 'Psychological skills training for secondary school sports in Singapore', *Journal of the International Council for Health, Physical Education, Recreation, Sport and Dance*, 36, 53–6.

Smith, RE 1988, 'The logic and design of case study research', *The Sport Psychologist*, 2, 1–12.

Smith, RE & Johnson, J 1990, 'An organizational empowerment approach to consultation in professional baseball, *The Sport Psychologist*, 4, 347–57.

Smith, RE & Smoll, FL 2002, 'Youth sports as a behavior setting for psychosocial interventions', in JL Van Raalte & B Brewer (eds), *Exploring sport and exercise psychology*, 2nd edn, American Psychological Association, Washington, DC, pp. 341–72.

Smither, JW & Reilly, SP 2001, 'Coaching in organizations', in M London (ed.), *How people evaluate others in organizations*, Lawrence Erlbaum Associates, Mahwah, NJ, pp. 221–52.

Smoll, FL & Smith, RE 2001, 'Conducting sport psychology training programs for coaches: cognitive-behavioral principles and techniques', in JM Williams (ed.), *Applied sport psychology: personal growth to peak performance*, 4th edn, Mayfield, Palo Alto, CA, pp. 378–400).

Stewart, A 1990, *Psychology and motivation in football*, National Australian Football Council, Melbourne.

Suinn, RM 1986, *Seven steps to peak performance*, Hans Huber, Toronto.

Swoap, RA & Murphy, SM 1996, 'Eating disorders and weight management in athletes', in SM Murphy (ed.), *Sport psychology interventions*, Human Kinetics, Champaign, IL, pp. 307–30.

Taylor, J & Ogilvie, B 2001, 'Career transition among athletes: is there life after sports?', in JM Williams (ed.) 2001, *Applied sport psychology: personal growth to peak performance*, 4th edn, Mayfield, Mountain View, CA, pp. 480–96.

Taylor, J & Taylor, C 1995, *Psychology of dance*, Human Kinetics, Champaign, IL.

Tenenbaum, G (ed.) 2001, *The practice of sport psychology*, Fitness Information Technology, Morgantown, WV.

Thelwell, RC & Greenlees, IA 2001, 'The effects of a mental skills training package on gymnasium triathlon performance', *The Sport Psychologist*, 15, 127–41.

Thomas, PR 1990, 'An overview of performance enhancement processes in applied sport psychology', unpublished manuscript, United States Olympic Training Centre, Colorado Springs.

Thomas, PR & Fogarty, GJ 1997, 'Psychological skills training in golf: the role of individual differences in cognitive preferences', *The Sport Psychologist*, 11, 86–106.

Tingley, JS 1998, 'Mental skills training with competitive swimmers 12 years of age and under', unpublished master's thesis, University of Alberta.

Ulrich-Suss, KL 1999, 'An evaluation of the influence of psychological skills training on the self-esteem of adolescent female golfers', unpublished master's thesis, Prescott College.

US Olympic Committee 1983, 'US Olympic Committee establishes guidelines for sport psychology services', *Journal of Sport Psychology*, 5, 4–7.

Van Raalte, JL & Andersen, MB 2000, 'Supervision I: from models to doing', in MB Andersen (ed.), *Doing sport psychology*, Human Kinetics, Champaign, IL, pp. 153–66.

Van Raalte, JL & Brewer, B (eds) 1996, *Exploring sport and exercise psychology*, 1st edn, American Psychological Association, Washington, DC.

Van Raalte, JL & Brewer, B (eds) 2002, *Exploring sport and exercise psychology*, 2nd edn, American Psychological Association, Washington, DC.

Vealey, RS 1988, 'Future directions in psychological skills training', *The Sport Psychologist*, 2, 318–36.

Wann, DL & Church, B 1998, 'A method for enhancing the psychological skills of track and field athletes', *Track Coach*, 144, 4597–605.

Waxman, D 1989, *Hartland's medical and dental hypnosis*, 3rd edn, Balliere Tindall, London.

Weinberg, RS 1984, 'Mental preparation strategies', in JM Silva & RS Weinberg (eds), *Psychological foundations of sport*, Human Kinetics, Champaign, IL, pp. 145–56.

Weinberg, RS 1987, *The mental advantage*, Human Kinetics, Champaign, IL.

Weinberg, RS 1988, *The mental advantage*, Leisure Press, Champaign, IL.

Weinberg, RS & Williams, JM 1993, 'Integrating and implementing a psychological skills training program', in JM Williams (ed.), *Applied sport psychology: personal growth to peak performance*, 2nd edn, Mayfield, Mountain View, CA, pp. 274–98.

Weinberg, RS & Williams, JM 2001, 'Integrating and implementing a psychological skills training program', in JM Williams (ed.), *Applied sport psychology: personal growth to peak performance*, 4th edn, Mayfield, Mountain View, CA, pp. 347–77.

Weinberg, R & McDermott, M 2002, 'A comparative analysis of sport and business organizations: factors perceived critical for organizational success', *Journal of Applied Sport Psychology*, 14, 282–98.

Weinberger, J 1995, 'Common factors aren't so common: the common factors dilemma', *Clinical Psychology: Science and Practice*, 2, 45–69.

Wiese, DM, Weiss, MR & Yukelson, DP 1991, 'Sport psychology in the training room: a survey of athletic trainers', *The Sport Psychologist*, 5, 15–24.

Williams, JM (ed.) 1986, *Applied sport psychology*, 1st edn, Mayfield, Mountain View, CA.

Williams, JM (ed.) 1993, *Applied sport psychology*, 2nd edn, Mayfield, Mountain View, CA.

Williams, JM (ed.) 2001, *Applied sport psychology*, 4th edn, Mayfield, Mountain View, CA.

Williams, JM & Andersen, MB 1998, 'Psychosocial antecedents of sport injury: review and critique of the stress and injury model', *Journal of Applied Sport Psychology*, 10, 5–25.

Williams, JM & Krane, V 1993, 'Psychological characteristics of peak performance', in JM Williams (ed.), *Applied sport psychology*, 2nd edn, Mayfield, Mountain View, CA, pp. 137–47.

Williams, JM & Straub, WF 2001, 'Sport psychology: past, present, future', in JM Williams (ed.), *Applied sport psychology*, 4th edn, Mayfield, Mountain View, CA, pp. 1–10.

Wilson, GD 2002, *Psychology for performing artists*, 2nd edn, Whurr Publishers, London.

Winter, G & Martin, C 1991, *SASI Psych: basic training program*, South Australian Sports Institute, Adelaide.

Witherspoon, R & White, RP 1996, 'Executive coaching: a continuum of roles', *Consulting Psychology Journal: Practice and Research*, 48, 124–33.

Wolpe, J 1958, *Psychotherapy by reciprocal inhibition*, Stanford University Press, Palo Alto, CA.

Yukelson, DP 2001, 'Communicating effectively', in JM Williams (ed.), *Applied sport psychology: personal growth to peak performance*, 4th edn, Mayfield, Mountain View, CA, pp. 135–49.

Zizzi, S, Zaichkowsky, L & Perna, FM 2002, 'Certification in sport and exercise psychology', in JL Van Raalte & B Brewer (eds), *Exploring sport and exercise psychology*, 2nd edn, American Psychological Association, Washington, DC, pp. 459–78.

CHAPTER 10

GOAL SETTING PRACTICES FOR COACHES AND ATHLETES

Robert Weinberg

Through anecdotal reports we know that coaches, athletes and exercisers have long been setting goals to enhance their performance. However, there was little empirical support for goal setting in sport and exercise settings before the past 15 years. It wasn't until 1995 (when enough studies had been conducted — 36 were used in this analysis) that Kyllo and Landers conducted the first meta-analysis on goal setting in sport and exercise. The recent trend towards conducting studies in the sport and exercise area can be seen in the review by Burton, Naylor and Holliday (2001), who found approximately 56 published (and a number of unpublished) references to goal-setting research in sport and exercise contexts. This chapter focuses on defining different types of goals, reviewing the empirical evidence in organisational as well as sport and exercise settings, and applying the results to real-world situations. We will start by defining and specifying types of goals, especially those employed in sport and exercise settings.

WHAT IS A GOAL?

Although many definitions have been put forward, the most commonly accepted definition of a goal was proposed by Locke, Shaw, Saari and Latham (1981), who characterised a goal as attaining a specific level of proficiency in a task, usually within a specified time limit. However, it should be noted that although goals can help direct behaviour, they do not necessarily work at a conscious level all the time. For example, in an automated skill like the tennis serve, goals may help initiate action, but once initiated little conscious control is needed. In reality, goals typically focus on improving one's own performance or beating another person or team, and these types of goals will be discussed in the following pages.

Outcome, performance and process goals

In sport and exercise settings, three types of goals are discussed: outcome, performance and process goals. *Outcome goals* focus on the end result of a competition and are therefore primarily concerned with winning and losing. An athlete is not in total control of reaching his or her outcome goal, since winning or losing depends, at least in part, on the performance of the opponent. *Performance goals* refer to an individual athlete's performance independent of the other competitors or the team. For example, a performance goal might be to improve your free throw percentage from 68 per cent to 75 per cent. An athlete is in control of achieving a performance goal because the performance of other players or competitors does not affect the goal's attainment. *Process goals* are usually concerned with how an athlete performs a certain skill. These goals tend to be used during practice or training. For example, a process goal in baseball might involve getting down on one knee when fielding a sharp ground ball (percentages can be placed on these process goals to make them more specific).

All three types of goals can be effective in enhancing performance and positively affecting behaviour. Process and performance goals are particularly important since they are to a large extent under the individual athlete's control.

WHY IS GOAL-SETTING THEORY IMPORTANT?

According to goal-setting theory, an individual's conscious goals while trying to perform a task actually regulate task performance (Locke 1966, 1968, 1978; Locke et al. 1981; Locke & Latham 1990a, 1990b). Thus it is thought that goals are formed by using internal comparisons and standards to evaluate performance. Athletes can achieve a higher performance level if specific, hard goals are created. Research indicates that easy goals, no goals or generalised 'do your best' goals are not as effective. But the theory also suggests that a number of variables mediate this performance, including personality factors, monetary incentives, degree of commitment, knowledge of results, time limits, participation in decision making, and competition. Locke (1968) also argued against a simple causative relationship between goals and behaviour, stating that a number of factors (e.g. ability to attain the goal) influence effective goal setting.

Much of the early work on goal setting originated from two main sources, one academic and one industrial/organisational. Using these early sources, Locke and his colleagues developed their theory of goal setting, which has been the central theory in industrial and organisational settings as well as in sport and exercise settings.

Sport and exercise literature on goal setting

More than 600 goal-setting studies have been conducted in industrial and organisational settings, testing aspects of goal setting such as goal specificity, goal proximity, goal commitment and goal type. However, while considerable research has been conducted in industrial and organisational settings over the past 40 years, it is only in the past 15 to 20 years that sport and exercise psychology researchers have systematically studied the area. Given the objective nature of the performance outcome in most sport settings, sport would appear to be an excellent context in which to study goal-setting effects (Locke & Latham 1985). Goal effectiveness in competitive sport settings has been studied using a variety of surveys. Results have revealed that goal-setting strategies were perceived to be effective by leading sport psychology consultants working with US Olympic athletes (Gould, Greenleaf, Guinan & Chung 2002; Weinberg, Burton, Yukelson & Weigand 2000). In addition to using goal setting as part of their daily training regimen, Olympians reported that goals were one of the most often used psychological interventions (Gould, Tammen, Murphy & May 1989; Orlick & Partington 1988; Sullivan & Nashman 1998).

These surveys tend to indicate that goal setting is effective in enhancing athletic performance. This conclusion is supported by recent reviews in sport and exercise, although even stronger effects are found in the organisational literature. More specifically, both in terms of meta-analysis focusing on the strength of the relationship between goals and performance (.34 for sport/exercise versus .42 to .80 for organisations), as well as in general reviews (78 per cent effectiveness in sport versus approximately 90 per cent effectiveness for industry), results in the sport/exercise psychology literature are not as convincing as those in the industrial/organisational literature. However, as more studies accumulate, the consistency of goal-setting effects in sport/exercise is increasing. But even given this increase, the strength of the goal-setting performance relationship is still less than that found in the organisational literature (see Burton et al. 2001 for a detailed review).

The disparity in these findings has generated a good deal of debate and discussion in the literature (Burton et al. 2001; Locke 1991, 1994; Weinberg & Weigand 1993, 1996). It is beyond the scope of the present chapter to discuss fully the potential methodological differences that might have led to the goal-setting differences across domains, as these can be found in the studies referenced above. However, it appears that athletes and exercise participants and industrial/organisational participants have different motivations and perform under different task conditions. So the critical question for researchers is not whether there are differences between sport and organisational settings but, rather, under which conditions are goal-setting techniques most effective? Along these lines, a number of studies (many of them interventions across an entire athletic season) have recently been conducted using athletes (as opposed to laboratory studies using predominantly college students). In general, results have revealed goal setting to be positively related to enhanced performance (Burton, Weinberg, Yukelson & Weigand 1998; Filby, Maynard & Graydon 1999; Kingston & Hardy 1997; Swain & Jones 1995; Weinberg, Burton, Yukelson & Weigand 2000; Weinberg, Stitcher & Richardson 1994). Some specific consistent findings are listed below (Weinberg 2002):

- Performance is enhanced when goals are moderately difficult, challenging and realistic.
- Goal setting provides athletes with direction and focus.
- Motivation will be higher if athletes are committed to their goals and accept them.
- Goals plus feedback produce better performance than either goals alone or feedback alone.
- Goals should be given priorities.
- Goals should generally be emphasised because they come under the athlete's control.
- Time pressures, stress, tiredness, academic pressures and social relationships negatively affect goal achievement.
- Both short-term and long-term goals are important. Long-term goals provide direction and short-term goals provide motivation as well as making long-term goals seem more achievable, since sometimes the 'whole' can be daunting.
- While action plans help to implement goal-setting strategies, many athletes do not use them.
- Athletes using multiple goal strategies have the best performance.
- While many athletes and coaches think about and image their goals, they are not consistent in writing them down.

PRINCIPLES OF GOAL SETTING

When discussing the principles of effective goal setting, it is important to emphasise the distinction between the 'science' and the 'art' of setting goals. Researchers can provide practitioners with the science of goal setting, which leads to certain principles. But situational constraints and individual differences always play a role; thus coaches need to know their teams and individual athletes to maximise goal-setting effectiveness. It is important to keep in mind that all motivational techniques are affected by the interaction between individuals and their situation. It is with these cautionary notes that some recommendations and principles for developing a goal-setting program are introduced.

Setting specific goals

Reviews and meta-analyses in the organisational literature have found that specific goals consistently enhanced performance when compared with more general, 'do your best' goals (Latham & Lee 1986; Locke & Latham 1990a, 1990b; Mento, Steel & Karren 1987), although it is often hard to separate out goal specificity from goal difficulty findings since many researchers use specific, difficult goals in testing goal-setting effects. For example, combining goal specificity and goal difficulty, reviewers (Chidester & Grigsby 1984; Hunter & Schmidt 1983; Locke & Latham 1990a, 1990b; Mento, Steel & Karren 1987; Tubbs 1986; Wood, Mento & Locke 1987) have agreed that specific, challenging goals result in higher levels of task performance than 'do your best' goals, easy goals or no goals.

Besides being specific, goals should be measurable so individuals know if they are making progress towards achieving them. To achieve maximum performance, a weight-lifter, for example, might set a goal to improve on the weight lifted by 10 per cent for each of the next six months. In addition, a process goal specifying how he might accomplish this gain would also be useful. In this way, he would have something specific to shoot for and would receive feedback on exactly how much he had improved in attempting to reach this goal.

Using short-term and long-term goals

Athletes and exercisers typically set outcome-oriented and long-term goals, focusing on such things as winning a division championship or losing 12 kilograms over the next six months. These long-term goals are critical, as they provide individuals with a direction and destination, and can act as dream goals. However, research has revealed that both short- and long-term goals are needed to maintain motivation and performance (Weinberg, Butt & Knight 2001; Weinberg et al. 1993, 2000; Kane, Baltes & Moss 2001). Short-term goals help individuals focus on small improvements and also provide continuous feedback.

Making goals challenging but realistic

Goal-setting theory predicts that the more difficult the goal, the better the performance. Of 192 organisational/industrial studies reviewed, 175 (91 per cent) provided support for harder goals producing higher levels of task performance than easy goals with performance increments of 8 per cent to 16 per cent (Chidester & Grigsby 1984; Mento, Steel & Karren 1987; Tubbs 1986). This relationship holds until performers reach the limits of their ability and performance levels off. If goals are too hard, they can produce either a levelling off or a decline in performance.

Individuals should set goals that are challenging yet realistically achievable; in essence, the goals should be moderately difficult, as opposed to moderate or difficult. If goals are too easy, individuals have a tendency to become complacent, not trying hard or putting in consistent effort, since they feel that they can reach the goal without great effort. Conversely, if goals are too difficult, individuals will have a tendency to become frustrated, lose motivation and possibly give up when they become discouraged by falling short of their goal.

Dream goals can be used to replace unrealistic goals. For example, many young athletes dream of playing professionally, but fewer than 1 per cent of competitive athletes at high-school level will make it to professional level (Coakley 1997). One approach is to set this ambition as a dream goal but to set a more realistic performance goal that focuses on improving your skills. In essence, a balance needs to be struck between striving to achieve the dream goal and focusing on short-term performance improvement (Weinberg 2002).

From a practical point of view, an important question is 'how does one determine a goal that is realistic and challenging?' Here is where the art of coaching comes in; it is imperative that coaches know each individual athlete in order to determine what is challenging for that athlete. This requires knowledge of the capabilities of each athlete as well as the demands of the task in optimally 'pushing' athletes to reach their respective challenging goals.

Recording goals

While several sport psychology researchers have found it important to record goals, research has also revealed that coaches and athletes generally do not write down their goals, or at least do not do so in a systematic fashion (Weinberg et al. 2001). In-depth interviews with coaches (Weinberg et al. 2001; Weinberg, Butt, Knight & Perritt 2001) have shown that coaches will often use elaborate goal-setting procedures to set goals but then never look at the goals again. Goals should be displayed in a place where they can be easily seen, such as inside lockers or on a noticeboard in a prominent place. What is essential is that the goals remain first and foremost in athletes' minds and remain salient to them.

Using a combination of process, performance and outcome goals

Although the emphasis in sport is often on competition and winning, competitive anxiety increases when too much emphasis is placed on outcome goals (i.e. winning). It appears that the best way to win is to focus on performance or process goals (Gould, Finch & Jackson 1993; Orlick & Partington 1988). Interestingly, interviews with athletes have revealed that achieving one or two of these goals helps achieve the third. For example, the three most often stated goals were winning, improving performance and having fun. For some athletes, if they played well they would most likely win, and winning was fun. Therefore you did not have to achieve one goal at the expense of another. In fact, all three could work together to produce an optimal performance and result.

The lesson in this is that outcome goals need to be balanced by performance and process goals. As many coaches note, if teams meet their performance goals, winning will usually take care of itself. But the bottom line is still to win, and in many cases only lip-service is paid to performance and process goals. So both coaches and athletes need to use a combination of process and performance goals to maximise effectiveness.

Using individual and team goals

Individual goals for team sport athletes are appropriate as long as they do not conflict with team goals. For example, if a baseball player sets a goal of hitting 25 home runs for the season, this personal ambition could conflict with team goals if the player becomes more concerned with hitting home runs than with helping the team win.

Using practice goals

Given the large amounts of time athletes spend practising, it is important that goals be set for both practice and competition (Weinberg et al. 2001). Setting practice goals is a good way to keep an athlete motivated during practice sessions. They can also help athletes focus on improving skills that may not ordinarily be worked on.

Observing expert coaches, Cote, Salmela and Russell (1993) found that one of the things these coaches did consistently was set goals for practice. These coaches recognised the importance of setting practice goals to keep athletes focused and motivated. Similarly, Orlick and Partington (1988) found that setting practice goals was one key factor that differentiated successful and unsuccessful Olympic athletes. Research with US high-school and college coaches (Weinberg et al. 2001, 2002) has confirmed that coaches feel it is important to set goals both in practice and in competition. In fact, some research suggests that practice goals could be more important than competition goals (Filby et al. 1999).

Practice goals should focus more on developing skills and working on improving weak areas than on outcome. For example, a baseball coach might want his players to make good decisions about when to swing and when not to swing (disregarding bad pitches out of the strike zone), and not be overly worried about getting a base hit (performance goal). Therefore, a practice goal might be to make good decisions when hitting 80 per cent of time. Thus, the focus is on the process (i.e. the decision), rather than the outcome of that decision (i.e. whether the ball was hit hard or not). In addition, practice goals might include issues such as getting to practice on time, encouraging team-mates and displaying specific leadership behaviours (Weinberg 2002).

Practice goals can also affect skill improvement and psychological preparedness. For example, a tennis player may set a goal of hitting 10 consecutive serves, to the deuce and advantage sides of the court at the end of practice. This goal helps the player focus on his serve, and as he gets closer to hitting 10 in a row the pressure starts to build, because he does not want to start all over again. This pressure is similar to the pressure of real game situations. Thus this one practice goal could have a variety of positive effects on stroke production and the psychology of hitting serves.

Developing plans to reach goals

Research indicates that most coaches and athletes do not use plans and seem to believe that simply having goals will improve performance. However, it has been proposed that relevant learning strategies can help achieve goals that enhance performance (Locke 1968). For example, chipping a bucket of golf balls onto a practice green three days a week is a strategy to help achieve the goal of lowering your handicap by three shots. Participating in a walking program that burns 2 500 calories a week is a strategy to achieve a weight loss of 12 kilograms in five months. Strategies need to be specific and should involve definite numbers (e.g. how much, how many, how often). Finally, in setting these goal achievement strategies, it is a good idea to build in some flexibility. For instance, it is better to have a goal to lift weights three days a week than to say that you will lift weights on Mondays, Wednesdays and Fridays. In this way, if there is a barrier to lifting on a specific day, you can still achieve your goal by lifting another day.

Consider participant's personality

Although there are general principles to follow when setting goals, it is always important to individualise goal-setting practices. For example, individuals are typically motivated either to focus on their own improvement (mastery goal) or to focus on performing better than their competitor (competitive goal). A motivational climate that matches the motives of the individual (given that this is also the orientation of the coach) would help produce maximum motivation. But since research has indicated more positive outcomes in mastery-goal environments than in competitive-goal environments, a coach or exercise leader could create a mastery motivational climate by fostering learning, progress and improvement in striving to reach goals.

Providing and encouraging social support

There is strong evidence in psychological research to show that social support helps keep motivation and persistence high, particularly when goals are difficult to reach (Albrecht & Adelman 1984; Cohen 1988). The same findings have been made in sport and exercise psychology literature (Hardy, Richman & Rosenfeld 1991). For example, in fitness settings, Dishman (1988) found that individuals were more likely to keep to an exercise program if their spouse or significant other supported the program. Unfortunately, too often in the past spouses and significant others were not included as part of exercise and weight loss programs, which might in part explain the huge dropout rate that is typically seen in exercise programs. More recent programs inform spouses of ways in which they can support their partner in achieving his or her goals. In a sport context, social support, which can come from parents, teachers or friends, should focus on achieving goals, not winning or losing. Support and reinforcement at home can go a long way to keeping young athletes motivated and focused on behaviours espoused by the coach.

Evaluating goals

Coaches and athletes are often not very good at persisting with a goal-setting program and, especially, evaluating it afterwards; evaluation, however, is critical for effective goal setting. One way this evaluation can be provided is through goal evaluation meetings, which might be held during the season, or towards the end of the season. Most coaches have an informal process for goal re-evaluation during the season, and at times this occurs very regularly (Weinberg, Butt & Knight 2001; Weinberg, Butt, Knight & Perritt 2001). These meetings should evaluate how individuals are progressing towards their goals, so that the goals can be re-evaluated and adjusted upward or downward, providing the players with new motivation and commitment.

Besides assessing performance, there are other areas relating to the development of psychological skills, as well as enhanced fun, satisfaction and intrinsic motivation, that are important to assess. Goals in these areas tend to be more subjective and thus are typically harder to monitor and evaluate, but nonetheless they should be incorporated into goal-setting programs. For example, Gould (2000) suggested an athlete with a goal to improve his overall satisfaction in playing the sport could evaluate this goal by rating his satisfaction on a 1–10 scale on a weekly basis and describe the things that enhanced or detracted from his satisfaction.

In summary, this section has noted that setting goals does not in itself automatically imply that increased performance will occur. Rather, effective goal setting requires an understanding of the literature so that the principles gathered from research can be applied in practice. Taking a research-to-practice orientation will make it more likely that your goal-setting program will be effective and produce the results you intended.

POTENTIAL PROBLEMS IN GOAL SETTING

It is clear that goals can enhance performance and other responses such as satisfaction, enjoyment and intrinsic motivation. However, they need to be set in such a way as to maximise positive outcomes. Knowledge of the goal-setting process is essential, but common pitfalls and problems faced by practitioners also need to be recognised if effective goals are to be set. If practitioners understand and anticipate these problems, then the potential drawbacks of goal setting can be avoided.

Convincing participants to set goals

Sometimes it is difficult to get performers to set goals in the first place because of a variety of negative attitudes about goals. Some individuals believe that goal setting takes too much time or have previous negative experiences with goal setting, the perception that they will become a public failure if they don't reach certain goals, and the feeling that goal setting is too structured and won't work with 'spontaneous' people. Performers need to be reassured that if performance (as opposed to outcome) goals are set, these objectives are under the performer's control and thus should produce less worry about failure. Similarly, setting goals actually *saves* time, as it makes people more focused and efficient. A coach or exercise leader can inform performers that the common concerns that inhibit people from setting goals in the first place are really myths, and that goal setting has been proven to help performance and efficiency in a number of ways.

Too many goals

A common mistake made by practitioners who initiate goal-setting programs is setting up too many goals. The common assumption is that, with lots of motivation and drive, more is better. However, one can be overwhelmed by the time and effort it takes to monitor and track these goals across time. Monitoring a variety of goals belonging to a group of athletes or exercise participants can be very difficult unless you have the help of assistant coaches, managers or other helpers. As a result, it is good practice to start small, choosing only those goals that are the highest priority (and that can be tracked and measured relatively easily). For example, for a person just starting an exercise program, a simple goal of exercising for 20 to 30 minutes three to four times a week would be sufficient. Similarly, for a runner, a goal might simply involve running a certain number of laps or a required distance.

Goal re-evaluation

We know that performers have good intentions when their goals are originally set. But as time goes on, goals set at the beginning of a season or an exercise program can at times be forgotten. Sometimes a goal is not written down or is just not kept in the forefront of an individual's mind; it is easy to lose sight of the original goal. Other times, situations can occur that act as barriers to reaching a goal, such as an injury or personal crisis that serves to limit sport performance as well as exercise participation. For this reason goals should be re-evaluated regularly. If a coach is integral in setting these goals, then regularly scheduled meetings should be set up to revisit and possibly adjust these goals.

For example, a swimmer might have had a goal of reducing her 100-metre time from 60 to 58 seconds, but because of nagging injuries she has not been able to practise regularly to build up her speed and endurance. As a result, her time has actually increased to 64 seconds, which could result in frustration and a decrease in motivation. In this situation her goal should be re-evaluated. She may start out by simply swimming for 30 minutes so as not to aggravate her injury, while undergoing physical therapy three days a week. When (and if) she completes rehabilitation, she may slowly reset her goals, swimming for longer and then swimming faster (with specific times for these different goals). Eventually, as she gets stronger and continues to improve, she can reset her goal to 62 seconds and then to 60 seconds. As her goals are re-evaluated, a written record of this re-evaluation should be made and posted in a prominent place so that she sees it regularly. This will show her progress and provide feedback on how she is progressing towards her goals.

Forgetting to cater for individual differences

One of the principles of sport/exercise psychology (as well as general psychology) is that individual differences need to be considered when investigating the effects of different variables on performance and behaviour. In essence, 'one size does not fit all'. Some generalisations (such as the principles noted earlier) can be proposed, and these propositions fundamentally represent the science of goal setting. To use goal setting effectively, however, requires an understanding of the 'art' of goal setting. The research tells us generally what we can expect, but it does not account for individual differences. Coaches need to know their athletes so that goals can be customised according to the specific nature of the individual.

In our research, for example, we find that some athletes prefer moderately difficult goals, some prefer difficult goals and others choose moderate goals. Similarly, some athletes have as their primary goal to improve their performance, whereas others are primarily motivated to win or to have fun. This may be related to athletes' goal orientations (i.e. *task* versus *ego*), which can make a significant difference in the specific goals that are effective for them (Garland, Weinberg, Bruya & Jackson 1988). In fact, research (Giannini, Weinberg & Jackson 1988) indicates that task-oriented individuals are most motivated by self-improvement goals and thus might focus on performance improvement or enjoyment, whereas ego-oriented individuals are most motivated by outcome goals such as winning.

Another important individual difference factor related to goal setting is self-efficacy (Bandura 1986, 1997). Research has shown that high self-efficacy is associated with high goal attainment (Bandura 1986, 1997). Weinberg and Jackson's (1990) research with tennis players has revealed the importance of self-confidence (used here interchangeably with self-efficacy) in achieving goals. If an athlete sets and achieves her goals, then her self-efficacy increases because she has been successful in achieving her goals. This, in turn, would make her more likely to set and attain more difficult goals, which would again enhance her feeling of self-efficacy.

Setting 'do your best' goals

A fundamental principle of goal setting is that goals should be specific and measurable, as opposed to the more general, 'do your best' goals. Athletes often set goals that are too general. For example, their goals might include 'improving my consistency in tennis' or 'just doing the best I can in each competition' or 'improving my jump shot in basketball'. To be effective, such general goals must be made more specific and measurable. For example, the goal of improving your jump shot could be re-expressed as 'improving my jump shot percentage from 40 per cent to 45 per cent'. Since this is a performance goal, the player would need a process goal in the form of a strategy (or a couple of different strategies) to help achieve the 45 per cent objective. A process goal could be to make sure you follow through on all your shots. To help determine if this goal was met, the player could be rated by a coach from 1 (*did not follow through consistently*) to 10 (*followed through consistently*). Alternatively a player might resolve to shoot an extra 200 shots from 15 to 20 feet in practice each day. Again, the goal needs to be specific and measurable to enhance its effectiveness.

THE COMPONENTS OF A GOAL-SETTING PROGRAM

Once the coach is familiar with the principles of goal setting and understands some of the inherent problems in setting goals, the next step is to implement a goal-setting program with three stages — preparation, education and acquisition, and implementation and evaluation.

Preparation stage

Goal setting in sport or physical activity requires preparation and planning, including a specific action plan to enhance the potential effectiveness of the program. The practitioner should assess both the individual's and the team's needs. Although this assessment can be done by athletes, it is usually best undertaken by the coach. Coaches can use returning players or, if most members are new, can determine their needs through pre-testing and talking with previous coaches. While an assessment focuses on developing specific skills or conditioning (Weinberg et al. 2001), other needs should also be considered, such as enjoyment, satisfaction and intrinsic motivation. (For example, one middle-school coach had felt there was so much sarcastic commentary among the team the previous year that he decided to set as a goal 'increasing the number of positive statements about each other'.) Such needs then form the basis on which specific goals are set.

Once the goals are determined, it is of critical importance that coaches plan on specific strategies to help achieve the goals set for the coming season. Similarly, exercisers should develop strategies to meet their goals, such as lifting weights three days a week to improve upper body strength. For athletes, these strategies will be provided during the education and acquisition phase of implementation, but coaches consider these strategies when they think about goals during the off-season.

Education and acquisition stage

Once the goals have been determined on the basis of a needs assessment, and you have planned the goal strategies, you are ready to educate the athlete directly on the most effective way to set goals. In a competitive context, coaches would provide basic goal-setting information and principles to participants as well as have them set their specific goals.

Schedule meetings

A formal meeting or a series of brief, informal meetings should be scheduled before practices or classes begin. In these meetings coaches and athletes can identify examples of effective and ineffective goals, along with basic information about different types of goals, since most performers know only part of what makes goals most effective. However, at this point participants should not be expected to be able to list their specific goals immediately. Rather, players should think about setting goals in specific areas, as well as implementation strategies. This will help them set their own goals as well as team goals and will provide them with an opportunity to think about different options instead of having to come up with goals and strategies on the spot.

After the initial meeting, and athletes are given time to think about their goals, a second meeting should be scheduled. First, team goals are discussed and decided upon by the coach and team. More specifically, coaches should steer athletes towards goals to which both parties agree so that the athletes 'own' their goals. In addition to the team meetings, the coach should meet individually with all participants to set up their specific goals in one-on-one meetings, again in such a way that the athletes feel they 'own' the goals they agree to. All goals, both team and individual, should be written down and displayed in a prominent place (e.g. taped on lockers or on the locker-room wall) so they are seen by everyone every day, as this public disclosure increases commitment to the goals.

Provide athletes with goal strategies

As noted in the preparation and planning phase, coaches should give their athletes strategies to reach their goals. It is not enough to set a goal; specific strategies must be put into place so the performer knows what to do to reach a specific goal. For example, if a baseball player has a goal to increase his batting average from .275 to .300, this might include stepping into the ball (as opposed to stepping away (called stepping 'in the bucket'), which would be a process goal. In fact, given that no single strategy will work equally well on all tasks, for all occasions and across time, self-regulated athletes need to make continuous adjustments when planning and selecting their strategies (Zimmerman 2000). Finally, unless they have lots of experience with goal setting, athletes should focus on only one or two individual goals. The coach can help athletes choose the goals they really want to focus on along with appropriate strategies to achieve these goals.

Implementation and the goal evaluation stage

When a psychological skills program is implemented it is always important to evaluate its effectiveness and determine if it produced the positive changes that were intended. Without good evaluation we simply do not know the effectiveness of the program and what might have worked or did not work. This stage is the most difficult, because inevitably coaches become busy with other tasks, and goal setting becomes a less important priority. There are, however, strategies that can be used to keep up the excitement over goals felt at the outset of the season.

Goal evaluation is much more likely to succeed if it is well planned for from the beginning. For example, a specific time should be established when goals are objectively evaluated. This could occur at the end of the season or possibly during the season to check whether the program is working as expected. To make the feedback process less time-consuming for the coach, an assistant coach or manager may be enlisted to help keep a daily track of the goals as a normal part of feedback to athletes. In a physical education setting, performance or skill tests can be set to monitor goal progress.

Research (Weinberg, Butt & Knight 2001; Weinberg, Butt, Knight & Perritt 2001) has found that while many coaches specifically planned sessions for goal re-evaluation, others were more haphazard in their approach. It is important that goals be re-evaluated, as conditions can change throughout the year owing to a variety of circumstances. Goals may need to be revised upwards or downwards. Using an exercise example, a person may have set a goal to 'lose 10 kilos in 10 weeks' but find after five weeks she has lost only 3 kilos. She could choose to lower her goal to, say, losing 5 kilos in 10 weeks, or the time frame could be changed to create a new goal of losing 10 kilos in 15 weeks.

Research from a variety of sources has consistently indicated the importance of social support to enhance adherence to various behaviours. Besides support from friends and family, coaches and exercise leaders need to publicly encourage individuals' goal progress. Participants are more likely to achieve their goals and maintain high motivation if they are enthusiastically supported throughout the goal-setting process.

FUTURE DIRECTIONS

Early in the chapter some future directions for research were indicated. Much of the succeeding discussion focused on the practice of goal setting, both the principles involved and the practical implications of initiating a goal-setting program. What might the future have in store for the practice of goal setting?

First of all, goal-setting research offers much practical information for the practitioner wishing to make goal setting more effective. As we learn more through research, this knowledge filters down and helps inform our practice. It has been my observation working with coaches and athletes, as well as conducting qualitative research with coaches (Weinberg et al. 2001, in press), that there is a great deal of variability in the application of goal-setting principles to actual sport and exercise settings. Some coaches and athletes seem to apply very sophisticated and detailed models, while others are very haphazard. Over time, more of the goal-setting research will be conveyed to practitioners, and they will be more systematic in the implementation of these ideas in their practice.

One interesting question is how specific or structured goal setting will become in the future. There have been some very specific, formula-based approaches (e.g. O'Block & Evans 1984) and some very subjective approaches (Orlick 2000). It appears that a more subjective approach is gaining a foothold, with many practitioners reluctant to be confined by specific formulas. More practical applications may be expected in the area of overcoming barriers. To date, when confronted by barriers, practitioners have either given up or just 'flown by the seat of their pants' while trying to figure out how to overcome the obstacle. Specific strategies (possibly gleaned from new research) will be developed to help cope more effectively with barriers to goal setting. In summary, as the research on goal setting grows, so will the practice. It is an extremely valuable applied area, and there should remain close links between the research and practice of goal setting.

CONCLUSIONS

A vast amount of research conducted in sport and business organisations confirms that goal setting can have a positive influence on performance. Most people at some stage set themselves informal goals, but in many cases these goals are not set in ways that will maximise performance and other desired behaviours. One goal of this chapter was to discuss the research and the different types of goals that can be set and why, in fact, goal setting works in the first place. Another, more important goal was to outline the principles of effective goal setting along with the associated problems, as well as to describe a goal-setting system that can be used by coaches (and other practitioners) in real-life settings. In essence, a research-to-practice orientation was followed; the focus was to integrate research to best practice. This is the way goals work, but only if they are implemented in ways that follow the research and ensuing principles developed.

SUMMARY

The main purpose of this chapter was to present the theory and empirical research on goal setting in sport and exercise environments and then to apply them to practical settings. First, a goal was defined. Second, distinctions were made between performance, process and outcome goals with particular emphasis on how much control individuals have in achieving their goals. Third, Locke's theory of goal setting was presented, its focus being that specific, difficult, challenging goals lead to higher levels of task performance than easy goals, no goals, or 'do your best' goals. Fourth, empirical research testing Locke's seminal research and theory was presented, with a particular emphasis on goal difficulty and goal specificity. Next, the focus shifted to goal setting in sport and exercise settings: the results, although not as robust as those in the industrial literature, nonetheless supported the effectiveness of goal setting.

The basic goal-setting principles were then presented, including setting realistic and challenging goals; setting both short- and long-term goals; setting specific, measurable goals; prioritising goals; writing goals down; providing support for goal achievement; and providing for goal evaluation. Moving from general principles, a specific goal-setting system for coaches was presented, which included preparation, education and acquisition, and evaluation phases. Although certain general principles regarding goal-setting were proposed, it is important to remember that the motivations of the specific individuals involved and the task being performed also influence the efficacy of any goal-setting program. The chapter concluded with a discussion of some of the common problems that might arise when implementing a goal-setting program.

 ## REVIEW QUESTIONS

1   What is the difference between process, performance and outcome goals? Give examples of each to compare and contrast them.

2   What are the three basic steps to consider in designing a goal-setting system? What should happen during each stage?

3   According to Locke's mechanistic model, why and how do goals work? Give examples where appropriate to substantiate your points.

4   Discuss five principles of goal setting including how you would use them in establishing a goal-setting program with a team or exercise group.

5   Identify four common problems when setting goals.

6   A number of goal-setting intervention studies have been conducted. Briefly list five consistent findings from these studies.

7   You are a new coach and you want to set up a goal-setting system for your sport (you choose the sport). Briefly outline the system you would develop based on the principles and process of goal setting discussed in this chapter.

References

Albrecht, TL & Adelman, MB 1984, 'Social support and life stress: new directions for communication research', *Human Communications Research*, 2, 3–22.

Bandura, A 1986, *Social foundations of thought and action: a social cognitive theory*, Prentice Hall, Englewood Cliffs, NJ.

Bandura, A 1997, *Self-efficacy: the exercise of control*, Freeman, New York.

Burton, D, Naylor, S & Holliday, B 2001, 'Goal setting in sport: investigating the goal effectiveness paradox', in R Singer, H Hausenblas & C Janelle (eds), *Handbook of sport psychology*, John Wiley & Sons, New York, pp. 497–528.

Burton, D, Weinberg, R, Yukelson, D & Weigand, D 1998, 'The goal effectiveness paradox in sport: examining the goal practices of collegiate athletes', *The Sport Psychologist*, 12, 404–19.

Chidester, JS & Grigsby, WC 1984, 'A meta-analysis of the goal setting performance literature', in A Pearce & RB Robinson (eds), *Proceedings of the 44th annual meeting of the Academy of Management*, Academy of Management, Ada, OH, pp. 202–6.

Coakley, J 1997, *Sport in society: issues and controversies*, 5th edn, Times Mirror/Mosby College, St Louis, MO.

Cohen, S 1988, 'Psychosocial models of the role of social support in the etiology of physical disease', *Health Psychology*, 7, 269–97.

Cote, J, Salmela, J & Russell, S 1993, 'The knowledge of high-performance gymnastic coaches: competition and training considerations', *The Sport Psychologist*, 9, 76–95.

Dishman, RK 1988, *Exercise adherence: its impact on public health*, Human Kinetics, Champaign, IL.

Filby, CD, Maynard, IW & Graydon, JK 1999, 'The effect of multiple-goal strategies on performance outcomes in training and competition', *Journal of Applied Sport Psychology*, 11, 230–46.

Garland, H, Weinberg, RS, Bruya, LD & Jackson, A 1988, 'Self-efficacy and endurance performance: a longitudinal field test of cognitive mediation theory', *Applied Psychology: An International Review*, 37, 381–94.

Giannini, J, Weinberg, RS & Jackson, A 1988, 'The effects of mastery: competitive and cooperative goals on the performance of simple and complex basketball skills', *Journal of Sport & Exercise Psychology*, 10, 408–17.

Gould, D 2000, 'Goal setting for peak performance', in J Williams (ed.), *Applied sport psychology: personal growth to peak performance*, 2nd. edn, Mayfield, Mountain View, CA, pp. 190–228.

Gould, D, Greenleaf, C, Guinan, D & Chung, Y 2002, 'A survey of U.S. Olympic coaches: variables perceived to have influenced athletic performance and coach effectiveness', *The Sport Psychologist*, 16, 229–50.

Gould, D, Finch, L & Jackson, S 1993, 'Coping strategies used by national figure skating champions', *Research Quarterly for Exercise and Sport*, 64, 453–68.

Gould, D, Tammen, V, Murphy, S & May, J 1989, 'An examination of U.S. Olympic sport psychology consultants and the services they provide', *The Sport Psychologist*, 3, 300–12.

Hardy, C, Richman, JM & Rosenfeld, LB 1991, 'The role of social support in the life-stress/injury relationship', *The Sport Psychologist*, 5, 128–39.

Hunter, JE & Schmidt, FL 1983, 'Quantifying the effects of psychological interventions on employee job performance and work force productivity', *American Psychologist*, 38, 473–8.

Kane, TD, Baltes, TR & Moss, MC 2001, 'Causes and consequences of free-set goals: an investigation of athletic self-regulation', *Journal of Sport & Exercise Psychology*, 23, 55–75.

Kingston, K & Hardy, L 1997, 'Effects of different types of goals on processes that support performance', *The Sport Psychologist*, 11, 277–9.

Kyllo, LB & Landers, DM 1995, 'Goal setting in sport and exercise: a research synthesis to resolve the controversy', *Journal of Sport & Exercise Psychology*, 17, 117–37.

Latham, GP & Lee, TW 1986, 'Goal setting', in EA Locke (ed.), *Generalizing from laboratory to field settings: research findings from industrial-organizational psychology, organizational behavior, and human resource management*, Heath, Lexington, MA, pp. 101–17.

Locke, EA 1966, 'The relationship of intentions to level of performance', *Journal of Applied Psychology*, 50, 60–6.

Locke, EA 1968, 'Toward a theory of task motivation incentives', *Organizational Behavior and Human Performance*, 3, 157–89.

Locke, EA 1978, 'The ubiquity of the technique of goal setting in theories of and approaches to employee motivation', *Academy of Management Review*, 3, 594–601.

Locke, EA 1991, 'Problems with goal-setting research in sports — and their solution', *Journal of Sport & Exercise Psychology*, 8, 311–16.

Locke, EA 1994, 'Comments on Weinberg and Weigand', *Journal of Sport & Exercise Psychology*, 16, 212–15.

Locke, EA & Latham, GP 1985, 'The application of goal setting to sports', *Journal of Sport Psychology*, 7, 205–22.

Locke, EA & Latham, GP 1990a, *A theory of goal setting and task performance*, Prentice Hall, Englewood Cliffs, NJ.

Locke, EA & Latham, GP 1990b, 'Work motivation and satisfaction: light at the end of the tunnel', *Psychological Science*, 1, 240–6.

Locke, EA, Shaw, KN, Saari, LM & Latham, GP 1981, 'Goal setting and task performance', *Psychological Bulletin*, 90, 125–52.

Mento, AJ, Steel, RP & Karren, RJ 1987, 'A meta-analytic study of the effects of goal setting on task performance: 1966–1984', *Organizational Behavior and Human Decision Processes*, 39, 52–83.

O'Block, F & Evans, F 1984, 'Goal-setting as a motivational technique', in J Silva and R Weinberg (eds), *Psychological foundations of sport*, Human Kinetics, Champaign, IL.

Orlick, T 2000, *In pursuit of excellence*, 3rd edn, Human Kinetics, Champaign, IL.

Orlick, T & Partington, J 1988, 'Mental links to excellence', *The Sport Psychologist*, 2, 105–130.

Sullivan, PA & Nashman, HW 1998, 'Self-perceptions of the role of USOC sport psychologists in working with Olympic athletes', *The Sport Psychologist*, 12, 95–103.

Swain, A & Jones, G 1995, 'Effects of goal setting interventions on selected basketball skills: a single-subject design', *Research Quarterly for Exercise and Sport*, 66, 51–63.

Tubbs, ME 1986, 'Goal setting: a meta-analytic examination of the empirical evidence', *Journal of Applied Psychology*, 71, 474–83.

Weinberg, R 2002, 'Goal setting in sport and exercise', in J Van Raalte and B Brewer (eds), *Exploring sport and exercise psychology*, 2nd edn, American Psychological Association Press, Washington, DC, pp. 25–48.

Weinberg, R, Burton, D, Yukelson, D & Weigand, D 1993, 'Goal setting in competitive sport: an exploratory investigation of practices of collegiate athletes', *The Sport Psychologist*, 7, 275–89.

Weinberg, RS, Burton, D, Yukelson, D & Weigand, D 2000, 'Perceived goal-setting practices of Olympic athletes: an exploratory investigation', *The Sport Psychologist*, 14, 280–96.

Weinberg, RS, Butt, J & Knight, B 2001, 'High school coaches' perceptions of the process of goal setting', *The Sport Psychologist*, 15, 20–47.

Weinberg, RS, Butt, J, Knight, B & Perritt, N 2001, 'Collegiate coaches' perceptions of their goal setting practice: a qualitative investigation', *Journal of Applied Sport Psychology*, 13, 374–99.

Weinberg, R & Jackson, A 1990, 'Building self-efficacy in tennis players: a coach's perspective', *Journal of Applied Sport Psychology*, 2 161–71.

Weinberg, RS, Stitcher, T & Richardson, P 1994, 'Effects of a seasonal goal setting program on lacrosse performance', *The Sport Psychologist*, 8, 166–75.

Weinberg, RS & Weigand, D 1993, 'Goal setting in sport and exercise: a reaction to Locke', *Journal of Sport & Exercise Psychology*, 15, 88–95.

Weinberg, RS & Weigand, D 1996, 'Let the discussions continue: a reaction to Locke's comments on Weinberg and Weigand', *Journal of Sport & Exercise Psychology*, 18, 89–93.

Wood, RE, Mento, AJ & Locke, EA 1987, 'Task complexity as a moderator of goal effects: a meta-analysis', *Journal of Applied Psychology*, 72, 416–25.

Zimmerman, BJ 2000, 'Attaining self-regulation: a social-cognitive perspective', in M Boekaerts, PR Pinrich & M Zeidner (eds), *Handbook of self-regulation*, Academic Press, San Diego, pp. 13–39.

CHAPTER 11

ANXIETY AND COPING IN SPORT: THEORETICAL MODELS AND APPROACHES TO ANXIETY REDUCTION

Ronald E Smith & Frank L Smoll

A setting that provides challenges, opportunities and potential threats to both physical and psychological wellbeing, the sport environment is capable of eliciting a wide range of motivational and emotional states, including anxiety. High levels of anxiety can be experienced at all ages and competitive levels, from youth leagues to the professional ranks.

Performance pressures increase in intensity at elite levels of competition. Smith (1980) collected survey data on the frequency and intensity of anxiety reactions experienced before, during and after games from more than 200 athletes on major college football teams. More than 40 per cent of the respondents reported frequently experiencing high levels of anxiety that they felt interfered with their performance. The potentially disruptive effects of heightened anxiety on the performance of college athletes have been objectively demonstrated by Weinberg and Genuchi (1980). They found that collegiate golfers who were high in competitive anxiety performed significantly more poorly during tournament rounds than did low-anxiety players of comparable ability, as defined by scores during practice rounds.

There is also evidence that the stress produced by life changes that require re-adjustment (e.g. academic, athletic and personal relationship concerns and disruptions) is linked to an increased susceptibility to sport-related injuries (Bramwell, Masuda, Wagner & Holmes 1975; Cryan & Alles 1983; Williams & Roepke 1993), particularly when the athlete's social support and coping skills are low (Smith, Smoll & Ptacek 1990). A more recent study of ballet dancers revealed that those high in performance anxiety were at significantly greater risk for injury when under life stress. Both somatic and cognitive components of anxiety increased injury vulnerability (Smith, Ptacek & Patterson 2000).

Because of the potentially negative effects that anxiety can have on athletes' performance, physical health and psychological wellbeing, sport psychologists are interested in reducing maladaptively high levels of anxiety. In the survey study of anxiety reactions in college football players cited on the previous page, fully 80 per cent of those who reported experiencing high anxiety expressed interest in receiving stress management training. Moreover, one of the most highly prized characteristics within the sport community, 'mental toughness', is generally regarded as involving the ability to deal with stress and adversity in such a way that performance does not suffer (or even peaks) under conditions that place high physical and psychological demands on the competitor. It is therefore not surprising that anxiety reduction and control strategies are prominently discussed in recent books on psychological skills training for athletes and coaches (e.g. Smith & Smoll 2001; Williams 2001). From a scientific perspective, considerable interest exists in theoretical analyses of sport anxiety and their implications for the development of effective anxiety reduction approaches.

This chapter describes current conceptual models of anxiety as well as the anxiety reduction approaches they have inspired. We also illustrate how these approaches might be employed to reduce maladaptive anxiety responses in athletes. Because there is as yet no substantive research literature on the use of some of these techniques with athletes, we selectively review outcome studies of anxiety reduction performed with other client populations, as well as animal and human research bearing on the processes that appear to mediate anxiety reduction.

THE NATURE OF SPORT PERFORMANCE ANXIETY

Before discussing the nature of sport performance anxiety, distinctions should be drawn between the related concepts of arousal, stress and anxiety. These terms are often used interchangeably, resulting in no small measure of confusion within the literature.

Arousal is the most general of the three terms. Cannon (1929) used the term to refer to physiological and energy mobilisation in response to situations that threaten the physical integrity of the organism. The concept of arousal has also occupied a prominent position in the theoretical formulations of Berlyne (1960), Duffy (1962), Hebb (1949), Malmo (1959) and others. If behaviour is viewed as varying along two dimensions of direction and intensity, then arousal is the intensity dimension. Arousal, often used interchangeably with other intensity-related terms such as tension, drive and activation, can vary on a continuum ranging from deep sleep to peak excitement.

The term *stress* is used in two different but related ways. First, it is used in relation to situations (termed *stressors*) that place significant demands on the organism. This situational definition of stress is frequently couched in terms of the balance between situational demands and the resources the individual can bring to bear on them (e.g. Lazarus & Folkman 1984). When situational demands greatly exceed an individual's coping resources, the situation is said to be stressful. The second use of the term stress refers to the responses of individuals to stressors. Used in this sense, stress refers to a cognitive-affective response involving appraisal of threat and increased physiological arousal, as well as behavioural coping responses (Lazarus & Folkman 1984; Spielberger 1989). Although some authors (e.g. Selye 1976) have viewed stress as being either positive or negative in its effects on behaviour and wellbeing, contemporary researchers typically use the term to incorporate a range of subjectively aversive emotional states, including anxiety, depression and anger. In any case, the stress response is not as global a concept as arousal.

Anxiety is one variety of stress response, and it too is a multifaceted construct. The term can refer either to a transitory state or to a dispositional trait that expresses itself across situations. On the one hand, then, anxiety can be a momentary aversive emotional *state* that can fluctuate over time. This 'A-state' is characterised by current worry and apprehension concerning the possibility of physical or psychological harm, together with increased physiological arousal resulting from the appraisal of threat. State anxiety also has motivational properties. As a motivational state, anxiety can be viewed as an avoidance motive that helps strengthen successful coping and/or avoidance responses through negative reinforcement (i.e. the strengthening of behaviours that result in an avoidance or reduction of anxiety).

As a *trait*, sport performance anxiety (A-trait) is a relatively stable individual difference personality variable. More specifically, it involves a predisposition to respond with state anxiety to competitive sport situations in which the adequacy of the athlete's performance can be evaluated. Although a number of specific sources of threat (including the possibility of physical harm) may reside in the sport situation, probably the most salient sources of threat are the possibilities of failure and of disapproval by significant others who are evaluating the athlete's performance in relation to some standard of excellence (e.g. Dunn 1999). Athletic performance anxiety is thus part of a family of performance-related fear-of-failure constructs that include test anxiety, speech anxiety and the 'stage fright' that actors, musicians and dancers can experience within their evaluative performance situations (Kendrick, Craig, Lawson & Davidson 1982; Steptoe & Fidler 1987).

Like other forms of anxiety, sport performance anxiety has separate but functionally related cognitive, physiological and behavioural components. Burton (1998) has reviewed the literature on sport-related state anxiety and its measurement, and Smith, Smoll and Wiechman (1998) have provided a similar review of the trait anxiety literature. Well-validated sport-specific measures, such as the Competitive State Anxiety Inventory–2 (Martens, Burton, Vealey, Bump & Smith 1990) are now available to measure the cognitive and somatic components of state anxiety. At the trait level, measures such as the Sport Anxiety Scale (Smith, Smoll & Schutz 1990) can be used to measure individual differences in the tendency to respond with cognitive and somatic anxiety states in competitive sport situations.

A conceptual model of athletic performance anxiety is presented in figure 11.1. This model includes both the trait–state distinction and the differentiation between situational, cognitive, physiological and behavioural components of the anxiety response. The model also accounts for a distinction that is sometimes made between anxiety states that are viewed by athletes as having negative effects on performance (debilitative anxiety) and those that seem to positively affect performance (facilitative anxiety).

The cognitive and somatic components of sport A-state are shown within the appraisal and physiological response panels of the figure. The intensity and duration of the A-state response are assumed to be influenced by three major factors. The first of these factors is the nature of the competitive situation in which the athlete is involved. Obviously such situations differ in the demands they place on the athlete, as well as the degree of threat they pose to successful performance. Such factors as strength of opponent, importance of the contest, presence of significant others, and degree of social support received from coaches and team-mates can affect the amount of threat that the situation is likely to pose for an athlete. It should also be noted that A-trait influences the situations to which people will expose themselves. Thus, people with excessively high performance anxiety may choose to avoid the sport situation altogether. As an individual difference variable, A-trait therefore represents a relatively stable set of cognitive and affective tendencies that interact with the situation to determine the level of A-state experienced.

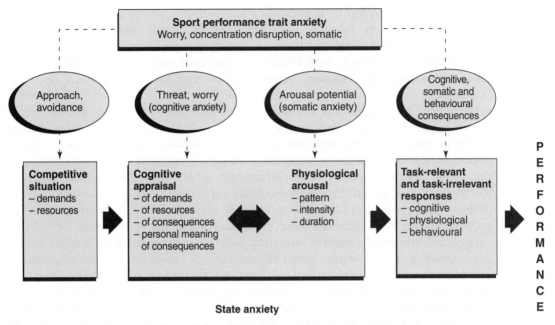

Figure 11.1 A conceptual model of sport performance anxiety, indicating the influence of cognitive and somatic trait anxiety on situational, cognitive, physiological and behavioural state anxiety components

(*Source:* Smith, Smoll & Passer, in press)

The objective situation and the performer's level of A-trait are assumed to influence the performer's appraisal processes. Four classes of appraisal are particularly important: (a) appraisal of the situational demands; (b) appraisal of the resources available to deal with them; (c) appraisal of the nature and likelihood of potential consequences if the demands are not met (i.e. the expectancies and valences relating to potential consequences); and (d) the personal meaning that the consequences have for the individual (Smith 1986). The meanings attached to the consequences derive from the person's belief system, and they often involve the individual's standards for self-worth (Ellis 1962; Rogers 1959). Thus an athlete who defines the present situational demands as overwhelming, who appraises her resources and skills as insufficient to deal with the demands, who anticipates failure and/or social disapproval as a result of the demands/resources imbalance, and who defines her self-worth in terms of success and/or the approval of others will clearly perceive this competitive situation as threatening or dangerous. We assume that differences in the worry component of cognitive trait anxiety are especially important determinants of the kinds of appraisals that are made. Worriers perceive an unfavourable balance between demands and resources, and expect the worst to occur.

Negative appraisals are likely to generate high levels of physiological arousal, and this arousal, in turn, feeds back into the ongoing process of appraisal and re-appraisal (Lazarus 2000). High levels of arousal may convince the athlete that he or she is 'falling apart' and help generate even more negative appraisals. Athletes clearly vary in the amount of physiological arousal they report, and individual differences in the trait of somatic anxiety are likely to predispose athletes to differ in this regard. As behaviour genetics research is demonstrating, some portion of the variance in somatic anxiety potential is attributable to genetically based constitutional factors (e.g. Buss 1995).

Since the relationship between anxiety and performance has always been a central focus of sport anxiety research, our model should include mechanisms assumed to mediate positive and negative effects of anxiety on performance. As Mandler and Sarason (1952) have noted, motivational and emotional states may generate two broad classes of task-related responses. Some of these responses (task-relevant responses) facilitate task performance, whereas others (task-irrelevant responses) are detrimental to performance. We suggest that the task-relevant and task-irrelevant responses may be cognitive, physiological or behavioural in nature. Thus, cognitive responses, such as perceived control over the situation, positive expectations of goal attainment, concentration on the task and strategic planning may be considered task-relevant responses that would contribute positively to performance. These cognitive responses (including the appraisal that the affective response being experienced is a 'psyching up' that will facilitate performance) are assumed to underlie some performers' reports that anxiety improves rather than degrades their performance (e.g. Jones & Swain 1995). Conversely, task-irrelevant cognitive responses, such as expectations of an inability to cope and impending failure, worries about the reactions of others and catastrophic thinking can interfere with task performance by disrupting attentional and problem-solving processes. Both the worry and the concentration-disruption components of A-trait (as measured by the Sport Anxiety Scale) are assumed to be negative predisposing factors of debilitative anxiety (Smith 1996). Likewise, depending on the nature of the task (especially its complexity, degree of mastery and precision of required movements), certain classes and intensities of physiological responding might facilitate task performance, whereas other types and intensities of physiological responding might interfere with task performance (Jones 1995). Thus, high physiological arousal may enhance a sprinter's performance, which requires relatively simple and overlearned running responses, while negatively affecting a golfer's more precise and complex task behaviours (e.g. Weinberg & Genuchi 1980). Finally, behavioural responses such as persistence and smooth execution of motor responses would facilitate performance, whereas impulsive or inappropriate behaviours would interfere with it. These task-irrelevant responses contribute to debilitative anxiety effects. The balance between task-relevant and task-irrelevant responses and the manner in which they are affected by the performer's anxiety level will therefore affect the adequacy of performance. It should also be noted that ongoing appraisal of performance adequacy can influence the four basic cognitive appraisal elements shown in the figure. For example, when athletes are performing poorly, they are likely to view the situation as more demanding and their coping resources as less adequate, and they may therefore expect negative consequences.

It should be noted that at both the state and trait levels, important individual differences may exist among athletes in their customary pattern of cognitive, affective and behavioural anxiety responses. For example, one athlete may be more prone to excessive worry and cognitive interference, whereas another may react with relatively higher physiological arousal. Within the cognitive, physiological and behavioural domains, individual differences also exist. For example, the principle of autonomic response stereotypy (Lacey & Lacey 1958) tells us that people with similarly high levels of somatic trait anxiety may differ in their specific patterns of physiological arousal when exhibiting state anxiety. Thus, one athlete may exhibit high cardiovascular reactivity and relatively lower muscle tension, whereas another athlete may show the opposite arousal pattern. Likewise, the specific thoughts, self-statements and images involved in cognitive performance anxiety vary among athletes. Such differences have important implications when teaching athletes stress management coping skills (Smith 1980).

Implications for anxiety reduction

According to the model presented in figure 11.1, anxiety may be reduced at any of the major points in the model. At the situational, or stressor, level, any development or intervention that reduces situational demands or increases resources will decrease the stress potential of the situation. For example, relationships with coaches can be a potent source of performance anxiety. Within the youth sport environment, coaches can play an especially influential role in the processes that affect the development and maintenance of performance anxiety. Critical or punitive feedback from coaches can evoke high levels of negative affect in youngsters who fear failure and disapproval, thereby contributing to a threatening and unnecessarily demanding athletic situation (Baker, Cote & Hawes 2000; Passer 1988). In contrast, children who perceive their coaches as supportive of their efforts experience higher levels of sport enjoyment (Scanlan & Lewthwaite 1986; Smoll, Smith, Barnett & Everett 1993). Support from coaches and team-mates constitutes an important resource that helps counteract the stressful aspects of competition. In one intervention designed to decrease punitive behaviours and increase supportive ones, coaches were administered Coach Effectiveness Training (CET), an educational workshop designed to help coaches create a more positive sport environment for children (Smith, Smoll & Curtis 1979; Smoll & Smith 2001). A control group of coaches was given a workshop on how to teach children sport skills. Youngsters who subsequently played for CET coaches showed a significant reduction in sport performance A-trait over the course of the season, whereas no significant decline was found in children who played for untrained coaches (Smith, Smoll & Barnett 1995).

The interacting nature of the model components in figure 11.1 is shown by what occurs when athletes become more proficient in sport skills. At the situational level, increased skilfulness positively affects the demands/resources balance, for skills are personal resources that help decrease situational demands and increase the likelihood of successful performance. Skill attainment also affects cognitive appraisals of personal resources, increasing self-efficacy and thereby reducing anxiety (Bandura 1997). Thus, skill improvement at the behavioural 'output' level increases task-relevant response capabilities, but such effects also modify the situation and the athlete's appraisal of the situation, personal efficacy and expectations of success. Other interventions that reduce anxiety-arousing cognitive appraisals effectively short-circuit the process of anxiety. For example, peak performers tend to view competitive 'pressure' situations as challenges and opportunities, rather than threats (Smith 1986).

Interventions can also be directed at the physiological component of the anxiety response. As we shall see, coping skills such as the ability to relax the body can help athletes prevent or control physiological arousal that might affect their performance adversely. Other anxiety reduction measures reduce physiological arousal through deconditioning methods derived from learning theory. We now turn to the major theoretical approaches and methods that can be used to change the cognitive and emotional components of the anxiety response.

Four models of anxiety reduction have been particularly influential in psychological research on anxiety and anxiety reduction. Two models derived from the psychology of learning, the *extinction model* and the *counterconditioning model*, conceive of anxiety as a conditioned emotional response. Based on these models, two techniques employed to reduce anxiety, exposure and systematic desensitization, have been developed. A third model of anxiety reduction, known as the *cognitive mediational model*, addresses the thought processes that underlie anxiety and is aimed at modifying affect-eliciting cognitions. A fourth and increasingly influential model of anxiety reduction is the *coping skills model*, which underlies several approaches designed to increase the individual's self-regulation ability by teaching active coping skills.

THE EXTINCTION MODEL

Theoretical models derived from the psychology of learning view anxiety as a conditioned emotional response (Rachman 1990). Anxiety responses are elicited by formerly neutral stimuli through a process of classical conditioning. By virtue of being paired with aversive or painful stimuli (unconditioned stimuli, or UCS), certain sport-related stimuli become conditioned stimuli (CS) capable of eliciting a conditioned anxiety response. An example of this process occurred when a professional baseball player was struck in the face by a pitched ball and suffered painful fractures and an eye injury. After recovering from his injuries, that athlete found that going to bat evoked intense anxiety. The previous pairing of the stimuli associated with stepping up to bat with the traumatic experience of being hit in the face with the baseball had created a conditioned fear response to going up to bat.

In many instances, people develop anxiety responses to particular situations when there is no history of their undergoing aversive classical conditioning themselves. It is possible for anxiety responses to develop through vicarious classical conditioning, in which the CS–UCS pairing is observed to occur to someone else (Berger 1962). For example, a gymnast began to experience intense anxiety that prevented her from attempting a difficult dismount after seeing another gymnast fracture her back while attempting a similar routine.

Once a conditioned anxiety response is established through direct or vicarious classical conditioning, it becomes capable of motivating and reinforcing avoidance responses. That is, because anxiety is an aversive state, people (and animals) are motivated to reduce, escape or avoid it. When successful avoidance responses occur, the resulting reduction in anxiety constitutes a negative reinforcement that serves to strengthen the avoidance responses (Rescorla & Solomon 1967). This is one reason why the tendency to avoid anxiety-arousing stimuli often appears to become stronger over time even though no further CS–UCS pairings occur.

Extinction is the process whereby classically conditioned responses are eliminated by repeatedly presenting the CS in the absence of the UCS. In Pavlov's (1927) classic studies of conditioning of salivary responses in dogs, the conditioned salivary response was extinguished by presenting the CS (i.e. the bell) repeatedly in the absence of food. According to the extinction model, then, one way to reduce a conditioned anxiety response is to expose the individual to anxiety-arousing stimuli in the absence of the primary aversive stimuli with which they were originally paired. Undoubtedly this process occurs in some people who are able to face up to their fears and remain in an anxiety-arousing situation until their anxiety is overcome. In many other people, however, the natural process of extinction is prevented from occurring because avoidance responses remove the individual from the exposure to the CS before extinction can occur. In animal studies, forced exposure to the CS, together with prevention of the avoidance response (e.g. by restraining the animal), has been successfully employed in extinguishing anxiety responses (see Mineka 1979). The human therapeutic counterparts to this forced exposure procedure are known as flooding and graded exposure.

Flooding and graded exposure techniques

Flooding refers to the general technique of exposing the individual to anxiety-provoking stimuli while preventing the occurrence of avoidance responses. Clinically the technique usually involves the use of imagined scenes, although *in vivo* (real-life) exposure to the actual feared stimuli or situations can also be used, either alone or as an adjunct to the imaginal exposure. It is assumed that prolonged exposure to the anxiety-arousing stimuli in the absence of an aversive UCS will extinguish the anxiety. A large number of clinical and experimental studies provide evidence that this does indeed occur, whereas brief exposures do not produce extinction (Marshall 1985; Staub 1968). Accordingly, the client is 'flooded' with the CS and the anxiety they elicit until the anxiety no longer occurs.

Flooding procedures are a part of several other treatment techniques as well, such as eye movement desensitisation and reprocessing (EMDR), in which clients relive previous traumatic events while their therapist induces eye movements by moving her or his finger back and forth in front of the client's face (Shapiro 1991). Recent evidence suggests that the stimulus exposure is the primary factor in improvement when it occurs, whether or not eye movements are induced as well (e.g. Carrigan & Levis 1999).

Since flooding can arouse considerable anxiety during treatment, the client's informed consent should always be obtained before beginning the procedure. This can be accomplished by carefully explaining to the client the concepts discussed above: anxiety as a conditioned response, the concept of extinction, and the nature of and rationale for the treatment that will be used. The client should be told that he or she will probably experience intense anxiety for a period of time before it diminishes. The client's informed commitment to the treatment technique is likely to enhance his or her willingness and ability to experience the aversive scenes and the anxiety they elicit.

Given the client's consent to the procedure, a careful assessment should be made of the kinds of situations that are distressing and the specific aspects of the situations that trigger the anxiety. In conjunction with the assessment phase, clients may be given imagery training in which they are asked to vividly experience events in the visual, auditory, kinesthetic and olfactory-gustatory sensory modalities. The training that follows involves the prolonged presentation of scenes that are highly anxiety arousing to the athlete, as illustrated in the case study that follows.

ANXIETY EXTINCTION THROUGH FLOODING: A CASE STUDY

The most common sources of anxiety in athletes are fears of failure and resulting social disapproval or rejection (Smith 1980). To illustrate the use of flooding, let us consider the treatment of a highly anxious male basketball player who had a tendency to 'choke' in pressure situations. After establishing through interview what the most fearful situations might be, the athlete was asked to close his eyes and imagine a series of scenes involving his responding to pressure game situations with paralysing fear, failing miserably in the clutch, and anticipating the disapproval and possible rejection of team-mates, the coach, spectators and significant others such as parents, relatives and (former) friends. Each scene was presented in vivid detail (with the athlete frequently asked to provide additional details to enhance involvement) and involved as many sensory modalities as possible. For example, the athlete was asked to imagine standing at the foul line waiting to shoot crucial free throws late in the game. He could vividly see every aspect of the scene — the crowd, with all eyes focused on him; opponents smiling confidently at him; his team-mates avoiding his eyes; his parents watching intently and looking anxious. He could also hear the crowd screaming and one of his opponents muttering, 'No way. You're going to choke.' Kinaesthetic cues (e.g. the trembling of his knees, his pounding heart, the weight of the ball in his slippery, sweaty hands) and olfactory-gustatory stimuli, such as the smell of sweaty bodies and the taste of sweat as he licked his lips with his dry, cotton-like tongue, were also presented. Predictably, such scenes elicited intense anxiety, and they were prolonged until a visible and reported reduction of anxiety was observed. Flooding sessions typically lasted from 30 to 40 minutes, with an additional 15 to 20 minutes spent discussing the athlete's experiences during the flooding. Five sessions of the exposure-based treatment resulted in a marked reduction in self-reported anxiety and an improvement in performance.

In the behaviour therapy literature, the terms flooding and exposure are often used interchangeably. However, other researchers and therapists distinguish between them in terms of stimulus presentation. *Graded exposure*, unlike flooding, does not immediately expose clients to stimuli that arouse high anxiety. Instead, exposure occurs in a gradual manner as clients are exposed initially to stimuli (either imaginal or real) that do not arouse much anxiety, presumably allowing extinction of these low-level anxiety responses to occur before proceeding to stimuli that arouse stronger anxiety (hence the term 'graded' exposure). Graded exposure is therefore easier on the client than is flooding. On the other hand, the treatment may take longer, for once extinction occurs to the intense stimuli of flooding, it should not be necessary to extinguish lower-level stimuli, given that they are very similar to those situations that have already been dealt with in earlier exposures. Surprisingly, few studies in the clinical literature have directly compared the two approaches, but there is some evidence that flooding may be more effective in some cases (Dua 1980). To this point, no research has been done with athletes to compare the two stimulus-exposure approaches.

The effectiveness of exposure techniques for anxiety reduction in athletes cannot currently be appraised owing to a paucity of clinical reports and experimental outcome studies with this treatment population. In one case study, a woman athlete avoided triathlons because of a lifelong fear and avoidance of swimming in the ocean. Seven *in vivo* exposure and response prevention sessions during which she entered the ocean and swam eliminated her fear, and she subsequently swam successfully in a major triathlon (Farkas 1989). However, much experimental evidence with clinical populations suffering from severe anxiety indicates the efficacy of exposure techniques (Antony & Swinson 2000; O'Leary & Wilson 1998), suggesting that they can be successfully applied to athletes as well.

THE COUNTERCONDITIONING MODEL

An alternative to extinguishing a conditioned emotional response is to condition a state that is incompatible with physiological arousal responses to the anxiety-arousing cues. The general principle, according to Joseph Wolpe, who was the chief proponent of the counterconditioning approach, is as follows:

> If a response antagonistic to anxiety can be made to occur in the presence of anxiety-evoking stimuli so that it is accompanied by a complete or partial suppression of the anxiety responses, the bond between these stimuli and the anxiety responses will be lessened. (1958, p. 21)

According to Wolpe, anxious people have learned through a process of classical conditioning to experience excessively high levels of sympathetic nervous system arousal in the presence of certain stimuli. The goal of treatment is to replace sympathetic activity with competing behaviours that have a predominance of parasympathetic innervation, a process Wolpe termed *reciprocal inhibition*.

Systematic desensitisation

Systematic desensitisation, the treatment devised by Wolpe, is designed to permit the gradual counterconditioning of anxiety using relaxation as the incompatible response. Theoretically, other incompatible responses (Wolpe suggested assertion, sexual activity, vigorous muscular activity, carbon dioxide inhalation and eating as possibilities) could also be used, but not as easily or dependably as relaxation. The process of systematic desensitisation is carried out in such a way that the client should experience little if any anxiety, a feature that differentiates this approach from exposure techniques, particularly flooding.

The client is first trained in deep muscle relaxation, using a variant of Jacobson's (1938) progressive relaxation procedure. Relaxation is learned through a process of tensing and voluntarily relaxing the major muscle groups of the body. At the same time that relaxation is being mastered, the trainer and client begin to construct a stimulus hierarchy of scenes related to the client's anxiety. The hierarchy typically consists of 10 to 15 scenes arranged in terms of the intensity of anxiety they elicit. Hierarchies may be constructed along one or more of a variety of gradients, including time (gradually approaching a highly feared event), distance, seriousness and so forth. Much care should be taken constructing the hierarchy in collaboration with the client, so that the steps are gradual and roughly equivalent in the increments of anxiety they elicit.

Returning to the anxious basketball player discussed earlier in connection with flooding, sample items in his hierarchy (arranged from most to least anxiety arousing) might include scenes like the following:

- Preparing to shoot a free throw, with 1 second left in a championship game and your team trailing by 1 point (very high anxiety scene)
- Listening to the coach's final instructions in the huddle, just before tip-off (high anxiety scene)
- Sitting in the locker room before the game as your coach tells you how important this game is (moderately high anxiety scene)
- Walking towards the arena where the game will be played (moderate anxiety scene)
- Waking in the morning and thinking of the game that evening (moderately low anxiety scene)
- Thinking about the fact that the game will be played in two days (low anxiety scene).

A complete hierarchy would obviously have other scenes interspersed between the above scenes. Note that these scenes are basically arranged along an intensity dimension and a time dimension.

When the client has mastered the relaxation skill and the hierarchy has been developed, treatment begins. The client is deeply relaxed and asked to imagine the lowest (least anxiety-arousing) in the hierarchy for perhaps 3 seconds. If any anxiety is experienced, the client is instructed to signal the clinician, who terminates the scene immediately and reinstates relaxation. However, if the client is deeply relaxed, the relaxation should inhibit the low level of anxiety aroused by a well-chosen initial hierarchy item. If no anxiety is experienced, the scene is presented again for a slightly longer interval, perhaps 5 seconds. If again successful, the scene is presented for 10 seconds, then for 15. Each time the client is able to imagine the scene without experiencing anxiety, it is assumed that some of the total anxiety is being deconditioned through reciprocal inhibition, and the anxiety reduction is assumed to generalise to the items higher in the hierarchy.

After the first item has been counterconditioned, the relaxation may well be sufficient to inhibit the reduced amount of anxiety now elicited by the second item. In this way the clinician proceeds up the hierarchy. If the client cannot make the transition from a mastered item to the next highest item, the clinician may intersperse a new item to bridge the gap. Wolpe emphasised that great care should be taken to prevent anxiety from occurring, since this could partially undo the deconditioning that has already occurred. As in flooding, it is assumed that the reduction of anxiety that occurs to imagined stimuli generalises to corresponding life situations.

Probably no behaviour therapy technique has been as widely researched as systematic desensitisation, and its efficacy as an anxiety-reduction technique is well established. More than 100 controlled studies have found desensitisation to be superior to placebo or untreated controls with a wide range of anxiety-based disorders (Spiegler & Guevremont

1998; Stuart 2001). The technique has proven very effective in the treatment of test anxiety, a form of performance anxiety analogous to that experienced by many athletes. Positive changes have been observed on self-report test anxiety measures as well as on performance measures, such as grade point average (e.g. Smith & Nye 1973). There is every reason to believe that the technique would be valuable for athletes, as indicated in a case study by Heyman (1987), but additional research is clearly needed.

Because the extinction and counterconditioning models both focus on deconditioning arousal responses to specific classes of stimuli, we should not expect substantial generalisation of treatment gains to other areas of anxiety. Indeed, little generalisation has been demonstrated with either flooding or desensitisation (O'Leary & Wilson 1998). The generalisation of treatment effects is a significant issue when considering the concepts of treatment efficacy and efficiency (Smith 1999). Eliminating anxiety responses to specific situations may in itself be a very worthwhile goal for many clients, and the issue of generalisation of treatment gains to other areas of the individual's life may be a moot one. However, some treatment approaches provide for the development of generalisable coping skills that are relevant not only to the specific anxiety-arousing situations that are the focus of treatment, but also to problem situations that may confront the individual in other circumstances or in the future, or even to other emotional responses, such as anger or depression.

THE COGNITIVE MEDIATIONAL MODEL

The extinction and counterconditioning models are based on a concept of anxiety as a classically conditioned emotional response. Radical behaviourists such as Wolpe (1978) eschew the use of cognitive concepts in accounting for the development, maintenance and reduction of anxiety responses. Other theorists, such as Aaron Beck (1984), Albert Ellis (Ellis & Grieger 1977) and Richard Lazarus (2000), have given cognitive mediational processes a prominent role in their theories of emotion. These theorists assume that, as suggested in the model shown in figure 11.1, emotional arousal is triggered by thoughts, images and other cognitions, rather than being elicited directly by environmental cues. From this perspective, then, a powerful means of reducing maladaptive emotional responses, including anxiety, is to modify the cognitions that elicit and perpetuate emotionality.

According to Ellis (1962), many maladaptive emotions are the result of certain irrational beliefs that are learned early in life and reinforced within our culture. Irrational beliefs that are likely to underlie anxiety include the following:

1. One must be thoroughly competent, adequate and achieving in every way in order to be worthwhile.
2. It is a dire necessity to be loved or approved of by virtually every other significant person.
3. It is catastrophic when things are not the way we would like them to be.
4. Unhappiness and anxiety are externally caused and we have no control over our feelings.
5. If something is threatening or dangerous, one must keep thinking that it might happen.

Cognitive restructuring

Cognitive restructuring is a method derived from Ellis's (1962) rational emotive therapy. The intervention, directed towards the modification of self-defeating and irrational anxiety-eliciting cognitions, typically involves four related stages. The first step is to help the athlete recognise that his or her beliefs, assumptions, perceptions or ideas (i.e. cognitions) mediate emotional arousal. These cognitions have typically become automatised; they are, after all, overlearned habitual ways of thinking and tend to occur without the athlete's awareness. Once the athlete accepts this tenet, the sport consultant proceeds to a second stage, helping the athlete to identify some of the underlying ideas and to recognise their irrational and self-defeating nature. In the third phase, the athlete is helped to actively attack the irrational ideas and replace them with cognitions that prevent or reduce maladaptive anxiety. Finally, the athlete is helped to practise and rehearse the new modes of thinking and to apply them to the relevant life situations.

As stated earlier, the most common irrational beliefs among highly anxious athletes are that one must be thoroughly competent to be worthwhile (a belief that leads to fear of failure), and that one must be loved and approved of by everyone who is a significant other (which leads to fear of social disapproval). Cognitive restructuring has proven effective in reducing a related form of performance anxiety, test anxiety, which is typically mediated by similar beliefs (Goldfried, Linehan & Smith 1978) and with many other emotion-based problems (Antony & Swinson 2000). Rushall (1993) and Silva (1982) have published case studies describing successful use of cognitive restructuring with athletes, but controlled experimental outcome studies are lacking. We should note, however, that cognitive modification techniques are also integral parts of the coping skills interventions to be described in the next section of this chapter.

Cognitive restructuring approaches are likely to be very useful in reducing anxiety in athletes, particularly those who are fairly insightful and psychologically minded. As cognitive theorists have argued, the type of intervention likely to have the greatest impact in preventing maladaptive emotional arousal from occurring would be directed at modifying the cognitive mediators of emotionality. We should also expect that the modification of key irrational beliefs and self-statements will result in generalisation across related anxiety-arousing situations.

Self-instructional training

In *self-instructional training*, the focus is on helping athletes develop and use specific task-relevant self-commands that direct attention and enhance performance of the task at hand. Athletes are trained to give themselves adaptive instructions in dealing with preparing for the stressor, confronting and handling it, coping with feelings of being overwhelmed with anxiety, and evaluation and self-reinforcement (Meichenbaum 1985). Examples of adaptive self-statements at each of these four junctures are presented in the following highlighted feature.

SELF-INSTRUCTIONAL TRAINING

As applied to stress management training, Meichenbaum's (1985) self-instructional training helps individuals 'talk to themselves' in ways that reduce anxiety and focus attention on the task at hand. Clients are also trained to explicitly evaluate the effectiveness of their coping efforts after the episode, and to positively reinforce themselves for successful coping efforts. Here are examples of self-statements that can be applied at four phases of the coping process.

Preparing for the stressor
- What is it I have to do?
- I can work out a plan to deal with it.
- Just rehearse in your mind how you're going to deal with it.

(continued)

Confronting the stressor
- Don't think about fear, just about what I have to do.
- Take a deep breath and relax. Ah ... good.
- My nervousness is just a cue to focus on the task. I can meet this challenge.

Coping with high levels of anxiety
- Relax and slow things down.
- Keep your focus on the present. What is it I have to do?
- Don't try to eliminate all the stress. Just keep it manageable.

Post-event evaluation and self-reinforcement
- OK, what worked and what didn't?
- It didn't work this time, but I'll make the right adjustment next time.
- Way to go! I handled that pretty well.

(*Source:* After Meichenbaum 1985)

THE COPING SKILLS MODEL

Consistent with the definition of a stress-inducing situation shown in figure 11.1, Lazarus and Folkman (1984) have described coping as 'constantly changing cognitive and behavioural efforts to manage specific demands that are appraised as taxing or exceeding the resources of the person' (p. 141). There are, of course, countless ways that people might respond to a stressor. In a comprehensive review of the sport-related coping literature, Crocker, Kowalski and Graham (1998) noted that the categorisation and measurement of sport-related coping strategies has varied from as few as two global or higher-order categories, such as engagement/disengagement (Haney & Long 1995) and approach/avoidance (Anshel & Wells 2000), to a dozen or more specific strategies (Crocker & Isaak 1997; Gould, Finch & Jackson 1993). Factor analyses of coping strategies provide little uniformity in identifying the structure of coping because their results depend on the specific questions or scales that go into the analysis. In figure 11.2, we present a conceptual grouping of coping strategies in three relatively uncorrelated classes, each of which contains more specific coping methods. *Problem-focused coping* strategies attempt to confront and directly deal with the demands of the situation, or to change the situation so that it is no longer stressful. Examples include seeking out written information on sport strategies or skill development, going directly to a coach or fellow athlete to work out a misunderstanding, signing up for a course in time management in order to deal with time pressures, or engaging in extra practice in order to master a physical skill that reduces the demands of the athletic situation.

Rather than dealing directly with the stressful situation, *emotion-focused coping* strategies attempt to manage the emotional responses that result from it. As figure 11.2 shows, some forms of emotion-focused coping involve appraising the situation in a way that minimises its emotional impact. An athlete might deal with the stress created by an interpersonal conflict with a team-mate or coach by denying that any problem exists. Other forms involve avoidance or acceptance of the stressful situation. Thus, an athlete might seek escape from anxiety about an upcoming meet by going to a party, getting drunk and forgetting about it. Informed that her injury will prevent her from competing for a starting position on a team, an athlete may simply accept grim reality, realising that there is nothing that can be done to change the situation. Or an athlete may develop coping skills that allow for the self-control of anxiety responses in performance situations.

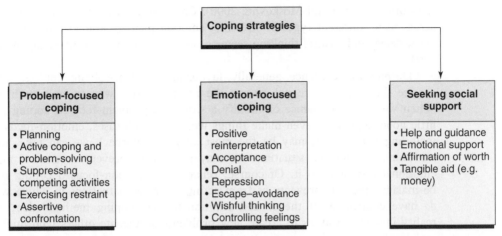

Figure 11.2 Categorisation of coping strategies into three general classes: (1) problem-focused methods, involving active attempts to change or control the anxiety-arousing situation; (2) emotion-focused coping directed at minimising emotional distress; and (3) seeking or accepting social support from others

(*Source:* Smith 1993)

A third class of coping strategies involves *seeking social support* — that is, turning to others for assistance and emotional support in times of stress. Thus, an athlete may seek a coach's or team-mate's help in mastering a skill or dealing with the emotional stress of a slump. In team sports, an important resource is the support that athletes and coaches can provide for one another.

We should note that our tripartite categorisation of coping strategies is based in part on findings of low correlations (less than .25) between them in previous research (e.g. Ptacek, Smith, Espe & Raffety 1994). This does not mean, however, that they are mutually exclusive. For example, support seeking that takes the form of asking a coach for technical assistance with a sport skill can be seen as a form of problem-solving, whereas seeking emotional support from a team-mate during a slump may be done in the service of reducing negative emotions. Similarly, a coping phenomenon labelled 'detach-ment' (Roger, Jarvis & Najarian 1993) or 'transcendence' (Yoo 2000) has been described as a distinctive coping response. The athlete reports an emotional detachment from the stressful aspects of the competitive situation and a total focus on task demands. Detach-ment can be viewed as serving both problem-focused and emotion-focused functions. The athlete detaches emotionally from the stressful situation (emotion-focused coping), but also focuses on the task demands and responds with task-relevant responses (problem-focused coping).

Much research has been done on the effectiveness of the various coping strategies. Holahan and Moos (1990) studied coping patterns and psychological outcomes in more than 400 California adults over a one-year period. First, they found that people used different coping strategies to deal with different classes of situations. They also found that problem-focused coping methods and seeking social support were more often associated with favourable adjustment to stressors. In contrast, emotion-focused strat-egies that involved avoiding feelings or taking things out on other people predicted depression and poorer adjustment. Other research indicates that problem-focused coping, positive reappraisal of demands and infusing ordinary events with positive meaning (e.g. focusing on the enjoyment deriving from an interaction with a friend) helped generate positive emotional responses that countered distress created by life stressors (Folkman and Moskowitz 2000). Conversely, in both children and adults, and across many different types of stressors, emotion-focused strategies that involve avoidance, denial and wishful thinking seem to be related to less effective adaptation (Aldwin 1994).

Despite the evidence generally favouring problem-solving coping, attempts to change the situation are not always the most adaptive way to cope with a stressor. When we cannot influence or modify a situation, problem-focused coping may do us little good, and could even make things worse. In such cases, emotion-focused coping, including detachment, may be the most adaptive approach we can take, for even if we cannot master the situation, we may be able to prevent or control maladaptive emotional responses to it. Of course, reliance on emotion-focused coping is likely to be maladaptive if it prevents us from acting to change situations in which we actually *do* have control, or if the chosen emotion-focused coping methods deny or distort reality in such a way as to create new problems or alienate others who might provide social support.

On the other hand, there exists a class of adaptive emotion-focused strategies, such as identifying and changing irrational negative thinking, thinking in a task-relevant fashion and learning relaxation skills to control arousal. These emotion-focused methods can reduce stress responses without avoiding or distorting reality and can be healthy ways of dealing with stress (Meichenbaum 1985; Smith 1980). We now describe several cognitive-behavioural approaches designed to teach athletes adaptive emotion-focused self-regulation skills for coping with competitive anxiety.

The coping skills model differs in important ways from the extinction and counter-conditioning models, in which the client is viewed as the passive recipient of a deconditioning procedure carried out by the trainer. Fundamentally, something is done *to* the client to undo past anxiety-conditioning experiences. In contrast, cognitive modification approaches give the athlete a far more active role and greater responsibility for developing and applying new modes of thinking about problem situations. Not surprisingly, therefore, several coping skills approaches have incorporated cognitive methods to teach people how to cope with the maladaptive modes of thinking that often underly performance anxiety.

The coping skills approach was stimulated in part by several influential reconceptualisations of the conditioning-based technique of systematic desensitisation. For example, Goldfried (1971) suggested that systematic desensitisation could be reconstrued as a procedure for learning and practising relaxation as an active coping skill for the self-control of anxiety. At about the same time, Suinn introduced an approach called anxiety management training, which was based on a similar conception of relaxation as an active coping skill (Suinn & Richardson 1971). In this treatment, clients practised using relaxation to reduce anxiety elicited by imagining stressful situations. In his technique of induced affect, Sipprelle (1967) used relaxation as an active coping skill to help clients gain self-control over strong emotional responses evoked by the therapist's suggestions of increasingly stronger feelings and the verbal reinforcement and encouragement of emotional expression. (This technique will be described in greater detail in a later section.)

Cognitive-affective stress management training

An illustrative coping skills approach is cognitive-affective stress management training (Smith 1980; Smith & Ascough 1985). This program has been successfully applied to a variety of populations, including test-anxious college students (Smith & Nye 1989), problem drinkers (Rohensenow, Smith & Johnson 1985), stressed-out medical students (Holtzworth-Munroe, Munroe & Smith 1985) and athletes (e.g. Crocker 1989; Ziegler, Klinzing & Williamson 1982). In a series of studies of high-performance volleyball players, Crocker and co-workers found decreases in negative thoughts and improved performance among athletes who were trained in the procedures, but no effects on state or trait anxiety at post-treatment (Crocker, Alderman & Smith 1988). In a six-month follow-up, performance gains were maintained and decreased anxiety was now found, but only in female athletes (Crocker 1989). In another study with athletes (Ziegler et al. 1982) it was found that, compared with an untrained control group with whom they were matched on baseline endurance measures, trained athletes exhibited enhanced endurance during a post-training sub-maximal treadmill run as defined by heart rate and oxygen consumption measures. This difference was attributed to the acquisition of coping skills, which the trained athletes reported using to cope with the discomfort experienced during the endurance task.

The cognitive-affective program represents an attempt to combine a number of effective clinical techniques into an educational program for self-regulation of emotional responses. These include cognitive restructuring, self-instructional training, somatic and cognitive relaxation skills for arousal control, and an adaptation of Sipprelle's (1967) induced affect technique for skill rehearsal under affective arousal. Athletes have proven to be a good target population for the program because they are able to acquire a number of the coping skills (e.g. muscle relaxation) somewhat more quickly than other populations. Moreover, they are typically exposed to the stressful athletic situations frequently enough to permit careful monitoring of their progress, and behavioural performance measures are readily available for assessment and research purposes.

The training package can be administered in either an individual or a group format. The rehearsal technique used to practise coping skills to reduce high emotional arousal is more effectively carried out in individual sessions, where trainees are less likely to inhibit emotional arousal. Virtually all of the outcome studies with athletes have used group sessions, and athlete studies that optimise rehearsal in individual sessions are badly needed.

For descriptive purposes, the program as administered on an individual basis can be divided into five partially overlapping phases: (a) pre-training assessment, (b) training rationale, (c) skill acquisition, (d) skill rehearsal, and (c) post-training evaluation.

Pre-training assessment

When the program is administered to individual athletes, several sessions may be devoted to assessing the nature of their stress responses, the circumstances under which they occur, the manner in which performance is affected, and the coping responses that are currently being used. This phase is also directed towards assessing the athlete's cognitive and behavioural strengths and deficits, so that the program can be tailored to the individual's specific needs. For example, the focus of training for an athlete who already has fairly good relaxation skills but has little control over self-defeating thought processes will tend to be focused on developing cognitive skills. On the other hand, a primary focus on the development of relaxation and self-instructional skills may be the preferred approach for a chronically tense child athlete.

A variety of assessment techniques can be employed during this phase, including careful interviewing, administration of questionnaires and rating scales, and self-monitoring by the athlete. For example, we frequently employ a 100-point 'tension thermometer', which can be completed in seconds and allows us to obtain 'readings' from the athlete at various times before and during competition. Athletes can also be asked to monitor the frequency with which certain kinds of thoughts occur before, during and after competition. Measures such as the Irrational Beliefs Test (Jones 1968) can also be useful in targeting specific self-defeating ideas for cognitive restructuring.

Training rationale

In any behaviour change program, initial conceptualisation of the problem is of crucial importance in obtaining compliance and commitment to the program. The conceptualisation should be shared by the athlete and the trainer, it should be understandable and plausible, and it should have clear intervention implications.

We have found it fairly easy to ensure that athletes arrive at our basic conceptual model of anxiety simply by asking them to describe a recent stressful incident. This description should contain situational, cognitive, physiological and behavioural components, and these can usually be elicited by follow-up questions if not mentioned spontaneously (e.g. 'What kinds of thoughts went through your mind?' or 'What kinds of body sensations did you experience?'). Labelling these elements and the relations among them provides an entry to the conceptual model and its intervention components. An overview of the training program is then presented in relation to the athlete's specific needs. This procedure provides a credible rationale and a conceptual framework for the athlete.

Two important points are emphasised during the conceptualisation phase and throughout training. One is that the program is not psychotherapy, but an educational program designed to increase 'mental toughness', or self-control of emotion. We emphasise that the components of mental toughness (a quality highly valued by athletes) are specific skills that can be learned in the same way that other sport skills are learned. The second point emphasised is that the results of the program will be determined by the amount of commitment the athlete shows to acquiring the skills. The goal is to place the locus of responsibility on the athlete so that positive changes are attributed to the athlete rather than to the trainer. This should enhance both self-efficacy and the durability of change (Bandura 1997; Davison & Valins 1969), and it is consistent with the self-regulation orientation of the program.

Skill acquisition

The skill acquisition phase focuses on the cognitive appraisal and emotional arousal components of the anxiety framework presented in figure 11.1. The training program involves the acquisition and rehearsal of relaxation skills to control physiological arousal and the development of cognitive coping responses through cognitive restructuring and/ or self-instructional training.

The mastery of relaxation skills is faster and easier for most people than are the cognitive modification procedures. For this reason, we begin with training in somatic and cognitive relaxation skills. Relaxation skills are useful in controlling the physiological arousal component of the stress response so that the athlete can prevent an increase in arousal beyond the optimal arousal level for performance of the task at hand.

Somatic relaxation training is carried out using an abbreviated version of Jacobson's (1938) progressive muscle relaxation technique. During relaxation training, an association is formed between the exhalation phase of the breathing cycle, a cognitive trigger word such as 'relax', and voluntary relaxation of muscular tension so that exhaling and mentally saying the trigger word become conditioned cues for relaxation.

A second relaxation technique that produces both physical and mental relaxation is Benson's (1976) meditation approach. Meditation cannot readily be used as a coping skill in stressful situations, as somatic (progressive) relaxation can, but it can be extremely useful as a means of dealing with pre-event anxiety, conserving energy and combating worry and other dysfunctional thought processes. Many athletes who have sleep problems find this a helpful technique in conjunction with somatic relaxation.

Training in cognitive coping skills begins with a didactic description of the manner in which emotional responses are elicited by ideas, images and self-statements. Because such thought patterns are well-practised and automatised, athletes often have limited awareness of the appraisal elements that underlie their dysfunctional emotional responses. To facilitate identification of stress-inducing cognitions and development of adaptive self-statements, athletes are given written materials to read as well as daily homework forms on which they list a situation that they found upsetting, the emotion they experienced, what they must have told themselves about the situation in order to have upset themselves, and what they might have told themselves instead that would have prevented or minimised their upset. This cognitive restructuring procedure is designed to help athletes identify, rationally evaluate and replace any dysfunctional and irrational ideas that evoke anxiety.

The most common sources of maladaptive stress in athletes are fear of failure and fear of disapproval. For many of them, athletic success has been their major source of recognition and self-esteem, so that feelings of self-worth are closely linked to the adequacy with which they perform. Successful cognitive restructuring of these fears usually involves separating self-worth from successful outcome and focusing on maximum effort (e.g. 'All I can do is give 100 per cent. No one can do more.'). Written materials on identifying and challenging irrational beliefs, discussions with the trainer and the homework assignments form the basis for an 'anti-stress log' in which athletes list their irrational self-statements and an 'anti-stress' substitute for each. The latter form the basis for later practice and rehearsal. In most cases, however, both cognitive restructuring and self-instructional training (see feature on pages 305–6) are employed.

Skill rehearsal

Stress coping skills are no different from any other kind of skill. In order to be most effective, they must be rehearsed and practised under conditions that approximate the real-life situations in which they will eventually be employed. In the cognitive-affective program, a variant of a psychotherapeutic procedure known as induced affect (Sipprelle 1967) is used to generate high levels of emotional arousal. The athlete then practises 'turning off' the emotional arousal using the coping skills learned in the preceding phase of the program (Smith & Ascough 1985). Induced affect is designed to allow rehearsal of coping responses in the presence of two kinds of cues: (a) imaginal representations of external cues that tend to elicit stress, and (b) internal cues resulting from emotional arousal. While the external cues are fairly specific to certain situations, the internal cues are probably common to differing emotional responses that may occur across a variety of situations. Practice in dealing with the latter class of cues should help to maximise the generalisation of the coping skills across a wide variety of stressful situations (Goldfried 1971; Suinn & Richardson 1971). The theoretical and research literature pertaining to the induced affect technique is summarised in Smith and Ascough (1985).

A word of caution is in order: The induced affect technique is never employed until the trainer is certain that the athlete has learned the coping skills well enough to ensure success in controlling the level of arousal that is generated. During initial use of the technique, arousal is kept at a moderate level to ensure successful control and is increased as the athlete demonstrates greater control. During skill rehearsal, athletes are asked to imagine as vividly as possible a stressful situation (e.g. getting ready to shoot a free throw in a critical situation). They are then asked to redirect their attention inside and to focus on the feeling that the situation elicits. The trainer suggests that the feeling will begin to grow and to become stronger and stronger. The suggestions continue as the athlete begins to respond with increased emotional arousal, and indications of arousal are verbally reinforced and encouraged by the trainer. At intervals during the induced affect, the trainer asks the athlete what kinds of thoughts are occurring, and this information is used to elaborate on the arousal. It also provides information (often previously unreported by the athlete) concerning the cognitions that accompany (and, it is hypothesised, mediate) the arousal.

When the appropriate level of arousal is obtained, the athlete is instructed to 'turn it off' with his or her coping responses. Initially, relaxation alone is used as the active coping skill. Later, to rehearse the cognitive coping responses derived from cognitive restructuring and self-instructional training, self-statements from the athlete's 'anti-stress log' are used to reduce arousal. Finally, the cognitive and somatic coping responses are combined into the 'integrated coping response', which ties both the self-statements and the relaxation response into the natural breathing cycle (see figure 11.3). During the inhalation phase, the athlete emits a stress-reducing or task-oriented self-statement. At the peak of inhalation, she or he says the word 'so' or 'and'; and during exhalation gives the self-instruction 'relax' while inducing muscular relaxation. Recall that during relaxation training, exhalation, the mental command to relax, and voluntary relaxation are repeatedly associated with one another in a contiguity-based conditioning procedure to establish the mental command as a cue that will automatically evoke relaxation. The self-statements in the integrated coping response can be modified as appropriate, and the total coping response can be employed repeatedly in the stressful situation without disrupting ongoing behaviour.

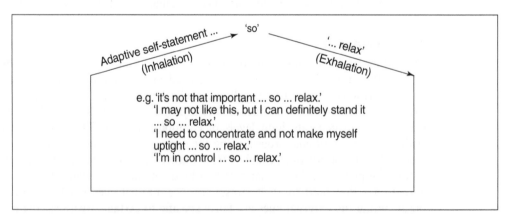

e.g. 'it's not that important ... so ... relax.'
'I may not like this, but I can definitely stand it ... so ... relax.'
'I need to concentrate and not make myself uptight ... so ... relax.'
'I'm in control ... so ... relax.'

Figure 11.3 The 'integrated coping response' includes anxiety-reducing self-statements acquired through cognitive restructuring and self-instructional training, combined with relaxation training. The coping skills are integrated into the breathing cycle as indicated.

(*Source:* Smith 1998)

Post-training evaluation

A variety of measures can be used to assess the effectiveness of the intervention. These include self-monitoring of emotional states and cognitive events by the athlete, performance measures that might be expected to improve with stress reduction, and standardised psychological test scores. All of these classes of measures have shown positive changes in the research studies of the cognitive-affective program cited above, and they can also be employed in a single-subject design when individual athletes are trained. Comprehensive evaluation of outcome with individual athletes can be extremely valuable not only for scientific purposes, but also in planning and supplementing the program with other psychological skill programs such as goal setting and mental rehearsal.

Stress inoculation training

Like the cognitive-affective approach, Meichenbaum's (1985) stress inoculation training provides a comprehensive treatment package that incorporates both cognitive and physiological coping skills. Meichenbaum conceives of the stress inoculation package as a kind of buffet of coping skills that clients can master and apply as needed to deal with stressful situations. The coping skills are muscle relaxation and adaptive self-statements learned through self-instructional training.

As the name suggests, stress inoculation is aimed at allowing clients to practise using their coping skills to cope with low and manageable doses of anxiety. The rehearsal phase takes the form of asking clients to imagine anxiety-arousing situations and to imagine themselves using their coping skills successfully in these situations, a procedure known as covert rehearsal. This imaginal procedure can be combined with graded exposure to real-life stressors that approximate those that are dealt with through mental rehearsal. The notion is that practising their coping skills to manage low levels of anxiety will help to 'inoculate' clients against higher levels of anxiety in actual life situations. This assumption is contrary to that of the cognitive-affective procedure, whose underlying rationale is that learning to master high levels of arousal ensures that lower levels can also be controlled, whereas the converse is not necessarily the case. Only one study has directly compared the efficacy of induced affect and covert rehearsal in the rehearsal of relaxation skills and stress-reducing self-statements (Smith & Nye 1989). In this comparative study of cognitive-affective and stress inoculation approaches to the reduction of severe test anxiety in college students, both treatments yielded significant reductions in test anxiety, but the test-anxious students who were administered the cognitive-affective program showed larger anxiety decreases and expressed stronger post-treatment self-efficacy beliefs in their ability to cope with test situations than did students who rehearsed their coping skills with the stress inoculation procedures. Those in the cognitive-affective program also showed a significant increase in academic grades, whereas those treated with stress inoculation did not. Another comparative study (Ziegler et al. 1982) found the techniques to be approximately equal in effectiveness. Unfortunately both of the cited studies involved group administration of the programs, which typically result in appreciably lower levels of arousal during induced affect. Clearly more research, particularly with athletes, is needed to assess the effectiveness of these two coping skills rehearsal techniques.

The stress inoculation procedure has been employed successfully in a wide range of client populations to reduce anxiety and anger, as well as to increase pain tolerance, and many controlled studies attest to its effectiveness as an intervention approach (O'Leary & Wilson 1998; Spiegler & Guevremont 1998). It has also been applied successfully with athletes to reduce anxiety, pain and other stress responses (e.g. Kerr & Goss 1996; Ross & Berger 1996; Whitemarsh & Alderman 1993). In one study, anxiety levels increased after stress inoculation, but because performance also increased, the authors concluded that the increased anxiety was facilitative rather than debilitative (Kerr & Leith 1993).

Figure 11.4 summarises the specific interventions used by coping skills approaches to modify the cognitive and physiological components of the anxiety response. When successful, these interventions result in effective cognitive and physical (somatic) coping skills for the self-regulation of anxiety.

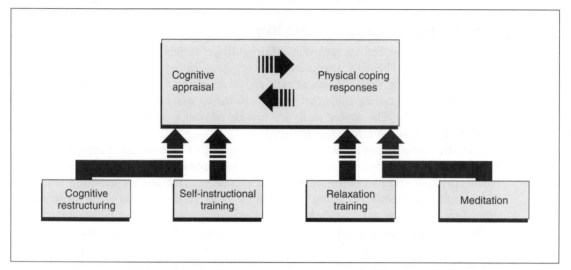

Figure 11.4 Coping skills training programs employ a variety of approaches to modify the cognitive appraisal and physiological arousal components of the anxiety response through the acquisition of cognitive and physical (somatic) self-regulation skills.

(*Source:* Smith 1998)

The coping skills approach to anxiety reduction in athletes, as typified in the cognitive-affective and stress inoculation approaches, offers two potential advantages over the extinction and counterconditioning approaches. First, rather than being the passive recipient of a deconditioning procedure, the athlete assumes major responsibility for developing the coping skills needed to reduce anxiety and is more likely to attribute improvement to his or her efforts. This should enhance maintenance of treatment gains, since self-attributed changes are better maintained than changes attributed to external agents (Davison & Valins 1969). Psychotherapy research has also shown that the more a specific treatment approach increases self-efficacy (belief in one's own ability to cope successfully) the more behavioural improvement is shown (see Bandura 1997).

The second advantage of coping skills approaches over those based on conditioning models relates to the issue of generalisation introduced earlier. Neither flooding nor Wolpe's systematic desensitisation produces gains that generalise readily to other areas of anxiety. In contrast, training athletes in the mastery of general and flexible coping skills that can be applied to a variety of situations should result in greater treatment generalisation (Bandura 1997; Smith 1999). Evidence to support this prediction comes from findings that students treated for test anxiety using a self-control variant of desensitisation developed by Goldfried also showed a reduction in untreated speech anxiety, whereas students treated with traditional desensitisation showed no speech anxiety reduction (Goldfried 1971). Likewise, Smith and Nye (1989) found evidence for generalisation of test anxiety reduction to general nonspecific anxiety in students treated with the cognitive-affective approach. Thus, as applied to athletes, we should expect the coping skills they learn to control sport performance anxiety to be useful over a wider range of both athletic and non-athletic situations.

CONCLUSIONS AND FUTURE DIRECTIONS

Theory development and research on sport-specific anxiety has been a major focus of sport psychology for more than two decades. Recent conceptualisations have focused on cognitive–somatic and debilitative–facilitative distinctions, and research on both state and trait anxiety has become more sophisticated.

The study of coping strategies is a more recent development, one that mirrors the explosion of work in this area in mainstream psychology. Two major directions seem apparent. One line of research, assisted by the development of several new sport-specific coping scales, studies the structure of coping and the variety of strategies used by athletes, as well as how strategy use relates to performance outcomes and psychological wellbeing. The second direction involves the attempt to measure how effectively an athlete can apply performance-enhancing coping skills, using instruments such as the Athletic Coping Skills Inventory (Smith, Smoll, Schutz & Ptacek 1995). This research suggests that individual differences in the use of such skills can account for as much, and sometimes appreciably more, performance variance than do differences in physical skills (e.g. Smith & Christensen 1995). We can expect to see continued research on both coping strategies and their effectiveness.

The scientific study of intervention techniques designed to reduce anxiety in athletes is still in its infancy. What are needed are controlled outcome studies with well defined and competently administered treatment procedures, dependent variable measures that tap behavioural, physiological and self-report outcome indices, and appropriate control groups (including attention-placebo control conditions that are as credible as the treatment conditions). Clearly the problem of anxiety is sufficiently widespread among athletes to justify the application and assessment of current anxiety-reduction techniques and the development of more powerful and cost-effective ones in the future.

On a more general level, concepts like 'mental toughness' are being operationally defined in terms of specific psychological skills, such as the ability to control emotional arousal and focus attention in a task-relevant fashion under conditions of intense competitive demands and adversity. The development of an educational technology to train athletes in these and other psychological skills is one of the most exciting frontiers of sport psychology.

SUMMARY

The nature of sport performance anxiety was discussed, distinguishing anxiety from arousal and stress and state anxiety from trait anxiety. Anxiety represents a process involving situational factors and cognitive, physiological and behavioural responses that can be either task-relevant or task-irrelevant and thereby either enhance or degrade performance. Sport performance trait anxiety represents the potential to exhibit anxiety states in evaluative athletic situations. We then considered implications of the model for anxiety reduction, presenting extinction, counterconditioning, cognitive and coping skills models. The coping skills model requires an understanding of methods of coping and the effectiveness with which they are carried out. We described several coping-skill enhancement procedures, such as cognitive-affective stress management training and stress inoculation training.

REVIEW QUESTIONS

1 Differentiate between (a) arousal, stress and anxiety; (b) state and trait anxiety; and (c) cognitive and somatic anxiety.

2 Summarise the components and processes in the cognitive-affective model of sport anxiety shown in figure 11.1.

3 Compare and contrast the extinction, counterconditioning and cognitive mediational models, and describe the specific anxiety reduction approaches they have each inspired.

4 What forms can athletic coping take? What evidence exists for the efficacy of various coping strategies?

5 What procedures are used in cognitive-affective approaches to coping skills training? How are the skills learned and how are they rehearsed?

6 What evidence exists that the anxiety reduction techniques described in this chapter produce positive changes?

References

Aldwin, CM 1994, *Stress, coping, and development: an integrative perspective*, Guilford Press, New York.

Anshel, MH & Wells, B 2000, 'Sources of acute stress and coping styles in competitive sport', *Anxiety, Stress, and Coping*, 13, 1–26.

Antony, MM & Swinson, RP 2000, *Phobic disorders and panic in adults: a guide to assessment and treatment*, American Psychological Association, Washington, DC.

Baker, J, Cote, J & Hawes, R 2000, 'The relationship between coaching behaviors and sport anxiety in athletes', *Journal of Science and Medicine in Sport*, 3, 110–19.

Bandura, A 1997, *Self-efficacy: the exercise of control*, Freeman, New York.

Beck, AT 1984, 'Cognitive approaches to stress', in R Woolfolk & P Lehrer (eds), *Principles and practice of stress management*, Guilford Press, New York, pp. 162–87.

Benson, H 1976, *The relaxation response*, Morrow, New York.

Berger, SM 1962, 'Conditioning through vicarious instigation', *Psychological Review*, 69, 450–66.

Berlyne, DE 1960, *Conflict, arousal, and curiosity*, McGraw-Hill, New York.

Bramwell, ST, Masuda, M, Wagner, NN & Holmes, TH 1975, 'Psychosocial factors in athletic injuries: development and application of the Social and Athletic Readjustment Rating Scale (SARRS)', *Journal of Human Stress*, 1, 6–20.

Burton, D 1998, 'Measuring competitive state anxiety', in JL Duda (ed.), *Advancements in sport and exercise psychology measurement*, Fitness Information Technology, Morgantown, WV, pp. 129–48.

Buss, AH 1995, *Personality: temperament, social behavior, and the self*, Allyn & Bacon, Boston, MA.

Cannon, WB 1929, 'The mechanism of emotional disturbance of bodily functions', *New England Journal of Medicine*, 198, 877–84.

Carrigan, MH & Levis, DJ 1999, 'The contributions of eye movements to the efficacy of brief exposure treatment for reducing fear of public speaking', *Journal of Anxiety Disorders*, 13, 101–18.

Crocker, PRE 1989, 'A follow-up of cognitive-affective stress management training', *Journal of Sport & Exercise Psychology*, 11, 236–342.

Crocker, PRE & Isaak, K 1997, 'Coping during competitions and training sessions: are youth swimmers consistent?', *International Journal of Sport Psychology*, 28, 355–69.

Crocker, PRE, Alderman, RB & Smith, FMR 1988, 'Cognitive-affective stress management training with high performance youth volleyball players: effects on affect, cognition, and performance', *Journal of Sport & Exercise Psychology*, 10, 448–60.

Crocker, PRE, Kowalski, KC & Graham, TR 1998, 'Measurement of coping strategies in sport', in JL Duda (ed.), *Advancements in sport and exercise psychology measurement*, Fitness Information Technology, Morgantown, WV, pp. 149–61.

Cryan, PD & Alles, WF 1983, 'The relationship between stress and college football injuries', *Journal of Sports Medicine*, 23, 52–8.

Davison, GC & Valins, S 1969, 'Maintenance of self-attributed and drug-attributed behavior change', *Journal of Personality and Social Psychology*, 11, 25–33.

Dua, JK 1980, 'Counterconditioning, hierarchy, and CS exposure in extinction of human avoidance responding', *Psychological Reports*, 46, 1139–50.

Duffy, E 1962, *Activation and behavior*, John Wiley & Sons, New York.

Dunn, JGH 1999, 'A theoretical framework for structuring the content of competitive worry in ice hockey', *Journal of Sport & Exercise Psychology*, 21, 259–79.

Ellis, A 1962, *Reason and emotion in psychotherapy*, Lyle Stuart, New York.

Ellis, A & Grieger, R 1977, *Handbook of rational emotive therapy*, Springer, New York.

Farkas, GM 1989, 'Exposure and response prevention in the treatment of an okeanophobic triathlete', *The Sport Psychologist*, 3, 189–95.

Folkman, S & Moskowitz, JT 2000, 'Positive affect and the other side of coping', *American Psychologist*, 55, 647–54.

Goldfried, MR 1971, 'Systematic desensitization as training in self-control', *Journal of Consulting and Clinical Psychology*, 37, 228–34.

Goldfried, MR, Linehan, MM & Smith, JL 1978, 'The reduction of test anxiety through cognitive restructuring', *Journal of Consulting and Clinical Psychology*, 46, 32–9.

Gould, D, Finch, L & Jackson, S 1993, 'Coping strategies utilized by national championship figure skaters', *Research Quarterly for Exercise and Sport*, 64, 453–68.

Haney, CJ & Long, BC 1995, 'Coping effectiveness: a path analysis of self-efficacy, control, coping, and performance in sport situations', *Journal of Applied Social Psychology*, 25, 1726–46.

Hebb, DO 1949, *The organization of behavior*, John Wiley & Sons, New York.

Heyman, SR 1987, 'Research and interventions in sport psychology: issues encountered in working with an amateur boxer', *The Sport Psychologist*, 1 208–23.

Holahan, CJ & Moos, RH 1990, 'Life stressors, resistance factors, and improved psychological functioning: an extension of the stress resistance paradigm', *Journal of Personality and Social Psychology*, 58, 909–17.

Holtzworth-Munroe, A, Munroe, MS & Smith, RE 1985, 'Effects of a stress management training program on first- and second-year medical students', *Journal of Medical Education*, 60, 417–19.

Jacobson, E 1938, *Progressive relaxation*, University of Chicago Press, Chicago, IL.

Jones, G 1995, 'More than just a game: research developments and issues in competitive anxiety in sport', *British Journal of Psychology*, 86, 449–78.

Jones, G & Swain, A 1995, 'Predisposition to experience debilitative and facilitative anxiety in elite and nonelite performers', *The Sport Psychologist*, 9 201–11.

Jones, RG 1968, *A factored measure of Ellis' irrational belief systems with personality and maladjustment correlated*, Test Systems, Inc., Wichita, KS.

Kendrick, MJ, Craig, KD, Lawson, DM & Davidson, PO 1982, 'Cognitive and behavioral therapy for musical-performance anxiety', *Journal of Consulting and Clinical Psychology*, 50, 353–62.

Kerr, G & Goss, J 1996, 'The effects of a stress management program on injuries and stress levels', *Journal of Applied Sport Psychology*, 8, 109–17.

Kerr, G & Leith, L 1993, 'Stress management and athletic performance', *The Sport Psychologist*, 7, 221–31.

Lacey, JI & Lacey, BC 1958, 'Verification and extension of the principle of autonomic response stereotypy', *American Journal of Psychology*, 71, 50–73.

Lazarus, RS 2000, 'How emotions influence performance in competitive sports', *The Sport Psychologist*, 14, 229–52.

Lazarus, RS & Folkman S 1984, *Stress, appraisal, and coping*, Springer, New York.

Malmo, RB 1959, 'Activation: a neurophysiological dimension', *Psychological Review*, 66, 367–86.

Mandler, G & Sarason, SB 1952, 'A study of anxiety and learning', *Journal of Abnormal and Social Psychology*, 47, 166–73.

Marshall, WL 1985, 'The effects of variable exposure in flooding therapy', *Behaviour Therapy*, 16, 117–35.

Martens, R, Burton, D, Vealey, RS, Bump, LA & Smith, DE 1990, 'Development and validation of the Competitive State Anxiety Inventory–2 (CSAI-2)', in R Martens, RS Vealey & D Burton (eds) 1990, *Competitive anxiety in sport*, Human Kinetics, Champaign, IL.

Meichenbaum, D 1985, *Stress inoculation training*, Pergamon Press, New York.

Mineka, S 1979, 'The role of fear in theories of avoidance learning, flooding, and extinction', *Psychological Bulletin*, 86, 985–1010.

O'Leary, KD & Wilson, GT 1998, *Behavior therapy: applications and outcome*, Prentice Hall, Paramus, NJ.

Passer, MW 1988, 'Determinants and consequences of children's competitive stress', in FL Smoll, RA Magill & MJ Ash (eds), *Children in sport*, 3rd edn, Human Kinetics, Champaign, IL, pp. 203–27.

Pavlov, I 1927, *Conditioned reflexes*, Clarenden Press, London.

Ptacek, JT, Smith, RE, Espe, K & Raffety, B 1994, 'Limited correspondence between daily coping reports and retrospective coping recall', *Psychological Assessment*, 6, 41–9.

Rachman, S 1990, 'The determinants and treatment of simple phobias', *Advances in Behaviour Research and Therapy*, 12, 1–30.

Rescorla, RA & Solomon, RL 1967, 'Two-process learning theory: relationships between Pavlovian conditioning and instrumental learning', *Psychological Review*, 74, 151–82.

Roger, D, Jarvis, G & Najarian, B 1993, 'Detachment and coping: the construction and validation of a new scale for measuring coping strategies', *Personality and Individual Differences*, 15, 619–26.

Rogers, CR 1959, 'A theory of therapy, personality and interpersonal relationships as developed in the client-centered framework', in S Koch (ed.), *Psychology: a study of a science*, vol. 3, McGraw-Hill, New York, pp. 67–102.

Rohensenow, DJ, Smith, RE & Johnson, S 1985, 'Stress management training as a prevention for heavy social drinkers: cognitions, affect, drinking, and individual differences', *Addictive Behaviors*, 10, 45–54.

Ross, MJ & Berger, RS 1996, 'Effects of stress inoculation training on athletes' post-surgical pain and rehabilitation after orthopedic injury', *Journal of Consulting and Clinical Psychology*, 64, 406–10.

Rushall, BS 1993, 'The restoration of performance capacity by cognitive restructuring and covert positive reinforcement in an elite athlete', in JR Cautela & AJ Kearney (eds), *Covert conditioning casebook*, Brooks/Cole, Pacific Grove, CA, pp. 47–57.

Scanlan, TK & Lewthwaite, R 1986, 'Social psychological aspects of competition for male youth sport participants: IV. Predictors of enjoyment', *Journal of Sport Psychology*, 8, 25–35.

Selye, H 1976, *The stress of life*, 2nd edn, McGraw-Hill, New York.

Shapiro, F 1991, 'Eye movement and desensitization and reprocessing procedure: from EMD to EMD/R — a new treatment model for anxiety and related traumata', *The Behavior Therapist*, 15, 133–5.

Silva, JM 1982, 'Competitive sport environments: performance enhancement through cognitive intervention', *Behavior Modification*, 6, 443–63.

Sipprelle, CN 1967, 'Induced anxiety', *Psychotherapy: Theory, Research, and Practice*, 4, 36–40.

Smith, RE 1980, 'A cognitive-affective approach to stress management training for athletes', in CH Nadeau, WR Halliwell, KM Newell & GC Roberts (eds), *Psychology of motor behavior and sport — 1979*, Human Kinetics, Champaign, IL, pp. 54–72.

Smith, RE 1986, 'A component analysis of athletic stress', in MR Weiss & D Gould (eds), *Sport for children and youths*, Human Kinetics, Champaign, IL, pp. 107–11.

Smith, RE 1993, *Psychology*, West Publishing, St Paul, MN.

Smith, RE 1996, 'Performance anxiety, cognitive interference, and concentration enhancement strategies in sports', in IG Sarason, GR Pierce & BR Sarason (eds), *Cognitive interference: theories, methods, and findings*, Lawrence Erlbaum Associates, Mahwah, NJ, pp. 261–84.

Smith, RE 1997, *Enhancing human performance: a psychological skills approach*, Performance Enhancement Associates, Seattle, WA.

Smith, RE 1999, 'Generalization effects in coping skills training', *Journal of Sport and Exercise Psychology*, 21, 189–204.

Smith, RE & Ascough, JC 1985, 'Induced affect in stress management training', in S Burchfield (ed.), *Stress: psychological and physiological interactions*, Hemisphere Press, New York, pp. 150–72.

Smith, RE & Christensen, DS 1995, 'Psychological skills as predictors of performance and survival in professional baseball', *Journal of Sport & Exercise Psychology*, 17, 399–415.

Smith, RE & Nye, SL 1973, 'A comparison of implosive therapy and systematic desensitization in the treatment of test anxiety', *Journal of Consulting and Clinical Psychology*, 41, 37–42.

Smith, RE & Nye, SL 1989, 'A comparison of induced affect and covert rehearsal in the acquisition of stress-management coping skills', *Journal of Counseling Psychology*, 36, 17–23.

Smith, RE, Ptacek, JT & Patterson, E 2000, 'Moderator effects of cognitive and somatic trait anxiety on the relation between life stress and physical injuries', *Anxiety, Stress, and Coping*, 13, 269–88.

Smith, RE & Smoll, FL 2001, *Way to go, coach!: a scientifically-proven approach to coaching effectiveness*, 2nd edn, Warde Publishers, Portola Valley, CA.

Smith, RE, Smoll, FL & Barnett, NP 1995, 'Reduction of children's sport performance anxiety through social support training and stress-reduction training for coaches', *Journal of Applied Developmental Psychology*, 16, 125–42.

Smith, RE, Smoll, FL & Curtis, B 1979, 'Coach effectiveness training: a cognitive-behavioral approach to enhancing relationship skills in youth sport coaches', *Journal of Sport Psychology*, 1, 59–75.

Smith, RE, Smoll, FL & Passer, MW (in press), 'Sport performance anxiety in young athletes', in FL Smoll & RE Smith (eds), *Children and youth in sport: a biopsychosocial perspective*, 2nd edn, Kendall/Hunt Publishers, Dubuque, IA.

Smith, RE, Smoll, FL & Ptacek, JT 1990, 'Conjunctive moderator variables in vulnerability and resiliency research: life stress, social support and coping skills, and adolescent sport injuries', *Journal of Personality and Social Psychology*, 58, 360–70.

Smith, RE, Smoll, FL & Schutz, RW 1990, 'Measurement and correlates of sport-specific cognitive and somatic trait anxiety: the Sport Anxiety Scale', *Anxiety Research*, 2, 263–80.

Smith, RE, Smoll, FL, Schutz, RW & Ptacek, JT 1995, 'Development and validation of a multidimensional measure of sport-specific psychological skills: the Athletic Coping Skills Inventory–28', *Journal of Sport & Exercise Psychology*, 17, 379–98.

Smith, RE, Smoll, FL & Wiechman, SA 1998, 'Measurement of trait anxiety in sport', in JL Duda (ed.), *Advances in sport and exercise psychology measurement*, Fitness Information Technology, Morgantown, WV, pp. 105–27.

Smoll, FL & Smith, RE 2001, 'Conducting sport psychology training programs for coaches: cognitive-behavioral principles and techniques', in JM Williams (ed.), *Applied sport psychology: personal growth to peak performance*, 4th edn, Mayfield, Mountain View, CA, pp. 378–400.

Smoll, FL, Smith, RE, Barnett, NP & Everett, JJ 1993, 'Enhancement of children's self-esteem through social support training for youth sport coaches', *Journal of Applied Psychology*, 78, 602–10.

Spiegler, MD & Guevremont, DC 1998, *Contemporary behavior therapy*, Brooks/Cole, Forest Grove, CA.

Spielberger, CD 1989, 'Stress and anxiety in sports', in D Hackfort & CD Spielberger (eds), *Anxiety in sports: an international perspective*, Hemisphere, New York, pp. 3–17.

Staub, E 1968, 'Duration of stimulus exposure as a determinant of the efficacy of flooding procedures in the elimination of fear', *Behavior Research and Therapy*, 6, 131–2.

Steptoe, A & Fidler, H 1987, 'Stage fright in orchestral musicians: a study of cognitive and behavioural strategies in performance anxiety', *British Journal of Psychology*, 78, 241–9.

Stuart, R 2001, *Behavior therapy*, Allyn & Bacon, Boston, MA.

Suinn, RM & Richardson, F 1971, 'Anxiety management training: a nonspecific behavior therapy program for anxiety control', *Behavior Therapy*, 2, 498–510.

Weinberg, RS & Genuchi, M 1980, 'Relationship between competitive trait anxiety, state anxiety, and performance: a field study', *Journal of Sport Psychology*, 2, 148–54.

Whitemarsh, BG & Alderman, RB 1993, 'Role of psychological skills training in increasing athletic pain tolerance', *The Sport Psychologist*, 7, 388–99.

Williams, JM (ed.) 2001, *Applied sport psychology: personal growth to peak performance*, 4th edn, Mayfield, Mountain View, CA.

Williams, JM & Roepke, N 1993, 'Psychology of injury and injury rehabilitation', in RN Singer, M Murphey & LK Tennant (eds), *Handbook of research on sport psychology*, Macmillan, New York, pp. 815–39.

Wolpe, J 1958, *Psychotherapy by reciprocal inhibition*, Stanford University Press, Stanford, CA.

Wolpe, J 1978, 'Cognition and causation in human behavior and its therapy', *American Psychologist*, 33, 437–46.

Yoo, J 2000, 'Factorial validity of the coping scale for Korean athletes', *International Journal of Sport Psychology*, 31, 391–404.

Ziegler, SG, Klinzing, J & Williamson, K 1982, 'The effects of two stress management training programs on cardiorespiratory efficiency', *Journal of Sport Psychology*, 4, 280–9.

CHAPTER 12

BUILDING CONFIDENCE IN SPORT

Keith Henschen & Maria Newton

Confidence is to performance as batteries are to a flashlight.

The concept of confidence has remained an elusive one since the general field of psychology was recognised as an important behavioural science. Ask any graduate student or lecturer in either psychology or sport psychology and they will readily define this phenomenon; but the problem is that each definition will be slightly different. As with many psychological constructs, there is general agreement on a global understanding of the idea, but the actual specifics remain less than concrete. This chapter will attempt to define the concept of confidence (especially in sport situations); examine various theories concerning confidence; discuss how confidence interrelates with other areas of the self; present research on confidence in sport; examine misconceptions concerning confidence; and, finally, present methods that can be used to develop and/or increase confidence. We will begin with a theoretical perspective and conclude with practical applications.

DEFINITIONS

Athletes and sport psychologists alike agree that self-confidence is central to optimal performance. Despite its being a key ingredient to performance, sport psychologists have long struggled with clearly defining confidence and understanding the antecedents and the mechanisms underlying variations in confidence. Review the dictionary definitions and terms such as 'assurance', 'belief' and 'certitude' emerge. Clearly, self-confident athletes hold high levels of conviction and certainty relative to their ability to perform. This was exemplified by tennis great Jimmy Conners when he stated, 'I go out to every match convinced that I'm going to win' (cited in Weinberg 1988, p. 127).

Goldsmith and Sweetenham (2000) asked a number of Australian coaches and athletes to define and discuss the importance of confidence. Forbes Carlile, a master coach, observed that 'Attitudes such as belief, optimism, high aspirations and anticipation of the best possible result — all these positive states of mind add up to confidence, the keystone for success' (Goldsmith & Sweetenham 2000, p. 20). Jackie Gallagher, a world triathlon champion, added, 'I think confidence is all about believing in your ability to achieve a particular task or goal' (Goldsmith & Sweetenham 2000, p. 19).

Feelings of optimism have also been associated with confidence (Zinsser, Bunker & Williams 2001). Optimistic individuals view the glass as half full as opposed to half empty. They view the world of sport in terms of possibilities rather than hindrances and obstacles. Confident athletes look forward to competition, expect to perform well, and accept the challenges and adversities they encounter while competing.

Conceiving of self-confidence in terms of self-efficacy, sport confidence and collective efficacy is particularly useful because each provides insight into the mechanisms underlying confidence in sport. In other words, they help us to understand 'why' self-confidence underpins optimal performance and 'how' self-confidence can be fostered. Self-efficacy (Bandura 1977) represents an athlete's belief that she or he has the requisite abilities to perform a specific behaviour. For instance, a setter in volleyball may have high self-efficacy in her ability to set the ball to the outside hitter. In contrast, she might have low self-efficacy relative to her ability to perform a weakside set to a hitter in the back row. Thus, self-efficacy refers to situation-specific self-confidence. Bandura suggested that an individual's efficacy expectations might vary greatly within specific domains and within specific situations. Thus, athletes' self-efficacy may vary for the multitude of skills they possess in one sport and may ebb and flow within a particular competitive match or game.

While self-efficacy is clearly instrumental in our understanding of self-confidence in sport, Vealey (1986, 2001) has suggested that the unique nature and context of competitive sport should be incorporated into our conceptualisation of the construct. The term *sport confidence* was coined to represent a sport-specific form of self-confidence (Vealey 1986). Sport confidence is defined as the 'belief or degree of certainty that individuals possess about their ability to be successful in sport' (Vealey 2001, p. 551). Gould and colleagues' study of teams that failed to meet or met/exceeded their 1996 Olympic aspirations offers a fine example of high sport confidence. One athlete, on a team that was expected to win a gold medal and did so at the Games, commented that, 'we are winning this, no doubt about it' (Gould, Guinan, Greenleaf, Medbery & Peterson 1999, p. 382).

Furthermore, sport confidence may be viewed as more trait- or state-like depending on the temporal reference point of interest (Vealey 2001). For instance, one can consider an athlete's sport confidence 'right now' (representation of *state sport confidence*) or an athlete's 'typical' sport confidence (indicator of *trait sport confidence*). Sport confidence and self-efficacy both represent the extent to which an athlete believes that they can get the job done. Sport confidence and the conceptual model that emanates from it (discussed in the following section), however, were specifically developed with the athlete and competitive sport in mind.

Interestingly, the issue of confidence in sport is not only a phenomenon of individual performance but also of critical importance in team situations. For instance, the self-confidence levels of individual athletes on a basketball team or bobsled team are obviously critical, but possibly of equal importance is the confidence of the team as a unit. Bandura first referred to a group's perception of collective competency and expectations for success as *collective efficacy* (1982). A more precise definition suggests that collective efficacy entails 'a sense of collective competence shared among individuals when allocating, coordinating, and integrating their resources in a successful concerted response to specific situational demands' (Zaccaro, Blair, Peterson & Zazanis 1995, p. 309). Thus, collective efficacy refers to the shared efficacy or confidence a team feels when they are striving as a unit to perform optimally.

Collective efficacy is distinct from self-efficacy on many levels (Carron & Hausenblas 1998). Firstly, and most obviously, collective efficacy pertains to groups and teams rather than individuals. Secondly, collective efficacy depends on the extent to which feelings of efficacy are shared by team members. A team with high collective efficacy, or team confidence, shares positive beliefs about the team's ability to perform. Thirdly, collective efficacy depends on the team's ability to coordinate and balance their individual talents so that the team performance is optimised. Lastly, collective efficacy depends on the team believing that they have the necessary resources, skills and abilities to be successful (Carron & Hausenblas 1998).

In summary, confidence as it relates to individual and team sport performance may best be understood in terms of self-efficacy, sport skill/ability and collective efficacy. Our understanding of confidence benefits not only from the clear operational definitions that the above terms provide but also from the conceptual frameworks that accompany each.

SELF-CONFIDENCE TERMS

Concept	Source	Key terms or phrases
Confidence	Dictionary	Assurance, belief, certitude
Self-efficacy	Self-efficacy theory Bandura (1977)	Belief in ability to perform a specific behaviour
		Situation-specific self-confidence
Sport confidence	Vealey (2001)	Belief or degree of certainty that individuals possess about their ability to be successful in sport
Collective efficacy	Zaccaro et al. (1995)	Sense of competence shared by group members that they can respond successfully

SELF-CONFIDENCE CONCEPTUAL FRAMEWORKS

The conceptual frameworks that relate to self-efficacy, sport confidence and collective efficacy are all based on social cognitive theory. A social cognitive perspective emphasises that behaviour, in this case the indicators of confidence, occurs in a social context and emphasises the critical role that cognitions and thought processes play in filtering, perceiving and comprehending information (Bandura 1977, 1982). Chris Stephenson, a noted ultramarathoner, clearly understands the power of cognitions when he states, 'Where the mind goes, the body will follow. Flesh is dumb' (Goldsmith & Sweetenham 2000, p. 19). In essence, the situation and the cognitive processes of the athlete act as interacting determinants of confidence (Bandura 1986). High and low confidence, in turn, are evidenced behaviourally (e.g. task choice, levels of exerted effort and persistence), cognitively (e.g. coping skills and self-talk) and affectively (e.g. variations in attitude and emotional responses). According to social cognitive theory, behaviour is better understood within each situation rather than across situations. For example, in order to understand self-confidence it is more beneficial to examine the varied characteristics of situations and cognitions that both positively and negatively affect confidence than it is to study how athletes differ in levels of trait-like self-confidence (Vealey 2001).

Self-efficacy theory

Bandura (1977, 1982, 1986) proposed self-efficacy as a situation-specific form of self-confidence, a belief that one has the ability to perform whatever is necessary in a particular situation. Given the requisite skills and incentives, Bandura's theory suggests, self-efficacy is the critical mediating variable that will predict actual performance. Self-efficacy theory is particularly instructive because it proposes four primary means by which confidence can be altered: self-confidence can be enhanced or hindered by performance accomplishments, vicarious experiences, verbal persuasion and emotional arousal (see figure 12.1).

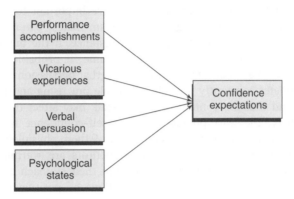

Figure 12.1   Sources of confidence: self-efficacy theory

Performance accomplishments are the most powerful source of confidence because they are experiential in nature. If an athlete is trying to build confidence in his or her ability to hit a flop shot in golf, no better strategy exists than physically practising and performing that skill. Positive performance outcomes will enhance confidence, whereas negative performance experiences will tend to undermine confidence. It is logical to assume, however, that the characteristics of the performance experience will influence the relationship. Success at difficult tasks will affect confidence to a greater extent than success at easy tasks. In a parallel way, a negative outcome against an easy opponent will upset confidence more than a loss to a formidable opponent. Similarly, success with little effort will have less impact on an athlete's confidence than success achieved through hard work. It is common practice for coaches to schedule relatively easy opponents early in the season to foster confidence. But if the task difficulty and effort required are not optimally challenging, the impact of those successful experiences may not be as potent as believed.

Self-efficacy can also be fostered through vicarious experience, or watching others perform the skill successfully. *Vicarious experiences*, also referred to as modelling influences (Bandura 1982, 1986), tend to take two forms — live modelling and symbolic modelling. Live modelling refers to watching an actual performer attempt the skill, whereas symbolic modelling may include watching videotape or computer simulations. Vicarious experiences can be a critically important source of confidence for beginning athletes and athletes attempting a new skill. For instance, a ski aerialist attempting a new skill, such as a double flip in the layout position with a full twist, may be able to develop a base level of personal confidence by watching a more experienced skier successfully complete the jump. The model's impact is influenced by the extent to which the performer perceives the more experienced model to be similar to himself. If the performer perceives the more experienced model to be similar in age, sex, ethnicity, background and general appearance, it is likely that the impact on his confidence would be greater than had the model been perceived as dissimilar. Because vicarious experiences are not based on personal mastery attempts, they tend not to affect confidence to the same extent as performance accomplishments.

The third most important source of self-confidence according to self-efficacy theory, is verbal persuasion. *Verbal persuasion* refers to the persuasive comments that others and athletes themselves use to encourage performance. For example, a coach may say to an athlete, 'You are better than that. Show us how you can really play'. An athlete may interpret such a statement as encouragement and experience a boost in confidence. On the other hand, the advice may be perceived as degrading and may hurt the athlete's self-confidence. Additionally, the source of the comments is important. Verbal persuasion from significant others who are important to the athlete, credible and have some level of expertise (e.g. coaches, team-mates, parents or recruiters) will influence confidence to the greatest extent. For instance, if the bus driver made the above comment to the player on the way to the game, it probably would not affect the player's confidence level to any great measure. Verbal persuasion may also take the form of self-talk. Athletes constantly use self-talk while practising and performing. It is important to understand that the content of the self-talk may affect the athlete's self-confidence.

Finally, the least potent source of self-confidence is emotional arousal. *Emotional arousal* refers to athletes' interpretation of their physiological and emotional state. For instance, suppose two badminton competitors are warming up for their competition. Both objectively experience butterflies in their stomach and sweaty palms. One athlete may interpret these physiological reactions as positive correlates of competition and experience a boost in confidence. The other, however, may perceive these as signs of not being adequately prepared and suffer a slump in confidence.

Self-efficacy theory is incredibly informative and instructive with regard to self-confidence in sport. It offers us insight into how confidence can be both fostered and undermined.

Collective efficacy

The concept of *collective efficacy* is based on self-efficacy theory (Bandura 1982, 1986, 1997). The sources of collective efficacy include the three most powerful sources of self-efficacy. Performance accomplishments, vicarious experiences and verbal persuasion are central antecedents of collective efficacy (Bandura 1977, 1982, 1986, 1997; Zaccaro et al. 1995). However, the frame of reference for collective efficacy is the group rather than the individual. Prior positive team performances and outcomes, watching similar teams perform successfully, and being supported and encouraged by others all foster confidence in team settings.

In addition to the traditional efficacy sources, Zacarro et al. (1995), Watson and Chemers (1998), and Carron and Hausenblas (1998) suggested three additional sources of collective efficacy: *group cohesion*, *group leadership* and *group size*. Cohesive groups are likely to be more effective. Additionally, leaders who focus on developing the coordinative and integrative functioning of the team as a whole appear to increase collective efficacy. For example, a coach who emphasises how each team member's skills and abilities are integral to success, and who promotes a shared understanding of how the team must work together in order to succeed, may increase confidence. Finally, group size may influence team confidence. A large group may have more talent, skills and abilities to draw from in pursuit of success. As group size increases, however, the task of coordinating and integrating capabilities and sharing a common belief system becomes exponentially more difficult (Carron & Hausenblas 1998). Frameworks related to self-efficacy and collective efficacy have driven a majority of the self-confidence research. Vealey (1986, 2001), drawing from the areas of self-efficacy, perceived competence, movement confidence and expectancy theory, has attempted to extend our current understanding of self-confidence by developing the sport confidence model.

Sport confidence model

Recently Vealey and colleagues (Vealey, Hayashi, Garner-Holman & Giacobbi 1998; Vealey 2001) reconceptualised her model of sport confidence. Vealey's sport confidence model is based on social cognitive principles and draws heavily on Bandura's self-efficacy theory (see figure 12.2). Vealey (1986) defined sport confidence as a sport-specific form of self-efficacy and developed her model to be sensitive to the uniqueness of sport and competition. Three primary alterations were made to the original model (Vealey 1986, 2001). First, the bifurcation of sport confidence into trait and state components was eliminated. A single construct, which could be conceptualised as either state- or trait-like depending on the time reference of interest, was created. Second, Vealey aligned her model more closely with its social cognitive roots by incorporating the influence of the context to a greater extent. The current model incorporates characteristics of the organisational climate and culture as sources of sport confidence. Finally, Vealey undertook an involved investigation to determine the most salient sources of confidence that were unique to sport (Vealey et al. 1998).

Three categories, which include nine specific sources of sport confidence, are proposed in the sport confidence model (Vealey et al. 1998). The first category, *achievement*, includes fostering confidence through mastery experiences and demonstrations of ability. Achievement sources of confidence parallel Bandura's performance accomplishments. Identification of two distinct sources suggests that, in sport performance, confidence may be achieved through improvement of skills and demonstration of sport ability to others, or showing that one has more ability than others. For example, suppose a tennis player learns how to hit a topspin second serve. Her confidence may be fostered in two manners. Firstly, mastering the technique of the serve positively affects her confidence. Secondly, the act of successfully performing the serve in front of others in practice or competition also enhances her confidence.

The second category, *self-regulation*, includes two specific sources of sport confidence, namely physical/mental preparation and physical self-presentation. Physical/mental preparation refers to feeling physically and mentally prepared to practise and/or compete in sport. Athletes' confidence levels can be fostered by feeling in peak condition, physically prepared, and mentally positive and energised. Self-presentation is linked with athletes' perception of their body image. Sport entails public display of the body. Athletes' confidence is influenced by their subjective appraisal of the appearance of their body. Confidence is enhanced when athletes hold positive views about their body and the public display of their body.

The final category of sources of sport confidence is called *social climate*. Five specific sources comprise this category: social support, vicarious experience, coach's leadership, environmental comfort and situational favorableness. Social support (conceptually similar to verbal persuasion in self-efficacy theory) refers to perceiving encouragement and support about sport-related pursuits from significant others. Vicarious experiences, or watching others perform successfully, is utilised in a manner similar to that in self-efficacy theory. Coach's leadership refers to athletes' belief and trust in their coach's ability to successfully provide leadership and direction. Environmental comfort is derived from feeling at ease or comfortable performing at a specific competition or practice site. A golfer's confidence may be fostered by playing their home course because they are knowledgeable about the layout of the holes, the hazards and how the greens run. Similarly, tennis players competing in a tournament at an unfamiliar site may not be optimally confident because they are uncertain about the quickness of the court surface and how wind and sun will affect play. The final source of sport confidence, situational favourableness, stems from athletes' perceiving that things are going their way. For instance, in sport it sometimes seems as though the ball bounces only your way, the rim on the basketball goal is soft only for your shots, calls go only in your direction, and all the let cords are falling for you. Situational favourableness is synonymous with a belief that the sporting gods are on your side.

The three categories and nine specific sources of sport confidence reside in a broader model detailing the conceptual underpinnings of sport confidence, as shown in figure 12.2 (Vealey 2001). The core of the model contains the three sources of sport confidence, the sport confidence construct itself and three primary indices of sport confidence — namely, affect, behaviour and cognitions. In line with the social cognitive perspective, how athletes feel (affect), behave and think (cognitions) are viewed as being reciprocally determined (Bandura 1978). Additionally, sport confidence, according to Vealey (2001), functions as a 'mental modifier' (p. 556), suggesting that variations in sport confidence affect affect, behaviour and cognitions. Thus, the core of the model suggests that how the athlete thinks, behaves and feels (relative to sport confidence) is mediated by variations in sport confidence. Sport confidence is thought to be derived from three general sources — achievement, self-regulation and the social climate.

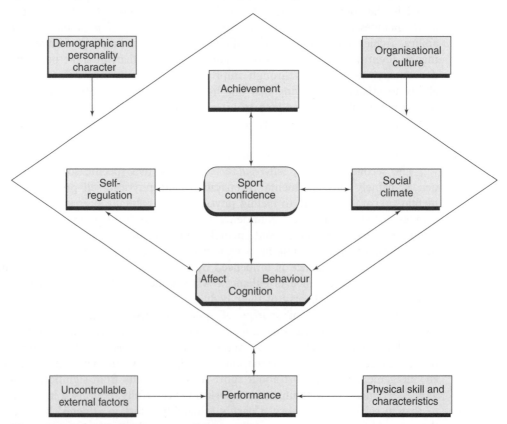

Figure 12.2 Vealey's (2001) sport confidence model

The sport confidence model also contains a number of secondary influences that are unique to sport. The organisational culture and demographic and personality characteristics are hypothesised to have an impact on the model's core processes (Vealey 2001).

Organisational culture refers to the manner in which the culture of sport is structured. For example, suppose a youth hockey player is involved in a very competitive developmental league. The culture that surrounds his or her participation (parental involvement and influence, pressure to perform, elitism of junior sport, etc.) may affect sport confidence. Demographic variables, such as sex, age and ethnicity, are also seen as influencing sport confidence.

Finally, the extent to which variations in sport confidence affect objective performance, it is proposed, is influenced by physical skill, athlete characteristics (e.g. size, fatigue and nutritional status) and external factors such as luck, weather and the opponent's skill level. Vealey's (2001) model of sport confidence was created to 'serve as an organizational framework to elicit meaningful extensions to the research examining confidence in sport, and it should also serve as a foundation for interventions designed to enhance confidence in athletes' (p. 555). This model offers researchers and practitioners clear and distinct paths to pursue in terms of both empirical examinations and performance enhancement strategies.

CONFIDENCE AND THE OTHER ASPECTS OF SELF

The 'self' is a fascinating concept that is a true example of synergy. All the various aspects of self add up to the total self-concept that Fitts (1965) attempted to identify and measure using the Tennessee Self-Concept Scale (TSCS). Summing all of the components of the self gives an insight into how individuals perceive their own strengths and weaknesses. Figure 12.3 illustrates in a linear way how the selves are interrelated.

Notice the inner core of the self is self-efficacy, which is the situation-specific component of self-confidence. The self can be pictured as an onion with many different layers, some thicker or stronger than others. Confidence, with its subcategory of self-efficacy, either can make the entire self-concept a stable and strong entity or it can cause an erratic and weak self-concept. The importance of confidence is therefore self-evident (no pun intended).

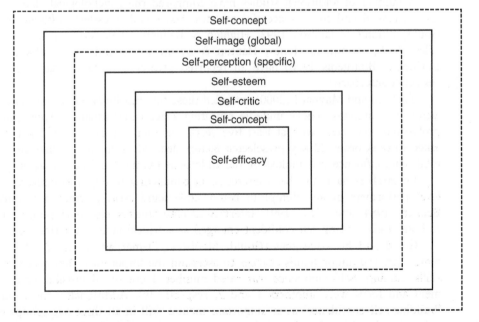

Figure 12.3 The 'self' diagram

RESEARCH ON CONFIDENCE

Research examining confidence has taken five primary approaches. First, a line of work has attempted to discern those psychological characteristics that best distinguish highly successful from less successful performers. Second, tangentially, researchers have attempted to identify the psychological characteristics most associated with peak performance. Third, a majority of the theoretically grounded research has utilised self-efficacy theory. Researchers have examined the influence of the four sources of efficacy expectations on self-efficacy. In turn, the strength of the association between efficacy and various behavioural, affective and cognitive patterns has been examined. Fourth, initial research examining Vealey's (1986) sport confidence model resulted in the reformulation of the framework (Vealey 2001). Little research exists as yet either supporting or refuting the reconceptualisation. Lastly, those interested in the construct of collective efficacy have begun to examine the relationships suggested by Zaccaro et al. (1995).

Williams and Krane (2001) summarised the role of confidence in peak performance as follows: 'The most consistent finding is higher levels of self confidence for the more successful competitors. Without exception, the researchers reported that the better athletes believed in themselves more than the less successful athletes' (p. 168). The work of Mahoney and colleagues (Mahoney & Avener 1977; Mahoney, Gabriel & Perkins 1987) was critical in initially attempting to characterise the psychological profile of peak performers. Mahoney and Avener (1977) examined the psychological characteristics of 13 male gymnasts attempting to make the 1976 Olympic team. Comparison of qualifiers and non-qualifiers suggested that the qualifiers indicated greater self-confidence during the trials.

Using a much larger and more diverse sample, Mahoney et al. (1987) examined the psychological skills of pre-elite, elite and non-elite athletes. Analysis of data from the Psychological Skills Inventory for Sports questionnaire indicated that the elite and pre-elite athletes reported greater and more stable confidence than the non-elite performers. The elite and pre-elite athletes did not differ.

A number of additional studies have compared the psychological characteristics of less successful and more successful athletes. Successful wrestlers (Eklund 1994, 1996; Gould, Eklund & Jackson 1992; Highlen & Bennett 1979; Meyers, Cooke, Cullen & Liles 1979), swimmers (Jones, Hanton & Swain 1994) and rodeo athletes (Meyers, LeUnes & Bourgeois 1996) have all reported greater confidence than their less successful counterparts.

Thelwell and Maynard (2000) extended these findings by attempting to identify those factors that athletes believe underlie repeating a good performance. Approximately 200 professional cricketers with at least five years' experience participated. Each athlete was asked to rank order 22 key preselected factors deemed essential to achievement. Having total self-confidence was ranked by the athletes as the most influential factor.

Researchers have also been interested in conducting in-depth examinations of high-level performers in an attempt to better understand peak performance. Garfield and Bennett (1984) and Cohn (1991) interviewed elite athletes regarding peak performance. In both studies, being self-confident emerged as a critical factor in performing optimally.

Gould and his colleagues (Gould, Medbery, Damarjian & Lauer 1999) surveyed more than 150 junior tennis coaches to ascertain the importance they placed on mental skills training. Self-confidence was rated number 3 out of 24 possible choices (enjoyment and focus were numbers 1 and 2, respectively). Additionally, the coaches rated 'building self-confidence' as an important mental skill in all three age groups examined (12 and under, 14 and under, and 16 and under). Interestingly, when asked to rate their level of comfort in teaching specific mental skills, the coaches rated the instruction of self-confidence skills as more difficult than teaching enjoyment or focus mental skills.

These studies are generally descriptive in nature and lack a theoretical basis. We are much better able to describe and identify characteristics underlying peak performance. Unfortunately, however, we are less well informed about how confidence 'works'. That is, the mechanisms underlying variations in confidence tend not to be illuminated in descriptive work. In chapter 7, Vealey and Morris provide an excellent discussion of the research based on self-efficacy theory. Readers are also encouraged to refer to excellent reviews provided by Feltz (1988; Feltz & Lirgg 2001).

The concept of collective efficacy has been examined in a select number of studies. Feltz and Lirgg (1998) examined the relative influence of team/collective efficacy versus individual aggregated self-efficacy on performance in hockey teams. Two interesting findings were reported. First, in the highly interactive sport of hockey, collective efficacy, as opposed to self-efficacy, predicted performance. Second, wins and losses affected levels of collective efficacy, but not self-efficacy. Thus, collective efficacy was found to be both an antecedent and a consequence of performance outcomes.

Spink (1990) examined cohesion and collective efficacy in recreational and elite volleyball teams. Elite teams with high collective efficacy reported greater cohesion and performed better than elite teams with low collective efficacy. No differences with respect to cohesion or performance were noted for the recreational volleyball teams.

Levels of collective efficacy were manipulated in a laboratory setting by Hodges and Carron (1992). High and low collective efficacy triads were created by presenting members of each group with bogus feedback regarding their general strength. Each triad then competed against a team of confederates in a contest in which a medicine ball was held aloft. The weight of the ball was manipulated so that in each competition the outcome was controlled. The group of confederates won. The dependent variable was performance as measured by time. The high collective efficacy group performed better than the low collective efficacy group during the first performance. Following the initial defeat, the performance differences between the groups became much more amplified. The high collective efficacy group actually tried harder in the second competition, whereas the low collective efficacy group reduced their effort. These results were partially supported in the laboratory setting by Lichacz and Partington (1996).

Collective efficacy is an area ripe for research. Given that much of sport contains a team element, research in this area might be very applicable to enhancing not only performance but also the experience of athletes at all levels.

Although there have been five primary approaches in the research concerning confidence, the concept of confidence itself remains ambiguous to many researchers and athletes. Confidence is surrounded by a number of misconceptions, which need to be recognised before this phenomenon is accurately or fully understood. Knowing what confidence is or is not is essential if it is to be studied and improved.

MISCONCEPTIONS CONCERNING CONFIDENCE

Zinsser, Bunker and Williams (2001) presented five common misconceptions concerning confidence. These are:
(a) Either you have it or you don't.
(b) Only positive feedback can build confidence.
(c) Success always builds confidence.
(d) Confidence equals outspoken arrogance.
(e) Mistakes inevitably destroy confidence.

Rather than attempt to discuss these misconceptions, we will ask you, the reader, to review your own thoughts and perceptions. Building on the list provided by Zinsser et al., the following are three further misconceptions concerning confidence for your examination.

Misconception 1: Confidence is a global trait.

It is our contention that confidence is not only situationally specific but also a state of mind. It is commonly believed that the nature of confidence is such that once you have it, it becomes normal manifested behaviour. Actually, while confidence in one area is often prevalent, this confidence does not readily transfer to other aspects of an individual's life. The individual's state of mind is a precursor to confidence. Some athletes may be confident on offence, but less so on defence, for example. The idea that confidence is a generalised trait is yet to be supported by research.

Misconception 2: Cockiness indicates confidence.

This is very seldom true. When watching almost all levels of competition (age groups to professional) you will witness much outlandish and cocky behaviour. This type of behaviour is more frequently manifested by males than by females. Displaying such behaviours is commonly not an indication of confidence but rather the opposite: it is a sign of insecurity. Athletes who are truly confident allow their actions to speak for themselves and do not need to resort to intimidation or attempts to bring undue recognition to themselves. A few confident athletes are probably cocky, but very few cocky athletes are really confident.

Misconception 3: There are easy and standard methods to develop confidence.

Because it is a state of mind, confidence is very difficult to develop, and a technique that works for one individual may not work for another. Confidence is such a fleeting phenomenon and individuals are unique, so there are no sure methods that are successful for all athletes. Confidence is so fragile that most athletes need occasional 'booster shots' to guarantee its continued existence. The challenge to the sport psychology consultant is to know the athlete well enough that effective confidence-building techniques can be designed uniquely for that individual.

Because the concept of confidence is ambiguous to begin with, many researchers, coaches and athletes have misconceptions in this area. To fully understand this phenomenon, to ensure that the same variable(s) are being discussed or researched, the terminology and parameters need to be crystal clear.

ENHANCING CONFIDENCE IN SPORTS

All the theories that attempt to define confidence and understand or explain how it works, and all the research on how important confidence is to performance, establish an interesting and much-needed foundation, but they do not take us far enough. Sport psychology practitioners need to transfer the findings of the research and the theoretical concepts into meaningful practical applications for developing and/or increasing confidence in sports. The following suggestions for enhancing confidence can be employed individually or in combination, depending on the situation and individuals involved. These practical suggestions originate in the research on confidence but are ideas based on the authors' own experiences while working with athletes.

Cooperative activities

Interestingly, research has indicated that children learn more, retain more information and derive more enjoyment in cooperative activities than in competitive situations. The reason cooperative activities are so productive for children is that they are able to test themselves and enjoy the activities without the negative consequences inherent in competition (negative emotions such as fear, guilt and ego mitigation). Cooperative activities may involve more experienced athletes working with less experienced ones, for example. Competition results in winners and losers, but cooperation is a win–win endeavour. Confidence is increased with success and satisfaction. Cooperation enhances confidence over time; competition increases confidence only when you are winning.

COOPERATION VS COMPETITION

At the beginning of each year the women's soccer team from the University of Utah schedules a two-day retreat somewhere in the Wasatch Mountains, 50 miles from their campus. During these two days the team and the coaches do everything cooperatively as a group. They cook meals, plan team objectives, and participate in planned games and activities (e.g. a rope course and rock climbing) that force team members to depend on one another and develop cooperation. Team members learn many important characteristics concerning their team-mates and develop confidence in each other as well as in themselves and their importance to the team.

Emotion management

A common mistake many people make is to commit a lot more emotional energy to their mistakes than to their successes. In other words, we treat mistakes, from an emotional perspective, as more important than doing something correctly or well. Coaches (who are error correction specialists) and parents spend more time correcting errors than reinforcing what is being done in the right way. The constant attention to errors actually continually reinforces these behaviours. Research has reported that 70 per cent of coaches' instruction is directed towards error correction and only 30 per cent to positive reinforcement. Consequently, the confidence of the performer is diminished because of this constant negative reinforcement. How can a young athlete develop confidence if most of the reinforcement received from significant others is negative? Because of this continued negative feedback, most athletes develop a powerful tendency to self-criticism instead of strong confidence. This process is depicted in figure 12.4.

Figure 12.4 Self-criticism

   When self-criticism is repeatedly reinforced, athletes learn to devote little emotional energy on what they are doing right, but rather to focus on their mistakes. Of course, this type of cognitive dysfunction will never develop confidence, and the opposite type of learning approach should be promoted. Athletes should be encouraged to enjoy their successes first and work on their weaknesses second. Far too many athletes take their successes for granted while berating themselves for their failures. Building confidence is much easier with a positive rather than a negative focus.

   An athlete who becomes emotionally upset over an aspect of his or her performance must overcome this emotionality before being capable of correcting the performance.

EMOTIONAL MANAGEMENT

Jamie, an excellent 12-year-old pitcher, rarely gives up a hit, but in one particular game he became a little wild and walked two consecutive batters. His coach came to the mound and yelled at him for not striking out the batters. Jamie's father also became agitated, berating his son in front of the spectators and his team-mates. Jamie responded by becoming defensive, angry and frustrated. He hit the next batter and then threw his glove down on the ground. The rest of the inning was a disaster for Jamie as he continued to walk batters and the opposing team scored five runs. Jamie's emotionality had destroyed his confidence.

Jamie's story is all too common. Performers need to be encouraged to value what they are doing correctly instead of focusing on mistakes. The following simple technique will help performers to develop confidence and will mitigate negative emotions. Each day have the athletes pick something they want to accomplish. These objectives should be reasonable — challenging, but not impossible to achieve. When they have achieved their objective, have them reward themselves with something tangible (e.g. a yogurt or a milkshake). This reward will elicit positive emotions and make them feel good about what they have accomplished. Their confidence will increase because they feel good about themselves.

Emotionality is an inevitable outcome of intense involvement; but negative emotions kill confidence. Performers must learn to favour positive emotions over negative emotions if confidence is to prevail. This point will be discussed further later in the chapter.

Self rewards

Athletes can build confidence by embracing patience and taking small steps. All athletes want to be exceptional; many want to be perfect or the best there ever was in their sport. These are admirable goals but are most likely unreasonable and unattainable. A cardinal principle of goal setting is to take small steps towards the ultimate goal. Thinking this way is a challenge to most of us because of the current norm of instant gratification.

Achieving athletic excellence is a slow and painful process. With rare exceptions, it is attained only by those who demonstrate an exceptional work ethic and extremely strong intrinsic motivation. To negotiate this pathway to excellence, the future superstar must take small steps and manifest the patience to succeed. Each successful step needs to be self-rewarded.

A THOUSAND SMALL STEPS

As a young man, I developed new shots in basketball by using a simple system. I would tell myself that I could drink my soft drink only if I made ten shots in a row. Sometimes it would take me a long time to accomplish the task, and once in a while I did not reach it. The soft drink remained unopened until I accomplished what I had set out to do. A few days I drank water and took the soft drink home with me, only to bring it back the next day. On the days I accomplished my self-imposed task, I thoroughly enjoyed the taste of that soft drink. I felt good about myself and was ready for the next challenge. I taught myself early on that shooting a basketball was a fine art and could not be perfected if I got too emotional. Each journey comprises a thousand small steps, so rewards along the way are crucial if the experience is to be enjoyable. Bribing yourself is an acceptable form of reinforcement to develop confidence. Only you know what you truly desire.

Keith Henschen

Mental skills training

A growing body of empirical literature demonstrates the effectiveness of mental skills training for helping in athletic performance (Greenspan & Feltz 1989; Vealey 1994; Weinberg & Comar 1994). One of the benefits frequently touted, but not empirically tested, is that mental skills training increases the confidence of most performers. What mental skills aid in the development of confidence, and precisely what is done to accomplish this end?

The Greenspan and Feltz (1989) study, which investigated the effectiveness of various psychological interventions reported in about 20 different published articles, found that 23 different interventions had been used. However, many of these interventions are not used in the normal settings; also, many such interventions are clinical variations and are not applicable to confidence-building situations. Most comprehensive mental skills training programs include such techniques as anxiety management, concentration training, imagery, self-talk and mental routines (Weinberg & Williams 2001). Confidence training is normally included as one of the interventions, but under closer scrutiny confidence building is revealed as a combination of other interventions and does not stand alone as a mental skills intervention.

It seems reasonable to conclude that if an athlete develops a variety of mental skills and has their utilisation under control, then raised confidence will be a logical result. Mental skills training teaches performers to control their environment, rather than having the environment control them. Being in control builds personal confidence, especially when performance turns out well.

Mental skills training accomplishes both A and B and thus increases your confidence and self-efficacy. Let us now examine how each of these skills contributes to confidence building.

Anxiety management techniques

Techniques such as Chinese breathing methods, progressive relaxation, autogenic training and various meditation exercises have proven beneficial in mitigating the effects of stress and anxiety (Benson 1975; Jacobson 1964; Linden 1993; Mason 1980; McGuigan 1993). One method is not necessarily superior to another; rather, the critical factor is that the individual practising the method enjoys the experience and believes in its effectiveness. When athletes find an anxiety management technique that works for them and they learn to feel in control of themselves, their confidence begins to increase. Being in control translates into positive, confident feelings. Confidence is a state of mind and not a permanent, unchanging trait.

Concentration training

The single most frequent cause of errors during performance is the wrong attentional state. Once athletes learn how to control their attentional styles, they will make fewer mistakes and thus feel more confident in their performances. Nideffer (1981) proposed five attentional styles for all athletes to master if they are to achieve good performance. These are broad–external (e.g. reading the game), broad–internal (e.g. planning and stragegy), narrow–external (e.g. focusing on the ball/opponent), narrow–internal (e.g. monitoring your own heartbeat), and switching (e.g. moving from planning a golf chip, based on past experience, the slope and speed of the green, the location of bunkers and water, the lie of the ball, the wind and moisture, to focusing on the ball as the shot is played). Attentional styles are discussed in more detail in chapter 4. Most applied sport psychology consultants use a variety of exercises to develop these five attentional styles. Mastering concentration techniques provides continual positive reinforcement during competition and thus contributes to confidence building.

Confidence is a precursor of arousal and attention control.

- As anxiety inreases, concentration goes out the window.
- As arousal increases, concentration narrows.
- Performers who are confident can handle higher levels of arousal.

Imagery

One of the most wonderful skills with which the human animal is blessed is the ability to imagine. Each of our senses has imagining capabilities (seeing = visual, hearing = auditory, feeling = kinesthetic, etc.). We create images while we sleep (dreams) and when we are awake (daydreams). The beauty of this natural process is that using imaging can help us gain, maintain and increase self-confidence (Short, Afremow & Overby 2001). We are able to boost our confidence by imagining our previously successful performances from both feeling (kinesthetic) and seeing (visualisation) perspectives. The following simple exercise can be useful for developing imagery skills among athletes seeking to enhance confidence:

> Close your eyes and see yourself at the bottom of a set of stairs. At the top of these stairs (about 15 of them) is a door. In your mind, see yourself walk up the stairs and open the door. Once you open the door, you see a big empty room. For the next two minutes I want you to decorate this room. You can put anything you want in this room. (After about two minutes I will continue to direct the imagery.) Now sit in a chair in your happiness room and place the newest type of television on one of your walls. It is about five feet by five feet and an inch thick and hangs on the wall. Take the remote control and turn on the television. When you turn on the television, I want you to see yourself performing — perfectly. See how you look. Watch yourself for about five minutes. Now turn off the television, go over to the door, turn around and see how happy your room makes you. Close the door and walk down the steps. When you get to the bottom, open your eyes.

The athlete is then instructed to return to his happiness room each night for ten minutes and watch himself perform perfectly. This exercise builds confidence because the athlete constantly sees himself performing excellently (Bandura 1977).

Self-talk

According to Zinsser, Bunker & Williams (2001), 'The key to cognitive control is self-talk'. We all talk to ourselves almost continually, and the content of this internal dialogue is extremely important. Positive self-talk contributes to the enhancement of all our selves (see figure 12.3), as well as to better performance. Self-talk keeps the mind occupied, and thus the body can act automatically. Conversely, negative self-talk creates less than positive emotions and detracts from the task at hand. Negative self-talk quickly results in negative emotions and strong self-criticism, which prompts your mind to search for what you are doing wrong instead of focusing on what is going right. When the critic takes centre stage, over-analysis naturally follows, and automatic movements are replaced by carefully considered movements that lack flow or rhythm. Confidence is replaced by doubt and emotionality, and performance is doomed.

The best way to perform is thought free (out of your head!), trusting yourself and not allowing self-talk to override automatic responses. Another technique that has produced effective results is to replace negative self-talk with positive cue words. The following example should illustrate the point.

RESTORING CONFIDENCE THROUGH POSITIVE SELF-TALK

During the training camp just before the 2000 Olympic Games in Sydney, a couple of 400-metre runners from the United States approached one of the authors and requested help. During practice, they explained, when they reached the 300-metre mark they started to feel uncomfortable physiologically and then to talk to themselves negatively. They needed help in order to finish the last 100 metres strongly. Both of these individuals were world-class athletes in this event. The author asked them to select two words they found positive and uplifting, and, from the 300-metre point, to repeat these words over and over again until they crossed the finish line. They went on to practise this technique in a couple of pre-Olympic meets.

Each of these athletes ran excellently at the Olympics; each won a medal. This simple technique allowed them to occupy their minds positively rather than succumbing to negative self-talk during their races. Their confidence was restored.

Mental routines

Systematic pre-competitive routines enhance performances by allowing performers to prepare mentally for the competition. Many of the previously discussed mental skills are incorporated into a short routine in order for the athlete to enter their ideal mental state for performance (e.g. pre-shot free throw routines in basketball or pre-shot routines in golf). Routines provide consistency and security, which translate into confidence and self-efficacy. Normally such pre-competition routines constitute part of the athlete's warm-up procedure, immediately (5–10 minutes) before competing. Mental routines should allow the athlete to mentally switch to 'automatic pilot' — to 'lose themselves to find themselves'.

Embracing pressure

Pressure is a phenomenon that is created in the athlete's own mind in anticipation of a future negative result. In this sense, it is a form of fear. Athletes can learn to feel pressure or they can learn to embrace challenging situations rather than focusing on possible failure. This variable appears to separate athletes at all levels. The best performers approach defining situations in the competitive atmosphere with pleasure rather than trepidation. They enjoy challenges and relish these opportunities. Cognitively restructuring an athlete's perception of pressure is important in developing confidence. There is a reason that some athletes always seem to perform at their best in crucial situations — they love the pressure and refuse to be handicapped by focusing on possible negative outcomes. Would Michael Jordan have approached championship games with negative thoughts, or would he have embraced the pressure?

Dealing with failure

'He who has never lost has never faced competition.' Dealing with failure is a lot like embracing pressure. Failure is a natural and essential consequence of competition. Again, depending on the *perception* of the athlete, failure can either be devastating or, if handled properly, have little negative effect. One of the main distinctions between good and great athletes is how they handle failure or mistakes. Many players respond to failure by over-analysing their performance and becoming tentative and wary as the competition continues. In other words, their egos become involved and negative emotions (embarrassment, anger, guilt etc.) are allowed to surface. Great performers make mistakes and experience failure just as all athletes do. The difference lies in how mistakes are handled, during and after competition. The great ones just 'play on'. Analysis must wait until after the competition has concluded. They do not become overly emotional or critical of themselves at the wrong time. They remain in control, and their confidence is not affected. Much can be gained from properly dealing with mistakes and failures. Great athletes make mistakes too, but they do not focus on these mistakes during competition. They wait until half-time or after the game and *then* analyse what happened. They think about how to perform differently in future instead of dwelling on the consequences of the mistake. Most importantly, they do not carry about the negative mental baggage of a mistake. They simply learn from the incident and 'play on'.

Early-season success

There is no doubt that success raises confidence more than failure does. Many coaches have learned to schedule competition with this in mind. Scheduling competition early in the season where the chances of being successful are high is a common plan. A devastating and humiliating defeat early in the season can destroy confidence for a long time. Coaches should also realise that rough and demeaning handling of athletes early in the season can affect confidence for months. You cannot humiliate anyone into greatness, because in the process confidence is destroyed.

Mastery tapes

Mastery audio- and videotapes are excellent tools for enhancing confidence. Listening to yourself and/or watching yourself is very uplifting for most performers, and athletes are no exception. They enjoy being centre stage, especially when performing successfully. Watching themselves perform well soothes their vanity and makes them feel good. All types of positive reinforcement increase confidence.

Attuning

Attuning is a process that helps to provide the most thorough and total preparation for competition. Being well prepared and knowing that your preparation is of a high level will enhance confidence. Attuning can be applied a few days, a few hours or even a few minutes in advance of competition. The following are some suggested procedures for attuning.

ATTUNING

A. Attune to the environment:
Get the 'big picture'; check out the sport venue; find the changing rooms; find a quiet place; determine where the coach will be; make it like home.

B. Attune to opponents:
Fellow athletes and spectators are people too! Acknowledge their presence without focusing on them.

C. Attune to your team-mates:
Insulate yourself from unexpected distractions; treat team-mates as a resource for support, not an obstacle or distraction.

D. Attune to yourself:
Physically and psychologically take an inner body scan.

E. Attune to your objective:
Why are you here?

F. Attune to your strategy:
How will you get the job done? Affirm yourself. TRUST!!!

Intrinsic motivation

Lasting confidence cannot be based on extrinsic motivation or materialistic rewards; rather, it needs to be grounded on intrinsic motivation; if your confidence depends on external rewards, it will be as fleeting as the frequency of these rewards. Confidence as a relatively permanent trait, rather than a transient state, depends on your gaining responsibility, accountability and trust for and of yourself. Learning to take pride in effort and a performance well done, rather than focusing only on the results (winning or losing) will increase confidence. Confidence that is grounded on intrinsic motivation is more stable and long lasting than confidence based on external incentives. Zinsser, Bunker & Williams (2001) stated that 'confidence has relatively little to do with what happens to an individual. Instead, confidence is a result of how one thinks, what one focuses on, and how one reacts to the events in one's life' (p. 287). This statement is only partly correct, because what happens to you as an individual affects how you think and react and whether you trust yourself.

Increasing confidence is a major challenge for the sport psychology consultant. Coaches and athletes frequently ask, 'How can we increase confidence?' In this last section we have presented a number of techniques that can be used to address this question. Remember, though, that each athlete is unique and what works for one may not be effective with another. Finding the technique that is appropriate for the individual athlete is the art of sport psychology application.

FUTURE DIRECTIONS

There is no doubt that confidence will remain a critical concept in relation to performance. Greater definitional clarity will open many doors in terms of the questions researchers seek to answer and the techniques practitioners employ to increase confidence in sport. The development of models designed specifically to enhance our understanding of confidence will raise many new questions and can be expected to lead to much insight into the variability of confidence. Vealey's (2001) model offers many pathways that deserve to be investigated. The model also presents interesting interactions — such as those between achievement gains or losses, the social climate and personality — whose examination will no doubt unravel some of the complexity surrounding confidence.

Collective efficacy as it pertains to the confidence of a team is a particularly interesting area for future research. We only have to consider our society's love for soccer, rugby and countless other team games to appreciate the significance of an understanding of collective efficacy.

It is also important for us to broaden our focus to begin to examine and understand other aspects of the self. For instance, what are the origins of the self-critic, and how does the self-critic influence confidence? Similarly, do variations in confidence influence other aspects of the self and visa versa?

As our knowledge and understanding of confidence grows, the effectiveness of our interventions will likewise be positively affected. It is critical that practitioners and researchers maintain a dialogue regarding confidence. Researchers must continue to examine the efficacy of the techniques that practitioners employ. Practitioners must adapt and integrate the most recent research into their consultations with athletes. Only through such interplay will true advances in optimising the confidence of athletes occur.

CONCLUSIONS

The bottom line for confidence involves the proverbial good news – bad news dichotomy. The bad news is that confidence is a very complex phenomenon, and while everyone has a general working definition, few agree on the particulars. Confidence is a behavioural quagmire. Definitions of the concept frequently depend on the perspective of the definer.

The good news is that we are making progress. Some of the definitions offer useful distinctions, and Vealey's model is a step forward for both research and practice. The misconceptions surrounding confidence are being unravelled, and effective applied techniques for enhancing confidence are being identified. The paradox of confidence and performance continues to perplex the sport psychology profession but more and more answers seem to be within our grasp.

SUMMARY

Confidence is a key psychological construct influencing performance. Definitional ambiguity plagued early understanding of confidence. Recent clarification has identified sport confidence as the construct that is most relevant to athletes, coaches and the field of sport psychology. Sport confidence (Vealey 2001) may be viewed as either state- or trait-like, and has been defined as the belief or degree of certainty that individuals possess about their ability to be successful in sport. Conceptually, self-efficacy theory (Bandura 1977, 1982, 1986) provides tremendous insight into the possible antecedents of self-efficacy and confidence. Bandura (1977) identified prior performance accomplishments, vicarious experiences, verbal persuasion and emotional arousal as the primary sources of confidence. Vealey's (2001) sport confidence model is a social cognitive framework that is drawn from Bandura's work in self-efficacy. Vealey's model suggests three primary sources of confidence. Variations in confidence can be directly linked to achievement opportunities, the social climate and self-regulatory skills. The model also contains two secondary sources that influence sport confidence. The organisational climate and personality/demographic characteristics influence the three primary sources of confidence. The term used to characterise group or team confidence is collective efficacy. The literature that examines extracting more from less successful athletes, antecedents of peak performance, self-efficacy theory, the sport confidence model and collective efficacy is reviewed.

The following misconceptions about confidence are discussed: 'either you have it or you don't', 'only positive feedback can build confidence', 'success always builds confidence', 'confidence equals outspoken arrogance' and 'mistakes inevitably destroy confidence'. Enhancing the confidence of athletes depends on practitioners transferring the findings of research into meaningful practical applications. A number of methods of enhancing confidence are discussed in detail. It is suggested that cooperative activities can foster confidence as well as teaching emotional management. Teaching athletes to use self rewards as well as learning and integrating mental skills into athletic preparation and performance help to build confidence. Some of the more effective mental skills employed to foster confidence include anxiety management, concentration enhancement, self-talk, mental routines, learning to embrace pressure, and learning how to deal with failure. It is also critical to provide early-season successes and opportunities for athletes to attune to their performance. Confidence is clearly necessary but insufficient in itself for success; it is as unique as every individual performer. The process of how to develop and/or increase confidence generates great interest, but our understanding of this area is far from definitive.

REVIEW QUESTIONS

1   Provide a number of definitions of confidence specific to the sports situation.
2   Name and describe four theories of confidence.
3   How do the various aspects of 'self' interrelate, and particularly how do self-confidence and self-efficacy correlate with the other selves?
4   What is the difference between self-confidence and self-efficacy?
5   What have researchers in sport psychology reported concerning self-confidence? Name the researchers and discuss the findings of their investigations.
6   What are the misconceptions surrounding the concept of self-confidence?
7   Which techniques presented for developing and/or increasing self-confidence do you believe would be most effective? Why?

References

Bandura, A 1977, 'Self-efficacy: toward a unifying theory of behavioral change', *Psychological Review*, 84 191–215.

Bandura, A 1978, 'The self-system in reciprocal determinism', *American Psychologist*, 33, 344–58.

Bandura, A 1982, 'Self-efficacy mechanism in human agency', *American Psychologist*, 37, 122–47.

Bandura, A 1986, *Social foundation of thought and action: a social cognitive theory*, Prentice Hall, Englewood Cliffs, NJ.

Bandura, A 1997, *Self-efficacy: the exercise of control*, Freeman, New York.

Benson, H 1975, *The relaxation response*, Avon Books, New York.

Carron, AV & Hausenblas, HA 1998, *Group dynamics in sport*, 2nd edn, Fitness Information Technology, Morgantown, WV.

Cohn, PJ 1991, 'An exploratory study on peak performance in golf', *The Sport Psychologist*, 5, 1–14.

Eklund, RC 1994, 'A season long investigation of competitive cognition in collegiate wrestlers', *Research Quarterly for Exercise and Sport*, 65, 169–83.

Eklund, RC 1996, 'Preparing to compete: a season-long investigation with collegiate wrestlers', *The Sport Psychologist*, 10, 111–31.

Feltz, DL 1988, 'Self-confidence and sports performance', in KB Pandolf (ed.), *Exercise and sport sciences reviews*, Macmillan, New York, pp. 423–57.

Feltz, DL & Lirgg, CD 1998, 'Perceived team and player efficacy in hockey', *Journal of Applied Sport Psychology*, 83, 557–64.

Feltz, DL & Lirgg, CD 2001, 'Self-efficacy beliefs of athletes, teams, and coaches', in RN Singer, HA Hausenblas & CM Janelle (eds), *Handbook of sport psychology*, 2nd edn, John Wiley & Sons, New York, pp. 340–61.

Fitts, WH 1965, *Tennessee Self-Concept Scale: manual*, Western Psychological Services, Los Angeles.

Garfield, CA & Bennett, HZ 1984, *Peak performance: mental training techniques of the world's greatest athletes*, Tarcher, Los Angeles.

Goldsmith, W & Sweetenham, B 2000, 'What our Australian athletes and coaches tell us about confidence', *Sports Coach*, summer, 18–21.

Gould, D, Eklund, RC & Jackson, SA 1992, '1988 U.S. Olympic wrestling excellence: I. mental preparation, precompetitive cognition, and affect', *The Sport Psychologist*, 6, 358–82.

Gould, D, Guinan, D, Greenleaf, C, Medbery, R & Peterson, K 1999, 'Factors affecting Olympic performance. Perceptions of athletes and coaches from more and less successful teams', *The Sport Psychologist*, 13, 371–94.

Gould, D, Medbery, R, Damarjian, N & Lauer, L 1999, 'A survey of mental skills training knowledge, opinions, and practices of junior tennis coaches', *Journal of Applied Sport Psychology*, 11, 28–50.

Greenspan, MJ & Feltz, DF 1989, 'Psychological interventions with athletes in competitive situations: a review', *The Sport Psychologist*, 3, 219–36.

Highlen, PS & Bennett, BB 1979, 'Psychological characteristics of successful and non-successful elite wrestlers: an exploratory study', *Journal of Sport Psychology*, 1, 123–37.

Hodges, L & Carron, A 1992, 'Collective efficacy and group performance', *International Journal of Sport Psychology*, 23, 48–59.

Jacobson, E 1964, *Self-operators control: a manual of tension control*, National Foundation for Progressive Relaxation, Chicago.

Jones, G, Hanton, S & Swain, ABJ 1994, 'Intensity and interpretation of anxiety symptoms in elite and non-elite sports performers', *Personal Individual Differences*, 17, 657–63.

Lichacz, FM & Partington, JT 1996, 'Collective efficacy and true group performance', *International Journal of Sport Psychology*, 27, 146–58.

Linden, W 1993, 'The autogenic training method of JH. Schultz', in PM Lerner & RL Woolfolk (eds), *Principles and practice of stress management*, 2nd edn, The Guilford Press, New York, pp. 205–29.

Mahoney, MJ & Avener, M 1977, 'Psychology of the elite athlete: an exploratory study', *Cognitive Therapy and Research*, 1, 135–42.

Mahoney, MJ, Gabriel, TJ & Perkins, TS 1987, 'Psychological skills and exceptional athletic performance', *The Sport Psychologist*, 1, 181–99.

Mason, LJ 1980, *Guide to stress reduction*, Peace Press, Culver City, CA.

McGuigan, FJ 1993, 'Progressive relaxation: origins, principles, and clinical applications', in PM Lerner & RL Woolfolk (eds), *Principles and practice of stress management*, 2nd edn, The Guilford Press, New York, pp. 17–52.

Meyers, AW, Cooke, CJ, Cullen, J & Liles, L 1979, 'Psychological aspects of athletic competitors: a replication across sports', *Cognitive Therapy and Research*, 3, 361–6.

Meyers, MC, LeUnes, A & Bourgeois, AE 1996, 'Psychological skills assessments and athletic performance in collegiate rodeo athletes', *Journal of Sport Behavior*, 19, 132–46.

Nideffer, RM 1981, *The ethics and practice of applied sport psychology*, Movement Publications, Ithaca, NY.

Paskevich, DM 1995, 'Conceptual and measurement factors of collective efficacy in its relationship to cohesion and performance outcome', unpublished doctoral dissertation, University of Waterloo, Canada.

Short, SE, Afremow, J & Overby, L 2001, 'Using mental imagery to enhance children's motor performance', *Journal of Physical Education, Recreation & Dance*, 72 (2) 19–23.

Spink, KS 1990, 'Group cohesion and collective efficacy of volleyball teams', *Journal of Sport & Exercise Psychology*, 12, 301–11.

Thelwell, RC & Maynard, IW 2000, 'Professional cricketers' perceptions of the importance of antecedents influencing repeatable good performance', *Perceptual and Motor Skills 2000*, 90, 649–58.

Vealey, RS 1986, 'Conceptualization of sport-confidence and competitive orientation: preliminary investigation and instrument development', *Journal of Sport Psychology*, 8, 221–46.

Vealey, RS 1994, 'Current status and prominent issues in sport psychology interventions', *Medicine and Science in Sport and Exercise*, 26, 495–502.

Vealey, RS 2001, 'Understanding and enhancing self-confidence in athletes', in RN Singer, HA Hausenblas & CM Janelle (eds), *Handbook of Sport Psychology*, 2nd edn, John Wiley & Sons, New York, pp. 550–65.

Vealey, RS, Hayashi, SW, Garner-Holman, G & Giacobbi, P 1998, 'Sources of sport-confidence: conceptualization and instrument development', *Journal of Sport & Exercise Psychology*, 20, 54–80.

Watson, CB & Chemers, MM 1998, 'The rise of shared perceptions: a multilevel analysis of collective efficacy', paper presented at the Organizational Behavior Division for the Academy of Management Meeting, San Diego, CA.

Weinberg, RS 1988, *The mental advantage: developing your psychological skills in tennis*, Human Kinetics, Champaign, IL.

Weinberg, RS & Comar, W 1994, 'The effectiveness of psychological interventions in competitive sport', *Sports Medicine Journal*, 18, 406–18.

Weinberg, RS & Williams, JM 2001, 'Integrating and implementing a psychological skills training program', in JM Williams (ed.), *Applied sport psychology: personal growth to peak performance*, 4th edn, Mayfield, Mountain View, CA, pp. 347–77.

Williams, JM & Krane, V 2001, 'Psychological characteristics of peak performance', in JM Williams (ed.), *Applied sport psychology: personal growth to peak performance*, 4th edn, Mayfield, Mountain View, CA, pp. 162–8.

Zaccaro, SJ, Blair, V, Peterson, C & Zazanis, M 1995, 'Collective efficacy', in JE Maddux (ed.), *Self-efficacy, adaptation and adjustment: theory, research, and application*, Plenum Press, New York, pp. 308–30.

Zinsser, N, Bunker, L & Williams, JM 2001, 'Cognitive techniques for building confidence and enhancing performance', in JM Williams (ed.), *Applied sport psychology: personal growth to peak performance*, 4th edn, Mayfield, Mountain View, CA, pp. 284–311.

CHAPTER 13

MENTAL IMAGERY IN SPORT

Tony Morris, Michael Spittle & Clark Perry

Images can be powerful tools in enhancing sporting performances. Imagery has long been a subject of research interest in psychology, motor learning and sport psychology. It was already a central pillar of applied sport psychology practice more than 15 years ago. Gould, Tammen, Murphy and May (1989) found it to be the most widely used technique among United States Olympic sport psychology consultants; Jowdy, Murphy and Durtschi (1989) discovered that imagery techniques were used regularly by all consultants they sampled, 90 per cent of athletes, and 94 per cent of coaches. Ten years later, Gould and colleagues reported that imagery, as part of mental training, was an important component in the preparation of US Olympic athletes (Gould, Guinan, Greenleaf, Medbery & Petersen 1999).

The popularity of imagery probably has a number of origins. It is certainly intuitively appealing, as many people daydream and mentally prepare themselves for future action, for example giving someone bad news, driving the best route to a particular location or playing a tune on the piano. It is readily accepted that greater success is likely if one rehearses an activity mentally before performing it. Anecdotal reports from elite sports performers provide another basis for the implementation of formal imagery programs (e.g. Defrancesco & Burke 1997), as does the research on mental practice and mental imagery in the psychological literature (e.g. Cumming & Hall 2002). Consistent with many other areas of psychological skills training, it could be claimed that the use of imagery techniques in applied sport psychology represents the systematic application of processes that most sports performers already use in a 'naïve' form. In the long history of theory and research, psychologists have aimed to clarify the processes that constitute imagery and to determine the factors that influence the imagery process.

Although this is a chapter about the use of imagery in practice, for imagery techniques to be applied effectively it is important to appreciate the underlying theory and research. Because there is no corresponding theoretical chapter on imagery in part 1 of this book, in the first part of the chapter we briefly reflect on major aspects of theory and research as a background to the discussion of practice. Theoretical issues can only be summarised. For additional information, there are several recent review chapters on imagery in sport (e.g. Gould, Damarjian & Greenleaf 2002; Hall 2001; Murphy & Martin 2002; Vealey & Greenleaf 2001), but to address in detail all aspects of imagery applied to sport requires a book (see Morris, Spittle & Watt, in press). More attention will be paid to several issues that have a direct bearing on the use of imagery. We first consider definitions of imagery then review theories proposed to explain how imagery works. We discuss the measurement of imagery then summarise the research on imagery. The chapter then moves on to consider the application of imagery, including discussion of common uses of imagery, how it can be introduced to athletes and how it can be effectively integrated into competition to enhance performance. We provide examples of the application of imagery, then we consider the use of technical aids to facilitate imagery. Finally, we reflect on future directions in imagery research and practice.

DEFINITION OF MENTAL IMAGERY

Defining mental imagery remains one of the more contentious issues in sport psychology. Corbin (1972) defined mental practice as the 'repetition of a task, without observable movement, with the specific intent of learning' (p. 94). Most reviewers of mental imagery refer to a substantial amount of mental practice research. A problem with Corbin's definition is its all-encompassing nature. Although it excludes actual movement, it nonetheless inherently embraces a very wide range of mental processes, including verbal repetition of a movement sequence, thinking one's way through a movement, and mental problem-solving. In addition, the reference to intent of learning excludes several common uses of imagery, such as imagery for stress management, for the control of physiological functions, for pre-game mental warm-up or for injury rehabilitation.

Richardson (1969) considered the term mental imagery to apply to 'all those quasi-sensory and quasi-perceptual experiences of which we are self-consciously aware and which exist for us in the absence of those stimulus conditions that are known to produce their genuine sensory or perceptual counterparts' (pp. 2–3). Yet this definition does not clearly distinguish imagery from a range of other mental phenomena. Murphy and Jowdy (1992) argued that the element of conscious awareness in the definition does distinguish mental imagery from dreaming and daydreaming, but daydreams are typically experienced in a fully conscious state. A more pertinent distinction might be that imagery is under volitional control; that is, the imager intends to generate the experience. There are still problems here, as the degree of control over generated images can vary.

A number of other terms have been used almost interchangeably with mental practice and mental imagery. These include mental rehearsal, visualisation, imaginal practice, imagery rehearsal, symbolic rehearsal, ideomotor training and visual motor behaviour rehearsal. Popular among these terms is visualisation; this expression, however, fosters the misapprehension that imagery is totally or largely visual in nature. Imagery rehearsal and visual-motor or visuo-motor behaviour rehearsal (VMBR) are two terms proposed by Suinn (1983, 1984a, 1984b). VMBR refers to a specific imagery technique whereby the imagery process is preceded by a relaxation exercise. Suinn (1984b, 1993) made a very clear distinction between imagery rehearsal and mental practice. Referring to the Corbin (1972) definition of mental practice, Suinn noted that 'this broad definition considers the term as a generic one, covering a diverse set of activities' (1993, p. 498). In contrast, imagery rehearsal, which includes neuromuscular, physiological and emotional involvement, is a covert activity in which a person experiences sensory-motor sensations that reintegrate reality experiences (1993). Suinn (1984b) proposed that the rich, multi-modal (i.e. involving all the sense modalities) imagery rehearsal process can closely replicate the original experience, even arousing similar emotions to those associated with victory and defeat, success and failure.

Operationally, imagery rehearsal in research and applied work can be distinguished from mental practice research in a number of ways. Protocols in mental practice research typically involve one session lasting half an hour or less. The most common design involves a pre-test on the task in question, a mental practice exercise of 10 to 20 minutes' duration and a post-test of performance on the task. Much of the literature involves laboratory studies using analogue tasks, which are artificial tasks constructed for use in the laboratory, usually with the intent that participants will not be familiar with them. Because the tasks don't require real-world skills of any importance to the participants, motivation and ego-involvement can often be low. Additionally, many studies have not selected elite or even competitive sports performers as participants, so generalisation to real-world situations seems limited.

Conversely, imagery rehearsal, as used in preparation for sports performance, frequently involves weeks or months of practice, several times a week. As the practical part of this chapter describes, this practice, especially in the early stages, involves education and training in how to go about generating rich, multi-modal imagery and why it is a valuable skill to develop. This sort of application is typically done with skilled athletes in their own sport or a particularly important aspect of it. Thus, commitment and motivation are likely to be high, and because their sport closely reflects many elite athletes' self-concept, the ego-involvement of these performers is also high for these tasks. This operational distinction between mental practice and imagery rehearsal not only reflects on the issue of defining imagery, but also presents a strong argument for the need to study skilled athletes using imagery rehearsal for actual practice of and competitive performance in their own sport.

Conceptual models of imagery in sport

The difficulties with efforts to define imagery have also been evident in conceptualising imagery in sport. Without adequate conceptual models, it has proved difficult to develop coherent research programs. Martin, Moritz and Hall (1999) have developed a framework to 'guide the application of where and why to use imagery' (Hall 2001, p. 544). This framework, which is illustrated in figure 13.1, involves four components. First is the situation in sport or exercise that represents the *where* of imagery use. Next is the function of imagery — that is, *why* imagery is being employed. As proposed by Martin et al., the desired outcome of the imagery, or *what*, is the third component in a sequence. The final element of the framework is imagery ability, which is depicted to intervene between the function and the outcome of imagery. The framework developed by Martin et al. appears to be of value in understanding how to apply imagery and could stimulate a range of research.

Hall (2001) uses the what, where, why and how questions as a way to structure discussion of the work on imagery in sport. In that chapter, Hall also employs the framework proposed by Paivio (1985) of motivational and cognitive types of imagery that can be general or specific in nature. We explain these terms in more detail in the measurement section of the present chapter. In this chapter, cognitive specific imagery relates most closely to the learning and practice of sports skills. Cognitive general imagery refers more to the development of strategies to guide performance. Motivational specific imagery is concerned with the goals that are set, a topic that is not discussed in depth in this chapter. Motivational general imagery is primarily about arousal, so it relates to our discussion of stress management and anxiety.

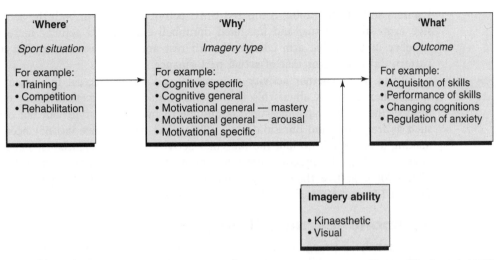

Figure 13.1 The applied model of imagery use in sport   (*Source:* Martin et al. 1999)

Murphy and Martin (2002) proposed another way of looking at the variety of issues related to imagery in sport. They suggested that imagery can be studied at three levels. Level 1 is concerned with understanding the nature of imagery. This involves examination of the physiological and cognitive processes that occur during imagery. Level 2 is concerned with the use of imagery to achieve performance goals. The focus here should be on examining how imagery influences sports performance. Level 3 deals with the meaning of the image to the athlete. Very little research in sport has addressed the phenomenology of the imagery experience for the imager. For detailed descriptions of these useful models and their capacity to help direct research, see Martin et al. (1999), Hall (2001), and Murphy and Martin (2002).

WHAT MAKES IMAGERY WORK?

A number of theories have been proposed to explain what makes imagery work in physical activity settings. Grouios (1992) described twelve theories on the relationship between mental practice and motor performance alone. The theories of imagery that are most commonly discussed in sport are described here.

Psychoneuromuscular theory

The psychoneuromuscular theory evolved largely out of Carpenter's (1894) ideomotor principle, which he proposed as far back as 1855. Start and Richardson (1964) were the first researchers actually to mention the psychoneuromuscular explanation, based on early psychophysiological studies, such as those of Jacobson (1930, 1931), Shaw (1938, 1940), and Allers and Scheminsky (1926). According to psychoneuromuscular explanations, imagery assists motor skill learning and performance by activating neuromuscular activity patterns that are similar to those generated in actual performance, but of a smaller magnitude. These impulses, although usually not even of a sufficient level to produce movement, help create a 'muscle memory' of the correct movement pattern (Vealey & Walter 1993). The theory has been supported by a number of studies that have reported increased neuromuscular activity during imagery in those muscles that would be used to perform the skills (Bird 1984; Hale 1982; Harris & Robinson 1986; Jacobson 1930, 1931; Suinn 1976; Wehner, Vogt & Stadler 1984). Some research, however, might suggest that the effect is not localised (Shaw 1938, 1940). Recently, Slade,

Landers and Martin (2002) compared EMG activity patterns in both the active and passive arms during actual and imagined dumbbell curls. EMG activity increased during imagery in the active arm compared with rest and the passive arm, but this activity pattern did not mirror that of actual performance.

Aside from whether activity is localised and mirrors actual movement, there are some other concerns about this theory. For instance, the methodologies employed in most of the studies have measured amplitude of muscular activity but not other aspects such as frequency and duration (Hale 1994); skill performance has not been measured, making it impossible to link the muscular activity to skill enhancement; and reviews of imagery and mental practice research support a cognitive explanation by finding larger effects for cognitive than strength and motor tasks (Driskell, Copper & Moran 1994; Feltz & Landers 1983; Feltz, Landers & Becker 1988).

Symbolic learning theory

The symbolic learning theory provides a cognitively oriented theory of how imagery works to enhance skill learning and performance. Sackett (1934, 1935) proposed that imagery symbolises in the brain the movements needed to perform skills. When an athlete is learning a new skill, imagery helps create a mental map or blueprint of the movements required (Vealey & Walter 1993). There is research to support the symbolic/cognitive theory (Hird, Landers, Thomas & Horan 1991; Minas 1980; Morrisett 1956; Ryan & Simons 1981, 1983; Wrisberg & Ragsdale 1979), and meta-analyses of the research literature have reported larger effect sizes for cognitive rather than motor or strength tasks, which would be expected according to such a cognitive explanation (Driskell, Copper & Moran 1994; Feltz & Landers 1983; Feltz, Landers & Becker 1988) and physical tasks. There are concerns with this theory and questions that it fails to answer. For example, the theory does not predict that imagery should enhance performance of motor and strength tasks. Although meta-analyses have suggested larger effects for cognitive tasks, they have still found a smaller effect for strength and motor tasks. The theory accounts for the use of mental practice in initial skill acquisition, but fails to adequately explain how imagery enhances performance of already well-established skills, since this level of performer would already have a well-established 'mental blueprint'.

Bio-informational theory

Bio-informational theory developed from Lang's (1977, 1979) research on imagery and the psychophysiology of phobias and anxiety disorders. Lang proposed an information-processing model that specified that images are sets of functionally organised propositions stored in long-term memory. The model comprises two main types of propositions: stimulus propositions that describe specific characteristics of the imagery scene and response propositions that describe typical behavioural outcomes, such as cognitive, physiological and emotional responses to the imagined scene. For instance, a footballer might imagine the crowd, the opponents and the game situation (stimulus propositions), and the feeling of his heart pounding and the movement of the muscles as he kicks for goal and the relief he experiences when the ball goes through for a goal (response propositions). Lang argued that learning and performance involve the linking of appropriate stimulus and response propositions, and that imagery is a process that allows strengthening of these links. To be effective in enhancing performance, images should thus contain both stimulus and response propositions. For example, in Lang's work with fear and the techniques of desensitisation and flooding, the more realistic the imagery, and the more fear that is produced in it, the better the individu. cope with the real fearful situation.

Research evidence for the bioinformational theory outside of sport is quite strong in demonstrating that the type of propositions will determine physiological responses (Cuthbert, Vrana & Bradley 1991). In sport psychology, studies have suggested that there is a greater physiological response to scripts weighted in response rather than stimulus propositions (Bakker, Boschker & Chung 1996; Hale 1982; Hecker & Kaczor 1988). Unfortunately, the effect on performance was not linked in these studies to the physiological data. Other studies that have tried to link performance enhancement to stimulus and response propositions have found equivocal results (Ziegler 1987; Kremer & Pressing 1998) More research in sport is required, as well as studies that link the theory to actual performance outcome and not just efferent activity.

Triple code theory

Ahsen's (1984) triple code (ISM) theory is a model that sets out three components of imagery that are important in the imaginal process. The first component is the image itself (I), a centrally aroused sensation that is internal but possesses all the attributes of a sensation. The second component is the somatic response (S), imagery that causes psychophysiological changes in the body. The third component is the meaning of the image (M) — individuals bring their own background and history with them into imagery, so even if people receive the same imagery instructions, the imagery experi- ence will be different for each individual. For example, for a sprinter who imagines running the 100-metre final at the Olympics, the image (I) might include the kinaes- thetic feel of running the race, the sound of the crowd, the vision of the other runners, and all the other sensory experiences of an Olympic final. The somatic response (S) might be an increased heart rate as the imager actually feels that he or she is there and begins to feel nervous. The meaning (M) of the image is crucial in this example. If the sprinter had been to the Olympics four years ago and performed poorly, the imagery experience would probably be different from that of the Olympic champion or someone who has not been to the Olympics before. The meaning is also important because an athlete might use imagery of the same activity for different purposes, such as motiv- ation, confidence or skill acquisition, and this might change the effect of the imagery on performance. Murphy and Jowdy (1992) outlined three important aspects of Ahsen's (1984) model for imagery practice: the description of the imagery script and examin- ation of the resultant imaginal experience; the measurement of various physiological systems in response to imagery; and the evaluation of the meaning the image has for the individual. The triple code model has had limited empirical or applied evaluation in relation to sport imagery.

Psychological state explanations

Other potential explanations that sport psychologists have put forward consider how imagery affects the athlete's psychological state, which in turn influences performance. For example, imagery of winning a gold medal in front of a large crowd, or even simply per- forming a skill correctly, can affect the athlete's arousal motivation or self-confidence, and this change leads to an increase in performance.

Attention-arousal set

According to attention-arousal set theory, imagery functions as a preparatory set that assists in achieving an optimal arousal level. This optimal level of arousal allows the athlete to focus attention on task-relevant cues and screen out task-irrelevant or ng cues. The attention-arousal set theory has not received any direct al support (Hecker & Kaczor 1988; Murphy, Woolfolk & Budney 1988), but some research to support such a theory. For instance, some researchers (e.g. 982; Harris & Robinson 1986; Jacobson 1931; Ryan, Blakeslee & Furst 1986; 1940) have found low-level muscle innervations associated with imagery. It (1982) proposed that these innervations might be indications of the performer 'preparing for the action, setting the arousal level, and generally getting prepared for good performance' (p. 520). Feltz and Landers (1983) suggested that this minimal tension helps prime the muscles and lower the sensory threshold to assist in producing focused attention. Wilkes and Summers (1984) found a post-hoc relationship between self-reports of attentional focus and performance following imagery, providing indirect support for an attention-arousal set theory. In opposition to these findings, Lee (1990) found that task-relevant imagery produces greater improvement than irrelevant imagery, but that imagery effects were not a result of affective mood states. The evidence does not provide adequate support for an attention-arousal explanation of imagery effects. In addition, this sort of explanation does not adequately explain the facilitative effects found for imagery training programs that do not use imagery only as a pre-performance readiness tool, but rather as a part of daily training programs.

Self-efficacy and self-confidence explanations

Self-confidence or self-efficacy theory (Bandura 1977) has been proposed to explain imagery's effect on performance (Budney, Murphy & Woolfolk 1994; Grouios 1992; Perry & Morris 1995). The idea is that imaging oneself performing a task successfully is similar to observing someone else perform the skill (modelling) or overtly performing the skill (past performance success), and therefore provides reinforcement and expectations of success. Several studies on imagery in sport or motor skills have suggested that imagery can influence self-efficacy or self-confidence (Callery & Morris 1993, 1997a, 1997b, 1997c; Feltz & Riessinger 1990; Garza & Feltz 1998; Hale & Whitehouse 1998; Martin & Hall 1995; McKenzie & Howe 1997; She & Morris 1997; Short et al. 2002; Woolfolk, Murphy, Gottesfeld & Aitken 1985), although few of these studies have tested causal links between imagery, self-efficacy and performance, a notable exception being the structural equation modelling analysis conducted by Callery and Morris (1997b), which determined that, in the study of football goal-kicking, imagery independently affected self-efficacy and performance; there was no relationship between self-efficacy and performance. Other studies have been more equivocal in their findings of a relationship between imagery and self-efficacy (Callow & Hardy 1997; Moritz, Hall, Martin & Vadocz 1996).

Motivational explanations

It is also possible that imagery can increase the motivation of an athlete, for instance by imaging achieving goals or successful performance. Paivio's (1985) framework for imagery, described earlier, suggests imagery plays a motivational role and a cognitive role at a general or specific level. Research on Paivio's model has come recently through Hall and his colleagues (Hall 1998, 2001; Hall, Mack, Paivio & Hausenblas 1998; Martin, Moritz & Hall 1999), who designed the Sport Imagery Questionnaire (SIQ), which is reviewed later in this chapter. Research using this model suggests that athletes do engage in imagery for motivational functions (Callow and Hardy 1997; Salmon, Hall & Haslam 1994; White and Hardy 1998). Paivio's theory has promise because it incorporates a cognitive theory along with motivational explanations.

Functional equivalence and neurophysiological explanations

Newer and more sophisticated neurophysiological measures (such as positron emission tomography and regional cerebral blood flow) have allowed researchers to gain a greater understanding of the relationship between imagery and movement. Interestingly, recent research seems to suggest that imagery and movement are very similar, and some researchers have gone so far as to suggest that motor imagery and motor preparation are functionally equivalent (Decety 1996a, 1996b; Jeannerod 1994, 1995). The hypothesis of functional equivalence is that imagery and movement recruit common structures and/or processes (Finke 1980, 1985; Finke & Shephard 1986). In essence, imagery enhances performance because imagery and performance are the same in their preparation, but during imagery execution is blocked. Imagery practice is therefore just like actual physical practice but does not involve the final execution of the motor commands, although the commands are generated centrally, in the brain. There is a reasonable amount of evidence in support of a functional equivalence (Annett 1996; Berthoz 1996; Decety 1996a, 1996b; Jeannerod 1994). For instance, studies have found that cortical activation during motor imagery occurs in areas related to motor control and that the activity follows a specific pattern that closely resembles action execution (e.g. Cunnington, Iansek, Bradshaw & Phillips 1996; Hallett, Fieldman, Cohen, Sadato & Pascual-Leone 1994; Lang, Cheyne, Hollinger, Gerschlager & Lindinger 1996; Stephan et al. 1995). We have yet to produce central neurophysiological studies of a complex sports movement.

This section has considered a number of attempts to explain the mechanisms through which imagery might facilitate performance and, to a lesser extent, confidence and motivation. Unfortunately, none of the large amount of research has managed to clarify the roles of low-level muscle innervation or symbolic representation, although the theories of Jacobson (1931) and Sackett (1934) have been considered for 60 years. The psychoneuromuscular theory and the symbolic learning theory were developed to explain skill learning. Imagery use in sport psychology encompasses a much wider range of applications than the acquisition of relatively simple movements. The alternative theories have to date not been subjected to rigorous study. Research must continue to seek a well-substantiated theoretical basis for imagery. It is evident that none of the theories discussed here has sufficient support as a definitive theory of imagery functioning in sport.

MEASUREMENT OF IMAGERY

The measurement of imagery is important in research and in applied work. In research, various aspects of imagery might moderate the effect of imagery programs. For example, individuals low in imagery ability are likely to experience limited success from the use of imagery programs. Few of the many studies of imagery in the literature have measured such imagery characteristics, so the conclusions of some studies might be misleading. Two aspects of applied work that can be influenced by understanding how each individual images are imagery training and individualised imagery program design. Measurement of relevant aspects of imagery can identify individuals who need training to develop their imagery skills before they can gain optimal benefit from an imagery program. For example, one golfer might use visual imagery most effectively, whereas another uses kinaesthetic imagery. Knowing this, a practitioner can individually tailor two imagery scripts for putting, one describing watching the putter head swinging smoothly through the ball, which then rolls steadily into the hole (visual), the other referring to settling over the putt in a well-balanced way and the feel in the arm and shoulder muscles as the putter swings smoothly through the ball (kinaesthetic).

Measuring imagery is important, but perhaps it is unfair to criticise most of the research on imagery for not using measures of imagery or claim that practitioners who don't measure imagery are not doing their job as effectively as they could. This is because until recently there have been no sport-specific measures of aspects of imagery that have met acceptable psychometric standards. Most of the measures that have been available originated in mainstream psychology. They typically measured one or some of the components of imagery ability, but few were comprehensive. In this section, we briefly review these measures, because for many years any measurement of imagery in sport employed those instruments, along with measures of movement imagery. Over the past decade Hall and his colleagues have developed a measure of imagery use in sport (see Hall 2001 for a review). Recently a measure of imagery ability in sport has been developed and validated (Watt, Morris & Andersen, in press). These sport-specific measures will be discussed in more detail.

The practical and conceptual problems associated with the area have meant that psychologists have largely ignored the issue of measuring imagery. Those who have addressed the question have primarily adopted self-report methods; that is, they have devised questionnaires that simply ask individuals to estimate how proficient they are at imagery, usually by selecting a number on a scale. It is these measures that we now address.

Non-sport measures of imagery

Despite these difficulties, a number of tests of imagery have been developed. The first was published more than 80 years ago, when the Betts (1909) Questionnaire on Mental Imagery (QMI) appeared. A version that substantially reduced the 150 items of the original, the Shortened Questionnaire on Mental Imagery (SQMI), developed by Sheehan (1967), has been popular in research. It is a 35-item measure, with self-report responses given on a Likert scale. The SQMI measures vividness of imagery across a range of sense modalities.

Another test that has been used for some years, both in its original and adapted form, is Gordon's (1949) Test of Imagery Control (GTIC), which was modified by Richardson (1969). It is a relatively short scale consisting of only 12 items, which are designed to measure controllability by requiring unusual mental manipulations of real objects, for example imaging a car standing on its end.

Whereas the QMI/SQMI and the GTIC have been used in research relevant to sport, two interesting measures that have not attracted much attention in research are the Individual Differences Questionnaire (IDQ) (Paivio 1971) and the Group Test of Mental Rotations (GTMR) (Vandenberg & Kuse 1978). The IDQ measures individual differences in verbalising and visualising, which are the two representational systems proposed in Paivio's (1971) dual code theory. The GTMR is claimed to be an objective test of spatial visual ability, after the style of Shephard and Metzler's (1971) mental orientation test. In the GTMR, the orientations of three-dimensional drawings must be judged. There are 40 items, each containing a target and four alternatives, two of which are correct. All the instruments in this section have a degree of reliability and validity. Moran (1993) reported on this. One weakness that has been claimed for use of these measures in sport is that their content is general and sport-specific tests are likely to be more effective (Martens 1987).

The most popular imagery measure in general psychology research in recent times is the Vividness of Visual Imagery Questionnaire (VVIQ) (Marks 1973). Marks (1989) published a substantial bibliography of research using the scale. The VVIQ is a 16-item measure derived from the visual component of Betts' (1909) QMI. It is scored on Likert-type scales. The VVIQ measures only vividness of imagery, so it is only the vividness of visual imagery that is assessed. Most of the items do not refer to movement, so its relevance to sport can be questioned.

Non-sport movement focused measures

Hall and Pongrac (1983) developed the Movement Imagery Questionnaire (MIQ) with an orientation to motor skill and sport. It consists of 18 items, describing nine short movement sequences. Each sequence is executed physically twice, once followed by instructions to recreate the experience using visual imagery, and once with kinaesthetic imagery instructions. After each imagery episode, the person rates the quality of the imagery on a Likert scale. The nine visual scores provide one total and the nine kinaesthetic items generate another total. These scores are claimed to reflect independent capacities to see and to feel movements through imagery. A strength of the MIQ is the involvement of active imagery of relevant activities, as a basis for the assessment of imagery. Intuitively this would appear to make the judgements of respondents more grounded than in tests in which people simply rate their ability to image a range of objects, actions or events. Recently Hall and Martin (1997) revised the MIQ, reducing the number of items from 18 to 10. The MIQ and the MIQ-R face the criticism that it is not clear to what extent it should be expected that a measure of very simple body movements will predict complex behaviour in sport, which often entails a rich and constantly varying environment, including opponents, as well as various physical implements to manage and spectators' activities to contend with.

Some time after the VVIQ was published, an equivalent with a kinaesthetic focus, the Vividness of Movement Imagery Questionnaire (VMIQ) (Isaac, Marks & Russell 1986) was developed. Isaac et al. claimed that the VMIQ measures the visual imagery associated with movement itself, as well as the kinaesthetic sensations. Isaac (1992) revised the VMIQ. The VMIQ items, even in the revised version, are movement-rather than sport-related.

Sport imagery measures

The Sport Imagery Questionnaire (SIQ) (Martens 1982) presents descriptions of four experiences common in sport. These are practising alone, practising with others, watching a team-mate and playing in a contest. After spending a minute imaging each scene, ratings are made on 5-point Likert scales, from *no image* to *clear, vivid image*, for three sense modalities — vision, hearing and kinaesthesis — and for emotions. Vealey and Walter (1993) added controllability to these four response dimensions. This is assessed on a 5-point scale, from *no control* to *complete control.* They also added an internal-imagery-perspective question, which asks, for each experience, whether it could be seen from inside the body, with a *yes/no* response choice. Vealey and Greenleaf (2001) have further modified the SIQ and changed its name to Sport Imagery Evaluation (SIE). The SIE has seven scales that probe vision, hearing, feeling of movement, feeling of emotions, ability to see from inside the body, ability to see from outside the body, and controllability. Although the SIQ, or SIE, has been widely used in applied work, there has been no attempt to validate it. The SIQ/SIE was the first sport-specific imagery measure. This is consistent with Martens' (1975) proposition that sport-specific tests are more sensitive.

Measurement of imagery use in sport

The Sport Imagery Questionnaire has both theoretical and research foundations (Hall, Mack, Paivio & Hausenblas 1998). Paivio (1985) proposed a simple framework for the categorisation of imagery activities, consisting of two dichotomies. First, Paivio proposed, imagery could be used for motivational or cognitive purposes; second, imagery could be general or specific. Combining these produces four kinds of imagery use: motivational general imagery, motivational specific imagery, cognitive specific imagery and cognitive general imagery use. Hall et al. (1998) employed Paivio's framework, as well as a substantial amount of research that Hall and his colleagues conducted on imagery use, employing the Imagery Use Questionnaire (IUQ) (Hall, Rodgers & Barr 1990). The IUQ is not a questionnaire in the strict sense, because its items measure a variety of aspects of imagery use in different ways. More precisely, the IUQ is a survey of when people use imagery (e.g. before, during or after competition or practice, before or in bed at night), what perspectives they employ (internal, external), and how imagery sessions are structured. Work with the IUQ for Rowing (Barr & Hall 1992), the IUQ for Figure Skating (Rodgers, Hall & Buckolz 1991) and the IUQ for Soccer Players (IUQ-SP) (Salmon, Hall & Haslam 1994) provided useful background for the development of the SIQ. The SIQ consists of 30 items taking the form 'I can consistently control the image of a physical skill' and 'I make up new plans/strategies in my head'. Athletes respond on a 7-point Likert scale, from 1 (*rarely*) to 7 (*often*). Hall and colleagues have employed the SIQ widely in recent years to examine imagery use in a range of sport contexts (see Hall 1998, 2001 for detailed reviews). Recently Hall has applied the SIQ to dance training, calling the modified scale the Exercise Imagery Questionnaire (EIQ) (Hausenblas, Hall, Rodgers & Munroe 1999), and dance training and performance, calling this version the Dance Imagery Questionnaire (DIQ) (Fish, Cumming & Hall, in press). Hall and colleagues have also developed a measure of imagery use in exercise, the Exercise Imagery Questionnaire (EIQ) (Hausenblas, Hall, Rodgers & Munroe 1999). Originally the EIQ was developed as a 23-item scale, based on a preliminary open-ended study of uses of imagery in exercise. Hausenblas et al. found that this version of the EIQ did not have good fit indices in a Confirmatory Factor Analysis (CFA) in Phase 3 of the research. They developed a 9-item version, based on the modification indices in the CFA. The 9-item scale has three items measuring technique imagery, three items measuring energy imagery and three items measuring appearance imagery, based on the three factors that emerged from an Exploratory Factor Analysis in Phase 2 of this research. Examinations of the relationship between imagery use and outcomes, such as performance and confidence, are beginning to appear. These are important, because it cannot be assumed that particular kinds of imagery are effective simply because they are the most widely used.

Measurement of imagery ability in sport

Watt, Morris and colleagues have developed an instrument to measure imagery ability that has several key features of Martens' (1982) original SIQ, but its construction and validation go well beyond any other measures of imagery ability in sport to date. Like the SIQ, the Sport Imagery Ability Measure (SIAM) (Watt, Morris & Andersen, in press) was developed on the principle of athletes actively imaging scenes from their sport and then rating their imagery. The SIAM includes generic scene descriptions, with athletes asked to think of a specific example from their own experience. Respondents image each scene for up to a minute. Then they respond to 12 items by placing a cross on a 100 mm analogue rating scale for each item. Six items refer to sense modalities (visual, auditory, kinaesthetic, tactile, olfactory and gustatory senses); five items refer to dimensions (vividness, control, ease, speed and duration of imagery); and the twelfth item relates to the emotion associated with the imagery.

The original six-scene version of the SIAM (Watt, Morris and Andersen, in press) was examined for test–retest reliability, internal consistency and factor structure, using exploratory factor analysis, in 633 male and female Australian sports performers aged 12 to 55 years and ranging from elite to club level. Along with other minor modifications, it was reduced to four scenes. Watt and Morris (1999) examined test–retest reliability internal consistency and factor structure, using confirmatory factor analysis, in a study of Australian sports performers from club to elite level. To test the construct validity of the SIAM, Watt, Morris and colleagues performed several studies. Watt and Morris (1999) examined concurrent validity by comparing a sample of elite-level performers ($n = 272$) with non-elite athletes ($n = 361$). Watt and Morris (2001) examined the convergent and discriminant validity of the SIAM in Australian athletes, who completed the SIAM, the VMIQ, the SQMI and tests of spatial memory and reasoning. Watt and Morris have carried out further examination of the SIAM in the culture and language of Finland. Many of the findings with Australian samples were replicated in Finland (Peltomaki, Watt, Jaakkola & Morris 2003; Watt, Morris, Lintunen, Elfving & Riches 2001).

Measurement of imagery has been a continuing problem for the development of research and the effective application of imagery programs in practice. The development of the SIQ (Hall et al. 1998) and the SIAM (Watt et al., in press) offers opportunities for researchers and practitioners in sport psychology to measure imagery use and imagery ability using well-validated, sport-specific measures.

RESEARCH ON IMAGERY IN SPORT

Aspects of imagery in human movement and sport have been studied for more than a century (e.g. Carpenter 1894). Imagery is such a flexible concept that the range of contexts in which it has been examined is broad and the extent of the research is vast. Various conceptual frameworks have been proposed to present imagery research (for recent examples, see Martin et al. 1999; Murphy & Martin 2002), but none easily captures all imagery research. Another reason for this is that researchers have not investigated imagery systematically; rather, many different researchers have each explored their own interest related to imagery. In the present brief summary, we can offer only a flavour of the main research topics involving imagery. Much of the imagery research in sport can be classified as study of aspects of the effectiveness of imagery and investigation of variables that affect imagery processes.

Effectiveness of imagery
Mental practice for learning and performance

The relationship between the terms *imagery* and *mental practice* (MP) was discussed in the definitions section of this chapter. A large amount of MP research has been conducted mainly in laboratory settings, often employing motor tasks that were not part of competitive sports, and frequently using tasks that were novel to participants. The evidence from those studies indicated that MP rarely produced gain scores for learning motor skills as high as those resulting from physical practice (e.g. McBride & Rothstein 1979, Mendoza & Wichman 1978). At the same time, MP consistently produced higher gain scores than no practice (e.g. Kohl & Roenker 1983; Wrisberg & Ragsdale 1979). When combined with physical practice, MP typically produced gain scores that were equivalent to physical practice alone (e.g. Oxendine 1969; Stebbins 1968) and sometimes produced significantly greater effects than physical practice alone (e.g. McBride & Rothstein 1979; White, Ashton & Lewis 1979). Little has changed since Feltz & Landers (1983) published their classic meta-analysis on mental practice and the update on it (Feltz et al. 1988), although motor learning researchers continue to work in the 'mental practice' paradigm (e.g. Boschker, Bakker & Rietberg 2000; Boschker, Hendriks & Bakker 2002; Dawson & Immink 2002; Waskiewicz & Zajac 2001). With the advent of imagery as a central component of psychological skills training in the 1980s, the emphasis switched to examining whether, how and under what circumstances imagery programs were effective in enhancing the performance of real sports skills. One approach that gained popularity in this context was the single-case research design.

Single-case studies

As applied sport psychologists needed answers to questions related to the most effective application of imagery in elite sport, much of the pre-existing research was criticised. In addition to the points listed in the previous section, critics noted that many studies involved very short amounts of imagery practice (less than five minutes on one occasion). Such studies also often included no training in how to image, and no demonstrations of the effects of imagery, as are recommended later in this chapter to enhance belief or confidence in the imagery process. Even the studies that examined learning and performance of sports skills frequently employed field study designs in which specific skills were examined out of their sport context. Researchers often expressed the concern that they could not do studies in real sports competition, because coaches would not allow some players to form a control group or permit other stringencies required by traditional experimental designs. Some researchers began to promote single-case designs (Bryan 1987; Morris 1991). In single-case designs, there is no separate control group, as each person performs for some time in a baseline condition, where the intervention is not introduced, thus providing their own control. Baselines differ in length, so that different participants start to undertake the intervention on different occasions, minimising the chance that a coincidental event on the single intervention introduction occasion, such as a stirring team talk, will mimic an imagery effect. Also, baselines and intervention stages last for several occasions each, giving sufficient time for Hawthorne effects to subside and real changes to stabilise.

Single-case studies of the effects of imagery on sports performance have generally produced positive results. Some researchers have examined the effect that imagery, as part of a psychological skills training package, had on performance. Kendall, Hrycaiko, Martin and Kendall (1990) studied a defensive task in female college basketballers over a season. Spittle and Morris (1997) investigated a pre-ball bowling routine, comprising brief relaxation, imagery and concentration, with five male junior cricketers. Thelwell and Greenlees (2001) found that a goal-setting, relaxation, imagery and self-talk package enhanced five participants' triathlon performance. Others have employed packages including imagery to influence variables other than performance. Hanton and Jones (1999) found that a goal-setting, imagery and self-talk package enhanced facilitative interpretations of anxiety symptoms and had a positive effect on performance in three swimmers. Nagel (2002) reported that a package of relaxation, imagery and video observation reduced stroke errors in six 10- to 14-year-old female swimmers. Pates and colleagues found that a package of relaxation, imagery and hypnotic induction enhanced flow as well as performance in three studies, one on golf chipping in three golfers (Pates & Maynard 2000), another on putting in five players (Pates, Oliver & Maynard 2001) and a third in three-point shooting of five collegiate basketballers (Pates, Cummings & Maynard 2002).

Although the package research is informative, especially for practice, it is not clear what element(s) of the package was effective. Single-case studies of imagery programs throw more light on this. Gough (1989) found that imagery of baseball hitting enhanced performance in two of three varsity players. Callery and Morris (1993) reported that an imagery program enhanced kick-passing performance across a season in eight of ten elite professional Australian Rules footballers. Callery and Morris (1997c) replicated this with eight players from another professional club, and She and Morris (1997) found similar benefits for nine A-grade baseball batters. Shambrook and Bull (1996) found improvement for only one of four female basketballers in free-throw shooting. Positive effects have typically been found for outcomes other than performance, such as arousal control (Medbery 1995), self-efficacy (Callery & Morris 1997a, 1997b, 1997c; McKenzie & Howe 1997; She & Morris 1997) and sport confidence (Callow, Hardy & Hall 1998). Carboni, Burke, Joyner, Hardy and Blom (2002) found that an imagery program focusing on concentration enhancement with five intercollegiate basketball players did not improve concentration but did increase self-efficacy for some players.

Single-case studies have shown imagery to be effective in enhancing performance, as well as a range of psychological processes, in performers from early adolescence upwards, representing a range of levels from limited skill (e.g. McKenzie & Howe 1997) up to elite professional level (e.g. Callery & Morris 1993, 1997a, 1997b, 1997c). Some studies were conducted in artificial environments, but several involved imagery programs applied in real, high-level competition, over long periods, such as a season (e.g. Callery & Morris 1993, 1997c).

Outcomes of imagery

The studies described in the previous section examine the effects of imagery programs on outcome variables including performance, self-confidence, anxiety, concentration and flow, typically reporting positive effects. Other kinds of research have also been undertaken to examine the impact of imagery on important outcomes like these. Often these were field studies in which athletes performed a skill from their sport, but outside the sport context, allowing for comparisons to be made with control conditions. Early studies of this kind are exemplified by Kolonay's (1977) study of relaxation and imagery, using Suinn's (1976) visuo-motor behaviour rehearsal (VMBR) approach. The combination treatment was found to be superior to relaxation, imagery alone, and a control condition, for free-throw shooting in basketball. Lane (1978) in basketball, Lane (1980) in baseball and Noel (1980) in tennis found similar results, whereas Weinberg, Seabourne and Jackson (1981) found less support in karate. A comparison of high- and low-ability players in Noel's study did find that, whereas the former improved with imagery, the low-ability players' performance dropped. This is consistent with a study by Woolfolk, Parrish and Murphy (1985), who found that a negative (incorrect) imagery condition produced decrements in performance, relative to a control condition, whereas a positive imagery condition led to an improvement in golf putting. Lower ability performers are more likely to rehearse incorrect skills in imagery, unless imagery content is carefully controlled. More recently imagery has been applied successfully in a widening range of contexts. Millard, Mahoney and Wardrup (2001) examined a kayak skill; Callery and Morris (1997b) conducted a field study in Australian football goal kicking. Using Structural Equation Modelling, they found that imagery enhanced performance and self-efficacy independently. O'Donoghue and Ormsby (2002) studied the similar task of taking free kicks in Gaelic football. Golf putting is still popular, however, with studies by Gervais (2000), Short et al. (2002), and Taylor and Shaw (2002).

In terms of other outcomes, Callery and Morris (1997b) also found that imagery enhanced self-efficacy in their field study of football goal kicking. Short et al. (2002) and Taylor and Shaw (2002) reported that negative imagery was detrimental to confidence in golf putting. Like Callery and Morris, Beauchamp, Bray and Albinson (2002) found that imagery enhanced self-efficacy as well as performance in varsity golfers, reporting that self-efficacy predicted performance in a regression analysis. Carter and Kelly (1997) supported the use of imagery to reduce somatic state anxiety in basketball free-throw shooting among collegiate players. Hale and Whitehouse (1998) gave pressure and challenge imagery scripts to soccer players and found that somatic and cognitive state anxiety intensity and direction were higher with pressure imagery. Page, Sime and Nordell (1999) found a trend for positive imagery to reduce pre-competition anxiety in 40 female intercollegiate swimmers. Thus the evidence is also mounting from field studies to support the impact of appropriate imagery on performance and psychological processes.

Variables that affect imagery

Researchers have examined a wide range of variables that have been proposed to affect imagery effectiveness. A question that has been raised is whether the influence of imagery varies depending on the type of task. One distinction that was addressed in Feltz and Landers' (1983) meta-analysis of mental practice research was whether imagery is more effective for learning motor or cognitive elements of tasks. Feltz and Landers reported that imagery effects are typically greater for cognitive components of motor tasks, such as sports. Care should be taken in interpreting this frequently cited result. Effect sizes were bigger for cognitive components of tasks in direct comparison, but this does not mean that imagery cannot enhance performance of tasks that are primarily motor, as all the studies of golf putting and basketball free-throw shooting demonstrate. More recent meta-analyses should also be examined (e.g. Driskell, Copper & Moran 1994; Hinshaw 1991). Another task variable that has been examined is the open–closed skill distinction. This is discussed in the later section on internal and external imagery perspectives, because the inconsistent findings of previous research might be explained by variations in the effects of imagery perspective. In a recent study, Spittle and Morris (2000) reported that performance of a closed skill, darts, was enhanced more by an internal than an external perspective, whereas an open skill, table tennis, showed greater facilitation by external imagery.

Sport psychologists have considered whether imagery is more useful for beginners or experts. Again, Feltz and Landers' (1983) meta-analysis produced an early position on this question, concluding that imagery can be effective for learners or skilled performers, but that the content of the imagery needs to match the stage of development of the skill. The research of Noel (1980) and Woolfolk et al. (1985), reported in a previous section, supports this position. When asked to image a skill, performance of low-ability individuals declined, whereas that of high-ability players improved. This seems to be because low-ability performers or beginners are more likely to image incorrect performance, thus reinforcing their errors. One anomaly should be noted here. Lutz, Landers and Linder (1999) found that elite golfers' putting performance declined when they were required to perform imagery specific to the research. Post-study inquiry revealed that these golfers had well-established pre-performance routines that were disrupted by the introduction of the imagery.

Another issue that has received some attention from researchers concerns the best way to deliver imagery. Landers (1999) espoused a dose-response approach to research on imagery (he still referred to 'MP' throughout this paper). Based on the drug

research model, Landers argued that researchers should determine wh
increase as people do larger amounts (doses) of imagery. For example, I
(1999) found no effect of no, one or two imagery trials. Etnier and Landers
found that 1- and 3-minute MP sessions were more effective for performance
3-minute basketball shooting task than 0-, 5- and 7-minute sessions. Etnier and Landers
also found that MP was more effective before than after physical practice. This research
is again based on the MP paradigm, but the point applies equally to imagery research.
There is little in the imagery literature that has examined whether imagery should be
practised before or after physical practice, or even away from physical practice, the
length of imagery sessions, the number of times the task is imaged in a session, or the
optimal number or frequency of imagery sessions.

Many other factors have been examined in the wide-ranging imagery literature
(including mental practice), but these are beyond the scope of this chapter. Few variables have been studied in depth, so there is plenty of room for researchers to focus on
researching the role of one personal or situational aspect of imagery. One example of a
variable that has been studied in some detail is internal and external imagery perspectives. We briefly review the literature on this issue next.

Imagery perspective

An aspect of imagery that sport psychologists have claimed acts as a mediator between
imagery practice and performance enhancement is the imagery perspective the individual adopts; however, the actual influence of the imagery perspective is still unclear.
Mahoney and Avener (1977) defined perspective in terms of whether the image is
internal or external. They proposed that external imagery occurs when the subjects
view themselves from the perspective of an external observer (much like watching
themselves on television). Mahoney and Avener considered that internal imagery
involves the person imagining being inside his or her body and experiencing those sensations that might occur while performing in the real situation. Sport psychologists and
researchers in the past generally considered that internal imagery was superior to
external imagery for performance enhancement (e.g. Rushall 1992; Vealey 1986).
Recent textbooks have been more circumspect, suggesting that which perspective is
used will depend on the athlete and the situation (e.g. Vealey & Greenleaf 2001; Weinberg & Gould 2003).

Generally, research on imagery perspectives has been of three types: questionnaire
studies, electromyography (EMG) studies and performance task studies. The questionnaire findings have been mixed. Some studies have found that elite performers, or
more successful elite performers, used more internal imagery than less elite or successful athletes (e.g. Barr & Hall 1992; Carpinter & Cratty 1983; Doyle & Landers
1980; Mahoney & Avener 1977). Some studies have found no difference between the
use of internal and external imagery by these categories of performer (e.g. Hall,
Rodgers & Barr 1990; Highlen & Bennett 1979; Meyers, Cooke, Cullen & Liles 1979;
Rotella, Gansneder, Ojala & Billing 1980). Still others have concluded that elite athletes
used more external imagery (e.g. Ungerleider & Golding 1991). EMG studies have
generally suggested that internal imagery produces greater muscular activity than
external imagery (e.g. Bakker, Boschker & Chung 1996; Hale 1982; Harris & Robinson
1986; Jacobson 1931). It appears that some researchers have interpreted this as
meaning that internal imagery is superior for performance enhancement; however, the
generation of greater muscular activity or kinaesthetic experience does not mean that
the imagery will enhance performance more. None of the EMG studies reported
actually tested to see if this increased EMG activity had any effect on subsequent

in sport

ether effects
utz et al.
(1996)
of a
rs

359

1 addition, even in the empirical EMG studies that have shown greater iternal imagery than external imagery, the distinction between internal iagery and kinaesthetic and visual imagery has been confused, so that internal imagery emphasise kinaesthetic sensations, whereas external phasise visual instructions (Hardy 1997). So it is not a surprise that rnal imagery produces greater muscular activity than non-kinaesthetic y. Studies that have examined performance change due to imagery actice in different perspectives have also produced mixed findings (Epstein 1980; Gordon, Weinberg & Jackson 1994; Mumford & Hall 1985; Neisser 1976). The research is therefore equivocal and clearly does not support the contention that internal imagery is superior to external imagery for performance enhancement with every individual or for all skills.

It has been suggested that individual preference for one perspective or another may influence perspective use (Hall 1997); however, no studies have examined this aspect. In fact, several studies have suggested that it is probably very difficult to categorise participants as internal or external imagers, because many report extensive switching between the two perspectives both between imagery trials and within imagery trials (Epstein 1980; Gordon, Weinberg & Jackson 1994; Harris & Robinson 1986; Mumford & Hall 1985; Spittle & Morris 1999b; Wang & Morgan 1992). A tentative theoretical paper by Morris and Spittle (2001) has speculated that internal imagery might be the default perspective and that individuals learn the external perspective with experience. Thus, internal imagery may be more natural to us, but external imagery might add something new and different to our experience. This new perspective might actually make external imagery more beneficial in some cases. This relates closely to the explanation suggested by Hardy (1997) that the beneficial effect of imagery practice on motor skills depends on the extent to which the imagery adds to the useful information that is otherwise available, and that using internal and external imagery might provide different information.

Recently researchers and theorists have suggested that the type of task might influence which perspective is more appropriate for the efficacious application of imagery (Hardy 1997; Spittle & Morris 2000). Hardy and colleagues (Hardy 1997; Hardy & Callow 1999; White & Hardy 1995) have proposed that external imagery is better for skills that rely on form for successful execution, and that internal imagery is better for skills that depend on spatial elements, such as perception and anticipation. This is supported by research on form-based tasks, such as gymnastics, karate and rock-climbing (Hardy & Callow 1999; White & Hardy 1995); however, Cumming and Ste-Marie (2001) found no difference between imagery perspective on synchronised figure-skating that emphasised form and body position.

Another aspect of task type that has been investigated is the open–closed skill continuum. It has been suggested that closed skills might benefit most from internal imagery, whereas open skills might benefit most from external imagery (Annett 1995; Harris 1986; Mclean & Richardson 1994). Spittle and Morris (1999a, 1999b, 2000) have conducted a series of studies examining the relationship between imagery perspective and open and closed sport skills. In an initial study (Spittle & Morris 1999b), participants experienced more internal imagery than external imagery across imagination of eight generic sport skills, but reported experiencing more external imagery in imagining the closed skills than the open skills. In two follow-up training studies (Spittle & Morris 1999a, 2000) before training, participants experienced more internal imagery than external imagery in imagining both skills; however, participants experienced more external imagery in imagination of the open skill (table tennis) than the closed skill (darts). Spittle and Morris (2000) went a step further and explored the influence of imagery perspective training of the performance of an open skill, table tennis, and a closed skill, darts. Participants were assigned to a control group or mismatched imagery perspective training groups, with those reporting lower on internal imagery use assigned to internal training and those lower on external imagery use assigned to external training. Following training, there was a change in perspective use by the two training groups, resulting in participants using their mismatched perspective more than they did before training. There was no difference between the perspective training groups on performance gains; however, both training groups improved performance on the darts and table tennis skills significantly more than the control group. In addition, an analysis of actual reported use of imagery perspective, irrespective of training group, revealed that internals improved performance significantly more on the darts skill than externals, whereas for the table tennis task externals improved performance significantly more than internals. Consequently the research reviewed on task type suggests that different tasks influence the efficacy of perspective use; however, it is still not clear just what this relationship is. Clearly more research is needed on the influence of imagery perspectives on performance of sport skills. There is a need for studies to address issues of task type, imagery perspective preference, the influence of imagery purpose on the functions of imagery, and imagery training effects on perspective use.

USES OF IMAGERY IN SPORT

Probably one of the most appealing aspects of imagery rehearsal is that it is an extremely versatile technique that can be used in a wide range of situations in sport. This section introduces some of these ways of using imagery. It is by no means comprehensive; in fact, the uses of imagery are probably limited only by the imaginations of athletes, coaches and sport psychologists. Each use mentioned in this section is explained only briefly, given the space constraints of this chapter.

Skill learning and practice

Skill learning

One of the most common uses of imagery is as mental practice for skill learning and practice. Imagery can be used to mentally practise a skill in an effort to learn the skill on its own or combined with physical practice. For example, a beginner learning a tennis serve could couple physical practice of the skill with mental practice to assist skill learning and speed up the learning process.

Skill practice

Just as we keep physically practising skills to retain them, well-developed skills can also benefit from mental practice to reinforce the skill and keep them well tuned. One example of this is during long overseas trips, when many hours may be spent on a plane or bus, where there is no opportunity for physical practice.

Error-detection and correction

Imagery can also be used to examine a skill, to detect a problem and then to correct it in readiness for the next physical practice session or competitive performance. A gymnast who is an experienced imager can use internal and external perspectives to help identify a difficulty in a beam routine. Running through the skill at normal pace in imagery to locate the part where the problem occurs could be followed by a slow-motion rerun for detailed examination of the precise difficulty.

Perceptual and cognitive skills

Strategy development

Players and coaches can use imagery as a means to develop or create new strategies to get the best out of themselves or their team or to combat specific opponents before getting to the competition.

Strategy learning

Once new strategies have been created, athletes can use imagery to rehearse them in an attempt to learn them before the competition. To familiarise themselves with the roles of all their team-mates, as well as to fit their own part in with those of the others, both temporally and spatially, a basketball team might each use imagery to enhance performance of a new offensive strategy.

Strategy practice

A common situation in team games is that alternative strategies must be adopted against each opposing team, because they all play using different styles. In soccer, for instance, the B team is often drafted to play like next week's opposition, but their speed and competence cannot match the real thing. Imaging strategy implementation against the actual opposition can help players sharpen that strategy during the week before the match.

Problem solving

Just as it is possible to use imagery to review performance, and detect and correct errors, imagery might be used to solve problems in performance. A player who is in a slump might use imagery to compare their current performance with when they were performing at their best to find the factor causing the slump.

Competition and performance

Pre-event familiarisation of competition sites

To help the athlete feel more comfortable and reduce distractions on the day of competition, athletes can imagine themselves competing at the venue. For instance, footballers or cricketers might go out to the ground the night before or on the morning of the match and stand in the middle of the ground and imagine themselves performing on the ground later. Or if they have played at the ground in previous years, they might use this memory to recreate the scene in the weeks leading up to the game.

Mental warm-up

It is important that athletes are mentally ready to give maximum effort in the vital first few minutes of the match, and imagery can be used to prepare in the lead-up to the match to focus attention, control anxiety, and build motivation and confidence.

Pre-performance routine

Imagery may be used as part of a pre-performance routine to help the athlete focus on the performance. For instance, the high jumper might run through the execution of the jump at the top of the run-up to help focus on the relevant cues in the performance.

Preview

Mental warm-up is a technique most applicable to open-skill sports, in which the player does not know exactly what the opponent will do within the parameters of the game. In closed skills, such as gymnastics, figure skating or trampoline, the performer knows exactly what the performance involves. Imaging the whole routine can help to automatise performance.

Review

After performance, imagery can be used to 'replay' the whole performance or a part of it. With practice it is possible to 'fast forward' through uninteresting phases of a badminton game, 800-metre swim or lacrosse match and then to examine the critical parts in 'slow motion', as if watching a video of the event. Review using imagery should emphasise positive aspects of performance, but should not neglect the negative. Detecting weaknesses and errors, which are then replaced by the correct response, should help future performance. Because positive and negative emotions are often aroused by performance and outcome, it is usually recommended that review be left until a few hours after the event, when a more objective assessment can be made. In long events with substantial breaks, such as cricket batting, tennis or golf, players often review each shot and immediately image corrections to it.

Psychological skills

Stress management

Imagining a relaxing scene can generate feelings of relaxation. A pistol shooter suffering somatic anxiety before and during competition will not perform well with trembling arms. The shooter can decide on a scene that he or she finds pleasant and relaxing, such as lying in soft, white sand on a beach, with the waves gently rolling in and the sun making him or her feel warm and comfortable (but not drowsy). Where the anxiety is cognitive, not producing bodily reactions but raising self-doubts about performance, imaging a scenario in which the person is coping with the performance situation effectively may help reduce the anxiety.

Developing attentional focus

To learn to remain focused in performance, athletes can imagine the upcoming performance and all the potential distracters that might be present and develop coping strategies to deal with them before they become a problem on the day of competition.

Building confidence

As noted earlier in this chapter, imagery has been widely canvassed as a means of enhancing self-confidence. For example, a netball goal-shooter who has had a couple of consecutive poor shooting percentages might begin to doubt her ability. Imagery of being in shooting positions against the next opponents, being well defended, but still feeling relaxed and confident and netting the ball might boost confidence.

Increasing motivation

Imagery can also be used as a means to increase motivation. Athletes can imagine successful performance or imagine doing well in major competitions that they are preparing for to keep them going when training gets tough. For instance, the distance runner who is having trouble getting out of bed in the morning to go for a run in the middle of winter might imagine the satisfaction she will feel when she completes the marathon in a few months' time. Or the exerciser working out at the gym can imagine how he will look and feel in a few months if he continues his program of weights.

Recovery from injury or heavy training

Imagery can be employed to facilitate physical recovery from injury, especially to soft tissue. The same process can be applied to the soreness associated with heavy training.

Physically, recovery is promoted by greater blood flow to an injured area, as well as warmth in the locality of damaged tissue. It has been shown that imagery of increased blood flow and warmth can lead to measurable increases in an area as specific as a finger (Blakeslee 1980). A long-jumper with a pulled hamstring or a sprinter after a heavy training or weights session could image the flow of warm, rich, bright-red blood to flood the affected muscles. With many athletes now using hyperbaric chambers to assist recovery, athletes could use the down time spent in the chamber to apply imagery to relax and recover from training or to mentally practise aspects of performance, as outlined earlier. A more substantial example, which also uses the special properties of flotation, is presented in a later section of the chapter. Other potential uses of imagery with injury include maintenance of confidence and motivation, coping with pain and anxiety associated with the injury, and mentally practising sport skills to keep them fine-tuned when unable to practise physically. Injured athletes could also use imagery to develop aspects of their game they might not have had time to concentrate on; for instance, athletes could use the time to imagine new strategies or learn and adjust skills or techniques.

HOW DO WE BEGIN AN IMAGERY TRAINING PROGRAM?

Introducing imagery

It was noted in the discussion of the motivational explanation of the effect of imagery on performance that many practitioners consider belief to be a prerequisite for effective imagery. More specifically, it seems important that an athlete believes that thoughts can influence behaviour, not so much to 'make the imagery process work', but to persuade the performer to add yet another discipline to a largely dedicated life, especially when the level of commitment to practise imagery must be high if it is to be effective. In order to persuade athletes of the effectiveness of imagery training, a number of exercises have been devised to add to the explanations of theory, citations of research and anecdotes of successful athletes, because athletes are often doers, so talk does not impress them as much as action.

Arm as iron bar

In chapter 14, Bond and Sargent describe one exercise called the 'Arm as Iron Bar', which they call 'The Unbendable Arm'. As a demonstration of imagery, the only modification needed is to ensure that in the second part of that exercise when giving the instruction to image the arm as an iron bar reaching out and fixed to the wall, the emphasis is on the involvement of the imagery process. Another two, widely used techniques for the introduction of mind–body links, described briefly here, are the string-and-bolt exercise and the biofeedback of arousal.

String and bolt

Despite its name, this exercise can be done with any type of thread (e.g. string, cord, wool, cotton or metal) and any small weight (e.g. a nut, bolt, paperclip or screw). The weight is tied to the end of the piece of string, forming a pendulum about 20 centimetres long. The person is instructed to place his or her elbow on a solid surface, with the forearm at an angle of around 45 degrees, to keep his or her arm still, and to image the pendulum swinging to and fro. Soon it starts to swing. The amount varies between people, but very few get no movement. Once it is swinging, the instruction is to image the pendulum standing still. For most people this will soon happen, or at least it will

slow down a lot. Then the person is instructed to image it swinging towards
from them; then stopped again. Then they image it describing a clockwise circ
it, then an anticlockwise circle and stop again. The reactions of athletes as they w
the pendulum is akin to one's reaction to a magic trick. It is important that the psychol
ogist then notes that the only trick being played is by the athlete's brain. Nothing
moves without a force being applied to it, so small movements of the arm are being
made, but many people feel they are holding their arm so rigid that it aches. The crucial point to make is that although the person is actively trying to stop the arm from
moving, the imagery still gets the message through to the muscles to act. Another interesting point can be made by asking how one stops a swinging pendulum in two to three
swings, as often happens here. Most people don't know — aside from using the free
hand, of course! Thus, under imagery conditions, it is also possible to carry out actions
or skills for which directions are not consciously accessible.

Biofeedback of arousal

Another exercise that is particularly pertinent to the use of imagery to manage arousal
level, but that can be invoked to make a general point about the mind and the body, is
to give heart rate, galvanic skin response or other feedback of physiological arousal level
while an athlete images emotive events. The events can be guided, for example by
instructing the athlete to select the final few minutes of a very close, tense game they
have played, or to imagine an especially pleasant and relaxing experience. The athlete
can then be shown how arousal changed as he or she imaged the two contrasting scenes.
An alternative or follow-up is simply to instruct performers to image something they
believe will make their arousal level increase or decrease. In addition to making the
point that they can control their arousal level by learning to use imagery, it is also possible to make the more general point that this is just one example of how the mind can
control the body, thus linking the demonstration to imagery used for skill enhancement,
concentration, confidence and other purposes. Once the point is made by any of these
techniques, imagery training can commence with an enhanced likelihood of adherence.

General imagery training

When beginning imagery training with athletes, it is helpful to start with an assessment
of their abilities in a number of areas. First, it is important to ascertain a basic level of
competence in the motor skill. If the athlete has no knowledge of the appropriate movements required to perform the task, chances are their imagery will not closely approximate
the physical skills needed for enhanced performance. In this case, imagery may actually
be detrimental to performance because the individual will be mentally rehearsing movements that may not be appropriate to the successful completion of the task. Imagery should
be used as an adjunct to physical training. As the athlete's physical talents improve, the
complexity of the imagery may also increase. That is not to say that the imagery must
always be based on current performance levels. Imagery that is grounded on sound principles based on the requirements of the sport will help in the acquisition of the skill. For
example, a swimmer may watch world champion Ian Thorpe's technique in order to
improve his or her arm pull under water. This swimmer may not be at the same level of
performance as Thorpe at the time, but by watching the film and internalising the image,
improvement of the underwater arm pull can occur.

Additionally, it is important to assess the imagery abilities of the athlete. Dimensions of imagery commonly mentioned in the literature are quality, vividness and controllability. The quality of the imagery involves the utilisation of the various senses. As
mentioned earlier, there are six major senses that should be used in imagery training:

), olfactory (smell), auditory (hearing), gustatory (taste), tactile (touch) and (body awareness). As more senses are used, the quality of the image ience the effectiveness of imagery for enhancing performance also improves. e have found that athletes have a dominant or preferred sense — some are 'see' themselves competing but are able to feel the leather of the football in s. The term 'visualisation' has been used extensively in the literature, but it ur experience that many athletes have difficulty creating a visual picture. At times, these athletes feel as if they have failed and quit on the idea of imagery, unless their ability to image in other sense modalities is quickly tapped. Despite vivid descriptions of the green of the rink and the tracks of the balls rolling across to the jack, a bowler could not generate a visual image of the bowling green at all. She reported a strong kinaesthetic image, so focus was kept on smooth delivery in kinaesthetic imagery. This worked very well for that performer. Thus we must have a more balanced approach to the presentation of imagery training. The overall quality of the image may actually be greater even if the athlete can't visualise. For example, a basketball player may feel the bumps and seams on a ball, smell the odour of the ball or perspiration on the skin, hear the echoes of the gym as the ball bounces on the floor, feel the coolness of the air on his or her body, or feel as if his or her arms moved while imaging taking a shot. It is the goal of the person doing imagery training to acquire a rich experience in as many senses as possible.

The issue of vividness pertains to the 'sharpness' of the image. It is the removal of all the 'noise' that can be associated with mentally rehearsing skills, as if you have focused a fuzzy picture on the television, or quieted a room full of people to hear someone speak, or perhaps lifted the lid off a pot of homemade spaghetti sauce and taken in the delicious aroma. By eliminating all extraneous stimuli, you can concentrate more clearly on the important information. As athletes work on their concentration skills (see chapter 14), they find that the vividness of their images improves. This improvement in vividness enhances the mental picture and creates a more accurate representation of life.

Finally, controllability allows the individual to be creative and manipulate the mental picture. Especially when creating images that have not actually occurred in reality, the individual has to take known events and manipulate them in the mind to represent the ideal condition. As athletes move items and themselves within their image they learn to exercise more control over outcomes. This not only enhances the effectiveness of the imagery, it also increases athletes' self-confidence as they see and feel that they are able to achieve success. Just as quality and vividness are learned skills, controllability may be improved through practice.

Once these abilities have been assessed, a personalised training program is designed. In group imagery sessions, it is important to allow for a wide variation in abilities. Be sure to include a gradation of skill levels, use all the senses, present a variety of vivid images, and allow the athlete an opportunity to control and change the image. Individually, be sure that the athlete practises and develops all phases of physical and mental skills to enhance his or her imagery effectiveness.

WHEN AND WHERE DO WE DO IT?

Imagery is a skill that can be utilised at any time and in any place for a wide variety of reasons. Imagery is extremely effective in the acquisition of skills. The 'mental maps' set the groundwork for future physical acts. Depending on the physical and imagery ability level of the athlete, we would prescribe different types of imagery, timing and locations.

In the early stages, incorporating imagery at the end of a quality relaxation session is advocated. This relaxation session removes unwanted distractions, such as thoughts, emotions, tension and so on, and allows the athlete to concentrate more effectively on the images. In these developmental stages, this can be done away from the training or competition venue, which again assists in minimising distractions. For beginners, it is common to start with images of well-known objects, such as the house they grew up in, a family pet, or a favourite location like the beach or mountain. These are recollections that are fairly easy for most people and, with practice, can be manipulated to enhance controllability of images.

Once the athletes show some proficiency in these skills, the focus is moved on to more sport-specific examples. Again, the athletes can practise these at the end of a relaxation session away from the venue. They should be guided to use as many senses as possible when re-creating themselves playing their sport. The images can be restricted to actions that have already taken place so as to tap into the memory portion of their minds. As they gain confidence in these skills, more self-directed imagery of possible changes to the mental picture can be introduced.

After achieving sport-specific imagery, athletes need to practise the imagery at the training site. It is important for the athletes to progress to the level of producing mental pictures without the need for total relaxation. They need to be able to block out all distractions at a moment's notice and to focus solely on the task at hand. In order to attain this level, they must begin to practise in distracting conditions. It is important for the athletes to practise imagery skills before, during and after physical training sessions. They can learn to internalise images by performing a task and by immediately noticing the feelings that were internally generated during the movement: for example, a swimmer doing butterfly, with eyes closed, focuses on the sounds below and above the water; feels the water as it rolls over the head and down the back; smells the chlorine as he or she comes up to take a breath; feels the movement of the arms and legs as they propel themselves through the water. By programming these images into the brain while they are actually being physically executed, there is an increased likelihood of retrieving them during imagery training away from the pool.

As mentioned earlier, imagery is a vital tool in preparing oneself just before competition. Therefore it needs to be practised at all competitions, regardless of the importance of the outcome. Some athletes have been heard to say that it is only important to practise imagery before big competitions. It is argued here, however, that if it is not practised before *all* competitions, it won't be there when you need it before big competitions. Imagery is a skill that should be practised as often as the individual deems necessary. It can be used in very small doses many times a day or once a day for 20 to 30 minutes before going to bed. Once the performer is proficient, there is no particular time or place where athletes should practise imagery. It is a life skill that should be used to assist individuals to plan and achieve success.

HOW DO WE USE IMAGERY? EXAMPLES OF THE USE OF IMAGERY IN SPORT

In the previous section, a number of factors were discussed that are pertinent to the introduction of imagery to an athlete. Once these general and basic aspects of the imagery procedure have been addressed, the imagery program designed must be specific to the sport and the individual. It is not possible to describe every aspect of every program. Instead, a number of specific examples are now presented in order to illustrate the range of issues and the nature of the imagery rehearsal that might be used in each case.

Learning a new gymnastics routine

Julie, a developing gymnast, is learning a new floor routine. This routine will include movements from a previous program and some new pieces her coach has introduced.

1. In practising imagery of this routine, Julie will call up her memory of her previous program to recollect those components that are familiar to her. If this is done properly, Julie will use as many of her senses as possible to recollect that image. She should see the colour of the mat, feel the mat under her feet and hands, hear the music being played, smell the aroma of the gym, be aware of her body position as she moves, perhaps even taste dryness, moistness or flavours in her mouth. Using as many senses as possible enhances the 'picture' that is generated in the mind. As you add each of the senses, it is similar to taking a black and white photo and converting it to state-of-the-art virtual reality. Julie can 'examine' a black and white photo but she can 'relate to' virtual reality.

2. When imaging new movements, Julie must call up her knowledge of gymnastics and how things move in order to create the appropriate picture. She has memories of the visual pictures and colours in the gym, what the mat feels like, the smells in the air, the various possible tastes, the feel of her body in space as she performs gymnastic movements. She must now take this knowledge of her sport and create images of these new, unperfected elements. By using multisensory imagery, Julie's new program will be learned more quickly and efficiently. Julie could also use internal and external perspectives to view and experience the new routine from multiple angles to get a better understanding of the form and spatial elements of the routine.

Improving imagery ability in freestyle swimming

To improve the athlete's ability to use imagery, it is often effective to have them experience the real sensory input and then immediately re-create it. In some cases, such as swimming, this might actually happen in the pool, as the automatised strokes are done in the following example.

1. After a standard warm-up, the swimmer swims 50 metres of freestyle at a controllable speed that allows for maximal technique without undue fatigue.

2. The next 50 metres is swum four strokes with eyes open and a broad focus of attention, four strokes with eyes closed, practising imagery of the senses used for the four previous strokes.

3. This rotation is continued for 400 metres, alternating between awareness of internal and external conditions, and imaging those same conditions with eyes closed.

4. At the conclusion of 400 metres, 7 to 8 minutes is spent imaging the 400-metre freestyle in its entirety, without actually swimming.

5. Once out of the pool, the swimmer repeats the imagery of the full 400-metre swim several times a day.

    This drill will enhance the swimmer's imagery ability in a number of areas. It will:
    - assist the swimmer in acquiring an internal perspective of imagery in cooperation with the external perspective
    - encourage multisensory imagery

- improve controllability by allowing the swimmer to change images and senses during an actual swim
- increase vividness by recreating sensory experiences currently in short-term memory
- assist in transfer of images from short-term memory for storage in long-term memory by immediate rehearsal and programming for future recall
- enhance the ability to create images instead of just recreating images.

Minimising muscle soreness in the heavy training phase of a middle-distance runner

This exercise is undertaken in a flotation tank. This provides three advantages. First, there is a direct physical effect, whereby the removal of a large part of gravity allows more rapid healing. (This is in contrast to lying on a bed, where part of the body, including many important muscle groups, is still under pressure.) Second, flotation facilitates physical, as well as mental relaxation, and relaxing the muscles also enhances their recovery. Third, flotation reduces sensory stimulation, so that one can focus on the imagery-rehearsal process without distractions, which leads to more vivid, sustainable and controllable imagery.

1. The runner visits the flotation facility every day, not too long after training. At first, short floats are used to permit orientation, as initially the tank and the experience can be distracting. Length of sessions increases, perhaps 15 minutes to start, then 25, 35 and 45 minutes may be used. Once the runner has been able to attain and maintain a relaxed state, imagery is introduced to sessions. (Time to achieve this will vary between athletes.)

2. Full 45- to 60-minute sessions are used. For the first 20 minutes the runner simply settles into a deeply relaxed state.

3. At around the 20-minute mark the runner commences an imagery protocol based on the physiological processes involved in recovery of soft tissue:
    - A stream of bright-red, oxygenated blood is imaged flowing to a specific major-muscle group, say in the lower legs.
    - As the blood flows through these muscles, its colour changes to dark red, signifying that the impurities (such as lactic acid) that cause muscle soreness are being taken up by the blood. This removes soreness and stiffness, while the oxygen in the blood is being supplied to the muscles to re-energise them.
    - As the fresh, clean, bright-red blood flows in and the deoxygenated blood carrying the impurities flows away, the runner feels the warmth of the cleansing, re-energising process in the muscles.
    - The athlete must be introduced to this concept of blood cleaning muscles during imagery training, which takes place while phase 1, the non-imagery, orientation phase, is in progress. The athlete is also trained to become sensitive to signals from the body. Then, once the runner is skilled at the imagery, he or she can take responsibility for the focus of the imagery, spending more time on those muscle groups that are signalling more soreness on any occasion.

4. Imagery lasts 15 to 20 minutes, leaving 10 to 20 minutes at the end of the session to relax and enjoy the flotation experience. Auditory signals can be used to indicate approximate times to start and conclude imagery, but they should not be too intense or high pitched.

While this exercise may appear to depend on an expensive piece of technology not accessible to many, in fact flotation facilities are to be found around most cities and towns in Australia. Access to flotation facilities is also possible at major sport psychology centres such as the Australian Institute of Sport (AIS), the South Australian Sports Institute (SASI) and Victoria University.

Developing a pre-performance routine for golf

There are often opportunities to use imagery to great effect in or close to performance. In the build-up to an open-skill team game such as basketball, a pre-competition routine can be developed; this would include imagery used for warming up mentally against the style of the present opposition and for rehearsing set moves against them. A pre-performance routine could be developed, whereby imagery is used by a gymnast to preview her floor exercise. In games with breaks from play or closed sport skills, a pre-shot or pre-point routine can be developed, with imagery of the intended shot used on every occasion. For instance, for service and return in racquet games, for each shot in archery, darts, pistol and rifle shooting and before each shot in golf or each delivery in cricket or set shot in Australian Rules football or penalty shot in soccer or hockey. A pre-performance routine incorporating imagery can be very effective for helping the athlete focus on performance of the skill. The following might be an appropriate pre-shot routine developed to improve consistency in a golfer's performance.

1. The golfer is trained in rapid muscular relaxation, using a technique such as centring or breathing. Whether or not relaxation enhances the effectiveness of imagery, it should be used before the performance of each golf shot to ensure that the player's muscles are loose for shot execution.

2. Imagery will vary depending on the shot required. To simulate this, a range of shots can be listed and the one used on each occasion is then selected at random. Practice of the relaxation and imagery combination can then take place each day off the course until the player is comfortable with the procedure and reports effective imagery.

3. An individual's routine must incorporate psychological skills or they will be distracting. Examination of the current pre-shot routine leads to the identification of a way to introduce the relaxation and imagery with minimum disruption. For example, imagine that the player's current pre-shot routine is: check location of the hole or a desired target on the fairway or green; decide on the best club to use and the type of shot; pick the club from the golf bag; walk behind the ball and check the shot down the fairway or across the green; address the ball; do a couple of practice swings; then adjust stance and play the stroke. Relaxation and imagery might fit best at the point at which the player stands behind the ball, having decided on club and stroke. It might be decided that it is suitable to take two or three deep breaths, to image the feel of the shot, using an internal imagery perspective, then image the ball travelling to its desired destination. The rest of the routine is maintained.

4. The player then starts to use the relaxation and imagery in the full routine for every shot during practice. This continues until the revised routine becomes habitual.

5. Only at this point is the routine introduced into competition, and even then it would be used only in less important events, such as club pennant tournaments. When the player reports being unaware of consciously executing the relaxation and imagery, but observation indicates that it was happening for every shot, then the new routine can be applied in major events.

Note that it might be best to introduce such a technique during a period when major competition is not occurring regularly. This is because there will be a transition period during which some confusion may arise, while the new routine is becoming habitual.

TECHNICAL AIDS TO ENHANCE IMAGERY EFFECTIVENESS

Like any skill, untrained imagery varies considerably between individuals. Some athletes automatically imagine themselves performing effectively. Nobody has told them to use imagery; it just happens. For other athletes imagery comes less easily. Those who train athletes to use imagery search for any techniques that will help all athletes to employ imagery effectively. Several technical aids have been proposed to facilitate imagery use. Video modelling and flotation, for example, have been used to enhance imagery.

Video modelling as an aid to imagery

Video modelling of performance can be an effective aid to imagery. One argument for this is that experiencing correct performance facilitates imagery. In video modelling, the individual watches an expert performer execute the skill. For elite athletes, the video-tape simply comprises edited examples of their own best performances. The edited tape can repeat those really excellent examples over and over again. The idea is to ensure that the ideal or near ideal performance of the skill becomes the image used in the mental rehearsal, as research suggests (e.g. Short et al. 2002; Woolfolk et al. 1985).

National organisations where athletes prepare for competition, as well as professional clubs, often provide facilities for video modelling. For example, the Australian Institute of Sport has a video-editing suite, where athletes can produce their own examples for imagery. Such video modelling is commonly used at the AIS in conjunction with flotation. Floating for 20 minutes or so induces a very relaxed state in many athletes. Then the video modelling is introduced via a monitor mounted into the top of the tank, so the person can view the screen from the supine position. The video shows the athlete's best performances of the skill, immediately after which imagery rehearsal is used to recreate the images viewed on screen. Alternatively, blank spaces can be left in the edited video to allow the athlete to re-create each example.

The use of video modelling, although based on substantial literature in the modelling field, is an applied technique that has yet to be investigated thoroughly by research in sport psychology. Hall and Erffmeyer (1983) included video modelling in a study of relaxation and imagery with 10 female college basketball players. The modelling group watched a player perform 10 consecutive successful foul shots on video, then imaged themselves performing the perfect 10. The video modelling group improved significantly more than the group that did imagery and relaxation without video modelling. Suinn (1993) noted that with the small sample and the absence of other evidence, the result is interesting but 'can only be considered suggestive' (p. 495). Another study by Gray (1990) provides support for the findings. Out of a class of 24 novice racquetball players, significantly greater improvement was found in the performance of those participants who received relaxation, imagery and modelling than those who received relaxation and imagery, but no modelling. Gray and Fernandez (1993) replicated the Hall and Erffmeyer result with varsity basketball players performing free throws. Should the early research be supported, future studies might test the conditions under which video modelling is most effective and determine the basis for its influence.

Flotation REST as an aid to imagery

The idea of flotation in an enclosed tank containing a salt solution dense enough to support the body was developed by Lilly (1977) out of an area of research and practice termed restricted environmental stimulation therapy (REST). The whole topic is based on the finding from early studies on sensory deprivation that, although long periods of reduced sensory input were distressing, causing hallucinations, irrational fear and the like, participants often reported very pleasant, relaxing experiences during the first one to two hours. REST attempts to utilise that early feeling of relaxation. Flotation was introduced because it permits all the usual sensory restriction, but also reduces the sensation of gravity — that is, the pressure of one's body on the couch — by virtue of floating in an Epsom salts solution dense enough to support the body.

Research has suggested that flotation REST can activate a range of positive physical, behavioural and psychological changes. Among these, it appears to be a potent environment for imagery. Several studies support the claim that imagery is effective in the flotation environment. Lee and Hewitt (1987) compared visualisation in a flotation tank, imagery on a mat, and a no-practice control condition. After the treatment, the athletes in the flotation condition had significantly higher gymnastics competition scores than those in either of the other conditions. Wagaman, Barabasz and Barabasz (1991) compared imagery during flotation REST with an imagery 'control' condition, with 22 college basketballers as participants. Those in the float condition showed significantly higher scores on the objective measure of performance after the training. McAleney, Barabasz and Barabasz (1990) found similar results with 10 male and 10 female varsity tennis players on the service shot, and Suedfeld and Bruno (1990) showed a significant effect in basketball foul-shooting with 30 university students. This study compared flotation to imagery in an alpha chair (another high-technology, sensory-reduction environment).

All these studies supporting the use of imagery in flotation were executed by major figures in the flotation field. This is not surprising since they have the facilities to conduct such research. Still, it will be interesting to see similar work done by sport psychology groups. The AIS and the SASI use flotation facilities. The AIS has developed substantial anecdotal support from its athletes for practice of imagery in flotation tanks. Aldridge, Morris and Andersen (2003) recently reported a study that examined imagery in flotation. They criticised earlier studies for not monitoring level of relaxation attained. Aldridge et al. compared free-throw shooting after imagery during three 55-minute flotation sessions with the same pattern and duration of autogenic training sessions in 18 junior A-grade players. Shooting gain scores in the imagery and flotation condition were significantly larger than for the same imagery script delivered in the autogenic training condition. Monitoring of heart rate showed that participants in both conditions became more relaxed during the progression of each session and from session 1 to session 3. Level of relaxation achieved was deeper and maximal relaxation was attained earlier in sessions for the imagery and flotation condition. Although this study is suggestive, it cannot be concluded that deeper relaxation leads to more effective imagery, in terms of free-throw shooting performance.

The flotation environment does seem to offer a good laboratory for the examination of a number of issues in imagery research, and the development of research programs in these facilities is awaited with interest. Although elite performers make substantial use of such facilities, tanks are not portable, so athletes cannot take them to events. One response to this is that the impact of flotation is sufficiently strong that it transfers to competition. All the studies cited earlier involved relatively small numbers of sessions and performance that was executed at a different time, away from the flotation environment, sometimes actually during competition. Nonetheless, performance effects were observed. While athletes perceive there to be benefits, whether in terms of relaxation, concentration or some other altered state, no doubt they will continue to use flotation techniques to support imagery rehearsal, wherever they can access flotation facilities.

Relaxation and imagery

There has been a tradition in mainstream psychology to employ relaxation as part of therapies. For example, Wolpe (1958) combined progressive relaxation with increasingly realistic and physically close experiences of an anxiety-provoking stimulus, a technique called systematic desensitisation. Some of the progressive stimuli in systematic desensitisation could be images. Suinn (1976) proposed the combination of imagery with relaxation in his visuo-motor behaviour rehearsal (VMBR) technique. In VMBR, relaxation is seen as a base for the imagery, so it precedes imagery rehearsal. Note that the imagery technique is typically being used to enhance performance of motor or sports skills. A number of studies using VMBR showed it to be effective for performance enhancement (e.g. Lane 1978, 1980; Noel 1980), but only Kolonay's (1977) study included a direct comparison of imagery with and without relaxation. Kolonay found that a group that used only imagery and a group that used only relaxation did not differ from a control group, but the basketball free-throw shooting of the VMBR group was significantly superior to all other groups.

Murphy and Jowdy (1992) cited a study by Weinberg, Seabourne and Jackson (1981, p. 230) as support for their contention that in research examining the role of relaxation in imagery, 'None of the studies conducted to date have found any significant benefits to using relaxation with imagery' (Gray, Haring & Banks 1984; Hamberger & Lohr 1980; Weinberg, Seabourne & Jackson 1981, 1987). This conclusion seems premature. Without giving any justification, Murphy and Jowdy (1992) did not include Kolonay's study and, as was noted earlier, Suinn (1993) interpreted the Weinberg et al. (1981) study as providing partial support for VMBR. Kremer, Morris and Allen (1994) argued that although Kolonay's study has methodological weaknesses, so do those of Gray et al. (1984) and Hamberger and Lohr (1980). Murphy and Jowdy (1992) made the point that many studies of imagery have produced significant results without the inclusion of relaxation procedures (e.g. Clark 1960; Corbin 1967; Woolfolk, Parrish & Murphy 1985). They concluded that 'while relaxation may interact with imagery, it is not a critical variable in producing imagery effects upon performance' (p. 230). This seems a reasonable conclusion in the light of present evidence. It can be noted that Vealey's (1986) seminal chapter on the application of imagery included a section on relaxation, whereas recent revisions (Vealey & Greenleaf 2001; Vealey & Walter 1993) mention relaxation only once when introducing a specific exercise on relaxation imagery. Despite these reactions, practitioners should be cautious before discarding relaxation. For example, it is possible that in some studies, participants who were not instructed to relax did so naturally as a precursor to, or concomitant of, imaging; or that when this occurred, studies found significant results. There remains a need to examine the role relaxation plays. Aldridge et al. (2003) did find that imagery was enhanced more by flotation than by autogenic training, and flotation reduced heart rate more quickly and to lower levels. This study did not permit a conclusion about cause and effect to be drawn, but the research demonstrates the kind of design needed, where arousal level is monitored throughout imagery sessions. Until the issue of the role of relaxation is empirically resolved, it seems sensible to advise sports performers to relax before using imagery, but not to expend a great amount of time or effort trying to induce relaxation.

FUTURE DIRECTIONS

Although imagery has long been recognised as the most widely practised psychological skill (e.g. Jowdy et al. 1989), and has been the subject of a large amount of research in motor performance and sport (Hall 2001; Murphy & Martin 2002), there is still much that is not clearly understood about this ubiquitous mental process. Basic research is needed to clarify the mechanisms underlying the imagery process and to determine more precisely the concomitants of effective imagery. Such research can answer questions to facilitate applied work. Nonetheless, more practice-oriented research is also needed. Issues include the most effective conditions for imagery; the usefulness of aids, such as video modelling and flotation; and aspects of the nature of sessions, such as their optimal length and the most appropriate timing for imagery rehearsal sessions.

After 60 years the psychoneuromuscular theory and the symbolic learning theory are still the major theoretical perspectives in the area, but little more is known about them. Well-designed studies need to be conducted to clarify the role of muscular innervation and symbolic representation, such as by measuring muscle innervation in a range of muscles during imagery of a task, in which performance is also measured. Sophisticated brain mapping technology could be applied to study the functional location in the brain of imagery during sport skills. More systematic examination of Lang's (1977) bioinformational theory and Ahsen's (1984) triple code theory is also overdue. Further exploration of the relationship between confidence and imagery would also be valuable. Understanding how imagery works in the context of performance enhancement is essential for the most effective use of imagery processes in applied work.

Thoughtful examination of those factors that appear to influence the operation of imagery is another direction for future research. Major issues in imagery research include the role of motivation; expectancy or belief in the imagery process; and the interaction between skill level and the nature of the imagery presented. The role of imagery ability in successful imagery is an important issue to study, based on valid measurement. The role of relaxation is still relevant, not as a necessary condition for imagery, but as a factor enhances the experience greatly in some circumstances.

The development of a promising measure of imagery use in sport, the SIQ (Hall, Mack, Paivio & Hausenblas 1998), and a measure of imagery ability in sport, the SIAM (Watt, Morris & Andersen, in press) opens up a range of areas for research. These include the moderating roles that imagery use and imagery ability might play in the effective application of imagery, especially when used to enhance performance. Imagery is such a rich and complex phenomenon that there are many directions for future research that have not been recorded here. Practitioners and many theorists clearly consider it a premier psychological skill. The range of uses of imagery in stress management, confidence building and recovery from injury, as well as in direct performance enhancement, should reassure students that well-designed research on aspects of imagery will be greatly welcomed.

CONCLUSIONS

There can be little doubt about the value of imagery as a resource in the practice of applied sport psychology. Imagery techniques have been used systematically in psychological skills training since the early peak performance research of Mahoney and Avener (1977) and Ravizza (1977), and practically oriented texts including Suinn (1980) and Orlick (1980). Imagery use in sport continues to grow. Similarly there appears to be little waning of interest in the study of imagery to optimise its use in sport. To date there has been more anecdotal and research evidence that imagery works, particularly in terms of enhancing performance, than there has been clarification of the underlying mechanisms that account for its effectiveness, the concomitants that affect its action or the ancillary techniques that aid in its operation.

Because imagery remains a pre-eminent means of enhancing performance, solving problems, reviewing skills, building confidence, coping with stress, focusing attention, easing pain, and facilitating recovery from injury or heavy exercise, many important questions still await answers. As the previous section intimated, the ideal approach is to solve theoretical and practical problems together. In fact, most of the theoretical issues have bearing on practical problems. Collaboration between practitioners working with elite and non-elite athletes and researchers, who have access to the infrastructure, including equipment and facilities, will also facilitate progress in this field.

While research goes on, so must the application of imagery in sport. The under-lying theory and research reviewed here, and the guidance on the use of imagery, should reflect current best practice. We will enhance the 'academic' experience only by working with athletes. By doing this, students will soon appreciate that while general principles are useful, what works with some athletes doesn't necessarily prove effective with others. Sensitivity to the needs of the individual, and a creative imagination that matches those needs to the content of imagery training and practice, will continue to produce positive experiences for athletes using imagery.

SUMMARY

This chapter considered the theoretical base and the application of imagery in sport. After defining imagery and related terms, and discussing conceptual frameworks pro-posed to examine imagery, we considered theories of imagery. We then considered the issue of measuring imagery. We presented a brief summary of research on imagery, then, moving from research to practice, we described a number of uses for imagery in sport. Next we presented procedures for the introduction of imagery and its use. This section led on to a range of examples of imagery programs for different purposes. We then addressed the use of technical aids. The relationship between relaxation and imagery was then examined. Finally we proposed a number of future directions for research and practice.

REVIEW QUESTIONS

1   What is imagery and how would you distinguish it from mental practice?

2   Describe three ways in which the field of imagery has recently been conceptualised.

3   Why has no theory of imagery attained ascendancy? Critique the psychoneuromuscular theory, symbolic learning theory, bioinformational theory and triple code theory.

4   What are the five factors proposed in the Sport Imagery Questionnaire (SIQ)?

5   What is the importance of measuring imagery ability in research and practice?

6   How is imagery affected by task type, level of skill and individual differences?

7   What are the two imagery perspectives and how does research suggest that they relate to performance of sports skills?

8   Name and describe six uses for imagery in sport.

9   How would you design an effective imagery script?

10   What is flotation REST and how effective is it for imagery rehearsal?

References

Ahsen, A 1984, 'ISM: the triple code model for imagery and psychophysiology', *Journal of Mental Imagery*, 8, 15–42.

Aldridge, T, Morris, T & Andersen, MB 2003, 'A comparison of flotation and autogenic relaxation for the facilitation of imagery of basketball shooting', in R Stelter (ed.), *New approaches to exercise and sport psychology: theories, methods and applications*, Proceedings of the 11th European Congress of Sport Psychology, CD-ROM (3-page full paper), University of Copenhagen, Copenhagen, Denmark.

Allers, R & Scheminsky, F 1926, 'Uber Aktionsstrome der Muskeln bei motorischen und verwandten Vorgangen', *Pflugers Archiv fur die gestamte Physiologie*, 212, 169–82.

Annett, J 1995, 'Imagery and motor processes: editorial overview', *British Journal of Psychology*, 86, 161–7.

Annett, J 1996, 'On knowing how to do things: a theory of motor imagery', *Cognitive Brain Research*, 3, 65–9.

Bakker, FC, Boschker, MSJ & Chung, T 1996, 'Changes in muscular activity while imagining weightlifting using stimulus or response propositions', *Journal of Sport & Exercise Psychology*, 18, 313–24.

Bandura, A 1977, 'Self-efficacy: toward a unifying theory of behavioral change', *Psychological Review*, 84, 191–215.

Barr, KA & Hall, CR 1992, 'The use of imagery by rowers', *International Journal of Sport Psychology*, 23, 243–61.

Beauchamp, MR, Bray, SR & Albinson, JG 2002, 'Pre-competition imagery, self-efficacy and performance in collegiate golfers', *Journal of Sports Sciences*, 20, 697–705.

Berthoz, A 1996, 'The role of inhibition in the hierarchical gating of executed and imagined movements', *Cognitive Brain Research*, 3, 101–13.

Betts, GH 1909, *The distribution and functions of mental imagery*, Teachers College, Columbia University, New York.

Bird, EI 1984, 'EMG quantification of mental practice', *Perceptual and Motor Skills*, 59, 899–906.

Blair, A, Hall, C & Leyshon, G 1993, 'Imagery effects on the performance of skilled and novice soccer players', *Journal of Sport Sciences*, 11 (2) 95–101.

Blakeslee, TR 1980, *The right brain*, Anchor Press, New York.

Boschker, MSJ, Bakker, FC & Rietberg, MB 2000, 'Retroactive interference effects of mentally imagined movement speed', *Journal of Sports Sciences*, 18, 593–603.

Boschker, MSJ, Hendriks, B & Bakker, FC 2002, 'Changing existing preferences of movement execution by imagery', in *Proceedings of 12th Commonwealth International Sport Conference*, Manchester, pp. 340–1.

Bryan, AJ 1987, 'Single-subject designs for evaluation of sport psychology interventions', *The Sport Psychologist*, 1, 283–92.

Budney, AJ, Murphy, SM & Woolfolk, RL 1994, 'Imagery and motor performance: what do we really know?', in AA Sheikh & ER Korn (eds), *Imagery in sports and physical performance*, Baywood Publishing, Amityville, NY, pp. 97–120.

Callery, P & Morris, T 1993, 'The effect of mental practice on the performance of an Australian Rules football skill', in S Serpa, J Alves, V Ferreira & A Paula-Brito (eds), *Proceedings of VIIIth World Congress of Sport Psychology*, International Society of Sport Psychology, Lisbon, pp. 646–51.

Callery, PJ & Morris, T 1997a, 'Imagery, self-efficacy and goal kicking performance', in R Lidor & M Bar-Eli (eds), *Proceedings of the IXth World Congress of Sport Psychology*, International Society of Sport Psychology, Netanya, Israel, pp. 169–71.

Callery, PJ & Morris, T 1997b, 'Modelling imagery, self-efficacy and performance', in R Lidor & M Bar-Eli (eds), *Proceedings of the IXth World Congress of Sport Psychology*, International Society of Sport Psychology, Netanya, Israel, pp. 172–4.

Callery, PJ & Morris, T 1997c, 'The effects of an imagery program on self-efficacy and performance of an Australian Rules football skill', in R Lidor & M Bar-Eli (eds), *Proceedings of the IXth World Congress of Sport Psychology*, International Society of Sport Psychology, Netanya, Israel, pp. 175–7.

Callow, N & Hardy, L 1997, 'Types of imagery associated with high sport confidence and self-efficacy', in R Lidor & M Bar-Eli (eds), *Proceedings of the IXth World Congress of Sport Psychology*, International Society of Sport Psychology, Netanya, Israel, pp. 178–80.

Callow, N, Hardy, L & Hall, C 1998, 'The effect of a motivational-mastery imagery intervention on the sport performance of three elite badminton players', *Journal of Applied Sport Psychology*, 10, S135.

Callow, N, Hardy, L & Hall, C 2001, 'The effects of a motivational general-mastery imagery intervention on the sport confidence of high-level badminton players', *Research Quarterly for Exercise and Sport*, 72, 389–400.

Carboni, J, Burke, KL, Joyner, AB, Hardy, CJ & Blom, LC 2002, 'The effects of brief imagery on free throw shooting performance and concentrational style of intercollegiate basketball players: a single-subject design', *International Sports Journal*, 6, 60–7.

Carpenter, WB 1894, *Principles of mental physiology*, 4th edn, Appleton, New York.

Carpinter, PJ & Cratty, BJ 1983, 'Mental activity, dreams and performance in team sport athletes', *International Journal of Sport Psychology*, 14, 186–97.

Carter, JE & Kelly, AE 1997, 'Using traditional and paradoxical imagery interventions with reactant intramural athletes', *The Sport Psychologist*, 11, 175–89.

Clark, LV 1960, 'The effect of mental practice on the development of a certain motor skill', *Research Quarterly for Exercise and Sport*, 31, 560–9.

Corbin, C 1967, 'Effects of mental practice on skill development after controlled practice', *Research Quarterly for Exercise and Sport*, 38, 534–8.

Corbin, C 1972, 'Mental practice', in WP Morgan (ed.), *Ergonomic aids and muscular performance*, Academic Press, New York, pp. 94–116.

Cumming, J & Hall, CR 2002, 'Athletes' use of imagery in the off-season', *The Sport Psychologist*, 16, 160–72.

Cumming, JL & Ste-Marie, DM 2001, 'The cognitive and motivational effects of imagery training: a matter of perspective', *The Sport Psychologist*, 15, 276–88.

Cunnington, R, Iansek, R, Bradshaw, JL & Phillips, JG 1996, 'Movement-related potentials associated with movement preparation and motor imagery', *Experimental Brain Research*, 111, 429–36.

Cuthbert, BN, Vrana, SR & Bradley, MM 1991, 'Imagery: function and physiology', *Advances in Psychophysiology*, 4, 1–42.

Dawson, A & Immink, MA 2002, 'The correspondence of motor imagery to response programming processes', *Proceedings of the North American Society for the Psychology of Sport and Physical Activity (NASPSPA) Annual Conference*, Hunt Valley, MD.

Decety, J 1996a, 'The neurological basis of motor imagery', *Behavioural Brain Research*, 77, 45–52.

Decety, J 1996b, 'Do imagined and executed actions share the same neural substrate?', *Cognitive Brain Research*, 3, 87–93.

Defrancesco, C & Burke, KL 1997, 'Performance enhancement strategies used in a professional tennis tournament', *International Journal of Sport Psychology*, 28, 185–95.

Doyle, LA & Landers, DM 1980, 'Psychological skills in elite and sub-elite shooters', unpublished manuscript, Arizona State University.

Driskell, JE, Copper, C & Moran, A 1994, 'Does mental practice enhance performance?', *Journal of Applied Psychology*, 79, 481–92.

Epstein, ML 1980, 'The relationship of mental imagery and mental rehearsal to performance on a motor task', *Journal of Sport Psychology*, 2, 211–20.

Etnier, JL & Landers, DM 1996, 'The influence of procedural variables on the efficacy of mental practice' *The Sport Psychologist*, 10, 48–57.

Feltz, DL & Landers DM 1983, 'The effect of mental practice on motor skill learning and performance: a meta-analysis', *Journal of Sport Psychology*, 2, 211–20.

Feltz, DL, Landers, DM & Becker, BJ 1988, 'A revised meta-analysis of the mental practice literature on motor skill learning', in D Druckman & J Swets (eds), *Enhancing human performance: issues, theories and techniques*, National Academy Press, Washington DC, pp. 1–65.

Feltz, DL & Riessinger, CA 1990, 'Effects of in vivo emotive imagery and performance feedback on self-efficacy and muscular endurance', *Journal of Sport & Exercise Psychology*, 12, 132–43.

Finke, RA 1980, 'Levels of equivalence of mental images and perception', *Psychological Review*, 87, 113–32.

Finke, RA 1985, 'Theories relating mental imagery to perception', *Psychological Bulletin*, 98, 236–59.

Finke, RA & Shephard, RN 1986, 'Visual functions of mental imagery', in KR Boff, L Kaufman & JP Thomas (eds), *Handbook of perception and human performance*, John Wiley & Sons, New York, pp. 37–55.

Fish, L, Cumming, J & Hall, CR (in press), 'What are confident dancers imagining?', *Journal of Applied Sport Psychology*.

Garza, DL & Feltz, DL 1998, 'Effects of selected mental practice on performance, self-efficacy, and competition confidence of figure skaters', *The Sport Psychologist*, 12, 1–15.

Gervais, PD 2000, 'Golf putting and preferences for cognitive training', unpublished master's thesis, Springfield College.

Gordon, R 1949, 'An investigation into some of the factors that favour the formation of stereotyped images', *British Journal of Psychology*, 39, 156–267.

Gordon, S, Weinberg, R & Jackson, A 1994, 'Effect of internal and external imagery on cricket performance', *Journal of Sport Behavior*, 17, 60–75.

Gough, D 1989, 'Improving batting skills with small college baseball players through guided visual imagery', *Coaching Clinic*, 27, 1–6.

Gould, D, Damarjian, N & Greenleaf, C 2002, 'Imagery training for peak performance', in JL Van Raalte & B Brewer (eds), *Exploring sport and exercise psychology*, 2nd edn, American Psychological Association, Washington, DC, pp. 49–74.

Gould, D, Guinan, D, Greenleaf, C, Medbery, R & Peterson, K 1999, 'Factors affecting Olympic performance: perceptions of athletes and coaches from more or less successful teams', *The Sport Psychologist*, 13, 371–94.

Gould, D, Tammen, V, Murphy, SM & May, J 1989, 'Life at the top: the experiences of U.S. national champion figure skaters', *The Sport Psychologist*, 7, 354–74.

Gray, JJ, Haring, MJ & Banks, NM 1984, 'Mental rehearsal for sport performance: exploring the relaxation imagery paradigm', *Journal of Sport Behavior*, 7, 68–78.

Gray, SW 1990, 'Effect of visuo-motor rehearsal with videotaped modelling on racquet ball performance of beginning players', *Perceptual and Motor Skills*, 70, 379–85.

Gray, SW & Fernandez, SJ 1993, 'Effects of a visuo-motor behavior rehearsal with videotaped modeling on basketball shooting performance', *Psychology: A Journal of Human Behavior*, 26, 41–7.

Grouios, G 1992, 'Mental practice: a review', *Journal of Sport Behavior*, 15, 42–59.

Hale, BD 1982, 'The effects of internal imagery on muscular and ocular concomitants', *Journal of Sport Psychology*, 4, 379–87.

Hale, BD 1994, 'Imagery perspectives and learning in sports performance', in AA Sheikh & ER Korn (eds), *Imagery in sports and physical performance*, Baywood Publishing, Amityville, NY, pp. 75–96.

Hale, BD & Whitehouse, A 1998, 'The effects of imagery-manipulated appraisal on intensity and direction of competitive anxiety', *The Sport Psychologist*, 12, 40–51.

Hall, CR 1997, 'Lew Hardy's third myth: a matter of perspective', *Journal of Applied Sport Psychology*, 9, 310–13.

Hall, CR 1998, 'Measuring imagery abilities and imagery use', in JL Duda (ed.), *Advances in sport and exercise psychology measurement*, Fitness Information Technology, Morgantown, WV, pp. 165–72.

Hall, CR 2001, 'Imagery in sport and exercise', in RN Singer, HA Hausenblas & CM Janelle (eds), *Handbook of research on sport psychology*, 2nd edn, John Wiley & Sons, New York, pp. 529–49.

Hall, CR, Mack, DE, Paivio, A & Hausenblas, HA 1998, 'Imagery use by athletes: development of the Sport Imagery Questionnaire', *International Journal of Sport Psychology*, 29, 73–89.

Hall, CR & Martin, KA 1997, 'Measuring movement imagery abilities: a revision of the Movement Imagery Questionnaire', *Journal of Mental Imagery*, 21, 143–54.

Hall, CR & Pongrac, J 1983, *Movement imagery questionnaire*, University of Western Ontario, London, ON.

Hall, CR, Rodgers, WM & Barr, KA 1990, 'The use of imagery by athletes in selected sports', *The Sport Psychologist*, 4, 1–10.

Hall, EG & Erffmeyer, ES 1983, 'The effect of visuo-motor behavior rehearsal with videotaped modeling on free throw accuracy of intercollegiate female basketball players', *Journal of Sport Psychology*, 5, 343–6.

Hallett, M, Fieldman, J, Cohen, LG, Sadato, N & Pascual-Leone, A 1995, 'Involvement of primary motor cortex in motor imagery and mental practice', *Behavioral and Brain Sciences*, 17, 210.

Hamberger, K & Lohr, J 1980, 'Relationship of relaxation to the controlability of imagery', *Perceptual and Motor Skills*, 51, 103–10.

Hanton, S & Jones, G 1999, 'The effects of a multimodal intervention program on performers: II. Training the butterflies to fly in formation', *The Sport Psychologist*, 13, 22–41.

Hardy, L 1997, 'The Coleman Robert Griffiths Address: three myths about applied consultancy work', *Journal of Applied Sport Psychology*, 9, 277–94.

Hardy, L & Callow, N 1999, 'Efficacy of external and internal visual imagery perspectives for the enhancement of performance on tasks in which form is important', *Journal of Sport & Exercise Psychology*, 21, 95–112.

Harris, DV 1986, 'A comment to a comment...much ado about nothing', *Journal of Sport Psychology*, 8, 349.

Harris, DV & Robinson, WJ 1986, 'The effects of skill level on EMG activity during internal and external imagery', *Journal of Sport Psychology*, 8, 105–11.

Hausenblas, HA, Hall, CR, Rodgers, WM & Munroe, KJ 1999, 'Exercise imagery: its nature and measurement', *Journal of Applied Sport Psychology*, 11, 171–80.

Hecker, JE & Kaczor, LM 1988, 'Application of imagery theory to sport psychology: some preliminary findings', *Journal of Sport & Exercise Psychology*, 10, 363–73.

Highlen, P & Bennett, B 1979, 'Psychological characteristics of successful and non-successful elite wrestlers: an exploratory study', *Journal of Sport Psychology*, 1, 123–37.

Hinshaw, KE 1991, 'The effects of mental practice on motor skill performance: critical evaluation and meta-analysis', *Imagination, Cognition and Personality*, 11, 3–35.

Hird, JS, Landers, DM, Thomas, JR & Horan, JJ 1991, 'Physical practice is superior to mental practice in enhancing cognitive and motor task performance', *Journal of Sport & Exercise Psychology*, 13, 281–93.

Isaac, AR 1992, 'Mental practice: does it work in the field?', *The Sport Psychologist*, 6, 192–8.

Isaac, AR, Marks, DF & Russell, DG 1986, 'An instrument for assessing imagery of movement: the Vividness of Movement Imagery Questionnaire (VMIQ)', *Journal of Mental Imagery*, 10, 23–30.

Jacobson, E 1930, 'Electrical measurement of neuromuscular states during mental activities', *American Journal of Physiology*, 94, 24–34.

Jacobson, E 1931, 'Electrical measurement of neuromuscular states during mental activities', *American Journal of Physiology* , 96, 115–21.

Jeannerod, M 1994, 'The representing brain: neural correlates of motor intention and imagery', *Behavioral and Brain Sciences*, 17, 187–202.

Jeannerod, M 1995, 'Mental imagery in the motor context', *Neuropsychologia*, 33, 1419–32.

Jowdy, D, Murphy, SM & Durtschi, SK 1989, *An assessment of the use of imagery by elite athletes: athlete, coach and psychological perspectives*, Olympic Sports Committee, Colorado Springs.

Kendall, G, Hrycaiko, D, Martin, GL & Kendall, T 1990, 'The effects of an imagery rehearsal, relaxation, and self-talk package on basketball game performance, *Journal of Sport & Exercise Psychology*, 12, 157–66.

Kohl, RM & Roenker, DL 1983, 'Mechanism involvement during skill imagery, *Journal of Motor Behaviour*, 15, 179–90.

Kolonay, BJ 1977, 'The effects of visuo-motor behaviour rehearsal on athletic performance', unpublished master's thesis, Hunter College, City University of New York.

Kremer, P, Morris, T & Allen, N 1994, 'Mental imagery and mental relaxation in sport psychology', unpublished manuscript, University of Melbourne.

Kremer, PJ & Pressing, JL 1998, 'A test of the bio-informational theory of mental imagery in sport', paper presented at the 33rd Australian Psychological Society Conference, Melbourne, October.

Landers, DM 1999, 'Mental practice/imagery and performance: research findings guiding application', in *Proceedings of the 3rd Asian South Pacific Association of Sport Psychology International Congress of Sport Psychology*, ASPASP, Wuhan, China, pp. 1–7.

Lane, JF 1978, 'Four studies of visuo-motor behavior rehearsal', unpublished manuscript.

Lane, JF 1980, 'Improving athletic performance through visuo-motor behavior rehearsal', in R Suinn (ed.), *Psychology in sports: methods and applications*, Burgess, Minneapolis, MN, pp. 316–20.

Lang, PJ 1977, 'Imagery in therapy: an informational processing analysis of fear', *Behavior Therapy*, 8, 862–86.

Lang, PJ 1979, 'A bio-informational theory of emotional imagery', *Psychophysiology*, 16, 495–512.

Lang, W, Cheyne, D, Hollinger, P, Gerschlager, W & Lindinger, G 1996, 'Electric and magnetic fields of the brain accompanying internal simulation of movement', *Cognitive Brain Research*, 3, 125–9.

Lee, AB & Hewitt, J 1987, 'Using visual imagery in a flotation tank to improve gymnastic performance and reduce physical symptoms', *International Journal of Sport Psychology*, 18, 223–30.

Lee, C 1990, 'Psyching up for a muscular endurance task: effects of image content on performance and mood state', *Journal of Sport & Exercise Psychology*, 12, 66–73.

Lilly, JC 1977, *The deep self*, Simon & Schuster, New York.

Lutz, R, Landers, DM & Linder, DE 1999, 'Procedural variables and skill level influences on pre-performance mental practice efficacy', paper presented at a meeting of the American Psychological Society, Denver, CO.

Magill, RA 2003, *Motor control and learning: concepts and applications*, 7th edn, McGraw-Hill, Dubuque, IA.

Mahoney, MJ & Avener, M 1977, 'Psychology of the elite athlete: an exploratory study', *Cognitive Therapy and Research*, 3, 361–6.

Marks, DF 1973, 'Visual imagery differences in the recall of pictures', *British Journal of Psychology*, 64, 17–24.

Marks, DF 1989, 'Bibliograpy of research utilizing the vividness of visual imagery', *Perceptual and Motor Skills*, 69, 707–18.

Martens, R 1975, 'The paradigmatic crisis in American sport personology', *Sportwissenschaft*, 1, 9–24.

Martens, R 1982, 'Imagery in sport', paper presented at the Medical and Scientific Aspects of Elitism in Sport Conference, Brisbane, September.

Martens, R 1987, 'Science, knowledge, and sport psychology', *The Sport Psychologist*, 1, 29–55.

Martin, K & Hall, C 1995, 'Using mental imagery to enhance intrinsic motivation', *Journal of Sport & Exercise Psychology*, 17, 54–69.

Martin, KA, Moritz, SE & Hall, CR 1999, 'Imagery use in sport: a literature review and applied model', *The Sport Psychologist*, 13, 245–68.

McAleney, PJ, Barabasz, A & Barabsz, M 1990, 'Effects of flotation restricted environmental stimulation on intercollegiate tennis performance', *Perceptual and Motor Skills*, 71, 1023–8.

McAuley, E 1985, 'Modeling and self-efficacy: a test of Bandura's model', *Journal of Sport Psychology*, 7, 283–95.

McBride, ER & Rothstein, AL 1979, 'Mental and physical practice and the learning and retention of open and closed skills', *Perceptual and Motor Skills*, 49, 359–65.

McKenzie, AD & Howe, BL 1997, 'The effect of imagery on self-efficacy for a motor skill', *International Journal of Sport Psychology*, 28, 196–210.

McLean, N & Richardson, A 1994, 'The role of imagery in perfecting already learned physical skills', in AA Sheikh & ER Korn (eds), *Imagery in sports and physical performance*, Baywood Publishing, Amityville, NY, pp. 59–73.

Medbery, RE 1995, 'The use of imagery as a strategy for arousal control with youth soccer players', unpublished master's thesis, Purdue University.

Mendoza, D & Wichman, H 1978, 'Inner darts: effects of mental practice on performance of dart throwing', *Perceptual and Motor Skills*, 47, 1195–9.

Meyers, AW, Cooke, CJ, Cullen, J & Liles, L 1979, 'Psychological aspects of athletic competitors: a replication across sports', *Cognitive Therapy and Research*, 3, 361–6.

Millard, M, Mahoney, C & Wardrop, J 2001, 'A preliminary study of mental and physical practice on the kayak wet exit skill', *Perceptual and Motor Skills*, 92, 977–84.

Minas, SC 1980, 'Mental practice of a complex perceptual-motor skill', *Journal of Human Movement Studies*, 4, 102–7.

Moran, A 1993, 'Conceptual and methodological issues in the measurement of mental imagery skills in athletes', *Journal of Sport Behaviour*, 16, 156–70.

Moritz, SE, Hall, CR, Martin, KA & Vadocz, E 1996, 'What are confident athletes imaging? An examination of image content', *The Sport Psychologist*, 10, 171–9.

Morris, T 1991, 'Single-case designs to study treatment effects in sport psychology', paper presented at the annual conference of the Australian Sports Medicine Federation, Canberra, October.

Morris, T & Spittle, M 2001, 'Internal and external imagery: a case of default theory?', in A Papaioannou, M Goudas & Y Theodorakis (eds), *Proceedings of the Xth World Congress of Sport Psychology, Volume 5*, International Society of Sport Psychology, Athens, Greece, pp. 11–13.

Morris, T, Spittle, M & Watt, AP (in press), *Imagery in sport: the complete picture*, Human Kinetics, Champaign, IL.

Morrisett, LN 1956, 'The role of implicit practice in learning', unpublished doctoral dissertation, Yale University, New Haven, CT.

Mumford, P & Hall, C 1985, 'The effects of internal and external imagery on performing figures and figure skating', *Canadian Journal of Applied Sport Sciences*, 10, 171–7.

Murphy, SM & Jowdy, DP 1992, 'Imagery and mental practice', in TS Horn (ed.), *Advances in sport psychology*, Human Kinetics, Champaign, IL, pp. 221–50.

Murphy, SM & Martin, KA 2002, 'The use of imagery in sport', in T Horn (ed.), *Advances in sport and exercise psychology*, 2nd edn, Human Kinetics, Champaign, IL, pp. 405–39.

Murphy, SM, Woolfolk, RL & Budney, AJ 1988, 'The effects of emotive imagery on strength performance', *Journal of Sport & Exercise Psychology*, 10, 334–45.

Nagel, CF 2002, 'The effect of relaxation training, video-observation, and mental imagery upon the reduction of freestyle swimming errors of youth competitive female swimmers', unpublished master's thesis, Western Washington University.

Neisser, U 1976, *Cognition and reality: principles and implications of cognitive psychology*, WH Freeman, San Francisco.

Noel, RC 1980, 'The effect of visuo-motor behavior rehearsal on tennis performance', *Journal of Sport Psychology*, 2, 220–6.

O'Donoghue, PG & Ormsby, D 2002, 'The effectiveness of mental imagery training in enhancing the taking of free kicks in Gaelic football', *Journal of Sports Sciences*, 20, 70.

Orlick, T 1980, *In pursuit of excellence*, 1st edn, Human Kinetics, Champaign, IL.

Oxendine, JB 1969, 'Effect of mental and physical practice on the learning of three motor skills', *Research Quarterly*, 40, 755–63.

Page, SJ, Sime, W & Nordell, K 1999, 'The effects of imagery on female college swimmers' perceptions of anxiety', *The Sport Psychologist*, 13, 458–69.

Paivio, A 1971, *Imagery and verbal processes*, Holt, Rinehart and Winston, New York.

Paivio, A 1985, 'Cognitive and motivational functions of imagery in human performance', *Canadian Journal of Applied Sport Sciences*, 10, 22–8.

Pates, J, Cummings, A & Maynard, IW 2002, 'The effects of hypnosis on flow states and three-point shooting performance in basketball players', *The Sport Psychologist*, 16, 34–47.

Pates, J & Maynard, IW 2000, 'Effects of hypnosis on flow states and golf performance', *Perceptual and Motor Skills*, 9, 1057–75.

Pates, J, Oliver, R & Maynard, IW 2001, 'The effects of hypnosis on flow states and golf-putting performance', *Journal of Applied Sport Psychology*, 13, 341–54.

Peltomaki, V, Watt, A, Jaakkola, T & Morris, T 2003, 'Examination of imagery ability and imagery use in athletes from individual and team sports', in R Stelter (ed.), *New approaches to exercise and sport psychology: theories, methods and applications*, Proceedings of the 11th European Congress of Sport Psychology, CD-ROM (3-page full paper), University of Copenhagen, Copenhagen, Denmark.

Perry, C & Morris, T 1995, 'Mental imagery in sport', in T Morris & J Summers (eds), *Sport psychology: theory, applications & issues*, John Wiley & Sons, Brisbane, pp. 339–85.

Ravizza, K 1977, 'Peak experiences in sport', *Journal of Humanistic Psychology*, 17, 35–40.

Richardson, A 1969, *Mental imagery*, Springer, New York.

Rodgers, W, Hall, CR & Buckolz, E 1991, 'The effect of an imagery training program on imagery ability, imagery use, and figure skating performance', *Journal of Applied Sport Psychology*, 3, 109–25.

Rotella, RJ, Gansneder, B, Ojala, D & Billing, J 1980, 'Cognitions and coping strategies of elite skiers: an exploratory study of young developing athletes', *Journal of Sport Psychology*, 2, 350–4.

Rushall, BS 1992, *Mental skills training for sports*, Sports Science Associates, Canberra, ACT.

Ryan, DE, Blakeslee, T & Furst, M 1986, 'Mental practice and motor skill learning: an indirect test of the neuromuscular feedback hypothesis', *International Journal of Sport Psychology*, 17, 60–70.

Ryan, ED & Simons, J 1981, 'Cognitive demand imagery and frequency of mental practice as factors influencing the acquisition of mental skills', *Journal of Sport Psychology*, 4, 35–45.

Ryan, ED & Simons, J 1983, 'What is learned in mental practice of motor skills: a test of the cognitive motor hypothesis', *Journal of Sport Psychology*, 5, 419–26.

Sackett, RS 1934, 'The influences of symbolic rehearsal upon the retention of a maze habit', *Journal of General Psychology*, 10, 376–95.

Sackett, RS 1935, 'The relationship between amount of symbolic rehearsal and retention of a maze habit', *Journal of General Psychology*, 13, 113–28.

Salmon, J, Hall, C & Haslam, I 1994, 'The use of imagery by soccer players', *Journal of Applied Sport Psychology*, 6, 116–33.

Schmidt, RA 1982, *Motor control and learning: a behavioral emphasis*, Human Kinetics, Champaign, IL.

Shambrook, CJ & Bull, SJ 1996, 'The use of a single-case research design to investigate the efficacy of imagery training', *Journal of Applied Sport Psychology*, 8, 27–43.

Shaw, WA 1938, 'The distribution of muscular action-potentials during imaging', *Psychological Record*, 2, 195–216.

Shaw, WA 1940, 'The relation of muscular action potentials to imaginal weight lifting', *Archives of Psychology*, 247, 50.

She, W & Morris T 1997, 'Imagery, self-confidence, and baseball hitting', in R Lidor & M Bar-Eli (eds), *Proceedings of the IXth World Congress of Sport Psychology*, International Society of Sport Psychology, Netanya, Israel, pp. 626–8.

Sheehan, P 1967, 'A shortened form of Bett's Questionnaire upon mental imagery', *Journal of Clinical Psychology*, 23, 386–9.

Shepard, RN & Metzler, J 1971, 'Mental rotation of three-dimensional objects', *Science*, 171, 700–3.

Short, SE, Bruggeman, JM, Engel, SG, Marback, TL, Wang, LJ, Willadsen, A & Short, MW 2002, 'The effect of imagery function and imagery direction on self-efficacy and performance on a golf-putting task', *The Sport Psychologist*, 16, 48–67.

Slade, JM, Landers, DM & Martin, PE 2002, 'Muscular activity during real and imagined movements: a test of inflow explanations', *Journal of Sport & Exercise Psychology*, 24, 151–67.

Spittle, M & Morris, T 1997, 'Concentration skills for cricket bowlers', *Sports Coach*, 20, 32. Summary and Journal Documentation Service No. 97/06/027 for full paper.

Spittle, M & Morris, T 1999a, 'Training of imagery perspectives', *Proceedings of the 5th International Olympic Committee World Congress on Sport Sciences*, Sydney, November, p. 142.

Spittle, M & Morris, T 1999b, 'State and trait measurement of imagery perspectives', *Proceedings of the 3rd International Congress of the Asian South Pacific Association of Sport Psychology*, ASPASP, Wuhan, China, pp. 327–9.

Spittle, M & Morris, T 2000, 'Imagery perspective preferences and motor performance', *Australian Journal of Psychology*, 52S, 112.

Start, KB & Richardson, A 1964, 'Imagery and mental practice', *British Journal of Education Psychology*, 34, 280–4.

Stebbins, RJ 1968, 'A comparison of the effects of physical and mental practice in learning a motor skill', *Research Quarterly*, 39, 728–34.

Stephan, KM, Fink, GR, Passingham, RE, Silbersweig, D, Ceballous-Bauman, AO, Frith, CD & Frackowiak, RSJ 1995, 'Functional anatomy of the mental representation of upper extremity movements in healthy participants', *Journal of Neurophysiology*, 73, 373–86.

Suedfeld, P & Bruno, T 1990, 'Flotation REST and imagery in the improvement of athletic performance', *Journal of Sport and Exercise Psychology*, 12, 82–5.

Suinn, RM 1976, 'Visual motor behavior rehearsal for adaptive behavior', in J Krumboltz & C Thoresen (eds), *Counseling methods*, Holt, Rinehart & Winston, New York.

Suinn, RM 1980, 'Psychology and sports performance: principles and applications', in R Suinn (ed.), *Psychology in sports: methods and applications*, Burgess, Minneapolis, pp. 26–36.

Suinn, RM 1983, 'Imagery and sports', in AA Sheikh (ed.), *Imagery: current theory research and applications*, John Wiley & Sons, New York, pp. 507–34.

Suinn, RM 1984a, 'Visual motor behavior rehearsal: the basic technique', *Scandinavian Journal of Behavior Therapy*, 13, 131–42.

Suinn, RM 1984b, 'Imagery and sports', in WF Straub & JM Williams (eds), *Cognitive sports psychology*, Sport Science Associates, New York, pp. 253–71.

Suinn, RM 1993, 'Imagery', in RN Singer, M Murphey & LK Tennant (eds), *Handbook of research on sport psychology*, Macmillan, New York, pp. 492–510.

Taylor, JA & Shaw, DF 2002, 'The effects of outcome imagery on golf-putting performances', *Journal of Sports Sciences*, 20, 607–13.

Thelwell, RC & Greenlees, IA 2001, 'The effects of a mental skills training package on gymnasium triathlon performance', *The Sport Psychologist*, 15, 127–41.

Ungerlieder, S & Golding, JM 1991, 'Mental practice among Olympic athletes', *Perceptual and Motor Skills*, 72, 1007–17.

Vandenberg, S & Kuse, AR 1978, 'Mental rotations: a group test of three dimensional spatial visualisation', *Perceptual and Motor Skills*, 47, 599–604.

Vealey, RE 1986, 'Imagery training for performance enhancement', in JM Williams (ed.), *Applied sport psychology: personal growth to peak performance*, 1st edn, Mayfield, Mountain View, CA, pp. 209–231.

Vealey, RE & Walter, SM 1993, 'Imagery training for performance enhancement and personal development', in JM Williams (ed.), *Applied sport psychology: personal growth to peak performance*, 2nd edn, Mayfield, Mountain View, CA, pp. 200–24.

Vealey, RE & Greenleaf, C 2001, 'Seeing is believing: understanding and using imagery in sport', in JM Williams (ed.), *Applied sport psychology: personal growth to peak performance*, 4th edn, Mayfield, Mountain View, CA, pp. 247–83.

Wagaman, JD, Barabasz, AF & Barabasz, M 1991, 'Flotation REST and imagery in the improvement of collegiate basketball performance', *Perceptual and Motor Skills*, 79, 119–22.

Wang, Y & Morgan, WP 1992, 'The effect of imagery perspectives on the psychophysiological responses to imagined exercise', *Behavioural Brain Research*, 52, 167–74.

Waskiewicz, Z & Zajac, A 2001, 'The imagery and motor skills acquisition', *Biology of Sport*, 18, 71–83.

Watt, AP & Morris, T 1999, 'Reliability, factor structure, and criterion validity of the Sport Imagery Ability Measure (SIAM)', in *Proceedings of the 3rd International Congress of the Asian–South Pacific Association of Sport Psychology*, ASPASP, Wuhan, China, pp. 130–2.

Watt, AP & Morris, T 1999, 'Reliability, factor structure, and criterion validity of the Sport Imagery Ability Measure (SIAM)', *Proceedings of the 3rd Asian South Pacific Association of Sport Psychology International Congress of Sport Psychology*, Wuhan, China, pp. 330–2.

Watt, AP & Morris, T 2001, 'Criterion validity of the Sports Imagery Ability Measure (SIAM)', in A Papaioannou, M Goudas & Y Theodorakis (eds), *Proceedings of the Xth World Congress of Sport Psychology, Volume 2*, International Society of Sport Psychology, Athens, Greece, pp. 60–2.

Watt, AP, Morris, T & Andersen, MB (in press), 'Issues of reliability and factor structure of sport imagery ability measures', *Journal of Mental Imagery*.

Watt, T, Morris, T, Lintunen, T, Elfving, T & Riches, D 2001, 'Factor structure of the Sports Imagery Ability Measure (SIAM)', in A Papaioannou, M Goudas & Y Theodorakis (eds), *Proceedings of the Xth World Congress of Sport Psychology, Volume 4*, International Society of Sport Psychology, Athens, Greece, pp. 167–9.

Wehner, T, Vogt, S & Stadler, M 1984, 'Task-specific characteristics during mental training', *Psychological Research*, 46, 389–401.

Weinberg, RS & Gould, D 2003, *Foundations of sport and exercise psychology*, 3rd edn, Human Kinetics, Champaign, IL.

Weinberg, RS, Seabourne, T & Jackson, A 1981, 'Effects of visuo-motor behaviour rehearsal, relaxation and imagery on karate performance', *Journal of Sport Psychology*, 3, 228–38.

Weinberg, RS, Seabourne, T & Jackson, A 1987, 'Arousal and relaxation instructions prior to the use of imagery', *International Journal of Sport Psychology*, 18, 205–14.

White, KD, Ashton, R & Lewis, S 1979, 'Learning a complex skill: effects of mental practice, physical practice, and imagery ability', *International Journal of Sport Psychology*, 10, 71–8.

White, A & Hardy, L 1995, 'Use of different imagery perspectives on the learning and performance of different motor skills', *British Journal of Psychology*, 86, 169–80.

White, A & Hardy, L 1998, 'An in-depth analysis of the uses of imagery by high-level slalom canoeists and artistic gymnasts', *The Sport Psychologist*, 12, 387–403.

Wilkes, RL & Summers, JJ 1984, 'Cognitions, mediating variables, and strength performance', *Journal of Sport Psychology*, 6, 351–9.

Wolpe, J 1958, *Psychotherapy by reciprocal inhibition*, Stanford University Press, Stanford, CA.

Woolfolk, RL, Murphy, SM, Gottesfeld, D & Aitken, D 1985, 'Effects of mental rehearsal of task motor activity and mental depiction of task outcome on motor skill performance', *Journal of Sport Psychology*, 7, 191–7.

Woolfolk, RL, Parrish, W & Murphy, SM 1985, 'The effects of positive and negative imagery on motor skill performance', *Cognitive Therapy and Research*, 9, 235–341.

Wrisberg, CA & Ragsdale, MR 1979, 'Cognitive demand and practice level: factors in the mental rehearsal of motor skills', *Journal of Human Movement Studies*, 5, 201–8.

Ziegler, S 1987, 'Comparison of imagery styles and past experience in skills performance', *Perceptual and Motor Skills*, 64, 579–86.

CHAPTER 14

CONCENTRATION SKILLS IN SPORT: AN APPLIED PERSPECTIVE

Jeffrey Bond & Gregory Sargent

> We can practice for hours and hours, but if our hearts aren't in it, we're not going to get much out of it. We need to bring FOCUS and CONCENTRATION to all our warm-ups.
>
> (Farley & Curry 1994)

This chapter offers an operational definition of concentration that athletes, coaches and applied sport psychologists can relate to, and provides practical suggestions on how concentration may be enhanced. The approach is intentionally practical, drawing on the authors' collective experiences as applied sport psychologists at the Australian Institute of Sport and beyond. It is hoped that readers will find this approach valuable in assisting athletes who have problems with concentration. Other chapters focus on the more theoretical issues arising from the investigation of attention and concentration in sport — issues emerging from the research and theory that continue to contribute to our understanding of these concepts. They discuss a variety of important topics such as definition, the distinction between controlled and automatic processing, the direction of attentional focus, width of attention, and intensity and flexibility in attention. This chapter also discusses important developments in the applied work on concentration since the first edition of this text was published.

The importance of attention or concentration in sporting performance is acknowledged in both training and competition. Coaches and athletes use the terms interchangeably and frequently. We often hear about 'lapses' in concentration, about the need to 'concentrate harder' and so on. Most of us would accept that our concentration levels are generally well under 100 per cent; this is true for elite athletes too. Nevertheless, our brains have an amazing capacity to process information: given the number of cues we focus on, the speed with which our focus can change and the number of irrelevant things we take in seems almost limitless. Adopting an applied perspective demands a focus on skills that can be employed by practitioners, measured and then changed via intervention.

The first section of this chapter examines the importance of concentration from a performance perspective and briefly reviews studies of the components of peak sporting performances. These studies reinforce the central role concentration plays in high-quality sporting performances. The second section examines an applied model of concentration that continues to demonstrate utility for the practising applied sport psychologist. The theoretical constructs underpinning the Nideffer (1976a, 1993a, 1993b) model of attention will be discussed, as will their application in high-performance sport. Nideffer's model has had a great impact on applied sport psychology around the world, notably in terms of the models approach to attention generally, the concept of attentional style and the types of exercises that can be used to develop concentration. The third section of this chapter presents Nideffer's assessment device, the Test of Attentional and Interpersonal Style (TAIS). Psychometric properties, how attentional style is measured, explanations of attentional factors important in sport performance, as well as the test's value as a diagnostic tool in the development of attentional training exercises are presented. In the fourth section we review various concentration exercises that have been found to be useful when working with elite athletes in a variety of sports. These exercises offer a number of different ways in which athletes can be assisted to enhance their control of attentional skills. These drills are readily adaptable to a wide range of sports and can be used by the athlete, coach or applied sport psychologist. They are presented in two parts: those that are specifically linked to sport and those that are not. The final section discusses future approaches to the issue of concentration in applied sport psychology.

THE IMPORTANCE OF FOCUSING ON THE RIGHT THING AT THE RIGHT TIME

Our performances on virtually all tasks depend on our attentional capacity (the ability to focus on the right thing at the right time), yet the efficient application of these capacities is volatile, difficult and at times fragile. The slightest distraction can sometimes have a crucial impact on performance. The following cases illustrate the central importance of concentration skills in high-performance situations.

THE IMPORTANCE OF CONCENTRATION SKILLS

At the 2000 Sydney Olympics, Australian and world 400 m champion Catherine Freeman was expected to win gold in front of her home crowd and under immense worldwide media and public attention. Having lit the cauldron in the massive Olympic stadium to open the games, Cathy had to contend with huge popular expectations to complete the fairytale. It is now history how Cathy coped with the hopes of a nation, successfully focusing on her pre-race plan, blocking out all distractions and allowing the countless hours of training to pay off with a fabulous victory. Many Australians were deeply moved by Cathy's extraordinary effort and felt some of the relief that she experienced as she collapsed on the track after the run. Many other high achievers, such as outstanding swimmers and gold medallists Kieran Perkins, Ian Thorpe and Grant Hackett, have shown a similar commitment and ability to focus under extraordinary pressure.

At the 2003 World Athletic Championships, Australian Jana Pittman displayed incredible stamina and focus to stick with her race plan and defeat the favoured world record holder, Yuliya Pechonkina of Russia, in the women's 400 m hurdles final. It was later reported that Pechonkina had worked hard to upset Pittman's concentration in the period before the final, as reflected in a number of actions. Mike Hurst describes how Pechonkina had moved from across the track to warm up just five metres from Pittman; had warmed up over the same three hurdles that Pittman had laid out; stood in front of Pittman's warm-up group as they rounded the track; and on two occasions sat down next to Pittman in the call-up room, even after Pittman had moved away (Hurst 2003). 'Mind games,' commented Pittman's coach. 'Jana dealt with all of that as well as keeping her cool in the race.' This is the cauldron of elite sport, where concentration and focus are put to the ultimate test.

While there are many such illustrations of the importance of attentional factors on outcomes in elite sport, these cases illustrate the need for sportspeople to fully appreciate the role of concentration and/or attention in performance.

Several practitioners have stressed the importance of attention as a component of performance (e.g. Boutcher 1990, 1992; Nideffer 1976b). Much of the discussion centres on theoretical and research questions. While this theoretical work is important, there is a strong case supporting an applied approach model that will produce positive outcomes for athletes and coaches. This chapter presents information accumulated over many years of applied sport psychology experience with elite athletes across all types of sports and situations. Important theoretical and research issues have been discussed elsewhere (as in chapter 4 of the current text). Our focus here will be on issues with a more intuitive, practical and experiential appeal for the athlete and coach, in the hope that this will help to bridge the much-criticised gap between theory/research and applied practice.

The terms *concentration* and *attention*, as we have noted, are so often used interchangeably by athletes and coaches and in the literature (e.g. Moran 2003) that for the purposes of this chapter we will treat them as synonyms. So what is concentration? Moran (2003) suggests that concentration is the conscious experience of orienting mental effort when perceiving information selectively. (For example, long jumpers focus exclusively on the take-off board as they approach the jump.) In this view, concentration directs a 'spotlight' on the 'target' area (whether objective or subjective). Alternatively, concentration is the ability to focus attention on the set task or what is vital in a situation.

As a skill, concentration is often linked with exceptional athletic performances. Many anecdotal examples may be gleaned from post-performance interviews and other qualitative analyses. Garfield and Bennett (1984), investigating the components of exceptional performances, proposed eight physical and mental capacities described by elite athletes as associated with those moments when they perform extraordinarily well. Of these eight, three were particularly associated with high levels of concentration. These were 'mentally relaxed' (an inner calm, a sense of control and a high degree of concentration), 'a sense of being focused in the present with a feeling of "harmony between the mental and physical"' (being absorbed in the present with no thoughts about the past or future), and 'a feeling of being in a state of extraordinary awareness' (acute awareness of their body as well as the space around them). The importance of concentration and attention is further emphasised by Garfield and Bennett's peak performance 'compass', with attention having a major role.

Vanden Auweele, de Cuyper, van Mele and Rzewnicki (1993) described eight further studies investigating peak performance. Consistently, factors such as being centred on a limited stimulus field, being in a cocoon, displaying a clear knowledge of task demands and a determination to complete a task were reported in these studies. Once again, concentration appeared to be a central element of all these facets. Butler and Hardy's (1992) work with performance profiles also reinforced the central role of concentration as a major component of elite performance. Jones (1993) applied a performance profiling methodology when assessing the effectiveness of a cognitive behavioural intervention with an international racket ball player. Significant improvements were reported in the ability to cope with pressure at three and six months after intervention, with changes in concentration being the most significant.

We can conclude from research, from reports from athletes and coaches, and also intuitively that concentration on the right thing at the right time is a crucial component of a highly skilled sporting performance. Moran (2003) stated that both anecdotal and empirical evidence support its efficacy. His empirical evidence was drawn from studies with sprinters: those advised to focus on task-relevant cues ran faster compared with those who did not. Anecdotal testimonials from a range of athletes further support this view. Furthermore, interesting information from other sources such as psychophysiological research again emphasises the importance of concentration and attention. For example, Hatfield, Landers and Ray (1984) investigated left- and right-brain EEG activity in a sample of elite shooters while either shooting or performing other mental tasks. The authors found that elite shooters possessed more highly tuned attentional foci, and that they could effectively reduce conscious mental activities of the left hemisphere and thereby minimise distraction. These findings clearly highlight the role that attentional control plays in elite sport.

CONCENTRATION SKILLS AS A CENTRAL COMPONENT OF HIGH-LEVEL PERFORMANCE

A landmark study conducted by Orlick and Partington (1988) investigated qualitative elements that contributed to the success and mental readiness of a Canadian Olympic squad. The role of concentration as a central component of performance was repeatedly reinforced, as the following comments make clear. On *quality training*: 'When I'm training, I'm focused ... By focusing all the time on what you're doing when you're training, focusing in a race becomes a by-product ...' (p. 111). On *mental preparation for competition*: 'Most pre-competition plans included ... reminders to focus on what had previously worked well ... and doing the best we could. I concentrated on that a lot' (p. 115). On a *competition focus plan*: 'My focus was very concentrated throughout the race. We have a short plan, and in it I concentrate only on the first few strokes. I've found that if I concentrate beyond that, those first strokes won't be strong enough' (p. 116). On *competition evaluation*: 'If the performance was off ... I tried to assess why, paying particular attention to my mental state or focus before and during competition' (p. 116). On *distraction control*: 'I [performed] better if I concentrated on my [performance] instead of concentrating on everyone else ... I decided to stop looking at everyone else, just be prepared for my next [effort]' (pp. 117–18).

From the applied sport psychologist's perspective, and in the interests of performance enhancement, it is essential that we identify useful and applicable models from the theoretical and research literature. A critical issue for practitioners is the existence of a model of attention that can be applied in sporting situations, that can be readily understood and accepted by athletes and coaches, and that will lead to an enhanced understanding, prediction and control over attentional capacities in high-performance situations.

THE NIDEFFER ATTENTION MODEL

Robert Nideffer's background in martial arts and competitive diving led him to the development of a model of attention and a theory of attentional and interpersonal style that he suggests would aid in the understanding, prediction and control of behaviour (Nideffer 1976a, 1981). Nideffer's attention model proposes the existence of two dimensions of concentration: direction and width. We can, he suggests, direct our attention in one of two ways in order to attend to relevant performance cues. We can focus our attention on external cues (e.g. a target, ball, team-mate, opponent) or internal cues (e.g. thoughts, images, feelings, kinaesthetic sensations). This dimension of direction is often seen as a dichotomy according to which attentional focus is either external or internal, not somewhere between. By contrast, Nideffer (1981) proposed that we can choose to attend to a large or small number of cues, and that this dimension probably extends along a continuum. There are therefore a possible four types of attention (see figure 14.1). Additionally, although our main emphasis in sport is often visual, Nideffer's model is not simply a model of visual attention. Attention actually involves the use of each of the human senses of sight, sound, feel, taste and smell.

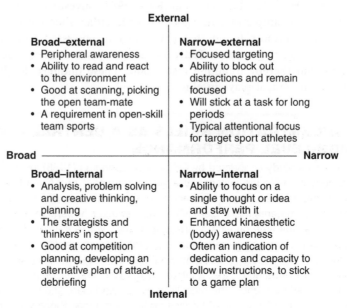

External

Broad–external
- Peripheral awareness
- Ability to read and react to the environment
- Good at scanning, picking the open team-mate
- A requirement in open-skill team sports

Narrow–external
- Focused targeting
- Ability to block out distractions and remain focused
- Will stick at a task for long periods
- Typical attentional focus for target sport athletes

Broad ———————————————————— **Narrow**

Broad–internal
- Analysis, problem solving and creative thinking, planning
- The strategists and 'thinkers' in sport
- Good at competition planning, developing an alternative plan of attack, debriefing

Narrow–internal
- Ability to focus on a single thought or idea and stay with it
- Enhanced kinaesthetic (body) awareness
- Often an indication of dedication and capacity to follow instructions, to stick to a game plan

Internal

Figure 14.1   Nideffer's (1981) model of attention

Athletes who adopt a broad–external focus of attention in response to the demands of a performance situation attend to a large number of cues relating to the external environment. There are some sports (e.g. many team and open-skill sports) in which one would intuitively expect such an attentional focus to be preferable for a significant part of the game. In team sports involving fast ball activities, such as the various football codes, basketball, netball, and field and ice hockey, one major attentional requirement is commonly referred to as *field* or *peripheral awareness*. This type of awareness is not exclusively the realm of open-skill sports, as there are identifiable times in static, target sports when the ability to read and react to the environment is essential for high-level performance. When we observe that athletes have above-average ability to be aware of what is occurring around them (e.g. knowing where their team-mates and opponents are), we are describing a broad–external focus. These athletes quickly read a situation and instantly can find the best passing option; in contact sports they are rarely hit. They seem to have an extra sense that makes them special athletes.

When adopting a broad–internal focus of attention, the athlete shifts the focus of concentration towards internal thoughts, feelings, images and self-talk. There are many situations in sport in which it is necessary for the athlete to use a broad–internal focus. These typically involve planning, problem-solving, reminding oneself of specific coaching instructions, imagining or visualising aspects of the performance, and debriefing after a performance. Nideffer (1981) described this as an analytical, thinking type of concentration. Most of us can probably identify an athlete we know who is a master strategist, a great problem-solver and extremely analytical. This same athlete was probably very good at planning and writing creative essays in school. They are the thinkers in sport and perform exceptionally well in those areas of sport that demand a high capacity for analysis and creativity.

Some sports demand that athletes adopt a narrow–external focus of attention at specific times. Target sports such as archery and shooting require a good deal of narrowing in order to be successful. Even open-skill team sports have clearly identifiable times when the athlete must narrow down and block out distractions in order to be successful (e.g. when shooting for goal or passing the ball). Athletes who have an exceptional capacity to focus in a narrow–external way are very good at keeping the blinkers on, at remaining focused despite distractions, and at targeting for extended periods of time. These athletes will often be oblivious to spectator noise and movements around them.

Nideffer's (1981) narrow–internal focus of attention is required on those occasions when an athlete must remember a single coaching point (e.g. 'keep in front!'), must focus on a specific kinaesthetic feeling or must flash up an immediate image of part of the action. This type of attention is internal in that it involves an instant of thought, feeling, self-talk or image, and narrow because it is focused on very few attentional cues.

Nideffer (1981) drew attention to the relationship between attentional efficiency and level of arousal. Under conditions of ideal arousal (physiological and psychological), Nideffer postulated that an athlete will effectively match the attentional demands of the performance with an appropriate focus of attention. An athlete who has achieved an ideal arousal level is able to shift attention very quickly, and without the need for conscious thought, to match the rapidly changing demands of the performance situation. This is confirmed in the reports of athletes who have experienced peak performances and described being in an almost trance-like state in which there was little conscious thought. Such a state is often associated with flow (see chapter 15). It seems that prior experience in identical situations, a thorough knowledge of and control over the skill requirements, superior levels of physical conditioning and an appropriate level of achievement motivation might combine with an ideal arousal level and effective matching of the attentional demands to provide the antecedents for an intuitive level of optimal performance.

Attentional errors

Most concentration problems in sport appear to arise because performers fail to pay attention to the optimal cues or are distracted by other cues. Nideffer (1976b, 1981), Nideffer and Pratt (1981), and Griffiths (1999) have suggested that athletes can make the following kinds of attentional errors.

Attentional mismatch

Nideffer (1976b, 1981) proposed that individuals possess a unique attentional style characterised by specific strengths and weaknesses in the various areas of attention. An individual's developmental background, including long-term involvement in specific activities requiring specific types of attentional focus, and specific personality traits may contribute to the development of a unique attentional style. This suggestion by Nideffer conforms with the view of those theorists who have developed trait personality theories (e.g. Cattell 1957).

Because an athlete may have a dominant attentional style — for example, a high-level broad–external focus — it is feasible that under stressful conditions the athlete will subconsciously return to that style of attention in circumstances in which a different attentional focus might be more appropriate. This involuntary return to an existing attentional strength may occur because the athlete has successfully used his or her attentional strength to advantage in previous high-stress situations. The broad–external athlete may mismatch the attentional demands of the performance situation and become too influenced by the surrounding environment. Behaviourally, a coach would observe an athlete who was very distractible under stress. How often do we see a professional tennis player during a critical point in a major tournament interrupt a service action because someone has moved in the back corner of the spectator area (nowhere near the line of sight for the serve)?

The broad–internal athlete is likely to mismatch the attentional requirements of a performance because he or she is focused on a range of internal cues at a time when other cues, whether external or more narrow, are more important. Under high-stress conditions this athlete will become very analytical, and will therefore be slow to react to external cues. This athlete may not 'read' the passing options or may overlook an appropriate cue. Some years ago an AFL footballer who was within kicking distance and running towards goal during a particularly intense and important part of the game, was knocked unconscious by an opponent in a fair tackle on open ground. The 100 000 spectators in the stands could see the tackle coming, but the player was presumably reminding himself of the importance of this potentially match-winning goal (and perhaps on the consequences of a missed kick at goal). The player was unable to focus in a way that would have revealed his opponent running at full speed straight at him from a shallow angle. This clear example of attentional mismatch may have been related to the inappropriate return to an attentional (broad–internal) strength under pressure.

The athlete whose attentional style is characterised by a strength in either of the narrowing areas is likely to use that type of focus under high-stress conditions and make mistakes because he or she misses important information by being too narrow or by focusing narrowly on the wrong cue. During the 1988 Calgary Winter Olympics the team sport psychologist was approached by an alpine skier immediately before a race with a request to assist in blocking out a real fear of injury/accident. It was apparent that the skier's focus had inappropriately narrowed onto a cue that was likely to increase the likelihood of a fall. The intensity of that particular cue was so great that the athlete was unable to clear his mind and focus on more positive aspects of his performance. Athletes who find it impossible to shift their focus from an existing injury while performing experience similar concerns.

Inability to adopt or maintain appropriate attentional focus

This inability may occur because the athlete has not sufficiently developed a particular type of attentional focus. For example, an athlete who has below-average capacity to effectively narrow attention (perhaps the individual has a developmental background that has enhanced other attentional capacities) may find it difficult to produce a narrow focus when required in a performance. Such athletes will very likely make mistakes because they are unable to narrow appropriately onto the cues important for successful performance of the skill. Many athletes train for long periods of time to improve their ability to narrow onto appropriate cues. Coaches can of course assist athletes to identify the appropriate cue and then design specific drills to enhance the athlete's capacity to utilise this attentional focus.

Internal and external overloads

In high-stress situations, athletes produce errors because their attentional capacity is exceeded by the overwhelming nature of the stimuli. Internal overloads occur because the athlete simply has too much internal information clogging up the attentional system. There are too many coaching points, too many 'what ifs' or too much self-talk. Examples of internal overload are common in sporting situations in which the stakes are high, the consequences of failure are extremely significant, or the athlete feels externally controlled and dominated by a need to please others. External overloads occur under stressful circumstances in which the athlete is bombarded by too much external information. This typically occurs in major competitions, where large numbers of athletes compete, large crowds are watching and a significant media presence is apparent. Olympic Games are a trap for the uninitiated and inexperienced young athlete unused to such a flood of potentially distracting information.

Involuntary internal narrowing

Under critical stress conditions, Nideffer (1976b, 1981) predicted that athletes will ultimately focus inwards in a very narrow way and make mistakes because they are 'paralysed' by the situational stresses. Athletes who find themselves in life-threatening situations often experience an involuntary narrowing that may be part of a final-stage protective survival mechanism. In life-threatening, 'fire in the theatre' situations, people may have been killed because they narrowed their attention so much that they ignored other alternative exits.

Choking

One of the ugliest labels in sport is that of 'the choker', according to Mack and Casstevens (2001). Yet it is a situation many athletes experience at some stage in their careers. Many perceive choking as a normal human reaction to a high-pressure situation and as a physiological response to a perceived psychological threat. It is characterised by a loss of control or focus, and is typically associated with contests of high emotional importance to the athlete (such as the eighteenth hole of a golf tournament or the last game of a tough five-setter in tennis). Choking is often described as feeling extreme pressure, muscle tightening, respiration increase, dry mouth and damp palms leading to attention changes and performance decrement. Choking also provides real-life examples of attentional errors linked to an overapplication of internal narrowing.

THE IMPACT OF CHOKING ON PERFORMANCE

Top golf professionals often lose tournaments worth millions of dollars because they inadvertently shift their focus from the shot they are about to hit to the consequences of making a mistake at an important moment of the round. Those who watched the 1999 British Open might remember Belgian Jean Van de Velde's agonising performance in the last few holes as he lost his commanding lead to hand Scot Paul Lawrie an extraordinary and unexpected victory. Did Van de Velde lack the required technical skills, or was it a case of an ineffective attentional focus? One can only imagine the extreme levels of stress that contributed to an inward shifting of focus, so that he became overly analytical, unable to accurately read the situation and make 'rational' decisions. Once in this negative spiral initiated by a simple mistake at a crucial time, Van de Velde's game seemed to fall apart. This case illustrates sadly how all the technical and physical ability in the world cannot make up for an inefficient application of concentration under the pressure of high-performance sport. The case of Jana Novotna in the 1993 Women's Wimbledon tennis final offers a similar example of a classic psychological 'choke' situation. (See chapter 3 for an alternative perspective of these cases.)

Marchant and Sargent (2002) presented a number of tips to address choking. These include challenging negatives and replacing them with positives; recognising that athletes internally verbalise incorrect thinking when under pressure and that such negative self-talk needs to be reversed; developing routines to assist with coping under pressure to ensure that distractive self-talk is replaced by task-relevant cues; utilising effective brief relaxation procedures in order to control the anxiety linked to choking; and encouraging athletes to accept that pressure is partly self-imposed, so by changing thought patterns they have in their control an effective tool to change the perception of pressure. Internalisation of such tips will hopefully reduce the impact of such an experience.

Using the model

In applied sport psychology settings, the Nideffer attentional model has been used to enhance understanding of the nature of concentration and how it might explain what happens in performances (Bond 1984). There have been many occasions when work with elite athletes has been enhanced by the use of this model. It makes intuitive sense to coaches and athletes, who can relate the model directly to sporting situations. Furthermore, the model assists with post-performance analyses, which centre on those factors influential in a performance. For some athletes a clear and applied description of the Nideffer model is sufficient for them to develop their own self-help attentional strategies.

An example of the latter involved a volleyball player who sought assistance with a problem she was having related to her spiking skill. She could spike well in practice, but under the stress of a game she misdirected her spikes into the waiting opposition blockers. Initially this recurring error was analysed as a technical problem. After considerable practice there was little change in the percentage improvement of successful spikes. It seemed that the harder she tried, the worse things became. The player, it transpired, described herself as having an attentional style dominated by a narrow–external focus. Following detailed discussion of the Nideffer model, she decided to adjust her attentional focus during spiking. She believed she had been focusing on the ball too narrowly (a legacy of the traditional coaching instruction to 'keep your eye on the ball') and could probably improve her awareness of the position of the opposition blockers if she looked when approaching the hitting zone at a point between the ball and the position of the blockers' hands. Because she understood the importance of a controlled level of arousal during spiking, she practised taking a preliminary centring breath before starting her run in, and relaxing her upper body as she jumped for the spike. This, combined with the shift in visual focus, produced a significant improvement in her spiking statistics.

APPLYING THE NIDEFFER ATTENTIONAL MODEL

Scully and Kremer (2000) presented a recent application of the Nideffer attentional model when discussing the sequence of attention required for a golf shot. Golfers begin in the *preliminary phase*, in which the player moves from broad–external (gathering information needed to assess the requirements of the shot), to broad–internal (examining his or her personal abilities and preferences), then narrow–external focus (club selection). Next, in the *set-up phase* players adopt narrow–external (concentrating on the target) then narrow–internal (feeling the perfect shot) and then narrow–external focus (thinking through the immediate target about a metre in front of the ball in line with the final goal). Finally, in the *swing phase* players use narrow–external (observing the results), then narrow–internal (capturing the feeling of the shot), then broad–external (analysing the shot relative to previous correct or poor decisions) and finally narrow–internal (experiencing the feeling of the correct swing). This sequence serves to demonstrate the complex attentional demands of a sport skill requiring continual changing across the attentional styles. These changes were actually incorporated into the individual's pre-performance routine in order to enhance subsequent performance.

THE TEST OF ATTENTIONAL AND INTERPERSONAL STYLE (TAIS)

The Test of Attentional and Interpersonal Style (TAIS) was developed by Nideffer as a means of measuring a number of attentional and interpersonal characteristics that might be applicable in a range of situations, including high-performance sport (Nideffer 1976a, 1976b). The instrument was designed to examine behaviourally relevant characteristics, is multidimensional and looks at cognitive styles (attentional processes) as well as interpersonal characteristics. Nideffer (1990) postulated that both attentional and interpersonal characteristics have state and trait components, and that these can be examined by manipulating arousal.

The TAIS has been used extensively in Australian sport over the past 25 years as a means of identifying individual elite athlete characteristics related to high-performance sport. In the past the TAIS has demonstrated internal consistency and good test–retest reliability (Nideffer 1976a). Other studies have confirmed construct validity (e.g. Antonelli, Caldarone & Gatti 1982; DePalma & Nideffer 1977; Feifel, Strack & Nagy 1987), while support for its predictive validity has been described frequently (e.g. Bond & Nideffer 1992; Landers & Richards 1980; Reis & Bird 1982). A number of studies have questioned the validity of the TAIS factor structure and its predictive utility, and argued for the development of more sport-specific versions of the test. Interest in the model underlying the attentional subscales of the TAIS has prompted the development of a number of sport-specific versions, including for tennis (Van Schoyck & Grasha 1981), baseball and softball batting (Albrecht & Feltz 1987), and basketball (Vallerand 1983). For a rebuttal to the studies that have criticised various aspects of the TAIS, the reader is referred to Nideffer (1990).

Applied sport psychologists use the TAIS as a means of assisting athletes to understand their attentional style and as a diagnostic tool for helping to explain performance-related phenomena that affect the athlete and/or coach. This is clearly demonstrated in Griffith's recent (1999) publication. On the basis of further consensual validation of the TAIS subscale scores (from coach reports, athlete interviews, structured observations and performance statistics), attentional training strategies are designed with the coach and athlete.

Figure 14.2 provides an example from the attentional subscale portion of a full TAIS completed by an elite athlete with a response set based on the following assumptions: answers given would be as honest and accurate as possible; there were no right or wrong answers; the results would not be used for selection purposes; and the results would remain confidential and be returned directly to the athlete as a means of enhancing performance. Athletes should always be directed to relate the behavioural descriptions in the TAIS questionnaire to their own training and competition situations in such a way that the 'average' athlete in their group would respond 'sometimes' to most of the questions.

This athlete's attentional profile shows a clear strength in the capacity to use a broad–external focus of attention (high BET). This was confirmed by the athlete via a number of examples from training and competition situations. There was discussion about a prediction that arose from this attentional strength — that during times of increased arousal the athlete might subconsciously revert to the use of this type of focus at the expense of a concentration focus that would be more appropriate to high-quality performance. Further discussion centred on learning to control arousal levels before entering that type of situation in competitions. Also, the athlete was encouraged to focus on identifying attentional cues appropriate to that specific situation. The coach was advised to develop a drill requiring that the athlete adopt a specific type of focus (NAR), and to progressively increase the competitive intensity as a way of 'testing' the athlete's ability to maintain the appropriate focus.

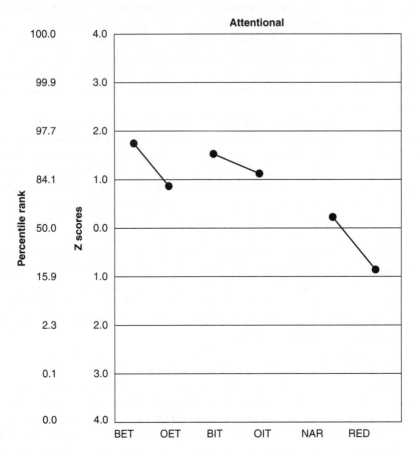

Note: For the purpose of discussion, only the six subscales from the complete TAIS are shown here — see below. A more complete TAIS diagnostic interpretation is obtained by using all of the 19 TAIS attentional and interpersonal subscales.

Attentional subscales — brief description

BET Broad External Focus — measures the ability to assess the environment: to read, react to and integrate multiple environmental cues at once.

OET Overloaded by External Stimuli — measures the tendency to become distracted and overloaded by too many environmental cues.

BIT Broad Internal Focus — measures the ability to analyse, plan, anticipate and deal with multiple internal cues.

OIT Overloaded by Internal Stimuli — measures the tendency to make mistakes because of an overly analytical focus, or thinking about too many things at once.

NAR Narrow focus — measures the ability to narrow attention when required and to avoid distraction.

RED Reduced Attentional Focus — measures the tendency to make mistakes because of a failure to attend to all task-relevant cues, a failure to shift from an external focus to an internal one, and vice versa.

Figure 14.2 Example of an effective attentional subscale portion of a TAIS for an elite athlete

Figure 14.3 shows an attentional style that demonstrates a tendency to experience external and internal overloads (high OET and OIT) under pressure and an inability to narrow attention (low NAR) when required. Following further validation of the examples, which the athlete discussed during an individual TAIS feedback session, the athlete and sport psychologist discussed the need for improved arousal control strategies (centring breath), an investigation of some of the cognitive components contributing to the excessive anxiety the athlete typically experienced in this situation, and the identification of specific cues important in the efficient execution of the specific skill required. These strategies were further enhanced by the use of carefully structured imagery sessions and a transfer to training and low-level competition situations.

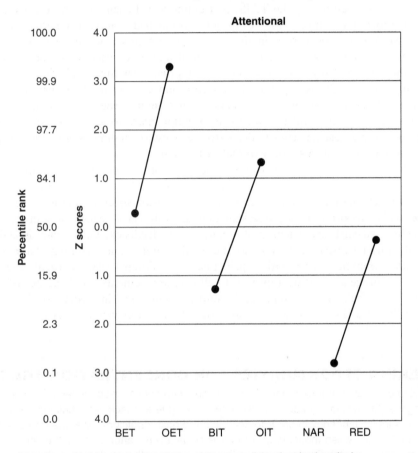

(*See figure 14.2 for a brief description of the above attentional subscales.*)

Figure 14.3 Example of overloaded attentional subscales on the TAIS for an elite athlete

SPECIFIC ATTENTIONAL TRAINING EXERCISES FOR ATHLETES

German international soccer player Jurgen Klinsman stated that 'you have to concentrate all the time so when a chance comes you're going to take it' (Moran 2003, p. 166). Tennis great Martina Navratilova commented that 'concentration is born on the practice court ... you must mentally treat your practice sessions as matches, concentrating on every ball you hit' (Mack & Casstevens 2001, p. 166). These observations remind us that concentration is a skill that can be improved and worked on just like a physical skill (e.g. Jones 1993).

A recent study by Nideffer, Sagal, Lowry and Bond (2001), involving an analysis of the TAIS data of some 4500 elite athlete scholarship holders at the Australian Institute of Sport, 142 Olympic and World Championship medallists and a non-sport standardised comparison group, highlighted the positive development of attentional abilities over time (presumably as a result of combined learning, experience and age maturation). The TAIS data were derived from longitudinal, cross-sectional and test–retest testing, and confirmed the importance of concentration characteristics in high performance. As predicted, the combined attentional, intra- and interpersonal characteristics measured by the TAIS differentiated membership of the three groups (non-sport, AIS athlete and Olympic/World Championship medallists). Importantly, the cognitive and intra- and interpersonal characteristics (as measured by the TAIS) that define world champions were consistent across gender, sport and culture). Athletes in both groups had significantly better concentration skills than the average person in the non-sport comparison group. This study confirms that, given access to appropriate psychological and elite coaching support and training programs, elite athletes' concentration skills improve over time. This finding underscores the importance of the recognition of concentration as a set of skills that can respond to specific aspects of a performance enhancement training program. This important study also showed that elite athletes can focus attention more exactly, can effectively narrow attention to task-relevant cues under extreme stress (including fatigue and competition), and can block out internal and external distractions.

This study also reminds us of the importance of considering a range of other factors that are important to the development of mental skills such as concentration. These include practising mental skills (athletes must set aside specific time for exercises, while the coach's support is vital); assessing mental skills via a variety of sources (including individual self-analysis, coaching observations and feedback, video analysis and psychological profiling instruments such as the TAIS); timing and planning elements of concentration training (periodisation principles (see Bompa 1983; Sargent 1997; Spence 2001) encourage a scientific approach to all training elements); and the need for athletes to be fully trained in coping and control techniques in order to deal with any demanding situation (such as being able to reduce and elevate arousal levels as the situation demands).

SEEKING OPPORTUNITIES FOR CONCENTRATION TRAINING

Athletes experience frequent periods in training when concentration is tested. These include during weight training or endurance work (when fatigue and lactic acid build-up lead to a 'back off just a touch' tendency in order to complete the next repetition), or at the end of a long training session (when thoughts turn towards social events after training, the warm shower, dinner arrangements). Similar opportunities occur across the whole range of training activities. Tougher situations provide tests of mental toughness in which internal conflict between avoiding injury and striving for success need to be balanced. They also provide opportunities for intense focusing on appropriate technical cues for successful completion of the set task, rather than succumbing to the negative internal voice that could lead to a mistake or tailing off of performance. These situations reflect the demands experienced during lengthy competitions that require athletes to practise lifting their concentration up a notch to task-relevant or specific technical cues. Athletes are also encouraged to actively seek out opportunities for concentration training and to regularly practise them. With a positive approach and appropriate reflection, athletes will become more skilled at utilising the most appropriate attentional focus when under different types of stress, leading to enhanced confidence in their ability to cope in any situation.

We believe that an applied chapter such as this one should place a major emphasis on presenting appropriate exercises for the development of attentional skills. The next two sections deal with some of the exercises (sport and non-sport related) that have been described in the literature and some additional drills that we use on a regular basis with elite Australian athletes. Any list of training exercises can never be complete, so readers are encouraged to be creative in developing specific concentration exercises to include in their own programs. Such creativity should also be applied when altering exercises previously used in other sports or circumstances.

Sport-related activities

This section deals first with exercises highlighting cognitive aspects of sport-related activities, before moving on to those requiring thought with body movement, then preparation along the lines of mental skills, and finally group and individual activities.

Sport object focusing

For this exercise, athletes require a specific object from their particular sport on which to concentrate (e.g. a racquet, ball, shoe or piece of clothing). The task demands examination of the object in as much detail as possible while at the same time ensuring that distractions from the immediate environment or beyond do not inhibit this concentration. As with many of these tasks, athletes may initially find this difficult to do, and it may be necessary to begin by working in 30-second periods followed by rest. Athletes assume a relaxed position in an environment free of obvious or potential distractions. They then hold the object in front of them while repeating a meaningful cue word that relates to that object. (A slight variation is to use an object that is not directly related to their sport.) The object can then be taken away and the athlete instructed to use the cue word to 'return' the object to consciousness.

The use of specific cue words during actual performance to block out irrelevant thoughts or when concentration is waning is often reported by elite athletes. With practice, athletes should aim to retain focus for up to five minutes. At this level, athletes can be extended so that they alternate between a narrow concentration on the object and a broadening of focus to other objects in the field of vision before a return to the narrow focus again. Introducing other distractions can add to task difficulty. Additionally, Moran (2003) suggested that coaches check what information players describe during observation activities: Was the ball spinning in a certain way? Did it land where you thought it would? This feedback encourages players to become more attuned to their focusing.

Using specific cues

Cues have been found to be most beneficial for athletes in regaining concentration when distracted or ensuring that they remain properly focused. Many sport psychologists have emphasised the value of cues or triggers. Bull and his colleagues (Bull, Albinson & Shambrook 1996; Bull 2000) stressed the importance of cues to assist athletes in switching to high attentional intensity. Cues help athletes to focus on the key factors that contribute to optimal performance. For example, track athletes might use cue words (self-talk instructions) such as 'relax', 'see a tunnel', 'stay in touch' or 'rhythmic movements' to assist them in remaining properly focused. Other athletes might develop a series of cue types, including verbal ('focus', 'switch on', 'ready'); visual (watch your opposition about to serve, look at the strings on your racquet); and physical (wipe your hand on your shirt, tap the bat on the home plate). It is important that players develop individualised cues. It is also imperative that cues are practised consistently in order that they become automatic and effective in competition. (Coaches often ask players to 'watch the ball' as a concentration tip, which seems somewhat vague.)

Positive self-talk

A technique (borrowed from meditation practice and the use of positive affirmations) that is used regularly in the applied sport setting is the repetition of positive statements in a self-talk format (e.g. 'I am feeling fit and ready to go' or 'I feel relaxed and happy with my form'). These statements are often listed in a poster-style format and displayed in athletes' rooms for continual referral. This type of affirmation helps ensure that athletes are in a focused frame of mind when preparing for training or competition. The poster style can also be adopted for the display of other reminders to athletes to stay in a correct concentrational mode. A list of daily mental goals, inspirational quotes and uplifting songs have also been presented in this way and have proved valuable for many athletes.

Switching on and off

This technique requires athletes to identify appropriate points at which to 'switch on' (when ready to train or compete) and 'switch off' (when to shift to non-sport thoughts) in their daily schedule. For example, athletes may use entering the locker room or starting a pre-training stretch as the 'switch on' point for a training session, and stepping into the shower as the 'switch off' point after the session. The daily schedule consists of a series of 'switch on' and 'switch off' triggers. The emphasis, of course, is on the need to be effectively focused during the 'switch on' period while still allowing for recovery (of concentration and mental energy) during the 'switch off' periods.

'Parking' thoughts

A very effective behavioural tool for dealing with intruding thoughts is to 'park' them. This effectively means putting them aside for another time, typically by using a rational self-talk instruction or form of visualisation that places the troublesome thought in a safe and non-distracting place until after the performance. This device is extremely effective for athletes who tend to bring outside issues into competition situations. Sometimes athletes are advised to record distractions (literally or metaphorically in their imagination) and then to put them in some safe locked place (this 'parking' component could be a box or an imaginary vault). After performing, the athletes 'unpark' the issues and deal with them. The technique ensures that competition is not distracted by extraneous intrusions, which are dealt with more appropriately after the event.

Murray (1999) described an exercise used successfully with tennis players as an alternative to the usual 'parking' approach. Murray calls it 'build a home on the tennis court', and it effectively describes a place to go during a game in times of need. Some players go to the extent of marking off a one-metre square, using a towel to construct the boundaries. This 'home' functions as a sanctuary where, between points and change-overs, you know you will be protected from any distraction. Your home just may give you that important edge on the court.

Murray (1999) described 'thought freezing' as a way of examining player focus. To examine concentration, players are asked to describe the content of their focus at any stage that a coach yells out 'freeze'. The exercise is effective in ensuring athletes are kept in touch with their feelings, thoughts and concentration, while encouraging them to learn more about how they process information during a game, how to exert control over their attention and whether their focus is optimal. Thought freezing is similar to the thought stoppage approach often described in texts.

Distraction training

Distractions, a problem that is central to any study of concentration, can be either internal or external. External environmental factors include crowd noise, obstructed view or gamesmanship. The latter is a tactic often used to distract and upset concentration. Moran (2003) described a number of examples of this ploy including sledging (trash talking or taunting), physical intimidation, provocative tactics (spitting, pinching or manhandling) and even physical obstruction. Internal distractions, which stem from thoughts, feelings or body sensations, include overanalyses, regretting mistakes made, feeling anxious or tired, and worrying about performance evaluation.

Inventive practitioners have developed many different ways to distract athletes in training through the use of loud noise, fatigue, heightened arousal, visual distractions and so on. The purpose of introducing these distractions during training is to enhance the athletes' ability to maintain their focus on task-relevant/process execution cues and to train them to switch focus more effectively. For example, a coach might introduce an exercise in which athletes perform specific technical skills when already fatigued by running or even after sleep deprivation. In one recent example, the AIS archery squad agreed to be subjected to an extended period of sleep deprivation followed by an intra-squad competition shoot. In another case, the national netball squad were awoken at 2 am to do push-ups and other running activities before being woken again at 6 am for physical challenges requiring clear thought and teamwork.

On other occasions AIS and national teams have trained with loud noises in the background. Regular training sessions have been conducted with the AIS tennis players using high-powered radios set to produce annoying static. Players are then given the task of serving to stay in the set or match (i.e. serving from 15–40 down). Before they serve, they are required to undergo a short burst of physical activity to elevate their heart rate and muscle tension. Servers then have to step up to the service line and serve to avoid the service break. Blocking out the annoying loud noise, maintaining composure by controlling their elevated arousal, narrowing their focus to the service target and their regular routine while ensuring the 'feel' for their best service action takes considerable effort. To add even further stress to the situation, line umpires are sometimes asked to make wrong calls as a way of testing out the coping ability of players. Over time, the players become more and more accustomed to dealing with elevated arousal and distraction.

Similar types of distraction training have been adapted for a wide variety of sports. Glad and Beck (1999) described golfers being required to play a round while other players intentionally tried to distract them from their game, for example through talking at inappropriate times. Importantly, after any of these tasks players must fully debrief and discuss how they coped, what impact the distractions had on their performances and what they might do in the future should a similar situation arise. Glad and Beck also described a technique for fine-tuning focus ability. The authors suggested using a radio, TV, DVD or video player to sharpen attention and concentration skills. Players are required to watch a set period of television (about four minutes of videotape or DVD) and then to recall as much detail as possible. The task can be made more difficult by introducing different distractions. To determine how much introduced sounds affect their degree of concentration, athletes might then be required to do the same activity while a radio is playing.

Centring

Many concentration activities are time-consuming. The attraction of the centring exercise is that it is very quick and specifically designed to be used at the sporting site. Centring is an example of a relaxation technique that doubles as a form of attentional shifting or refocusing (Nideffer 1976b, 1981, 1989). This one- or two-breath technique serves as a form of preparation for more effective and appropriate concentration.

An Australian tennis champion used centring techniques as a way of clearing his thoughts before serving and waiting to return service. Part of this player's pre-service routine involved a centring breath to bring in the focus of attention (narrow–internal) as a blocking-out technique. In order to feel his centre of gravity sink down as he breathed out, he could not be thinking about other details or attending to external cues. The centring breath also reduced his arousal level and minimised upper body muscle tension (to the levels optimal for a fluid service action). Following the centring breath the player shifted his focus onto the service target (a specific mark on the service court) and from there to the position of the ball toss before serving.

Routines and segmenting before and during performance

One of the building blocks of consistent high-quality performances is the development of high-quality routines both before and during performance (Bond 1985; Clarkson 1999; Orlick 1986a, 1986b; Rushall 1979). Many athletes have been assisted towards successful competition outcomes by having them prepare specific performance plans, which are in fact attentional cue sequences perceived by both athlete and coach as a significant part of a successful performance. An effective routine includes a refocusing section as part of the package. Once the routine is established, the athlete is assisted to learn it through mental practice (visualisation), by writing it down, by placing the point-by-point description in a visible place, by recording it on audiotape and listening to the audiotape in a variety of situations (including salt-water flotation sessions), and by physically practising the routines in training sessions, competition simulations and low-level competitions.

Cohn (1990) examined both the theoretical and empirical factors surrounding the creation of routines. Among his conclusions were that the chosen routine should reflect the tempo and feel of the activity in order to prepare the appropriate mind-set. The routine should also take into account some awareness of the learning stage of the performer, which might indicate more clearly defined cognitive steps or something more automatic. Chosen cue words could also reflect this difference to encourage direct concentration on important aspects while retaining optimal arousal. Cohn also advocated an awareness of performers' specific individual characteristics to ensure that routines reflect their dominant perceptual style as well as any coping difficulties.

RESEARCH REINFORCING THE EFFICACY OF PRE-PERFORMANCE ROUTINES

Farrow and Kemp (2003) discussed the efficacy of pre-performance routines from a number of different research perspectives. First, they reported on routines used in a variety of sports — namely, golf, tennis and basketball. The shorter the time of the routine (regardless of the number of behaviours in that routine), they reported, the more successful the performance. Second, the high use of routines in Australian Rules football is indirectly reflected by the fact that the time to take a set shot at goal has increased by 54 per cent (from 17.6 seconds to 27.1 seconds) over the past 40 years since the use of routines became popular. Finally, the accuracy of performance has not increased at the same rate as this change in the use of routines. Only super goal-kicker Matthew Lloyd of Essendon has a conversion rate approaching 75 per cent. He also has one of the most recognised routines, as evidenced by his trademark flinging of grass in to the air, even when playing indoors! In a recent discussion about his routine (Timms 2003), Lloyd described how it had taken a long time to fine-tune his routine and that he does the routine pretty much automatically and without thought.

Response to errors

Many athletes report that after they make a mistake they find it difficult to refocus and 'get back on track'. A useful technique is to use the error as an opportunity to learn by very quickly analysing why the error was made and then mentally rehearsing the skill again, except this time ensuring that it is done perfectly. In this way the athlete learns from the experience, and also sees any errors as challenges (to be turned into a positive self-instruction) rather than as negative and emotion-disturbing mistakes. Such a rationalisation is effective for retaining confidence and a high self-image. Injured athletes can also use this thought switching approach by not concentrating on the negative aspects of the injury but, rather, using it as an opportunity to learn so that in the future the same situation will not occur.

Playing it in your head — visualisation

Many players report the benefits of playing the game in their head before the actual game (see chapter 13 for a longer discussion of imagery and visualisation). Imagery is an effective tool for facilitating concentration and minimising distractions. Many athletes have recorded that they visualise their event in every way possible before competition as a way of minimising distraction and improving concentration. Visualisation can be enhanced in a number of ways, salt-water flotation being a particularly ideal environment (Bond 1987).

Schmid and Peper (1993) presented an interesting variation on mental rehearsal. They organised team members into pairs in which one member relaxes and mentally rehearses while the other attempts to cause distractions to this rehearsal by any method except touch. The roles are then switched. On completion of the activity, both members are required to evaluate their concentration on a rating scale. Over time, participants report an improved ability to concentrate by dissociating themselves from distractions and remaining focused on the mental rehearsal task. Part of this training could also include athletes being required to regain concentration after being distracted.

Goal setting

A useful technique for developing concentration is to encourage athletes to set specific, measurable goals during training and competition (see chapter 10 on goal setting for a more detailed discussion of this area). For example, a netball goal shooter may decide on a goal of 85 per cent shooting accuracy during training, or that she will not complete her shooting training until she has shot 20 in a row. To make this activity more realistic, the player should ensure that she includes some of the same movement patterns required in the game (e.g. dodging defenders, whose court positions may be indicated by appropriately placed chairs) and that a number of shots are taken from various positions in the circle. These specific goals serve to keep the athlete focused on the set task, even in the event of distractions such as a build-up of fatigue or when other players leave the court after finishing their training.

Group discussion — controlling the controllables

Athletes find it very beneficial to discuss important factors that affect their performance. First, they are required to list all the factors likely to affect their performance (one column for the positive factors and another for the negative). Discussion may be facilitated by employing instructive subheadings such as 'tactical', 'psychological' and 'technical'. Next, responses are collated and the athletes are invited to discuss which factors they have control over (e.g. execution of skills, maintaining an ideal level of arousal or concentrating effectively) and which ones they do not (e.g. weather conditions, the presence of spectators or the media, or environmental noise). Athletes are often distracted by such things as the score, their competitive situation or other thoughts. They need to examine which factors distract them and to identify the best coping strategies to deal with them. One of these is to accept that some factors are beyond their control and therefore not worth being concerned about. There will be a range of other responses, including the importance of focusing on the present and the task at hand.

Athletes need to consider all the 'what ifs' that may be associated with a particular competition, or all the possible factors that may affect a situation, and then to devise coping strategies to deal with each of them. In this way, if (and when) these problems do arise, the athlete will be armed with effective coping responses, rather than being distracted by them, and will remain optimally focused. However, there are appropriate and inappropriate times to consider these 'what ifs'. It is important to address them when something can be done about them — that is, when effective coping strategies can be put in place at some time before competition. They should not be considered on race or event day, as this can seriously disrupt an optimal concentration mode for that competition.

APPLICATION OF 'WHAT IF' EXERCISES IN A PRACTICAL SETTING

The Australian netball team examined a range of 'what ifs' during their usual preparation for major tournaments such as the Commonwealth Games and the World Championships. Interestingly, one of the 'what if' scenarios often discussed was dealing with a blackout in the stadium. Playing the heavily supported Jamaicans in front of their parochial home crowd in an important late-round match, the Australians were exposed to exactly that scenario: the stadium lights went out. The Australian press subsequently reported how the Australians coped very well with this interruption at a crucial time in the match and went on to record an impressive victory. This success was partly attributed to the extensive planning that the coaching staff had undertaken before the tournament.

Group discussion should also address how athletes can maintain their own momentum and control the opposition. Miller (1997) described interesting examples of team focusing utilised by many elite teams. Squads devise tactics to address game periods when the opposition appear to be 'on a roll' — that is, when they have the momentum. Many team sports feature ebbs and flows in performance across a game, and it is essential that teams ride out the storm of opposition pressure and then reassert their own pressure. Individual players are designated as callers of some sign as a cue word signifying 'danger' and warning the rest of the team that the opposition have the momentum and that the focus should be on low-risk, conservative play for the next few minutes in order to arrest it. This ensures that players focus on appropriate processes during predictable phases of high pressure during a match. Further, when the momentum is with their own team, the players should seize any opportunities to discuss strategies on how to maintain it in light of similar disruptive tactics used by the opposition. For example, many teams group together during major unexpected disruptions (e.g. loss of power in an indoor arena, major injury on court, broken equipment) in order to maintain optimal focus and the game momentum that they may have built.

Game simulation activity

> The best athletes make extensive use of simulation training ... approach[ing] training ... in practice as if they were in competition, often wearing what they would wear and preparing like they would prepare ...
>
> (Orlick & Partington 1988, p. 114)

The idea behind developing game simulations is to minimise the negative effects of novelty and the pressures often associated with high-level competition. Many authors have examined the value of simulations (e.g. Orlick & Partington 1988; Hardy et al. 1996), which have been discussed under a variety of different names, including *adversity training*, *dress rehearsal*, *simulated practice* and *distraction training*. (Moran 2003). The assumption underlying this approach is that if athletes can practise in an environment approximating the game situation, then they will be able to develop enhanced coping strategies for the actual game. It has been argued from a cognitive perspective that stressors such as anxiety, fatigue, pain and controversial officiating calls are situation specific. Different stressors have different effects on attention and performance. Therefore it is appropriate to simulate as many different conditions as possible in order to fully prepare the athlete. The closer the simulation to the 'real thing', the better. It is vital to organise the scenario so that players approach it as if it was a 'real' game. This will involve paying attention to as many details as possible, such as wearing the correct game uniform, ensuring the usual pre-game routine, warm-up and pre-match discussion, using appropriate announcements and music, setting up a typical change-room, inviting real referees to officiate, and using a crowd noise tape or organising a crowd to attend.

Glencross (1993) utilised simulations when preparing the Australian women's Olympic hockey team for the 1992 Barcelona Olympics. The aim of the pre-Olympic camp was to simulate the situation and conditions that the team was likely to confront in an attempt to develop coping strategies for the Games. Glencross included the following factors in the simulation: climatic conditions, competition schedule, opponents and their styles of play, umpire rulings, playing conditions, tournament rules and regulations, spectators and crowd bias, transport conditions, accommodation and meals, and media exposure. Unexpected situations (e.g. a bomb scare) were also introduced. In order to fully test athletes' coping abilities, distractions are often chosen to go beyond typical expectations. This type of simulation program has been used successfully with a range of different sports.

One of the current authors employed simulations when preparing the 2002 Commonwealth gold medal Australian netball team for their World Championship defence in Jamaica in 2003. Jamaican crowd noise was played at training camps before departure. During the camp a large sound system was set up to play the ebb and flow of noise of a parochial Jamaican crowd. Testing exercises might also focus on coping with travel problems, lost luggage and blackouts in the stadium. Players vary in their ability to cope with these kinds of pressures; some athletes are unsettled by them, but all athletes gain from this sort of attention 'overtraining' exercise.

Leadership activities

A particularly good concentration exercise that has been used frequently with athletes is an activity that combines leadership qualities with communication, trust and concentration. This activity requires that all participants be blindfolded except for one person, the leader (either a prescribed leader or someone needing to develop leadership qualities). All participants in the team link hands with the leader, who takes up a position at the front of the group. The leader then leads the group around an obstacle course (comprising chairs, hurdles, trees and so on), warning them about impending dangers. It is imperative that the leader is clear about the type of information that he or she gives to the rest of the group, and that each team member concentrate in order to accurately interpret this communication. This activity has been particularly well accepted by athletes, as it results in a compensatory shift in attentional focus when the blindfold is in place. It seems that when vision is impaired, other senses are enhanced in order for us to make sense of our surroundings.

Designing individualised sport exercises

With some imagination, it is possible to design effective exercises that ensure that any athlete can practise moving from one attentional focus to another. Consideration might be given to the specific circumstances of a particular sport in which athletes are required to use one attentional style and then shift to another. For example, it is common practice in basketball to require players to dribble the ball while wearing special blinker glasses that effectively force the athlete to look ahead rather than at the ball. As players dribble the ball down the court, the coach calls out to them, asking them how many fingers he has raised in the air.

Non-sport activities

For most of these concentration activities it is assumed that the athlete has adopted a comfortable and relaxed position. In the following exercises, therefore, only the more important concentration aspects of the exercises are described, with no mention of the relaxation component. Cognitive aspects will be dealt with first, then exercises requiring vision with thinking, then those needing muscular involvement, and finally flow or meditation-like activities.

Passive thinking (Albinson & Bull 1988)

This particular exercise evaluates how ideas tend to flow freely in and out of the conscious mind. Initially, athletes are required to practise one minute of 'free-flow' thought (letting ideas just flow in and out without holding on to them) followed by one minute of rest. Athletes can then reflect on the sort of thoughts they have difficulty letting go, those thoughts that lead to further associations and distracting thoughts. This can be a difficult exercise as it runs counter to our daily lives, which seem to consist of rationalisation and serious concentration. However, it is important for athletes to understand how their thought processes operate. This is especially true for those who are easily distracted or who find that thoughts keep intruding into their task-relevant focus — for example, the player who dwells on the last umpiring decision or error rather than focusing on the developing game. The task may be difficult to begin with, so the period of free flow will be brief to begin with. Over time, athletes should be able to work from an initial one minute to up to five minutes of free-flow thinking and control practice. To increase task difficulty, athletes might like to practise with their eyes open or in different environments (e.g. at training, in their room or in a crowded place). This also ensures that athletes make the connection to the sport setting in which they may need the skill.

Focusing and refocusing in the present

Many athletes find it difficult to refocus and constantly perform below their best because of this problem. The key to resolving this concern is to ensure that athletes focus on the 'now', rather than on the past or the future, while at the same time being able to move from negative thinking to a more constructive, positive approach. Techniques that have proved valuable in enhancing concentrational style include the following.

Video and computer games

These games are especially helpful in training athletes to remain in the present, while also helping them get their minds off stressful events. Many elite swimmers have used electronic games as a way of enhancing their concentration through the immediate feedback such games provide. Nideffer's (1994) interactive CD-ROM *Focus for success* was initially developed as an interactive attentional development program to improve concentration skills. Participants are advised first to take an assessment (the Concentration and Personality Profile) before interacting with a series of tasks designed to look at how we concentrate, some techniques designed to improve concentration in order to perform better, and a final reassessment of the gains achieved from the program. A number of games designed to test concentration are included in the program. Many athletes find these games interesting and enjoyable. Other CD-ROMs are now available that test concentration, although possibly more indirectly than this program. One interesting reported use of the program has baseballers or softballers sitting in the dugout between innings playing the CD-ROM in order to enhance their focus on the ball before their hit.

The concentration grid exercise

The grid exercise is another technique used to evaluate and enhance focusing and refocusing. The grid is typically a box of ten rows and ten columns drawn up into cells. Each cell has a random two-digit number placed in it, ranging from 00 to 99. The athlete is required to mark in ascending numerical sequence as many numbers as possible in a given time (usually one minute). Scores in the high twenties and thirties have been suggested as indicative of good concentration skills (Burke 1992). Variations of this task include changing the numbers in each of the cells, using different orders and sequences, using letters instead of numbers, or even using specific sport pictures as targets within each cell. In order to increase the difficulty of the task once mastered, distractions may be introduced. For example, the use of background noise such as loud talking, television programs and direct questioning of the performer while undertaking the test place the athlete's attention under pressure. The grid has been used successfully with a variety of athletes under different pressure conditions.

VARIATION ON THE CONCENTRATION GRID

Blundell (1995) described a further variation of the concentration grid that many athletes might enjoy. Blundell takes one player in a competitive environment and 'trains him up' on the grid, or so the other player thinks. In fact, all that is done is that the 'trained' athlete acts supremely confident (as though trained in a new technique) by working through the grid at a feverish pace, acting as if he is 'killing the grid', while at the same time showing pleasure in newfound success by laughing excitedly in front of his opponent. The 'untrained' player either gives up in frustration before this performance or becomes more competitive in trying to beat his opponent. Either way, the 'extra training' façade tends to plant doubt in the 'untrained' player's mind, placing further pressure on his ability to concentrate on the task. Needless to say, the 'untrained' player needs to be properly debriefed after the exercise, thus learning how his concentration might be upset by such deceit.

Awareness exercise (Schmid & Peper 1993)

After achieving a relaxed state, athletes are instructed to listen to the environment (*scanning*), first identifying any sound (*targeting*), then listening without identification to these sounds and finally just letting all of these noises blend together. The same process is then followed when listening to bodily sensations, then with thoughts and feelings, and finally identifying specific aspects of bodily functioning or single thoughts or feelings. In another variation, athletes may introduce a sport-relevant piece of equipment, which is placed in front of them. The athlete is then instructed to focus on specific features of that object, then switch to being more aware of other details by using his or her peripheral vision. This zooming and changing of concentration is an effective technique for developing the ability to switch from one focus of attention to another as the situation changes.

Expanding awareness (Schmid & Peper 1993)

This is an excellent exercise for ensuring that athletes experience different attentional styles, as discussed earlier in this chapter. Originally developed by Gauron (1984), it has been adapted successfully for a range of athletes. The advantage of this exercise is that it trains the athlete to move from a narrow to a broad focus while also demonstrating the difference between external and internal concentration. It also helps athletes determine which style of concentration they are most comfortable with and which style causes them most difficulty.

The first step is to focus on breathing, alternating between normal and a deeper, slower breathing. It is important to assume a relaxed state during this breathing exercise; biofeedback monitoring equipment may be used to gauge physiological relaxation. The second step involves attending to specific sounds that are present, identifying and labelling each. The athlete is then required to simultaneously listen to all the sounds blending together without attempting any identification. Alternating between a specific (narrow) and broad awareness is then repeated for the athlete's bodily experiences and then for emotions and thoughts. Within the thought phase, the athlete is instructed not to force any feeling or thought and to remain calm. The goal is to empty the mind of all thoughts and feelings. In the final stage of the exercise the athlete concentrates on an object while using peripheral vision to be aware of other features in the environment. The athlete is then asked to imagine a narrow funnel centring on the chosen object before gradually widening the funnel to take in everything in the room. This task is another example of the *zooming* activity that many athletes have found a valuable training technique for dealing with any subsequent distraction to their optimal focus.

'Soft eyes – hard eyes'

When we focus intently on a specific external cue it is possible to feel a tightening of the muscles around our eyes and a 'hardening' of the eye itself (a tightening of the muscles and eyelid may produce a feeling of increased pressure, or hardening, within the eye). When we attempt to focus on peripheral cues, it is possible for some individuals to feel their eyes become 'soft' as they relax the muscles around their eyes. Athletes can be shown how to practise narrowing by making their eyes slightly harder, and to broaden their visual focus by relaxing the muscles around their eyes and allowing their eyes to become soft. Another simple technique we have developed involves the athlete holding one thumb up at arm's length (in a thumbs-up position) and practising a narrow focus on a specific mark or part of the thumbnail, then shifting to a broad–external focus taking in the background detail of the surroundings, before moving back to the narrow focus, and so on. Athletes can be encouraged to practise this attentional switching technique in a variety of situations outside their sport.

Watching the clock face (Albinson & Bull 1988)

This is another activity that athletes have found valuable for developing an ability to maintain focus on a particular object. The idea is to focus attention on a clock face and to watch the second hand sweep. At prescribed times athletes are required to blink or tap their fingers. This requirement may involve a simple sequence to begin with, such as every five seconds; greater demands can be made later. Different sequence patterns can be adopted, such as changing from every five seconds to every ten seconds then back to five. Athletes are instructed to examine how their thoughts moved in and out of their mind during the exercise, paying special attention to the longer time intervals between blinks/taps, as these are when distractions are most likely to occur. Again, the difficulty of the task can be increased by attempting it while listening to music (progressing to more intrusive types of music) or to a television program, or while someone is talking loudly.

The stork stand

This particularly novel task requires the athlete to stand on one leg with both arms outstretched to the sides and eyes closed. The task involves maintaining balance for as long as possible, the trial finishing when balance is lost. This exercise can be attempted a number of times and is good for developing concentration. The exercise can be varied by first concentrating on cues (physical or kinaesthetic) that assist with balance. Athletes are then required to discuss the value of the cueing exercise and its usefulness in assisting with balance. An experienced and successful Olympic yachtsman described how he managed to draw his focus of attention into his boat immediately before the start of a race. When he noticed that his focus had broadened too much or he was feeling too anxious through thinking about the consequences of a poor performance, he stood up in his boat with one foot on each side of the hull. Naturally, the boat initially behaved in a very unstable way, but he was able to bring the boat to a stable state by consciously relaxing and centring himself until he felt at one with the boat. This exercise proved to be very effective primarily because it forced him to focus on himself and the movement of the boat (blocking out external factors and thoughts). The settling effect of centring breathing combined with the attentional shift to bring about the desired result.

The unbendable arm

Athletes are asked to pair up, with one athlete seated on a chair holding one arm out in front at shoulder height. The partner stands beside the seated athlete and is instructed to place one hand around the wrist of the seated athlete's outstretched arm and the other hand on top of the outstretched elbow. The task is for the standing athlete to bend the seated athlete's arm by pressing down on the elbow and pulling up on the wrist of the outstretched arm. The seated athlete is instructed to tense the arm muscles to prevent the outstretched arm from being bent. The standing athlete can usually bend the outstretched arm fairly easily, presumably because the seated athlete typically tenses up antagonistic muscles (such as biceps and triceps) in an attempt to brace the elbow. In doing so the seated athlete in fact makes it more difficult to maintain a straight arm as the biceps, for example, work against the natural action of the triceps in locking the elbow. The second stage of this exercise is to instruct the seated athlete to tense only the triceps by pointing the outstretched arm towards the wall of the room or some other immovable object and imagining there is a steel beam stretching from the shoulder of the outstretched arm to the immovable object, making it impossible for the arm to be bent. If this instruction is followed to the letter, and preceded by one or two centring breaths, it will be extremely difficult for the standing athlete to bend the outstretched arm. We use this exercise to demonstrate the strength of an appropriate attentional focus in tapping into physical functions.

Using biofeedback equipment

Athletes can improve control over their concentration by using biofeedback devices. These instruments may be used to demonstrate how thoughts can affect the body, how relaxation is reflected physiologically and which components of imagery appear to be stressful. They show alterations in autonomic arousal that are reflected in skin conductance changes, or in other indicators such as heart rate, muscle tension or temperature. The feedback device typically shows this alteration through a change in pitch (raised pitch showing when conductivity and arousal increase, and vice versa) or through changes in a lighting display or click frequency. Biofeedback devices can also be used to show how thoughts affect performance by demonstrating a corresponding physiological effect. Even asking athletes to think of a stressful situation can change the feedback from the instrument. This demonstration is valuable in helping athletes identify and stop disturbing thoughts and self-talk by creating a connection to altered psychophysiological states. The subsequent challenge is to alter this self-talk to something more positive. Athletes have also used these instruments to gain valuable feedback about their mental rehearsal. Using biofeedback during mental rehearsal, athletes can identify stressful cues by the way the pitch changes. This may reflect some psychophysiological change (possibly muscle tightening or increased anxiety) during a particularly stressful movement sequence. After subsequent intervention, athletes are able to approach these sequences in a more controlled way during their mental rehearsal as well as in real practice and performance situations.

Flow state

There has been a great deal of interest in the flow experience sometimes reported by athletes when performing exceptionally well. Csikszentmihalyi (1990) and others (Jackson 1992; Jackson & Roberts 1992; Jackson & Csikszentmihalyi 1999; Kimiecik & Stein 1992; Sargent 2001a, 2001b, 2001c, 2002) have described a number of elements that seem to characterise the flow state. These elements include the merging of action and awareness (the activity is spontaneous and almost automatic), the setting of clear goals and unambiguous feedback (a direction must be set, as well as some kind of feedback about progress), a loss of self-consciousness (complete immersion in a task without being forced, so that concentration can be directed completely to the task), a paradox of control (performers feel in control without being concerned about losing it) and a complete concentration on the task at hand, with all distractions shut out. Concentration is clearly an important component of the flow state.

NLP and meditation

Another area relevant to concentration is neuro-linguistic programming, or NLP. Although the scientific support is at present unclear, NLP is an area that seems to be providing interesting insights into applied sport psychology. For example, O'Connor (2001) identified NLP as particularly well suited to sports performance. In an interesting alternative to typical sport psychology literature, O'Connor (2001) looked at the zone and dealing with distractions as two areas relevant to concentration. In terms of a zone, the author examined critical concentration points (those important points in a game when concentration must be optimal and when the athlete typically loses focus), creating anchors for taking one to the required concentration state (triggers or rituals used by athletes to establish consistency), and setting neutral anchors for dealing with moments of high emotional intensity that may distract.

THE STAGES AND EFFECTS OF MEDITATION

Heathcote (1996) described the 11 stages of Zen meditation. These include *counting* (while exhaling, count at the same rate), *rhythm* (as you inhale, say 'I will breathe in', and during exhalation, say 'I shall breathe out'), *waves* (as you inhale, imagine waves lapping on the shoreline; focus on the rhythm of the waves), *feather* (imagine having a tiny feather on the end of your nose, and ensure your breathing is so gentle that the feather is not dislodged) and *music* (listen to appropriate music and try to lose yourself in it as you breathe gently; flute, pan pipes, nature music or baroque music is often suggested). Heathcote (1996) described further stages of moving Zen (relaxed walking at a breathing rhythm in tune with one's steps), *hara* (nose breaths while mentally pushing down on the lower abdomen), *tanden* (breathe and push as in *hara* but focus on the *tanden*, 3 cm above the navel), *polishing* (make large circular sweeping movements with your hand flat on a table while focused on breathing and the *tanden* spot) and *blankness* (allow your mind to go blank as distractions come and go).

Heathcote (1996) described how meditation can help with breathing and rhythm. Short periods of meditation are suggested at a number of times before a race. (In one case, an international swimmer described how the exercise led him to being so much 'in the zone' that he was not even aware of other, more famous performers lining up beside him.) Practising meditation in the morning for 5 to 10 minutes before breakfast helps to energise the athlete for the day. Furthermore, practising across the day for 5 minutes can ensure optimal focusing. Meditation may also be used while walking or stretching or even when changing clothes at the competition site. When meditating, it is suggested that the athlete count up for each exhalation while using cues such as 'in' for inhalations and 'out' for exhalations. Meditation is very useful when preparing for potentially stressful situations, such as just before a race or before dealing with the media. There has been some argument about how similar meditation is to other breathing and centring techniques, although experienced meditators would insist that they are very different. Meditation is a valuable tool worth examining by those interested in enhancing concentration.

Meditation bubble (Murphy 1996)

After relaxing, athletes are required to become one with their environment and to let go of intruding thoughts, or any thought at all. Even after becoming quite adept at quieting the mind, thoughts will continue to 'flow'. The trick in this exercise is to put these thoughts into a 'bubble' and to then see the bubble floating away, with that thought gone. This exercise involves peaceful observation and is not to be used when a problem needs to be solved. Murphy suggested that after some experience, athletes should be able to stay with this task for up to half an hour. A variation is to focus on a single object at the expense of everything else.

Concentration exercises from other areas

Concentration as a skill is also used extensively in training games and life coaching. For example, Kroehnert (1999) described a game called 'powers of concentration'. The game requires participants to follow instructions while blindfolded, such as folding some paper in a certain way and tearing off the right-hand corner. The exercise also doubles as an effective communication tool, as it clearly illustrates how people can interpret instructions in different ways. Kroehnert (1999) described another activity in which participants are required to make comparisons between two pictures that have a number of differences, ensuring that they focus on the task for a set time period. Stibbard (1998) described a game called 'magnetic chair' in which participants, working in pairs, try to focus on strong goals: one participant sits on a chair and tries to rise from the chair while the other presses lightly on the seated person's shoulders. The seated person is required to focus on a goal just beyond reach while trying to rise from the chair. This interesting activity illustrates the power of a strong focus on one's goals and the importance of setting challenging objectives to work towards. Other exercises in similar publications require participants to examine a range of important factors related to teamwork, concentration, dealing with distractions, energising, listening, introductions and so on. This is another area of great interest for applied practitioners in sport psychology.

FUTURE DIRECTIONS

Concentration is the ability to think about absolutely nothing when it is absolutely necessary.

(Ray Knight, in Farley & Curry 1994)

The future for concentration training is indeed exciting. Given the central importance of concentration for sport performance, there remain a number of issues to be resolved in research and applied domains. These include further development and refinement in assessment, analysis and feedback. The TAIS continues to provide valuable information, although other assessment devices, for example those described by Ostrow (1990), also seem promising. A recent tool is Thomas's Test of Performance Strategies (Thomas et al. 1999), which includes a concentration scale within its assessment of mental skills that looks very promising. Abernathy (1998) has also suggested the need for a diagnostic model that includes a self-report scale (like the TAIS), behavioural measures (tasks in which athletes are required to divide their attention between different actions) and psychophysiological indices. Such a multidimensional approach might hold a great deal of practical utility for applied work in the future. Future development in interactive technology may also offer worthwhile insights.

Improved technology, and further application of what is currently available, should ensure that the simulations designed for athletes reflect the real environment with ever greater accuracy. Creative use of multiple-camera video feedback will ensure that athletes are able to experience more closely the appropriate attentional demands of competition situations. When this process is used in conjunction with controlled environments, such as saltwater flotation tanks, its efficiency will further increase. Development of three-dimensional holograms may even allow the athlete to experience the concentration requirements of a game situation within the confines of a training venue or professional's office.

There has also been considerable interest in the planning of mental training programs to ensure that all skills are scientifically addressed. Bompa's (1983) periodisation principles continue to challenge practitioners. To this stage little attempt has been made in the literature to address the relationship of Bompa's approach with mental skill development, although this issue has been discussed by one of the present authors (see Sargent 1997). Furthermore, specific mental training programs have been created that further demonstrate how concentration skills can be effectively improved. Gordon (1990) presented a program based on the mental demands of cricket that employs an educational approach in a workbook setup. In the area of concentration, Gordon emphasised the importance of focusing on one thing at a time, selective attention to important cues, focusing in the present as well as developing the ability to maximise the quality of required periods of optimal concentration, and shifting attentional focus as a form of concentration 'relaxation'. The 'switching off' requirement reflected the immense time demands of the sport and was addressed by the use of checklists, cue words and refocusing plans similar to the type presented by Orlick (1986a, 1986b). Gordon also developed commercially available audiotapes designed to enhance concentration skills. There has been some concern about the value of commercially prepared tapes that are not individualised to the athlete and his or her sport, although they do provide an interesting template worth consideration.

More recent mental training programs have been developed. A plethora of coaching manuals and books have been prepared presenting mental training programs for a wide range of sports, including golf (e.g. Glad & Beck 1999; Cohn & Winters 1995), tenpin bowling (Hinitz 2003), lawn bowls (Salter & Bliss 1997), tennis (Murray 1999; Blundell 1995) and soccer (Morrow 2001), to name a few. Savoy (1993) presented a program for college basketball. Of particular interest was the applied nature of her approach, as well as the inclusion of the TAIS as an assessment tool along with anxiety questionnaires and stress scales. Her report further reinforced the value of inventories when analysing attentional capacity. Savoy used a case design to examine the efficacy of her program as well as weaknesses in dealing with distractions and getting psyched up for practice. For the distraction/concentration area, Savoy describes a program to control the tendency to be overloaded by both external and internal information. This was presented in the form of an imagery worksheet and a mental checklist for game-like situations. This extremely practical approach again demonstrates how these procedures can be adopted in the sport setting through a blend of theory and practice. The effectiveness of such programs is still unclear. Examination of the impact of parts of such programs has also received some interest, but with confusing results. For example, the efficacy and validity of such tried and accepted tools as the concentration grid have been seriously questioned. Interestingly, Jones (1993) used a sport psychological skills package to evaluate changes in a number of skills including concentration. Scores for a number of skills showed vast improvement after three months and at a six-month follow-up, with concentration showing the most marked change.

Implications for the development of concentration can be drawn from a wide variety of other areas. For example, the corporate world has shown an interest in how sportspeople cope with the demands of their sport, as reflected by Winter and Hamilton (1992), Macqueen (2001), Parkin, Bourke and Gleeson (2001) and Gilson, Pratt, Roberts and Weymes (2000). Furthermore, the performing arts have also borrowed from work in sport, as reflected by Taylor and Taylor's (1995) work on applications of psychological principles in dance. Recent dance magazines have included specific sections designed to tackle mental preparation and have even employed a sport psychologist in their preparation.

Moran (2003) proposed several significant areas for concentration research, including further investigation into the phenomenon of distraction and in particular why elite athletes become distracted, and evaluation of concentration models and the different techniques suggested. More research is needed to examine what attentional demands are required in different activities. A slightly different approach was suggested by Andersen (2000) in his 'cookbook' descriptions of applied sport psychology in which he identified the exact processes and dialogues in a variety of domains. Kolt (2000) described a multidimensional approach to assisting injured athletes, with an emphasis that includes concentration and focusing. Kolt described a number of techniques including an approach called 'moment-for-moment' or 'staying in present time'. This technique encourages focusing on one task at a time while ignoring all uncontrollables. While this idea is not particularly new to applied work, the presentation of a client–practitioner interaction offers insights for practitioners.

IMPACT OF AN OFFICIAL ERROR ON CONCENTRATION SKILLS AT THE OLYMPICS

The research area of concentration remains full of potential. Grandjean, Taylor and Weiner (2002) presented some extremely interesting, fortuitous research that looked at the ability of women gymnasts to cope with a major error in the setup of the vault (set 5 cm too low) at the Sydney Olympics. The authors examined confidence and concentration on competitive performance in a natural environment. Discussion centred on whether or not the low vault affected the gymnasts' performance. Many of the world's media and many coaches suggested that the impact was significant; the authors, on the other hand, suggested that there was no impact at all, concluding that world-class competitors involved in a closed skill are adept at blocking out distractions from the environment. Elite athletes master such concentration skills far better than the average athlete. Their highly developed mental skills allow these athletes to cope with potential confidence-sapping mishaps on one apparatus and then cope well enough to succeed on the next one. These results suggest that concentration may be just as important as confidence, and that momentum seems to be a major factor in open skills but not in closed skills like gymnastics. This example again points to the key role played by concentration in the performance of elite athletes in closed-skill sports such as gymnastics.

Further areas of interest in concentration investigation are gamesmanship, working with children and the ideal performance state (IPS). Moran (2003) discussed gamesmanship and why athletes lose concentration. External threats to concentration seem to be linked closely to gamesmanship factors (including verbal abuse, sledging, physical intimidation, provocative tactics, physical obstruction and diving). Internal threats, on the other hand, are more cognitively based (on thoughts, feelings, fear of failure, anxiety). Little is known about the nature and operation of other distractions and how they influence gamesmanship and athletic performance. Orlick (1993) addressed important issues in the mental development and enhancement of concentration in children, describing a number of activities and games designed to enhance concentration and improve ability to shift attention. The IPS is another area of great interest. It seems that attention is a central aspect of the IPS, although the essential conditions required to create it are still unclear.

Moran (2003) suggested a number of practical implications for coaches that should be considered closely. First, coaches need to move from a general admonition ('Concentrate!') to something more specific, such as stipulating precisely what performers need to focus on in a given situation. Next, coaches should ensure that athletes focus on actions that are relevant to their situation as well as under their control. Third, coaches must ensure that they fully understand the distractions that athletes experience in their sport and then simulate such distractions in training regimes. Fourth, coaches must continue to employ 'what if' practices to ensure that athletes are developing appropriate plans and routines for their sport and are thus empowered in their performances.

CONCLUSIONS

This chapter examined the theoretical bases of attention while endorsing an applied model of concentration when working in sport. Readers are urged to acknowledge the significance of concentration when addressing athletic excellence. Nideffer's model continues to have applied value in individual work with athletes and in a broader educational sense with teams. The model remains useful for understanding and (in conjunction with psychometric profiles and other measures) predicting strategies for change in the area of concentration and sport performance. Nideffer's Test of Attentional and Interpersonal Style (TAIS) also continues to prove useful in applied work with athletes and coaches, an aspect reinforced by Griffith's (1999) recent work. Applied sport psychologists are encouraged to use the TAIS as a part of their repertoire. In conjunction with other measures, the TAIS is an excellent way to assess and educate athletes and coaches on attentional issues.

The attentional exercise section of the chapter provided only a starting point for use by applied sport psychologists, coaches and athletes when designing individualised training programs. The future development of resources, programs and strategies in the area of concentration remains exciting. In particular, the continued development of interactive software will further increase the effectiveness of concentration training. Continued interest in diverse areas such as flow states and the relationship between ideal arousal levels and effective concentration remains promising. Finally, readers are encouraged to be creative when addressing concentration training in sport, for instance in the use of video simulations and in the application of training guidelines such as periodisation. Applied sport psychology will continue to benefit from new quantitative and qualitative research on attention and concentration. Many unanswered questions about attention and concentration remain to be addressed.

SUMMARY

This chapter addressed the importance of attention to the serious athlete and coach. While there exists some definitional confusion with the term concentration, this chapter provided an operational definition of utility to practitioners. There appear to be many opportunities for intervention by the applied sport psychologist, coach and athlete. Some of these have been suggested by the work of Nideffer through his attentional model. Nideffer has provided the practitioner with a means of enhancing the understanding, explanation, prediction, control and change of attentional factors. While there have been some criticisms of the Nideffer model, it remains a workable, easily understood applied diagnostic approach of practical significance. A reasonably extensive list of general and sport-specific attentional exercises has been described. These should prove useful for those with a creative mind intent on stimulating the further development of concentration training activities. The final section of the chapter examined some areas of future interest relating to attention and concentration. It should be re-emphasised that further research in the applied area of attention is still needed.

We close this chapter with a quotation to encourage others to continue investigating this vital area of applied performance psychology:

> Concentration helps us focus and, in effect, turn off our minds. Thinking too much can hamper our performance ... concentrating helps us turn off the mental chatter that can distract us. It can also help to eliminate extra babble — when we are focused we are not thinking ... we are completely involved in our game ... we will discover the time passing without our even noticing ... (Farley & Curry 1994)

REVIEW QUESTIONS

1 Explain the four attentional styles proposed by Nideffer and give an example of the kind of situation in which each occurs.

2 Explain the ways in which attentional errors occur, based on the Nideffer model.

3 Pick a skill from your favourite sport and prepare an attentional sequence that would make sense to an athlete and provide the basis for part of a performance plan.

4 Briefly explain what is meant by each of the following:
   (a) Parking
   (b) 'Soft and hard eyes'.

5 Explain the ineffective attentional sequence involved in the following example.
   A footballer kicking for goal in an important game misses the shot (and loses the game for his team) because a train rattled past the rear of the stadium as he jogged in on his shooting attempt. What attentional/arousal strategies would you suggest to the coach/athlete to address the issue?

6 An athlete in your charge displays a major performance decrement as the pressure mounts in a competition (similar to that experienced by golfer Jean Van de Velde in a case described in the chapter). Provide a possible arousal/attentional diagnosis and some tips for the athlete in dealing with this situation.

7 Identify one or more of the attentional training strategies presented in this chapter that would appear to be most suited to your specific sporting situation.

8 Provide details of the ways in which you would include attentional training under pressure in your typical sporting training program.

References

Abernathy, B 1998, 'Attention', in RN Singer, M Murphey & LK Tennant (eds), *Handbook of research on sport psychology*, Macmillan, New York, pp. 57–9.

Albinson, JG & Bull, SJ 1988, *A mental game plan: a training program for all sports*, Spodym, London, Ontario.

Albrecht, RR & Feltz, DL 1987, 'Generality and specificity of attention related to competitive anxiety and sport performance', *Journal of Sport Psychology*, 9, 231–48.

Andersen, MB (ed.) 2000, *Doing sport psychology*, Human Kinetics, Champaign, IL.

Antonelli, F, Caldarone, L & Gatti, M 1982, 'Profile psychologique du gymnastic national Italien', in T Orlick, JT Partington & JH Salmela (eds), *Mental training for coaches and athletes*, Coaching Association of Canada, Ottawa, pp. 100–1.

Blundell, N 1995, *So you want to be a tennis pro?*, Lothian, Port Melbourne.

Bompa, T 1983, *Theory and methodology of training: the key to athletic performance*, Kendall/Hunt Publishing Co., Iowa.

Bond, JW 1984, 'Concentration: focusing on the right thing at the right time', unpublished manuscript, Australian Institute of Sport.

Bond, JW 1985, 'Segmenting or performance planning for success in sport', unpublished manuscript, Australian Institute of Sport.

Bond, JW 1987, 'Flotation therapy: theoretical concepts', *Sports Science and Medicine Quarterly*, 4, 2–4.

Bond, JW & Nideffer, RM 1992, 'Attentional and interpersonal characteristics of elite Australian athletes', *Excel*, 8, 101–10.

Boutcher, SH 1990, 'The role of performance routines', in G Jones & L Hardy (eds), *Stress and performance in sport*, John Wiley & Sons, Chichester, UK, pp. 231–45.

Boutcher, SH 1992, 'Attention and athletic performance: an integrated approach', in TS Horn (ed.), *Advances in sport psychology*, Human Kinetics, Champaign, IL, pp. 251–65.

Bull, SJ 2000, 'The immersion approach', in R Butler (ed.), *Sports psychology in performance*, Arnold, London, pp. 177–202.

Bull, SJ, Albinson, JG and Shambrook, CJ 1996, *The mental game plan: getting psyched for sport*, Sports Dynamics, Eastbourne, UK.

Burke, KL 1992, 'Concentration', *Sport Psychology Bulletin*, 4 (1) 1–8.

Cattell, RB 1957, *Personality and motivation structure and measurement*, World Book Company, Yonkers-on-Hudson, NY.

Clarkson, M 1999, *Competitive fire: insights to developing the warrior mentality of sports champions*, Human Kinetics, Champaign, IL.

Cohn, PJ 1990, 'Pre-performance routines in sport: theoretical support and practical applications', *The Sport Psychologist*, 4, 301–12.

Cohn, PJ & Winters, RK 1995, *The mental art of putting: using your mind to putt your best; the psychology of great putting*, Taylor Trade, Lanham, USA.

Csikszentmihalyi, M 1990, *Flow: the psychology of experience*, Harper & Row, New York.

DePalma DM & Nideffer, RM 1977, 'Relationships between the Test of Attentional and Interpersonal Style and psychiatric subclassification', *Journal of Personality Assessment*, 41, 622–31.

Farley, KL & Curry, SM 1994, *Get motivated: daily psych ups*, Simon & Schuster; New York.

Farrow, D & Kemp, J 2003, *Run like you stole something (the science behind the score line)*, Allen & Unwin, Sydney.

Feifel, H, Strack, S & Nagy, VT 1987, 'Degree of life-threat and differential use of coping modes', *Journal of Psychosomatic Research*, 31 (1) 91–9.

Garfield, CA & Bennett, HZ 1984, *Peak performance: mental training techniques of the world's greatest athletes*, Warner, Los Angeles, CA.

Gauron, EF 1984, *Mental training for peak performance*, Sport Science Associates, Lansing, NY.

Gilson, C, Pratt, M, Roberts, K & Weymes, E 2000, *Peak performance: business lessons from the world's top sports organizations*, HarperCollins Business, London.

Glad, W & Beck, C 1999, *Focused for golf: proven mental techniques and strategies for serious players*, Human Kinetics, Champaign, IL.

Glencross, B 1993, 'Simulation camp', *Sports Coach*, 16 (1) 7–10.

Gordon, S 1990, 'A mental skills training program for the Western Australia state cricket team', *The Sport Psychologist*, 4, 386–99.

Grandjean, BD, Taylor, PA & Weiner, J 2002, 'Confidence, concentration and competitive performance of elite athletes: a natural experiment in Olympic gymnasts', *Journal of Sport & Exercise Psychology*, 24, 320–7.

Griffiths, R 1999, *Modern psychology for cricket and other Australian sports*, Odlum & Garner, Sydney.

Hardy, L, Jones, G & Gould, D 1996, *Understanding psychological preparation for sport: theory and practice of elite performers*, John Wiley & Sons, Chichester, UK.

Hatfield, BD, Landers, DM & Ray, WJ 1984, 'Cognitive processes during self-paced motor performance: an electroencephalographic profile of skilled marksmen', *Journal of Sport Psychology*, 6, 42–59.

Heathcote, F 1996, *Peak performance: Zen and the sporting zone*, Wolfhound Press: Harpenden, UK.

Hinitz, D 2003, *Focused for bowling: mental skills to master every shot*, Human Kinetics, Champaign, IL.

Hurst, M 2003, 'Cool Jana silences Russian's "rattle"', *Sunday Herald-Sun News Pictorial*, August 31, p. 73.

Jackson, SA 1992, 'Athletes in flow: a qualitative investigation of flow states in elite figure skaters', *Journal of Applied Sport Psychology*, 4, 161–80.

Jackson, SA & Csikszentmihalyi, M 1999, *Flow in sports: the keys to optimal experiences and performances*, Human Kinetics, Champaign, IL.

Jackson, SA & Roberts, GC 1992, 'Positive performance states of athletes: toward a conceptual understanding of peak performance', *The Sport Psychologist*, 6, 156–71.

Jones, G 1993, 'The role of performance profiling in cognitive behavioural interventions in sport', *The Sport Psychologist*, 7, 160–72.

Kimiecik, JC & Stein, GL 1992, 'Examining flow experiences in sport contexts: conceptual issues and methodological concerns', *Journal of Applied Sport Psychology*, 4, 144–60.

Kolt, G 2000, 'Doing sport psychology with injured athletes', in Andersen, MB (ed.), *Doing sport psychology*, Human Kinetics, Champaign, IL, pp. 223–36.

Kroehnert, G 1999, *101 more training games*, McGraw-Hill, Sydney.

Landers, DM & Richards DE 1980, 'Test of attentional and interpersonal style scores of shooters', in GC Roberts & DM Landers (eds), *Psychology of motor behaviour and sport*, Human Kinetics, Champaign, IL, p. 94.

Louder, J 2001, 'Think success, bring success', *Bicycling Australia*, May, 64–5.

Mack, G & Casstevens, D 2001, *Mind gym: an athlete's guide to inner excellence*, Contemporary Books, Sydney.

Macqueen, R 2001, *One step ahead: on the field and in the boardroom*, Random House, Sydney.

Marchant, D & Sargent, GI 2002, 'Turning the tables on choking', *Sports Coach*, 24 (4) 14–15.

Miller, B 1997, *Gold minds: the psychology of winning in sport*, The Crowood Press, Marlborough.

Moran, A 2003, 'Improving concentration skills in team-sport performers: focusing techniques for soccer players', in R Lidor & KP Henschen, *The psychology of team sports*, Fitness Information Technology: Morgantown, WV, pp. 161–90.

Morrow, K 2001, *'It's what's up here that counts': winning the mental game of soccer*, Morrow Psychological Consulting, Melbourne.

Murphy, S 1996, *The achievement zone*, Putnam, New York.

Murray, JF 1999, *Smart tennis: how to play and win the mental game*, Jossey-Bass, San Francisco.

Nideffer, RM 1976a, 'Test of Attentional and Interpersonal Style', *Journal of Personality and Social Psychology*, 34, 394–404.

Nideffer, RM 1976b, *The inner athlete*, Thomas Crowell, New York.

Nideffer, RM 1981, *Predicting human behaviour: a theory and test of attentional and interpersonal style*, Enhanced Performance Associates, San Diego, CA.

Nideffer, RM 1987, 'Issues in the use of psychological tests in applied settings', *The Sport Psychologist*, 1, 18–28.

Nideffer, RM 1989, *Attention control training for athletes*, Enhanced Performance Services, Oakland, CA.

Nideffer, RM 1990, 'Use of the Test of Attentional and Interpersonal Style (TAIS) in sport', *The Sport Psychologist*, 4, 285–300.

Nideffer, RM 1993a, 'Attention control training', in R Singer, M Murphey & LK Tennant (eds), *Handbook of research on sport psychology*, Macmillan, New York, pp. 542–56.

Nideffer, RM 1993b, 'Concentration and attention control training', in J Williams (ed.), *Applied sport psychology: personal growth to peak performance*, 2nd edn, Mayfield, Palo Alto, CA, pp. 243–61.

Nideffer, RM 1994, *Focus for success* [CD-ROM], Compton's New Media Inc., Tribune New Media.

Nideffer, RM & Bond, J 1989, 'Test of attentional and interpersonal style — cultural and sexual differences', paper presented at the XXI International Conference on Psychology, Sport and Health Promotion, Banff, Canada.

Nideffer, RM & Pratt, RW 1981, *Taking care of business: a manual to guide the refinement of attention control training*, Enhanced Performance Associates, San Diego, CA.

Nideffer, RM, Sagal, M, Lowry, M & Bond, J 2001, 'Identifying and developing world class performers', in G Tenenbaum (ed.), *The practice of sport psychology*, Fitness Information Technology, Morgantown, WV, pp. 129–44.

O'Connor, J 2001, *NLP in sport*, Arnold, London.

Orlick, T 1986a, *Psyching for sport: menial training for athletes*, Leisure Press, Champaign, IL.

Orlick, T 1986b, *Coaches' training manual for psyching for sport*, Leisure Press, Champaign, IL.

Orlick, T 1993, *Free to feel great — teaching children to excel at living*, Creative Bound Inc., Carp, Ontario.

Orlick, T 1998, *Embracing your potential*, Human Kinetics, Champaign, IL.

Orlick, T & Partington, J 1988, 'Mental links to excellence', *The Sport Psychologist*, 2, 105–30.

Ostrow, AC 1990, *Directory of psychological tests in the sport and exercises sciences*, Fitness Information Technology, Morgantown, WV.

Parkin, D, Bourke, P & Gleeson, R 2001, *Working with pumped up people*, Information Australia, Melbourne.

Reis, J & Bird, A 1982, 'Cue processing as a function of breadth of attention', *Journal of Sport Psychology*, 4, 64–72.

Rushall, BS 1979, *Psyching in sport*, Pelham Books, London.

Salter, B & Bliss, J 1997, *The A to Zen of lawn bowls*, Ironbark, Pan Macmillan, Sydney.

Sargent, G 1997, 'Developing a mental skills training program. Part 6: periodising mental training programs', *Sports Coach*, 20 (2) 24–5.

Sargent, G 2001a, 'Being in flow: part one', *Sports Coach*, 24 (1) 35.

Sargent, G 2001b, 'Being in flow: part two', *Sports Coach*, 24 (2) 28–9.

Sargent, G 2001c, 'More tips on achieving the elusive state of flow', *Sports Coach*, 24 (3) 32–3.

Sargent, G 2002, 'Being in flow: part four', *Sports Coach*, 25 (1) 30 & 32.

Savoy, C 1993, 'A yearly mental training program for a college basketball player', *The Sport Psychologist*, 7, 173–90.

Schmid, A & Peper, E 1993, 'Training strategies for concentration', in J Williams (ed.), *Applied sport psychology: personal growth to peak performance*, 2nd edn, Mayfield, Mountain View, CA, pp. 262–73.

Scully, D & Kremer, J 2000, 'An educational approach: the design, implementation and evaluation of a psychological skills training programme', in R Butler (ed.), *Sports psychology in performance*, Arnold, London.

Spence, P 2001, 'An integrated approach to planning', in FS Pyke (ed.), *Better coaching: advanced coach's manual*, 2nd edn, Human Kinetics, Champaign, IL.

Stibbard, J 1998, *Training games from the inside: the secret to what works and what doesn't*, Business and Professional Publishing, NSW.

Taylor, J & Taylor, C 1995, *Psychology of dance*, Human Kinetics, Champaign, IL.

Thomas, P, Murphy, S & Hardy, L 1999, 'The test of performance strategies: development and preliminary validation of a comprehensive measure of athlete psychological skills', *Journal of Sports Sciences*, 17 (9).

Timms, D 2003, 'Pain-in-the-grass routine here to stay', *Herald-Sun News Pictorial*, 11 August, p. 89.

Vallerand, RJ 1983, 'Attention and decision making: a test of the predictive validity of the Test of Attentional and Interpersonal Style (TAIS) in a sport setting', *Journal of Sport Psychology*, 5, 449–59.

Vanden Auweele, Y, de Cuyper, B, van Mele, V & Rzewnicki, R 1993, 'Elite performance and personality: from description and prediction to diagnosis and intervention', in RN Singer, M Murphey & LK Tennant (eds), *Handbook of research on sport psychology*, Macmillan, New York, pp. 257–89.

Van Schoyck, RS & Grasha, AF 1981, 'Attentional style variations and athletic ability: the advantages of a sport specific test', *Journal of Sport Psychology*, 3, 149–65.

Winter, G & Hamilton, C 1992, *The business athlete: winning the inner game of business*, Pan Macmillan, Sydney.

CHAPTER 15

OPTIMAL EXPERIENCE IN SPORT: CURRENT ISSUES AND FUTURE DIRECTIONS

Susan A Jackson & William J Wrigley

In recent times the psychological study of human behaviour has seen a surge in the investigation of positive human states with a concomitant interest in prevention. This has followed from an earlier, heavy focus on psychological ill-health, weakness and suffering (Ryan & Deci 2001) and has recognised that 'psychology is not just the study of pathology, weakness, and damage; it is also the study of strength and virtue. Treatment is not just fixing what is broken; it is nurturing what is best.' (Seligman & Csikszentmihalyi 2000, p. 7). The move towards positive psychology has focused on the investigation of internal states that include wellbeing, happiness, optimism and flow (Buss 2000; Kogan 2001; Myers 2000; Seligman & Csikszentmihalyi 2000).

This shift of focus has been mirrored in the domain of sport and exercise psychology. An earlier focus on negative performance states such as performance anxiety has more recently been counterbalanced by a growing body of research investigating positive states and experiences such as flow, enjoyment and peak experiences.

As Csikszentmihalyi (1992) has suggested, in sport enjoyment, satisfaction and feeling in control are emotions that keep an athlete's participation active and consistent. Performing in a state where mind and body are one is the optimal internal experience to which most performers aspire. Understanding the quality of athletes' experiences, optimal and otherwise, and how they are linked to their peak performance achievements is therefore important for those involved in sport. As Kimiecik and Jackson (2002) stated, 'If we are interested in understanding athletes in a sport context, we must describe and understand the quality of their experience' (p. 501)

The purpose of this chapter is to examine the construct of optimal experience from the perspective of flow and the body of research that supports it. Optimal experience can be considered from other perspectives. However, the concept of flow has received the most attention in the sport literature and, we argue, comes closest to a clear understanding of optimal experience.

This chapter is divided into five sections. First, a conceptual definition of optimal experience will be explored, its association with peak performance and peak experience will be examined, and its compatibility with the concept of flow will be proposed. Second, there will be an overview of flow research in sport. The third area to be addressed will be the measurement of optimal experience. This will be followed by a description of factors facilitating flow, and, finally, future research directions will be explored.

At the time this chapter was first written a survey of researchers known to be involved in the study of flow in sport and exercise was conducted. The results obtained from the survey provide a picture, albeit incomplete, of the types of flow research questions being raised and addressed by researchers around the world. Information obtained from these surveys will be referred to throughout the chapter as personal communications where the research was not published at the time of the communications. It should be noted that there was an uncontrollable time lag between when the communications were obtained and the publication of this chapter. Thus it is likely that there is substantial research into flow in sport and exercise that is not reported here. The information summarised in this chapter provides examples of what has been investigated and ideas for future flow research.

WHAT IS AN OPTIMAL EXPERIENCE?

The challenge to describe and understand optimal experiences in sport and exercise psychology has mirrored a broader struggle in mainstream psychology with determining the elements of positive states such as subjective wellbeing, enjoyment and satisfaction. By examining the constructs of this broader effort, the understanding and conception of optimal experience in sport may be advanced.

Recently Ryan and Deci (2001) provided a thoughtful and compelling theoretical clarification of the psychological study of positive states to date that has particular relevance to the understanding and study of optimal experience in sport. They outline two research streams within which the predominant construct of wellbeing has been considered — the hedonistic and eudemonic.

The hedonistic psychology stream (Diener 2000; Kahneman, Diener & Schwarz 1999) has considered wellbeing as a subjective experience involving the desire for pleasure, fun or happiness as against displeasure or pain. Hedonistic wellbeing involves the seeking of highest happiness and is related to feeling relaxed and happy and being away from problems. The eudemonic (meaning 'true self') position rejects subjective happiness as a principal criterion of wellbeing (Waterman 1993). It promotes the idea of psychological wellbeing (PWB) and enjoyment as being related to personal growth and development, being challenged, exerting effort and actualising human potential (Ryan & Deci 2001).

The distinction between these two views highlights a qualitative difference — namely, striving to hedonistically attain desires or to eudemonically work towards becoming fully functional. In an effort to reconcile these different approaches, Ryan and Deci (2001) proposed a multidimensional viewpoint as the most useful position that incorporates both hedonistic and eudemonic viewpoints.

If the multidimensional framework proposed by Ryan and Deci (2001) is utilised, the concept of optimal experience in sport and exercise psychology can be clarified further. Optimal experience in sport has not referred exclusively simply to attaining the desire of pleasure or highest happiness, as proposed by the hedonist position. The construct can be more closely aligned to the eudemonic position that reflects a state of functionality and actualisation of self in which the participant feels intensely alive and authentic, and in which high states of joy or happiness may or may not occur.

Csikszentmihalyi (1990; Seligman & Csikszentmihalyi 2000) has clearly distinguished between hedonistic happiness, or what he refers to as pleasure states, and a eudemonic definition of enjoyment.

ENJOYMENT LEADS TO PERSONAL GROWTH

'Pleasure is the good feeling that comes from satisfying homeostatic needs such as hunger, sex and bodily comfort. Enjoyment, on the other hand, refers to good feelings people experience when they break through the limits of homeostasis — when they do something that stretches them beyond what they were — in an athletic event, an artistic performance, a good deed, a stimulating conversation. Enjoyment, rather than pleasure, is what leads to personal growth and long-term happiness ...'

(Seligman & Csikszentmihalyi 2000, p. 12)

Crucially, it is flow that makes experience enjoyable, according to Csikszentmihalyi (1990).

The concept of optimal experience in sport fits nicely within a research-supported, multidimensional perspective that includes both hedonic and eudemonic conceptions of wellbeing as outlined by Ryan and Deci (2001). Optimal experience will be used here as an umbrella term that refers to the multidimensional aspects of positive experiences in sport and exercise performance that provide not only strong positive feelings associated with highest happiness (hedonistic psychology) but also, and primarily, experiences that are self-fulfilling and come as a result of exerting effort (eudemonic psychology).

OPTIMAL EXPERIENCE DEFINED

'Yet we have all experienced times when, instead of being buffeted by anonymous forces, we do feel in control of our actions, masters of our own fate. On the rare occasions that it happens, we feel a sense of exhilaration, a deep sense of enjoyment that is long cherished and that becomes a landmark in memory for what life should be like. This is what we mean by *optimal experience* ... moments like these, the best moments in our lives, are not the passive, receptive, relaxing times ... The best moments usually occur when a person's body or mind is stretched to its limits in a voluntary effort to accomplish something difficult and worthwhile. Optimal experience is thus something we *make* happen.'

(Csikszentmihalyi 1990, p. 3)

Optimal experience, peak experience and peak performance

Over the past fifteen years, sport and exercise psychology research has focused considerable attention on ascertaining the psychological correlates of peak performance. The three significant constructs to emerge from this body of research have been peak performance, peak experience and flow. There has been considerable confusion in the use of terminology, which requires elucidation. Jackson and colleagues (Jackson 1996, 2000; Kimiecik & Jackson 2002) discuss this issue, and we now address it briefly.

Peak performance

Researchers in sport psychology have been drawn to the question of whether there is an optimal psychological state that occurs when athletes perform at their peak. To address this question, researchers have asked athletes to recall their subjective perceptions when performing optimally; they have compared the experiences of elite/successful with non elite/less successful athletes; and they have interviewed top athletes and coaches (Williams & Krane 1997).

After reviewing the results of a number of researchers in the area, including Ravizza (1977), Loehr (1984), Orlick and Partington (1988), Gould et al. (1992a, 1992b, 1993a, 1993b), Jackson (1992, 1995) and Eklund (1994, 1996), Williams and Krane (1997) concluded that 'regardless of the source of data or the nature of the sport, a certain psychological profile appears to be linked with successful performance' (p. 174). The general profile contained the following commonalities: the self-regulation of arousal, higher self-confidence, better concentration, feeling in control but not forcing it, a positive preoccupation with sport, determination and commitment.

More recently, Hanin (2000) has added to this tradition of exploring the psychological states accompanying peak performance. Through his study of optimal pre-competition anxiety, he proposed his Individual Zones of Optimal Functioning (IZOF) approach, which he later developed into a multidimensional model of positive and negative emotions in individual optimal performance.

The study of psychological states such as optimal experience from the perspective of peak performance has elucidated some useful parameters from which to better understand the performer's internal experience. However, this approach has also led to conceptual confusion and inaccuracy in the study of optimal experience in sport. For example, peak performance has been used interchangeably with optimal experience through the frequent use of the term 'peak performance states'.

Peak performance refers to an outcome or achievement of superior functioning rather than to an internal experience of optimal feelings and perceptions. Optimal experience describes an inner psychological state while engaged in an effortful and challenging activity, whereas peak performance refers to the outcome or accomplishment as a consequence of that person's effort and sustained concentration. Simply put, peak performance refers to an outcome rather than an experience.

Although a peak performance may bring with it an optimal experiential state in the performer, it is not synonymous with that internal experience. While an optimal experience may be a precursor to a peak performance, it may not necessarily accompany it. An athlete may be in flow and not necessarily be achieving a peak performance. This does not mean that the concept of flow is less useful to the world of sport and exercise psychology. It is important that the study of the flow experience not be limited to its potential associations with peak performance outcomes. In commenting on his aversion to focusing on the flow experience for what it can produce in terms of performance outcomes, Csikszentmihalyi (1988) stated, 'As soon as the emphasis shifts from the experience per se to what you can accomplish with it, we are back in the realm of everyday life ruled by extrinsic considerations' (p. 374).

Peak experience

Abraham Malsow (1968, 1970, 1973), the initiator of the psychological concept of self-actualisation in the late 1950s and 1960s, was the first psychologist to devote considerable study to the phenomenon of peak experiences across a number of life domains. He asked groups of people such questions as what was 'the single most joyous, happiest, most blissful moment of your life' (1973, p. 182). He found that almost all people have peak experiences or ecstasies and that they can be 'purely and exclusively emotional' (1973, p. 366). He also argued that self-actualising people were likely to have more peak experiences than those who were less fully functioning.

Maslow (1968, 1970) suggested that a peak experience was a self-validating moment containing 14 characteristics that reflected a variety of emotional and cognitive changes. These changes included a feeling of being detached from concerns, a strong concentration, an egoless and unselfish perception, disorientation in time and space, and a feeling of life being meaningful, beautiful and desirable. More recently, McInman and Grove (1991) suggested that 'Peak experiences are characterized by feelings of bliss, great joy, and illumination. There is a strong sense of self and freedom from outer restrictions. They are very often unexpected, rare and extraordinary' (p. 340).

Ravizza (1977, 1984) was the first researcher to conduct an in-depth examination of the peak experience within the sport context. He found similarity with some of the characteristics proposed by Maslow. Ravizza (1984) suggested that the peak experiences of athletes were temporary, involuntary and unique. 'Athletes gave their experiences total attention, resulting in temporary ego loss, union with the experience as a whole, and disorientation in time and space' (Ravizza 1977, p. 39). Athletes experienced a total immersion in the activity, a narrow focusing of attention with the immediate activity, and a feeling that everything was perfect. 'With no conscious effort the participant is in total control of the situation with no fears of failure' (Ravizza 1977, p. 38).

However, Ravizza (1977) found that the sport peak experiences did not contain a number of the cognitive qualities described by Maslow (1968) and were not reported as experiences of central importance in respondents' whole lives, as Maslow found.

Since then, Privette and colleagues (1981, 1982, 1983; Privette & Bundrick 1987, 1991, 1997; Privette, Bundrick & Hwang 1997; Privette & Landsman 1983) have been the most prolific in examining peak experience and its links to peak performance. From their perspective, peak experience has been considered as an intense, positive and enjoyable experience of highest happiness. They have found that in performance-dominated sport events, peak performance was often, but not necessarily, accompanied by the feeling-dominated state of peak experience (Privette & Bundrick 1997). This view of peak experience substantially removed the cognitive components of peak experience as proposed by Maslow (1968, 1970), and can be considered more consistent with the hedonistic feeling state of attaining desire.

Research has suggested that flow and peak experience are overlapping constructs and can co-occur (Jackson 1996, 2000; McInman & Grove 1991; Privette & Bundrick 1997). However, the notion of peak experience appears to be conceptually different in two significant ways from the optimal experience model of flow. While peak experience is aligned with the hedonistic viewpoint, the central components of the flow construct reflect the eudemonic position of effort, functionality, challenge and self-actualisation. Also, the optimal experience model consists not only of an affective component but also of several important cognitive components, such as intense concentration, clear goals, and a balance of skills and challenge (Csikszentmihalyi 1990).

Along with this richer perspective, the flow construct is grounded in a multidimensional theory of optimal experience with a substantive empirical base drawn from a variety of life domains such as work, school, leisure and sports (Kowal & Fortier 1999). These conceptual differences suggest that the optimal experience of flow provides a central and unifying construct with regard to positive experiences in sport (Jackson 2000). It may therefore be more useful to consider the notion of peak experience as a component of the multidimensional construct of optimal experience in which pleasurable moments of highest happiness occur within the potential for a eudemonically enjoyable experience such as flow. As Csikszentmihalyi (1997) has described, 'It is the full involvement of flow, rather than happiness, that makes for excellence in life' (p. 32).

What is flow?

Csikszentmihalyi (1975) first developed the concept of flow after investigating the experiences of a diverse group of people including rock climbers, surgeons, dancers and chess players. The term flow came from descriptions of involving experiences by the participants. He went on to study optimal experiences in other domains such as work and leisure activities and found consistency in how the involving experience was reported. This experience became known as flow (Csikszentmihalyi & Csikszentmihalyi 1988).

Flow is an internal, conscious process that lifts our experience from the ordinary to the optimal. It is the experiencing of several characteristics together that makes the flow experience so special (Jackson & Csikszentmihalyi 1999). Flow is a state of consciousness that involves total focus, involvement and absorption in what we are doing, to the exclusion of all other thoughts and emotions. Our mind and body are working together effortlessly so that there is an intrinsic experience of harmonious enjoyment and pleasure (Jackson & Csikszentmihalyi 1999). This leads us to feeling that we are so involved in the activity that nothing else seems to matter and we continue in it 'even at great cost, for the sheer sake of doing it' (Csikszentmihalyi 1990, p. 4).

Csikszentmihalyi has found from his studies that flow is accessible by all people in a variety of activities.

ALMOST ANY ACTIVITY CAN PRODUCE FLOW

'Flow is generally reported when a person is doing his or her favourite activity — gardening, listening to music, bowling, cooking a good meal. It also occurs when driving, talking to friends, and surprisingly often at work ... almost any activity can produce flow provided the relevant elements are present ...'

(Csikszentmihalyi 1997, pp. 33–4)

Flow is something we make happen through participation and striving towards mastery in an activity (Csikszentmihalyi 1990). Rarely do we experience flow in passive leisure activities, such as watching television or relaxing.

The degree of flow occurs on a continuum. At one end of the continuum are simple, absorbing moments of enjoyment or microflow events (Csikszentmihalyi 1992), while at the other end are defining moments of optimal experience that are 'truly memorable occasions of *deep flow*' (Csikszentmihalyi 1992, p. 183).

A central element of the flow construct is the need for the challenges of an activity to be balanced with the skills of the participant. This challenge–skill balance is depicted in figure 15.1.

However, the person's *perception* of the level of challenge and degree of skill and the balance between them are essential to the concept of flow (Csikszentmihalyi 1990). When our perceived challenge of the activity is in balance with our perceived skill we are setting ourselves up for an experience of flow. This means it is not so much what the objective challenges or skills are in a situation that determine the quality of the experience, but what we *think* of the level of challenge of a situation and how skilled we *believe* we are to meet the challenge.

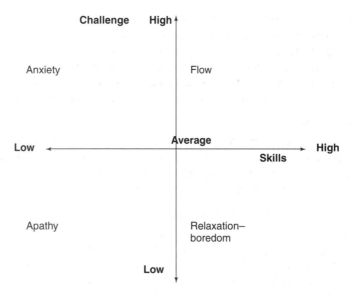

Figure 15.1 Model of the flow state   (*Source:* Adapted from Jackson & Csikszentmihalyi 1999)

The focus of this chapter is the flow experience in sport. The idea of an optimal experiential state while performing in sport has been referred to by athletes as being 'in the groove', 'in the zone' and even 'flowing' (Jackson & Csikszentmihalyi 1999). As described in the quotation below, the best athletes can bring about this optimal state of flow.

ATHLETES IN FLOW

'They know what to do and believe they can succeed. There is order in their consciousness, with clear goals focusing their thoughts so intensely that not enough attention is left over to even worry about themselves or their problems. Concentration is directed totally toward the activity. The players are so in tune with what they are doing that they quickly notice the finest nuances of their game and make adjustments to stay in the groove.'

(Jackson & Csikszentmihalyi 1999, p. 8)

The dimensions of flow

Csikszentmihalyi (1990, 1997) has proposed a model of optimal experience in which the central concept is an inner experience called the *flow state*. From his research he has proposed nine experiential dimensions that define the concept of flow. A fuller explanation of these dimensions can be captured in Csikszentmihalyi (1990), and with reference to sporting contexts in Jackson and Csikszentmihalyi (1999).

Challenge–skill balance

The most central concept that defines flow is the need for us to experience a balance between our perceived challenges and our perceived skills. Our perception of both the challenge of the situation and our skills to meet the challenge needs to be at personally high levels in order for us to be primed to experience flow: 'it is not enough for challenges to equal skills; both factors need to be extending the person, stretching them to new levels' (Jackson & Csikszentmihalyi 1999, p. 16). The balance depends more on 'what you *believe* you can do' (p. 17) and how you perceive the situation than on the actual demands or your abilities per se.

Merging of action and awareness

Flow also involves the experience of our actions merging with our awareness. Our total absorption in the activity means that we cease to be aware of ourselves as separate from our actions and experiences of the activity. Our mind is not looking at our body from the outside. Instead, there is a feeling of total immersion and oneness with the task. There is a sense of effortless ease and fluency in our movements.

Holding clear goals

In flow we feel very clear about what we are doing and what we need to achieve. We have clear goals or a blueprint that has been set in advance of what we need to do, together with an awareness while undertaking the activity of knowing, moment by moment, what to do next (Jackson & Csikszentmihalyi 1999, p. 21).

Receiving unambiguous feedback

Having clear goals means that we are likely to develop the flow state further by experiencing unambiguous feedback while undertaking the activity. This feedback can involve tuning into the information from our body or from external factors that tell us how we are going, such as other competitors, the coach or the audience. The flow state requires us to appraise the success of our actions in an ongoing way during the performance process. The unambiguous feedback provides a clear idea of the next action and enables us to know we are on track towards achieving our goals.

Total concentration on the task at hand

One of the clearest indications of flow is the ability to hold complete and full focus on the activity in which we are immersed. 'In flow there is no room for any thoughts other than what you are doing and feeling right at the moment, the "now"' (Jackson & Csikszentmihalyi 1999, p. 25). Flow requires a full and sustained concentration — the ability to exclude irrelevant or unhelpful thoughts from your consciousness and instead to tune in to the task at hand. In flow, this focus becomes effortless.

Sense of control

Athletes in flow report a clear sense of their ability to exercise control over their performance so that they experience a sense of empowerment for the challenging activity to be undertaken. This sense of control frees them from any fear of failure or lack of confidence. They believe they have the required skills, trust in them and know the task is achievable. As a result they have a strong sense of power, confidence and calm.

Loss of self-consciousness

Because in flow you are totally absorbed in the activity and experiencing a merging of action and awareness in which you are one with the activity, there is no room for worry about self or about the evaluations of others. Csikszentmihalyi (2000) has stated that 'what is lost in flow is not the "I", but the "me"' (p. 1163). Flow therefore frees you from the negative thoughts that produce self-doubt and fear.

Transformation of time

Because you are deeply absorbed in an activity, you can lose sense of the ordinary passage of time so that time is transformed in some way. The activity can seem to pass by very quickly, so that time speeds up and hours pass by like minutes; sometimes the reverse is reported — you feel as if time slows down and you have all the time in the world for your actions to be performed. This is perhaps the least experienced of the flow dimensions. It may not always be experienced in the flow state (Csikszentmihalyi 1990). Qualitative research (e.g. Jackson 1996) and quantitative research (Jackson, Kimiecik, Ford & Marsh 1998; Jackson, Thomas, Marsh & Smethurst 2001) has found time transformation to be the least experienced flow dimension in the sport setting.

Autotelic experience

The flow state is an intrinsically rewarding and enjoyable experience, one that we choose for its own sake and that provides its own reward. As Kimeicik and Harris (1996, p. 256) state, 'An enjoyable activity is one that is done not with the expectation of some future benefit, but simply because the doing itself is the reward'. This is what is known as an autotelic experience. We experience high levels of intrinsic satisfaction or enjoyment from engaging in the activity. This dimension has been described by athletes as being on a high, being fun, feeling exhilarated, a buzz.

The autotelic flow dimension is the end product of the convergence of all the other dimensions (Csikszentmihalyi 1990). 'It is a dimension that athletes endorse strongly, and it is what makes flow so enticing that, once experienced, it is sought after again and again' (Jackson & Csikszentmihalyi 1999, p. 30).

OVERVIEW OF FLOW RESEARCH IN SPORT
The beginnings

Empirical study of the flow state in sport began in a concerted way with in-depth investigations by Jackson in the early 1990s (Jackson & Roberts 1992; Jackson 1992). The primary foci were to examine the subjective meaning of the flow experience for athletes, to determine the degree of consistency of athletes' descriptions of the flow experience with the dimensional model of flow espoused by Csikszentmihalyi (1990), and to ascertain the relationship of the flow state to positive performance. Elite athletes were chosen as the initial subject of study because of their expected familiarity with optimal performance and flow experiences (Jackson 1996).

An initial study of elite athletes by Jackson and Roberts (1992) examined the association between peak performance and flow with 200 athletes from a wide-ranging sample of sports that included gymnastics, swimming, golf, track and field, cross-country running, tennis and diving. The authors investigated whether peak performance was related to flow and motivational constructs by examining the relationships between athletes' goals of action, their perception of flow, their perceived ability and the quality of their competitive performance. Results showed a significant association between flow and peak performance. Flow was experienced to a greater degree in the athletes' best performance than when they generally competed. They also found that athletes who were higher in orientation towards mastery of the task before them experienced flow more frequently than athletes low in mastery orientation.

A subsequent study by Jackson (1992) was one of the first of its kind to examine from an interpretive qualitative perspective the manner in which flow was described and experienced and to compare this with the flow model proposed by Csikszentmihalyi (1990). The nature of the flow experience was examined with 16 national champion figure skaters. Results showed a close agreement between the skaters' perceptions of flow and the theoretical descriptions of the flow construct as proposed by Csikszentmihalyi (1990). Factors perceived as important for attaining flow were identified, as were factors seen to prevent or disrupt flow.

These studies provided promising research possibilities for the further exploration of optimal experiences in sport. In this context Kimiecik and Stein (1992) provided a significant and timely contribution regarding conceptual and methodological issues of flow research in sport contexts.

Expansion of flow research

In the early 1990s Kimiecik and Stein (1992) noted that research needed to go beyond descriptions of the elements of the flow experience to examine the interactions between person and situation variables that were associated with the flow state — that is, 'how, when, where and what person factors ... such as self-efficacy, trait anxiety and concentration skills ... interact with situation factors to produce flow, boredom, anxiety or apathy in athletes?' (p. 149). The situation factors they proposed included the type of sport, whether it was self-paced (such as golf) or reactive (such as tennis), whether the sport was individual or team focused, the importance of the activity and the impact of environmental factors.

Studies of the flow experience in sport have been forging new paths in some of the directions suggested by Kimiecik and Stein (1992). A more concerted effort to examine the flow experiences of non-elite athletes has occurred, together with the inclusion of a variety of physical activities such as exercise, circuit training, yoga and aerobics. There were also efforts to tease out the nuances of the flow dimensions, to determine the influence of situational variables and to illuminate factors that facilitate flow. Jackson (1996) examined the descriptions of 28 elite athletes from seven sports to assess whether these descriptive accounts coincided with Csikszentmihalyi's (1990) dimensional model of flow. Results showed a consistency in flow experience descriptions with Csikszentmihalyi's model and with the figure skating sample from her 1992 study.

Jackson (1995) also investigated antecedent flow factors in greater depth and with a larger, more diverse sample of athletes than her initial 1992 study. Results were consistent with the earlier study, identifying some similar factors such as confidence as being key antecedent factors. The 1995 study by Jackson also generated additional antecedent and preventive flow factors such as pre-competitive/competitive plans and preparation and level of motivation.

Stein, Kimiecik, Daniels and Jackson (1995) undertook three studies to examine the relationships between flow, goal orientations, perceptions of confidence and competence in a sample of recreational tennis players, basketballers and golfers. Their results showed that optimal experiences did occur in recreational sports. However, the mechanisms influencing these experiences remained unknown as their results showed that neither goals, competence nor confidence predicted the flow experience. However, these associations have since been found (Catley & Duda 1997; Kowal & Fortier 1999).

Catley and Duda (1997) undertook a quantitative examination of the findings of the Jackson studies (1992, 1995) with a non-elite, non-competitive sport sample of 163 recreational golfers. They tested psychological states both before and during the golf round and found consistency with the Jackson (1995) study. Their findings of confident readiness, positive focus and pessimism, having the strongest relationship with flow, demonstrated that antecedent factors not found by Stein et al. (1995) did occur in their sample.

In a confirmation of the findings with regard to flow and task orientation by Jackson and Roberts (1992), Kowal and Fortier (1999) found with 203 masters' level swimmers that those who were motivated in a self-determined way by engaging in swimming for their own pleasure, satisfaction or benefit reported the highest instances of flow. Also, they found that the situational determinants of perceived competence, autonomy and relatedness were positively and significantly related to flow experiences.

Grove and Lewis (1996) examined the association between flow, personal factors of the participants and hypnotic susceptibility in a sample of participants engaged in the non-competitive, recreational, self-paced activity of circuit training. Results showed that participants with higher hypnotic susceptibility and a prior history of more than six months of circuit training reported more flow-like experiences.

Jackson and colleagues (Jackson, Kimiecik, Ford & Marsh 1998) examined the flow experience in non-elite, older athletic participants in four sports of the World Masters Games — swimming, triathlon, cycling, and track and field. Using a dispositional version of the Flow State Scale (Jackson & Marsh 1996), their findings gave support to the idea suggested by Csikszentmihalyi (1990) of an autotelic personality in which participants choose to undertake an activity for its own sake and that provides its own reward. Factors found to be predictive of state and dispositional flow were perceived ability, intrinsic motivation and anxiety.

Recent advances in flow research

The period from the latter half of the 1990s to the present has seen further advances and exciting developments in the study of the flow experience among athletes. Studies have been able to consider more closely the definition of the flow dimensions. There has been research to clarify the relationship of the flow state to person variables such as subjective feelings, hypnotic susceptibility and personality variables. Situational variables such as sport setting and organisational levels have also been examined.

Furthermore, consistent with Kimiecik and Stein's (1992) recommendations, the measurement of flow has become more flexible and robust with the development of two quantitative scales that operationalise the flow experience. The development of the Flow State Scale–2 (FSS-2) (Jackson & Eklund 2002) provides a quantitative measure of the flow experience for a participant during an activity. The Dispositional Flow Scale–2 (DFS-2) (Jackson & Eklund 2002) operationalises the general dispositional tendency of that participant to experience flow. This development will be explored more fully in the next section.

Evidence is emerging that the experience of flow dimensions is not homogeneous across sports, situations and participants. It appears that some dimensions are more relevant than others in the achievement of flow in sport contexts, and not all flow elements may be experienced to the same extent (Jackson et al. 1998; Jackson, Thomas, Marsh & Smethurst 2001). In earlier qualitative research, Jackson (1996) found that the flow dimensions of autotelic experience, action-awareness merging, concentration on the task at hand and sense of control formed the core elements of the experience from analysis of athletes' flow experiences. Similarly, Jackson and colleagues (1998) found in a quantitative study that the most predominant dimensions across both state and dispositional flow were challenge–skill balance, concentration on the task at hand, sense of control and unambiguous feedback. In a recent study of 236 athletes involved in orienteering, surf life saving and road cycling, Jackson and colleagues (2001) found that the four dimensions of challenge–skill, concentration on the task at hand, sense of control and clear goals emerged as the strongest factors in associational analyses with other psychological variables. Jackson et al. (1998) also found that the dimensions of action-awareness merging and time transformation failed to demonstrate substantial relationships with the predictor variables of perceived ability, intrinsic/extrinsic motivation, goal orientation and trait anxiety.

Jackson (1996) found that the dimensions of loss of self-consciousness and time transformation received relatively lower endorsement by athletes in qualitative research, and lower loadings on higher order factors in quantitative studies (Jackson & Marsh 1996; Jackson et al. 1998; Jackson et al. 2001; Jackson & Eklund 2002). Kowal and

Fortier (1999) found that these dimensions were not significantly associated with the different types of situational motivation as compared with the other flow characteristics. They suggested that this might be because these two dimensions were less salient for their sample of swimmers. Jackson (1996) raised this as a general possibility after her qualitative study with athletes, and again following quantitative analyses of the flow dimensions as assessed by the flow scales (Jackson & Marsh 1996; Jackson & Eklund 2002).

Similarly, other studies (Vlachopoulos, Karageorghis & Terry 2000; Russell 2001) found that the time transformation subscale was less associated with global flow than the other flow dimensions. Bennett and Kremer (2000) found it to be weakly evident among elite surfers and Vlachopoulos and colleagues (2000) raised the possibility that in their sample of aerobic exercisers the dimension of time was inappropriate to the demands of their task. An awareness of time in athletic situations where flow occurs has been identified by Jackson and colleagues (Jackson & Marsh 1996; Jackson & Eklund 2002) as a potential reason for lack of relationship between this factor and global flow scores.

The lack of robust support for the loss of self-consciousness dimension of flow found in research by Jackson and colleagues (Jackson 1996; Jackson & Marsh 1996; Jackson et al. 1998; Jackson et al. 2001; Jackson & Eklund 2002) has similarly been found in others' research (e.g. Bennett & Kremer 2000; Vlachopoulos et al. 2000). Vlachopoulos and colleagues (2000) suggested that this dimension may vary according to the situational variable of the extent to which participants engage in a group activity or in public. Under these circumstances the tendency to self evaluate rather than be aware of self may increase or become more blurred. Jackson and Eklund (2002) discuss how a certain degree of self-consciousness may be a necessary part of the sport flow experience. However, Jackson and colleagues (1998, 2001) did find that the loss of self-consciousness dimension, when measuring state flow, was moderately predictive of other psychological factors such as perceived ability, intrinsic motivation and self-concept in two different sport samples. Future research may be able to clarify the relationship of the loss of self-consciousness and time transformation dimensions to the physical activity flow experience.

Summary of research findings investigating correlates of flow

Some interesting research has investigated the association between the flow experience and particular person or situational variables such as the length of sport involvement, self-concept, use of psychological skills, positive subjective feelings and the sport setting.

Person variables

Length of sport involvement

Grove and Lewis (1996) found that participants with a longer history of involvement in an activity experienced more flow-like characteristics. They found that persons with a prior history of six months of gymnasium circuit training reported more flow-like experiences than those with less than six months' prior history. Fletcher (2002) found that number of years playing rugby predicted dispositional flow scores, using the DFS-2.

Gender

Do males and females experience flow differently? Research by Jackson and colleagues (e.g. Jackson & Marsh 1996; Jackson et al. 1998, 2001) has not found substantial differences in the ways in which males and females respond to the flow scales. Russell (2001) used quantitative and qualitative methods with 42 college athletes drawn from a variety of sports to examine the effect of gender with the flow experience. He did not find any significant differences, which suggested the athletes experienced flow in a similar manner whether they were male or female. Lack of gender differences was also found in a study of male and female aerobic exercise participants by Vlachopoulos et al. (2000). However, in an Italian sample across a variety of sport types, gender differences were found in three of the flow dimensions — challenge–skill balance, unambiguous feedback and concentration on task at hand (Muzio, Nitro, Lecchi, in press). Curry and colleagues (personal communication, 5 July 2001) similarly found gender differences in their sample of US college athletes, using the Dispositional Flow Scale–2 (Jackson & Eklund 2002). Future research is needed to clarify the question of gender differences in flow experience.

Self-concept and psychological skills

Jackson and colleagues (2001) examined relationships between self-concept, use of psychological skills by athletes and their flow experiences. Using both state and dispositional forms of the flow scale with a sample of 236 athletes, their results showed that the more proficient athletes were at using psychological skills and the more positive their perceptions of self, the more likely they experienced flow.

Although using a small sample size, Straub (1996, reported in Kimiecik & Jackson 2002) found that a mental imagery program helped increase frequency of flow states in college wrestlers. Stock (1997) reported an educational program he applied in a single case study to help an athlete induce flow.

Positive subjective feelings

Csikszentmihalyi (1990) described flow as an optimal psychological state in which the experience itself is so enjoyable that it becomes autotelic. Kimiecik and Harris (1996) have proposed that flow acts within a motivational cycle in which flow promotes positive internal feelings that become an intrinsic motivator to undertake the activity again and again. Hence the activity becomes autotelic.

Studies have found that athletes experience a strong feeling of enjoyment when in flow (Jackson 1996; Jackson et al. 2001). There has been some investigation of the association between the subjective feelings of enjoyment and flow in exercise. Karageorghis et al. (2000) found in their sample of 1231 aerobic dance exercise participants a positive and significant association between levels of flow and the post-exercise feelings of revitalisation, tranquillity and positive engagement. This suggested that the optimal experience of flow is likely to encourage adherence to physical activity regimes through the experience of positive post-exercise feelings. Extrapolating their findings to the physical education setting, they suggested that school students would benefit by assistance from their physical educator to facilitate flow experiences.

Autotelic experience

The autotelic experience (enjoying the activity for its own sake) has been found to be an important element of the flow experience in sport and exercise (Jackson 1992, 1996; Jackson et al. 1998; Jackson et al. 2001; Bennett & Kremer 2000). Ellis, Voelkl & Morris (1994) found that variation in flow experience could be partly explained by variables that represented the autotelic nature of the person. This supports the notion put forward by Csikszentmihalyi (1975, 1990) that some individuals may be better equipped to create flow experiences in their lives, and that this individual capacity could be linked to an autotelic personality trait of intrinsic enjoyment or openness to absorbing experiences.

Hypnotic susceptibility

Grove and Lewis (1996) studied a non-competitive sport sample of university gymnasium circuit training participants and found an association between hypnotic susceptibility and 'flow-like' states. Their results showed that highly hypnotic susceptible participants showed greater changes in their flow-like states than those with low susceptibility.

Performance

Relationships between flow and performance levels are obviously of interest to those who wish to understand and maximise peak performance, although we reiterate the need to not limit the flow phenomenon to only its links with performance accomplishments. Jackson and colleagues (1998) found preliminary support for a positive association in demonstrating links between flow and self-reported performance levels. In a subsequent study, Jackson et al. (2001) found that flow state predicted a small amount of variance in an objective performance measure, finishing position, as well as positive associations between self-reported performance and flow.

Situational factors

In her initial research, Jackson (1995) found situational factors that were perceived as non-favourable by elite athletes, such as non-optimal conditions, unwanted crowd response and influences from uncontrollable events, were major disruptors of flow. Jackson et al. (2001) discussed the ways in which the type of sport may influence experience of flow. In their study, the sports included were competitive, continuous rather than stop–start events, endurance-based and subject to variable environmental conditions. The authors suggested that these and other sport-related factors may influence whether, and how, flow is experienced.

A group of Italian researchers have been investigating the flow experience across a variety of sport settings (e.g. Muzio, Nitro & Lecchi, in press). They have reported differences on an Italian version of the Flow State Scale (FSS) (Jackson & Marsh 1996) between fencers, skiers, swimmers, cyclists, and track and field athletes. The fencers were the most different from the other groups, which the researchers explained in terms of the high importance assigned to immediate feedback cues in fencing bouts. There was close similarity between the swimming, cycling, and track and field groups.

Russell (2001), in his study of college athletes, used a combination of qualitative and quantitative methods that included interviews and the FSS to examine the effect of the situational variable of sport setting on the experience of flow. The qualitative results supported those found quantitatively with the FSS and were consistent with previous, similar research (Jackson 1995, 1996). Using the FSS, Russell (2001) did not find any significant differences between participants from a variety of individual and team sports. This suggested that this group of college athletes experienced flow in a similar manner irrespective of whether they engaged in a team or individual sport. Because the FSS was mailed to participants and was not given immediately after the activity, further study of sport setting influences on flow will be needed to confirm this finding. In an earlier qualitative study, Jackson (1995) found that an important factor unique to team athletes that influenced the occurrence of flow was how well the team was playing and interacting.

A further interesting situational variable has been investigated by Gilson, Pratt, Roberts and Weymes (2000). They qualitatively examined the organisational structures of ten consistently high-performing elite sports clubs world wide, including the Chicago Bulls, Women's Hockey Australia and the Williams Formula One motor racing team and developed a model of organisational flow from their findings. They proposed three interrelated principles that promote organisational peak performance and described the conditions necessary to achieve these principles. 'Peak purpose provides meaning and direction for people within organizations. Peak practices create the organizational context for people to prepare for peak performance, while peak flow explains how people work together to achieve it.' (Gilson et al. 2000, p. 241). This recent research provides encouragement and direction in examining flow within the more complex situation domains of team and organisational settings and their interrelationships.

The impact of situational variables on the flow experience of sports participants has received limited attention. The results to date show that further delineation of influential situation-specific variables under varying conditions will enhance the understanding and utility of the flow experience.

MEASUREMENT OF OPTIMAL EXPERIENCE

Because of the complexity of this psychological state and his fear that the flow spirit would be broken, Csikszentmihalyi (1992) expressed some reluctance to operationalise the flow state. He believed that any measure of flow would be a 'partial reflection' of the human experience (Csikszentmihalyi 1992, p. 183), and refers to the history of psychology as being replete with 'examples of how barren important ideas become as soon as they are precisely "measured" ' (p. 182).

Because flow is a subjective, experiential phenomenon and susceptible to the problems of empirical measurement as alluded to in Csikszentmihalyi's (1992) comments above, no one measurement method can provide a comprehensive assessment of flow. Kimiecik and Stein (1992), together with Jackson and colleagues (Jackson 2000; Jackson & Marsh 1996; Jackson, et al. 1998), have argued for a multi-modal approach that incorporates both qualitative and quantitative methods of measurement. This approach has been suggested so as to ensure that a broad and rich amount of information can be gathered and methods can be refined to understand and explain the 'what' and 'how' questions posed by the unique phenomenon of the flow experience.

The measurement approaches that have been developed and described below are tools to tap into the flow experience and are presented with the understanding that no one empirical tool can fully capture flow.

Use of qualitative methods

Csikszentmihalyi's (1975) early research that brought to light the flow concept involved qualitative interviews with people from a variety of life domains. In a similar vein, initial research of flow in sport (Jackson 1992, 1995, 1996) used qualitative methods to assess the flow experience. This involved in-depth interviews of participants and inductive content analysis of their descriptions to tease out the higher-order factors inherent in their experiences. A qualitative approach was adopted in this early research because it was felt that this would facilitate the understanding of athletes' flow experiences, particularly as little prior research had been conducted in the area. By interviewing athletes about their flow experiences, it was possible to explore the understanding and meaning of flow from the eyes of the elite athlete.

The development of quantitative methods

Csikszentmihalyi (1975) developed his model of flow through the use of experience sampling (Csikszentmihalyi & Larson 1987). A concomitant quantitative approach has been more recently developed in sport by Jackson (e.g. Jackson & Marsh 1996; Jackson

& Eklund 2002) through the development of both the dispositional and flow state scales. These quantitative scales were developed to facilitate the examination of the flow experience among sport and exercise participants and to assist with teasing out those factors that may be associated with its occurrence. Both the Experience Sampling Method and Jackson's flow scales are described below.

The Experience Sampling Method (ESM)

The Experience Sampling Method (ESM) involves the systematic measurement of people's everyday experiences as they are interacting in their natural environment (Csikszentmihalyi & Larson 1987; Hormuth 1986). The usual method is for participants to carry a beeper or wristwatch, which provides them with a randomly occurring signal several times during their day. At each time they receive the signal they complete a questionnaire with regard to their momentary experiences in the situation at the time. These measures are generally taken over a period of one week.

EXAMPLE QUESTIONS FROM CSIKSZENTMIHALYI'S ESM FORM

- How well were you concentrating?
- How self-conscious were you?
- Did you feel good about yourself?

(*Source:* Csikszentmihalyi & Larson 1987)

Analysis of the ESM data provides a description of the patterns of people's individual daily experiences and as a result can yield evaluations of the commonality of experience in particular situations (Csikszentmihalyi & Larson 1987). Csikszentmihalyi and Larson (1987) stated, 'ESM data allow examination of the magnitude, duration, and sequences of states, as well as an investigation of correlations between the occurrences of different experiences' (p. 533).

The ESM has been considered a reliable and valid tool for assessing flow (Csikszentmihalyi & Larson 1987) and has been used for this purpose in many varied life settings (see Csikszentmihalyi & Csikszentmihalyi 1988). The ESM offers several advantages that are particularly useful in the study of flow. Measures of momentary thoughts and feelings and their effects can be gathered in the person's natural environment without too much disruption. It is also an ecologically valid method. The ESM methodology is able to detect fine-grained temporal relationships between affects and changeable antecedents (Cerin, Szabo & Williams 2001).

The difficulties with implementing the ESM approach in naturalistic sport settings have been discussed elsewhere (e.g. Jackson 2000; Kimiecik & Stein 1992). There are obvious problems to be encountered with the idea of interrupting a sport performance. Creative ways of applying the ESM approach will enable the benefits of this type of assessment to be realised in physical activity settings. One issue not frequently addressed is the potential for the ESM to produce invalid results as a result of priming effects (Cerin et al. 2001). The repeated measuring of psychological variables in itself could cause changes in a person's experience. Cerin et al. (2001) addressed this issue by studying the pre-competitive experience of 22 athletes. Their results found strong evidence for the validity of the ESM for the analysis of emotions within the competitive sport context, and evidence of priming effects were not found.

Flow State Scale–2 (FSS-2)

Based on both qualitative and quantitative methods, Jackson and Marsh (1996) developed a self-report scale, called the Flow State Scale (FSS), so as to open up the possibilities for quantitative investigations of the flow state in sport settings. Recently Jackson and Eklund (2002) developed a revision of the FSS, which they have called the FSS-2.

The FSS-2, like its predecessor, is a 36-item self-report questionnaire designed to measure the state of flow when participating within a specific sport or physical activity. It is designed to be given immediately or soon after a participant has completed an activity. The questionnaire has nine subscales, each with four items, to assess the nine flow dimensions. Respondents indicate the extent to which they agree with each statement on a five-point Likert scale, ranging from 1 (Strongly disagree) to 5 (Strongly agree).

SAMPLE ITEMS FROM THE FSS-2

- I made the correct movements without thinking about trying to do so.
- I had a sense of control over what I was doing.
- It was no effort to keep my mind on what was happening.

(*Source:* Jackson & Eklund 2002)

Dispositional Flow Scale–2 (DFS-2)

A dispositional version of the flow scale was developed to measure the frequency with which one typically experiences flow in sport or physical activity (Jackson et al. 1998). The DFS was based on preliminary validation of the FSS developed by Jackson and Marsh (1996). Recently Jackson and Eklund (2002) developed a revision of the DFS and have called it the DFS-2. The DFS-2 was developed to aid in the understanding of the autotelic personality, which could be a factor in explaining individual differences in the propensity to experience flow in sport (Jackson et al. 1998).

The DFS-2 is essentially a parallel version of the FSS-2. Like the FSS, it is a 36-item self-report questionnaire. However, items are reworded to assess to what degree an individual *generally* experiences the flow state while participating in physical activity. It is therefore designed to be answered away from an immediate involvement in one's activity. The questionnaire has nine subscales with four items each, corresponding to the nine flow dimensions. Respondents indicate the frequency of each statement on a five-point Likert scale, ranging from 1 (Never) to 5 (Always).

Flow scale reliability

Both the FSS-2 and the DFS-2 and their predecessors have demonstrated acceptable reliability. The FSS was shown to have alphas ranging from .72 to .91 across three studies by Jackson and colleagues (Jackson & Marsh 1996; Jackson et al. 1998; Jackson et al. 2001). The DFS was shown to have alphas ranging from .70 to .89 across two studies by Jackson and colleagues (Jackson et al. 1998; Jackson et al. 2001). Karageorghis, Vlachopoulos and Terry (2000), in a study of aerobic dance exercise participants using the FSS, found alphas over .70 for all subscales except Time Transformation, which yielded an alpha of .65. Kowal and Fortier (1999), using the FSS with masters' swimmers, found alphas ranging from .76 to .89. Pates and Maynard (2000) investigated the association between hypnotic states and flow using the FSS and found a mean alpha of .83 with the nine subscales. In initial validation research, the FSS-2 has yielded alphas ranging from .80 to .92, with the DFS-2 range being .78 to .90 (Jackson & Eklund 2002).

Flow scale validity

Within- and between-network studies (Marsh & Jackson 1999) have been undertaken for the purpose of evaluating support for the construct validity of the FSS-2 and DFS-2 and their predecessors. Jackson and Marsh (1996) demonstrated acceptable fit values for the FSS, as did Marsh and Jackson (1999) for the FSS and DFS. In both these studies, a nine-factor first-order model and a hierarchical model with one global flow factor were evaluated. The first-order model has received stronger support, and caution was advised in using total scores from the scales owing to the slightly weaker fit of the hierarchical model.

Vlachopoulos and colleagues (2000), using confirmatory factor analysis, examined the factor structure of the FSS with exercise participants. They concluded that the data provided inadequate support for both a nine-factor first-order model and a hierarchical model. However, these conclusions were based on application of Hu and Bentler's (1999) revised and stringent recommendations regarding fit values in confirmatory factor analyses, which have not received unequivocal support as appropriate benchmarks for multifactor rating instruments (Marsh 2000).

The issue of fit values and the range of acceptable values for confirmatory factor analyses is complex and beyond the scope of this chapter. Jackson and Eklund (2002) discuss the issue in their paper, which examines the factor structure and fit of the FSS-2 and DFS-2. The revisions to the flow scales were undertaken to try to improve the factor structure of the weaker performing loss of self-consciousness and time transformation dimensions, as well as to seek to replace a small number of problematic items from the original versions of the scales. Jackson and Eklund (2002) discuss the replacement items and subsequent improvements to the factor structure of the scales. The authors found that both new versions of the scale demonstrated acceptable fit patterns and an overall improvement in the measurement of flow from the original FSS and DFS.

FACILITATING FLOW

INCREASING THE OCCURRENCE OF FLOW

'It is not possible to make flow happen at will ... and attempting to do so will only make the state more elusive. However, removing obstacles and providing facilitating conditions will increase its occurrence ...'

(Jackson & Csikszentmihalyi 1999, p. 138)

A number of facilitating factors have been suggested by research to increase the likelihood of experiencing flow during a performance. Knowing what these factors are and how to implement them will allow athletes to increase the likelihood of achieving the rewarding optimal experience of flow in their performances.

Facilitative factors

While Jackson (1992) found that elite figure skaters generally experienced flow infrequently when competing, there were certain factors that helped and hindered the achievement of this state. Skaters were more likely to achieve flow when they had a positive mental attitude, experienced positive pre-competitive and competitive affect, maintained appropriate focus, felt physically ready and experienced a unity with their dance partner. Skaters' experience of flow was more likely to be prevented or disrupted if they experienced physical problems and made mistakes, had an inability to maintain focus, had a negative attitude or experienced a lack of audience response.

In an extension of her 1992 study, Jackson (1995) considered the factors that facilitated, disrupted and prevented the experience of flow together with the perceived controllability of flow with a larger and more diverse range of elite athletes across seven sports. Results showed considerable consistency with results from her previous research with figure skaters (Jackson 1992). They suggested that athletes may have more control over the occurrence of flow than had been suggested. Ten factors (see boxed example 15.8) were described by the athletes to influence their development of flow that included physical, psychological, nutritional and situational variables. Support for the multidimensional nature of antecedent and preventive flow factors was provided by the findings.

FACTORS INFLUENCING FLOW

1. Being motivated to perform well.
2. Achieving an optimal arousal level before performing.
3. Having pre-competitive and competitive plans so that the performer felt totally prepared and knew clearly what to do.
4. Knowing they had done the training and felt physically ready.
5. Optimal environmental and situational conditions and influences.
6. Feeling good during a performance.
7. Holding strong focus and concentration.
8. Feeling confident and having a positive mental attitude.
9. Having positive team play and interaction.
10. Feeling experienced as a competitor and in having experienced flow in the past.

(*Source:* Jackson 1995)

Karageorghis et al. (2000) made some suggestions to facilitate the flow experience among school students. They suggested that students 'set personal goals which are attainable, challenging and well-defined', 'give pupils a choice from time to time in the activities they engage in' to increase their autotelic experience and use 'skill-learning techniques' to encourage persistence in mastering the tasks to increase their sense of control (p. 243).

Perceived skill level

It has been shown that perceived ability is an important predictor of flow (Jackson et al. 1998, 2001; Jackson & Roberts 1992). Consistent with earlier research (Jackson 1995; Stein et al. 1995), Jackson and colleagues (1998) studied an older, non-elite athlete sample and found that a high perception of their sporting ability was a crucial factor facilitating flow. Similarly, Jackson et al. (2001) found a positive relationship between self-concept and flow in a competitive athlete sample. Earlier Jackson and Roberts (1992) had examined the challenge–skill dimension and found that flow was more likely to be achieved if athletes adopted a self-referenced perspective about their ability that focused on mastery. These findings led Jackson (Jackson et al. 2001) to suggest that the perceived skills component of the challenge–skill balance that defines flow is a critical aspect in the acquisition of the flow state in sport.

Anxiety

The model of flow proposed by Csikszentmihalyi (1990) (see figure 15.1) underscores the important balance between the perceptions of skill and challenge in a situation and the relationship of imbalance of these factors to anxiety. When the challenges are greater than perceived skills, anxiety is the predicted outcome in this flow model. Considerable research (Jackson 1995; Jackson & Roberts 1992; Jackson et al. 1998; Stein et al. 1995; Taylor 2001) has shown that anxiety is a preventative flow factor and, further, that the cognitive rather than the physiological components of anxiety are seemingly more detrimental to the flow experience. Taylor (2001) suggested that facilitative appraisal of somatic anxiety may have a role in regulating flow experiences.

Intrinsic motivation

Flow appears to be best facilitated when the participant holds self-determined, intrinsic motivation (Kowal & Fortier 1999). Extrinsic forms of motivation may have detrimental influences on flow states. A study by Jackson and colleageus (1998) using a multidimensional measure of intrinsic motivation showed that only an intrinsic motivation factor demonstrated substantial relationships with flow. The extrinsic factors were unrelated to flow. Further research may shed light on how different forms of motivation are related to flow.

Hypnosis training and skill

Two studies have suggested that flow may be enhanced by hypnotic capacity and training. The results of a study by Grove and Lewis (1996) showed that the flow state can be enhanced by the capacity for hypnotic susceptibility. They found that high-susceptibility exercisers had greater increases in flow than low-susceptibility participants.

Exploratory studies by Pates and Maynard (2000) and Pates, Cummings and Maynard (2002) examined the effects of hypnotic intervention on flow states with golf chipping performance and three-point shooting in basketball. Although their studies were limited in generalisability by a small sample size (three golfers and five basketballers respectively), they found that hypnotic interventions using imagery, relaxation, hypnotic induction, regression and triggers enhanced their experience of and personal control over flow.

FUTURE DIRECTIONS

The way forward for research into the optimal experience of flow appears promising and exciting. Many interesting and fruitful aspects of the flow experience that await research attention are likely to significantly broaden and deepen the understanding of flow and its utility for people engaged in sporting endeavours.

There are a number of broad research areas that remain a high priority in the development of knowledge about the flow experience. The four areas we focus on here are to:

* tease out more of the correlates of flow and their interaction
* further clarify the dimensional flow model, in particular the relative contribution of each of the flow dimensions and the interaction between them
* investigate the utility of different measurement tools for investigating flow
* expand investigation into other performance domains such as music, dance, theatre and leisure time.

Each of these research directions will now be considered more fully.

The correlates of flow

While there has been a promising beginning in drawing out the antecedent correlates of flow (e.g. Jackson 1992; Jackson & Roberts 1992; Jackson et al. 1998; Jackson et al. 2001; Karageorghis et al. 2000), there is scope for research to explore this area further (Jackson et al. 2001). An important focus that requires closer attention is the study of the ways in which the person within as well as situational variables singly and together may affect the flow experience.

From the person perspective, an important question to study is to what degree and in what ways does the athlete's disposition influence his or her ability to experience flow? Variables that could be considered include the athlete's:

- general level of capacity to experience enjoyment and fun
- general disposition for and frequency of flow experiences
- emotional and personality characteristics, such as the autotelic personality trait
- motivational orientations
- cognitive styles and processes, including the capacity to concentrate and immerse oneself in an activity
- links between the concepts of trust and flow (J. Fournier, personal communication, 22 June 2001)
- experience with and use of psychological skills
- physiological correlates, such as respiratory and heart rate, electroencephalogram (EEG) and brain scan patterns (Grove & Lewis 1996).

A research proposal from France (J. Fournier, personal communication, 22 June 2001) envisages undertaking an examination of the links between brainwave activity and the flow experience with elite archery participants. Information from studies such as this may provide some much-needed clarification of physiological correlates of flow.

Situational factors that include environmental and sport setting variables also require research attention. In what ways do such variables as the following impact on the experience of flow?

- Sport settings, such as competitive and recreational environments. Research is needed to better understand the relationship between non-competitive and competitive sport contexts and flow experiences. It may be that competition, with its emphasis on winning, shifts the focus of concentration to external factors and, as a result, decreases the capacity for loss of self-consciousness (see Kimiecik & Jackson 2002).
- Activity types, such as team compared with individual; organised sport compared with physical activities such as exercise.
- Within-sport related factors such as practice conditions and conditioning methods.
- Continuing the research that has begun to investigate whether mental skills training programs can facilitate flow.
- Social factors such as coaching and team-mate styles and relationships. For example, is there a 'collective flow' in team sports? (J. Fournier, personal communication, 22 June 2001). Fletcher (2002) recently conducted a study with rugby union players in New Zealand using the DFS-2 to investigate the antecedent and preventative factors created by the coach in the game and practice sessions that influence the achievement of flow in players. He concluded that the coaching process might be an active element in the achievement of flow, and may provide the impetus for it to develop over time. However, his results did not conclusively show that the coaching process was an active element in the achievement of flow. Fletcher recommended that future research use a multi-method approach to assess the impact of the coaching process on flow, arguing that the coaching process plays a critical role in establishing an

optimal environment that may foster the right conditions for an athlete to achieve flow (S Fletcher, personal communication, 9 September 2002).

- Organisational contexts such as the influence of organisational cultures and administration styles.
- Environmental factors such as the crowd/audience and performance conditions.

One of the most important research pursuits for the future will be the unravelling of the complex interplay between these person and situational variables. How do certain dispositional characteristics of the athlete interact with situational variables to affect the experience of the nine dimensions of flow? The recent development of both state and dispositional measures of flow in the FSS-2 and DFS-2 (Jackson & Eklund 2002) will assist researchers in examining this question.

The dimensional flow model

Csikszentmihalyi (e.g. 1990, 1993) has delineated nine dimensions of flow. This dimensional model has been confirmed in sport research (e.g. Jackson 1996; Jackson & Marsh 1996; Jackson & Eklund 2002; Kowal & Fortier 1999; Russell 2001). However, it remains unclear how some of the nine dimensions operate in different performance domains. Future research is required to tease out the relative importance of each of the nine dimensions and the pattern of relationships between them within different sporting contexts and individuals (Jackson et al. 1998, 2001). For example, as has been discussed earlier in this chapter, the loss of self-consciousness and time transformation dimensions have been found to receive lower endorsement and lower factor loadings (Jackson 1996; Jackson & Marsh 1996; Kowal & Fortier 1999; Vlachopoulos et al. 2000). One future research direction would be to investigate how these two dimensions are experienced in different settings. In one study, Kershaw (1999) investigated the links between self-consciousness and the attainment of flow states in elite and non-elite karate athletes. He concluded that it might be useful to view self-consciousness as being composed of different dimensions, some of which need to be gained while others need to be lost for flow to occur. Csikszentmihalyi (2000) has distinguished between the 'me', which he suggests is lost in flow, and the 'I', which remains active. Future research may be able to clarify how these more complex flow dimensions are experienced in physical activity.

In the dimensional model of flow, the challenge–skill balance operates as one of the most important nine factors. Research to date (Jackson & Roberts 1992; Jackson 1995; Jackson et al. 1998; Jackson et al. 2001) has supported the centrality of the challenge–skill dimension in the flow experience. The skill component of the equation appears to be the most critical (Jackson et al. 1998, 2001). However, the role of the degree of challenge in sport and exercise contexts remains less clear. Jackson and colleagues (1998) and Stein and colleagues (1995) found no relationship between ratings by competitive athletes of the degree of challenge of an activity and the flow subscales. Stein et al. (1995) did, however, find an association with recreational athletes. Further research is needed to define the challenge–skill balance more precisely within different physical activity contexts. For example, what degree of competence and what degree of challenge must be perceived before flow can be experienced (Ellis et al. 1994; Kimiecik & Stein 1992)? Also, is the high skill – high challenge mix, as suggested by Csikszentmihalyi (1990), a necessary condition for all optimal experiences in sport settings? Bennett and Kremer (2000) did not find a balance between challenge and skill in the peak performances of elite surfers. In what ways does this mix vary according to different sports settings, such as within competitive or recreational sports? In what ways might the challenge–skill mix vary within the other channels of the flow model, such as boredom or anxiety?

Ellis and colleagues (1994) have suggested that the specific measurement of the physical, emotional and cognitive aspects of the challenge and skill elements of an activity may further broaden our understanding of the role of this dimension in facilitating flow.

The recent study by Jackson et al. (2001) has suggested that the unambiguous feedback dimension of flow may require closer research analysis to determine the type of feedback that will maximise the flow experience. Csikszentmihalyi (1990) indicated that the important elements of this dimension were that the feedback be clear and immediate. However, Jackson et al. (2001) found that feedback that focused on errors rather than the positive aspects of the performance generated more errors. This suggested that the degree to which the feedback was positive or negative might also affect the achievement of flow.

The measurement of flow

The ESM of Csikszentmihalyi (Csikszentmihalyi & Larson 1987) and Jackson's flow scales are the primary tools used for quantitative assessments of flow. There is a need to continue investigating creative and reliable ways of using these instruments in a variety of physical activity settings.

The ESM

The ESM has been the central method used by Csikszentmihalyi and colleagues (e.g. Csikszentmihalyi & Csikszentmihalyi 1988; Csikszentmihalyi & Nakamura 1989) to assess flow. While it provides an in-situ measurement of the flow experience, the method has been underutilised in psychological research in sport.

Stein and colleagues (1995) used the ESM to study the flow experience with basketballers. Over a nine-week academic quarter at an American university, a research assistant entered the gymnasium, stopped the activity (such as a game or drill) and the students immediately filled out the experience sampling forms. They reported that the ESM was a practical method for use in recreational sports. Similarly, Jones, Hollenhorst, Perna and Selin (2000) successfully used a modified version of the ESM on-site with 52 competitive whitewater kayak participants to assess the flow model.

In a recent study, Cerin and colleagues (2001) randomly assigned 66 male competitive tae kwon do practitioners into three different measurement groups to ascertain their emotional states. While this study did not measure the flow experience, it provided strong evidence that the ESM can be used to assess dynamic psychological states during competitive sport.

As previously discussed, working out creative and effective ways to adapt and apply the ESM approach to physical activity settings has the potential to open up greater understanding of flow through this dynamic measurement approach.

The flow scales

The flow scales have been the primary tools used by Jackson and colleagues (e.g. Jackson et al. 1998; Jackson et al. 2001) to assess flow in physical activity settings. The FSS-2 and DFS-2 provide valid and reliable tools for assessing post-event and general tendency to experience flow respectively. Despite the substantial base of confirmatory factor analysis studies of the flow scales, continuing research is required to validate the new scales in different settings. Research using the FSS-2 and DFS-2 will be able to assess the dimensional model of flow questions addressed above. The DFS-2 facilitates investigation of correlates of flow, while the FSS-2 provides assessment of experience of flow characteristics within an event. The Flow State Scale–2 (FSS-2) is best administered as soon after the activity as possible (Jackson & Marsh 1996; Jackson & Eklund 2002). Jackson et al. (1998, 2001) have recognised from their research that this can be difficult to achieve in some sport settings in which control over when the participants complete the state assessment can be variable. Gaining immediate post-performance assessments with the FSS-2 will provide insights into how flow is experienced by different individuals in different situations.

Jackson and Eklund (in press) have recently written a flow scale test manual that details the use, scoring and interpretation of the DFS-2, FSS-2.

Examining flow in other performance domains

Interestingly, Csikszentmihalyi (1975) initially began investigating flow through interviewing performers in varied domains and was struck by the consistency of the flow experience across domains. There is tremendous scope for broadening the understanding of flow through continuing to explore the flow experience across different performance domains. To this end, research is beginning to examine the flow experience in other performance domains, including the following:

* In the performing arts domain, such as among musicians, singers, dancers and actors, empirical study of positive psychological performance states, while extremely relevant and likely to prove of immense utility, is extremely sparse. A doctoral dissertation is under way to examine the association of the flow state with examination performances of music students at an Australian conservatorium of music (Wrigley 2001). In the initial validation studies of the FSS-2 and DFS-2, Jackson and Eklund (2002) included a variety of dance performers in their samples.
* An interesting development in the understanding of flow has been the examination of its relevance and application in computer-mediated environments, especially web instruction and design (e.g. Chen, Wigand & Nilan 1999; Novak, Hoffman & Yung 2000; Roberts 2001). Given the growing importance of computer technology, this is a timely and potentially productive direction in which the study of flow can move.
* While Ellis and colleagues (1994) cite a number of research studies up to the early 1990s that have examined the flow experience in leisure activities, replication and extension of these is required to deepen our understanding of the flow model, especially the apathy, anxiety and boredom dimensions.

CONCLUSIONS

Flow is an exciting area to research, and the work that we have described in this chapter has opened up diverse possibilities in terms of research questions as well as approaches to the study of optimal experience. Seeking to further understand the flow experience is important for those interested in researching or fostering the positive side of physical activity. We close with a quote from Jackson and Csikszentmihalyi (1999) regarding the perspective that the flow experience in sport can provide us as researchers, practitioners and participants:

> What is true for life as a whole is true in the more limited domain of sport. Winning, getting medals, improving one's time, or beating a record are important to get us motivated at the beginning, but if we take these goals too seriously — so that their pursuit blinds us to the experience along the way — then we miss the main gift that sport can give.

(Jackson & Csikszentmihalyi 1999, p. 163)

SUMMARY

In this chapter we have argued that optimal experience in sport contexts is best considered within the framework of the flow model. This is consistent with a multidimensional approach to studies of wellbeing within the broader domain of positive psychology, where hedonistic and eudemonic perspectives (Ryan & Deci 2001) are outlined. We covered five main areas related to the study of optimal experience. We began with a conceptual definition of optimal experience and related this to other constructs. We then undertook an overview of the research that has been conducted on flow in sport and followed this with a discussion of measurement options and issues. The factors that have been found to facilitate and hinder the flow experience were explored and, finally, suggestions for future research directions were outlined.

REVIEW QUESTIONS

1 What is the difference between hedonistic and eudemonic views of wellbeing?
2 Which view does optimal experience fit more closely with and why?
3 What is the main difference between a peak experience and a peak performance?
4 What is the main difference between a peak experience and an optimal experience, as we define the terms in this chapter?
5 Define the concept of flow in your own words.
6 How many dimensions describe flow? Can you name them?
7 Name three recent advances in flow research.
8 What are two person factors that have been correlated with flow?
9 Describe the ESM approach for measuring flow.
10 What is the difference between the FSS-2 and the DFS-2?

References

Bennett, R & Kremer, P 2000, 'The psychology of peak performance among elite surfers', paper presented at the 2nd annual Monash University Sport Psychology Conference, July 3.

Buss, DM 2000, 'The evolution of happiness', *American Psychologist*, 55 (1) 15–23.

Catley, D & Duda, JL 1997, 'Psychological antecedents of flow in golfers', *International Journal of Sport Psychology*, 28, 309–22.

Cerin, E, Szabo, A & Williams, C 2001, 'Is the Experience Sampling Method (ESM) appropriate for studying pre-competitive emotions?', *Psychology of Sport and Exercise*, 2, 27–45.

Chen, H, Wigand, RT & Nilan, MS 1999, 'Optimal experience of web activities', *Computers in Human Behavior*, 15, 585–608.

Csikszentmihalyi, M 1975, *Beyond boredom and anxiety*, Jossey-Bass, San Francisco.

Csikszentmihalyi, M 1988, 'The future of flow', in M Csikszentmihalyi & I Csikszentmihalyi (eds), *Optimal experience: psychological studies of flow in consciousness*, Cambridge University Press, New York, pp. 364–83.

Csikszentmihalyi, M 1990, *Flow: the psychology of optimal experience*, Harper & Row, New York.

Csikszentmihalyi, M 1992, 'A response to the Kimiecik & Stein and Jackson papers', *Journal of Applied Sport Psychology*, 4, 181–3.

Csikszentmihalyi, M 1993, *The evolving self*, Harper & Row, New York.

Csikszentmihalyi, M 1997, *Finding flow: the psychology of engagement with everyday life*, HarperCollins, New York.

Csikszentmihalyi, M 2000, 'Happiness, flow and economic equality', *American Psychologist*, 55, 1163–4.

Csikszentmihalyi, M & Larson, R 1987, 'Validity and reliability of the experience-sampling method', *Journal of Nervous and Mental Disease*, 175, 526–36.

Csikszentmihalyi, M & Csikszentmihalyi, I 1988, 'Measurement of flow in everyday life: introduction to part IV', in M Csikszentmihalyi & I Csikszentmihalyi (eds), *Optimal experience: psychological studies of flow in consciousness*, Cambridge University Press, New York, pp. 251–65.

Csikszentmihalyi, M & Nakamura, J 1989, 'The dynamics of intrinsic motivation: a study of adolescents', in C Ames & R Ames (eds), *Research on motivation in education, Vol. 3: Goals and cognitions*, Academic Press, New York, pp. 45–71.

Diener, E 2000, 'Subjective wellbeing', *American Psychologist*, 55 (1) 34–43.

Eklund, RC 1994, 'A season long investigation of competitive cognition in collegiate wrestlers', *Research Quarterly for Exercise and Sport*, 65, 169–83.

Eklund, RC 1996, 'Preparing to compete: a season-long investigation with collegiate wrestlers', *The Sport Psychologist*, 10, 111–31.

Ellis, G, Voelkl, J & Morris, C 1994, 'Measurement and analysis issues with explanation of variance in daily experience using the flow model', *Journal of Leisure Research*, 26, 337–56.

Fletcher, S 2002, 'Achieving flow: evaluating how the coaching process influences flow in rugby union players', unpublished master's thesis, University of Otago, Dunedin, NZ.

Gilson, C, Pratt, M, Roberts, K & Weymes, E 2000, *Peak performance: business lessons from the world's top sports organizations*, HarperCollins, London.

Gould, D, Eklund, R & Jackson, S 1992a, '1988 USA Olympic wrestling excellence I: mental preparation, pre-competitive cognition, and affect', *The Sport Psychologist*, 6 (4) 358–82.

Gould, D, Eklund, R & Jackson, S 1992b, '1988 USA Olympic Wrestling Excellence II: competitive cognition and affect', *The Sport Psychologist*, 6 (4) 383–402.

Gould, D, Eklund, RC & Jackson, SA 1993a, '1988 USA Olympic Wrestling Excellence: coping strategies used by U.S. Olympic Wrestlers', *Research Quarterly*, 64 (1) 83–93.

Gould, D, Finch, LM & Jackson, SA 1993b, 'Coping strategies utilized by national champion figure skaters', *Research Quarterly for Exercise and Sport*, 64 (1) 83–93.

Grove, JR & Lewis, MA 1996, 'Hypnotic susceptibility and the attainment of flowlike states during exercise', *Journal of Sport & Exercise Psychology*, 18, 380–91.

Hanin, YL 2000, 'Individual zones of optimal functioning (IZOF) model: emotion performance relationships in sport', in YL Hanin (ed.), *Emotions in sport*, Human Kinetics, Champaign, IL, pp. 65–89.

Hormuth, SE 1986, 'The sampling of experiences in situ', *Journal of Personality*, 54, 262–93.

Hu, L & Bentler, PM 1999, 'Cutoff criteria for fit indexes in covariance structure analysis: conventional criteria versus new alternatives', *Structural Equation Modelling*, 6, 1–55.

Jackson, SA 1992, 'Athletes in flow: a qualitative investigation of flow states in elite figure skaters', *Journal of Applied Sport Psychology*, 4, 161–80.

Jackson, SA 1995, 'Factors influencing the occurrence of flow states in elite athletes', *Journal of Applied Sport Psychology*, 7, 135–63.

Jackson, SA 1996, 'Toward a conceptual understanding of the flow experience in elite athletes', *Research Quarterly for Exercise and Sport*, 67, 76–90.

Jackson, SA 2000, 'Joy, fun, and flow state in sport', in Y Hanin (ed.), *Emotions in sport*, Human Kinetics, Champaign, IL, pp.135–56.

Jackson, SA & Csikszentmihalyi, M 1999, *Flow in sports: the keys to optimal experiences and performances*, Human Kinetics, Champaign, IL.

Jackson, SA & Eklund, RC 2002, 'Assessing flow in physical activity: the FSS-2 and DFS-2', *Journal of Sport and Exercise Psychology*, 24, 133–50.

Jackson, SA & Eklund, RC (in press), *The flow scale manual*, Fitness Information Technology, Morgantown, WV.

Jackson, SA, Kimiecik, J, Ford, S & Marsh, HW 1998, 'Psychological correlates of flow in sport', *Journal of Sport & Exercise Psychology*, 20, 358–78.

Jackson, SA & Marsh, HW 1996, 'Development and validation of a scale to measure optimal experience: the flow state scale', *Journal of Sport & Exercise Psychology*, 18, 17–35.

Jackson, SA & Roberts, GC 1992, 'Positive performance states of athletes: toward a conceptual understanding of peak performance', *The Sport Psychologist*, 6, 156–71.

Jackson, SA, Thomas, PR, Marsh, HW & Smethurst, CJ 2001, 'Relationships between flow, self-concept, psychological skills, and performance', *Journal of Applied Sport Psychology*, 13, 154–78.

Jones, CD, Hollenhorst, SJ, Perna, F & Selin, S 2000, 'Validation of the flow theory in an on-site whitewater kayaking setting', *Journal of Leisure Research*, 32 (2) 247–61.

Kahneman, D, Diener, E & Schwarz, N (eds) 1999, *Wellbeing: the foundation of hedonic psychology*, Russell Sage Foundation, New York.

Karageorghis, CI, Vlachopoulos, SP & Terry, PC 2000, 'Latent variable modelling of the relationship between flow and exercise-induced feelings: an intuitive appraisal perspective', *European Physical Education*, 6 (3) 230–48.

Kershaw, A 1999, 'Self-consciousness and the attainment of flow states in elite and non-elite karate athletes', unpublished BSc (Hons) thesis, University of Glamorgan, Pontypridd, Wales.

Kimiecik, J & Harris, A 1996, 'What is enjoyment? A conceptual/definitional analysis with implications for sport and exercise psychology', *Journal of Sport & Exercise Psychology*, 18, 247–63.

Kimiecik, JC & Jackson, SA 2002, 'Optimal experience in sport: a flow perspective', in TS Horn (ed.), *Advances in sport psychology*, 2nd edn, Human Kinetics, Champaign, IL, pp. 501–27.

Kimiecik, J & Stein, G 1992, 'Examining flow experiences in sport contexts: conceptual issues and methodological concerns', *Journal of Applied Sport Psychology*, 4, 144–60.

Kogan, M 2001, 'Where happiness lies', *Monitor on Psychology*, January, 74–6.

Kowal, J & Fortier, M 1999, 'Motivational determinants of flow: contributions from self-determination theory', *Journal of Social Psychology*, 139 (3) 355–68.

Loehr, JE 1984, 'How to overcome stress and play at your peak all the time', *Tennis*, March, 66–76.

Marsh, HW 2000, 'Conventional fit criteria too restrictive. Formal discussion initiation to Structural Equation Modeling Discussion Group', http://bama.ua.edu/archives/semnet.html (accessed 30 August 2000).

Marsh, HW & Jackson, SA 1999, 'Flow experience in sport: construct validation of multidimensional, hierarchical state and trait responses', *Structural Equation Modelling*, 6, 343–71.

Maslow, AH 1968, *Toward a psychology of being*, 2nd edn, Van Nostrand, New York.

Maslow, AH 1970, *Religions, values and peak-experiences*, Viking, New York.

Maslow, AH 1973, *The farther reaches of human knowledge*, Pelican (Penguin), New York.

McInman, AD & Grove, JR 1991, 'Peak moments in sport: a literature review', *Quest*, 43, 333–51.

Muzio, M, Nitro, G & Lecchi, R (in press), 'Flow e peak performance: discipline sportive a confronto', in M Muzio (a cura di), *Flow e prestazione eccellente nello sport — dai modelli teorici all'applicazione sul campo*, F. Angeli Ed., Milano.

Myers, DG 2000, 'The funds, friends, and faith of happy people', *American Psychologist*, 55 (1) 56–67.

Novak, TP, Hoffman, DL & Yung, YF 2000, 'Measuring the customer experience in online environments: a structural modeling approach', *Marketing Science*, 19, 21.

Orlick, T & Partington, J 1988, 'Mental links to excellence', *The Sport Psychologist*, 2, 105–30.

Pates, J & Maynard, I 2000, 'Effects of hypnosis on flow states and golf performance', *Perceptual and Motor Skills*, 91, 1057–75.

Pates, J, Cummings, A & Maynard, I 2002, 'Effects of hypnosis on flow states and three-point shooting performance in basketball players', *The Sport Psychologist*, 16, 34–47.

Privette, G 1981, 'The phenomenology of peak performance in sports', *International Journal of Sport Psychology*, 12, 51–60.

Privette, G 1982, 'Peak performance in sports: a factorial typology', *International Journal of Sport Psychology*, 13, 242–9.

Privette, G 1983, 'Peak experience, peak performance, and flow: a comparative analysis of positive human experiences', *Journal of Personality and Social Psychology*, 45, 1361–8.

Privette, G & Bundrick, CM 1987, 'Measurement of experience: construct and content validity of the experience questionnaire', *Perceptual and Motor Skills*, 65, 315–32.

Privette, G & Bundrick, CM 1991, 'Peak experience, peak performance, and flow', *Journal of Social Behavior and Personality*, 6, 169–88.

Privette, G & Bundrick, CM 1997, 'Psychological processes of peak, average, and failing performance in sport', *International Journal of Sport Psychology*, 28, 323–34.

Privette, G, Bundrick, CM & Hwang, K 1997, 'Cross-cultural measurement of experience: Taiwanese and Americans' peak performance, peak experience, misery, failure, sport and average events', *Perceptual and Motor Skills*, 84, 1459–82.

Privette, G & Landsman, T 1983, 'Factor analysis of peak performance: the full use of potential', *Journal of Personality and Social Psychology*, 44 (1) 195–200.

Ravizza, K 1977, 'Peak experiences in sport', *Journal of Humanistic Psychology*, 17 (4) 35–40.

Ravizza, K 1984, 'Qualities of the peak experience in sport', in J Silva & R Weinberg (eds), *Psychological foundations of sport*, Human Kinetics, Champaign, IL, pp. 452–61.

Roberts, AG 2001, 'Establishing and maintaining flow within a CSCL business education community', PhD dissertation in progress.

Russell, WD 2001, 'An examination of flow state occurrence in college athletes', *Journal of Sport Behavior*, 24 (1) 83–99.

Ryan, RM & Deci, EL 2001, 'On happiness and human potentials: a review of research on hedonic and eudaimonic wellbeing', *Annual Review of Psychology*, 52, 141–66.

Seligman, ME & Csikszentmihalyi, M 2000, 'Positive psychology: an introduction', *American Psychologist*, 55 (1) 5–14.

Stein, G, Kimiecik, J, Daniels, J & Jackson, SA 1995, 'Psychological antecedents of flow in recreational sport', *Personality and Social Psychology Bulletin*, 21, 125–35.

Stock, M 1997, 'Educating an athlete to induce the flow state', unpublished master's thesis, University of Wales Institute, Cardiff.

Straub, C 1996, 'Effects of a mental imagery program on psychological skills and perceived flow states of collegiate wrestlers', unpublished master's thesis, Miami University, Oxford, OH.

Taylor, MK 2001, 'The relationships of anxiety intensity and direction of flow in collegiate athletes', unpublished master's thesis, University of North Carolina at Greensboro, NC.

Vlachopoulos, SP, Karageorghis, CI & Terry, PC 2000, 'Hierarchical confirmatory factor analysis of the Flow State Scale in exercise', *Journal of Sport Sciences*, 18, 815–23.

Waterman, AS 1993, 'Two conceptions of happiness: contrasts of personal expressiveness (eudaimonia) and hedonic enjoyment', *Journal of Personality and Social Psychology*, 64, 678–91.

Williams, JM & Krane, V 1997, 'Psychological characteristics of peak performance', in JM Williams (ed.), *Applied sport psychology: personal growth to peak performance*, 3rd edn, Mayfield, Mountain View, CA, pp. 158–70.

Wrigley, WJ 2001, 'The association between flow and excellence in music performance', PhD dissertation in progress, Griffith University, Queensland.

CHAPTER 16

THE EVOLUTION OF TRAINING AND SUPERVISION IN SPORT PSYCHOLOGY

Mark B Andersen

Sport psychology research and practice can be traced back to the work of Triplett (1897) and Griffith (1928). A major landmark in the field occurred with the establishment of the International Society of Sport Psychology (ISSP) in 1965. Five years later the first academic sport psychology periodical, the *International Journal of Sport Psychology*, appeared under the auspices of the ISSP. While applied sport psychology research progressed, inquiry into professional practice remained in its infancy. It would be over a decade before the debate about the training and education of sport psychologists began in earnest, and it took until the early 1990s before the word 'supervision' gained any more than a cursory mention in the literature. In applied training and supervision, sport psychology remained in arrested development for a long time. Now this area of our field seems to be growing up.

TRAINING AND IDENTITY

The first major growth spurt on the issue of training is intimately tied to questions about the identity for researchers and applied practitioners in the field. Much of what follows is an account of developments in North America, where much of the debate on professional practice and training took place. In the early 1980s it seemed as though the discipline was undergoing an Eriksonian psychosocial adolescent crisis of 'identity versus role confusion' (Erikson 1968), as exemplified in Brown's (1982) article titled 'Are sport psychologists really psychologists' and in Dishman's (1983) article. The identity issue may perhaps be explained by the diverse backgrounds of those involved, which included physical education, exercise science, and clinical and counselling psychology. The turf wars about who could practise what, and who was trained for what raged through the 1980s. Clinicians argued that physical educationists were not properly trained to do some of the things they were doing. The exercise science people responded that the clinicians did not understand sport and were overpathologising athlete concerns. Some sport psychology meetings degenerated into shouting matches over these issues — adolescent identity crisis indeed. There was, however, some 'balm in Gilead', although in this case the balm came from Colorado Springs.

The United States Olympic Committee (USOC) established a tripartite taxonomy of sport psychology service providers, along with a registry for people who met their classification guidelines (USOC 1983). The USOC classified the world of sport psychologists into researchers, educators and clinicians. The research sport psychologist would be permitted to study USOC athletes with a view to providing scientific evidence of the usefulness of various psychological interventions. The educational sport psychologist would teach mental skills (e.g. relaxation, imagery and goal setting) to athletes with the primary aim of enhancing performance, and the clinical sport psychologist would deal with athletes with issues relating to mental health and adjustment. The educational category was designed to include those with physical education backgrounds, so that they might practise applied sport psychology techniques, even though they were not licensed as psychologists. The USOC also had relatively clear guidelines on the academic and experiential backgrounds required for each of these classifications (e.g. a PhD in clinical or counselling psychology for clinical sport psychologists).

In time the USOC scheme, by giving each group a specific area of expertise, helped ease some of the tensions between the different practitioners. The scheme also profoundly influenced how people in the field thought about themselves, spoke about themselves and viewed their training. Even today one can still hear people say, 'I am an educational sport psychologist'; such self-appellations stem directly from the USOC guidelines. In the 1980s, when the question of what training a sport psychologist should have arose, the answer was, 'It depends on whether you want to be a clinical, educational or research sport psychologist'. The USOC academic requirements for registry membership for the three categories became the unofficial guidelines for training in many schools in the US (see McCullagh & Noble 1996).

Today, however, the USOC trinity appears arbitrary and naïve. Andersen (1992) argued that the research category was the only clear one, and that the distinction between educational and clinical sport psychologists was hazy at best. He suggested that an educational sport psychologist who works with a team over a long period, teaches players mental skills, travels with the team, helps the athletes and coaches communicate better, and so forth, really fills the role of a team counsellor, and is acting in a therapeutic capacity. A decade later some of Andersen's comments also appear naïve. The sorts of behaviours and actions that constitute 'research' these days further cloud the tripartite distinction. A researcher conducting a study on autogenic training and sport performance is delivering a powerful therapeutic intervention. A clinician who assembles and presents a well-documented case study is engaged in a time-honoured research process. The educational psychologist could be seen to be involved in a type of action research. In Piagetian terms, the USOC scheme seems to have emerged during a concrete operational stage of the field's development. Recently Simons and Andersen (1995) reported (in quite 'formal operational' terms) the observations of Giges, one of the elder statesmen of applied sport psychology, which transcended the whole issue of what folks call themselves and what they do:

> What we know, and what we do, need not be limited by what we call ourselves. Is helping someone learn a new behavior, change a belief, or change thinking considered education, counseling, or therapy? I believe it is a part of each and all three, therefore it can be done by an educator, counselor, or therapist who has acquired the necessary knowledge, skill, and experience to do so. (p. 464)

It is knowledge and competencies that define the boundaries for practice, not labels. The turf wars over this issue now seem like a lot of sound and fury signifying little more than adolescent growing pains. Nevertheless, the USOC registry sparked significant debate (Clarke 1984; Feltz 1987; Heyman 1984). Feltz suggested that for those interested in service delivery for athletes, an education predominantly in psychology would be most appropriate, but for those wishing to do research and assume academic positions, exercise science would be a better path.

AAASP certification

The next significant influence on training in sport psychology came with the Association for the Advancement of Applied Sport Psychology (AAASP) certification of consultants and their certification guidelines (the current version is available online at www.aaasponline.org; see also appendix A). AAASP first began certifying sport psychology consultants in 1992. Currently there are almost 120 certified consultants listed on the AAASP website, approximately 100 of them working in the United States.

AAASP stipulates several principles and criteria that must be met in order to become a certified consultant. The criteria for certification include a doctoral degree, graduate course work in the sport sciences (e.g. sport psychology, biomechanics, exercise physiology, motor learning, sport sociology and philosophy) and psychology (e.g. counselling, psychopathology and assessment) and supervised experience. As a result of AAASP certification guidelines, doctoral students began to request more interdisciplinary training in order to be eligible for certification on completing their degrees. Some doctoral programs in sport psychology offered within the sport sciences have begun to offer students credit for work in psychology departments (e.g. the University of North Carolina, Greensboro). A recent endorsement of AAASP certification by the USOC (certification by AAASP is required to be eligible for USOC Registry listing) may further increase the numbers of those seeking certification, at least in North America. Although AAASP is an international organisation, its membership base is primarily North American, and the certification process and guidelines seem rather Amerocentric. For example, on the AAASP website, only seven consultants from outside the US and Canada are listed.

Although there is much to applaud in the certification criteria, some aspects do seem questionable. Criterion 8 (see appendix A) specifies 400 supervised hours 'with a qualified person (i.e. one who has an appropriate background in applied sport psychology)'. The definition of 'qualified' and 'an appropriate background' is left vague at best. Also, 400 hours is the equivalent of 10 weeks' full-time work; this term seems minimal, and many other service delivery professionals (e.g. psychologists, athletic trainers and hairdressers) would consider 400 hours only a 'good start'.

AAASP certification will probably continue to influence training in the foreseeable future, especially in North America. Its relevance outside North America, however, is probably limited. For example, in Flanders (western Belgium) sport psychologists are registered psychologists (Wylleman, De Knop, Delhoux & Vanden Auweele 1999). A similar pattern is emerging in Australia (Morris 1995).

In a related area of sport psychology training, the accreditation of applied sport psychology graduate programs has recently been advocated (Silva, Conroy & Zizzi 1999). These authors have suggested that the advancement of applied sport psychology as a profession has been hindered by a variety of issues and that accreditation of graduate programs will go far to 'assure academic credibility and public confidence in the standards of training and practice' (p. 298). Although this proposal is well-intentioned, the field of sport psychology is still overwhelmingly an academic field. There are few full-time practitioners, and extremely limited public demand for services (see Andersen, Williams,

Aldridge & Taylor 1997). As Hale and Danish (1999) suggested, calling for accreditation at this point may be an idea ahead of its time, and could actually be counterproductive.

Other certification systems

In the United Kingdom, the British Association of Sport and Exercise Sciences (BASES) has an accreditation system for sport psychology researchers and applied sport psychology practitioners. Requirements for practitioners include undergraduate and postgraduate degrees in sport science or psychology, or other relevant qualifications. In Canada, the Canadian Mental Training Registry helps coaches and athletes identify practitioners with qualifications to work on the mental aspects of training and performance. Requirements for registry include an academic background in the field as well as past experience in sport and supervised work with athletes and coaches. Other countries have less formal recognition of practitioners (see Morris, Alfermann, Lintunen & Hall 2003, for a thorough review of the training of sport psychologists worldwide).

The Australian model

In Australia, some training in sport psychology is also taking place in exercise science/human movement departments, but those programs are research oriented, and the major activity of graduate students is the completion of theses and dissertations. The training of sport psychology practitioners, however, occurs primarily in psychology departments. Currently there are four universities in Australia that offer master's of applied psychology degrees (professional degrees that lead to registration as psychologists) that are sport and exercise oriented. All these programs are accredited by the Australian Psychological Society. So in Australia major doctoral and master's level research in sport psychology occurs within the traditional department of origin, but applied sport psychology is found in the parent discipline of the field, psychology. The message here in Australia is quite clear. If you want to practise sport psychology, you need to be a psychologist. Sport psychology is much younger in Australia than it is in North America, and the arrangements for training here seem to have helped the field avoid the sometimes acrimonious debate over who can practise and what is appropriate training that occurred in the US and Canada.

SUPERVISION

The word *supervision* probably needs a little clarification. In Australia and throughout the British Commonwealth, supervision in the training of sport psychologists applies to two different realms. Both research and practice are 'supervised' by qualified university staff members. In North America, the person who oversees student research projects is called a thesis or dissertation 'advisor'. The person who oversees applied practice with individual clients and groups is the 'supervisor'. For this part of the chapter, the former usage (covering both research and practice) will apply.

Formal discussion and research on the quality of research supervision in sport psychology is currently at the conference presentation stage, with little published research. Butki and Andersen (1994) examined sport psychology students' perceptions of the quality of the guidance they received from their research supervisors regarding publishing their work and presenting at conferences. They found that most students felt they had received good advice and guidance from their supervisors in these areas, but there was also a substantial number of students who were not pleased with the quality of this important aspect of supervision. This study is the only data-based work on research supervision in sport psychology.

The first discussion on supervision in sport psychology service delivery appears to be a 1992 conference presentation at AAASP in Colorado Springs (Carr, Murphy & McCann 1992), but only an abstract exists. It is curious that supervision made such a late entry onto the sport psychology scene given that its roots are in physical education. Supervision for physical education (PE) teachers (e.g. student teaching) has been a major part of training for decades and is thoroughly integrated into the education of all PE teachers. That tradition of engaging in intense supervision processes, however, did not carry over into a profession that, in its beginnings, was primarily interested in teaching mental skills. Why supervision did not appear osmotically in the sport psychology literature from the PE field is an open question. One reason may be that there is a huge population of PE teachers serving the public, and their competence is of great importance for public health, safety and welfare. The population of practising sport psychologists, however, is very small and their perceived impact on public health is minimal. So the demands of competence, quality assurance and public safety did not receive serious consideration as it did with PE teachers. Every mother's son and every father's daughter comes into contact with PE teachers. In comparison, few of them see sport psychologists.

Sachs (1993) mentioned the usefulness of supervision in two short paragraphs in a book chapter on professional ethics. Also that year the first published article dedicated to supervision appeared. Van Raalte and Andersen (1993) presented a paper on supervising sport psychology trainees at the International Society of Sport Psychology meeting in Lisbon. The paper was published in the congress proceedings, but those proceedings did not circulate much beyond the conference attendees.

Andersen, Van Raalte and Brewer (1994), drawing on a survey of supervisors and supervisees in applied sport psychology service, reported on the skills of supervisors and experiences of supervision in the field. They surveyed AAASP professional and student members, using the Sport Psychology Supervisory Skills Inventory (see highlighted feature opposite). The results of that survey were not encouraging. Although most students were satisfied with the quality of supervision they received, the median number of supervised contact hours they had with clients (at less than 200 hours) was about half that required for AAASP certification. Also, about half of the supervisors surveyed had never received any supervision of their own work with athletes. This last point is of concern in terms of the quality of supervision applied sport psychology graduates are receiving. The low levels of supervision for both supervisees and supervisors suggest that the training in applied sport psychology (as of 1994) is notably deficient.

Andersen and Van Raalte (1994) expanded the issues of supervision into an area in which a lot of 'psychology' takes place with university athletes in North America — that is, academic athletic counselling in US university sports programs. Athletic counsellors act as helpers for athletes, guiding them through the university processes, providing support for adjustment to university life and acting as sounding boards for athletes. Academic athletic counsellors, like sport psychologists, hear about performance issues, problems with coaches, problems with team-mates, homesickness, academic frustrations and other personal concerns. They, too, need supervision, but the supervisory relationships in academic athletic counselling are probably less structured than in sport psychology.

Supervision plays many roles in the development of a competent sport psychologist; one of its useful roles is as a stage for the discussion of ethical issues in service delivery. Andersen (1994) presented an article on ethical issues in the supervision of sport psychology graduate students (cf. Andersen, Van Raalte & Brewer 2001). The main thrust of the article concerned the central role played by supervision in helping graduate students put ethical principles into practice. This article was the first in applied sport psychology to provide case examples of ethical issues in supervision and to show ethical quandaries in the real world of consulting. Andersen addressed such issues as the competence of the supervisor (a serious concern given that many supervisors in sport psychology either had no supervision training or had received no supervision of their own work, or both), referral for problems beyond the scope of the student and the supervisor, intimate behaviour, and exploitation.

SPORT PSYCHOLOGY SUPERVISORY SKILLS INVENTORY

Evaluate your supervisor (or if you are a supervisor, evaluate yourself) on each of the following items by circling the number that best represents your opinion of your supervisor (yourself). Circle NA only if the item is in no way applicable to you or your supervisory experience; otherwise use a 5-point scale in which:

1 = unsatisfactory, 2 = marginally satisfactory, 3 = satisfactory, 4 = very satisfactory
and 5 = outstanding.

I. Providing information and technical support

1. Conveys practicum requirements to the students.   1 2 3 4 5 NA
2. Conveys understanding of the sport psychology supervisor's role to the students.   1 2 3 4 5 NA
3. Provides information to supplement the students' theoretical knowledge.   1 2 3 4 5 NA
4. Communicates knowledge effectively.   1 2 3 4 5 NA
5. Suggests appropriate outside reading material.   1 2 3 4 5 NA
6. Demonstrates sufficient sport psychology expertise with the presenting concerns of athletes.   1 2 3 4 5 NA
7. Provides direct suggestions for interventions when needed or requested.   1 2 3 4 5 NA
8. Demonstrates intervention techniques when needed or requested.   1 2 3 4 5 NA
9. Provides guidance in implementing diagnostic procedures.   1 2 3 4 5 NA
10. Provides guidance for maintaining records and report writing tasks.   1 2 3 4 5 NA

II. Fulfilling supervisory responsibilities

11. Remains up to date regarding graduate students' ongoing cases.   1 2 3 4 5 NA
12. Provides adequate direct supervision.   1 2 3 4 5 NA
13. Conveys opinions regarding graduate students' specific consulting/counselling strengths.   1 2 3 4 5 NA
14. Conveys opinions regarding graduate students' specific consulting/counselling weaknesses.   1 2 3 4 5 NA
15. Suggests ways for students to improve areas of weakness.   1 2 3 4 5 NA
16. Appropriately confronts students for not fulfilling practicum/internship requirements.   1 2 3 4 5 NA
17. Provides opportunities for sufficient number of supervisory conferences.   1 2 3 4 5 NA
18. Provides comprehensive supervisory evaluations periodically.   1 2 3 4 5 NA
19. Evaluates students' performance fairly.   1 2 3 4 5 NA

(continued)

III. Facilitating interpersonal communication

20. Encourages students' expression of feelings and opinions
relevant to their development as sport psychologists/counsellors. 1 2 3 4 5 NA
21. Listens attentively to students. 1 2 3 4 5 NA
22. Demonstrates empathy and respect towards students. 1 2 3 4 5 NA
23. Communicates at a level consistent with the students'
professional development. 1 2 3 4 5 NA
24. Maintains emotional stability during supervisory encounters. 1 2 3 4 5 NA
25. Exhibits an appropriate sense of humour. 1 2 3 4 5 NA
26. Allows the students sufficient opportunity to interact during
the supervisory conferences. 1 2 3 4 5 NA
27. Encourages student feedback concerning the supervisory
process. 1 2 3 4 5 NA

IV. Fostering student autonomy

28. Remains receptive to student ideas concerning intervention
strategies. 1 2 3 4 5 NA
29. Shows flexibility in permitting a variety of valid procedures
for psychological intervention. 1 2 3 4 5 NA
30. Motivates the students to develop consulting and/or
counselling skills. 1 2 3 4 5 NA
31. Encourages the students' self-appraisals of their consulting
and/or counselling skills. 1 2 3 4 5 NA
32. Encourages students to become increasingly independent
and autonomous professionals. 1 2 3 4 5 NA

V. Providing professional model

33. Exhibits an appropriate ethical responsibility to the athletes
served. 1 2 3 4 5 NA
34. Maintains confidentiality regarding the students' performance
in practicum/internship. 1 2 3 4 5 NA
35. Discusses with the students the ethical standards regarding
interactions with clients. 1 2 3 4 5 NA
36. Discusses with the students ethical behaviour regarding
supervisor–supervisee interactions. 1 2 3 4 5 NA
37. Demonstrates interest and enthusiasm regarding the profession. 1 2 3 4 5 NA
38. Provides an appropriate model of speech and language. 1 2 3 4 5 NA
39. Maintains an appropriate professional appearance. 1 2 3 4 5 NA
40. Provides an appropriate professional model overall. 1 2 3 4 5 NA

(*Source:* Reprinted with permission from Andersen, Van Raalte & Brewer 1994, 'Assessing
the skills of sport psychology supervisors', *The Sport Psychologist*, 8 (3) 238–47)

Supervision models and core issues

The first major overview of supervision models from counselling and clinical psychology, and how they might apply to sport psychology service delivery, was offered by the Andersen and Williams-Rice (1996) article. They described psychodynamic (Mueller & Kell 1972; cf. Strean & Strean 1998), phenomenological (Rogers 1957), behavioural (Delaney 1972), cognitive behavioural (Kurpius & Morran 1988) and developmental (Stoltenberg 1981) models of supervision. A description of these models is beyond the scope of this chapter; the reader might wish to refer to this article for more details.

Andersen and Williams-Rice suggested that the more concrete, skill-based models (behavioural and cognitive-behavioural) might be most appropriate for sport psychology, at least in the early stages of training. The more advanced psychotherapeutic models of supervision (phenomenological and psychodynamic) might be more valuable later in one's career (e.g. during peer supervision). Andersen and Williams-Rice also discussed the training of supervisors (see Barney, Andersen & Riggs 1996, below) and the process of metasupervision (i.e. the supervision of supervision), two serious issues in professional development that still do not receive much attention.

Andersen and Williams-Rice (1996) also raised the issues of transference and countertransference in service delivery. These topics had previously received only brief attention in the sport psychology literature (e.g. Hellstedt 1987; Henschen 1991; Yambor & Connelly 1991). There are many misconceptions about transference and countertransference (e.g. they are unhealthy; they represent misalliances; they should be avoided), and because these service delivery phenomena are rarely discussed, such misunderstandings continue to cloud what are powerful and potentially beneficial aspects of working with athletes. Transference occurs when athletes begin to respond to the sport psychologist as they have responded (behaviourally, emotionally, cognitively) to significant others, or fantasised significant others, in their lives. A prime example from the sport world is athletes who see their coaches as the idealised mother or father they never had. Henschen wrote specifically about young gymnasts seeing him as a father figure, a dynamic that lies at the heart of transference. Countertransference relates to similar phenomena when they occur with the psychologist. Andersen (2000) has written about 'big brother' feelings towards younger athletes and wanting to protect and nurture them. These phenomena are ubiquitous in service delivery, and supervision is the ideal place to discover how they occur, how to understand them, and how to make sure such feelings help, rather than hinder, the working alliance between the psychologist and the athlete. Petitpas, Danish and Giges (1999) emphasised the importance of the psychologist–athlete relationship and suggested that future training in applied sport psychology should have a significant component that helps graduate students understand their interpersonal dynamics — what they bring (for good or ill) to working relationships, and how the psychologist's understanding of the instrument of service (i.e. him- or herself) is a central aspect of becoming a competent applied sport psychologist.

Andersen and Williams-Rice (1996) also discussed the role of supervision in exploring the ethical issues of misalliances (e.g. sport psychologist and athlete in a counterproductive relationship), boundary blurring (e.g. over-identification with the athlete) and dual role problems (e.g. team buddy, friend, psychologist). These pitfalls of service delivery cover exactly the material that is appropriate and necessary to bring up in supervision. Finally, they discussed the role of supervision in the process of referral. Sport psychologists and graduate students who are getting out of their depths with a client's issues should refer that client to an appropriate professional. The referral process is not a simple one. To refer an athlete to someone else after rapport and a working alliance have been established is fraught with sensitive problems. The athlete may have become comfortable enough, for example, to reveal an internal conflict or traumatic history (e.g. sexual abuse), and then be faced with a psychologist who cannot deal with those issues and is sent off to someone else to start the process all over again. Such referral may be perceived as rejection, and actually lead to a shutting down of the therapeutic process. Supervision is a place to help the student (and peer) handle such situations in the most salubrious manner (see Van Raalte & Andersen 2002 and Andersen 2001a for more on the processes of referral).

Supervision training model

Barney, Andersen and Riggs (1996) described a model for preparing sport psychology graduate students for their future roles as supervisors of applied work. Their model, based on earlier work in clinical supervision (e.g. Dowling 1986; Hart 1982), involves advanced doctoral graduate students in sport psychology undertaking course work in supervision processes and engaging in supervision internships with beginning master's students in their first applied sport psychology placements. The doctoral students act as supervisors for the master's students and then receive metasupervision (supervision of their supervision) from their professors (and peers in group metasupervision) on their work as neophyte supervisors. Barney et al. offered probably the most advanced models of training in sport psychology, but the key word here is 'advanced'. It is doubtful whether such a model of training has been put in place in many universities, given the limited amount of regular supervision that appears to be taking place in the field. Their model is more an ideal training program than a reality in current applied sport psychology graduate education.

Problems in supervision

Van Raalte and Andersen (2000) covered similar ground as Andersen and Williams-Rice (1996), but they expanded the discussion to include some of the recurring problems in the supervision process. For example, supervisees may be afraid of the supervisor and the evaluative atmosphere of supervision. Such fears may lead supervisees to report only their perceived successes and avoid their problems with athletes in order to appear competent. If the supervisor is not aware of such supervisee difficulties, the future growth of the supervisee as a practitioner will be compromised. Another problem may arise when supervisors are not willing to confront supervisees on sensitive issues, either because they do not want to intimidate supervisees or because they themselves are uncomfortable with such issues (e.g. supervisee over-identification with athletes). Such limitations of supervisors also limit trainee development. The problem of supervisor–supervisee transference and countertransference has already been raised. Dealing with these complex dynamic interpersonal issues in the supervisory process may be beyond either person's capabilities. Supervisors and supervisees get along or do not get along with each other for a variety of reasons (e.g. different theoretical orientations). Some interpersonal problems stem from past relationship patterns with significant others. Training in the dynamics of supervisor–supervisee relationships (part of the Barney et al. 1996 model), however, is not a common feature of applied sport psychology education. Van Raalte and Andersen briefly touched on the issue of graduate students becoming impaired while under supervision, and Andersen, Van Raalte and Brewer (2000) expanded on this concern.

A graduate student (or a practitioner) can become an impaired deliverer of services to athletes and coaches for a number of reasons. Impairment may arise as a result of personality disorders of the trainee, adjustment disorders, bereavement, substance abuse, incompetence or violations of ethical standards (themselves usually the result of one of the previous conditions). People enter the applied sport psychology field for a large number of reasons. Some truly want to help; others want to 'fix' problems in their own sport histories by helping others. Still others want to rub shoulders with the elite and bask in the reflected glory of their clients. Even more pathological are those who wish to exploit athletes for their own financial, social or sexual interests. Finally, there are those who are simply not competent to deliver services and who have no desire to remedy their incompetencies.

The primary concern of a supervisor is the health and welfare of the client (athlete, coach, team). When the practice of a sport psychology graduate student (or seasoned practitioner) is impaired, for example by a personality disorder, grief or substance abuse or because of serious boundary blurring, then that welfare is in jeopardy. How one goes about confronting the impaired sport psychologist or student, what constitutes due process, how to address impairment in the most ethical manner, and how to refer the student or psychologist to appropriate professionals for remediation or psychotherapy are all sensitive issues within supervision and training. See Andersen, Van Raalte and Brewer (2000) for more details on handling impairment in sport psychology service delivery.

The levels of discussion

The types of research into supervision in applied sport psychology have not progressed beyond the descriptive stage (e.g. Andersen et al. 1994; Butki & Andersen 1994), and most articles on the topic are at the level of discussion papers with some case examples.

Detailed case studies in sport psychology are relatively rare. Many of the 'case studies' in the literature might be better described as case examples. The difference between these two classes of reporting is usually a question of depth. For example, case examples in sport psychology usually deal with a presentation of the athlete's concern, the formulation of what is going on, the introduction of an intervention aimed at the problem and an evaluation of the effectiveness of that intervention (see Rotella, Boyce, Allyson & Savis 1998; Thompson, Vernacchia & Moore 1998). Case studies usually involve a deeper exploration of the athlete's world, take place over a relatively long period of time, and delve into the intra- and interpersonal dynamics of the individual (and often the personal reflections of the practitioner involved). In the area of supervision, there are a few case examples (e.g. Andersen 1994; Andersen, Van Raalte & Brewer 2000), but only one book chapter in print (Andersen, Van Raalte & Harris 2000) could classify as a case study. In this study, the authors described a year-long supervisory relationship that covered issues of supervision intake interview processes and supervisee needs (e.g. need to help, need for recognition, identification with and introjection of the supervisor, fear of supervisor judgement, understanding self in service, transference and countertransference). In an upcoming book chapter, Andersen (in press) has taken the case study approach to describe a supervisee caught up in the quagmire of erotic transference and countertransference with an athlete in his care. Much of the chapter involves the description and interpretation of the supervisory sessions between the graduate student and his supervisor. This topic has not been broached in any significant way in sport psychology service except in a study by Petrie and Buntrock (1995), which revealed that a substantial minority of sport psychologists admitted to being sexually attracted to clients, and a small minority acted on those feelings. Training in how to deal with erotic transference and countertransference has not been a topic of discussion at sport psychology conferences until recently (Andersen 2001b), and the central role of competent supervision in helping trainees handle such powerful feelings cannot be overestimated.

Outside the work of Van Raalte, Andersen and colleagues, supervision is beginning to emerge as a leitmotif in many works on sport psychology professional practice. Poczwardowski, Sherman and Henschen (1998), in their description of central factors in service delivery, cited the importance of supervision as an ongoing professional endeavour. Holt and Strean (2001) recounted the experiences of a neophyte practitioner and how his development and understanding of himself and his client were facilitated by supervision. The importance of supervision is being recognised more and more in the field and should be a topic of discussion and research for many years to come. Recently the status of supervision in sport psychology was highlighted by an entry in the *Encyclopedia of Social and Behavioral Sciences* dedicated solely to supervision and training (Andersen 2001c). As applied sport psychology moves from adolescent concerns over identity into issues of intimacy in young adulthood, the discussion of supervision and training in sport psychology is moving closer to the heart of the matter in service delivery: the intimate working alliance between practitioners and the people they serve, the athletes and coaches.

FUTURE DIRECTIONS

In the past decade there has been substantial discussion of the training and supervision of applied sport psychology service providers. That discussion, still in its early stages, needs to continue. Research into training and supervision should proceed along several fronts. There is a need for large survey-based studies aimed at evaluating supervisors and experiences in supervision in order to discover the 'state of the field'. Idiographic, in-depth case studies of the experiences of individual supervisors and supervisees would be welcome additions to the discussion. The discussion of the models, training and philosophical orientations needs to be translated into the real-life experiences of students in graduate programs and peers in collegial consultation. These experiences should then be brought into workshops and symposia at national and international conferences. In the training area, the question 'Training for what?' remains to be answered. For those interested in academic or research positions, that training may involve little if any applied sport psychology work in graduate school. But here is the rub: future advertisements for academic sport psychology positions in academia may include in their job descriptions 'ability to supervise applied sport psychology practica'. It may be that those interested primarily in academia will also need to have skills in applied sport psychology and supervision in order to increase their opportunities of landing a job. Coordinators of sport psychology programs might want to consider incorporating supervision training similar to that suggested by Barney et al. (1996) to increase the competence (and employability) of their graduates.

Among those training programs that offer applied experience, past research has shown that supervision has ranged from thorough and extensive to ad hoc or non-existent. It would be fine indeed if the central feature of training, the activity that probably shapes future sport psychologists more than any other — that is, supervision — actually acquired a position of centrality in all programs.

CONCLUSIONS

To return to Erikson's developmental psychosocial challenges, sport psychologists have watched the field grow from infancy to childhood to adolescence to its current status in young adulthood. A major challenge of young adulthood is establishing, understanding and appreciating intimacy. The psychosocial metaphor of the Eriksonian challenge of intimacy versus isolation is mirrored in the experience of researchers in the field currently addressing the core of service delivery, the intimate relationships between sport psychologists and those they serve. It probably does not matter whether a CBT, REBT, behavioural or gestalt approach is chosen in working with athletes and coaches. For some athletes I have worked with, even Primal Scream therapy might have been a viable option. What does matter is how we connect with each other, how we form working alliances, how we respect each other — in sum, how we establish intimacy. In relation to the supervision and training of sport psychologists, our young adulthood has just started. But Erikson's stages can overlap. In his next stage the mature adult faces the challenge of generativity versus stagnation. It is in this stage that one gives back to the next generation. Many in the field of sport psychology are in positions to give back to the new generation, helping to train and supervise them better than they themselves were trained and supervised. We can continue with old, varied and inconsistent models of training, or we can seize the issues by the horns and help equip our students for an increasingly challenging and competitive world.

SUMMARY

This chapter traced the history of the training and supervision of applied sport psychology practitioners. From its beginnings in physical education departments, sport psychology has branched out to include a wide variety of practitioners trained along several different paths. These differences have led to disparate views about the qualifications needed to practise. The early USOC classification of educational, research and clinical sport psychologists brought some stability. Further work by AAASP in North America and organisations in other countries brought some standardisation to training.

The professional practice and training issue of supervision began to receive attention in the mid 1990s, when the applicability of various supervision models to applied sport psychology was examined. Supervision is a central feature of training and practice, and this chapter covered topics such as ethical issues in supervision (boundary blurring, dual roles), common problems encountered in supervision (fear of supervisor, poor communication) and what happens when supervisees become impaired.

Future directions include the translation of supervision models into real-life training and the continued examination of precisely what we are training future sport psychologists to do. The chapter ends with an appeal for the relocation of supervision as a central feature in future training in applied sport psychology.

REVIEW QUESTIONS

1 What were the basic training and identity issues in the field of sport psychology as they emerged in the 1980s?

2 What are some of the problems with the USOC division of sport psychologists into research, education and clinical categories?

3 What are the AAASP criteria for certification as a consultant? Why might the supervision criterion be a problem?

4 What might be a reason the topic of supervision is a late entry into the sport psychology literature?

5 What is the working alliance, and why is it important?

6 What are some of the ethical problems inherent in the process of supervision?

7 What is metasupervision? Describe it in the context of supervision training.

References

Andersen, MB 1992, 'Sport psychology and procrustean categories: an appeal for synthesis and expansion of services', *Association for the Advancement of Applied Sport Psychology Newsletter*, 7, 8–9, 15.

Andersen, MB 1994, 'Ethical considerations in the supervision of applied sport psychology graduate students', *Journal of Applied Sport Psychology*, 6, 152–67.

Andersen, MB 2000, 'Beginnings: intakes and the initiation of relationships', in MB Andersen (ed.), *Doing sport psychology*, Human Kinetics, Champaign, IL, pp. 3–16.

Andersen, MB 2001a, 'When to refer athletes for counseling and psychotherapy', in JM Williams (ed.), *Applied sport psychology: personal growth to peak performance*, 4th edn, Mayfield, Mountain View, CA, pp. 401–15.

Andersen, MB 2001b, 'Erotic transference and countertransference in sport psychology service delivery', in A Papaioannou, M Goudas & Y Theodorakis (eds), *International Society of Sport Psychology (ISSP) 10th World Congress of Sport Psychology: programme and proceedings*, vol. 3, Christodoulidi, Thessaloniki, Greece, pp. 221–3.

Andersen, MB 2001c, 'Training and supervision in sport psychology', in T Wilson, *International encyclopaedia of the social and behavioural sciences*, vol. 22, Elsevier Science, Oxford, UK, pp. 14 929–32.

Andersen, MB (in press), 'What a babe! Sex and the sport psychologist', in MB Andersen (ed.), *Practicing sport psychology*, Human Kinetics, Champaign, IL.

Andersen, MB & Van Raalte, JL 1994, 'Supervising academic athletic counselling trainees', *Academic Athletic Journal*, 9, 1–10.

Andersen, MB, Van Raalte, JL & Brewer, BW 1994, 'Assessing the skills of sport psychology supervisors', *The Sport Psychologist*, 8, 238–47.

Andersen, MB, Van Raalte, JL, Brewer, BW 2000, 'When sport psychology consultants and graduate students are impaired: ethical and legal issues in training and supervision', *Journal of Applied Sport Psychology*, 12, 134–50.

Andersen, MB, Van Raalte, JL & Brewer, BW 2001, 'Sport psychology service delivery: staying ethical while keeping loose', *Professional Psychology: Research and Practice*, 32, 12–18.

Andersen, MB, Van Raalte, JL & Harris, G 2000, 'Supervision II: a case study', in MB Andersen (ed.), *Doing sport psychology*, Human Kinetics, Champaign, IL, pp. 167–80.

Andersen, MB, Williams, JM, Aldridge, T & Taylor, J 1997, 'Tracking the training and careers of graduates of advanced degree programs in sport psychology 1989–1994', *The Sport Psychologist*, 11, 326–44.

Andersen, MB & Williams-Rice, BT 1996, 'Supervision in the education and training of sport psychology service providers', *The Sport Psychologist*, 10, 278–90.

Barney, ST, Andersen, MB & Riggs, CA 1996, 'Supervision in sport psychology: some recommendations for practicum training', *Journal of Applied Sport Psychology*, 8, 200–17.

Brown, JM 1982, 'Are sport psychologists really psychologists?', *Journal of Sport Psychology*, 4, 13–17.

Butki, BD & Andersen, MB 1994, 'Mentoring in sport psychology: students' perceptions of training in publication and presentation guidelines', *The Sport Psychologist*, 8, 143–8.

Carr, CM, Murphy, SM & McCann, S 1992, 'Supervision issues in clinical sport psychology', workshop presented at the annual conference of the Association for the Advancement of Applied Sport Psychology, Colorado Springs, CO, October.

Clarke, KS 1984, 'The USOC Sport Psychology Registry: a clarification', *Journal of Sport Psychology*, 6, 365–6.

Delaney, DJ 1972, 'A behavioral model for the practicum supervision of counselor candidates', *Counselor Education and Supervision*, 12, 46–50.

Dishman, RK 1983, 'Identity crisis in North American sport psychology: academics in professional issues', *Journal of Sport Psychology*, 5, 123–34.

Dowling, S 1986, 'Supervisory training: impetus for clinical supervision', *The Clinical Supervisor*, 4 (4) 27–34.

Erikson, E 1968, *Identity: youth and crisis*, Norton, New York.

Feltz, DF 1987, 'The future of graduate education in sport and exercise science: a sport psychology perspective', *Quest*, 39, 217–23.

Griffith, CR 1928, *The psychology of athletics*, Scribner, New York.

Hale, BD & Danish, SJ 1999, 'Putting the accreditation cart before the AAASP horse: a reply to Silva, Conroy and Zizzi', *Journal of Applied Sport Psychology*, 11, 321–8.

Hart, GM 1982, *The process of clinical supervision*, University Park Press, Baltimore.

Hellstedt, JC 1987, 'The coach/parent/athlete relationship', *The Sport Psychologist*, 1, 151–60.

Henschen, KP 1991, 'Critical issues involving male consultants and female athletes', *The Sport Psychologist*, 5, 313–21.

Heyman, SR 1984, 'The development of models for sport psychology: examining the USOC guidelines', *Journal of Sport Psychology*, 6, 125–32.

Holt, NL & Strean, WB 2001, 'Reflecting on initiating sport psychology consultation: a self-narrative of neophyte practice', *The Sport Psychologist*, 15, 188–204.

Kurpius, DJ & Morran, DK 1988, 'Cognitive-behavioral techniques and interventions for application in counselor supervision', *Counselor Education and Supervision*, 27, 368–76.

McCullagh, P & Noble, JM 1996, 'Education and training in sport and exercise psychology', in JL Van Raalte and BW Brewer (eds), *Exploring sport and exercise psychology*, American Psychological Association, Washington, DC, pp. 377–94.

Morris, T 1995, 'Sport psychology in Australia: a profession established', *Australian Psychologist*, 30, 128–35.

Morris, T, Alfermann, D, Lintunen, T & Hall, H 2003, 'Training and selection of sport psychologists: an international review', *Journal of Sport & Exercise Psychology*, 1, 139–54.

Mueller, WJ & Kell, BL 1972, *Coping with conflict: supervising counselors and psychotherapists*, Appleton-Century-Crofts, New York.

Petitpas, AJ, Danish, SJ & Giges, B 1999, 'The sport psychologist–athlete relationship: implications for training', *The Sport Psychologist*, 13, 344–57.

Petrie, T & Buntrock, C 1995, 'Sexual attraction and the profession of sport psychology' (abstract), *Journal of Applied Sport Psychology*, 7 (Suppl.) S98.

Poczwardowski, A, Sherman, CP & Henschen, KP 1998, 'A sport psychology service delivery heuristic: building on theory and practice', *The Sport Psychologist*, 12, 191–207.

Rogers, CR 1957, 'Training individuals to engage in the therapeutic process', in CR Strother (ed.), *Psychology and mental health*, American Psychological Association, Washington DC.

Rotella, B, Boyce, BA, Allyson, B & Savis, JC 1998, *Case studies in sport psychology*, Jones & Bartlett, Sudbury, MA.

Sachs, ML 1993, 'Professional ethics in sport psychology', in RN Singer, M Murphey & LK Tennant (eds.), *Handbook of research on sport psychology*, Macmillan, New York, pp. 921–32.

Silva, JM, III, Conroy, DE & Zizzi, SJ 1999, 'Critical issues confronting the advancement of applied sport psychology', *Journal of Applied Sport Psychology*, 11, 298–320.

Simons, JP & Andersen, MB 1995, 'The development of consulting practice in applied sport psychology: some personal perspectives', *The Sport Psychologist*, 9, 449–68.

Stoltenberg, C 1981, 'Approaching supervision from a developmental perspective: the counselor complexity model', *Journal of Counseling Psychology*, 28, 59–65.

Strean, WB & Strean, HS 1998, 'Applying psychodynamic concepts to sport psychology practice', *The Sport Psychologist*, 12, 208–22.

Thompson, MA, Vernacchia, RA & Moore, WE (eds) 1998, *Case studies in sport psychology: an educational approach*, Kendall/Hunt, Dubuque, IA.

Triplett, N 1897, 'The dynamogenic factors in pacemaking and competition', *American Journal of Psychology*, 9, 507–53.

United States Olympic Committee 1983, 'US Olympic committee establishes guidelines for sport psychology services', *Journal of Sport Psychology*, 5, 4–7.

Van Raalte, JL & Andersen, MB 1993, 'Special problems in sport psychology: supervising the trainee', in S Serpa, J Alves, V Ferreira & A Paulo-Brito (eds), *Proceedings: VIII World Congress of Sport Psychology*, International Society of Sport Psychology, Lisbon, pp. 773–6.

Van Raalte, JL & Andersen, MB 2000, 'Supervision I: from models to doing', in MB Andersen (ed.), *Doing sport psychology*, Human Kinetics, Champaign, IL, pp. 153–66.

Van Raalte, JL & Andersen, MB 2002, 'Referral processes in sport psychology', in JL Van Raalte & BW Brewer (eds), *Exploring sport and exercise psychology*, 2nd edn, American Psychological Association, Washington, DC, pp. 325–37.

Wylleman, P, De Knop, P, Delhoux, J & Vanden Auweele, Y 1999, 'Current status and future issues of sport psychology consultation in Flanders', *The Sport Psychologist*, 13, 99–106.

Yambor, J & Connelly, D 1991, 'Issues confronting female sport psychology consultants working with male student athletes', *The Sport Psychologist*, 5, 304–12.

APPENDIX A

Criteria for standard AAASP certification

Certification by AAASP requires current membership in the Association at the time of application and having attended at least two AAASP conferences. Continuing AAASP certification is contingent upon maintaining active membership status in the Association.

A. Background information

Applicant's status in AAASP, home and work information should be provided.

B. Education

Completion of a doctoral degree from an institution of higher education accredited by one of the regional accrediting bodies recognised by the Council of Postsecondary Accreditation is required. In Canada, an institution of higher education must be recognised as a member, in good standing, of the Association of Universities and Colleges of Canada. Programs leading to a doctoral degree must include the equivalent of three full-time academic years of graduate study:

- two years of which are at the institution from which the doctoral degree is granted.
- one year of which is in full-time residence at the institution from which the doctoral degree is granted.

C. Course of study

Sport psychology is a unique subdiscipline which requires specialised education and training in both the exercise and sport sciences and in psychology. The necessary, but sufficient, areas of training and knowledge are outlined below. Certification by AAASP does require documentation of necessary levels of training and expertise in each area as specified on the application form. Necessary levels of preparation in the substantive content areas generally require successful completion of at least three graduate semester hours or their equivalent (e.g. passing suitable exams offered by an accredited doctoral program). However, up to four upper-level undergraduate courses may be substituted for this requirement (unless specifically designated as requiring graduate credit only). It is not always necessary to take one course to satisfy each requirement. However, one course or experience cannot be used to satisfy more than one criterion except for Criterion #1 (Knowledge of professional ethics and standards).

1. Knowledge of professional ethics and standards. This requirement can be met by taking one course on these topics or by taking several courses in which these topics comprise parts of the courses or by completing other comparable experiences.

2. Knowledge of the sport psychology subdisciplines of intervention/performance enhancement, health/exercise psychology and social psychology, as evidenced by three courses or two courses and one independent study in sport psychology (two of these courses must be taken at the graduate level).

3. Knowledge of the biomechanical and/or physiological bases of sport (e.g. kinesiology, biomechanics, exercise physiology).

4. Knowledge of the historical, philosophical, social or motor behaviour bases of sport (e.g. motor learning/control, motor development, issues in sport/physical education, sociology of sport history and philosophy of sport/physical education).

5. Knowledge of psychopathology and its assessment (e.g. abnormal psychology, psychopathology).

6. Training* designed to foster basic skills in counselling (e.g. graduate course work on basic intervention techniques in counselling, supervised practica in counselling, clinical or industrial/organisational psychology).

7. Knowledge of skills and techniques within sport or exercise (e.g. skills and techniques courses, clinics, formal coaching experiences or organised participation in sport or exercise).

8. Knowledge and skills* in research design, statistics and psychological assessment. At least two of the following four criteria must be met through educational experiences that focus on general psychological principles (rather than sport-specific ones).

9. Knowledge of the biological bases of behaviour (e.g. biomechanics/kinesiology, comparative psychology, exercise physiology, neuropsychology, physiological psychology, psychopharmacology, sensation).

10. Knowledge of the cognitive–affective bases of behaviour (e.g. cognition, emotion, learning, memory, motivation, motor development, motor learning/control, perception, thinking).

11. Knowledge of the social bases of behaviour (e.g. cultural/ethnic and group processes, gender roles in sport, organisation and system theory, social psychology, sociology of sport).

12. Knowledge of individual behaviour (e.g. developmental psychology, exercise behaviour, health psychology, individual differences, personality theory).

* Graduate level only

D. Professional experience: supervised and unsupervised

1. *Supervised practica.* In this section, document the supervised practicum experiences that you have completed including a total number of hours in group and individual work, the inclusive dates of each practicum, a description of the type of applied sport psychology services provided and the supervisor's evaluation of your practicum experience. Applicants must have completed 400 hours of supervised experience with a qualified person (i.e. one who has an appropriate background in applied sport psychology) during which the individual receives training in the use of sport psychology principles and techniques (e.g. supervised practica in applied sport psychology in which the focus of the assessments and interventions are participants in physical activity, exercise or sport).

2. *Unsupervised consultation experience.* List any additional consultation experiences in applied sport psychology that you have completed or that are ongoing. Evaluation of effectiveness of consultation must be provided. (*Note:* A presentation to a group/ team does not constitute a consultation.)

E. References

Provide the names, job titles, addresses and phone numbers of three individuals familiar with your work in applied sport psychology, who would be willing to provide a recommendation for you.

F. Ethical standards

Applicants must read and sign the statement of ethical standards.

G. Certification

In order to be certified, all of the above conditions must be met and approval must be received by a two-thirds vote of a quorum of the Certification Review Committee. The

Certification Review Committee will review applications at the next application review meeting. The Chair of the committee will contact applicants following each meeting to inform them of their status. If deficiencies were determined, the Chair will recommend a course of action to receive certification. If the applicant is not satisfied with the determination of the Certification Review Committee, the applicant may appeal the decision to the Executive Committee of AAASP.

(*Source:* Andersen, Van Raalte & Brewer 1994, pp. 246–7)

PART 3

CURRENT ISSUES IN SPORT PSYCHOLOGY

>>

Sport and exercise psychology is a relatively young but rapidly growing discipline. The previous edition of this book reflected this vigorous growth by including in part 3 a range of emerging topics — that is, topics that lacked even the 30-year history of such areas as personality, anxiety or motivation research. Most of these current issues have since become well-established areas of theory and practice in the profession. In part 3 of this edition, we have collected those issues that have drawn more recent attention in the field and that have somewhat different origins from the theory and practice themes addressed in parts 1 and 2. Work in physical activity and exercise has expanded dramatically over the past decade. Consequently we have included two chapters on exercise psychology; still, this area of the discipline can only be summarised. In chapter 17, Courneya considers factors that affect involvement in physical activity, a particularly theory-driven topic. In chapter 18, Grove and Zillman discuss the outcomes of physical activity participation, including some drawbacks along with the many benefits of physical activity. Injury is a serious concern in sport and exercise, and it has become evident that psychological factors play an influential role here. In chapter 19, Petrie and Perna address the sport psychology research and practice that have developed around efforts to prevent injuries from occurring, or at least to reduce their incidence substantially, and psychological aspects of recovery from injury. In chapter 20, Tremayne and Tremayne discuss the commitment of the profession to the involvement of children in sport and exercise. The nexus between physical activity and psychophysiology has substantially expanded recent research and application of psychophysiology in our field. In chapter 21, Boutcher introduces an overview of the application of psychophysiology to sport and exercise psychology. More and more people with physical and intellectual disabilities are being encouraged to participate in competitive sports and physical activity for wellbeing. In chapter 22, Hanrahan considers the application of sport and exercise psychology to people with disabilities. The significance of issues related to transitions in sport, such as from junior to senior athlete and from elite to retired performer, have now been widely recognised. This has led to substantial research, the development of programs that prepare athletes for major transitions, and counselling for performers who experience transition problems. In chapter 23, Gordon and Lavallee review this now considerable topic. In chapter 24, Morris concludes with some reflections on future directions in sport and exercise psychology. He raises a range of issues still to be addressed, including the often-tenuous links between theory and practice, some directions in which the profession is expanding and the related need for a sustainable career structure. He also celebrates the vibrancy of sport and exercise psychology.

CHAPTER 17

PSYCHOLOGICAL CONSEQUENCES OF EXERCISE: BENEFITS AND POTENTIAL COSTS

J Robert Grove & Nadine Zillmann

Scholarly interest in the psychological aspects of health-related behaviour has increased substantially during the past two decades. This increase in scientific scrutiny has come about for at least two reasons. Firstly, scientists and the general public have become aware that exercise can produce substantial physical benefits, although, at the same time, they have begun to realise that these benefits cannot be obtained if people do not participate on a regular basis. Secondly, scientists and the public have become curious about the potential for exercise to produce psychological benefits that parallel its widely acknowledged physical benefits. Consequently the behavioural principles that underlie exercise adoption and maintenance have been analysed and elucidated, and the psychological consequences of exercise have also been examined. In chapter 18 Courneya presents an overview of the psychological antecedents of exercise. In this chapter we review research findings on the psychological consequences of exercise. Given the extensive literature in this area, our coverage will necessarily be selective. At the same time, we will attempt to present a balanced discussion of the psychological benefits as well as the potential psychological costs of regular exercise.

PSYCHOLOGICAL BENEFITS OF EXERCISE

Claims for the psychological benefits of exercise are certainly not new. According to Ryan (1984), Hippocrates believed that exercise had positive psychological consequences and prescribed it for mental health purposes. In more recent times others have held similar views, but the structure of society, as well as philosophic and scientific trends towards mind–body dualism meant that the systematic examination of what was viewed as essentially a 'background phenomenon' was not undertaken until the second half of the twentieth century (Blair 1988; Dishman 1986). Even then much of the research lacked scientific rigour and produced conclusions that were difficult to justify given the types of designs, samples and measures employed (Morgan 1988). Since the early 1980s, however, scholars have become more sophisticated in their approaches to research and their analyses of the findings. In general, these more rigorous investigations have substantiated the positive impact of exercise on self-perceptions, mood states and mental health (Leith 1994). We review some of this evidence here.

Self-perceptions

Self-concept and self-esteem are multidimensional constructs that include perceptions of intellectual, social, emotional and physical aspects of the self (Shavelson, Hubner & Stanton 1976). Early work on the physical domain typically viewed it as consisting of either a single dimension related to body satisfaction (Secord & Jourard 1953) or a limited number of subdomains related to physical ability and physical appearance (Marsh & Shavelson 1985; Ryckman, Robbins, Thornton & Cantrell 1982). However, Fox and Corbin (1989) suggested that a more complex structure could characterise physical self-perceptions (figure 17.1, panel A). Specifically, these investigators found evidence that the physical self-worth of young adults was influenced by perceptions of sport/athletic ability, physical condition/stamina/fitness, body attractiveness and physical strength.

Fox (1990, 1997) further suggested that the perceived importance of each subdomain determined its impact on higher-order constructs, and that the relative importance of specific subdomains could change across the life span. Although the development of this model was based on samples of young adults, subsequent research has supported its generalisability by demonstrating positive correlations between all four of the domains and participation in exercise among middle-aged and older adults (Sonstroem, Speliotis & Fava 1992). Evidence also suggests that higher levels of exercise are associated with stronger beliefs in the importance of these four physical self-concept dimensions, and that self-perceptions of condition/stamina/fitness, in particular, are strongly linked to exercise involvement (Fox 1997; Marsh & Sonstroem 1995).

Marsh and colleagues have proposed an even more detailed model of physical self-perceptions (Marsh, Richards, Johnson, Roche & Tremayne 1994; Marsh & Redmayne 1994). This model (figure 17.1, panel B) is hierarchical and includes nine subdomains (appearance, strength, endurance/fitness, flexibility, health, coordination, activity, body fat and sport competence) that contribute to general physical self-perceptions, which, in turn, contribute to global self-esteem. Initial research with high-school students provided support for this model among both males and females (Marsh et al. 1994), and subsequent research has confirmed that specific subdomains are positively correlated with actual physical performance in a domain-specific manner (Marsh 1997). More specifically, Marsh (1996a) reported substantial positive correlations between self-perception of endurance capabilities and actual performance on a continuous 1.6 km of 20-metre shuttle run tests. In a more comprehensive study along the same lines, Marsh (1996b) demonstrated significant positive correlations between objective body composition measures and self-perceptions of body fatness; self-reports of past, present and intended exercise involvement and self-perceptions of activity capabilities; multiple field tests of strength and self-perceptions of strength capabilities; and performance on a sit-and-reach test and self-perceptions of flexibility.

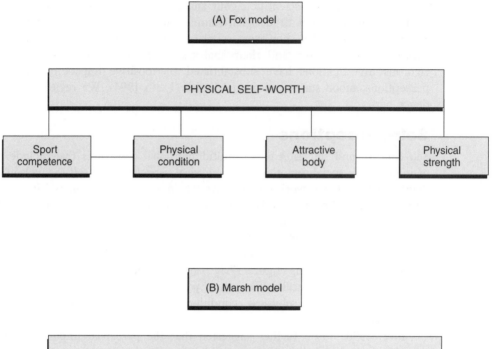

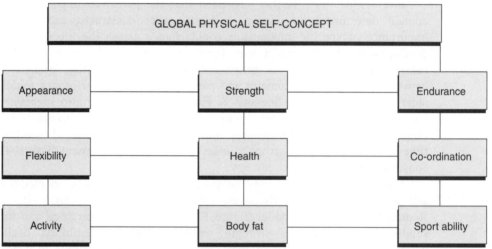

Figure 17.1 Proposed dimensions of the physical self

(*Source:* Based on Fox & Corbin 1989; Marsh et al. 1994)

Mood states

The effect of aerobic exercise on mood has been one of the most widely researched areas within exercise psychology. In the first edition of this book we noted that some investigators had failed to find changes in mood as a result of involvement in this type of exercise (e.g. Hughes 1984), but that most of the evidence favoured a relationship between participation in aerobic activity and more positive mood (Plante & Rodin 1990). Indeed, measures taken immediately after exercise have documented decreases in a variety of negative mood states as well as increases in positive mood states such as vigour and exhilaration (Berger & Owen 1988; LaFontaine, DiLorenzo, Frensch, Stucky-Ropp, Bargman & McDonald 1992; McInman & Berger 1993; Morgan 1985;

Steptoe & Cox 1989). Although the long-term benefits of exercise on mood are not as well documented as the short-term benefits (Plante & Rodin 1990), several studies have obtained findings that suggest a beneficial effect. For example, correlational research by Hayden and Allen (1984) and Lobstein, Mosbacher and Ismail (1983) found that regular exercisers were less anxious and depressed than non-exercisers. Experimental studies have also shown positive mood effects from exercise interventions ranging in length from six weeks to twelve months (Blumenthal, Williams, Needels & Wallace 1982; Goldwater & Collis 1985; King, Taylor & Haskell 1993).

The beneficial effect of exercise on stress-related emotions and perceived stress has been an area of particular interest in recent years. Comprehensive reviews have consistently documented exercise-induced decreases in the stress-related emotions of anxiety and depression (e.g. Landers & Petruzzello 1994; Morgan 1994; North et al. 1990; Petruzzello et al. 1993; Raglin 1997). More specifically, both acute and chronic exercise are associated with small to moderate reductions in state anxiety, with the beneficial effects of acute exercise appearing to last for two to four hours. Similar benefits are evident with respect to depression, and the effects appear to be greater for more severely depressed individuals (McDonald & Hodgdon 1991; North et al. 1990). For this reason, exercise is viewed as a useful tool in the treatment of clinical depression (Babyak et al. 2000; Morgan 1994; Tkachuk & Martin 1999). Studies of stress reactivity and perceived stress have also found beneficial effects from exercise (Aldana et al. 1996; Bulbulian & Darabos 1986; Fillingim & Blumenthal 1992). Interestingly, women appear to be especially receptive to the use of exercise as a stress reduction strategy (Campbell et al. 1992; Rogers & Gauvin 1998).

In a review of the anxiety-related findings, Raglin (1997) noted that the reductions in anxiety symptoms associated with exercise are comparable to those produced by cognitive-behavioural therapies such as stress inoculation training. He also cited evidence that these changes cannot be explained in terms of the perceived importance of exercise (e.g. Simons & Birkimer 1988). At the same time, however, he called attention to two issues that need further scrutiny in connection with the effects of exercise on anxiety. Specifically, it appears that initial levels of anxiety need to be taken into account because the benefits of exercise may be greater for individuals with high baseline levels of anxiety (De Gues, Van Doornen & Orlebeke 1993). Possible differences in the effects of resistance exercise and aerobic exercise should also be investigated because of inconsistency in the findings related to this form of exercise. For example, some researchers have reported significant *increases* in blood pressure and state anxiety following resistance exercise (Koltyn, Raglin, O'Connor & Morgan 1995; Raglin, Turner & Eksten 1993), while others have found these increases to be transitory and followed by improvements in mood (Bartholomew 1999).

Mechanisms

Self-perception effects

Sonstroem and colleagues provide an explanation of the psychological processes responsible for the relationships between involvement in physical activity and self-perceptions. According to Sonstroem and Morgan (1989), exercise-induced changes in measurable physical attributes (e.g. aerobic capacity, flexibility, strength/endurance, body composition) give rise to task-specific judgements of physical self-efficacy. Improvements in task-specific competencies then produce broader feelings of mastery/control and a perception of general physical competence. Feelings of physical acceptance (i.e. satisfaction or dissatisfaction with the physical self) may also be influenced by task-specific physical self-efficacies and/or perceptions of physical competence. The effects of exercise on global self-concept or self-esteem are hypothesised to depend on the amount of change in physical self-efficacies, physical competence and physical acceptance as well as the perceived importance of these constructs for the individual (cf. Fox 1990, 1997). A diagram of this process is shown in figure 17.2.

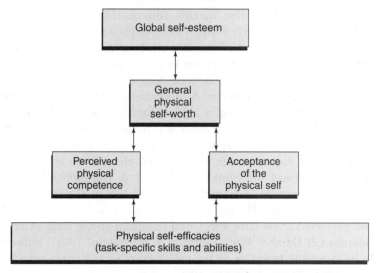

Figure 17.2   Sonstroem and Morgan's (1989) Exercise and Self-esteem Model

(*Source:* Based on Sonstroem & Morgan 1989)

This model was tested in a study by Sonstroem, Harlow, Gemma and Osborne (1991), and the results were generally favourable. Although physical acceptance was not included in this investigation, exercise-related self-efficacy was positively correlated with perceptions of physical competence, which was, in turn, positively correlated with global self-esteem. The direct path between physical self-efficacy and global self-esteem was not significant. Adaptations of the original model were also tested by Sonstroem, Harlow and Salisbury (1993) and Sonstroem, Harlow and Josephs (1994). In the first of these studies, data from high-school swimmers on three separate occasions confirmed the validity of the proposed hierarchical structure when physical competence was assessed in a unidimensional manner. Additional confirmation was obtained in the Sonstroem et al. (1994) study when physical competence was operationalised in a multi-dimensional way using the four subdomains from Fox and Corbin's (1989) physical self-perception model. Although the physical-acceptance component of the Sonstroem and Morgan (1989) model has not been examined as extensively as the physical-competence component (Sonstroem 1998), available data support the proposed hierarchical model. More specifically, involvement in physical activity appears to improve task-specific competencies, which, in turn, improve self-perceptions of differentiated physical sub-domains. Enhanced self-perceptions within these subdomains then have positive effects on more general feelings about physical self-worth and the global self. Moreover, these follow-on effects appear to be independent of gender, age classification and form of exercise (McDonald & Hodgdon 1991).

Mood effects

It has been noted that the nature of exercise-induced mood changes may depend on the previous fitness status of the individual, the type of exercise undertaken, the intensity of exercise, and/or the time lag between exercise and the assessment of mood (Boutcher & Landers 1988; Raglin, Turner & Eksten 1993; Raglin, Wilson & Morris 1993; Steptoe & Cox 1989). The potential for mood enhancement may also be related to characteristics of the exercise activity itself and may occur for a number of reasons. Berger and Owen (1988) suggest that positive psychological outcomes are most likely to occur when exercise is pleasant/enjoyable, noncompetitive, repetitive/rhythmical and temporally/ spatially certain. Regular participation (three or four times a week) at a moderate intensity (60 to 75 per cent of estimated maximum heart rate) for 20 to 60 minutes also contributes to positive mood effects. Although much of the research on exercise and mood deals with aerobic activities, there is some question as to the necessity for an aerobic component (Berger & Owen 1992).

Potential mechanisms for exercise-related mood enhancement are summarised in figure 17.3, and include both physiological and psychological processes (Boutcher 1993; Hatfield 1991; Petruzzello, Landers, Hatfield, Kubitz & Salazar 1991; Tuson & Sinyor 1993). With respect to the physiological mechanisms, it is possible that the increases in core temperature associated with exercise produce reductions in cortical activation as a result of changes in hypothalamic and thalamic activity. Reduced cortical activation may, in turn, result in a relaxed state of mind (Koltyn 1997). Another possibility is that the repetitive and rhythmical physical feedback associated with exercise has a dampening effect on brainstem activity and a calming effect on the overall system. This notion (known as the visceral afferent feedback hypothesis) is consistent with Berger and Owen's (1988) observation that the mood state benefits from exercise occur most often for repetitive, rhythmical, closed-loop activities.

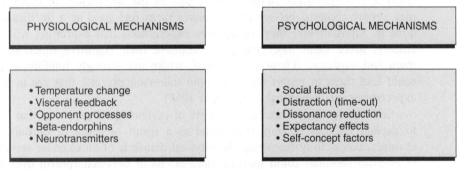

Figure 17.3 Proposed mechanisms for the effects of exercise on mood

The opponent-process model provides a third physiological explanation for positive mood changes as a result of exercise. Also called 'autonomic rebound', this explanation is based on the observation that stressful experiences are typically followed by an opposing, pleasurable state of mind upon cessation of the stress. In other words, the system experiences heightened activation during exercise but then 'rebounds' below baseline activation in a compensatory fashion when exercise ends. With repeated exposure, the system habituates to the sympathetically mediated stress of exercise, and the opposing process (i.e. parasympathetically mediated positive affect) becomes stronger. Some researchers have suggested that increases in beta-endorphins could be responsible for this rebound effect (Hatfield 1991). Exercise-induced increases in the levels of neurotransmitters such as norepinephrine, dopamine and serotonin could also play a role in mood enhancement following exercise. The levels of these substances tend to be reduced during depressive states and increased by treatments and/or medications that are effective in reducing depression. The levels of these substances have also been shown to increase during exercise, so it is possible that such increases play a role in exercise-induced mood changes.

Psychological explanations for the enhancement of mood via exercise include social factors, distraction, dissonance reduction, expectancy effects and changes in self-concept. With respect to social factors, physical activity can provide opportunities to avoid loneliness and isolation, to affiliate with friends, to make new acquaintances and/or to receive public recognition for taking positive steps towards a healthy lifestyle. These types of motives are frequently cited as reasons for exercising, and there is also evidence that people enjoy exercise more when it is undertaken along with others (Ingledew, Markland & Medley 1998; Markland & Ingledew 1997; Willis & Campbell 1992). The distraction hypothesis was originally proposed by Bahrke and Morgan (1978) in an attempt to explain why acute exercise, meditation and quiet rest all had similar effects on state anxiety. Given that all three of these procedures provided a break from routines, worries and hassles, it was suggested that 'time out' may have been responsible for the observed reductions in anxiety. This notion was tested in a study of high-anxious women by Breus and O'Connor (1998), in which distraction was prevented during some exercise sessions but not others. The findings supported the validity of the time-out hypothesis.

Cognitive dissonance occurs when there are inconsistencies between thoughts and behaviours. People prefer to avoid these inconsistencies, and they can do so by altering either their behaviour or their cognitions (Festinger 1957). Petruzzello et al. (1991) suggest that feelings of positive affect following exercise could, in part, result from unconscious attempts to reduce dissonance through an emotional justification for the time, effort and commitment required to engage in the behaviour. In other words, people may simply come to believe that it makes them feel good as a justification for having done it. Alternatively, they might have expectations that exercising will reduce stress/anxiety, make them more energetic, improve their cognitive functions and/or make them feel euphoric. These expectations, which are strongly reinforced by the media, could lead them to report states of mind following exercise that are in line with these expectancies (cf. Rosenthal & Jacobson 1968).

Self-concept factors include a variety of psychological processes that could also help to explain findings of improved mood as a result of acute or chronic exercise. For example, successfully managing the physical demands of an exercise session (or a series of exercise sessions) could increase perceptions of personal control over one's lifestyle and health, which, in turn, could have a beneficial effect on mood states (Rodin 1986; Steptoe 1989). Similarly, completion of individual exercise sessions, effortful physical tasks or exercise programs undoubtedly contributes to a sense of mastery competence with concomitant effects on positive affect (Harter 1978; Ryan & Deci 2000). Finally, improvements in task-specific physical capabilities, strength, fitness and/or physique resulting from exercise could have a positive impact on mood and self-esteem by improving self-perceptions of general physical competence. This is, of course, precisely the point that Sonstroem and colleagues make in their exercise and self-esteem model (figure 17.2), and it represents an interesting overlap between the explanations offered for exercise-related changes in self-concept and exercise-related changes in mood.

PSYCHOLOGICAL COSTS OF EXERCISE

The previous sections clearly document the potential for exercise to deliver psychological benefits. At the same time, however, it is important to recognise that exercise also has the potential to extract a psychological toll. An appreciation of this 'darker side' to the psychological consequences of exercise can be gained through an examination of the literature on overtraining/staleness and exercise dependence.

Overtraining and staleness

Involvement in a very heavy exercise schedule (i.e. overtraining) is sometimes accompanied by persistent declines in performance capabilities as well as negative physiological and psychological changes. These systemic changes include muscle soreness/ damage, neuroendocrinological imbalance, suppressed immunity, lethargy, loss of appetite/weight, mood disturbance, insomnia and alterations of movement biomechanics (Fry, Morton & Keast 1991; Kuipers & Keizer 1988; Myers & Whelan 1998; O'Connor 1996; Raglin & Wilson 2000). Although individual differences are apparent in susceptibility to this 'overtraining syndrome' (Costill et al. 1988; Morgan, Costill, Flynn, Raglin & O'Connor 1988), insufficient recovery time between exercise sessions is the primary predisposing factor for both acute and chronic episodes (Fry et al. 1991; Mackinnon & Hooper 1991; Raglin 1993). Additional stresses related to diet/sleep, travel and competition may exacerbate the effects of insufficient recovery time (Costill et al. 1988; O'Connor & Morgan 1990). Because endurance athletes often undertake planned overtraining in an attempt to produce 'superadaptation effects', they may be especially prone to the overtraining syndrome. For example, studies of long distance runners and swimmers suggest a yearly incidence rate of 5 to 10 per cent and a career incidence rate of approximately 60 per cent for these athletes (Morgan, Brown, Raglin, O'Connor & Ellickson 1987; Morgan, O'Connor, Ellickson & Bradley 1988; Morgan, O'Connor, Sparling & Pate 1987).

Raglin and Wilson (2000) view overtraining as a process and use the term 'staleness' to describe the consequences of this process (i.e. the overtraining syndrome). They note that psychological measures are typically more consistent indices of staleness than physiological measures, and they also suggest that the Profile of Mood States (POMS) (McNair, Lorr & Droppelman 1971) has proven to be one of the more reliable psychological measures for this purpose. Indeed, increases in total mood disturbance (TMD) scores on the POMS have been linked to corresponding increases in training loads for periods ranging from a few days to several months (Fry, Grove, Morton, Zeroni, Gaudieri & Keast 1994; Morgan, Brown et al. 1987; O'Connor, Morgan & Raglin 1991; O'Connor, Morgan, Raglin, Barksdale & Kalin 1989). These changes in TMD have been observed in a variety of sport groups including swimmers, runners, speed skaters, rowers and basketball players (Raglin 1993; Raglin & Wilson 2000). When individual POMS subscales are examined, increases in fatigue and decreases in vigour seem to account for much of the change in TMD among athletes who are exposed to training stress but who are not stale (Raglin, Morgan & O'Connor 1991). For stale athletes, however, substantial increases in depression and/or anger may also occur (Raglin 1993; Raglin & Morgan 1994). Most POMS subscales return to baseline levels when exercise workloads are decreased to 'normal' training levels, but residual elevations during recovery have been found for tension and fatigue (Fry et al. 1994; Raglin et al. 1991).

Although mood state assessment via the POMS has been the predominant approach used to monitor the psychological effects of heavy exercise loads, other approaches have also been employed. For example, Rushall (1990) suggests that, in order to understand responses to the specific stress of training, it is necessary to monitor sources of stress within other areas of life as well. Towards this end, he developed an instrument called the Daily Analyses of Life Demands for Athletes (DALDA) as a means of assessing the extent to which an individual is experiencing stress as well as the factors leading to the stressed condition. The DALDA contains two sections and assesses sources of stress as well as stress symptoms at a particular point in time. The potential sources of stress include events related to diet, home life, work, friends, training and sleep, and a symptom checklist contains common stress reactions. Rushall suggests that an increase in self-reported sources of stress and/or stress symptoms can provide an early warning sign that the individual is training too hard.

A MULTI-COMPONENT ASSESSMENT OF RESPONSES TO HEAVY TRAINING

Studies conducted by Shepherdson (2000) illustrate the value of using measures other than mood disturbance to assess the effects of training load on mental and physical states. Participants in an initial study were 17 swimmers who were preparing to compete in state and national meets. These swimmers were monitored over a nine-week period that included a normal training phase as well as an overload phase and a taper phase. The measures consisted of brief questionnaires designed to assess mood as well as perceived stress and training-specific symptoms such as those noted by Fry et al. (1994). Weekly training distances were noted, and questionnaire responses obtained during heavier-than-average weeks were compared with those obtained during lighter-than-average weeks. The results showed that mood states were not the only measure affected by the differential training loads. More specifically, both mood disturbance and perceived stress were significantly higher during heavy training weeks than during light training weeks. Training-specific symptoms such as lethargy and muscle soreness also tended to be higher during the heavier training periods than during the lighter training periods. A follow-up study subsequently found that relationships between training state scores and swimming performance were stronger when all three measures were combined rather than used separately.

Kellmann and colleagues (Kellmann & Günther 2000; Kellmann & Kallus 2001) also adopt a stress perspective in their research on the psychological effects of heavy training. These authors use the term 'recovery-stress state' to indicate the extent to which someone is physically and/or mentally stressed but, at the same time, capable of using various strategies to buffer the effects of the stress (i.e. to recover). Kellmann believes that, in order to fully understand the psychological effects of heavy exercise loads, it is necessary to adopt a multidimensional approach that gives consideration not only to the cognitive/emotional aspects of the issue, but also to the behavioural/performance and social aspects of the issue. In line with this belief, Kellmann and Kallus (2001) report on the development of an instrument called the Recovery-Stress Questionnaire for Athletes (RESTQ-Sport) that assesses stress-recovery status using 12 general and 7 sport-related subscales. These subscales are designed to quantitatively assess the level of current stress while also taking into account regeneration capabilities, thereby providing an indication of the potential for staleness at a given point in time. Like the DALDA, the REST-Q addresses the sources of stress, which means that it provides useful information for identifying interventions that are likely to reduce the negative emotional consequences of heavy training (Steinacker et al. 1999).

Exercise dependence

It is natural for people to spend time doing things they enjoy. However, the amount of time spent pursuing enjoyable activities can sometimes increase to a point where the pursuit of those activities becomes compulsive and interferes with adequate functioning in other areas. If this occurs, the individual may have a dependence problem. The criteria for evaluating behavioural dependence are summarised in figure 17.4 and include tolerance, withdrawal symptoms, excessive time investment, suppression of other activities and continued involvement despite awareness of negative consequences (American Psychological Association 1994). A number of researchers have suggested that people could become dependent on specific exercise activities or exercise in general, and their analyses typically make reference to one or more of these criteria. Withdrawal symptoms are perhaps the most widely researched phenomenon in this regard.

DSM-IV CRITERIA FOR EVALUATION OF DEPENDENCE

- Tolerance
- Withdrawal symptoms
- Excessive time investment
- Suppression of unrelated activities
- Negative consequences from involvement
- Continued involvement despite awareness of negative consequences

Figure 17.4 The American Psychological Association's criteria for evaluating dependence

Restriction of physical activity has been shown to produce a number of psychological symptoms in regular exercisers. Some of the more common symptoms are guilt, depression, irritability, increases in tension/anxiety and somatic complaints (Sachs 1991; Szabo 1995). Baekeland (1970) was one of the first to call attention to the possible negative effects of exercise deprivation. In his study, undergraduate students who were accustomed to regular exercise were prohibited from exercising for a month. Analysis of their sleep patterns and self-report data suggested that tension and anxiety increased considerably during the deprivation period. Subsequent studies have corroborated these findings and have also shown that deprivation periods as short as 24 hours can produce psychological symptoms in habitual exercisers (Sachs & Pargman 1979; Thaxton 1982). In a study of 345 male and female runners who averaged 20–25 miles a week, Robbins and Joseph (1985) observed that the symptoms experienced following a missed workout typically fell into three categories: anxiousness, feelings of loss and fatigue. Similar findings were obtained in studies of runners conducted by Blumenthal, O'Toole and Chang (1984) and by Acevedo, Dzewaltowski, Gill and Noble (1992).

Experimental studies in which exercise involvement has been manipulated provide even stronger evidence for withdrawal symptoms as a result of removing the exercise stimulus. Morris, Steinberg, Sykes and Salmon (1990) examined anxiety as well as other negative mood states in a study involving middle-aged male runners. This study lasted for six weeks, with a two-week baseline followed by a two-week experimental phase in which the participants were randomly assigned to exercise deprivation or control groups. The deprivation group abstained from regular exercise during the experimental phase of the study, but the control group maintained their normal training schedule. Results revealed that runners who stopped exercising experienced increases in both perceived stress and anxiety during the deprivation period. Similar findings were obtained in a quasi-experimental study by Mondin and colleagues (1996). Participants in that study were 10 individuals who engaged in aerobic activities such as jogging, cycling and/or swimming for a minimum of 45 minutes per day on six days each week. These regular exercisers completed daily assessments of anxiety and other mood states over a five-day period during which their exercise involvement was manipulated. Significant changes over time were noted for measures of tension and anxiety, with both measures peaking on the second day of exercise withdrawal and then returning towards baseline at follow-up.

Other investigators have elaborated on the manifestations of additional dependence criteria among habitual exercisers. For example, the physiological adaptations that occur as a result of training are, in themselves, a form of tolerance and necessitate increases in 'dosage' to achieve desired physical and mental effects (Cockerill & Riddington 1996; Pierce, McGowan & Lynn 1993). The time demands of some physical activities also mean that they (or the activities that surround them) occupy a large portion of the person's day. This may be especially true for physical activities characterised by both high performance demands and strong expectations for a particular physical appearance (Pierce, Daleng & McGowan 1993). As a result, it is not uncommon for highly committed exercisers to reduce their commitment and/or involvement in important but conflicting familial, social and occupational activities (Cockerill & Riddington 1996; Morgan 1979). Finally, there is ample evidence that many highly committed exercisers will refuse to cut back on their involvement in this activity despite an awareness of negative social and physical consequences (Little 1969; Polivy 1994; Stannish 1984; Tuckman 1999). In these instances, the refusal to stop may be a means of asserting inner strength, self-regulation and control, all of which appear to be strong incentives for participation (Yates 1991).

Numerous general and activity-specific assessment procedures have been used to assess exercise dependence, but two of these procedures deserve special mention because of their divergent approaches but, at the same time, their similarity of content. De Coverley-Veale (1987) proposed a clinical checklist for the diagnosis of exercise dependence that included the following criteria: (a) engaging in exercise once or more per day; (b) a narrow (i.e. stereotyped) exercise pattern; (c) tolerance and an associated need/desire to increase the amount of exercise undertaken; (d) withdrawal symptoms following cessation or deprivation; (e) rapid reinstatement of the previous pattern of exercise after a period of abstinence; (f) relief of withdrawal symptoms as a result of resuming exercise; and (g) awareness of a compulsion to exercise. Associated features that were considered to be outgrowths of dependence rather than its core elements included continuation of exercise despite negative physical, social or occupational consequences and self-inflicted weight loss in an effort to improve exercise performance.

A brief pen-and-paper instrument designed specifically to assess exercise dependence was developed and validated by Ogden, Veale and Summers (1997). Eighty-six potential items for the scale were first generated from statements made by 131 highly committed exercisers about their exercise-related thoughts and feelings. Data from a second sample of 449 regular exercisers were then factor analysed to produce a 29-item questionnaire that consisted of eight subscales. These subscales reflected social/occupational interference, perceived positive reward, withdrawal symptoms, weight concerns, awareness of problem, social affiliation motives, fitness/health motives and stereotyped behaviour. Internal consistencies were above .70 for all of these subscales except for the stereotyped behaviour subscale measure (which contained only two items). Correlations with external criteria indicated that total scores on the instrument as well as scores on individual subscales were related in meaningful ways to measures of eating attitudes, negative emotionality and exercise involvement.

FUTURE DIRECTIONS

Although a great deal of research has been conducted into the psychological consequences of exercise, there are a number of interesting and important avenues for future research. For example, now that the multidimensional nature of the physical self has been established, it will be possible for researchers to become more focused when evaluating relationships between exercise involvement and self-perceptions. Early research in this area had the difficult task of documenting associations between exercise participation and general self-concept, but current and future research has the advantage of being able to isolate specific aspects of the physical self that are likely to be associated with participation in specific types of exercise. Increasing specificity will undoubtedly characterise mood state research as well. For example, does high-frequency but low-intensity exercise (e.g. daily walking) produce mood state benefits similar to those produced by aerobic exercise? Does resistance exercise produce a different pattern of post-exercise mood state response than aerobic exercise? Evidence is beginning to emerge on these issues, but considerably more work needs to be done.

With respect to overtraining and staleness, there is likely to be both a refinement of the existing POMS paradigm (cf. Raglin & Morgan 1994) and an attempt to develop complementary measures. The stress-oriented measure developed by Rushall (1990) and the stress-recovery instrument published by Kellmann and Kallus (2001) could provide a starting point for this work. Unlike the POMS, these measures provide information about the psychological state of the performer as well as the potential sources of stress. Consideration could also be given to the social consequences of intensive training schedules, especially among young athletes. With increasing specialisation at an early age, children are sometimes expected to forgo important developmental activities in order to meet their training commitments. The impact of these adult-like demands on the child's social development deserves research attention.

CONCLUSIONS

A physically active lifestyle is within the grasp of most people, and the attainment of such a lifestyle is likely to provide significant benefits at both an individual and societal level. From an individual perspective, regular physical activity is associated with positive mood states, improvements in self-concept, reduced risk of chronic disease and enhanced quality of life. From a societal perspective, physical activity represents a cost-effective means of improving economic productivity, enhancing the physical and mental health of the general population, and reducing public health-care costs. These potential benefits have prompted government agencies and scientists alike to call for the development of strategies to increase physical activity levels within society at large (Centers for Disease Control 1996; Sparling, Owen, Lambert & Haskell 2000). We fully endorse such efforts, but we also believe they can only be successful if they are based on a thorough understanding of the personal consequences of specific forms of exercise for specific types of people. In this chapter, we have attempted to point out that exercise has the potential to provide important psychological benefits but, at the same time, also carries with it the risk of psychological costs. Acknowledgement of both possibilities and an awareness of the circumstances surrounding them is an important step towards effective implementation of interventions at both individual and societal level.

SUMMARY

Exercise offers numerous psychological benefits. These benefits include positive changes in perceptions of the physical self, acute improvements in mood, and reductions in clinically relevant emotions such as anxiety and depression. A number of physiological and psychological mechanisms have been proposed to explain these effects, and it is likely that several of these mechanisms act interdependently to produce the observed benefits. At the same time, however, research evidence also indicates that it is possible to get 'too much of a good thing' with respect to exercise. That is, excessive exercise can be associated with mood disturbance, increases in perceived stress, 'staleness' and, in extreme cases, behavioural dependence. These negative consequences need not be feared, but it is important to recognise when they might occur and how they might be manifested.

 REVIEW QUESTIONS

1 Outline the models of the physical self proposed by Fox and Corbin (1989) and by Marsh et al. (1994).

2 Explain the exercise and self-esteem model as described by Sonstroem and Morgan (1989).

3 List and describe four *physiological* mechanisms that have been suggested to explain the beneficial effects of exercise on mood.

4 List and describe four *psychological* mechanisms that have been suggested to explain the beneficial effects of exercise on mood.

5 Distinguish between 'overtraining' and 'staleness'.

6 How is staleness usually assessed? What alternatives have been proposed to this traditional assessment approach?

7 What criteria do psychologists use to evaluate dependence, and how have these criteria been used in connection with exercise behaviour?

References

Acevedo, EO, Dzewaltowski, DA, Gill, DL & Noble, JM 1992, 'Cognitive orientations of ultramarathoners', *The Sport Psychologist*, 6, 242–52.

Aldana, SG, Sutton, LD, Jacobson, BH & Quirk, MG 1996, 'Relationship between leisure time physical activity and perceived stress', *Perceptual and Motor Skills*, 82, 315–21.

American Psychological Association 1994, *Diagnostic and statistical manual of mental disorders*, 4th edn, American Psychiatric Association, Washington, DC.

Babyak, M, Blumenthal, JA, Herman, S, Khatri, P, Doraiswamy, M, Moore, K, Craighead, WE, Baldewicz, TT & Krishnan, KR 2000, 'Exercise treatment for major depression: maintenance of therapeutic benefit at 10 months', *Psychosomatic Medicine*, 62, 633–8.

Baekeland, F 1970, 'Exercise deprivation: sleep and psychological reactions', *Archives of General Psychiatry*, 22, 365–9.

Bahrke, MS & Morgan, WP 1978, 'Anxiety reduction following exercise and meditation', *Cognitive Therapy and Research*, 2, 323–33.

Bartholomew, JB 1999, 'The effect of resistance exercise on manipulated pre-exercise mood states for male exercisers', *Journal of Sport & Exercise Psychology*, 21, 39–51.

Berger, BG & Owen, DR 1988, 'Stress reduction and mood enhancement in four exercise modes: swimming, body conditioning, hatha yoga, and fencing', *Research Quarterly for Exercise and Sport*, 59, 148–59.

Berger, BG & Owen, DR 1992, 'Mood alteration with yoga and swimming: aerobic exercise may not be necessary', *Perceptual and Motor Skills*, 75, 1331–43.

Blair, SN 1988, 'Exercise within a health lifestyle', in RK Dishman (ed.), *Exercise adherence: its impact on public health*, Human Kinetics, Champaign, IL, pp. 75–89.

Blumenthal, JA, O'Toole, LC & Chang, JL 1984, 'Is running an anologue of anorexia nervosa? An empirical study of obligatory running and anorexia nervosa', *Journal of the American Medical Association*, 252, 520–3.

Blumenthal, JA, Williams, S, Needels, TL & Wallace, AG 1982, 'Psychological changes accompany aerobic exercise in healthy middle-aged adults', *Psychosomatic Medicine*, 44, 529–35.

Boutcher, SH 1993, 'Emotion and aerobic exercise', in RN Singer, M Murphey & LK Tennant (eds), *Handbook of research on sport psychology*, Macmillan, New York, pp. 799–814.

Boutcher, SH & Landers, DM 1988, 'The effects of vigorous exercise on anxiety, heart rate, and alpha activity of runners and nonrunners', *Psychophysiology*, 25, 696–702.

Breus, MJ & O'Connor, PJ 1998, 'Exercise-induced anxiolysis: a test of the "time-out" hypothesis in high anxious females', *Medicine & Science in Sports & Exercise*, 30, 1107–12.

Bulbulian, R & Darabos, BL 1986, 'Motor neuron excitability: the Hoffmann reflex following exercise of low and high intensity', *Medicine & Science in Sports & Exercise*, 18, 697–702.

Campbell, RL, Svenson, LW & Jarvis, GK 1992, 'Perceived level of stress among university undergraduate students in Edmonton, Canada, *Perceptual and Motor Skills*, 75, 552–4.

Centers for Disease Control 1996, *Physical activity and health: a report of the Surgeon General*, U.S. Department of Health and Human Services, Atlanta, GA.

Cockerill, IM & Riddington, ME 1996, 'Exercise dependence and associated disorders: a review', *Counselling Psychology Quarterly*, 9, 119–29.

Costill, DL, Flynn, MG, Kirwan, JP, Houmard, JA, Mitchell, JB, Thomas, R & Park, SH 1988, 'Effects of repeated days of intensified training on muscle glycogen and swimming performance', *Medicine & Science in Sports & Exercise*, 20, 249–54.

de Coverley Veale, DMW 1987, 'Exercise dependence', *British Journal of Addiction*, 82, 735–40.

De Gues, EJC, Van Doornen, LJP & Orlebeke, JF 1993, 'Regular exercise and aerobic fitness in relation to psychological make-up and physiological stress reactivity', *Psychosomatic Medicine*, 55, 347–63.

Dishman, RK 1986, 'Mental health', in V Seefeldt (ed.), *Physical activity and well-being*, American Association for Health, Physical Education and Recreation, Reston, VA, pp. 304–40.

Dishman, RK 1988, *Exercise adherence: its impact on public health*, Human Kinetics, Champaign, IL.

Festinger, L 1957, *A theory of cognitive dissonance*, Stanford University Press, Stanford, CA.

Fillingim, RB & Blumenthal, JA 1992, 'Does aerobic exercise reduce stress responses?', in RJ Turner et al. (eds), *Individual differences in cardiovascular response to stress: perspectives on individual differences*, Plenum, New York, pp. 203–17.

Fox, KR 1990, *The physical self-perception profile manual*, Office for Health Promotion, Northern Illinois University.

Fox, KR 1997, *The physical self: from motivation to well-being*, Human Kinetics, Champaign, IL.

Fox, KR & Corbin, CB 1989, 'The physical self-perception profile: development and preliminary validation', *Journal of Sport & Exercise Psychology*, 11, 408–30.

Fry, RW, Grove, JR, Morton, AR, Zeroni, P, Gaudieri, S & Keast, D 1994, 'Psychological and immunological correlates of acute overtraining', *British Journal of Sports Medicine*, 28, 241–6.

Fry, RW, Morton, AR & Keast, D 1991, 'Overtraining in athletes: an update', *Sports Medicine*, 12, 32–65.

Goldwater, BC & Collis, ML 1985, 'Psycholgic effects of cardiovascular conditioning: a controlled experiment', *Psychosomatic Medicine*, 47, 174–81.

Harter, S 1978, 'Effectance motivation reconsidered: toward a developmental model', *Human Development*, 21, 34–64.

Hatfield, BD 1991, 'Exercise and mental health: the mechanisms of exercise-induced psychological states', in L Diamant (ed.), *Psychology of sports, exercise, and fitness: social and personal issues*, Hemisphere, New York, pp. 17–49.

Hayden, RM & Allen, GJ 1984, 'Relationship between aerobic exercise, anxiety, and depression: convergent validation by knowledgeable informants', *Journal of Sports Medicine*, 24, 69–74.

Hughes, JR 1984, 'Psychological effects of habitual aerobic exercise: a critical review', *Preventive Medicine*, 13, 66–78.

Ingledew, DK, Markland, D & Medley, AR 1998, 'Exercise motives and stages of change', *Journal of Health Psychology*, 3, 477–89.

Kellmann, M & Günther, KD 2000, 'Changes in stress and recovery in elite rowers during preparation for the Olympic games', *Medicine & Science in Sports & Exercise*, 32, 676–83.

Kellmann, M & Kallus, KW 2001, *Recovery-Stress Questionnaire for Athletes: user manual*, Human Kinetics, Champaign, IL.

King, AC, Taylor, CB & Haskell, WL 1993, 'Effects of differing intensities and formats of 12 months of exercise training on psychological outcomes in older adults', *Health Psychology*, 12, 292–300.

Koltyn, KF 1997, 'The thermogenic hypothesis', in WP Morgan (ed.), *Physical activity and mental health*, Taylor & Francis, Washington, DC, pp. 213–26.

Koltyn, KF, Raglin, JS, O'Connor, PJ & Morgan, WP 1995, 'Influence of weight training on state anxiety, body awareness, and blood pressure', *International Journal of Sports Medicine*, 16, 266–9.

Kuipers, H & Keizer, HA 1988, 'Overtraining in elite athletes: review and directions for the future', *Sports Medicine*, 6, 79–92.

LaFontaine, TP, DiLorenzo, TM, Frensch, PA, Stucky-Ropp, RC, Bargman, EP, McDonald, DG 1992, 'Aerobic exercise and mood: a brief review 1985–1990', *Sports Medicine*, 13, 160–70.

Landers, DM & Petruzzello, SJ 1994, 'Physical activity, fitness, and anxiety', in C Bouchard, RJ Shephard & T Stephens (eds), *Physical activity, fitness, and health: international proceedings and consensus statement*, Human Kinetics, Champaign, IL, pp. 868–82.

Leith, LM 1994, *Foundations of exercise and mental health*, Fitness Information Technology, Morgantown, WV.

Little, JC 1969, 'The athlete's neurosis: a deprivation crisis', *Acta Psychiatrica Scandinavica*, 45, 187–97.

Lobstein, DD, Mosbacher, BJ & Ismail, AH 1983, 'Depression as a powerful discriminator between physically active and sedentary middle-aged men', *Journal of Psychosomatic Research*, 27, 69–76.

Mackinnon, LT & Hooper, S 1991, *State of the art review no. 26: overtraining*, Australian Sports Commission, Canberra.

Markland, D & Ingledew, DK 1997, 'The measurement of exercise motives: factorial validity and invariance across gender of a revised Exercise Motivations Inventory', *British Journal of Health Psychology*, 2, 361–76.

Marsh, HW 1996a, 'Construct validity of Physical Self-Description Questionnaire responses: relations to external criteria', *Journal of Sport & Exercise Psychology*, 18, 111–31.

Marsh, HW 1996b, 'Physical Self-Description Questionnaire: stability and discriminant validity', *Research Quarterly for Exercise and Sport*, 67, 249–64.

Marsh, HW 1997, 'The measurement of physical self-concept: a construct validation approach', in K Fox (ed.), *The physical self: from motivation to well-being*, Human Kinetics, Champaign, IL, pp. 27–58.

Marsh, HW & Redmayne, RS 1994, 'A multidimensional physical self-concept and its relation to multiple components of physical fitness', *Journal of Sport & Exercise Psychology*, 16, 45–55.

Marsh, HW, Richards, GE, Johnson, S, Roche, L & Tremayne, P 1994, 'Physical Self-Description Questionnaire: psychometric properties and a multitrait–multimethod analysis of relationships to existing instruments', *Journal of Sport & Exercise Psychology*, 16, 270–305.

Marsh, HW & Shavelson, RJ 1985, 'Self-concept: its multifaceted, hierarchical structure', *Educational Psychologist*, 20, 107–25.

Marsh, HW & Sonstroem, RJ 1995, 'Importance ratings and specific components of physical self-concept: relevance to predicting global components of physical self-concept and exercise', *Journal of Sport & Exercise Psychology*, 17, 84–104.

McDonald, DG & Hodgdon, JA 1991, *Psychological effects of aerobic fitness training: research and theory*, Springer-Verlag, London.

McInman, AD & Berger, BG 1993, 'Self-concept and mood changes associated with aerobic dance', *Australian Journal of Psychology*, 45, 134–40.

McNair, DM, Lorr, M & Droppelman, LF 1971, *Profile of Mood States manual*, Educational and Industrial Testing Service, San Diego.

Mondin, GW, Morgan, WP, Piering, PD, Stegner, AJ, Stotesbery, CL, Trine, MR & Wu, M-Y 1996, 'Psychological consequences of exercise deprivation in habitual exercisers', *Medicine & Science in Sports & Exercise*, 28, 1199–203.

Morgan, WP 1979, 'Negative addiction in runners', *Physician and Sportsmedicine*, 7, 56–63, 67–70.

Morgan, WP 1985, 'Affective beneficence of vigorous physical activity', *Medicine & Science in Sports & Exercise*, 17, 94–100.

Morgan, WP 1988, 'Exercise and mental health', in RK Dishman (ed.), *Exercise adherence: its impact on public health*, Human Kinetics, Champaign, IL, pp. 91–121.

Morgan, WP 1994, 'Physical activity, fitness, and depression', in C Bouchard, RJ Shephard & T Stephens (eds), *Physical activity, fitness, and health: international proceedings and consensus statement*, Human Kinetics, Champaign, IL, pp. 851–67.

Morgan, WP, Brown, DR, Raglin, JS, O'Connor, PJ & Ellickson, KA 1987, 'Psychological monitoring of overtraining and staleness', *British Journal of Sports Medicine*, 21, 107–14.

Morgan, WP, Costill, DL, Flynn, MG, Raglin, JS & O'Connor, PJ 1988, 'Mood disturbance following increased training in swimmers', *Medicine & Science in Sports & Exercise*, 20, 408–14.

Morgan, WP, O'Connor, PJ, Ellickson, KA & Bradley, PW 1988, 'Personality structure, mood states, and performance in elite male distance runners', *International Journal of Sport Psychology*, 19, 247–63.

Morgan, WP, O'Connor, PJ, Sparling, PB & Pate, RR 1987, 'Psychologic characterization of the elite female distance runner', *International Journal of Sports Medicine*, 8, 124–31.

Morris, M, Steinberg, H, Sykes, EA & Salmon, P 1990, 'Effects of temporary withdrawal from regular running', *Journal of Psychosomatic Research*, 34, 493–500.

Myers, AW & Whelan, JP 1998, 'A systematic model for understanding psychosocial influences in overtraining', in RB Kreider, AC Fry & ML O'Toole (eds), *Overtraining in sport*, Human Kinetics, Champaign, IL, pp. 335–69.

North, TC, McCullagh, P & Tran, ZV 1990, 'The effect of exercise on depression', *Exercise and Sport Science Reviews*, 18, 379–415.

O'Connor, PJ 1996, 'Overtraining and staleness', in WP Morgan (ed.), *Physical activity and mental health*, Taylor & Francis, Washington, DC, pp. 145–60.

O'Connor, PJ & Morgan, WP 1990, 'Athletic performance following rapid traversal of multiple time zones: a review', *Sports Medicine*, 10, 20–30.

O'Connor, PJ, Morgan, WP & Raglin, JS 1991, 'Psychobiologic effects of 3 days of increased training in female and male swimmers', *Medicine & Science in Sports & Exercise*, 23, 1055–61.

O'Connor, PJ, Morgan, WP, Raglin, JS, Barksdale, CN & Kalin, NH 1989, 'Mood state and salivary cortisol levels following overtraining in female swimmers', *Psychoneuroendocrinology*, 14, 303–10.

Ogden, J, Veale, D, Summers, Z 1997, 'The development and validation of the Exercise Dependence Questionnaire', *Addiction Research*, 5, 343–56.

Petruzzello, SJ, Landers, DM & Salazar, W 1993, 'Exercise and anxiety reduction: examination of temperature as an explanation for affective change', *Journal of Sport & Exercise Psychology*, 15, 63–76.

Petruzzello, SJ, Landers, DM, Hatfield, BD, Kubitz, KA & Salazar, W 1991, 'A meta-analysis on the anxiety-reducing effects of acute and chronic exercise: outcomes and mechanisms', *Sports Medicine*, 11, 143–82.

Pierce, EF, Daleng, ML & McGowan, RW 1993, 'Scores on exercise dependence among dancers', *Perceptual and Motor Skills*, 76, 531–5.

Pierce, EF, McGowan, RW & Lynn, TD 1993, 'Exercise dependence in relation to competitive orientation of runners', *Journal of Sports Medicine and Physical Fitness*, 33, 189–93.

Plante, TG & Rodin, J 1990, 'Physical fitness and enhanced psychological health', *Current Psychology: Research & Reviews*, 9, 3–24.

Polivy, J 1994, 'Physical activity, fitness, and compulsive behaviors', in C Bouchard, RJ Shephard & T Stephens (eds), *Physical activity, fitness, and health: international proceedings and consensus statement*, Human Kinetics, Champaign, IL, pp. 883–97.

Raglin, JS 1993, 'Overtraining and staleness: psychometric monitoring of endurance athletes', in RN Singer, M Murphey & LK Tennant (eds), *Handbook of research on sport psychology*, Macmillan, New York, pp. 840–50.

Raglin, JS 1997, 'Anxiolytic effects of physical activity', in WP Morgan (ed.), *Physical activity and mental health*, Taylor & Francis, Washington, DC, pp. 107–26.

Raglin, JS & Morgan, WP 1994, 'Development of a scale for use in monitoring training-induced distress in athletes', *International Journal of Sports Medicine*, 15, 84–8.

Raglin, JS, Morgan, WP & O'Connor, PJ 1991, 'Changes in mood states during training in female and male college swimmers', *International Journal of Sports Medicine*, 12, 585–9.

Raglin, JS, Turner, PE & Eksten, F 1993, 'State anxiety and blood pressure following 30 min of leg ergometry or weight training', *Medicine & Science in Sports & Exercise*, 25, 1044–8.

Raglin, JS & Wilson, GS 2000, 'Overtraining in athletes', in Y Hanin (ed.), *Emotions in sport*, Human Kinetics, Champaign, IL, pp. 191–207.

Raglin, JS, Wilson, MW & Morris, MJ 1993, 'State anxiety and blood pressure following 20-minutes of leg ergometry at differing intensities', *Medicine & Science in Sports & Exercise*, 25 (Suppl.) S46 (abstract).

Robbins, JM & Joseph, P 1985, 'Experiencing exercise withdrawal: possible consequences of therapeutic and mastery running', *Journal of Sport Psychology*, 5, 314–31.

Rodin, J 1986, 'Aging and health: effects of the sense of control', *Science*, 233, 1271–6.

Rogers, W & Gauvin, L 1998, 'Heterogeneity of incentives for physical activity and self-efficacy in highly active and moderately active women exercisers', *Journal of Applied Social Psychology*, 28, 1016–29.

Rosenthal, R & Jacobson, L 1968, *Pygmalion in the classroom: teacher expectations and pupils' intellectual development*, Holt, Rinehart & Winston, New York.

Rushall, BS 1990, 'A tool for measuring stress tolerance in elite athletes', *Journal of Applied Sport Psychology*, 2, 51–66.

Ryan, AJ 1984, 'Exercise and health: lessons from the past', in MH Eckert & HJ Montoye (eds), *Exercise and health: American Academy of Physical Education Papers*, 17, Human Kinetics, Champaign, IL, pp. 3–13.

Ryan, RM & Deci, EL 2000, 'Self-determination theory and the facilitation of intrinsic motivation, social development, and well-being', *American Psychologist*, 55, 68–78.

Ryckman, RM, Robbins, MA, Thornton, B & Cantrell, P 1982, 'Development and validation of a physical self-efficacy scale', *Journal of Personality and Social Psychology*, 42, 891–900.

Sachs, ML 1991, 'Running — a psychological phenomenon', in L Diamant (ed.), *Psychology of sports, exercise, and fitness: social and personal issues*, Hemisphere, New York, pp. 237–47.

Sachs, ML & Pargman, D 1979, 'Running addiction: a depth interview examination', *Journal of Sport Behavior*, 2, 143–55.

Secord, PF & Jourard, SM 1953, 'The appraisal of body-cathexis: body-cathexis and the self', *Journal of Consulting Psychology*, 17, 343–7.

Shavelson, RJ, Hubner, JJ & Stanton, GC 1976, 'Self-concept: validation of construct interpretations', *Review of Educational Research*, 46, 407–41.

Shepherdson, AJ 2000, 'Psychometric properties of a training state scale and the relationship of training state to performance', unpublished honours thesis, Department of Human Movement and Exercise Science, University of Western Australia.

Simons, CW & Birkimer, JC 1988, 'An exploration of factors predicting the effects of aerobic conditioning on mood state', *Journal of Psychosomatic Research*, 32, 63–75.

Sonstroem, RJ 1998, 'Physical self-concept: assessment and external validity, *Exercise and Sport Science Reviews*, 26, 133–64.

Sonstroem, RJ, Harlow, LL, Gemma, LM & Osborne, S 1991, 'Test of structural relationships within a proposed exercise and self-esteem model', *Journal of Personality Assessment*, 56, 348–64.

Sonstroem, RJ, Harlow, LL & Josephs, L 1994, 'Exercise and self-esteem: validity of model expansion and exercise associations', *Journal of Sport & Exercise Psychology*, 16, 29–42.

Sonstroem, RJ, Harlow, LL & Salisbury, KS 1993, 'Path analysis of a self-esteem model across a competitive swim season', *Research Quarterly for Exercise and Sport*, 64, 335–42.

Sonstroem, RJ & Morgan, WP 1989, 'Exercise and self-esteem: rationale and model', *Medicine & Science in Sports & Exercise*, 21, 329–37.

Sonstroem, RJ, Speliotis, ED & Fava, JL 1992, 'Perceived physical competence in adults: an examination of the Physical Self-perception Profile', *Journal of Sport & Exercise Psychology*, 14, 207–21.

Sparling, PB, Owen, N, Lambert, EV, Haskell, WL 2000, 'Promoting physical activity: the new imperative for public health', *Health Education Research*, 15, 367–76.

Stannish, WD 1984, 'Overuse injuries in athletes: a perspective', *Medicine & Science in Sports & Exercise*, 16, 1–7.

Steinacker, JM, Kellmann, M, Bohm, BO, Liu, Y, Opitz-Gress, A, Kallus, KW, Lehmann, M, Altenburg, D & Lormes, W 1999, 'Clinical findings and parameters of stress and regeneration in rowers before world championships', in M Lehmann, C Foster, U Gastmann, H Keizer & JM Steinacker (eds), *Overload, fatigue, performance incompetence, and regeneration in sport*, Plenum, New York, pp. 71–80.

Steptoe, A 1989, 'The significance of personal control in health and disease', in A Steptoe & A Appels (eds), *Stress, personal control and health*, John Wiley & Sons, New York, pp. 309–18.

Steptoe, A & Cox, S 1989, 'Acute effects of aerobic exercise on mood', *Health Psychology*, 7, 329–40.

Szabo, A 1995, 'The impact of exercise deprivation on well-being of habitual exercisers', *Australian Journal of Science and Medicine in Sport*, 27, 68–75.

Thaxton, L 1982, 'Physiological and psychological effects of short-term exercise addiction on habitual runners', *Journal of Sport Psychology*, 4, 73–80.

Tkachuk, GA & Martin, GL 1999, 'Exercise therapy for patients with psychiatric disorders: research and clinical implications', *Professional Psychology: Research & Practice*, 30, 275–82.

Tuckman, B 1999, 'I cried because I had no shoes ... a case study of motivation applied to rehabilitation', in D Pargman (ed.), *Psychological bases of sport injuries*, 2nd edn, Fitness Information Technology, Morgantown, WV, pp. 321–32.

Tuson, KM & Sinyor, D 1993, 'On the affective benefits of acute aerobic exercise: taking stock after twenty years of research', in P Seraganian (ed.), *Exercise psychology: the influence of physical exercise on psychological processes*, John Wiley & Sons, New York, pp. 80–121.

Willis, JD & Campbell, LF 1992, *Exercise psychology*, Human Kinetics, Champaign, IL.

Yates, A 1991, *Compulsive exercise and eating disorders: toward an integrated theory of activity*, Brunner/Mazel, New York.

CHAPTER 18

ANTECEDENT CORRELATES AND THEORIES OF EXERCISE BEHAVIOUR

Kerry S Courneya

It is difficult to overstate the established health benefits of regular exercise. Moreover, the list of documented health benefits seems to grow on an almost daily basis. We have known for some time, for example, that exercise and physical fitness are important in the prevention and rehabilitation of various chronic disease/health conditions including cardiovascular disease, diabetes, osteoporosis and obesity (Bouchard, Shephard & Stephens 1994). More recently, we have discovered that exercise may also be useful in cancer prevention (Friedenreich 2001) and rehabilitation (Courneya, Mackey & Jones 2000). In chapter 17 we learned of the extensive psychological benefits of exercise including reduced depression, anxiety and stress, as well as enhanced self-confidence, self-esteem and cognitive functioning. Indeed, it is indisputable that exercise is a foundational behaviour for human health and wellbeing.

EXERCISE MOTIVATION

Obviously, then, everyone exercises regularly — or so one might expect. In fact, the data show that despite the known benefits of regular exercise, most individuals in developed countries remain sedentary or insufficiently active (Stephens & Caspersen 1994). For example, more than 80 per cent of the 18- to 65-year-old population in the United States do not exercise at sufficient levels of intensity, frequency and duration to accrue positive health and fitness benefits (Centers for Disease Control 1994). Moreover, a recent Australian survey found that the proportion of physically inactive Australians increased between 1997 and 1999 from 13 per cent to 15 per cent (Armstrong, Bauman & Davies 2000). These low exercise participation rates are also evident in Europe (Caspersen, Merritt & Stephens 1994) and support what might be called 'the first law of exercise motivation' — that is, 'a body at rest will continue at rest unless compelled to change that state by a net force'.

Moreover, like most health behaviours, regular exercise must be maintained over a lifetime for optimal benefits to be realised. Unfortunately the data show that even when individuals are motivated enough to adopt a regular exercise program, as many as 50 per cent will drop out within the first three to six months (Dishman 1988; Robison & Rogers 1994). This drop-out rate cuts across all contexts regardless of the demographic profile of the group or the purpose of the exercise (Robison & Rogers 1994). These data support what might be called 'the second law of exercise motivation' — 'a body in motion will not necessarily continue in motion unless it is compelled to maintain that state by a net force'.

TWO LAWS OF EXERCISE MOTIVATION

1. A body at rest will continue at rest unless compelled to change that state by a net force.
2. A body in motion will not necessarily continue in motion unless it is compelled to maintain that state by a net force.

Motivating individuals to adopt and maintain regular exercise, therefore, is a major challenge for health professionals. Moreover, the development of interventions to promote exercise is facilitated by a sound understanding of the determinants of exercise. That is, unless we know the factors that influence exercise adoption and maintenance, we will not be able to intervene in any effective way. The purpose of this chapter is to provide an overview of the factors related to exercise behaviour, with a specific focus on the major theoretical models that have been applied in the exercise domain.

CORRELATES OF EXERCISE BEHAVIOUR

A common first step in understanding a behaviour is to determine the antecedent variables that are correlated with it. The term *correlate* is used to denote a reproducible association (but not necessarily a causal relationship) between a variable and exercise behaviour (Dishman 1988). Early research into the correlates of exercise behaviour adopted an approach that is termed 'atheoretical' (Dishman 1988). That is, researchers would assess a large collection of eclectic variables and examine each in turn for its correlation with exercise behaviour, but they would make no attempt to understand how the various correlates might be interrelated. This approach can be useful when very little is known about a behaviour. Unfortunately what we have learned from this approach is that an infinite number of diverse and complex variables are associated with exercise behaviour. Systematic reviews of this literature have been presented elsewhere (Dishman 1991; Dishman & Sallis 1994; King et al. 1992; Rhodes, Martin, Taunton, Rhodes, Donnelly & Elliot 1999; Sallis, Prochaska & Taylor 2000; Young & King 1995) but a partial listing of the correlates will provide the general idea. To date, documented antecedent correlates of exercise behaviour include age, sex, education, income, ethnicity, body weight, climate, smoking status, health status, attitudes, perceived control, self-efficacy, intentions, motivation, commitment, perceived barriers, knowledge, skills, distance from a fitness facility, having home exercise equipment, amount of park space, time spent outdoors, spousal support, number of children at home, extroversion, neuroticism, exercise intensity, exercise type, cohesion, group norms, class size, muscle fibre type and genetic predispositions. Clearly there is a very large and diverse number of variables that are (and will be) correlated with exercise behaviour.

The problem with the atheoretical or 'shotgun' approach to understanding the antecedent correlates of exercise behaviour is that eventually there are too many bricks in the brickyard to be understood in any coherent manner. Moreover, our understanding of the correlates becomes characterised as 'a mile wide and an inch deep' — that is, we know a little about a lot of exercise correlates but not a lot about any correlate in particular. How are we to make sense of this large number of correlates of exercise behaviour and gain a deeper understanding of the most important ones? A common second step in exercise behaviour research has been to organise exercise correlates into categories based on similarity. Categories that exercise researchers have created include biological, demographics, personality, social cognitive, other behaviours, social environment, physical environment and exercise characteristics (Dishman & Sallis 1994; King et al. 1992; Rhodes et al. 1999). Although such *organisational* models or frameworks are a good start, we ultimately need *theoretical* models both *within* and *among* the categories of correlates if we are to obtain a comprehensive yet parsimonious understanding of exercise behaviour that is capable of guiding intervention strategies.

The importance of theory in guiding the development of interventions is generally well recognised by researchers. Accordingly, most recent research into the antecedents of exercise behaviour has adopted a theoretical model to guide the inquiry. To date, the two categories of exercise correlates that have received the most theoretical attention are the psychological or 'cognitive' and the interpersonal or 'social'. Models that combine these two categories have been labelled *social cognitive* models. Personality is another category that has received significant theoretical attention, resulting in a number of personality models. Finally, ecological models are relatively new in the exercise domain but they have sparked a great deal of interest (Sallis & Owen 1997). These models attempt to examine multiple levels of exercise correlates in one broad framework. An overview of these three approaches to understanding exercise behaviour is now provided.

SOCIAL COGNITIVE MODELS APPLIED TO EXERCISE BEHAVIOUR

Many of the currently popular theoretical models applied to exercise behaviour are social cognitive theories — that is, the models theorise primarily about the relationships among variables contained within the social and cognitive categories of exercise correlates. Other determinants of exercise (e.g. demographics, personality, physical environment) are typically considered external to these models and beyond their theoretical scope. Sometimes the social cognitive variables are labelled 'proximal' determinants of behaviour, whereas the other categories are labelled 'distal' determinants of behaviour. These models have led to an excellent understanding of the social cognitive correlates of exercise behaviour but a limited understanding of the broader correlates of exercise. We shall return to this concern later in the chapter.

The social cognitive models that have been applied to exercise behaviour are many and varied and include protection motivation theory (Rogers & Prentice-Dunn 1997), the health belief model (Rosenstock 1990), attribution theory (Weiner 1986), locus of control (Rotter 1966), relapse prevention model (Marlatt & Gordon 1980), self-determination theory (Deci & Ryan 1985), personal investment theory (Maehr & Braskamp 1986) and the theory of reasoned action (Ajzen & Fishbein 1980; Fishbein & Ajzen 1975). Although reviewing all of these theories is beyond the scope of this chapter, the reader is referred to the theorists for a full explication of their models. Currently the three theories that have garnered the most research attention in the exercise domain are social cognitive theory (Bandura 1986), the transtheoretical model (Prochaska & Velicer 1997), and the theory of planned behaviour (Ajzen 1991).

Social cognitive theory

Bandura's (1986, 1997) social cognitive theory (SCT) has been a major force in exercise behaviour research (McAuley & Blyssmer 2002; McAuley, Pena & Jerome 2001). SCT is based on the concept of reciprocal determinism wherein behaviour is viewed as a function of the dynamic interaction among the person, the behaviour and the environment. More specifically, SCT posits a multifaceted causal structure in which self-efficacy beliefs operate in concert with biological processes, cognised goals, outcome expectations and perceived environmental impediments/facilitators in the regulation of human motivation, affect and behaviour (Bandura 2000). Self-efficacy is considered the key organising construct within SCT and is defined as 'beliefs in one's capabilities to organize and execute the courses of action required to produce given levels of attainment' (Bandura 2000, p. 300). Self-efficacy is theorised to influence the activities that individuals choose to approach, the effort expended on such activities, and the degree of persistence demonstrated in the face of failure or aversive stimuli (Bandura 1986).

Another important construct in SCT is outcome expectation, which refers to the expected outcomes associated with the performance of a behaviour. Outcome expectations serve as incentives when the anticipated outcomes are positive, and disincentives when the anticipated outcomes are negative. Bandura (2000) describes three major forms of outcome expectations, which he labels physical, social and self-evaluative. Physical outcome expectations include the physical effects of a behaviour such as pain, injury or disease risk. Social outcomes consist primarily of social reactions towards the behaviour, such as disapproval or chastisement. The third class of outcomes, self-evaluative reactions, focus on one's own reaction to performing a given behaviour (e.g. guilt, pride or embarrassment). A schematic representation of the difference between self-efficacy and outcome expectations is provided in figure 18.1.

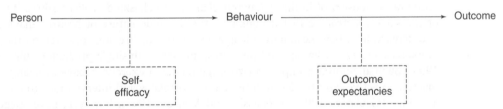

Figure 18.1   A schematic representation of the distinction between self-efficacy beliefs and outcome expectations

(*Source:* Modified from Bandura 2000, p. 306)

A major strength of SCT is that it also explicates the mechanisms by which behaviour change occurs through self-efficacy. Bandura (1986) highlights four major sources of self-efficacy, which he labels *past performance accomplishments*, *vicarious experiences*, *social persuasion* and *physiological arousal*. The strongest determinant of self-efficacy is past mastery experiences at the specific task. Early successes lead to a robust sense of self-efficacy whereas early failures result in self-doubt. Vicarious experiences refer primarily to efficacy information obtained through observing others perform the task (i.e. modelling) but can also include imagining oneself performing the task. Social or verbal persuasion is self-efficacy information derived from having others or yourself (i.e. self-talk) suggest that you are capable of performing a given task. It is probably the most common technique for bolstering self-efficacy but is generally the least powerful (Bandura 1986). Finally, physiological or emotional arousal can influence self-efficacy. That is, emotional states such as anxiety, fatigue and pain in a given situation can be interpreted as an indication of one's ability to perform the task.

Research in the exercise domain has demonstrated overwhelmingly the importance of self-efficacy to exercise behaviour. After comprehensive reviews of this literature, McAuley and colleagues (McAuley & Blyssmer 2002; McAuley et al. 2001) have concluded that self-efficacy predicts exercise behaviour in diseased and asymptomatic populations, in large-scale community studies, and in training studies. Moreover, McAuley & Blyssmer (2002) have noted that self-efficacy appears to play a particularly important role in those circumstances where exercise is the most challenging, such as in the initial stages of adoption, the long-term maintenance of activity, and for persons with chronic diseases. Clearly, a strong perception of self-efficacy is fundamental to exercise behaviour adoption and maintenance.

Paradoxically, the primary criticism of social cognitive theory has been its breadth and complexity (Baranowski, Perry & Parcel 1997); that is, it is a difficult theory to operationalise, test in a simple path model and ultimately disconfirm. Consequently, despite Bandura's (2000) admonition to measure the full set of determinants posited by SCT, many researchers have reduced SCT to self-efficacy. Moreover, many other researchers and theorists have incorporated self-efficacy into other simpler and more parsimonious models, making the complexity of SCT less attractive to researchers and practitioners. Thus SCT may prove to be a better theoretical exercise than an exercise theory.

The transtheoretical model

Prochaska's introduction of the transtheoretical model (TTM) (Prochaska & DiClemente 1984, 1986; Prochaska & Velicer 1997) has been another important theoretical advance in our understanding of when, how and why people change their exercise behaviour. The most popular construct from the TTM has been the stages of change, which reflects the temporal dimension of health behaviour change (Prochaska & Velicer 1997). The strength of the stage construct is that it highlights the dynamic nature of health behaviour change and demarcates when meaningful change has occurred. Previous research on the correlates of exercise behaviour has applied theoretical models with single prediction rules (Courneya 1995). Such an approach implies a two-stage model of exercise behaviour change (i.e. from inactive to active) and has led to a search for correlates and interventions to facilitate such a change (Courneya 1995). Prochaska and Velicer (1997), however, have suggested that individuals may progress through multiple stages when changing their behaviour and that each stage transition may have different determinants and require different intervention strategies.

Currently the TTM proposes six stages of change, which have been labelled precontemplation, contemplation, preparation, action, maintenance and termination. In the first stage, *precontemplation*, the person is not performing the health behaviour and has no intention of changing in the foreseeable future. In the *contemplation* stage, the person has formed an intention to change in the distant future (i.e. within six months) but still has not attempted the behaviour change. The third stage, *preparation*, is reached when the person intends to take action in the immediate future (i.e. within one month), has a detailed plan for taking action and may have taken some small steps towards behaviour change. The *action* stage is achieved when behaviour has been initiated to the target level that is recommended for that behaviour (e.g. exercising three times a week for at least 30 minutes at vigorous intensity). Once this level of behaviour has been maintained for six months, the person is considered to be in the *maintenance* stage. The sixth and final stage, *termination*, is reached when the risk of returning to the previous unhealthy behaviour has been completely eliminated (i.e. the risk is zero). The person has no temptation to engage in the old behaviour and 100 per cent self-efficacy in all previously tempting situations. Although no definitive behavioural guideline exists, Prochaska (1995; Prochaska & Marcus 1994; Prochaska & Velicer 1997) has suggested that five years of continuous maintenance is likely to result in termination.

The TTM's original goal was to explain *how* health behaviour change occurs. To this end, 10 processes of change were identified that consist of strategies and techniques that people use to change their behaviour (Prochaska, Velicer, DiClemente & Fava 1988). These processes include overt and covert activities that individuals use to modify their experiences and environments in order to modify their behaviour (Prochaska & Velicer 1997). The 10 processes of change can be divided into two higher order factors labelled cognitive/experiential (i.e. consciousness raising, dramatic relief, environmental reevaluation, self-reevaluation and social liberation) and behavioural/environmental (i.e. counterconditioning, helping relationships, contingency management, self-liberation and stimulus control). The 10 processes of change are defined in table 18.1.

TABLE 18.1 Definitions of the processes of change

Process	Definition
Experiential/cognitive	
Consciousness raising	Efforts by the individual to seek new information and to gain understanding and feedback about the problem behaviour.
Dramatic relief	Affective aspects of change, often involving intense emotional experiences related to the problem behaviour.
Environmental reevaluation	Consideration and assessment by the individual of how the problem affects the physical and social environments.
Self-reevaluation	Emotional and cognitive reappraisal of values by the individual with respect to the problem behaviour.
Social liberation	Awareness, availability and acceptance by the individual of alternative, problem-free lifestyles in society.
Environmental/behavioural	
Counterconditioning	Substitution of alternative behaviours for the problem behaviour.
Helping relationships	Trusting, accepting and utilising the support of caring others during attempts to change the problem behaviour.
Reinforcement management	Changing the contingencies that control or maintain the problem behaviour.
Self-liberation	Choosing to, and committing to, change the problem behaviour, including the belief that one *can* change.
Stimulus control	Controlling situations and other causes that trigger the problem behaviour.

(*Source:* Adapted from Marcus, Banspach et al. 1992, p. 387)

Self-efficacy, decisional balance (pros and cons) and temptation are also key constructs of the TTM (DiClemente, Prochaska, Fairhurst, Velicer, Valasquez & Rossi 1991; Prochaska & Velicer 1997). These constructs appear to be included to help explain *why* health behaviour change occurs. Self-efficacy was taken from Bandura's (1986) SCT and reflects a person's confidence in performing the health behaviour change. The pros and cons were borrowed from Janis and Mann's (1977) decisional balance theory and reflect the costs and benefits of health behaviour change. Temptation reflects the intensity of urges to engage in the old behaviour (Prochaska & Velicer 1997).

More than 50 studies have examined the TTM in the exercise domain (see Buxton, Wyse & Mercer 1996; Cardinal 1995; Marcus & Simkin 1993; Prochaska & Marcus 1994 for partial reviews) and these studies have provided support across a wide range of populations including different worksite groups (e.g. medical, industrial, retail and government), age groups (e.g. children, adolescents, older adults), places of residence (e.g. rural, urban), medical conditions (e.g. cardiac patients) and countries (e.g. United States, Canada, Britain, Australia). Similar to research on the TTM in other health domains, however, research in the exercise domain has relied almost exclusively on cross-sectional designs (Herzog, Abrams, Emmons, Linnan & Shadel 1999). Such designs provide the weakest evidence for a stage model and the weakest test of the attendant explanatory constructs (Weinstein, Rothman & Sutton 1998). Although some recent studies have employed intervention designs in the exercise domain (e.g. Calfas, Sallis, Oldenburg & French 1997; Marcus, Banspach, Lefebvre, Rossi et al. 1992; Marcus et al. 1998), they have not assessed the hypothesised social cognitive constructs thought to induce stage changes. Longitudinal designs with repeated assessments of these constructs are only beginning to emerge in the exercise domain (Plotnikoff, Hotz, Birkett & Courneya 2001).

One primary criticism of the TTM is that it is atheoretical, or at least it is lacking in theoretical sophistication (Courneya 1995). That is, the TTM does not offer explicit theoretical predictions concerning the relationships *among* the 14 independent constructs in the model or even simply *between* the independent constructs and the dependent construct (Courneya 1995; Courneya & Bobick 2000). An interesting consequence of this lack of theoretical development is that of the more than 50 studies testing the TTM in the exercise domain, only two have examined all the constructs at one time (Gorely & Gordon 1995; Nigg & Courneya 1998). This piecemeal examination of the TTM is accepted in the literature because there is no theoretical basis that makes it necessary to include all the constructs. Each construct can be examined in univariate analysis with the stages of change construct. Moreover, of the two studies that did include all the TTM constructs, neither discussed the relationships among the constructs, although one did employ multivariate analysis to examine redundancies in predicting stage of change (Gorely & Gordon 1995). Consequently, the primary contribution of the TTM appears to be the notion that people move through a series of stages, phases or steps when attempting to change a health behaviour, and that the determinants and interventions for each stage transition may be different.

The theory of planned behaviour

Ajzen's (1991) theory of planned behaviour (TPB) has also received significant research attention in the exercise domain (figure 18.2). The TPB proposes that a person's intention to perform a behaviour is the central determinant of that behaviour because it reflects the level of motivation and willingness to exert effort. Intention, in turn, is determined by attitude, subjective norm and perceived behavioural control (PBC). PBC, defined as the perceived ease or difficulty of performing the behaviour, may also directly predict behaviour if it accurately reflects the person's actual control over the behaviour. Attitude is reflected in a positive or negative evaluation of performing the behaviour (e.g. good/bad, favourable/unfavourable) whereas subjective norm is intended to reflect the perceived social pressure that individuals feel to perform or not perform the behaviour.

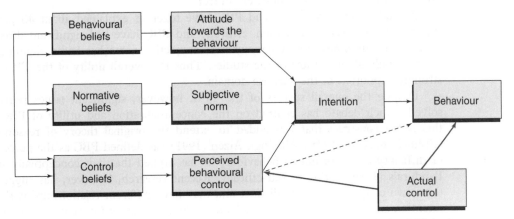

Figure 18.2 A schematic representation of the relationships among theory of planned behaviour constructs

(*Source:* Modified from Ajzen 1991, p. 182)

The TPB also proposes that attitude, subjective norm and PBC are determined by underlying accessible beliefs in an expectancy-value formulation (Ajzen 1991). Attitude is believed to be a function of *behavioural* beliefs, which refer to the perceived advantages and disadvantages of performing the behaviour. Subjective norm is thought to be determined by *normative* beliefs, which centre on whether or not specific individuals or groups who are important to the individual think the individual should perform the behaviour. Finally, *control* beliefs are theorised to underlie PBC and focus on the opportunities and resources available for performing the behaviour and their power in influencing the behaviour. Summary propositions of the TPB are provided in the highlighted text below.

SUMMARY PROPOSITIONS OF THE THEORY OF PLANNED BEHAVIOUR

1. People will perform a behaviour when they intend to do so and have control over it.
2. People will intend to perform a behaviour when they evaluate it positively, perceive social pressure to perform it, and believe it to be under their own control.
3. People will evaluate a behaviour positively when they believe it will lead to more positively valued outcomes than negatively valued outcomes.
4. People will perceive social pressure to perform a behaviour when they believe that important others in their lives think they should perform it.
5. People will perceive a behaviour to be under their control when they believe that potential obstacles to the behaviour are either unlikely to occur or easy to overcome.

A number of meta-analytic reviews of the TPB in the exercise domain have been conducted (Godin & Kok 1996; Hausenblas, Carron & Mack 1997; Spence, Courneya, Blanchard, Wilson & Becker 2001). The latest review by Spence et al. (2001) located more than 50 studies on exercise. Overall, these meta-analytic reviews report that intention and PBC explain approximately 30 to 35 per cent of the variance in exercise behaviour. Intention has had a significant direct effect on exercise in all studies, whereas PBC has had a significant direct effect on exercise in about half of the studies. Clearly the road to health is paved with good intentions! Moreover, navigating that paved road often requires strong perceptions of control.

Attitude, subjective norm and PBC have together explained about 40 per cent of the variance in exercise intention. Attitude and PBC have had significant direct effects on intention in almost all studies, whereas subjective norm has had a significant direct effect in only about a third of the studies. Thus the overall utility of the TPB has been strongly supported in the exercise domain.

Despite the overall success of the TPB, however, significant issues remain unresolved. Much debate has centred on the conceptualisation and utility of PBC because this is the construct that was added to extend the original theory of reasoned action (Fishbein & Ajzen 1975). Although Ajzen (1991) has defined PBC as the perceived ease or difficulty of performing a behaviour, he has argued that it is conceptually similar to Bandura's (1986) notion of self-efficacy. Recent research, however, has suggested that these two constructs may be distinct and may have different relationships with exercise intention and behaviour (Terry & O'Leary 1995; Rhodes & Courneya, in press).

Moreover, subjective norm has come under attack in the exercise domain because of its limited utility. Some researchers have suggested that social support may be the more theoretically relevant social influence construct in the exercise domain (Courneya & McAuley 1995; Courneya, Plotnikoff, Hotz & Birkett 2000). The conceptual distinction between these two social influence constructs is that subjective norm refers to the perceived pressure to perform a behaviour that comes from observing what important others say and/ or do, whereas social support implies some sort of assistance in performing the behaviour (Courneya, Plotnikoff et al. 2000). For behaviours such as exercise that are not under complete volitional control (i.e. they can be done at will and are free of practical constraints), it is likely that assistance from others in performing the behaviour (social support) would be helpful beyond knowing that they approve of the behaviour (i.e. subjective norm). Some empirical research has supported the superiority of social support over subjective norm in the exercise domain (Courneya, Plotnikoff et al. 2000; Rhodes, Jones & Courneya 2002) although more recent research has suggested that the relative importance of each construct may depend on the stage transition in question (Courneya, Plotnikoff, Hotz & Birkett 2001).

Lastly, although the TPB is not an authentic stage model, it does distinguish between an 'intention' and 'behaviour' stage. Nevertheless, researchers from the exercise domain have applied the TPB to the stages of change from the TTM (Courneya 1995; Courneya, Nigg & Estabrooks 1998; Courneya, Plotnikoff et al. 2000; Courneya et al. 2001). Overall, it appears that the TPB may provide a more comprehensive and sophisticated theoretical understanding of the stages of change in the exercise domain.

PERSONALITY MODELS APPLIED TO EXERCISE BEHAVIOUR

Personality traits can be defined as dimensions of individual differences in tendencies to show consistent patterns of thoughts, feelings and actions (McCrae & Costa 1990). The more of a trait people possess, the more likely they are to display behaviours predisposed by that trait. Given their motivational properties, long-term stability and consistency across situations, personality traits may be a significant influence on exercise behaviour over time and across contexts. Although many single specific personality traits have been examined in the exercise domain (e.g. optimism, self-motivation, locus of control), the focus of the present review is on models or frameworks of personality. Cattell's (1947) 16 personality factor (PF) model, Eysenck's (1967) personality inventory (EPI) and the more recent five factor model (FFM) are briefly reviewed here.

The 16 personality factor model

Cattell (1947) was one of the early pioneers in applying factor analysis to personality research. He adopted the lexical approach of personality trait development, which argues that the importance of a trait is based on how many words are used to describe it. Using this approach, Cattell (1947) argued for 16 personality dimensions, which he labelled cool–warm, concrete–abstract thinking, affected by feelings–emotionally stable, submissive–dominant, sober–enthusiastic, expedient–conscientious, shy–bold, tough–tender minded, trusting–suspicious, practical–imaginative, forthright–shrewd, self-assured–apprehensive, conservative–experimenting, group-oriented–self-sufficient, undisciplined–controlled and relaxed–tense. Further, Cattell (1947) argued for two second or higher order factors, which he labelled extroversion and anxiety/neuroticism. These 16 dimensions and two second order factors are measured using the 16 Personality Factor (16PF) Questionnaire (Cattell, Eber & Tatsuoka 1977). Unfortunately, other independent researchers have not been able to replicate the 16 factor structure (Digman 1990), and only two studies have examined the 16PF in the exercise domain, with inconsistent results (Rhodes 2001).

Eysenck's personality inventory

Unlike the lexical approach used by Cattell (1947), Eysenck (1967) based his trait model on biological functioning of the nervous system. Eysenck (1967) argued for two super-traits of personality, which he labelled extroversion (e.g. sociability, craving for excitement, liveliness, activeness and dominance) and neuroticism (e.g. emotional stability with distress, moodiness, anxiety and depression). He added a third super-trait called psychoticism (i.e. a tendency towards psychopathic and psychotic behaviour), but it has received far less attention than extroversion and neuroticism (Eysenck & Eysenck 1976). These super-traits are measured with the Eysenck personality inventory (EPI) (Eysenck & Eysenck 1975). A number of studies have examined the EPI in the exercise domain, the general findings being that neuroticism is negatively related to exercise behaviour, extroversion is positively related to exercise behaviour, and psychoticism is unrelated to exercise behaviour (Rhodes 2001).

The five factor model

The most recent advance in the personality domain is the growing consensus that there are five major traits of personality functioning. Consequently the so-called 'big five' or five factor model (FFM) has emerged as the dominant framework for studying personality (Digman 1990; McCrae & John 1992). Moreover, its potential utility in the exercise domain has been duly noted (Courneya & Hellsten 1998). The FFM is a version of trait theory that views human nature from the perspective of consistent and enduring individual differences (McCrae & John 1992). The five personality dimensions of the

FFM, as highlighted by Costa and McCrae (1992), are neuroticism (the tendency to experience negative affect), extroversion (i.e. sociable, active, talkative, energetic, optimistic), openness to experience (active imagination, preference for variety, curiosity), agreeableness (altruistic, sympathetic, cooperative) and conscientiousness (purposeful, strong-willed, determined).

A major advantage of the FFM is that it provides a comprehensive yet parsimonious taxonomy of personality traits at the highest hierarchical level of trait description (Digman 1990; McCrae & John 1992). FFM theorists do not believe that the five factors exhaust personality description but rather that they represent personality at the highest hierarchical level of trait description (McCrae & John 1992). Moreover, FFM adherents argue that if none of the five factors is related to the criterion of interest, it may be time to abandon the search for personality determinants of that criterion (McCrae & John 1992). Importantly, unlike other major models of personality, the FFM does not utilise only one measurement instrument. Several researchers have developed inventories for FFM assessment, such as the NEO-PI-R and NEO-FFI (Costa & McCrae 1992), Hogan Personality Inventory (Hogan 1986), Goldberg's 100 unipolar markers (Goldberg 1992), Saucier's mini markers (Saucier 1992), and an extension of Wiggins' interpersonal circumplex model (Trapnell & Wiggins 1990).

Four recent studies have applied the FFM to exercise behaviour (Courneya & Hellsten 1998; Courneya, Bobick & Schinke 1999; Rhodes, Courneya & Bobick 2001; Rhodes, Courneya & Jones, in press), while one has correlated the FFM with measures of physical fitness (Hogan 1989). The results have been consistent in showing that extroversion and conscientiousness are positively associated with exercise, whereas neuroticism is negatively associated with exercise. Moreover, these personality dimensions also correlate with other determinants of exercise such as exercise motives and barriers (Courneya & Hellsten 1998). A final interesting finding is that openness to experience seems to be associated more with exercise preferences for context and structure rather than with the quantity of exercise (Courneya & Hellsten 1998).

ECOLOGICAL MODELS

One class of models that has recently gained currency in the study of exercise behaviour is the ecological model. The term 'ecological' refers to models, frameworks or perspectives rather than a specific set of variables (Sallis & Owen 1997). The primary focus of ecological models is to explain how environments and behaviours affect each other (Sallis & Owen 1997). Moreover, these models attempt to encompass the multiple levels of influence on behaviour including intrapersonal (e.g. biological, psychological), interpersonal (e.g. family, friends), institutional (e.g. schools, worksites, fitness facilities), community (e.g. institutional relationships) and policy (e.g. laws at all levels) (McLeroy, Bibeau, Steckler & Glanz 1988). Therefore, ecological models can be viewed as 'overarching' models of behaviour.

Nevertheless, despite the multilevel approach of ecological models, Sallis and Owen (1997) have argued that physical environments are really the hallmark or defining feature of ecological models. This feature is important because most social cognitive models theorise only about the cognitive and social correlates of behaviour, not the role of the physical environment. Consequently the unique contribution of ecological models to social cognitive models is the identification of physical environment factors (Sallis & Owen 1997). The five major principles of ecological models proposed by Sallis and Owen (1997) are provided in the highlighted feature opposite.

FIVE MAJOR PRINCIPLES OF ECOLOGICAL MODELS

1. *Multiple dimensions of influence on behaviours.* Ecological models include multiple categories of correlates, which sets them apart from models that focus on only one or two categories.
2. *Interactions of influences across dimensions.* Ecological models should predict and explain how the multiple categories of correlates interact.
3. *Multiple levels of environmental influences.* Ecological models propose multiple levels of environmental influences including family, organisations, communities, institutions and public policies. Their unique contribution is in highlighting the role of the physical environment.
4. *Environments directly influence behaviours.* Ecological models include the proposition that environmental factors directly influence behaviours, which puts them at odds with social cognitive models.
5. *Behaviour-specific ecological models.* Specific ecological models will be needed to guide research and intervention for each health behaviour (e.g. exercise).

Physical environments can be divided into natural (e.g. weather, climate, geography) and constructed (e.g. homes, communities, worksites, malls, transportation systems). The general thesis of ecological models of behaviour is that environments restrict the range of behaviour by promoting or demanding certain actions and by discouraging or prohibiting other actions (Wicker 1979). Indeed, research is available to show that some characteristics of the physical environment do, in fact, correlate with exercise behaviour. For example, at least four studies have found that the number of pieces of home exercise equipment is significantly correlated with exercise (Jakicic, Wing, Butler & Jeffrey 1997; Sallis, Hovell & Hofstetter 1992; Sallis et al. 1989, Sallis, Johnson, Calfas, Caparosa & Nichols 1997). Although many of the specifics remain to be documented, there seems to be little doubt that the physical environment can play a role in promoting or inhibiting exercise behaviour.

The more provocative claim by proponents of ecological models, however, is that the physical environment can have direct effects on exercise behaviour above that provided by intrapersonal and interpersonal (i.e. social cognitive) models (Sallis, Bauman & Pratt 1998). This feature of ecological models is in direct opposition to social cognitive models, which acknowledge that the physical environment can affect behaviour but hypothesise that physical environmental influences are mediated through social cognitive variables. Consequently the claim that the physical environment can directly affect behaviour independent of social cognitive variables needs to be demonstrated empirically and, perhaps more importantly, argued theoretically. Related to this point, but more broadly applied, it is important that ecological models do not take us 'back to the future' in exercise behaviour research by investigating large numbers of correlates from multiple categories without a theoretical model. The atheoretical approach to understanding exercise behaviour has been abandoned by proponents of social cognitive models and should not be embraced once again just because multiple categories of correlates are being examined. Although a daunting task, the challenge for exercise researchers is to build theories not only within but across categories of correlates.

Adventures in theory building

The introduction of ecological models into the exercise domain is a good jumping-off point to discuss theory building. Despite the utility of current models for understanding exercise behaviour, there is always a desire for 'better' theories. Virtually all theory building involves extensions of current theoretical models and/or theoretical integrations rather than theorising from scratch. However, some theorists (e.g. Ajzen 1991; Fishbein, Triandis, Kanfer, Becker, Middlestadt & Eichler 2001) seem more open to this approach than others (e.g. Bandura 2000). For example, Ajzen (1991) has stated that in principle he is open to extensions of the TPB as long as it can be demonstrated that the new construct(s) explains additional variance in intention or behaviour beyond the current TPB constructs. Conversely, Bandura (2000) appears critical of this approach, arguing that bringing constructs together from various theories results in 'cafeteria style' theorising. More specifically, Bandura (2000, p. 300) has argued that 'there is a marked difference between expanding the scope of an integrative theory and creating conglomerates from different theories with problems of redundancy and fractionation of predictors and theoretical disconnectedness'.

Bandura's (2000) concern is well founded and should be heeded. Integrating a weak, redundant or theoretically disconnected construct with an extant validated theory will not likely be helpful. It is analogous to those breakfast cereal commercials that place their bowl of sugary cereal among various fruits, bran muffins and milk/juice products and then claim that the cereal is 'part of this complete breakfast'. Of course, the breakfast was complete before the sugary bowl of cereal was added and, paradoxically, the addition of the sugary bowl of cereal may actually reduce its (health) value. Similarly, researchers must be careful not to add weak, redundant or disconnected constructs to a validated theoretical model and then claim that the new constructs are 'part of this complete theory'.

Nevertheless, the solution to the problems of redundancy, fractionation and theoretical disconnectedness is to engage in theory integration properly, not to abandon it. The theory builder must *theorise* on how the new construct differs from current constructs in a model and also how it relates to those constructs. Conner and Armitage (1998) have noted that such theoretical additions should (a) specify the process by which the new variable influences intention/behaviour, (b) describe its relationship to current constructs in the model, and (c) specify the boundary conditions of the new construct. If these guidelines are heeded, theory integration may result in an improved theoretical model for our understanding of exercise behaviour. Simply testing a collection of constructs from different theories (or categories) is not theoretical integration. It is an atheoretical approach that inevitably leads to precisely the problems that Bandura (2000) has cautioned against.

Integrating personality and social cognitive models in the exercise domain

For one example of theory integration across different categories of exercise correlates, we can look to personality and social cognitive research. To date, most research on personality and social cognitive models in the exercise domain has been conducted independently (Courneya et al. 1999). As a result, it is not known if the relationship between personality and exercise behaviour is mediated by social cognitive constructs, as is hypothesised by most social cognitive models. The answer to this question has both theoretical and practical implications. Theoretically, social cognitive models are one attempt to account for the relationship between personality and exercise, but they have never been tested empirically. If social cognitive models do not provide an adequate explanation of this relationship, then alternative theoretical models will need to be developed and tested. From a practical perspective, most exercise practitioners do not consider the role of personality in influencing behaviour or moderating the success of interventions. If social cognitive models do not adequately account for the relationship between personality and exercise, there may be a need to consider personality differences when developing and administering interventions.

Courneya and colleagues (Courneya et al. 1999; Rhodes, Courneya et al., in press) have examined the adequacy of the TPB in mediating the relationship between the FFM and exercise behaviour. Courneya et al. (1999) presented two studies to examine this question including one that used a cross-sectional design with self-reported exercise behaviour and one that used a prospective design with objective attendance records. As expected from the personality literature, extroversion, conscientiousness and neuroticism were significantly related to exercise behaviour. Contrary to the social cognitive hypothesis, however, the relationship between personality and exercise behaviour was only partially mediated by the TPB. Specifically, extroversion had a direct relationship with exercise behaviour in both studies even after controlling for the TPB. Moreover, Rhodes, Courneya et al. (in press) found that it was one particular facet of extroversion (i.e. the activity facet) that had a direct effect on exercise behaviour independent of global extroversion and the social cognitive constructs within the TPB. These researchers concluded that personality, as operationalised by the FFM, may need to be integrated into social cognitive models applied to exercise behaviour.

FUTURE DIRECTIONS

The good news for young academics interested in the antecedents of exercise is that a complete understanding of exercise behaviour is unlikely before their tenure decisions. Much theorising and theory testing remains to be done. The directions of future research will vary depending on the category of variables under study. For categories that contain very few known correlates of exercise (e.g. biological, physical environment), identification of additional exercise correlates is warranted. For categories with a sufficient number of known exercise correlates (e.g. demographics, personality), the development of preliminary theoretical models would be useful. For categories with multiple validated theoretical models (e.g. social cognitive), theory refinements, comparisons and integrations are justified. Finally, when validated theoretical models exist within multiple categories of exercise correlates (e.g. personality and social cognitive models), then 'cross-categorical' theorising will move the field forward. Ultimately, the 'grand theory' of exercise behaviour will theorise within and across all known categories of correlates and rightly warrant the label *transtheoretical*.

There are many challenges, however, to the pursuit of a grand theory of exercise behaviour. First, it is already evident that the importance of various exercise correlates varies dramatically across population characteristics (e.g. age, sex, ethnicity, chronic diseases), contexts (e.g. worksites, supervised programs, home-based, group-based), and characteristics of the exercise activity itself (e.g. type, intensity, duration). Consequently, it is challenging enough to develop a comprehensive and useful theory that applies to a given exercise behaviour, in a given context, in a given population. Developing a grand theory that cuts across these characteristics may be too much to ask.

Moreover, measurement is sometimes referred to as the Achilles heel of the behavioural and social sciences, and exercise is not immune to this criticism. Better measures of all categories of exercise correlates, including exercise itself, is an ongoing challenge. Finally, although developing and implementing intervention strategies (e.g., cognitive-behavioural, social, physical environment) that map on to theoretical models of exercise behaviour is the ultimate goal of exercise behaviour research, it is a daunting challenge and not for the faint-hearted.

CONCLUSIONS

Researchers have made great strides in understanding when, why and how meaningful exercise behaviour change occurs. The greatest progress has been in our understanding of the social cognitive correlates of exercise behaviour. We also have a good understanding of the personality and social influences that modify exercise behaviour. Ecological models promise to provide a greater understanding of the role of the physical environment and to stimulate theorising across categories of correlates. Such theorising within and among categories of exercise correlates will enhance our understanding of exercise behaviour immeasurably, and will provide us with a sound basis for developing effective interventions at the clinical, community and population levels.

SUMMARY

The implications of exercise for public health are enormous, yet most people do not exercise regularly throughout life. Exercise motivation is a huge challenge for self-changers and health professionals alike. Understanding the correlates of exercise is the foundation of effective intervention strategies. Early research took an atheoretical approach to examining the correlates of exercise. More recent research has applied social cognitive models to the study of exercise including social cognitive theory, the transtheoretical model and the theory of planned behaviour. Personality models have also received research attention, and with the development of the FFM there is renewed interest in personality and exercise. Finally, ecological models have only recently been introduced into the exercise domain but they are sparking a lot of interest from researchers and practitioners. The challenges of this research are many but the impact on public health promises to be commensurate with the effort.

 REVIEW QUESTIONS

1   What are the two 'laws of exercise motivation'? Provide statistics to support each law.

2   List at least 10 different antecedent correlates of exercise behaviour from at least three different categories of correlates.

3   What are the differences between theoretical and atheoretical research?

4   Which three social cognitive models have most often been applied to exercise behaviour?

5   Describe the five major theoretical tenets of the theory of planned behaviour.

6   What are the 'big five' personality traits and which traits are most consistently related to exercise behaviour?

7   What is the unique contribution and primary focus of ecological models?

8   What is the most provocative claim made by proponents of ecological models, and how would proponents of social cognitive models respond?

9   Select two distinct categories of exercise correlates and theorise about their relationships to each other and to exercise behaviour.

References

Ajzen, I 1991, 'The theory of planned behaviour', *Organizational Behaviour and Human Decision Processes*, 50, 179–211.

Ajzen, I & Fishbein, M 1980, *Understanding attitudes and predicting social behaviour*, Prentice Hall, Englewood Cliffs, NJ.

Armstrong, T, Bauman, A & Davies, J 2000, *Physical activity patterns of Australian adults. Results of the 1999 National Physical Activity Survey*, Australian Institute of Health and Welfare, Canberra.

Bandura, A 1986, *Social foundations of thought and action: a social cognitive theory*, Prentice Hall, Englewood Cliffs, NJ.

Bandura, A 1997, *Self-efficacy: the exercise of control*, Freeman, New York.

Bandura, A 2000, 'Health promotion from the perspective of social cognitive theory', in P Norman, C Abraham & M Connor (eds), *Understanding and changing health behaviour from health beliefs to self-regulation*, Harwood Academic Publishers, Amsterdam, pp. 299–339.

Baranowski, T, Perry, CL & Parcel, GS 1997, 'How individuals, environments, and health behaviour interact', in K Glanz, FM Lewis & BK Rimer (eds), *Health behaviour and health education: theory, research, and practice*, Jossey-Bass, San Francisco, pp. 153–78.

Bouchard C, Shephard, RJ & Stephens, T 1994, *Physical activity, fitness, and health: international proceedings and consensus statement*, Human Kinetics, Champaign, IL.

Buxton, K, Wyse, J & Mercer, T 1996, 'How applicable is the stages of change model to exercise behaviour? A review', *Health Education Journal*, 55, 239–57.

Calfas, KJ, Sallis, JF, Oldenburg, B & French, M 1997, 'Mediators of change in physical activity following an intervention in primary care: PACE', *Preventive Medicine*, 26, 297–304.

Cardinal, BJ 1995, 'The transtheoretical model of behaviour change as applied to physical activity and exercise: a review', *Journal of Physical Education and Sport Sciences*, 8, 32–45.

Caspersen, CJ, Merrit, RK & Stephens, T 1994, 'International physical activity patterns: a methodological perspective', in RK Dishman (ed.), *Advances in exercise adherence*, Human Kinetics, Champaign, IL, pp. 73–110.

Cattell, RB 1947, 'Confirmation and clarification of primary personality factors', *Psychometrica*, 12 197–220.

Cattell, RB, Eber, HW & Tatsuoka, MM 1977, *Handbook for the 16 Personality Factor Questionnaire*, IPAT, Champaign, IL.

Centers for Disease Control and Prevention 1994, *1994 BRFSS summary prevalence report*, US Department of Health and Human Services, Atlanta, GA.

Conner, M & Armitage, CJ 1998, 'Extending the theory of planned behaviour: a review and avenues for further research', *Journal of Applied Social Psychology*, 28, 1429–64.

Costa, PT Jr & McCrae, RR 1992, *Revised NEO Personality Inventory (NEO-PI-R) professional manual*, Psychological Assessment Resources, Odessa, FL.

Courneya, KS 1995, 'Understanding readiness for regular physical activity in older individuals: an application of the theory of planned behaviour', *Health Psychology*, 14, 80–7.

Courneya, KS & Bobick, TM 2000, 'Integrating the theory of planned behaviour with the processes and stages of change in the exercise domain', *Psychology of Sport and Exercise*, 1, 46–56.

Courneya, KS, Bobick, TM & Schinke, RJ 1999, 'Does the theory of planned behaviour mediate the relation between personality and exercise behaviour', *Basic and Applied Social Psychology*, 21, 317–24.

Courneya, KS & Hellsten, LM 1998, 'Personality correlates of exercise behaviour, motives, barriers, and preferences: an application of the five-factor model', *Personality and Individual Differences*, 24, 625–33.

Courneya, KS, Mackey, JR & Jones, LW 2000, 'Coping with cancer: can exercise help?', *The Physician and Sportsmedicine*, 28, 49–73.

Courneya, KS & McAuley, E 1995, 'Cognitive mediators of the social influence–exercise adherence relationship: a test of the theory of planned behaviour', *Journal of Behavioural Medicine*, 18, 499–515.

Courneya, KS, Nigg, CR & Estabrooks, PA 1998, 'Relationships among the theory of planned behaviour, stages of change, and exercise behaviour in older persons over a three year period', *Psychology and Health*, 13, 355–67.

Courneya, KS, Plotnikoff, RC, Hotz, SB & Birkett, NJ 2000, 'Social support and the theory of planned behaviour in the exercise domain', *American Journal of Health Behaviour*, 24, 300–8.

Courneya, KS, Plotnikoff, RC, Hotz, SB & Birkett, NJ 2001, 'Predicting exercise stage transitions over two consecutive six month periods: a test of the theory of planned behaviour in a population-based sample', *British Journal of Health Psychology*, 6, 135–50.

Craig, CL, Russell, SJ, Cameron, C & Beaulieu, A 1999, *Foundations for joint action: reducing physical inactivity*, Canadian Fitness and Lifestyle Research Institute, Ottawa, ON.

Deci, EL & Ryan, RM 1985, *Intrinsic motivation and self-determination in human behaviour*, Plenum, New York.

DiClemente, CC, Prochaska, JO, Fairhurst, SK, Velicer, WF, Velasquez, MM & Rossi, JS 1991, 'The process of smoking cessation: an analysis of precontemplation, contemplation, and preparation stages of change', *Journal of Consulting and Clinical Psychology*, 59, 295–304.

Digman, JM 1990, 'Personality structure: emergence of the five-factor model', *Annual Review of Psychology*, 41, 417–40.

Dishman, RK 1988, *Exercise adherence: its impact on public health*, Human Kinetics, Champaign, IL.

Dishman, RK 1991, 'Increasing and maintaining exercise and physical activity', *Behaviour Therapy*, 22, 345–78.

Dishman, RK & Sallis, JF 1994, 'Determinants and interventions for physical activity and exercise', in C Bouchard, RJ Shephard & T Stephens (eds), *Physical activity, fitness and health: consensus statement*, Human Kinetics, Champaign, IL, pp. 214–38.

Eysenck, HJ 1967, *The biological basis of personality*, Charles C Thomas, Springfield, IL.

Eysenck, HJ & Eysenck, SBG 1975, *Manual of the Eysenck Personality Inventory*, EDITS, San Diego, CA.

Eysenck, HJ & Eysenck, SBG 1976, *Psychoticism as a dimension of personality*, Hodder & Stoughton, London.

Fishbein, M & Ajzen, I 1975, *Beliefs, attitude, intention, and behaviour: an introduction to theory and research*, Addision-Wesley, Reading, MA.

Fishbein, M, Triandis, HC, Kanfer, FH, Becker, M, Middlestadt, SE & Eichler, A 2001, 'Factors influencing behaviour and behaviour change', in A Baum, TA Revenson & JE Singer (eds), *Handbook of health psychology*, Lawrence Erlbaum Associates, Mahwah, NJ.

Friedenreich, CM 2001, 'Physical activity and cancer prevention: from observational to intervention research', *Cancer Epidemiology, Biomarkers & Prevention*, 10, 287–301.

Godin, G & Kok, G 1996, 'The theory of planned behaviour: a review of its applications to health-related behaviours', *American Journal of Health Promotion*, 11, 87–98.

Goldberg, LR 1992, 'The development of markers for the big-five factor structure', *Psychological Assessment*, 4, 26–42.

Gorely, T & Gordon, S 1995, 'An examination of the transtheoretical model and exercise behaviour in older adults', *Journal of Sport & Exercise Psychology*, 17, 312–24.

Hausenblas, HA, Carron, AV & Mack, DE 1997, 'Application of the theories of reasoned action and planned behaviour to exercise behaviour: a meta-analysis', *Journal of Sport & Exercise Psychology*, 19, 36–51.

Herzog, TA, Abrams, BB, Emmons, KM, Linnan, LA & Shadel, WG 1999, 'Do processes of change predict smoking stage movements? A prospective analysis of the transtheoretical model', *Health Psychology*, 18, 369–75.

Hogan, R 1986, *Hogan Personality Inventory manual*, National Computer Systems, Minneapolis, MN.

Hogan, J 1989, 'Personality correlates of physical fitness', *Journal of Personality and Social Psychology*, 56, 284–8.

Jakicic, JM, Wing, RR, Butler, BA & Jeffrey, RW 1997, 'The relationship between presence of exercise equipment in the home and physical activity level', *American Journal of Health Promotion*, 11, 363–5.

Janis, IL & Mann, L 1977, *Decision-making: a psychological analysis of conflict, choice and commitment*, The Free Press, New York.

King, AC, Blair, SN, Bild, DE, Dishman, RK, Dubbert, PM, Marcus, BH, Oldridge, NB, Paffenbarger, RS, Powell, KE & Yeager, KK 1992, 'Determinants of physical activity and interventions for adults', *Medicine & Science in Sports & Exercise*, 24, S221–36.

Maehr, ML & Braskamp, LA 1986, *The motivation factor: a theory of personal investment*, Lexington Press, Lexington, MA.

Marcus, BH, Banspach, SW, Lefebvre, RC, Rossi, JS et al. 1992, 'Using the stages of change model to increase adoption of physical activity among community participants', *American Journal of Health Promotion*, 6, 424–9.

Marcus, BH, Emmons, KM, Simkin-Silverman, LR, Linnan, LA, Taylor, ER, Bock, BC, Roberts, MB, Rossi, JS & Abrams, DB 1998, 'Evaluation of motivationally tailored vs. standard self-help physical activity interventions at the workplace', *American Journal of Health Promotion*, 12, 246–53.

Marcus, BH & Simkin, LR 1993, 'The stages of exercise behaviour', *Journal of Sports Medicine and Physical Fitness*, 33, 83–8.

Marlatt, GA & Gordon, JR 1980, 'Determinants of relapse: implications for the maintenance of behaviour change', in: P Davidson & S Davidson (eds), *Behavioural medicine: changing health lifestyles*, Brunner-Mazel, New York, pp. 410–52.

McAuley, E & Blyssmer, B 2002, 'Self-efficacy and attributional processes in physical activity', in T Horn (ed.), *Advances in sport and exercise psychology*, Human Kinetics, Champaign, Il.

McAuley, E, Pena, MM & Jerome, GJ 2001, 'Self-efficacy as a determinant and an outcome of exercise', in GC Roberts (ed.), *Advances in motivation in sport and exercise*, Human Kinetics, Champaign, IL, pp. 235–62.

McCrae, RR & Costa, PT Jr 1990, *Personality in adulthood*, 2nd edn, Guilford Press, New York.

McCrae, RR & John, OP 1992, 'An introduction to the five-factor model and its applications', *Journal of Personality*, 60, 175–215.

McLeroy, KR, Bibeau, D, Steckler, A & Glanz, K 1988, 'An ecological perspective on health promotion programs', *Health Education Quarterly*, 15, 351–77.

Nigg, CR & Courneya, KS 1998, 'Transtheoretical model: examining adolescent exercise behaviour', *Journal of Adolescent Health*, 22, 214–24.

Plotnikoff, RC, Hotz, SB, Birkett, NJ & Courneya, KS 2001, 'Exercise and the transtheoretical model: a longitudinal test of a population sample', *Preventive Medicine*, 33, 441–52.

Prochaska, JO 1995, 'Why do people behave the way they do?', *Canadian Journal of Cardiology*, 11 (Suppl. A) 20A–25A.

Prochaska, JO & DiClemente, CC 1984, *The transtheoretical approach: crossing traditional boundaries of therapy*, Brookes/Cole, Pacific Grove, CA.

Prochaska, JO & DiClemente, CC 1986, 'Toward a comprehensive model of change', in WE Miller & N Heather (eds), *Treating addictive behaviours*, Plenum, London, pp. 3–27.

Prochaska, JO & Marcus, BH 1994, 'The transtheoretical model: applications to exercise', in RK Dishman (ed.), *Advances in exercise adherence*, Human Kinetics, Champaign, IL, pp. 161–80.

Prochaska, JO & Velicer, WF 1997, 'The transtheoretical model of health behaviour change', *American Journal of Health Promotion*, 12, 11–12.

Prochaska, JO & Velicer, WF, DiClemente, CC, Fava, J 1988, 'Measuring processes of change: applications to the cessation of smoking', *Journal of Consulting and Clinical Psychology*, 56, 521–8.

Prochaska, JO, Velicer, WF, Rossi, JS, Goldstein, MG, Marcus, BH, Rakowski, W, Fiore, C, Harlow, L, Redding, CA, Rosenbloom, D & Rossi, SR 1994, 'Stages of change and decisional balance for twelve problem behaviours', *Health Psychology*, 13, 39–46.

Rhodes, RE 2001, 'Personality and social cognitive determinants of exercise in cancer survivors: a structural equation modelling approach', unpublished doctoral dissertation, Faculty of Physical Education, University of Alberta, Edmonton, AB, Canada.

Rhodes, RE & Courneya, KS (in press), 'Investigating multiple components of attitude, social influence, and perceived control: a conceptual examination of the theory of planned behaviour in the exercise domain', *British Journal of Social Psychology*.

Rhodes, RE, Courneya, KS & Bobick, TM 2001, 'Personality and exercise participation across the breast cancer experience', *Psycho-oncology*, 10, 380–8.

Rhodes, RE, Courneya, KS & Jones, LW (in press), 'Personality, the theory of planned behaviour, and exercise: a unique role for extraversion's activity facet', *Journal of Applied Social Psychology*.

Rhodes, RE, Jones, LW & Courneya, KS 2002, 'Extending the theory of planned behaviour in the exercise domain: a comparison of social support and subjective norm', *Research Quarterly for Exercise and Sport*, 73, 193–9.

Rhodes, RE, Martin, AD, Taunton, JE, Rhodes, EC, Donnelly, M & Elliot, J 1999, 'Factors associated with exercise adherence among older adults: an individual perspective', *Sports Medicine*, 28, 397–411.

Robison, JI & Rogers, MA 1994, 'Adherence to exercise programmes: recommendations, *Sports Medicine*, 17, 39–52.

Rogers, RW & Prentice-Dunn, S 1997, 'Protection motivation theory', in DS Gochman (ed.), *Handbook of health behaviour research I: personal and social determinants*, Plenum, New York, pp. 113–32.

Rosenstock, IM 1990, 'The health belief model: explaining behaviour through expectancies', in K Glanz, FM Lewis & BK Rimer (eds), *Health behaviour and health education*, Jossey-Bass, San Francisco, pp. 39–62.

Rotter, JB 1966, 'Generalized expectancies for internal versus external control of reinforcement', *Journal of Consulting and Clinical Psychology*, 43, 56–67.

Sallis, JF, Bauman, A & Pratt, M 1998, 'Environmental and policy interventions to promote physical activity', *American Journal of Preventive Medicine*, 15, 379–97.

Sallis, JF & Hovell, MF, Hofstetter, CR, Faucher, P, Elder, JP, Blanchard, J, Caspersen, CJ, Powell, KE & Christenson, GM 1989, 'A multivariate study of determinants of vigorous exercise in a community sample', *Preventive Medicine*, 18, 20–34.

Sallis, JF, Hovell, MF & Hofstetter, CR 1992, 'Predictors of adoption and maintenance of vigorous physical activity in men and women', *Preventive Medicine*, 21, 237–51.

Sallis, JF, Johnson, MF, Calfas, KJ, Caparosa, S & Nichols, J 1997, 'Assessing perceived physical environment variables that may influence physical activity', *Research Quarterly for Exercise and Sport*, 68, 345–51.

Sallis, JF & Owen, N 1997, 'Ecological models', in K Glanz, FM Lewis & BK Rimer (eds.), *Health behaviour and health education: theory, research, and practice*, Jossey-Bass, San Francisco, pp. 403–24.

Sallis, JF, Prochaska, JJ & Taylor, WC 2000, 'A review of correlates of physical activity of children and adolescents', *Medicine & Science in Sports & Exercise*, 32, 963–75.

Saucier, G 1992, 'Benchmarks: integrating affective and interpersonal circles with the big-five personality factors', *Journal of Personality and Social Psychology*, 62, 1025–35.

Spence, JC, Courneya, KS, Blanchard, C, Wilson, P & Becker, BJ 2001, 'The theory of planned behaviour and physical activity: a meta-analysis', *Annals of Behavioural Medicine*, 23, S045.

Stephens, T & Caspersen, CJ 1994, 'The demography of physical activity', in C Bouchard, RJ Shephard & T Stephens (eds), *Physical activity, fitness and health: consensus statement*, Human Kinetics, Champaign, IL, pp. 204–13.

Terry, DJ & O'Leary, JE 1995, 'The theory of planned behaviour: the effects of perceived behavioural control and self-efficacy', *British Journal of Social Psychology*, 34, 199–220.

Trapnell, PD & Wiggins, JS 1990, 'Extension of the interpersonal adjective scales to include the big five dimensions of personality', *Journal of Personality and Social Psychology*, 59, 781–90.

Weiner, B 1986, *An attributional theory of motivation and emotion*, Springer-Verlag, New York.

Weinstein ND, Rothman, AM & Sutton, SR 1998, 'Stage theories of health behaviour: conceptual and methodological issues', *Health Psychology*, 17, 290–9.

Wicker, AW 1979, *An introduction to ecological psychology*, Brooks/Cole, Pacific Grove, CA.

Young, DR & King, AC 1995, 'Exercise adherence: determinants of physical activity and applications of health behaviour change theories', *Medicine Exercise Nutrition & Health*, 4, 335–48.

CHAPTER 19

SPORT AND EXERCISE PSYCHOPHYSIOLOGY

Stephen H Boutcher

Psychophysiology is the study of psychological processes inferred from the examination of physiological measures (Sternback 1966). Originating in the field of physiological psychology, it was not until the 1960s that psychophysiology was recognised as a distinct domain (Hatfield & Landers 1983). Today psychophysiologists use non-invasive techniques to study psychophysiological phemonena in humans. Areas of study in psychophysiology include emotion, attention, cognitive functioning, stress reactivity and sleep. Measuring techniques include electroencephalography (brain activity), impedance cardiography (cardiac activity), electrocardiography (the ECG), electromyography (muscle activity), electrodermal analysis (skin response) and endocrine response. For an overview of the different areas under study in psychophysiology and a description of the techniques used, see Coles, Donchin and Porges (1986).

Psychophysiology studies in sport were undertaken throughout the 1950s and 1960s, but it was not until the 1970s that sport psychophysiology laboratories were established and started to produce systematic programs of research. The first research sport psychophysiology research programs were established by Dan Landers and Brad Hatfield, who carried out a series of studies examining the psychophysiology of closed-skill performance. The main area of study in sport psychophysiology has been examination of attentional characteristics of athletes such as shooters, archers and golfers. Analysis of electroencephalographic (EEG) patterns before and during performance has been the predominant research strategy. The relationship between attention and heart rate deceleratory and acceleratory patterns has also been examined, as have breathing patterns before and during performance. The psychophysiological concomitants of imagery and mental rehearsal have been investigated. Researchers have tried to find out if imaging sport skills results in muscular activity similar to that recorded when physically performing the imaged skill. Other psychophysiologists have focused their efforts on the exercise area. For example, a growing number of studies have examined the effects of physical activity on emotion by examining post-exercise brainwave patterns. Also the ability of regular and acute exercise to attenuate the cardiovascular physiological response to mental stress has been investigated. Researchers have also examined the effect of exercise on sleep quality.

This chapter will summarise and describe the major findings of the sport and exercise psychophysiological research. The first section will review the sport psychophysiology literature and will focus on the psychophysiology of closed-skill performance and the muscular response to imagery. The second section will focus on a review of exercise psychophysiology and will summarise the literature on exercise and emotion, exercise and stress reactivity, and sleep.

SPORT PSYCHOPHYSIOLOGY

Closed-skill performance

The main area of interest of sport psychophysiologists has been the study of closed-skill performance such as shooting, archery and golf. Before the emergence of psychophysiology, researchers investigating the psychological aspects of sport performance had been restricted to questionnaires, interviews and video analysis. The use of psychophysiological techniques has allowed greater insight into the cognitive processes underlying athletic performance. For example, Hatfield, Landers and Ray (1984) recorded left- and right-brain alpha EEG activity of elite rifle shooters while shooting. They then compared the shooter's EEG to that recorded while performing a series of mental tasks. Authors were interested in finding out which parts of the brain were more or less active before and during shooting performance. Results showed that seconds before pulling the trigger, shooters exhibited more alpha activity in their left hemisphere compared with their right (increased alpha activity is associated with reduced mental activity). Authors suggested that elite marksmen have such a highly developed attentional focus that they can reduce conscious mental activities of the left hemisphere, thus reducing task-irrelevant cognitions.

Studying golfers, Crews and Landers (1992) found similar increases in left hemispheric alpha EEG activity immediately before striking the ball in putting. Unlike shooters, however, golfers also showed decreased right hemispheric alpha activity before putting. Researchers suggested that the decreased right hemispheric alpha activity might be a consequence of the need for both hands to be actively involved in putting. Landers et al. (1994) have also shown that as novice archers improve performance their EEG asymmetries increasingly resemble those of elite archers. With improved performance novice archers showed an increase in left hemisphere alpha activity before releasing the arrow. Interestingly, too much of an increase in left hemisphere activity was correlated with poorer performance. Also, heart rate of the novice archers was observed to decelerate seconds before shooting after a 15-week archery class. The authors suggested that heart rate deceleration and EEG asymmetries are markers of attention that are modified with learning.

Other sport psychophysiologists have examined evoked response potentials (ERP) before and during rifle shooting. In this research area multiple ERPs are recorded and then separated from other electrocortical noise by signal averaging techniques. For example, Konttinen and Lyytinen (1992) and Konttinen, Lyytinen and Konttinen (1995) examined an ERP known as the slow wave. They found that increase in frontal negative shifts correlated with better performance. The authors suggest that their results reflect the ability of elite shooters to eradicate task-irrelevant motor activity while concentrating on visual-spatial processing. However, even among elite shooters there appears to be individual variability in EEG response during shooting. For example, Konttinen and Lyytinen (1993) examined pre-shot brain slow potential shifts from frontal, central, centro-lateral and occipital areas of elite shooters while shooting. Results indicated that the slow wave profiles differed from subject to subject, indicating that the shooters had differing styles. Although shooters typically possessed systematic slow wave profiles, occasionally the slow wave pattern varied even though performance was maintained. The researchers suggested that occasional corrective procedures during shooting might be associated with different slow wave profiles. Recently gaze behaviour and cortical activation of elite and non-elite shooters has also been compared (Janelle et al. 2000). When compared with non-experts, experts exhibited superior shooting performance, less eye movement activity and the usual increase in left hemisphere alpha activity. The authors suggested that the reduced eye movement of the experts reflected the optimal organisation needed to achieve elite performance. Lawton, Hung, Saarella and Hatfield (1998) have summarised the EEG research and sport performance literature and have also provided suggestions for future research in this area.

Collectively, these data confirm that there are general processing differences between the left and right cerebral hemispheres of the brain. For example, studies of lateral eye movements (Schwartz, Davidson & Maer 1975; Tucker, Shearer & Murray 1977) and split brain patients' EEG patterns (Le Doux, Wilson & Gazzinga 1977; Sperry 1968) have demonstrated that verbal and linguistic processing generally occurs in the left cerebral hemisphere, whereas spatial cognitive processing occurs in the right hemisphere. Also, the right hemisphere appears to process information holistically in a gestaltic fashion, whereas the left hemisphere processes information analytically, breaking down a concept into parts (Tucker, Shearer & Murray 1977).

Because a large body of research indicates that brainwave activity can be self-regulated, sport-specific EEG biofeedback would seem to be a way of enhancing athletes' concentration skills during performance. For instance, research has established that individuals can learn to suppress cortical activity by learning to enhance alpha waves (Bauer 1976; Elder et al. 1985; Jackson & Eberly 1982). Furthermore, other studies have trained subjects to develop both symmetrical and asymmetrical EEG patterns (Schwartz, Davidson & Pugwash 1976; Suter, Griffin, Smallhouse & Whitlach 1981). In the sport context, the effect of brainwave biofeedback on archery performance has been one of the few areas to be examined. For example, Landers et al. (1991) administered right hemispheric alpha feedback, left hemispheric alpha feedback or no feedback to three groups of archers. Results indicated that the left hemisphere group improved performance, whereas the right hemisphere group exhibited significantly worse performance. Although the efficacy of these EEG biofeedback techniques has yet to be established in sport, the increasing use of biofeedback techniques in a variety of athletic situations suggests that biofeedback will play an increasingly important role in sport performance enhancement.

Another variable that has been used to explore attentional states in closed-skill performance is heart rate deceleration. Lacey and Lacey (1974) have shown that immediately before reactive motor performance (e.g. a reaction time task) subjects' heart rate typically decelerates. These authors have designated this interaction between cardiovascular activity and the brain and its effect on sensorimotor performance as the intake-rejection hypothesis (Lacey & Lacey 1974). The Laceys have proposed that decreases in cardiac activity facilitate attentional processes by decreasing feedback to the brain. In the same study they found that the greater the cardiac deceleration during the fore period of a reaction time task, the greater brain activity. Thus, greater heart rate deceleration and enhanced brain activity were accompanied by faster reaction times.

A number of studies have found significant heart rate deceleration with elite rifle marksmen just before the trigger was pulled (Konttinen & Lyytinen 1993; Landers, Christina, Hatfield, Doyle & Daniels 1980). Similar results have been found with archers, who recorded a progressive heart rate deceleration seconds before arrow release (Landers et al. 1994). Interestingly, Salazar et al. (1990) examined heart rate deceleration of elite archers but did not find heart rate deceleration before arrow release. The authors suggested that the absence of heart rate deceleration in their elite archers was due to the physiological strain caused by drawing a 14 to 22 kg bow. They proposed that cardiac deceleration should be used only as an attentional index when the preparatory performance state is not physiologically demanding.

Similar deceleration effects have been found during putting in elite and beginning golfers (Boutcher & Zinsser 1990). Both groups displayed heart rate deceleration during the performance of four- and twelve-foot putts. However, the elite golfers showed significantly greater deceleration and less variable pre-shot routines. The authors suggested that the different heart rate deceleration patterns reflect the more efficient attentional control possessed by the elite golfers. Examinations of old and young golfers have found similar results (Molander & Backman 1989).

> Studies have shown that closed-skill athletes record reduced left hemisphere brain activity and heart rate deceleration immediately before initiating performance.

Another performance-related variable examined by sport psychophysiologists has been breathing patterns during shooting performance. In this sport it is essential that breathing is controlled so that movement of the chest does not result in movement of the gun barrel. Even a shallow breath during the trigger pull can be detrimental to shooting performance (Landers 1985). Wilkinson, Landers and Daniels (1980) compared breathing patterns of elite shooters to that recommended by the US Army Marksmanship Training Unit's manual, which was to take a deep breath before pulling the trigger. In contrast, Wilkinson et al. (1980) showed that the great majority of shooters took an inhalation followed by shallow breathing up to a breath hold before the trigger pull. The authors suggested that this pattern is advantageous because breath inhalation occurred well before the trigger pull and thus was less disruptive. Optimal breathing patterns in other sports such as golf, snooker, darts and penalty taking in rugby and soccer appear to be undetermined.

Imagery and motor performance

Sport psychophysiologists have also been interested in examining physiological responses to imagery and mental rehearsal. Imagery has been used extensively in sports (see chapter 13 in this book). From a psychophysiological perspective perhaps most interesting is the effect of imagery or mental rehearsal on electromyography (EMG) activity. For example, the psychoneuromuscular theory suggests that imaged events can produce muscle innervations similar to those produced during actual physical practice of the event (Jacobson 1931). Thus, imaging a sports skill such as the golf swing should activate actual but reduced muscle activity whose pattern is similar to that experienced during actual swinging of the club (Perry & Morris 1996).

Preliminary evidence to support the psychoneuromuscular theory was provided by Suinn (1984), who found that electrical activity in the leg muscles of downhill skiers during imagery training was similar to that expected during skiing itself. Suinn recorded the EMG activity of US alpine ski team members while imaging downhill skiing and found that increased EMG activity matched the skiers' description of the course they were imaging. A similar finding was reported by Bird (1984), who found that increases in muscular activity during mental practice occurred at times when increased EMG activity would be expected during actual performance.

Hale (1982) examined EMG responses to differing imagery perspectives. The two most common ways of visualising are through external and internal imagery. The external imagery perspective refers to the experience of seeing oneself from outside, as if on television. The internal perspective describes the image you would see if you were actually carrying out the activity (see figures 1.1a and 1.1b). Hale predicted that external images primarily would invoke an ocular (eye movement) response whereas internal images would invoke a muscular response. During an imagined biceps curl results showed support for the relationship between internal imagery and muscular activity but failed to show any relationship between visual imagery and ocular amplitude. In an extension of the Hale study, Bakker, Boschker and Chung (1996) compared muscular activity in both biceps during imaginary lifting of 4.5 and 9 kg weights. The authors hypothesised that imaging a 9 kg bicep curl would result in more bicep EMG activity than imaging a 4.5 kg bicep curl. They also hypothesised that better, as compared with lower, ability imagers would produce muscular activity patterns closer to those expected during actual movements. Results showed that muscular activity in the imaged arm was greater than that of the passive arm. In the active arm, however, the difference found in muscular activity between the 4.5 and 9 kg weights was not significant. No relationship between imagery ability and EMG activity was found.

Overall, the effect of imagery on muscle activity at this time is unclear. Several authors have pointed out the serious conceptual and methodological flaws that are common to the imagery literature (see Collins & Hale 1997). Perhaps the most serious limitation of past research in this area has been the use of limited EMG sites and the reliance on muscle amplitude to reflect muscle activity. If imagery does produce a pattern of EMG response that is similar to the skill imaged, then temporal and specificity aspects of muscle activity must be considered (Collins & Hale 1997). Thus, the EMG response to imagery recorded by prior studies in this area may be just a generalised muscle response to the image. For example, skiers imaging a downhill event may naturally tense their leg muscles when they image a turn or jump. Consequently the EMG response may bear little relation to the EMG produced by actually performing the skill. The way forward in this area of research has been suggested by Collins and Hale (1997), who have called for the use of comparisons of EMG traces of real and imaged performance. They have also suggested that future research in this area should utilise a variety of measures such as EEG and measures of cerebral blood flow.

Sport psychophysiologists have studied closed-skill performance by monitoring cortical and autonomic responses. EEG studies have indicated that elite athletes in sports such as rifle shooting, golf and archery can effectively reduce conscious mental activities of the left hemisphere. This cognitive reduction may help performance of the task by reducing the interfering effect of non-task cognitions. Heart rate has been found to consistently decelerate during the preparatory stage in closed-skill sports such as shooting and golf. Results from imagery research are equivocal because of the reliance of past studies on EMG amplitude from a limited number of sites and the failure to differentiate between actual and reflex EMG responses to the skill being imaged.

EXERCISE PSYCHOPHYSIOLOGY

The main areas of interest in exercise psychophysiology have been the study of the acute effects of physical activity on emotion, the effects of chronic and acute aerobic exercise on cardiovascular reactivity to mental challenge, and the effect of exercise on quality of sleep.

Physical activity and emotion

An important question from a mental health perspective is, does involvement in exercise make people feel better? Results of surveys have confirmed that exercising individuals do constantly 'feel better' after participation in physical activity (Brunner 1969). How they feel better, however, is undetermined (Boutcher 1993). As feeling better is an emotion, this phenomenon probably reflects an interaction between cognitive and physiological processes. From the psychophysiological perspective, one of the obvious ways of assessing emotional change to exercise is by measuring EEG. As previously mentioned, brain activation can be indexed by recordings of spontaneous EEG. Typically, studies in this area have recorded EEG before and after exercise and then have quantified the amount of alpha activity. Increased alpha activity reflects reduced mental activity and is associated with relaxed states. For example, Boutcher and Landers (1988) compared the brain alpha activity and state anxiety of aerobically trained and untrained males after a 20-minute vigorous bout of treadmill running. On another occasion the same subjects underwent a 20-minute quiet reading session. Results showed that trained compared with untrained subjects recorded significantly less anxiety after exercise. In contrast, the anxiety levels of the untrained did not change. Alpha levels of both groups were increased after exercise, whereas brainwave activity and state anxiety for both groups remained unchanged after quiet reading. Similar results have been found after cycle ergometry exercise. For example, Kubitz and Pothakas (1997) randomly assigned subjects to a cycle exercise and a non-exercise condition and measured brain activation (indexed by alpha and beta band activity) before and after both conditions (greater beta activity indicates greater brain activity). The authors found that higher levels of alpha activity and lower levels of beta activity were found after the exercise compared with the control condition. Other studies have produced similar results (Brasil-Neto et al. 1993; Travis et al. 1996).

> Studies have shown that individuals typically record less cortical brain activity after vigorous aerobic exercise such as running and cycling.

Cardiovascular reactivity

In the cardiovascular reactivity area researchers have been interested in examining the ability of aerobic exercise to decrease cardiovascular hyperreactivity to mental stress. Hyperreactivity to mental challenge has been shown to be an important contributor to both coronary heart disease and hypertension (Julius 1993). Typically researchers in this area have compared the heart rate change of aerobically trained and untrained individuals to mental challenge (e.g. the Stroop task, mental arithmetic, interview). Results of both cross-sectional and longitudinal studies with normal populations are equivocal. For example, in cross-sectional research comparing reactivity of trained and untrained subjects approximately half of the studies showed reduced relative heart rate reactivity to laboratory stressors in trained subjects, whereas in other studies no differences have been found. Relative reactivity is assessed by subtracting the baseline values from those responses measured during mental challenge.

However, cross-sectional studies have also shown that aerobically trained individuals, who possess low resting heart rates, have a reduced absolute heart rate response to mental challenge (Boutcher et al. 1998). Absolute reactivity is assessed by measuring the absolute values during mental challenge. The reduced absolute heart rate response to mental challenge has also been confirmed by longitudinal studies (Blumenthal et al. 1988; Stein & Boutcher 1992). These lower heart rates during rest and mental challenge may reflect an exercise-induced cardio-protective effect. For example, Beere, Glagov and Zarins (1984) surgically reduced heart rates of cynomolgus monkeys and then fed the monkeys an atherogenic high cholesterol diet for six months. Coronary atherosclerosis of the low heart rate monkeys was less than half that of control monkeys possessing normal heart rates. The authors suggested that a lowered average heart rate results in more total time spent in diastole when changes in the rate of flow and departures from laminar unidirectional flow are least. Such a relationship, they proposed, could explain the protective effect of regular physical activity on coronary artery disease.

Other studies have compared the pattern of heart rate increase of trained and untrained individuals to mental challenge. Heart rate increase to mental challenge can be brought about by parasympathetic withdrawal, an increase in sympathetic activity or a combination of decreased parasympathetic and increased sympathetic activity. It is feasible that greater parasympathetic dominance of the heart at rest results in reduced sympathetic cardiac activity during cardiovascular challenge. Typically, aerobically trained individuals possess lower resting heart rates and greater parasympathetic influence on the heart than untrained individuals (Boutcher et al. 1998). Thus aerobically trained individuals may have a more benign autonomic response to cardiac challenge by responding more in the parasympathetic and less in the sympathetic limb. Increasing heart rate to mental challenge through parasympathetic withdrawal is more attractive than increasing heart rate to mental challenge through increased sympathetic activity, as increased sympathetic activity results in significant elevations of catecholamines. Stress-induced catecholamine excretion has been associated with atherosclerosis and hypertension (Manuck, Muldoon, Adams & Polefrone 1989). Thus regular exercise may have a protective effect on the heart through a catecholamine sparing effect during mental challenge.

A number of studies examining mental challenge provide preliminary support for this notion. For example, Boutcher et al. (1998) have shown that aerobically trained individuals possess a different pattern of cardiac autonomic response to laboratory stress than untrained males. These authors compared the parasympathetic response to mental challenge of trained adult males with that of sedentary controls. Trained males had a 38 per cent greater reduction in parasympathetic withdrawal to mental challenge (the Stroop task) compared with the parasympathetic withdrawal of sedentary males. Parasympathetic activity was assessed by time series analysis of heart period variability (for an overview, see Stein & Kleiger 1999). The greater parasympathetic withdrawal to mental challenge of trained individuals does not appear to be affected by age, as similar patterns have been found in trained pre-adolescent children (Franks & Boutcher 2003) and trained postmenopausal women (Nurhayati & Boutcher 1998). Thus aerobically trained individuals may have a more benign autonomic response to mental challenge by responding in the parasympathetic and less in the sympathetic limb. Studies measuring both parasympathetic activity and catecholamine excretion to mental challenge are needed to verify this relationship.

Studies have shown that trained compared with untrained individuals possess a smaller absolute heart rate response and greater parasympathetic withdrawal to mental challenge.

Other researchers have examined the cardiovascular pattern of response to stress by recording such variables as cardiac output, stroke volume, cardiac contractility, blood pressure and total peripheral resistance in order to provide a more comprehensive picture of the cardiovascular response to mental challenge. For example, de Geus, van Doornen, De Visser and Orlebeke (1990) initially used a correlational design to study the relationship between aerobic fitness and cardiovascular reactivity. Changes in heart rate, cardiac output, stroke volume, total peripheral resistance and blood pressure during tasks were not significantly related to fitness level. Subjects were then randomly assigned to a running and indoor fitness training program or a wait-listed control group. Results also showed no effect of endurance training on the reactivity of any variable. Other studies have confirmed that patterns of cardiovascular reactivity to mental challenge of trained and untrained young adults are similar. However, as subjects in these studies have typically been moderately fit it is feasible that aerobic training will induce reactivity changes only in low fitness subjects, or those who are highly reactive, such as older males and females, and clinical groups such as hypertensive patients.

For example, using impedance cardiography Boutcher, Nurhayati and McLaren (2001) have shown that certain aspects of the cardiovascular reactivity response to mental stress of older aerobically trained males were greater, not smaller, than the response of older untrained males. Results showed that highly trained older males possessed significantly greater heart rate and cardiac contractility response to stress. Researchers have also shown that pre-adolescent boys (Franks & Boutcher 2003) and postmenopausal women (Boutcher, Craig & Nurhayati 1999) were also more reactive to mental challenge than their untrained counterparts. Trained compared with untrained boys recorded greater heart rate response, whereas trained postmenopausal compared with untrained women recorded greater cardiac contractility response to mental challenge.

Differences in patterns of cardiovascular reactivity in trained and untrained subjects have also been found in clinical groups. For example, Georgiades et al. (2000) examined the effect of chronic exercise on stress reactivity in hypertensive subjects and found that systolic and diastolic blood pressure, total peripheral resistance and heart rate were significantly reduced during mental stress after six months of aerobic exercise training. Other researchers have compared the effect of aerobic training and fitness on the cardiovascular reactivity of high risk groups such as offspring hypertensives. Individuals with a history of hypertension in the family show significantly increased risk of becoming hypertensive. Holmes and Cappo (1987) have shown that aerobic fitness plays a role in preventing high levels of stress reactivity in offspring hypertensives. They assigned normotensive collegiate males into three categories — the most fit offspring hypertensives, the least fit offspring hypertensives and controls with normotensive parents. Heart rate and blood pressure reactivity were measured during a series of mental challenges (recall of digits, a vocabulary test, mental arithmetic, a Stroop test and a mathematical information task). The authors found that during stress challenge offspring hypertensives who were classified as highly fit demonstrated similar levels of reactivity compared with controls, and both groups recorded lower reactivity levels compared with those of the offspring hypertensive low fitness group.

Buckworth, Dishman and Cureton (1994) recruited offspring hypertensive females and classified them by fitness and activity level. Heart rate and blood pressure were measured during mental arithmetic and cold face testing, and on a separate occasion the same tests were performed while the carotid-cardiac baroreflex was stimulated. Assessment of the carotid-cardiac baroreflex reflects autonomic control of the heart. No differences were observed in heart rate or blood pressure reactivity responses to mental arithmetic or the cold-face test, however, despite the lack of difference in reactivity, the highly fit women had longer R-R intervals compared with the moderately fit women during stimulation of the carotid-cardiac baroreflex at rest. Also, the carotid-cardiac baroreflex was attenuated during mental arithmetic compared with rest in both the moderately active and moderately fit women but not in the highly active and highly fit groups. These findings suggest that physical activity and cardiorespiratory fitness may help regulate blood pressure during stress by enhancing parasympathetic tone. Thus physical activity may prevent baroreflex control abnormalities that characterise offspring hypertensives.

In a follow-up study, Buckworth, Convertino, Cureton and Dishman (1997) conducted an eight-week exercise program and then detrained subjects for a further six to eight weeks. Heart rate and blood pressure response to mental arithmetic and forehead cold exposure, and the carotid-cardiac vagal baroreflex after the training period, were compared with responses after detraining. Following an 11.5 per cent decrease in maximal oxygen uptake after detraining in the experimental group, mean arterial blood pressure response to the mental arithmetic task and systolic blood pressure response during cold head exposure were both elevated. However, despite higher submaximal exercise heart rates after detraining, the experimental group showed no change in the carotid-cardiac vagal baroreflex, or heart rate response to autonomic challenge. The lack of significant findings is likely due to the length of training period employed, as Raven (1993) has suggested that cardiovascular adaptations associated with exercise training take far longer than eight to ten weeks.

Other researchers have examined the muscle vasodilation response to mental challenge in physically active and inactive offspring hypertensives. An exaggerated skeletal muscle vasodilation response to mental challenge is thought to play a major role in the development of hypertension by initiating a vascular remodelling process. Skeletal muscle vasodilation is typically measured non-invasively by assessing limb blood flow through occlusion plethysmography (Hamer, Boutcher & Boutcher 2002). For example, less fit and active male offspring hypertensives demonstrated a significantly higher level of forearm blood flow reactivity to mental challenge compared with that of highly active, fitter males (Hamer, Boutcher & Boutcher 2002). The mechanism underlying the exaggerated blood flow reactivity of individuals with hypertensive relatives is likely to be cardiopulmonary baroreceptor sensitivity, as Hamer, Boutcher and Boutcher (2003) have shown that the exaggerated forearm blood flow reactivity to mental challenge of offspring hypertensives is significantly reduced when the cardiopulmonary baroreceptors are impeded.

In summary, evidence is emerging to suggest that fitness and physical activity may decrease stress reactivity, thus decreasing the risk of hypertension among normotensive individuals who are already at risk because of familial history of hypertension.

Acute exercise effects on stress reactivity

The rationale behind studying the effects of acute exercise on stress reactivity is that acute exercise effects may accumulate over a training program to bring about lowered hyperreactivity. For example, the acute reduction of blood pressure that follows vigorous exercise is well documented (Kenney & Seals 1993). Thus the repeated exposure to hypotensive episodes through exercise training are hypothesised to reduce total hemodynamic load, producing cardiovascular benefits. There seems to be more evidence to support an acute exercise (rather than chronic exercise) stress reactivity lowering effect, possibly because of the absence of the confounding variable genetic fitness, which has plagued cross-sectional chronic exercise studies. For example, the majority of studies in this area have shown a stress reactivity lowering effect to mental challenge after an acute bout of exercise (e.g. Steptoe, Kearsley & Walters 1993). A minority of studies, however, have shown no effect. The stress reactivity lowering effects of acute exercise have been mainly observed as a reduction in blood pressure reactivity, although West, Brownley and Light (1998) also noted a post-exercise reduction in total peripheral resistance. Also, the exaggerated blood flow reactivity of male offspring hypertensives, mentioned previously, has been found to be significantly reduced after one bout of exercise. Hamer and Boutcher (2003) exposed offspring hypertensives to 20 minutes of hard cycle ergometry exercise and found that post-exercise forearm blood flow reactivity to mental challenge was significantly blunted compared with a control condition. Probst, Bulbulian and Knapp (1997) found reduced heart rate reactivity to stress in a post-exercise condition. However, this may have been due to the higher initial pre-stress heart rate level from the exercise, which may have blunted the stress response. The lack of significant findings in some studies may be related to the intensity and duration of exercise employed and the variation in timing of the post-exercise reactivity test. It seems those studies reporting significant findings have generally employed higher intensity exercise (more than 60 per cent maximal oxygen uptake) for at least 20 minutes and have completed reactivity testing within the first hour of exercise recovery. For example, Steptoe et al. (1993) employed two different exercise intensities (50 per cent and 70 per cent maximal oxygen uptake) but found a significant stress reactivity lowering effect only for the higher intensity.

Physical activity and sleep

Another area of exercise psychophysiology is examination of the effects of physical activity on the quality of sleep. Sleep problems are prevalent in Western societies; indeed it has been estimated that the majority of adults have suffered from some form of sleep problem (Ford & Kamerow 1989). There is also a significant relationship between sleep problems and mental illness (Ford & Kamerow 1989). Given the enormous toll that sleep problems take on public health it would be particularly attractive if physical activity improved sleep quality. Exercise is cheap and available and, unlike many sleep-inducing drugs, has few side effects. Study of the effect of exercise on sleep quality is also important for theoretical reasons (e.g. why do we sleep?).

Epidemiological, cross-sectional, longitudinal and acute studies have examined the ability of exercise to improve the quality of sleep (for an overview, see O'Connor & Youngstedt 1996). For example, Urponen, Vuori, Hasan and Partinen (1988) conducted a large survey in Finland that asked males and females about the perceived benefits of exercise on sleep. Thirty-three per cent of the males and 30 per cent of the females reported that exercising was their most important sleep-promoting factor. Cross-sectional studies in this area have typically compared the sleep of athletes and fit individuals with that of unfit individuals. For example, Trinder, Paxton, Montgomery and Fraser (1985) compared the quality of sleep of runners, power athletes, sprinters and unfit controls. Sleep quality was assessed by analysing the amount of slow wave sleep, measured through EEG recording during sleep. Results indicated that the aerobically trained runners recorded significantly greater amounts of slow wave sleep than the other groups. A number of other cross-sectional studies have produced similar results (see O'Connor & Youngstedt 1996).

Although this evidence is promising, no firm conclusions regarding the effect of exercise on sleep can be made based on cross-sectional results because of the inherent methodological problems of this approach. Because subjects are not randomised to conditions, a number of nuisance variables may have influenced the results (e.g. diet, body mass, sleep history, lifestyle). Although longitudinal studies get around these threats to internal validity, few such studies have been conducted examining exercise and sleep.

Results of those longitudinal studies that have been carried out are mixed and have generally involved older subjects. The final approach in examining the effect of exercise on sleep has been the acute exercise experiment that has measured sleep quality after subjects have performed daytime exercise. Results have indicated that exercise is associated with a small but significant increase in sleep quality (i.e. increased slow wave sleep). The mechanisms that underlie exercise-associated increases in slow wave sleep are unknown.

Although physical activity is generally thought to enhance sleep quality, the evidence is primarily provided by cross-sectional results. Given the limitations of this approach already described, it is important that better controlled studies are carried out to confirm these positive preliminary findings.

Exercise psychophysiologists have examined the effect of aerobic exercise on emotion by monitoring EEG responses before and after exercise. EEG studies have indicated that aerobic exercise such as running and cycling is associated with reduced mental activity in the right and left hemispheres of the brain. Results from cardiovascular reactivity research has shown that aerobically trained compared with untrained individuals have a lower absolute heart rate response to mental challenge. Trained subjects may also possess a more benign autonomic response to mental challenge by responding to stress more in the parasympathetic and less in the sympathetic limb. Exposing hypertensive and offspring hypertensive individuals to exercise training has been found to attenuate cardiovascular reactivity to mental challenge. Exposing individuals to mental challenge after acute aerobic exercise has been found to attenuate blood pressure response. Studies have shown that aerobic athletes typically have better quality sleep than non-athletes and that moderately vigorous aerobic exercise increases the quality of sleep.

FUTURE DIRECTIONS

Research into sport and exercise psychophysiology has only recently been initiated. However, the benefits of using physiological measures as indicators of psychological processes have already been demonstrated. It would be beneficial if future research in the sport and health areas used sport and exercise psychophysiological measures along with other questionnaire and behavioural assessment. This multidimensional approach is fitting for the sport and exercise psychophysiological area, as this research is multifactorial in nature. From a practical perspective the application of psychophysiology techniques (i.e. biofeedback) to improve sport performance and influence health has tremendous potential.

CONCLUSIONS

Elite shooters, golfers and archers may enhance performance by consciously reducing left hemisphere mental activity. These athletes also consistently decelerate their heart rate immediately before performance. Results from research examining the effects of imagery on muscle activity is equivocal because of methodological problems. Aerobic exercise such as running and cycling effectively reduces mental activity in the right and left hemispheres of the brain. Aerobically trained compared with untrained individuals have a lower absolute heart rate response to mental challenge and may also possess a more benign autonomic response by responding to stress more in the parasympathetic and less in the sympathetic limb. Aerobic athletes typically have better quality sleep than non-athletes. Moderately vigorous in contrast to mild aerobic exercise results in greater increases in quality of sleep.

SUMMARY

This chapter has attempted to outline research examining different aspects of sport and exercise psychophysiology. Sport psychophysiologists have studied closed-skill performance by monitoring cortical and autonomic responses. EEG studies have indicated that elite athletes in sports such as rifle shooting, golf and archery can effectively reduce conscious mental activities of the left hemisphere. This cognitive reduction may help performance of the task by reducing the interfering effect of non-task cognitions. Heart rate has been found to consistently decelerate during the preparatory stage in closed-skill sports such as shooting and golf. Results from imagery research is equivocal because of the reliance of past studies on EMG amplitude from a limited number of sites and the failure to differentiate between actual and reflex EMG responses to the skill being imaged.

Exercise psychophysiologists have examined the effect of aerobic exercise on emotion by monitoring EEG responses before and after exercise. EEG studies have indicated that aerobic exercise such as running and cycling effectively reduces mental activity in the right and left hemispheres of the brain. Results from cardiovascular reactivity research have shown that aerobically trained compared with untrained individuals have a lower absolute heart rate response to mental challenge. Trained subjects may also possess a more benign autonomic response to mental challenge by responding to stress more in the parasympathetic and less in the sympathetic limb. Exposing hypertensive and offspring hypertensive individuals to exercise training has been found to attenuate cardiovascular reactivity to mental challenge. Exposing individuals to mental challenge after acute aerobic exercise has been found to attenuate blood pressure and muscle blood flow response. Studies have shown that aerobic athletes typically have better quality sleep than non-athletes and that moderately vigorous aerobic exercise increases the quality of sleep.

REVIEW QUESTIONS

1   What happens to the left hemispheric EEG activity of elite shooters, golfers and archers seconds before they perform their skills?

2   Does heart rate decelerate or accelerate immediately before closed-skill performance such as shooting and golf putting?

3   True or False: The psychoneuromuscular theory suggests that imagined events can produce muscular innervations similar to those produced during actual performance of a skill.

4   Does moderately vigorous running and cycling increase or decrease cortical brain activity?

5   True or False: Studies have shown that trained compared with untrained adults possess a smaller absolute heart rate response and greater parasympathetic withdrawal to mental challenge.

6   What does an acute bout of vigorous exercise lasting more than 30 minutes do to cardiovascular reactivity to mental challenge?

7   What effect does an acute bout of aerobic exercise have on the quality of sleep the following night?

References

Bakker, FC, Boschker, MSJ & Chung, T 1996, 'Changes in muscular activity while imagining weight lifting using stimulus or response propositions', *Journal of Sport & Exercise Psychology*, 18, 313–24.

Bauer, RH 1976, 'Short-term memory: EEG alpha correlates and the effect of increased alpha', *Behavioral Biology*, 17, 425–33.

Beere, PA, Glagov, S & Zarins, CK 1984, 'Retarding effect of lowered heart rate on coronary atherosclerosis', *Science*, 226, 180–2.

Bird, EI 1984, 'EMG quantification of mental rehearsal', *Perceptual and Motor Skills*, 59, 899–906.

Blumenthal, JA, Emery, CF, Walsh, MA 1988, 'Exercise training in healthy Type A middle-aged males: effects on behavioral and cardiovascular responses', *Psychosomatic Medicine*, 50, 418–33.

Boutcher, SH 1993, 'Exercise and emotion', in R Singer, M Murphe & K Tennant (eds), *Handbook of research on sport psychology*, Macmillan, New York.

Boutcher, SH, Craig, G & Nurhayati, Y 1999, 'Cardiovascular response of aerobically trained and untrained postmenopausal females to mental challenge', *Medicine & Science in Sports & Exercise*, 31 (5) S290.

Boutcher, SH & Landers, DM 1988, 'The effects of vigorous exercise on anxiety, heart rate, and alpha activity of runners and nonrunners', *Psychophysiology*, 25, 696–702.

Boutcher, SH, Nugent, FW, McLaren, P & Weltman, A 1998, 'Parasympathetic response to psychological stress of individuals possessing low resting heart rate', *Psychophysiology*, 35, 16–22.

Boutcher, SH, Nurhayati, Y & McLaren, P 2001, 'Cardiovascular response to mental challenge in trained and untrained older males', *Medicine & Science in Sports & Exercise*, 3 (4) 659–64.

Boutcher, SH & Zinsser, N 1990, 'Cardiac deceleration of elite and beginning golfers during putting', *Journal of Sport Psychology*, 12, 37–47.

Brasil-Neto, JP, Pascual-Leone, A, Valls-Sole, J, Cammarota, A, Cohen, LG & Hallett, M 1993, 'Postexercise depression of motor-evoked potentials: a measure of central nervous system fatigue', *Experimental Brain Research*, 93, 181–4.

Brunner, BC 1969, 'Personality and motivating factors influencing adult participation in vigorous physical activity', *Research Quarterly*, 3, 464–9.

Buckworth, J, Dishman, RK & Cureton, KJ 1994, 'Autonomic responses of women with parental hypertension', *Hypertension*, 24, 576–84.

Buckworth, J, Convertino, VA, Cureton, KJ & Dishman, RK 1997, 'Autonomic responses of women with parental hypertension', *Hypertension*, 24, 576–84.

Coles, MGH, Donchin, E & Porges, S 1986, *Psychophysiology: systems, processes, and applications*, The Guildford Press, New York.

Collins, D & Hale, BD 1997, 'Getting closer . . . but still no cigar. Comments on Bakker, Boschker & Chung (1996)', *Journal of Sport & Exercise Psychology*, 19, 207–12.

Crews, DJ & Landers, DL 1992, 'Electroencephalographic measures of attentional patterns prior to the golf putt', *Medicine & Science in Sports & Exercise*, 25, 116–26.

de Geus, EJC, van Doornen, LJP, De Visser, DC & Orlebeke, JF 1990, 'Existing and training induced differences in aerobic fitness: their relationship to physiological response patterns during different types of stress', *Psychophysiology*, 27, 457–78.

Elder, ST, Grenier, C, Lashley, J, Martyn, S, Regenbogen, D & Roundtree, G 1985, 'Can subjects be trained to communicate through the use of EEG biofeedback?', *Biofeedback and Self-Regulation*, 10, 88–9.

Ford, DE & Kamerow, DB 1989, 'Epidemiological study of sleep disturbances and psychiatric disorders', *Journal of the American Medical Association*, 262, 1479–84.

Franks, P & Boutcher, SH 2003, 'Cardiovascular response to mental challenge in trained and untrained pre-teenage boys', *Medicine & Science in Sports & Exercise*, 35, 1429–35.

Georgiades, A, Sherwood, A, Gullette, EC, Babyak, MA, Hinderliter, A, Waugh, R, Tweedy, D, Craighead, L, Bloomer, R & Blumenthal, J 2000, 'Effects of exercise and weight loss on mental stress-induced cardiovascular responses in individuals with high blood pressure', *Hypertension*, 36, 171–6.

Hale, B 1982, 'The effects of internal and external imagery on muscular and ocular concomitants', *Journal of Sport Psychology*, 4, 378–9.

Hamer, M & Boutcher, S 2003, 'Acute exercise reduces vascular reactivity to mental challenge in offspring of hypertensives', *Medicine & Science in Sports & Exercise*, 35 (5) S26.

Hamer, M, Boutcher, Y & Boutcher, SH 2002, 'Cardiovascular and renal reactivity to mental challenge in trained and untrained offspring hypertensives', *Journal of Human Hypertension*, 16, 319–26.

Hamer, M, Boutcher, YN & Boutcher, SH 2003, 'The role of cardiopulmonary baroreceptors during the forearm vasodilation response to mental stress in humans', *Psychophysiology*, 40, 249–53.

Hatfield, BD & Landers, DM 1983, 'Psychophysiology — a new direction for sport psychology', *Journal of Sport Psychology*, 5, 243–59.

Hatfield, BD, Landers, DM & Ray, WJ 1984, 'Cognitive processes during self-paced motor performance: an electroencephalographic profile of skilled marksmen', *Journal of Sport Psychology*, 6, 42–59.

Holmes, DS & Cappo, BM 1987, 'Prophylactic effect of aerobic fitness on cardiovascular arousal among individuals with a family history of hypertension', *Journal of Psychosomatic Research*, 31, 601–5.

Jackson, GM & Eberly, DA 1982, 'Facilitation of performance on an arithmetic task as a result of the application of a biofeedback procedure to suppress alpha wave activity', *Biofeedback and Self-Regulation*, 7, 211–21.

Jacobson, E 1931, 'Electrical movements of neuromuscular states during mental activities', *American Journal of Physiology*, 96, 115–21.

Janelle, C, Hillman, CH, Apparies, RJ, Murray, NP, Meili, L, Fallon, EA & Hatfield, B 2000, 'Expertise differences in cortical activation and gaze behavior during rifle shooting', *Journal of Sport & Exercise Psychology*, 22 (2) 167–82.

Julius, S 1993, 'Sympathetic hyperactivity and coronary risk in hypertension', *Hypertension*, 21, 886–93.

Kenney, MJ & Seals, DR 1993, 'Postexercise hypotension: key features, mechanisms, and clinical significance', *Hypertension*, 22, 653–64.

Konttinen, N & Lyytinen, K 1992, 'Physiology of preparation: brain slow waves, heart rate, and respiration preceding triggering in rifle shooting', *International Journal of Sports Psychology*, 23, 110–27.

Konttinen, N & Lyytinen, K 1993, 'Individual variability in brain slow profiles in skilled sharpshooters during the aiming period in rifle shooting', *Journal of Sport & Exercise Psychology*, 15 (3) 275–89.

Konttinen, N, Lyytinen, K & Konttinen, R 1995, 'Brain slow potentials reflecting successful shooting performance', *Research Quarterly for Exercise and Sport*, 66, 64–72.

Kubitz, KA & Pothakos, K 1997, 'Does aerobic exercise decrease brain activation?', *Journal of Sport & Exercise Psychology*, 19, 291–301.

Lacey, JI & Lacey, BC 1974, 'Studies of heart rate and other bodily processes', in PA Obrist, AH Black, J Brener & LV DiCara (eds), *Cardiovascular Psychophysiology*, Aldine, Chicago, pp. 538–64.

Landers, DM 1985, 'Psychophysiological assessment and biofeedback: application for athletes in closed-skill sports', in J Sandweiss & S Wolf (eds), *Biofeedback and sports science*, Plenum, New York, pp. 65–105.

Landers, DM, Christina, R, Hatfield, BD, Doyle, LA & Daniels, FS 1980, 'Moving competitive shooting into the scientists' lab', *American Rifleman*, 128, 36–7, 76–7.

Landers, DM, Han, M, Salazar, W, Petruzzello, SJ, Kubitz, KA & Gannon, TL 1994, 'Effects of learning on electroencephalographic and electrocardiographic patterns in novice archers', *International Journal of Sport Psychology*, 25, 313–30.

Landers, DM, Petruzzello, SJ, Salazar, W, Kubitz, CA & Crews, DJ, Kubitz, KA, Gannon, TL, Han, M 1991, 'The influence of electrocortical biofeedback on performance in pre-elite archers', *Medicine & Science in Sports & Exercise*, 23, 123–9.

Lawton, GW, Min Hung, T, Saarella, P & Hatfield, B 1998, 'Electroencephalography and mental states associated with elite performance', *Journal of Sport & Exercise Psychology* 20(1) 35–53.

Le Doux, JE, Wilson, DH & Gazzinga, MS 1977, 'Manipulo-spatial aspects of cerebral lateralization: clues to the origin of lateralization', *Neuropsychologica*, 15, 743–50.

Manuck, SB, Muldoon, MF, Adams, JR & Polefrone, JM 1989, 'Coronary artery atherosclerosis and cardiac response to stress in cynomolgus monkeys', in AW Siegman & TM Dembroski (eds), *In search of coronary-prone behavior: beyond type A*, Lawrence Erlbaum Associates, Hillsdale, pp. 207–27.

Molander, B & Backman, L 1989, 'Age differences in heart rate patterns during concentration in a precision sport: implications for attentional functioning', *Journal of Gerontology: Psychological Sciences*, 44, 80–7.

Nurhayati, Y & Boutcher, SH 1998, 'Vagal response to mental challenge in aerobically trained and untrained postmenopausal females', *Medicine & Science in Sports & Exercise*, 30, S119.

O'Connor, PJ & Youngstedt, SD 1996, 'Influence of exercise on human sleep', *Exercise and Sport Science Reviews*, 23, 105–34.

Perry, C & Morris, T 1996, 'Mental imagery in sport', in T Morris & J Summers (eds), *Sport psychology; theory, applications, and issues*, John Wiley & Sons, New York, pp. 339–79.

Probst, M, Bulbulian, R & Knapp, C 1997, 'Hemodynamic responses to the Stroop and cold pressor tests after submaximal cycling exercise in normotensive males', *Physiology and Behavior*, 62, 1283–90.

Raven, PB 1993, 'An overview of the problem: exercise training and orthostatic intolerance', *Medicine & Science in Sports & Exercise*, 25, 702–4.

Salazar, W, Landers, DM, Petruzzello, SJ, Han, M, Crews, DJ & Kubitz, KA 1990, 'Hemispheric asymmetry, cardiac response, and performance in elite archers', *Research Quarterly for Exercise and Sports*, 61, 351–9.

Schwartz, GE, Davidson, RJ & Maer, F 1975, 'Right hemispheric specialization for emotion: interactions with cognitions', *Science*, 190, 286–90.

Schwartz, GE, Davidson, RJ & Pugwash, E 1976, 'Voluntary control of patterns of EEG parietal asymmetry: cognitive concomitants', *Psychophysiology*, 13, 498–504.

Sperry, RW 1968, 'Hemisphere deconnection and unity in conscious awareness', *American Psychologist*, 23, 723–33.

Stein, P & Boutcher, SH 1992, 'The effect of participation in an exercise training program on cardiovascular reactivity in sedentary middle-aged men', *International Journal of Psychophysiology*, 13, 215–23.

Stein, PK & Kleiger, RE 1999, 'Insights from the study of heart rate variability', *Annual Review of Medicine*, 50, 249–61.

Steptoe, A, Kearsley, N & Walters, N 1993, 'Cardiovascular activity during mental stress following vigorous exercise in sportsmen and inactive men', *Psychophysiology*, 30, 245–52.

Sternback, RA 1966, *Principles of psychophysiology*, Academic Press, New York.

Suinn, RM 1984, 'Imagery and sports', in WF Straub & JF Willaims (eds), *Cognitive sport psychology*, Sports Science Associates, Lansing NY.

Suter, S, Griffin, G, Smallhouse, P & Whitlach, S 1981, 'Biofeedback regulation of temporal EEG alpha asymmetries', *Biofeedback and Self-Regulation*, 6, 45–56.

Trinder, J, Paxton, S, Montgomery, I & Fraser, G 1985, 'Endurance as opposed to power training: their effect on sleep', *Psychophysiology*, 22, 668–73.

Tucker, DM, Shearer, SL & Murray, JD 1977, 'Hemispheric specialization and cognitive behavior therapy', *Cognitive Therapy and Research*, 1, 263–73.

Travis, F, Blasdell, K, Liptak, R, Zisman, S, Daley, K & Douillard, J 1996, 'Invincible athletics program: aerobic exercise and performance without strain', *International Journal of Neuroscience*, 85, 301–8.

Urponen, H, Vuori, I, Hasan, J & Partinen, M 1988, 'Self-evaluation of factors promoting and disturbing sleep: an epidemiological survey in Finland', *Social Science & Medicine*, 26, 443–50.

West, SG, Brownley, KA & Light, KC 1998, 'Postexercise vasodilation reduces diastolic blood pressure response to stress', *Annals of Behavioral Medicine* 20, 77–83.

Wilkinson, MO, Landers, DM & Daniels, FS 1980, 'Respiration patterns and their influence on rifle shooting', *The American Marksman*, August, 6, 8–9.

CHAPTER 20

CHILDREN AND SPORT PSYCHOLOGY

Patsy Tremayne & Bob Tremayne

Children's early experiences in sport will have a major impact on their participation and enjoyment of movement activities throughout their lives. How many unpleasant memories of childhood — being left on the bench for the final, the embarrassment of one's clumsy execution of a skill that seemed so easy for everyone else — have adversely influenced an individual's later participation? How many hours of adult enjoyment, whether spent playing a social game of tennis or golf or otherwise maintaining an acceptable standard of health and wellbeing, have derived from rewarding childhood experiences?

Sport, incorporating play, leisure and physical education, affects children's development in a number of ways. Many of these are related to physical development, but there are social, intellectual and emotional effects that also need to be recognised. The subject of sport for children is not without its problems. This chapter considers children's development in the area of movement and analyses some of the emerging issues associated with it.

CHILDREN'S DEVELOPMENT

The childhood years between ages 3 and 12 are generally characterised by gradual increases in height, weight and muscle mass (Gallahue & Ozmun 1995; Kirchner 1992; Payne & Isaacs 1999). Childhood tends to be a steadying time between the rapid growth stages of infancy and adolescence. The child has the opportunity to become familiar with his or her body and how it operates, learning greater degrees of control and coordination. Bone development is not yet complete; because bones are soft, contact sports and excessive weight bearing should be avoided. In this pre-puberty stage, there appears to be little difference between boys and girls in size, weight, strength and cardiovascular function. This suggests that there are no physical reasons why boys and girls should not participate in the same sports activities. However, physical fitness and motor tests indicate that boys are stronger and perform better in cardiovascular terms and in motor skills performance (Walkley, Holland, Treloar & Probyn-Smith 1993). These differences may be due to social factors, as boys tend to be more active than girls and are provided with more opportunities to participate in sports.

Children enter this stage with limited movement skills but a desire to move. They have an egocentric view of the world around them, as they lack the experience of other worlds and other viewpoints. They depend to a great extent on caregivers to organise matters and make decisions. Childhood is a period in which opportunities need to be provided for individuals to develop their movement abilities, so they can make decisions for themselves about their participation in activities according to their own needs. It is also a time for them to develop interpersonal skills as they relate to those around them, fostering respect and consideration of others, while at the same time promoting independence and an ability to think for themselves in preparation for the demands of adolescence and adulthood. The availability of opportunities to develop these attributes may depend on cultural and socioeconomic factors. However, optimal conditions for children's development need to involve sound nutritional practices, safe and appropriate exercise activities, and a supportive environment (Gallahue & Ozmun 1995; Kirchner 1992).

Factors affecting motor skills acquisition

Motor skills development usually follows the sequential pattern set out in table 20.1.

TABLE 20.1 Motor skills development from birth to late childhood

Babyhood	Early childhood	Middle childhood	Late childhood
1 month – 2 years	3–7 years	8–9 years	10–12 years
Rudimentary skills such as sitting, crawling and standing	Fundamental movement skills such as walking, running, skipping, stretching, throwing, catching and striking	Refined movement skills combining movements such as running and jumping, landing and rolling, and dribbling and kicking	Specific sports and specialised skills such as running, long jumping, and performing specific dance steps and gymnastic movements.

(*Source:* Adapted from Kirchner 1992, p. 24)

As children get older, the level of difficulty of the movements they perform increases and their motor skills generally improve. However, this development is affected by a number of factors. Some individual differences between children and their ability to move are based on genetic attributes — the abilities they have inherited from their parents, and their 'readiness' to learn (Gallahue & Ozmun 1995). Environmental influences have an increasing effect on development. Opportunities to practise, encouragement from significant others, feedback, motivation, enjoyment and a sense of competence are examples of environmental factors (Magill 1993; Walkley et al. 1993; Wankel & Kreisel 1985a). Correct approaches to teaching and coaching are a significant factor in motor skills acquisition. Hay and Cote (1998) indicated the importance of teachers and coaches recognising the difficulty of tasks and the skills of the learner, and then organising and implementing instruction appropriately. To achieve this, teachers and coaches need to control the attention of the learner by using cues and by limiting external distractions. In this way tasks are made simpler and practices are so organised that the learner accommodates the demands and achieves successful outcomes.

Such factors highlight the importance of school programs in movement education, especially in the light of evidence that the best times to learn motor skills are the preschool and primary years (Walkley et al. 1993). Schools play a vital role in children's motor skills development; for some children, it is their only experience of physical activity. However, the school situation is not without problems, and this issue will be returned to in the discussions about children and physical activity.

Psychological and sociological considerations

Psychological and sociological considerations regarding motor skills acquisition also need to be considered at this stage. Children are moving from a dependence on caregivers to the relative independence of the peer group (Kirchner 1992; Spink 1990). At this stage social play and games provide situations that are crucially important to children's sense of identity and their ability to socialise (Harter 1978). This period may also be important for moral development, and games are especially effective in providing models of social interaction and 'fair play'. Team games, in particular, provide an opportunity for children to share power and to experience collective achievements. In fact, part of the appeal and security of games organised by children lies in the fact that there is no fear or loss of love because of performance — they are simply fun (Orlick 1978; Spink & Longhurst 1990). They also provide children with opportunities in which they need to place the team goals above their personal goals. This represents a significant development from the egocentricity of earlier childhood years. Team participants learn to share tasks, help others, abide by rules, and recognise strengths and weaknesses — all skills that are necessary in the adolescent and adult worlds (Payne & Isaacs 1999).

Participation in sports and the ability to perform competently have important significance for children in their peer relationships. Many boys enjoy higher peer status as a result of their athletic ability, and with this come more opportunities to fulfil leadership positions and to develop and maintain friendships (Weiss, Smith & Theeboom 1996). On the other hand, some children endure the painful experience of 'picking teams', in which the less competent are continually left until the end and are often disregarded in the others' haste to get on with the game. In many cases, the child who most needs the opportunity to be active and involved is the one who is either left out or 'cut' first.

WHY DO CHILDREN MOVE?

Children move in order to bring organisation to the multitude of stimuli with which they are confronted. From this organisation individuals can start to exert a degree of control over their environment in order to make life more comfortable and efficient (Gallahue & Ozmun 1995).

Infants' efforts at stabilisation (sitting and standing), locomotion and manipulation represent early attempts to come to terms with their environment. These rudimentary skills lead to the fundamental movement abilities of childhood that see children running, jumping, throwing and catching. Movement becomes much more vigorous as children become more competent and controlled in their execution of motor skills. This more vigorous movement often takes the form of play, an important developmental activity for children. Play allows them to handle new stimuli, practise new skills and interact with new people, all on their own terms and at their own pace.

Biological explanations for play and physical activity in children are inconclusive (McManus 2000). However, as is discussed later in the chapter, concerns have been raised about children's physical activity levels and the consequent adverse health effects in later life.

CHILDREN'S PARTICIPATION IN SPORT

Sport takes many forms in our society. It is almost impossible to live one's life in modern times without being exposed to media coverage of elite sports, with their highly organised competitions, personalities, sponsors' messages and dressing-room stories. For most people, reading about it in the newspaper, glimpsing it on the TV news, taking part in 'expert' discussions with friends or attending a game at the stadium are as close to participation at this level of sports as they will get. Nonetheless, many people identify strongly with a sport, club or identity, and maintain an interest in what is happening at the professional level. Many follow sports activities in other parts of the world, encouraged by international television coverage and commentary. Some continue to participate in sports, sustaining the competence they have enjoyed for years, or embracing new activities as their interests and status change. Levels of performance become increasingly difficult to maintain, but interest and enjoyment in participation often remain.

Despite our society's obsession with sport, participation rates appear to be reasonably low. Using data from the 1996–97 Australian Bureau of Statistics survey, Dale (1998) showed that only 25.8 per cent of people living in New South Wales participated in organised sport or physical activity, compared with a national figure of 29 per cent. As one would expect, participation rates declined with age, with 61 per cent of 5- to 14-year-olds playing sport, while only 17 per cent of those aged over 65 were involved. In a study of reasonably affluent and mainly white college students in the United States, Martin (1997) found that just over half of them had maintained participation in sports throughout their high-school years.

Children, too, are exposed through the media to a wide variety of sporting experiences from a range of countries and competitive settings, and enjoy a similar spectrum of participation. Some children are involved at an elite level, experiencing intensive training, manifesting high degrees of competence and performing in competitive situations. Others take part in less demanding settings more in keeping with their skills and/or commitment. Some have little involvement in sports activities.

Payne and Isaacs (1999) believed American youth's participation in sports to be increasing because of the trend towards involvement at an earlier age, an increase in female participants, an expansion of the range of options available and an increase in opportunities for involvement by people with disabilities.

Some benefits

It is traditionally accepted that sport has a number of benefits for children. Sporting organisations, parents and children use this argument to justify participation in sports. The European Federation of Sport Psychology (FEPSAC) (1996) summarised a number of these benefits in its position statement on children's participation. Sport presents opportunities to experience enjoyment, to improve skills and to enhance one's physical development. Children can also build on their personal qualities of initiative, independence and self-esteem, their social attributes of cooperation and relating to others, and their moral development in recognising and accepting common rules of behaviour through sports involvement.

Alderman and Wood's (1976) early study of incentive motivation found that children enjoyed sport for friendship, the personal satisfaction of performing skills and the excitement of being involved. Wankel and Kreisel (1985b) later identified improving, performing and testing skills as important features of children's participation in sport. These intrinsic reasons for continued participation — having fun, improving competence and performing good skills — appear to be more important to children than winning trophies or pleasing others (Payne & Isaacs 1999). Friendship also appears to be an important factor. In a study of a group of 8- to 16-year-olds and their relationships in sport, Weiss, Smith and Theeboom (1996) identified 12 'friendship dimensions', including companionship, self-esteem enhancement, emotional support and conflict resolution. Weiss and Smith (1999) cited research that indicated that playing sports promoted the development of friendships, general wellbeing and positive outlooks, while poor sports performance hindered friendship formation.

RESEARCH STUDY

(to be marked out of 50)

Conduct your own research study to investigate participation and non-participation by children in sport. Your task is to:

- survey 10 participants regarding their participation or non-participation in sport as a child
- present your findings to the group.

Your presentation must outline the research methodology, such as design of survey questions, selection of respondents, characteristics of respondents and analysis of data. (Methodology is marked out of 20.)

What implications can be drawn from the study? (Implications are marked out of 20.)

How will you present your findings to the group? (Presentation is marked out of 10.)

Some problems

There are some concerns about children's participation in sport because of potentially detrimental effects on their development. The physical risks, the psychological stress that accompanies competitive sports, the emphasis on winning and the resultant disappointments of losing, and the roles of coaches, teachers and parents are issues to be considered in conjunction with the benefits of sport.

Physical risks

Children are exposed to physical risks as a result of events that arise directly from the field of play. These events may include injuries caused by tackles, incorrect landings and/or collisions with equipment. Injury may also arise during preparation for participation as a result of poor training techniques and/or overuse. Payne and Isaacs (1999) provided a summary of some American sports and their injury statistics relating to children. Injury rates were considered to be fairly low for children aged 8 to 15 — for example, only 5 per cent in American football, and soccer too was considered 'a fairly safe activity' (p. 326). In Australia, sporting violence and injuries may catch the headlines, but there is a feeling that the problems are perhaps overemphasised. The chief executive of Sports Medicine Australia argued that 'playing any organized sport is still safer than playing in the backyard' (Arndt 1999, p. 8).

Overuse injuries appear to be increasing. It is uncertain whether this is due to the increase in participation among children generally, increase at an earlier age, and/or specialisation in such 'early-achiever' activities as gymnastics, dance and swimming (Hammond 1994; Payne & Isaacs 1999; Robinson 1996). Such concerns have serious significance for training techniques and the design of training programs for children in schools and the community.

Stress

The physical demands on children's bodies may be accompanied by stress on their psychological development. The highly organised and competitive nature of some children's participation in sport may be a significant source of stress, especially in light of the evidence mentioned earlier concerning children's intrinsic motives for involvement. External expectations from coaches, teachers and parents can impose pressure on children involved in sport. Some children are challenged and motivated by participation in sport, but it is generally those who already have a reasonable level of proficiency that fall into this category. What of the others? Arguments concerning the role of competitive sport in schools arise with regular frequency. Judith Whelan (1996) raised some of the issues in a Sydney newspaper article:

> Some argue that competitive school sport bolsters the outdated male — an Anglo-Saxon-dominated ethos of the bronzed and brawny Australian hero. They also argue that too much emphasis on competitive sport leaves the untalented with low self-esteem and the tendency to shy away from sports because they feel they are failures. The result is that these students do not develop an exercise and relaxation program to take with them through life.
>
> There is little debate about the purpose of school sport. Advocates of competition at all levels and supporters of more lifestyle-based fitness training in schools see sport of some sort as vital to students' whole growth.
>
> They also agree that a school sport program should set up a child with a life-long approach to physical activity. What they disagree about is how those aims can be best achieved.

Roles of coaches, teachers and parents

However this debate is resolved, some children experience psychological stress due to the demands of competitive situations. This problem has been compounded by the emergence in recent years of the phenomenon of the 'ugly parent' and 'ugly coach', revealing aggressive behaviours of spectators at children's sports events. The Australian Sports Commission has attempted to tackle this issue by developing codes of conduct for stakeholders in children's sport and training courses for officials in 'harassment-free' sport (Aussie Sport Consultant 1998; Howell 1996; Lamont 2000).

These issues are of special significance for the role of coaches, teachers and parents in children's sports. Factors that coaches, teachers and parents need to carefully scrutinise in their own involvement in children's sport include providing a model of behaviour that they wish children to follow; exhibiting qualities of fairness and respect for others; accepting decisions that may be difficult to understand in the heat of the moment; and formulating plans that are appropriate and meaningful to all participants.

Some efforts have been made to deal with these issues in Australia. For instance, the Aussie Sports program, introduced in 1986 and enthusiastically embraced by primary schools, involved a series of modified sports with adapted equipment, playing fields, time arrangements and rules (Dry 1993). The program was designed to respond to the needs of children between the ages of 7 and 12, and to accommodate their participation in child-friendly activities. It addressed many of the criticisms levelled at children's participation in sport, such as inappropriate activities, injury risks and stressful situations, and community coaches and teachers were assisted in presenting activities to children.

In some cases, the Aussie Sports program took the place of physical education programs in schools (Tinning 1992). The fact that primary school teachers tended to be generalists (as opposed to specialist teachers dealing with specific curriculum areas) meant that many of them lacked expertise in movement education, and ready-made programs like Aussie Sports were used to overcome this shortcoming. These programs may have provided opportunities for children to be active, but they did not teach fundamental motor skills or correct poor movement ability. The problem was compounded by the reduction of time devoted to the curriculum area in teacher education degree courses and the growing demands on school time of basic skills testing in English and mathematics. All these factors raise the issue of the need for specialist physical education teachers in primary schools, an issue that has surfaced frequently in the past 20 years in Australia (Blanksby 1995).

Participation in sport by children needs to be considered in the context of the development of the concept of physical activity in recent times.

CHILDREN AND PHYSICAL ACTIVITY

Darlison used the term *physical activity* in its broadest sense, referring to 'the entire spectrum of "bodily movements" that each person can undertake in daily life, ranging from normal, active living conditions to "intentional", moderate physical activities, to structured and repetitive physical exercises, to physical exercises, to physical fitness and training sessions, to collective sport activities, including both high performance sport and leisure and recreational sports' (Darlison 2000, p. 11). In the educational literature there has been a shift towards use of the term to describe children's movement in schools and community settings. This usage reflects a change in thinking about the role of programs in these settings. There is still (and always will be) a strong emphasis on competitive sports. Many schools and community clubs receive a lot of publicity and recognition for the successes they enjoy. This emphasis mirrors the importance that the media place on such sports. However, there is a concern with programs that stress the 'product' (winning teams, championships and personal bests) as compared with those that develop the 'process' (promotion of regular physical activity). As Ernst, Pangrazi and Corbin (1998) put it, 'there was a shift in focus from fitness outcomes (product) toward regular physical activity (process)' (p. 29).

In line with this shift, the subject of Physical Education in schools is less dominated by sports activities and physical fitness tests, some of which are inappropriate and some of which are exceedingly demanding (Pangrazi 2000). Instead, the subject focuses increasingly on encouraging students to learn the skills needed to lead healthy lifestyles, according to their cultural and socioeconomic situations. In the New South Wales education system, the subject adopted the title Personal Development, Heath and Physical Education (PDHPE). Its aim 'is to develop in each student the knowledge and understanding, skills and values and attitudes needed to lead healthy, active and fulfilling lives. In doing so, the syllabus will form the basis for students to adopt a responsible and productive role in society' (Board of Studies NSW, 1999, p. 8).

This aim is reflected in a syllabus that deals with growth and development, relationships, health, safety, movement and the fostering of skills of problem-solving, communication, interacting and decision making. Movement is one part of a much broader educational lifestyle approach. Students' health is now considered from a holistic perspective, incorporating self-esteem, physical fitness and movement skills, and an ability to make informed healthy lifestyle decisions. It has relevance for all students, irrespective of their cultural, socioeconomic and ability backgrounds.

It should be pointed out that such a development in the approach to movement (and sport is included in this general term) has not been without opposition. There are still those who would prefer a more product-oriented approach in order to encourage and recognise those who can perform and achieve.

What are the benefits of physical activity for children?

Increased levels of adult physical activity are linked to reduced risk of such conditions as coronary heart disease, stroke, osteoporosis and some cancers (Brown & Brown 1996; Pangrazi 2000). It is therefore in the interests of individual and community health to encourage more physical activity. Concerns about this situation are seen in State and national efforts to encourage increased rates of exercise that foster improved individual and community wellbeing. In cold economic terms, Brown and Brown state that daily health-care savings of $6.46 million would be achieved 'if an additional 40 per cent of the Australian population undertook regular, moderate and effective exercise' (1996, p. 19). Using a broad definition of sport and recreational physical activities to include, for example, aerobics, walking and cycling, a National Centre for Culture and Recreation Statistics (NCCRS) survey in 1999–2000 found that only 55 per cent of Australians had participated in the previous 12 months (Australian Bureau of Statistics 2000).

One strategy is to encourage children to be more active. As some of the risk factors for adult medical conditions start in childhood (Brown & Brown 1996), and as activity rates in childhood are reflected in adulthood, it would seem logical to tackle the problem at the earliest possible stage (Pangrazi 2000).

There are immediate health benefits in physical activity for children. Brown and Brown (1996) indicated lower blood pressure and reduced blood lipids, leading to a lowering of the risk of cardiovascular disease, diabetes and obesity. The same authors cited research evidence regarding increased self-esteem in more active children, along with reduced risks of drug use and teenage pregnancy.

To achieve these benefits, children need to participate in regular physical activity. The impact of social factors on levels of participation has been noted. These factors include the restrictions urbanisation has placed on outdoor play, the number of leisure hours children spend in front of TV and computer screens, and the expense involved in some activities. Children's motor skill levels are another area of concern. These factors may be connected — children don't participate because their skills are not very good; children's skills are not very good because they don't participate.

Walkley et al. (1993) tested six fundamental motor skills in more than 1000 primary school children. The results showed an alarmingly low standard of performance in these skills, a marked inferiority of performance by girls in comparison to boys, and, in some cases, a deterioration of standards between year 6 (approximately 11 years of age) and year 8 students (approximately 13 years of age). Such results have significance for the individual's confidence in participating and relate to children's reasons for choosing to be involved or dropping out of organised sports (Ulrich 1987, cited in Walkley et al. 1993). Brown and Brown (1996) referred to New South Wales and Tasmanian studies that raise similar concerns about children's skill levels.

A study conducted by Booth, Macaskill et al. (1997), involving year 2 (approximately 7 years of age) to year 10 (approximately 15 years of age) students, reinforced the need to encourage children to improve their fundamental skills:

> For all six fundamental motor skills (with the exception of the run), the proportion of boys and girls in all year groups who displayed mastery of a skill did not exceed 40 per cent. This finding indicates only a moderate level of fundamental motor skills mastery among school students in New South Wales. It is reasonable to assume that most students, given appropriate learning opportunities, would be able to master these (and other) skills before the end of primary school. Fundamental motor skills mastery is integral to satisfying participation in a wide range of activities and may contribute substantially to improved self-esteem. (Booth et al. 1997, p. 62)

However, Pangrazi (2000) issued a note of caution about conclusions, stating that today's children are more unfit than earlier generations. American comparisons showed that children's performances in fitness tests are similar to past standards, but Pangrazi proposed the nature of the tests and teacher attitudes as explanations for some of these conclusions. Wright (1997) also suggested a need to consider the nature of the tests, especially when examining gender differences.

The movement towards emphasising physical activity, whether in school timetables or in community programs, in place of elite sport activities is an attempt to enable children to access the health benefits available as a result of participation. This is not to say that elite sport should be rejected; indeed, it has an extremely important role to play for those individuals who choose to be involved. Physical activity programs, however, need to provide meaningful and appropriate physical, social and intellectual opportunities for all children. In this way talented, obese, uncoordinated, capable, cooperative, unpopular, disabled, culturally diverse children — *all* children — will be challenged and stimulated to become involved in physical activity and to gain some of the benefits of this involvement.

PSYCHOLOGICAL SKILLS TRAINING FOR CHILDREN

Through involvement in physical activity children show improved physical health, fitness and psychological adjustment (Horn & Claytor 1993). These benefits are likely to occur more readily in unstructured physical activity and do not automatically transfer to a competitive sport setting. Children learn from significant adults and peers, and over time may assimilate both positive and negative behaviours and attitudes. For beneficial psychological, physical and social behaviours to occur in sport, they need to be taught and reinforced. With the accumulation of scientific evidence and the increasing body of knowledge about the growing child derived from various disciplinary areas (including the sport sciences, psychology, education and sociology), existing sport programs can be effectively restructured and conducted in ways that assist in the fulfilment of positive outcomes for children.

There has been considerable research on the factors that lead to positive or negative psychological outcomes in sport and exercise participation. These factors can be divided into two main areas. Environmental influences include self-concept, feedback and reinforcement, coaching and parental behaviours, mastery versus performance or ego orientation, modelling, intrinsic motivation and enjoyment. Individual learning strategies include goal setting, self-confidence, attribution retraining, self-talk, arousal regulation, imagery, anxiety management, coping skills, self-monitoring of progress, focusing/refocusing skills and relaxation.

Environmental influences

If a mental training program is to be effective with children, the interaction that takes place between the child and the environment needs to be taken into account (Danish & Hale 1981; Weiss 1991). Adults should be encouraged to focus on the desirable qualities or behaviours to be attained by children through sport, rather than on the outcomes of the sport. For instance, the comparisons children make with other children, the inferences they make based on the reactions of others and the direct feedback they receive from significant others provide important information that is incorporated into the developing self-concept of the child.

Physical activity has been shown to improve self-concept. For instance, Ebbeck and Gibbons (1998) investigated the effectiveness of a team-building program through physical challenges in 10- to 12-year-old physical education students in grades 6 and 7. Results indicated that the team-building program was effective in that children in the treatment group were significantly higher than the control group on perceptions of athletic competence, physical appearance, social acceptance and global self-worth.

According to Horn and Hasbrook (1987), young children rely primarily on feedback and reinforcement from significant adults such as coaches in order to judge their competency at sport, and it is important that this means of communication to children be evaluated regularly. Most young athletes have their first sport experiences in programs staffed by volunteer coaches, and these experiences have not always taken place in healthy psychological environments. In order to address this problem and increase the likelihood of youngsters having positive sporting experiences, several coaching education programs were developed during the 1980s and 1990s in the United States, Canada and Australia. These programs provide information for beginning coaches on sport psychology, sports medicine, physiology in the developing child, and specific sport skills and strategies.

However, coaching and parental behaviours are potent sources of anxiety for children involved in sport, because of perceived demands and expectations, negative evaluations, possible parental misbehaviour on the sidelines, and sometimes the parents' vicarious needs for the child to perform well. Strean (1995) considered how varying environmental contexts may affect coaching behaviour and its consequent effects on children. By using field observations, and formal and informal interviews with youth coaches, he examined contextual factors such as time, the role of parents, spectator location and rules. By examining coaches' comments about their work with children, and observing them during training sessions and at competitions, he found that, irrespective of the coaches' values and beliefs, the contexts in which they operated exercised significant influence on their coaching and might have a follow-on effect on children's sporting experiences.

A mastery versus performance orientation in coaching is also likely to have differing effects on children's sporting experiences (Duda 1992). For instance, a coaching style that encourages a performance- or ego-oriented climate, with the emphasis on winning, can lead to a child's increased worry and decreased enjoyment, and may well promote avoidance of or withdrawal from sport. A mastery-oriented climate in which the child is encouraged to concentrate on personal improvement may lead to higher levels of enjoyment, greater perceived competence and increased satisfaction.

Theeboom, De Knop and Weiss (1995) investigated the effectiveness of a performance- versus a mastery-oriented teaching program on children's motor skills development and psychological responses. Results indicated significantly higher levels of enjoyment, greater perceived competence and intrinsic motivation, and better motor skills of children in the mastery-oriented group, compared with the performance-oriented group. This study demonstrated that children are more likely to have positive experiences while learning new motor skills if there is a mastery motivational climate.

In addition to providing a mastery motivational climate, aspects of psychological skills training that may be useful for children include the development of a positive attitude to competition. By teaching youngsters to understand which aspects of competition are and are not in their control, and then helping them to focus on personally controllable goals, competition may be more enjoyable and less stressful. Weiss and Chaumeton (1992) concluded that children who remain in sport have high levels of perceived competence, whereas children who drop out of sport have lower perceptions of their abilities to learn and/or perform sport skills. Therefore it is essential that children learn to focus on aspects of competition that are within their control, and are encouraged to evaluate their own performances based on personal levels of improvement rather than outcomes such as winning or losing.

Modelling is another environmental factor that can have a profound effect on the development of motor skills, especially during childhood and adolescence. Children respond well to role models and, if chosen wisely, these models can have a marked positive psychological effect on children's self-perceptions, such as competence, control and confidence. These role models may be other children, athletes, coaches, teachers or parents (Gabbard 1992). As Orlick and McCaffrey (1991) pointed out, 'If well chosen, a role model can set a positive example to emulate with respect to mental skills, physical skills, a healthy perspective, persistence, or anything else one might want to pursue' (p. 332).

Weiss (1991) identified mastery models as an effective method of increasing physical proficiency and enhancing psychological skills, and also proposed the use of coping models as a way to target the learning of both psychological and physical skills. The coping model, she suggested, is one who starts out by displaying, both verbally and behaviourally, fears and uncertainties similar to those of the observing children. With instruction, this model gradually exhibits the ability to overcome these negative feelings and perform the skill effectively. This conveys to the children watching that with practice the skill can be learned; at the same time they are provided with motivating and confidence-enhancing skills.

Self-regulated individual learning strategies

Most mental skills training has been targeted towards elite athletes. While their physical skills are already well developed, coaches perceive that the use of psychological skills can help elite athletes to enhance or fine-tune performance (Weinberg & Williams 1998). However, some authors have proposed that mental skills training should also be introduced for children (Orlick & McCaffrey 1991; Weinberg & Williams 1998; Weiss 1991; Vealey 1988). This is an important issue, particularly when one considers that children engage in sport at an impressionable time in their lives, and their sporting experiences during this time will affect their attitudes towards physical activity throughout the life span. Well-planned sport psychology interventions are an opportunity to positively nurture children's personal development in competitive sport and to facilitate their growth in other areas of their life by generalising the use of these mental skills. There are several frameworks that can be adopted for the selection of interventions in sport psychology.

Vealey (1988) described a model that differentiates between skills, which are the desired qualities or behaviours, and the methods used to attain these skills. Vealey distinguished between *foundation skills* (e.g. volition, self-awareness, self-esteem and self-confidence), *performance skills* (e.g. optimal physical and mental arousal, and optimal attention) and *facilitative skills* (e.g. interpersonal and lifestyle management skills). Similarly, *foundation methods* include physical practice and education, while *mental training methods* include goal setting, imagery, physical relaxation and thought control.

Using a structured model such as this would enable a trained coach or teacher implementing mental skills training to focus on the skill to be acquired and to choose a method or methods by which this skill could be attained. These methods can be taught to children using simple verbal instructions, embellished with games and meaningful imagery, and include an element of fun. Verbal strategies used by coaches and teachers frequently include words that focus attention on the task (e.g. the child saying aloud 'step–hit' when practising a forehand in tennis).

Danish, Petitpas and Hale (1992) described a multidisciplinary developmental–educational model of intervention called Life Developmental Intervention (LDI) that fits the needs of practitioners from varied backgrounds and disciplines. The model looks at change from life situations (known as critical life events); the person's previous resources, level of preparation and past history in dealing with similar events; and the differing outcomes related to the critical life event. Practitioners using this model help the person prepare for the event, contend with the event during its occurrence and cope with it after its occurrence. Enhancement strategies used before the event include helping anticipate life events and teaching skills to cope with future events. LDI appears to be particularly useful for children and adolescents as it was developed out of a life-span human development framework that emphasised continuous growth and change.

Goal setting is a central teaching strategy of LDI, which is seen as a source of motivation and personal competence. Danish, Mash, Howard et al. (1992, cited in Smith & Smoll 1996) developed a goal-setting program specifically adapted for children, the training including games and imagery designed to be fun. According to Smith and Smoll (1996), this approach to skills training adapted to the child's level may encourage the development of important mental skills that could be transferred from one domain to another — for instance, from an educational setting to a sport or social setting.

Conversely, this approach, using a sport setting, may also promote the use of mental skills among youngsters resistant to life skills programs within the school setting. For instance, Danish, Nellen and Owens (1996) designed a sports-based life skills intervention program that teaches adolescents to apply a variety of skills to their athletic performance and to learn how to transfer these skills to other, non-sport settings. It was believed that youngsters would be more likely to practise mental skills in a sport setting in order to improve their sport, rather than in a school classroom when learning life skills.

Behavioural techniques are also a useful framework for psychological interventions with children. Smith, Smoll and Christensen (1996) reviewed a number of operant intervention studies, demonstrating that teaching coaches how to consistently apply behavioural techniques for improving and maintaining positive sporting behaviour can be very effective in enhancing children's performance and skill acquisition. These techniques include the use of shaping procedures (such as intermittent positive reinforcement and immediate rewards for progress), goal setting, behavioural contracting, modelling procedures, videotaped feedback and self-monitoring of behaviour. For example, Critchfield and Vargas (1991) investigated the impact of self-recording on the attendance and practice efficiency of young swimmers by observing them under four different conditions. Introduced sequentially, these conditions were no intervention, instructions to swim, instructions to self-monitor, and instructions to graph the results of their self-monitoring. At the same time, there was little or no feedback by the coach during any of these conditions. Results indicated that the third condition, self-monitoring, led to greater practice efficiency (more practice laps) than the other conditions.

There has been an increased international awareness of the usefulness of mental skills training for children. The school systems in Sweden (Solin 1991), and to a lesser extent in South Australia (P Wooller 1993, personal communication), have incorporated the teaching of relaxation, stress management, goal setting and imagery in order to improve physical fitness, self-esteem and self-confidence in relation to physical activity. Orlick (1990) and Orlick and McCaffrey (1991) have described the potential benefits of mental skills training for young children. They reported that mental training had been in effect in selected sport settings for approximately 20 years in Canada, and that a mental skills program using games and play has been introduced into elementary schools. The key elements of this program include the use of simple, concrete strategies, individualised and positive approaches, enjoyment, involvement of parents and the use of role models.

Orlick and McCaffrey (1991) also adapted aspects of their mental training program in sport for children fighting to overcome life-threatening illnesses. These children are taught relevant mental skills and positive perspectives in order to enhance their quality of living. Successful strategies include relaxation (e.g. pretending to feel like jello when about to have an injection); setting daily and long-term goals that are meaningful to the child; learning to cope during unpleasant procedures (e.g. through the use of music, personalised scripts, videos or imagery); and learning how to focus or refocus (e.g. putting worry in a matchbox or a tree).

Several empirical studies have tested the use of self-regulated individual learning strategies in children. Recent sport studies include goal setting for speed skaters (Wanlin, Hrycaiko, Martin & Mahon 1997), the use of imagery for table tennis players (Zhang, Ma, Orlick & Zitzelsberger 1992), and video modelling and imagery for tennis players (Atienza, Balaguer & Garcia Merita 1998).

The purpose of Wanlin et al.'s study was to assess the effectiveness of a goal-setting package on objective and subjective measures of speed skating performance in girls aged 12 to 17 years. Results indicated that, during training, laps and drills completed increased, while off-task behaviours decreased. Racing times obtained in practice and competition also improved. In the study by Zhang et al. (1992), the appropriateness of mental training for 7- to 10-year-old children playing table tennis was investigated. It was found that children who were given sessions in mental imagery, relaxation and video observation experienced significantly greater improvement in the accuracy and technical quality of their shots than children in the other two comparison groups. One group was given only the video observation component, and the control group was given no intervention. In the latter study, Atienza, Balaguer and Garcia Merita (1998) investigated the effects of video modelling and imagery training on tennis service performance in 12 young female tennis players aged between 9 and 12 years. The children were divided into three groups: a physical practice group; a physical practice/video-modelling group; and a physical practice/video modelling/imagery group. Results indicated that there was no significant difference between the two groups who were given video-modelling and video-modelling/imagery in addition to the physical practice. However, the tennis serve for participants in these two groups was significantly better than for the physical practice only group.

CASE STUDY

John is a 12-year-old swimmer competing successfully in sprint events at State level. His coach wants him to swim in the longer events, but John has a fear of competing in anything over 200 m. 'I'm scared I won't finish.' After chatting for a while, John divulged that three years ago, when he was nine, he swallowed water on the last turn in a 100 m race and struggled to breathe for the rest of the lap. He collapsed at the end in tears, very frightened by the experience. 'I just couldn't breathe — it was real scary.'

John later mentioned that he breathes very noisily when he is swimming time trials or races, and other kids have often remarked on it. I asked him to replicate his noisy breathing when he is really swimming hard — it was obvious while watching that his throat and neck muscles were very tense. We talked at length about his swimming since he had had that frightening experience, and after a while John realised that the fear of being unable to breathe when he swallowed water three years ago was still affecting his performance. 'Now I think about it, I guess it's in the back of my mind every time I race. I'm okay in the sprints, but I'm scared of longer events.'

Over the next two sessions we worked on breathing and relaxation techniques, imagery and specific cue words to encourage John to physically relax his neck muscles while swimming. There was an immediate improvement in his breathing technique and this, according to his mother and his coach, became more consistent over time when racing or doing time trials. Eventually John's fear of competing in the longer events subsided.

An earlier study by Wrisberg and Anshel (1989) investigated the effect of cognitive strategies on the free throw shooting performance of boys aged 10 to 12 years attending a sports camp. Results indicated that imagery and arousal regulation strategies were used effectively by young athletes to enhance performance.

Mental skills training in schools

There is an increasing emphasis on integrating personal development and health into physical education programs in schools. In these programs the focus is on personal growth and change, and gaining control over lifestyle, rather than just on skill development and performance enhancement. This focus provides an opportunity to introduce mental skills training by which children learn to develop positive attitudes towards competition in sport and other lifestyle activities.

Williams (1986) has noted that almost all coaches of elite athletes in Eastern European countries have been taught the use of mental skills training, as they have long been seen as key people in the process. In Australia coaches certified by the Australian Sports Commission have sport psychology included in their training programs, although training in the use of mental skills strategies is not always specifically provided. Some of the programs simply give an overview of the benefits of sport psychology.

Universities and colleges that have teacher education and sport science programs are appropriate settings in which to teach basic mental skills training because of the trend towards integration of personal development with physical education. Vealey (1988) reported that there is support in North America for this type of delivery system to be made available to college athletes and coaches. There appears to be a growing need for people other than sport psychologists to implement basic mental skills training. For instance, Smith and Johnson (1990) developed a consultation model along these lines that was used successfully in professional baseball.

Coaches and physical educators trained in psychological techniques and strategies would be the most appropriate people to teach mental skills training in schools, as these people often work full time in positions in which they advise and counsel youngsters in sport. In Australia there is an increase in the number of sports and performing arts high schools that specifically cater for talented children. These schools have special programs integrated into flexible timetables in order that children can do extra training in school time. Professional development is also encouraged for staff in the coaching and performing arts areas. As part of that development, counsellors and physical education teachers with a psychology background are being encouraged to enrol in accredited training programs in sport psychology while continuing to work at the schools.

FUTURE DIRECTIONS

There is a growing awareness of the importance of sport psychology for all children, elite and non-elite, in schools and the community. This increased awareness should encourage the development of physical activity and competitive sporting programs to cater for the physical, intellectual, social and psychological needs of all children.

Schools are developing programs that emphasise healthy lifestyle skills. The Australian Sports Commission and other, overseas organisations are introducing sport psychology to the training programs for coaches, and community organisations are catering for the psychological needs of their participants. However, qualified sport psychologists cannot satisfy these demands without assistance. Basic mental skills training for teachers and coaches is a way to overcome this strain on demand. Children are likely to have more effective, enjoyable and successful experiences if they are given the opportunity to participate regularly in a structured mental skills training program adjusted to their developmental level. In this way, children can receive psychological training that will help them to maximise their performance not only in the sport but in everyday settings.

CONCLUSIONS

Children must be treated differently from adults in physical movement training, which should reflect their developmental stage. They also need to be treated as individuals who range from the motivated and talented to the more leisure-oriented.

To provide the best opportunities for physical, social, emotional and intellectual development, the psychology of the child must be considered. Environmental factors that influence positive psychological outcomes and enhance children's enjoyment of physical activity must also be considered. The professional development of teachers and coaches in basic mental skills training would allow ongoing opportunities for children to develop their skills both in sporting performance and general living.

SUMMARY

This chapter provided a review of the existing research in the area of sport psychology and children. It examined some of the psychological and sociological factors affecting children's development from the years 3 to 12. The diverse reasons for children's involvement in sport were presented, and some of the benefits and problems were analysed. Physical activity was placed in the context of healthy living. Specific mental skills training for children was considered, taking into account some of the environmental influences and self-regulated individual learning strategies involved. Some frameworks and research studies were presented, and mental skills training in schools was discussed. The value of sport psychology was placed in the context of children's participation in enjoyable, meaningful and appropriate activity in sport and life generally.

 REVIEW QUESTIONS

1   What is the sequential pattern in motor development from birth to adulthood? Outline the distinctive features of each of the stages.

2   What are some of the benefits and risks associated with children's participation in sport?

3   What attempts have been made to increase the benefits and minimise the risks associated with children's participation in sport?

4   Explain how the physical activity approach promotes a healthy lifestyle.

5   Describe one of the models used for mental skills training.

6   Describe an empirical study that has tested the use of self-regulated individual learning strategies in children.

7   Give two examples of ways in which imagery can be made meaningful for young children.

References

Alderman, R & Woods, N 1976, 'An analysis of incentive motivation in young Canadian athletes', *Canadian Journal of Applied Sport Sciences*, 1, 169–76.

Atienza, FL, Balaguer, I & Garcia Merita, ML 1998, 'Video modeling and imaging training on performance of tennis serve of 9 to 12 year old children', *Perceptual and Motor Skills*, 87, 519–29.

Arndt, B 1999, 'Playing safe', *Sydney Morning Herald*, 29 May.

Aussie Sport Consultant 1998, *Codes of behaviour*, Australian Sports Commission, Canberra.

Australian Bureau of Statistics 2000, *National Centre for Culture and Recreation Statistics Survey*, www.abs.gov.au.

Blanksby, B 1995, 'The missing link: primary school physical education specialists', *ACHPER Healthy Lifestyles Journal*, Winter, 21–4.

Board of Studies NSW 1999, *Personal development, health and physical education K–6 syllabus*, Board of Studies NSW, Sydney.

Booth, M, Macaskill, P, McLellan, L, Phongsavan, P, Okely, T, Patterson, J, Wright, J, Bauman, A & Baur, L 1997, *NSW school fitness and physical activity survey 1997: summary*, NSW Department of Education, Sydney.

Brown, W & Brown, P 1996, 'Children, physical activity and better health', *ACHPER Healthy Lifestyles Journal*, 43 (4) 19–24.

Critchfield, TS & Vargas, EA 1991, 'Self-recording, instructions and public self-graphing: effects on swimming in the absence of coach verbal interaction', *Behavior Modification*, 15, 95–112.

Dale, D 1998, 'NSW wields the wooden spoon in a land of sport voyeurs', *Sydney Morning Herald*, 6 February.

Danish, SJ & Hale, BD 1981, 'Toward an understanding of the practice of sport psychology', *Journal of Sport Psychology*, 3, 90–9.

Danish, SJ, Nellen, VC & Owens, SS 1996, 'Teaching life skills through sport: community-based programs for adolescents', in JL Van Raalte & BW Brewer (eds), *Exploring sport and exercise psychology*, American Psychological Association, Washington, DC.

Danish, SJ, Petitpas, AJ & Hale, BD 1992, 'A developmental-educational intervention model of sport psychology', *The Sport Psychologist*, 6, 403–15.

Darlison, E 2000, 'The global relevance of physical activity in the new millennium', *ACHPER Healthy Lifestyles Journal*, 47 (3–4) 10–14.

Dry, J 1993, 'Why modify?', *Aussie Sport Action*, 4 (2) 16–17.

Duda, JL 1992, 'Motivation in sport settings: a goal perspective approach', in GC Roberts (ed.), *Motivation in sport and exercise*, Human Kinetics, Champaign, IL, pp. 47–91.

Ebbeck, V & Gibbons, SL 1998, 'The effect of a team building program on the self-conceptions of Grade 6 and 7 physical education students', *Journal of Sport & Exercise Psychology*, 20, 300–10.

Ernst, M, Pangrazi, R & Corbin, C 1998, 'Physical education: making a transition toward activity', *Journal of Physical Education, Recreation and Dance*, 69 (9) 29–32.

European Federation of Sport Psychology 1996, 'Position statement of the European Federation of Sport Psychology (FEPSAC II): children in sport', *The Sport Psychologist*, 10, 224–6.

Gabbard, C 1992, *Lifelong motor development*, Wm C Brown, Dubuque, IA.

Gallahue, D & Ozmun, J 1995, *Understanding motor development: infants, children, adolescents, adults*, 3rd edn, Wm C Brown, Madison, WI.

Hammond, P 1994, 'Burnt out babes', *Aussie Sport Action*, 5, 10–11.

Harter, S 1978, 'Effectance motivation reconsidered', *Human Development*, 21, 34–64.

Hay, J & Cote, J 1998, 'An interactive model to teach motor skills', *Physical Educator*, 55 (1) 50–7.

Horn, TS & Claytor, RP 1993, 'Developmental aspects of exercise psychology', in P Seraganian (ed.), *Exercise psychology: the influence of physical exercise on psychological processes*, John Wiley & Sons, New York, pp. 299–388.

Horn, TS & Hasbrook, C 1987, 'Psychological characteristics and the criteria children use for self-evaluation', *Journal of Sport Psychology*, 9, 208–21.

Howell, S 1996, 'The good, the bad and the ugly', *Aussie Sport Action*, 1, 10–11.

Kirchner, G 1992, *Physical education for elementary school children*, 8th edn, Wm C Brown, Dubuque, IA.

Lamont, L 2000, 'Blowing the whistle on parents from hell', *Sydney Morning Herald*, 28 October.

McManus, A 2000, 'Physical activity in children: meaning and measurement', *European Journal of Physical Education*, 5, 133–46.

Magill, R 1993, *Motor learning: concepts and applications*, 4th edn, Wm C Brown, Dubuque, IA.

Martin, D 1997, 'Interscholastic sport participation: reasons for maintaining or terminating participation', *Journal of Sport Behavior*, 20, 94–105.

Orlick, T 1978, *The cooperative sport and games book: challenge without competition*, Pantheon, New York.

Orlick, T 1990, *In pursuit of excellence*, Leisure Press, Champaign, IL.

Orlick, T & McCaffrey, N 1991, 'Mental training with children for sport and life', *The Sport Psychologist*, 5, 322–34.

Pangrazi, R 2000, 'Promoting physical activity for youth', *ACHPER Healthy Lifestyles Journal*, 47 (2) 18–21.

Payne, V & Isaacs, L 1999, *Human motor development: a lifespan approach*, 4th edn, Mayfield, Mountain View.

Robinson, M 1996, 'Sport, play and safety', *Aussie Sport Action*, 7, 12–13.

Smith, RE & Johnson, J 1990, 'An organizational empowerment approach to consultation in professional baseball', *The Sport Psychologist*, 4, 347–57.

Smith, RE & Smoll, FL 1996, 'Psychosocial interventions in youth sport', in JL Van Raalte & BW Brewer (eds), *Exploring sport and exercise psychology*, American Psychological Association, Washington, DC.

Smith, RE, Smoll, FL & Christensen, DS 1996, 'Behavioral assessment and interventions in youth sports: a review', *Behavior Modification*, 20, 3–44.

Solin, E 1991, 'Mental training in the Swedish school systems', paper presented at the First World Congress on Mental Training, University of Orebro, Sweden, in T Orlick & N McCaffrey (eds), 'Mental training with children for sport and life', *The Sport Psychologist*, 5, 322–34.

Spink, K 1990, *Give your kids a sporting chance: a guide for parents*, Sun Books, Melbourne.

Spink, K & Longhurst, K 1990, 'Participation motives of Australian boys involved in traditional and modified cricket', *Australian Journal of Science and Medicine in Sport*, 21 (1) 28–31.

Strean, WB 1995, 'Youth sport contexts: coaches' perceptions and implications for intervention', *Journal of Applied Sport Psychology*, 7, 23–37.

Theeboom, M, De Knop, P & Weiss, MR 1995, 'Motivational climate, psychological responses, and motor skill development in children's sport: a field-based intervention study', *Journal of Sport & Exercise Psychology*, 17, 294–311.

Tinning, R 1992, 'On speeches, dreams, and realities: physical education in the year 2001', *ACHPER National Journal*, Summer.

Vealey, R 1988, 'Future directions in psychological skills training', *The Sport Psychologist*, 2, 318–36.

Walkley, J, Holland, B, Treloar, R & Probyn-Smith, H 1993, 'Fundamental motor skill proficiency of children', *ACHPER National Journal*, 40 (3) 11–14.

Wankel, L & Kreisel, P 1985a, 'Methodological considerations in youth sport motivation research: a comparison of open-ended and paired comparison approaches', *Journal of Sport Psychology*, 7, 65–74.

Wankel, L & Kreisel, P 1985b, 'Factors underlying enjoyment of youth sports: sport and age group comparisons', *Journal of Sport Psychology*, 7, 51–64.

Wanlin, C, Hrycaiko, Q, Martin, D & Mahon, M 1997, 'The efficacy of a goal-setting package on the performance of speed skaters', *Journal of Applied Sport Psychology*, 9, 212–28.

Weinberg, RS & Williams, JM 1998, 'Integrating and implementing a psychological skills training program', in JM Williams (ed.), *Applied sport psychology: personal growth to peak performance*, 3rd edn, Mayfield, Mountain View, CA.

Weiss, MR 1991, 'Psychological skill development in children and adolescents', *The Sport Psychologist*, 5, 335–54.

Weiss, MR & Chaumeton, N 1992, 'Motivational orientations in sport', in TS Horn (ed.), *Advances in sport psychology*, Human Kinetics, Champaign, IL, pp. 61–99.

Weiss, M & Smith, A 1999, 'Quality of youth friendships: measurement development and validation', *Journal of Sport & Exercise Psychology*, 21, 145–66.

Weiss, M, Smith, A & Theeboom, M 1996, '"That's what friends are for": children's and teenagers' perceptions of peer relationships in the sport domain', *Journal of Sport & Exercise Psychology*, 18, 347–79.

Whelan, J 1996, 'Winning lessons', *Sydney Morning Herald*, 25 March.

Williams, JM 1986, *Applied sport psychology: personal growth to peak performance*, Mayfield, Palo Alto, CA.

Wright, J 1997, 'Fundamental motor skills testing as problematic practice: a feminist analysis', *ACHPER Healthy Lifestyles Journal*, 44 (4) 18–20.

Wrisberg, CA & Anshel, MH 1989, 'The effect of cognitive strategies on the free throw shooting performance of young athletes', *The Sport Psychologist*, 9, 95–104.

Zhang, L, Ma, Q, Orlick, T & Zitzelsberger, L 1992, 'The effect of mental imagery on performance enhancement with 7–10 year old children', *The Sport Psychologist*, 6, 230–41.

CHAPTER 21

PSYCHOLOGY OF INJURY: THEORY, RESEARCH AND PRACTICE

Trent A Petrie & Frank Perna

Every year millions of athletes, from recreational to competitive levels, are injured (e.g. Kraus & Conroy 1984). Research has suggested that in high schools and colleges, where sport participation is high, more than 30 per cent of student athletes will be injured in any given year and hundreds of millions of dollars will be spent on the treatment of those injuries (Meeuwisse & Fowler 1988; NCAA 1992; Requa 1991). Van Mechelen, Twisk, Molendijk, Blom, Snel and Kemper (1996) found that injury rates were almost five times higher during competitions than during training or practice and while playing unorganised sports. Contact and high-risk sports, such as football, gymnastics, wrestling and soccer, also have been identified as high-risk, with research reporting injury rates two to five times higher than those found in non-contact sports, such as baseball and softball (NCAA 1992). Although initial national injury surveys have consistently found greater incidence of injury among boys than girls (Kraus & Conroy 1984), as women's participation in sports has increased so have their rates of injury, in many instances equalling or exceeding men's (Elias 2001; Menckel & Laflamme 2000). Clearly injuries are a serious and costly health problem for all athletes that, despite improvements in equipment and physical conditioning techniques, has only increased over the years (Bergandi 1985).

Considerable research has focused on why athletes become injured. Van Mechelen, Hlobil and Kemper (1992) suggested that individual factors, such as age, previous injuries, body type and fitness level, and environmental factors, such as type of sport, playing conditions and equipment, play a role in the etiology of injury. For example, a soccer player who is not in top physical condition and is playing in a rainstorm on a field full of holes may be at greater risk for injury than a physically fit athlete who is playing on a level field on a sunny day. Clearly such physical and environmental factors influence an athlete's susceptibility to injury. They do not, however, adequately explain which athletes will be injured and when and in what situations those injuries will occur.

To better understand the complex processes that lead to injury, researchers have considered psychological factors.

Over the past 30 years psychological and social factors (referred to henceforth as *psychosocial factors*) have been implicated in the genesis of physical injuries. Initial investigations in this area focused on the effects of life-event stress, finding that injured football players often experienced higher levels of stress in the year leading up to their season than players who did not become injured (Bramwell, Masuda, Wagner & Holmes 1975; Holmes 1970; Coddington & Troxell 1980; Cryan & Alles 1983). These studies provided important initial information on the relationship of psychosocial variables to injury, yet they were limited by their atheoretical approach and singular focus on life stress. As a result, they failed to consider the complex interplay among psychosocial variables that was likely to underlie athletic injury.

In 1988 Andersen and Williams addressed these limitations and provided direction for future research. They presented a dynamic, multidimensional stress–injury model that suggested the simple, linear relationships defining earlier stress–injury methodologies were insufficient in explaining the injury process. In this model, Andersen and Williams acknowledged the importance of life stress, yet argued that it was only one of three important psychosocial factors to consider. They suggested that in addition to assessing athletes' history of stressors (e.g. life-event stress), researchers also needed to consider personality (e.g. competitive trait anxiety, locus of control) and coping resources (e.g. social support, psychological coping skills). In addition, Andersen and Williams hypothesised that the influence of these factors on athletic injury was not direct. Rather, their effects were mediated through a mechanism they referred to as the 'stress response'. In the end it was the athletes' physiological and attentional responses to acutely stressful situations that would determine whether or not they became injured.

In a recent review of the stress–injury model and related research, Williams and Andersen (1998) provided support for its basic tenets, arguing that it still provided the best way to understand the complex process of athletic injury. Further, they commented that injury prediction generally was enhanced through the consideration of psychosocial variables. Based on this support and other positive reviews (e.g. Williams 2001), we use Andersen and Williams' (1988) theoretical model as the organisational framework for our presentation on the psychology of injury. To begin, we overview the entire model and discuss how these variables interact to increase athletes' injury risk. Next we critically evaluate each of the model's components in detail, beginning with a historical overview of the research and then addressing current theoretical and empirical issues. We conclude by summarising research on psychological interventions that have been applied to reduce athletes' risk of injury. Throughout our presentation of this topic we offer ideas for future research and counselling interventions.

THE STRESS–INJURY MODEL: INTRODUCTION

As mentioned earlier, initial research concerning the influence of psychosocial variables on athletic injury focused on the direct effects of life stress. In their review of the life stress–injury research, however, Andersen and Williams (1988) suggested that the relationship between psychosocial variables and athletic injury was neither direct nor limited to life stress (see figure 21.1). Rather, three factors — history of stressors (e.g. life stress, previous injuries), personality (e.g. competitive trait anxiety, locus of control) and coping resources (e.g. social support, coping skills) — were hypothesised to influence athletes' susceptibility to injury indirectly through their effects on the stress response.

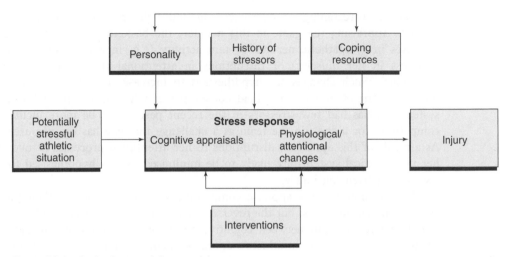

Figure 21.1   Revised stress–injury model

(*Source:* Andersen & Williams 1988; Williams & Andersen 1998. Copyright 1998 from *Journal of Applied Sport Psychology* by Jean Williams and Mark Andersen. Reproduced by permission of Taylor & Francis, Inc., www.routledge-ny.com)

In their initial model, Andersen and Williams (1988) suggested that the three psychosocial factors had direct influences on an athlete's stress response, the mechanism hypothesised to directly influence injury risk. They further suggested that personality and coping resources affected the stress response by moderating the influence of an athlete's history of stressors. For example, a wrestler's strong social support and low competitive anxiety might attenuate his stress response through two routes. First, these variables could positively influence how the wrestler viewed the competitive environment. Second, these variables could attenuate the effects of high levels of life stress, which in turn could lessen the strength of his response to stressful situations such as competitions. A more recent formulation of the stress–injury model, however, recognised the bidirectional influences that life stress is likely to have on the other psychosocial factors and that coping resources and personality are likely to influence one another (Williams & Andersen 1998). For example, an externally oriented athlete might feel less able to develop effective coping skills than a more internally oriented teammate. On the other hand, high levels of negative life stress might tax and weaken an athlete's support system, causing them to feel less supported in times of pressure. Clearly the current model (see figure 21.1) best represents the relationships that exist between the psychosocial variables.

The central mechanism in this model is the *stress response*, a bidirectional relationship between athletes' cognitive appraisals of demands, consequences and resources in the athletic situation and their physiological reactions (e.g. increased muscle tension) and attentional responses (e.g. narrowing of the visual field, distractibility). Andersen and Williams (1988) suggested that the stress response mediated the relationship between the psychosocial variables and athletic injury. As indicated in figure 21.1, the psychosocial variables influence how athletes' respond under acutely stressful situations, but only the athletes' response itself directly affects injury susceptibility. Depending on the extent to which the psychosocial variables are present or absent, the athletes' stress responsivity is attenuated or exacerbated. For example, during an important game, a basketball player who had pre-existing high levels of life stress, low levels of social support and high levels of competitive anxiety might view the situation as threatening or overwhelming and believe that she cannot perform as needed. Appraising the game in this manner, the basketball player might experience increases in sympathetic nervous system activity (e.g. increased HR, upset stomach, tightness in her muscles) or disruptions in attentional functioning (e.g. peripheral narrowing). Such changes are hypothesised to increase the athlete's susceptibility to injury. On the other hand, the field hockey player who has a well-established support system and has had few stressors in the recent past might be more inclined to view competition for a spot on the team as a challenge that she has the resources to meet. As a result of this appraisal, disruptions to her attentional processes or overactivity of her physiological systems are likely to be minimised. She is hypothesised to be at low risk for experiencing injury.

Clearly, how athletes appraise competitive situations influences their physiological and attentional processes, but the reverse is also true. As Andersen and Williams (1988) stated, the relationship between cognitive appraisals and physiological and attentional changes is bidirectional, an athlete's appraisals being as likely to influence her physiological/attentional processes as those processes are to influence how she thinks about the situation she is in. Take, for instance, the football player who, in the locker room before a game, notices that his hands are shaking a little and that the muscles in his shoulders feel 'tight'. Such awareness might lead him to wonder what is wrong. He may begin to question his physical readiness, his team's game plan or his ability to settle down and get focused ('What chance do we have against this team? They're undefeated!' or 'I haven't practised very well this week. I hope I don't screw up if I get to play'). In other words, he worries. He views the situation as threatening and overwhelming and questions his ability to perform. Such worry is likely to intensify his physiological and attentional responses, which in turn is hypothesised to cause further negative and debilitating appraisals. In such situations, the athlete's stress response is exacerbated and his susceptibility to injury increased.

The final component of the model concerns the interventions sport psychologists might use to assist athletes in reducing their risk of injury. As initially conceptualised by Andersen and Williams (1988, see figure 21.1), interventions are directed at the stress response itself. Cognitive behavioural in nature, these interventions are designed to help athletes cope more effectively with their reactions to stressful competitive situations. In general, the interventions help athletes either change how they appraise the situations they are in or learn to lessen the physiological reactions (e.g. muscle tightness) and the attentional changes (e.g. increased distractibility) they experience. Although most interventions are targeted at the athletes' stress responses, as we discuss later in this chapter the positive effects of some interventions might occur through their influence on the predisposing factors in the model, such as increasing athletes' support networks.

AN ATHLETE'S RESPONSE TO INJURY

Midway through the second game of an important volleyball match, Alyssa came down on the feet of an opponent and collapsed to the floor. Amid the chaos that followed, it became clear that she had injured her knee. Initially all Alyssa could sense was the physical pain — she had never felt anything quite like it before. After a while, though, as the pain lessened and she was being carried to the training room, she became numb. This could not be happening to her, could it? She knew from the look of the trainer that she was hurt badly, but she just could not believe that something like this had happened to her.

So how do athletes respond, both emotionally and behaviourally, to an athletic injury once the initial physical pain and emotional shock recede? Although researchers initially conceptualised athletes' responses to injury as a grief–loss process, more recent formulations suggest that athletes' reactions are very individualised and influenced by many of the same psychosocial factors that influence their susceptibility to being injured (Wiese-Bjornstal, Smith, Shaffer & Morrey 1998). Like injury-risk models, central to injury-response models is the athlete's cognitive appraisal of the injury itself. How the athlete views the injury is again influenced by psychosocial factors. Consider Alyssa's situation. If she views her knee injury as overwhelming or a threat to her position on the team or believes that she cannot effectively manage the rehabilitation process, she is likely to experience emotions such as anger, depression and tension, and behave in ways that interfere with recovery, such as missing physical therapy appointments or not adhering strictly to her rehabilitation regimen. If, on the other hand, Alyssa thinks about the injury more positively, perhaps as a challenge to be met or as a time to better strengthen her legs and knee joints, or she believes that she has the support of friends and team-mates, she is likely to maintain a positive mood state and make use of the resources available (e.g. counselling, physical therapy) to help her rehabilitate quickly and effectively. Clearly what an athlete experiences following injury extends far beyond the physical pain initially suffered.

THE STRESS–INJURY MODEL: OVERVIEW OF PSYCHOSOCIAL FACTORS

Because most stress–injury research has focused on the psychosocial factors, as opposed to the stress response itself, we discuss the research history associated with each set of psychosocial factors proposed by Andersen and Williams (1988). Although we present each factor independently, it is important to note that these variables do interact with one another to affect injury susceptibility (Petrie 1992; Smith, Smoll & Ptacek 1990). In addition, we provide directions for future research and address relevant methodological, statistical and measurement issues (for a more detailed discussion of these issues in injury research, see Petrie & Falkstein 1998).

History of stressors

Within this factor, Andersen and Williams (1988) identified life-event stress (hereafter referred to as life stress), daily hassles and prior injury. Of these, life stress has been the most thoroughly researched, extending from Holmes and Rahe's (1967) original work concerning the accumulation of life events and subsequent general health functioning. Early life stress–injury research (Bramwell, Masuda, Wagner & Holmes 1975; Coddington & Troxell 1980; Cryan & Alles 1983; Holmes 1970; Passer & Seese 1983) examined the extent to which football players who had experienced high levels of life stress during the one to two years before their seasons were more susceptible to injury than their low-stress counterparts. Consistently these studies found direct relationships between the amount of life stress experienced by the athletes and injuries suffered during their seasons. The explanation for these findings, later elaborated on by Andersen and Williams, was that experiencing life stress disrupted athletes' normal functioning and caused them to use existing resources to cope and adjust to the stressor. This adaptation process was hypothesised to place athletes at risk for injury or other adverse health outcomes.

Subsequent life stress–injury research (Brewer & Petrie 1995; Hardy, Richman & Rosenfeld 1991; Hardy & Riehl 1988; Petrie 1992, 1993a, 1993b; Thompson & Morris

1994) has corroborated these earlier studies. In fact, Williams (2001), in her review of the psychology of injury literature, found that 30 of 35 life stress–injury studies demonstrated at least some significant relationship between these two variables. She argued that 'this almost universal finding is itself compelling, but even more so considering it occurred across sports and competitive levels (youth to elite)' (p. 770). Clearly there is consistent and extensive support for the relationship between life stress, in particular negative life stress, and athletic injury.

Although not as thoroughly researched as life stress, daily hassles and previous injury are also important variables within the history of stressors factor. Daily hassles are the irritants or daily minor problems, such as being late for an appointment or not being able to find a parking space, that regularly occur in life. Sometimes stemming from major life events, such as moving to a new city to begin school or being promoted from a development- to an elite-level athletic team, daily hassles can increase athletes' susceptibility to illness and injury in much the same way as life stress. Initial research examining the effects of daily hassles (e.g. Blackwell & McCullagh 1990; Hanson, McCullagh & Tonymon 1992; Smith, Smoll & Ptacek 1990), however, found that they were unrelated to athletic injury. Although such findings suggest that daily hassles were not as salient as life stress in predicting athletic injury, a methodological limitation in the studies offered another viable explanation for the nonsignificant results (Williams 2001). Unlike life stress, daily hassles are likely to vary from week to week. Thus studies that measure daily hassles only at the beginning of an athletic season, such as these initial investigations, fail to accurately assess the dynamic nature of this variable. To determine if a relationship truly exists between daily hassles and athletic injury, hassles would have to be measured regularly throughout a season. In fact, recent research employing this type of repeated measures methodology has found support for the daily hassles–injury relationship (Byrd 1993; Fawkner, McMurray & Summers 1999).

As originally conceptualised, previous injury was thought to influence subsequent injury in one of two ways (Andersen & Williams 1988; Williams 2001). First, if athletes were not fully recovered from their injuries but returned to play anyway, their risk of re-injury was increased. Second, athletes may be physically recovered but not psychologically ready to return to competition, increasing the likelihood of their making negative appraisals. For example, an athlete who has had major reconstructive knee surgery may be physically cleared for practice by the training staff but still unable to play. Because of decreased levels of confidence in her playing ability, lack of psychological comfort with her knee brace or fear of re-injury, she may view returning to play as threatening and overwhelming, and not believe she has the ability to cope with the stress of intensive practice and competition. As a result, she may keep herself sidelined indefinitely or, if she does return to practice and competition, participate only sparingly. Although not unequivocal (e.g. Hanson et al. 1992), several studies have found support for the relationship between prior and subsequent injuries (e.g. Van Mechelen et al. 1996; Williams, Hogan & Andersen 1993), suggesting that this variable be considered in future investigations.

In considering the research on the *history of stressors* factor, there are two empirical issues that warrant discussion. The first issue concerns the measurement of life stress. Initial life stress–injury studies (e.g. Bramwell et al. 1975) used modifications of existing measures, such as the Social Readjustment Rating Scale (Holmes & Rahe 1967), which were simply compilations of life events that generally occurred in a specific population. Based on the stimulus perspective (Perkins 1982), these measures presumed that the 'stress' resided in the event itself and thus did not take into account an individual's experience of the event. More recent research (e.g. Petrie 1992; Smith et al. 1990), however, has taken a transactional approach to the measurement of life stress. Using measures such as the Life Events Scale for Collegiate Athletes (LESCA) (Petrie 1992), athletes are able to rate the impact of each event as they experienced it, ranging from extremely positive to extremely negative. This approach has received the most support and is conceptually most consistent with the Andersen and Williams (1988) model (Petrie & Falkstein 1998).

The second issue concerns when and how often measures are given in relation to the athletic season. There is strong support for the use of prospective designs (i.e. when measures of the psychosocial variables are taken at the beginning of the athletic season), because they allow for a better understanding of the cause and effect relationship between the psychosocial variables and the occurrence of injury (Petrie & Falkstein 1998). Thus life stress–injury research should incorporate this type of methodology whenever possible and ensure that, when measures are administered at the beginning of the athletic season, all participating athletes are medically cleared for practice and free of any time-loss injuries. Concerning how often measures are taken, recent research on daily hassles (e.g. Fawkner et al. 1999) and life stress (Petrie & Stoever 1995) indicate that these variables vary in intensity across an athletic season. Given the dynamic nature of these variables, single administrations taken at the beginning of an athletic season are likely to be inadequate in predicting the occurrence of injury three months later. Thus life stress–injury research should also adopt repeated measures designs, where measures are taken at prescribed times throughout the season. Clearly the time frame of the repeated measures will depend on the variable being assessed, with shorter time periods (e.g. one week) being necessary for constantly changing variables such as daily hassles.

Coping resources

Broadly, coping resources are the internal cognitions, behaviours and emotions, and the external social support networks that assist individuals in effectively handling the events, problems and stressors they experience in life (Andersen & Williams 1988; Williams 2001). According to Williams, these external and internal resources can decrease injury susceptibility either directly, by influencing how an athlete appraises a situation, or indirectly, by attenuating the negative effects associated with life stress or certain personality traits, such as competitive anxiety. For example, Jorge came from a caring family that provided him with many forms of support. When he was selected to join his country's national swimming team, he talked with his parents and siblings about the sacrifices he would have to make (e.g. moving away from home to live at the training site). When he made the decision to accept the invitation, his family helped him pack and move to the training centre. Once there, Jorge called his family every few days to discuss the rigours of training, the loneliness he sometimes felt and the transition to a new coach. As a result of this support, Jorge viewed this life transition more as a challenge than as a threat. He knew that he would face many stressors in the coming months, but he also believed he could handle them. In other words, the support provided by his parents helped him feel more confident in his abilities to cope with the changes that were occurring in his life.

Although Williams and colleagues (Andersen & Williams 1988; Williams 2001; Williams & Andersen 1998) have proposed a *direct effects model* for coping resource variables and athletic injury, empirical research has been equivocal. For example, in two studies (Hanson et al. 1992; Williams, Tonymon & Wadsworth 1986), the best predictor of injury was a low level of coping resources, which was measured by the amount of support and the number of self-care behaviours, such as eating, sleeping or taking time for self, in which the athletes engaged. Contrary to this finding, Blackwell and McCullagh (1990), Petrie (1993b), Rider and Hicks (1995), Smith, Smoll and Ptacek (1990) and Van Mechelen et al. (1996) found no relationship between coping and athletic injury. Concerning the direct effects of social support, the majority of studies have found no relationship with injury vulnerability or susceptibility (Lavallee & Flint 1996; Patterson, Smith, Everett & Ptacek 1998; Petrie 1992, 1993a; Rider & Hicks 1995; Smith et al. 1990). Williams and Andersen (1997), though, did report that lower levels of social support were related to more failures on a visual tracking task, a direct measure of the stress response.

More empirical support, though, exists for coping resource variables as moderators of the life stress–injury relationship (what is also termed an *indirect effects model*). Concerning social support, studies have generally found that high levels of support serve a protective or buffering function with respect to the deleterious effects of life stress (in particular negative life stress). Low levels of support, on the other hand, may actually exacerbate the effects of negative life stress, thus increasing athletes' vulnerability to injury (Andersen & Williams 1999; Hardy et al. 1991; Patterson et al. 1998; Petrie 1992, 1993a). For example, Petrie (1992) found that negative life stress was significantly related to the number of minor injuries, severe injuries, total injuries and days missed for low- but not high-support collegiate gymnasts. Similarly Patterson et al. (1998) found that under conditions of low but not high social support, high-life-stress dancers were significantly more susceptible to suffering an injury. Finally, in a study examining the relationship of psychosocial variables and the stress response to athletic injury, Andersen and Williams (1999) reported that for low-social-support athletes, high levels of negative life stress in conjunction with peripheral narrowing best predicted injury. As Williams (2001) noted, research clearly supports the conclusion that social support influences the life stress–injury relationship.

Research on the moderating effects of coping, however, has been less conclusive. For example, Smith et al. (1990) found that under conditions of low coping skills, negative life stress was positively related to athletic injury, accounting for just over 6 per cent of the variance. Under conditions of low coping skills and low social support, negative life stress accounted for almost 25 per cent of the injury variance. In a direct examination of the stress response, Williams and Andersen (1997) found that men with low support, low coping and high negative life stress had the lowest perceptual sensitivity of all groups. For women, low coping interacted with high negative life stress to decrease their ability to detect visual tracking cues. Petrie (1993b), however, found no significant moderator effects for coping skills in a sample of collegiate football players.

Although the research on coping has been inconclusive, there have been far too few studies to eliminate it as a possible moderator. In fact, additional research that examines both coping skills and social support, as was carried out in the Smith et al. (1990) study, is warranted, although such research will need to extend beyond the current ways in which coping has been measured, either by the number of resources a person has or by the psychological skills they possess. Neither approach incorporates the more traditional ways of measuring coping, such as that provided by Billings and Moos (1981). From this perspective, one considers the *method* and the *focus* of the coping. The method refers to how the person is trying to handle the situation. Are they actively trying to change something (e.g. cognitions or behaviours) or are they simply trying to avoid the situation that is causing distress? The focus, on the other hand, concerns the target of the coping behaviours. Is the focus a problem the person is trying to solve or is it the emotions that are occurring in response to the stressor? Such a measurement approach, which has been used extensively in general stress–coping research, may prove beneficial in delineating the stress–coping–injury relationship, although the one study that did incorporate this approach reported no significant results with respect to coping (Van Mechelen et al. 1996).

Personality

The final psychosocial factor in the Andersen and Williams (1988) model is personality. In their original article, Andersen and Williams identified hardiness, locus of control, sense of coherence, competitive trait anxiety and achievement motivation as measures worth consideration. Like coping resources, the personality measures were hypothesised to have either direct or indirect effects on athletes' stress responsivity. According to Williams (2001), however, only achievement motivation, locus of control and trait anxiety have been examined in life stress–injury studies.

Concerning motivation, the one study examining the effects of achievement motivation reported no relationship with injury (Van Mechelen et al. 1996). With self-motivation, though, McClay, Appleby and Plascak (1989) found a significant relationship with severe injuries. They suggested that self-motivated athletes might be more likely to overload themselves when training than less motivated athletes, thus setting up the condition of physical vulnerability. The results of studies examining the effects of locus of control, particularly those having an external locus, have been equivocal as well, with some research supporting a relationship with athletic injury (e.g. Pargman & Lunt 1989) and others not (Kerr & Minden 1988; Passer & Seese 1983).

With trait anxiety, studies using general measures of the construct have demonstrated no relationship with athletic injury (Kerr & Minden 1988; Passer & Seese 1983). When sport-specific measures have been used, however, competitive trait anxiety has related directly to athletic injury (Blackwell & McCullagh 1990; Hanson et al. 1992; Lavallee & Flint 1996) or moderated the life stress–injury relationship so that athletes with high levels of competitive trait anxiety and high levels of life stress were most vulnerable (Petrie 1993b). Although competitive trait anxiety appears to be a viable predictor and moderator in stress–injury research, it has been measured from a unidimensional perspective using the Sport Competition Anxiety Test (SCAT) (Martens 1977). Future research that examines competitive trait anxiety should do so using a multidimensional measure of the construct, such as the Sport Anxiety Scale (SAS) (Smith, Smoll & Shutz 1990). Unlike the SCAT, which primarily assesses somatic anxiety, the SAS measures three dimensions of competitive anxiety — somatic, worry and concentration disruption. Because anxiety has been hypothesised to influence attentional processes (which are cognitive responses) during stressful situations, stronger relationships with injury may be found using the cognitive components of the SAS. Clearly more research is needed to assess the effects of the different components of anxiety on athletic injury. In addition, future research may need to consider not only the intensity of the anxiety symptoms but also the extent to which athletes experience these symptoms as facilitating or debilitating (see Jones & Swain 1992).

Although not originally hypothesised by Andersen and Williams (1988), several other personality measures have been studied in relation to athletic injury, including self-concept (Kerr & Minden 1988; Pargman & Lunt 1989), sensation seeking (Smith, Ptacek & Smoll 1992), mood state (Brewer & Petrie 1995; Lavallee & Flint 1996; Thompson & Morris 1994), intrusive thoughts (Shuer & Dietrich 1997), positive states of mind (e.g. ability to stay focused and relaxed) (Williams et al. 1993), and attention and attentional style (Bergandi & Witting 1988; Thompson & Morris 1994). For example, Lavallee and Flint found that tension/anxiety and anger/hostility were related to injury severity, whereas Brewer and Petrie reported a direct relationship between injury status and elevated scores on a measure of depression. Similarly Thompson and Morris found that anger directed outwards increased the injury susceptibility of high-school football players. Finally, Williams et al. (1993) examined the extent to which athletes' ability to enter positive states of mind (e.g. ability to focus attention or be productive) was related to their experience of acute and chronic injuries. They found that athletes' ability to remain focused on tasks was negatively related to both types of injury. As Williams and Andersen (1998) noted, some of these variables, such as mood states, states of mind and self-concept, are likely to be intimately tied to coping responses and thus important to consider in conjunction with those psychosocial variables. Clearly these personality measures should be studied in more depth to determine the extent to which they independently or in combination influence athletes' stress response and susceptibility to injury.

STRESS–INJURY MODEL: THE STRESS RESPONSE

As discussed earlier in the chapter, Andersen and Williams' (1988) model has provided the framework for the majority of the research concerning psychosocial precursors to athletic injury. Central to this model is the bidirectional relationship between athletes' cognitive appraisals of life events and their stress responses. In this section we review cognitive appraisals, the multifaceted nature of the stress response, and psychophysiological mechanisms that may predispose highly stressed athletes to injury and illness.

Cognitive appraisals

A stressor acquires a *valence* (positive or negative) to the degree that the stressor is perceived as threatening, overwhelming or simply challenging to a person's wellbeing. This process is called the 'primary appraisal'. The stressor achieves a level of *intensity* in relation to the person's perceived ability to cope or respond to the threat (called the 'secondary appraisal') (Folkman, Lazarus, Dunkel-Schetter, Delongis & Gruen 1986). Thus, whenever individuals experience life events (or stressors), they go through this two-part appraisal process. First, they determine the extent to which the event is threatening/overwhelming or simply challenging. In the former the valence of the event is often negative. Second, they determine the extent to which they have the resources, whether internal or external, to cope effectively with the event/stressor. In general, when individuals believe they have the capacities to cope with the event, its intensity is diminished or attenuated.

The nature of primary and secondary appraisals also can be used to understand how responses to the same event, such as moving away from home to begin college, may differ in valence and intensity across individuals. For example, an athlete may see starting college as desirable or a positive challenge, whereas a team-mate might view it as threatening and overwhelming. Similarly even an undesirable (threatening) event such as the loss of a significant relationship may elicit different intensities of distress depending on factors, such as social support, that may alter a person's perceived ability to cope with the loss. Further, features of the stressor, such as whether it is an acute or chronic condition, and an athlete's response to a stressor can influence subsequent cognitive appraisals as well as stress responses. For example, an argument with a team-mate may elicit different stress responses if it is representative of an enduring conflictual relationship than if it was only an isolated event.

Stress response

As discussed earlier, the stress response is the bridge from an acute or chronic stressor to an adverse health reaction (e.g. injury or illness) and depends largely on the primary and secondary appraisals made by the individual. Andersen and Williams (1988) conceptualised the stress response as being physiological and attentional in nature. Although they hypothesised a variety of physiological changes (e.g. increased muscle tension and alteration of sympathetic and endocrine systems), their model and the preponderance of research have focused on attentional disturbances that affect cue recognition and distractibility (i.e. attentional changes).

Other researchers (Perna & McDowell 1995; Perna, Schneiderman & LaPerriere 1997), however, have characterised stress responses more broadly. Perna and colleagues argued that to fully understand an individual's stress response, one must consider effects to cognitive, emotional, behavioural and physiological systems (see figure 21.2). In addition to including a wider range of stress responses, this conceptualisation expands on the Andersen and Williams (1988) model in two distinct ways.

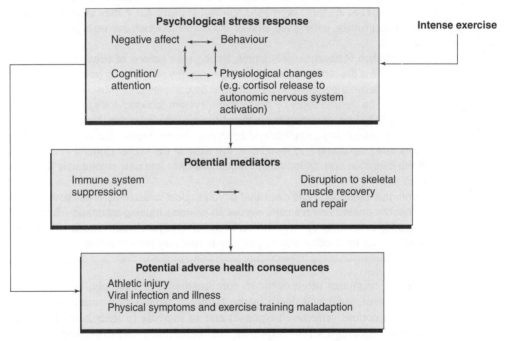

Figure 21.2 An extension of Andersen and Williams (1988) conception of the 'stress response'

First, stress responses are influenced not only by psychosocial factors, but also by their interaction with the intense and prolonged physical training generally required of athletes. A central tenet of this conceptualisation is that in addition to independent effects on health, psychosocially derived (dis)stress may combine additively with exercise-related stress to widen a *window of susceptibility* to injury and illness (Mackinnon, Ginn & Seymour 1991; Perna & McDowell 1995; Perna et al. 1997) (see the house analogy feature on page 558). Second, this conceptualisation expands psychosocial stress-induced outcomes beyond athletic injury to include other adverse health outcomes such as viral infection, physical symptoms and training maladaptation. We consider multiple health outcomes because each is affected by psychosocial stress and, ultimately, each affects athletes' availability to compete. Also, a complete understanding of potentially predisposing physiological factors to athletic injury requires an understanding of the physiological systems and how stress may alter the normal functioning of these systems.

A HOUSE ANALOGY TO EXPLAIN THE WINDOW OF SUSCEPTIBILITY

Think of skeletal muscle as a house that is being remodelled. These 'walls' can ultimately be strengthened by exercise, yet there will be a period during remodelling when the walls are weakened before being rebuilt. Heavy exercise, although necessary for athletes, causes the secretion of stress hormones, particularly cortisol. This reaction has been termed a catabolic cascade, and is analogous to the situation when the walls of our house are temporally weakened. The amount and duration of cortisol in response to exercise depend principally on the intensity of exercise and the athlete's physical condition. Intense exercise will result in relatively more cortisol secretion than moderate exercise, and a deconditioned athlete will secrete more cortisol to a standardised bout of exercise than an athlete measured during a relatively conditioned period of his or her training cycle. Because psychological stress also causes increases in stress hormones, cortisol in particular, it may extend the secretion of post-exercise cortisol (i.e. extend the time or the extent to which the walls are temporarily weakened).

The addition of psychological stress, through the actions of stress hormones (e.g. cortisol), may also affect the recovery period during which the remodelling (rebuilding) of muscle occurs. That is, there are a series of steps that must be completed for muscle to repair itself. Damaged tissue must be cleared away by the immune system (phagocytosis) — analogous to clearing away debris before rebuilding the walls of our remodelled home. New muscle cells must be generated through the secretion and actions of growth factors (i.e. an anabolic cascade) — analogous to rebuilding and reinforcing the walls of the home. Cortisol inhibits phagocytosis and the migration and differentiation of satellite cells into new myotubuals (beginning muscle fibres).

From this description it is clear that psychological stress may affect both the catabolic and the anabolic phases as an athlete makes an exercise training adaptation. Because the majority of the body's restorative processes occur at night, psychological stress-induced sleep disruption may be another way stress affects recovery from exercise.

Stress responses often occur in combination. For example, on experiencing a negative life event, such as a death in the family, a person may simultaneously experience a range of emotions (affective response) and an increase in their heart rate (a physiological response). Although stress responses are individually identified and may have independent effects, they often act and are experienced in synergistic fashion. For example, the athlete who views starting college as an overwhelming and threatening event may eventually have difficulty concentrating (cognitive response) and sleeping (behavioural response), which in turn may influence their emotional and physical state. All of these changes may, in turn, increase the athlete's chances of suffering an injury or experiencing other adverse health outcomes, such as developing a viral infection.

Affective responses

Although people can experience positive emotions in conjunction with life stressors, negative life stress has been more consistently associated with athletic injury and with illness in the general population than has total life stress (Cohen, Tyrrell & Smith 1991; McFarland, Norman, Streiner, Roy & Scott 1980; Petrie & Falkstein 1998; Smith, Smoll & Ptacek 1990). It is likely that the attendant affective experience predisposes a person to label a life event as negative or positive. Common negative affective states include anxiety, depression and anger. Fatigue is also frequently included as an emotional response, but it is most accurately characterised as a mixed response containing both mood and physical elements.

College athletes with high negative life stress reported experiencing significantly more depressed, angry and anxious moods than college athletes with low life stress (Perna, Antoni, Kumar, Cruess & Schneiderman 1998b). In a study of elite athletes attending a national team training camp that controlled for initial level of negative affect, Perna and McDowell (1995) found a higher rate of emotional symptoms one month after camp among high- as opposed to low-life-stress athletes. These data suggest that negative life stress is associated with a variety of unpleasant emotions and may also predispose athletes to future emotional symptoms.

Cognitive responses

Cognitive stress responses are those symptoms that interfere with thought and information processing, and may include disruptions in attention, concentration, speed at processing visual cues, rumination, and the experience of racing and unwanted thoughts. Elite and college athletes with high life stress have been found to experience more cognitive symptoms than low-life-stress athletes (Kovacs & Perna 1998; Perna & McDowell 1995).

A noteworthy line of research has examined the disruptions in attention and visual cue processing and the phenomenon of *peripheral narrowing (PN)* (Thompson & Morris 1994; Williams & Andersen 1997; Williams, Tonymon & Andersen 1990; Williams, Tonymon & Andersen 1991). PN refers to the diminished capacity to pick up stimuli in the peripheral field of vision during high-demand situations. PN studies are based on the notion that failure to recognise visual cues may predispose some athletes, particularly in contact sports, to athletic injury. The typical paradigm to test for PN involves classifying participants into high and low life-event stress groups and comparing their relative performances on a visual tracking task that requires them to identify a targeted stimulus under a baseline and a high-demand situation.

The high-demand condition is used to approximate the situation common to many sports in which an athlete must perform while being bombarded with extraneous stimuli. Williams and colleagues (1990, 1991) reported that in comparison to low-life-stress athletes, high-life-stress athletes experienced more state anxiety and PN in the high-demand situation. In a later study, Williams and Andersen (1997) found that in addition to PN, high-life-stress athletes were slower to respond to keyed targets in their central field of vision. Moreover, athletes with relatively lower social support, higher negative life stress and higher PN were at significantly greater risk for athletic injury compared with other athletes of similar ability. In a related outcome, Thompson and Morris (1994) found an increased athletic injury rate among athletes with high life stress and low vigilant attention.

Research involving cognitive symptoms, particularly PN and decreased vigilance as predisposing factors to injury, is promising. Investigators have been able to experimentally demonstrate decrements in cognitive and visual processing among high-life-stress athletes, and prospectively correlate life-stress and laboratory performance data with the actual occurrence of injury and posit plausible mechanistic explanations for these effects.

Behavioural responses

Behavioural stress responses are symptoms such as disruptions to sleep (e.g. increased sleep latency and unrestful sleep) and self-care routines that may predispose an athlete to injury or illness. For example, the bulk of metabolic recovery from exercise occurs at night (Savis 1994). Disruptions to sleep, particularly sleep onset disturbance, may impair muscle growth and repair processes, as described in the house analogy feature (page 558). Sleep deprivation and interrupted sleep are also known to cause decrements in attention and concentration, and in some cases athletic performance, that may also predispose individuals to athletic injury (Savis 1994). Although sleep parameters were not measured in the PN studies described previously, it is possible that sleep disturbance may mediate the association between life-event stress and PN.

A US Olympic Committee–sponsored Stress and Health Project, involving 103 elite men and women athletes, revealed a classic dose–response relationship between life-event stress and sleep onset disturbance (Perna 1995). After the study had controlled for a variety of exercise training factors and competitive anxiety, athletes in the highest quartile of life stress reported sleep onset disturbance in approximately half or more days a month, whereas athletes in the lowest life-stress quartile reported only one to two occasions of sleep onset disturbance in a month. The study suggests that although some sleep disturbance is common among most athletes, disturbances on seven or more nights in a month is atypical and warrants attention.

Although life stress has not been directly related to alterations in athletes' self-care, it is well known to interfere with self-regulatory behaviour (Heatherton & Penn 1995) that may have relevance for athletes. For example, many athletes adopt injury prevention measures such as maintaining adequate hydration, participating in stretching and strengthening routines, and engaging in preventative cryotherapy (e.g. a pitcher icing the arm after practice) that may be less likely to occur in the face of significant life stress. In one study, a vulnerability measure, which included several self-care behaviours, was not significantly associated with athletic injury (Hanson, McCullagh & Tonymon 1992). However, the vulnerability scale used was not a pure measure of self-care behaviour, and some of the behaviours (e.g. wearing seatbelts) were not relevant to athletic injury or illness.

Physiological responses

An assumption of biopsychosocial models, such as the Andersen and Williams (1988) model, is that psychological stressors and accompanying distress cause activation of the autonomic nervous system (ANS), yielding the release of neuroendocrines, neuropeptides and glucocorticoids (i.e. cortisol) (Perna et al. 1997). Many target organs (e.g. heart, vasculature, immune cells and muscle tissue) have receptors for neuroendocrines and glucocorticoids. Activation of the ANS affects target organs either through direct enervation by neurons of the sympathetic and parasympathetic nervous systems (SNS and PNS, respectively) or through hormonal action and receptor binding activity (Perna et al. 1997). That is, activation of the ANS is the first physiological phenomenon to occur that is causally related to the symptoms (e.g. changes in heart rate) observed when people are stressed. Direct enervation by the SNS and hormonal action provide the mechanistic links that have been used to explain how the brain and associated cognitive-affective processes (i.e. threat appraisal of a stressor) may influence other physical systems, and especially the immune system, within the body (Ader, Felten & Cohen 1991; Perna et al. 1997).

1. Types of physiological stress responses

Selye (1950) postulated that the stress response followed a single hormonal pattern and that it could be initiated by any number of events. Selye coined the term *general adaptation syndrome* (GAS) to describe a set pattern of events and a hormone profile thought to occur across stressors and individuals. Others (Frankenhaeuser 1990; Mason 1975; McCabe & Schneiderman 1985) observed differentiated hormonal profiles to diverse physical and psychological stressors that challenged the notion of a single nonspecific response pattern. Rather than the GAS, distinct stress hormone profiles have been delineated.

Relatively acute stressors elicit temporal increases in sympathoadrenal medulla (SAM) activity. SAM activity is characterised by catecholamine (epinephrine and norepinephrine) release and reductions in total peripheral resistance to blood flow (Frankenhaeuser 1990; Mason 1975; McCabe & Schneiderman 1985; Perna et al. 1997). On the other hand, activities/stressors that are chronic in nature, may lead to prolonged or repeated increases in SAM activity and an increase, rather than decrease, in total peripheral resistance, and especially to increased hypothalamic-pituitary-adrenal-cortex (HPA-axis) activation that initiates the release of cortisol and other stress hormones (Frankenhaeuser 1990; Hurwitz et al. 1993).

Frankenhaeuser (1990) and others (e.g. McCabe & Schneiderman 1985) suggest that increases in catecholamines reflect general SAM activation and *intensity of affect* associated with a stressor or challenge, whereas elevations in cortisol reflect *degree of distress* associated with a stressor. Frankenhaeuser has used the term *effort without distress* to describe coping associated with SAM activation but limited HPA-axis activation, and *effort with distress* to describe coping associated with SAM activation and pronounced HPA-axis activation. McCabe and Schneiderman (1985) have posited a similar position — namely, that cortisol release depends primarily on cognitive appraisal of a stress situation. Additionally, while an initial cortisol rise may be a necessary stress response, prolonged activation of the HPA axis is deleterious. Hence acute stress responses are associated with SAM activation, but HPA-axis activation depends on the intensity, duration and other characteristics of the stressor that influence affective tone and perceived ability to cope.

From our description of differential stress responses, one can also see how two individuals faced with the same stressor, but with different cognitive appraisals, may have divergent neuroendocrine responses that, in turn, may affect a host of other organs and bodily systems. Further, activation of the 'stress response' can be extremely useful and necessary. For example, activation of the physiological stress response does prepare people for challenging situations, and performance on cognitive and physical tasks is positively associated with catecholamine levels (Dienstbier 1991; Frankenhaeuser 1990). However, adverse health effects are most likely to occur when individuals (1) are often stressed and have frequent activation of the SAM system (e.g. perceive many life stressors); (2) are hypersensitive to stressors (e.g. are more prone to view situations as threatening) and have high reactivity of SAM (e.g. are by nature more prone to overreact to changes or stresses in their life); and (3) are under chronic stress and experience long-term distress that causes prolonged activation of the HPA axis. For example, a death in the family or a break-up of a significant relationship may be chronic stressors because people adjust to these events over time and may for some time have unpleasant daily reminders of these events. Two people may differ in their beliefs regarding their ability to 'get over' these events, or in the amount of social support they perceive, and these cognitive appraisals influence the intensity and length of distress associated with a chronic stressor.

2. Mechanisms potentially linking neuroendocrine responses to health outcomes

Many injuries in sport are chronic in nature and are not easily explained by cognitive mechanisms (e.g. PN). Similarly, the mechanisms by which social support may influence athletic injury have not been well articulated in the sport psychology literature, although a recent review indicates that social support may alter neuroendocrine response to psychological stress via emotional modulation (Uchino & Garvey 1997). The preceding observations suggest that sport psychology research related to athlete health, particularly with respect to chronic injury susceptibility, may be furthered by exploration of alternative non-perceptual mechanisms likely involving emotion and stress–hormone connections. Emotion (negative affect) linked increases in catecholamines and cortisol have been shown to have potent immunosuppressive and muscle catabolic effects that are of potential relevance to athlete health (Perna et al. 1998b; Perna & McDowell 1995; Perna et al. 1997).

With respect to immune function, both heavy training and negative affect have been associated with immunosuppression and increased risk of viral illness (Herbert & Cohen 1993; Shephard & Shek 1994; Weidner 1994). Immune suppression, particularly diminished *natural killer cell cytotoxicity* (NKCC), following high intensity exercise has been posited to be responsible for athletes' increased risk of upper respiratory illness (e.g. viral infection) (Nieman, Johanssen, Lee & Arabatzis 1990; Shephard & Shek 1994; Weidner 1994). Moreover, sub-clinical viral infection, which may produce symptoms but not necessarily cause an athlete to cease training, has been reported to decrease strength and aerobic capacity, potentially increasing illness or injury risk, especially when athletes continue to train without adequate rest (Roberts 1986). Stress-related neuroendocrine elevation is thought to be one mechanism linking stress (physical and psychological) with immune suppression. Specifically, cortisol and catecholamines have been shown to have immunosuppressive effects on NKCC and *T-lymphocyte* response (Cupps & Fauci 1982; Nieman et al. 1994). As mentioned, cortisol also impairs phagocytosis, a function of the immune system to rid the body of dead, damaged, defective or infected cells, which comes into play when exercise damages muscle fibre.

Although the physiological stress of training is largely responsible for normal temporary immune fluctuations and increases in negative affect and cortisol, a desirable adaptation over the course of exercise training would include mood and cortisol recovery (i.e. decreased cortisol and negative mood) (Perna et al. 1998b; Tharp 1975; Urhausen & Kinderman 1987). Several studies suggest that psychological stress may modulate cortisol, immune function and health parameters in general and athlete populations (Cohen et al. 1991; Perna et al. 1997; Perna 1995; Nieman et al. 1994; Shephard 1994). For example, Herbert and Cohen's (1993) meta-analysis found that negative affect was significantly related to immune suppression. Further, in a classic study in which people with varying degrees of negative life stress were exposed to a virus, a dose–response relationship between stress and rate of subsequent illness was found (Cohen et al. 1991).

Corroborating these findings, a study with elite athletes has found that in response to a standardised exercise stressor, high-life-stress athletes, in comparison to low-life-stress athletes, experienced prolonged post-exercise cortisol elevation, which was prospectively positively correlated with severity of physical symptoms (e.g. skeletal muscle pain) (Perna & McDowell 1995). This study was important because it demonstrated the importance of assessing psychological stress in predicting athletes' ability to recover from exercise and the extent of their adverse health a month later. Increases in stress hormones and decreases in immune response as athletes move from non-competitive to competitive days also have been partly attributed to psychological stress (e.g. competitive anxiety) (Mackinnon et al. 1991).

The cumulative findings of the studies reviewed in this section support the contention that psychological stress may be independent of exercise intensity in accounting for athletes' neuroendocrine and immune response to exercise. It has been suggested that adverse health effects associated with chronic psychological distress are likely to be most pronounced for those whose behaviour or medical status already poses a health risk (Kiecolt-Glaser & Glaser 1992). Considering that elite athletes endure long periods of high-intensity training, the presence of a high degree of uncontrollable life-event stress or a limited capacity to tolerate stress may exacerbate SAM and HPA-axis activation and compromise immune responses. All of these factors may impair athletes' ability to recover from high-intensity exercise and potentially increase their risk for injury or illness (Perna & McDowell 1995; Perna et al. 1997).

PSYCHOLOGICAL INTERVENTIONS TO FACILITATE EXERCISE TRAINING ADAPTATION AND ATHLETE HEALTH

Perna et al. (1998b) have suggested that one way sport psychology interventions may enhance performance is by facilitating athlete health. After genetic factors, the ability to undergo weeks and months of systematically planned training, uninterrupted by injury and illness, is central to achieving athletic goals. Because heavy training periods (e.g. high-intensity or prolonged bouts of exercise) are required to increase physical functioning, interventions that facilitate adaptation to exercise training and enhance recovery take on an increasingly important role in competitive athletics.

Cognitive behavioural stress management (CBSM) interventions employing relaxation training, imagery and cognitive restructuring have been shown to buffer psychological distress and immune function decrements (Antoni et al. 1991; Esterling, Antoni, Fletcher, Margulies & Schneiderman 1994; Green, Green & Santoro 1988). Similarly, psychological skills training, a form of CBSM, has been widely used to decrease competitive anxiety and improve performance among athletes (Daw & Burton 1994; Greenspan & Feltz 1989; Maynard & Cotton 1993; Maynard, Hemmings & Warwick-Evans 1995).

With respect to health outcomes among athletes, CBSM has been found to reduce post-surgical pain and anxiety and to speed physical recovery following arthroscopic surgery (Ross & Berger 1996). Enhanced physical recovery included quicker strength gains on the affected leg and a faster return to active sports participation among recreational athletes receiving two post-surgical sessions of CBSM.

As a preventative intervention, a seven-session CBSM helped improve collegiate athletes' adaptation to exercise training (Perna et al. 1998b). In comparison to a control group, rowers who received CBSM training experienced significant reductions in fatigue, depression and cortisol while maintaining a high level of training. Moreover, reductions in mood mediated the CBSM intervention effect on cortisol. These findings suggest that CBSM interventions may favourably alter athletes' physical and emotional responses to exercise training, which may in turn impart a health benefit (i.e. reduced illness/injury rate).

Further, in a controlled investigation, a 16-session CBSM intervention was found to significantly improve negative affect among high-level gymnasts, and the injury rate among gymnasts in the CBSM group was approximately half that of controls (Kerr & Goss 1996). Although the latter finding failed to reach statistical significance, the nonsignificant finding may have been due to a lack of statistical power rather than to a lack of intervention efficacy (Andersen & Stoove 1998; Kerr & Goss 1996). In a randomised, controlled clinical trial conducted as a follow-up to an earlier study (Perna et al. 1998b), athletes receiving CBSM had fewer post-intervention injury and illness days and fewer office visits as compared to controls (Perna, Antoni & Schneiderman 1998a). Mediation analyses also indicated that approximately half of the intervention effect on illness and injury was attributable to intervention-induced reductions in negative mood. Finally, Perna, Antoni, Baum, Gordon and Schneiderman (2003) examined the effectiveness of CBSM to reduce the frequency of injury and illness among collegiate rowers in a randomised, controlled clinical trial. Across the entire season, the CBSM group had fewer days ill or injured and half the number of health service visits compared with the control group. Perna et al. (2003) concluded that athlete-specific, time-limited interventions reduced the incidence of illness and injury.

Taken together, these data suggest that athletes can be taught a variety of skills to help them manage their stress. Using these techniques has helped injured athletes to return more quickly to their sports. There is also some evidence that teaching athletes these techniques may help them avoid injury or adapt better to their training. Either of these outcomes could be useful in helping athletes improve their performance as well as their health.

FUTURE DIRECTIONS

A criticism of health psychology interventions in general, and hence its application to sport, has been that while stress-induced changes in psychophysiological or biological markers are abundant, their meaningfulness to predict or lead to interventions that translate into observable behavioural phenomena (e.g. mortality, morbidity or quality of life) has been less bountiful. For example, what is the utility of knowing that psychological stress increases cortisol level or that CBSM reduces negative affect and cortisol unless those fluctuations can be associated with or causally linked to clinical changes (e.g. reductions in injury or performance improvements)? Although most scientists would generally agree with the merit of the above criticism, many would also maintain that sufficient evidence exists from general population studies and preliminary findings with athletes to warrant further investigation of psychophysiological mechanisms related to athlete health, and that these investigations may provide further empirical support for the interventions sport psychologists seek to employ.

Athlete health is a complex phenomenon, and our understanding and ability to promote it is likely to involve the interplay of biological, behavioural and psychosocial factors. A brief review of the peripheral narrowing literature provides an example of how systematic research can facilitate new inquiry and expand our understanding of the stress–health relationship among athletes. Unfortunately, with few exceptions, collaborative approaches employing systematic inquiry regarding the relationship between psychosocial, behavioural and physiological processes related to athlete health is lacking. Moreover, measurement of stress-related symptomatolgy (e.g. sleep, immune suppression, muscle pain) as health outcomes has not routinely occurred in the sport psychology literature; yet they all have relevance to athletes' quality of life and perhaps represent a prodromal phase to acute injury or prolonged illness. Similar to the call for a need for interdisciplinary training in sport psychology, which integrates exercise science and psychology, there is a need for interdisciplinary *science* investigating mechanisms potentially underlying psychological stress–health relationships.

CONCLUSIONS

In this chapter we used the Andersen and Williams (1988) stress–injury model as an organisational framework to discuss the current literature relating to the psychology of injury. We examined both the psychosocial factors hypothesised to influence athletes' stress response as well as the stress response itself. In discussing the stress response, we extended Andersen and Williams' original conceptualisation and included information regarding other behavioural, emotional and physiological mechanisms that underlie adverse health outcomes in athletes. From this review it is clear that sport psychologists' understanding of the psychosocial factors that influence injury susceptibility has increased considerably during the past 30 years. Still, as Williams and her colleagues (Williams 2001; Williams & Andersen 1998) have noted, additional research is needed to better understand the psychosocial variables that most strongly influence the stress response and the extent to which the various hypothesised mechanisms truly increase athletes' vulnerability to illness, injury or other adverse health outcomes. Further, if the Andersen and Williams model is to guide sport psychology practice, then research also needs to examine the efficacy of different injury intervention programs to determine which ones are most effective, under what circumstances and with which athletes. The base of knowledge concerning the psychology of injury is solid, but considerably more needs to be done to finish its structure.

SUMMARY

In this chapter we discussed the psychology of injury as it pertains to prediction and susceptibility. We began by presenting an overview of Andersen and Williams' (1988) and Williams and Andersen's (1998) theoretical model and then discussed each component of the model in depth. At the heart of this model was the 'stress response', which is defined as a bidirectional relationship between cognitive appraisals and physiological and attentional changes. We extended their conception of the stress response by discussing more broadly the physiological mechanisms that underlie an athlete's risk of becoming ill or sustaining an injury. We concluded the chapter by reviewing psychological strategies that have been used to reduce athletes' susceptibility to injury and discussing directions for future research.

 REVIEW QUESTIONS

1 What are the differences between the 'stimulus' and 'transactional' perspectives as they apply to the measurement of life stress?

2 List and discuss the key psychosocial components of Andersen and Williams' (1988) life stress–injury model.

3 According to the expanded stress-response model presented in this chapter, what are the four typical responses athletes might have during stressful situations and how might these responses increase athletes' risk of injury?

4 What is the relationship between athletes' appraisals and their responses to stressors?

5 How do prospective designs and repeated measures methodologies improve accuracy in predicting athletic injury?

6 Discuss how exercise-related stress interacts with psychosocial stressors to widen athletes' window of susceptibility.

7 How do the SAM and HPA systems respond to acute and chronic stressors and how do these responses increase or decrease athletes' susceptibility to injury and illness?

References

Ader, R, Felten, DL & Cohen, N 1991, *Psychoneuroimmunology*, 2nd edn, Academic Press, San Diego, CA.

Andersen, MB & Stoove, MA 1998, 'The sanctity of the p< .05 obfuscates good stuff: a comment on Kerr and Goss', *Journal of Applied Sport Psychology*, 10 (1) 168–75.

Andersen, M & Williams, J 1988, 'A model of stress and athletic injury: prediction and prevention', *Journal of Sport & Exercise Psychology*, 10, 294–306.

Andersen, M & Williams, J 1999, 'Athletic injury, psychosocial factors and perceptual changes during stress', *Journal of Sports Sciences*, 17, 735–41.

Antoni, M, Baggett, L, Ironson, G, August, S, LaPerriere, A, Klimas, N, Schneiderman, N & Fletcher, MA 1991, 'Cognitive behavioral stress management intervention buffers distress responses and elevates immunologic markers following notification of HIV-1 seropositivity', *Journal of Consulting and Clinical Psychology*, 59 (6) 906–15.

Bergandi, T 1985, 'Psychological variables relating to the incidence of athletic injury: a review of the literature', *International Journal of Sport Psychology*, 16, 141–9.

Bergandi, T & Witting, AF 1988, 'Attentional style as a predictor of athletic injury', *International Journal of Sport Psychology*, 19, 226–35.

Billings, A & Moos, R 1981, 'The role of coping responses and social resources in attenuating the stress of life events', *Journal of Behavioral Medicine*, 4, 139–57.

Blackwell, B & McCullagh, P 1990, 'The relationship of athletic injury to life stress, competitive anxiety and coping resources', *Athletic Training*, 25, 23–7.

Bramwell, S, Masuda, M, Wagner, N & Holmes, T 1975, 'Psychosocial factors in athletic injuries: development and application of the Social and Athletic Readjustment Rating Scale (SARRS)', *Journal of Human Stress*, 23, 52–8.

Brewer, B & Petrie, T 1995, 'A comparison between injured and uninjured football players on selected psychosocial variables', *The Academic Athletic Journal*, Spring, 11–18.

Byrd, B 1993, 'The relationship of history of stressors, personality and coping resources, with the incidence of athletic injuries', unpublished master's thesis, University of Colorado, Boulder.

Coddington, R & Troxell, J 1980, 'The effect of emotional factors on football injury rates — a pilot study', *Journal of Human Stress*, 6, 3–5.

Cohen, S, Tyrrell, DA & Smith, AP 1991, 'Psychological stress and susceptibility to the common cold', *New England Journal of Medicine*, 325, 606–12.

Cryan, P & Alles, W 1983, 'The relationship between stress and college football injuries', *Journal of Sports Medicine and Physical Fitness*, 23, 52–8.

Cupps, T & Fauci, A 1982, 'Corticosteroid-mediated immunoregulation in man', *Immunological Review*, 65, 133–55.

Daw, J & Burton, D 1994, 'Evaluation of a comprehensive psychological skills training program for collegiate tennis players', *The Sport Psychologist*, 8, 37–57.

Dienstbier, RA 1991, 'Behavioral correlates of sympathoadrenal reactivity: the toughness model', *Medicine & Science in Sports & Exercise*, 23, 846–52.

Elias, S 2001, '10-year trend in USA Cup soccer injuries: 1988–1997', *Medicine & Science in Sports & Exercise*, 33, 359–67.

Esterling, BA, Antoni, MH, Fletcher, MA, Margulies, S & Schneiderman, N 1994, 'Emotional disclosure through writing or speaking modulates latent Epstein-Barr virus antibody titers', *Journal of Consulting and Clinical Psychology*, 62, 130–40.

Fawkner, H, McMurray, N & Summers, J 1999, 'Athletic injury and minor life events: a prospective study', *Journal of Science and Medicine in Sport*, 2, 117–24.

Folkman, S, Lazarus, RS, Dunkel-Schetter, C, Delongis, A & Gruen, R 1986, 'Dynamics of a stressful encounter: cognitive appraisal, coping, and encounter outcomes', *Journal of Personality and Social Psychology*, 50, 992–1003.

Frankenhaeuser, M 1990, 'A psychobiological framework for human stress and coping', in MH Appley & R Trumbull (eds), *Dynamics of stress: physiological, psychological, and social perspectives*, Plenum, New York, pp. 105–11.

Green, RG, Green, ML & Santoro, W 1988, 'Daily relaxation modifies serum and salivary immunoglobulins and physiologic symptom severity', *Biofeedback & Self-Regulation*, 13, 187–99.

Greenspan, MJ & Feltz, DL 1989, 'Psychological interventions with athletes in competitive situations: a review', *The Sport Psychologist*, 3, 219–36.

Hanson, S, McCullagh, P & Tonymon, P 1992, 'The relationship of personality characteristics, life stress, and coping resources to athletic injury', *Journal of Sport & Exercise Psychology*, 14, 262–72.

Hardy, C & Riehl, R 1988, 'An examination of the life stress-injury relationship among noncontact sport participants', *Behavioral Medicine*, 14, 113–19.

Hardy, C, Richman, J & Rosenfeld, L 1991, 'The role of social support in the life stress/injury relationship', *The Sport Psychologist*, 5, 128–39.

Heatherton, TF & Penn, RJ 1995, 'Stress and the disinhibition of behavior', *Mind-Body Medicine*, 1, 72–81.

Herbert, T & Cohen, S 1993, 'Depression and Immunity: a meta-analytic review', *Psychological Bulletin*, 113, 472–86.

Holmes, T 1970, 'Psychological screening', in 'Football injuries', paper presented at a workshop sponsored by Subcommittee on Athletic Injuries, Committee on the Skeletal System, Division of Medical Sciences, National Research Council, February 1969, National Academy of Sciences, Washington, DC, pp. 211–14.

Holmes, TH & Rahe, RH 1967, 'The social readjustment scale', *Journal of Psychosomatic Research*, 11, 213–18.

Hurwitz, BE, Nelesen, RA, Saab, PG, Nagel, JH, Spitzer, SB, Gellman, MD, McCabe, PM, Phillips, DJ & Schneiderman, N 1993, 'Differential patterns of dynamic cardiovascular regulation as a function of task', *Biological Psychology*, 36, 75–9.

Jones, G & Swain, A 1992, 'Intensity and direction dimensions of competitive state anxiety and relationships with competitiveness', *Perceptual and Motor Skills*, 74, 467–72.

Kerr, G & Goss, J 1996, 'The effects of a stress management program on injuries and stress levels', *Journal of Applied Sport Psychology*, 8, 109–17.

Kerr, G & Minden, H 1988, 'Psychological factors related to the occurrence of athletic injuries', *Journal of Sport & Exercise Psychology*, 10, 167–73.

Kiecolt-Glaser, JK & Glaser, R 1992, 'Psychoneuroimmunology: can psychological interventions modulate immunity?', *Journal of Consulting and Clinical Psychology*, 60, 569–75.

Kovacs, AH & Perna, FM 1998, 'Life stress and health symptoms in competitive rowers', paper presented at the Annual Conference of the Association for the Advancement of Applied Sport Psychology, Hyannis, MA, September.

Kraus, J & Conroy, C 1984, 'Mortality and morbidity from injuries in sports and recreation', *Annual Review of Public Health*, 5, 163–92.

Lavallee, L & Flint, F 1996, 'The relationship of stress, competitive anxiety, mood state, and social support to athletic injury', *Journal of Athletic Training*, 31, 296–9.

Mackinnon, LT, Ginn, E & Seymour, G 1991, 'Effects of exercise during sports training and competition on salivary IgA levels', in AJ Husband (ed.), *Behavior and immunity*, CRC Press, Boca Raton, FL, pp. 169–77.

Martens, R 1977, *Sport competition anxiety test*, Human Kinetics, Champaign, IL.

Mason, JW 1975, 'A historical view of the stress field', *Journal of Human Stress*, 1, 22–36.

Maynard, IW & Cotton, PCJ 1993, 'An investigation of two stress management techniques in field settings', *The Sport Psychologist*, 7, 375–87.

Maynard, IW, Hemmings, B & Warwick-Evans, L 1995, 'The effects of a somatic intervention strategy on competitive state anxiety and performance in semiprofessional soccer players', *The Sport Psychologist*, 9, 51–64.

McCabe, PM & Schneiderman, N 1985, 'Psychophysiologic reactions to stress', in N Schneiderman & JT Tapp (eds), *Behavioral medicine: the biopsychosocial approach*, Lawrence Erlbaum Associates, Hillsdale, NJ, pp. 99–131.

McClay, M, Appleby, D & Plascak, F 1989, 'Predicting injury in young cross country runners with the self-motivation inventory', *Sports Training, Medicine, and Rehabilitation*, 1, 191–5.

McFarland, AH, Norman, GR, Streiner, DL, Roy, RG & Scott, DJ 1980, 'A longitudinal study of the influence of the psychosocial environment on health status: a preliminary report', *Journal of Health and Social Behavior*, 21, 124–33.

Meeuwisse, WH & Fowler, PJ 1988, 'Frequency and predictability of sports injuries in intercollegiate athletes', *Canadian Journal of Sport Sciences*, 13, 35–42.

Menckel, E & Laflamme, L 2000, 'Injuries to boys and girls in Swedish schools: different activities, different results?', *Scandinavian Journal of Public Health*, 28, 132–6.

National Collegiate Athletic Association 1992, *1991–1992 Women's volleyball injury surveillance system*, NCAA, Overland Park, KS.

Nieman, DC, Johanssen, LM, Lee, JW & Arabatzis, K 1990, 'Infectious episodes in runners before and after the Los Angeles marathon', *Journal of Sports Medicine and Physical Fitness*, 30, 316–28.

Nieman, DC, Miller, AR, Henson, DA, Warren, BJ, Gusewitch, G, Johnson, RL, Davis, JM, Butterworth, DE, Herring, JL & Nehlsen-Cannarelia, SL 1994, 'Effects of high-versus moderate-intensity exercise on lymphocyte subpopulations and proliferative response', *International Journal of Sports Exercise*, 26, 128–39.

Pargman, D & Lunt, SD 1989, 'The relationship of self-concept and locus of control to the severity of injury in freshman collegiate football players', *Sports Training, Medicine, and Rehabilitation*, 1 203–8.

Passer, MW & Seese, MD 1983, 'Life stress and athletic identity: examination of positive versus negative events and three moderator variables', *Journal of Human Stress*, 9, 11–16.

Patterson, W, Smith, R, Everett, J & Ptacek, J 1998, 'Psychosocial factors as predictors of ballet injuries: interactive effects of life stress and social support', *Journal of Sport Behavior*, 21, 101–12.

Perkins, DV 1982, 'The assessment of stress using life events scales', in L Goldberger & S Breznitz (eds), *Handbook of stress: theoretical and clinical aspects*, The Free Press, New York.

Perna, FM 1995, 'Competitive anxiety and sleep quality: an investigation of performance anxiety models in a health domain', paper presented at the Annual Conference of the Association for the Advancement of Applied Sport Psychology, New Orleans, LA.

Perna, F, Antoni, M & Schneiderman, N 1998a, 'Psychological intervention prevents injury/illness among athletes', *Journal of Applied Sport Psychology*, 10 (Suppl.) S53.

Perna, FM, Antoni, MH, Baum, A, Gordon, P & Schneiderman, N 2003, 'Cognitive behavioral stress management effects on injury and illness among competitive athletes: a randomized clinical trial', *Annals of Behavioral Medicine*, 25, 66–73.

Perna, FM, Antoni, MH, Kumar, M, Cruess, DH & Schneiderman, N 1998b, 'Cognitive-behavioral intervention effects on mood and cortisol during exercise training', *Annals of Behavioral Medicine*, 20, 92–8.

Perna, FM & McDowell, SL 1995, 'Role of psychological stress in cortisol recovery from exhaustive exercise among elite athletes', *International Journal of Behavioral Medicine*, 3, 13–26.

Perna, FM, Schneiderman, N & LaPerriere, A 1997, 'Psychological stress, exercise, and immunity', *International Journal of Sports Medicine*, 18 (Suppl. 1) S78–S83.

Petrie, T 1992, 'Psychosocial antecedents of athletic injury: the effects of life stress and social support on female collegiate gymnasts', *Behavioral Medicine*, 18, 127–38.

Petrie, T 1993a, 'The moderating effects of social support and playing status on the life stress-injury relationship', *Journal of Applied Sport Psychology*, 5, 1–16.

Petrie, T 1993b, 'Coping resources, competitive trait anxiety, and playing status: moderating effects on the life stress-injury relationship', *Journal of Sport & Exercise Psychology*, 15, 261–74.

Petrie, TA & Falkstein, DL 1998, 'Methodological, measurement and statistical issues in research on sport injury prediction', *Journal of Applied Sport Psychology*, 10, 5–25.

Petrie, T & Stoever, S 1995, 'Psychosocial antecedents of injury: a temporal analysis', paper presented at the annual meeting of the Association for the Advancement of Applied Sport Psychology, New Orleans, LA, October.

Requa, R 1991, 'The scope of the problem: the impact of sports-related injuries', Proceedings from the Conference on Sport Injuries in Youth: Surveillance Strategies, National Advisory Board for Arthritis and Musculoskeletal and Skin Diseases, National Institute of Arthritis and Musculoskeletal and Skin Diseases, and Centers for Disease Control Bethesda, MD, April.

Rider, SP & Hicks, RA 1995, 'Stress, coping, and injuries in male and female high school basketball players', *Perceptual and Motor Skills*, 81, 499–503.

Roberts, JA 1986, 'Viral illness and sports performance', *Sports Medicine*, 3, 296–303.

Ross, MJ & Berger, RS 1996, 'Effects of stress inoculation training on athletes' post-surgical pain and rehabilitation after orthopedic injury', *Journal of Consulting and Clinical Psychology*, 64, 406–10.

Savis, JC 1994, 'Sleep and athletic performance: overview and implications for sport psychology', *The Sport Psychologist*, 8, 111–25.

Selye, H 1950, *The physiology and pathology of exposure to stress*, Acta Inc., Montreal.

Shephard, RJ & Shek, PN 1994, 'Infectious disease in athletes: new interest for an old problem', *Journal of Sports Medicine and Physical Fitness*, 34, 11–22.

Shuer, M & Dietrich, M 1997, 'Psychological effects of chronic injury in elite athletes', *Western Journal of Medicine*, 166, 104–9.

Smith, RE, Ptacek, JT & Smoll, FL 1992, 'Sensation seeking, stress, and adolescent injuries: a test of stress-buffering, risk-taking, and coping skills hypotheses', *Journal of Personality and Social Psychology*, 62, 1016–24.

Smith, R, Smoll, F & Ptacek, J 1990, 'Conjunctive moderator variables in vulnerability and resiliency research: life stress, social support, coping skills and adolescent sport injuries', *Journal of Personality and Social Psychology*, 58, 360–9.

Smith, RE, Smoll, FL & Schutz, R 1990, 'Measurement and correlates of sport-specific cognitive and somatic trait anxiety: the sport anxiety scale', *Anxiety Research*, 2, 263–80.

Tharp, GD 1975, 'The role of glucocorticoids in exercise', *Medicine and Science in Sports*, 7, 6–11.

Thompson, NJ & Morris, RD 1994, 'Predicting injury risk in adolescent football players: the importance of psychological variables', *Journal of Pediatric Psychology*, 19, 415–29.

Uchino, BN & Garvey, TS 1997, 'The availability of social support reduces cardiovascular reactivity to acute psychological stress', *Journal of Behavioral Medicine*, 20, 15–27.

Urhausen, A & Kinderman, W 1987, 'Behavior of testosterone, sex hormone binding globulin, and cortisol before and after a triathlon competition', *International Journal of Sports Medicine*, 8, 305–8.

Van Mechelen, W, Hlobil, MG & Kemper HC 1992, 'Incidence, severity, etiology and prevention of sports injuries: a review of concepts', *Sports Medicine*, 14, 82–99.

Van Mechelen, W, Twisk, J, Molendijk, A, Blom, B, Snel, J & Kemper, H 1996, 'Subject-related risk factors for sports injuries: a 1-yr prospective study in young adults', *Medicine & Science in Sport & Exercise*, 28, 1171–9.

Weidner, TG 1994, 'Upper respiratory illness and sport and exercise', *International Journal of Sports Medicine*, 15, 1–9.

Wiese-Bjornstal, D, Smith, A, Shaffer, S & Morrey, M 1998, 'An integrated model of response to sport injury: psychological and sociological dynamics', *Journal of Applied Sport Psychology*, 10, 46–69.

Williams, JA 2001, 'Psychology of injury risk and prevention', in RN Singer, HA Hausenblas & C Janelle (eds), *Handbook of Sport Psychology*, 2nd edn, John Wiley & Sons, New York, pp. 766–86.

Williams, JA & Andersen, MB 1997, 'Psychosocial influences on central and peripheral vision and reaction time during demanding tasks', *Journal of Behavioral Medicine*, 26, 160–7.

Williams, JM & Andersen, MB 1998, 'Psychosocial antecedents of sport injury: review and critique of the stress and injury model', *Journal of Applied Sport Psychology*, 10, 5–25.

Williams, JM, Hogan, TD & Andersen, MB 1993, 'Positive states of mind and athletic injury risk', *Psychosomatic Medicine*, 55, 468–72.

Williams, JM, Tonymon, P & Andersen, MB 1990, 'Effects of life-event stress on anxiety and peripheral narrowing', *Journal of Behavioral Medicine*, 16, 174–81.

Williams, JM, Tonymon, P & Andersen, MB 1991, 'The effects of stressors and coping resources on anxiety and peripheral narrowing', *Journal of Applied Sport Psychology*, 3, 126–41.

Williams, JM, Tonymon, P & Wadsworth, WA 1986, 'Relationship of stress to injury in intercollegiate volleyball', *Journal of Human Stress*, 12, 38–43.

CHAPTER 22

SPORT PSYCHOLOGY AND ATHLETES WITH DISABILITIES

Stephanie J Hanrahan

Athletes with disabilities often have to deal with unique social, psychological and physical issues (Martin 1999). Some disabilities (e.g. neuromuscular diseases) are progressive and require individuals to cope with an active disease process as well as the impairments that result from the disease (Vash 1981). Athletes with dynamic disabilities (e.g. cerebral palsy) have to contend with changes in physical state or condition as a result of physical activity (Lockette & Keyes 1994). Approximately 85 per cent of athletes with disabilities have an acquired disability and, therefore, have had to confront the physical and/or psychological trauma associated with the illness or injury (Martin 1999). Many disabilities involve associated conditions that require rehabilitation or attention quite separate from the principal disability (Lockette & Keyes 1994). For example, athletes with physical disabilities may be confronted with problems with temperature regulation (Asken 1991). The processes by which athletes with disabilities are socialised into sport are often different from those for able-bodied athletes (Sherrill 1993). Accessibility of buildings, parking and transport can be an ongoing issue. Athletes competing in disability sport are confronted with a classification system that can be stressful (Tweedy 1998). Many athletes with disabilities also have to contend with various forms of prejudice in both sporting and non-sporting environments. For example, Sorenson (2001) found that sports participants with disabilities are disempowered compared with their able-bodied counterparts, and participants with and without disabilities agree that those with disabilities do not have a voice in society. The above list of issues is by no means complete but is intended to give the reader a glimpse of the factors that confront athletes with disabilities.

Because of these issues unique to athletes with disabilities, it is incorrect to assume that a psychological skills training program designed for able-bodied athletes is ideal for athletes with disabilities. Although the content of any mental skills training program should be designed on the basis of the needs of the athletes involved, the techniques and skills taught in these programs tend to be similar across sports and across athletes. It may be that athletes with disabilities are served best by comparable programs, but it is conceivable that modifications to some skills will enhance the effectiveness of psychological skills training programs.

Given the growth of both sport psychology and disability sport, it is surprising how little research has been accomplished in the adaptation of mental skills training for athletes with disabilities. Several investigators have noted this absence of research into how mental training programs can be developed and implemented for athletes with disabilities (Asken 1987, 1989; Goodling & Asken 1987; Henschen 1988; Sachs 1988). The good news is that research on mental training for athletes with disabilities is not as scarce as it once was. As research in the area slowly increases, so too has the frequency of 'how to' articles focusing on athletes with disabilities in publications aimed at coaches and athletes. For example, Banks (1992) provided recommendations for maximising athletic performance of Australians at the Barcelona Paralympics, including pre-departure, en route and post-arrival aspects. Similarly, Hedrick and Morse (1991, 1993, 1995) have supplied step-by-step instructions on how wheelchair basketball players can effectively set goals, and the role of specific pre-competition and competition plans for wheelchair racing and basketball.

DESCRIPTIVE PROFILES AND PSYCHOLOGICAL ASSESSMENT OF ATHLETES WITH DISABILITIES

In the 1980s and early 1990s the bulk of research in the area of sport psychology and disability focused on descriptive profiles of athletes with disabilities and/or the reliability of specific assessment tools that might be used with these athletes. Henschen, Horvat and French (1984), for example, found that wheelchair athletes were psychologically similar to able-bodied athletes, and Ewing, Dummer, Habeck and Overton (1987) presented an overview of selected psychological characteristics of athletes with cerebral palsy. Mastro, French, Henschen and Horvat (1985) reported that the State–Trait Anxiety Inventory is as suitably reliable for oral use with athletes who are visually impaired as it is for written use with sighted athletes. Elite male athletes with a visual impairment were found to have state and trait anxiety levels similar to the university norms for sighted individuals (Mastro & French 1985). In a similar study, however, blind male golfers were found to have higher levels of state and trait anxiety when compared with published norms for sighted university students (Mastro, French, Henschen & Horvat 1986). Higher levels of anxiety during competition have also been found for basketball players with intellectual disabilities, when compared with basketball players not classified as having an intellectual disability (Levine & Langness 1983).

Mastro et al. (1986) also studied mood states of the blind golfers and found their mood profiles to be similar to the published norms of the general population. It should be noted, however, that this investigation involved only six participants. A similar study contrasted 48 elite athletes who had a visual impairment with reported findings of sighted athletes on the Profile of Mood States (POMS) (Mastro, Sherrill, Gench & French 1987). Male athletes with a visual impairment demonstrated similar mood profiles to elite sighted athletes. The female athletes with a visual impairment, however, were below average in tension, depression, anger, fatigue and confusion, and above average in vigour, when compared with sighted athletes. Comparisons have also been made on the POMS between sighted and unsighted beep baseball players (Mastro, Canabal & French 1988). Unsighted players were significantly higher on tension and depression than sighted players, with no significant differences in the other moods measured by POMS. Obviously there is some discrepancy in the literature. An additional mood state comparison, this time between college able-bodied and wheelchair basketball players, found that the athletes with disabilities felt more vigour and less tension, depression, anger, fatigue and confusion than their able-bodied counterparts (Paulsen, French & Sherrill 1991).

Henschen, Horvat and Roswal (1992) have completed an additional investigation into the mood states of athletes with disabilities. This time, however, comparisons were made between individuals who made the US Wheelchair Basketball Paralympic team, and those who tried out for the team but were not selected. All of the participants completed the POMS before the beginning of tryouts. It was found that participants who made the team were significantly less tense and less angry than those who did not make the team. The same authors have also compared the POMS profiles of male wheelchair athletes before and after a major competition (Horvat, Roswal & Henschen 1991). They concluded that male competitors with disabilities demonstrate stable emotional sets throughout and after an entire competition, with the exception that fatigue increases significantly after a performance.

Although questionnaires about mood states and anxiety provide information about an individual's psychological wellbeing, they fail to indicate what psychological skills the athlete may use to enhance performance or enjoyment of participation. Cox and Davis (1992) administered the Psychological Skills Inventory for Sports (PSIS) to 31 international wheelchair competitors and 50 intercollegiate track athletes. The PSIS assesses an individual's psychological skills of anxiety control, concentration, confidence, mental preparation, motivation and emphasis on team goals. The wheelchair athletes were found to score significantly higher than the able-bodied athletes for the skills of anxiety control, confidence and motivation. These differences, however, may have been due to the differences in relative skill level (international versus intercollegiate), rather than to the presence or absence of disability.

Using a questionnaire designed to measure the key components of excellence as suggested by Orlick (2000), Setyadiputra and Ievleva (2001) completed a descriptive study of the perceived strengths and weaknesses of the Australian wheelchair basketball teams' mental skills. Although there were no able-bodied comparison teams and no normative comparison scores, the results indicated that these athletes had high levels of commitment, belief and constructive evaluation but were weaker in the areas of imagery, mental readiness and distraction control.

Overall, it is encouraging to see researchers in sport psychology expanding their population base to include athletes with disabilities. In many instances, however, these primarily descriptive studies have failed to provide any rationale as to why one might expect to find differences between athletes with and without disabilities in terms of the variables measured. These exploratory and somewhat speculative studies need to be followed up by vigorous and controlled research projects. If attempting to make comparisons between athletes with and without disabilities, researchers need to consider why differences might be expected and to control for numerous potentially confounding variables. In addition to considering competitive level (as previously mentioned), researchers should take into account experience, age, training and competitive opportunities, as well as phase of preparation (e.g. heavy training, tapering or off-season).

APPLICATION OF MENTAL SKILLS TRAINING

In a review of 11 articles about sport psychology for athletes with disabilities, Harlick and McKenzie (2000) found that mental skills training programs with these populations are similar to programs used by able-bodied athletes, but they argued that the unique needs of these individuals should be incorporated into the programs. Hanrahan (1995, 1996, 1998) and Martin (1999) agreed that, although there are many similarities between introducing mental skills to athletes with and without disabilities, sport psychologists will enhance their effectiveness when they are aware of information unique to athletes with disabilities. What follows are observations and findings regarding the use of various mental skills by athletes with disabilities.

Arousal control

Abdominal breathing, centring and progressive muscular relaxation (PMR) are common methods used to decrease levels of activation or arousal and are effective techniques for athletes with disabilities. For example, although athletes with little or no use of their abdominal muscles may find the physical mechanics of abdominal breathing difficult, they still tend to find abdominal breathing a useful exercise (Hanrahan 1995). Some have commented that they have benefited from the concentration aspects of the exercise (Hanrahan 1990a).

When practising centring in a standing position, athletes with no sight have a tendency to feel they are falling forward when they relax their necks, because of their reliance on vestibular feedback. Therefore, instead of allowing their necks to relax and their heads to fall slightly forward, they can maintain an erect posture. With the head erect, they still seem able to use the exercise to refocus their attention on the task at hand, suggesting that the slight difference in head angles between sighted and blind athletes is of little importance (Hanrahan, Grove & Lockwood 1990). Athletes who are blind or visually impaired can obtain the benefits of abdominal breathing or centring exercises, even though they are likely to report that distracting thoughts disrupt these exercises (Hanrahan 1996).

During group PMR exercises athletes with missing limbs or limbs with no muscular control may inadvertently be requested to tense and relax those muscles (Hanrahan 1990a). Stipulating in advance alternative activities when this occurs can minimise frustration. Individual tapes for PMR exercises can be made that exclude the parts of the body that the athletes either do not have or cannot control. When comparing standard PMR tapes with personalised PMR tapes that take into account muscle or limb losses, individual differences are apparent (Hanrahan 1995). Some athletes prefer the standard tape that includes all body parts; other athletes prefer the personalised tapes. One athlete stated that the tailor-made tape was too short because of the limited number of usable muscle groups he had. Future research should investigate the benefits of altering the content of personalised tapes while maintaining the duration of the standard version.

Individuals with mild to moderate intellectual disabilities can follow guided progressive muscular relaxation sessions; however, using the technique independently is very difficult for some (Hanrahan 1990a). For athletes with cerebral palsy who experience muscle spasms, the tensing phase of progressive muscular relaxation should be skipped (Hanrahan 1998). Alternatively, self-talk may be a more effective method of moderating arousal levels for these athletes (Martin 1999). Deaf athletes, who need to follow visual instructions for relaxation exercises, should be positioned so they can see without having to strain their neck or eyes (Hanrahan 1998).

Although in competitive situations most athletes need to learn to lower arousal levels, some athletes need to find ways to increase arousal levels. For example, because of limits in their ability to increase heart rate (Shephard 1994), quadriplegics may need to focus on methods of increasing arousal, rather than on relaxation.

Body awareness

Some amputee athletes have said that increasing body awareness resulted in their being more aware (and concerned) about muscle imbalances (Hanrahan 1990a). This can have potentially positive or negative effects. Some amputees may find body awareness exercises frustrating, if they cannot determine where their limbs end without actually looking. This suggests potentially interesting research in the area of phantom limbs and body awareness. On a more positive note, body awareness exercises may help athletes with physical disabilities determine exactly what muscles they can use. This increased awareness can lead to ideas for technique modifications in training. Increasing awareness also can help athletes with physical disabilities distinguish between pain from their disabilities and pain from injuries (Martin 1999).

What is and is not considered to be part of the body may vary. For example, a prosthesis is usually considered to be part of the athlete's body when the prosthesis is used during competition, but is not part of the body when it is not used when competing (Hanrahan 1995). Wheelchair athletes may consider the chair to be part of themselves and hence include it in body awareness exercises (Hanrahan 1998).

Imagery

For amputees, similar considerations need to be made for imagery as for body awareness exercises. If amputees perform in competition without a prosthesis, then imagery should be used when the prosthesis is off. Similarly, if athletes compete using a prosthesis, then imagery sessions should be completed while wearing the prosthesis (Hanrahan 1995). A prosthesis is different from a piece of sporting equipment (e.g. a golf club), because many athletes consider their prostheses to be part of them, part of who they are as athletes. Research needs to be done to explore this issue further. Does the wearing of a prosthesis affect kinaesthetic awareness, thereby influencing imagery, or can athletes with excellent imagery skills effectively image themselves performing with a prosthesis regardless of whether or not they are wearing it?

Imagery can be problematic for athletes with physical disabilities if they image themselves participating in their respective sports with full use of their bodies. One amputee swimmer vividly imaged herself swimming with good technique with two arms. When she returned to the water, she found it incredibly upsetting that she had only one arm. As with able-bodied athletes, unless imagery skills are highly controlled, mental practice may be potentially harmful for athletes. Other athletes with physical disabilities find imagery to be a very useful skill. It may be that any problems encountered are due solely to poor control of images, rather than anything inherent in their physical disability.

The use of imagery is not limited to sighted athletes. Blind athletes (even those totally blind from birth) are able to create images. In a small study of five athletes who were blind or visually impaired, four of the five could create vivid visual images, and all five could create movement images (Hanrahan 1996). One blind athlete pointed out that his visual images were based on what sighted people had described to him, and in fact might be very different from what would actually be seen. It would be interesting to investigate the vividness and controllability of imagery across various sensory modalities in blind and sighted athletes.

Imagery has been shown to enhance the motor performance of children with mild mental disabilities for both cognitive-oriented and motor-oriented tasks (Screws & Suburg 1997). Athletes with closed head injuries, however, may have cognitive damage. If long-term memory has been affected, imagery may be difficult (Martin

1999). Practitioners may find it useful to use a measure of imagery ability (e.g. the Sport Imagery Ability Measure) to determine existing imagery skills as well as to find out if imagery training is effective.

Goal setting

Generally the process of setting goals is exactly the same for athletes with and without disabilities. Individuals with poor writing skills (such as athletes who are blind or have severe cerebral palsy or an intellectual disability) should be encouraged to record their goals on tape (Hanrahan 1998). Some individuals may feel that their physical dependence on others requires them to rely on others when it comes to setting goals for their sport. The idea of setting goals over which they have personal control should be emphasised (as it should be with all athletes).

Self-confidence

Athletes with disabilities may have had fewer opportunities to develop the personal dispositions and skills, such as effective coping strategies and competitiveness, needed to effectively maintain self-confidence in competitive situations (Campbell & Jones 1997). On the other hand, participating in disability sport or recreation programs can help individuals develop confidence (Blinde & McClung 1997; Greenwood, Dzewaltowski & French 1990). If confidence levels are low, the interventions to enhance self-confidence are generally the same for athletes with and without disabilities.

Pre-competition preparation

Some athletes express concern about feeling in control of their own pre-competition preparation. Their partial dependence on others has led to a sense of not being in control. Where possible, athletes should be encouraged to take responsibility for themselves. In some instances, however, athletes must depend on others. In these situations it is suggested that the athletes take more control of the situation by having things that require help from others done as far in advance of competition as possible. It is also useful to set up alternate plans in case other people fail to do what they have promised, and to finalise all plans with other people well in advance, so that the athletes do not have to wait for others to realise what needs to be done. Even when some factors are beyond personal control, athletes can always be in control of their own mental preparation.

Difficulties need to be anticipated. Martin (1999) described a world-class event at which some wheelchair athletes missed the start because they were unable to find an empty lift from their upper-storey rooms. Advance planning can limit the effect of such inconveniences.

The use of audiocassettes as part of pre-competition preparation is fairly common and can be effective for athletes with disabilities. It should be noted, however, that it is rather less common for athletes who are blind to own and use personal cassette players (Hanrahan 1996). Because of their reliance on auditory cues when moving around, athletes who are blind need to find an appropriate time and place to listen to an audiotape containing affirmations, cue words, imagery scripts or music.

In summary, although sport psychologists do not need to make major changes to psychological skills training programs when working with athletes with disabilities, they should take into account some of the distinctive needs of these athletes to be most effective. Many of the studies upon which the aforementioned recommendations and findings were based had small sample sizes. These studies need to be replicated and extended to further guide practitioners when working in disability sport.

PRACTICAL CONSIDERATIONS FOR ATHLETES WITH DISABILITIES

The previous section focused on how specific psychological skills may be used by athletes with disabilities. This section presents practical considerations for working with athletes with disabilities and contains information that is relevant equally to coaches and to sport psychologists. What follows in the text applies to all athletes. See the features below and opposite for practical considerations focusing on the communication or education process for specific disabilities.

Regardless of the type or degree of disability, any training program, whether psychological or physical, should focus on the abilities of the athlete. Unfortunately, discussions that focus on disability (as does this chapter) may tend to centre readers' attention on the disabilities of specific individuals. Coaches, training partners, managers and sport psychologists should approach the individual as an athlete, rather than as a person with a disability. The reason a coach or sport psychologist is working with an individual is because that person is an athlete, not because that person has a sensory, intellectual or physical disability. Although every athlete should be treated as an individual, three important principles may be applied in any situation. Although they hold true both for athletes with disabilities and for able-bodied athletes, these considerations are often overlooked when working with athletes with disabilities.

First of all, ascertain the nature and extent of the athletes' abilities (Hanrahan 1990b). Just as people often assume that all rugby players are naturally aggressive or that short people cannot play basketball, it is also often believed that those who compete in blind competitions are totally without sight, or that all those in wheelchairs have the same amount of functional ability. Rather than make these generalisations or assumptions, determine the specific characteristics of each individual athlete.

Second, use the athletes as an information resource on themselves. They have been living with themselves all their lives. Instead of starting from scratch to ascertain what particular techniques or methods may be effective, ask the people involved.

Third, assist when and where requested, but do not offer sympathy when athletes experience temporary failure, frustration or confusion when learning new skills or increasing intensity levels (Hanrahan 1990b). An individual who has chosen to be a competitive athlete needs to develop the capacity to handle both success and failure. It is not the role of the sport psychologist or coach to protect the individual from failure.

SPECIFIC CONSIDERATIONS FOR WORKING WITH ATHLETES WITH SENSORY IMPAIRMENTS

Blind and visually impaired

- If holding sessions at a venue that is not familiar to the athletes, allow them time to explore the room, and avoid major changes in furniture arrangement.
- Ensure that all participants have access to information. This may require a variety of communication methods (e.g. large type, audiocassette recordings, Braille).
- When administering questionnaires, translate them into Braille, read them aloud and devise an answer sheet for the blind, or schedule times for athletes to complete the questionnaires individually with the consultant (Hanrahan et al. 1990). (Try to avoid having athletes complete inventories with the aid of coaches, other athletes or family members.)
- Make provisions for athletes to record their goals on cassettes or CDs.
- Provide athletes with access to personal cassette players.

Deaf and hearing impaired
- Maintain eye contact and attention of deaf athletes when communicating.
- The method of communication will vary with the athlete. Deaf athletes may communicate through sign language (which is not a single universal language), gestures, lip reading, speech, writing or a combination of methods (Clark & Sachs 1991).
- When speaking to deaf individuals, use facial expressions, body language and other visual means of communication, such as videotape, slides or demonstrations.
- When verbalising, speak clearly and slowly, but avoid over-enunciating or exaggerating words.

Keep in mind that even athletes who have lived in an English-speaking country their entire lives may not have English as a first language. Pencil and paper tests and inventories are not appropriate for use with deaf athletes whose first language may be American Sign Language (ASL) or another version of signing. If a great deal of work with deaf athletes is foreseen, learning the suitable sign language would be appropriate (Clark & Sachs 1991).

SPECIFIC CONSIDERATIONS FOR WORKING WITH ATHLETES WITH INTELLECTUAL OR PHYSICAL DISABILITIES

Intellectual disabilities
- The development of trust and rapport is critical (Travis & Sachs 1991).
- The sport psychologist must work at the individual's level of understanding.
- Soliciting help from relatives, case managers or residential staff is important (Travis & Sachs 1991).
- An athlete with an intellectual disability may be unable to think in abstract terms, lack the ability to make decisions, have poor short-term memory, have limited literacy or numeracy skills, and have inconsistent concentration spans (Hanrahan 1990b). With these possibilities in mind, instructions should be kept simple, skills should be broken down into smaller teaching components, and sessions should be fun and enjoyable with practice times on specific activities kept short.

Physical disabilities
- Ensure that venues are accessible.
- If working with a group of athletes in wheelchairs, communication can be improved by being on their level; in other words, sit in a chair.
- If the physical disability affects the control of muscles required for speech, be patient with verbal communication. Do not finish sentences for the athlete. If a carer or parent is present, allow that person to interpret, but be sure to speak directly to the athlete.
- Be aware of the temperature of the venue. Spinal lesions can involve the loss of autonomic control, limiting vasodilation, sweating and vasoconstriction (Shephard 1994).

Extra time may be required for athletes to transfer from their chairs to the floor for relaxation sessions. Alternatively, some athletes may prefer to stay in their chairs.

FUTURE DIRECTIONS

Providing applied sport psychology services for athletes with disabilities is a relatively new development. Most of the applied information presented in this chapter has been experiential or observational. The experimental studies that have been published usually have had small sample sizes. Obviously more research is needed. Many more questions than answers exist. A small list of questions that beg for active consideration by researchers follows.

- What method of communication is best when using questionnaires for assessing mental skills and evaluating programs when working with athletes with sensory impairments?
- Is there an ideal progressive muscular relaxation tape in terms of length and content for athletes with physical disabilities?
- Can longitudinal studies with precise methods of measuring body awareness ascertain the usefulness and success of becoming more aware of exactly which muscles can be controlled and used to improve performance in sport for athletes with physical or neurological disabilities?
- Is the general kinaesthetic awareness of athletes who are blind or visually impaired greater than that of sighted athletes?
- Are the imagery modality preferences of athletes with disabilities related to the type of disability? Similarly, are certain imagery modalities more effective for some disability types than others? For example, do athletes who are blind, deaf or paralysed find auditory, visual or kinaesthetic imagery most effective? Do sensory disabilities influence the effectiveness of internal versus external imagery?
- What alternatives to pre-competition audiotapes are effective for athletes who are deaf or hearing impaired? With the reliance of blind individuals on sound, does listening to pre-competition audiotapes ever have a negative effect, such as increasing feelings of isolation?
- How are phantom limb experiences influenced by body awareness or imagery exercises?
- What changes or additions could be made to the content or presentation of mental skills training programs that would make them more effective for athletes with intellectual disabilities?

CONCLUSIONS

At a time when sport psychology is expanding in terms of practice, recognition and research, it would be remiss to limit this growth to able-bodied athletes. Understanding the structure, use and potential benefits of mental skills training as applied to athletes with disabilities will allow these athletes to enhance their performance and enjoyment of sport. The dissemination of this information is as important as its collection.

No major changes to existing mental skills training programs are required when working with athletes with disabilities. Minor changes or adaptations of some skills and consideration of communication processes are all that is required. Although the evaluation of the overall effectiveness of mental skills training programs for athletes with disabilities has begun (e.g. Hanrahan 1995, 1996), research should evaluate different techniques or skills independently (Gould, Petlichkoff, Hodge & Simons 1990), particularly when modifications have been made. Research is needed that clearly outlines the effectiveness of various psychological skills in enhancing the performance and enjoyment of athletes with disabilities. These programs should cater to athletes with physical or sensory disabilities, as well as to those with intellectual disabilities.

SUMMARY

Athletes with disabilities often have to contend with unique social, psychological and physical issues. Because of these issues, psychological skills training programs designed for able-bodied athletes may or may not be ideal for athletes with disabilities. In the

1980s and early 1990s most publications in the area of sport psychology and athletes with disabilities focused on descriptive profiles and the reliability of assessment tools. Now there is research on mental skills training programs, as well as a range of applied articles aimed at coaches and athletes.

This chapter has presented observations and findings regarding athletes with disabilities and arousal control, body awareness, imagery, goal setting, self-confidence and pre-competition preparation. Issues related to communication and the educational process for specific types of disabilities have also been included. In addition, general considerations on working with athletes with disabilities have been provided. The chapter finished with a list of suggestions for future research.

 ## REVIEW QUESTIONS

1   Describe three unique issues with which athletes with disabilities have to contend.

2   What was the focus of the bulk of the research in the 1980s and early 1990s in the area of sport psychology and disability?

3   Discuss the pros and cons of using personalised progressive muscular relaxation (PMR) tapes that take into account muscle or limb losses.

4   When should prostheses be worn during body awareness and imagery exercises?

5   Can blind people use visual imagery?

6   How do issues of control relate to pre-competition preparation?

7   Describe the different communication issues related to working with athletes who are blind versus athletes who are deaf.

8   List three research questions that need to be addressed in future studies investigating applied sport psychology services for athletes with disabilities.

References

Asken, MJ 1987, 'Sport psychology: psychological effects of sport participation in physically disabled individuals', paper presented at the Conference on Sports Medicine and Science for Disabled Athletes, Bartlett, NH, March.

Asken, MJ 1989, 'Sport psychology and the physically disabled athlete: interview with Michael D Goodling, OTR/L', *The Sport Psychologist*, 3, 166–76.

Asken, MJ 1991, 'The challenge of the physically challenged: delivering sport psychology services to physically disabled athletes', *The Sport Psychologist*, 5, 370–81.

Banks, J 1992, 'Maximising athletic performance at the 1992 Paralympics, *Sports Coach*, July–December, pp. 18–24.

Blinde, EM & McClung, LR 1997, 'Enhancing the physical and social self through recreational activity: accounts of individuals with physical disabilities', *Adapted Physical Activity Quarterly*, 14, 327–44.

Campbell, E & Jones, G 1997, 'Precompetition anxiety and self-confidence in wheelchair sport participants', *Adapted Physical Activity Quarterly*, 14, 95–107.

Clark, RA & Sachs, ML 1991, 'Challenges and opportunities in psychological skills training in deaf athletes', *The Sport Psychologist*, 5, 392–8.

Cox, R & Davis, R 1992, 'Psychological skills of elite wheelchair athletes', *Palaestra*, 8 (3) 16–21.

Ewing, ME, Dummer, GM, Habeck, RV & Overton, SR 1987, 'Psychological character-istics of cognitions of athletes with cerebral palsy', paper presented at the Association for the Advancement of Applied Sport Psychology, Newport Beach, CA, September.

Goodling, MD & Asken, MJ 1987, 'Sport psychology and the physically disabled ath-lete', in JR May & MJ Asken (eds), *Sport psychology: the psychological health of the athlete*, PMA Publishing, New York, pp. 117–33.

Gould, D, Petlichkoff, L, Hodge, K & Simons, J 1990, 'Evaluating the effectiveness of a psychological skills educational workshop', *The Sport Psychologist*, 4, 249–60.

Greenwood, CM, Dzewaltowski, DA & French, R 1990, 'Self-efficacy and psychological well-being of wheelchair tennis participants and wheelchair non-tennis partici-pants', *Adapted Physical Activity Quarterly*, 7, 12–21.

Hanrahan, SJ 1990a, 'Psychological skills training for the disabled', paper presented at the Commonwealth and International Conference on Physical Education, Sport, Health, Dance, Recreation, and Leisure, Auckland, January.

Hanrahan, SJ 1990b, 'Coaching disabled individuals: some practical considerations', paper presented at the Commonwealth and International Conference on Physical Education, Sport, Health, Dance, Recreation, and Leisure, Auckland, January.

Hanrahan, SJ 1995, 'Psychological skills training for competitive wheelchair and amputee athletes', *Australian Psychologist*, 30 (2) 96–101.

Hanrahan, SJ 1996, 'Mental skills training for blind and visually impaired athletes', Australian Sports Commission, Canberra.

Hanrahan, SJ 1998, 'Practical considerations for working with athletes with disabilities', *The Sport Psychologist*, 12, 346–57.

Hanrahan, SJ, Grove, JR & Lockwood, RJ 1990, 'Psychological skills training for the blind athlete: a pilot program', *Adapted Physical Activity Quarterly*, 7, 143–55.

Harlick, M & McKenzie, A 2000, 'Psychological skills training for athletes with disabil-ities: a review', *New Zealand Journal of Sports Medicine*, 28 (3) 64–66.

Hedrick, B & Morse, M 1991, 'Setting goals in wheelchair basketball', *Sports 'n Spokes*, 17, 64–7.

Hedrick, B & Morse, M 1993, 'Preparation: a key to successful racing', *Sports 'n Spokes*, 19, 77–9.

Hedrick, B & Morse, M 1995, 'All psyched up', *Sports 'n Spokes*, 21, 70–1.

Henschen, KP 1988, 'More on sport psychology's neglected population', *Association for the Advancement of Applied Sport Psychology Newsletter*, 3 (2) 8.

Henschen, KP, Horvat, M & French, R 1984, 'A visual comparison of psychological profiles between able-bodied and wheelchair athletes', *Adapted Physical Activity Quarterly*, 1 (2) 118–24.

Henschen, KL, Horvat, M & Roswal, G 1992, 'Psychological profiles of the United States wheelchair basketball team', *International Journal of Sport Psychology*, 23 (2) 128–37.

Horvat, M, Roswal, G & Henschen, K 1991, 'Psychological profiles of disabled male athletes before and after competition', *Clinical Kinesiology*, 45, 14–18.

Levine, HG & Langness, LL 1983, 'Context, ability, and performance: comparison of competitive athletics among mildly mentally retarded and nonretarded adults', *American Journal of Mental Deficiency*, 87 (5) 528–38.

Lockette, KF & Keyes, AM 1994, *Conditioning with physical disabilities*, Human Kinetics, Champaign, IL.

Martin, JJ 1999, 'A personal development model of sport psychology for athletes with disabilities', *Journal of Applied Sport Psychology*, 11, 181–93.

Mastro, JR, Canabal, MY & French, R 1988, 'Psychological mood profiles of sighted and unsighted beep baseball players', *Research Quarterly for Exercise and Sport*, 59 (3) 262–4.

Mastro, J & French, R 1985, 'Sport anxiety and blind athletes', in C Sherrill (ed.), *Sport and disabled athletes*, Human Kinetics, Champaign, IL.

Mastro, J, French, R, Henschen, K & Horvat, M 1985, 'Use of the state-trait anxiety inventory for visually impaired athletes', *Perceptual and Motor Skills*, 61, 775–8.

Mastro, J, French, R, Henschen, K & Horvat, M 1986, 'Selected psychological characteristics of blind golfers and their coaches', *American Corrective Therapy Journal*, 40 (5) 111–14.

Mastro, JV, Sherrill, C, Gench, B & French, R 1987, 'Psychological characteristics of elite visually impaired athletes: the iceberg profile', *Journal of Sport Behavior*, 10 (1) 39–46.

Orlick, T 2000, *In pursuit of excellence*, 3rd edn, Human Kinetics, Champaign, IL.

Paulsen, P, French, R & Sherrill, C 1991, 'Comparison of mood states of college able-bodied and wheelchair basketball players', *Perceptual and Motor Skills*, 73, 396–8.

Sachs, ML 1988, 'Sport psychology's neglected population: persons with disabilities', *Association for the Advancement of Applied Sport Psychology Newsletter*, 3 (2) 8.

Screws, DP & Suburg, PR 1997, 'Motor performance of children with mild mental disabilities after using mental imagery', *Adapted Physical Activity Quarterly*, 14, 119–30.

Setyadiputra, E & Ievleva, L 2001, 'Paralympic case study in mental preparation: the Australian wheelchair basketball teams', in A Papaioannou, M Goudas & Y Theodorakis (eds), *International Society of Sport Psychology 10th World Congress of Sport Psychology Programme & Proceedings*, vol. 5, Christodoulidi, Thessaloniki, Greece, pp. 206–8.

Shephard, RJ 1994, 'Physiological aspects of physical activity for children with disabilities', *Physical Education Review*, 17, 33–44.

Sherrill, C 1993, *Adapted physical activity, recreation, and sport*, 4th edn, Wm C Brown, Dubuque, IA.

Sorensen, M 2001, 'Empowerment through sport for individuals with a disability: the role of motivational climate', in A Papaioannou, M Goudas & Y Theodorakis (eds), *International Society of Sport Psychology 10th World Congress of Sport Psychology Programme & Proceedings*, vol. 5, Christodoulidi, Thessaloniki, Greece, pp. 200–2.

Travis, CA & Sachs, ML 1991, 'Applied sport psychology and persons with mental retardation', *The Sport Psychologist*, 5, 382–91.

Tweedy, S 1998, 'B2 or not B2? A beginner's guide to classification and the Paralympics', *SportsMed News*, August, 10–11.

Vash, CL 1981, *The psychology of disability*, Springer, New York.

CHAPTER 23

CAREER TRANSITIONS IN COMPETITIVE SPORT

Sandy Gordon & David Lavallee

Career transitions as an area of research was generally overlooked by sport scientists in Australia until recently. Career retirement issues also received haphazard attention by sport administrators, coaches, athletes and those closely associated with athletes (e.g. family) who are nevertheless keenly aware of the complex personal adjustments and socio-psychological phenomena involved. This chapter attempts to provide an overview of the theoretical approaches and frameworks that help explain the phenomenon, a review of the existing literature and intervention strategies, and a summary of future directions for both research and career assistance programs.

The first section introduces the theoretical perspectives (summarised on page 588) that have been applied, more or less appropriately, to sport. The second section attempts to summarise the existing research conducted by sociologists and psychologists, including recent Australian research, and is followed by brief descriptions of current Australian career assistance programs. The fourth and fifth sections describe prevention and treatment interventions, and suggestions for further research, respectively.

THEORETICAL MODELS

Social gerontology theories

McPherson (1980), in his discussion of occupational and psychological adjustment problems in athletic retirement, suggested that certain theories associated with social gerontology (the study of ageing) might be usefully applied. Rosenberg (1981) discussed the merits and shortcomings of six such approaches — namely, activity, disengagement, subculture, continuity, social breakdown and reconstruction, and exchange theories.

Activity or substitution theory (Burgees 1960) maintains that lost roles are to be substituted for so that total activity continues. It proposed that high activity and maintenance of roles are positively related to self-concept and life satisfaction. Most older people, however, seem content to decrease their activity and do not retain patterns of activity associated with middle age, which is an anomaly that activity theory fails to explain. Disengagement theory (Cumming, Dean, Newell & McCaffrey 1960), a structural–functional theory, suggests that society and the ageing individual withdraw from one another to the mutual benefit and satisfaction of both. After retirement, society gets younger workers into the workforce and the elderly can enjoy their remaining years in leisure. While disengagement theory was developed to attack activity theory, neither theory provides mechanisms to predict whether activity or disengagement will result; both, therefore, are limited in their applied utility.

Building on activity theory, subculture theory (Rose 1965) adds the possibility of subcultural norms, which may be different from social norms, and according to which some elderly people may enjoy less activity but be well adjusted. Rosenberg (1981) sees some merit in this approach, since competitive athletes have fairly obvious and distinguishable subcultural characteristics. Unlike activity theory, continuity or consolidation theory (Atchley 1981) suggests that substitution is not necessary for lost roles. Time and energy can be redirected or redistributed among the roles remaining or towards new roles. However, if the lost role was an important role, consolidation or other activities might not provide the same basis for a meaningful existence and therefore might not provide a satisfactory solution.

Social breakdown theory (Kuypers & Bengston 1973) proposes that with any role loss (e.g. retirement or widowhood) individuals become susceptible to external labelling (e.g. 'hero to zero', Orlick 2000); and if the social evaluation of status is unfavourable, tendencies to withdraw or to reduce certain activities develop. To combat this negative downward-spiralling cycle out of activity, a 'social reconstruction' cycle is proposed to restore and maintain positive self-image through counselling and engagement in alternative activities that enhance self-reliance. Finally, exchange theory (Dowd 1975) can be adapted to illustrate how successful ageing can be achieved through rearrangement of social networks and activities to maximise return.

While all of these theories have relevance for sport retirement and warrant closer scrutiny than offered here, Rosenberg (1981) suggests that the latter two theories, social breakdown/reconstruction and exchange theories, are most salient. Anecdotal evidence alone, he believes, suggests that voluntary disengagement from sport is unlikely and that, contrary to disengagement theory, athletes typically try to hang on to sport, sometimes long after their skills have begun to deteriorate. Also, the main messages of the activity, subculture and continuity theories are, arguably, largely incorporated into social breakdown/reconstruction theory. For example, activity theory proposes concepts like role replacement and activity level maintenance; subculture theory acknowledges and identifies norms that are dysfunctional to retirement planning; and continuity theory is applicable in that commitment, sacrifice and self-concept from the competitive athlete role can be reallocated to remaining or new roles. Through understanding and counselling on these and other issues athletes can learn to minimise the potential for social breakdowns and take steps, through social reconstruction, to smooth out the transition period.

Exchange theory can help athletes to gradually understand their relationship with sport, and provide a perspective on what will happen to that relationship over time. For example, the athlete's resource — physical talent — is exchanged for meaningful rewards from the sport system, but that resource is finite and the inevitable deterioration in skill will affect the degree of control over the athlete/sport relationship. Rosenberg (1981) believes an exchange theory perspective 'would, in pre-retirement counseling, make a fitting prelude to a discussion of social breakdown' (p. 123).

Social death: thanatology

Both Rosenberg (1982) and Lerch (1982) have employed the concept of social death as a model for explaining the social and psychological changes involved in retirement from sport. Social death refers to the condition of being treated as if one were dead even while still physiologically and intellectually alive. It derives from the science of thanatology (study of death and dying), and although the concept of death is only an analogy, and there is a considerable difference between actual death and retirement from sport, the concept of social death is perceived as quite useful, particularly for designing career assistance and counselling programs. Lerch, for example, discussed two thanatological models that reveal interesting parallels between the socially dying retiring athlete and the physically dying hospital patient. These are the 'awareness context' notion of Glaser and Strauss (1965) and the 'stages of dying' of Kübler-Ross (1969).

Glaser and Strauss (1965) suggest four different types of awareness context: closed, suspicion, mutual pretence and open. In sport, the closed awareness category would apply when athletes are unaware of plans to cut, release or trade them from teams. Team-mates may have seen 'the axe' approaching but, because failures or deteriorations in form are rarely discussed in competitive sport, the athlete concerned is often surprised or even shocked when it happens. Suspicion awareness is more complicated, in that athletes may suspect a demotion is imminent through subtle changes in personal interactions with coaches and administrators. For example, less verbal and non-verbal (body language) communication is perceived by the athlete when in the presence of coaches and administrators. The next context, mutual pretence, is analogous to make-believe, a situation in which all concerned with the athlete — managers, coaches, trainers — know that no matter how well the athlete performs, her or his career is nearing its conclusion. If this awareness level is not sustained, mutual pretence can only switch to the final level, open awareness, at which both the athlete and others know that career end is inevitable and openly acknowledge the fact.

From interviews, Kübler-Ross (1969) identified certain reactions or coping mechanisms used by terminal patients to deal with impending death, and Lerch (1982) draws interesting parallels with athletes coping with social death. Similar reactions by athletes responding to and rehabilitating from sport injury have been reported by sport physiotherapists (e.g. Gordon, Milios & Grove 1991). The first stage is denial ('No it's not true') followed by anger ('Why me? Why now?'), bargaining ('I'll do anything to stay in the game'), depression ('This loss is unbearably sad') and finally acceptance or resignation ('It's happened. My competitive sport career is over. Now what?'). At the final stage, social death obviously lacks the finality of real death. Recovery from social death is therefore possible, although athletes themselves are likely to mourn the loss of their careers either publicly or privately in a cyclical fashion, drifting in and out of different stages of reaction. Regarded in this light, Rosenberg (1982) and Lerch (1982) maintain that the analogy of social death can be usefully applied particularly to involuntary rather than voluntary retirement. The consequences of voluntary retirement are less severe because the athlete retains control of his or her fate.

While models from social gerontology and thanatology dominate the literature, several researchers (e.g. Blinde & Greendorfer 1985; Greendorfer & Blinde 1985) have questioned the ability of those models to comprehensively capture the process of leaving sport. Crook and Robertson (1991) also criticise social gerontological models, specifically the analogy between athletic (functional) retirement and old age (chronological) retirement, and the inability of gerontological models to explain variations in athlete responses to retirement. The thanatological model is also criticised for stereotyping athlete reactions, and for portraying retirement in an overly negative light. Both models seem to assume that all retirement experiences require serious adjustment when, in reality, this may not always be the case.

Transition models

Whereas social gerontological models and thanatological models view retirement as a singular event, transition models characterise retirement as a process. A transition has been defined by Schlossberg (1981) as 'an event or non-event which results in a change in assumptions about oneself and the world and thus requires a corresponding change in one's behaviour and relationships' (p. 5). As such, a number of transition frameworks have been employed to examine the interaction of the retiring athlete and the environment, including Sussman's (1972) analytic model and Schlossberg's (1981) model of human adaptation to transition.

Although McPherson (1980) was perhaps the first to refer to the phenomenon of athletic career termination as a transition in the literature, Hill and Lowe (1974) initially suggested that Sussman's (1972) analytic model of retirement from the workforce may be useful in explaining adjustment to athletic retirement. In their article, Hill and Lowe (1974) asserted that the retirement process is a multidimensional conceptualisation; however, as suggested by Sussman himself, this particular process model does not apply to athletic retirement because athletes are aware of the brevity of their sport careers and thus can prepare for the inevitable transition.

The most frequently employed theory of transition, which has been outlined in the athletic career termination literature, has been the model of human adaptation to transition as discussed by Schlossberg and associates (Charner & Schlossberg 1986; Schlossberg 1981, 1984). In this model, three major sets of factors interact during a transition, including the characteristics of the individual experiencing the transition, the perception of the particular transition, and the characteristics of the pre-transition and post-transition environments. The variables that characterise the individual include attributes such as psychosocial competence, sex, age, state of health, race/ethnicity, socioeconomic status, value orientation and previous experience with a transition of a similar nature. These variables may show considerable differences across the population of athletes facing retirement from sport, and Coakley (1983) asserts that a diversity of factors influencing the athlete in transition must be acknowledged in order to understand the overall adjustment process.

Regarding the perception of a particular transition, Schlossberg (1981) has suggested that role change, affect, source, onset, duration and degree of stress are all important factors to consider. This aspect of the model emphasises the phenomenological nature of transitions, in that it is not just the transition itself that is important, but also the individual variables that have different salience depending on the transition. For retiring athletes, Sinclair and Orlick (1993) have acknowledged this position by suggesting that every career transition has the potential to be a crisis, a relief or combination of both, depending on the athlete's perception of the situation.

In considering the characteristics of the pre- and post-transition environments, Schlossberg (1981) acknowledged internal support systems, institutional support and physical settings. Although several researchers have examined social support networks among injured athletes (e.g. Ford & Gordon 1999; Udry 2001), little research has been conducted in this area with retired athletes. A number of theorists have outlined the obligations of coaches and sport associations in preparing athletes for retirement from high-level competition (e.g. Parker 1994; Thomas & Ermler 1988). Once again, however, few empirical investigations have been made in this area of athletic career termination.

Overall, the models of social gerontology, thanatology and transition that have been applied to retirement from sport have been instrumental in stimulating research on career transition and termination issues. All of these perspectives, however, possess limitations that indicate the need for further conceptual development in the area. As

Rotella and Heyman (1993) have stated, career transition research has often made generalisations across a number of athletes, and thus has not presented information about how to individualise approaches. Social gerontological and thanatological models do not indicate what factors influence the quality of adaptation to retirement from sport. In addition, transition models that have been applied to sport lack operational detail of the specific components related to the career transition and termination adjustment process (Taylor & Ogilvie 1994).

PERSPECTIVES REFERRED TO IN THE STUDY OF CAREER TRANSITIONS IN SPORT

Social gerontology (study of ageing)
Activity or substitution theory
Disengagement theory
Subculture theory
Continuity or consolidation theory
Exchange theory

Thanatology (study of death and dying)
Awareness context
Stages of dying

Transition models (process of retirement)
Analytical model of retirement from work
Model of human adaptation

Figure 23.1 is a conceptual model illustrating causal factors that initiate career transition, interacting and developmental factors related to retirement adaptation, tertiary factors that mediate adaptation, and potential sites for interventions or treatment modalities for career transition and career assistance.

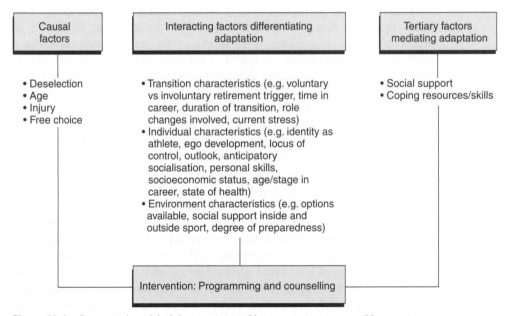

Causal factors	Interacting factors differentiating adaptation	Tertiary factors mediating adaptation
• Deselection • Age • Injury • Free choice	• Transition characteristics (e.g. voluntary vs involuntary retirement trigger, time in career, duration of transition, role changes involved, current stress) • Individual characteristics (e.g. identity as athlete, ego development, locus of control, outlook, anticipatory socialisation, personal skills, socioeconomic status, age/stage in career, state of health) • Environment characteristics (e.g. options available, social support inside and outside sport, degree of preparedness)	• Social support • Coping resources/skills

Intervention: Programming and counselling

Figure 23.1 Conceptual model of the career transitions process on competitive sport

In the following sections, first the international empirical research conducted on career transitions processes is reviewed. This survey is followed by investigations on how the overall quality of adjustment to athletic retirement is influenced by causal factors, developmental experiences and coping resources. A summary of specifically Australian research in these areas concludes the section.

CAREER TRANSITION RESEARCH

Transition processes

Studies of the process of transition are rare (McPherson 1980); however, four earlier investigations by Mihovilovic (1968), Haerle (1975), Werthner and Orlick (1986), and Allison and Meyer (1988) are among the most commonly cited.

Mihovilovic (1968) surveyed the reasons for career termination, and the ways the effects of retirement could be eased, among 44 male Yugoslavian soccer players using questionnaires and interviews. He found that only 5 per cent retired voluntarily and the remainder retired as a result of injury, age, club contract arrangements or deselection. More than half (52 per cent) reported retirement as a shock or sudden event that was closely related to illness, family factors or age. Only one-third (34 per cent) retired at their peak, while the remainder hung on until after their skills had begun to decline. Smoother transitions, it was suggested, could be facilitated by clubs' maintaining contact with players, including players in tournaments and public announcements, and using their experience and expertise in coaching or training.

Haerle (1975) surveyed 312 former baseball players and focused on their pre-retirement planning or preparations for retirement, and responses and attitudes when the event occurred. He reported that 75 per cent of the respondents did not consider retirement until their early thirties or the last quarter of their playing career, and 50 per cent were more psychologically oriented towards their past sporting career than to their future. At the time of retirement only 25 per cent were making plans for the future and had accepted their career end. In addition, while fame helped in securing the first post-playing job, educational attainment was more significant in predicting later careers. Interestingly, Haerle also reported that those who chose to stay in baseball experienced less stable career paths than those who quit the sport completely.

In Werthner and Orlick's (1986) study of the transitions of 28 Canadian Olympians, seven major factors that determined the nature of the transition emerged:

1. *A new focus.* Alternatives or options to sports participation allowed for a redirection of attention and energy.
2. *A sense of accomplishment.* Achieving goals in their sport (e.g. medals) facilitated transition.
3. *Coaches.* 'Lack of good coaches and conflicts with coaches or with coaching decisions ... often made the actual transition quite difficult' (Werthner & Orlick 1986 p. 354).
4. *Injuries/health problems.* Negative transition experiences were frequently precipitated by premature career termination due to injury.
5. *Politics/sport-association problems.* Canada's boycott of the 1980 Summer Olympics had a negative impact on the transition of many of the athletes. However, some also reported problems with the Sport Canada carding system that classifies amateur athletes into A, B and C categories as a basis for providing athletes with financial assistance.

6. *Finances.* The cost of continued training and preparation and the lack of funding, which together contributed to the decision to retire, often resulted in negative consequences for the athlete and a sense of bitterness.

7. *The support of family and friends.* Many athletes reported that the social support of family and friends was a positive factor in their transition. Athletes who did not receive such support reported more difficulties in the transition process.

Allison and Meyer (1988) surveyed 28 retired female tennis professionals and their experiences and perceptions of their competitive years and subsequent retirement. Results indicated that most subjects did not find disengagement from competitive sport traumatic, and in fact regarded it as an opportunity to re-establish more traditional social roles and lifestyles. This is perhaps not surprising since almost two-thirds (60 per cent) commented that they had not intended to become professionals in the first place and had continued playing much longer than they had planned. After experiencing significant levels of frustration touring, 50 per cent actually expressed relief upon retirement. One-third (30 per cent), however, did report initial adjustment problems (e.g. loss of identity, isolation) immediately following retirement.

In addition to the four studies just described, data from surveys conducted by Blann and Zaichkowsky (e.g. 1986, 1989) among American professional hockey and major league baseball players, and by Wylleman, de Knop, Menkehorst, Theeboom and Annerel (1993) with former Belgian Olympic athletes, highlight the perceived need of athletes for post-sport career planning programs. Using Blann's Professional Athletes Career Transition Inventory (PACTI), Blann and Zaichkowsky surveyed 117 National Hockey League (NHL) and 214 major league baseball (MBL) players. The two most helpful career planning programs perceived by players were seminars and individual counselling to help players understand their personal strengths, interests and skills related to careers; and all assistance to help players develop and carry out education/training programs and career action plans. The two least helpful types of services were arranging for jobs during the off-season, and help in developing and carrying out job search campaigns. Interestingly, these professional athletes believed that players' associations, and not management, were primarily responsible for the provision of such services. Wylleman et al., on the other hand, found that 45.5 per cent reported that 'lack of pre-retirement planning and the failing of official organizations such as the sport federations, the Olympic Committee, and the Flemish Bureau for Top-level Sport, had the most influence on the way in which their career termination and the following phase of adaptation and social integration evolved (mostly problematically)' (p. 904).

Taken together, Baillie and Danish (1992) believe that these and other earlier studies (e.g. Lerch 1981; Reynolds 1981; Rosenberg 1981) provide patterns of evidence that are useful in developing both career transition programs and directions for further research. For example, recurring themes include athletes being unprepared for retirement (financially or emotionally) while at the same time indicating a desire for more support; and secondly, a need for a gradual resocialisation out of athlete identities and sport and into non-sport participatory roles either through education or second careers or both.

More recent reviews of career transition processes by Lavallee and his colleagues (Lavallee, Sinclair & Wylleman 1998; Lavallee, Wylleman & Sinclair 1998) suggest that, while there is still considerable debate about how well athletes adapt to retirement, the factors most likely to determine whether the experience is positive or negative include the reasons for retirement, developmental experiences and coping resources (cf. Gordon 1995; Taylor & Ogilvie 2001).

Reasons for retirement: causal factors

Retirement from sport is likely to be a function of a variety of involuntary and voluntary reasons but, while actual causes are influenced by the structure of sport, studies have now demonstrated that the most common reasons are career-ending injuries, chronological age, deselection and personal choice.

An unexpected and sudden retirement from sport can result from serious sport injury, and adjustment difficulties can be expected because it is something for which individuals are seldom prepared (Werthner & Orlick 1986). Kleiber and Brock's (1992) study of competitive athletes who suffered career-ending injuries indicated that an injury may not even need to be severe to force athletes out of continued participation in competitive sport. As Ogilvie and Taylor (1993a) have suggested, because elite athletes perform at such a high level, even small reductions in their physical capabilities may be sufficient to make them no longer competitive at the highest level.

Research by Mihovilovic (1968) has shown that retirement from sport can also be a function of chronological age. In his study of former professional soccer players, decline in performance accompanying the ageing process was identified as one of the major causes for retirement. Taylor and Ogilvie (2001) suggest that age is one of the most significant reasons for retirement because psychological motivation, social status and physical capabilities can all complicate an individual's ability to continue competing at an elite level.

Associated with the physiological processes of ageing is the structural factor of an athlete failing to progress to the next-highest level of elite competition, namely deselection. Lavallee, Grove and Gordon's (1997) study showed that this involuntary reason is an important contributor to sports career termination in Australia.

The final notable reason for retirement from sport is that of choice. Research by Wylleman et al. (1993) demonstrated that many individuals freely elect to terminate their sporting career for a combination of personal and psychological reasons. Some athletes may decide to end their careers because of financial complications, ethnic or gender-related issues, or an overall lack of life satisfaction, whereas others may want to spend more time with their families and friends (Baillie 1993). Although a voluntary decision to retire from sport is perhaps the most attractive reason, it is important to recognise that ending a career voluntarily eases the career transition process (Taylor & Ogilvie 2001).

Developmental factors: athletic identity

With regard to developmental factors associated with the transition process, researchers have shown that athletic identity — that is, the degree to which an individual identifies with the athlete role (Brewer, Van Raalte & Linder 1993) — can have a significant effect on the quality of adjustment. Brewer and colleagues (Brewer et al. 1993; Good, Brewer, Petitpas, Van Raalte & Mahar 1993) discussed athletic identity within the framework of a multidimensional construct, and described a person with strong athletic identity as 'more likely to interpret a given event (e. g. an injury) in terms of its implications for that individual's athletic functioning than a person only weakly identified to the athlete role' (Brewer et al. 1993, p. 238). They also describe athletic identity as a social role, one that is heavily socialised by the influences of family, friends, coaches, teachers and the media.

While the benefits of strong athletic identity include adherence to and involvement in sport, exercise and health behaviours, development of athletic skills, sense of self, and confidence, the potential risks relate to difficulties athletes may experience during career transitions — specifically, problems associated with deselection, injury and athletic career termination (Baillie & Danish 1992; Murphy, Petitpas & Brewer 1996; Pearson & Petitpas 1990). A strong and exclusive athletic identity is thought to be a risk factor for emotional problems following career end because 'individuals who strongly commit themselves to the athlete role may be less likely to explore other career, education and lifestyle options due to their intensive involvement in sport' (Brewer et al. 1993 p. 241).

Earlier studies have provided indirect support for the hypothesis that strong exclusive athletic identity creates potential for emotional difficulties upon career end. For example, Werthner and Orlick (1986) found that former Canadian Olympians who had prearranged alternative career options and commitments adjusted to transitions out of the athlete role more effectively than those without prearranged alternatives. Kleiber, Greendorfer, Blinde and Samdahl (1987) demonstrated that intercollegiate athletes whose careers were terminated prematurely by injury reported lower post-collegiate life satisfaction than their student/athlete peers whose careers were not terminated by injury. Kleiber and Malik (1989), in their study of former Big 10 male football and basketball players, reported a significant relationship between academic involvement as a college student and post-collegiate life satisfaction and self-esteem, which suggests that a strong but not exclusive athletic identity affords more psychological benefits to competitive student/athletes. Finally, Chamalidis (1995) and Webb, Nasco, Riley and Headrick (1998) have demonstrated that those who ascribe great importance to their involvement in elite sport are more at risk of experiencing retirement-related difficulties than those who place less value on the athletic component of their self-identity.

Coping resources

Sport psychologists have examined ways in which coping resources influence the overall quality of adjustment to retirement from sport (e.g. Crook & Robertson 1991; Gordon 1995). A number of early studies reported that many high-performance athletes turn to alcohol as a way of coping with their career transition (e.g. Hallden 1965; Mihovilovic 1968), while others found that having a new focus after retirement predicts better adjustment (Baillie 1993; Werthner & Orlick 1986; Sinclair & Orlick 1993). In an individual's attempt to manage the career transition process, those high in coping resources tend to experience less stress than athletes possessing few coping skills (Murphy 1995; Pearson & Petitpas 1990).

A study by Reynolds (1981) with former professional football players in the United States was perhaps the first to outline the importance of social support as a significant coping resource among retired sports performers. In recent years other career transition researchers (e.g. Alfermann & Gross 1997) have also documented the importance of social support from friends, family, team-mates and coaches, and Kane's (1991) study of former professional male American athletes in the midst of a career transition demonstrated how social support networks can suffer following retirement.

Research in Australia

In the same year that Stronach (1993) commented on the role of coaches in the career transition process in New Zealand, Hawkins and Blann (1993) conducted Australia's first major survey of similar issues. Specifically, Hawkins and Blann surveyed the career transition needs of a sample of elite male and female athletes and coaches using the PACTI (Blann & Zaichkowsky 1986) adapted to suit Australian subjects, the Australian Athletes Career Transition Inventory (AACTI) and Australian Coaches Career Transition Inventory (ACCTI) (Hoskins & Hawkins 1992). The main purposes of this research were (1) to develop an instrument to assess Australian athletes' and coaches' career development and awareness needs; (2) to assess athletes' and coaches' levels of career awareness and their post-sport career planning involvement and career transition needs; and (3) to determine types of programs most useful in meeting career transition needs.

Results revealed that athletes in general had a higher awareness of the need for career development than coaches. Male athletes expected a prolonged athletic career, had more specific career goals, and were more interested in internship programs and specific job experiences than female athletes. Female athletes were more interested in assistance in identifying their personal qualities and the career that best matched those qualities. Both males and females agreed that programs using individual or small group counselling would be most effective, and that such programs would be most helpful if delivered both during and after their sport careers. Coaches, on the other hand, were reportedly less aware of transition issues than athletes and seemed more reluctant to consider careers outside coaching despite an expression of job insecurity. In general, coaches believed that the coaching profession was not greatly valued, that they (coaches) had limited opportunities for advancement in Australia, and that their profession left them limited time for relationships or personal development.

At about this time several other inquiries and postgraduate research projects appeared. Anderson (1993) prepared a report on career transitions and education programs for elite athletes in Canada, the USA and the UK as well as Australia. The following year she presented findings from a single-case study that examined the impact of an athlete career and education program on both athletic performance and mood states. Results revealed stability in perceived performance and a positive effect on mood (Morris & Anderson 1994a, 1994b). Mayocchi and Hanrahan (1994) reported results from studies on the influence of individual and work related factors on the use of transferable skills in non-athletic careers among elite-level athletes. In general, significant effects were found between job enthusiasm and the use of transferable skills, and several implications for career transition programs were discussed.

Hewett's (1994) case study of career orientations among five elite athletes suggested that a number of factors influenced vocational choices including the coach, age of entering the sport, life experiences outside sport and academic achievement. These triggers highlighted the importance of timing of interventions in career transition programs. Redmond (1994) examined career termination experiences among female netballers; results, discussed in the context of Schlossberg's (1984) model of transitions, revealed that retirement was an individual experience that included a phase of assimilation and a situation in which athletic identity remained on career termination. Fish (1994) explored the short- and long-term impact of deselection on retirement in cricket, field hockey and water polo. Results from in-depth interviews with 15 athletes (7 females, 8 males) revealed lack of understanding among sporting organisations, officials, team-mates and family members. Recommendations included greater professionalism in player relations, selection procedures and general athlete support.

The following year Lavallee, Grove and Gordon (1995) presented account-making as a treatment model for athletes who have experienced severe emotional adjustment to career termination. These authors also presented preliminary findings on the relationship between athletic identity and anxiety about career decision making (zeteophobia). Fortunato, Anderson, Morris and Seedsman (1995) published an outline of their research program, described the content of the Australian Athlete Career and Education (ACE) program and the results of a study conducted with Australian Football League (AFL) players. In the latter investigation, AFL players who had terminated their careers voluntarily experienced more positive transitions than those whose careers ended involuntarily (through injury or deselection). During the next year Fortunato (1996) completed her studies on role transitions in elite sport.

In the first of a series of studies, coordinated by Lavallee (1997), Lavallee, Gordon and Grove (1996) examined career beliefs and perceptions of life skills learned in sport that are transferable to post-athletic career occupations. Several areas of career development were relevant to elite athletes, and type of sport appeared to be related to subsequent career development. Lavallee, Gordon and Grove (1997) also examined the causes of retirement and the degree of adjustment required among former elite-amateur Australian athletes. Results revealed that involuntary career termination was related to significantly greater emotional and social adjustment, and those who experienced greatest adjustment difficulties also perceived least personal control over the reasons for retirement. Lavallee, Gordon and Grove (1997) later investigated the coping strategies of 15 former elite athletes (11 females, 4 males) during the career transition process, and the effects of career termination on athletic identity. Results suggested that confiding in others can moderate both stress and adjustment following career termination and changes in athletic identity. In a related investigation among 48 former elite-level Australian athletes (18 females, 20 males), Grove, Lavallee and Gordon (1997) collected data related to financial, occupational, emotional and social adjustment to retirement from sport, as well as athletic identity at the time of retirement. Results revealed that acceptance, positive reinterpretation, planning and active coping strategies were used more frequently. In addition, athletic identity at the time of retirement was significantly related to coping processes, emotional and social adjustment, pre-retirement planning and anxiety about career decision making.

The following year Lavallee, Grove, Gordon and Ford (1998) explored the concept of loss as it applied to elite athletes and symbolic losses associated with performance slumps, athletic injuries and retirement were reviewed. Grove, Lavallee, Gordon and Harvey (1998) then revisited the account-making model of Harvey, Weber and Orbuch (1990) as a framework for understanding negative emotional reactions to retirement from elite sport. A case study of Shane Gould Innes (former Australian Olympic gold medallist) was used to illustrate the central role of account making in the adjustment process. Also in that year Jackson (1998) and her colleagues (Jackson, Dover & Mayocchi 1998; Jackson, Mayocchi & Dover 1998) reported on the experiences of 18 former Olympic gold medallists (1984–1992) and 10 of their coaches. The qualitative results focused on Olympic experiences the year following the Olympics, performance and career issues following an Olympic gold medal win, and general experiences as a gold medallist.

At this time Anderson (1998) completed her study of the relationship between mood states among scholarship athletes from a number of sports and their participation in the Victoria Institute of Sport ACE program. Reduction of negative mood and self-reported stable and consistent performances among athletes in the ACE program, compared with non–ACE program athletes, suggested several benefits from a comprehensive life-skills program. Surprisingly, however, a national evaluation of the ACE program revealed that only 18 per cent of eligible Australian athletes were aware that the program offered retirement planning and support services (Gorely, Bruce & Teale 1998).

Fortunato (1998) and Fortunato and Marchant (1999) were the first to use grounded theory in examinations of the adjustment processes to involuntary retirement (injury and deselection) among AFL players. Results revealed themes relating to loss of identity, perceived control, financial issues and social support. Fish, Grove and Eklund (1999), in their investigation of changes in athletic identity due to non-selection, surveyed 47 women vying for selection at State level trials in basketball, volleyball and field hockey. Results revealed a statistically significant change in athletic identity among those not selected; interestingly, the authors suggested that changes in domain-specific self-concept may be driven more by self-protective rather than self-enhancement motives. In the following year Mayocchi (1999) completed her studies on transferable skills and the process of transfer in sport.

Recently Australian researchers have made other significant contributions to two major international publications in the area. Sandy Gordon served as reviewer to the European Federation of Sport Psychology (FEPSAC) monograph entitled *Career Transitions in Competitive Sport* edited by Wylleman, Lavallee and Alfermann (1999). Deidre Anderson and Tony Morris (athlete lifestyle programs), Lisa Mayocchi and Stephanie Hanrahan (transferable skills for career change), and Wendy Patton and Susan Ryan (career transitions among dancers) contributed chapters to Lavallee and Wylleman's (2000) text entitled *Career Transitions in Sport: International Perspectives*. Harriet Speed and Tony Morris (2001) also wrote a report, commissioned by the Victorian Minister for Racing on behalf of the Victorian Jockeys Association, titled *The Welfare of Retired Jockeys*. More current research projects include evaluations of career assistance programs (Bobridge, Gordon, Walker & Thompson 2002) and development of athletic identity (J Redmond, PhD, UWA).

AUSTRALIAN RESEARCH TOPICS IN CAREER TRANSITIONS

Athletic identity
  Development
  Identity foreclosure

Career assistance programs
  Mood
  Performance
  Career beliefs

Career termination
  Adjustment: occupational, financial, social, emotional
  Deselection
  Injury
  Loss

Prevention and treatment strategies
  Account making
  Ways of coping
  Career orientation

Transitions
  Surveys of need: athletes and coaches
  Transferable skills

AUSTRALIAN CAREER ASSISTANCE PROGRAMS

Table 23.1 identifies a selection of known career assistance programs internationally.

TABLE 23.1 Selected career transition programs

Program	Institution	Country
Athlete Career and Education Program (ACE)	Australian Institute of Sport	Australia
Athlete Career and Education Program (ACE UK)	United Kingdom Sports Institute	UK
British Athlete Lifestyle Assessment Needs in Career and Education (BALANCE) Program	University of Strathclyde	UK
Career Assistance Program for Athletes	US Olympic Committee	USA
CD Sports	Coyne Didsbury Sports	Australia
Making the Jump Program	Advisory Resource Centre for Athletes	USA
Olympic Athlete Career Centre — National Sports Centre	Olympic Athlete Career Centre	Canada
Olympic Job Opportunities Program	Australian Olympic Committee	Australia
Study and Talent Education Program	Vrije Universiteit Brussels	Belgium
The Retiring Athlete	Dutch Olympic Committee	Netherlands
Whole-istic	American College Athletic Association	USA
Women's Sports Foundation Athlete Service	Women's Sports Foundation	USA

Other programs are listed and discussed elsewhere (e.g. Anderson 1993; Anderson & Morris 2000; Gordon 1995; Lavallee, Wylleman & Sinclair 1998; Lavallee, Sinclair & Wylleman 1998). In Australia, following the 1988 Seoul Olympics, concerns relating to careers outside sport, primarily raised by athletes, prompted the introduction of the first Lifeskills for Elite Athletes Program (LEAP). It was renamed SportsLEAP in 1993 and merged with the Victorian Institute of Sport's Athlete Career and Education (ACE) program in 1995. From 1992 some elite-amateur Australian athletes have also made use of an Olympic Job Opportunity Program (OJOP), and since 1998 similar services have been available to professional athletes (Australian Football League and Cricket) through Coyne Didsbury Sports (CD Sports).

The Australian ACE program has been coordinated since 1995 by a national manager and advisers in each state institute/academy of sport. According to Anderson and Morris (2000), the overall aim of the program 'is to assist athletes to balance the demands of their sporting careers whilst enhancing their opportunities to also develop their educational and vocational skills' (p. 68). Eligible for program assistance are scholarship holders with the Australian Institute of Sport, state institute/academies of sport, or Olympic athlete program participants. The nine strategies of the program are:

1. Individual athlete assessment — a structured process to assess individual educational, vocational, financial and personal development needs.
2. Personal development training courses — provision of nationally accredited competency-based education programs.

3. Nationally consistent career and education planning — a process that facilitates management of individual vocational requirements.
4. Community recognition — promotion of the program and its ideals.
5. Transition program — career and education guidance for those experiencing a transition to a post-sporting career.
6. Program development — to ensure ACE personnel are appropriately trained to deliver ACE program services (since 1998 a graduate certificate in ACE management has been available through Victoria University of Technology).
7. Program integration — fostering integration of ACE personnel and services within ongoing programs offered by state institutes and academies of sport.
8. Direct athlete needs-based assessments — providing a structured assessment process for needs-based support.
9. Professional sports — provision of a nationally consistent and coordinated ACE program to professional sports. (Anderson & Morris 2000)

The Olympic Job Opportunity Program (OJOP), an Australian Olympic Committee (AOC) project, was initiated in 1992. It mirrors the American and South African OJOP programs and is sponsored by the international chartered accountancy firm of Ernst and Young. The program does not attempt to find short-term employment or 'fill-in' job opportunities, or focus on athlete education and development or similar career planning opportunities, which, it is assumed, would normally be provided by the employer and part of the athlete's conditions of employment. Eligible athletes are screened by both the AOC and Ernst and Young, and are either current Olympians or Olympic-calibre athletes and must be certified as such by their respective national federations. AOC and Ernst and Young State coordinators help eligible athletes identify future career goals and, subsequently, contact companies who can provide them with a career opportunity and, at the same time, allow athletes time off for training and competition without loss of either pay or career advancement. In addition to providing direct employer contact and identifying job positions, OJOP provides career analysis services, personality aptitude testing, interview skills training and résumé preparation advice.

More recently one of the most significant developments in athlete support has been in professional sport. The Australian Football League Players Association (AFLPA) and the Australian Cricketers Association (ACA), under the charter of player development and welfare, have initiated innovative support programs for their members. In conjunction with Coyne Didsbury Sports (CD Sports) both associations now provide an impressive range of career planning, player counselling and workshop-based training dealing with many of the life balance and personal issues that confront today's professional athlete. Since 1998 CD Sports has provided one-to-one and group-based sessions for athletes and their support networks. While they specialise in team-based sports, they also work with athletes from golf and tennis. CD Sports has a national network of skilled practitioners providing services that include self-management, personal development, leadership skills, presentation skills, business skills, career transition and money management. In addition, CD Sports provides a 24-hour helpline for athletes, allowing them to call and speak with a counsellor at any time should the need arise.

According to Terry Coyne (CD Sports co-director) the take-up rate among athletes and their support networks has been impressive. 'Players who may have originally been reluctant to seek assistance have found dealing with a third-party professional very beneficial. The ability to gain the support of an objective and professional ear that is not bound or directed by their club or organisation (i.e. their employer) can provide a valuable resource to assist them in a profession that has grown both in the public eye and in the personal demands of increasing professionalism.' (T Coyne, personal communication, 18 May 2001)

PREVENTION AND TREATMENT STRATEGIES

It is evident that prevention of crises associated with adjustments to career transitions and career retirement can be facilitated by the various career assistance programs described in the previous section. However, Ogilvie and colleagues (Ogilvie 1987; Ogilvie & Taylor 1993a, 1993b) stress the importance of targeting athletes as early as possible in their athletic development. They also emphasise the benefits of using a 'primary prevention model' — preventing problems before they occur. Pearson and Petitpas (1990) claim primary prevention approaches will work in sport because: '(a) the presence of widespread organisational structures that organise and implement sports programs make preventive programs a possibility, and (b) an ample literature supports the position that, in the long run, primary prevention-focused approaches offer the most efficient way of using limited human service resources' (p. 7).

These and other authors (e. g. Petitpas, Champagne, Chartrand, Danish & Murphy, 1997; Petitpas, Danish, McKelvain & Murphy 1992) are recommending that parents, coaches and youth sport administrators promote a holistic approach to youth participation in sport, an approach that de-emphasises success and winning (outcome orientation) and emphasises instead personal growth and social development (mastery and process orientation). The intention, therefore, is for young athletes to experience psychological and social phenomena in sport that promote, rather than inhibit, the development of coping behaviours that become necessary in non-sport aspects of their lives. In adopting a primary prevention model, long-term personal and social development hold precedence over short-term athletic success, allowing sports participation to become the vehicle through which young athletes develop general life skills that enable them to grow personally and socially and function in diverse situations. The adult manifestations associated with the single-minded pursuit of excellence and winning, and the socialisation of 'unidimensional' and 'cognitively simple' younger athletes, can be avoided using *primary prevention* in youth sports.

Pearson and Petitpas (1990) also believe that prevention-oriented programs can help identify individuals who are likely to experience transition difficulties. In Australia these 'at-risk' individuals, who can immediately be referred to preventive programs such as ACE and CD Sports, characteristically have strong sport identities and define their 'self' exclusively as 'athlete', have a considerable gap between their level of aspiration and level of ability, have little or no experience with sport transitions, are limited in general ability to adapt to change because of emotional or behavioural deficits, are limited in their ability to form and maintain support networks, and must make the transitions with meagre emotional and material resources that could be helpful (Pearson & Petitpas 1990).

For those athletes who already experience 'existential moments' (Who am I? Where am I heading?) and who become increasingly preoccupied with the spectre of career retirement or termination, the aforementioned career assistance programs can also help. Ogilvie and Taylor (1993b), however, further recommend the therapeutic assistance of sport psychologists who can help athletes clarify and modify their changing values, priorities, interests and goals. Broadening the athlete's social identity and role repertoire while maintaining or enhancing feelings of self-confidence and self-worth will also be helpful. Ogilvie and Taylor also refer to the significance of social systems for athletes leading up to and immediately following career termination and to the findings of Svoboda and Vanek (1982), who reported the significance of different methods of coping with career termination among 163 elite former athletes in Czechoslovakia. Social support was the predominant factor, with the family (37 per cent) perceived to be most important, followed by colleagues in the new profession (13 per cent), friends (8 per cent) and the coach (4 per cent). In that study it was interesting to note that even in a socialist society, in which elite athletes need not worry too much about finding a job, only 35 per cent reported that they coped immediately with the psychological adjustments associated with retirement, while 15 per cent coped in half a year, 8 per cent in a year, 17 per cent took up to 3 years, 4 per cent more than 3 years, and 18 per cent not at all.

Athletes in the middle of or approaching or at the end of their athletic careers are likely to experience crises that will adversely affect them cognitively, emotionally, behaviourally and socially (Ogilvie & Taylor 1993b). Subsequently, traditional therapeutic strategies such as cognitive restructuring (Beck 1979; Burns 1985; Ellis & Harper 1975) stress inoculation training (Meichenbaum 1985), and talking through stages of loss (Kübler-Ross 1969) and emotional expression (Yalom 1980) may be considered in this process. Shapiro's (1995) eye movement desensitisation and reprocessing psychomotor technique, which has been used in ameliorating undesirable beliefs and images associated with career-ending injuries (Sime 1998), is also a consideration. Similarly, the beneficial role of Harvey, Weber and Orbuch's (1990) account-making approach has been illustrated with samples of elite athletes who experienced greater post-retirement adjustment, to the extent that they engaged in productive confiding activity (Grove et al. 1998; Lavallee, Gordon & Grove 1997). Finally, consistent with this multi-site approach, Brammer and Abrego (1981) outside of sport, and Wolff and Lester (1989) inside sport, utilised an interactive coping model for dealing with transitions consisting of listening and confrontation, cognitive therapy (appraisal processes) and vocational guidance (planning for implementing change). In regard to the latter issue, long-term financial planning and money management, part of some but not all career assistance programs, would provide financial stability at the conclusion of careers that might bolster, at least temporarily, the negative effects of 'social death'.

Summary of prevention and treatment approaches
- Account making
- Cognitive restructuring
- Emotional expression
- Eye movement desensitisation and reprocessing psychomotor technique
- Interactive coping strategies — listen/confrontation, cognitive therapy, vocational guidance
- Primary prevention programs
- Social support
- Stages of loss
- Stress inoculation

FUTURE DIRECTIONS

In the past decade considerably more research attention has been given to career transitions and retirement, both internationally and in Australia. Previous sections mapped out where the research has come from, where it has been and where it is now. The following section outlines where the research is going or perhaps should go in the future.

1. The stage in a life cycle has not been formally incorporated into transition models when applied to sport. For example, is an athlete's decision to carry on in a particular sport influenced by school-age and parental pressure to focus on educational

or other occupational achievements? Do family commitments truncate sporting careers of both males and females? According to Professor Leonie Still (Graduate School of Management, University of Western Australia), career research suggests that women may handle sudden career termination better because they have other dimensions to their lives. On the other hand, single women who are career focused are likely to have the same reactions as men without adequate support systems (L Still, personal communication, 1 June 2001). Future research should examine the influence of 'stage in the life cycle' on sport career transitions and whether or not existing transition models accommodate both female and male experiences.

2. In addition to transitions out of elite sport, Coakley and Donnelly (1999) have identified several other transitions that should also receive attention. In the life span of an athlete inquiries could focus on transitions from play to competitive sport, becoming 'an athlete', becoming a sport specialist, and making the transition to intensive training, and also to elite/professional sport. Wylleman et al. (1999) have identified five stages in a sport career (SC) starting with the beginning of sport specialisation, moving to intensive training in a chosen sport, to the transition from amateur to elite/professional sport, the transition from the culmination to the end of SC, and finally termination of the SC. Since all transition experiences inevitably involve a network of social support providers, how each transition is experienced by family, friends and partners (e.g. husbands and wives) should also require examination. Implications for transition-specific SC assistance programs are discussed in item (15).

3. Early, intermediate and later transitions experienced by coaches and officials (e.g. umpires and referees), whose career patterns have generally been ignored, also require scrutiny. An 'occupational analysis' of sport (cf. Haerle 1975), and particularly the status of coaches and officials in Australia, would identify several critical incidents and triggers in the career pathways of both female and male participants. Similar recommendations were made almost a decade ago by Gordon (1995) and Hawkins and Blann (1993).

4. Professional sport team cultures now resemble the workplace, which is comprised of 'core employees', contractors to the core and casuals (L Still, personal communication, 1 June 2001). Players are contracted by management to fulfil performance demands (outcomes) and can subsequently be traded or moved among teams in a cartel (e.g. Australian Football League) when contracts expire. Investigation of the transitions created by inter-club trades is required, and could include comparisons between involuntary and voluntary trades and the adaptation processes to new club cultures and support systems.

Conceptual models such as figure 23.1, and that proposed by Taylor and Ogilvie (1994), illustrate all relevant concerns that can influence both the course of athletic retirement and the quality of subsequent adjustment.

5. Despite the use of several instruments designed to assess the adjustment process of career transitions, none have sufficiently captured the needs of athletes in transition. For this reason, Lavallee and Wylleman (1999) have developed the British Athlete Lifestyle Assessment Needs in Career and Education (BALANCE) Scale to identify individuals who are at risk of experiencing transition-related difficulties. This 12-item instrument focuses on the variables identified in the literature as being moderators of career transition adjustment (e.g. perception of control over the cause for retirement, identity foreclosure, provision of career transition support services). The scale itself requires further psychometric development if it is to be employed

by sport psychologists in order to predict the quality of adjustment to retirement. A better understanding of the specific variables that serve as a buffer following career termination is also needed.

6. Of the causal factors of career termination — age, injury, deselection, free choice — deselection remains the least examined. Surveys of how different sport associations deselect players and where these players go (e.g. first job post-playing career, second job etc.) would be useful. Are there differences and similarities across different sports, female, male and amalgamated organisations, and between semi-/full-time professional sports (e.g. AFL, baseball, basketball, cricket, rugby league, soccer) and elite amateur sports (including Olympic sports) organised through Institutes of Sport and major clubs?

7. The dual challenge of coping with retirement and a career-ending injury requires more attention (Heil 1993), in particular the relationship between injury, goal continuity and achievement of sport-related goals.

8. Studies of developmental factors should focus on the relationship between adjustment to retirement, athletic identity and identity foreclosure. Research on the concept of athletic identity and how it develops is required, as are further examinations of the psychometric properties of the Athletic Identity Measurement Scale (AIMS) (e.g. Hale 1995). Further empirical studies are also required on the relationships between athletic identity, identity foreclosure and social support. Lane, Eklund and Gordon (2001) recently replicated research by Good et al. (1993) and Murphy et al. (1996) in Australian netball, and more sport-specific studies should be encouraged.

9. There is a need to assess ways of coping and coping skills that are most beneficial during the course of transitions. Future research should take into account both long- and short-term effects of retirement-related coping processes. In Grove, Lavallee and Gordon's (1997) cross-sectional study some athletes may have reported generalised estimates of coping strategies used over a long period of continual adjustment. Others, on the other hand, may have reported how they coped during a briefer and more specific period. Longitudinal studies, therefore, are needed to determine if various coping strategies are employed at different points in time during the transition process. Such a program of research could result in a periodised approach to educating athletes how to use coping skills, similar to that proposed for sport injury rehabilitation personnel who educate athletes how to cope with athletic injury (e.g. Gordon, Potter & Hamer 2001).

10. A thorough analysis of the retirement process also requires prospective data. Pre- and post-event data would help determine whether retrospective accounts of thoughts and behaviours have been influenced by social desirability and/or selective memory. Qualitative methods such as those adopted by Gould and colleagues (Gould, Eklund & Jackson 1993; Gould, Finch & Jackson 1993) would be useful in delineating the sources of stress for retiring athletes and for comparisons with quantitative data on ways of coping.

11. To provide a better understanding of the extent to which continued involvement in sport serves as a buffer following retirement from elite competition, research by Curtis and Ennis (1988) should be replicated and extended. Female and male coaches, who have made transitions within competitive sport, could provide useful data on identification and use of transferable skills as well as the moderating effects of sport transfer (e.g. from athlete to coach). When contrasted with sport drop-outs these data could be used in both career assistance (prevention) and treatment programs. Empirical research on the benefits of confiding to others is

also recommended. Retiring athletes can often feel alienated from their sport upon career termination (Werthner & Olick 1986); consequently mentoring programs (cf. Perna, Zaichkowsky & Bocknek 1996) and those that incorporate account making (Grove et al. 1998; Harvey et al. 1990) could provide opportunities for athletes and coaches (e.g. Hurley 2000a, 2000b) to contribute meaningfully to the sport system as well as assist in their personal transition-adjustment process. Sinclair and Orlick (1993) have advised sport organisations to seek out former athletes for such roles since the knowledge retired athletes possess may be invaluable to those in various stages of the transition process. No empirical research has been devoted to the effects of such an arrangement on either retired or current athletes. Its focus should include how, when and with whom the account-making process is developed, as well as the dynamics associated with changes in athletic identity following retirement. Previous research outside sport (Lau 1984; Wong & Weiner 1981) suggests that the amount of time that has passed since retirement should also be taken into account.

While OJOP and the emergence of ACE and CD Sports reflects an 'acknowledgment of need' for career assistance programming among amateur and professional sport administrators and athletes in Australia, research activity on these programs has been restricted to the descriptive. The appropriateness of career assistance program content, including counselling, and its effects is yet to be determined.

12. Concomitant with the development of an 'athlete support industry', evidence-based research needs to be conducted upon which both the providers of programs and the sport industry (organisations, coaches and athletes) can rely. Research on transferable skills, pre-retirement planning and occupational decision making among amateur athletes could be compared with similar investigations in semi- and full-time professional sport.

13. Attention to the participation of athletes in retirement preparation programs is also warranted. Research outside sport suggests that a positive selectivity bias can exist in that those most likely to succeed in retirement are those given the opportunity to design post-retirement programs (e.g. Beck 1984; Campione 1988).

14. Existing career assistance programs might benefit from approaches Hewett (1994) took towards 'career orientations', which describes the awareness, priority and readiness of athletes for career assistance, and follows Prochaska and DiClemente's (1986) research on the transtheoretical model of behaviour change (TM). The TM, in this case, would theorise that both athletes and coaches may be individually located at different stages of career orientation (cf. Wylleman et al. 1999) and therefore are more or less 'ready' for services that ACE, OJOP and CD Sports offer. As Prochaska (1986) observed, 'we must quit pretending that all we have to do is deliver state-of-the-art action programs to the people and they will take advantage of them' (p. 32). TM provides both cognitive and behavioural processes (techniques) for athletes at different 'stages of change', which theoretically results in a gradual shift in attitude from, for example, 'I should attend career assistance programs' to 'I want to attend career assistance programs'.

CONCLUSIONS

This chapter has examined the process of desocialisation from competitive sport and career retirement or termination and has addressed the relevant research that has tried to understand, explain and predict both negative and positive consequences. Evidently the answer to whether career transitions or retirement are stressful is likely to be 'most likely yes, but sometimes no'; more Australian-based research, both quantitative and qualitative, is recommended to explicate culturally determined causal factors of transitions and how these affect responses to and, in turn, the consequences of, transitions at all levels of competitive sport. Commercial and rationalisation forces in elite amateur and professional sport can be accommodated if prevention-oriented programs are implemented by trained career assistance program coordinators in both Australia and overseas.

SUMMARY

This chapter referred to both the extant theoretical and applied literature on an important and topical area of sport psychology and sport sociology research in Australia — career transitions in competitive sport. First, social gerontological, thanatological and transitions theoretical models were described and their applied utility in terms of driving both future research and program development was discussed. Next, the research from Australia and overseas on career retirement and career termination was reviewed, followed by a summary of the current career assistance programs in Australia available to elite amateur athletes and some professional athletes. Finally, some approaches and proposals for prevention and treatment interventions were described, and the concluding section listed recommendations for both research and practice, specifically in Australia.

REVIEW QUESTIONS

1 Debate the 'retirement or rebirth?' argument discussed by Coakley (1983) in relation to career transitions in sport, and the relevance today of either opinion in Australian sport.

2 Discuss the strengths and weaknesses of three theoretical perspectives that have been used or referred to in the study of career transitions and retirement in sport.

3 Briefly describe the existing Australian research on career transitions and the recommendations made for career assistance programs targeting both coaches and athletes.

4 Describe the causes of career termination and how each can affect the nature and quality of adjustment to career transitions and career termination.

5 Discuss the concepts of athletic identity and identity foreclosure, and how they are related to athlete adaptation to career transition.

6 Factors that mediate the adaptation and quality of adjustment to career termination, such as social support and coping skills, were identified in the chapter. Discuss the implications from the research on these factors for career assistance programs.

7 Describe the Australian Career and Education (ACE) program and how it is delivered nationwide.

8 What are the characteristics of 'primary prevention approaches' to career assistance programs?

9 Describe the approaches and techniques sport psychologists can use when assisting athletes with career transitions, including retirement.

10 What are the main challenges in the future for both researchers and career assistance program managers in professional as well as amateur sport in Australia?

References

Alfermann, D & Gross, A 1997, 'Coping with career termination: it all depends on freedom of choice', in R Lidor & M Bar-Eli (eds), *Proceedings of the 9th World Congress of Sport Psychology*, International Society of Sport Psychology, Netanya, Israel, pp. 65–7.

Allison, MT & Meyer, C 1988, 'Career problems and retirement among elite athletes: the female tennis professional', *Sociology of Sport Journal*, 5, 212–22.

Anderson, D 1993, *Research tour — elite athlete education programs*, Victorian Institute of Sport, Melbourne.

Anderson, DK 1998, 'Lifeskill intervention and elite performances', unpublished master's thesis, Victoria University, Melbourne.

Anderson, DK & Morris, T 2000, 'Athlete lifestyle programs', in D Lavallee & P Wylleman (eds), *Career transitions in sport: International perspectives*, Fitness Information Technology, Morgantown, WV, pp. 59–80.

Atchley, RC 1981, *The social forces in later life*, Wadsworth, Belmont, CA.

Baillie, PHF 1993, 'Understanding retirement from sports: therapeutic ideas for helping athletes in transition', *The Counseling Psychologist*, 21, 299–410.

Baillie, PHF & Danish, SJ 1992, 'Understanding the career transition of athletes', *The Sport Psychologist*, 6, 77–98.

Beck, AT 1979, *Cognitive therapy and emotional disorders*, New American Library, New York.

Beck, SH 1984, 'Retirement preparation programs: differentials in opportunity and use', *Journal of Gerontology*, 39, 596–602.

Blann, W & Zaichkowsky, L 1986, 'Career/life transition needs of National Hockey League players', report prepared for the National Hockey League Players' Association.

Blann, W & Zaichkowsky, L 1989, 'National Hockey League and Major League baseball players' post-sport career transition surveys', final report for the National Hockey League Players' Association.

Blinde, EM & Greendorfer, SL 1985, 'A reconceptualization of the process of leaving the role of competitive athlete', *International Review for Sociology of Sport*, 20, 87–93.

Bobridge, K, Gordon, S, Walker, A & Thompson, R 2002, 'Evaluation of a career transition program for youth-aged cricketers', unpublished manuscript.

Brammer, LM & Abrego, PJ 1981, 'Intervention strategies for coping with transitions', *The Counselling Psychologist*, 9, 2 19–36.

Brewer, BW, Van Raalte, JL & Linder, DE 1993, 'Athletic identity: Hercules' muscles or Achilles' heel?', *International Journal of Sport Psychology*, 24, 237–54.

Burgees, E (ed.) 1960, *Aging in western societies*, University of Chicago Press, Chicago.

Burns, DD 1985, *Feeling good: the new mood therapy*, Penguin, New York.

Campione, WW 1988, 'Predicting participation in retirement preparation programs', *Journal of Gerontology*, 43, 91–5.

Chamalidis, P 1995, 'Career transitions of male champions', in R Vanfraechem-Raway & Y Vanden Auweele (eds), *Proceedings of the 9th European Congress on Sport Psychology*, European Federation of Sport Psychology, Brussels, pp. 841–8.

Charner, I & Schlossberg, NK 1986, 'Variations by theme: the life transitions of clerical workers', *The Vocational Guidance Quarterly*, 34, 212–24.

Coakley, JJ 1983, 'Leaving competitive sport: retirement or rebirth?', *Quest*, 35 (1) 1–11.

Coakley, J & Donnelly, P 1999, *Inside sports*, Routledge, London.

Crook JM & Robertson, SE 1991, 'Transitions out of elite sport', *International Journal of Sport Psychology*, 22, 115–27.

Cumming, E, Dean, LR, Newell, DS & McCaffrey, I 1960, 'Disengagement — a tentative theory of ageing', *Sociometry*, 13, 23.

Curtis, J & Ennis, R 1988, 'Negative consequences of leaving competitive sport? Comparison of findings for former elite-level hockey players', *Sociology of Sport Journal*, 5, 87–106.

Dowd, JJ 1975, 'Ageing as exchange: a preface to theory', *Journal of Gerontology*, 30, 584–94.

Ellis, A & Harper, RA 1975, *A new guide to rational living*, Prentice Hall, New York.

Fish, MB 1994, 'Non-selection as a factor contributing to retirement from Australian sport', unpublished honours thesis, Edith Cowan University, Perth.

Fish, MB, Grove, JR & Eklund, RE 1999, 'Changes in athletic identity following state team selection trials', paper presented at the 5th IOC World Congress on Sport Sciences, Sydney, November.

Ford, IW & Gordon, S 1999, 'Coping with sport injury: resource loss and the role of social support', *Journal of Personal and Interpersonal Loss*, 4 (3) 243–56.

Fortunato, V 1996, 'Role transitions in elite sports', unpublished doctoral dissertation, Victoria University of Technology, Melbourne.

Fortunato, V 1998, 'Getting the axe: adjustment process of delisted Australian rules footballers', *Journal of Applied Sport Psychology*, 10 (Suppl.) S119.

Fortunato, V, Anderson, D, Morris, T & Seedsman, T 1995, 'Career transition research at Victoria University of Technology', in R Vanfraechem-Raway & Y Vanden Auweele (eds), *Proceedings of the 9th European Congress on Sport Psychology*, European Federation of Sport Psychology, Brussels, pp. 533–43.

Fortunato, V & Marchant, D 1999, 'Forced retirement from elite football in Australia', *Journal of Personal and Interpersonal Loss*, 4, 269–80.

Glaser, B & Strauss, A 1965, *Awareness of dying*, Aldine, New York.

Good, AJ, Brewer, BW, Petitpas, AJ, Van Raalte, JL & Mahar, MT 1993, 'Identity foreclosure, athletic identity and college sport participation', *The Academic Athletic Journal*, Spring, 1–12.

Gordon, S 1995, 'Career transitions in competitive sport', in T Morris and J Summers (eds), *Sport psychology: theory, applications and issues*, 1st edn, John Wiley & Sons, Brisbane, pp. 474–501.

Gordon, S, Milios, D and Grove, JR 1991, 'Psychological aspects of the recovery process from sport injury: the perspective of sport physiotherapists', *Australian Journal of Science and Medicine in Sport*, 23 (2) 53–60.

Gordon, S, Potter, M & Hamer, P 2001, 'The role of the sport physiotherapist and sport trainer', in J Crossman (ed.), *Coping with sports injuries: psychological strategies for rehabilitation*, Oxford University Press, Melbourne, pp. 62–82.

Gorely, T, Bruce, D & Teale, B 1998, *Athlete Career and Education Program 1997 evaluation*, University of Queensland, Brisbane.

Gould, D, Eklund, RC & Jackson, SA 1993, 'Coping strategies used by more versus less successful US Olympic wrestlers', *Research Quarterly for Exercise and Sport*, 64, 83–93.

Gould, D, Finch, LM & Jackson, SA 1993, 'Coping strategies used by national champion figure skaters', *Research Quarterly for Exercise and Sport*, 64, 453–68.

Greendorfer, SL & Blinde, EM 1985, 'Retirement from intercollegiate sports: theoretical and empirical considerations', *Sociology of Sport Journal*, 2, 101–10.

Grove, JR, Lavallee, D & Gordon, S 1997, 'Coping with retirement from sport: the influence of athletic identity', *Journal of Applied Sport Psychology*, 9, 191–203.

Grove, JR, Lavallee, D, Gordon, S & Harvey, J 1998, 'Account-making as a treatment model for distressful reactions to retirement from sport', *The Sport Psychologist*, 12, 52–67.

Haerle, R 1975, 'Career patterns and career contingencies of professional baseball players: an occupational analysis', in DW Ball & JW Loy (eds), *Sport and social order*, Addison-Wesley, Reading, MA, pp. 457–579.

Hale, B 1995, 'Exclusive athletic identity: a predictor of positive or negative psychological characteristics', in R Vanfraechem-Raway & Y Vanden Auweele (eds), *Proceedings of the 9th European Congress on Sport Psychology*, European Federation of Sport Psychology, Brussels, pp. 466–72.

Hallden, O 1965, 'The adjustment of athletes after retiring from sports', in F Antonelli (ed.), *Proceedings of the 1st International Congress of Sport Psychology*, Rome, Italy, pp. 730–3.

Harvey, JH, Weber, AL & Orbuch, TL 1990, *Interpersonal accounts*, Basil Blackwell, Oxford.

Hawkins, K & Blann, FW 1993, *Athlete/coach career development and transition*, Australian Sports Commission, Canberra.

Heil, J 1993, *Psychology of sport injury*, Human Kinetics, Lower Mitcham, SA.

Hewett, K 1994, 'Career orientation of elite amateur athletes', unpublished honours thesis, University of Western Australia, Perth.

Hill, P & Lowe, B 1974, 'The inevitable metathesis of the retiring athlete, *International Review of Sport Sociology*, 4, 5–29.

Hoskins, D & Hawkins, K 1992, 'Career awareness and transition for Australian athletes and coaches: the design and validation of a measuring instrument', paper presented at the Annual Conference of the International Association for Physical Education in Higher Education, Melbourne.

Hurley, A 2000a, 'Life after coaching. Part 1: what skills do coaches possess to take them into the next life?', *Sports Coach*, 23 (3) 29–30.

Hurley, A 2000b, 'Life after coaching. Part 2', *Sports Coach*, 23 (4) 40–2.

Jackson, SA 1998, *Life after gold: the experiences of Australian Olympic gold-medallists 1984–1992*, Australian Sports Commission, Canberra.

Jackson, SA, Dover, JD & Mayocchi, LM 1998, 'Life after gold: 1. Experiences of Australian Olympic gold-medallists', *The Sport Psychologist*, 12 (2) 119–36.

Jackson, SA, Mayocchi, LM & Dover, JD 1998, 'Life after gold: 2. Coping with change as an Olympic gold-medallist', *The Sport Psychologist*, 12 (2) 137–55.

Kane, MA 1991, 'The metagonic transition: a study of career transition, marital stress and identity transformation in former professional athletes', unpublished doctoral dissertation, Boston University.

Kleiber, DA & Brock, SC 1992, 'The effect of career-ending injuries on the subsequent well-being of elite college athletes', *Sociology of Sport Journal*, 9, 70–5.

Kleiber, D, Greendorfer, S, Blinde, E & Samdahl, D 1987, 'Quality of exit from university sports and life satisfaction in early adulthood', *Sociology of Sport Journal*, 4, 28–36.

Kleiber, D, Malik, PB 1989, 'Educational involvement of college athletes and subsequent well-being in early adulthood', *Journal of Sport Behaviour*, 12 203–11.

Kübler-Ross, E 1969, *On death and dying*, Macmillan, New York.

Kuypers, JA & Bengston, VL 1973, 'Social breakdown and competence: a model of normal aging', *Human Development*, 16, 181–220.

Lane, G, Eklund, RC & Gordon, S 2001, 'Athletic identity, identity foreclosure and the female netball player', unpublished manuscript.

Lau, RR 1984, 'Dynamics of the attribution process', *Journal of Personality and Social Psychology*, 46, 1017–28.

Lavallee, D 1997, 'The process of adjustment to athletic career termination', unpublished doctoral dissertation, University of Western Australia, Perth.

Lavallee, D, Gordon, S & Grove, JR 1995, 'Athletic identity as a predictor of zeteophobia among retired athletes', paper presented by S Gordon at 12th Annual Conference on Counseling Athletes, Springfield College, Massachusetts, 1–4 June.

Lavallee, D, Grove, JR & Gordon, S 1995, 'Account-making as a treatment model for distressful reactions to athletic retirement', in R Vanfraechem-Raway & Y Vanden Auweele (eds), *Proceedings of the 9th European Congress on Sport Psychology*, European Federation of Sport Psychology, Brussels, pp. 857–64.

Lavallee, D, Gordon, S & Grove, JR 1996, 'A profile of career beliefs among retired Australian athletes', *Australian Journal of Career Development*, 5 (2) 35–8.

Lavallee, D, Gordon, S & Grove, JR 1997, 'Retirement from sport and the loss of athletic identity', *Journal of Personal and Interpersonal Loss*, 2, 129–47.

Lavallee, D, Grove, JR & Gordon, S 1997, 'The causes of career termination from sport and their relationship to post-retirement adjustment among elite-amateur athletes in Australia', *The Australian Psychologist*, 32, 131–5.

Lavallee, D, Grove, JR, Gordon, S & Ford, IW 1998, 'The experience of loss in sport', in JH Harvey (ed.), *Perspectives on loss: a sourcebook*, Taylor & Francis, Washington, DC.

Lavallee, D, Sinclair, DA & Wylleman, P 1998, 'An annotated bibliography on career transitions in sport: 2. Empirical references', *Australian Journal of Career Development*, 7 (3) 32–44.

Lavallee, D, Wylleman, P & Sinclair, DA 1998, 'An annotated bibliography on career transitions in sport: 1. Counselling-based references', *Australian Journal of Career Development*, 7 (2) 34–42.

Lavallee, D & Wylleman, P 1999, 'Toward an instrument to assess the quality of adjustment to career transition in sport: the British Athlete Lifestyle Assessment Needs in Career and Education (BALANCE) scale', paper presented at the 10th European Congress of Sports Psychology, Prague, July.

Lavallee, D & Wylleman, P (eds.) 2000, *Career transitions in sport: international perspectives*, Fitness Information Technology, Morgantown, WV.

Lerch, SH 1981, 'The adjustment to retirement of professional baseball players', in SL Greendorfer & A Yiannakis (eds), *Sociology of sport: diverse perspectives*, Leisure Press, West Point, NY, pp. 138–48.

Lerch, S 1982, 'Athlete retirement as social death', in N Theberge & P Donnelly (eds), *Sport and the sociological imagination*, Texas Christian University Press, Fort Worth, TX, pp. 259–72.

Mayocchi, L 1999, 'Transferable skills and the process of skill transfer: the athlete's experience', unpublished doctoral dissertation, University of Queensland, Brisbane.

Mayocchi, L & Hanrahan, S 1994, 'Transferable skills and high-performance athletes: research in progress', poster presented at the Australian Behaviour Modification Association update, Sunshine Coast, Queensland.

McPherson, BD 1980, 'Retirement from professional sport: the process and problems of occupational and psychological adjustment', *Sociological Symposium*, 30, 126–43.

Meichenbaum, D 1985, *Stress inoculation training*, Pergamon Press, Sydney.

Mihovilovic, M 1968, 'The status of former sportsmen', *International Review of Sport Sociology*, 3, 73–93.

Morris, T & Anderson, DK 1994a, 'Career education, perceived performance and mood state in elite athletes', paper presented at the 29th Annual Conference of the Australian Psychological Society, Wollongong, September.

Morris, T & Anderson, DK 1994b, 'Career education, perceived performance and mood state in elite athletes', paper presented at the 9th Annual Conference of the Association for the Advancement of Applied Sport Psychology, Lake Tahoe, October.

Murphy, GM, Petitpas, AJ & Brewer, BW 1996, 'Identity foreclosure, athletic identity, and career maturity in intercollegiate athletes', *The Sport Psychologist*, 10, 239–46.

Murphy, SM 1995, 'Transitions in competitive sport: maximizing individual potential', in SM Murphy (ed.), *Sport psychology interventions*, Human Kinetics, Champaign, IL, pp. 331–46.

Ogilvie, B 1987, 'Counseling for sports career termination', in JR May & MJ Asken (eds), *Sport psychology: the psychological health of the athlete*, PMA Publishing Corp, New York, pp. 213–30.

Ogilvie, B & Taylor, J 1993a, 'Career termination in sports: when the dream dies', in JM Williams (ed.), *Applied sport psychology: personal growth to peak performance*, Mayfield, Mountain View, CA, pp. 356–65.

Ogilvie, B & Taylor, J 1993b, 'Career termination issues among elite athletes', in RN Singer, M Murphey & LK Tennant (eds), *Handbook of research on sport psychology*, Macmillan, Sydney, pp. 761–75.

Orlick, T 2000, *In pursuit of excellence: how to win in sport and life through mental training*, 3rd edn, Human Kinetics, Lower Mitcham, SA.

Parker, KB 1994, ' "Has-beens" and wanna-bes: transition experiences of former major college football players', *The Sport Psychologist*, 8, 287–304.

Pearson, RE & Petitpas, AJ 1990, 'Transitions of athletes: developmental and preventive perspectives', *Journal of Counseling and Development*, 69, 7–10.

Perna, FM, Zaichkowsky, L & Bocknek, G 1996, 'The association of mentoring with psychosocial development among male athletes at termination of college career', *Journal of Applied Sport Psychology*, 8, 76–88.

Petitpas, A, Champagne, D, Chartrand, J, Danish, S & Murphy, S 1997, *Athlete's guide to career planning*, Human Kinetics, Lower Mitcham, SA.

Petitpas, A, Danish, S, McKelvain, R & Murphy, S 1992, 'A career assistance program for elite athletes', *Journal of Counseling and Development*, 70, 383–6.

Prochaska, J 1986, 'What causes people to change from unhealthy to health enhancing behaviour?', invited paper in the Proceedings of the American Cancer Society, Consensus Conference on the Current Unmet Research Need for Cancer Prevention.

Prochaska, J & DiClemente, C 1986, 'Toward a comprehensive model of change', in WE Miller & N Heather (eds), *Treating addictive behaviours*, Plenum Press, London, pp. 3–27.

Redmond, J 1994, 'Retirement experiences of former elite female netballers', unpublished master's thesis, Edith Cowan University, Perth.

Reynolds, MJ 1981, 'The effects of sports retirement on the job satisfaction of the former football player', in SL Greendorfer & A Yiannakis (eds), *Sociology of sport: diverse perspectives*, Leisure Press, West Point, NY, pp. 127–37.

Rose, A 1965, 'The subculture of the ageing: a framework in social gerontology', in A Rose & I Peterson (eds), *Older people and their social world*, FA Davis Company, Philadelphia.

Rosenberg, E 1981, 'Gerontological theory and athletic retirement', in SL Greendorfer & A Yiannakis (eds), *Sociology of sport: diverse perspectives*, Leisure Press, West Point, NY, pp. 119–26.

Rosenberg, E 1982, 'Athletic retirement as social death: concepts and perspectives', in N Theberge & P Donnelly (eds), *Sport and the sociological imagination*, Texas Christian University Press, Texas, pp. 245–58.

Rotella, RJ & Heyman, SR 1993, 'Stress, injury, and the psychological rehabilitation of athletes', in JM Williams (ed.), *Applied sport psychology: personal growth to peak performance*, Mayfield, Mountain View, CA, pp. 338–55.

Schlossberg, NK 1981, 'A model for analysing human adaptation to transition', *The Counseling Psychologist*, 9 (2) 2–18.

Schlossberg, NK 1984, *Counseling adults in transition*, Springer, New York.

Shapiro, F 1995, *Eye movement desensitization and reprocessing: basic principles, protocols, and procedures*, The Guilford Press, New York.

Sime, WE 1998, 'Injury and career termination issues', in MA Thompson, RA Vernacchia & WE Moore (eds), *Case studies in applied sport psychology: an educational approach*, Kendall/Hunt, Dubuque, IA, pp. 195–226.

Sinclair, DA & Orlick, T 1993, 'Positive transitions from high-performance sport', *The Sport Psychologist*, 7, 138–50.

Speed, H & Morris, T 2001, *The welfare of retired jockeys*, Victoria University Centre for Rehabilitation Exercise and Sports Science, Melbourne.

Stronach, A 1993, 'Life after sport: retirement from elite-level sport', *The New Zealand Coach*, 2, 10–11.

Sussman, MB 1972, 'An analytical model for the sociological study of retirement', in FM Carp (ed.), *Retirement*, Human Sciences, New York, pp. 29–74.

Svoboda, B & Vanek, M 1982, 'Retirement from high level competition', in T Orlick, JT Partington & JH Salmela (eds), *Mental training for coaches and athletes*, Fitness and Amateur Sport, Ottawa, pp. 166–75.

Taylor, J & Ogilvie, BC 1994, 'A conceptual model of adaptation to retirement among athletes', *Journal of Applied Sport Psychology*, 6, 1–20.

Taylor, J & Ogilvie, BC 2001, 'Career transitions among athletes: is there life after sports?', in JM Williams (ed.), *Applied sport psychology: personal growth to peak performance*, 4th edn, Mayfield, Mountain View, CA, pp. 480–96.

Thomas, CE & Ermler, KL 1988, 'Institutional obligations in the athletic retirement process', *Quest*, 40, 137–50.

Udry, E 2001, 'The role of significant others: social support during injuries', in J Crossman (ed.), *Coping with sports injuries: psychological strategies for rehabilitation*, Oxford University Press, Melbourne, pp. 148–61.

Webb, WM, Nasco, SA, Riley, S & Headrick, B 1998, 'Athletic identity and reactions to retirement from sports', *Journal of Sport Behavior*, 21, 338–62.

Werthner, P & Orlick, T 1986, 'Retirement experiences of successful Olympic athletes', *International Journal of Sport Psychology*, 17, 337–63.

Wolff, R & Lester, D 1989, 'A theoretical basis for counseling the retired professional athlete', *Psychological Reports*, 64 (3) 1043–6.

Wong, PTP & Weiner, B 1981, 'When people ask "why" questions, and the heuristics of attributional search', *Journal of Personality and Social Psychology*, 40, 650–63.

Wylleman, P, de Knop, P, Menkehorst, H, Theeboom, M & Annerel, J 1993, 'Career termination and social integration among elite athletes', in S Serpa, J Alves, V Ferreira & A Paula-Brito (eds), *Proceedings: VIII World Congress of Sport Psychology*, Lisbon, Portugal, 22–27 June, pp. 902–6.

Wylleman, P, Lavallee, D & Alfermann, D (eds) 1999, *Career transitions in competitive sports*, FEPSAC Monograph Series, European Federation of Sport Psychology.

Yalom, ID 1980, *Existential psychotherapy*, HarperCollins, New York.

CHAPTER 24

SPORT AND EXERCISE PSYCHOLOGY: INTO THE FUTURE

Tony Morris

Sport and exercise psychology is a relatively new field of research and practice. Its theoretical base and research methods are still in the process of development. Practice in sport and exercise psychology often borrows from more established fields. New methods and techniques typically emerge from the needs of particular consulting situations, rather than from theory and research. Reflection on the development of the field during the past thirty to forty years indicates that the paths down which sport and exercise psychology has travelled have not been easy to predict. At the same time, the rate of development, from slow beginnings, has increased dramatically. So much work is now in progress across so many aspects of the field that it is difficult for one person to keep abreast of all areas of discipline.

This mushrooming of theoretical and applied sport psychology is exciting for everyone involved in the discipline and the profession, but it signals a need for caution by anyone trying to predict the future. Precognition is not yet part of the training of sport psychologists, so this chapter makes no firm predictions about what the future of the field will hold. Rather, it reflects on what has been written in the present book about the way we do sport and exercise psychology. These reflections are accompanied by some observations on general directions that seem to hold value for the future of the profession. The contributors to this text have given their expert views, specific to their particular topics, on the directions that sport psychology should take. Rather than repeating their specific ideas, and entering into in-depth considerations of the issues raised, this chapter will address more general issues that are consistently reflected in these wide-ranging discussions. It is important, however, that issues of relevance to the future of the field are raised, and it is critical that they should be debated at length in more specialised forums.

This chapter addresses issues that relate to the way that theory and research are developing in the field. Concerns with the general focus of theory and research are introduced, as are methodological issues. Questions of importance to professional training and applied work are also raised. The artificial dichotomy of theory and practice, which is reflected in the structure of this book, raises a number of issues, which are considered in the following discussion.

FUTURE DIRECTIONS IN THEORY AND RESEARCH

Theories and concepts developed in sport and exercise psychology

A survey of the field of sport and exercise psychology indicates that few theories and models have been developed within the discipline. Many of the significant directions taken in sport psychology have been signposted by its parent discipline, psychology. Broad, paradigmatic shifts from the person-centred focus of early theory and research to interactional and then cognitive phenomenological approaches reflect developments that occurred in psychology some years earlier. More importantly perhaps, theoretical work on specific topics has often involved the application of a mainstream theory to sport and exercise — for example, Zajonc (1965) on social facilitation, Weiner (1974) on attribution theory, Deci (1975) on intrinsic motivation, Bandura (1977, 1986) on self-efficacy, and Spielberger (1966) on anxiety. But although sport and exercise psychology should always be alert to developments in the general discipline, there is a need for theories and models to be generated in the field of sport itself.

The sport-specific, theoretical approach proposed here is exemplified in sport and exercise psychology by the development of theory and research on anxiety in sport. Before 1975 researchers considered two main theories, drive theory and the inverted-U hypothesis, both emanating from mainstream psychology. This changed with the work of Martens and his colleagues, which led to the book *Competitive Anxiety in Sport* (Martens, Vealey & Burton 1990). That work originated in the application of Spielberger's state–trait theory and Martens' argument that we needed measures of anxiety that were specific to sport competition. It progressed through the development of two sport-specific measures, the Sport Competition Anxiety Test (SCAT) and the Competitive State Anxiety Inventory-2 (CSAI-2), to permit a more sensitive examination of anxiety in sport. The research that Martens and colleagues carried out culminated in the statement of a theoretical model of competitive anxiety that could be used to generate many hypotheses to further develop our understanding of sport competition anxiety.

The Martens et al. (1990) theoretical model of competitive anxiety in sport reflects another point that is crucial to the future development of theories and models in sport and exercise psychology. It is a point that comes up repeatedly in the chapters in the present text. To reflect the complexities of human behaviour, theories and models must be multifaceted; we need to develop multifactor theories because the single-factor theories of the past have not produced a high level of understanding and prediction of behaviour. Theories need to consider a range of dimensions and to operate on a number of levels. For example, psychophysiological and psychosocial factors should be considered alongside purely psychological dimensions. Martens et al. (1990) included a personal factor (trait anxiety), a situational factor (the objective situation) and cognitive phenomenological factors (perceived uncertainty and perceived importance) in their theory.

The development of sport-specific theory and research did not stop there. Much research was conducted using the measures to test anxiety–performance theories. During the 1990s Hardy and Fazey's (1987) application of catastrophe theory to the topic of anxiety in sport gained great popularity. This conceptualisation was also more complex, predicting that the effect of anxiety on performance depended on the specific combination of somatic and cognitive state anxiety. Yet research results were still not achieving the level of prediction that was expected. Jones and colleagues (Jones & Swain 1992; Swain & Jones 1996) made another major step forward in the sport field. Martens et al.'s sport-specific measures of anxiety, SCAT and CSAI-2, which were widely used in this research, examined intensity of anxiety — that is, how anxious a person feels, from 'not very' to 'very anxious'. Jones and Swain (1992) argued that to understand how anxiety affects a person, we also need to know its direction — that is, whether the person interprets the anxiety as facilitative or debilitative. So they added a directional scale to the existing CSAI-2 and the Sport Anxiety Scale (SAS) (Smith, Smoll & Schutz 1990), which is now used more widely than SCAT, because it is a multidimensional measure of sport-specific trait anxiety. Today, unless the focus is on only an aspect of intensity or direction of anxiety, it is expected that research on anxiety will employ the intensity and directional scales of sport-specific measures. These theoretical, conceptual and measurement developments have emerged within the field of sport and exercise psychology.

Structured sport and exercise psychology research programs

Generating a viable theory or model is not very useful if there are no structured research programs to address its propositions. A survey of the sport and exercise psychology literature reveals very few examples like that of anxiety, where a particular issue has been addressed systematically through long-term research programs that have progressed in a rational and systematic manner. The direction of such a program will inevitably shift as new knowledge leads to greater insight. This was the case in the original attempt, logical at the time, by Martens and his colleagues to develop a unitary measure of state anxiety, the Competitive State Anxiety Inventory (CSAI), based on the state scale of the STAI (Spielberger, Gorsuch & Lushene 1970). When this proved to be unsuccessful (Martens, Burton, Rivkin & Simons 1980), Martens and colleagues went back to theoretical perspectives on anxiety. Through the application of work by Liebert and Morris (1967) on worry and emotionality, and that of Davidson and Schwartz (1976) on cognitive and somatic anxiety, they produced the CSAI-2 (Martens, Burton, Vealey, Bump & Smith 1983). This measure distinguished between cognitive and somatic state anxiety applied specifically to sport competition and produced probably the most widely researched conceptualisation in sport psychology of the past 25 years. Further, as Martens et al. (1990) acknowledged, 'perhaps the "golden egg" of the CSAI-2 development was the fortuitous discovery of the state self-confidence component' (p. 213). It might be said that such 'good fortune' is much more likely to arise in the context of clear, structured, systematic research programs than in the one-off study of psychological processes or techniques that litter the sport and exercise psychology journals.

Theoretically based intervention research

The measurement and description of variables is an essential first stage in this process, but it should lead to the generation of theories and models that give rise to testable hypotheses or research questions. A range of research designs can be used to examine these questions and increase our understanding of the concepts and processes involved. Practice has often functioned in the absence of substantial testing of techniques in the sport context. Examination of the efficacy of applied interventions has been a recent and much-needed development in the field. Research involving interventions is an important direction for expansion in the future, but it should do more than test whether specific interventions work or whether one intervention is superior to another. Intervention research must help us to understand the underlying psychological mechanisms, so that the theory or model can be refined and applied to a range of potential interventions, thus advancing practice as well as theory.

Causal modelling

One approach to research that can focus and clarify thinking in this respect is causal modelling. The proposition of models is a favourite activity of sport psychologists, as exemplified by their generation at the conclusion of most contributions to the first edition of Horn's (1992) text, *Advances in Sport Psychology*. The testing of these models using causal modelling procedures, however, is infrequent, as noted by Schutz (1993). An informative example of the way it can be done was published some time ago, in McAuley's (1985) comparison of anxiety and self-efficacy as mediators between situation and behaviour. Carpenter, Scanlan, Simons and Lobel (1993) have pioneered the use of structural equation modelling in sport and exercise psychology. The use of causal modelling techniques to generate and modify conceptions of the relationships between variables in a particular area of sport psychology is especially useful for examining the role of mediating and moderating variables. Gould and Krane (1992) noted the need to move from correlational to causal research in the study of anxiety and performance. This suggestion applies much more widely in sport and exercise psychology, and causal modelling techniques should be of great value in facilitating this shift.

Gould and Krane (1992) also made the point that much research in sport and exercise psychology limits its theoretical value by testing only one theory in a particular study. Where two or more theories are tested in the same study, more information is gleaned. McAuley's (1985) study again exemplifies this point. Anxiety theorists, McAuley points out, have argued that it is not necessary to employ self-efficacy as an explanatory concept mediating between the stimulus components of the environment and participants' reactions. This theoretical perspective contends that anxiety explains such relationships and self-efficacy is simply a by-product of the process, so that as anxiety increases, confidence (self-efficacy) in the situation decreases. This accounts for any covariation of self-efficacy with performance. Self-efficacy theory (Bandura 1977), on the other hand, suggests that self-efficacy is the important mediating variable, and anxiety is simply a by-product of low self-efficacy for the task. McAuley was able to test both models using causal modelling, pitting them against each other in terms of their fit to the same data set. His results provided support for the contention that self-efficacy is the key variable, with stronger paths emerging when self-efficacy was the mediator in the causal model and anxiety was an outcome, than when anxiety was the mediator and self-efficacy one of the outcomes. This type of multi-theory research design is to be commended, but it has not been widely used in sport and exercise psychology research during the 20 years since McAuley's demonstration of its potential.

Longitudinal research

Sport psychology has been typically chracterised by the execution of cross-sectional research. There are few examples of studies that have considered the same group of participants over an extended period of time to understand development and change processes. Longitudinal research of this nature could answer many questions that remain unanswered from the cross-sectional work. An example can be drawn from the study of participation and drop-out from sport. Research on involvement in sport during teenage years has indicated that the high drop-out rate observed in American sport is primarily attributed to lack of time and failure to achieve desired goals (Weiss & Petlichkoff 1989). Studies often asked participants to consider their sport involvement retrospectively, which introduced the associated problems of memory and reconstruction. Studies also commonly asked superficial questions about reasons for dropping out. Weiss and Petlichkoff (1989) noted that deeper investigation by follow-up interviews has indicated that lack of time was often caused by the increasing demands of other sports in which the individuals were involved, while their limited goal achievement was also relative, rather than absolute — that is, comparatively greater success was being achieved in their other sports activities. Thus, it has been proposed that for many adolescents drop-out should be interpreted in a positive way, as indicating a focusing on strengths. Longitudinal study of the sports activities of teenagers could substantiate the pattern implied in previous research — that many children try out lots of activities and often enjoy most of them, but as success increases, the demands of each expand, until some enjoyable activities must be given up to gain the greater perceived satisfaction from another sport or sports. If this was found to be the case, then in-depth longitudinal research that involves interviewing adolescents about their motives as they drop out of one sport to give more time to another would be able to explore the processes underlying the decisions made by young athletes much more effectively than cross-sectional or retrospective research can do.

Lifespan research in sport and exercise psychology

Discussion of the changes in motives and sport behaviour that occur in a very short time during adolescence bring into sharp relief the need for lifespan research in sport and exercise psychology. As individuals move through life, their needs and priorities change and they perceive situations differently. It is important for sport psychology to be aware of the shifting background to sport and exercise behaviour and for researchers not to simply assume that values and processes operating in adolescents and/or college students, who commonly participate in the research, apply to all people. A simple example of this comes from research we completed, again in the area of participation motivation, that is reported in chapter 5. The study by Morris, Clayton, Power and Jin-Song (1996) used a modified 50-item version of the Participation Motivation Questionnaire (PMQ) (Gill, Gross & Huddleston 1983) to examine the reasons for participation of more than 2600 participants aged from 6 to over 70 years, who were involved in 14 activities. This lifespan study followed the original work of Brodkin and Weiss (1990) with a relatively small group of swimmers. One finding of the Morris et al. study was that adolescents and young adults rated a medical motive (participate to help an existing medical condition) very low, presumably because most of them had no medical problems, especially problems of a chronic nature. For adults in their middle years, the ranking of this medical item moved up to a moderate position, while for older adults it became one of the three most important reasons for doing the activity. It may seem obvious now that older adults suffer more frequently than others from chronic illnesses and other medical conditions that might be alleviated by exercise, and that this is likely to influence their motives for participation. Yet before the study by Brodkin and Weiss, sport and exercise psychology research on participation motivation exclusively examined adolescent samples, and whereas the researchers themselves were undoubtedly aware of the restrictions in generality of their findings, others may have assumed they applied to all participants in that sport or exercise activity.

It has long been noted that longitudinal research is relatively unattractive. This is largely because the organisations funding such research are interested in practical outcomes. Academics, who judge each other's work by published reports, also anticipate a rapid outcome, admittedly for different reasons. Regnier, Salmela and Russell (1993) reported on an alternative approach that permits a longitudinal view to be inferred but abbreviates the time frame. This technique, which combines cross-sectional and longitudinal research designs, is called the sliding populations approach. It involves measuring variables in what is called the 'pool population'. This refers to the younger age group of interest, for example 13-year-olds. A measuring instrument is devised to detect those athletes who will be successful at an older age, say 16 years, which is termed the 'target population'. The pool population is then followed to the target population age to test the predictive power of the instrument. By chaining together pool and target ages, for example following the 13- to 16-year-old phase, a 16-year-old pool population may be examined (using a different instrument) with an 18-year-old target population; based on statistical checks across these groups, inferences can then be made about 'longitudinal effects'. The target population for a younger pool population should not be used as the pool population for an older target population. This approach may not remove the need for longitudinal studies, but it does permit the reporting of much more rapid provisional conclusions to bodies such as national sports organisations — for example, when they need to make decisions on talent identification and development. It is to be hoped that longitudinal research will continue to confirm the sliding populations research conclusions.

Ecological validity and generalisability

Concern with generalising the results obtained from research underlies one of the most important issues for sport psychology to address. Much of the research in sport and exercise psychology has used adolescent and college student samples. Typically these individuals are competitive athletes. This presents little problem in research concerned with mass participation processes. In much of this research, however, inferences have been made from the results about other groups, particularly elite performers. It has been recognised that major differences exist in skills, motives, ego involvement and other psychological processes that invalidate generalising from competitive to elite performers (see chapter 13). Even when elite performers are used as participants, when they take part in laboratory-based studies using analogue tasks they are not using their skills and may not be highly motivated to do the task. In addition, they are not likely to feel personally threatened by possible failure at something that they have never done before and that they might view as a trivial task. Thus we cannot consider them 'experts' in any specific task. It is rather like expecting a lawyer to perform emergency surgery at a crash scene, because she is an 'expert'! Expertise is specific to tasks. Tiger Woods or Ian Thorpe would probably be novices at the task of table tennis or karate. Also, if these exceptional sports performers were asked to perform a mental arithmetic task, they might not feel they had to perform at a high level — that is, they would not be ego-involved — because moderate performance on the maths task would not tarnish their reputation, respectively, in golf or swimming (yardage and split-time calculations aside!).

Trite as it may seem, it must still be stressed that to understand the psychological processes underlying the behaviour of elite performers in their chosen sports it is essential for research to observe the elite performers in that environment. In two studies of imagery and performance, Callery and Morris (1993, 1997a) used multiple-baseline, single-case, A-B design studies to examine the effects of an imagery program on the skills of disposal of the ball by foot (Study 1) and taking the central position to receive the ball dropping from marking competitions (Study 2) in Australian Football (AFL). In the first study, 10 AFL players participated over most of a season. Eight AFL players from a different club took part in Study 2, which lasted for a whole season. In Study 1, performance of kick disposals during league matches was judged by three independent experts and inter-rater reliabilities exceeded 0.9. Eight of the 10 participants showed trends in the predicted direction, four revealing very clear positive effects of the imagery. Social validation questions at the end of the study indicated that the players felt more confident about the skill from an early stage of the study. Video analysis was used to assess performance in Study 2. All eight players in this study showed improvement in the skill in league games from baseline phase to imagery phase. This time we actually measured self-efficacy to test the claim that confidence for the specific task was enhanced. The results provided support for this claim. These findings led us to study the role of confidence as a mediator between imagery and performance in a causal modelling study, which indicated that imagery enhanced confidence and performance independently — that is, confidence was not a mediator of the imagery–performance relationship (Callery & Morris 1997b). Perhaps without studying elite performers doing tasks in competition that were critical to their performance, it would not have emerged that confidence is a critical factor for that group. It is also noteworthy that confidence in basic AFL tasks increased with imagery use among premier, professional exponents of that game.

One reason why much research has not been done with elite performers in competitive situations is that it is not ethically or practically acceptable to assign such individuals to a control group. Recognising that an understanding of elite performers, during practice as well as competition, depends on studying elite performers in these contexts is an important step for sport psychology. The problems associated with the traditional experimental design, in which an experimental group subject to some kind of manipulation is compared with a control group that does not receive an active intervention, will not go away. It is therefore essential that researchers in sport psychology recognise the value of alternative methods to the traditional experiment. The Callery and Morris (1993, 1997a, 1997b) studies employed one method that avoids most of the ethical and practical difficulties. In single-case designs, all participants receive the intervention but all spend time initially in a baseline condition, which means, in essence, that they act as their own controls. The multiple-baseline design has the added advantage that each participant starts to receive the intervention at a different time, say after four, five, six and seven weeks of baseline. One result of this is that any effects detected for each particiant shortly after starting the intervention are not attributable to the same extraneous event, such as a stirring team talk, as only one participant would have started the intervention at that time. Even so, the method has problems in practice. In our studies, participants assigned randomly to longer baselines became impatient to start the intervention when they perceived that their colleagues were benefiting from it. The single-case design, introduced to sport and exercise psychology by Kendall, Hrycaiko, Martin and Kendall (1990) in the context of college basketball, has a great deal of potential for research in real sport competition contexts. Elko and Ostrow (1991) employed it to study rational emotive therapy for anxiety management. More recently it has been employed to study imagery in basketball (Shambrook & Bull 1996) and elite badminton (Callow, Hardy & Hall 1998).

Other research methods also offer the opportunity to conduct research in the field with elite performers. Observational methods have not been widely used in sport psychology to date, but they can permit the researcher to participate in the competition environment. They are particularly effective for investigating interpersonal aspects of sport. Observational methods are often used in conjunction with other approaches to provide validation through the process of triangulation, whereby several methods are used independently and their correspondence indicates validity. Interview techniques have been more widely used in sport psychology research in recent times, perhaps because the interview has long been part of psychological practice. Methods have been established to systematically analyse the transcripts generated by in-depth interviews, and the findings emerging from use of these inductive methods are proving informative, as illustrated by the work of Gould and his colleagues (e.g. Gould, Eklund & Jackson 1992a, 1992b; Gould, Jackson & Finch 1993a, 1993b). Another approach to the interview is that of grounded theory (Glaser & Strauss 1967). This approach intentionally avoids theory leading to testable hypotheses, typically permitting the theory to emerge from the data gathered. Fortunato, Anderson, Morris & Seedsman (1995) reported the results of a grounded theory study of the career transition experiences of 45 recently retired professional footballers. They observed systematic differences between the relatively positive experiences of volunary retirees and the problems experienced by players whose top-level careers were ended by injury or deselection. Methods chosen should be appropriate to the question being asked. Use of a range of methods can provide different sorts of information and insights, and the picture created can have increased validity because of the reciprocal support of several independent research methods. Whatever the methods used, it is important for sport and exercise psychologists to be reflexive in their research processes. This means they must be aware of, and acknowledge, their own perspectives when they undertake research and interpret data.

An approach to research that should have relevance to the examination of practice is that of action research. Developed in other areas of psychology and education, action research has evolved to meet the needs of practitioners to initiate change. It comprises a combination of research and practice, in which the practitioner-researcher collaborates with the participants in identifying the subject of change and the methods, reporting on the process as well as the outcomes. Kellman and Beckmann (2003) stated that action research 'aims at maximum integration of the interests of participants, and thereby an integration of theory and practice' (p. 19). Kellman and Beckmann reported on action research at a training camp for junior world championship rowers. A promising sign for the future of action research in sport and exercise psychology was the debate between researcher-practitioners (Evans, Fleming & Hardy 2000; Gilbourne 2000) that followed publication of an article on action research in injury rehabilitation (Evans, Hardy & Fleming 2000) in the premier applied journal, *The Sport Psychologist*.

Researching sport at many levels

The emphasis in the previous section was on the need to study elite performers in the competitive environment. This was not meant to suggest that sport psychology should focus entirely on the elite. On the contrary, it must research sport and exercise at a wide range of levels and with a great variety of populations. Understanding human behaviour in sport and exercise cannot result from watching only those at the elite level. There are many other groups that sport psychologists must consider, if they are to convince the community that they can offer a service to everyone. Theory and research should address the needs of groups such as older adults, young children, people with disabilities, people with chronic diseases and people at risk for whom prevention is possible. A variety of ethnic and cultural factors should also be taken into account. With so many diverse groups to study, opportunities for this sort of research are legion. Also, the nurturing of sport psychology around the world offers great potential for cross-cultural research collaboration. Research programs that demonstrate that a particular psychological process is universal or that show how a process is influenced by cultural factors will surely be more convincing than narrowly based research in one culture.

Measurement in sport and exercise psychology

A final concern for theory and research, as well as for practice, is the role of measurement in sport and exercise psychology. Comments of contributors to the 1989 Olympic sports issue of *The Sport Psychologist* suggested that tests were not used much in applied work (see chapter 9). It is of some concern to note that practitioners have little faith in the tests their colleagues have developed, preferring to use their own judgement. The measures that are generally available, with the exception of the SCAT and the CSAI-2 (Martens et al. 1990), have not been substantially validated for research in the field. Validating tests is not the most attractive exercise in the eyes of many researchers, but there is still a long way to go in this area before we can look at the results of tests and predict in which activity the respondent is likely to participate, let alone whether an individual will do well under pressure, can switch attention effectively or has the ability to imagine sport-related situations in a rich, multimodal manner. These goals might never be attained, but sport psychology has hardly left the starting gate in sport-specific test development. In the latest edition of the *Directory of Tests in Sport and Exercise Psychology*, Ostrow (1996) listed nearly 400 entries. All of these were sport-specific instruments; tests such as the STAI (Spielberger, Gorsuch & Lushene 1970), the Profile of Mood States (POMS) (McNair, Lorr & Droppelman 1971) and the TAIS (Nideffer 1976) were not included.

Some measures from general psychology — for instance the STAI, the POMS and the TAIS — have been employed widely in sport and exercise psychology. A small number of sport-specific tests, including the CSAI-2 and the Task and Ego Orientation in Sport Questionnaire (TEOSQ) (Duda 1989), have also been widely used, but most measures in Ostrow's directory have limited validation and use in research. It is essential that we measure factors that could influence the variable of particular interest. For example, when an imagery intervention does not produce an improvement in performance, confidence or concentration, as intended, it cannot be concluded that this is because imagery doesn't 'work' if imagery itself has not been measured. It is possible that the participants had very low imagery ability, so they were not able to take advantage of a sound imagery program. Without reliable and valid tests to control for potential mediating and moderating variables, there are many areas of research in which it becomes difficult to draw definite conclusions. It is important for researchers to be prepared to spend some of their valuable time on the crucial activity of test validation.

FUTURE DIRECTIONS FOR THE SPORT PSYCHOLOGY PROFESSION

Research does not occur in a vacuum. The development of theories and their investigation through controlled research have a purpose beyond the better understanding of human behaviour in sport. That purpose is to provide more knowledge and skills for the professional sport psychologist to use to enhance the experience of people in sport and exercise contexts. Research is carried out in the service of the profession, so it is the responsibility of practitioners to identify and develop the range of practice situations in which research is needed. It should be the aim of sport psychologists to make sport and exercise psychology accessible to everyone in the community. In doing this, sport and exercise psychology practitioners will also expand the range of work available to the profession. Strategies need to be generated to involve more sectors of the community in sport and exercise psychology. Sport psychologists must be proactive in promoting their profession in all spheres of life. To facilitate this, research should be directed towards a much wider range of applications of sport psychology.

Creating sport and exercise psychology employment

Students in professional training need to be prepared for the process of creating sport psychology anew in areas of the community that have not previously had access to the field. Professional training has received little formal attention. There is a standing joke about the tendency of psychologists to spend much of their time analysing themselves, when there are better things for them to do. Although this overly reflexive view may have some general validity, there is a strong argument for sport psychologists to study the way they practise, so they can best train the practitioners of the future among their students. Fortunately, the largest single representative organisation of sport psychologists, the Association for the Advancement of Applied Sport Psychology (AAASP), has begun to do this. Chapter 16 addressed these issues in detail, indicating that the study of training and supervision of future professional sport and exercise psychologists is now being given the attention it deserves.

In chapter 9 we addressed the issue of how sport and exercise psychology practitioners can earn a living doing what they have trained for and, typically, what they love to do. (We can deduce that most people in our profession do the work for love by counting the number of our colleagues who have got rich out of sport psychology compared with the well-heeled dentists and accountants we meet. Sport psychologists are certainly not in this career for the money!) We noted in chapter 9 how applied sport and exercise psychology has expanded as it has evolved, so that much of the work done today involves counselling athletes rather than presenting psychological skills training programs. We also pointed out how sport and exercise psychology professionals have started to diversify into the performing arts and the world of business. We must expect these trends to continue. In addition, psychology practitioners seem to be the last professionals to get into the exercise field in a big way. This is an area with growing potential. Once we solve the problem of how to market sport and exercise psychology to make it attractive to the growing range of gyms, leisure centres and exercise groups, another substantial source of work will be opened up for the profession.

Understanding the psychologist's role

An important aspect of the training programs of the future will centre on perceptions about the sport psychologist's role in relation to clients. The potential for the client–practitioner relationship to become one of dependency has long been recognised. Frequently this entails clients becoming dependent on the psychologist, but it can also involve a need felt by the practitioner to maintain the professional relationship with the client. Sport psychologists working at the elite level are particularly vulnerable to this tendency. People commonly train in sport psychology because of their love of sport. Once trained, many are drawn to their favourite sports, in part perhaps because they feel they will present with greater credibility, given their knowledge of the game. Being associated with the Olympic squad in the sport one played as a club junior, or the professional team one supported as a youngster, has great potential to distract fledgling sport psychologists. They may enjoy basking in the reflected glory or simply feeling like one of the team. The message from this book is clear: the aim of applied work in sport psychology should be to create a self-regulating athlete who possesses the skills, techniques and self-understanding to cope with the stresses of heavy training and competition. Large sums of money and/or the hopes of a nation may depend on their performance. Self-managing exercisers must be able to handle the demands of a rigorous exercise regime, when pressures of family, work, weather or more attractive alternatives may tempt them to weaken. Sport psychologists should feel their job has been well done when clients do not need to see them any more.

Teaching and learning in sport and exercise psychology

Another aspect of the education question concerns mode of instruction. The didactic approach is just one method, and others must be considered. Workbooks, audiotapes and videos have emerged from a number of groups (see chapter 9), but their development has been slower than we might have expected. Multimedia technology is evolving very rapidly, however, and it is important that sport psychology is part of this technological revolution. Much of the subject matter to be learned is particularly suited to the interactive, computer-based educational tools currently used by students in school and at play. Multimedia technology can also make sport psychology practice more accessible to people in rural communities and individuals with limited money to spend on the frequent use of consultants. Although the Internet has produced many opportunities for online learning and distance education, we have yet to see a wide range of sport psychology programs offered on the Web. One reason for this may be the pre-eminent role of practical experience under supervision in the training of psychologists. As pointed out in chapter 9, learning about theories or models plays only a limited role in the development of expertise. There may be room for a really innovative sport psychologist to collaborate with a computing expert in developing a computer 'game' that presents scenarios in which the trainee sport psychologist interviews performers with problems.

Evaluation in applied sport and exercise psychology

Discussion of the range of teaching methods applicable to sport psychology introduces the issue of outcome evaluation. In chapter 9 we noted that many of the experts writing in the 1989 and 1990 issues of *The Sport Psychologist* reported that they had carried out evaluations of their interventions. At the same time, the assessment procedures themselves tended to be untested and, typically, ad hoc. Training in the formal procedures of evaluation is essential, but it should be guided by research work on the effectiveness of evaluation procedures in the sport and exercise psychology context. Evaluation is an important part of the learning process. Sports performers understand that feedback is a crucial component of learning. Evaluation procedures now feature in the applied publications in sport and exercise psychology, but it is not clear how widespread their application is. Perhaps only those writers wishing to publish an article are performing systematic evaluations of their work. In the future, formative and summative evaluation of programs should be an integral part of the sport psychologist's approach to practice. The feedback gleaned from this work should be used to enhance practice. (A more extensive discussion of the major issues for practice is presented in chapter 9.)

THE THEORY–PRACTICE NEXUS

In the past, theory and practice in sport psychology have been coordinated to only a limited extent. Whether this is a consequence of lack of communication between practitioners and researchers, the inapplicability of the orthodox research methods of sport psychology to real-world settings, the focus on issues of traditional concern in physical education, or a combination of other factors, for the future success of the applied field and sport psychology research it must not be permitted to continue. Theories that cannot be applied to real-world issues tend to be lifeless; comparisons of interventions with no systematic theory testing must ultimately consider *every* intervention, as no underlying principles can be deduced from ad hoc comparisons.

Models and theories must be generated to describe processes in real athletes involved in real sports competitions. For example, a theme running through this text is that a shift has taken place in many areas of sport and exercise psychology from an obsession with outcomes in sport to a focus on the psychological processes that lead to those outcomes. As more process-oriented applied work is undertaken, a great opportunity is presented to develop theory and research in concert with practice. These theories and models need to be tested in a systematic manner using a range of paradigms; in this way the theory can progress to the extent that it can be used to generate predictions about the best techniques to employ in particular situations. Theory and practice can thus grow together, with research carried out on the application of sport psychology, and practice guided by existing research. It is to be hoped that future editions of this book will adopt a thematic approach through which the topic, whether it be anxiety, imagery or confidence, can be addressed simultaneously in terms of both theory and practice.

One way in which researchers and practitioners might communicate more directly so researchers fully understand the pressing practical issues might be if a regular place in the applied journals was allocated to practitioners to write about the concerns they experience in the field. Through monitoring these 'problem pages', researchers might be better equipped to propose research that addresses the issues. In this way a dialogue could be initiated that might lead to collaborative studies involving both researchers and practitioners. Analyses of the implications for practice that emerge from such research collaboration should also find a place in the applied journals.

CONCLUSIONS

The field of sport and exercise psychology has developed rapidly over the past three decades and is now expanding faster than ever. There are so many interesting areas of research in sport psychology that it is difficult to choose the most rewarding in which to work. Collaboration and teamwork are practical ways to keep up with developments in the field, but it is becoming clear that few real-world issues will be resolved by a single disciplinary approach. Researchers need to collaborate with colleagues in the other sports sciences in addressing some of the most important practical issues. It is to be hoped that we will soon see multidisciplinary and multidimensional research programs, linking up researchers and practitioners all over the world. Collaborations that lead to research addressing major practical issues in a range of cultures will provide exciting opportunities for the profession in the future.

SUMMARY

In this chapter we reviewed some of the major themes for the future drawn from the analyses of the contributors to this text. A major thread in this review was the need for practice and research to move closer together. We proposed that there is a need for more sport-specific theories and structured research programs to test them. We noted a particular need for research on interventions. New research designs, paradigms and statistical techniques should be utilised, including causal modelling, qualitative paradigms, and longitudinal and lifespan research designs. We argued that research needs to examine a wide range of groups within the community and that whenever possible it should locate research in real competition or exercise contexts. We next suggested that there is a need to relate theory and practice more closely and to train new practitioners to a high standard. This requires that we conduct research on professional training and the supervision of practice. We also proposed that a range of alternative instructional methods and media should be used and that more attention should be given to researching program evaluation. Finally, we called for greater communication in the field between professionals and researchers and more direct research on the psychological processes of real athletes. Communication and collaboration between all professional and research sport psychologists is the most important theme in this book. We believe that the book, which has itself brought together such a large, disparate group of applied and academic sport psychologists, is a testimony to what can happen when there is a common will.

References

Bandura, A 1977, 'Self-efficacy: toward a unifying theory of behavior change', *Psychological Review*, 84, 191–215.

Bandura, A 1986, *Social foundations of thought and action*, Prentice Hall, Englewood Cliffs, NJ.

Brodkin, P & Weiss, MR 1990, 'Developmental differences in motivation for participating in competitive swimming', *Journal of Sport & Exercise Psychology*, 12, 248–63.

Callery, P & Morris, T 1993, 'Imagery training and the performance of a skill in elite sport', in S Serpa, J Alves, V Ferreira & A Paulo-Brito (eds), *Proceedings of the VIIIth World Congress of Sport Psychology*, International Society of Sports Psychology, Lisbon, June, pp. 648–51.

Callery, PJ & Morris, T 1997a, 'The effects of an imagery program on self-efficacy and performance of an Australian Rules football skill', in R Lidor & M Bar-Eli (eds), *Proceedings of the IXth World Congress of Sport Psychology*, International Society of Sports Psychology, Netanya, Israel, pp. 175–7.

Callery, PJ & Morris, T 1997b, 'Modelling imagery, self-efficacy and performance', in R Lidor & M Bar-Eli (eds), *Proceedings of the IXth World Congress of Sport Psychology*, International Society of Sports Psychology, Netanya, Israel, pp. 172–4.

Callow, N, Hardy, L & Hall, C 1998, 'The effect of a motivational-mastery imagery intervention on the sport performance of three elite badminton players', *Journal of Applied Sport Psychology*, 10, S135.

Carpenter, PJ, Scanlan, TK, Simons, JP & Lobel, M 1993, 'A test of the sport commitment model using structural equation modeling', *Journal of Sport & Exercise Psychology*, 15, 119–33.

Davidson, RJ & Schwartz, GE 1976, 'The psychobiology of relaxation and related states: a multi-process theory', in DI Mostofsky (ed.), *Behavior control and modification of physiological activity*, Prentice Hall, Englewood Cliffs, NJ, pp. 399–442.

Deci, EL 1975, *Intrinsic motivation*, Plenum, New York.

Duda, JL 1989, 'The relationship between task and ego orientation and the perceived purpose of sport among male and female high school athletes', *Journal of Sport & Exercise Psychology*, 11, 318–35.

Elko, PK & Ostrow, AC 1991, 'Effects of a rational-emotive education program on heightened anxiety levels of female collegiate gymnasts', *The Sport Psychologist*, 5, 235–55.

Evans, L, Fleming, S & Hardy, L 2000, 'Situating action research: a response to Gilbourne', *The Sport Psychologist*, 14, 296–303.

Evans, L, Hardy, L & Fleming, S 2000, 'Intervention strategies with injured athletes: an action research study', *The Sport Psychologist*, 14, 188–206.

Fortunato, V, Anderson, D, Morris, T & Seedsman, T 1995, 'Career education and career transition research at Victoria University', *Proceedings of the IXth European Congress of Sport Psychology*, FEPSAC (European Federation of Sport Psychology), Brussels, pp. 533–43.

Gilbourne, D 2000, 'Searching for the nature of action research: a response to Evans, Fleming, and Hardy', *The Sport Psychologist*, 14, 207–14.

Gill, DL, Gross, JB & Huddleston, S 1983, 'Participation motivation in youth sports', *International Journal of Sport Psychology*, 14, 1–14.

Glaser, B & Strauss, A 1967, *The discovery of grounded theory*, Aldine, Chicago.

Gould, D, Eklund, RC & Jackson, SA 1992a, '1988 USA Olympic wrestling excellence II: mental preparation, precompetitive cognition, and affect', *The Sport Psychologist*, 6 (4) 358–82.

Gould, D, Eklund, RC & Jackson, SA 1992b, '1988 USA Olympic wrestling excellence I: competitive cognition, and affect', *The Sport Psychologist*, 6 (4) 383–402.

Gould, D, Jackson, SA & Finch, LM 1993a, 'Life at the top: the experiences of U.S. national figure skaters', *The Sport Psychologist*, 7 (4) 354–74.

Gould, D, Jackson, SA & Finch, LM 1993b, 'Sources of stress in national champion figure skaters', *Journal of Sport & Exercise Psychology*, 15 (2) 134–59.

Gould, D & Krane, V 1992, 'The arousal-athletic performance relationship: current status and future directions', in TS Horn (ed.), *Advances in sport psychology*, Human Kinetics, Champaign, IL, pp. 119–42.

Hardy, L & Fazey, J 1987, 'The inverted-U hypothesis: a catastrophe for sport psychology?', paper presented at the Annual Conference of the North American Society for the Psychology of Sport and Physical Activity, Vancouver, Canada, June.

Horn, TS (ed.) 1992, *Advances in sport psychology*, Human Kinetics, Champaign, IL.

Jones, JG & Swain, ABJ 1992, 'Intensity and direction dimensions of competitive anxiety and relationships with competitiveness', *Perceptual and Motor Skills*, 74, 467–72.

Kellman, M & Beckmann, J 2003, 'Research and intervention in sport psychology: new perspectives on an inherent conflict', *International Journal of Sport & Exercise Psychology*, 1, 13–26.

Kendall, G, Hrycaiko, D, Martin, GL & Kendall, T 1990, 'The effects of an imagery rehearsal, relaxation, and self-talk package on basketball game performance', *Journal of Sport & Exercise Psychology*, 12, 157–66.

Liebert, RM & Morris, LW 1967, 'Cognitive and emotional components of test anxiety: a distinction and some initial data', *Psychological Reports*, 20, 975–8.

Martens, R, Burton, D, Rivkin, F & Simons, J 1980, 'Reliability and validity of the Competitive State Anxiety Inventory (CSAI)', in CH Nadeau, WR Halliwell, KM Newell & GC Roberts (eds), *Psychology of motor behavior and sport — 1979*, Human Kinetics, Champaign, IL.

Martens, R, Burton, D, Vealey, RS, Bump, LA & Smith, DE 1983, 'The Competitive State Anxiety Inventory–2', unpublished manuscript, University of Illinois at Urbana–Champaign, IL.

Martens, R, Vealey, RS & Burton, D (eds) 1990, *Competitive anxiety in sport*, Human Kinetics, Champaign, IL.

McAuley, E 1985, 'Modeling and self-efficacy: a test of Bandura's model', *Journal of Sport Psychology*, 7, 283–95.

McNair, DM, Lorr, M & Droppelman, LF 1971, *Profile of Mood States manual*, Educational and Industrial Testing Service, San Diego, CA.

Morris, T, Clayton, H, Power, H & Han Jin-song 1996, 'Age differences in participation motives', poster presented at the International Pre-Olympic Congress, Dallas, TX, August.

Nideffer, RM 1976, 'Test of Attentional and Interpersonal Style', *Journal of Personality and Social Psychology*, 34, 394–404.

Ostrow, AC 1996, *Directory of psychological tests in the sport and exercise sciences*, Fitness Information Technology, Morgantown, WV.

Regnier, G, Salmela, J & Russell, SJ 1993, 'Talent detection and development in sport', in RN Singer, M Murphey & LK Tennant (eds), *Handbook of research on sport psychology*, Macmillan, New York, pp. 290–313.

Schutz, RW 1993, 'Methodological issues and measurement problems in sport psychology', in S Serpa, J Alves, V Ferreira & A Paulo-Brito (eds), *Proceedings of the VIIIth World Congress of Sport Psychology*, International Society of Sport Psychology, Lisbon, June, pp. 119–31.

Shambrook, CJ & Bull, SJ 1996, 'The use of a single-case research design to investigate the efficacy of imagery training', *Journal of Applied Sport Psychology*, 8, 27–43.

Smith, RE, Smoll, FL & Schutz, RW 1990, 'Measurements and correlates of sport-specific cognitive and somatic trait anxiety', *Anxiety Research*, 2, 263–80.

Spielberger, CD 1966, *Anxiety and behavior*, Academic, New York.

Spielberger, CD, Gorsuch, R & Lushene, R 1970, *The State Trait Anxiety Inventory (STAI) test manual*, Consulting Psychologists Press, Palo Alto, CA.

Swain, ABJ & Jones, JG 1996, 'Explaining performance variance: the relative contribution of intensity and direction dimensions of competitive state anxiety', *Anxiety, Stress, and Coping: An International Journal*, 9, 1–18.

Weiner, B 1974, *Achievement motivation and attribution theory*, General Learning Press, Morristown, NJ.

Weiss, MR & Petlichkoff, LM 1989, 'Children's motivation for participation in and withdrawal from sport: identifying the missing links', *Pediatric Exercise Science*, 1, 195–211.

Zajonc, RB 1965, 'Social facilitation', *Science*, 149, 269–74.

Author index

Subject index